VOLUME 3: DISCIPLE

Chapter Thirteen   The Invisible Enemy 389

Chapter Fourteen   Let Me Protect You 419

Chapter Fifteen   Captive Women 451

Chapter Sixteen   The Priestess of Seiryu 481

Chapter Seventeen   Souls Drifting Apart 513

Chapter Eighteen   Only You.. 543

Sound Effects Glossary 574

Chinese-to-Japanese Glossary 586

Color Image Gallery 587

CAST OF CHARACTERS
PRESENT-DAY JAPAN

Miaka's Mom
She's a divorced single
mom who wants Miaka
to get into Johan, a
prestigious high school.

Miaka
Miaka is a chipper junior high
student who is studying for
high school entrance exams.
She loves food.

Yui
Yui is Miaka's best friend.
She gets better grades
than Miaka.

Keisuke
Keisuke is Miaka's
brother. He knows Miaka
is under a lot of pressure
from their mother.

ANCIENT CHINA

Tamahome
Tamahome is a dashing stranger who is obsessed with money.

Nuriko
Nuriko is a consort to the emperor of Hong-Nan.

Hotohori
Hotohori is a beautiful noble who lives in the palace of Hong-Nan.

Nakago
Nakago is a strong warrior from Qu-Dong.

Chichiri
Chichiri is a mysterious traveler who can appear and disappear at will.

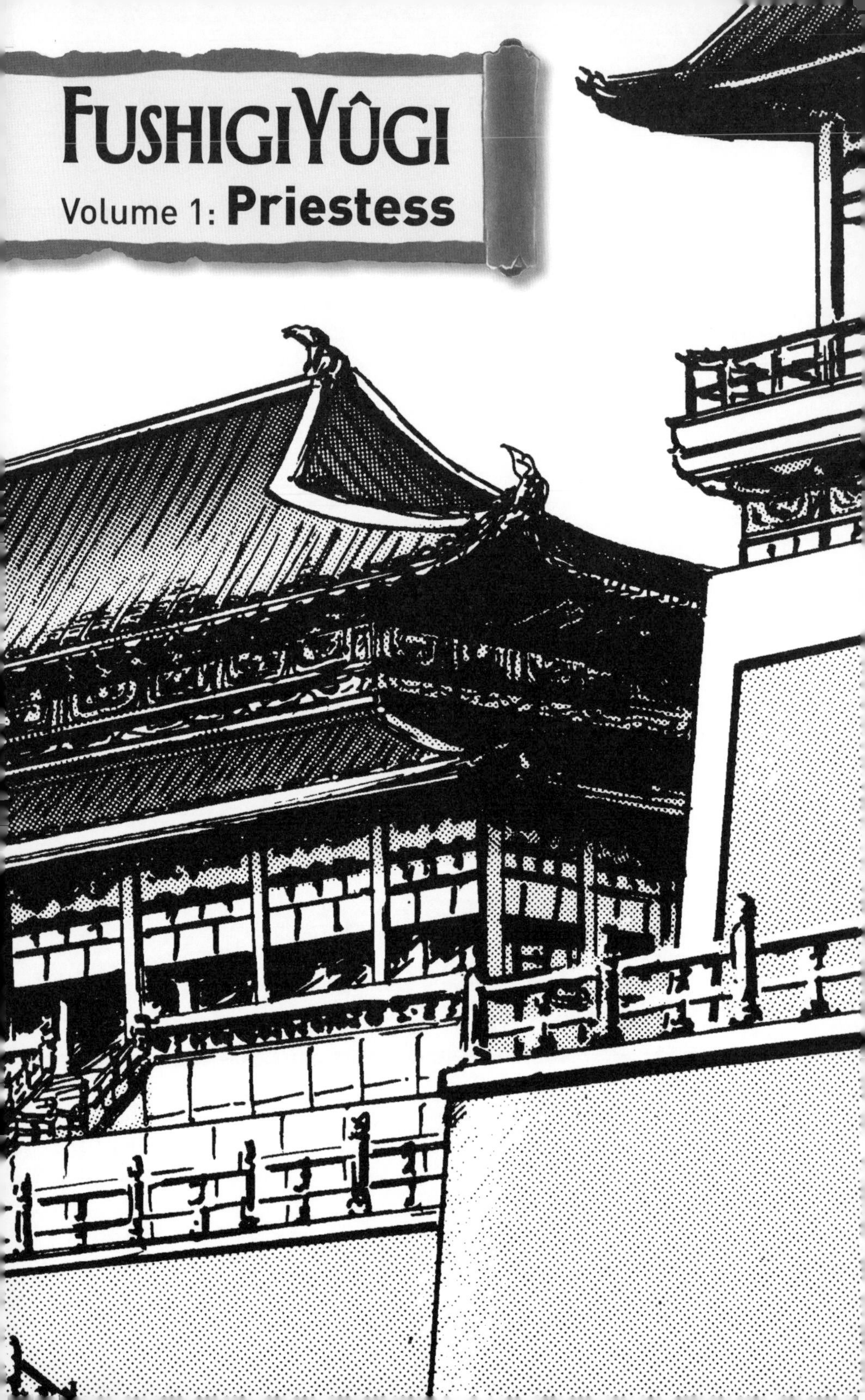
FUSHIGI YÛGI
Volume 1: Priestess

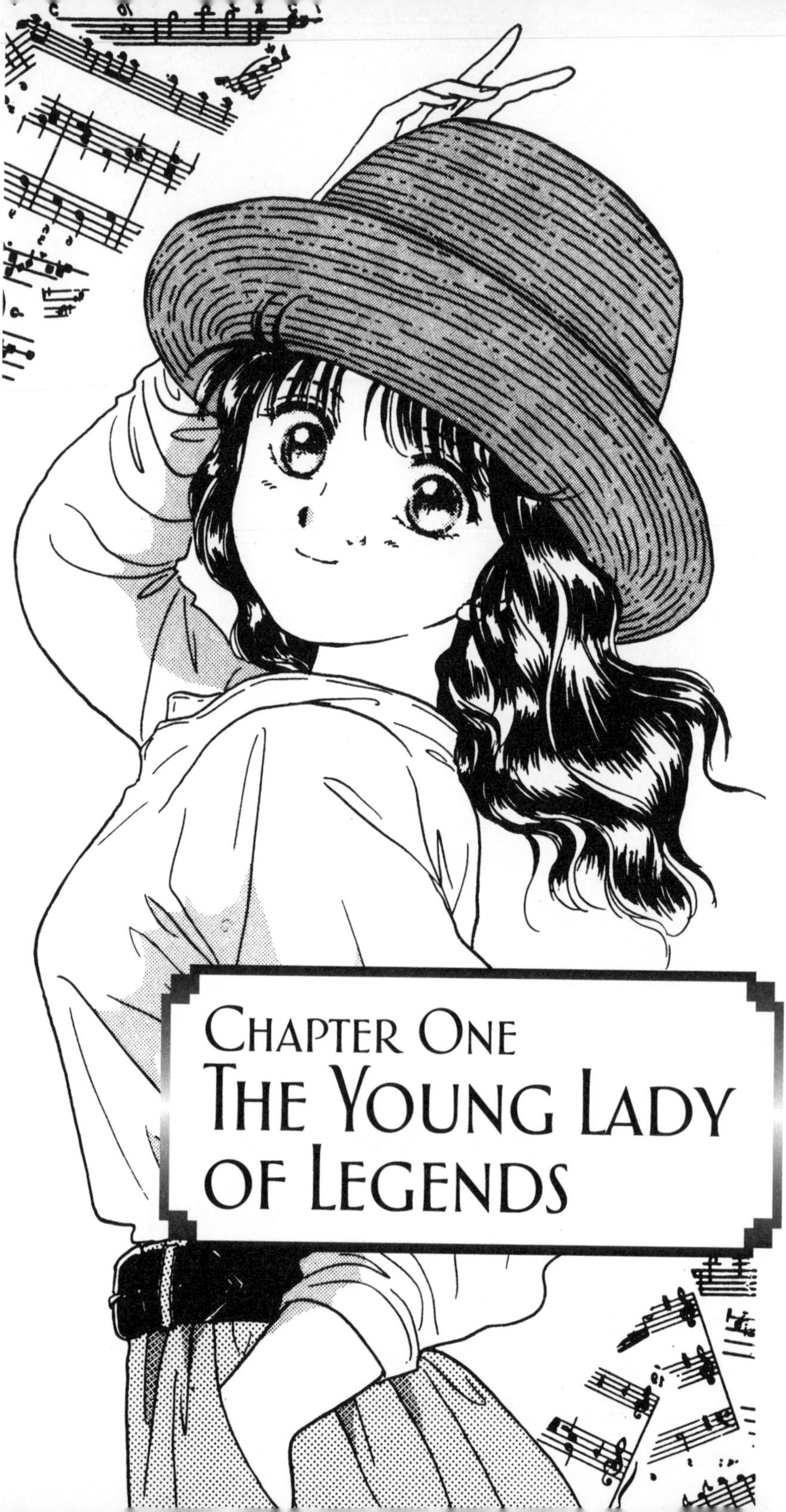

Chapter One
The Young Lady of Legends

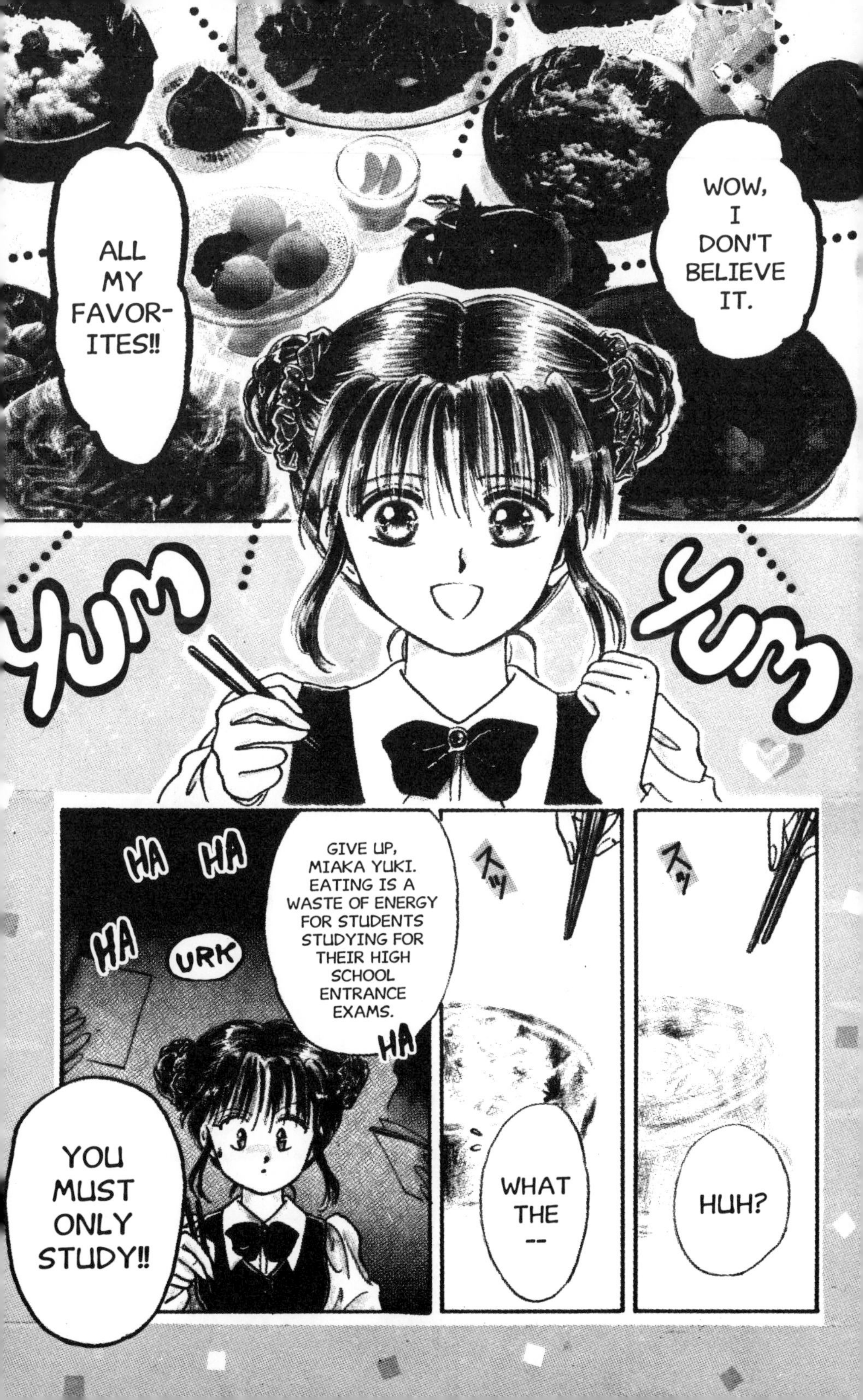
WOW, I DON'T BELIEVE IT.
ALL MY FAVOR-ITES!!
YUM
YUM
HUH?
WHAT THE --
GIVE UP, MIAKA YUKI. EATING IS A WASTE OF ENERGY FOR STUDENTS STUDYING FOR THEIR HIGH SCHOOL ENTRANCE EXAMS.
HA HA
HA
URK
HA
YOU MUST ONLY STUDY!!

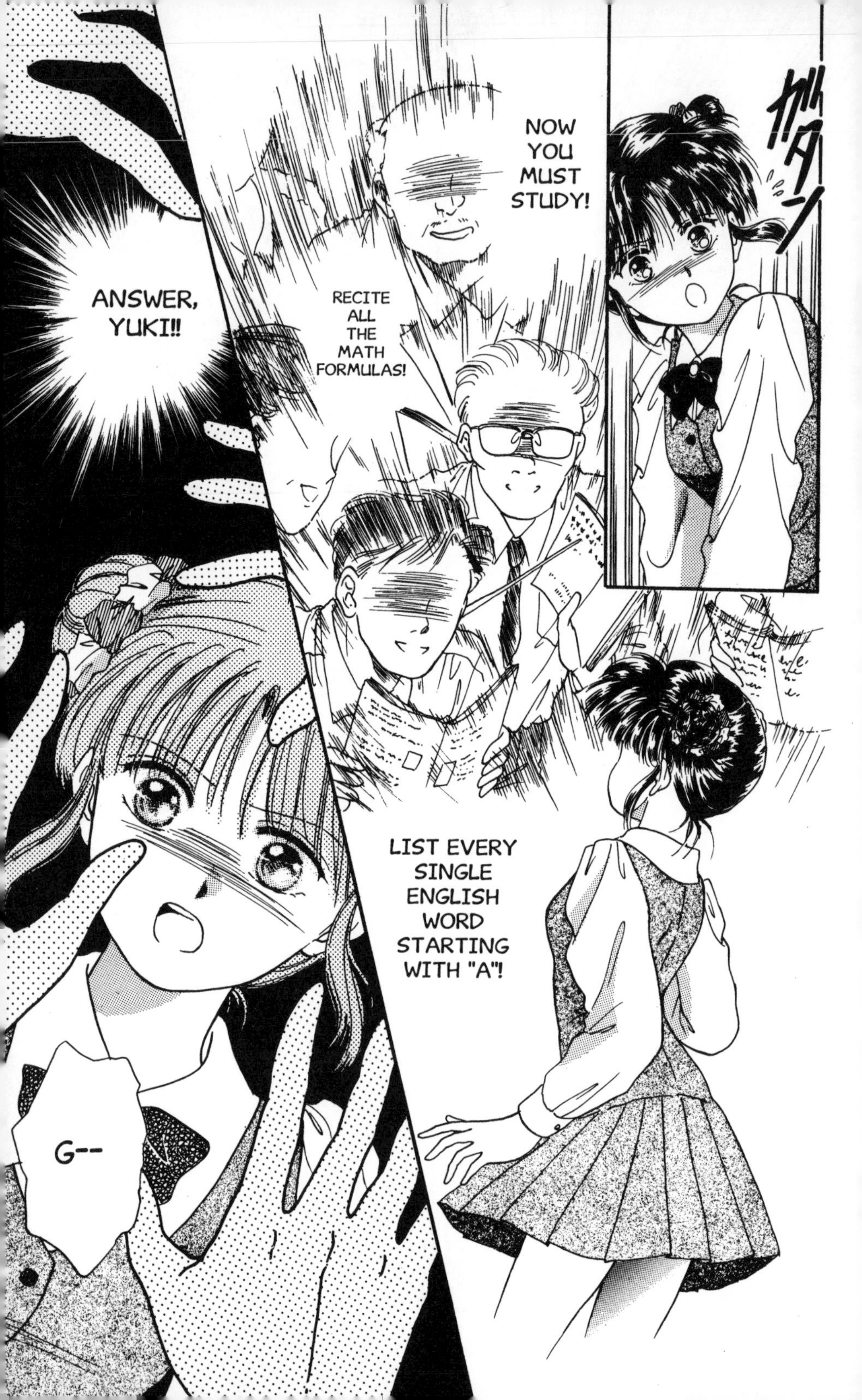
ガタン
NOW YOU MUST STUDY!
RECITE ALL THE MATH FORMULAS!
LIST EVERY SINGLE ENGLISH WORD STARTING WITH "A"!
ANSWER, YUKI!!
G--

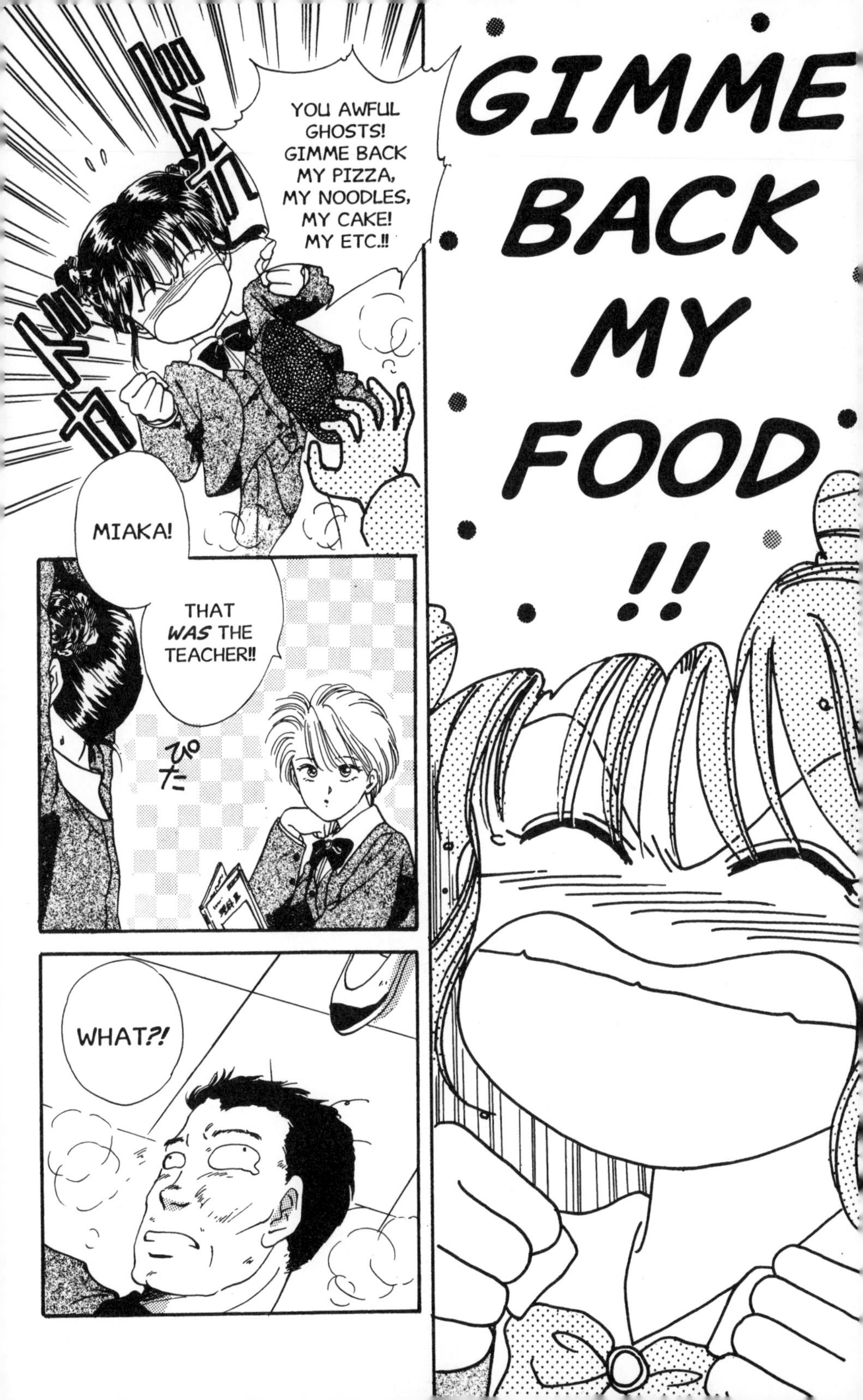
GIMME BACK MY FOOD!!
YOU AWFUL GHOSTS! GIMME BACK MY PIZZA, MY NOODLES, MY CAKE! MY ETC.!!
MIAKA!
THAT WAS THE TEACHER!!
WHAT?!

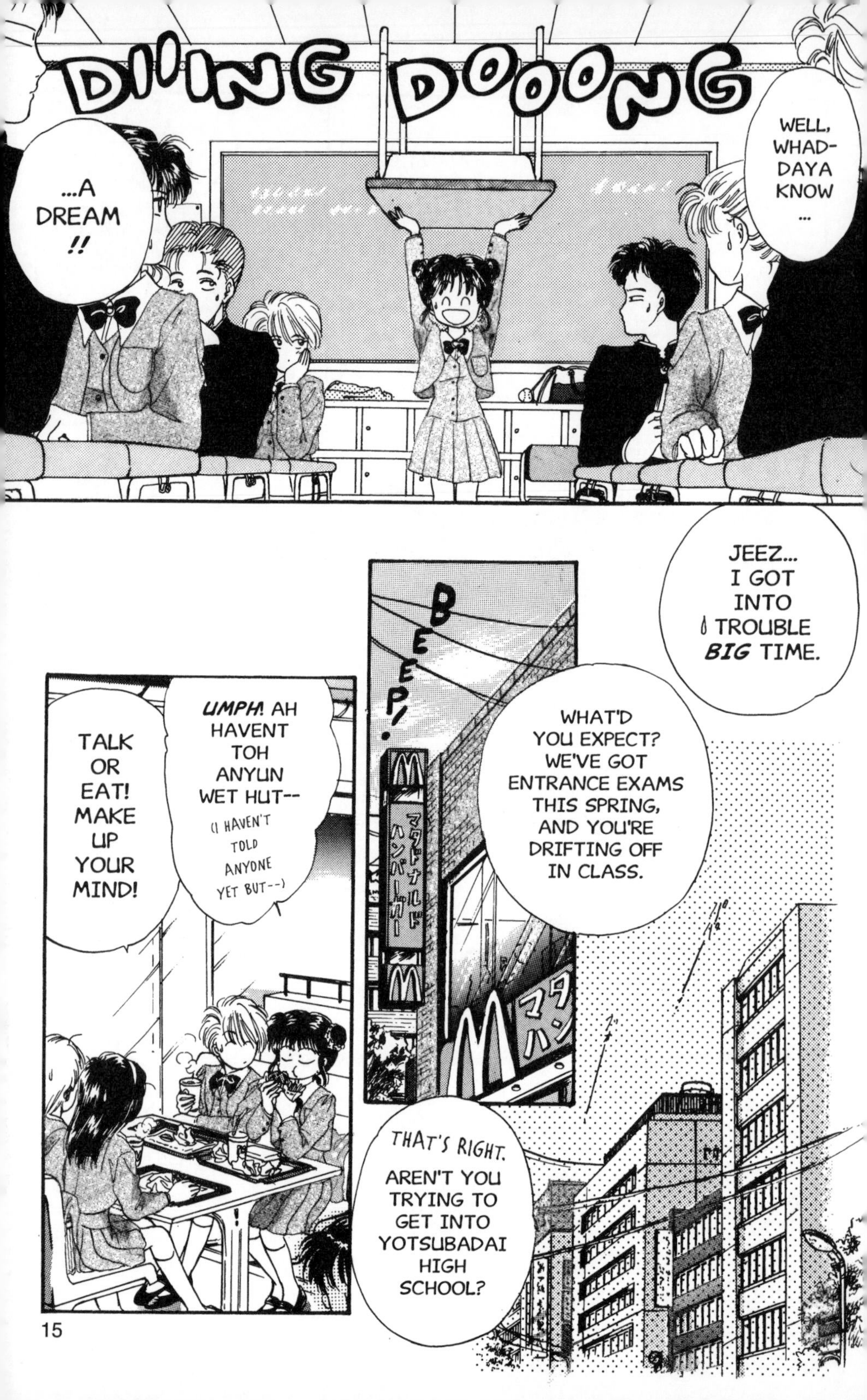
DIIING DOOOONG
WELL, WHAD-DAYA KNOW ...
...A DREAM !!
JEEZ... I GOT INTO TROUBLE BIG TIME.
WHAT'D YOU EXPECT? WE'VE GOT ENTRANCE EXAMS THIS SPRING, AND YOU'RE DRIFTING OFF IN CLASS.
THAT'S RIGHT. AREN'T YOU TRYING TO GET INTO YOTSUBADAI HIGH SCHOOL?
BEEP!
UMPH! AH HAVENT TOH ANYUN WET HUT--
(I HAVEN'T TOLD ANYONE YET BUT--)
TALK OR EAT! MAKE UP YOUR MIND!

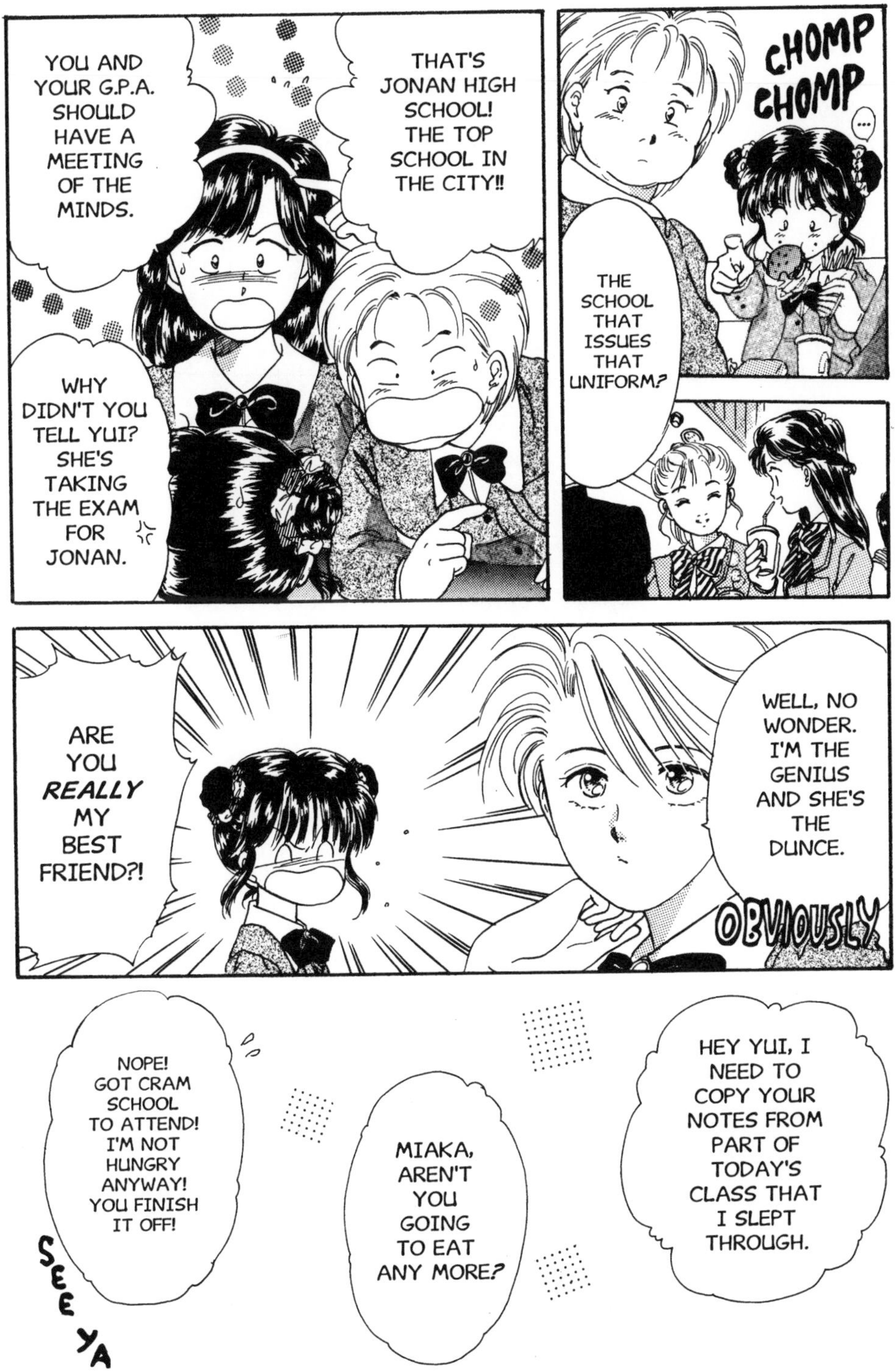
CHOMP CHOMP
...
THE SCHOOL THAT ISSUES THAT UNIFORM?
THAT'S JONAN HIGH SCHOOL! THE TOP SCHOOL IN THE CITY!!
YOU AND YOUR G.P.A. SHOULD HAVE A MEETING OF THE MINDS.
WHY DIDN'T YOU TELL YUI? SHE'S TAKING THE EXAM FOR JONAN.
WELL, NO WONDER. I'M THE GENIUS AND SHE'S THE DUNCE.
OBVIOUSLY
ARE YOU *REALLY* MY BEST FRIEND?!
HEY YUI, I NEED TO COPY YOUR NOTES FROM PART OF TODAY'S CLASS THAT I SLEPT THROUGH.
MIAKA, AREN'T YOU GOING TO EAT ANY MORE?
NOPE! GOT CRAM SCHOOL TO ATTEND! I'M NOT HUNGRY ANYWAY! YOU FINISH IT OFF!
SEE YA

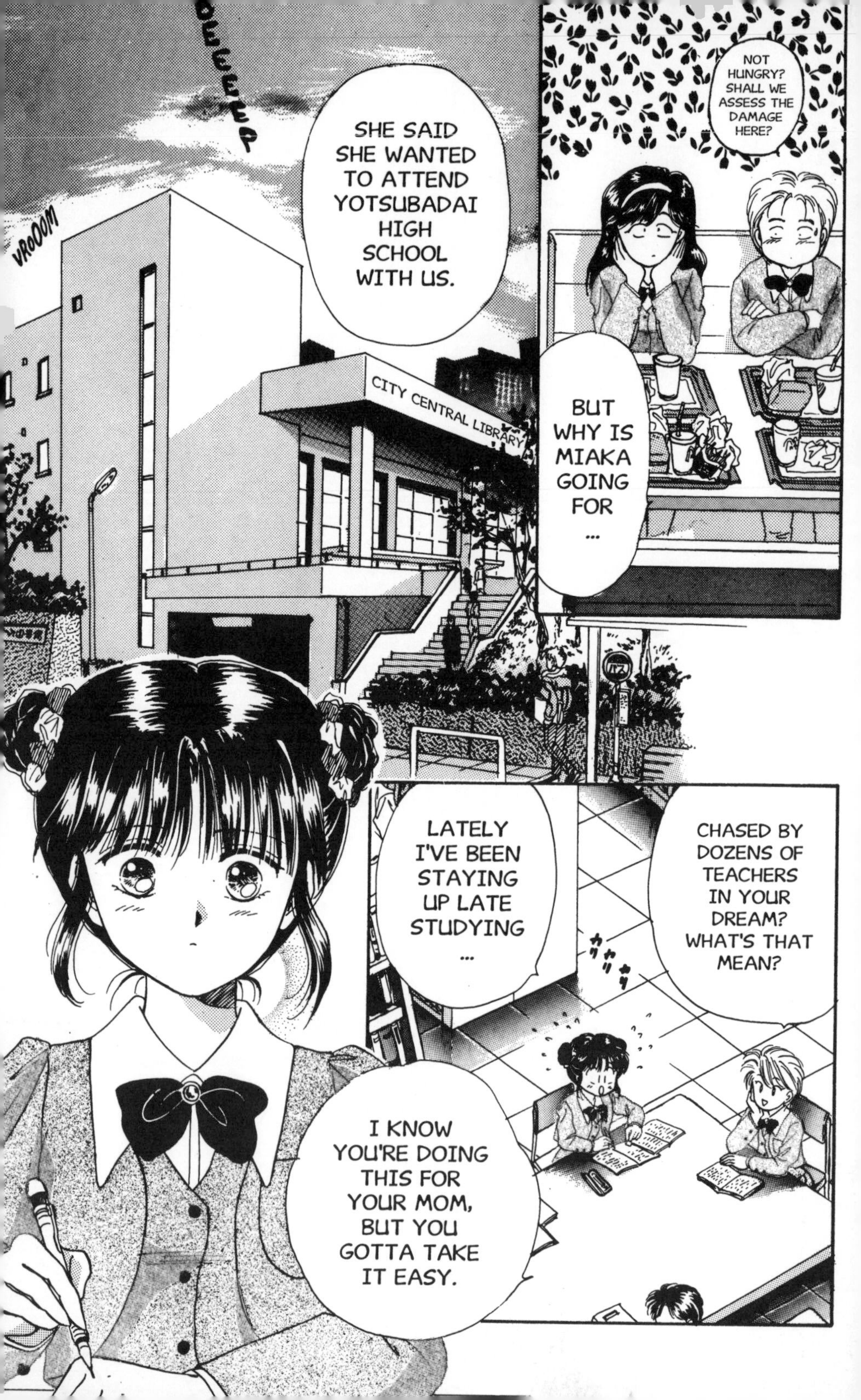
NOT HUNGRY? SHALL WE ASSESS THE DAMAGE HERE?
BUT WHY IS MIAKA GOING FOR ...
SHE SAID SHE WANTED TO ATTEND YOTSUBADAI HIGH SCHOOL WITH US.
BEEEEEP
VROOOM
CITY CENTRAL LIBRARY
CHASED BY DOZENS OF TEACHERS IN YOUR DREAM? WHAT'S THAT MEAN?
LATELY I'VE BEEN STAYING UP LATE STUDYING ...
I KNOW YOU'RE DOING THIS FOR YOUR MOM, BUT YOU GOTTA TAKE IT EASY.

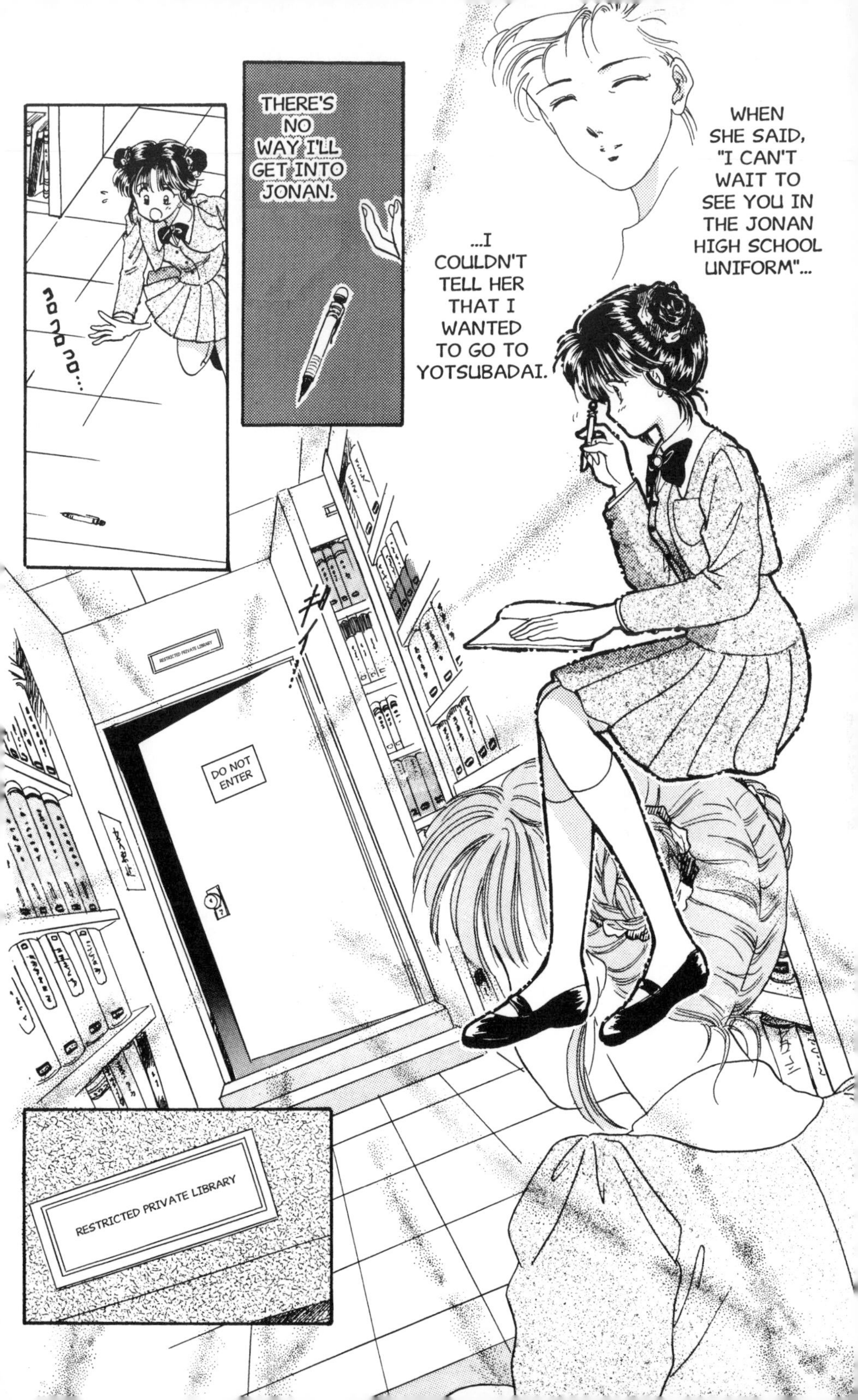
WHEN SHE SAID, "I CAN'T WAIT TO SEE YOU IN THE JONAN HIGH SCHOOL UNIFORM"...
...I COULDN'T TELL HER THAT I WANTED TO GO TO YOTSUBADAI.
THERE'S NO WAY I'LL GET INTO JONAN.
RESTRICTED PRIVATE LIBRARY
DO NOT ENTER
RESTRICTED PRIVATE LIBRARY

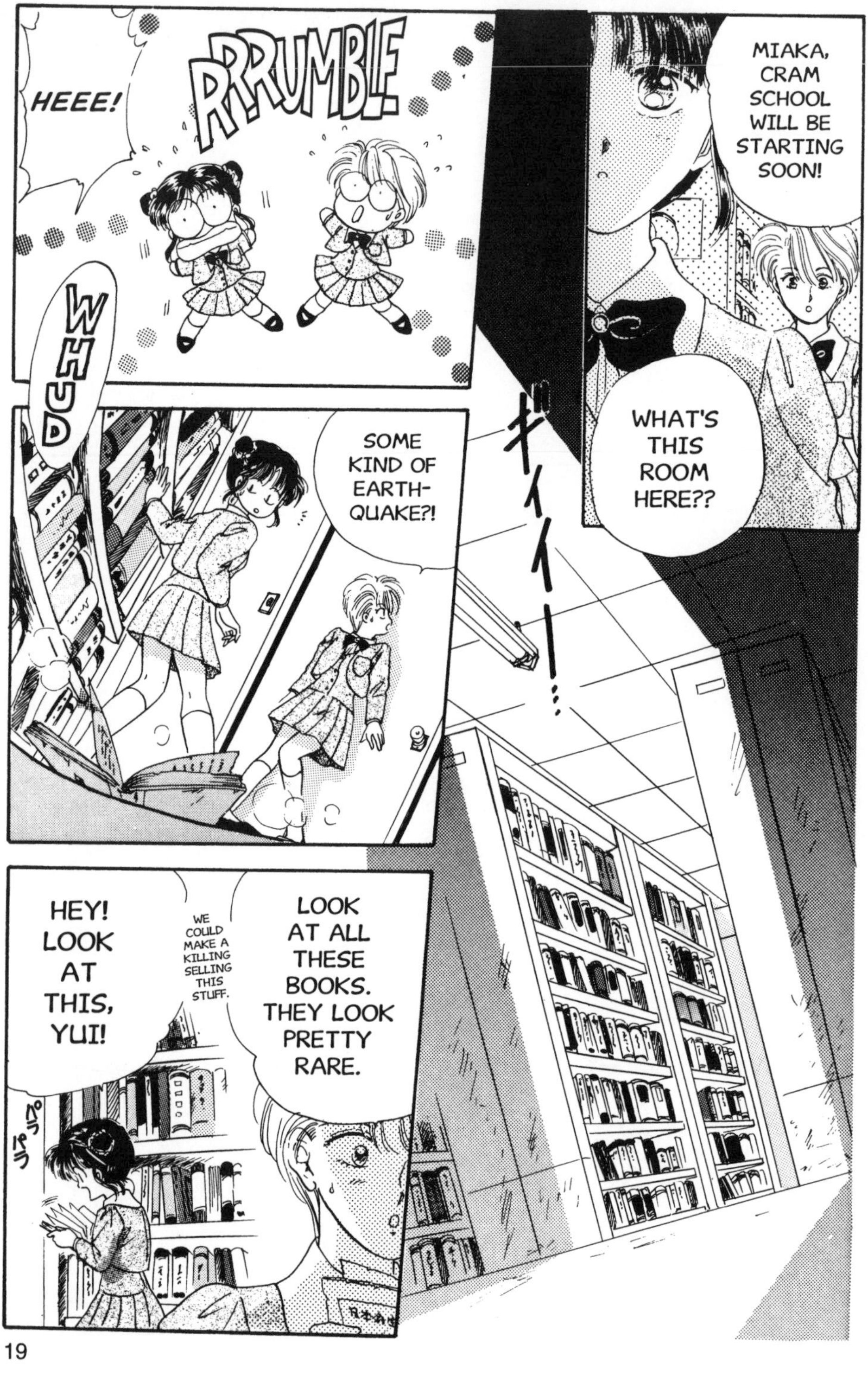
MIAKA, CRAM SCHOOL WILL BE STARTING SOON!
WHAT'S THIS ROOM HERE??
HEEE!
RRRUMBLE
WHUD
ギイイー…
SOME KIND OF EARTHQUAKE?!
LOOK AT ALL THESE BOOKS. THEY LOOK PRETTY RARE.
WE COULD MAKE A KILLING SELLING THIS STUFF.
HEY! LOOK AT THIS, YUI!

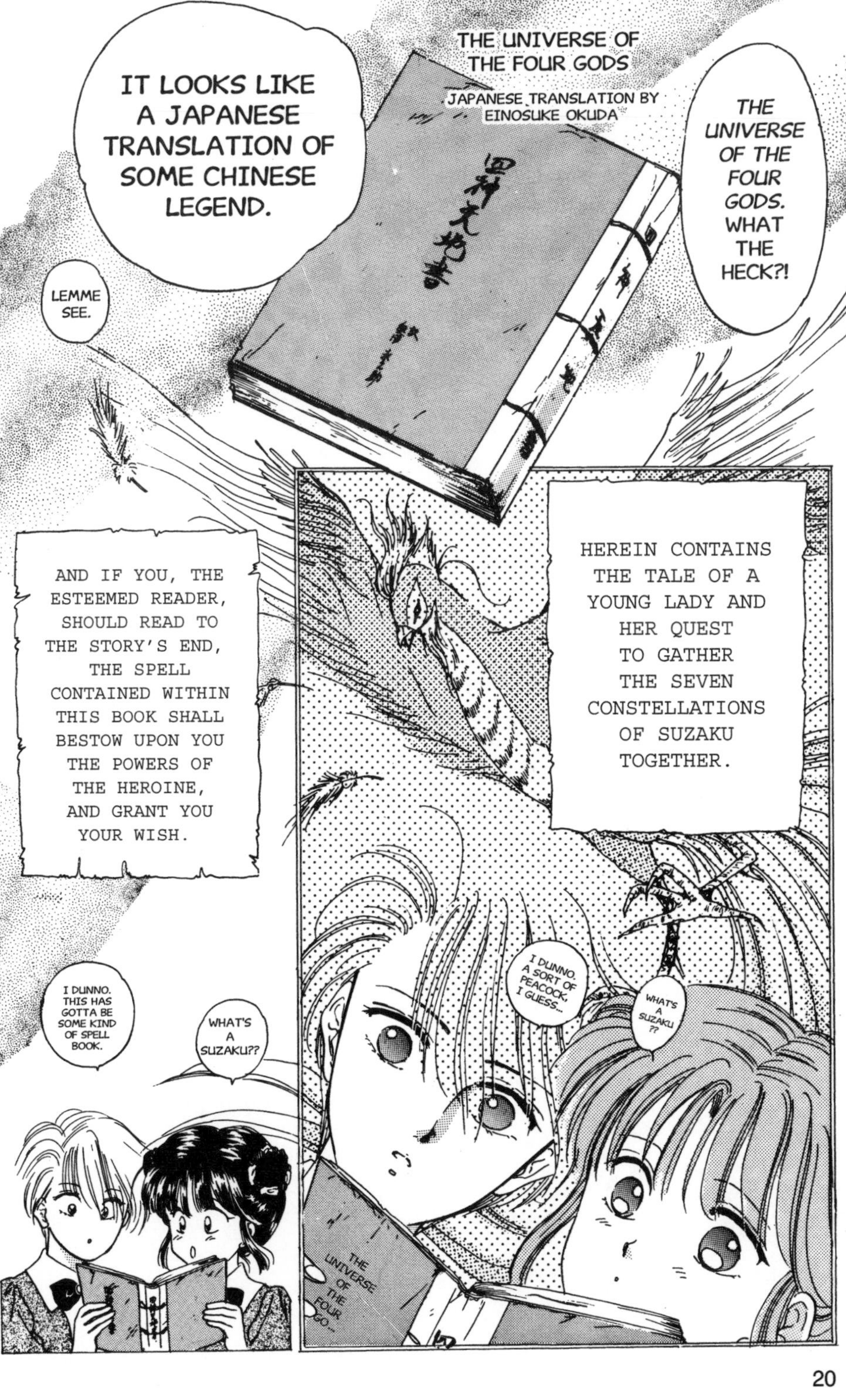
THE UNIVERSE OF THE FOUR GODS. WHAT THE HECK?!
THE UNIVERSE OF THE FOUR GODS
JAPANESE TRANSLATION BY EINOSUKE OKUDA
IT LOOKS LIKE A JAPANESE TRANSLATION OF SOME CHINESE LEGEND.
LEMME SEE.
HEREIN CONTAINS THE TALE OF A YOUNG LADY AND HER QUEST TO GATHER THE SEVEN CONSTELLATIONS OF SUZAKU TOGETHER.
AND IF YOU, THE ESTEEMED READER, SHOULD READ TO THE STORY'S END, THE SPELL CONTAINED WITHIN THIS BOOK SHALL BESTOW UPON YOU THE POWERS OF THE HEROINE, AND GRANT YOU YOUR WISH.
WHAT'S SUZAKU??
I DUNNO. A SORT OF PEACOCK, I GUESS...
THE UNIVERSE OF THE FOUR GO...
WHAT'S A SUZAKU??
I DUNNO. THIS HAS GOTTA BE SOME KIND OF SPELL BOOK.

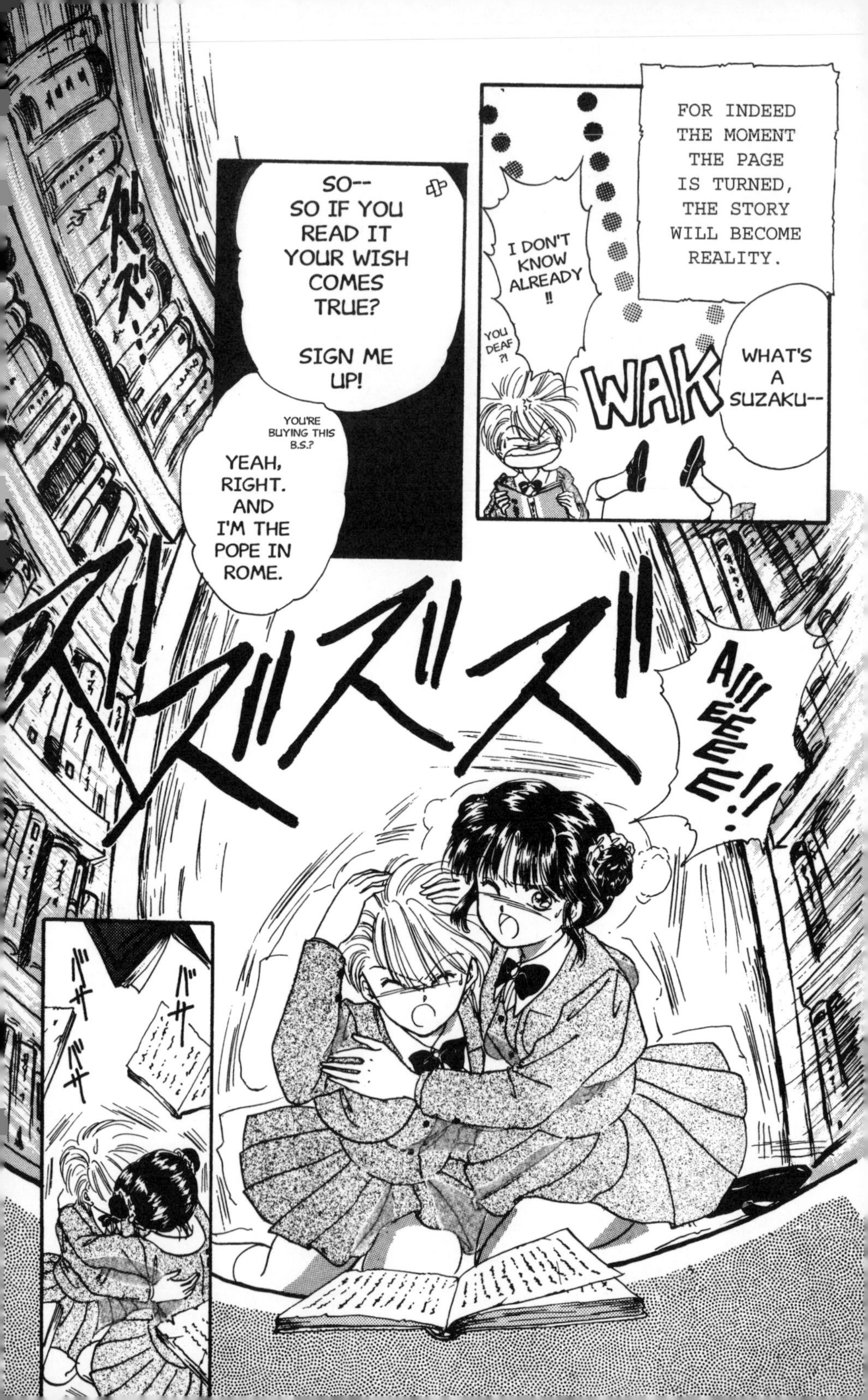
FOR INDEED THE MOMENT THE PAGE IS TURNED, THE STORY WILL BECOME REALITY.
WHAT'S A SUZAKU--
WAK
I DON'T KNOW ALREADY!!
YOU DEAF?!
SO-- SO IF YOU READ IT YOUR WISH COMES TRUE? SIGN ME UP!
YOU'RE BUYING THIS B.S.?
YEAH, RIGHT. AND I'M THE POPE IN ROME.
AIIIEEEE!!

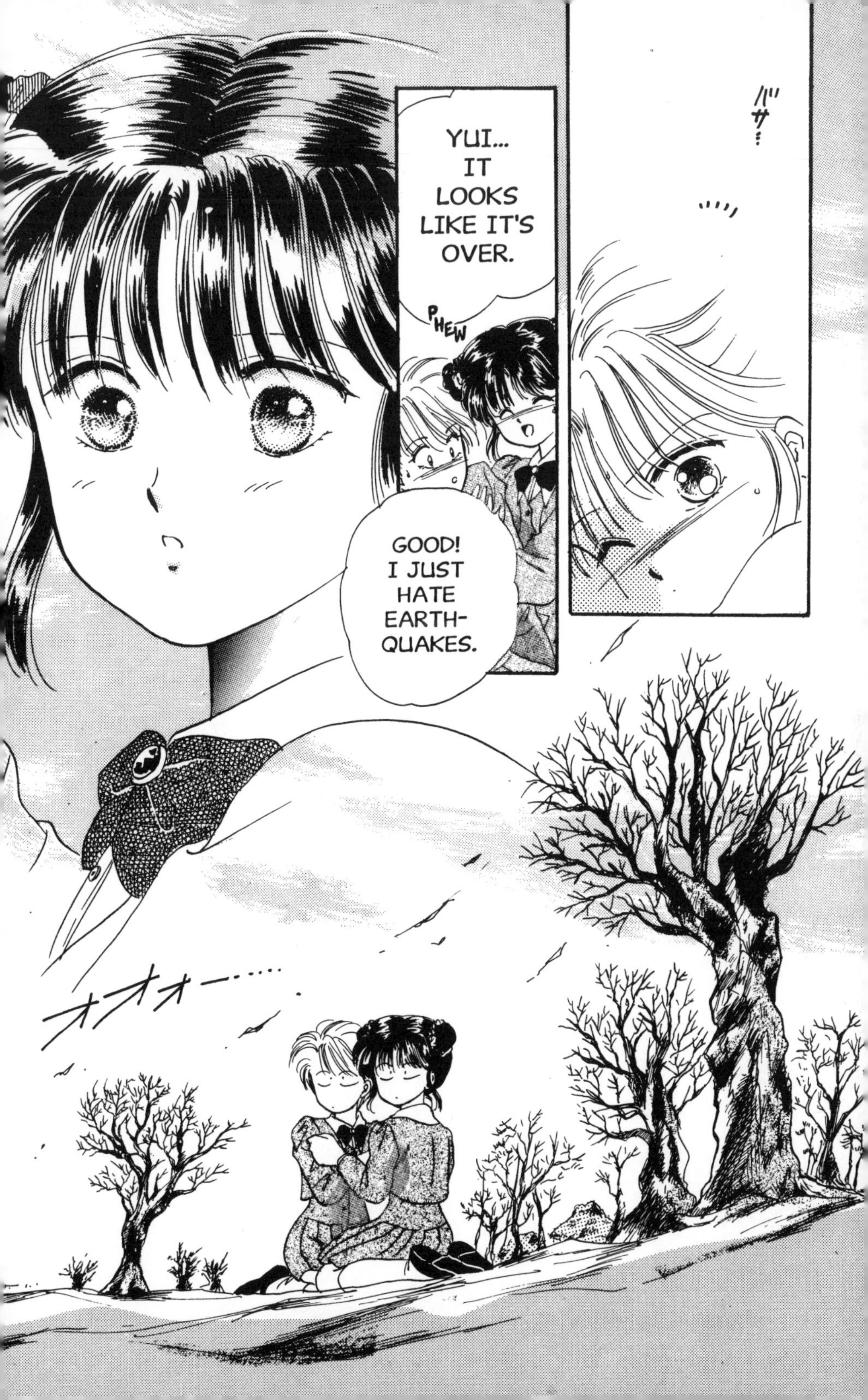
バサ
YUI... IT LOOKS LIKE IT'S OVER.
PHEW
GOOD! I JUST HATE EARTHQUAKES.
オオオー.....

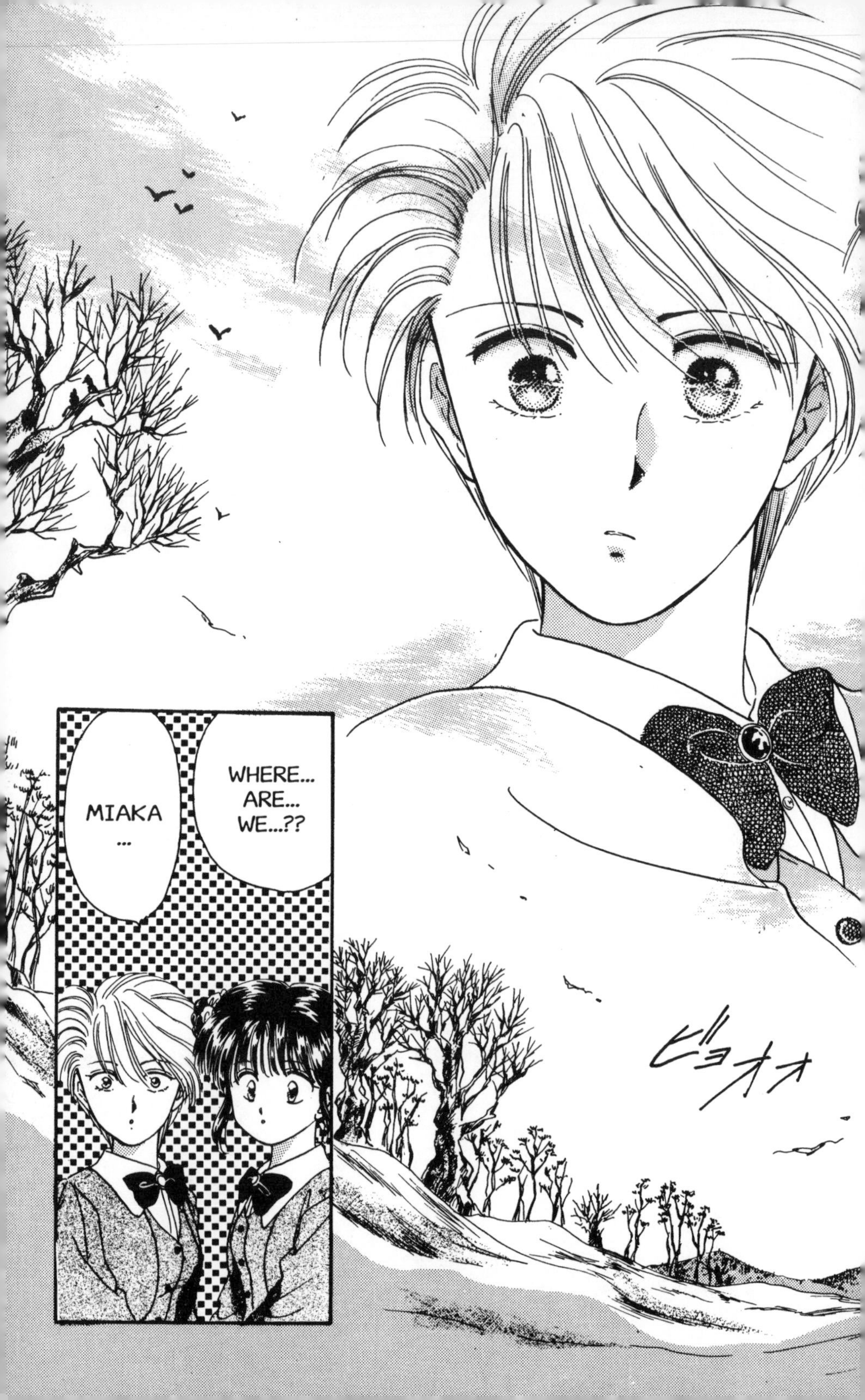
WHERE... ARE... WE...??
MIAKA ...
ビョオオ

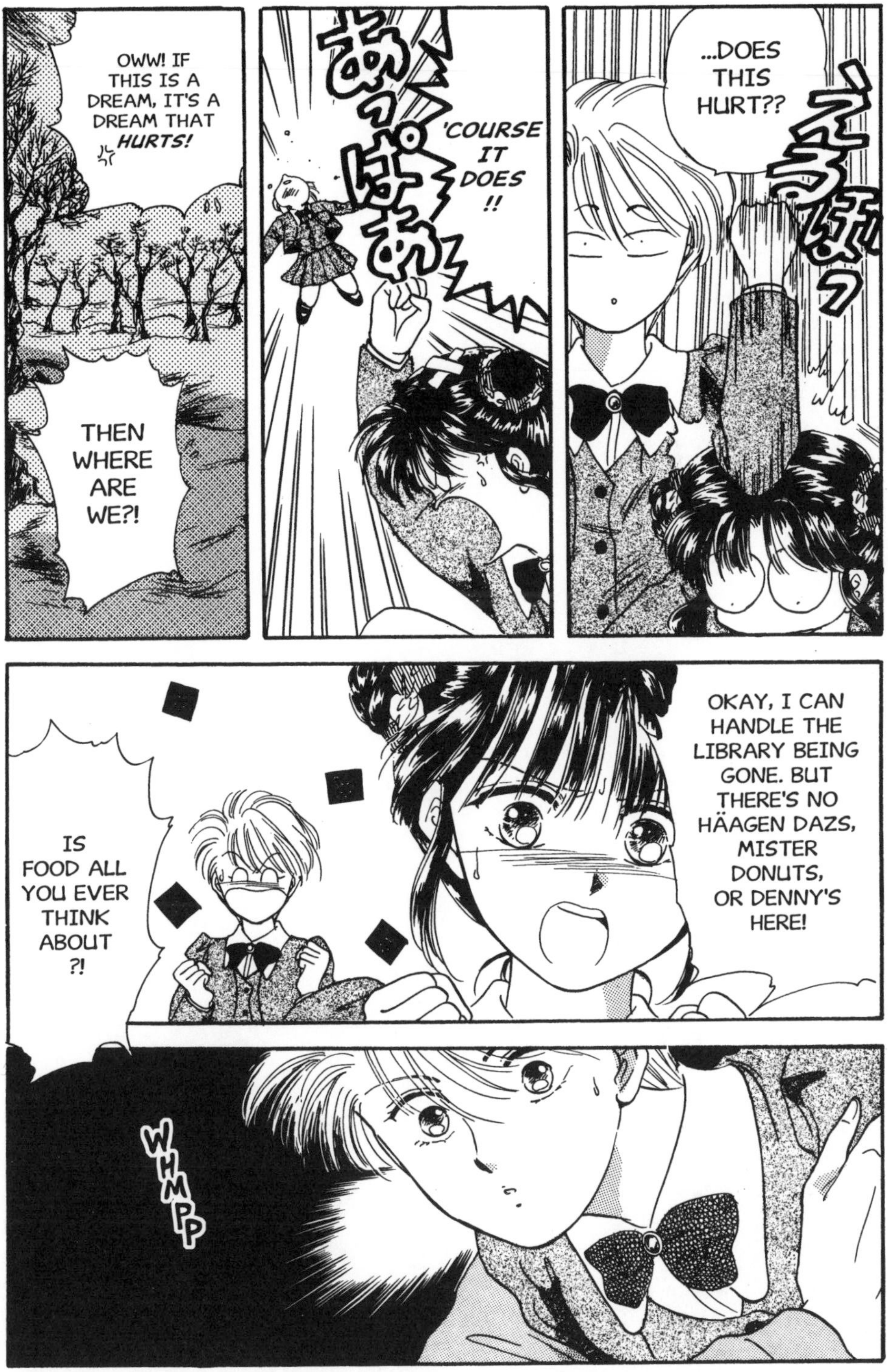
...DOES THIS HURT??
'COURSE IT DOES !!
OWW! IF THIS IS A DREAM, IT'S A DREAM THAT HURTS!
THEN WHERE ARE WE?!
OKAY, I CAN HANDLE THE LIBRARY BEING GONE. BUT THERE'S NO HÄAGEN DAZS, MISTER DONUTS, OR DENNY'S HERE!
IS FOOD ALL YOU EVER THINK ABOUT ?!
WHMPP

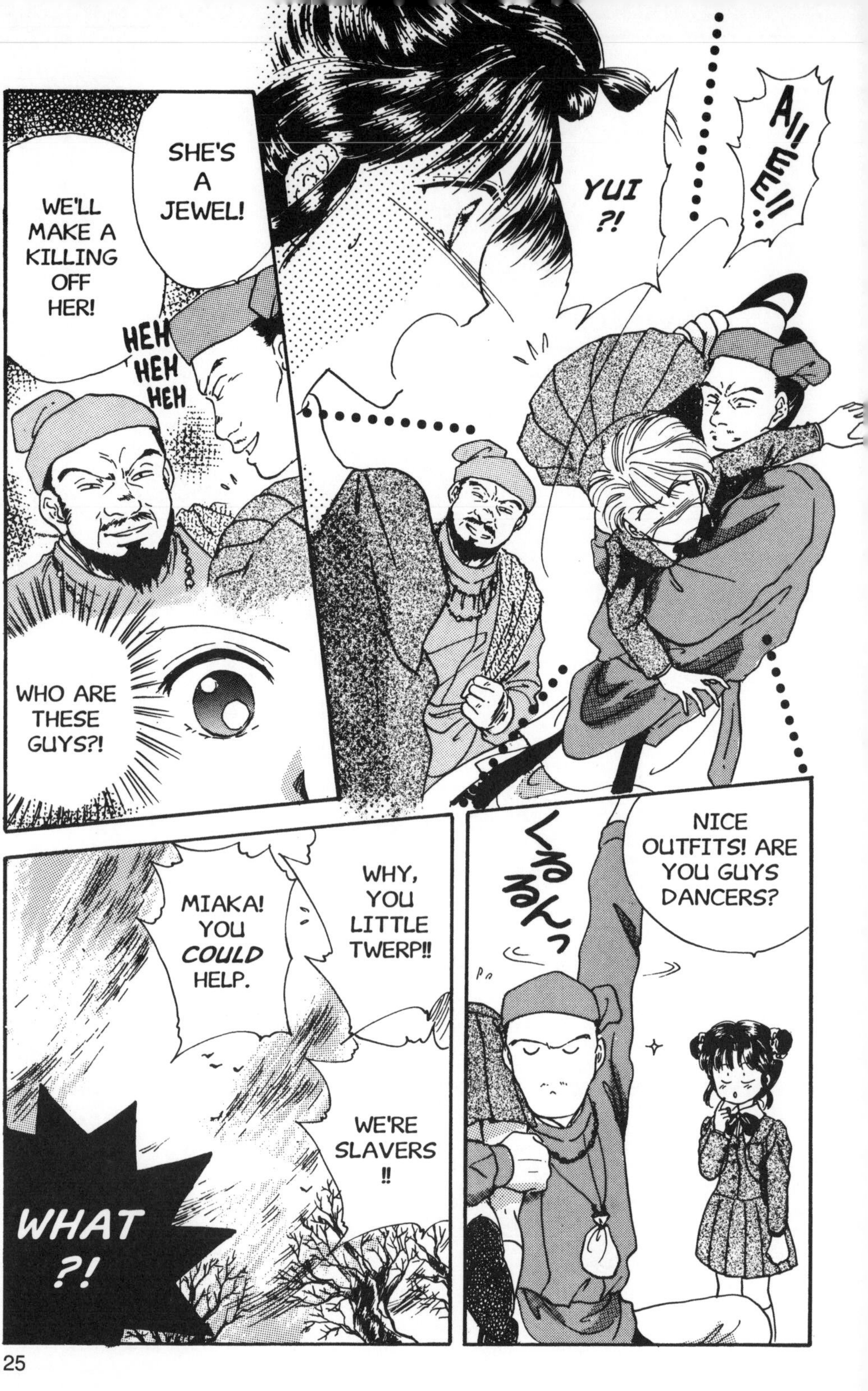
AIIEE!!
YUI?!
SHE'S A JEWEL!
WE'LL MAKE A KILLING OFF HER!
HEH HEH HEH
WHO ARE THESE GUYS?!
くるるんっ
NICE OUTFITS! ARE YOU GUYS DANCERS?
WHY, YOU LITTLE TWERP!!
MIAKA! YOU *COULD* HELP.
WE'RE SLAVERS!!
WHAT?!

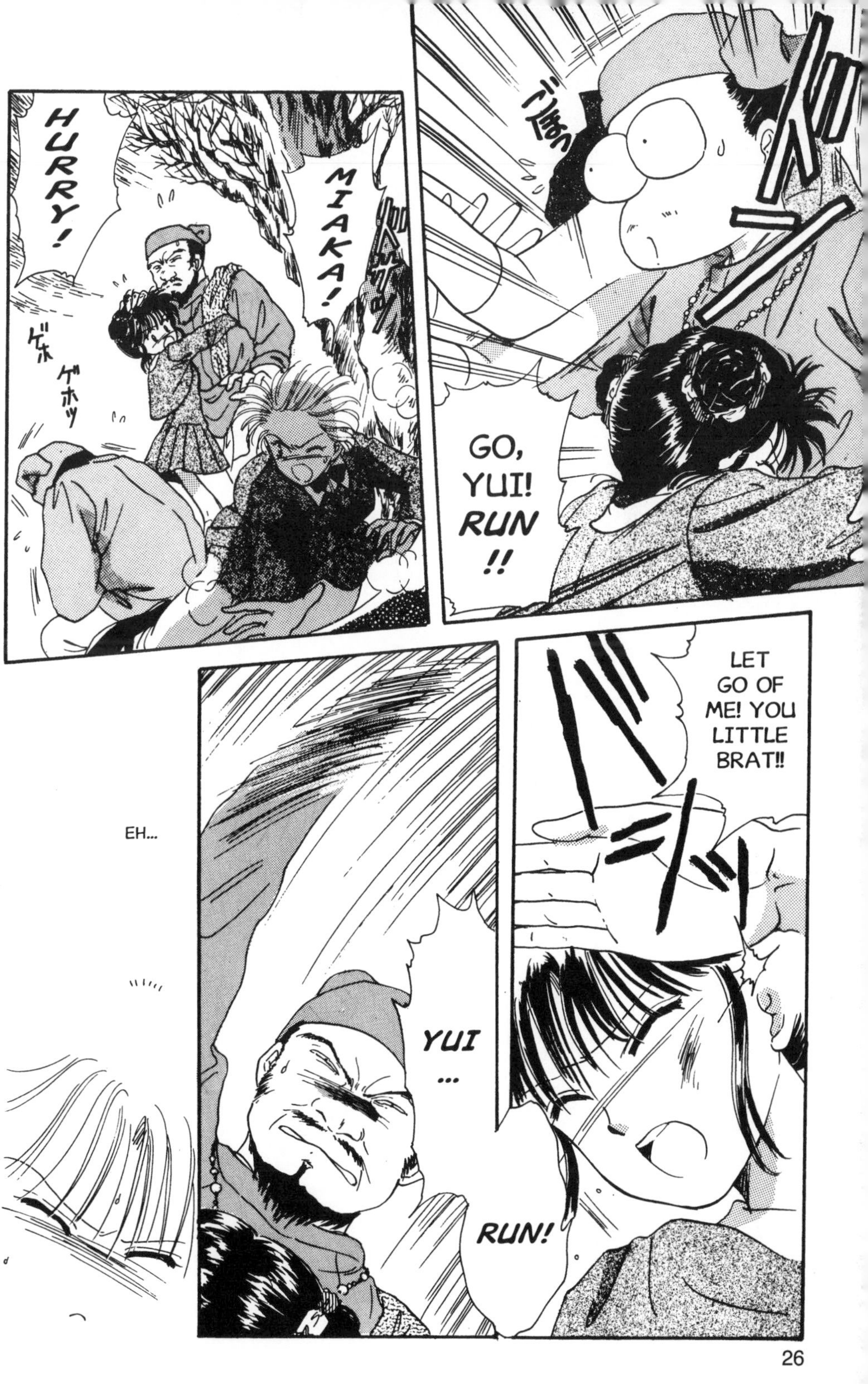
ごほっ
GO, YUI! RUN!!
MIAKA!
HURRY!
ゲホ
ゲホッ
LET GO OF ME! YOU LITTLE BRAT!!
YUI...
RUN!
EH...

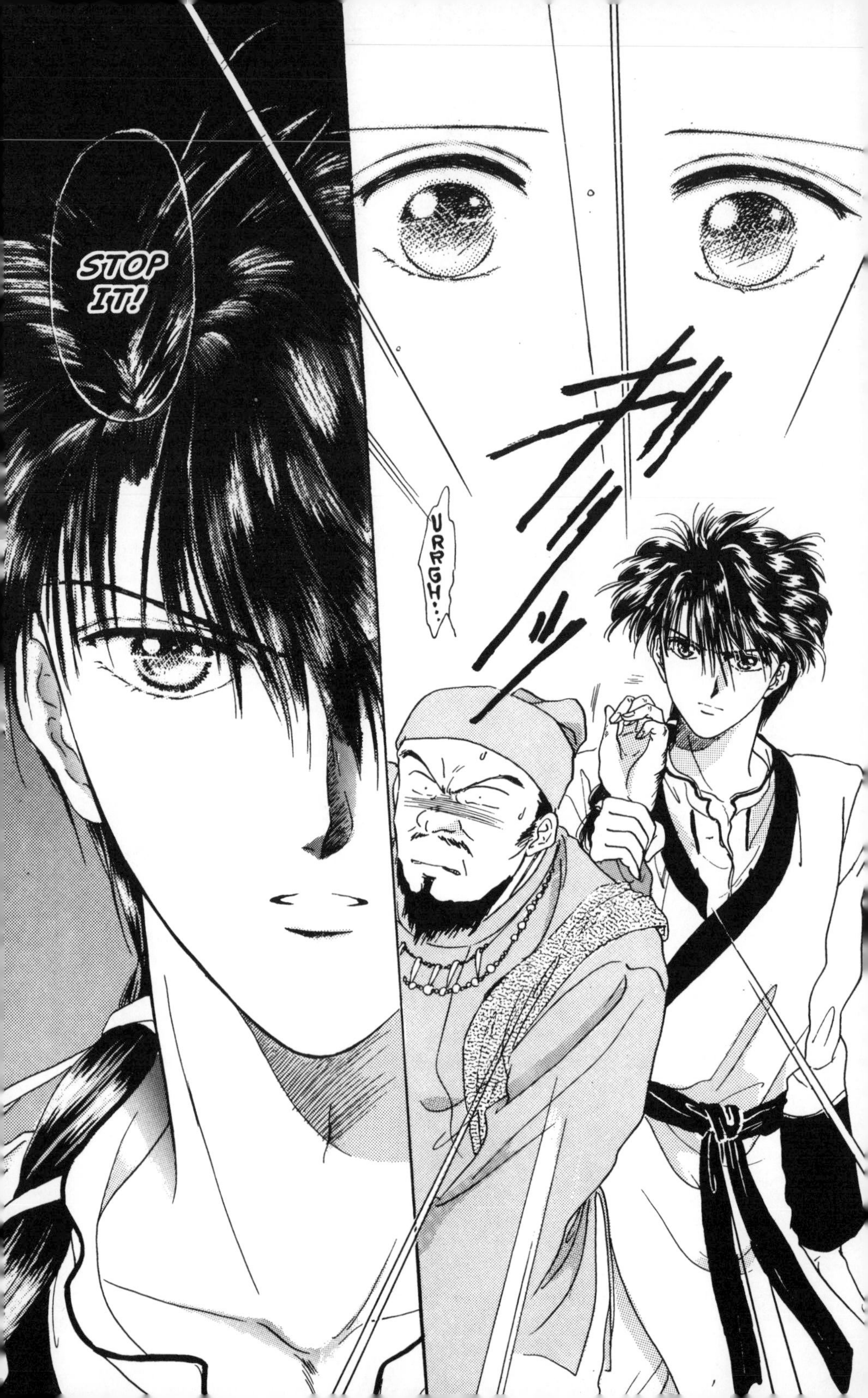
URRGH...
STOP IT!

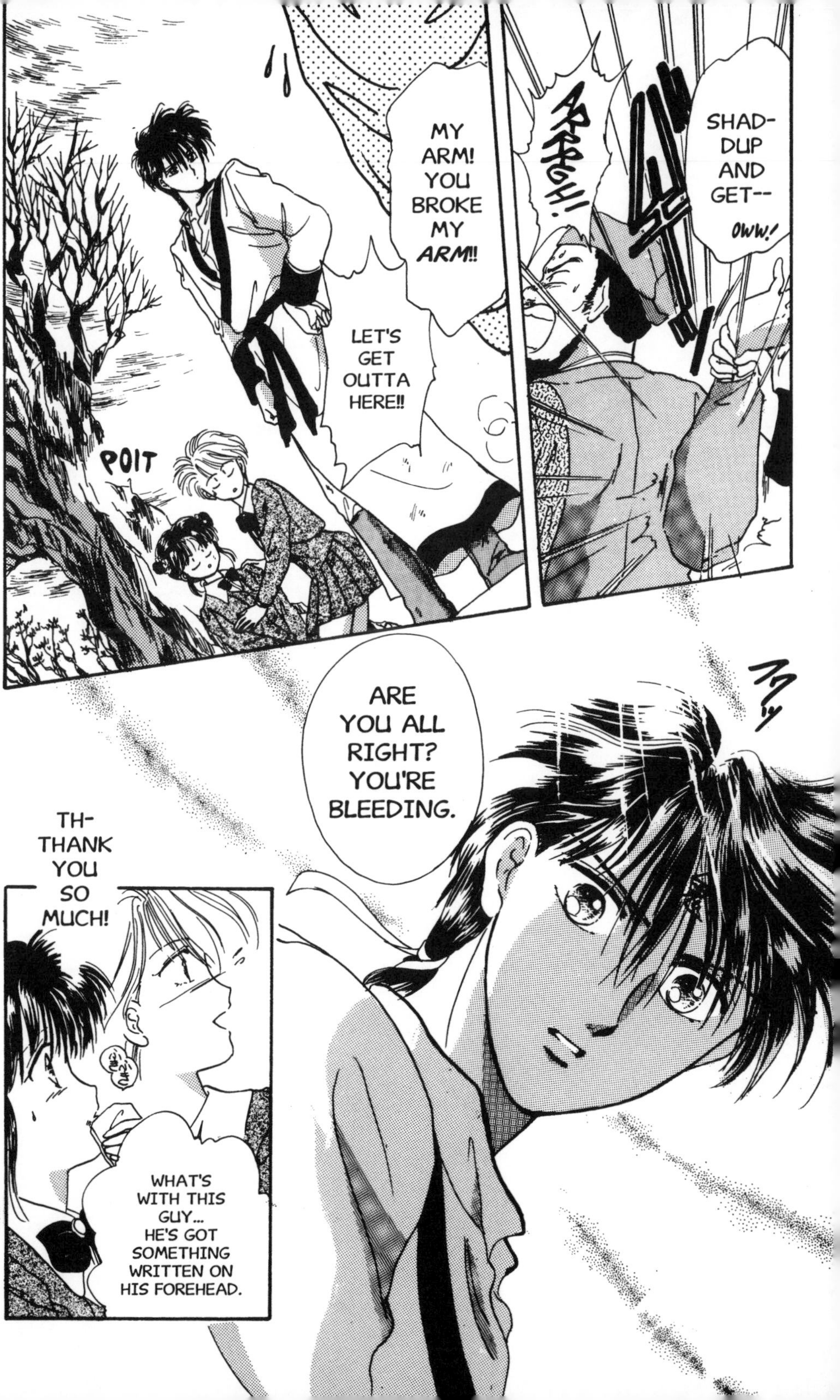
SHAD-DUP AND GET-- OWW!
MY ARM! YOU BROKE MY ARM!!
LET'S GET OUTTA HERE!!
POIT
ARE YOU ALL RIGHT? YOU'RE BLEEDING.
TH-THANK YOU SO MUCH!
WHAT'S WITH THIS GUY... HE'S GOT SOMETHING WRITTEN ON HIS FOREHEAD.

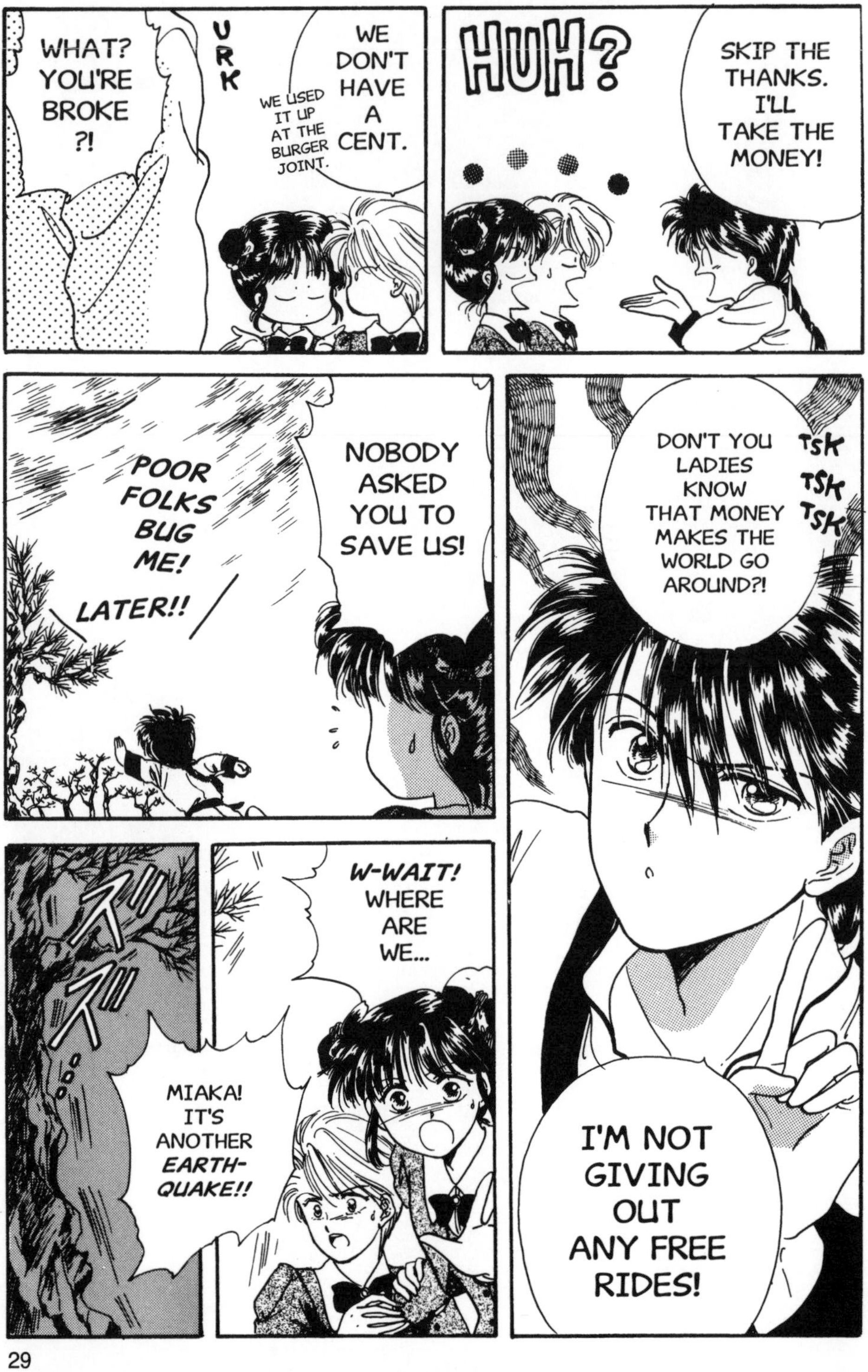
SKIP THE THANKS. I'LL TAKE THE MONEY!
HUH?
WE DON'T HAVE A CENT.
WE USED IT UP AT THE BURGER JOINT.
URK
WHAT? YOU'RE BROKE?!
DON'T YOU LADIES KNOW THAT MONEY MAKES THE WORLD GO AROUND?!
TSK TSK TSK
I'M NOT GIVING OUT ANY FREE RIDES!
NOBODY ASKED YOU TO SAVE US!
POOR FOLKS BUG ME!
LATER!!
W-WAIT! WHERE ARE WE...
MIAKA! IT'S ANOTHER EARTHQUAKE!!
ズズズ

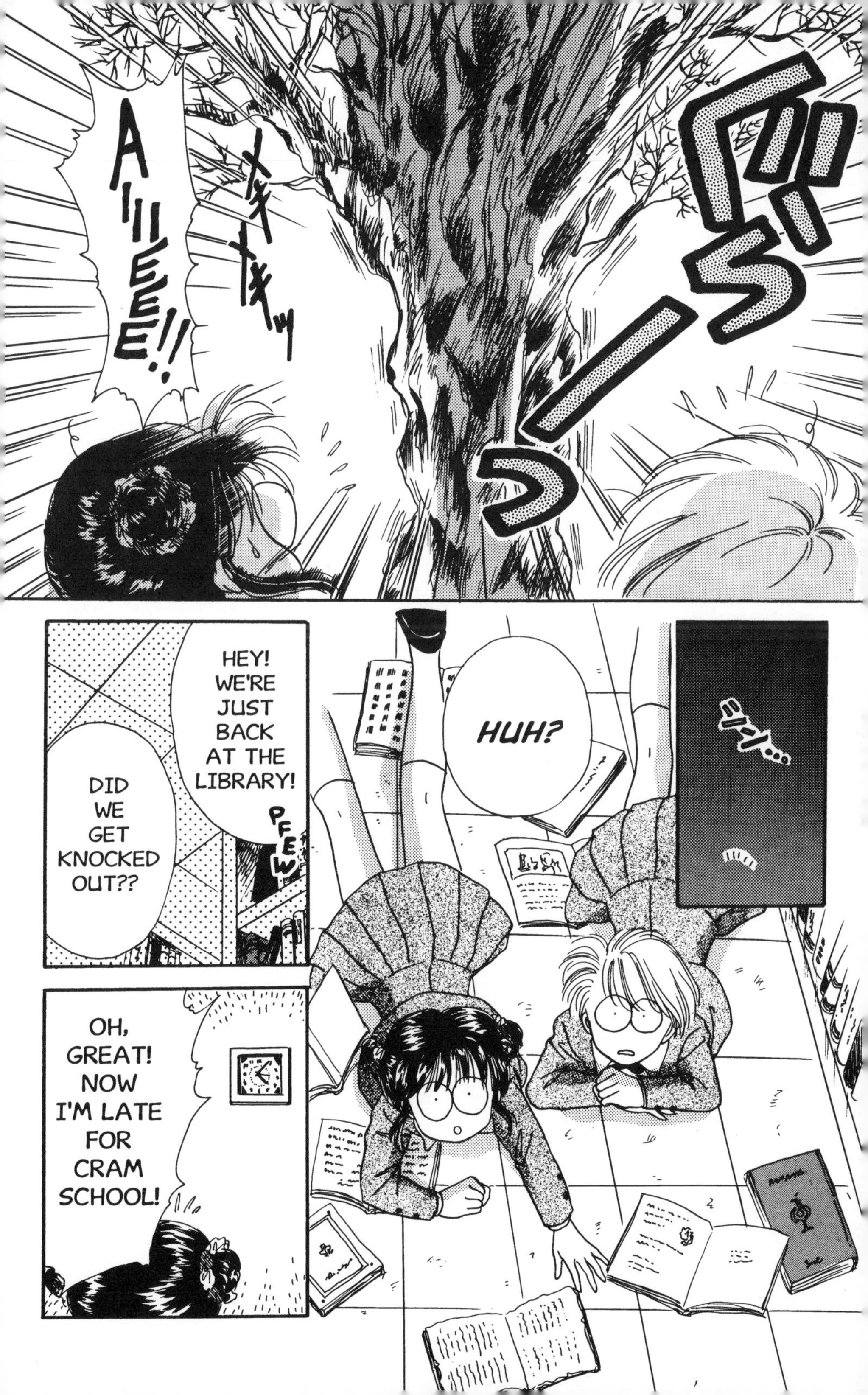
AIIIEEEE!!
HUH?
HEY! WE'RE JUST BACK AT THE LIBRARY!
DID WE GET KNOCKED OUT??
PFEW
OH, GREAT! NOW I'M LATE FOR CRAM SCHOOL!

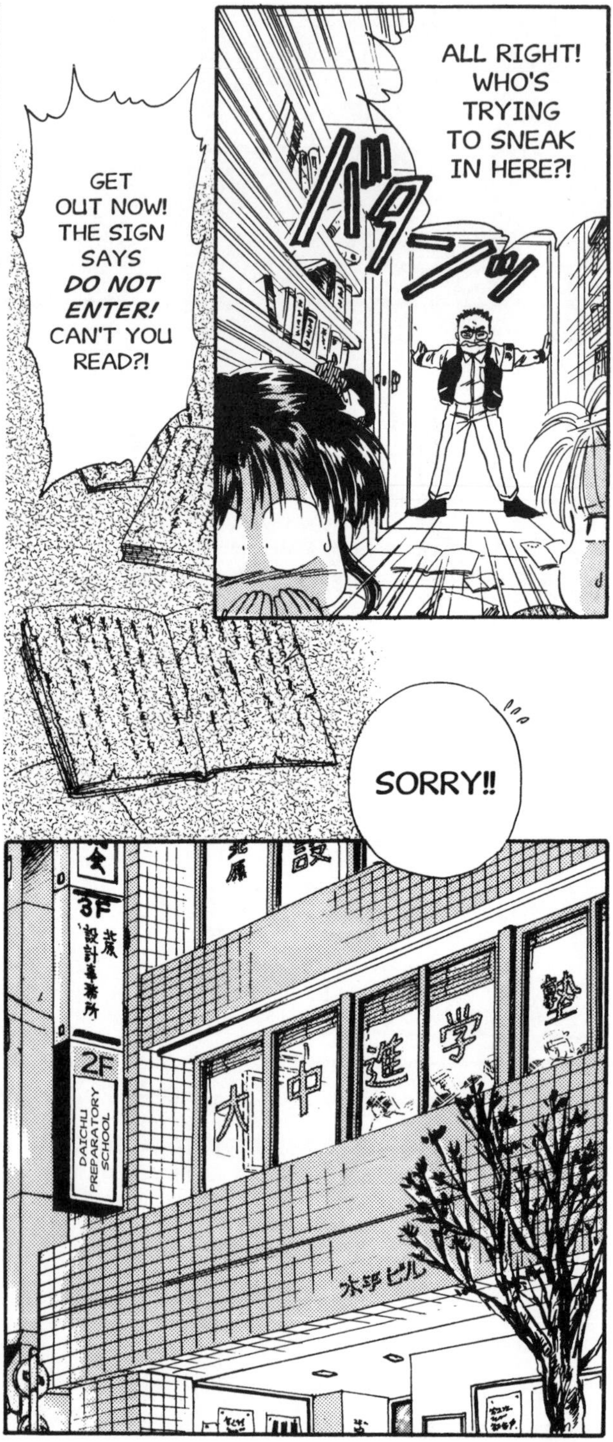
ALL RIGHT! WHO'S TRYING TO SNEAK IN HERE?!
GET OUT NOW! THE SIGN SAYS *DO NOT ENTER!* CAN'T YOU READ?!
SORRY!!
3F
2F
DAICHU PREPARATORY SCHOOL

Hello. It's me, Watase, and I'll be using this space to chat a little. I know, I know. You're complaining about my bad handwriting, sorry but I just scribble stuff down.

I don't like writing by hand. But since my writing is difficult enough to read I've decided to take some pains to write more legibly. Yeah right.

Now let's see, *Fushigi Yûgi*... when I was eighteen, before I got published, I looked up this incredibly thick *Buddhist Philosophy Encyclopedia* and was delighted to find how the character for "Oni" was read as "Tamahome." I discovered that "when the light of the Tamahome star in Suzaku's seven southern star constellations (out of a total of 28 constellations) fades, it is a sign of a bad harvest." As I came across this information, I came up with the idea for this story. I thought up the characters of Tamahome 鬼宿, and Hotohori 星宿, but Miaka still wasn't part of the picture. (I wanted to use the character for star rather than constellation which would make Tamahome 鬼星 (pronounced Kisei) but that would have made Hotohori 星星 (pronounced Seisei) so I decided against it). I submitted the FY story idea along with my *Shishunki Miman Okotowari* (No Interest in Prepubescence) idea. *Shishunki* was accepted instead of FY.

Although I've done my share of research on China for this story, it's still not a Chinese story. FY departs significantly from some basic historical facts. So please don't read it as if it were Chinese history. Who would? (For example, the emperor calls himself "Chin" so I decided against him using his real name.) I just want to let you know that I haven't been delinquent in my research. I read through 10 books before I began working on this series. If there are any discrepancies, they're being made with my knowledge.

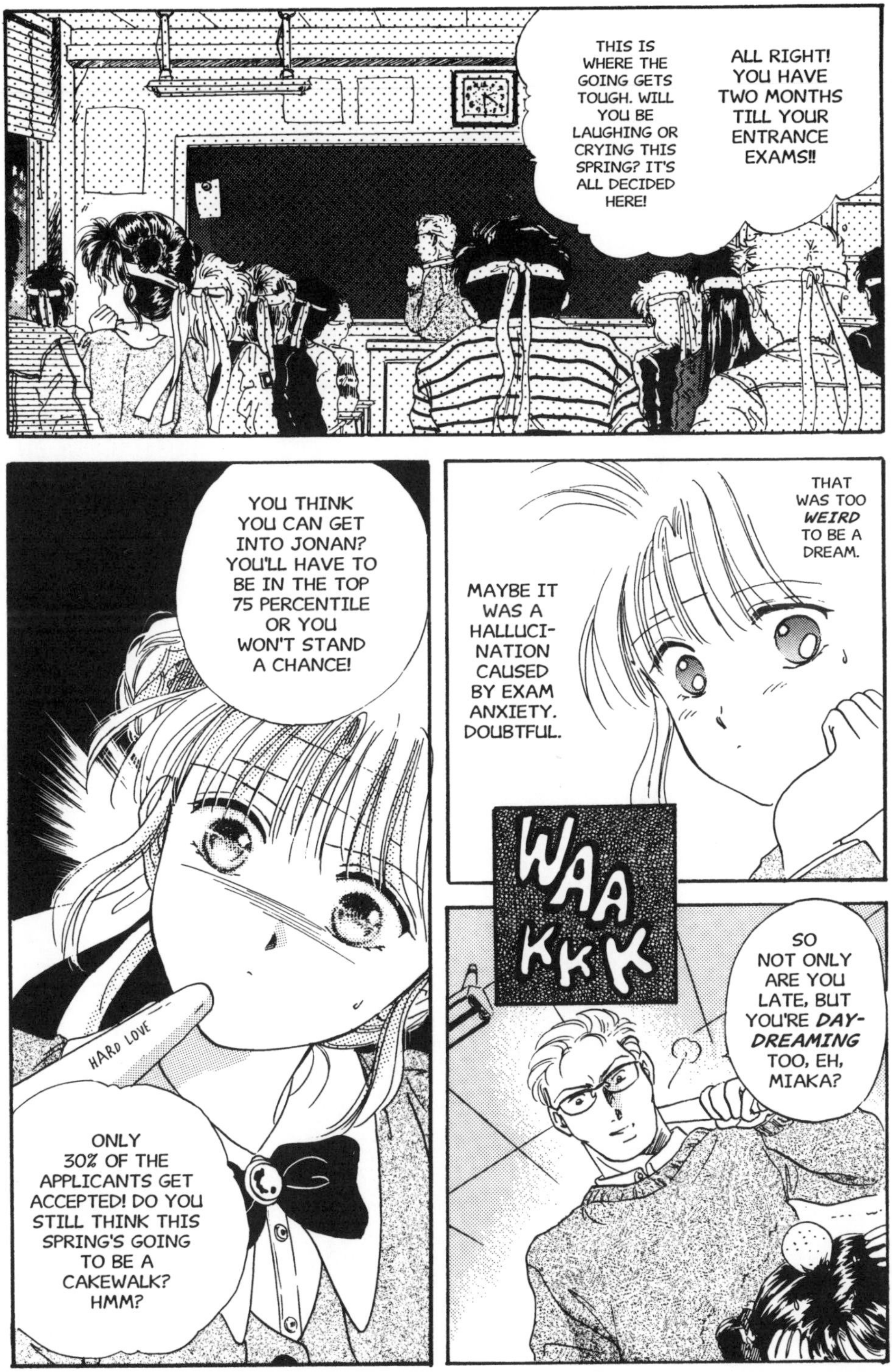
ALL RIGHT! YOU HAVE TWO MONTHS TILL YOUR ENTRANCE EXAMS!!
THIS IS WHERE THE GOING GETS TOUGH. WILL YOU BE LAUGHING OR CRYING THIS SPRING? IT'S ALL DECIDED HERE!
THAT WAS TOO *WEIRD* TO BE A DREAM.
MAYBE IT WAS A HALLUCI-NATION CAUSED BY EXAM ANXIETY. DOUBTFUL.
WAAKKK
SO NOT ONLY ARE YOU LATE, BUT YOU'RE *DAY-DREAMING* TOO, EH, MIAKA?
YOU THINK YOU CAN GET INTO JONAN? YOU'LL HAVE TO BE IN THE TOP 75 PERCENTILE OR YOU WON'T STAND A CHANCE!
HARD LOVE
ONLY 30% OF THE APPLICANTS GET ACCEPTED! DO YOU STILL THINK THIS SPRING'S GOING TO BE A CAKEWALK? HMM?

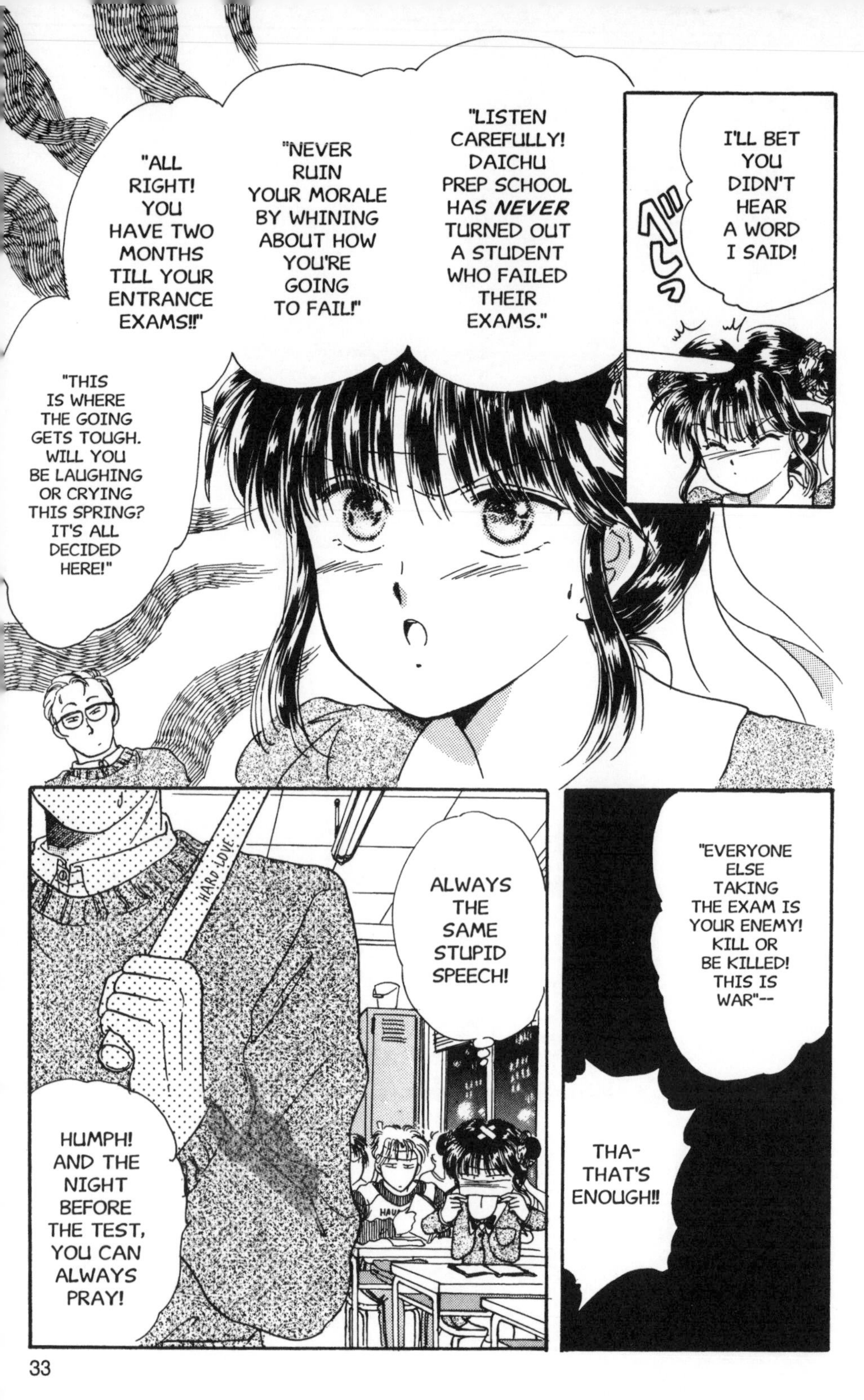
I'LL BET YOU DIDN'T HEAR A WORD I SAID!
"LISTEN CAREFULLY! DAICHU PREP SCHOOL HAS NEVER TURNED OUT A STUDENT WHO FAILED THEIR EXAMS."
"NEVER RUIN YOUR MORALE BY WHINING ABOUT HOW YOU'RE GOING TO FAIL!"
"ALL RIGHT! YOU HAVE TWO MONTHS TILL YOUR ENTRANCE EXAMS!!"
"THIS IS WHERE THE GOING GETS TOUGH. WILL YOU BE LAUGHING OR CRYING THIS SPRING? IT'S ALL DECIDED HERE!"
"EVERYONE ELSE TAKING THE EXAM IS YOUR ENEMY! KILL OR BE KILLED! THIS IS WAR"--
THA- THAT'S ENOUGH!!
HARD LOVE
ALWAYS THE SAME STUPID SPEECH!
HUMPH! AND THE NIGHT BEFORE THE TEST, YOU CAN ALWAYS PRAY!

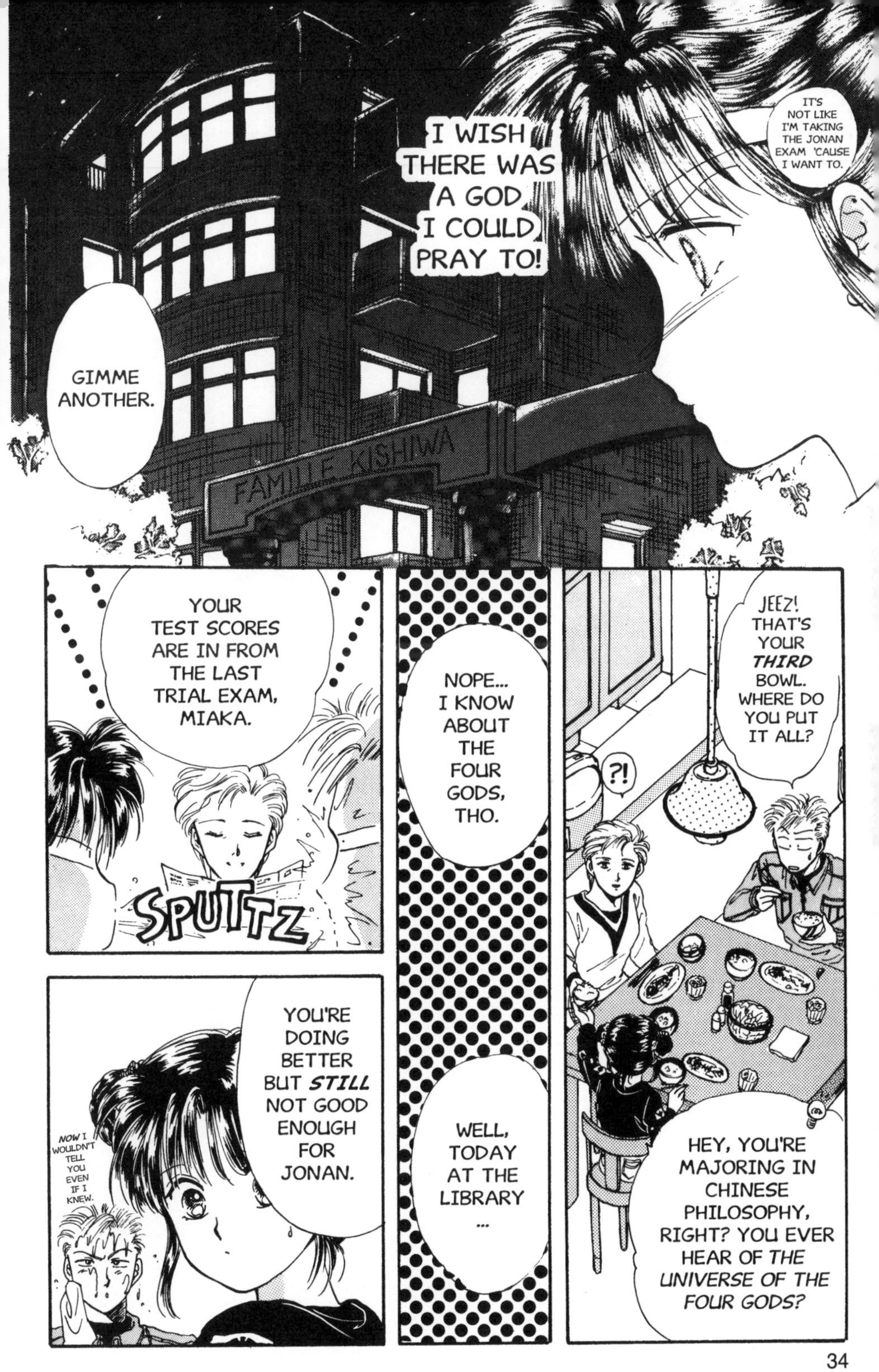
IT'S NOT LIKE I'M TAKING THE JONAN EXAM 'CAUSE I WANT TO.
I WISH THERE WAS A GOD I COULD PRAY TO!
GIMME ANOTHER.
FAMILLE KISHIWA
JEEZ! THAT'S YOUR THIRD BOWL. WHERE DO YOU PUT IT ALL?
?!
HEY, YOU'RE MAJORING IN CHINESE PHILOSOPHY, RIGHT? YOU EVER HEAR OF THE UNIVERSE OF THE FOUR GODS?
NOPE... I KNOW ABOUT THE FOUR GODS, THO.
WELL, TODAY AT THE LIBRARY ...
YOUR TEST SCORES ARE IN FROM THE LAST TRIAL EXAM, MIAKA.
SPUTTZ
YOU'RE DOING BETTER BUT STILL NOT GOOD ENOUGH FOR JONAN.
NOW I WOULDN'T TELL YOU EVEN IF I KNEW.

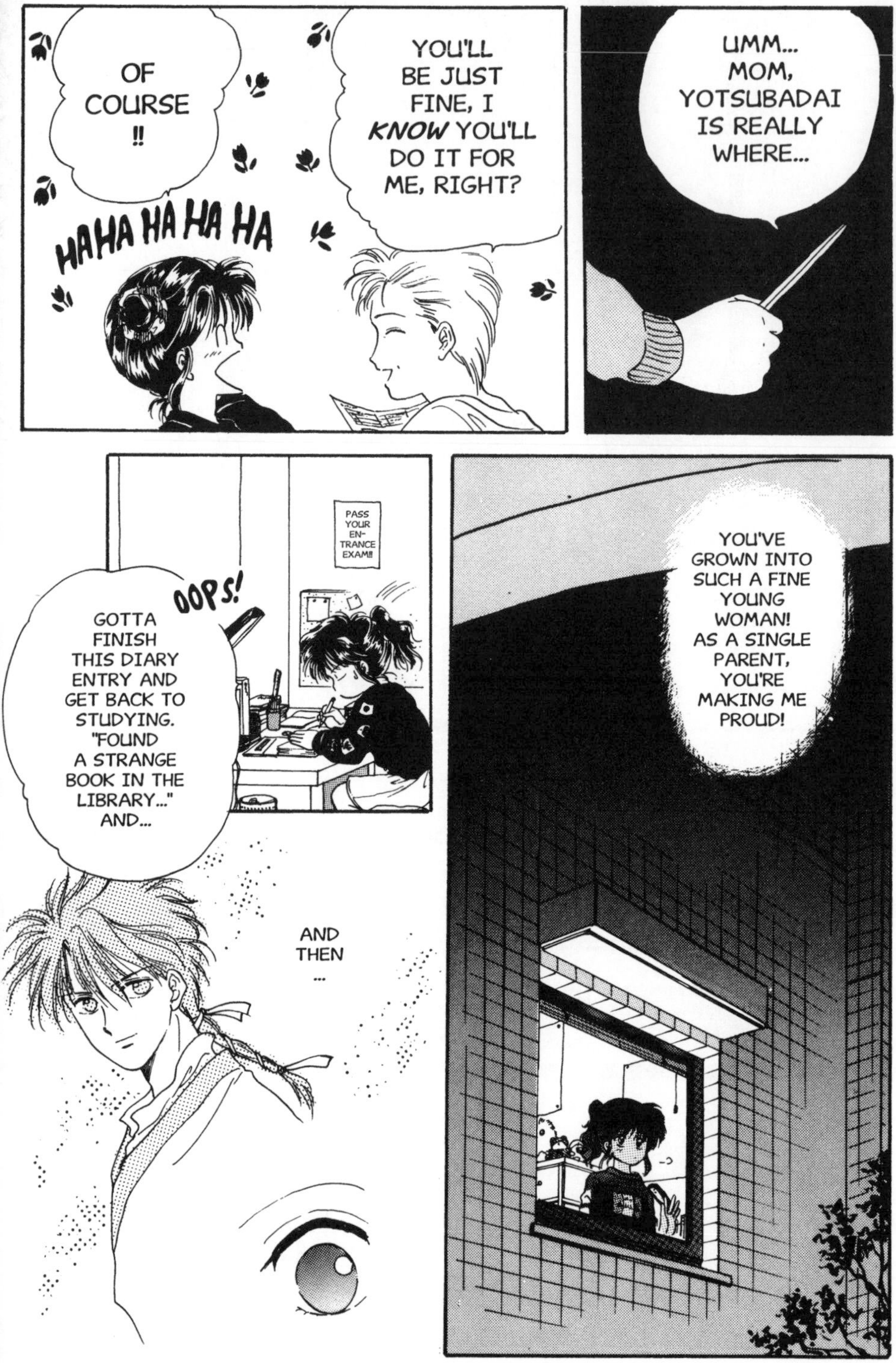
UMM... MOM, YOTSUBADAI IS REALLY WHERE...
YOU'LL BE JUST FINE, I *KNOW* YOU'LL DO IT FOR ME, RIGHT?
OF COURSE !!
HAHA HA HA HA
YOU'VE GROWN INTO SUCH A FINE YOUNG WOMAN! AS A SINGLE PARENT, YOU'RE MAKING ME PROUD!
PASS YOUR EN-TRANCE EXAM!!
OOPS!
GOTTA FINISH THIS DIARY ENTRY AND GET BACK TO STUDYING. "FOUND A STRANGE BOOK IN THE LIBRARY..." AND...
AND THEN ...

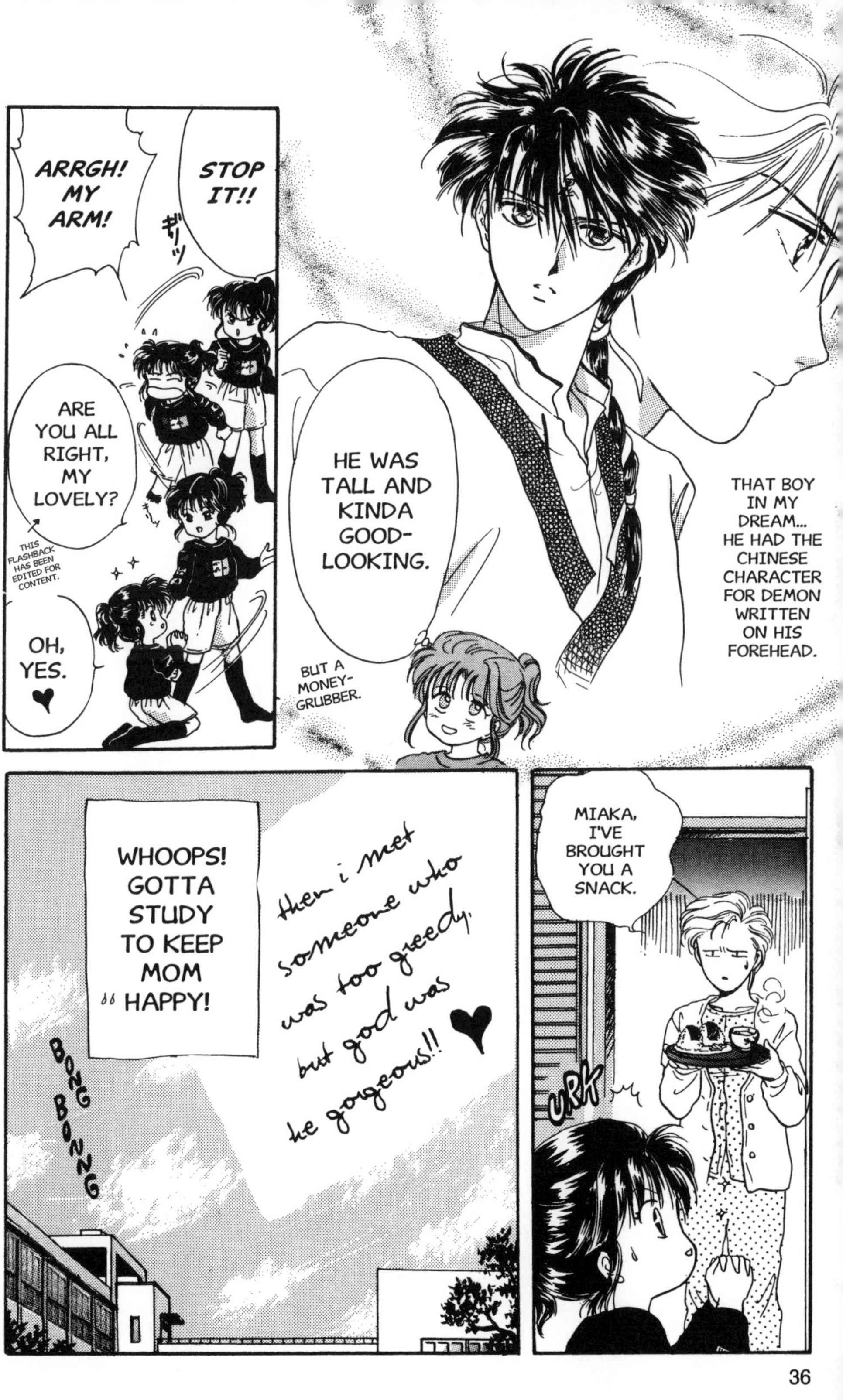

THAT BOY IN MY DREAM... HE HAD THE CHINESE CHARACTER FOR DEMON WRITTEN ON HIS FOREHEAD.
HE WAS TALL AND KINDA GOOD-LOOKING.
BUT A MONEY-GRUBBER.
STOP IT!!
ギリッ
ARRGH! MY ARM!
ARE YOU ALL RIGHT, MY LOVELY?
THIS FLASHBACK HAS BEEN EDITED FOR CONTENT.
OH, YES. ♥
MIAKA, I'VE BROUGHT YOU A SNACK.
URK
WHOOPS! GOTTA STUDY TO KEEP MOM HAPPY!
then i met someone who was too greedy, but god was he gorgeous!! ♥
BONG BONG

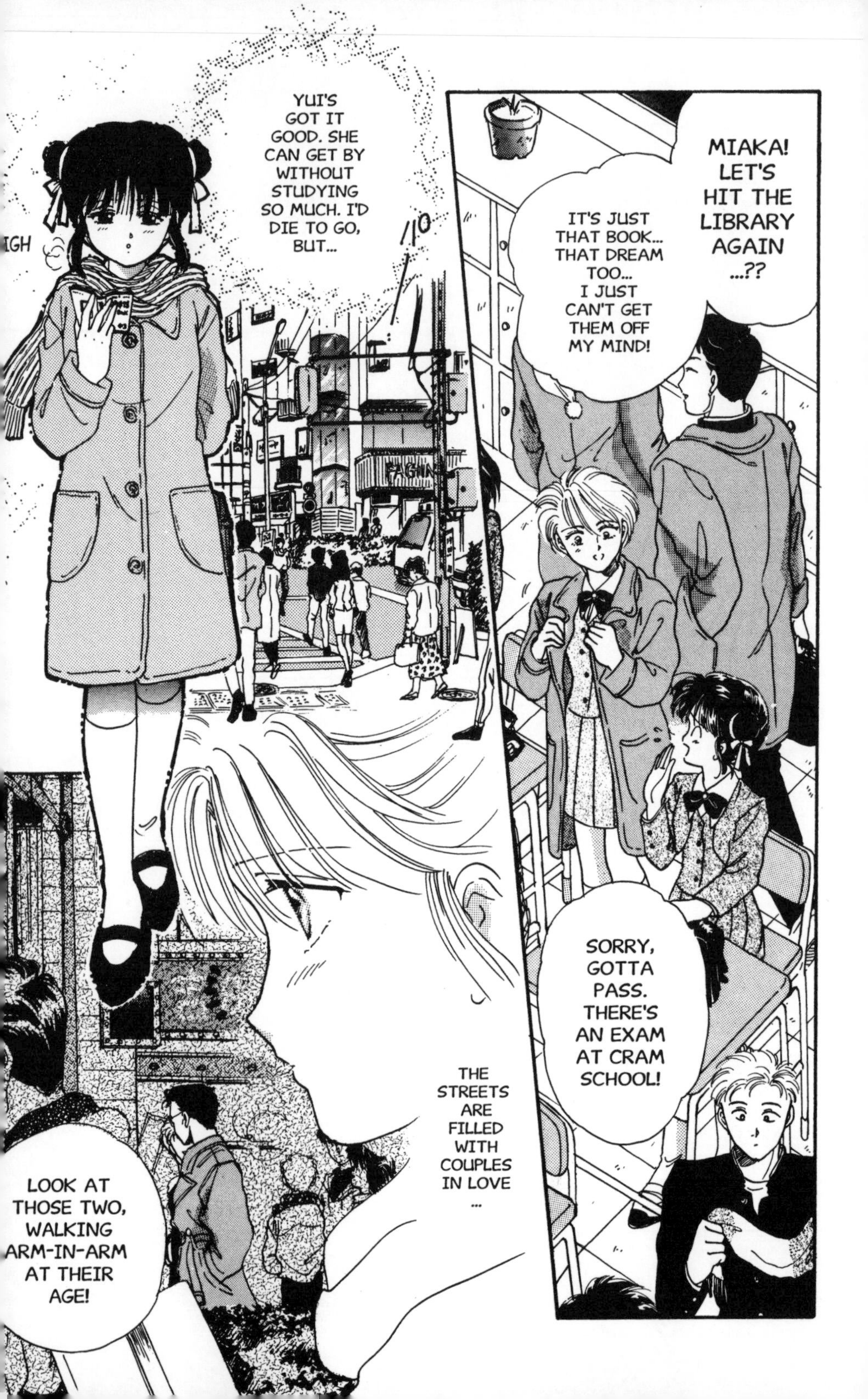
MIAKA! LET'S HIT THE LIBRARY AGAIN ...??
IT'S JUST THAT BOOK... THAT DREAM TOO... I JUST CAN'T GET THEM OFF MY MIND!
SORRY, GOTTA PASS. THERE'S AN EXAM AT CRAM SCHOOL!
YUI'S GOT IT GOOD. SHE CAN GET BY WITHOUT STUDYING SO MUCH. I'D DIE TO GO, BUT...
THE STREETS ARE FILLED WITH COUPLES IN LOVE ...
LOOK AT THOSE TWO, WALKING ARM-IN-ARM AT THEIR AGE!

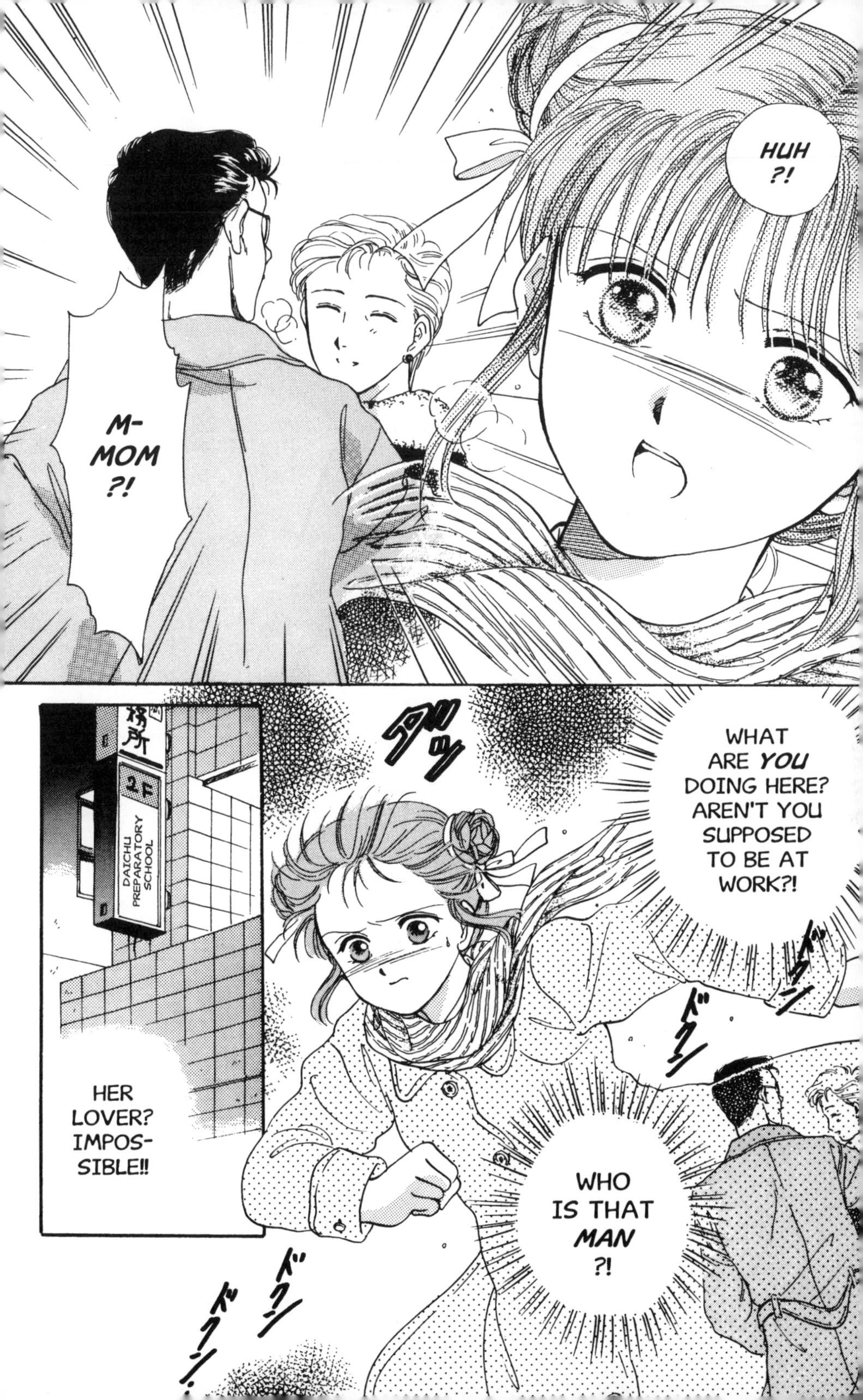
HUH ?!
M-MOM ?!
WHAT ARE *YOU* DOING HERE? AREN'T YOU SUPPOSED TO BE AT WORK?!
WHO IS THAT *MAN* ?!
DAICHU PREPARATORY SCHOOL
2F
HER LOVER? IMPOS-SIBLE!!

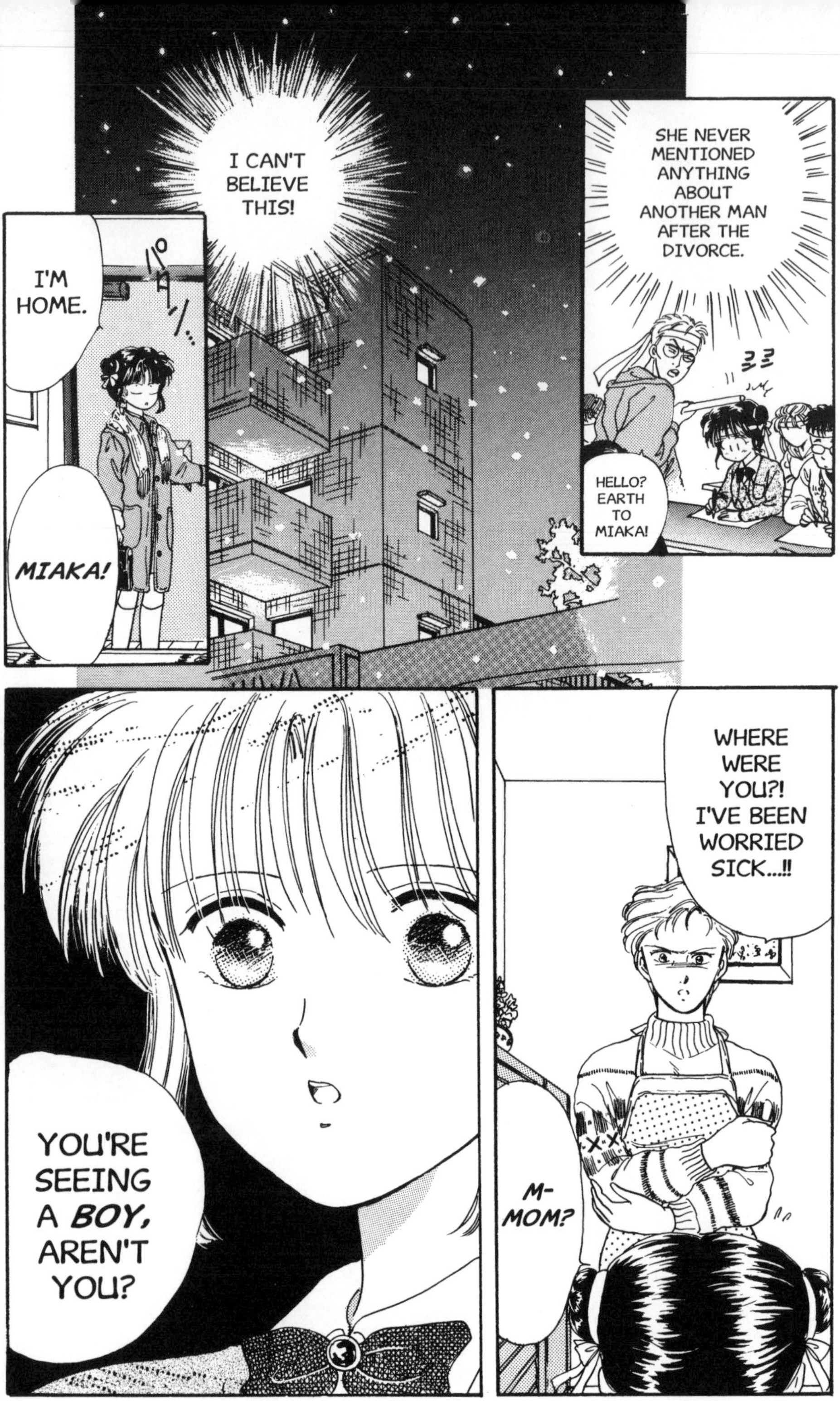

SHE NEVER MENTIONED ANYTHING ABOUT ANOTHER MAN AFTER THE DIVORCE.
HELLO? EARTH TO MIAKA!
I CAN'T BELIEVE THIS!
I'M HOME.
MIAKA!
WHERE WERE YOU?! I'VE BEEN WORRIED SICK...!!
M-MOM?
YOU'RE SEEING A *BOY,* AREN'T YOU?

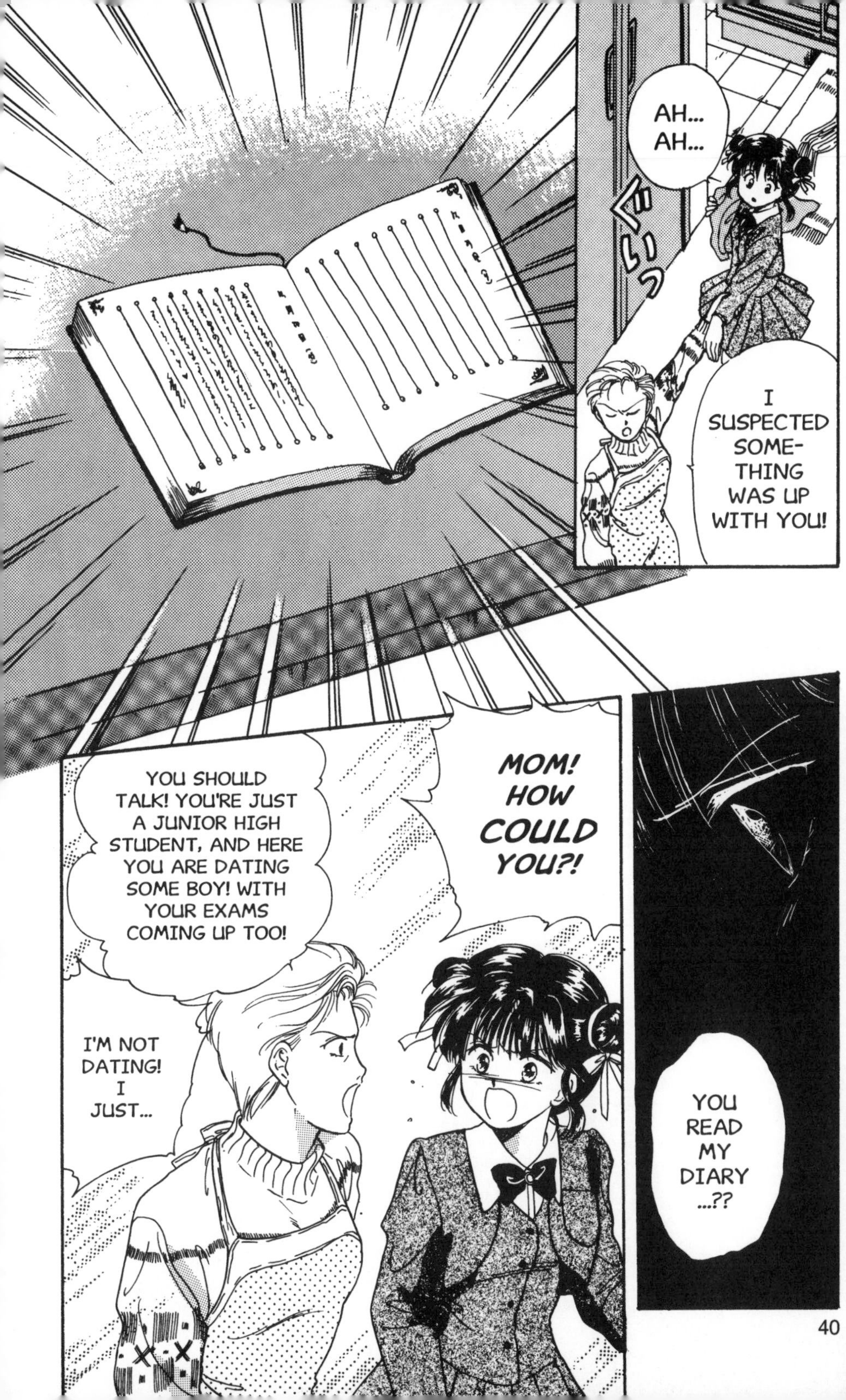
AH... AH...
ぐいっ
I SUSPECTED SOMETHING WAS UP WITH YOU!
YOU READ MY DIARY ...??
MOM! HOW COULD YOU?!
YOU SHOULD TALK! YOU'RE JUST A JUNIOR HIGH STUDENT, AND HERE YOU ARE DATING SOME BOY! WITH YOUR EXAMS COMING UP TOO!
I'M NOT DATING! I JUST...

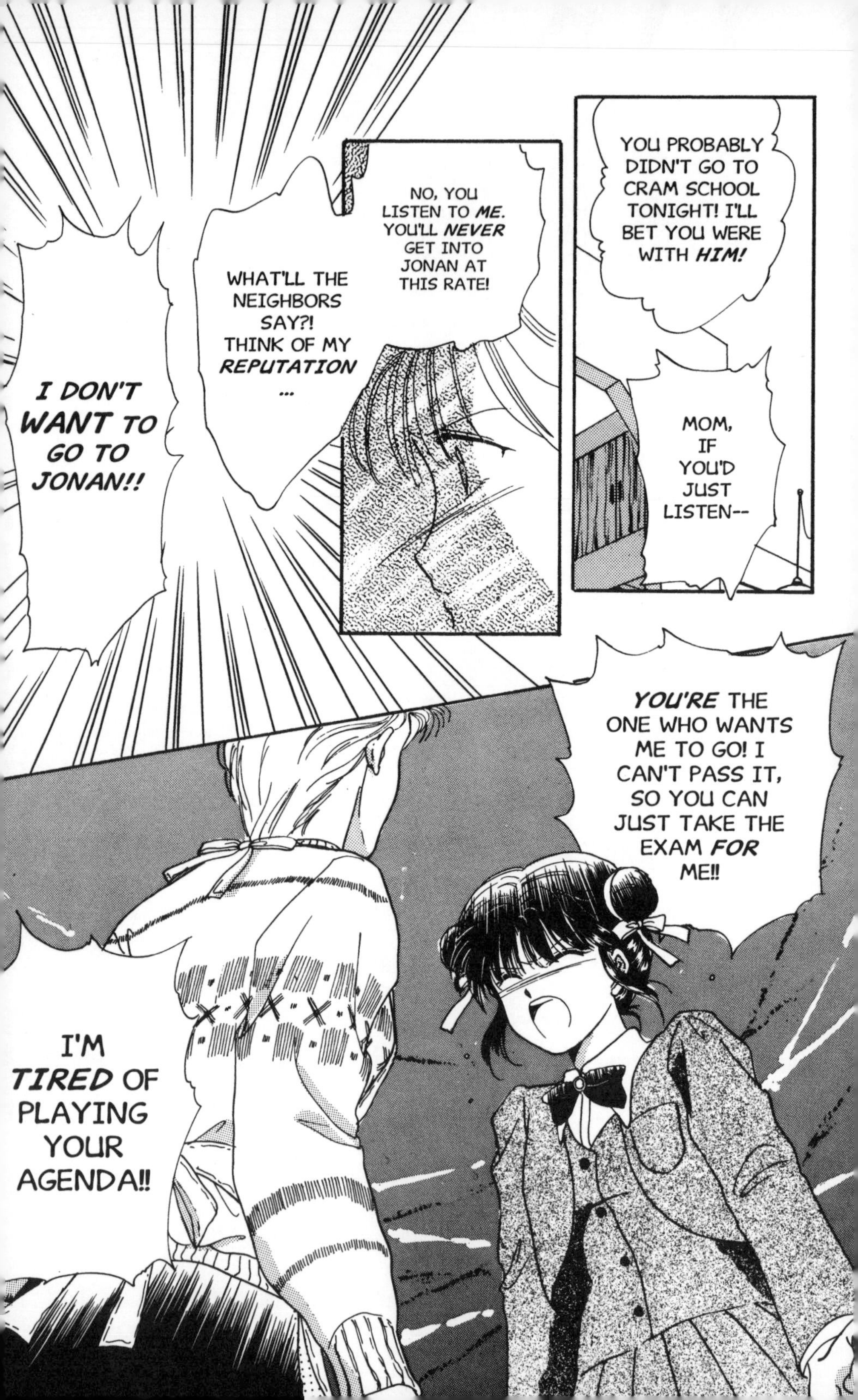

YOU PROBABLY DIDN'T GO TO CRAM SCHOOL TONIGHT! I'LL BET YOU WERE WITH *HIM!*
MOM, IF YOU'D JUST LISTEN--
NO, YOU LISTEN TO *ME*. YOU'LL *NEVER* GET INTO JONAN AT THIS RATE!
WHAT'LL THE NEIGHBORS SAY?! THINK OF MY *REPUTATION* ...
I DON'T WANT TO GO TO JONAN!!
YOU'RE THE ONE WHO WANTS ME TO GO! I CAN'T PASS IT, SO YOU CAN JUST TAKE THE EXAM *FOR* ME!!
I'M *TIRED* OF PLAYING YOUR AGENDA!!

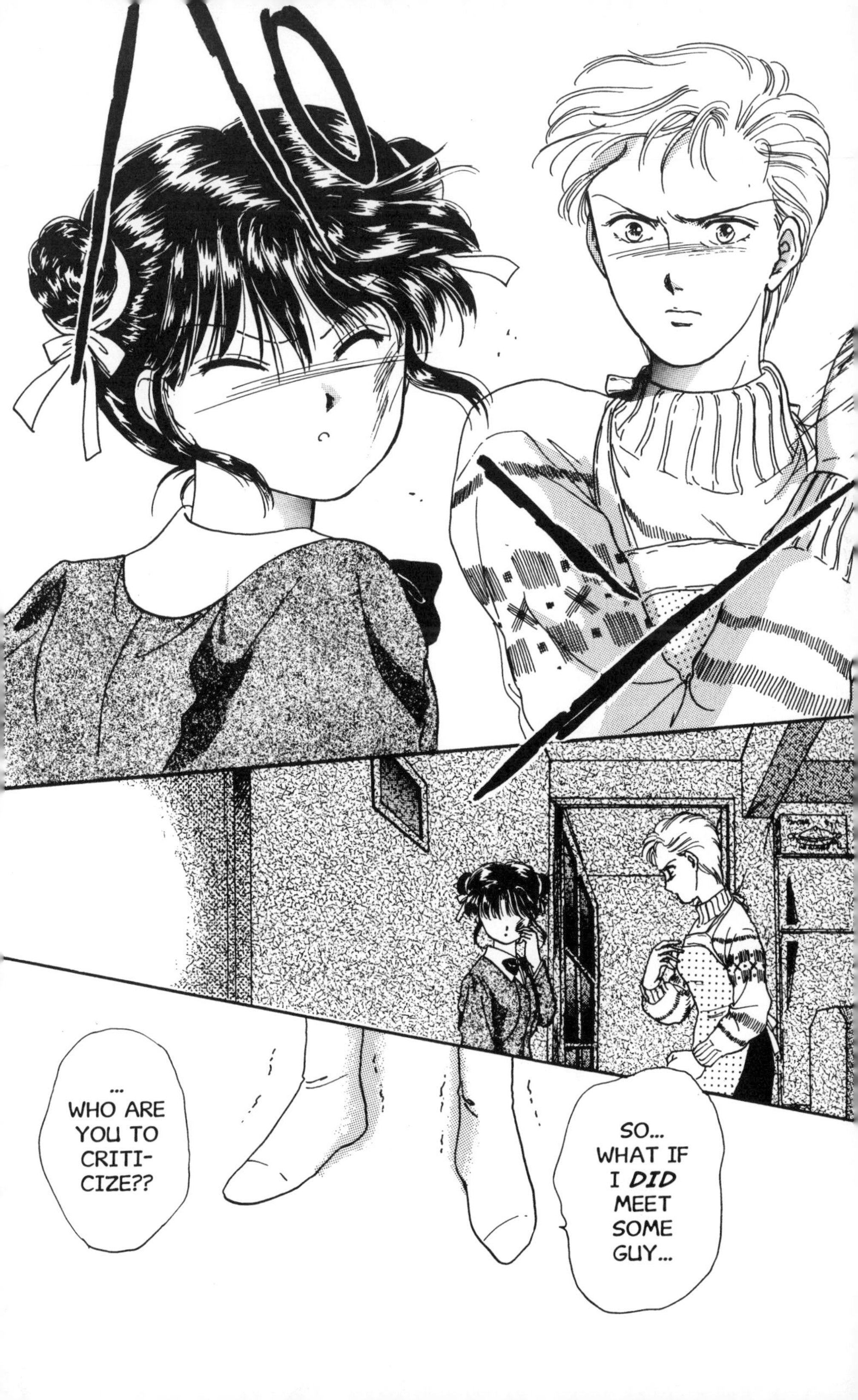
SO... WHAT IF I *DID* MEET SOME GUY...
... WHO ARE YOU TO CRITI-CIZE??

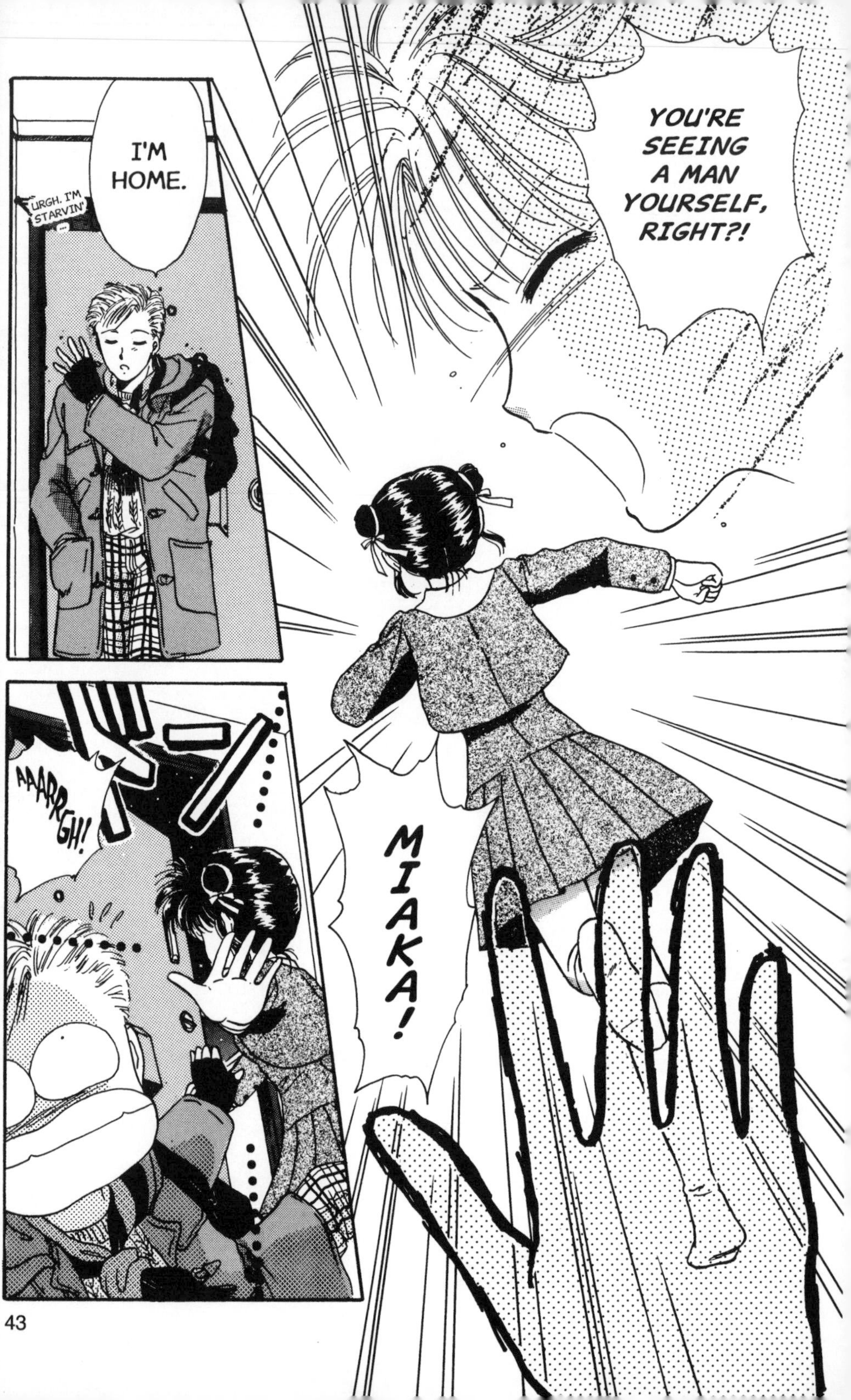
YOU'RE SEEING A MAN YOURSELF, RIGHT?!
MIAKA!
I'M HOME.
URGH. I'M STARVIN' ...
AAAARRGH!

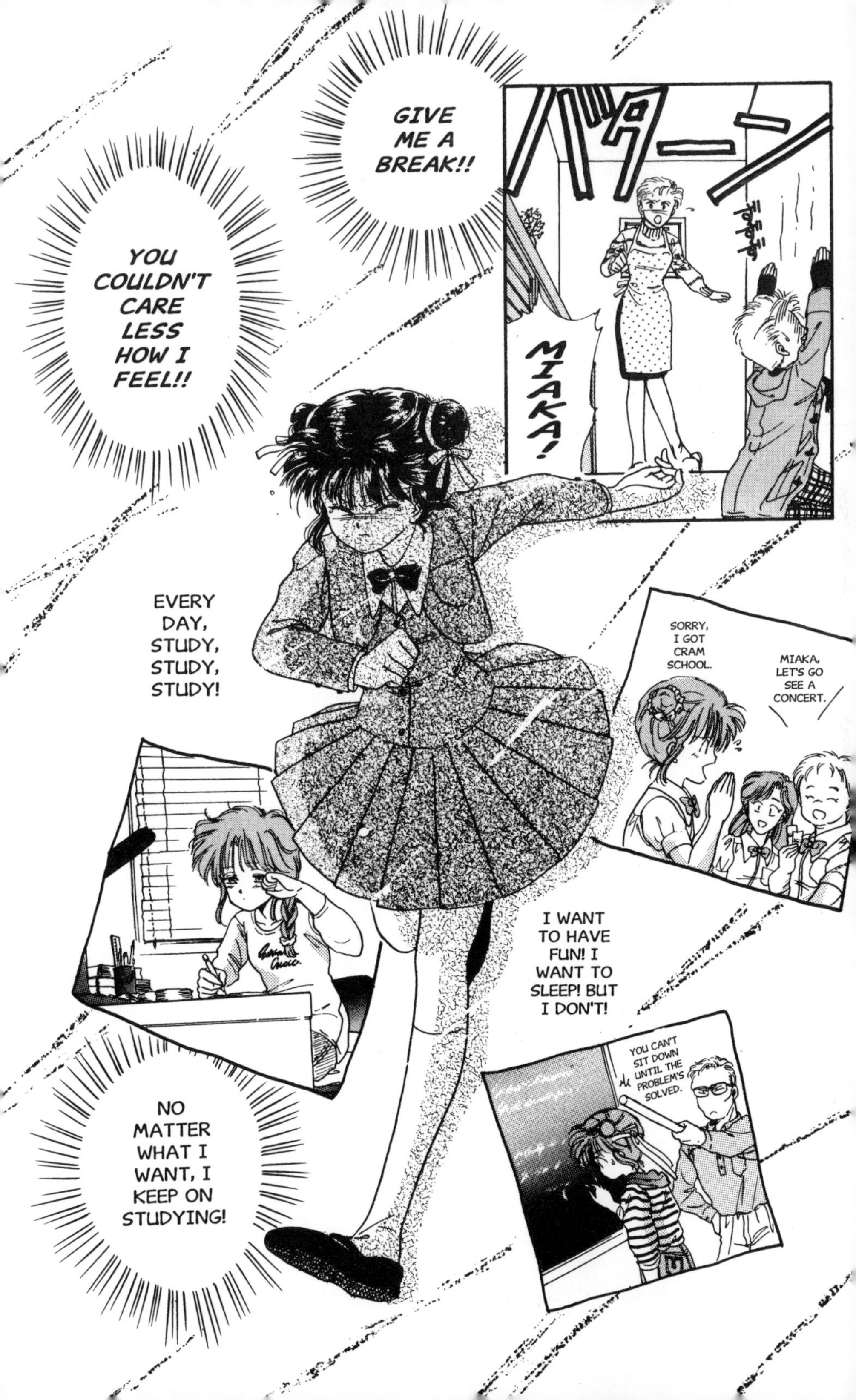
MIAKA!
GIVE ME A BREAK!!
YOU COULDN'T CARE LESS HOW I FEEL!!
MIAKA, LET'S GO SEE A CONCERT.
SORRY, I GOT CRAM SCHOOL.
EVERY DAY, STUDY, STUDY, STUDY!
I WANT TO HAVE FUN! I WANT TO SLEEP! BUT I DON'T!
YOU CAN'T SIT DOWN UNTIL THE PROBLEM'S SOLVED.
NO MATTER WHAT I WANT, I KEEP ON STUDYING!

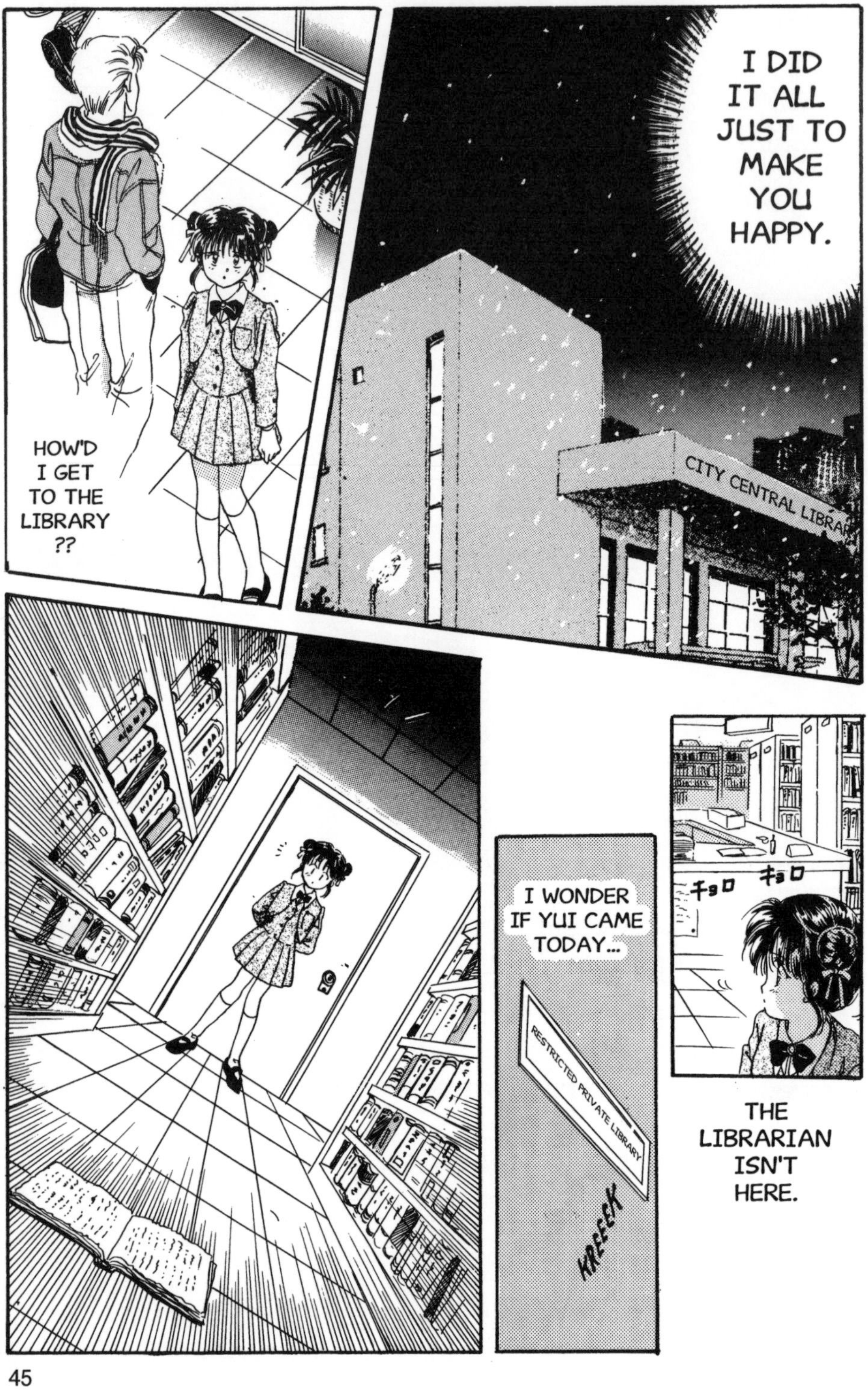
I DID IT ALL JUST TO MAKE YOU HAPPY.
CITY CENTRAL LIBRA
HOW'D I GET TO THE LIBRARY ??
キョロ キョロ
THE LIBRARIAN ISN'T HERE.
I WONDER IF YUI CAME TODAY...
RESTRICTED PRIVATE LIBRARY
KREEEK

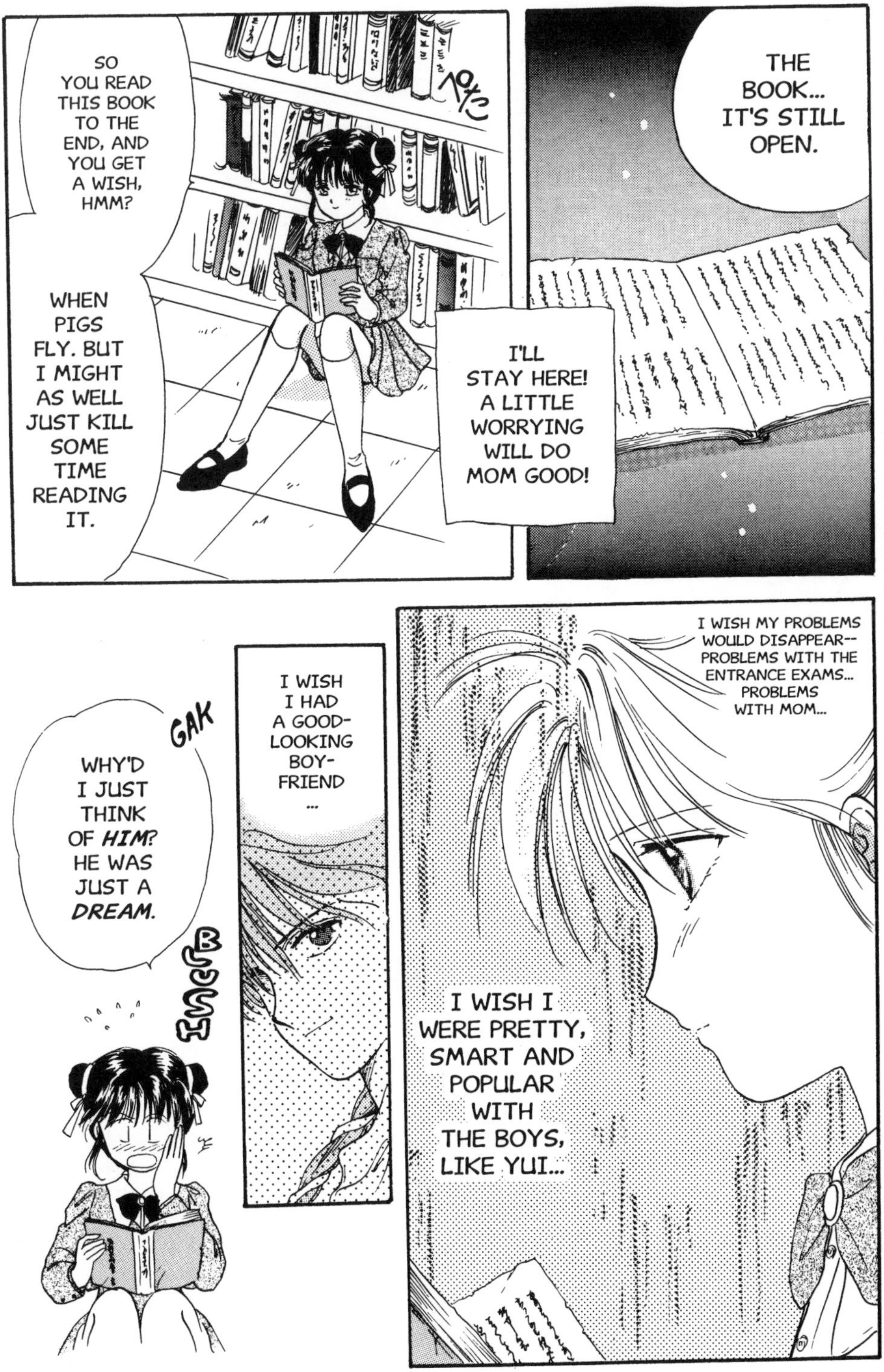
THE BOOK... IT'S STILL OPEN.
I'LL STAY HERE! A LITTLE WORRYING WILL DO MOM GOOD!
ぺたこ
SO YOU READ THIS BOOK TO THE END, AND YOU GET A WISH, HMM?
WHEN PIGS FLY. BUT I MIGHT AS WELL JUST KILL SOME TIME READING IT.
I WISH MY PROBLEMS WOULD DISAPPEAR-- PROBLEMS WITH THE ENTRANCE EXAMS... PROBLEMS WITH MOM...
I WISH I WERE PRETTY, SMART AND POPULAR WITH THE BOYS, LIKE YUI...
I WISH I HAD A GOOD-LOOKING BOY-FRIEND ...
GAK
WHY'D I JUST THINK OF *HIM*? HE WAS JUST A *DREAM*.
BLUSH

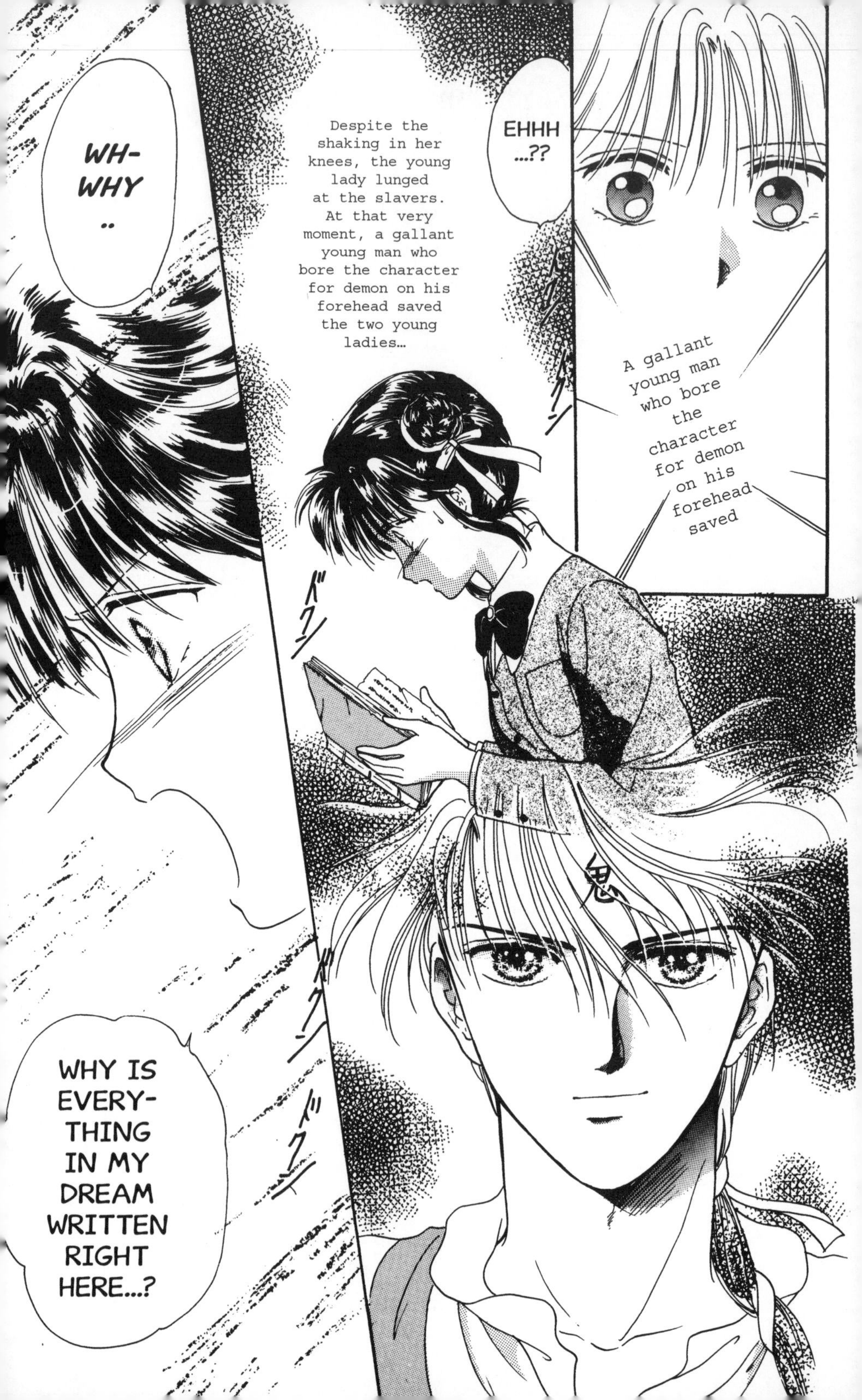
EHHH ...??
A gallant young man who bore the character for demon on his forehead saved
Despite the shaking in her knees, the young lady lunged at the slavers. At that very moment, a gallant young man who bore the character for demon on his forehead saved the two young ladies...
WH- WHY ..
WHY IS EVERYTHING IN MY DREAM WRITTEN RIGHT HERE...?

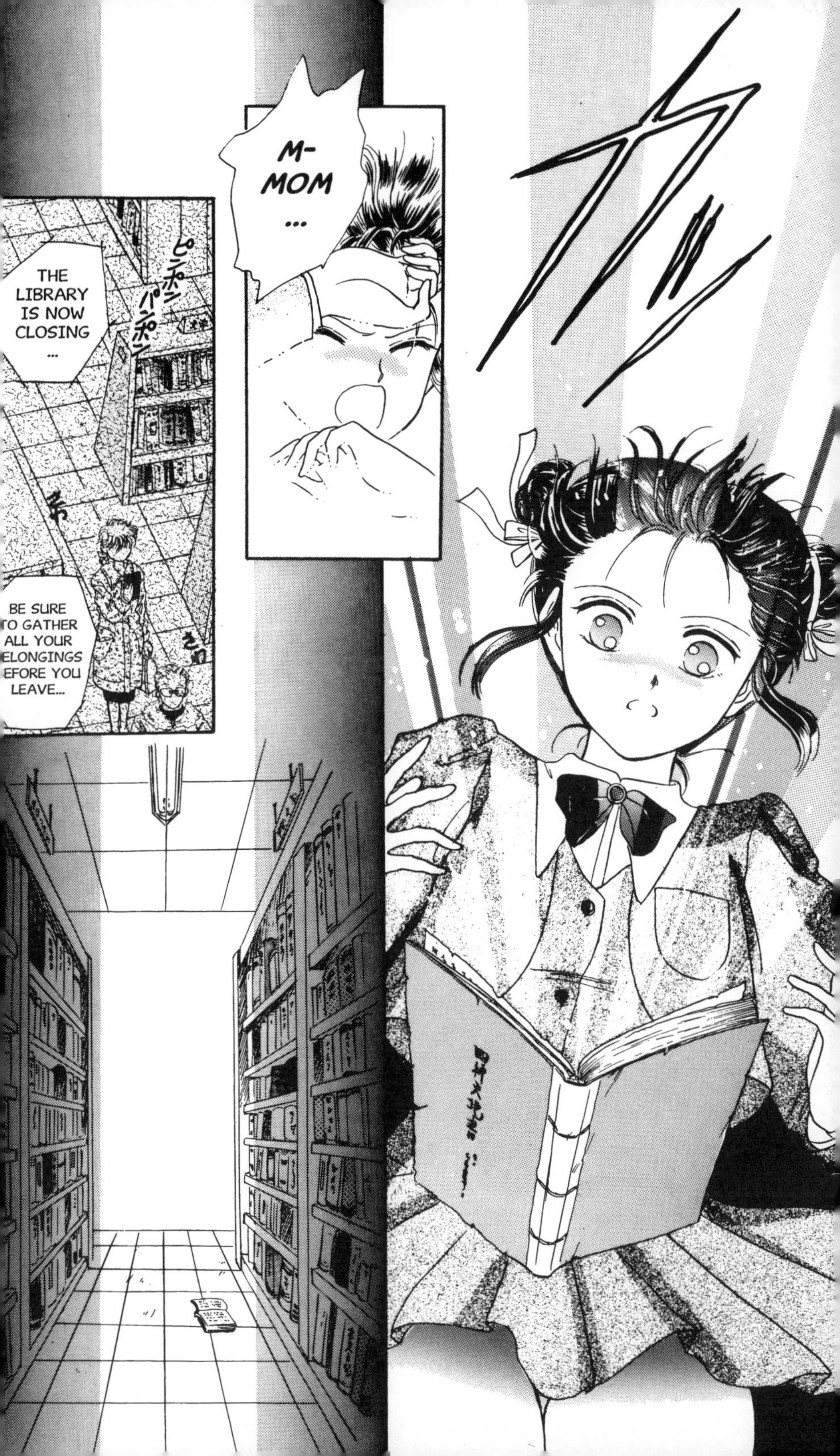
M- MOM ...
ピンポンパンポン
THE LIBRARY IS NOW CLOSING ...
BE SURE TO GATHER ALL YOUR ELONGINGS EFORE YOU LEAVE...

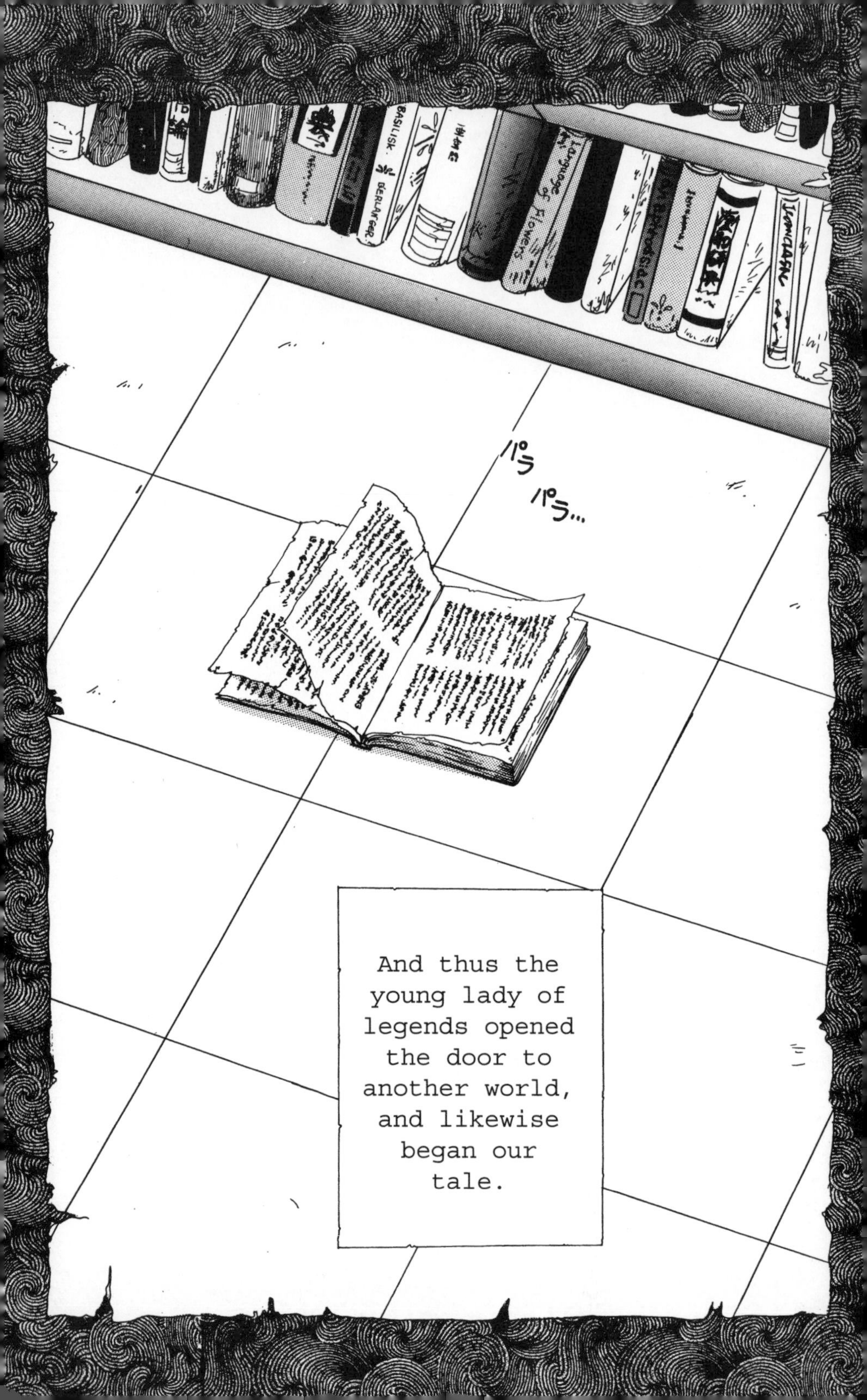
パラ
パラ…
And thus the young lady of legends opened the door to another world, and likewise began our tale.

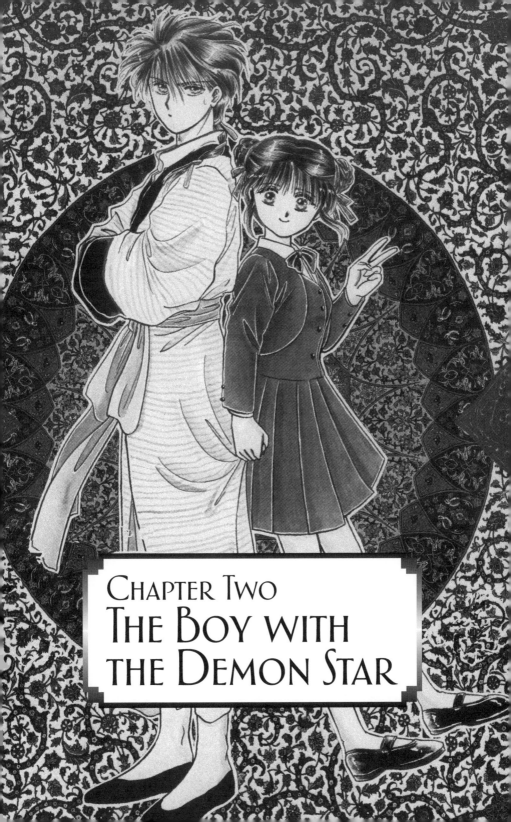

CHAPTER TWO
THE BOY WITH
THE DEMON STAR

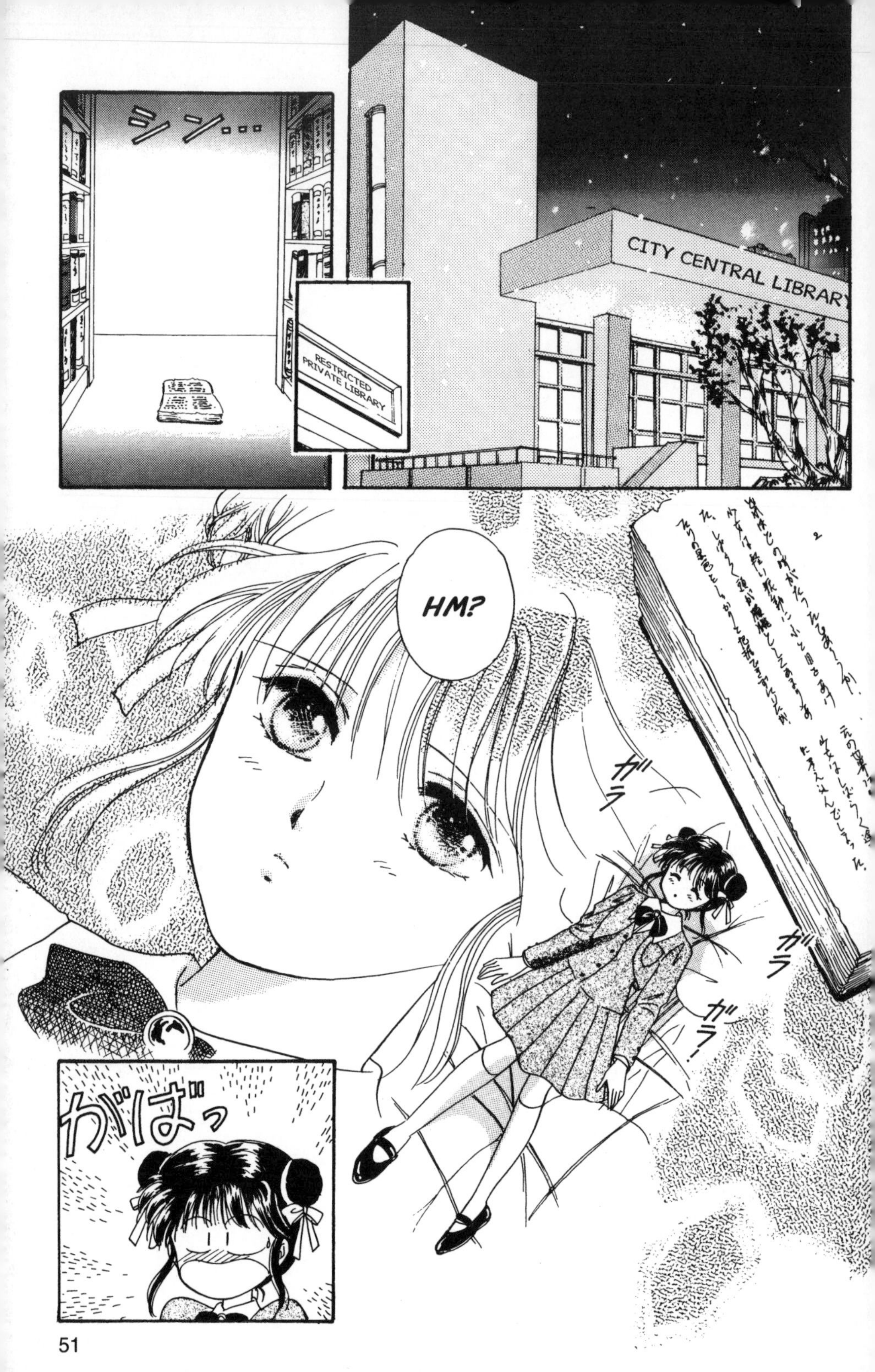
CITY CENTRAL LIBRARY
RESTRICTED PRIVATE LIBRARY
シン…
HM?
ガラ
ガラ
ガラ!
がばっ

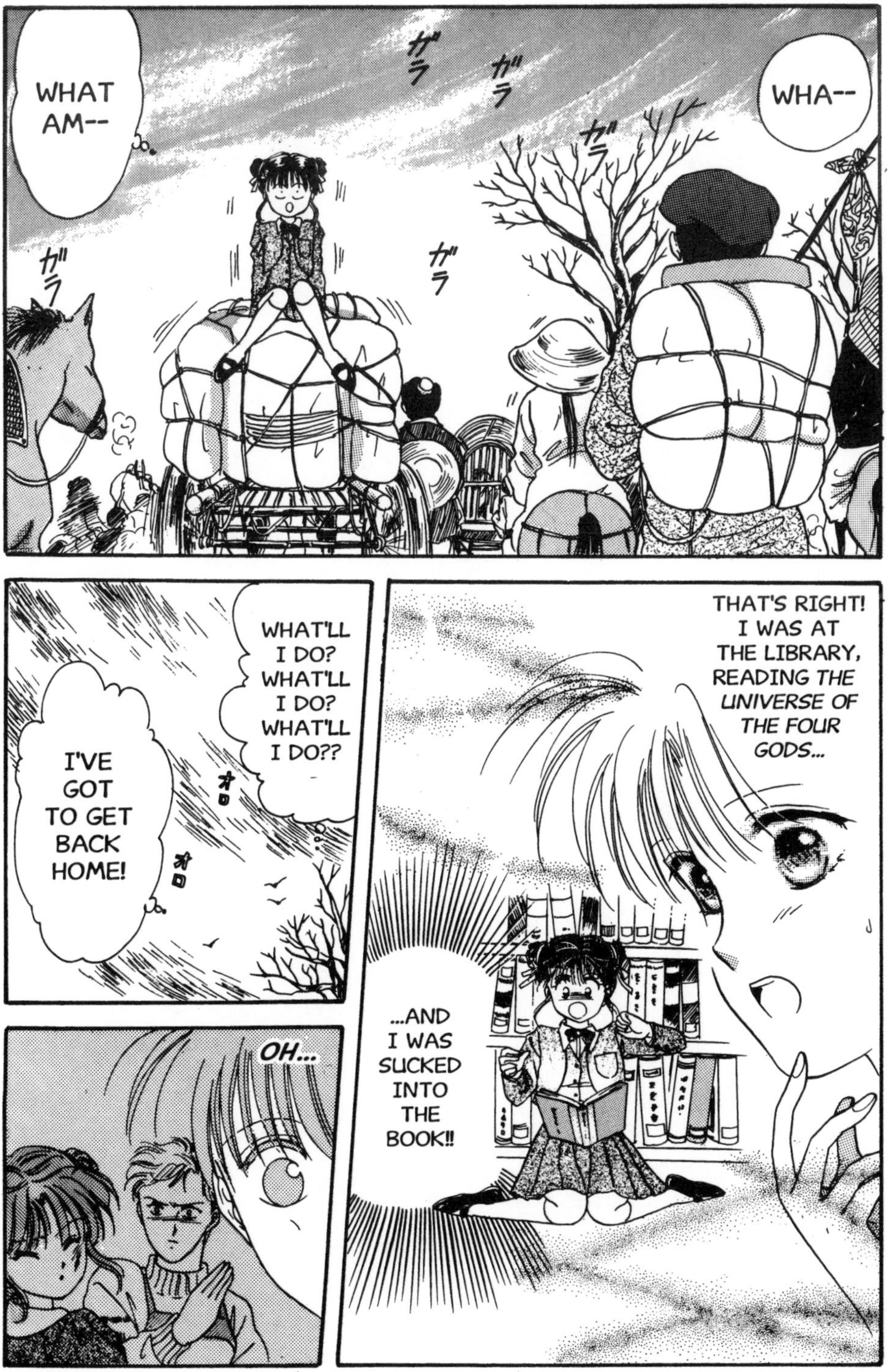
WHAT AM--
ガラ
ガラ
ガラ
ガラ
ガラ
WHA--
WHAT'LL I DO? WHAT'LL I DO? WHAT'LL I DO??
I'VE GOT TO GET BACK HOME!
オロ
オロ
OH...
THAT'S RIGHT! I WAS AT THE LIBRARY, READING *THE UNIVERSE OF THE FOUR GODS*...
...AND I WAS SUCKED INTO THE BOOK!!

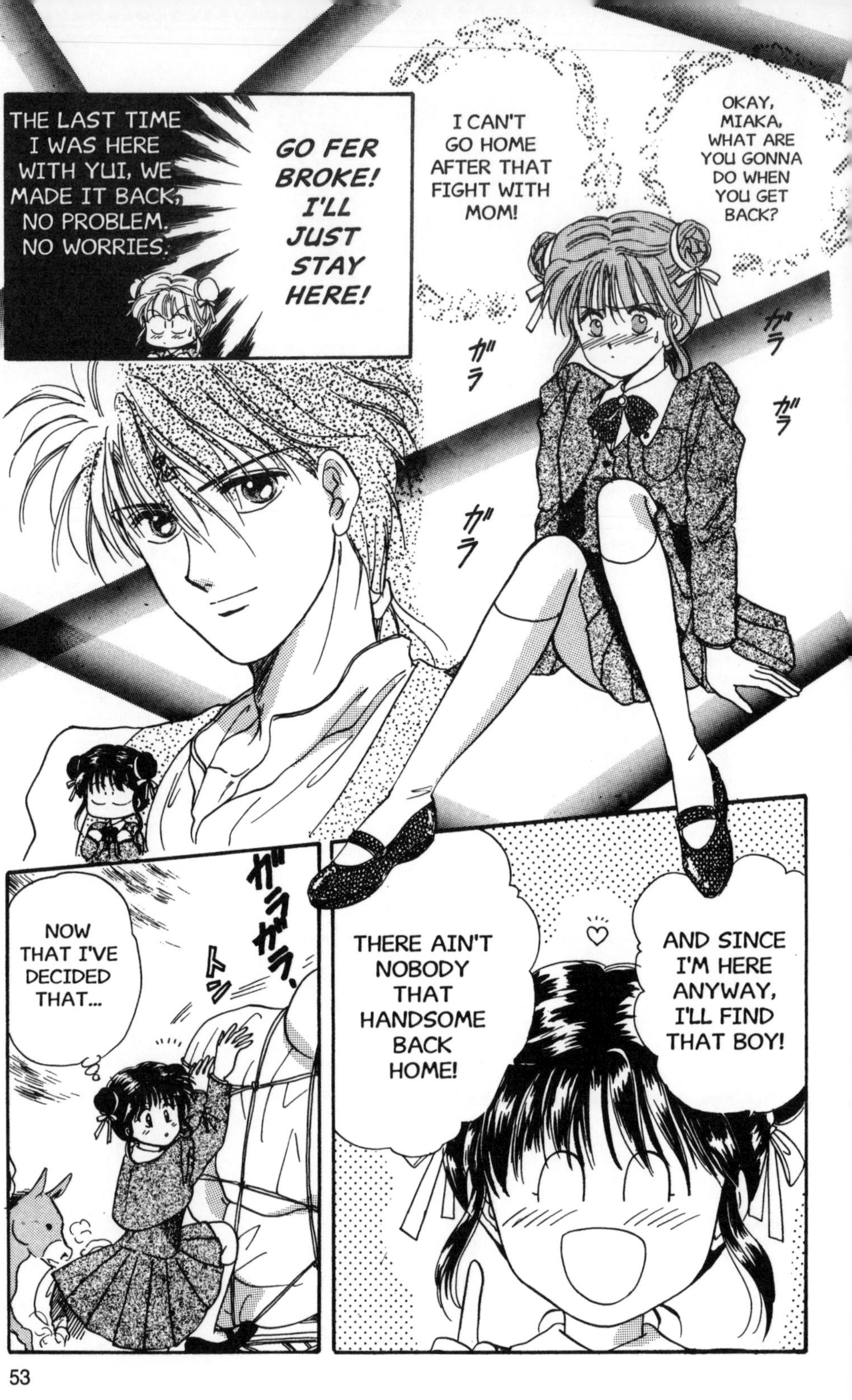
OKAY, MIAKA, WHAT ARE YOU GONNA DO WHEN YOU GET BACK?
I CAN'T GO HOME AFTER THAT FIGHT WITH MOM!
GO FER BROKE! I'LL JUST STAY HERE!
THE LAST TIME I WAS HERE WITH YUI, WE MADE IT BACK, NO PROBLEM. NO WORRIES.
ガラ
ガラ
ガラ
ガラ
AND SINCE I'M HERE ANYWAY, I'LL FIND THAT BOY!
THERE AIN'T NOBODY THAT HANDSOME BACK HOME!
ガラガラ、
トッ
NOW THAT I'VE DECIDED THAT...

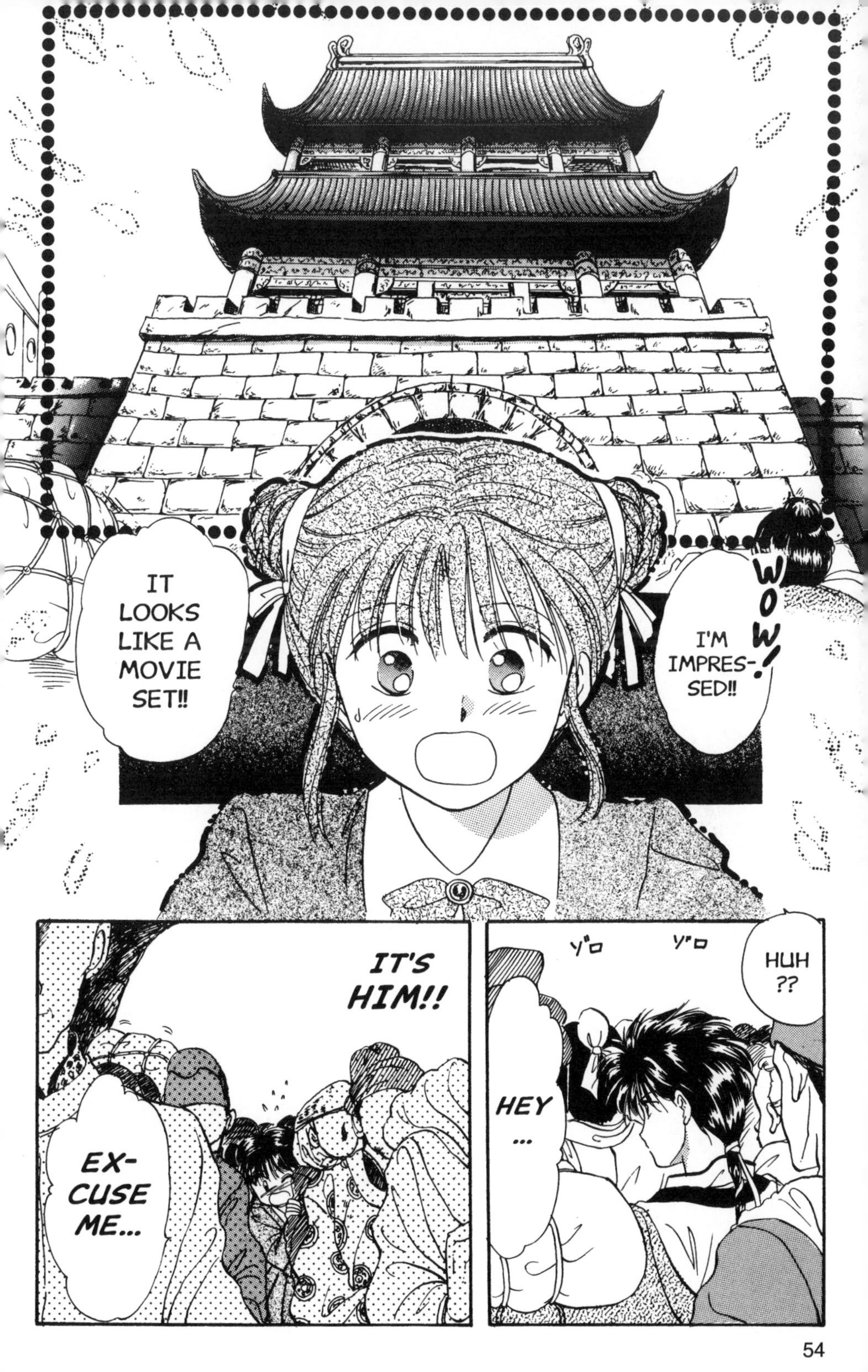
WOW!
I'M IMPRES-SED!!
IT LOOKS LIKE A MOVIE SET!!
HUH ??
ゾロ ゾロ
HEY ...
IT'S HIM!!
EX-CUSE ME...

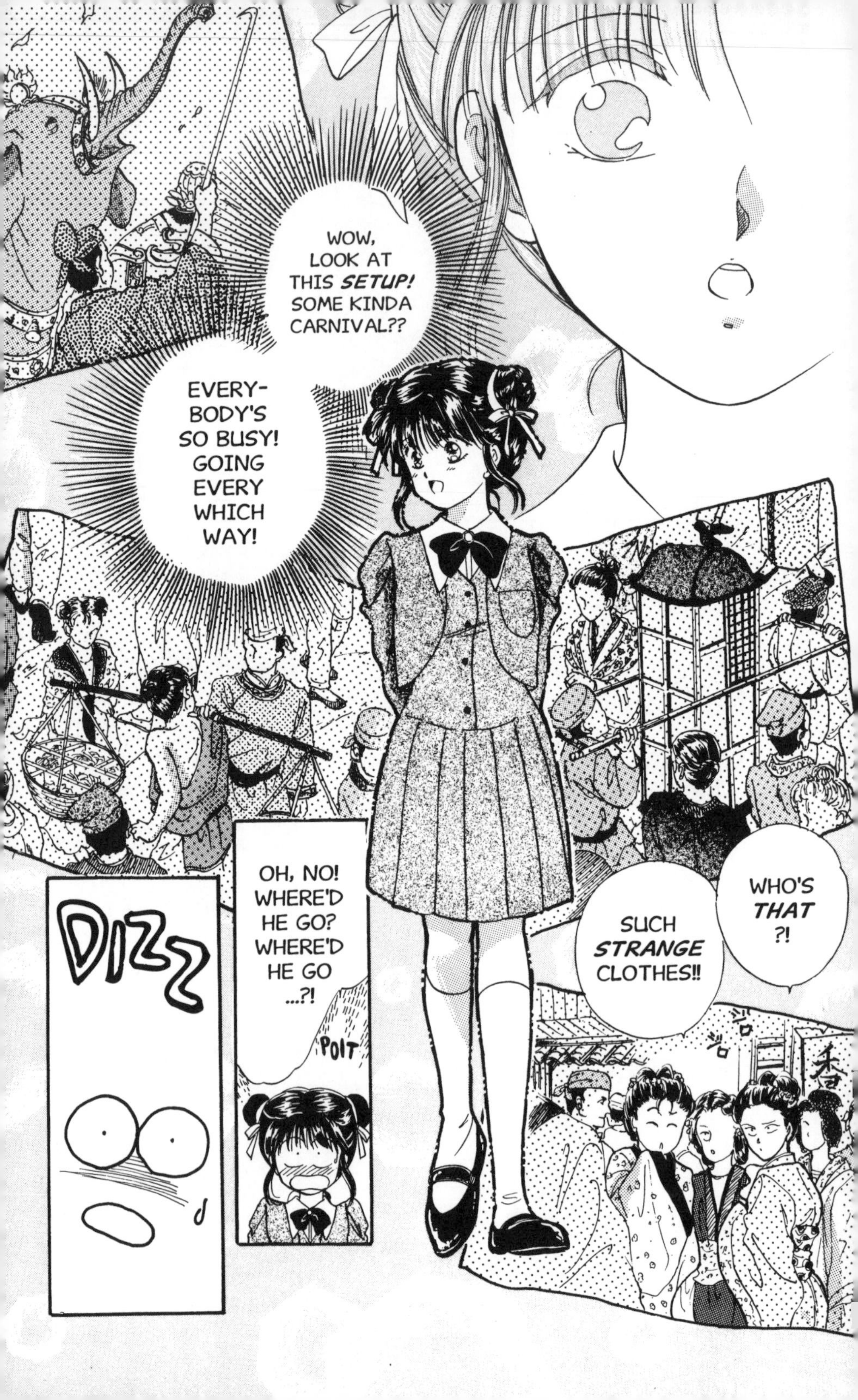
WOW, LOOK AT THIS *SETUP!* SOME KINDA CARNIVAL??
EVERY-BODY'S SO BUSY! GOING EVERY WHICH WAY!
WHO'S *THAT* ?!
SUCH *STRANGE* CLOTHES!!
ジロ ジロ
OH, NO! WHERE'D HE GO? WHERE'D HE GO ...?!
POIT
DIZZ

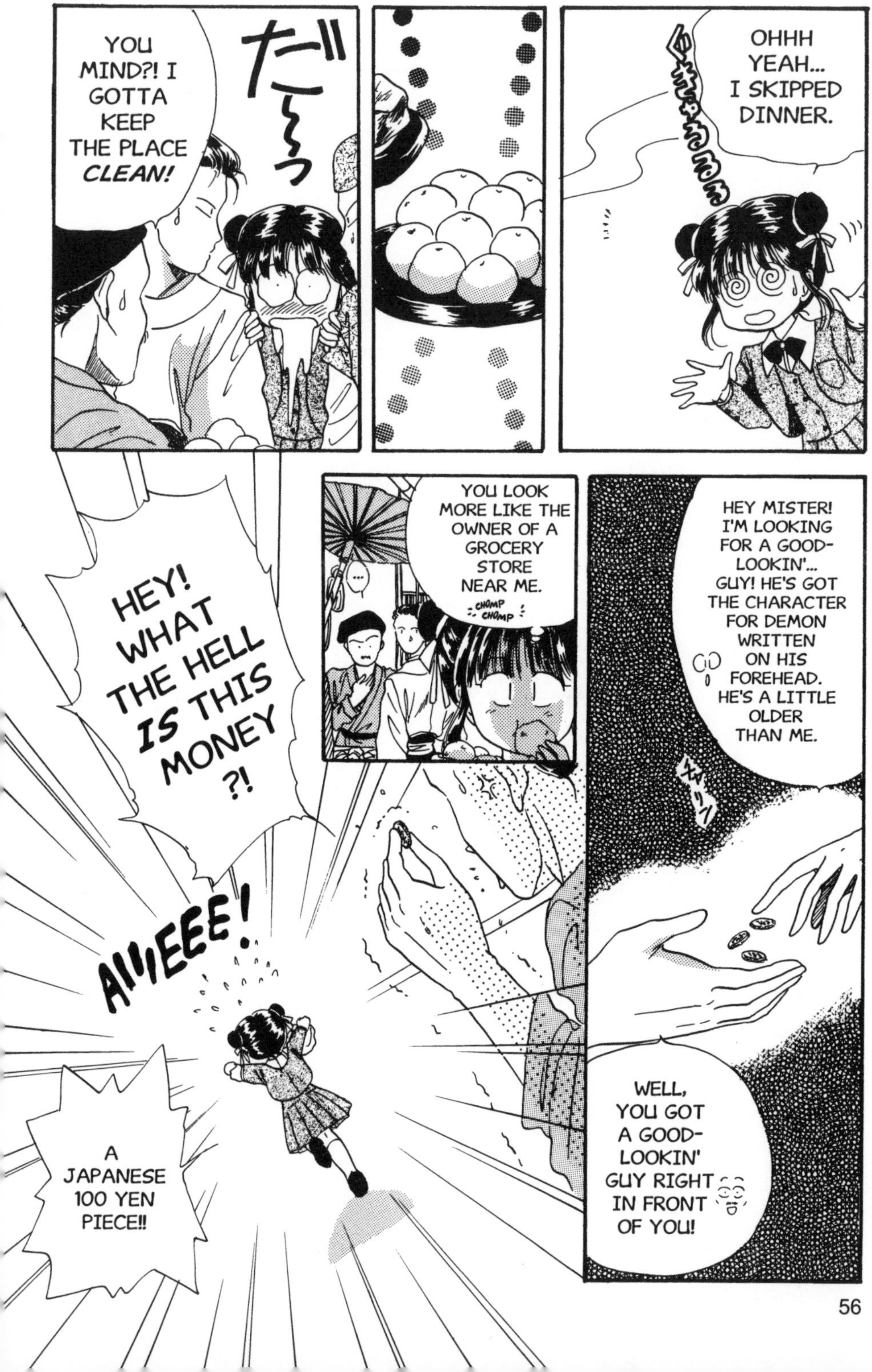
OHHH YEAH... I SKIPPED DINNER.
YOU MIND?! I GOTTA KEEP THE PLACE *CLEAN!*
HEY MISTER! I'M LOOKING FOR A GOOD-LOOKIN'... GUY! HE'S GOT THE CHARACTER FOR DEMON WRITTEN ON HIS FOREHEAD. HE'S A LITTLE OLDER THAN ME.
WELL, YOU GOT A GOOD-LOOKIN' GUY RIGHT IN FRONT OF YOU!
YOU LOOK MORE LIKE THE OWNER OF A GROCERY STORE NEAR ME.
CHOMP CHOMP
...
HEY! WHAT THE HELL *IS* THIS MONEY?!
AIIIEEE!
A JAPANESE 100 YEN PIECE!!

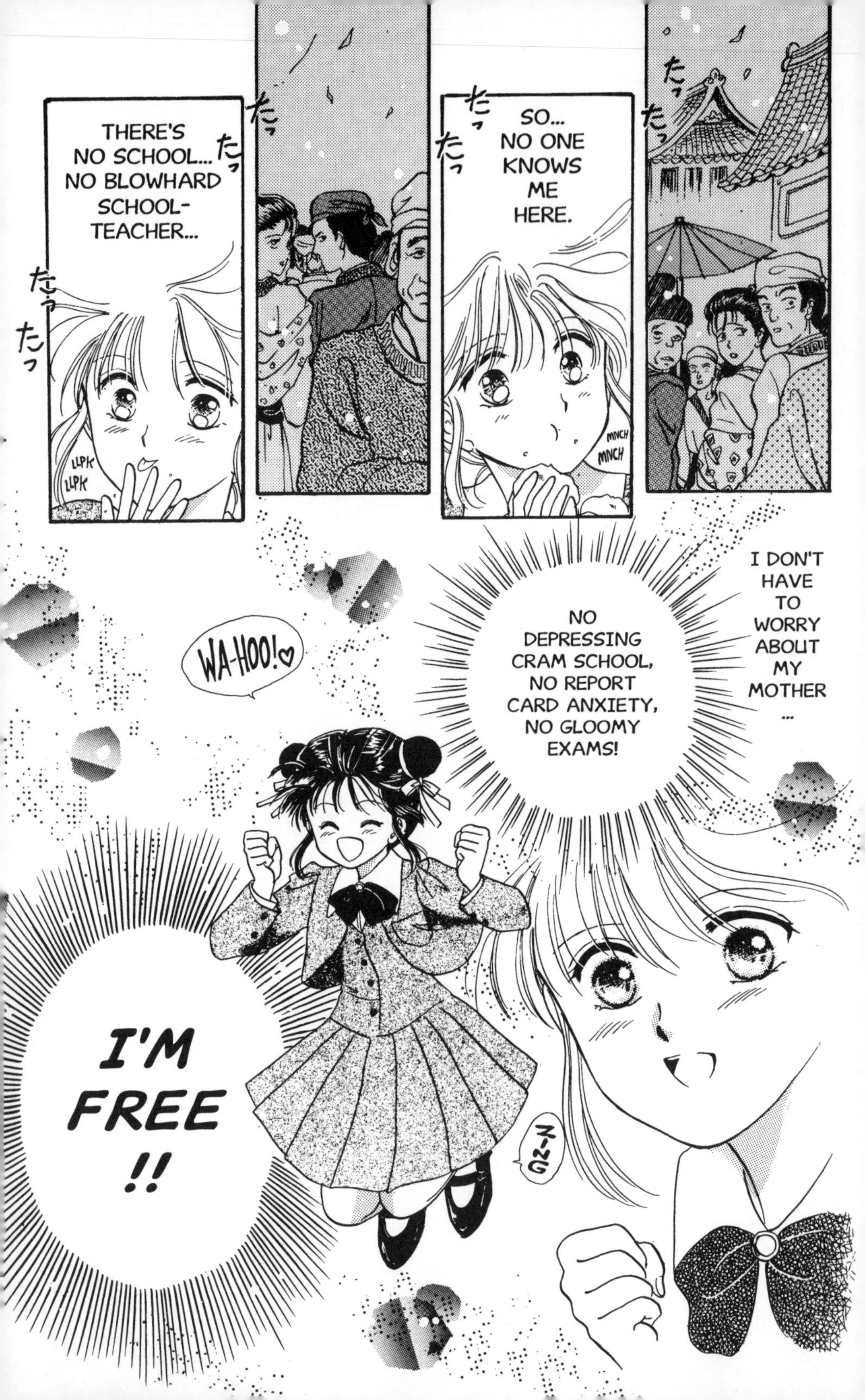
たっ
たっ
SO... NO ONE KNOWS ME HERE.
たっ
たっ
MNCH MNCH
たっ
たっ
THERE'S NO SCHOOL... NO BLOWHARD SCHOOL-TEACHER...
たっ
たっ
LLPK LLPK
I DON'T HAVE TO WORRY ABOUT MY MOTHER ...
NO DEPRESSING CRAM SCHOOL, NO REPORT CARD ANXIETY, NO GLOOMY EXAMS!
WA-HOO!♡
ZING
I'M FREE !!

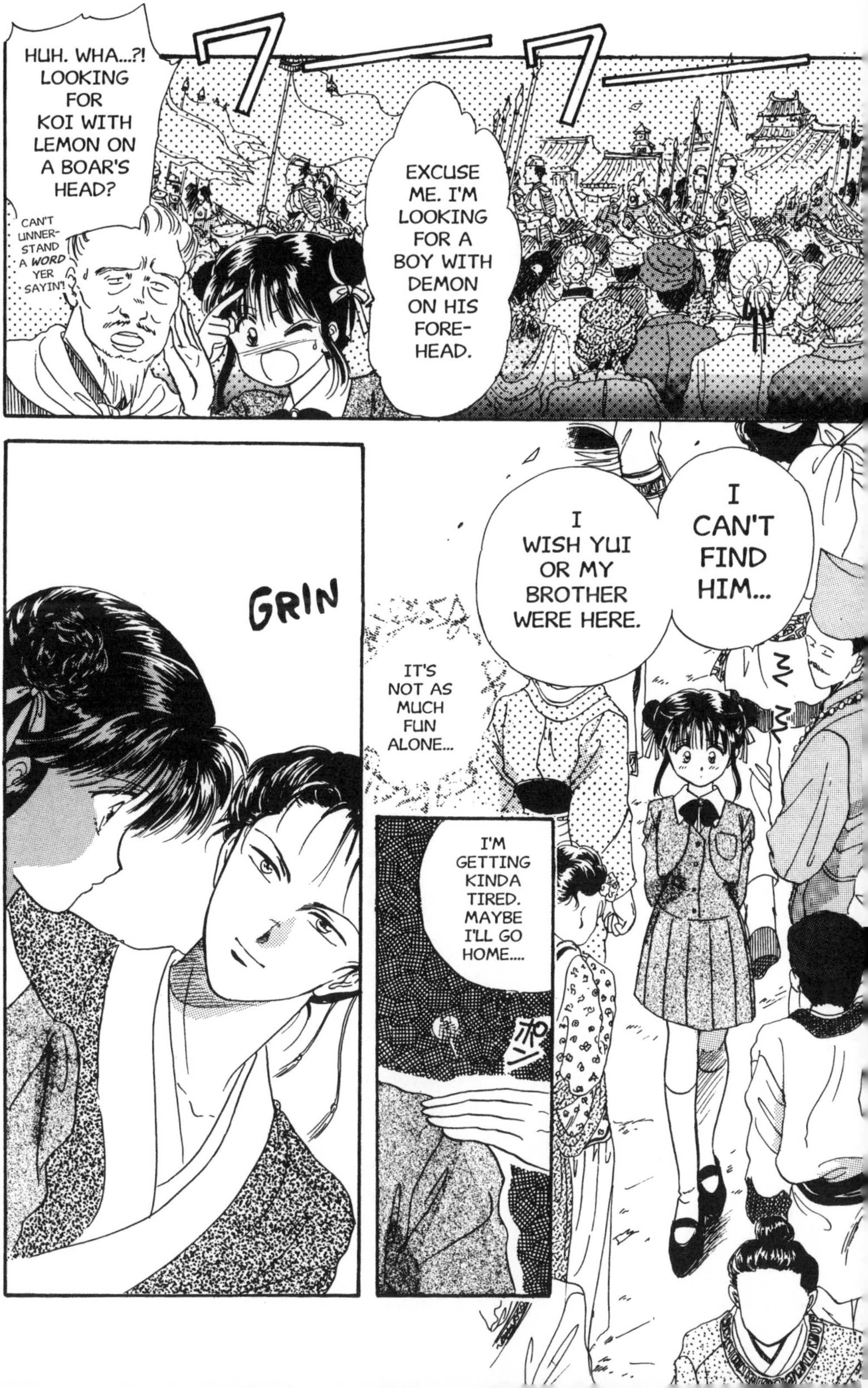
EXCUSE ME. I'M LOOKING FOR A BOY WITH DEMON ON HIS FORE-HEAD.
HUH. WHA...?! LOOKING FOR KOI WITH LEMON ON A BOAR'S HEAD?
CAN'T UNNER-STAND A WORD YER SAYIN'!
I CAN'T FIND HIM...
I WISH YUI OR MY BROTHER WERE HERE.
IT'S NOT AS MUCH FUN ALONE...
I'M GETTING KINDA TIRED. MAYBE I'LL GO HOME....
ポン
GRIN

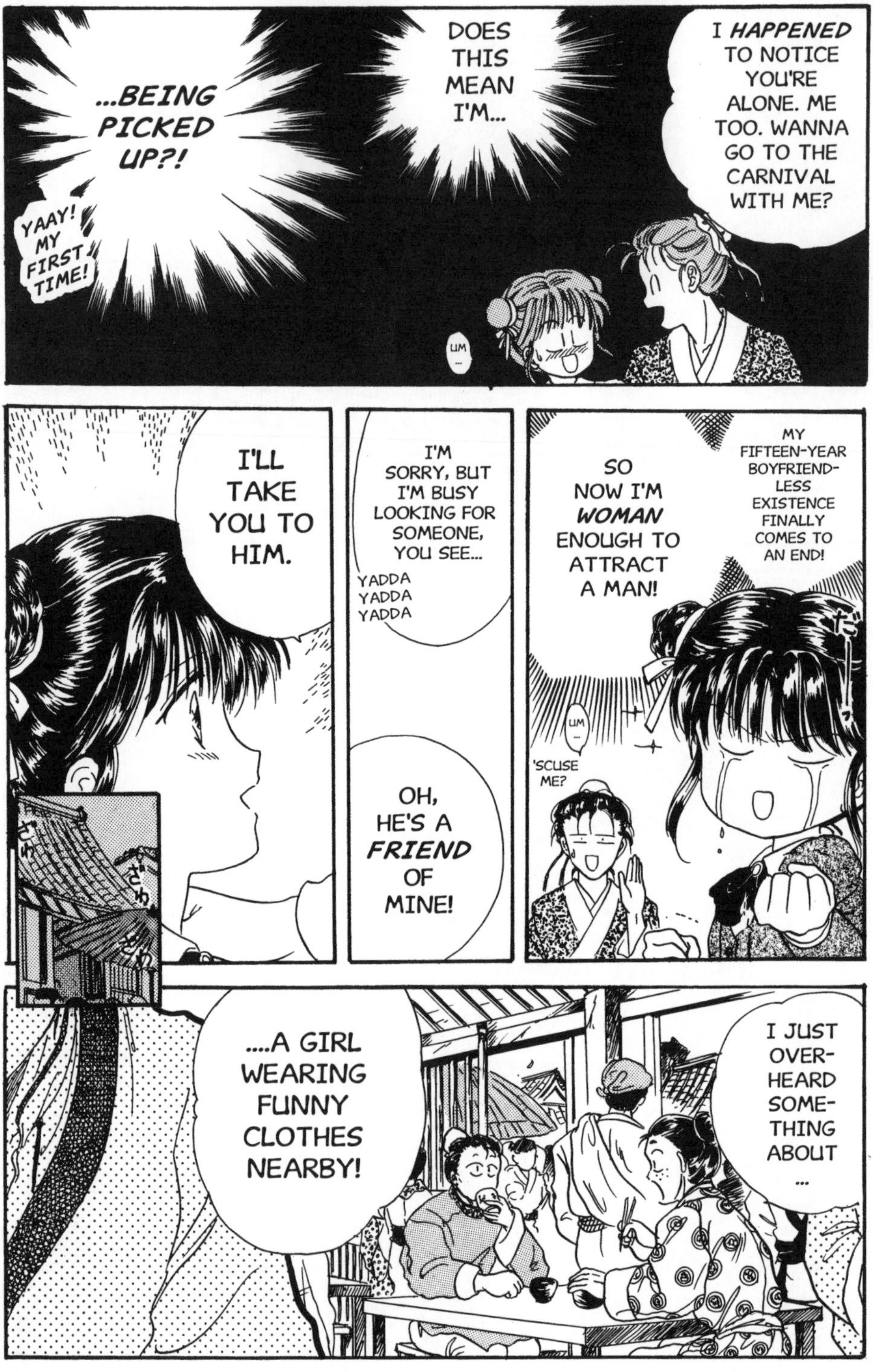
I HAPPENED TO NOTICE YOU'RE ALONE. ME TOO. WANNA GO TO THE CARNIVAL WITH ME?
UM...
DOES THIS MEAN I'M...
...BEING PICKED UP?!
YAAY! MY FIRST TIME!
MY FIFTEEN-YEAR BOYFRIEND-LESS EXISTENCE FINALLY COMES TO AN END!
SO NOW I'M WOMAN ENOUGH TO ATTRACT A MAN!
UM...
'SCUSE ME?
I'M SORRY, BUT I'M BUSY LOOKING FOR SOMEONE, YOU SEE...
YADDA YADDA YADDA
OH, HE'S A FRIEND OF MINE!
I'LL TAKE YOU TO HIM.
I JUST OVER-HEARD SOME-THING ABOUT...
....A GIRL WEARING FUNNY CLOTHES NEARBY!

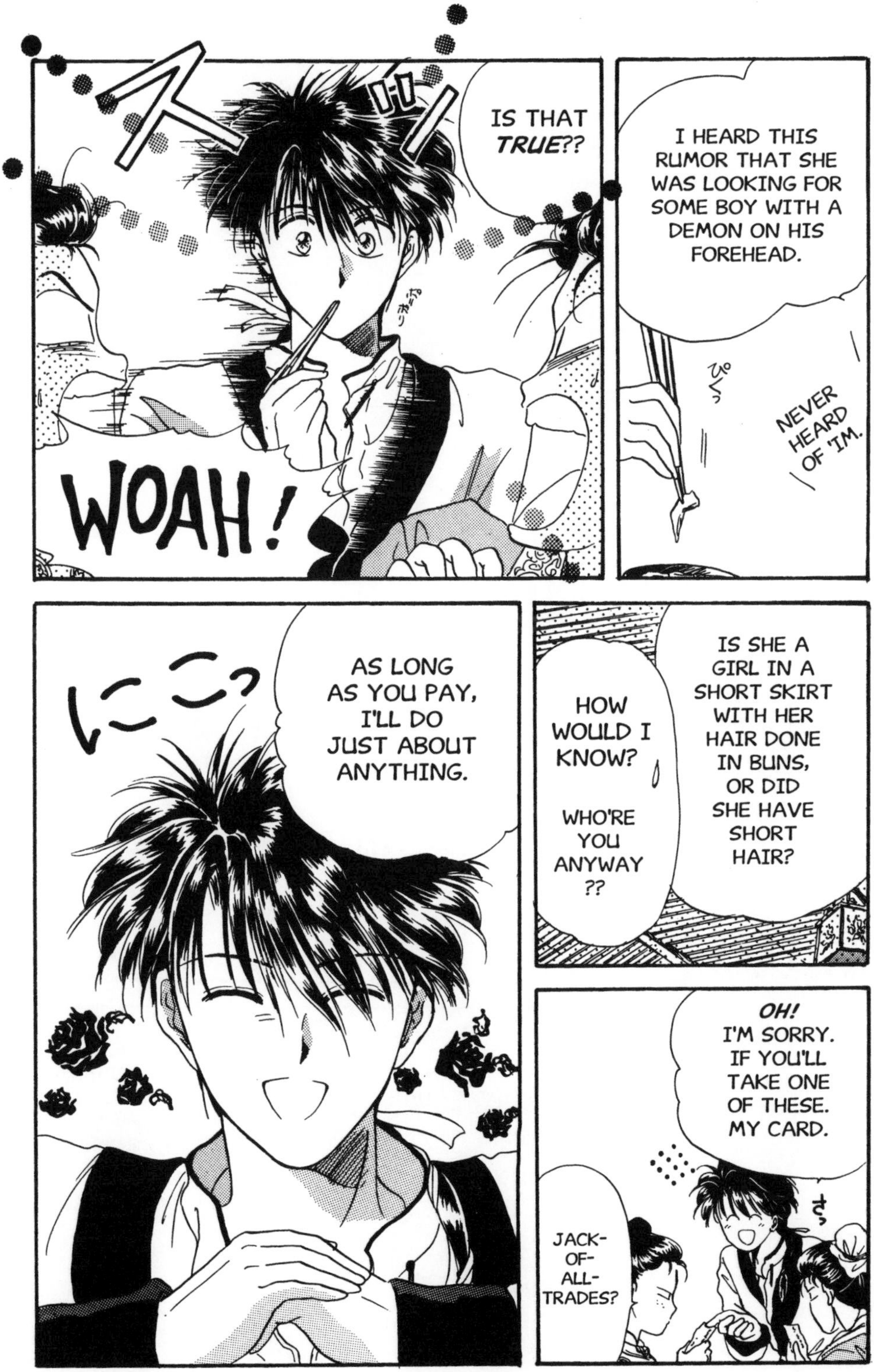
I HEARD THIS RUMOR THAT SHE WAS LOOKING FOR SOME BOY WITH A DEMON ON HIS FOREHEAD.
NEVER HEARD OF 'IM.
IS THAT *TRUE*??
WOAH!
IS SHE A GIRL IN A SHORT SKIRT WITH HER HAIR DONE IN BUNS, OR DID SHE HAVE SHORT HAIR?
HOW WOULD I KNOW?
WHO'RE YOU ANYWAY ??
OH! I'M SORRY. IF YOU'LL TAKE ONE OF THESE. MY CARD.
JACK-OF-ALL-TRADES?
にこっ
AS LONG AS YOU PAY, I'LL DO JUST ABOUT ANYTHING.

So I just want to clarify some things about my background. It seems I have to inform every reader that I'm a woman. ☺ As for how old I am...because I'm pretty young I'm not embarrassed about my age. Suffice to say I first got published at 18 and then *Prepubescence* came out when I was 20. You do the math.

I've had fans who tell me, "I want to be a manga artist just like you." Don't be just like me! "Lately I've been copying your drawings so much they look like yours." Well I suppose that's all right as long as you eventually acquire your own style. Every artist is always influenced by somebody else in the beginning. But I don't think it's such a good idea to continue copying other artists after you get published. Although they may seem the same, there's a big difference between being a big fan of an artist and unconsciously resembling that style, or parody, or reference, and PLAGIARISM. Lifting one or two ideas or scenes I can handle, but if you make a comic exactly like mine, I'll get mad at you!

I dunno, uh...

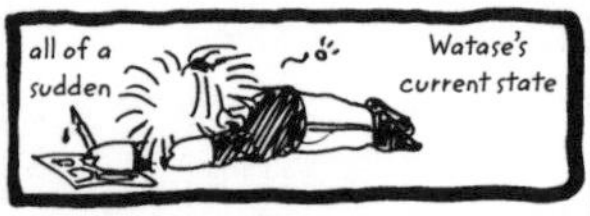
all of a sudden
Watase's current state

Now THAT'S something that can get me mad! (I'm still new to this.) I know that there are tons of ideas that resemble each other, but to steal a chapter verbatim... and when I get upset, it means I'm 10 times angrier than the average person. (Usually I'm laid back no matter what people say to me. Friends will say, "Why don't you get mad once in a while," and get mad at me!) Guess I haven't grown up. For the past two years, I haven't read any of my favorite manga artists who have influenced me! (Actually I haven't been reading much manga in general.) I want to shed my influences. I just want to draw manga my own way. But my drawings aren't getting better! And I'm working on it so hard!

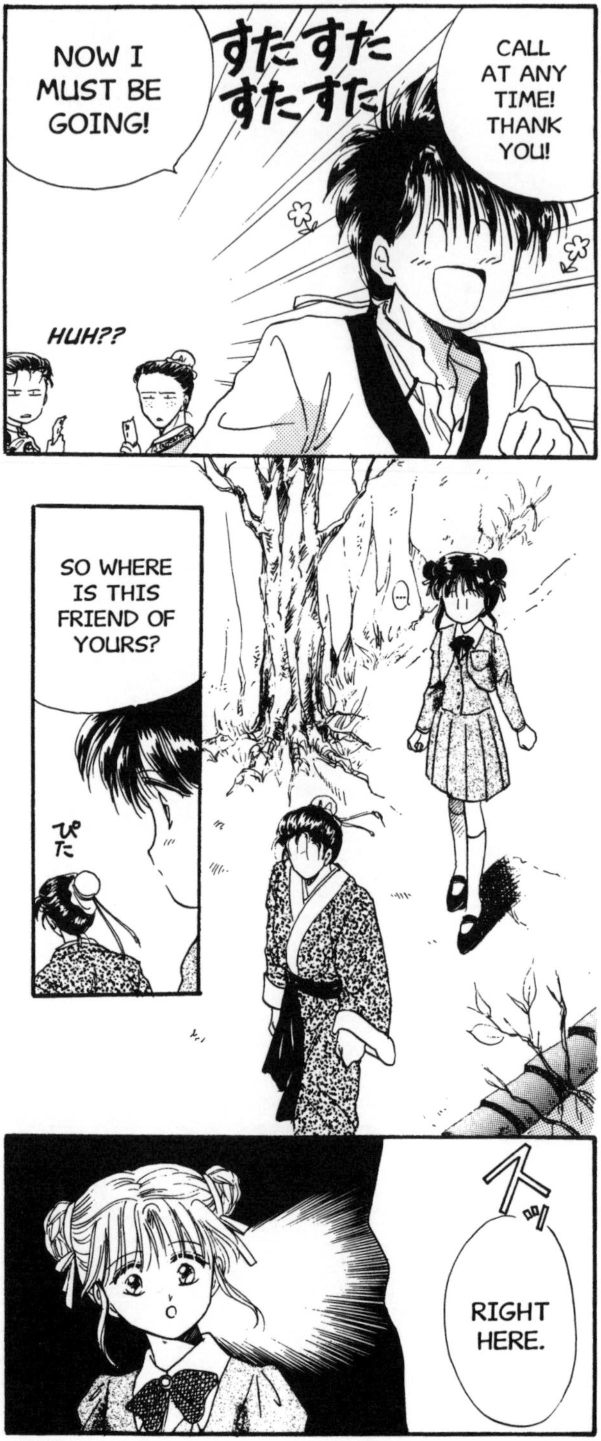
CALL AT ANY TIME! THANK YOU!
すたすたすたすた
NOW I MUST BE GOING!
HUH??
...
SO WHERE IS THIS FRIEND OF YOURS?
ぴた
RIGHT HERE.

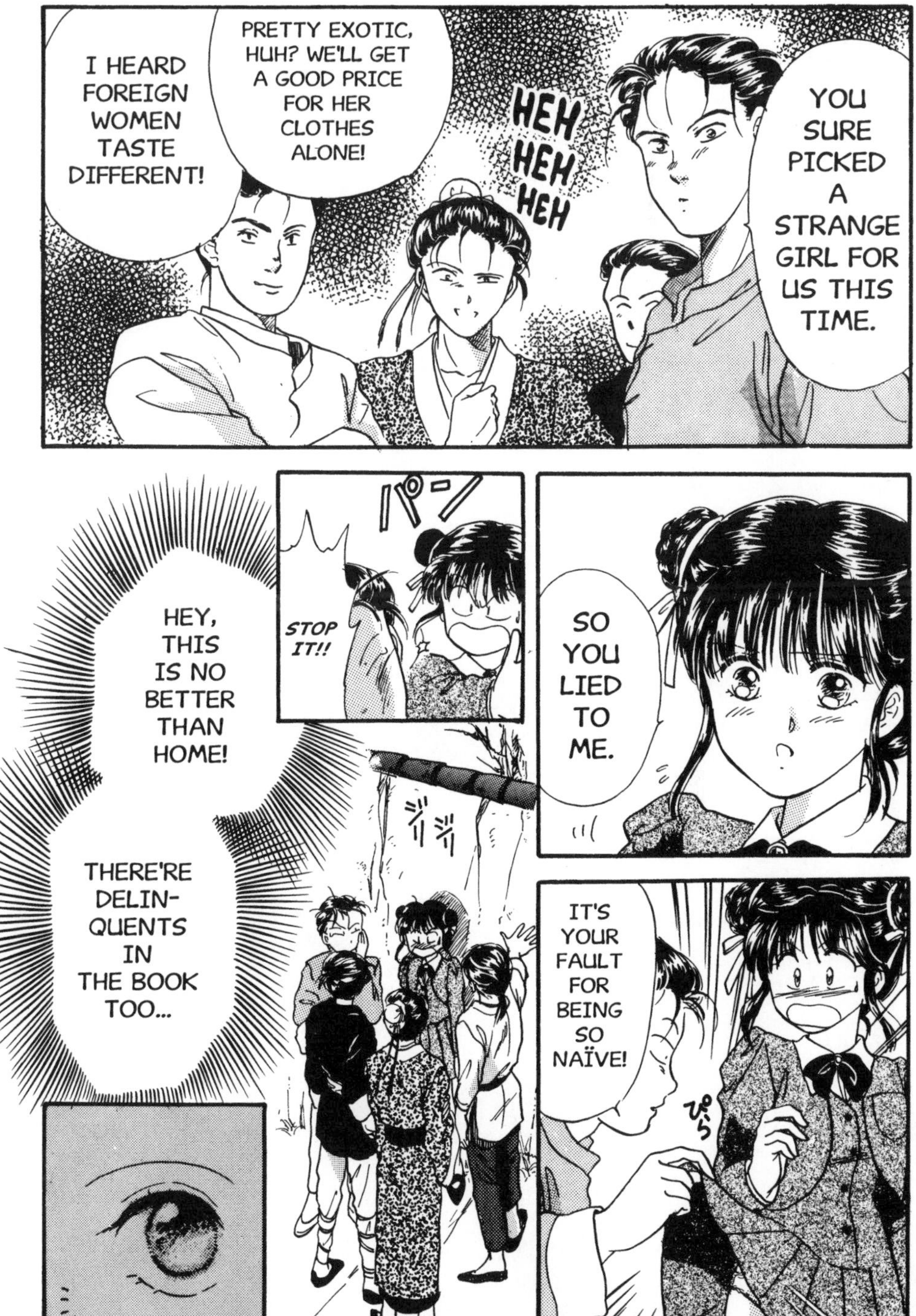
YOU SURE PICKED A STRANGE GIRL FOR US THIS TIME.
PRETTY EXOTIC, HUH? WE'LL GET A GOOD PRICE FOR HER CLOTHES ALONE!
HEH HEH HEH
I HEARD FOREIGN WOMEN TASTE DIFFERENT!
SO YOU LIED TO ME.
パーン
STOP IT!!
HEY, THIS IS NO BETTER THAN HOME!
IT'S YOUR FAULT FOR BEING SO NAÏVE!
ぴら
ジリジリ
THERE'RE DELIN-QUENTS IN THE BOOK TOO...

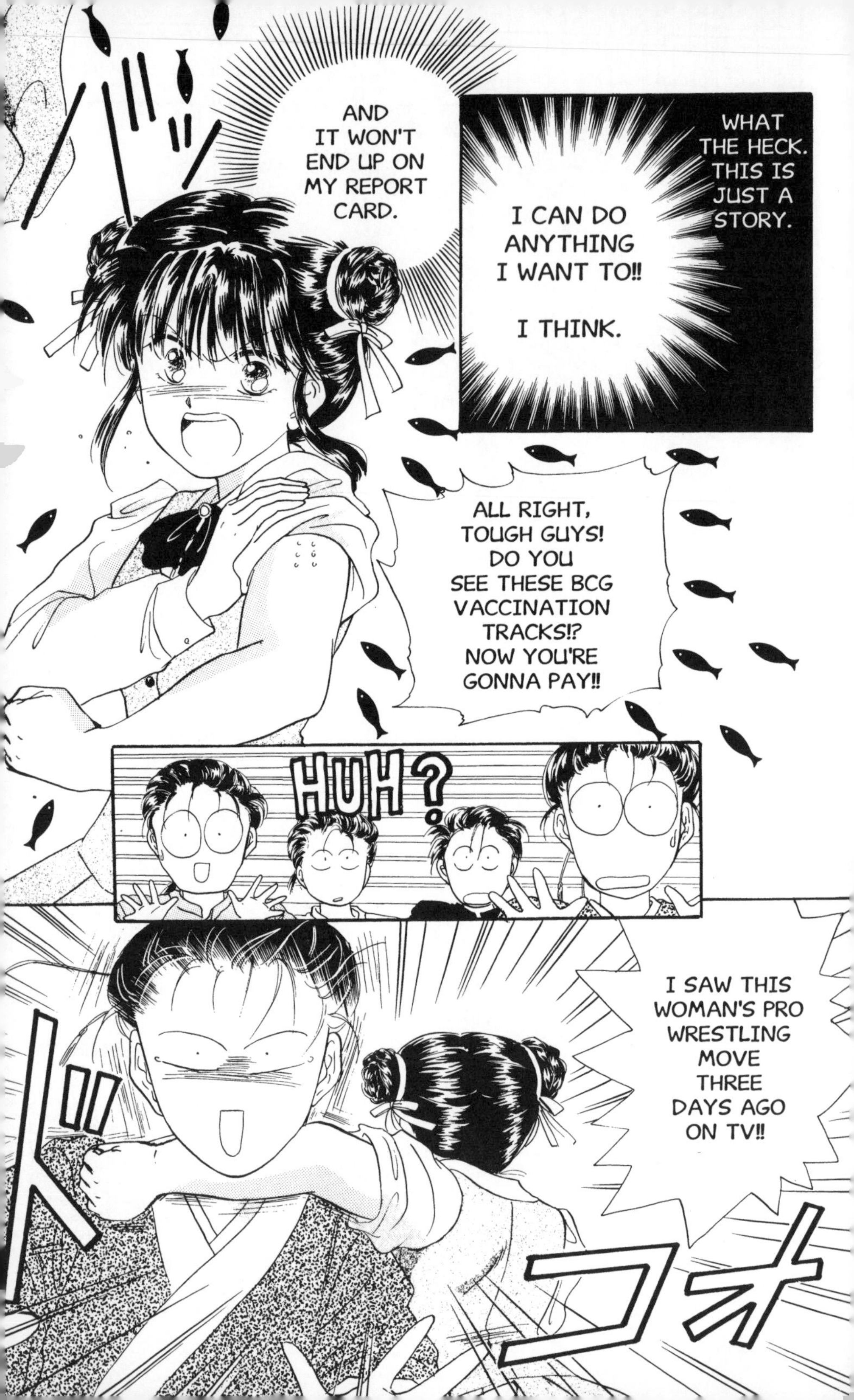
WHAT THE HECK. THIS IS JUST A STORY.
I CAN DO ANYTHING I WANT TO!!
I THINK.
AND IT WON'T END UP ON MY REPORT CARD.
ALL RIGHT, TOUGH GUYS! DO YOU SEE THESE BCG VACCINATION TRACKS!? NOW YOU'RE GONNA PAY!!
HUH?
I SAW THIS WOMAN'S PRO WRESTLING MOVE THREE DAYS AGO ON TV!!

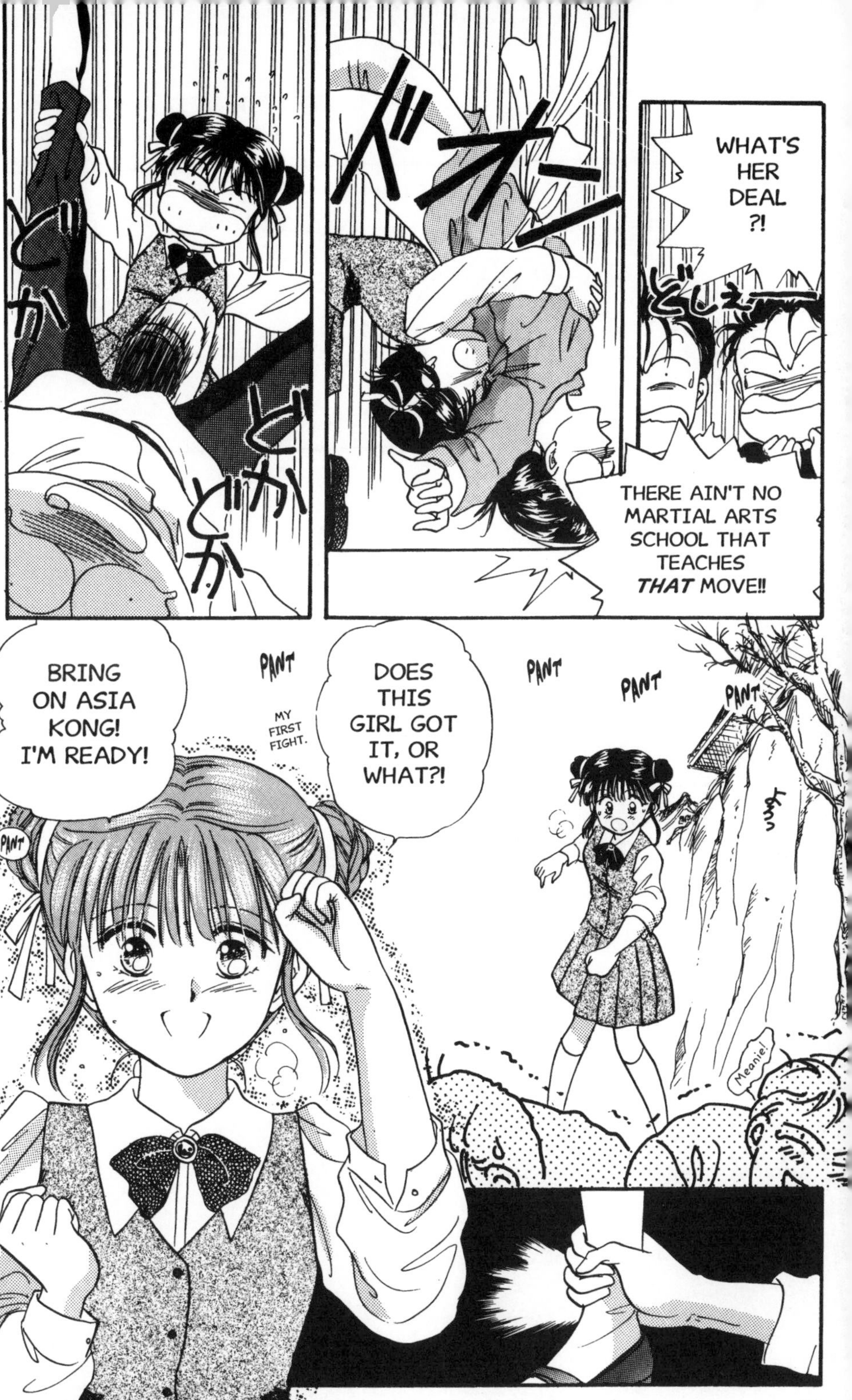
WHAT'S HER DEAL?!
どしぇー
THERE AIN'T NO MARTIAL ARTS SCHOOL THAT TEACHES ***THAT*** MOVE!!
ズオー
どかどかどか
どか
PANT
PANT
PANT
PANT
DOES THIS GIRL GOT IT, OR WHAT?!
MY FIRST FIGHT.
BRING ON ASIA KONG! I'M READY!
PANT
Meanie!

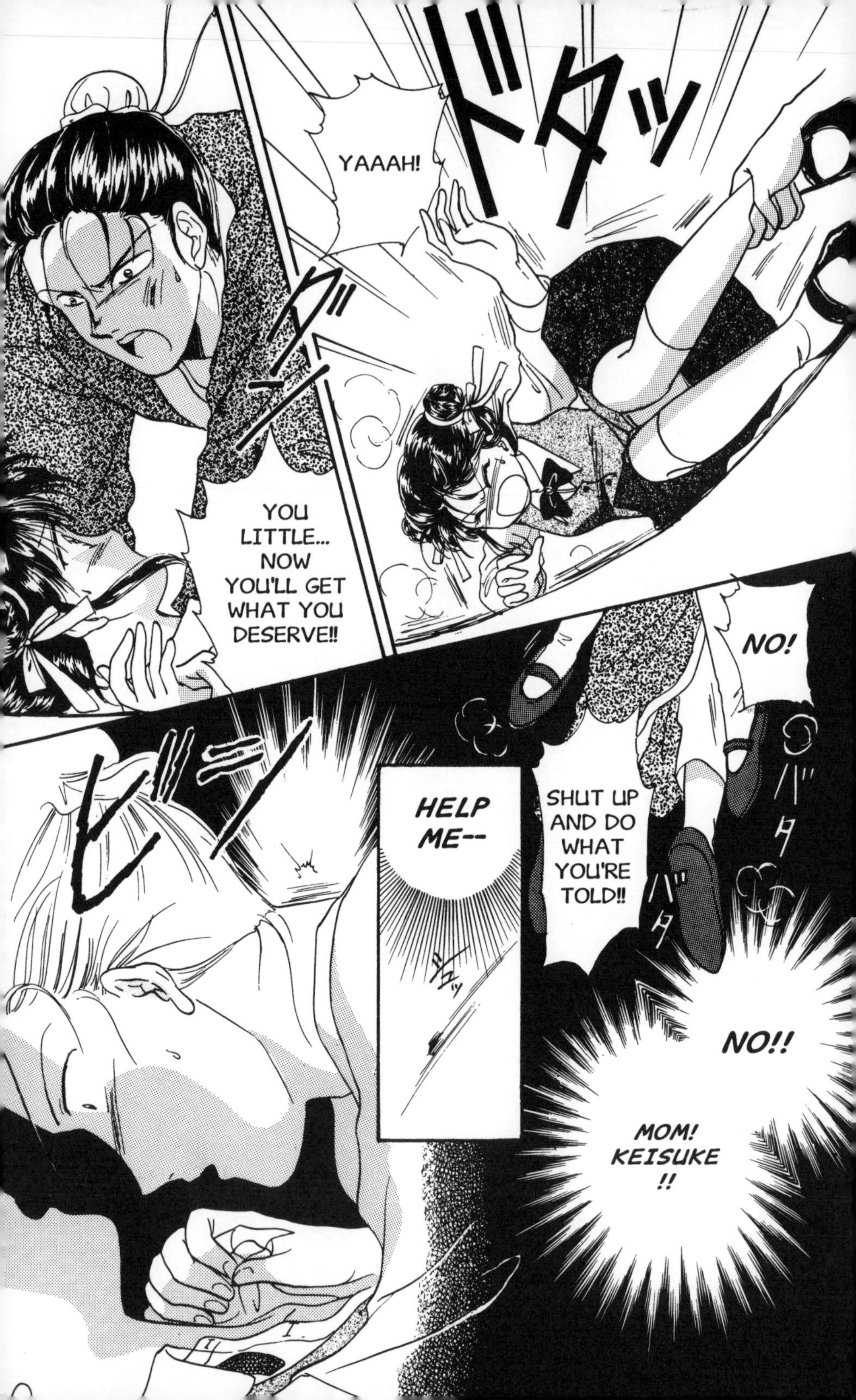
ドタッ
YAAAH!
YOU LITTLE... NOW YOU'LL GET WHAT YOU DESERVE!!
NO!
バタ
バタ
SHUT UP AND DO WHAT YOU'RE TOLD!!
HELP ME--
NO!!
MOM! KEISUKE !!

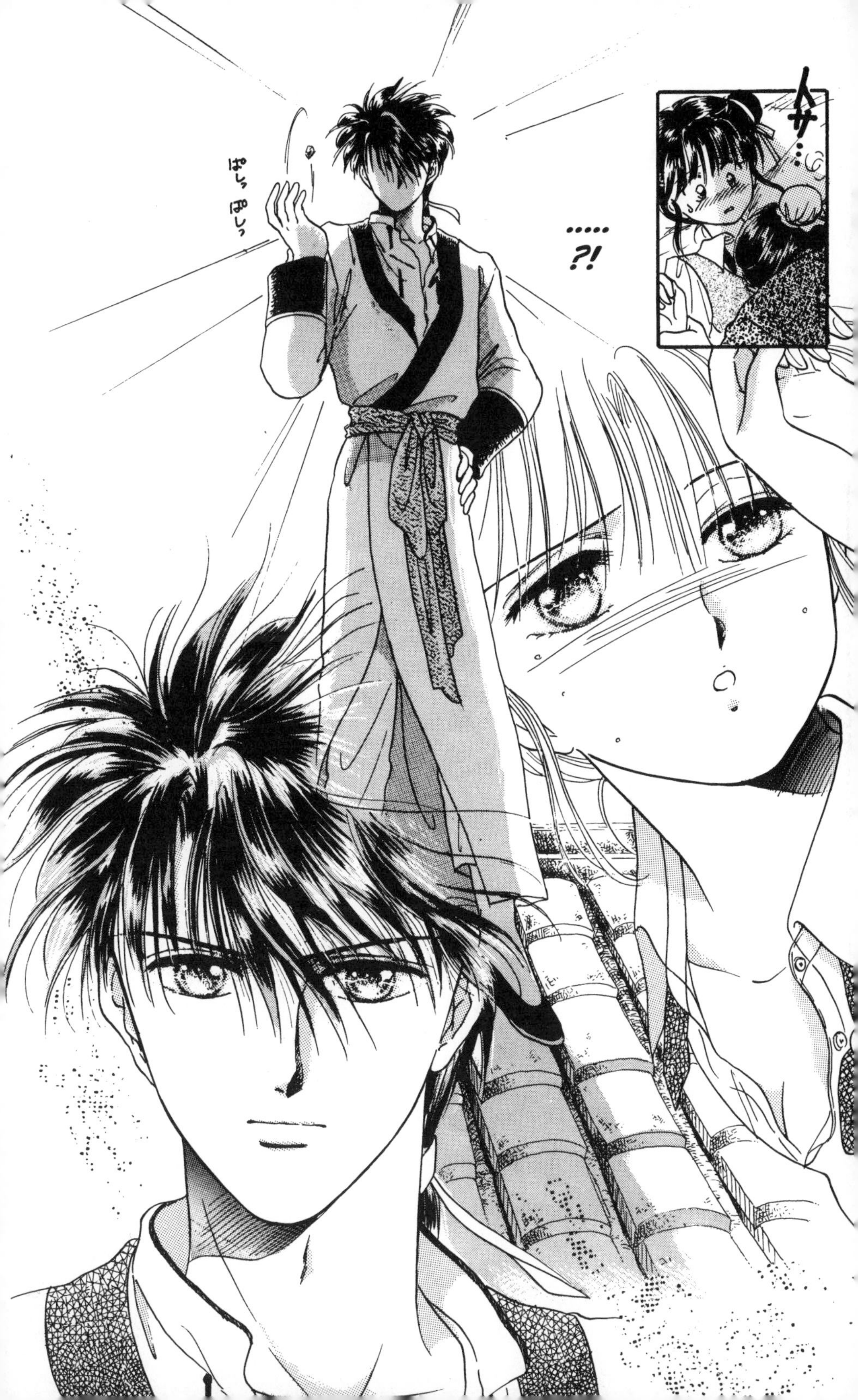
トサ…
.....
?!
ぱしっ ぱしっ

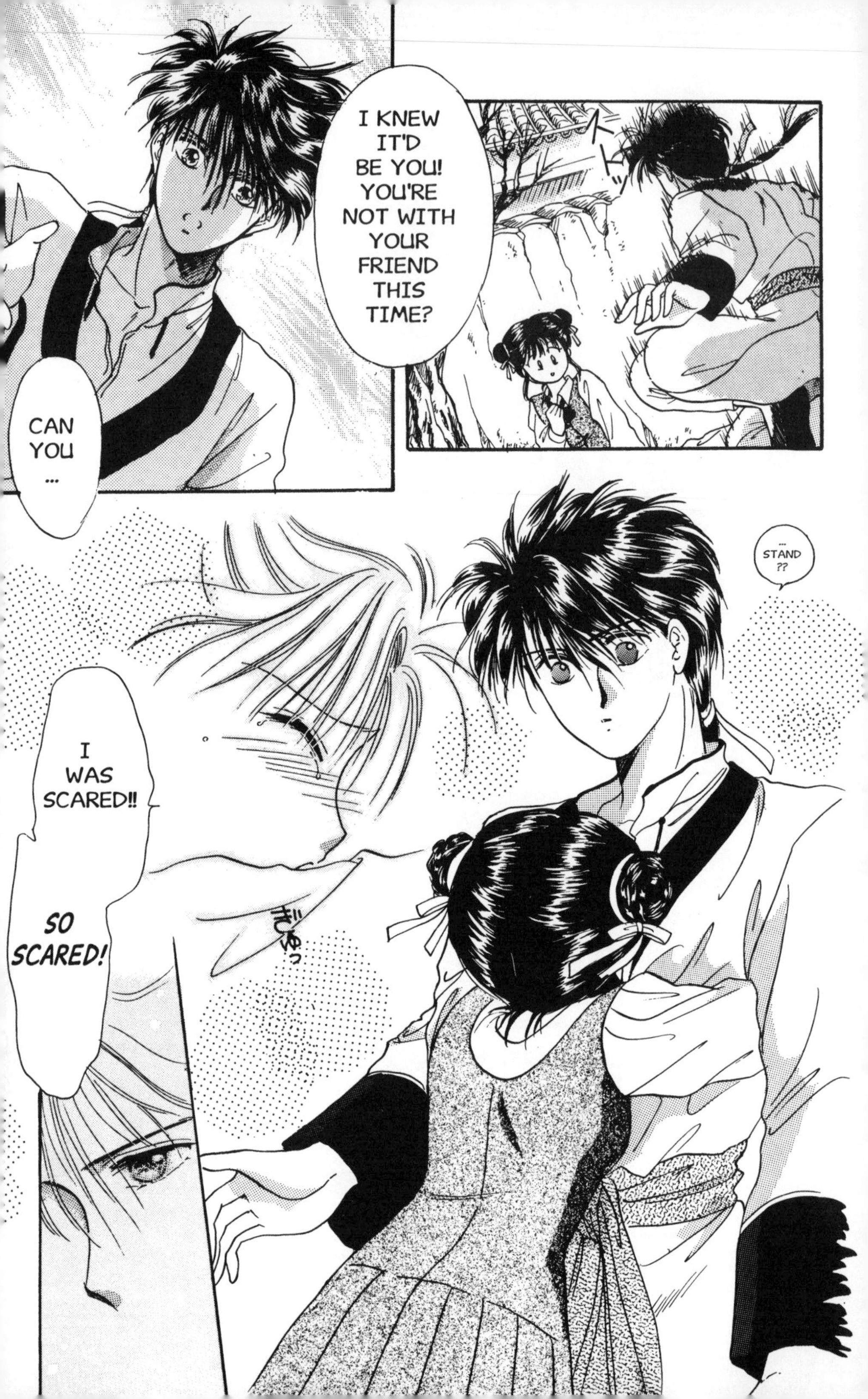
I KNEW IT'D BE YOU! YOU'RE NOT WITH YOUR FRIEND THIS TIME?
CAN YOU ...
... STAND ??
I WAS SCARED!!
SO SCARED!
ぎゅっ

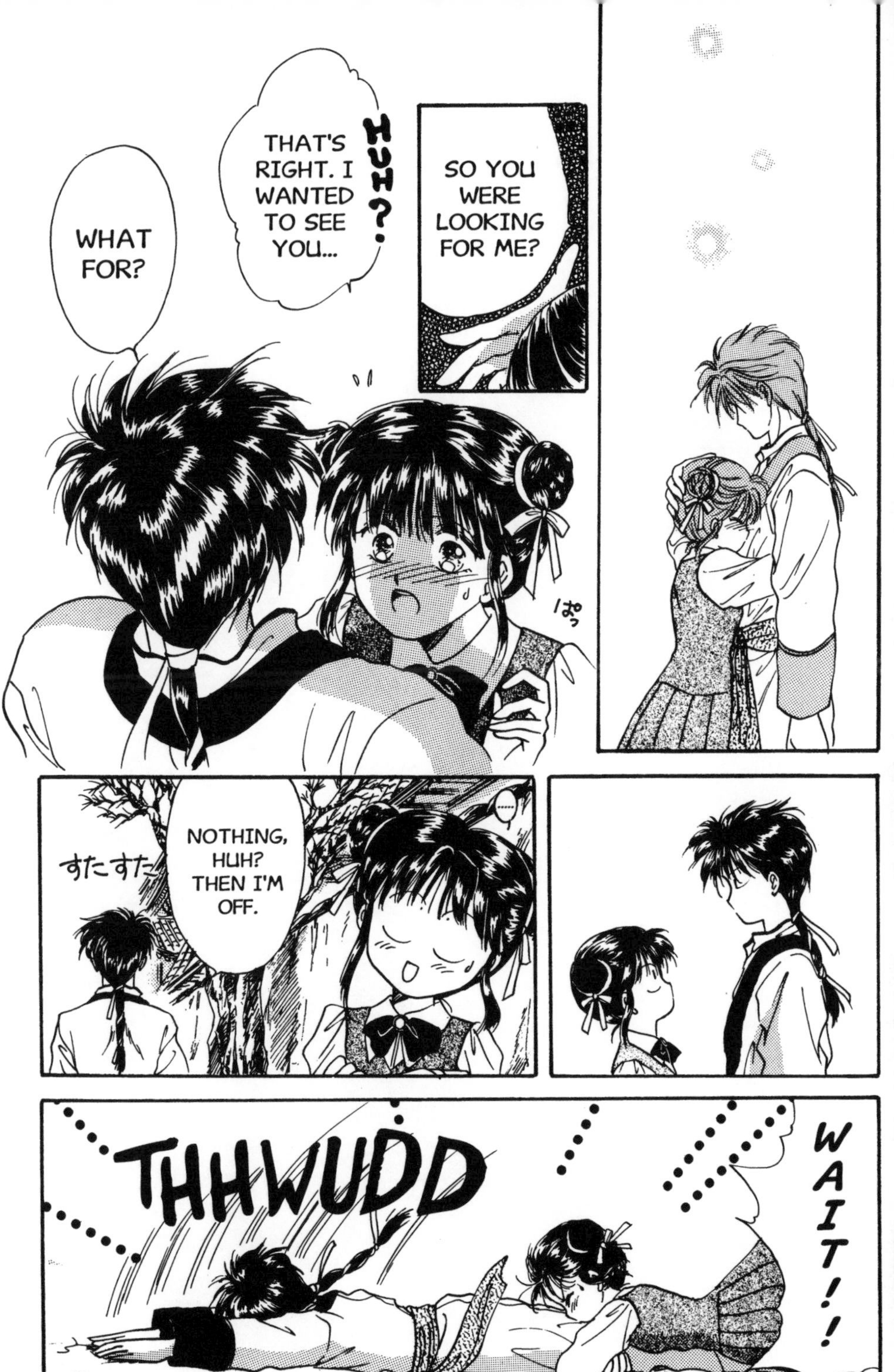
SO YOU WERE LOOKING FOR ME?
THAT'S RIGHT. I WANTED TO SEE YOU...
HUH?
WHAT FOR?
ぱっ
......
NOTHING, HUH? THEN I'M OFF.
すたすた
WAIT!!
THHWUDD

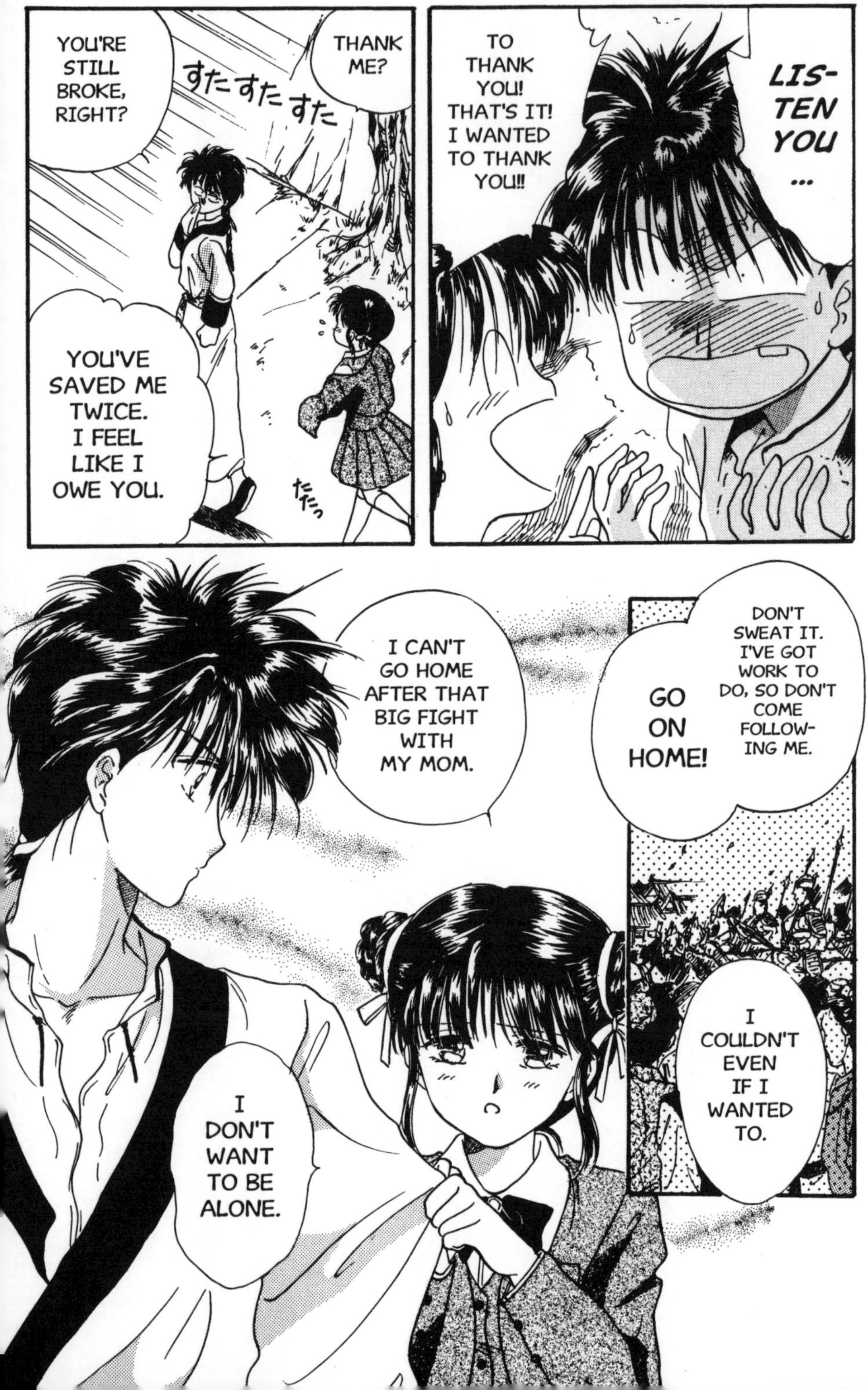
LISTEN YOU...
TO THANK YOU! THAT'S IT! I WANTED TO THANK YOU!!
THANK ME?
すたすたすた
YOU'RE STILL BROKE, RIGHT?
YOU'VE SAVED ME TWICE. I FEEL LIKE I OWE YOU.
たたっ
DON'T SWEAT IT. I'VE GOT WORK TO DO, SO DON'T COME FOLLOWING ME.
GO ON HOME!
I COULDN'T EVEN IF I WANTED TO.
I CAN'T GO HOME AFTER THAT BIG FIGHT WITH MY MOM.
I DON'T WANT TO BE ALONE.

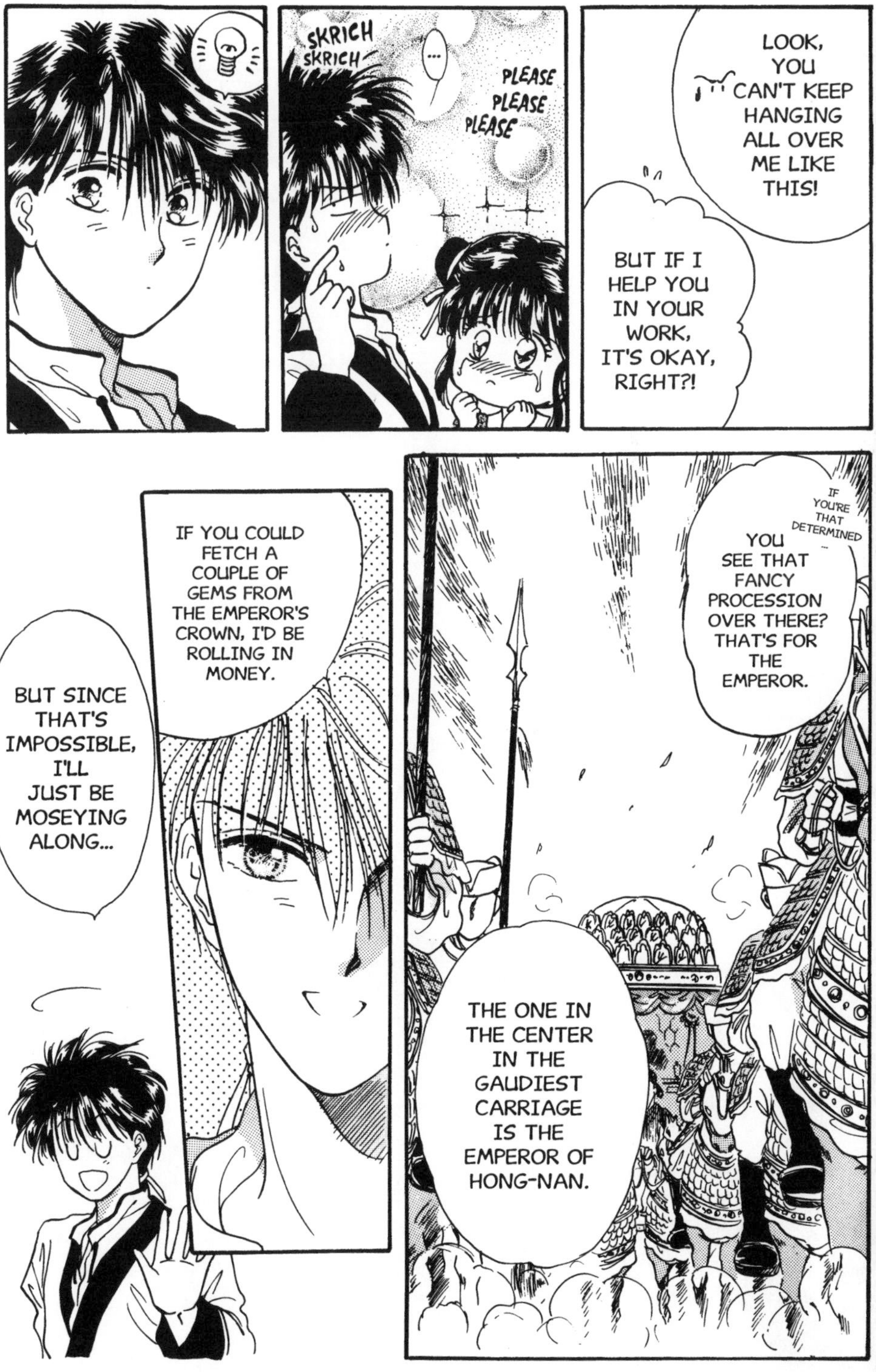
LOOK, YOU CAN'T KEEP HANGING ALL OVER ME LIKE THIS!
BUT IF I HELP YOU IN YOUR WORK, IT'S OKAY, RIGHT?!
SKRICH SKRICH
...
PLEASE PLEASE PLEASE
IF YOU'RE THAT DETERMINED...
YOU SEE THAT FANCY PROCESSION OVER THERE? THAT'S FOR THE EMPEROR.
THE ONE IN THE CENTER IN THE GAUDIEST CARRIAGE IS THE EMPEROR OF HONG-NAN.
IF YOU COULD FETCH A COUPLE OF GEMS FROM THE EMPEROR'S CROWN, I'D BE ROLLING IN MONEY.
BUT SINCE THAT'S IMPOSSIBLE, I'LL JUST BE MOSEYING ALONG...

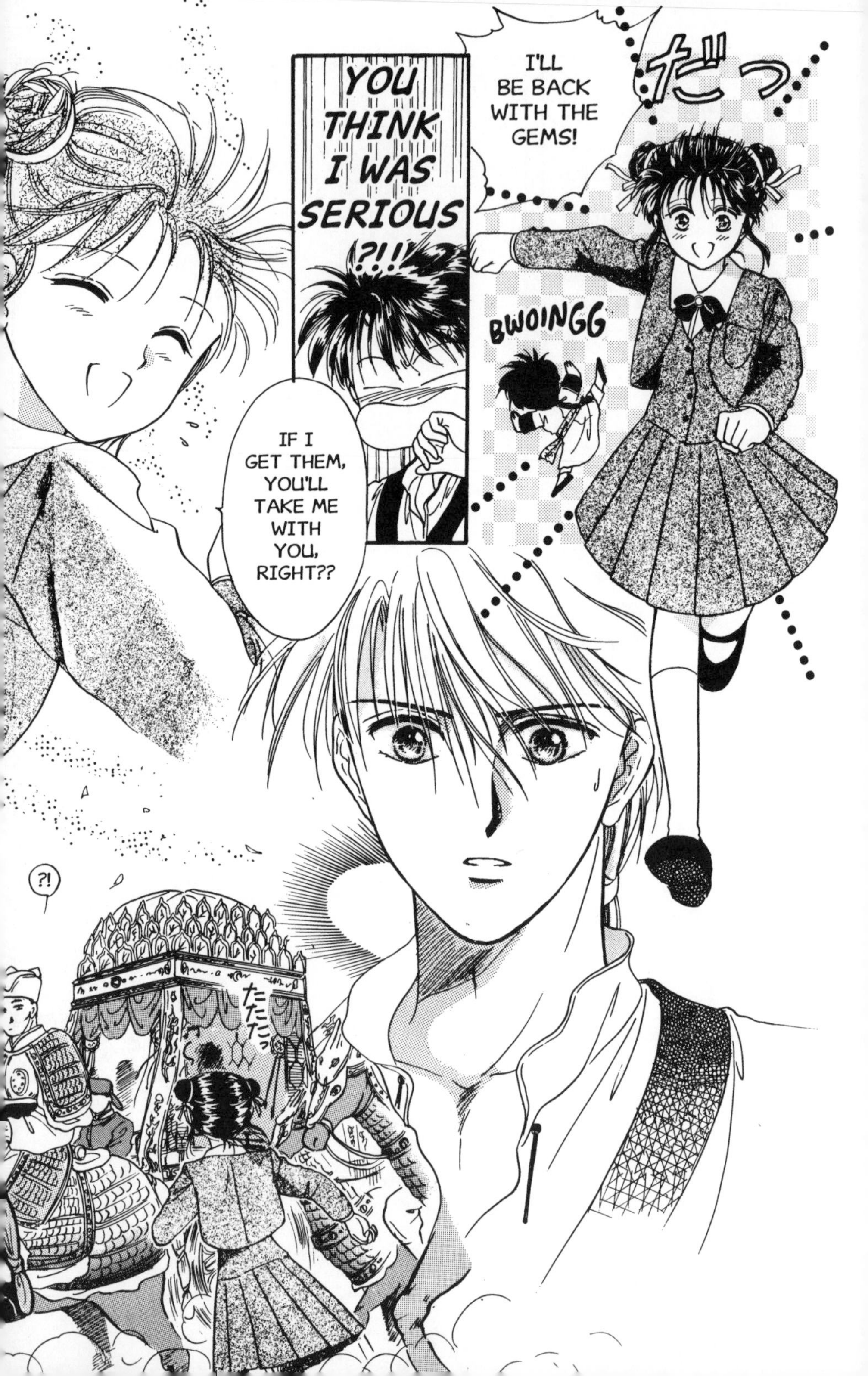
だっ
I'LL BE BACK WITH THE GEMS!
BWOINGG
YOU THINK I WAS SERIOUS ?!!
IF I GET THEM, YOU'LL TAKE ME WITH YOU, RIGHT??
?!
たたたっ

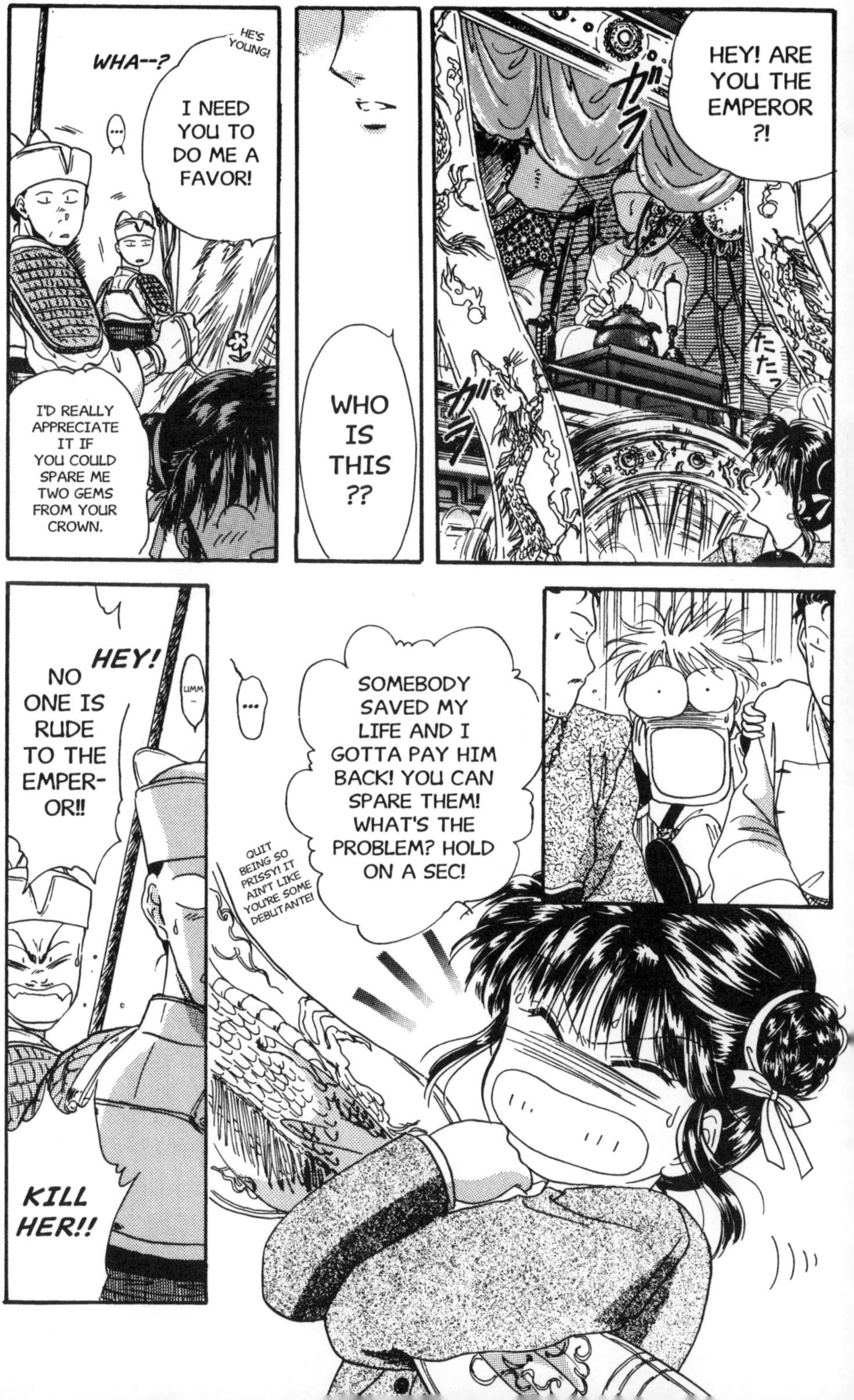
ガラ
HEY! ARE YOU THE EMPEROR ?!
ガラ
たたっ
WHO IS THIS ??
HE'S YOUNG!
WHA--?
I NEED YOU TO DO ME A FAVOR!
...
I'D REALLY APPRECIATE IT IF YOU COULD SPARE ME TWO GEMS FROM YOUR CROWN.
SOMEBODY SAVED MY LIFE AND I GOTTA PAY HIM BACK! YOU CAN SPARE THEM! WHAT'S THE PROBLEM? HOLD ON A SEC!
QUIT BEING SO PRISSY! IT AIN'T LIKE YOU'RE SOME DEBUTANTE!
...
UMM ...
HEY!
NO ONE IS RUDE TO THE EMPEROR!!
KILL HER!!

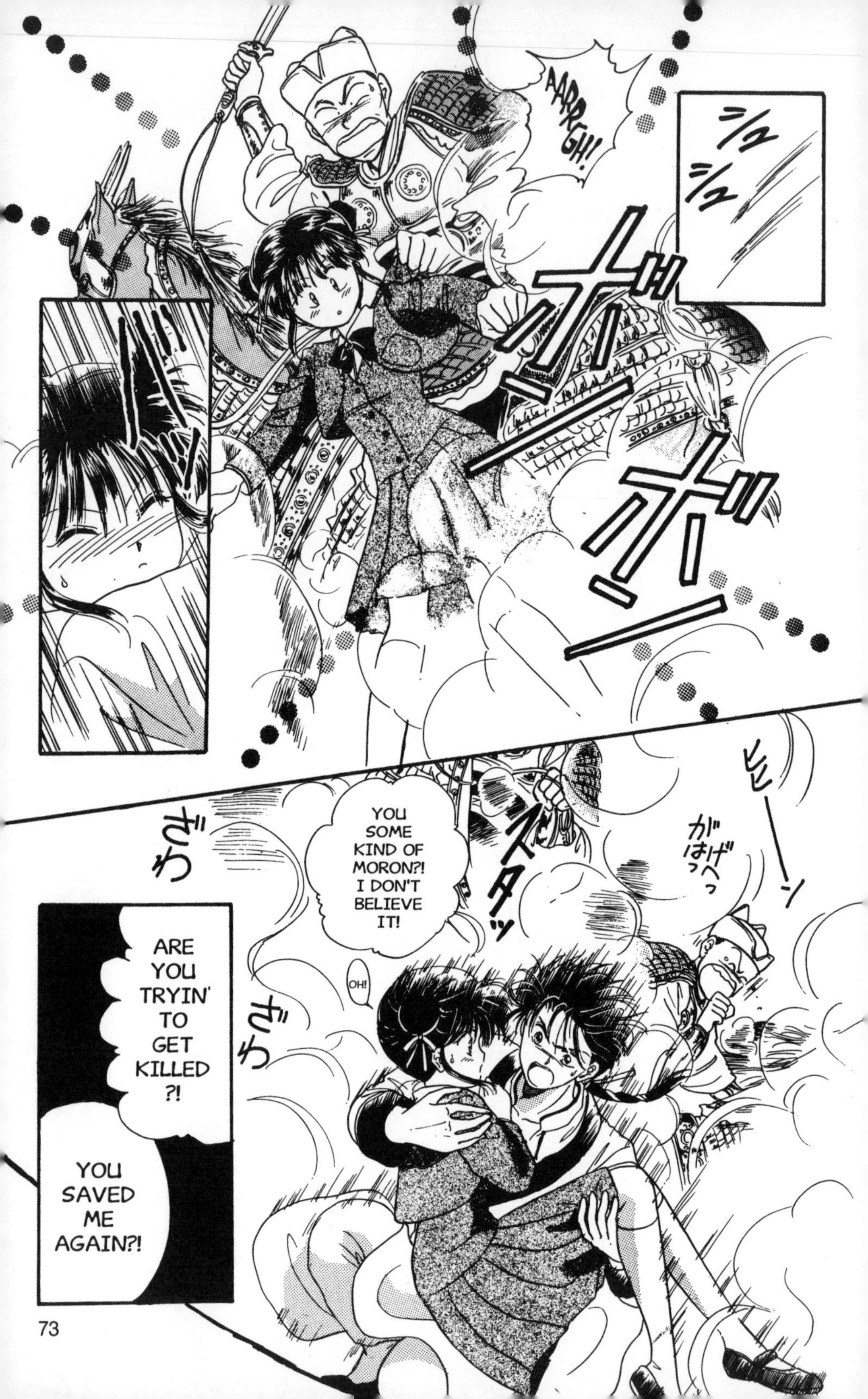
シュシュ
AARRGH!
ヒヒーン
がはげへっ
YOU SOME KIND OF MORON?! I DON'T BELIEVE IT!
スタッ
ざわ
OH!
ざわ
ARE YOU TRYIN' TO GET KILLED?!
YOU SAVED ME AGAIN?!

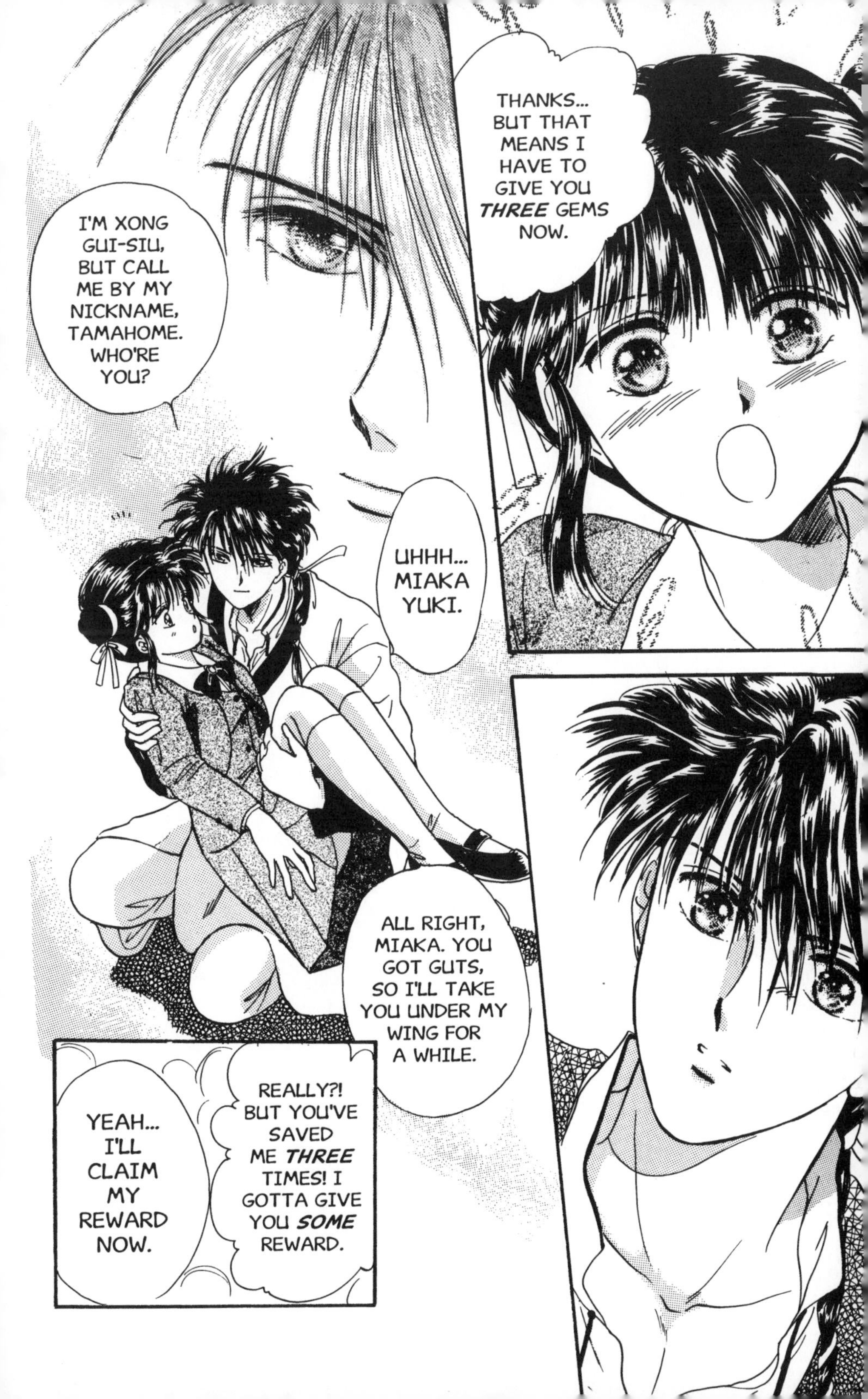
I'M XONG GUI-SIU, BUT CALL ME BY MY NICKNAME, TAMAHOME. WHO'RE YOU?
UHHH... MIAKA YUKI.
ALL RIGHT, MIAKA. YOU GOT GUTS, SO I'LL TAKE YOU UNDER MY WING FOR A WHILE.
REALLY?! BUT YOU'VE SAVED ME *THREE* TIMES! I GOTTA GIVE YOU *SOME* REWARD.
YEAH... I'LL CLAIM MY REWARD NOW.
THANKS... BUT THAT MEANS I HAVE TO GIVE YOU *THREE* GEMS NOW.

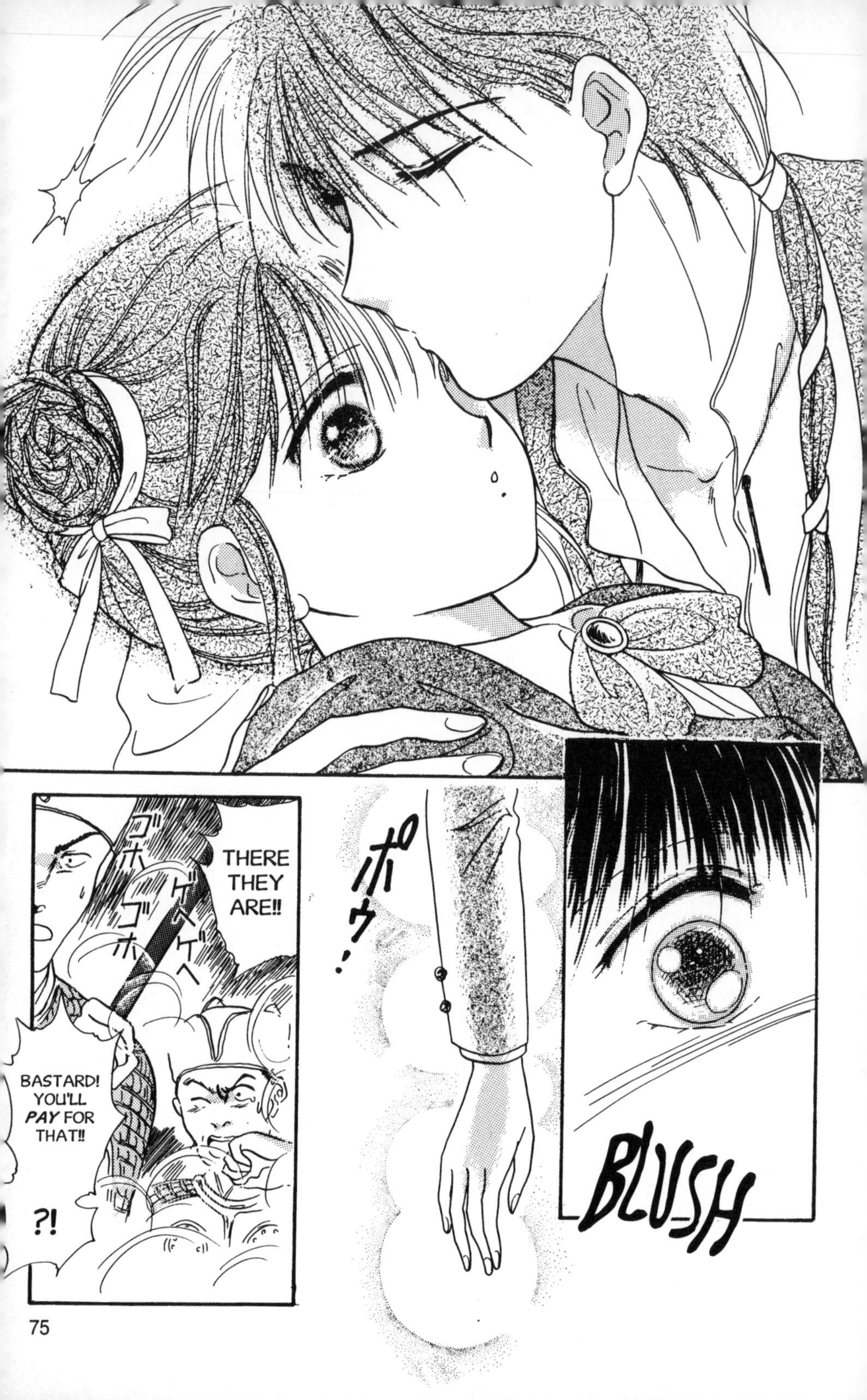
BLUSH
ポウッ!
THERE THEY ARE!!
ゲヘゲヘ
ゴホゴホ
BASTARD! YOU'LL *PAY* FOR THAT!!
?!

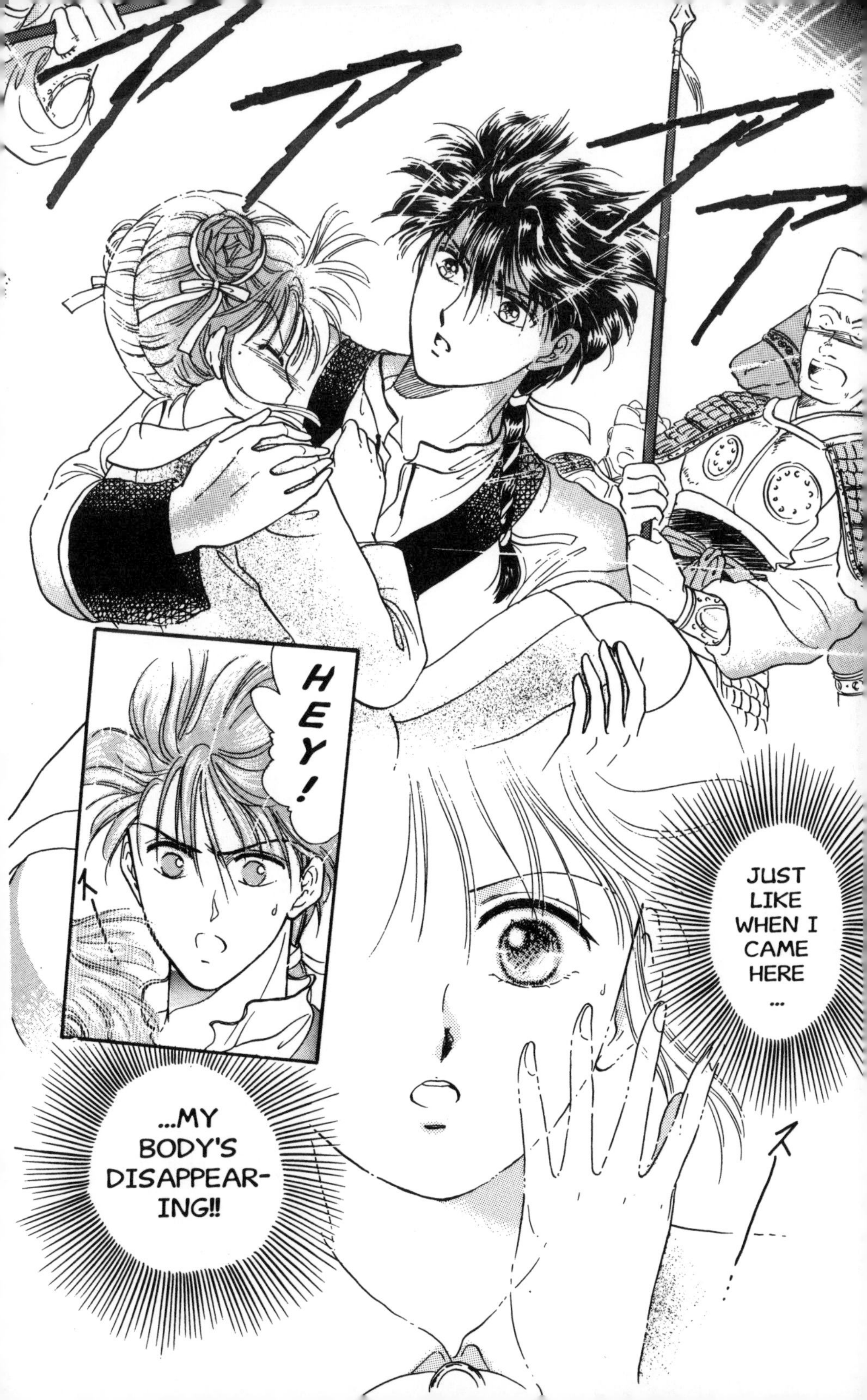
HEY!
JUST LIKE WHEN I CAME HERE ...
...MY BODY'S DISAPPEARING!!

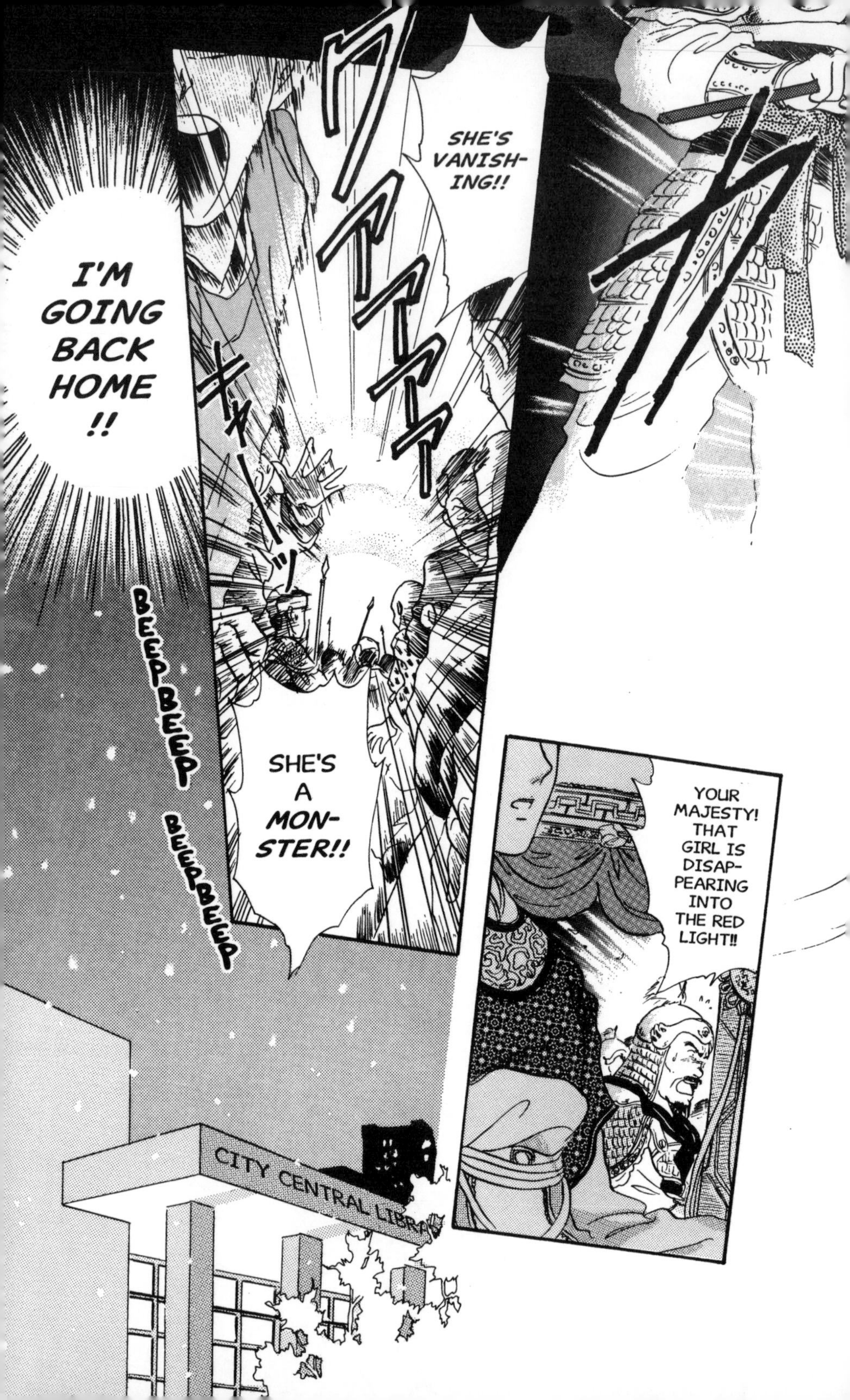
SHE'S VANISH- ING!!
SHE'S A MON- STER!!
I'M GOING BACK HOME !!
YOUR MAJESTY! THAT GIRL IS DISAP- PEARING INTO THE RED LIGHT!!
BEEPBEEP
BEEPBEEP
CITY CENTRAL LIBR

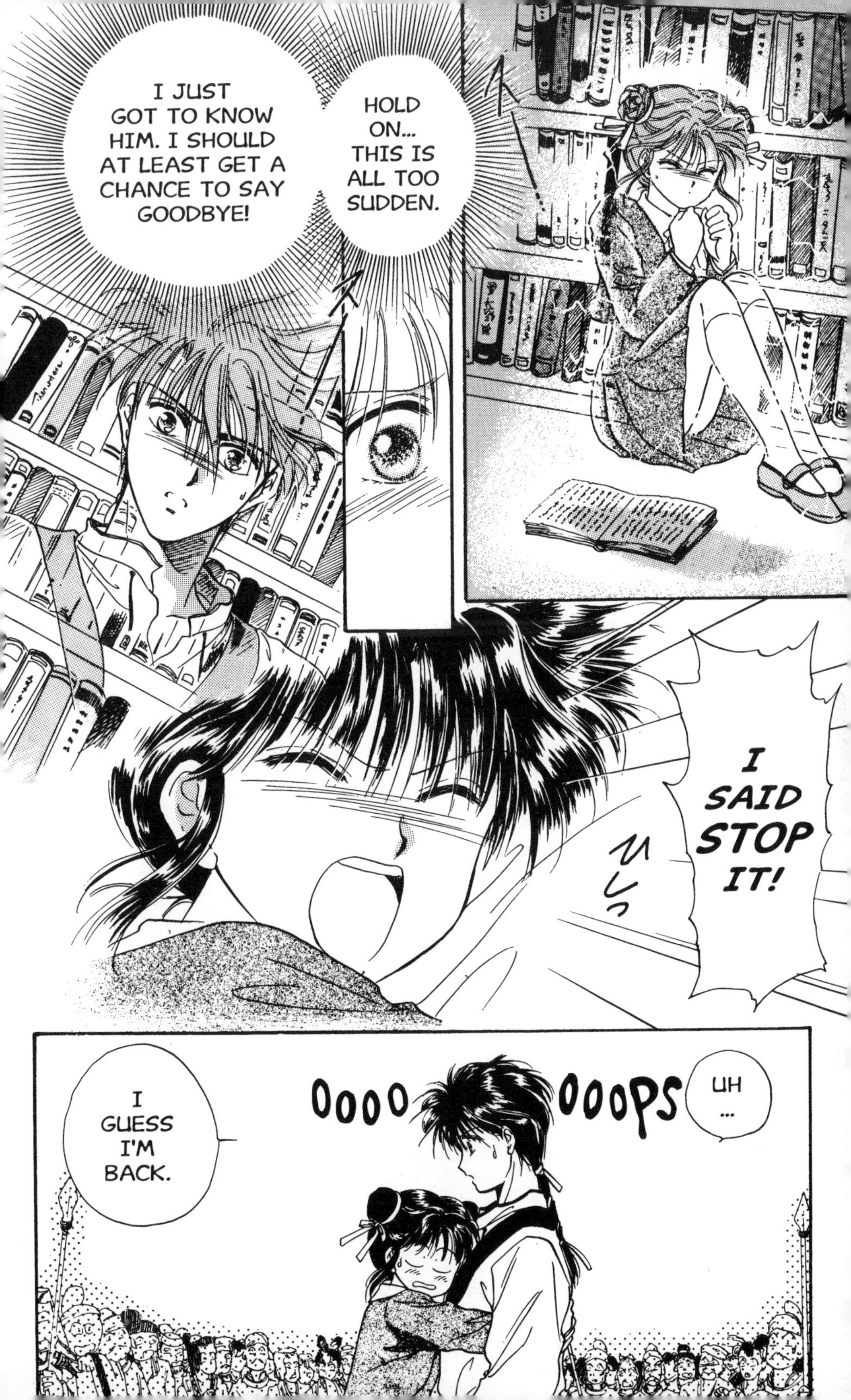
HOLD ON... THIS IS ALL TOO SUDDEN.
I JUST GOT TO KNOW HIM. I SHOULD AT LEAST GET A CHANCE TO SAY GOODBYE!
I SAID STOP IT!
ひしっ
UH ...
OOOO OOOPS
I GUESS I'M BACK.

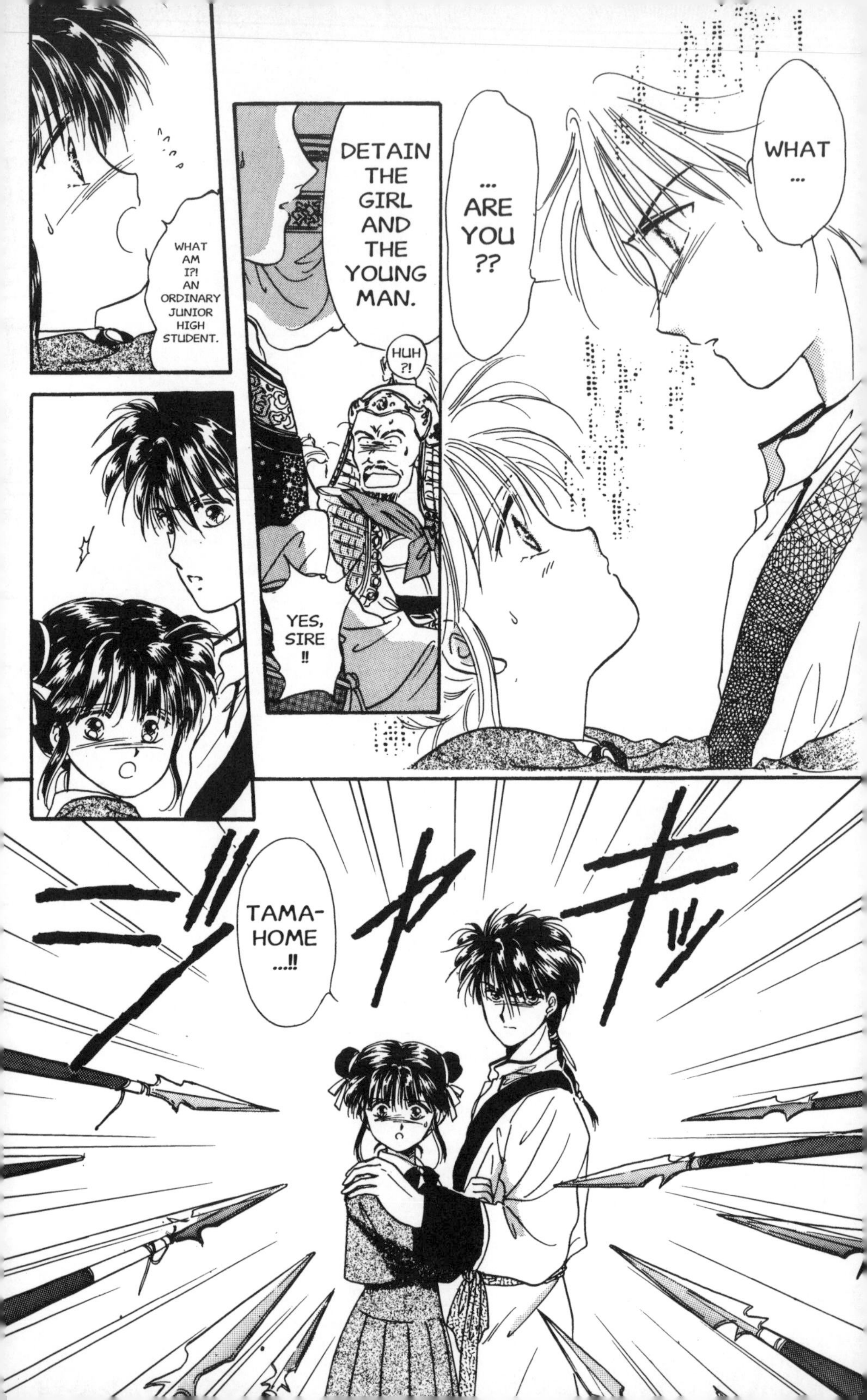
WHAT ...
... ARE YOU ??
DETAIN THE GIRL AND THE YOUNG MAN.
HUH ?!
YES, SIRE !!
WHAT AM I?! AN ORDINARY JUNIOR HIGH STUDENT.
TAMA-HOME ...!!

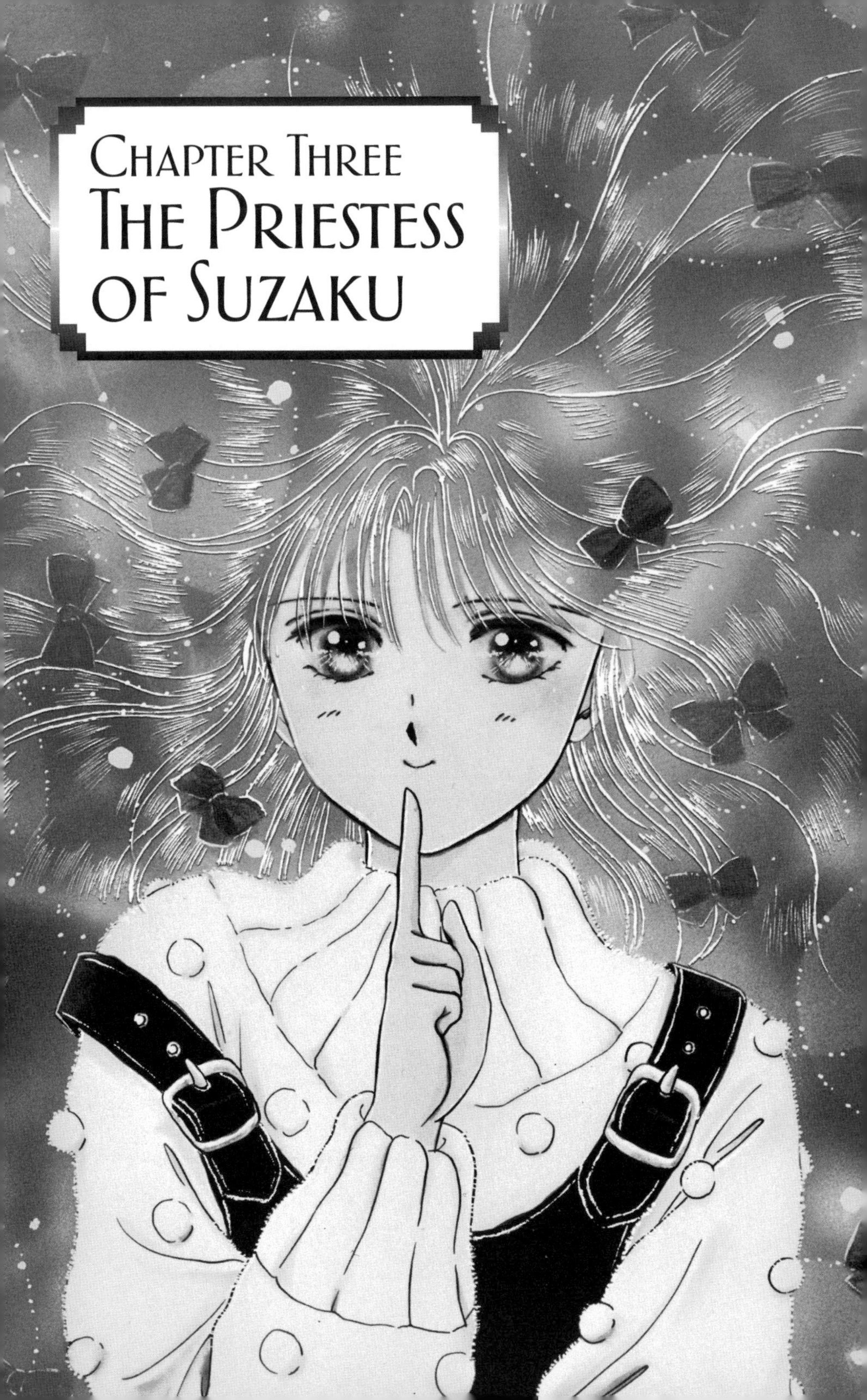
Chapter Three
The Priestess of Suzaku

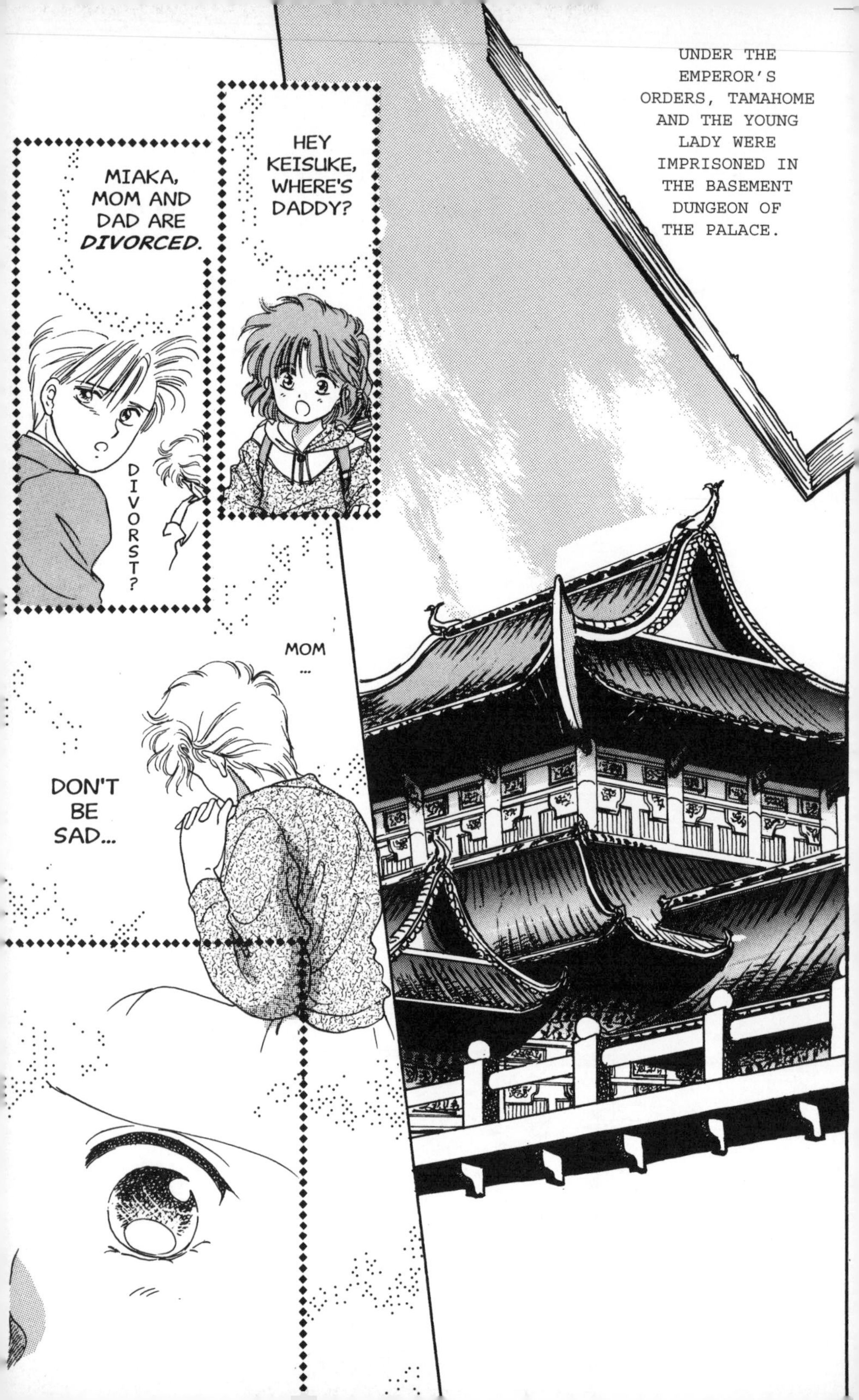
UNDER THE EMPEROR'S ORDERS, TAMAHOME AND THE YOUNG LADY WERE IMPRISONED IN THE BASEMENT DUNGEON OF THE PALACE.
HEY KEISUKE, WHERE'S DADDY?
MIAKA, MOM AND DAD ARE *DIVORCED*.
DIVORST?
MOM...
DON'T BE SAD...

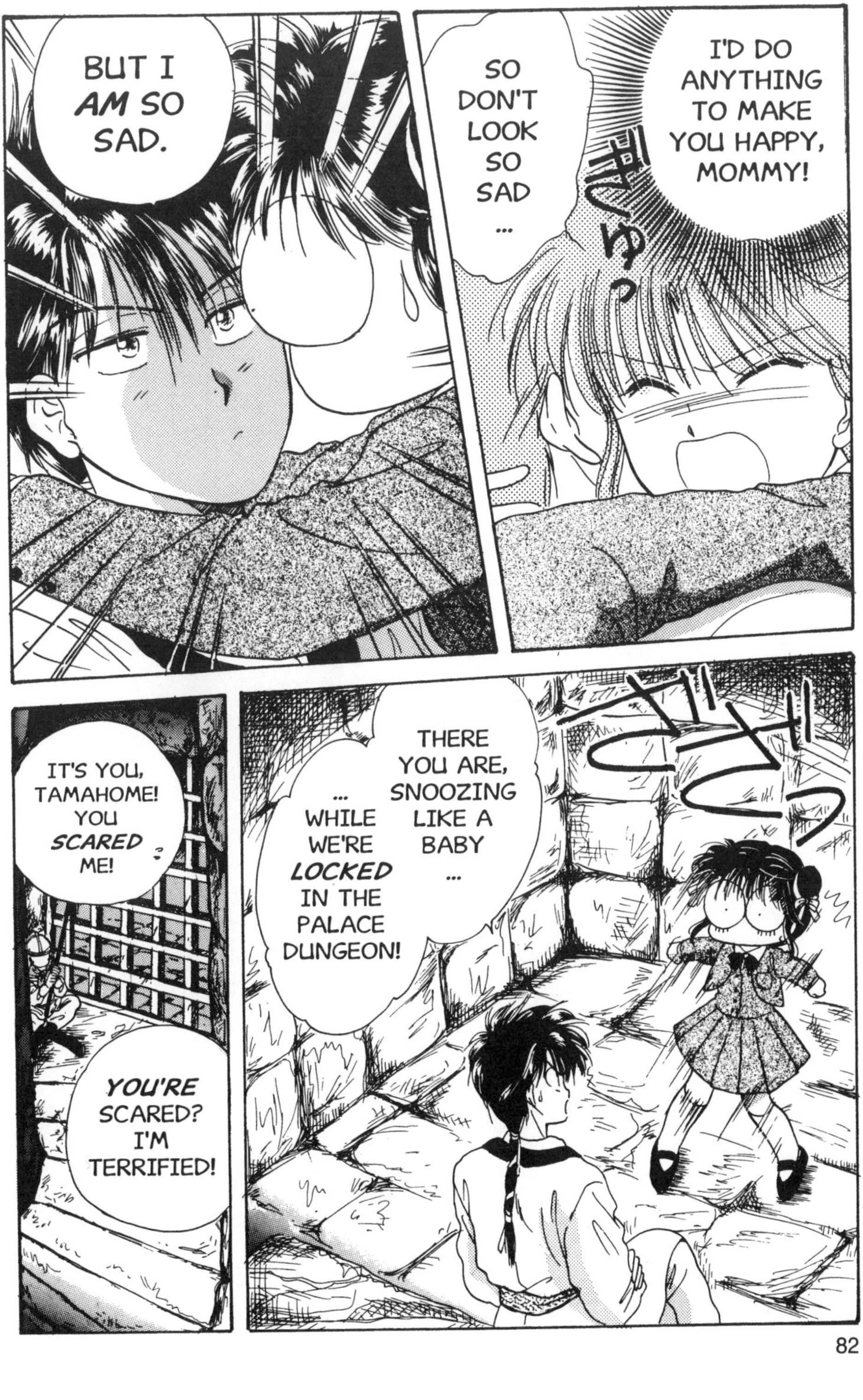
I'D DO ANYTHING TO MAKE YOU HAPPY, MOMMY!
ぎゅっ
SO DON'T LOOK SO SAD ...
BUT I *AM* SO SAD.
THERE YOU ARE, SNOOZING LIKE A BABY ...
... WHILE WE'RE *LOCKED* IN THE PALACE DUNGEON!
IT'S YOU, TAMAHOME! YOU *SCARED* ME!
YOU'RE SCARED? I'M TERRIFIED!

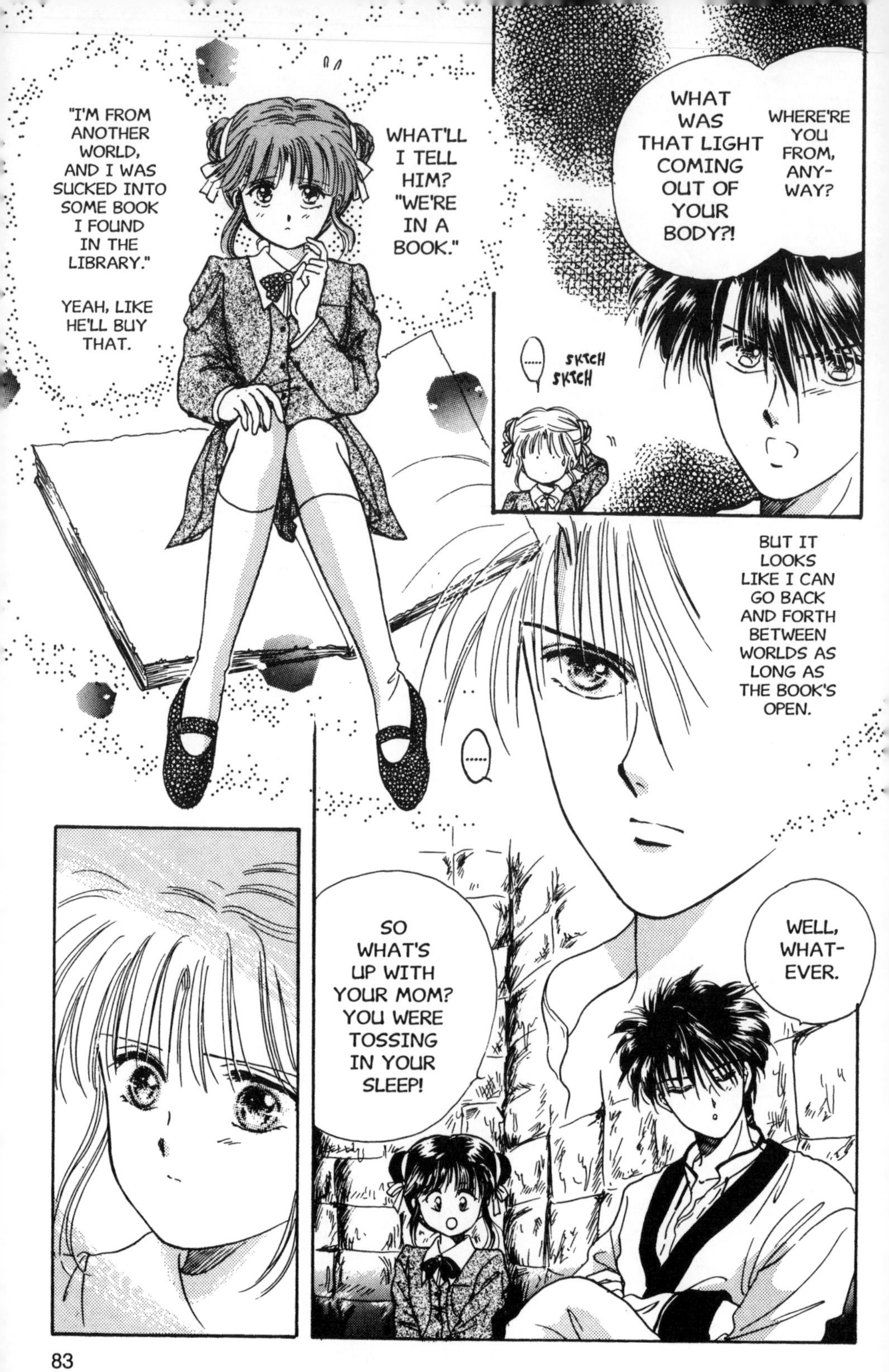
WHERE'RE YOU FROM, ANY-WAY?
WHAT WAS THAT LIGHT COMING OUT OF YOUR BODY?!
.....
SKTCH SKTCH
WHAT'LL I TELL HIM? "WE'RE IN A BOOK."
"I'M FROM ANOTHER WORLD, AND I WAS SUCKED INTO SOME BOOK I FOUND IN THE LIBRARY."
YEAH, LIKE HE'LL BUY THAT.
BUT IT LOOKS LIKE I CAN GO BACK AND FORTH BETWEEN WORLDS AS LONG AS THE BOOK'S OPEN.
.....
WELL, WHAT-EVER.
SO WHAT'S UP WITH YOUR MOM? YOU WERE TOSSING IN YOUR SLEEP!

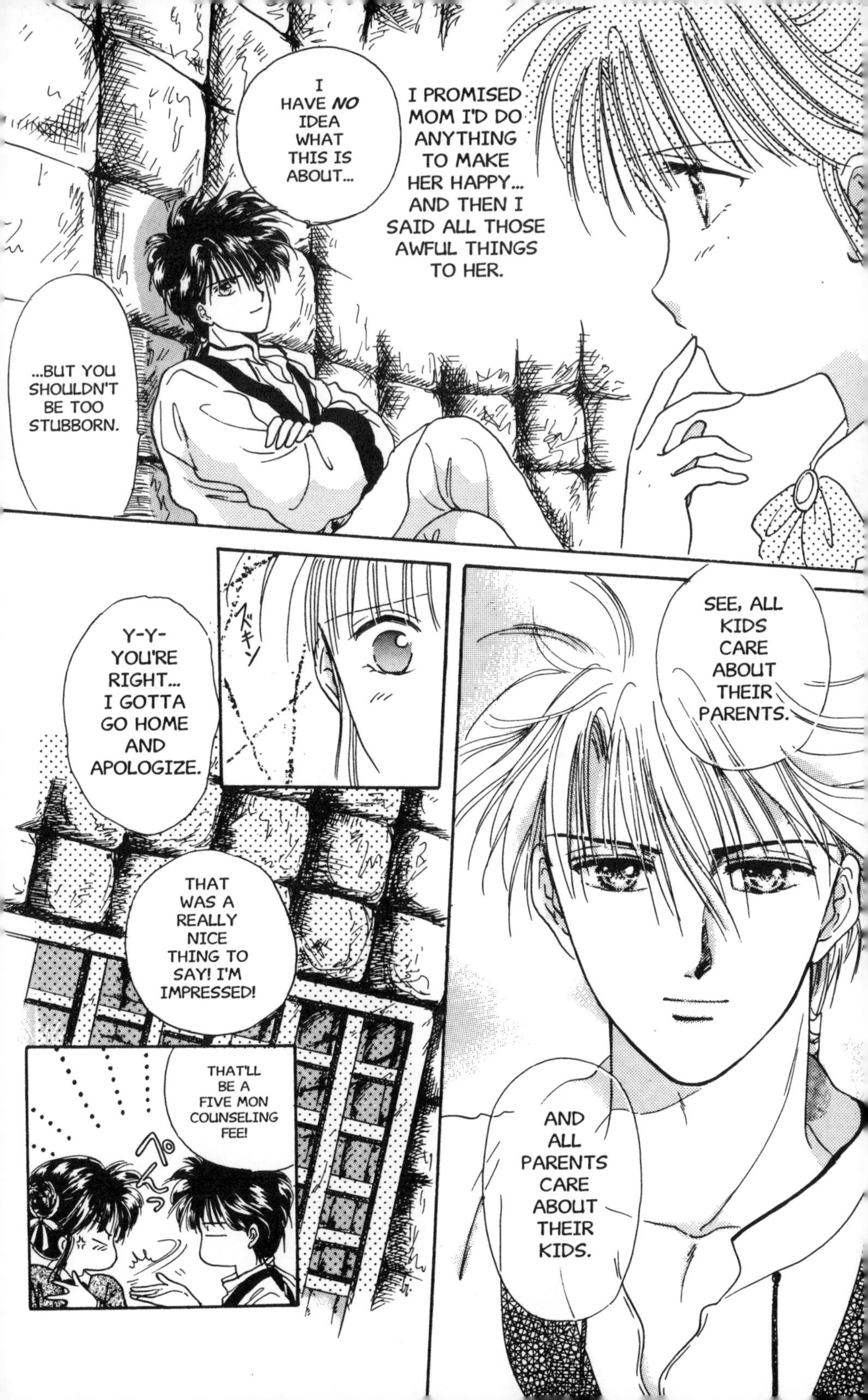

I PROMISED MOM I'D DO ANYTHING TO MAKE HER HAPPY... AND THEN I SAID ALL THOSE AWFUL THINGS TO HER.
I HAVE *NO* IDEA WHAT THIS IS ABOUT...
...BUT YOU SHOULDN'T BE TOO STUBBORN.
SEE, ALL KIDS CARE ABOUT THEIR PARENTS.
AND ALL PARENTS CARE ABOUT THEIR KIDS.
ズキン
Y-Y-YOU'RE RIGHT... I GOTTA GO HOME AND APOLOGIZE.
THAT WAS A REALLY NICE THING TO SAY! I'M IMPRESSED!
THAT'LL BE A FIVE MON COUNSELING FEE!

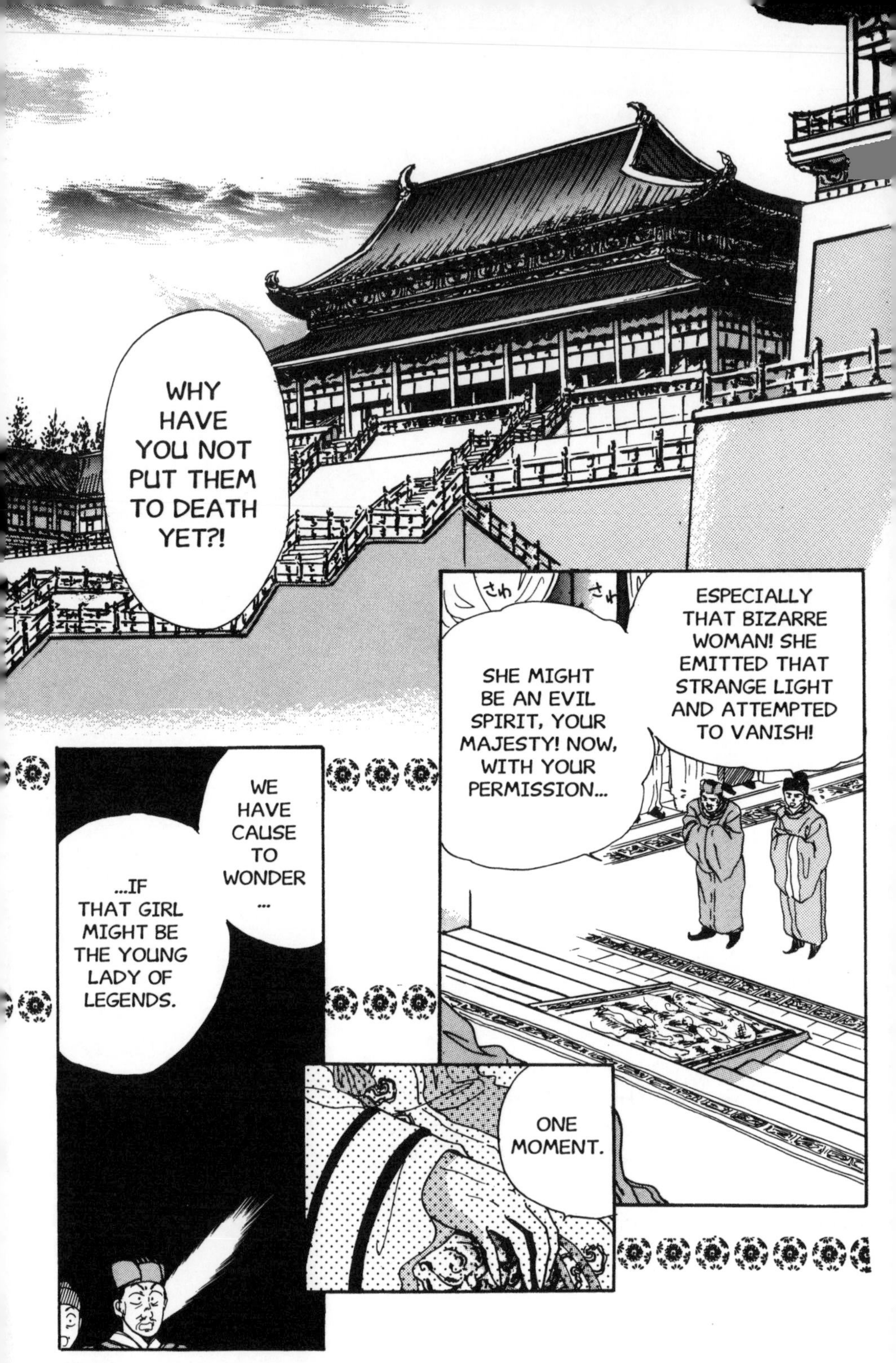
WHY HAVE YOU NOT PUT THEM TO DEATH YET?!
さわ
さわ
ESPECIALLY THAT BIZARRE WOMAN! SHE EMITTED THAT STRANGE LIGHT AND ATTEMPTED TO VANISH!
SHE MIGHT BE AN EVIL SPIRIT, YOUR MAJESTY! NOW, WITH YOUR PERMISSION...
ONE MOMENT.
WE HAVE CAUSE TO WONDER...
...IF THAT GIRL MIGHT BE THE YOUNG LADY OF LEGENDS.

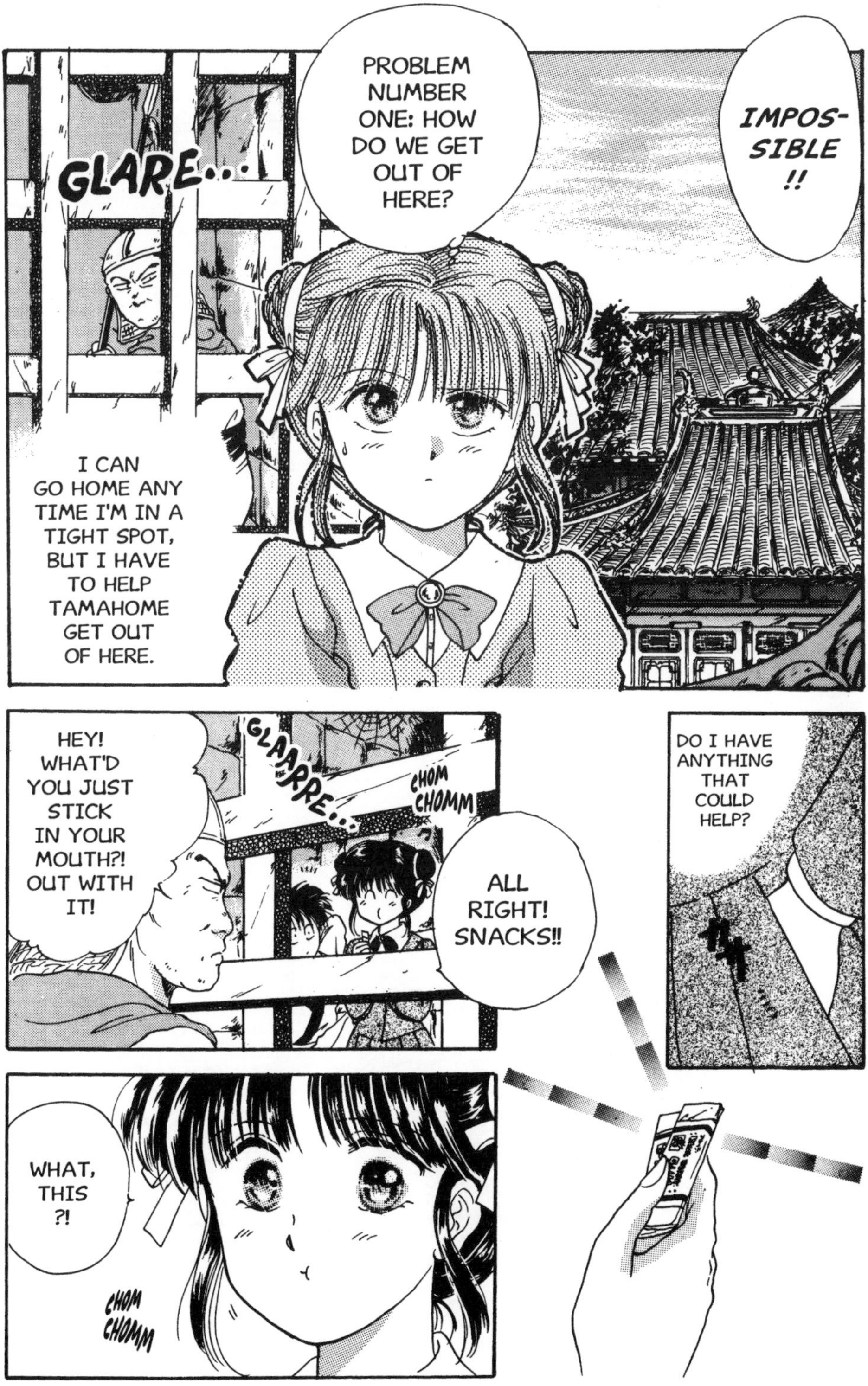
IMPOS-SIBLE !!
PROBLEM NUMBER ONE: HOW DO WE GET OUT OF HERE?
GLARE...
I CAN GO HOME ANY TIME I'M IN A TIGHT SPOT, BUT I HAVE TO HELP TAMAHOME GET OUT OF HERE.
DO I HAVE ANYTHING THAT COULD HELP?
CHOM CHOMM
GLAARRE...
ALL RIGHT! SNACKS!!
HEY! WHAT'D YOU JUST STICK IN YOUR MOUTH?! OUT WITH IT!
WHAT, THIS ?!
CHOM CHOMM

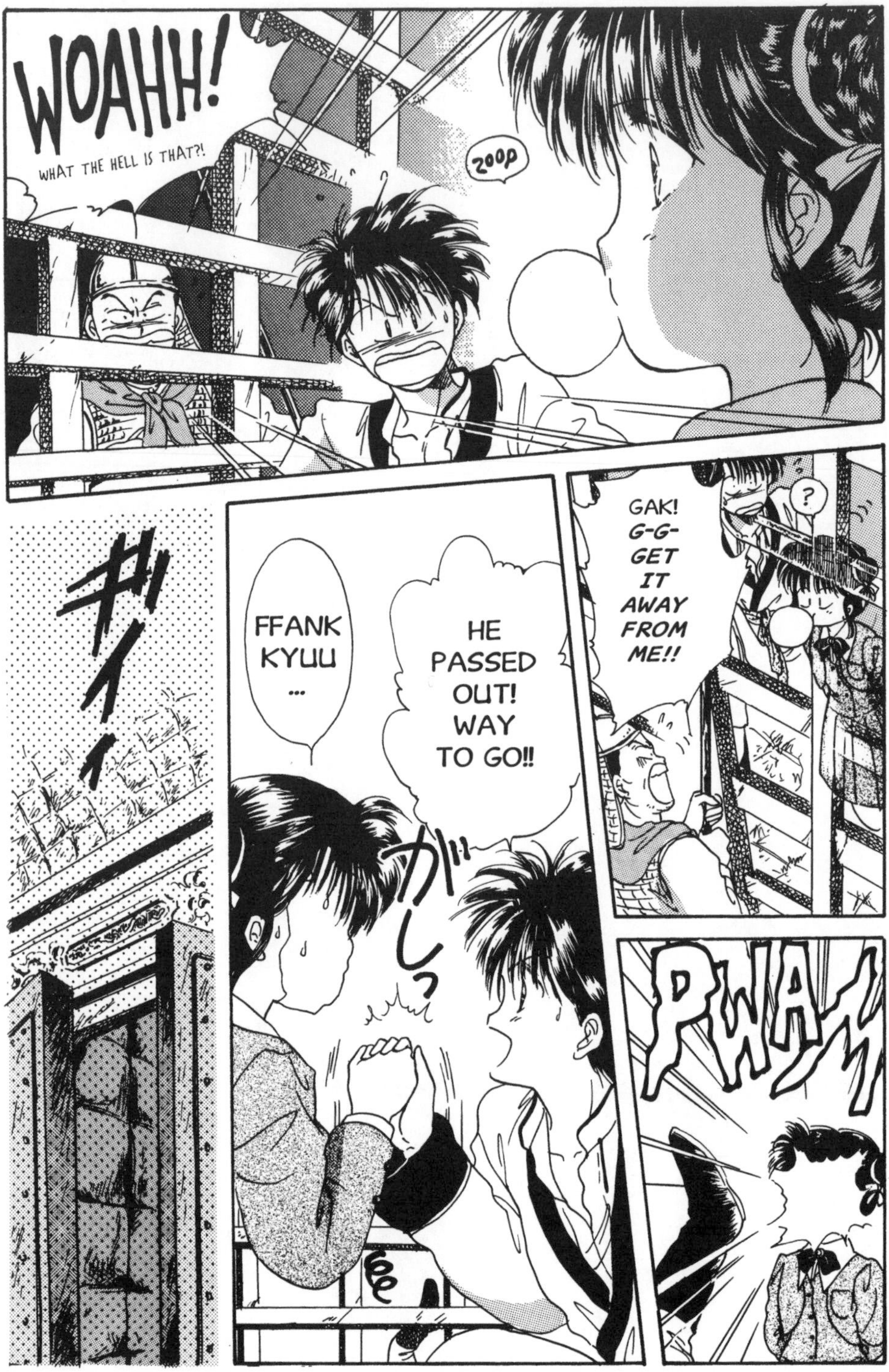
WOAHH!
WHAT THE HELL IS THAT?!
zoop
GAK! G-G-GET IT AWAY FROM ME!!
?
PWA
HE PASSED OUT! WAY TO GO!!
FFANK KYUU ...
がしっ
ガイイ

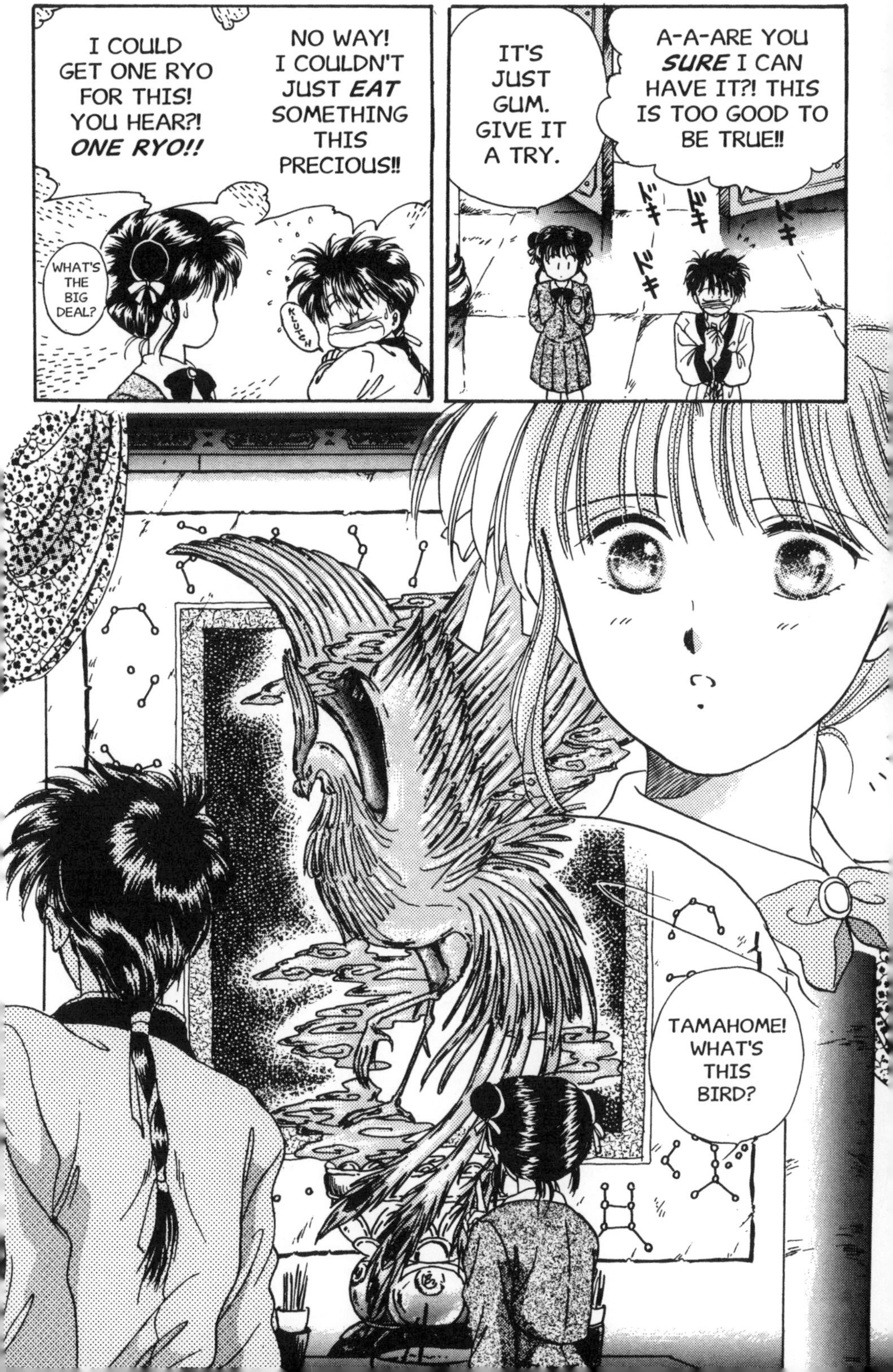

A-A-ARE YOU *SURE* I CAN HAVE IT?! THIS IS TOO GOOD TO BE TRUE!!
IT'S JUST GUM. GIVE IT A TRY.
ドキ ドキ ドキ ドキ
NO WAY! I COULDN'T JUST *EAT* SOMETHING THIS PRECIOUS!!
I COULD GET ONE RYO FOR THIS! YOU HEAR?! *ONE RYO!!*
KLUTCH
WHAT'S THE BIG DEAL?
TAMAHOME! WHAT'S THIS BIRD?

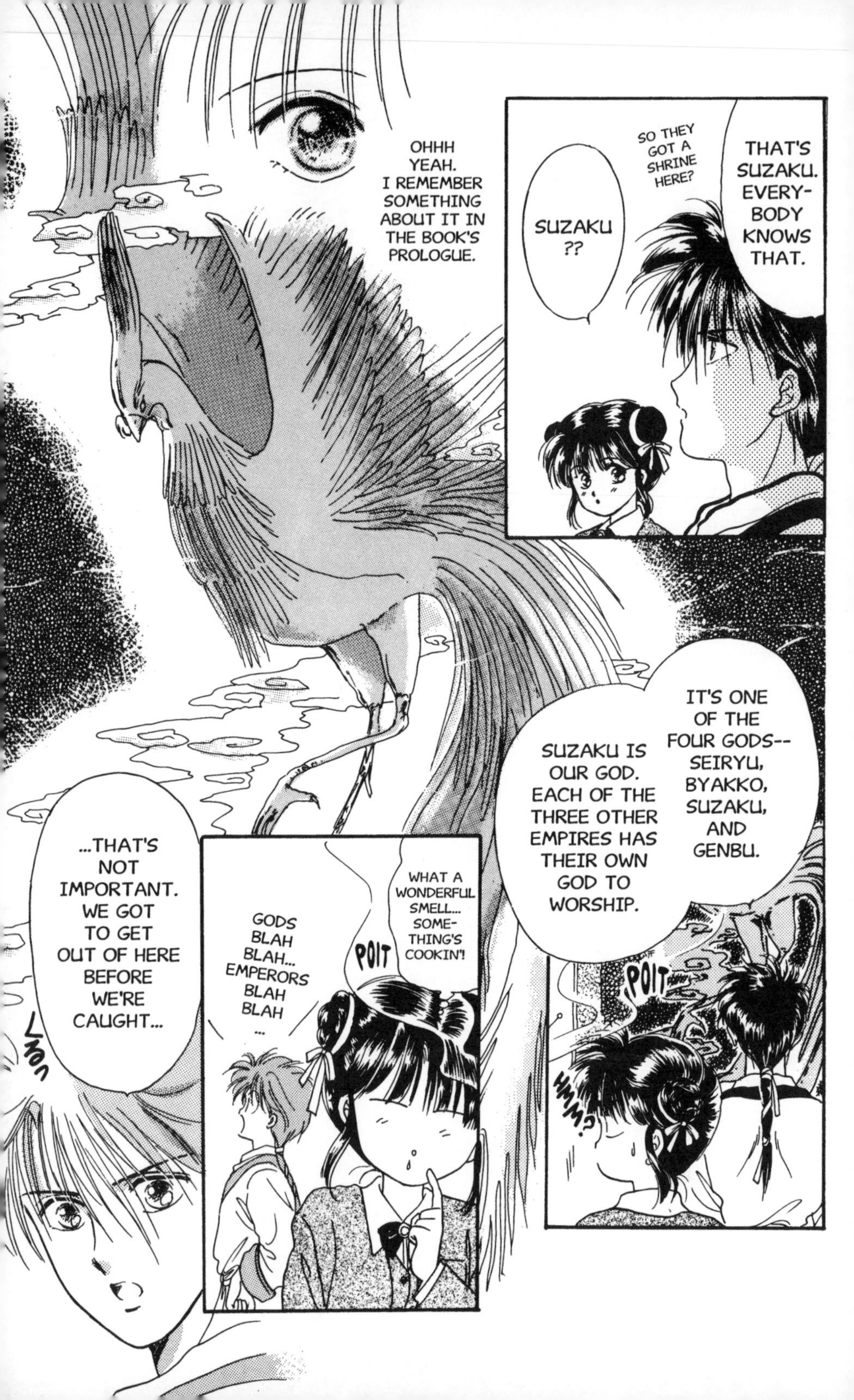
THAT'S SUZAKU. EVERYBODY KNOWS THAT.
SO THEY GOT A SHRINE HERE?
SUZAKU ??
OHHH YEAH. I REMEMBER SOMETHING ABOUT IT IN THE BOOK'S PROLOGUE.
IT'S ONE OF THE FOUR GODS-- SEIRYU, BYAKKO, SUZAKU, AND GENBU.
SUZAKU IS OUR GOD. EACH OF THE THREE OTHER EMPIRES HAS THEIR OWN GOD TO WORSHIP.
POIT
HMM?
WHAT A WONDERFUL SMELL... SOMETHING'S COOKIN'!
POIT
GODS BLAH BLAH... EMPERORS BLAH BLAH ...
...THAT'S NOT IMPORTANT. WE GOT TO GET OUT OF HERE BEFORE WE'RE CAUGHT...

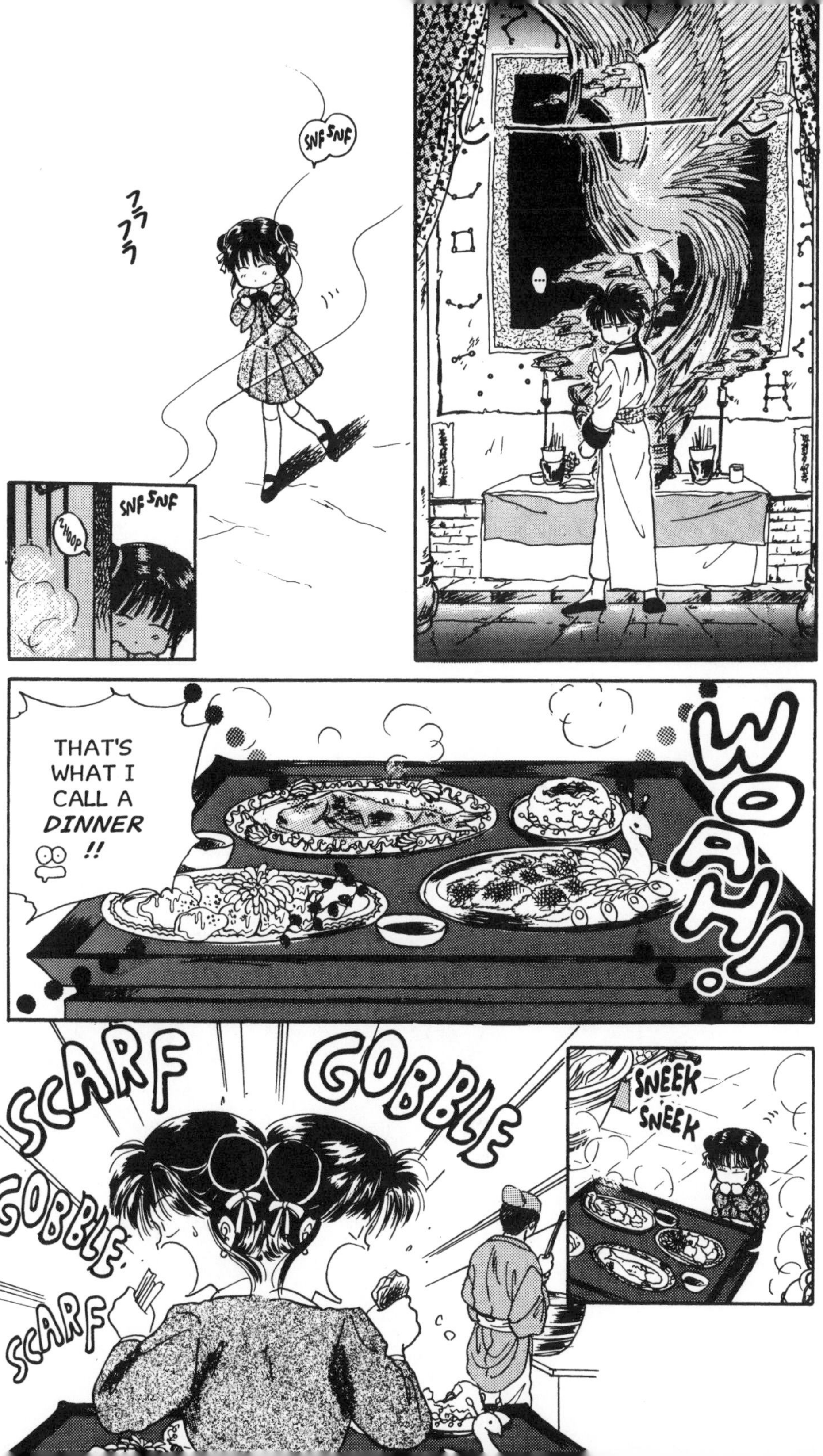
...
フラフラ
SNF SNF
SNF SNF
ZHOOP
WOAH!
THAT'S WHAT I CALL A *DINNER* !!
SNEEK SNEEK
GOBBLE
SCARF
GOBBLE
SCARF

Getting back to where we left off, I'm sure some of my work reminds the readers of other manga. Of course I never do it consciously! (Even I have some pride). Someone ends up pointing it out, and then I'm like, "Oh my God, wait!" *Magical Nan* was different. That came from a book my editor gave me. Although I tried to make my version totally different, due to limitations on the number of pages, I was told to imitate the book. I really do try not to copy scenes. During junior high and high school I was influenced mostly by people like Toyoo Ashida (director, animation director: *Yamato, Minky Momo* and *Vampire Hunter D*) and Akemi Takada (character designer: *Creamy Mami Urusei Yatsura, Kimagure Orange Road*) (My older drawings from *Prepubescence* vol. 3, I was really into Takada at the time) and Mutsumi Inomata (character designer: *Windaria, Leda, Brain-Powered*), anime artists rather than comic artists. Now I hardly get a chance to watch animation at all, so I don't know what's going on these days. I really loved animation. Seems so long ago. I tried to cram these animation influences into a shojo manga drawing style that never really existed before. (I've asked many people, and there's nobody else who draws like I do).

It's really hard to find a balance. I have many fellow artists who can give me advice, but I just can't change at this point.

I think that my own pictures are too complicated! I was really into boys' comics so everyone thought I'd be writing for shonen manga magazines such as *Shonen Sunday*. But can you believe that maybe after three years of hard work, I finally managed to draw shojo manga effectively? ♥ I still have a long way to go. Okay, okay, I'm getting a little long-winded here but most of my fan letters come from people who want to become comic artists, so you guys can use this as a reference (maybe). To sum up, I recommend you study and incorporate all the elements of artists you admire in your unique way into your own drawings (without ripping them off). I tend to discard those elements that don't fit with my style. You should also read as many novels, see as many films and dramas as possible. Remember the great Osamu Tezuka once said, "If you want to write a new manga then don't bother reading another manga!" Of course, this is coming from someone who bought his *How To Draw Manga* AFTER getting published! Sorry!

My friends razzed me about it. But I don't know how to do effects work. So sue me!!

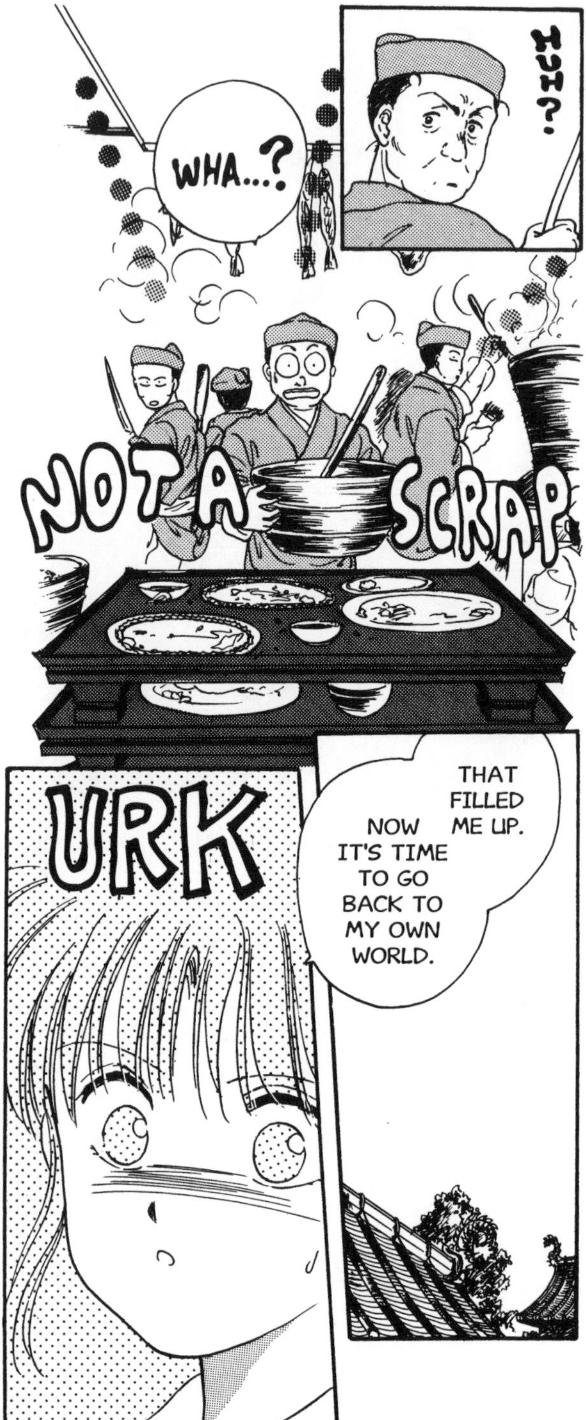
HUH?
WHA...?
NOT A SCRAP
THAT FILLED ME UP.
NOW IT'S TIME TO GO BACK TO MY OWN WORLD.
URK

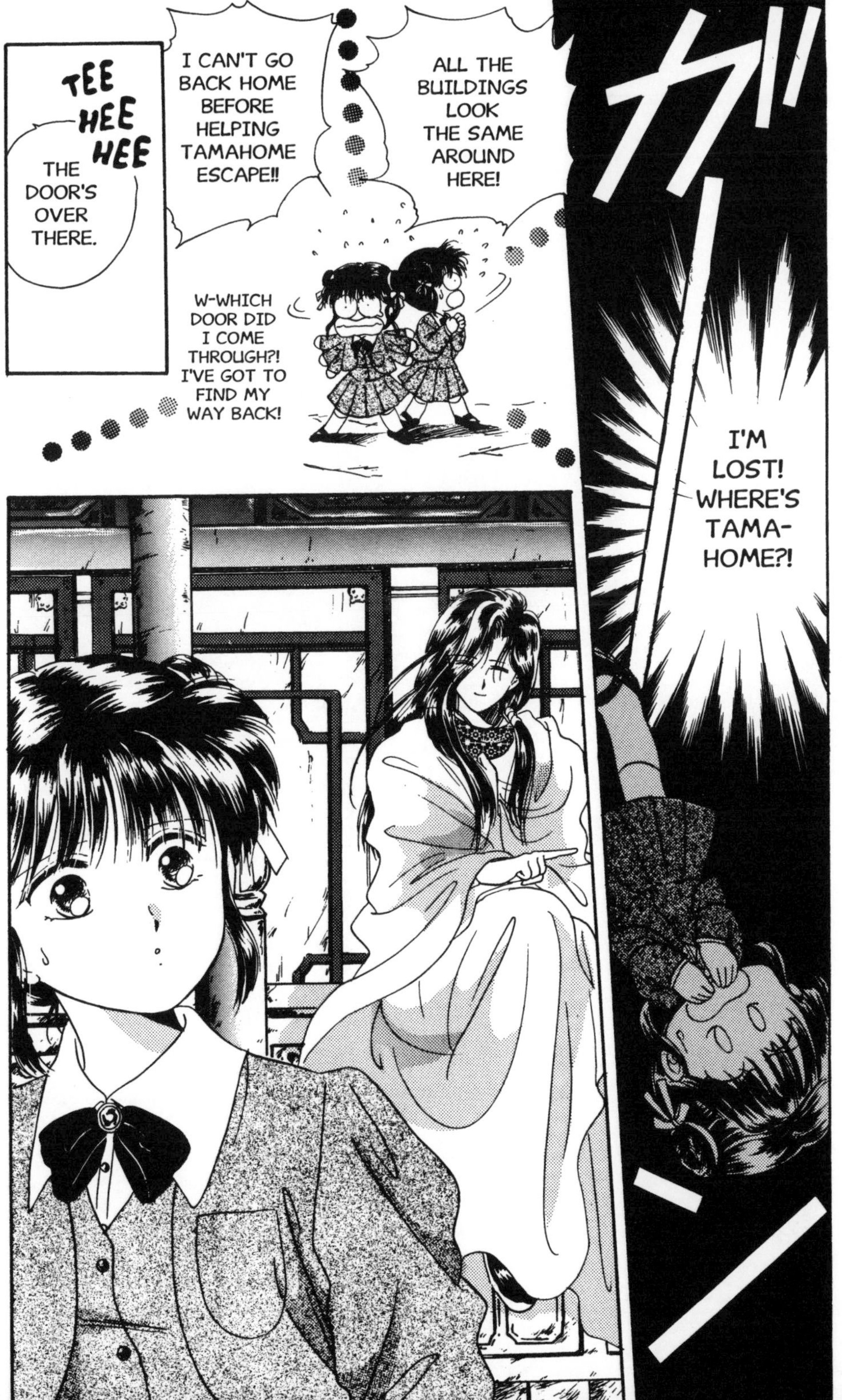
ガーン
I'M LOST! WHERE'S TAMA-HOME?!
ALL THE BUILDINGS LOOK THE SAME AROUND HERE!
I CAN'T GO BACK HOME BEFORE HELPING TAMAHOME ESCAPE!!
W-WHICH DOOR DID I COME THROUGH?! I'VE GOT TO FIND MY WAY BACK!
TEE HEE HEE
THE DOOR'S OVER THERE.

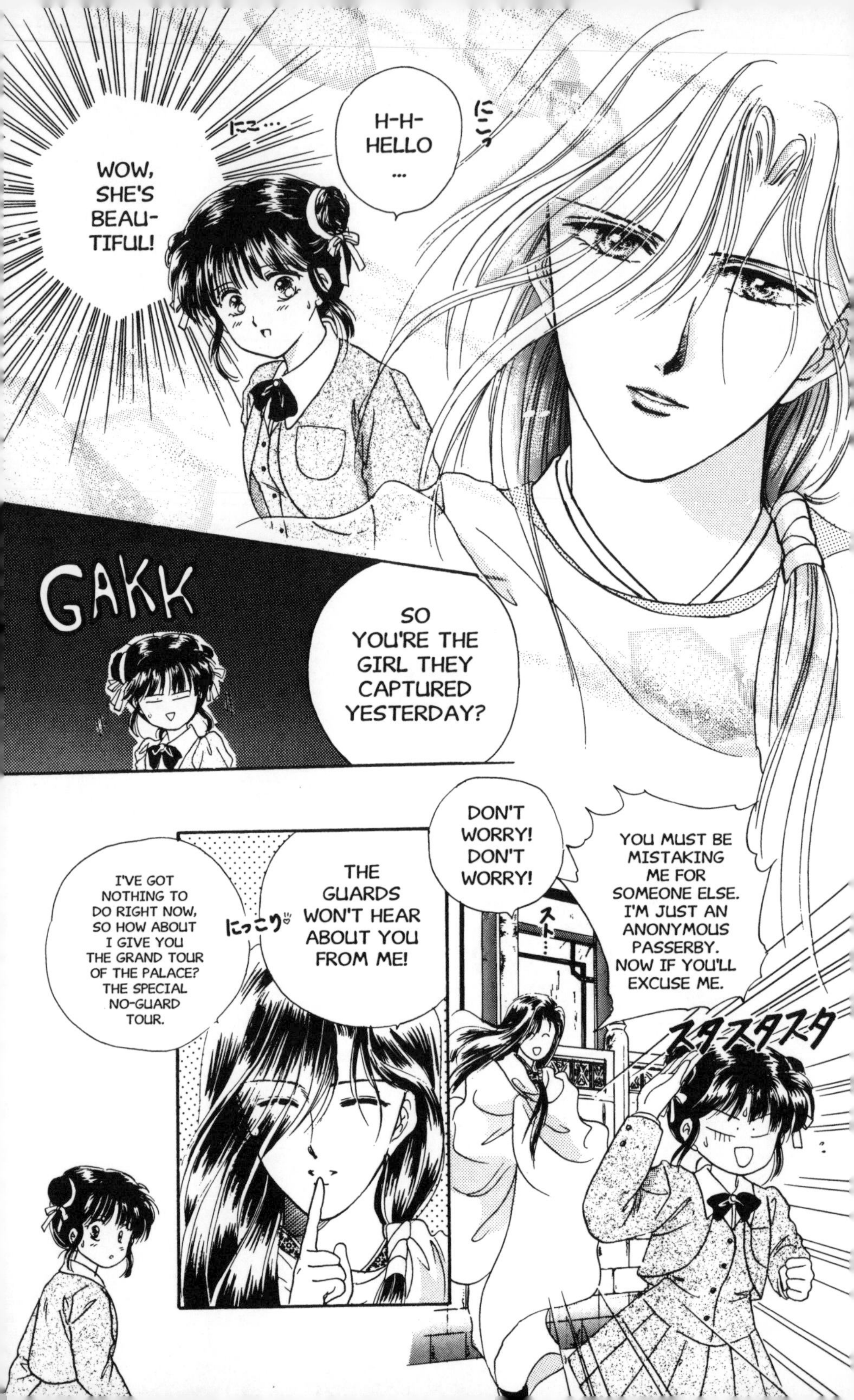
にこっ
H-H-HELLO...
にこ…
WOW, SHE'S BEAUTIFUL!
SO YOU'RE THE GIRL THEY CAPTURED YESTERDAY?
GAKK
YOU MUST BE MISTAKING ME FOR SOMEONE ELSE. I'M JUST AN ANONYMOUS PASSERBY. NOW IF YOU'LL EXCUSE ME.
スタスタスタ
DON'T WORRY! DON'T WORRY!
スト…
THE GUARDS WON'T HEAR ABOUT YOU FROM ME!
にっこり
I'VE GOT NOTHING TO DO RIGHT NOW, SO HOW ABOUT I GIVE YOU THE GRAND TOUR OF THE PALACE? THE SPECIAL NO-GUARD TOUR.

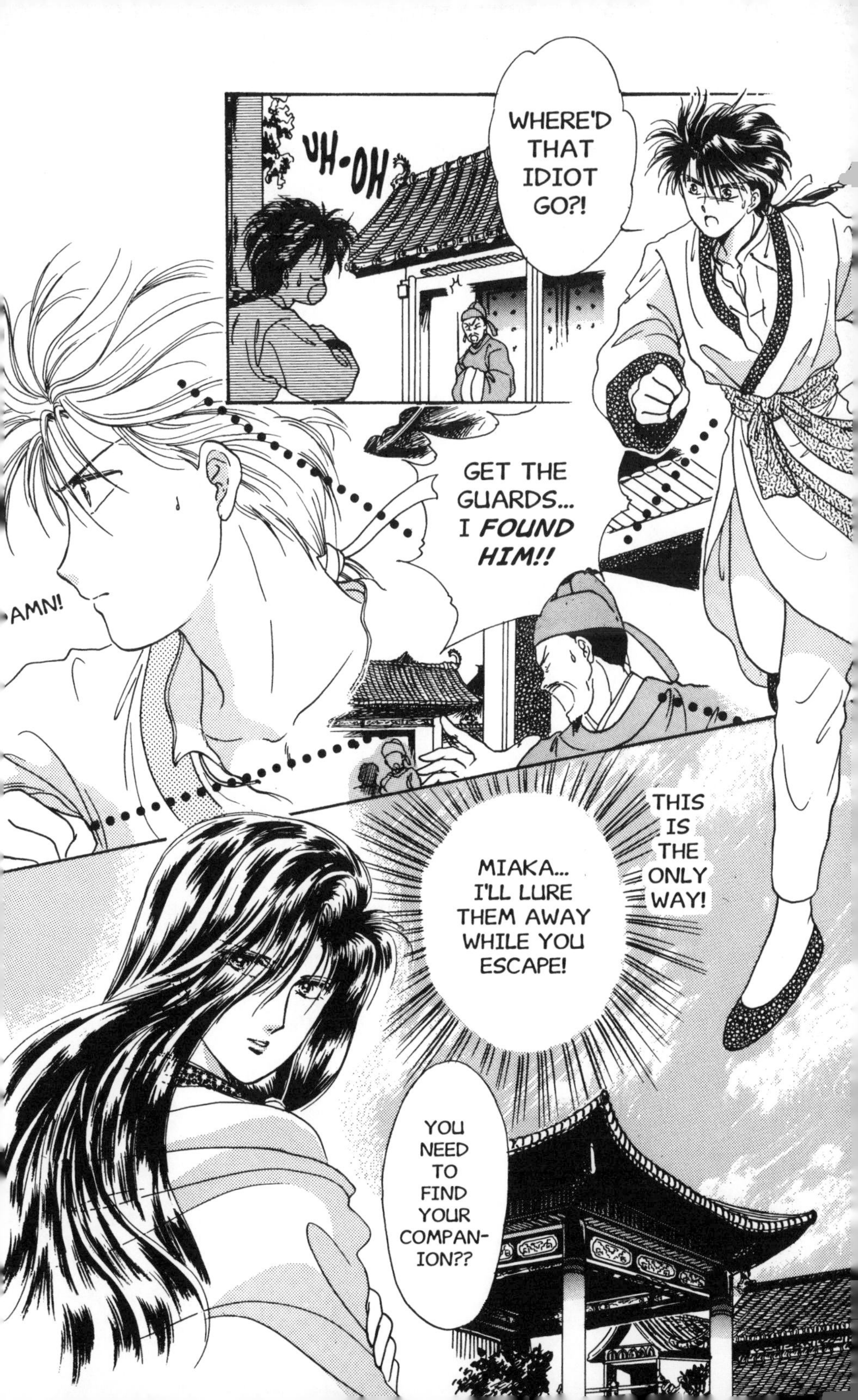
WHERE'D THAT IDIOT GO?!
UH-OH
GET THE GUARDS... I *FOUND HIM!!*
AMN!
THIS IS THE ONLY WAY!
MIAKA... I'LL LURE THEM AWAY WHILE YOU ESCAPE!
YOU NEED TO FIND YOUR COMPAN-ION??

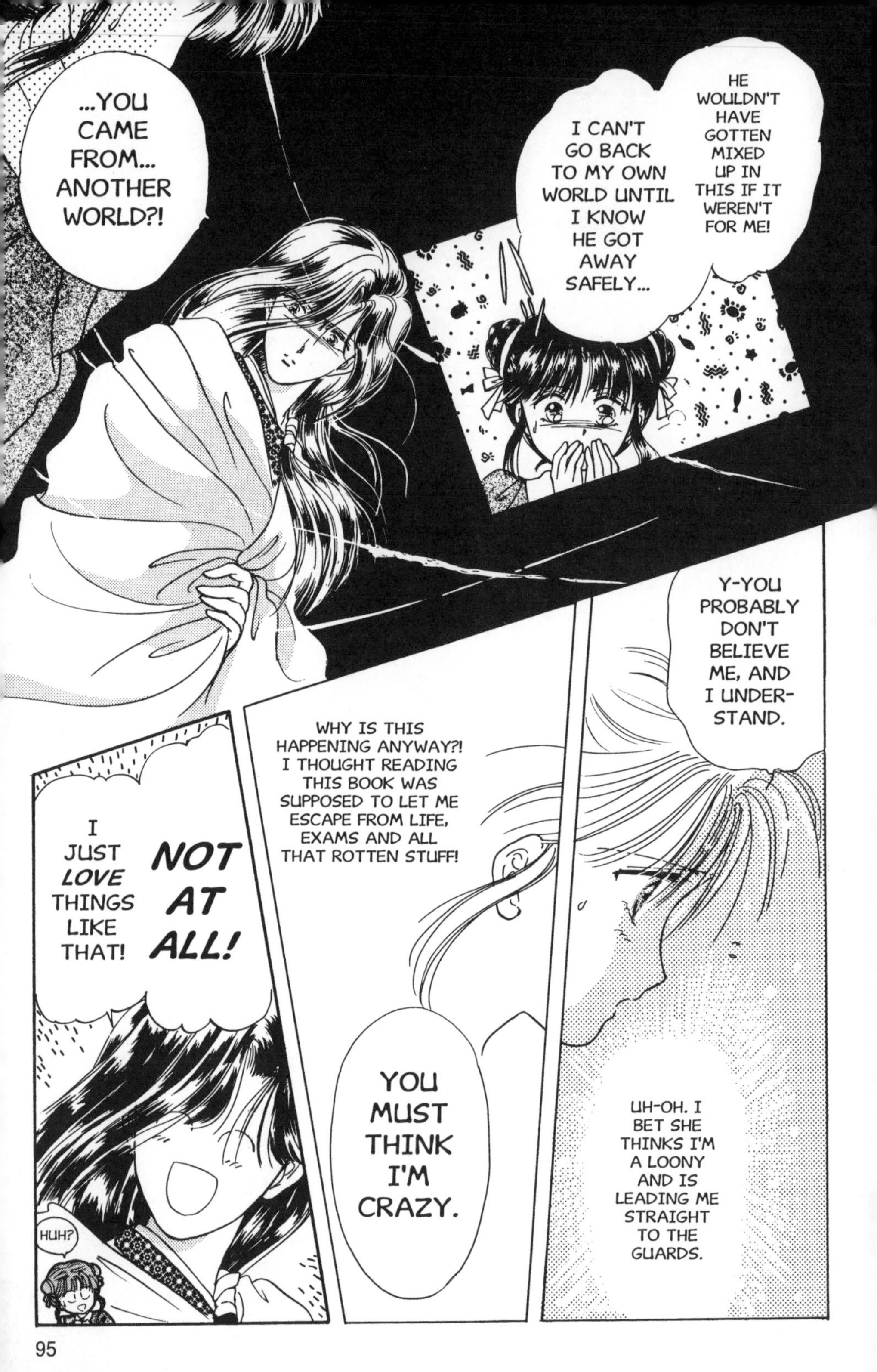
I CAN'T GO BACK TO MY OWN WORLD UNTIL I KNOW HE GOT AWAY SAFELY... HE WOULDN'T HAVE GOTTEN MIXED UP IN THIS IF IT WEREN'T FOR ME!
...YOU CAME FROM... ANOTHER WORLD?!
Y-YOU PROBABLY DON'T BELIEVE ME, AND I UNDER-STAND.
UH-OH. I BET SHE THINKS I'M A LOONY AND IS LEADING ME STRAIGHT TO THE GUARDS.
WHY IS THIS HAPPENING ANYWAY?! I THOUGHT READING THIS BOOK WAS SUPPOSED TO LET ME ESCAPE FROM LIFE, EXAMS AND ALL THAT ROTTEN STUFF!
YOU MUST THINK I'M CRAZY.
NOT AT ALL!
I JUST *LOVE* THINGS LIKE THAT!
HUH?

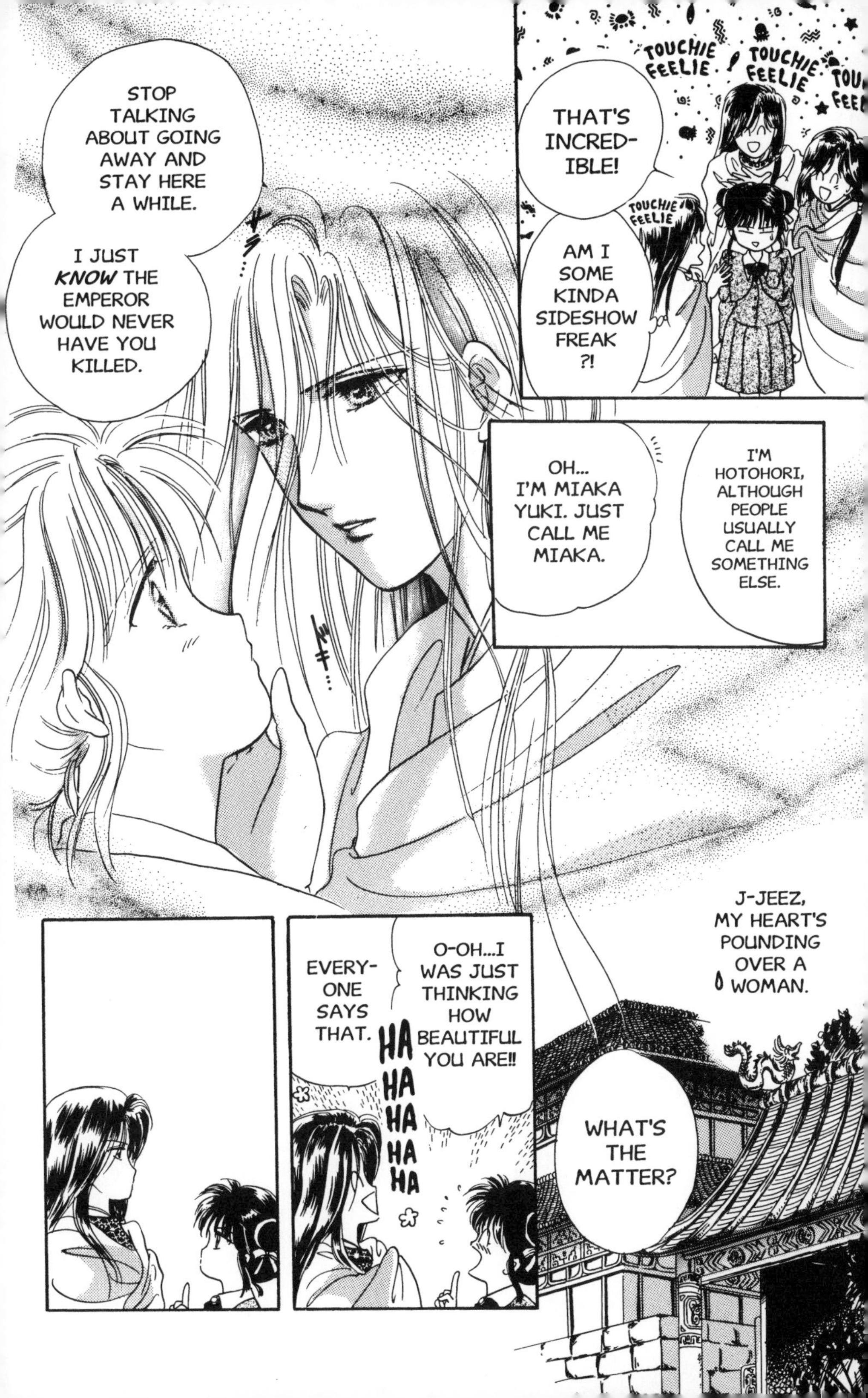
TOUCHIE FEELIE
TOUCHIE FEELIE
TOU FEE
THAT'S INCREDIBLE!
TOUCHIE FEELIE
AM I SOME KINDA SIDESHOW FREAK?!
STOP TALKING ABOUT GOING AWAY AND STAY HERE A WHILE.
I JUST *KNOW* THE EMPEROR WOULD NEVER HAVE YOU KILLED.
I'M HOTOHORI, ALTHOUGH PEOPLE USUALLY CALL ME SOMETHING ELSE.
OH... I'M MIAKA YUKI. JUST CALL ME MIAKA.
J-JEEZ, MY HEART'S POUNDING OVER A WOMAN.
WHAT'S THE MATTER?
O-OH...I WAS JUST THINKING HOW BEAUTIFUL YOU ARE!!
EVERYONE SAYS THAT.
HA HA HA HA HA HA

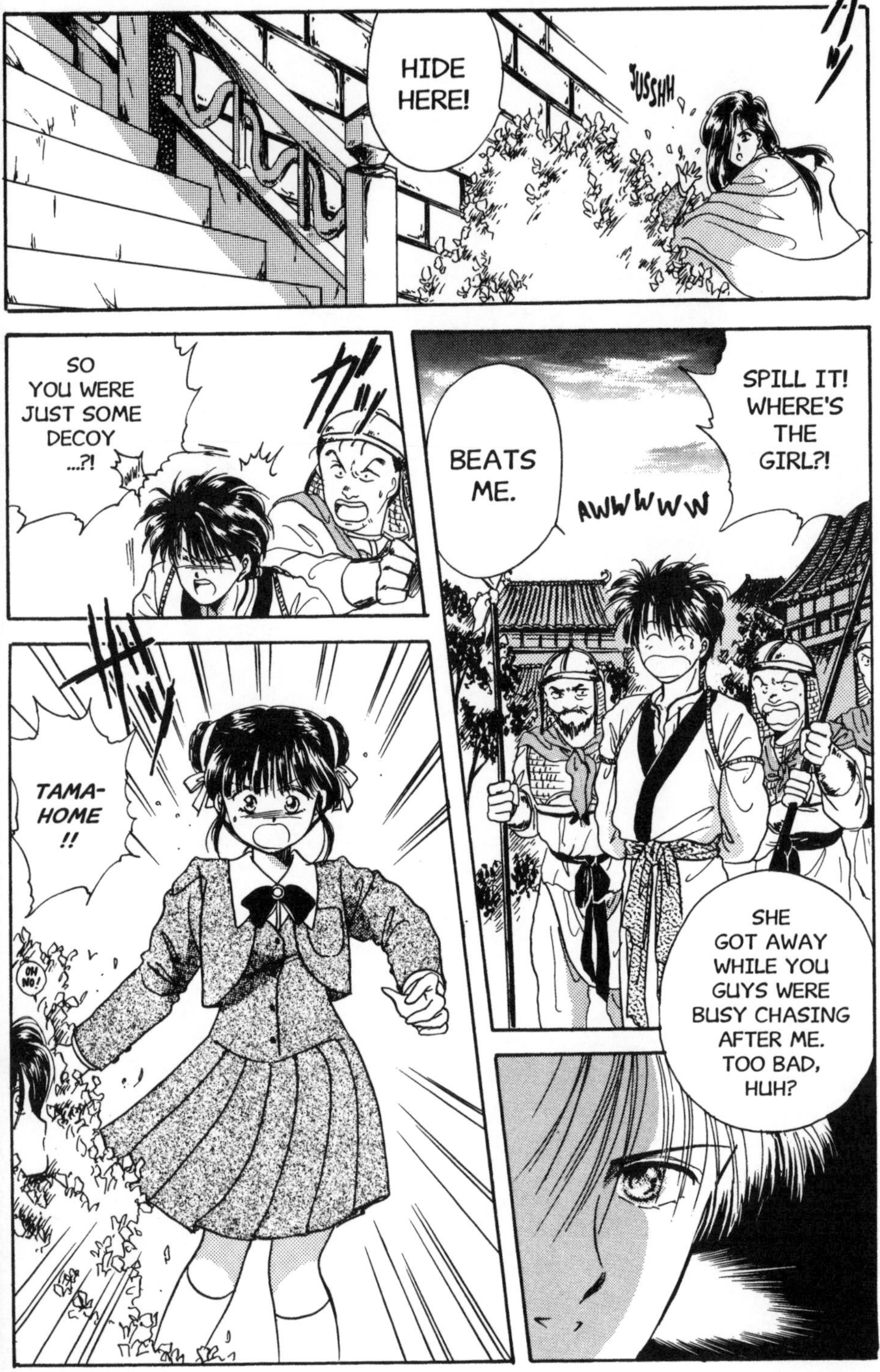
JUSSHH
HIDE HERE!
SPILL IT! WHERE'S THE GIRL?!
AWWWWWW
BEATS ME.
SHE GOT AWAY WHILE YOU GUYS WERE BUSY CHASING AFTER ME. TOO BAD, HUH?
SO YOU WERE JUST SOME DECOY ...?!
OWW!
TAMA-HOME !!
OH NO!

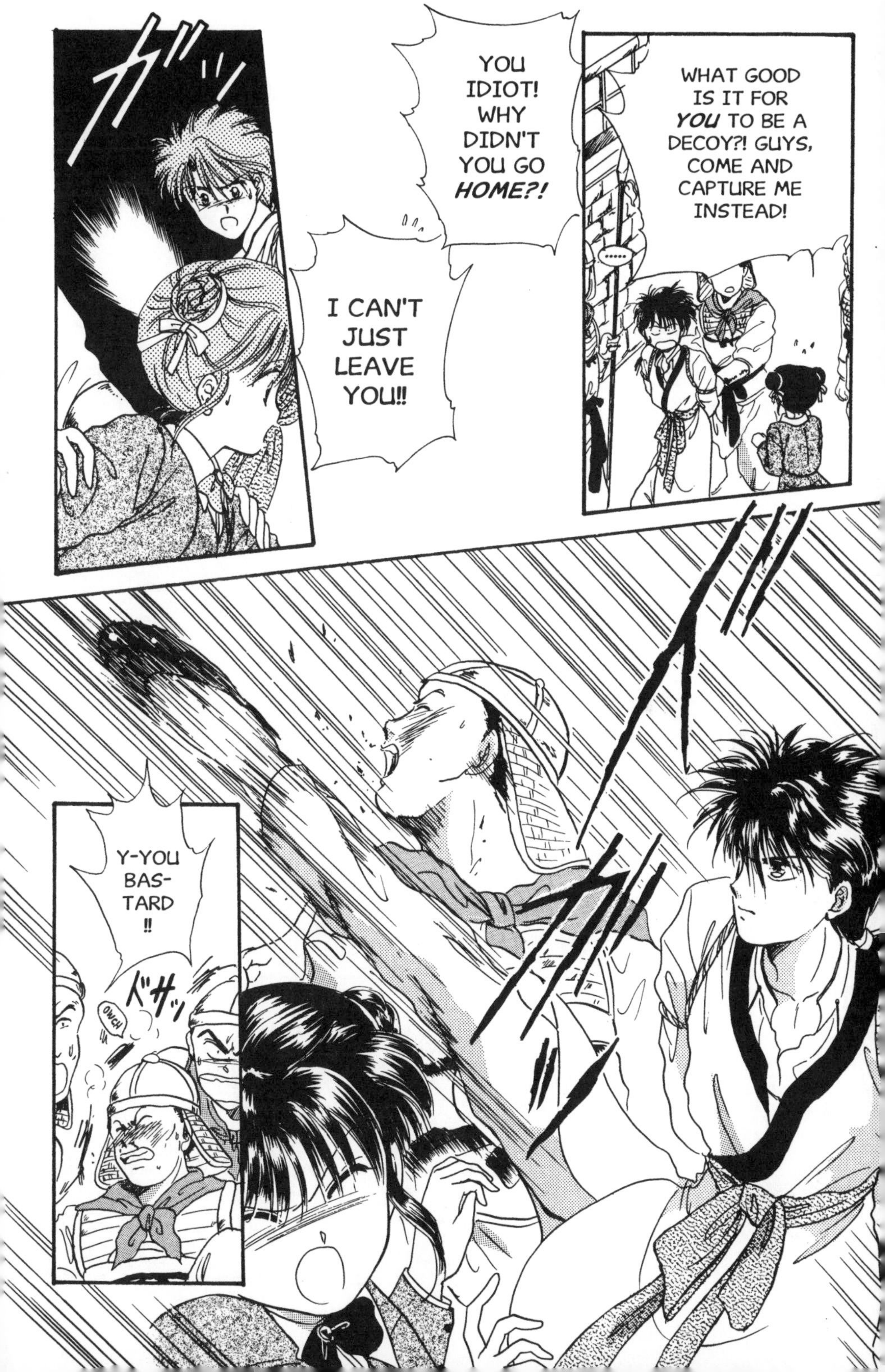
WHAT GOOD IS IT FOR *YOU* TO BE A DECOY?! GUYS, COME AND CAPTURE ME INSTEAD!
......
YOU IDIOT! WHY DIDN'T YOU GO *HOME?!*
ガッ
I CAN'T JUST LEAVE YOU!!
Y-YOU BAS-TARD!!
ドサッ
OWCH

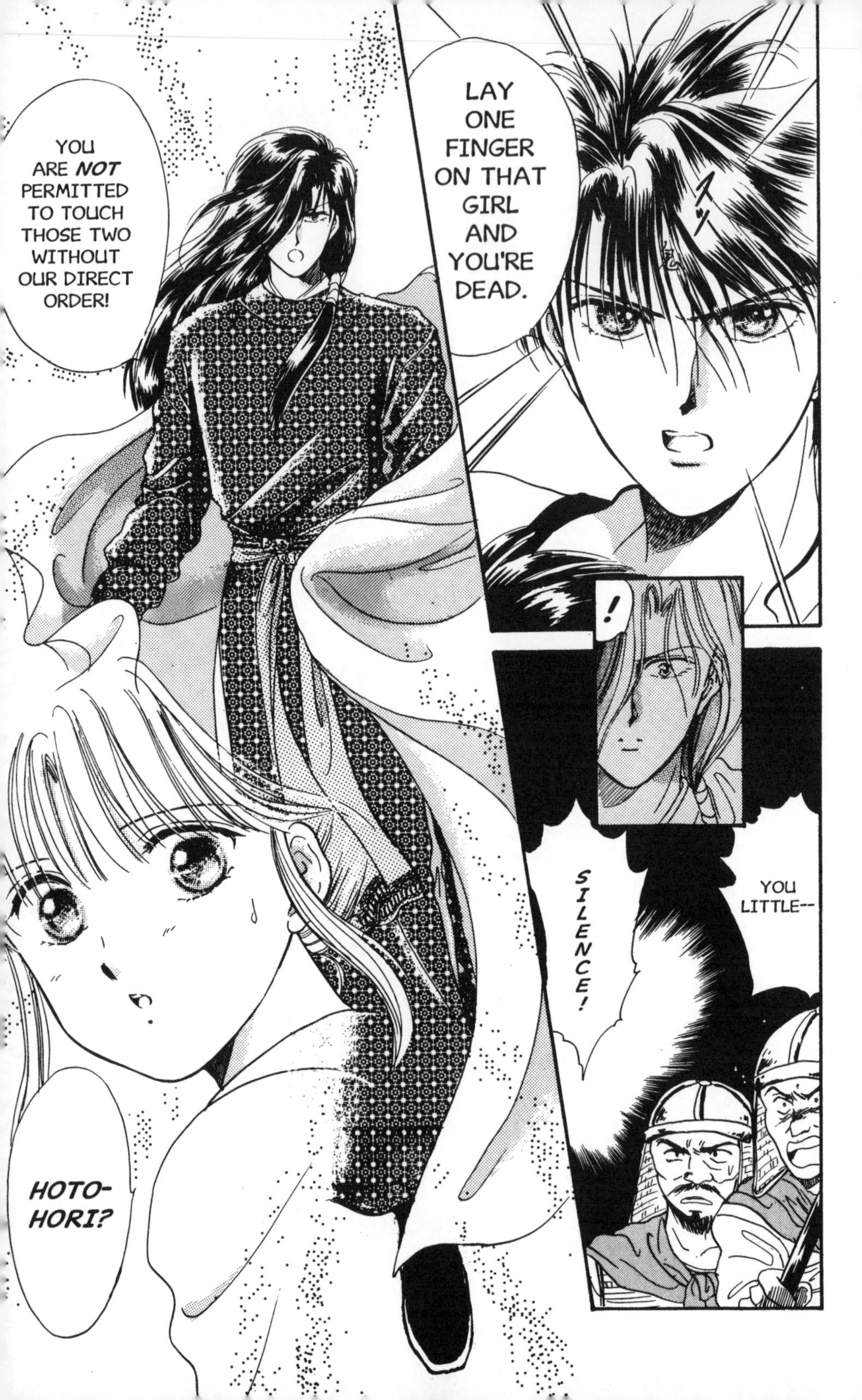

LAY ONE FINGER ON THAT GIRL AND YOU'RE DEAD.
!
YOU LITTLE--
SILENCE!
YOU ARE *NOT* PERMITTED TO TOUCH THOSE TWO WITHOUT OUR DIRECT ORDER!
HOTO-HORI?

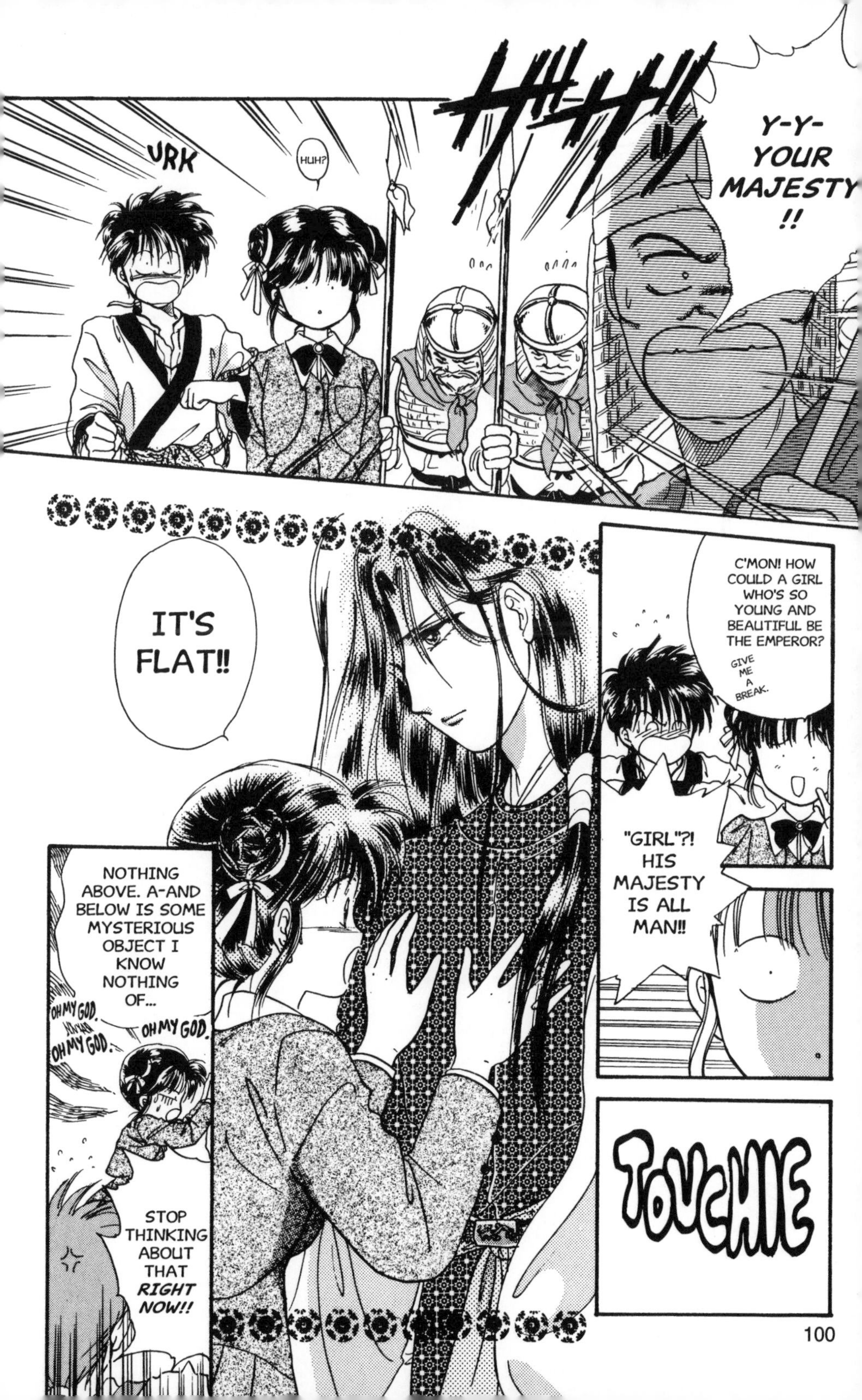
Y-Y-YOUR MAJESTY!!
HUH?
URK
C'MON! HOW COULD A GIRL WHO'S SO YOUNG AND BEAUTIFUL BE THE EMPEROR?
GIVE ME A BREAK.
"GIRL"?! HIS MAJESTY IS ALL MAN!!
TOUCHIE
IT'S FLAT!!
NOTHING ABOVE. A-AND BELOW IS SOME MYSTERIOUS OBJECT I KNOW NOTHING OF...
OH MY GOD.
OH MY GOD.
OH MY GOD.
STOP THINKING ABOUT THAT *RIGHT NOW!!*

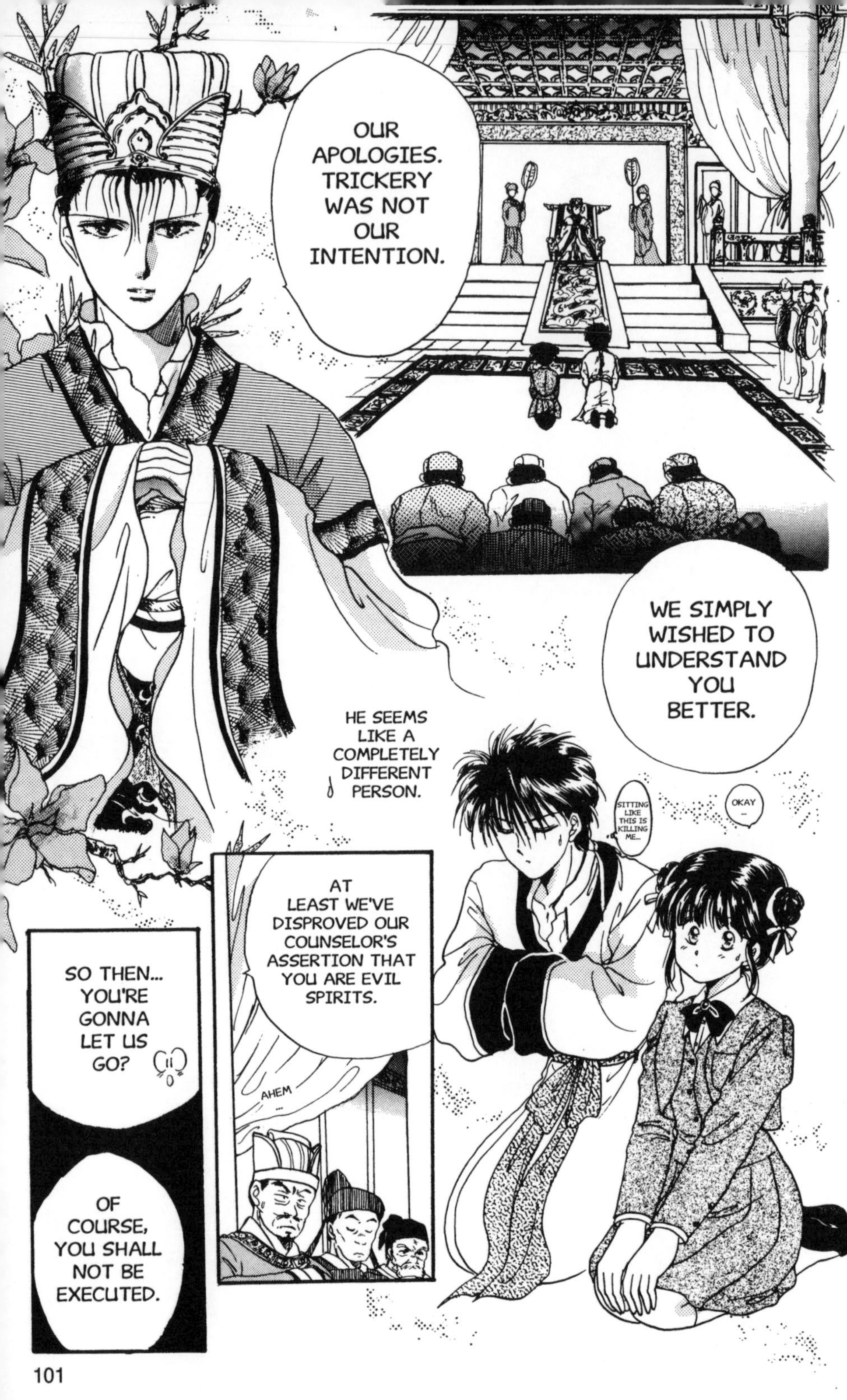
OUR APOLOGIES. TRICKERY WAS NOT OUR INTENTION.
WE SIMPLY WISHED TO UNDERSTAND YOU BETTER.
HE SEEMS LIKE A COMPLETELY DIFFERENT PERSON.
OKAY...
SITTING LIKE THIS IS KILLING ME...
AT LEAST WE'VE DISPROVED OUR COUNSELOR'S ASSERTION THAT YOU ARE EVIL SPIRITS.
AHEM...
SO THEN... YOU'RE GONNA LET US GO?
OF COURSE, YOU SHALL NOT BE EXECUTED.

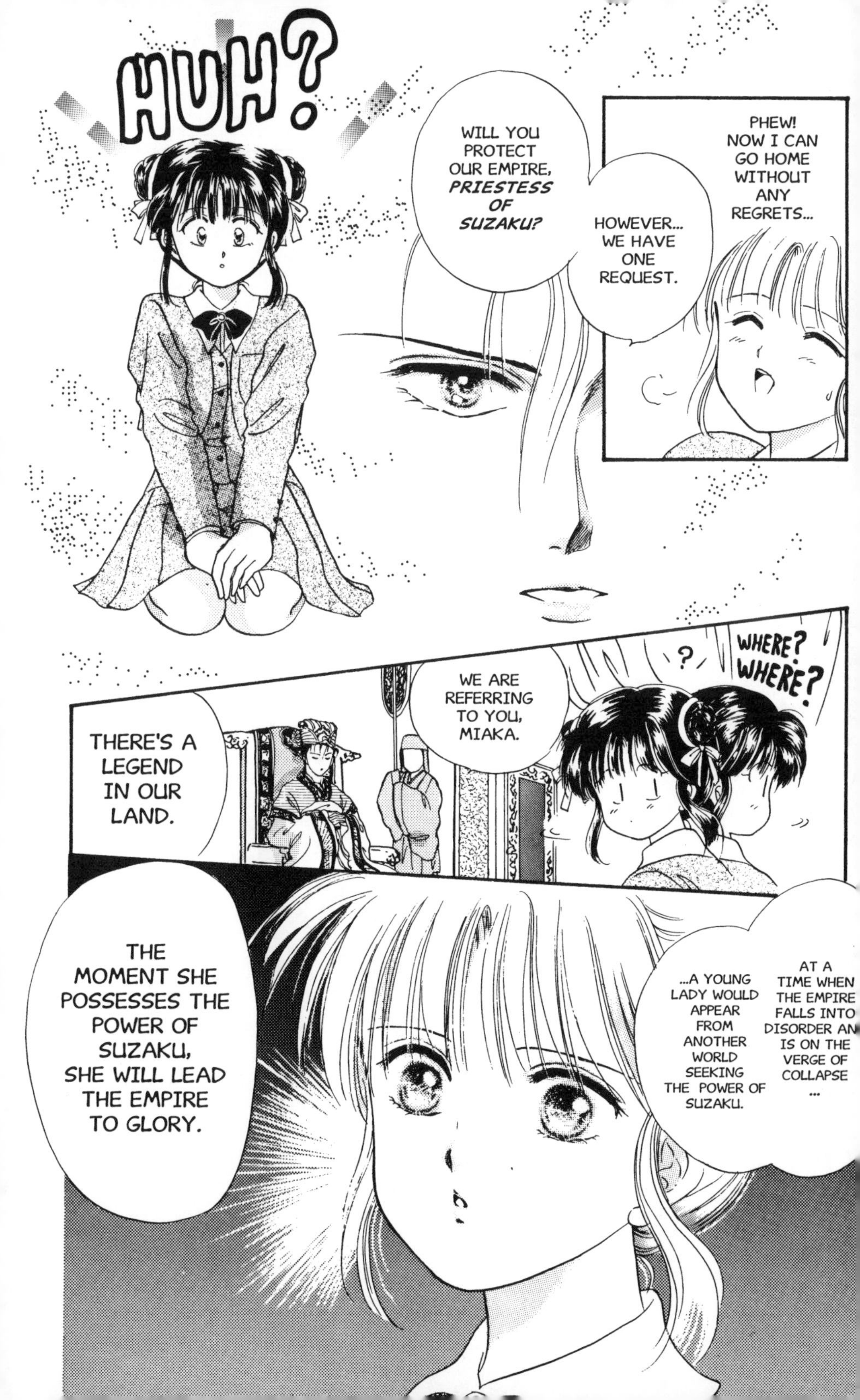
PHEW! NOW I CAN GO HOME WITHOUT ANY REGRETS...
HOWEVER... WE HAVE ONE REQUEST.
WILL YOU PROTECT OUR EMPIRE, *PRIESTESS OF SUZAKU?*
HUH?
WHERE? WHERE?
?
WE ARE REFERRING TO YOU, MIAKA.
THERE'S A LEGEND IN OUR LAND.
AT A TIME WHEN THE EMPIRE FALLS INTO DISORDER AN IS ON THE VERGE OF COLLAPSE ...
...A YOUNG LADY WOULD APPEAR FROM ANOTHER WORLD SEEKING THE POWER OF SUZAKU.
THE MOMENT SHE POSSESSES THE POWER OF SUZAKU, SHE WILL LEAD THE EMPIRE TO GLORY.

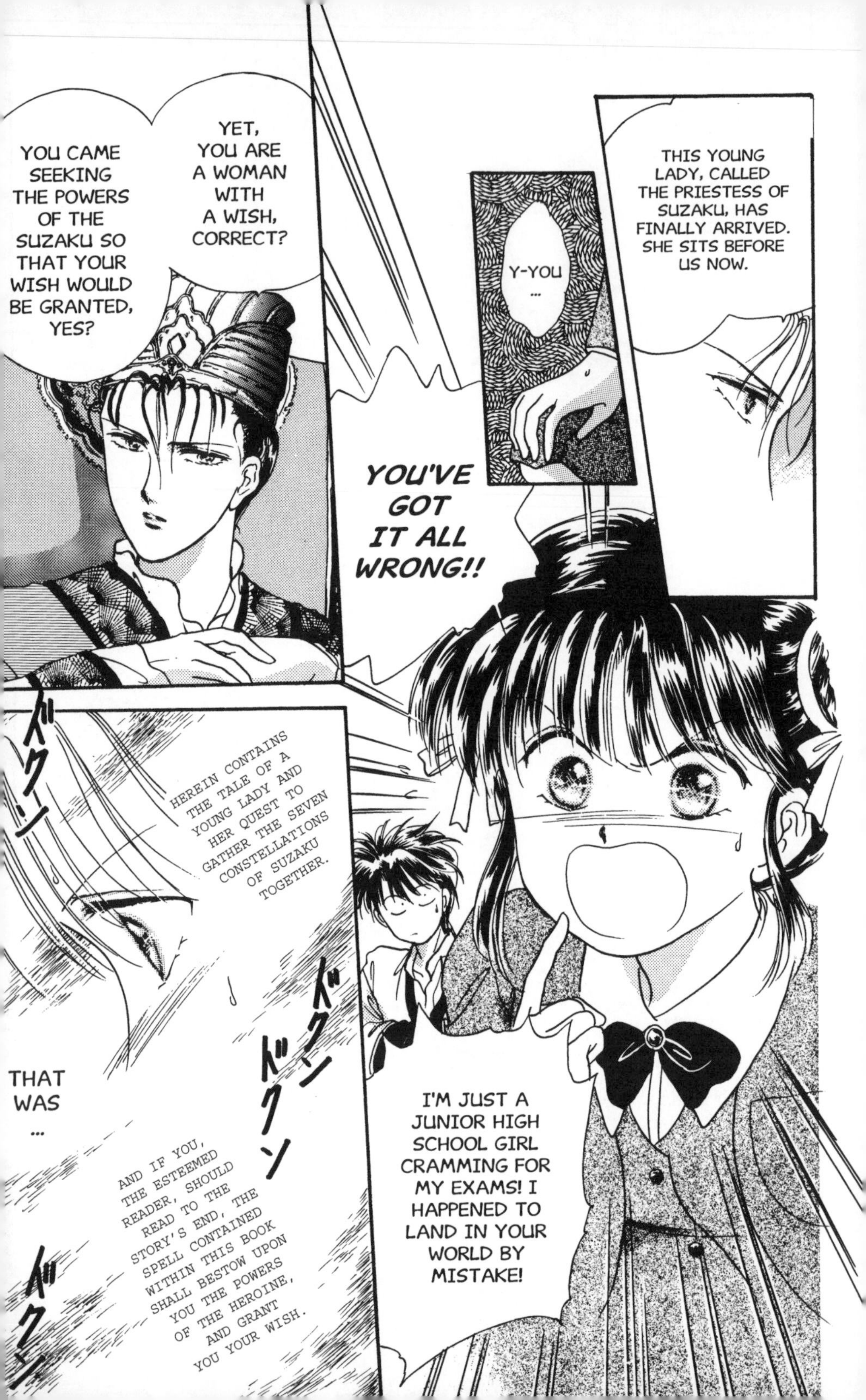

THIS YOUNG LADY, CALLED THE PRIESTESS OF SUZAKU, HAS FINALLY ARRIVED. SHE SITS BEFORE US NOW.
Y-YOU ...
YET, YOU ARE A WOMAN WITH A WISH, CORRECT?
YOU CAME SEEKING THE POWERS OF THE SUZAKU SO THAT YOUR WISH WOULD BE GRANTED, YES?
YOU'VE GOT IT ALL WRONG!!
I'M JUST A JUNIOR HIGH SCHOOL GIRL CRAMMING FOR MY EXAMS! I HAPPENED TO LAND IN YOUR WORLD BY MISTAKE!
HEREIN CONTAINS THE TALE OF A YOUNG LADY AND HER QUEST TO GATHER THE SEVEN CONSTELLATIONS OF SUZAKU TOGETHER.
AND IF YOU, THE ESTEEMED READER, SHOULD READ TO THE STORY'S END, THE SPELL CONTAINED WITHIN THIS BOOK SHALL BESTOW UPON YOU THE POWERS OF THE HEROINE, AND GRANT YOU YOUR WISH.
ドクン
ドクン
ドクン
THAT WAS ...

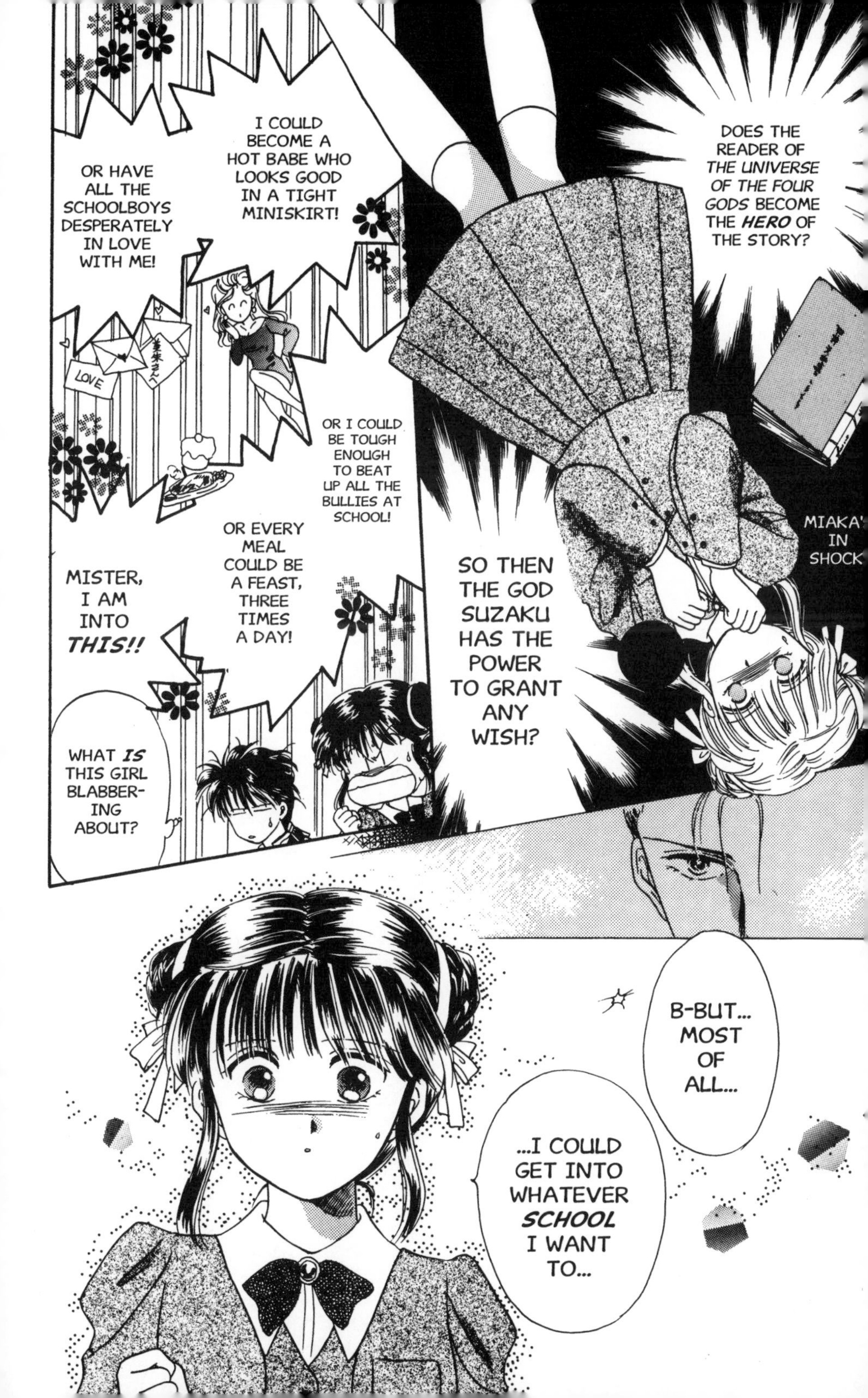
DOES THE READER OF *THE UNIVERSE OF THE FOUR GODS* BECOME THE ***HERO*** OF THE STORY?
MIAKA' IN SHOCK
SO THEN THE GOD SUZAKU HAS THE POWER TO GRANT ANY WISH?
I COULD BECOME A HOT BABE WHO LOOKS GOOD IN A TIGHT MINISKIRT!
OR HAVE ALL THE SCHOOLBOYS DESPERATELY IN LOVE WITH ME!
LOVE
OR I COULD BE TOUGH ENOUGH TO BEAT UP ALL THE BULLIES AT SCHOOL!
OR EVERY MEAL COULD BE A FEAST, THREE TIMES A DAY!
MISTER, I AM INTO ***THIS!!***
WHAT *IS* THIS GIRL BLABBERING ABOUT?
B-BUT... MOST OF ALL...
...I COULD GET INTO WHATEVER ***SCHOOL*** I WANT TO...

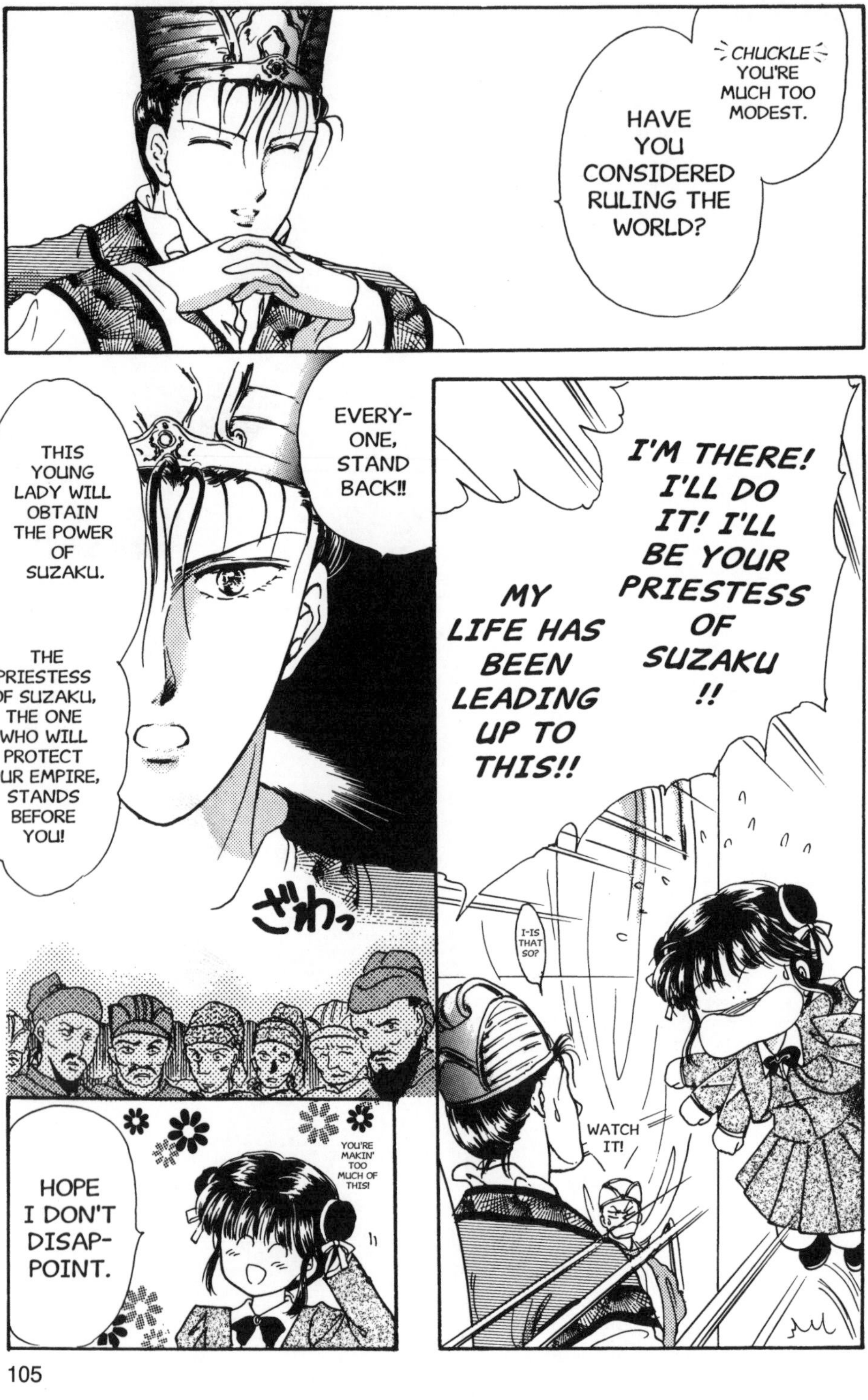
CHUCKLE YOU'RE MUCH TOO MODEST.
HAVE YOU CONSIDERED RULING THE WORLD?
I'M THERE! I'LL DO IT! I'LL BE YOUR PRIESTESS OF SUZAKU!!
MY LIFE HAS BEEN LEADING UP TO THIS!!
I-IS THAT SO?
WATCH IT!
EVERY-ONE, STAND BACK!!
THIS YOUNG LADY WILL OBTAIN THE POWER OF SUZAKU.
THE PRIESTESS OF SUZAKU, THE ONE WHO WILL PROTECT OUR EMPIRE, STANDS BEFORE YOU!
ざわっ
YOU'RE MAKIN' TOO MUCH OF THIS!
HOPE I DON'T DISAP-POINT.

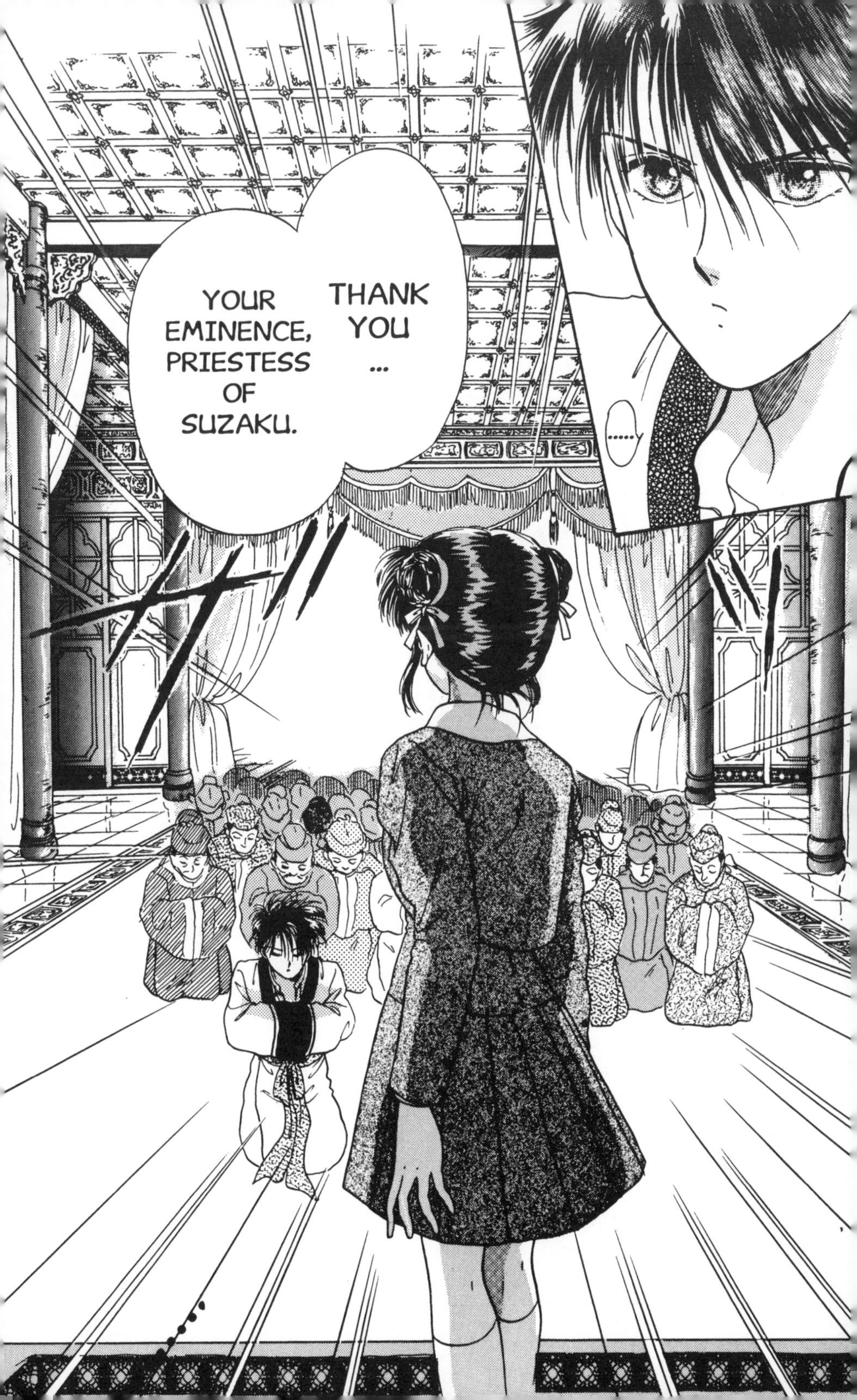
......
THANK YOU ...
YOUR EMINENCE, PRIESTESS OF SUZAKU.

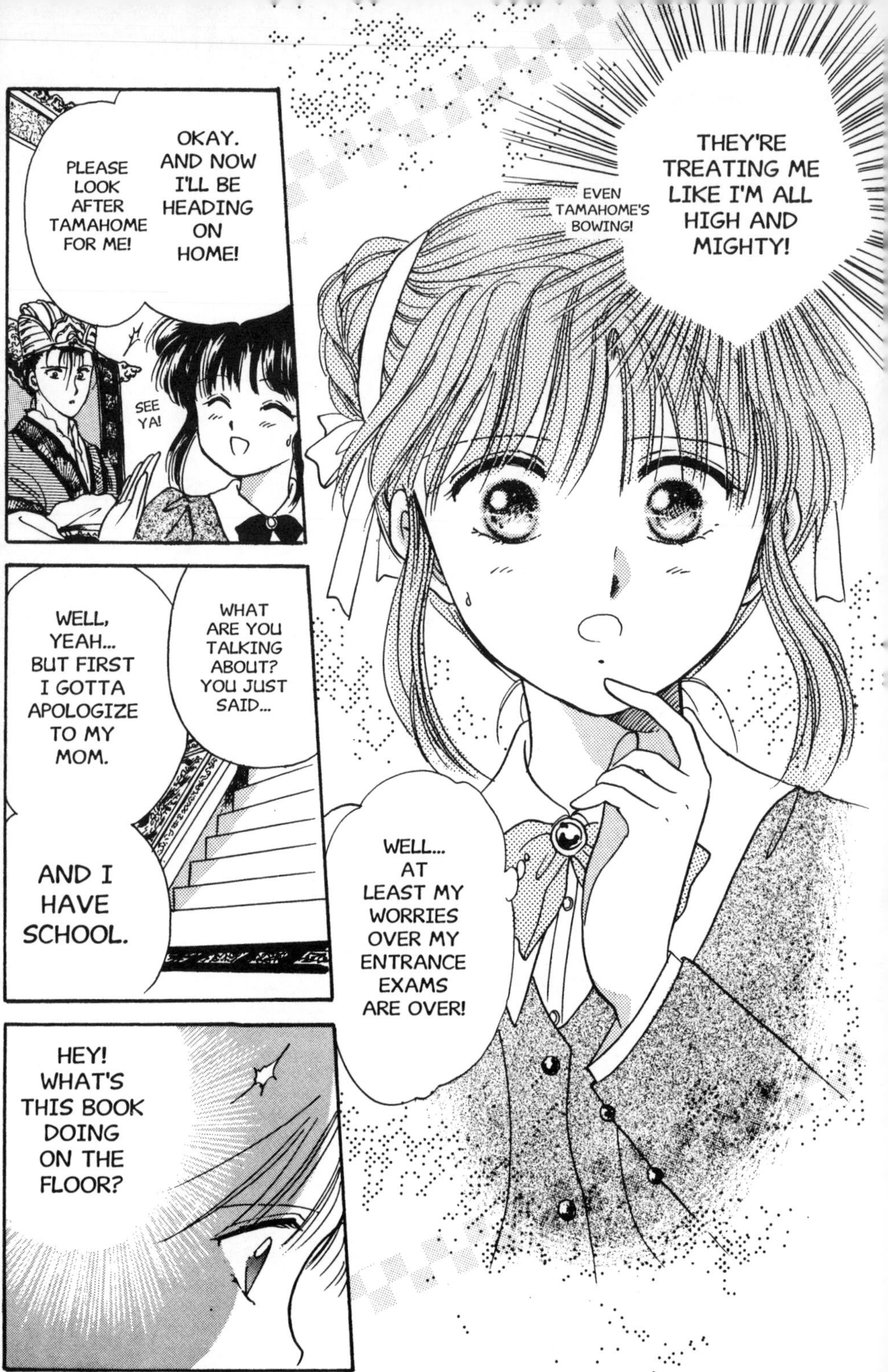
THEY'RE TREATING ME LIKE I'M ALL HIGH AND MIGHTY!
EVEN TAMAHOME'S BOWING!
WELL... AT LEAST MY WORRIES OVER MY ENTRANCE EXAMS ARE OVER!
OKAY. AND NOW I'LL BE HEADING ON HOME!
PLEASE LOOK AFTER TAMAHOME FOR ME!
SEE YA!
WHAT ARE YOU TALKING ABOUT? YOU JUST SAID...
WELL, YEAH... BUT FIRST I GOTTA APOLOGIZE TO MY MOM.
AND I HAVE SCHOOL.
HEY! WHAT'S THIS BOOK DOING ON THE FLOOR?

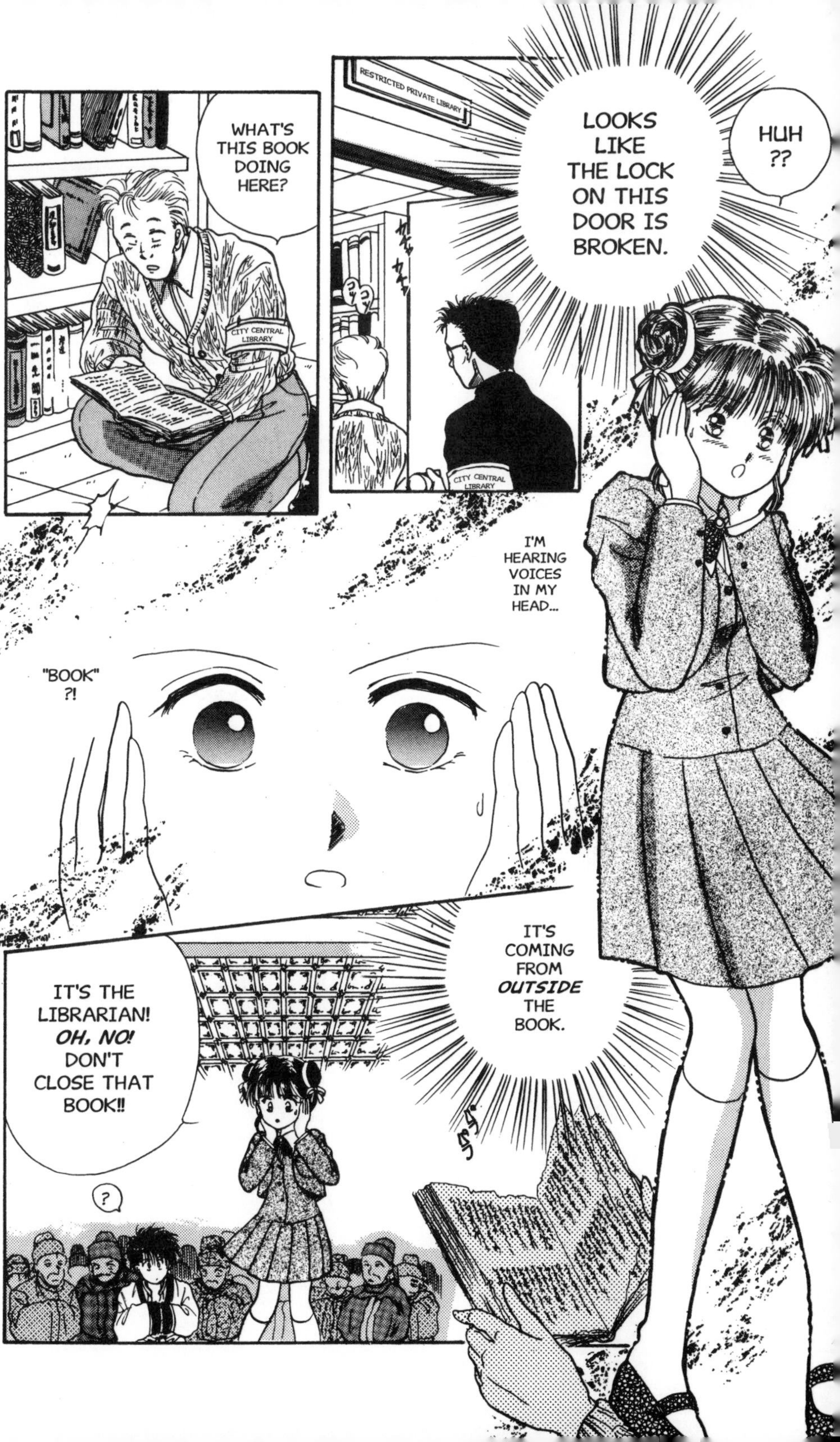
HUH ??
LOOKS LIKE THE LOCK ON THIS DOOR IS BROKEN.
RESTRICTED PRIVATE LIBRARY
CITY CENTRAL LIBRARY
WHAT'S THIS BOOK DOING HERE?
CITY CENTRAL LIBRARY
I'M HEARING VOICES IN MY HEAD...
"BOOK" ?!
IT'S COMING FROM *OUTSIDE* THE BOOK.
IT'S THE LIBRARIAN! ***OH, NO!*** DON'T CLOSE THAT BOOK!!
?

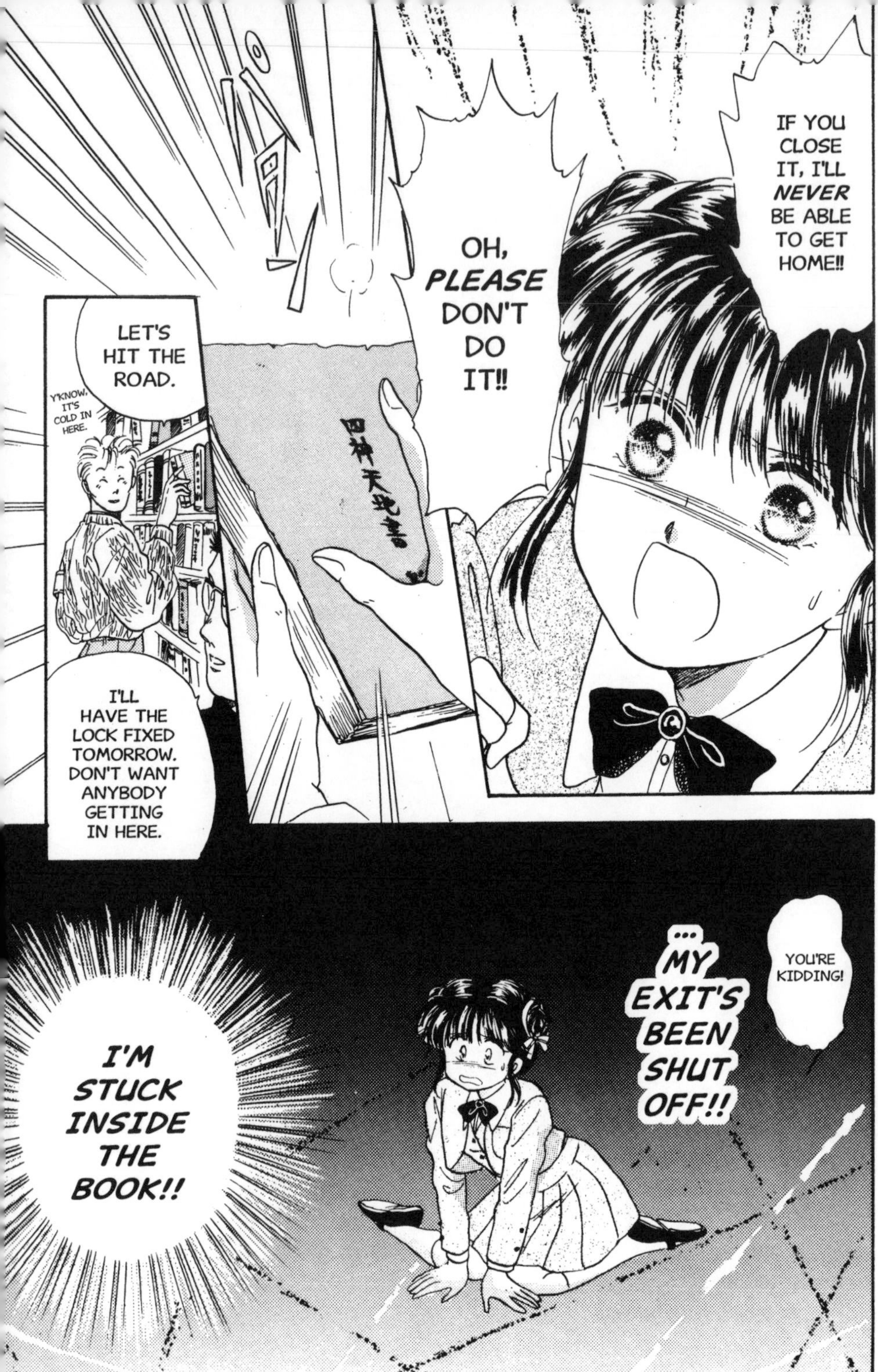

IF YOU CLOSE IT, I'LL *NEVER* BE ABLE TO GET HOME!!
OH, *PLEASE* DON'T DO IT!!
四神天地書
LET'S HIT THE ROAD.
Y'KNOW, IT'S COLD IN HERE.
I'LL HAVE THE LOCK FIXED TOMORROW. DON'T WANT ANYBODY GETTING IN HERE.
YOU'RE KIDDING!
...MY EXIT'S BEEN SHUT OFF!!
I'M STUCK INSIDE THE BOOK!!

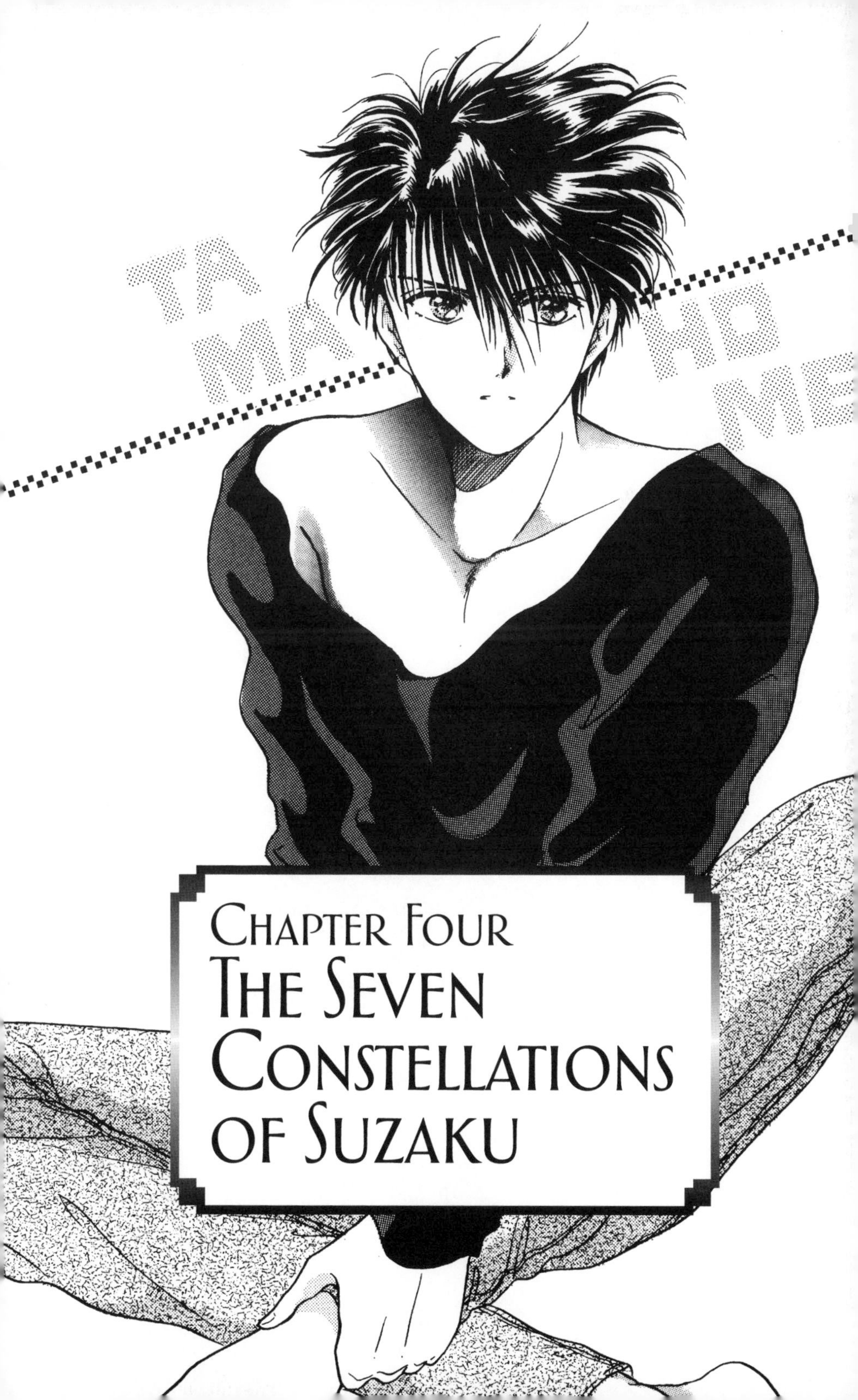

Chapter Four
The Seven Constellations of Suzaku

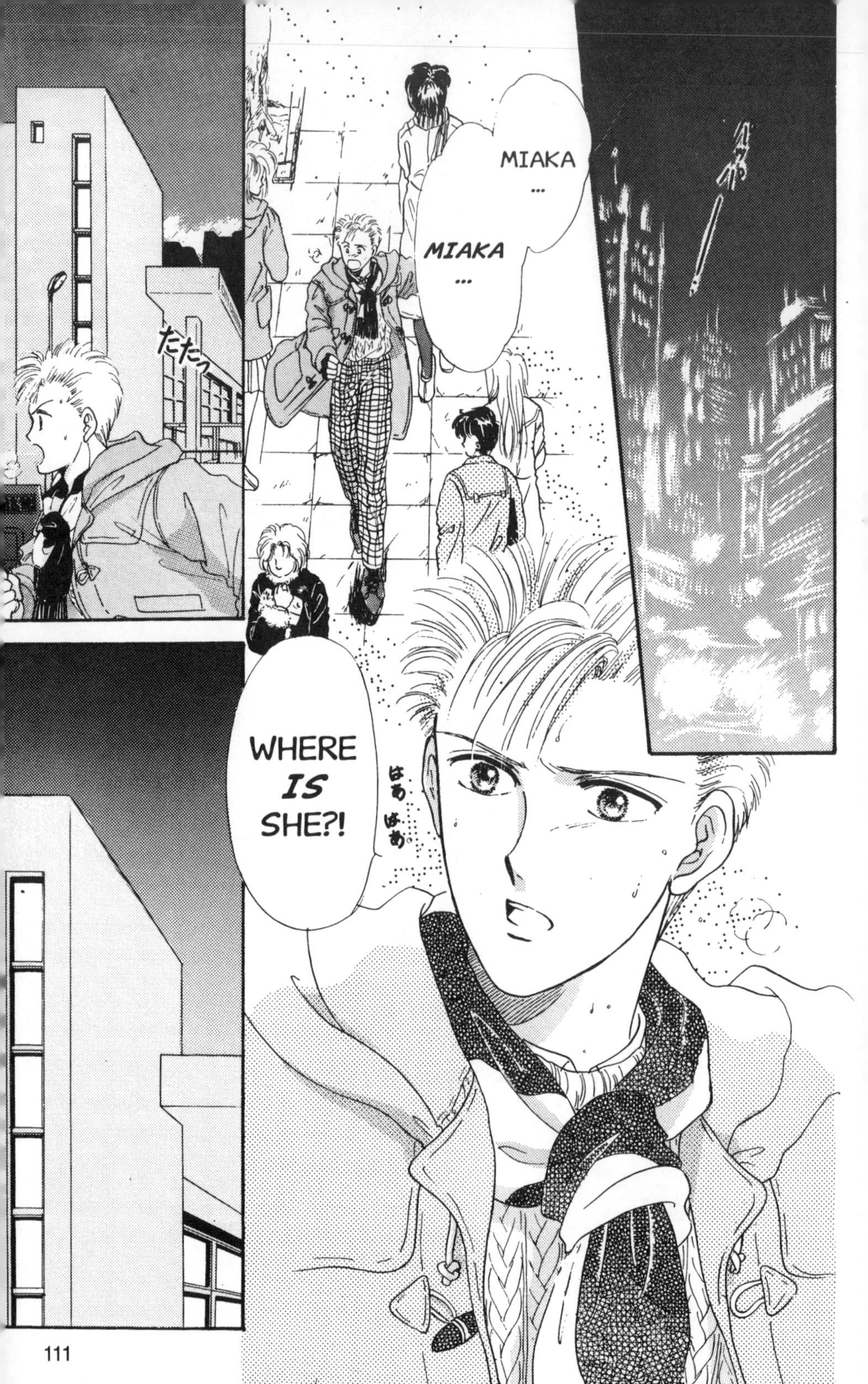
MIAKA ...
MIAKA ...
WHERE *IS* SHE?!
はあ はあ
たたっ

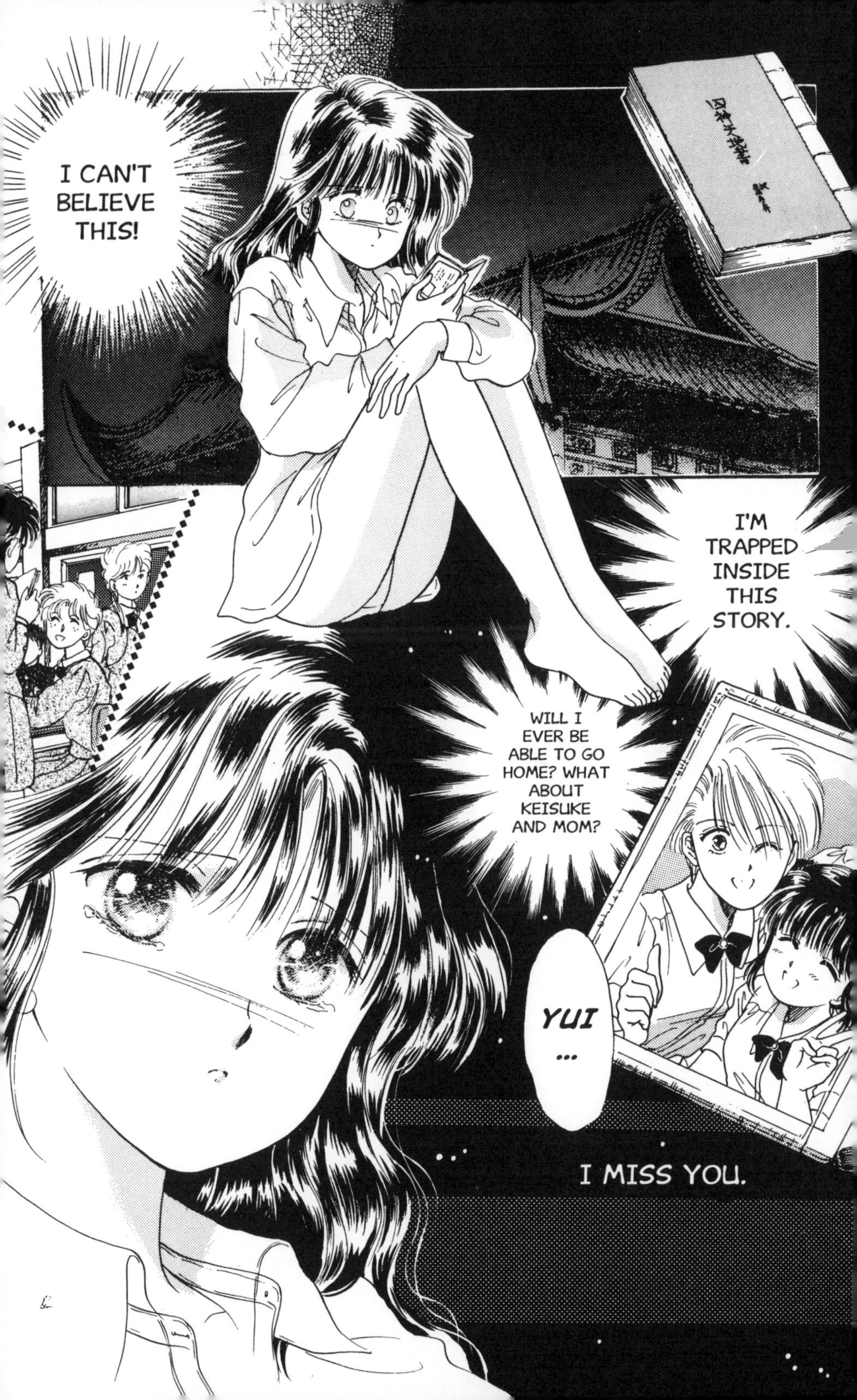
I CAN'T BELIEVE THIS!
I'M TRAPPED INSIDE THIS STORY.
WILL I EVER BE ABLE TO GO HOME? WHAT ABOUT KEISUKE AND MOM?
YUI ...
I MISS YOU.

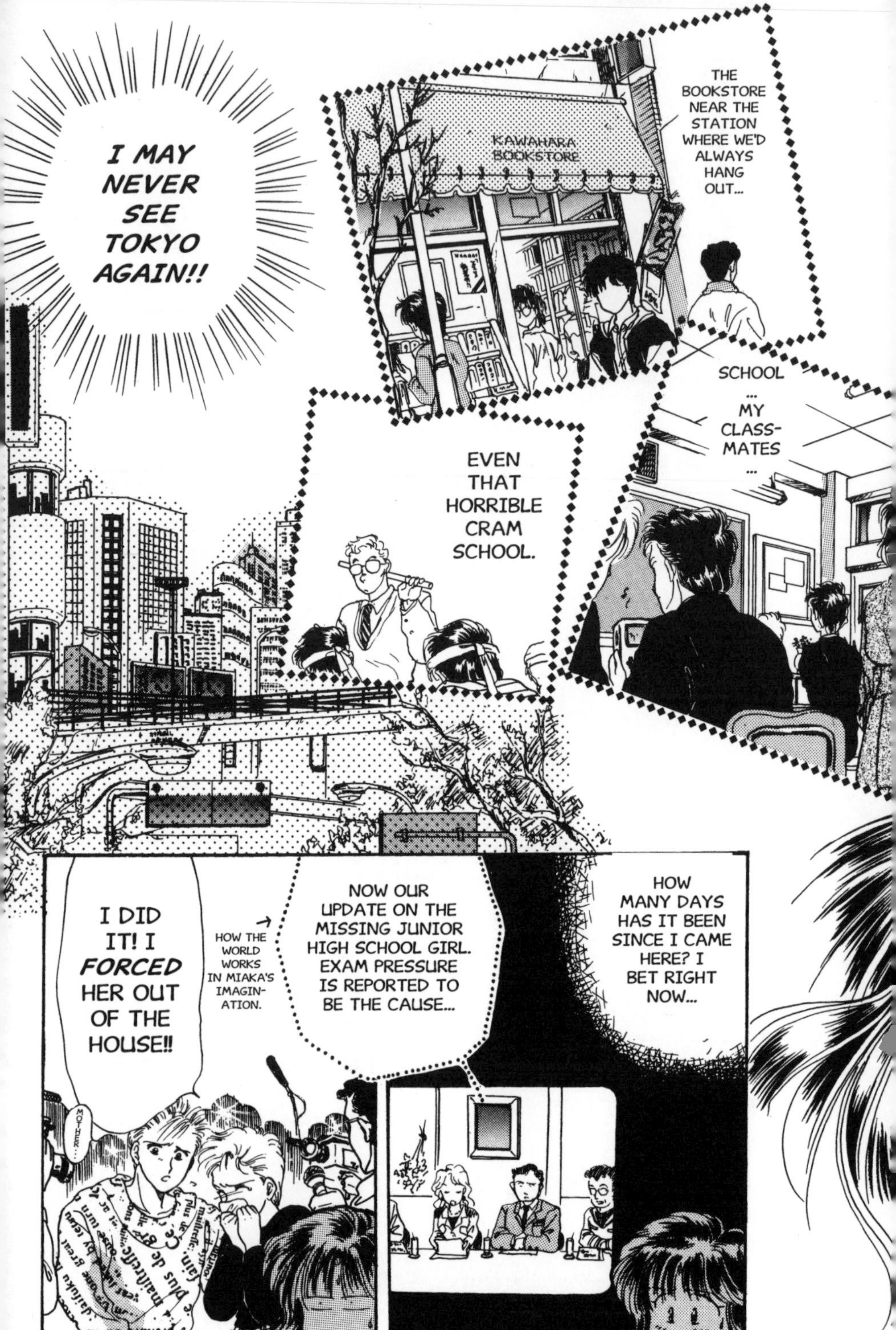
THE BOOKSTORE NEAR THE STATION WHERE WE'D ALWAYS HANG OUT...
KAWAHARA BOOKSTORE
SCHOOL ... MY CLASSMATES ...
EVEN THAT HORRIBLE CRAM SCHOOL.
I MAY NEVER SEE TOKYO AGAIN!!
HOW MANY DAYS HAS IT BEEN SINCE I CAME HERE? I BET RIGHT NOW...
NOW OUR UPDATE ON THE MISSING JUNIOR HIGH SCHOOL GIRL. EXAM PRESSURE IS REPORTED TO BE THE CAUSE...
HOW THE WORLD WORKS IN MIAKA'S IMAGINATION.
I DID IT! I FORCED HER OUT OF THE HOUSE!!
MOTHER...

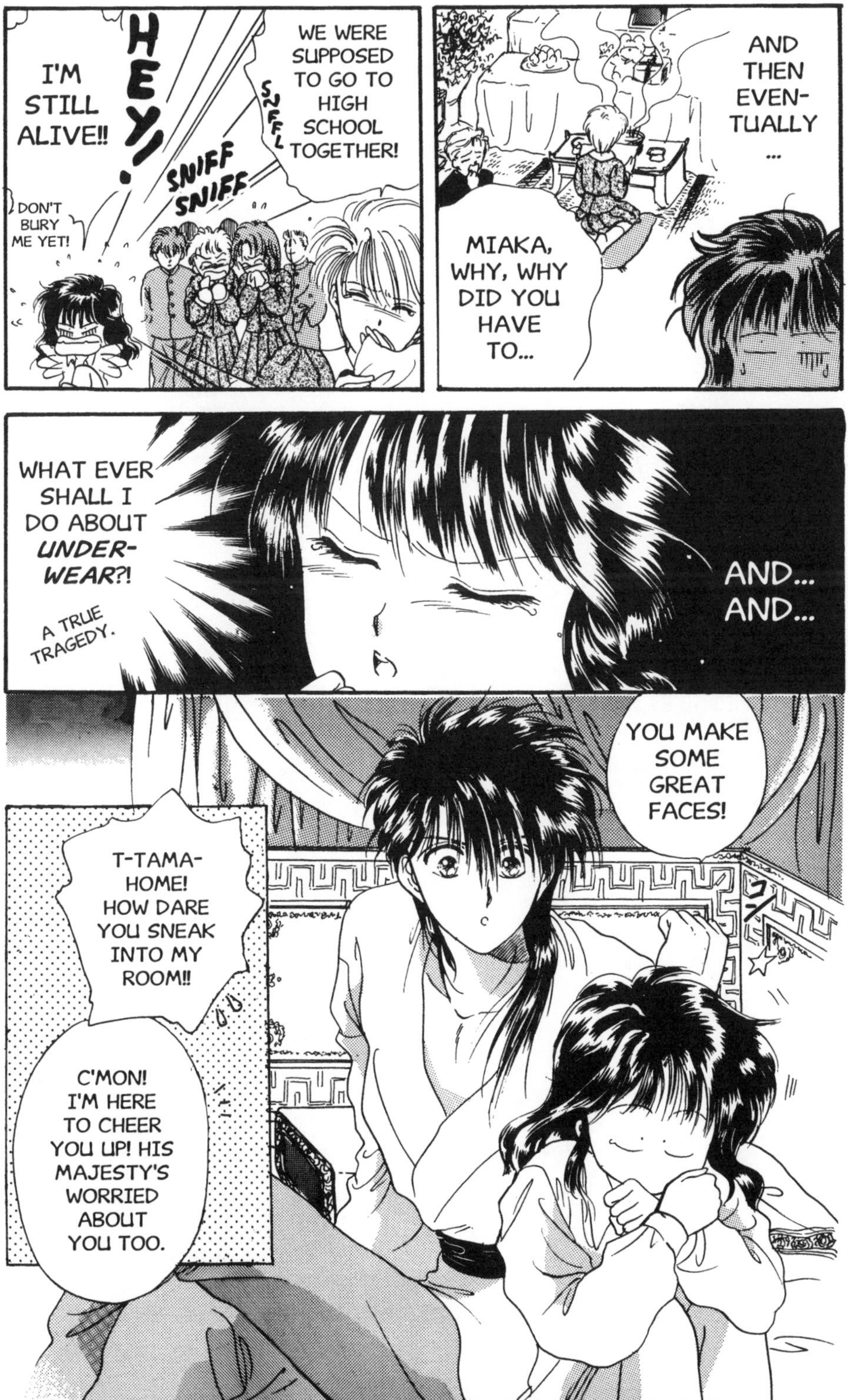
AND THEN EVEN-TUALLY ...
MIAKA, WHY, WHY DID YOU HAVE TO...
WE WERE SUPPOSED TO GO TO HIGH SCHOOL TOGETHER!
SNIFFL
SNIFF SNIFF
HEY!
I'M STILL ALIVE!!
DON'T BURY ME YET!
AND... AND...
WHAT EVER SHALL I DO ABOUT *UNDER-WEAR*?!
A TRUE TRAGEDY.
YOU MAKE SOME GREAT FACES!
T-TAMA-HOME! HOW DARE YOU SNEAK INTO MY ROOM!!
C'MON! I'M HERE TO CHEER YOU UP! HIS MAJESTY'S WORRIED ABOUT YOU TOO.

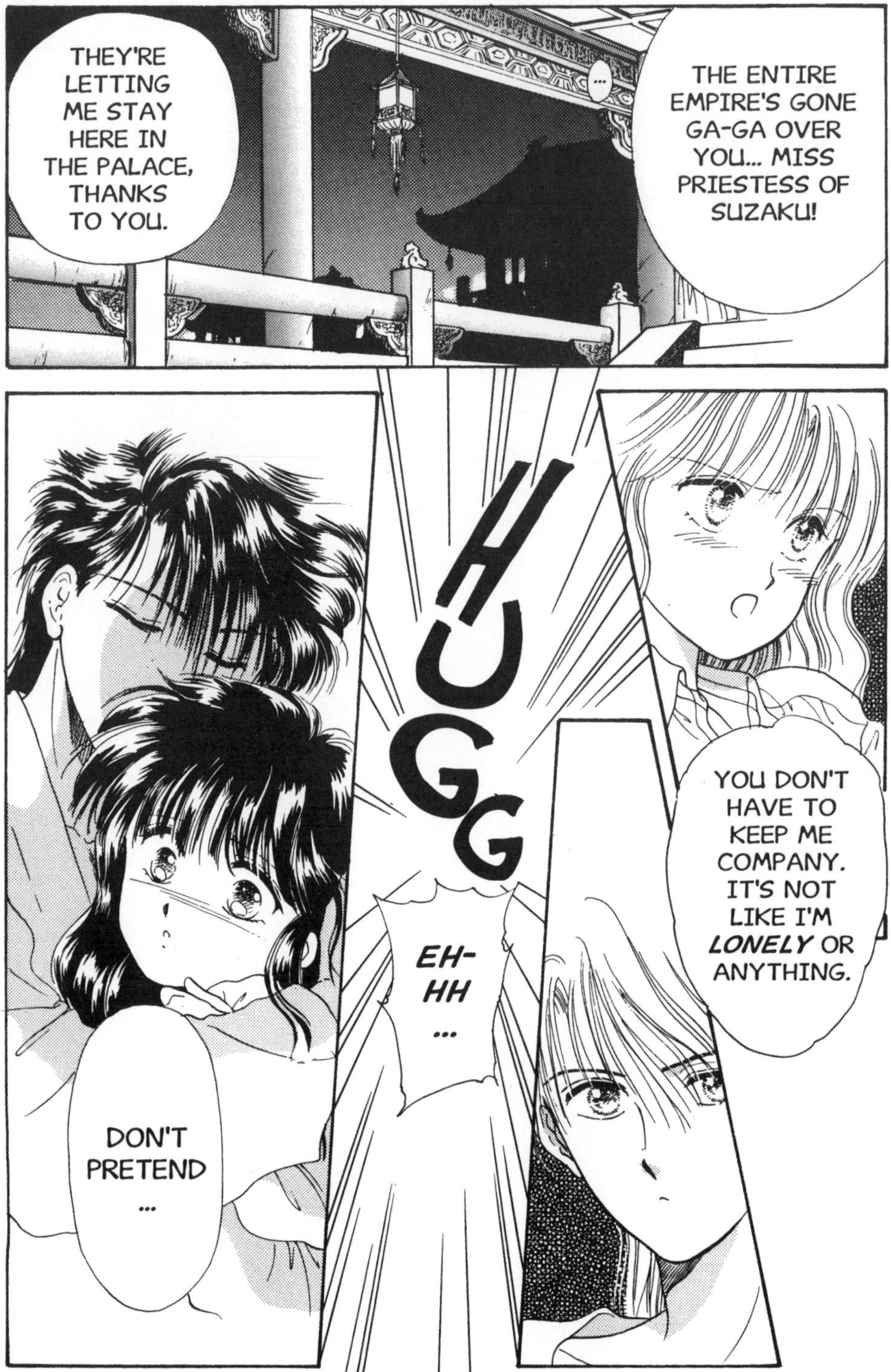
THE ENTIRE EMPIRE'S GONE GA-GA OVER YOU... MISS PRIESTESS OF SUZAKU!
...
THEY'RE LETTING ME STAY HERE IN THE PALACE, THANKS TO YOU.
YOU DON'T HAVE TO KEEP ME COMPANY. IT'S NOT LIKE I'M *LONELY* OR ANYTHING.
HUGG
EH-HH...
DON'T PRETEND...

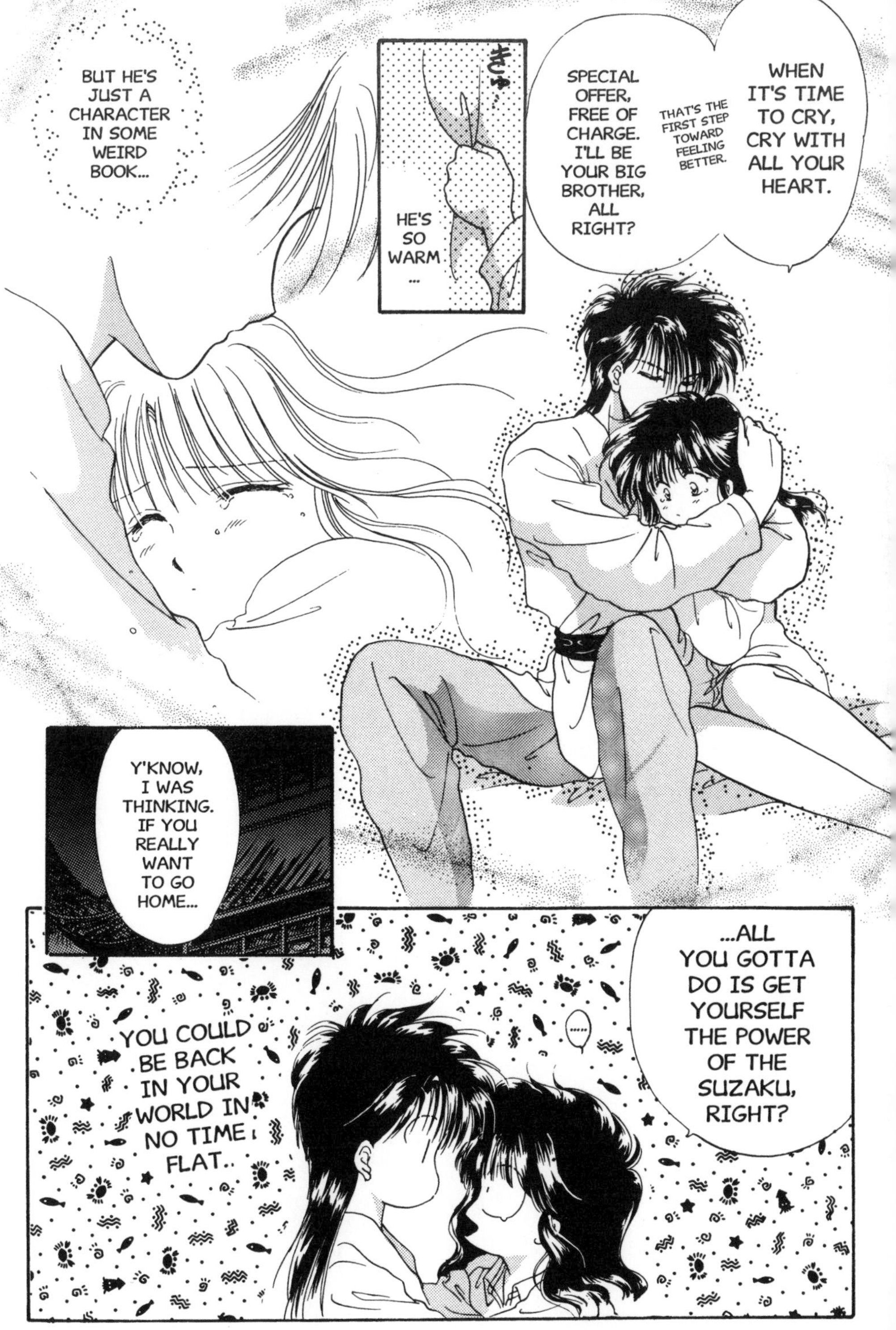
WHEN IT'S TIME TO CRY, CRY WITH ALL YOUR HEART.
THAT'S THE FIRST STEP TOWARD FEELING BETTER.
SPECIAL OFFER, FREE OF CHARGE. I'LL BE YOUR BIG BROTHER, ALL RIGHT?
きゅ…
HE'S SO WARM ...
BUT HE'S JUST A CHARACTER IN SOME WEIRD BOOK...
Y'KNOW, I WAS THINKING. IF YOU REALLY WANT TO GO HOME...
...ALL YOU GOTTA DO IS GET YOURSELF THE POWER OF THE SUZAKU, RIGHT?
......
YOU COULD BE BACK IN YOUR WORLD IN NO TIME FLAT..

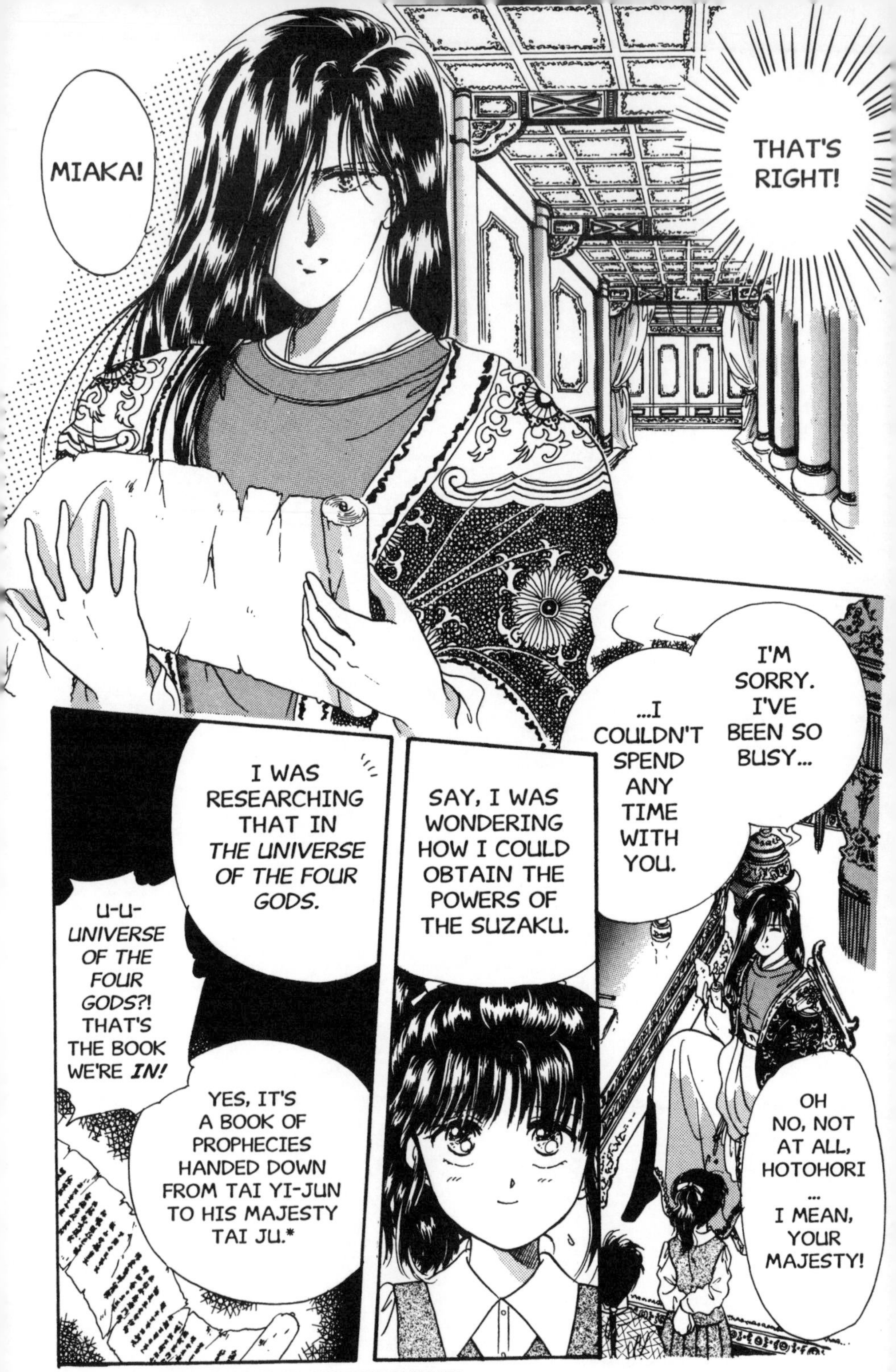
THAT'S RIGHT!
MIAKA!
I'M SORRY. I'VE BEEN SO BUSY...
...I COULDN'T SPEND ANY TIME WITH YOU.
OH NO, NOT AT ALL, HOTOHORI ... I MEAN, YOUR MAJESTY!
SAY, I WAS WONDERING HOW I COULD OBTAIN THE POWERS OF THE SUZAKU.
I WAS RESEARCHING THAT IN *THE UNIVERSE OF THE FOUR GODS.*
U-U-*UNIVERSE OF THE FOUR GODS?!* THAT'S THE BOOK WE'RE ***IN!***
YES, IT'S A BOOK OF PROPHECIES HANDED DOWN FROM TAI YI-JUN TO HIS MAJESTY TAI JU.*

*THE FIRST EMPEROR OF HOTOHORI'S DYNASTY.

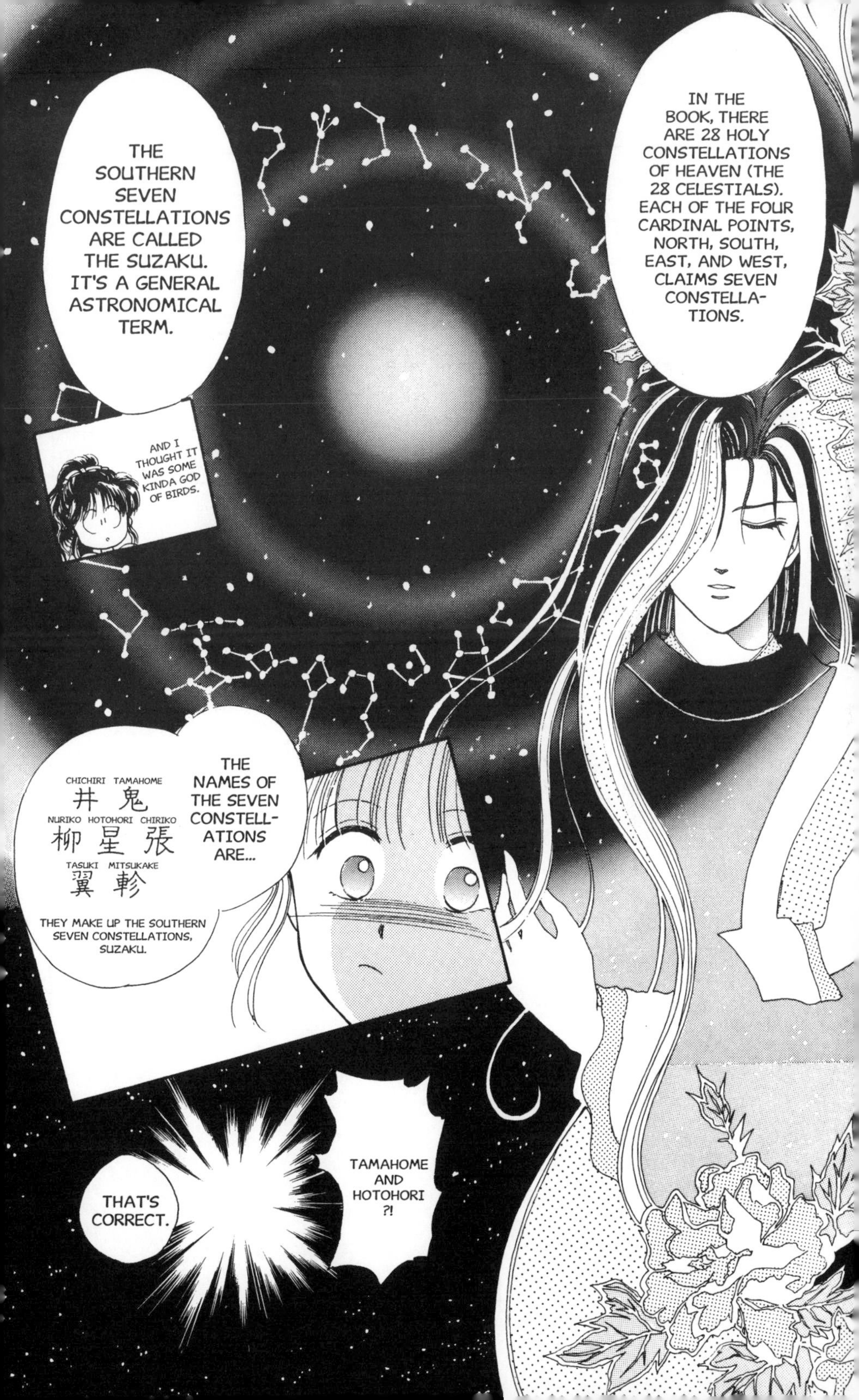
IN THE BOOK, THERE ARE 28 HOLY CONSTELLATIONS OF HEAVEN (THE 28 CELESTIALS). EACH OF THE FOUR CARDINAL POINTS, NORTH, SOUTH, EAST, AND WEST, CLAIMS SEVEN CONSTELLA- TIONS.
THE SOUTHERN SEVEN CONSTELLATIONS ARE CALLED THE SUZAKU. IT'S A GENERAL ASTRONOMICAL TERM.
AND I THOUGHT IT WAS SOME KINDA GOD OF BIRDS.
THE NAMES OF THE SEVEN CONSTELL- ATIONS ARE...
CHICHIRI TAMAHOME
井 鬼
NURIKO HOTOHORI CHIRIKO
柳 星 張
TASUKI MITSUKAKE
翼 軫
THEY MAKE UP THE SOUTHERN SEVEN CONSTELLATIONS, SUZAKU.
TAMAHOME AND HOTOHORI ?!
THAT'S CORRECT.

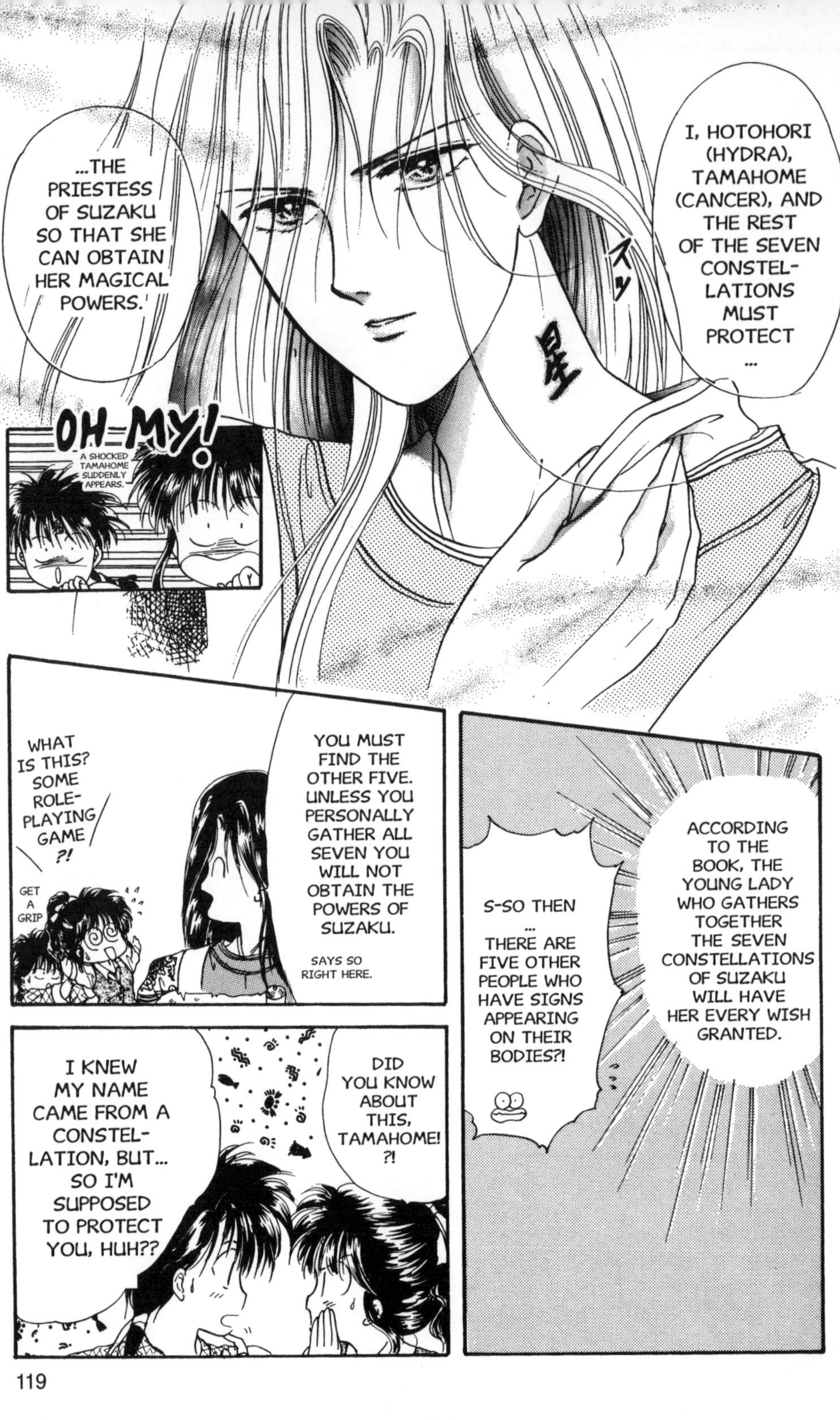
I, HOTOHORI (HYDRA), TAMAHOME (CANCER), AND THE REST OF THE SEVEN CONSTELLATIONS MUST PROTECT ...
スッ
星
...THE PRIESTESS OF SUZAKU SO THAT SHE CAN OBTAIN HER MAGICAL POWERS.
OH-MY!
A SHOCKED TAMAHOME SUDDENLY APPEARS.
ACCORDING TO THE BOOK, THE YOUNG LADY WHO GATHERS TOGETHER THE SEVEN CONSTELLATIONS OF SUZAKU WILL HAVE HER EVERY WISH GRANTED.
S-SO THEN ... THERE ARE FIVE OTHER PEOPLE WHO HAVE SIGNS APPEARING ON THEIR BODIES?!
YOU MUST FIND THE OTHER FIVE. UNLESS YOU PERSONALLY GATHER ALL SEVEN YOU WILL NOT OBTAIN THE POWERS OF SUZAKU.
SAYS SO RIGHT HERE.
WHAT IS THIS? SOME ROLE-PLAYING GAME?!
GET A GRIP
DID YOU KNOW ABOUT THIS, TAMAHOME!?!
I KNEW MY NAME CAME FROM A CONSTELLATION, BUT... SO I'M SUPPOSED TO PROTECT YOU, HUH??

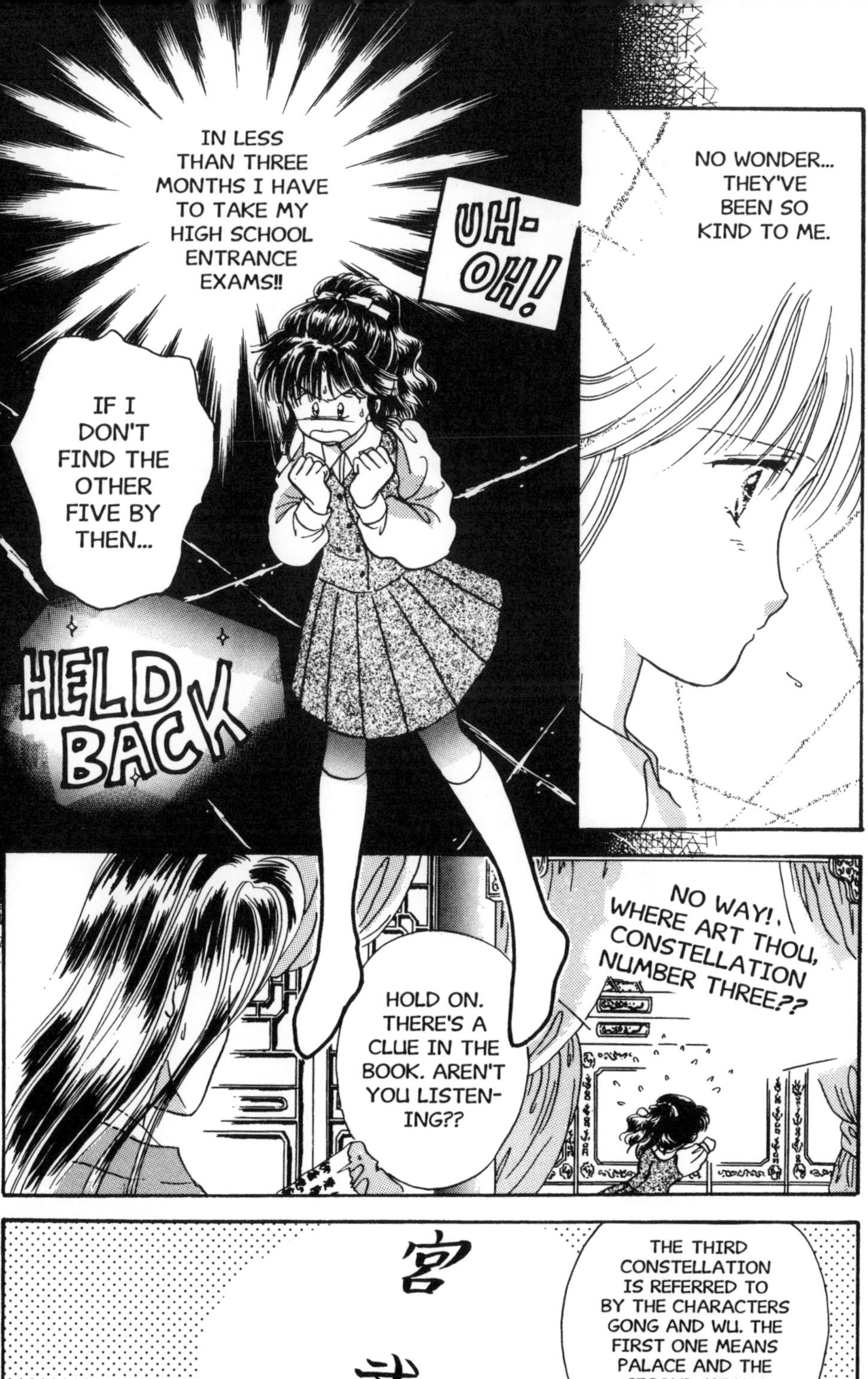
NO WONDER... THEY'VE BEEN SO KIND TO ME.
UH-OH!
IN LESS THAN THREE MONTHS I HAVE TO TAKE MY HIGH SCHOOL ENTRANCE EXAMS!!
IF I DON'T FIND THE OTHER FIVE BY THEN...
HELD BACK
NO WAY!. WHERE ART THOU, CONSTELLATION NUMBER THREE??
HOLD ON. THERE'S A CLUE IN THE BOOK. AREN'T YOU LISTEN-ING??
THE THIRD CONSTELLATION IS REFERRED TO BY THE CHARACTERS GONG AND WU. THE FIRST ONE MEANS PALACE AND THE SECOND MEANS FIERCE STRENGTH.
宮
武

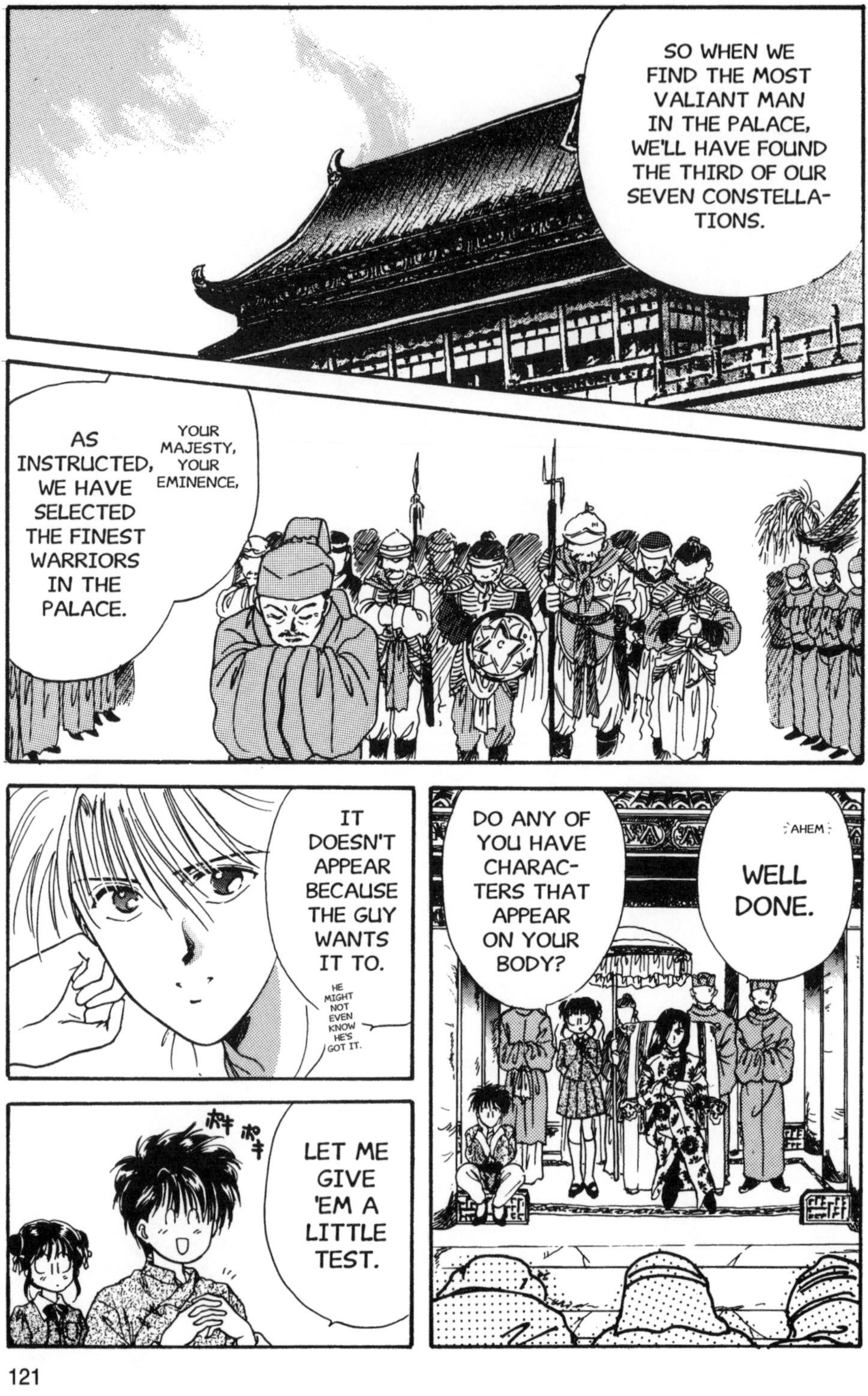
SO WHEN WE FIND THE MOST VALIANT MAN IN THE PALACE, WE'LL HAVE FOUND THE THIRD OF OUR SEVEN CONSTELLA-TIONS.
YOUR MAJESTY, YOUR EMINENCE,
AS INSTRUCTED, WE HAVE SELECTED THE FINEST WARRIORS IN THE PALACE.
AHEM
WELL DONE.
DO ANY OF YOU HAVE CHARAC-TERS THAT APPEAR ON YOUR BODY?
IT DOESN'T APPEAR BECAUSE THE GUY WANTS IT TO.
HE MIGHT NOT EVEN KNOW HE'S GOT IT.
ポキ ポキ
LET ME GIVE 'EM A LITTLE TEST.

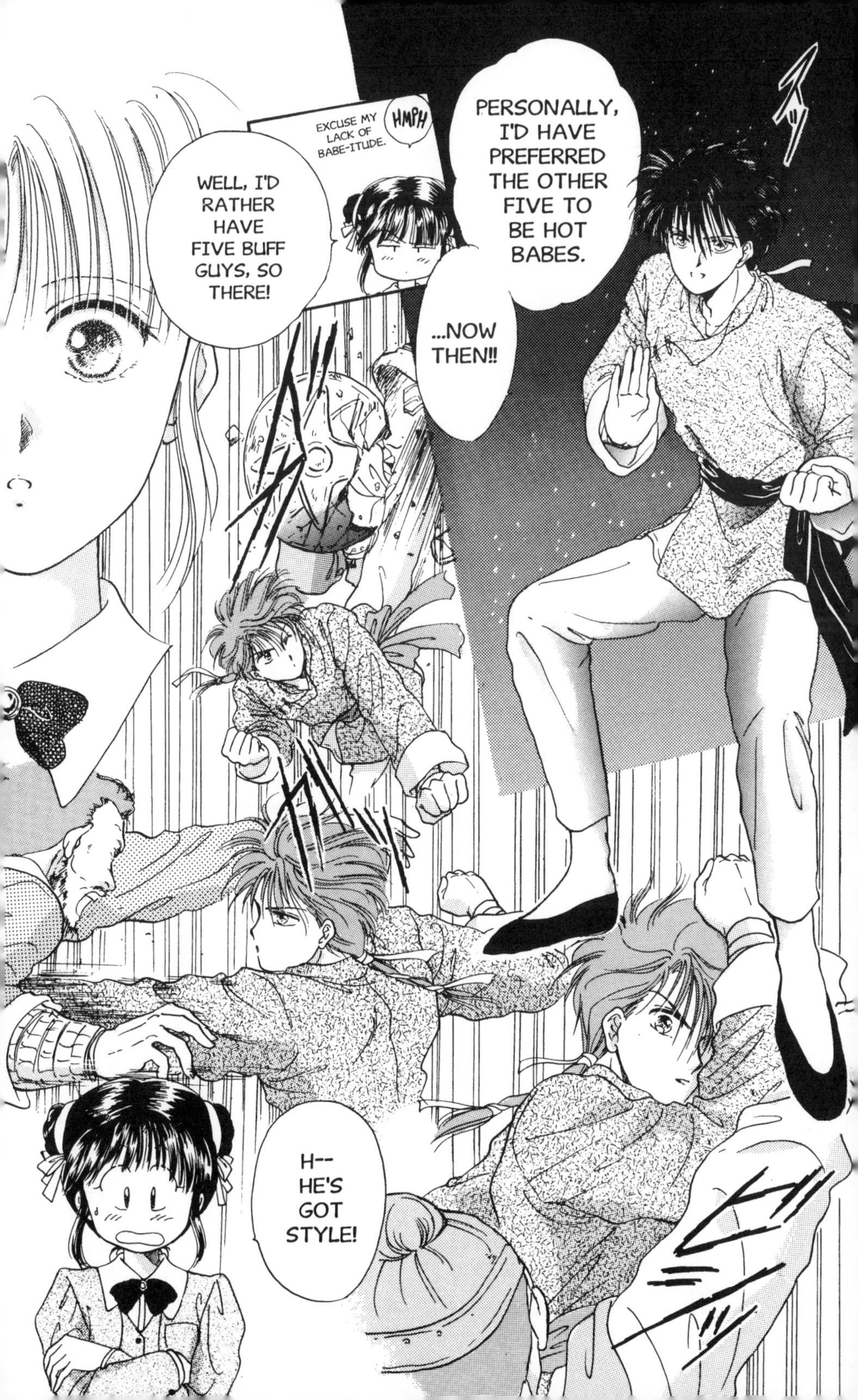
PERSONALLY, I'D HAVE PREFERRED THE OTHER FIVE TO BE HOT BABES.
HMPH
EXCUSE MY LACK OF BABE-ITUDE.
WELL, I'D RATHER HAVE FIVE BUFF GUYS, SO THERE!
...NOW THEN!!
H-- HE'S GOT STYLE!

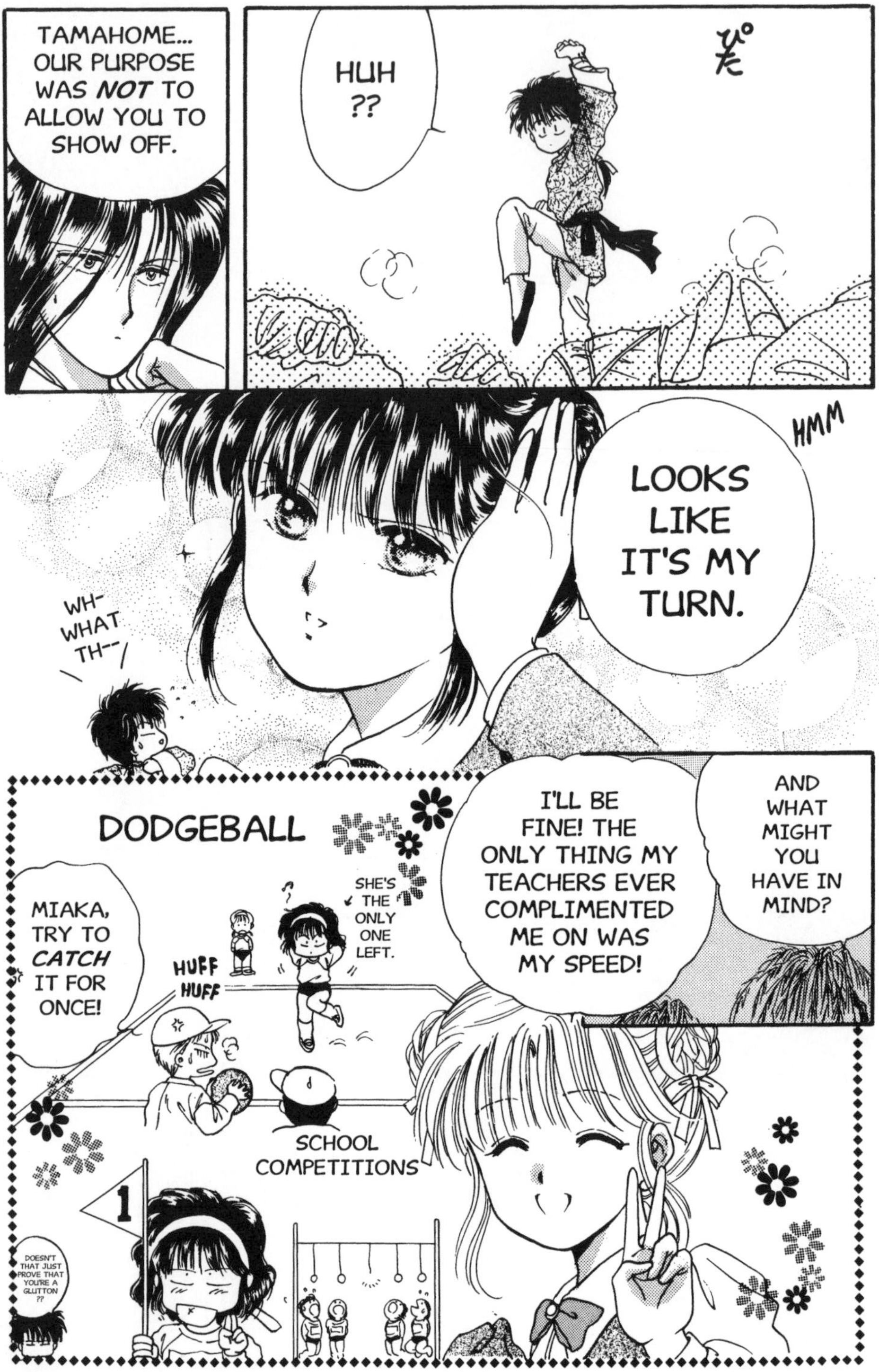
ぴた
HUH ??
TAMAHOME... OUR PURPOSE WAS *NOT* TO ALLOW YOU TO SHOW OFF.
HMM
LOOKS LIKE IT'S MY TURN.
WH-WHAT TH--
AND WHAT MIGHT YOU HAVE IN MIND?
I'LL BE FINE! THE ONLY THING MY TEACHERS EVER COMPLIMENTED ME ON WAS MY SPEED!
DODGEBALL
SHE'S THE ONLY ONE LEFT.
HUFF HUFF
MIAKA, TRY TO *CATCH* IT FOR ONCE!
SCHOOL COMPETITIONS
1
DOESN'T THAT JUST PROVE THAT YOU'RE A GLUTTON ??

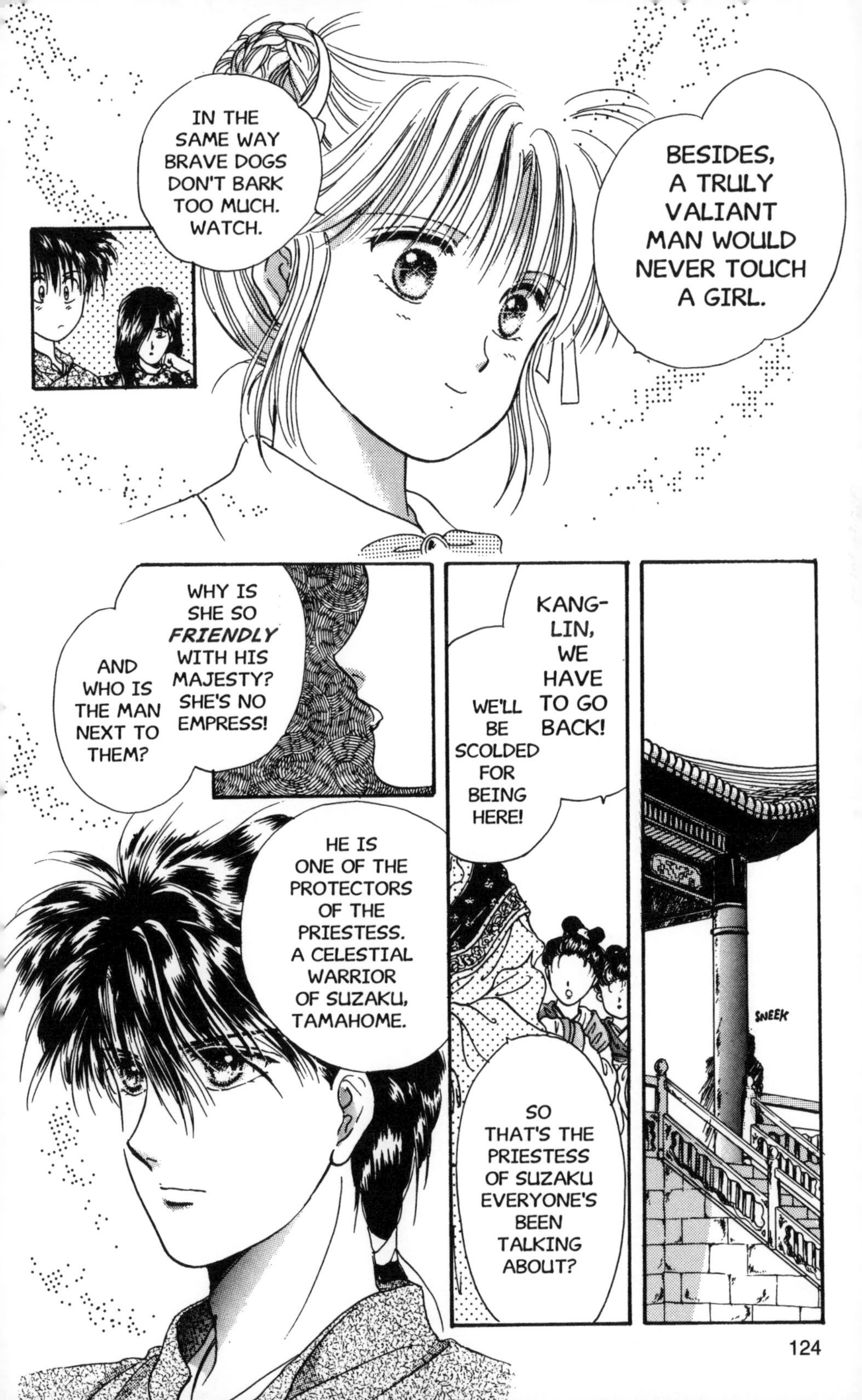
BESIDES, A TRULY VALIANT MAN WOULD NEVER TOUCH A GIRL.
IN THE SAME WAY BRAVE DOGS DON'T BARK TOO MUCH. WATCH.
SNEEK
KANG-LIN, WE HAVE TO GO BACK!
WE'LL BE SCOLDED FOR BEING HERE!
SO THAT'S THE PRIESTESS OF SUZAKU EVERYONE'S BEEN TALKING ABOUT?
WHY IS SHE SO *FRIENDLY* WITH HIS MAJESTY? SHE'S NO EMPRESS!
AND WHO IS THE MAN NEXT TO THEM?
HE IS ONE OF THE PROTECTORS OF THE PRIESTESS. A CELESTIAL WARRIOR OF SUZAKU, TAMAHOME.

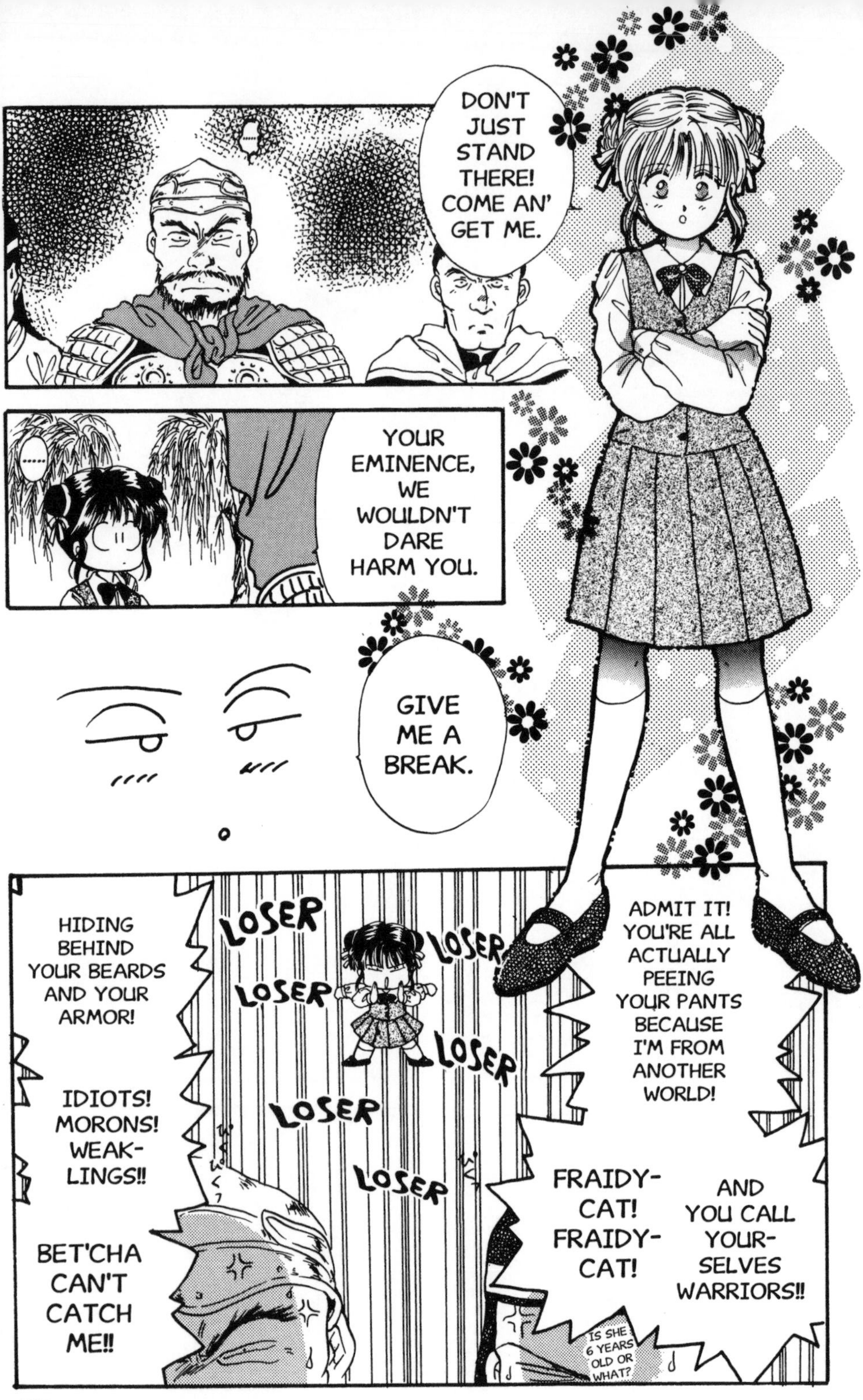
DON'T JUST STAND THERE! COME AN' GET ME.
YOUR EMINENCE, WE WOULDN'T DARE HARM YOU.
GIVE ME A BREAK.
ADMIT IT! YOU'RE ALL ACTUALLY PEEING YOUR PANTS BECAUSE I'M FROM ANOTHER WORLD!
AND YOU CALL YOUR-SELVES WARRIORS!!
FRAIDY-CAT! FRAIDY-CAT!
IS SHE 6 YEARS OLD OR WHAT?
LOSER
LOSER
LOSER
LOSER
LOSER
LOSER
HIDING BEHIND YOUR BEARDS AND YOUR ARMOR!
IDIOTS! MORONS! WEAK-LINGS!!
BET'CHA CAN'T CATCH ME!!

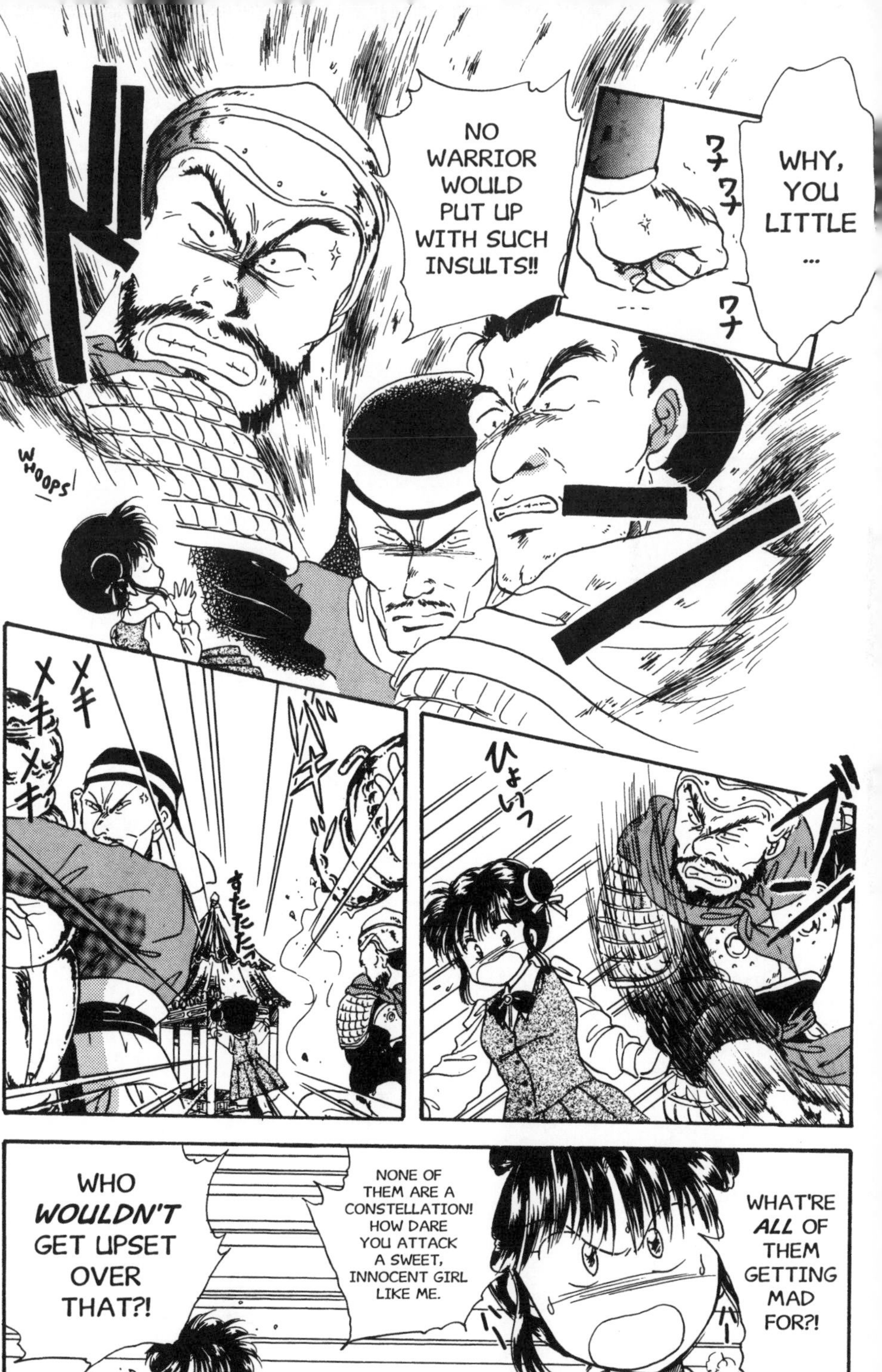
WHY, YOU LITTLE ...
ワナワナ
ワナ
NO WARRIOR WOULD PUT UP WITH SUCH INSULTS!!
WHOOPS
ひょいっ
メキメキ
すたたた
WHAT'RE ALL OF THEM GETTING MAD FOR?!
NONE OF THEM ARE A CONSTELLATION! HOW DARE YOU ATTACK A SWEET, INNOCENT GIRL LIKE ME.
WHO WOULDN'T GET UPSET OVER THAT?!

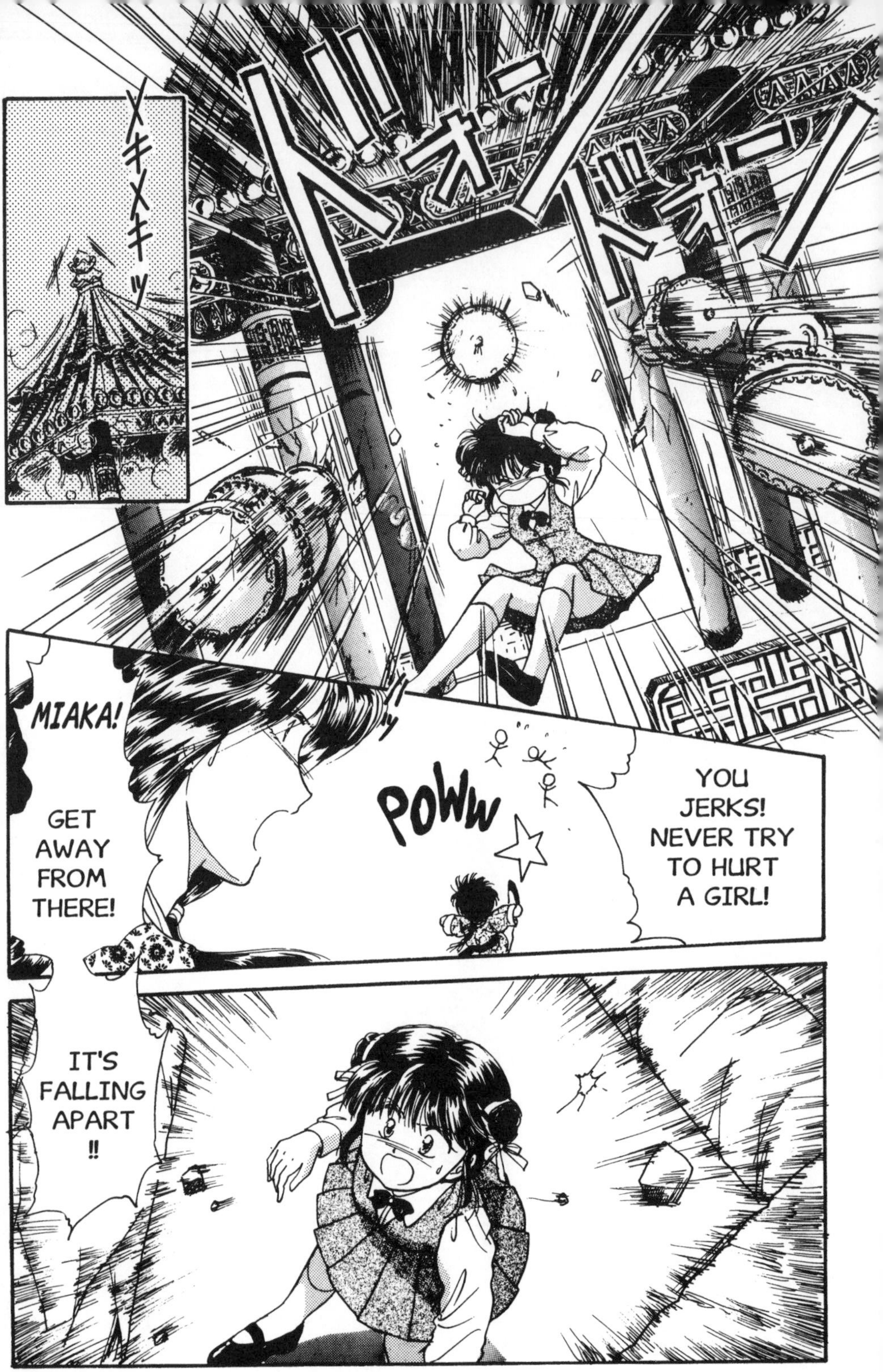
メキメキッ
YOU JERKS! NEVER TRY TO HURT A GIRL!
POWW
MIAKA!
GET AWAY FROM THERE!
IT'S FALLING APART !!

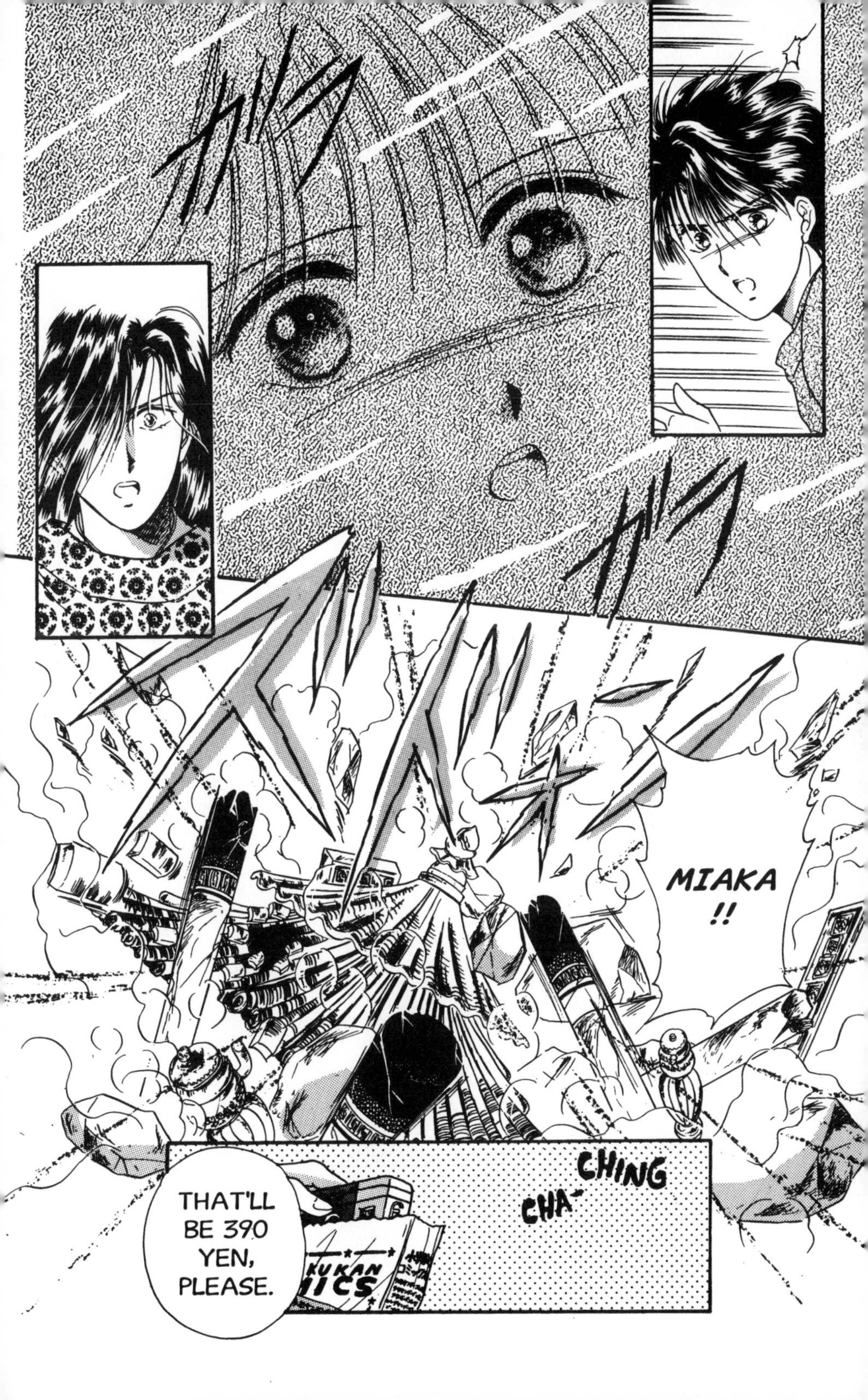
MIAKA!!
CHA-CHING
THAT'LL BE 390 YEN, PLEASE.

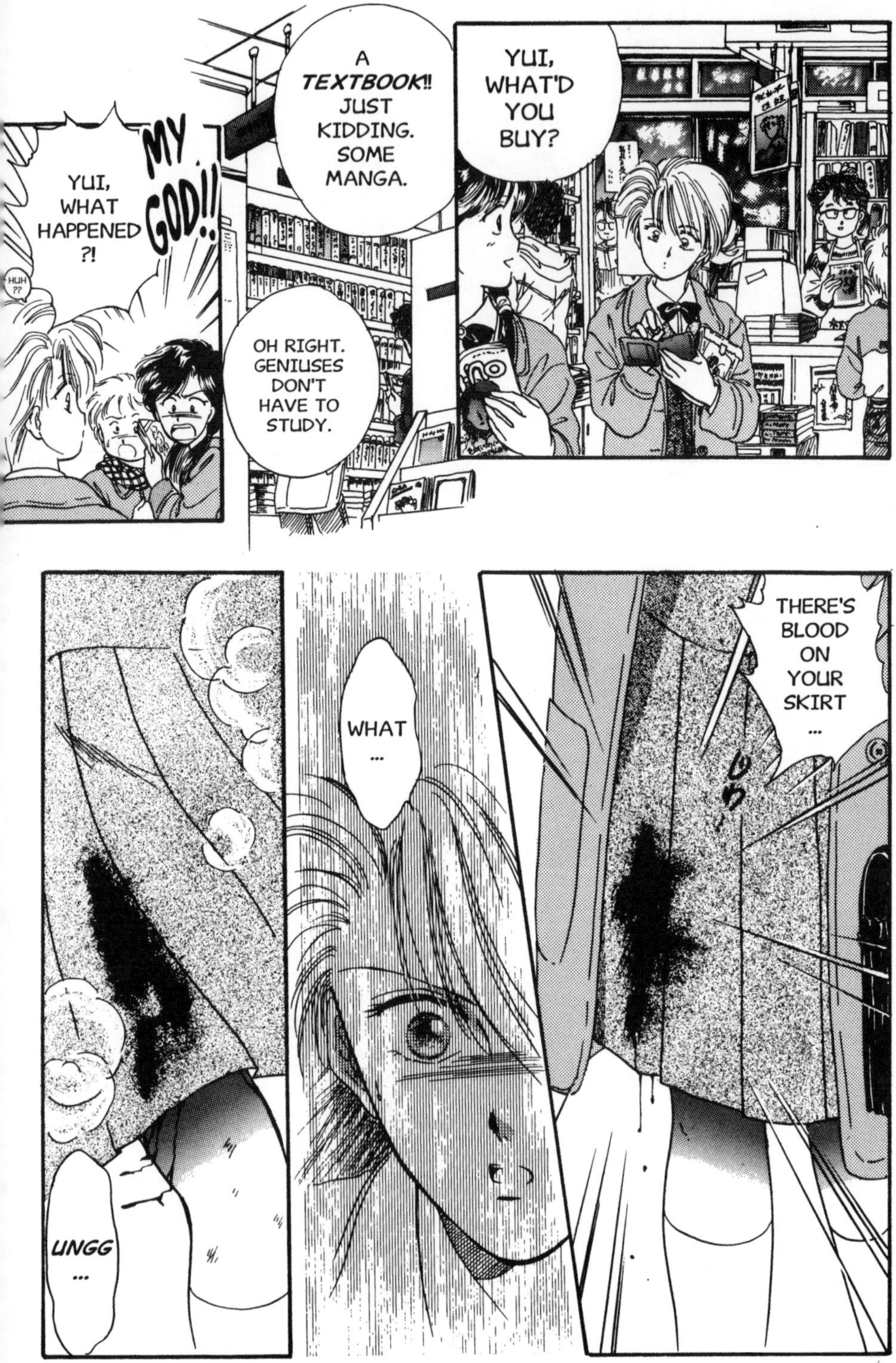
YUI, WHAT'D YOU BUY?
A TEXTBOOK!! JUST KIDDING. SOME MANGA.
OH RIGHT. GENIUSES DON'T HAVE TO STUDY.
MY GOD!!
YUI, WHAT HAPPENED ?!
HUH ??
THERE'S BLOOD ON YOUR SKIRT ...
WHAT ...
UNGG ...

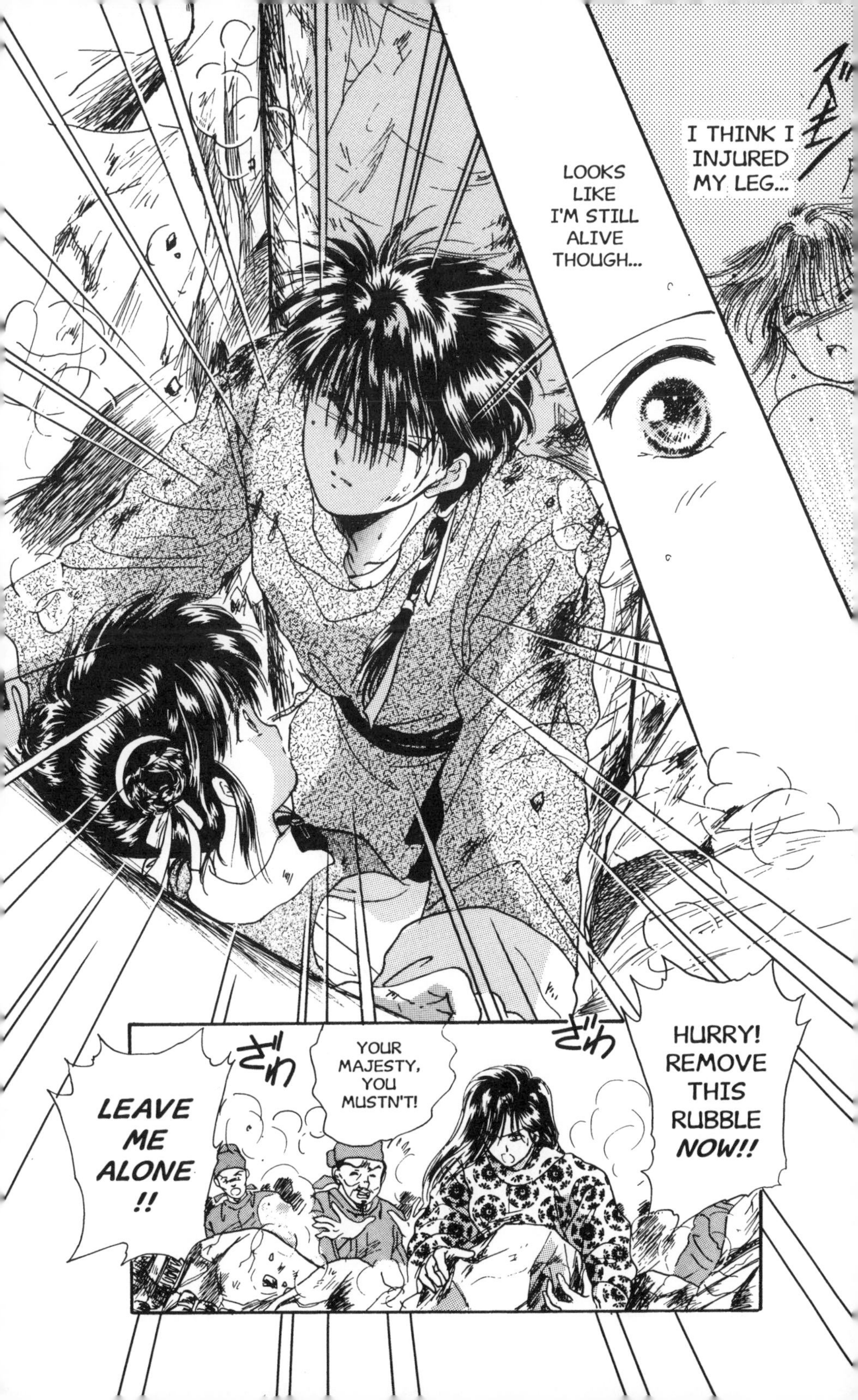

I THINK I INJURED MY LEG...
LOOKS LIKE I'M STILL ALIVE THOUGH...
ざわ
HURRY! REMOVE THIS RUBBLE NOW!!
YOUR MAJESTY, YOU MUSTN'T!
ざわ
LEAVE ME ALONE!!

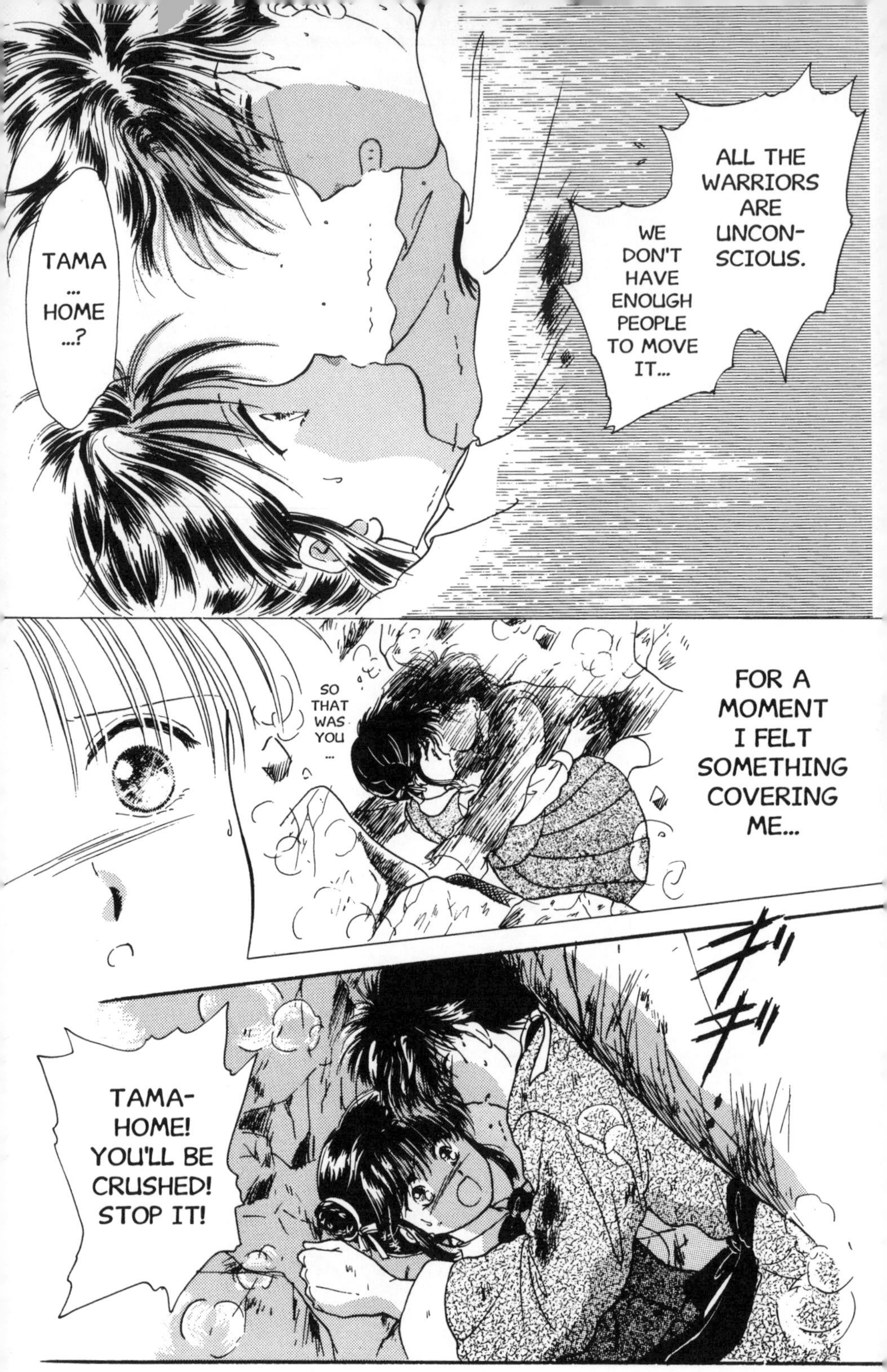
ALL THE WARRIORS ARE UNCON-SCIOUS.
WE DON'T HAVE ENOUGH PEOPLE TO MOVE IT...
TAMA... HOME...?
FOR A MOMENT I FELT SOMETHING COVERING ME...
SO THAT WAS YOU...
ギギ
TAMA-HOME! YOU'LL BE CRUSHED! STOP IT!

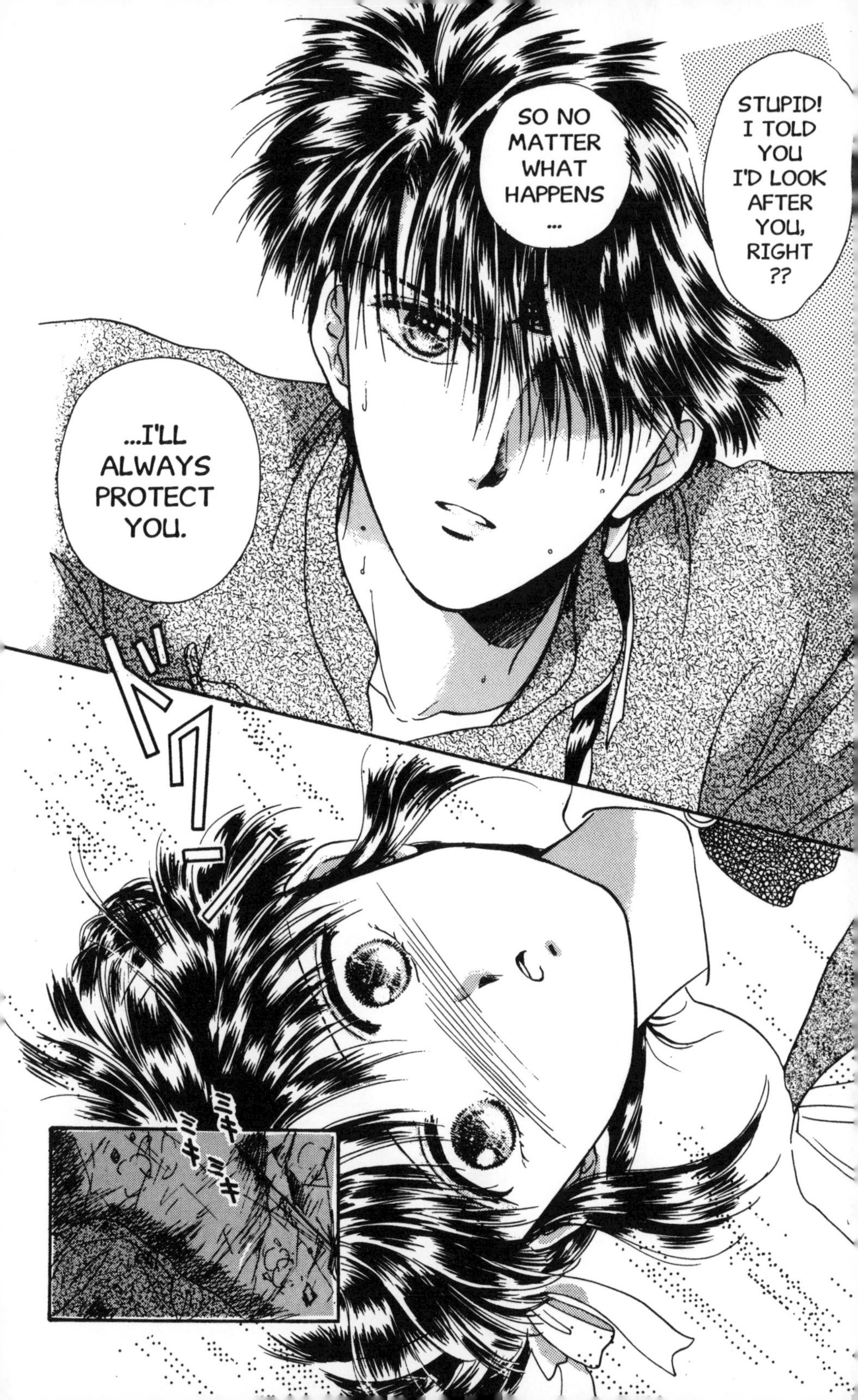
STUPID! I TOLD YOU I'D LOOK AFTER YOU, RIGHT ??
SO NO MATTER WHAT HAPPENS ...
...I'LL ALWAYS PROTECT YOU.
ミキ ミキ

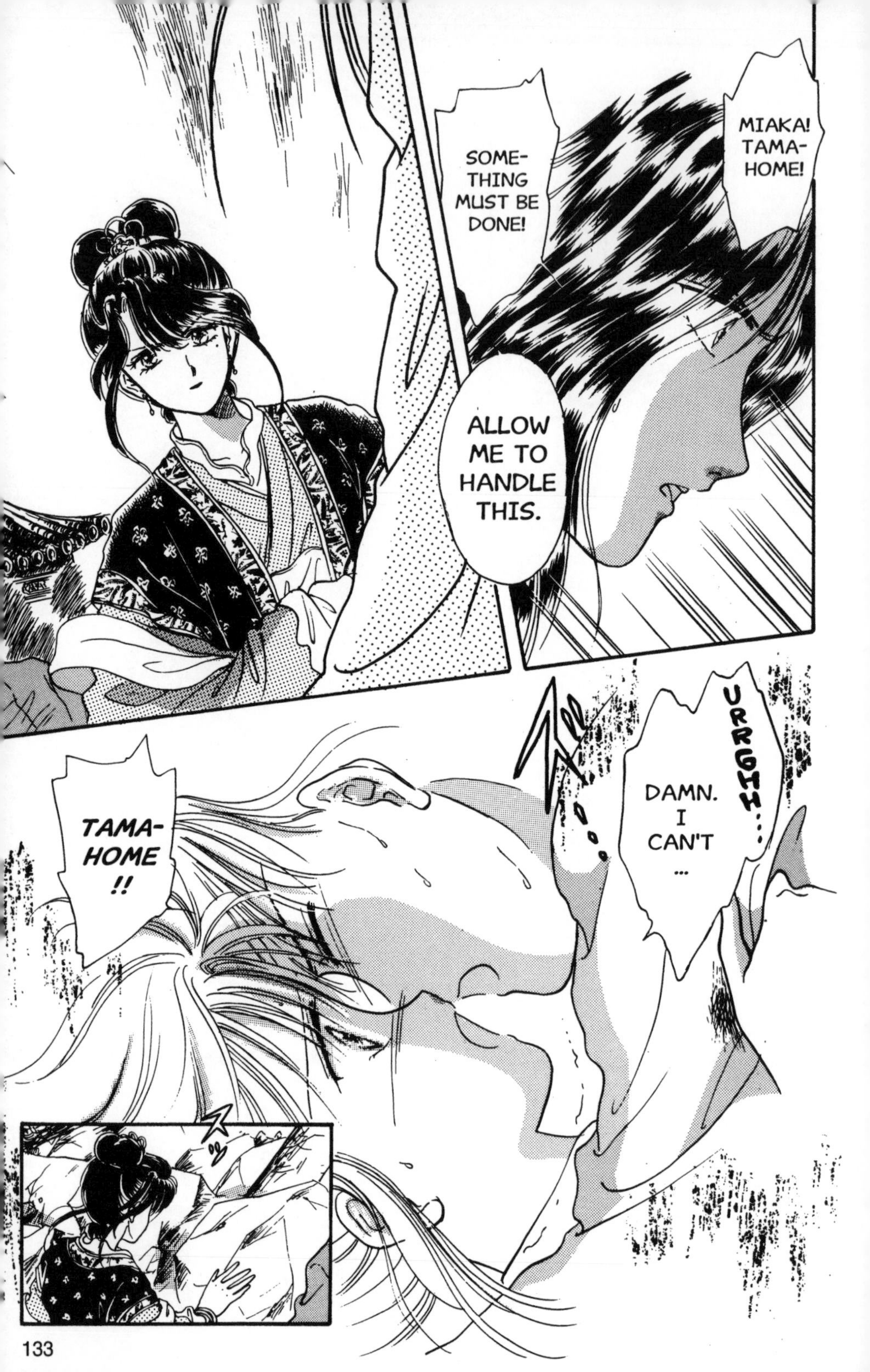
MIAKA! TAMA-HOME!
SOME-THING MUST BE DONE!
ALLOW ME TO HANDLE THIS.
URRGHH...
DAMN. I CAN'T ...
TAMA-HOME !!

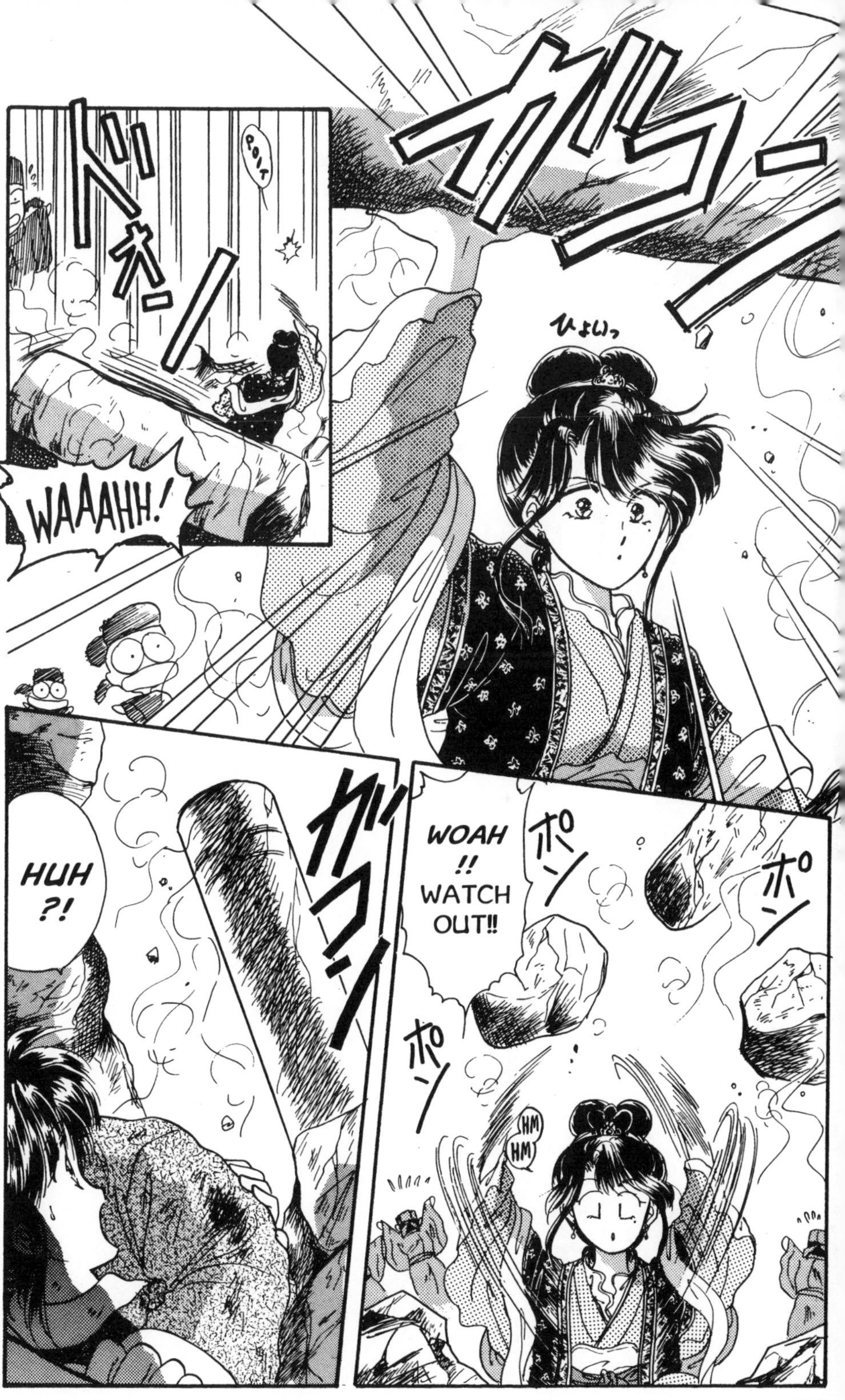

ひょいっ
POIT
WAAAHH!
ポン
ポン
WOAH!! WATCH OUT!!
ポン
HM HM
HUH?!

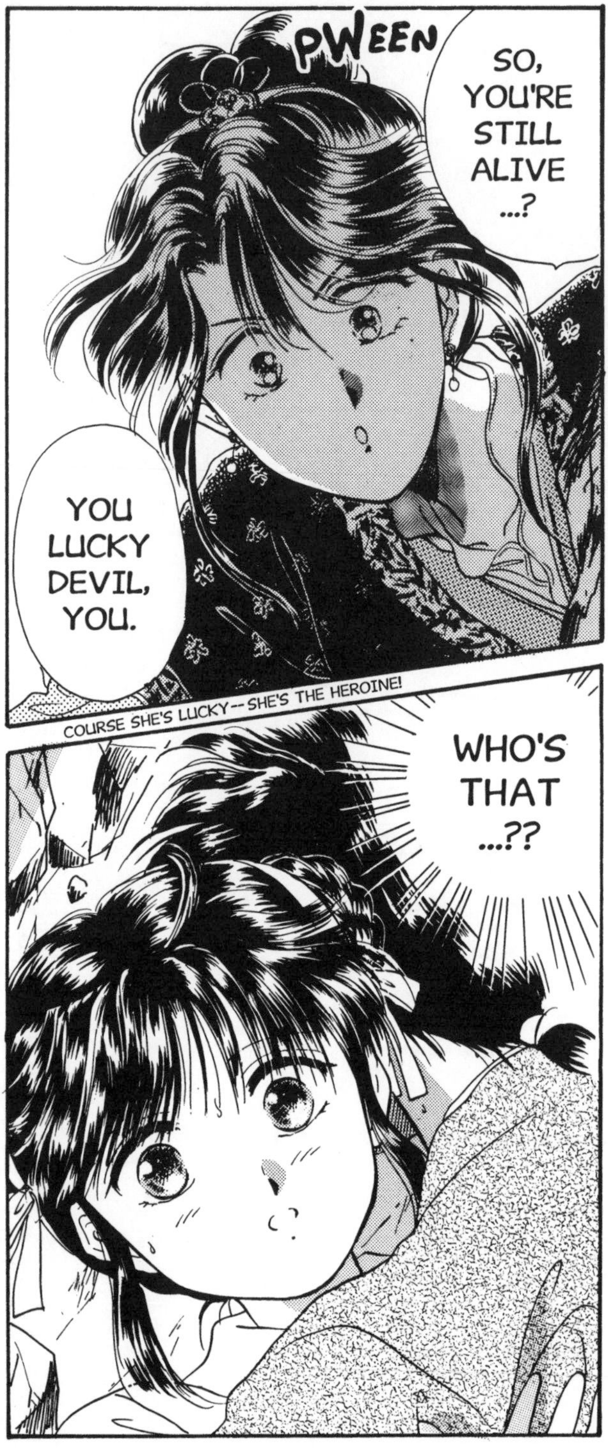
PWEEN
SO, YOU'RE STILL ALIVE ...?
YOU LUCKY DEVIL, YOU.
COURSE SHE'S LUCKY--SHE'S THE HEROINE!
WHO'S THAT ...??

Let me just say that drawing the buildings in this chapter was no easy task. I did all this research to draw them (although I didn't want it to look exactly the same as in my reference, so I'd alter some of the designs and layouts). It was a real pain for my assistants but also for me as well. (I do as much of the backgrounds as I possibly can.) Hey, Chinese architecture, why're you such a pain?! And these outfits are no easier. Not to mention the mob scenes. And I've had it up to here with the soldiers' armor! (I was gonna use *Romance of the Three Kingdoms* as reference material, but that story's set too far back in time. ♪ There's not a whole lot of changes over time in China but we're talking about a difference of a thousand years. ♪ At least I want the armor to be right. The armor is kind of a pastiche between different periods, mostly the period between the Sung and Ming dynasties, but also a little bit of Tang all mixed up together. But this China is supposed to be a work of the imagination. Even my editor's been telling me not to be too particular.

When I was in elementary school, I loved the TV live drama show *Saiyuki*. Then they started doing re-runs when I was eighteen. All of a sudden I realized how great the action, characters, and comedy were. So I'd look forward to 8 p.m. every Sunday. That's really the kind of project I'd like to work on.

By the way, I really wanted to have Tamahome wear an outfit with Chinese buttons, but the style only came into existence in modern China. I might eventually draw it in anyway. In the first graphic novel, maybe!

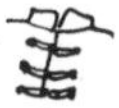

The kimono style just isn't much fun. When were the *Mr. Vampire* and *Chinese Ghost Story* series set? I'd like Tamahome to wear the same clothes worn by the guy in *Mr. Vampire*, but maybe that outfit would be too recent. I know, I know. I'm not supposed to be so particular, but I am. Oh, I also pay a lot of attention to hair. The bun style is just too boring.

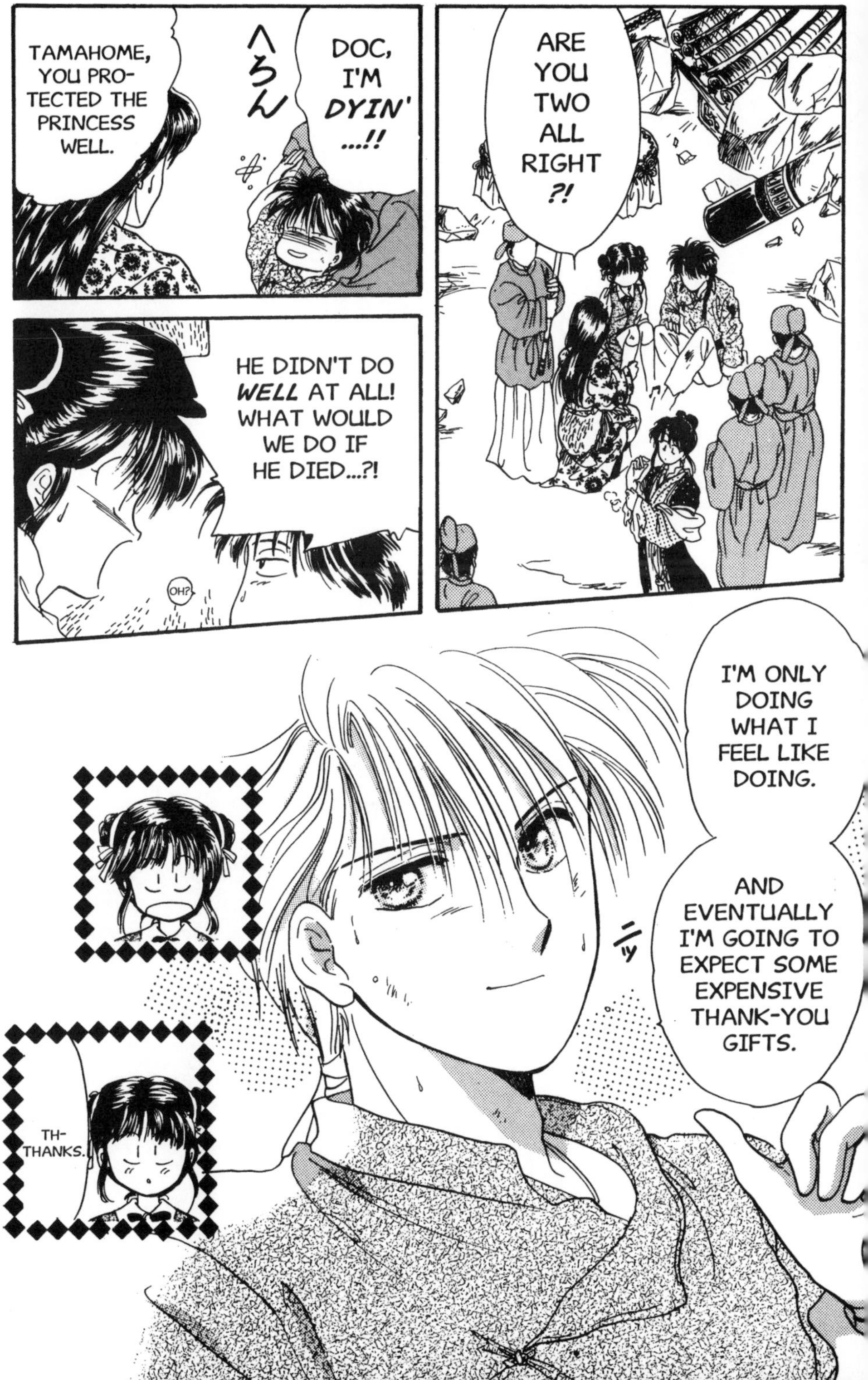
ARE YOU TWO ALL RIGHT?!
DOC, I'M *DYIN'*...!!
へろん
TAMAHOME, YOU PROTECTED THE PRINCESS WELL.
HE DIDN'T DO *WELL* AT ALL! WHAT WOULD WE DO IF HE DIED...?!
OH?
I'M ONLY DOING WHAT I FEEL LIKE DOING.
AND EVENTUALLY I'M GOING TO EXPECT SOME EXPENSIVE THANK-YOU GIFTS.
ニッ
TH- THANKS.

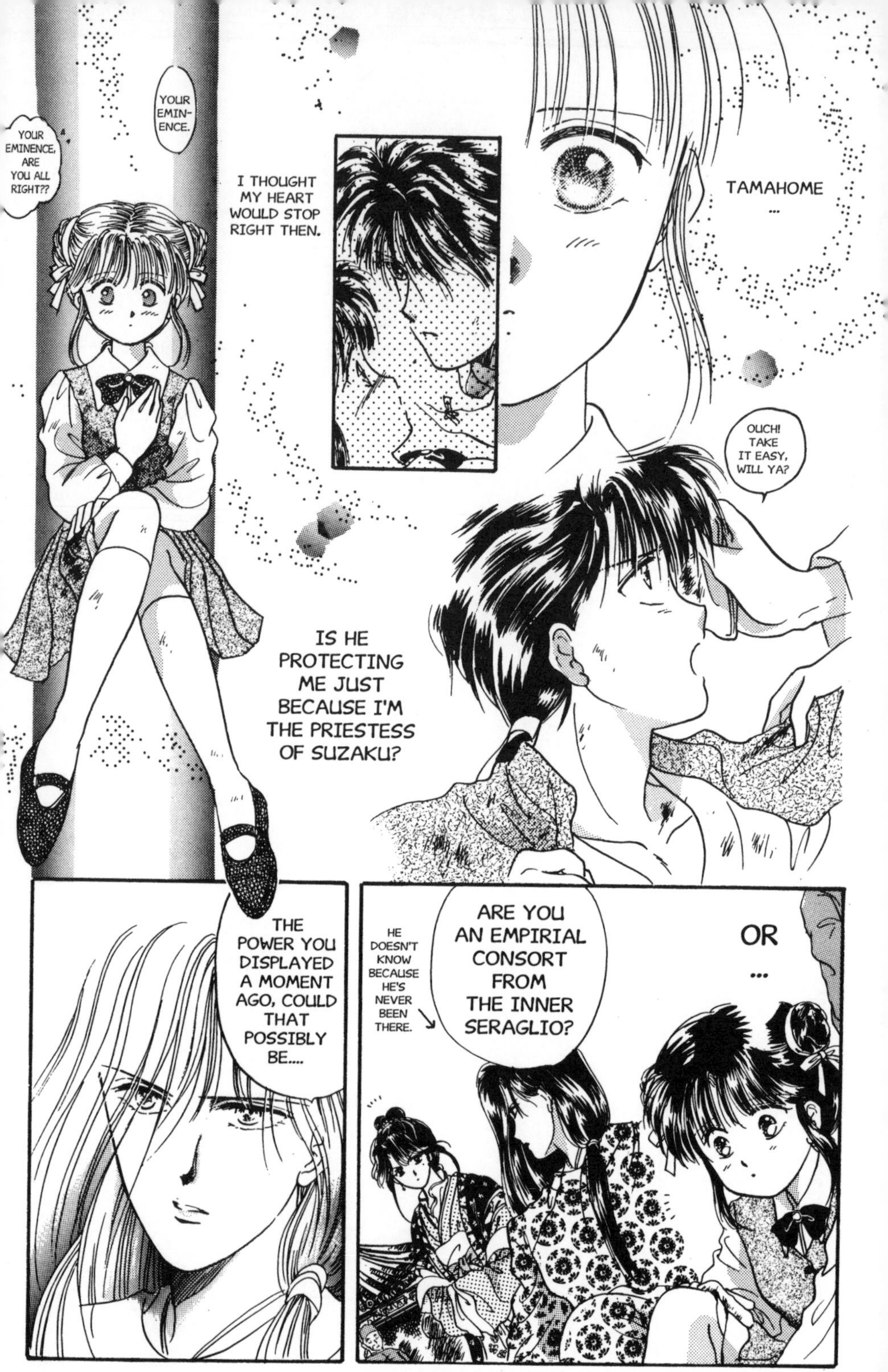
TAMAHOME ...
I THOUGHT MY HEART WOULD STOP RIGHT THEN.
YOUR EMINENCE.
YOUR EMINENCE, ARE YOU ALL RIGHT??
OUCH! TAKE IT EASY, WILL YA?
IS HE PROTECTING ME JUST BECAUSE I'M THE PRIESTESS OF SUZAKU?
OR ...
ARE YOU AN EMPIRIAL CONSORT FROM THE INNER SERAGLIO?
HE DOESN'T KNOW BECAUSE HE'S NEVER BEEN THERE.
THE POWER YOU DISPLAYED A MOMENT AGO, COULD THAT POSSIBLY BE....

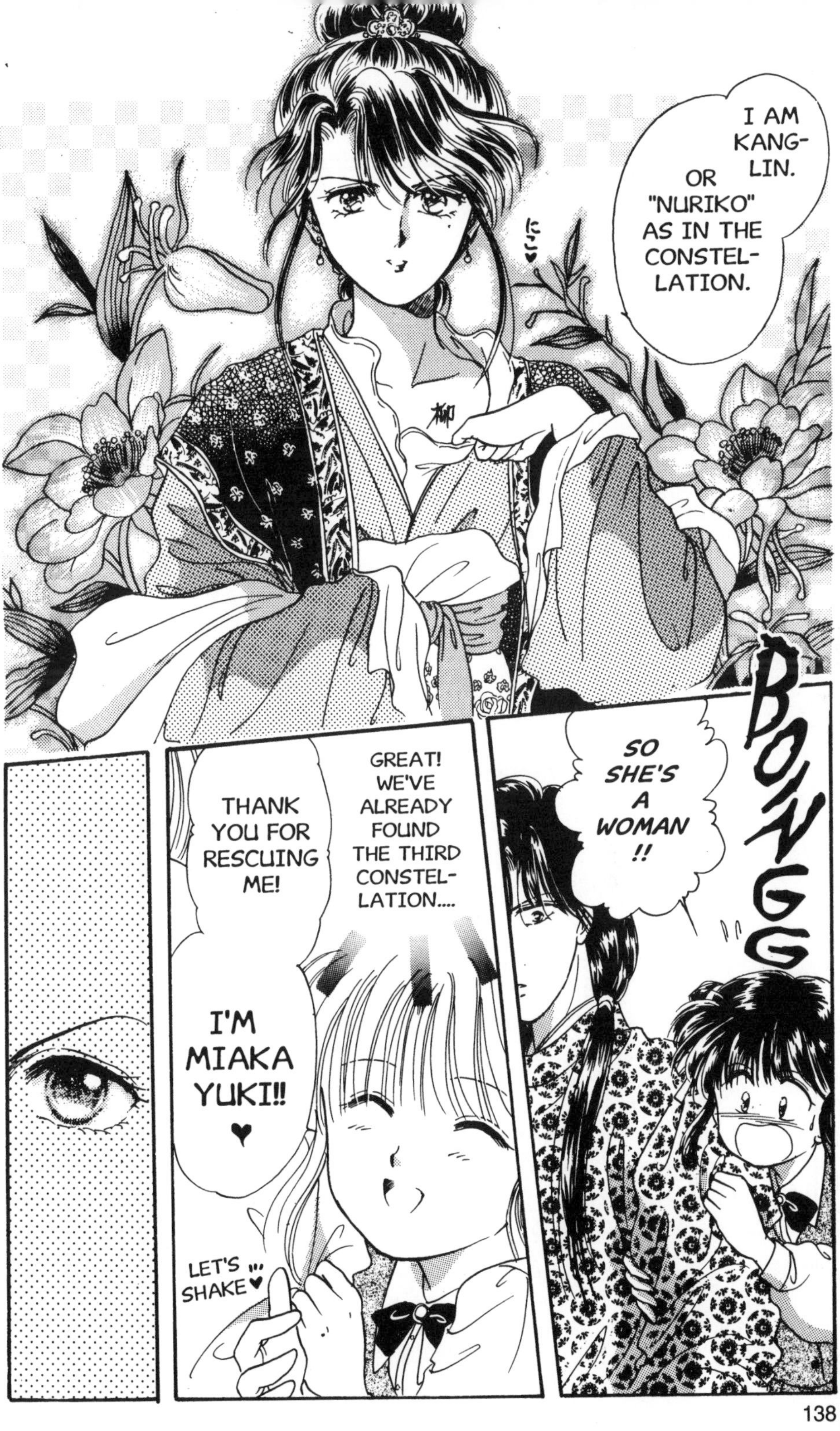
I AM KANG-LIN.
OR "NURIKO" AS IN THE CONSTELLATION.
BOINGG
SO SHE'S A WOMAN!!
GREAT! WE'VE ALREADY FOUND THE THIRD CONSTELLATION....
THANK YOU FOR RESCUING ME!
I'M MIAKA YUKI!! ♥
LET'S SHAKE ♥

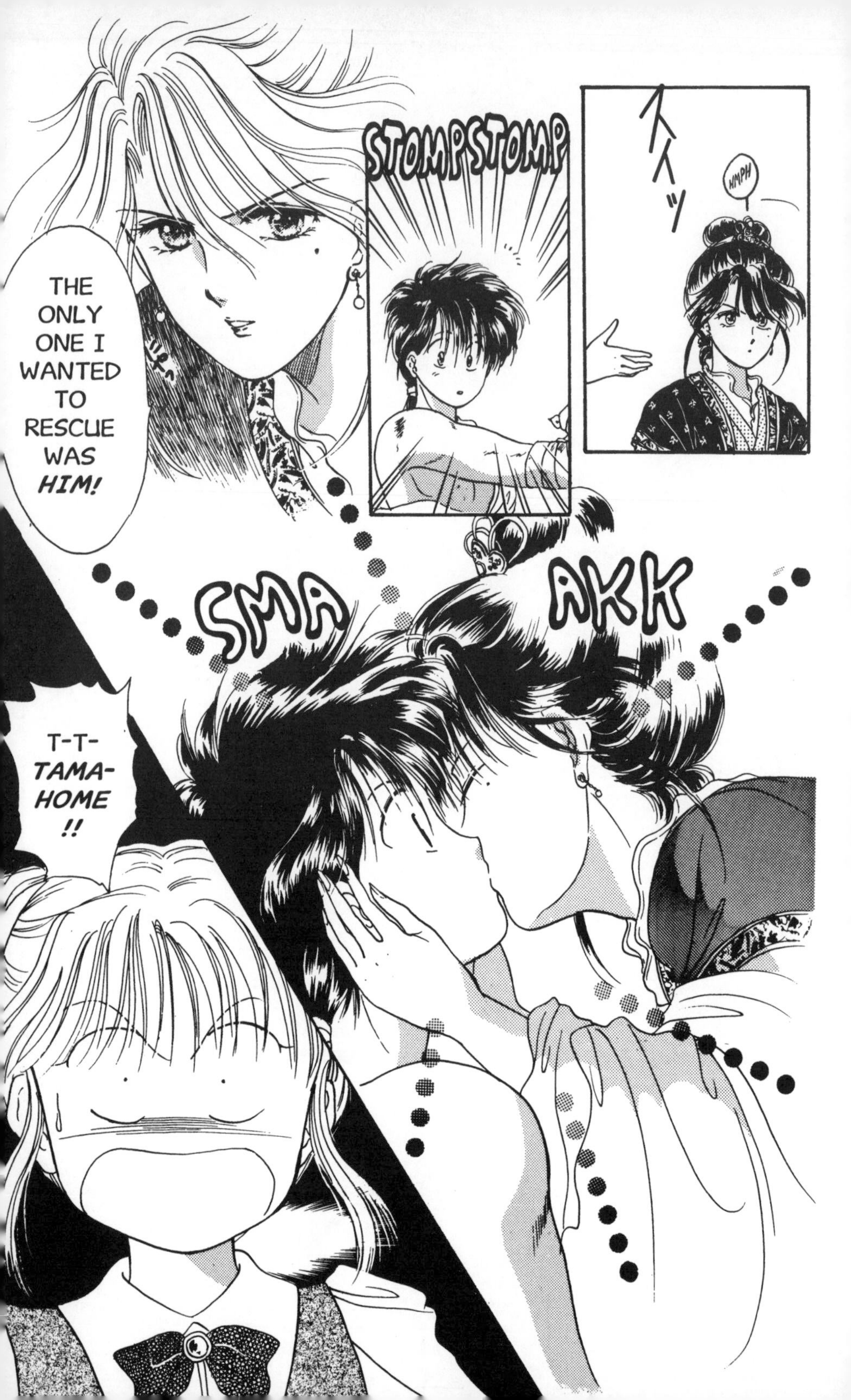
スイッ
HMPH
STOMPSTOMP
THE ONLY ONE I WANTED TO RESCUE WAS *HIM!*
SMA AKK
T-T-*TAMAHOME* !!

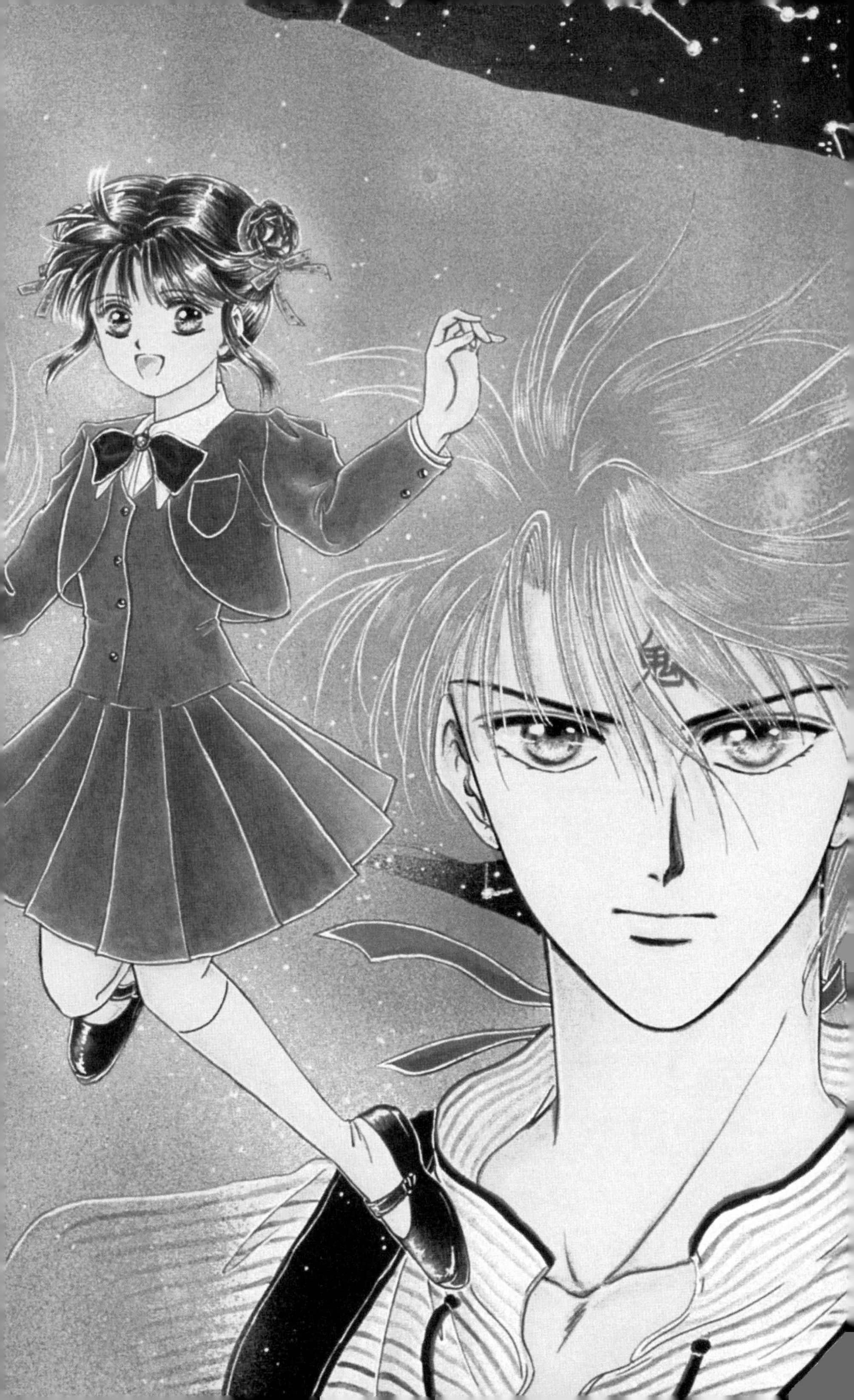
鬼

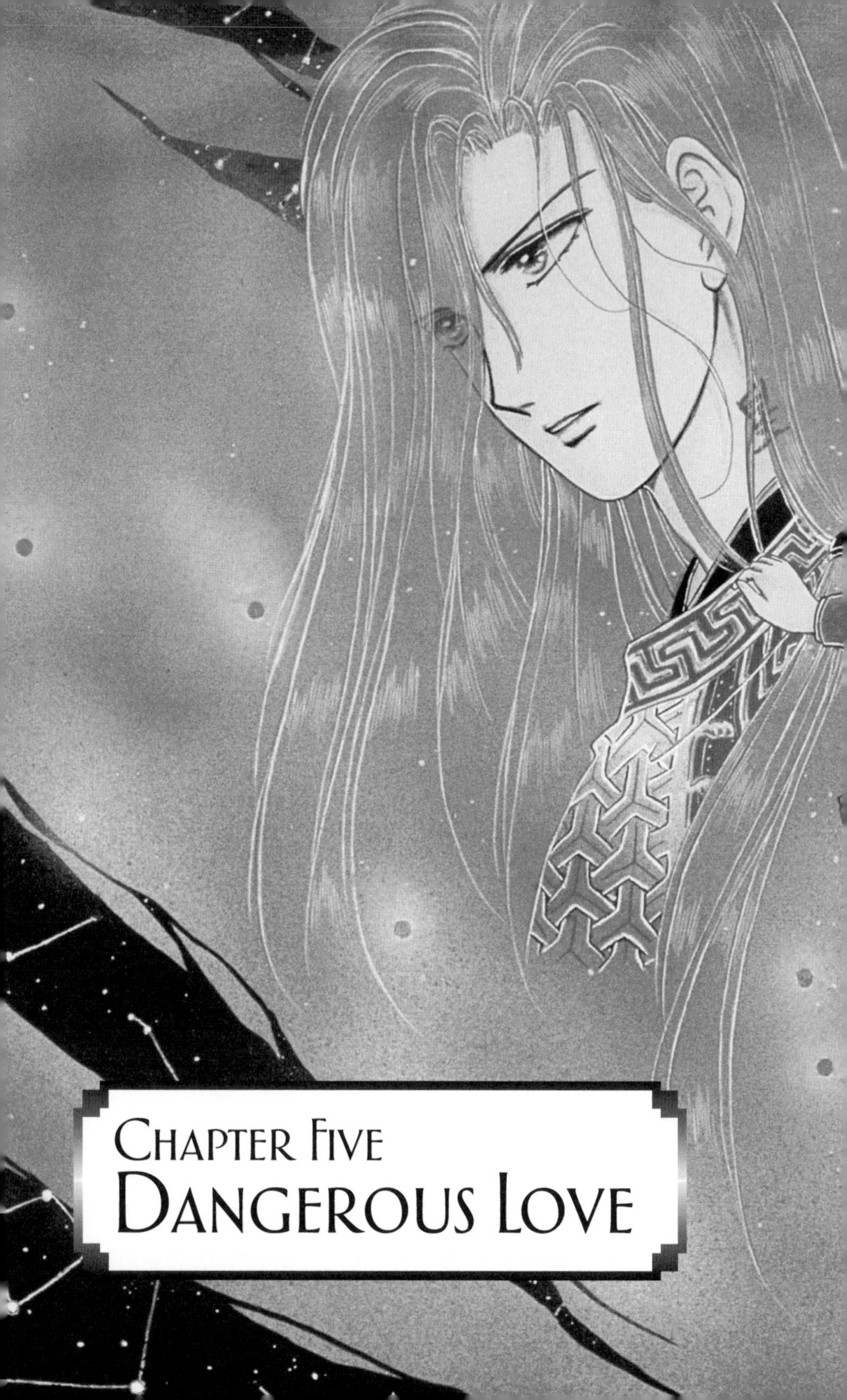
CHAPTER FIVE
DANGEROUS LOVE

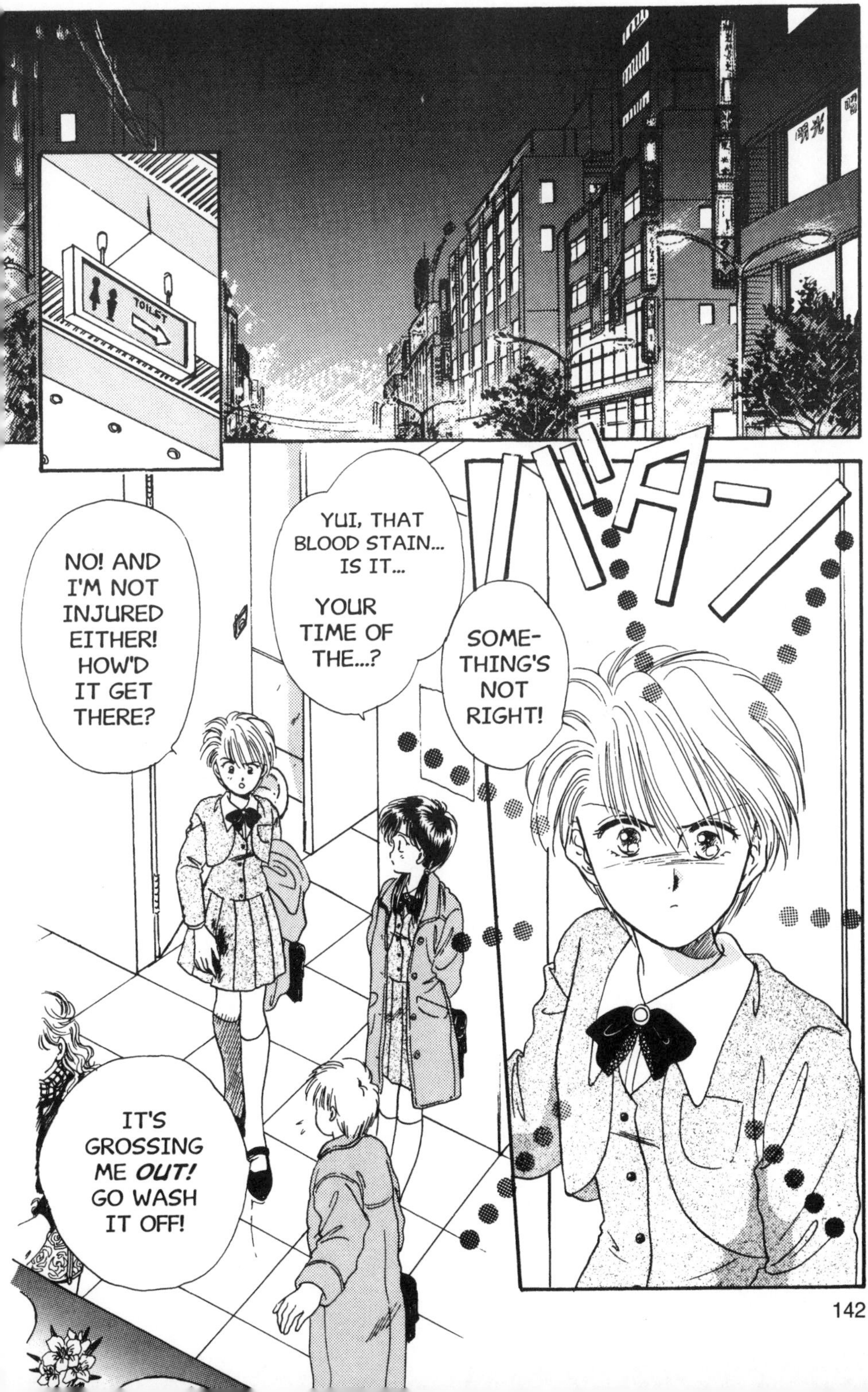
TOILET
バターン
SOME-THING'S NOT RIGHT!
YUI, THAT BLOOD STAIN... IS IT...
YOUR TIME OF THE...?
NO! AND I'M NOT INJURED EITHER! HOW'D IT GET THERE?
IT'S GROSSING ME *OUT!* GO WASH IT OFF!

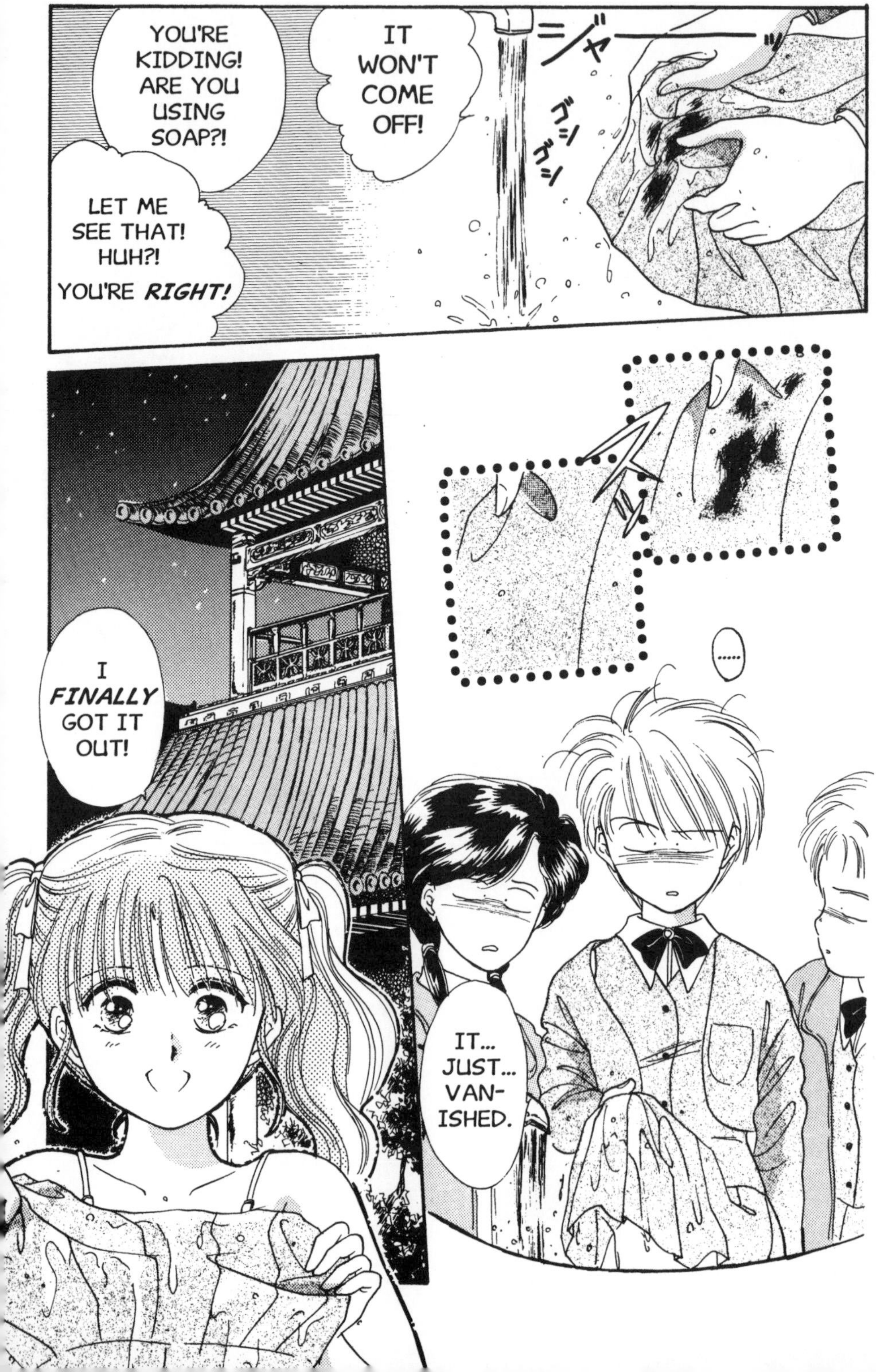
ジャーーーッ
ゴシゴシ
IT WON'T COME OFF!
YOU'RE KIDDING! ARE YOU USING SOAP?!
LET ME SEE THAT! HUH?! YOU'RE *RIGHT!*
スッ
......
IT... JUST... VAN-ISHED.
I *FINALLY* GOT IT OUT!

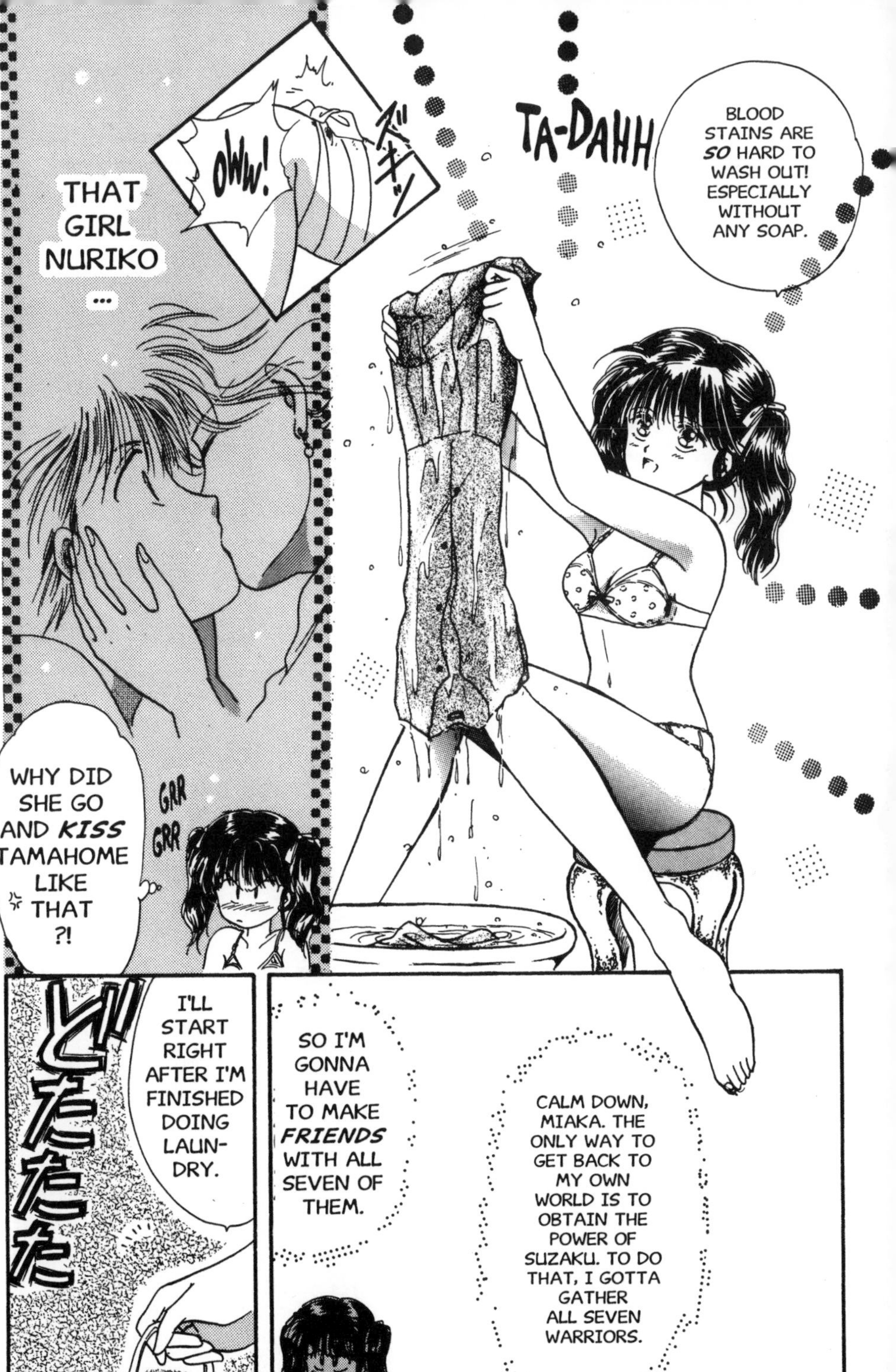
TA-DAHH
BLOOD STAINS ARE *SO* HARD TO WASH OUT! ESPECIALLY WITHOUT ANY SOAP.
OWW!
ズキッ
THAT GIRL NURIKO ...
WHY DID SHE GO AND *KISS* TAMAHOME LIKE THAT ?!
GRR GRR
CALM DOWN, MIAKA. THE ONLY WAY TO GET BACK TO MY OWN WORLD IS TO OBTAIN THE POWER OF SUZAKU. TO DO THAT, I GOTTA GATHER ALL SEVEN WARRIORS.
SO I'M GONNA HAVE TO MAKE *FRIENDS* WITH ALL SEVEN OF THEM.
I'LL START RIGHT AFTER I'M FINISHED DOING LAUN-DRY.
どたたたた

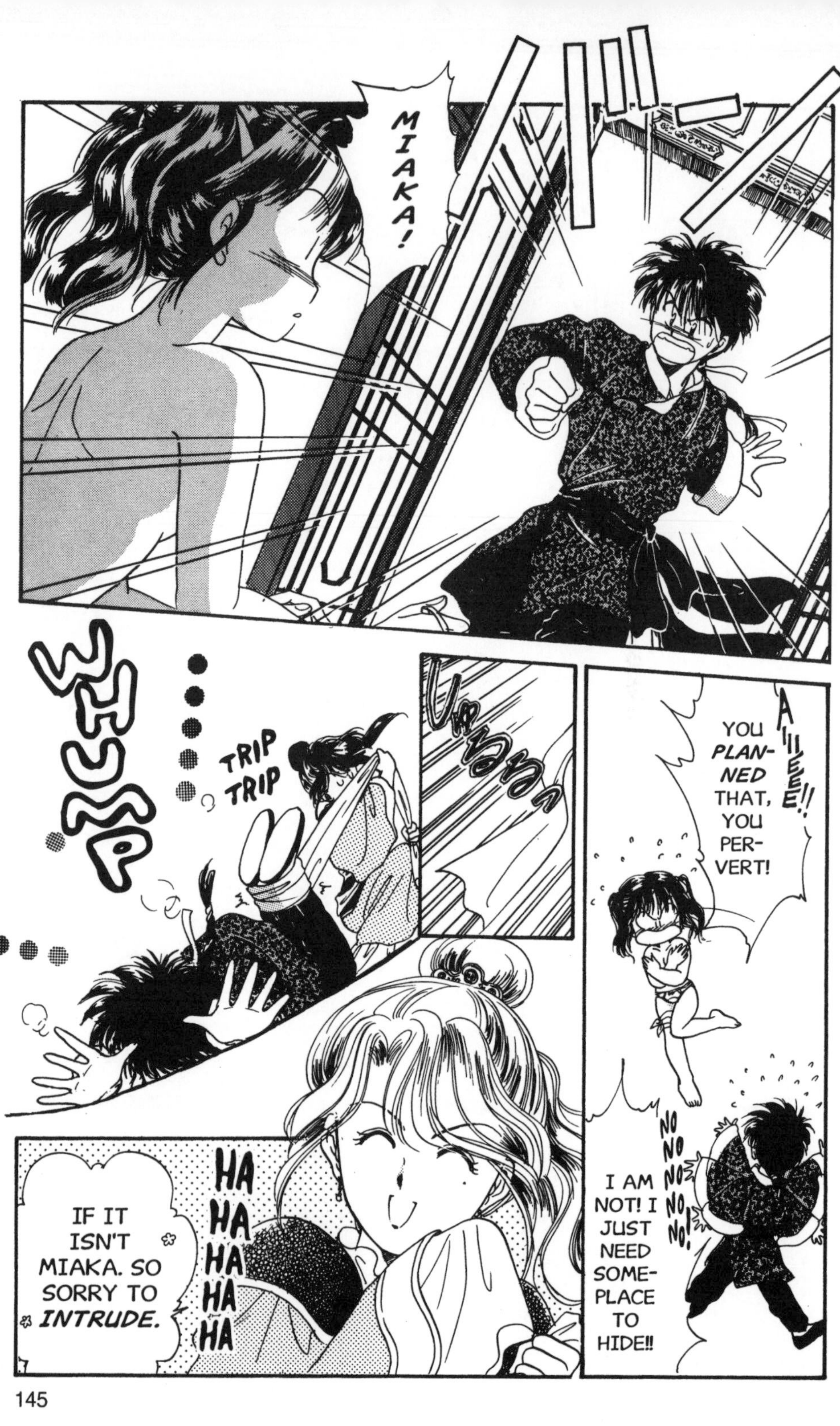
MIAKA!
AIIIEEE!!
YOU PLANNED THAT, YOU PERVERT!
I AM NOT! I JUST NEED SOMEPLACE TO HIDE!!
NO NO NO NO NO!
WHUMP
TRIP TRIP
...
...
HA HA HA HA HA
IF IT ISN'T MIAKA. SO SORRY TO INTRUDE.

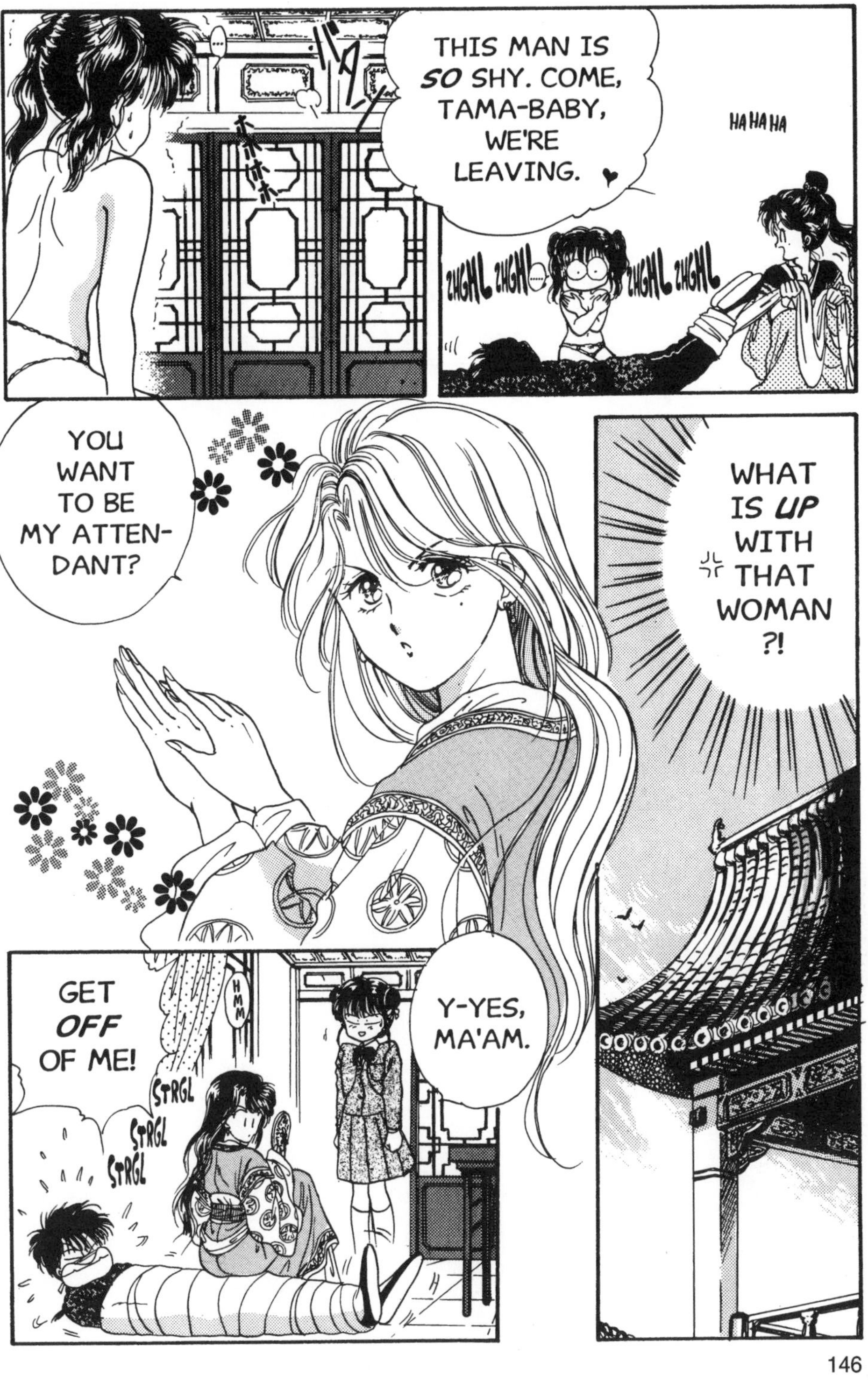
THIS MAN IS *SO* SHY. COME, TAMA-BABY, WE'RE LEAVING.
HA HA HA
ZHGHL ZHGHL
......
ZHGHL ZHGHL
...
WHAT IS *UP* WITH THAT WOMAN ?!
YOU WANT TO BE MY ATTEN-DANT?
Y-YES, MA'AM.
HMM
GET *OFF* OF ME!
STRGL
STRGL
STRGL

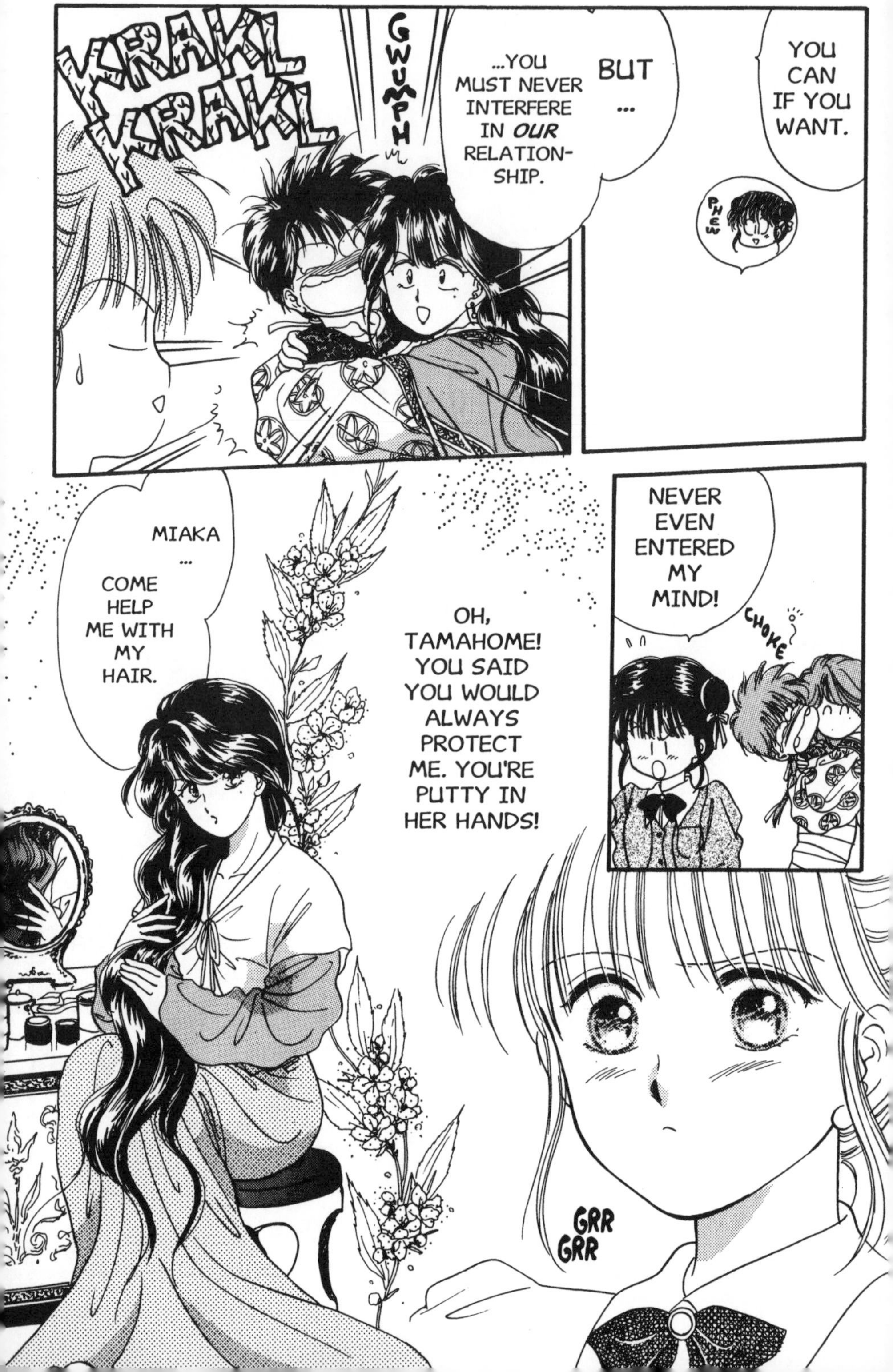
YOU CAN IF YOU WANT.
PHEW
BUT ...
...YOU MUST NEVER INTERFERE IN OUR RELATIONSHIP.
GWUMPH
KRAKL KRAKL
NEVER EVEN ENTERED MY MIND!
CHOKE
MIAKA ... COME HELP ME WITH MY HAIR.
OH, TAMAHOME! YOU SAID YOU WOULD ALWAYS PROTECT ME. YOU'RE PUTTY IN HER HANDS!
GRR GRR

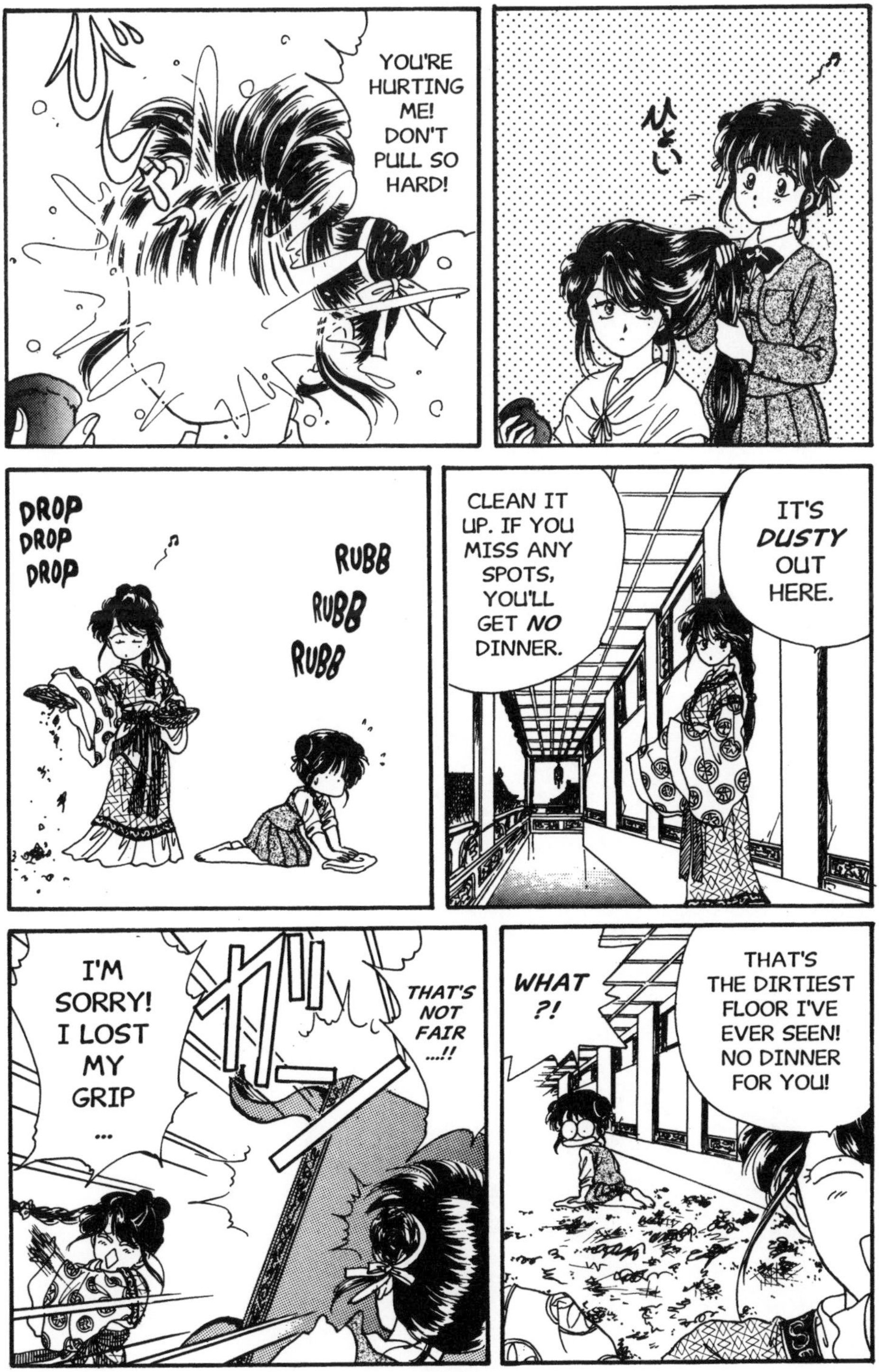

YOU'RE HURTING ME! DON'T PULL SO HARD!
IT'S *DUSTY* OUT HERE.
CLEAN IT UP. IF YOU MISS ANY SPOTS, YOU'LL GET *NO* DINNER.
RUBB RUBB RUBB
DROP DROP DROP
THAT'S THE DIRTIEST FLOOR I'VE EVER SEEN! NO DINNER FOR YOU!
WHAT?!
THAT'S NOT FAIR ...!!
I'M SORRY! I LOST MY GRIP ...

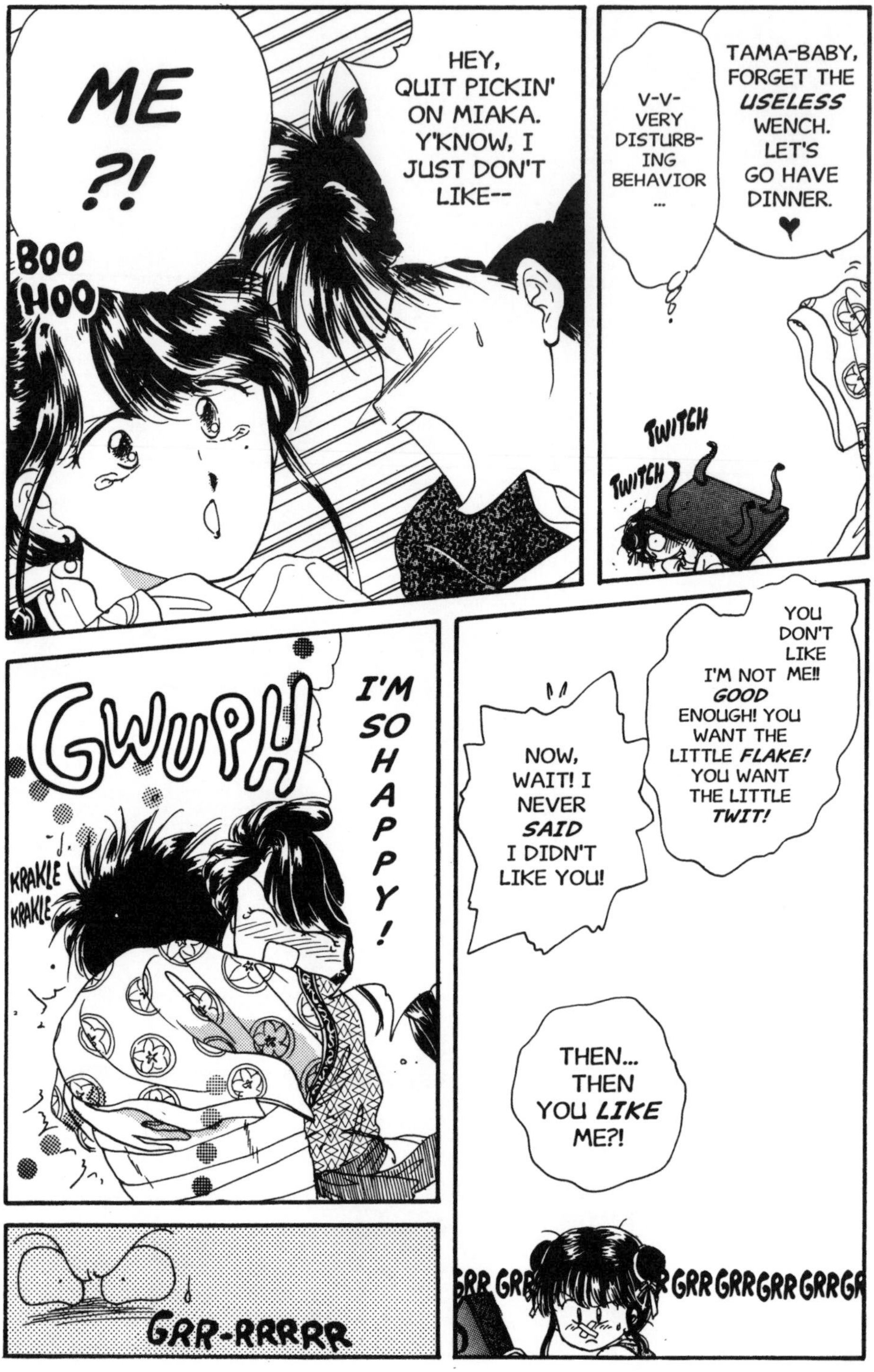
TAMA-BABY, FORGET THE USELESS WENCH. LET'S GO HAVE DINNER. ♥
V-V-VERY DISTURBING BEHAVIOR ...
TWITCH
TWITCH
HEY, QUIT PICKIN' ON MIAKA. Y'KNOW, I JUST DON'T LIKE--
ME ?!
BOO HOO
YOU DON'T LIKE ME!! I'M NOT GOOD ENOUGH! YOU WANT THE LITTLE FLAKE! YOU WANT THE LITTLE TWIT!
NOW, WAIT! I NEVER SAID I DIDN'T LIKE YOU!
THEN... THEN YOU LIKE ME?!
GRR GRR GRR GRR GRR GRR GR
I'M SO HAPPY!
GWUPH
KRAKLE KRAKLE
GRR-RRRRR

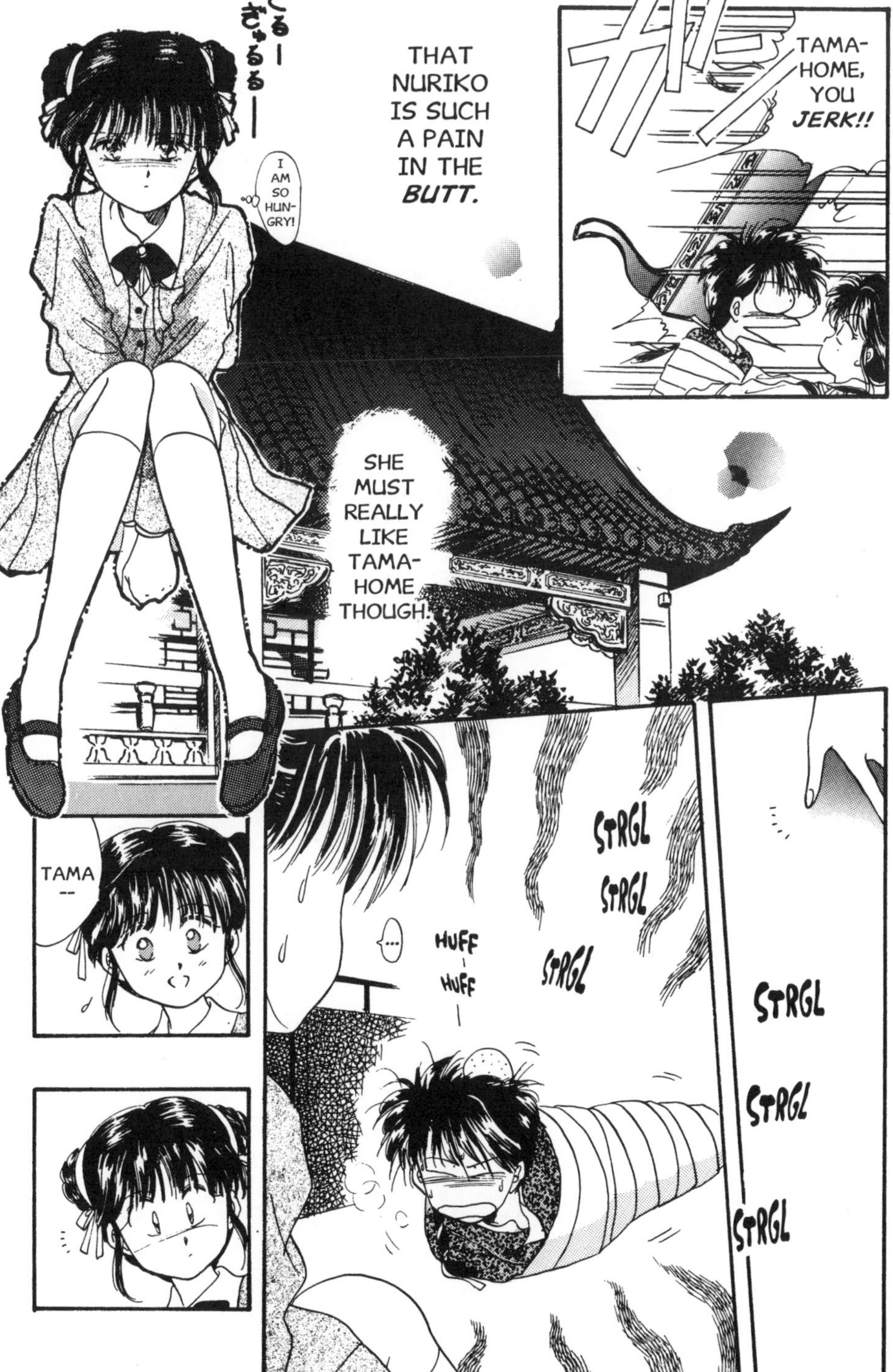
TAMA-HOME, YOU *JERK!!*
THAT NURIKO IS SUCH A PAIN IN THE *BUTT.*
くるー ぎゅるるー
I AM SO HUNGRY!
SHE MUST REALLY LIKE TAMA-HOME THOUGH.
STRGL
STRGL
STRGL
STRGL
STRGL
STRGL
HUFF HUFF
...
TAMA--

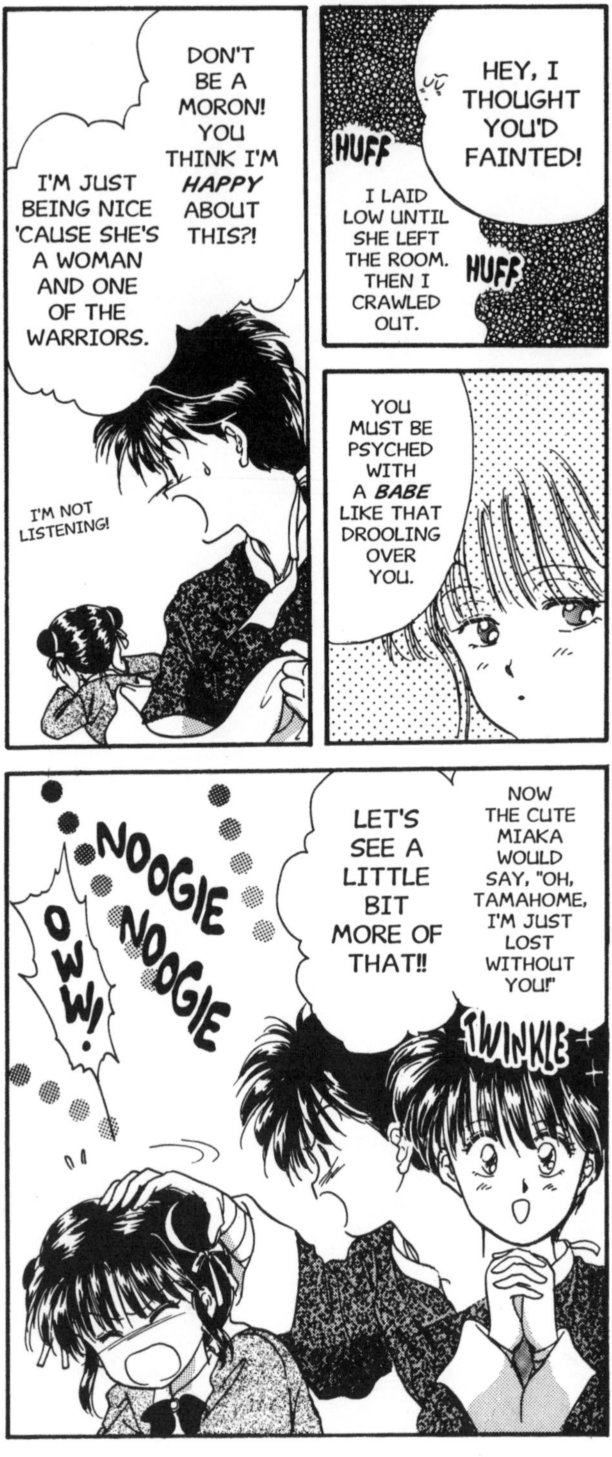
HEY, I THOUGHT YOU'D FAINTED!
HUFF
I LAID LOW UNTIL SHE LEFT THE ROOM. THEN I CRAWLED OUT.
HUFF
YOU MUST BE PSYCHED WITH A *BABE* LIKE THAT DROOLING OVER YOU.
DON'T BE A MORON! YOU THINK I'M *HAPPY* ABOUT THIS?!
I'M JUST BEING NICE 'CAUSE SHE'S A WOMAN AND ONE OF THE WARRIORS.
I'M NOT LISTENING!
NOW THE CUTE MIAKA WOULD SAY, "OH, TAMAHOME, I'M JUST LOST WITHOUT YOU!"
LET'S SEE A LITTLE BIT MORE OF THAT!!
TWINKLE
NOOGIE NOOGIE
OWW!

So I was reading some fan mail informing me that *Prebubescence* was voted second place in the top 20 manga poll in an anime magazine in Taiwan (I think). Can it really be true? A friend in the bookstore business told me that it was ranked in the top 10, 20, 30, or something. I dunno what it was, but I'm just happy to be ranked! sniffl sniffl Thank you everyone, so much! I received some fan mail from Taiwan, from a 15-year-old named Li. So I have readers abroad! Yui Len, a girl who is half Chinese and half Japanese, wrote me when I was working on *Treasure of the Heart.* I could have spelled her name wrong. She's studing martial arts with a real master. That's awesome! Her name is so cute, I'll have to use it in a future manga. I once got a letter from someone who's half British/half Japanese... very international. I have to admit I'm a little nervous about having native Chinese reading *Fushigi Yûgi.* Oh, and thanks so much for the tapes. I'm changing the subject. I listen to them all! There's B'z, TMN, *Ranma* soundtracks, recorded letters, *Lodoss* soundtracks, etc. Oh, when I mentioned COCO in *Prepubescence,* I had lots of people writing back! They're really popular! A special thanks to the people who made compilation tapes of COCO songs dedicated to scenes in *Prepubescence.* They were great! It's true that "Your Song, My Song" is really appropriate as Manato's song right around the "to live in the present" scene. "Melody" is perfect for the scene where Asuka is hiding in the rain, watching Manato. The best song though is "Circus Game"!! I was thinking how much I wanted it to be the theme song! But I found out that the *No Interest in Prepubescence* CD is coming out!! I'm on it too, so please listen to it. For those who are just now being introduced to my work, *No Interest in Prepubescence* is a three-volume manga. Check it out!!

But why wasn't the COCO tune "Why?" on the tape. "Why?" Oh, I get it, just so I'd make a silly pun.

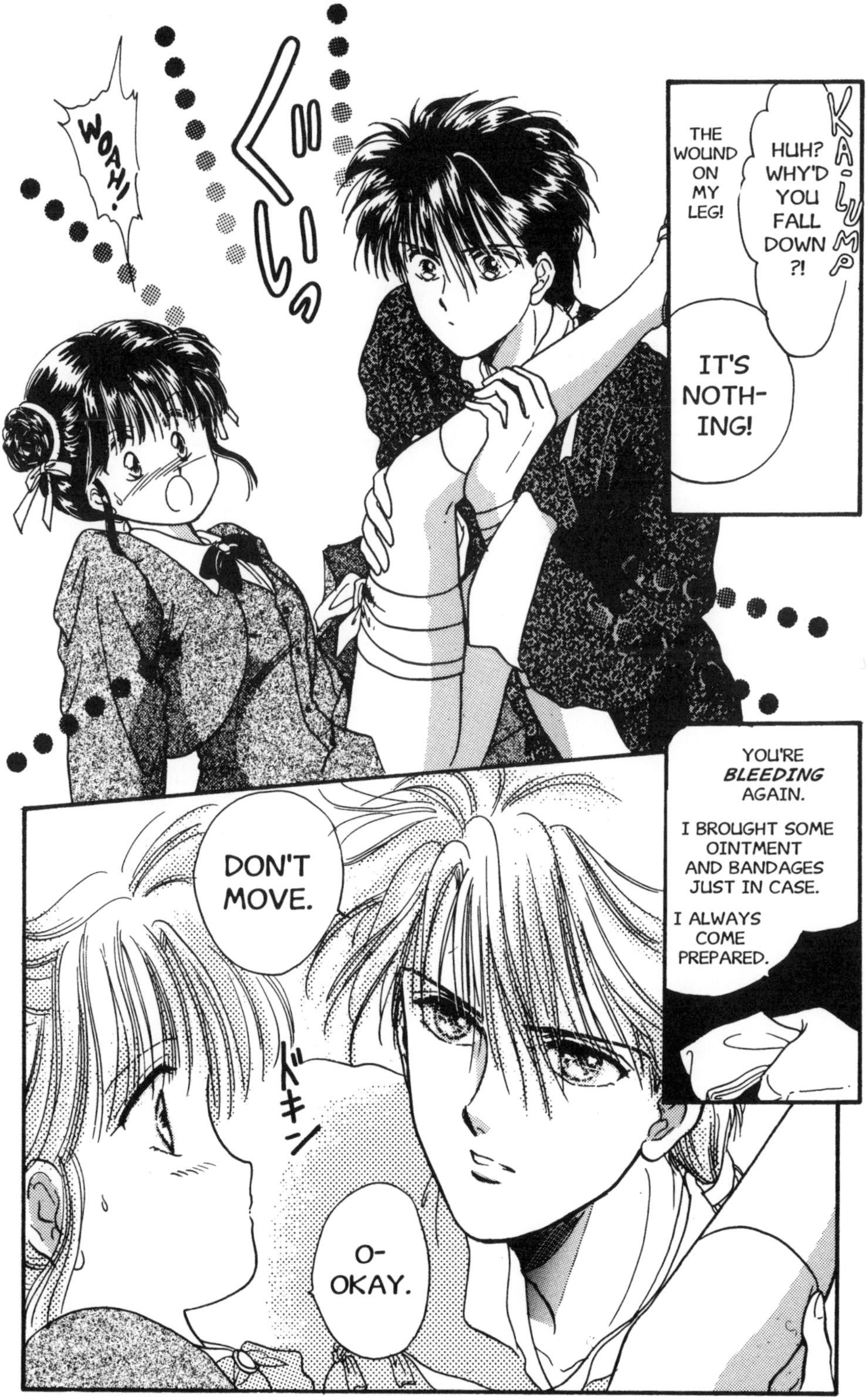
KA-LUMP
HUH? WHY'D YOU FALL DOWN?!
THE WOUND ON MY LEG!
IT'S NOTHING!
ぐいっ
WOAH!
YOU'RE *BLEEDING* AGAIN.
I BROUGHT SOME OINTMENT AND BANDAGES JUST IN CASE.
I ALWAYS COME PREPARED.
DON'T MOVE.
ドキン
O-OKAY.

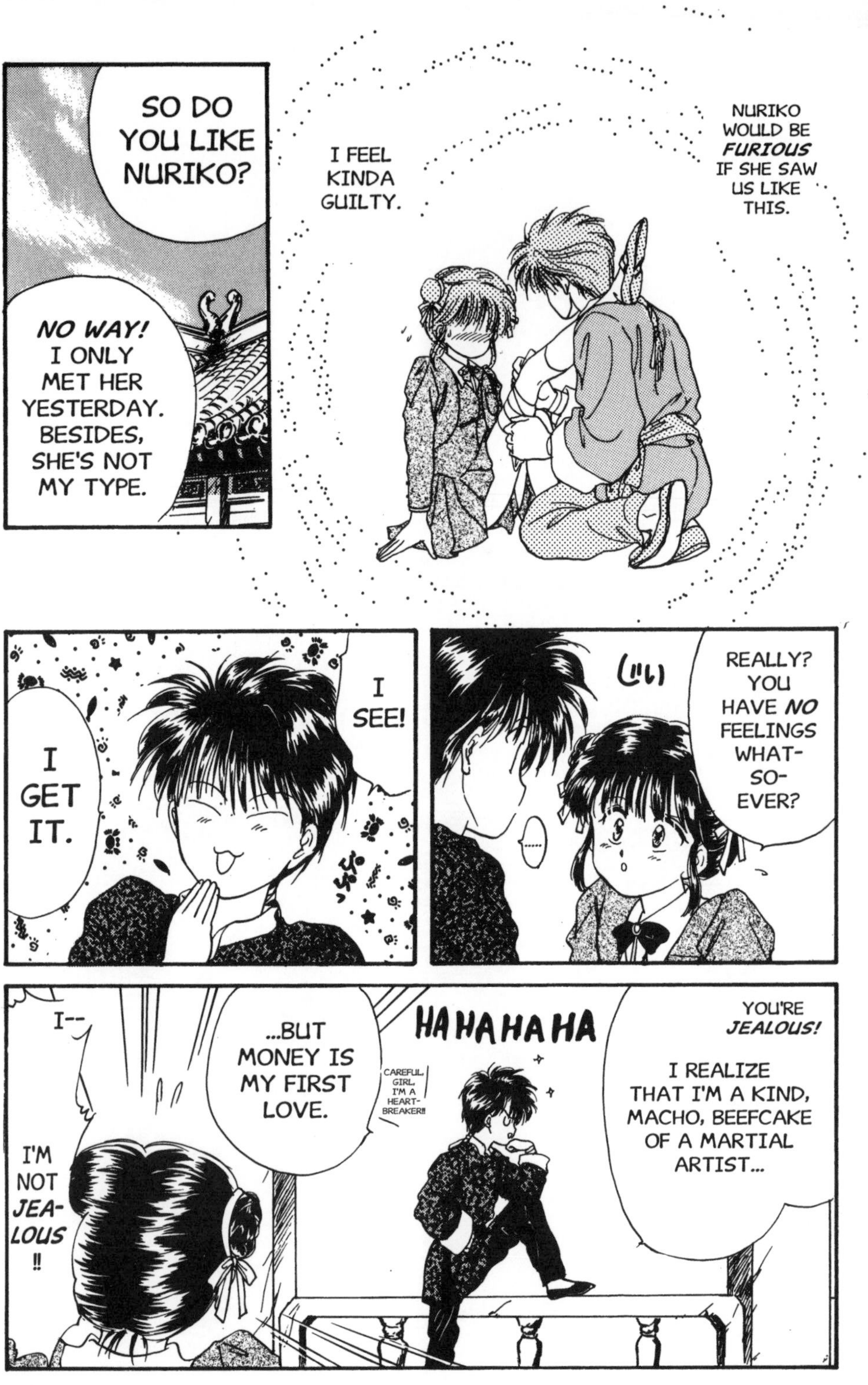
NURIKO WOULD BE FURIOUS IF SHE SAW US LIKE THIS.
I FEEL KINDA GUILTY.
SO DO YOU LIKE NURIKO?
NO WAY! I ONLY MET HER YESTERDAY. BESIDES, SHE'S NOT MY TYPE.
じぃ
REALLY? YOU HAVE NO FEELINGS WHATSOEVER?
......
I SEE!
I GET IT.
YOU'RE JEALOUS!
I REALIZE THAT I'M A KIND, MACHO, BEEFCAKE OF A MARTIAL ARTIST...
HAHAHAHA
CAREFUL, GIRL, I'M A HEARTBREAKER!!
...BUT MONEY IS MY FIRST LOVE.
I--
I'M NOT JEALOUS!!

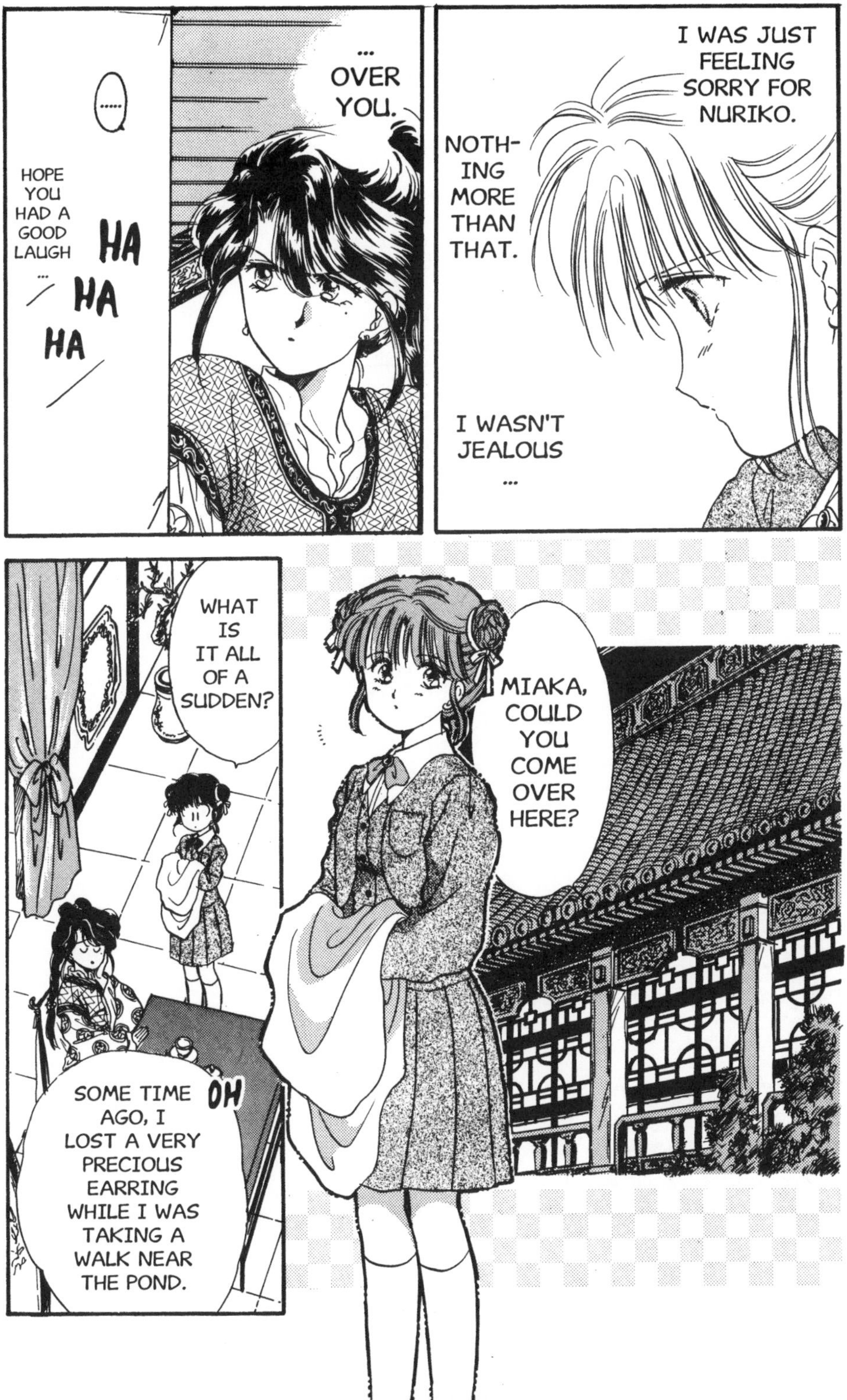
I WAS JUST FEELING SORRY FOR NURIKO.
NOTHING MORE THAN THAT.
I WASN'T JEALOUS ...
... OVER YOU.
......
HOPE YOU HAD A GOOD LAUGH ...
HA HA HA
MIAKA, COULD YOU COME OVER HERE?
WHAT IS IT ALL OF A SUDDEN?
OH
SOME TIME AGO, I LOST A VERY PRECIOUS EARRING WHILE I WAS TAKING A WALK NEAR THE POND.

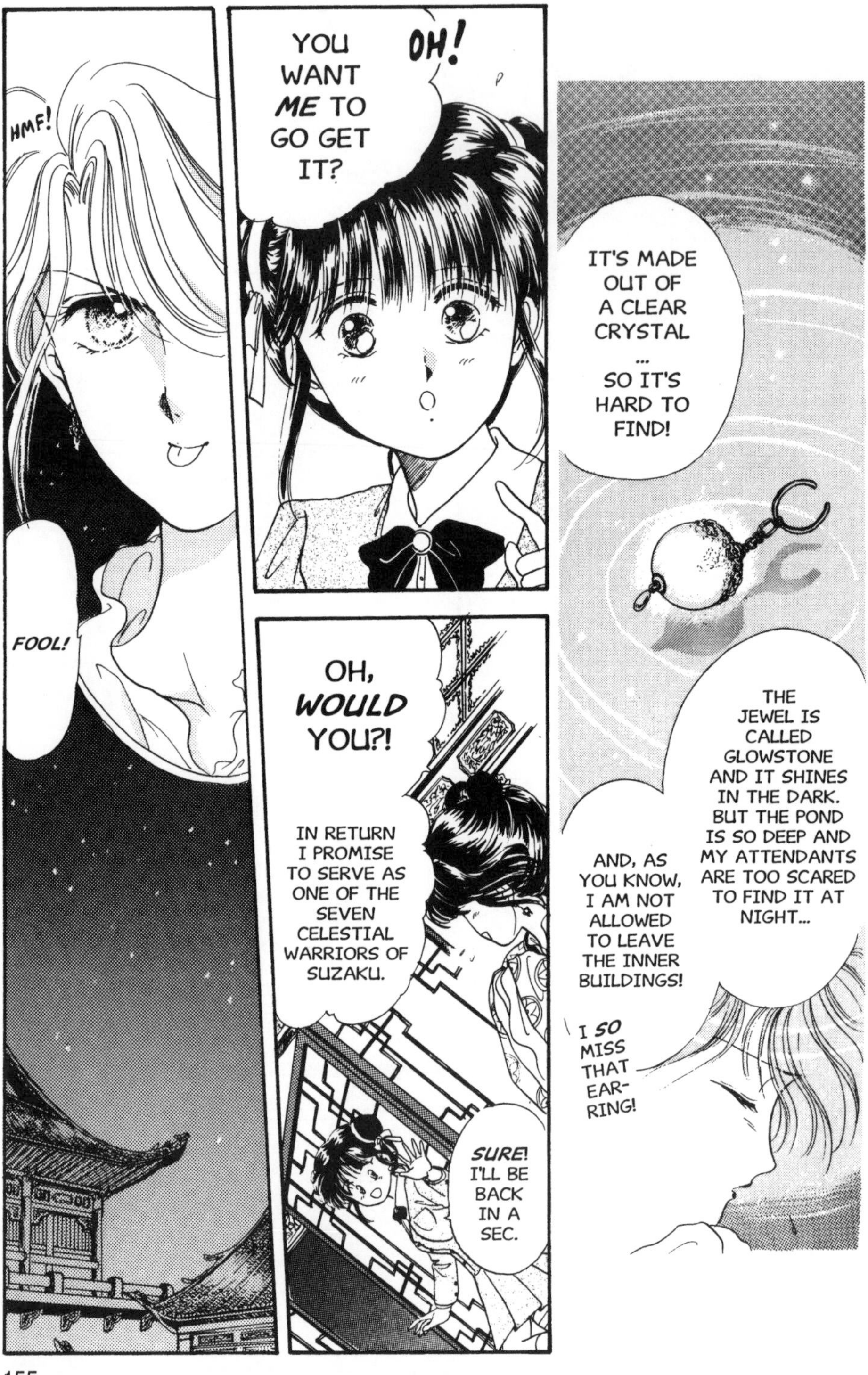

IT'S MADE OUT OF A CLEAR CRYSTAL ... SO IT'S HARD TO FIND!
THE JEWEL IS CALLED GLOWSTONE AND IT SHINES IN THE DARK. BUT THE POND IS SO DEEP AND MY ATTENDANTS ARE TOO SCARED TO FIND IT AT NIGHT...
AND, AS YOU KNOW, I AM NOT ALLOWED TO LEAVE THE INNER BUILDINGS!
I *SO* MISS THAT EAR-RING!
OH!
YOU WANT *ME* TO GO GET IT?
OH, *WOULD* YOU?!
IN RETURN I PROMISE TO SERVE AS ONE OF THE SEVEN CELESTIAL WARRIORS OF SUZAKU.
SURE! I'LL BE BACK IN A SEC.
HMF!
FOOL!

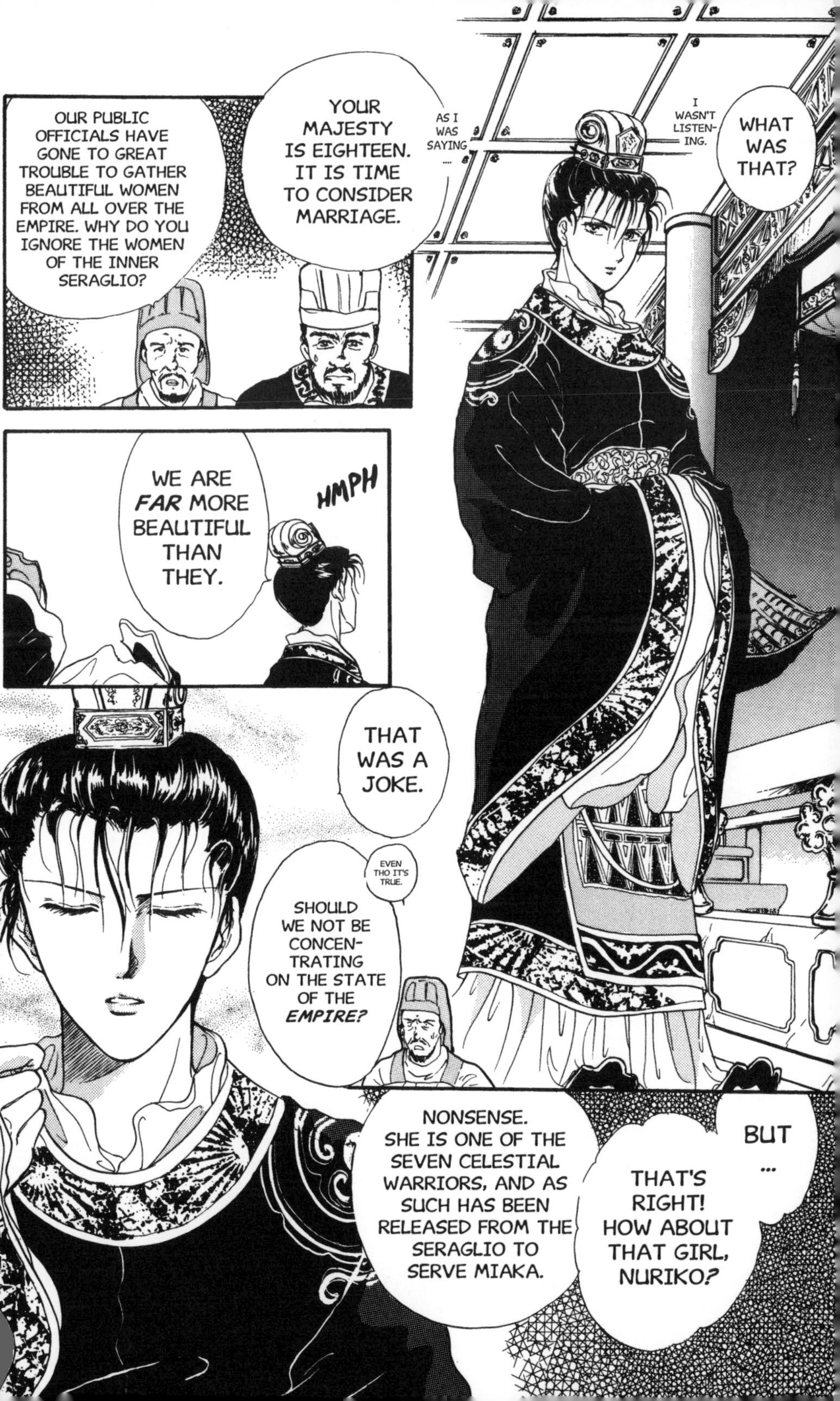
WHAT WAS THAT?
I WASN'T LISTEN-ING.
AS I WAS SAYING ....
YOUR MAJESTY IS EIGHTEEN. IT IS TIME TO CONSIDER MARRIAGE.
OUR PUBLIC OFFICIALS HAVE GONE TO GREAT TROUBLE TO GATHER BEAUTIFUL WOMEN FROM ALL OVER THE EMPIRE. WHY DO YOU IGNORE THE WOMEN OF THE INNER SERAGLIO?
HMPH
WE ARE *FAR* MORE BEAUTIFUL THAN THEY.
THAT WAS A JOKE.
EVEN THO IT'S TRUE.
SHOULD WE NOT BE CONCEN-TRATING ON THE STATE OF THE *EMPIRE?*
BUT ...
THAT'S RIGHT! HOW ABOUT THAT GIRL, NURIKO?
NONSENSE. SHE IS ONE OF THE SEVEN CELESTIAL WARRIORS, AND AS SUCH HAS BEEN RELEASED FROM THE SERAGLIO TO SERVE MIAKA.

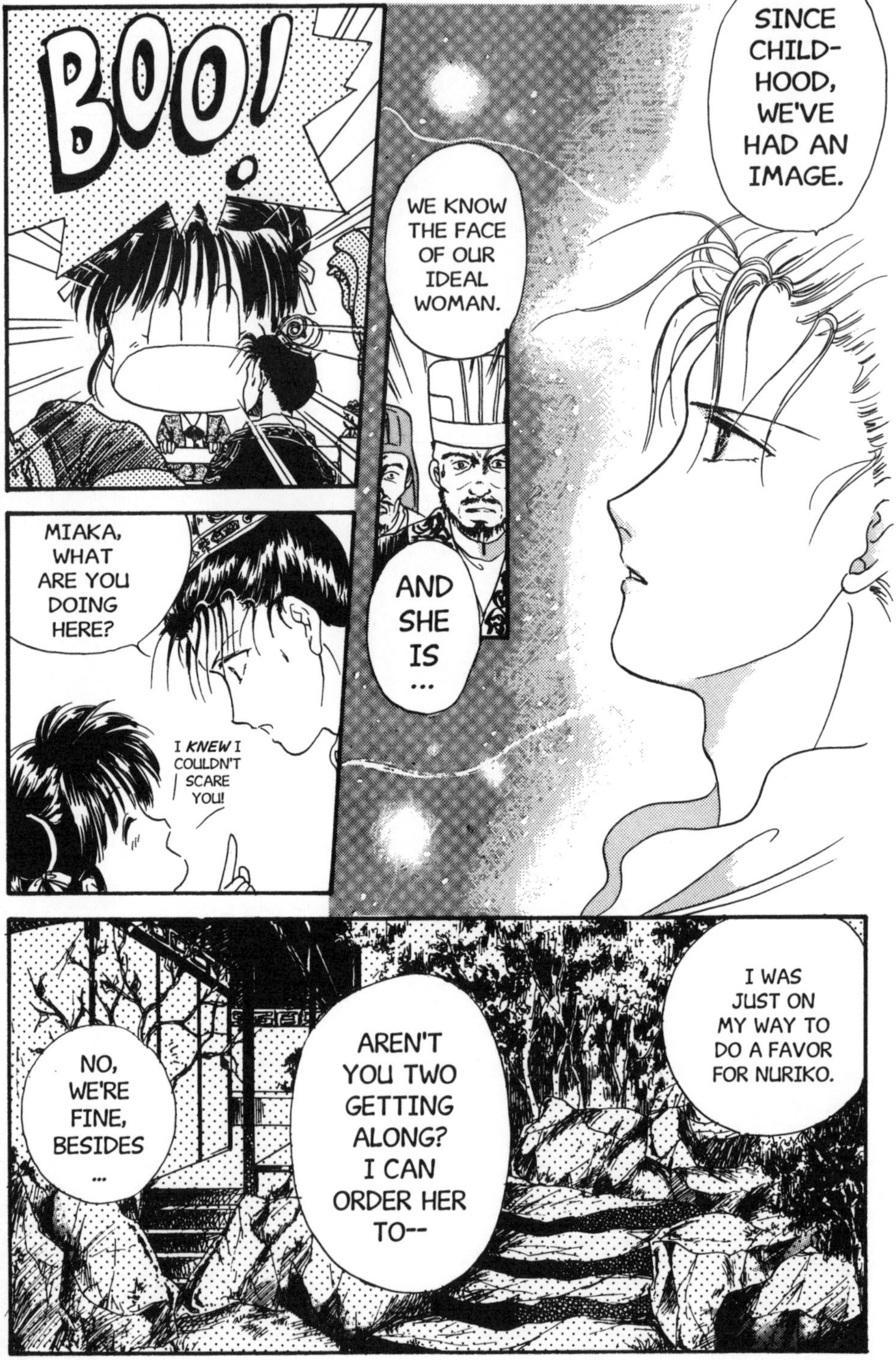
SINCE CHILDHOOD, WE'VE HAD AN IMAGE.
WE KNOW THE FACE OF OUR IDEAL WOMAN.
AND SHE IS ...
BOO!
MIAKA, WHAT ARE YOU DOING HERE?
I *KNEW* I COULDN'T SCARE YOU!
I WAS JUST ON MY WAY TO DO A FAVOR FOR NURIKO.
AREN'T YOU TWO GETTING ALONG? I CAN ORDER HER TO--
NO, WE'RE FINE, BESIDES ...

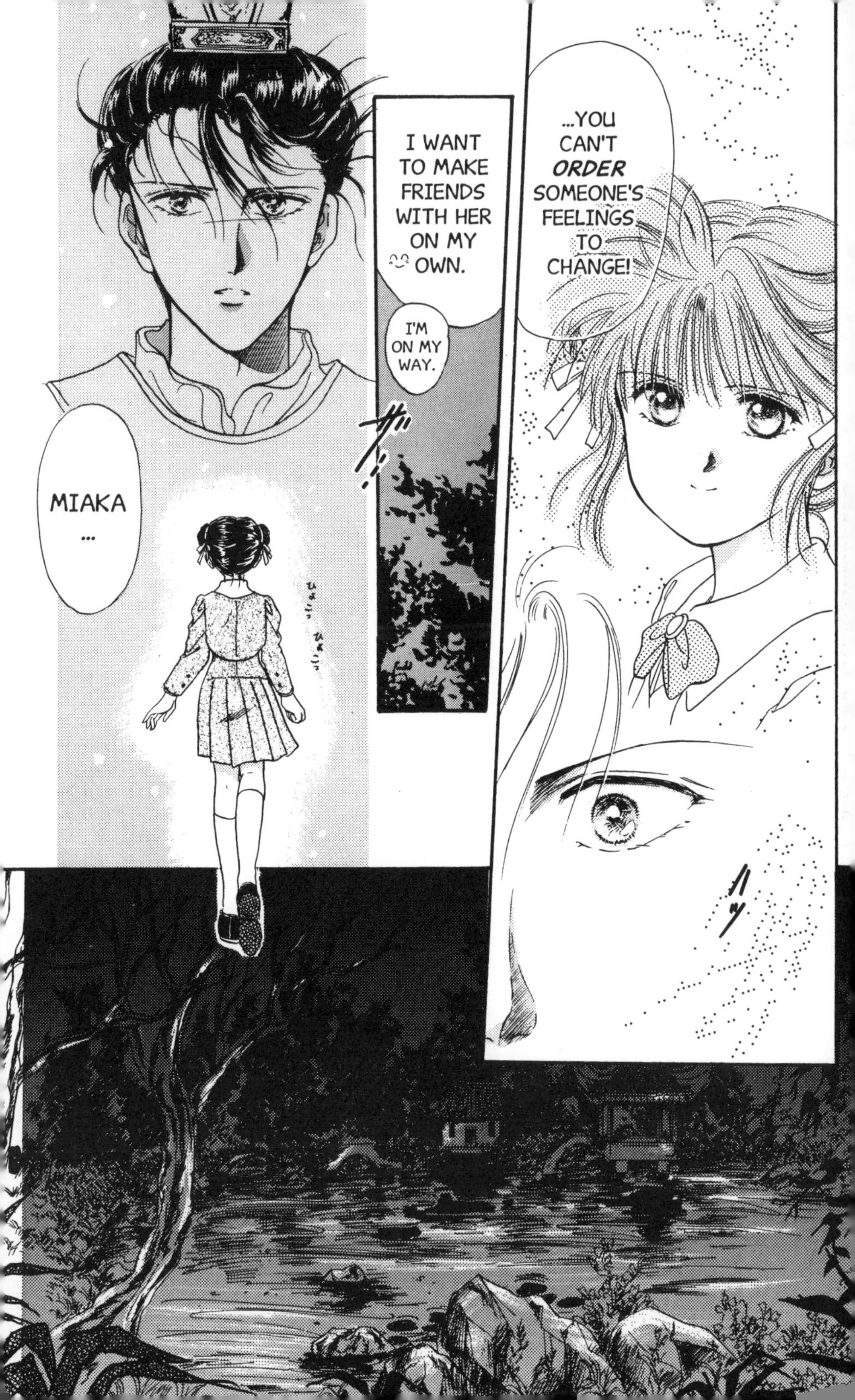
...YOU CAN'T ORDER SOMEONE'S FEELINGS TO CHANGE!
I WANT TO MAKE FRIENDS WITH HER ON MY OWN.
I'M ON MY WAY.
MIAKA ...

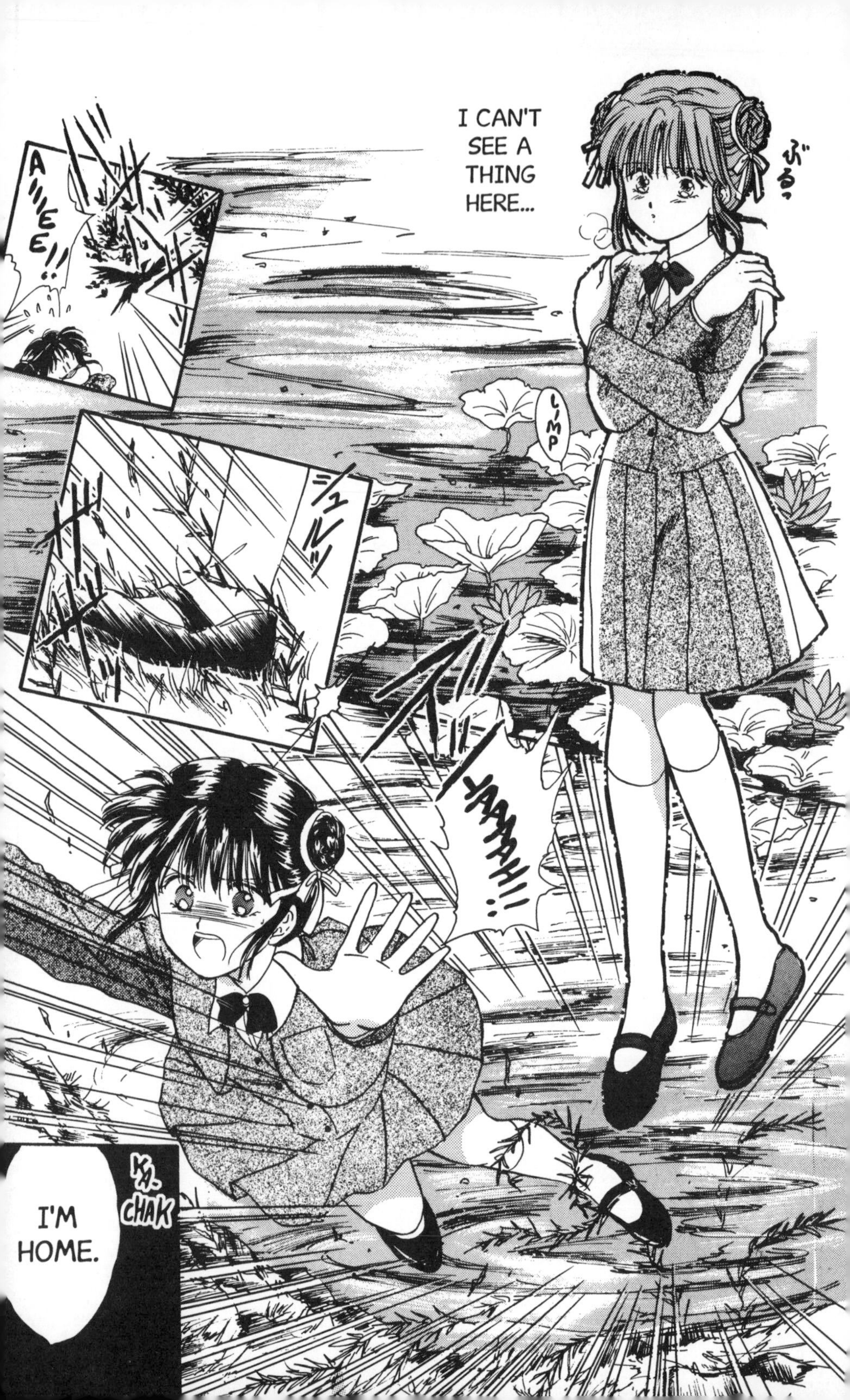

I CAN'T SEE A THING HERE...
ぶるっ
AIIEE!!
LIMP
シュルッ
YAAAAAH!!!
KA-CHAK
I'M HOME.

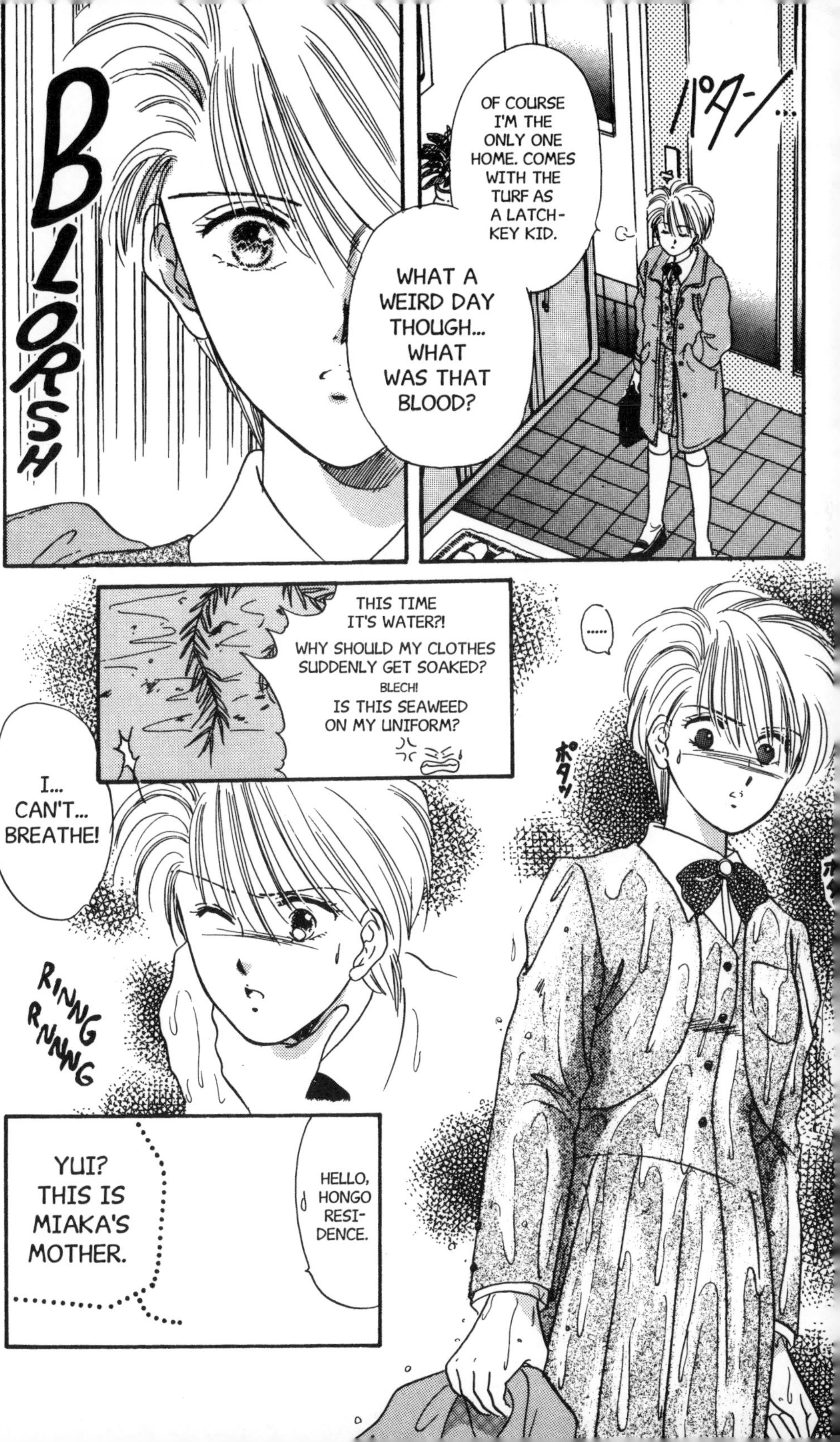
パタン…
OF COURSE I'M THE ONLY ONE HOME. COMES WITH THE TURF AS A LATCH-KEY KID.
WHAT A WEIRD DAY THOUGH... WHAT WAS THAT BLOOD?
BLORSH
......
ポタッ
THIS TIME IT'S WATER?!
WHY SHOULD MY CLOTHES SUDDENLY GET SOAKED?
BLECH!
IS THIS SEAWEED ON MY UNIFORM?
I... CAN'T... BREATHE!
RINNG RNNWG
HELLO, HONGO RESI-DENCE.
YUI? THIS IS MIAKA'S MOTHER.

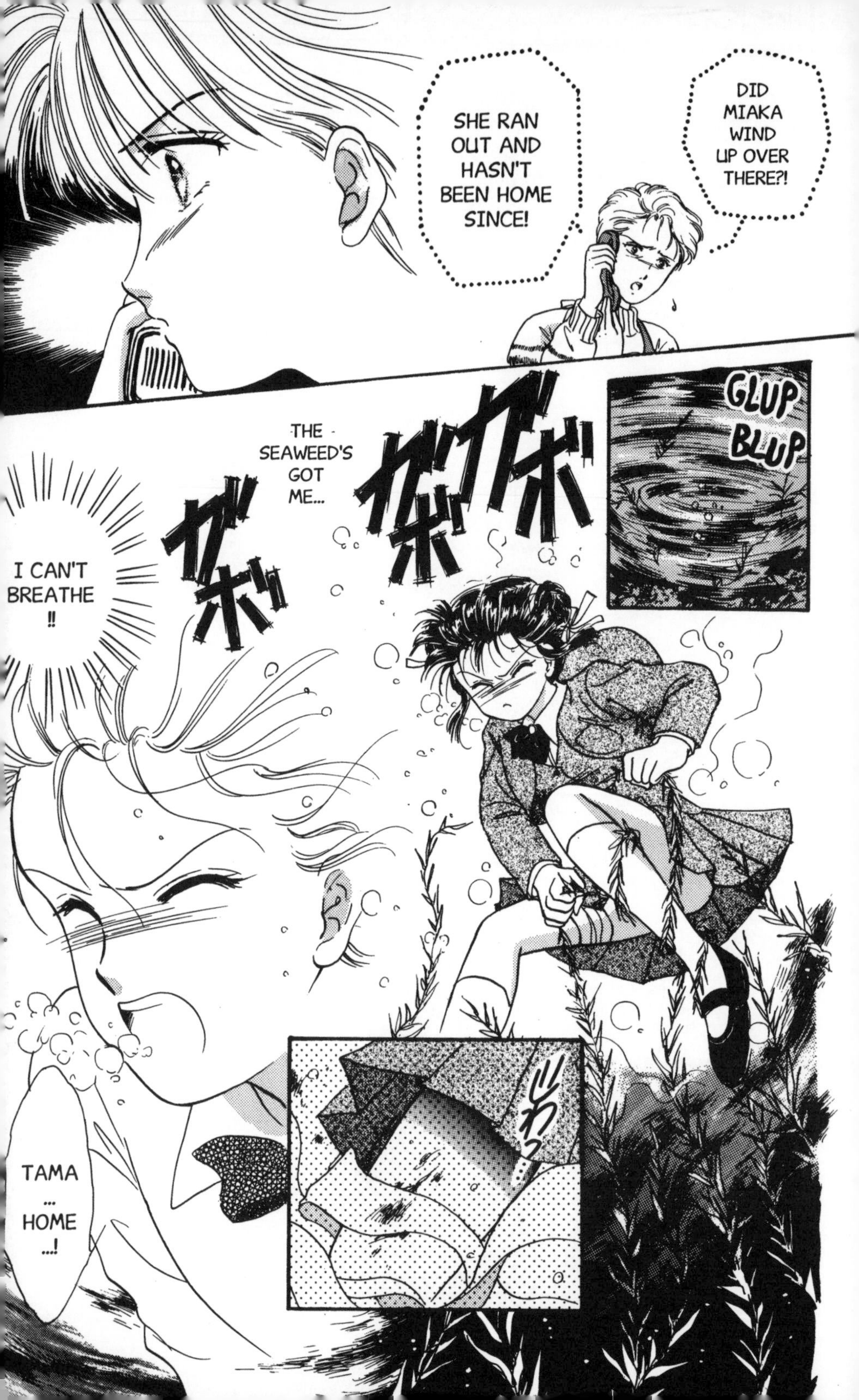
DID MIAKA WIND UP OVER THERE?!
SHE RAN OUT AND HASN'T BEEN HOME SINCE!
GLUP BLUP
ガボガボ
THE SEAWEED'S GOT ME...
ガボッ
I CAN'T BREATHE!!
じわっ
TAMA ... HOME ...!

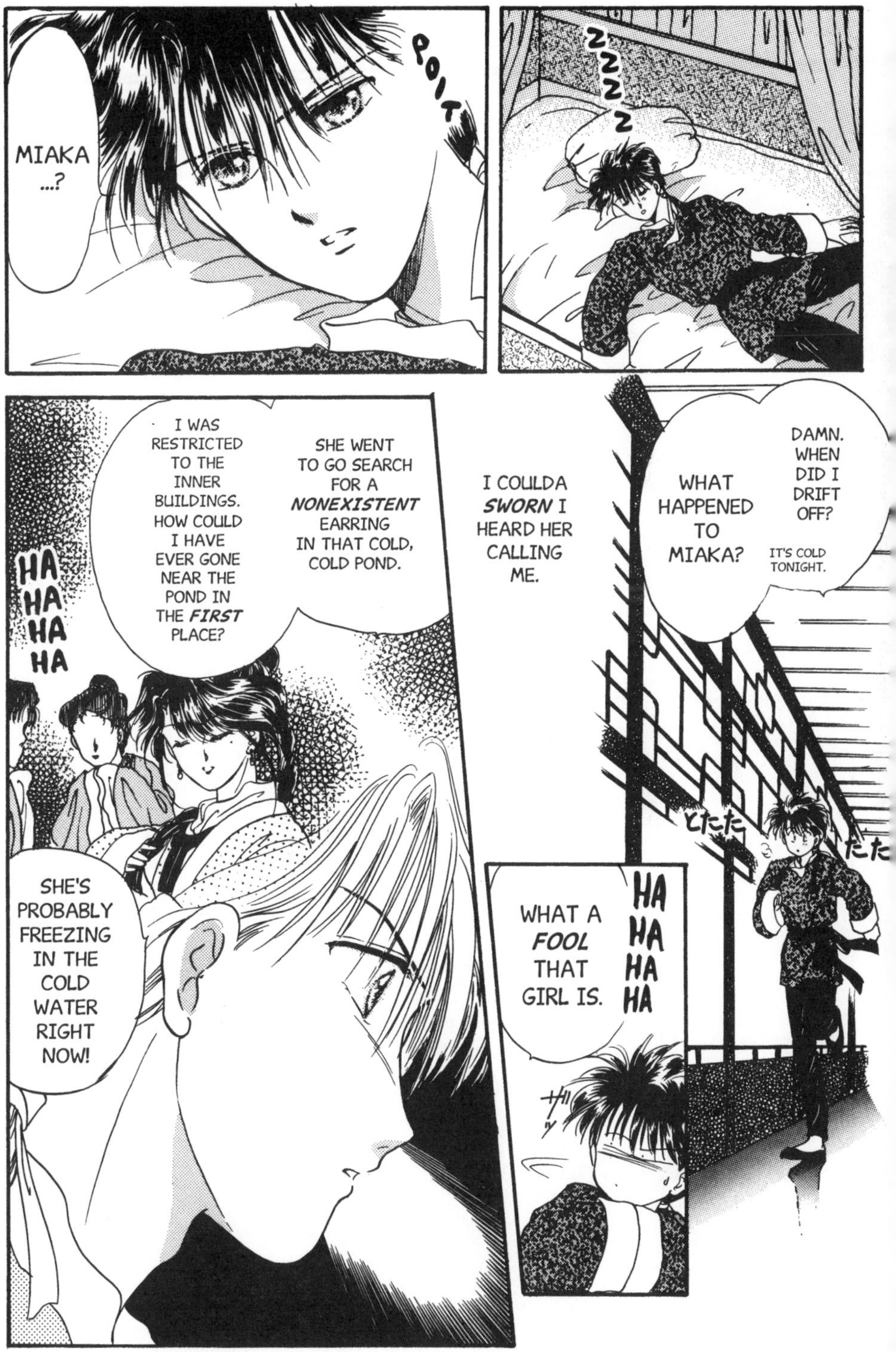
ZZZZ
POIT
MIAKA ...?
DAMN. WHEN DID I DRIFT OFF?
IT'S COLD TONIGHT.
WHAT HAPPENED TO MIAKA?
I COULDA *SWORN* I HEARD HER CALLING ME.
とたた
たた
HA HA HA HA
WHAT A *FOOL* THAT GIRL IS.
ザッ
SHE WENT TO GO SEARCH FOR A *NONEXISTENT* EARRING IN THAT COLD, COLD POND.
I WAS RESTRICTED TO THE INNER BUILDINGS. HOW COULD I HAVE EVER GONE NEAR THE POND IN THE *FIRST* PLACE?
HA HA HA HA
SHE'S PROBABLY FREEZING IN THE COLD WATER RIGHT NOW!

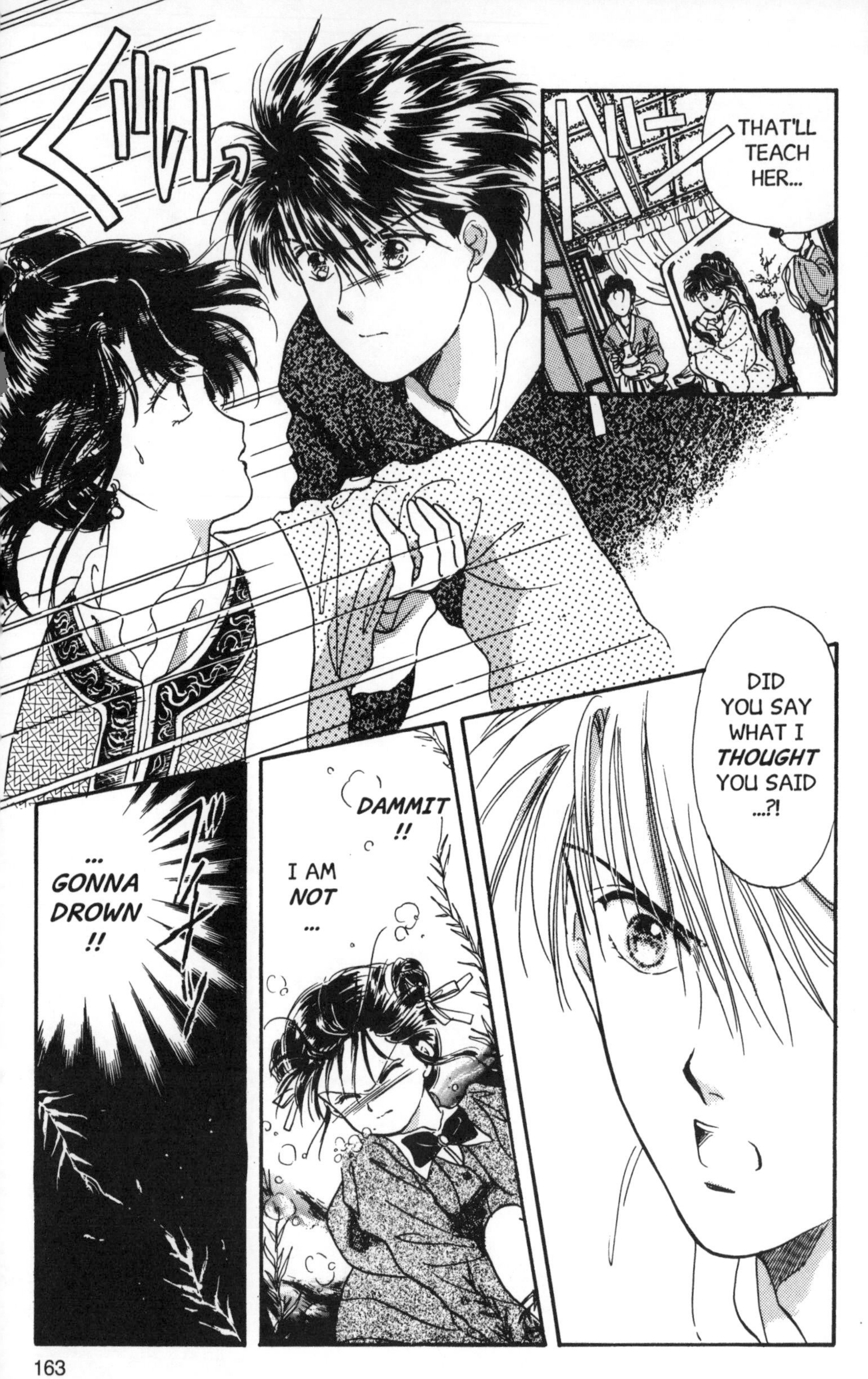
THAT'LL TEACH HER...
DID YOU SAY WHAT I THOUGHT YOU SAID ...?!
DAMMIT !!
I AM NOT ...
... GONNA DROWN !!

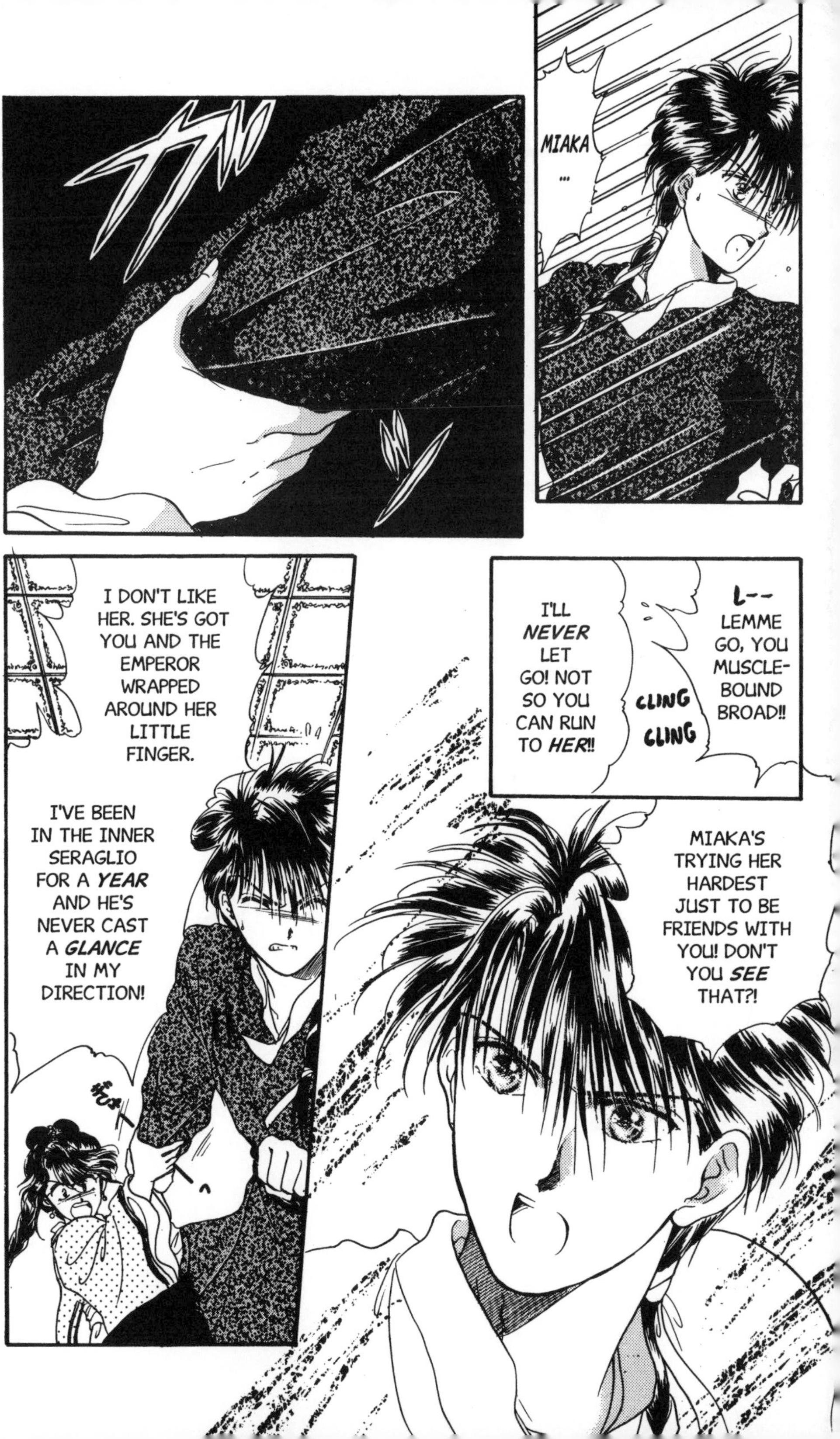
MIAKA ...
L-- LEMME GO, YOU MUSCLE-BOUND BROAD!!
CLING
CLING
I'LL *NEVER* LET GO! NOT SO YOU CAN RUN TO *HER*!!
MIAKA'S TRYING HER HARDEST JUST TO BE FRIENDS WITH YOU! DON'T YOU *SEE* THAT?!
I DON'T LIKE HER. SHE'S GOT YOU AND THE EMPEROR WRAPPED AROUND HER LITTLE FINGER.
I'VE BEEN IN THE INNER SERAGLIO FOR A *YEAR* AND HE'S NEVER CAST A *GLANCE* IN MY DIRECTION!

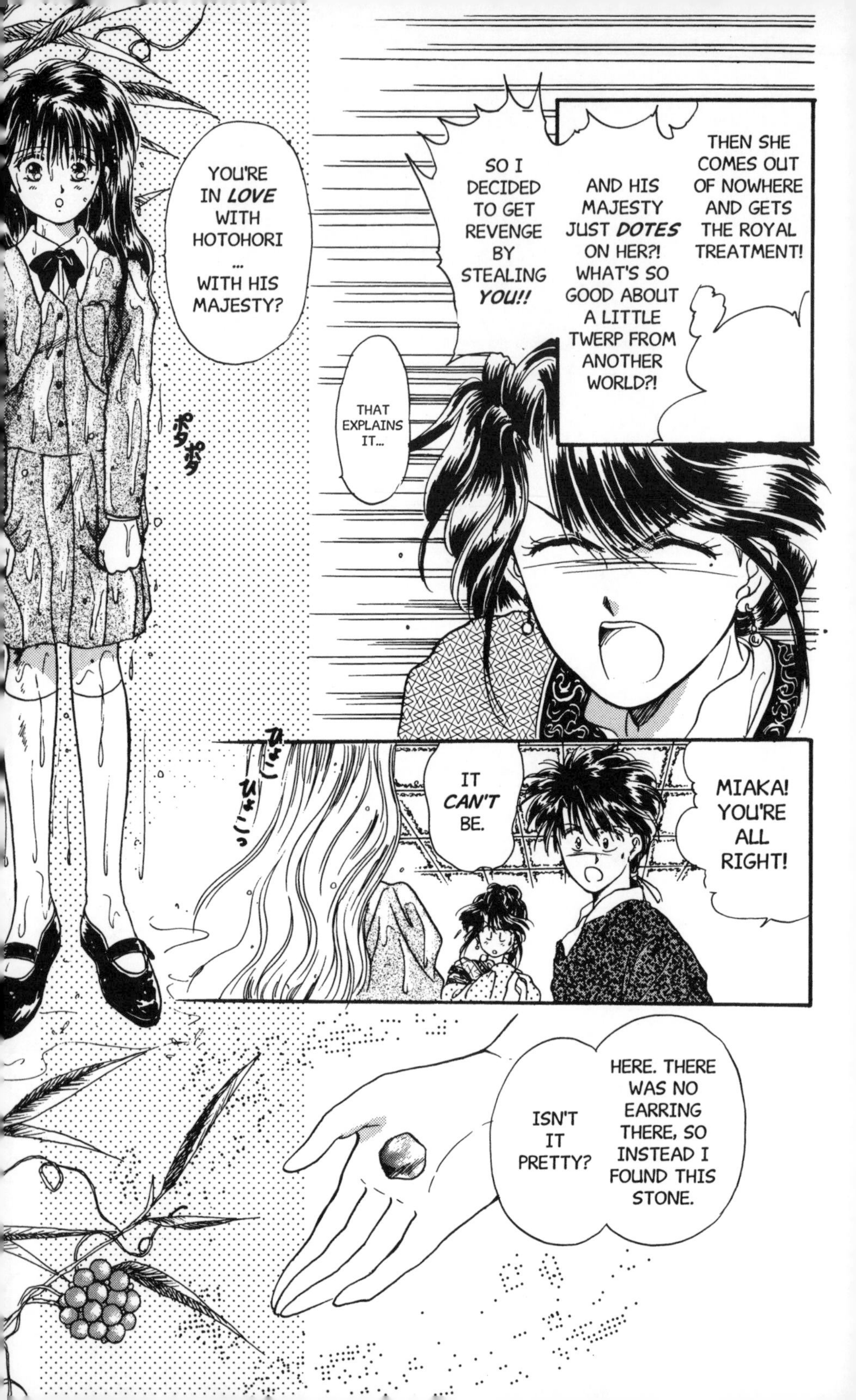

THEN SHE COMES OUT OF NOWHERE AND GETS THE ROYAL TREATMENT!
AND HIS MAJESTY JUST *DOTES* ON HER?! WHAT'S SO GOOD ABOUT A LITTLE TWERP FROM ANOTHER WORLD?!
SO I DECIDED TO GET REVENGE BY STEALING *YOU!!*
THAT EXPLAINS IT...
MIAKA! YOU'RE ALL RIGHT!
IT *CAN'T* BE.
ひょこ ひょこっ
YOU'RE IN *LOVE* WITH HOTOHORI ... WITH HIS MAJESTY?
ポタポタ
HERE. THERE WAS NO EARRING THERE, SO INSTEAD I FOUND THIS STONE.
ISN'T IT PRETTY?

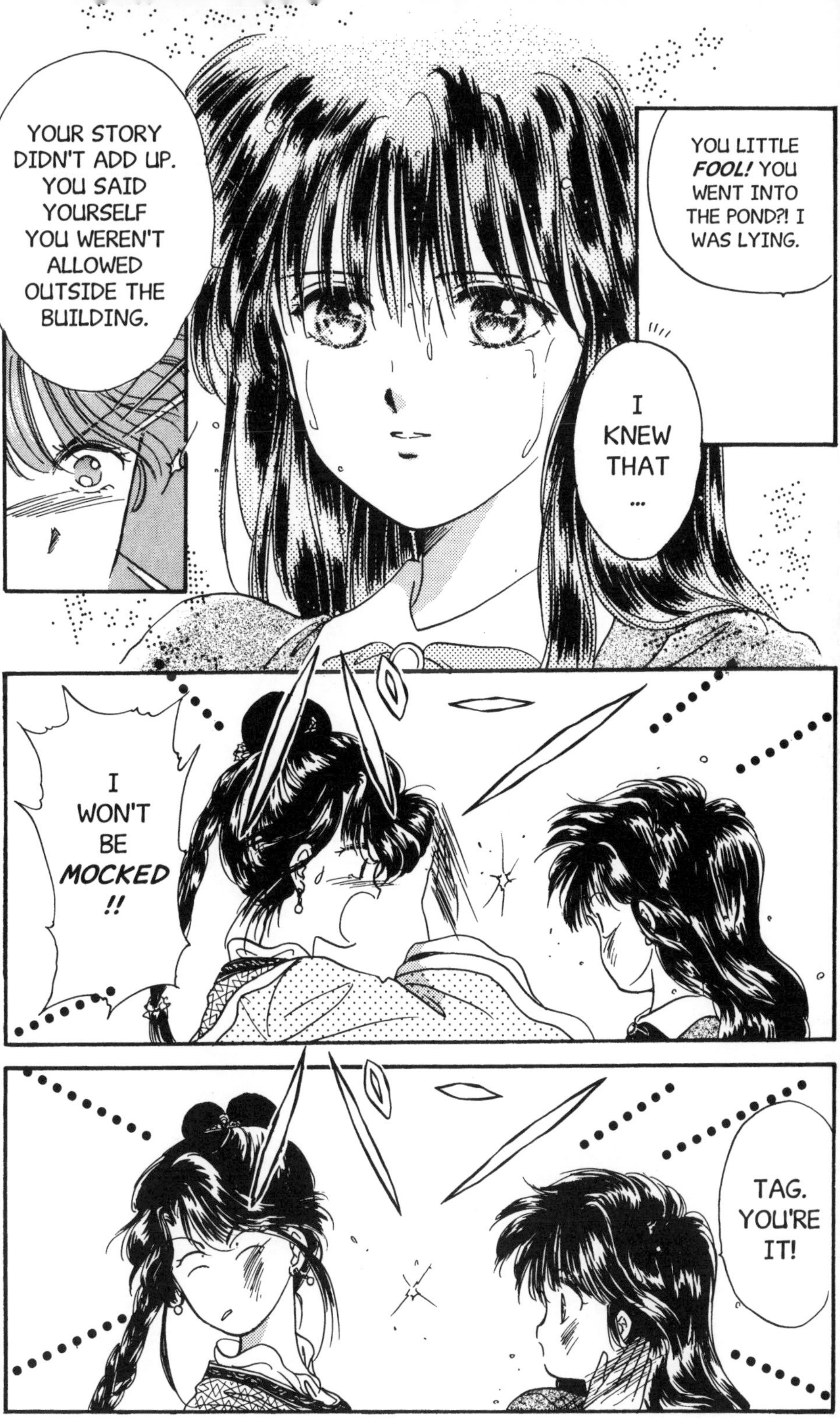
YOU LITTLE FOOL! YOU WENT INTO THE POND?! I WAS LYING.
I KNEW THAT...
YOUR STORY DIDN'T ADD UP. YOU SAID YOURSELF YOU WEREN'T ALLOWED OUTSIDE THE BUILDING.
I WON'T BE MOCKED!!
TAG. YOU'RE IT!

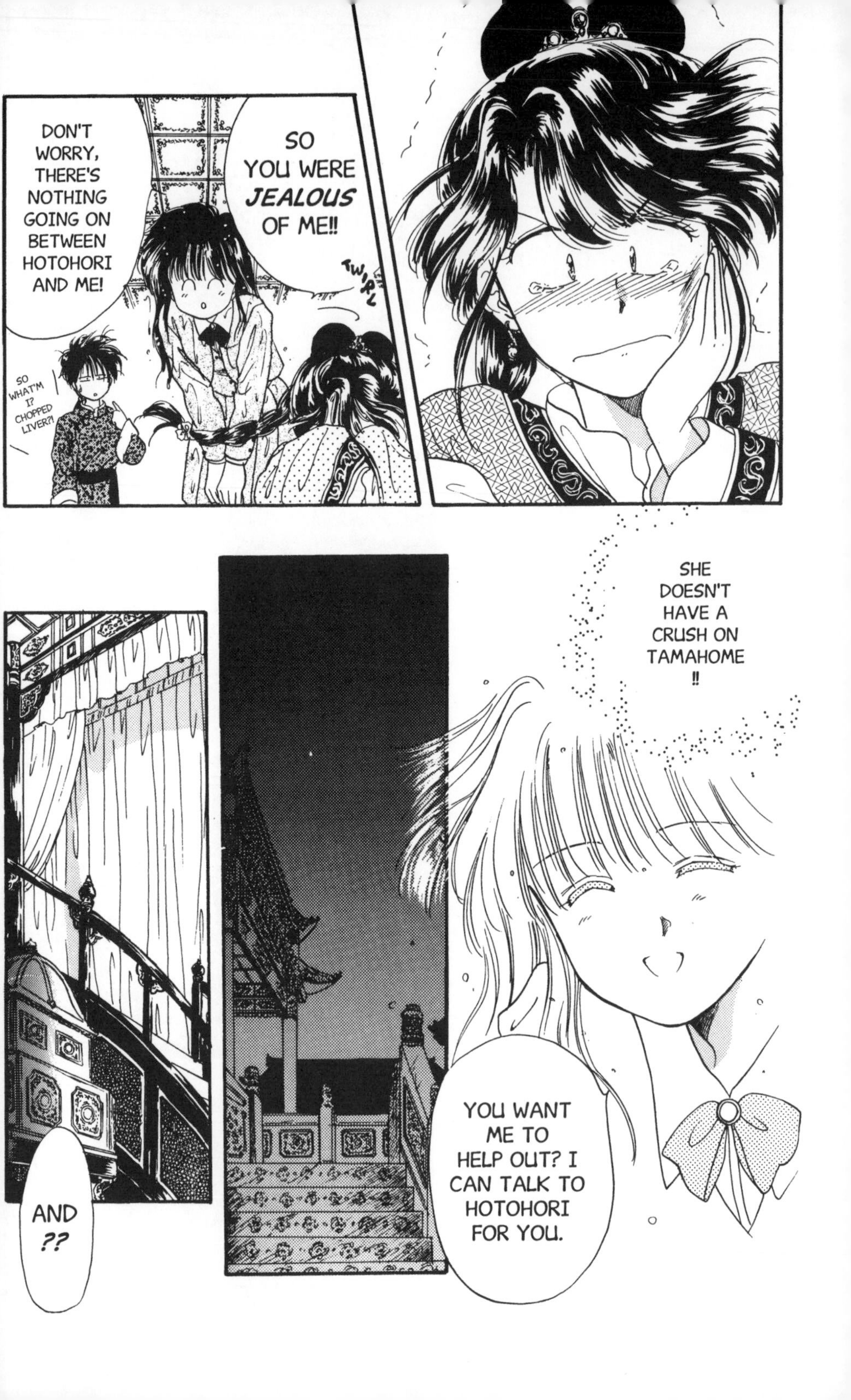
SO YOU WERE *JEALOUS* OF ME!!
DON'T WORRY, THERE'S NOTHING GOING ON BETWEEN HOTOHORI AND ME!
TWIRL
SO WHAT'M I? CHOPPED LIVER?!
SHE DOESN'T HAVE A CRUSH ON TAMAHOME !!
YOU WANT ME TO HELP OUT? I CAN TALK TO HOTOHORI FOR YOU.
AND *??*

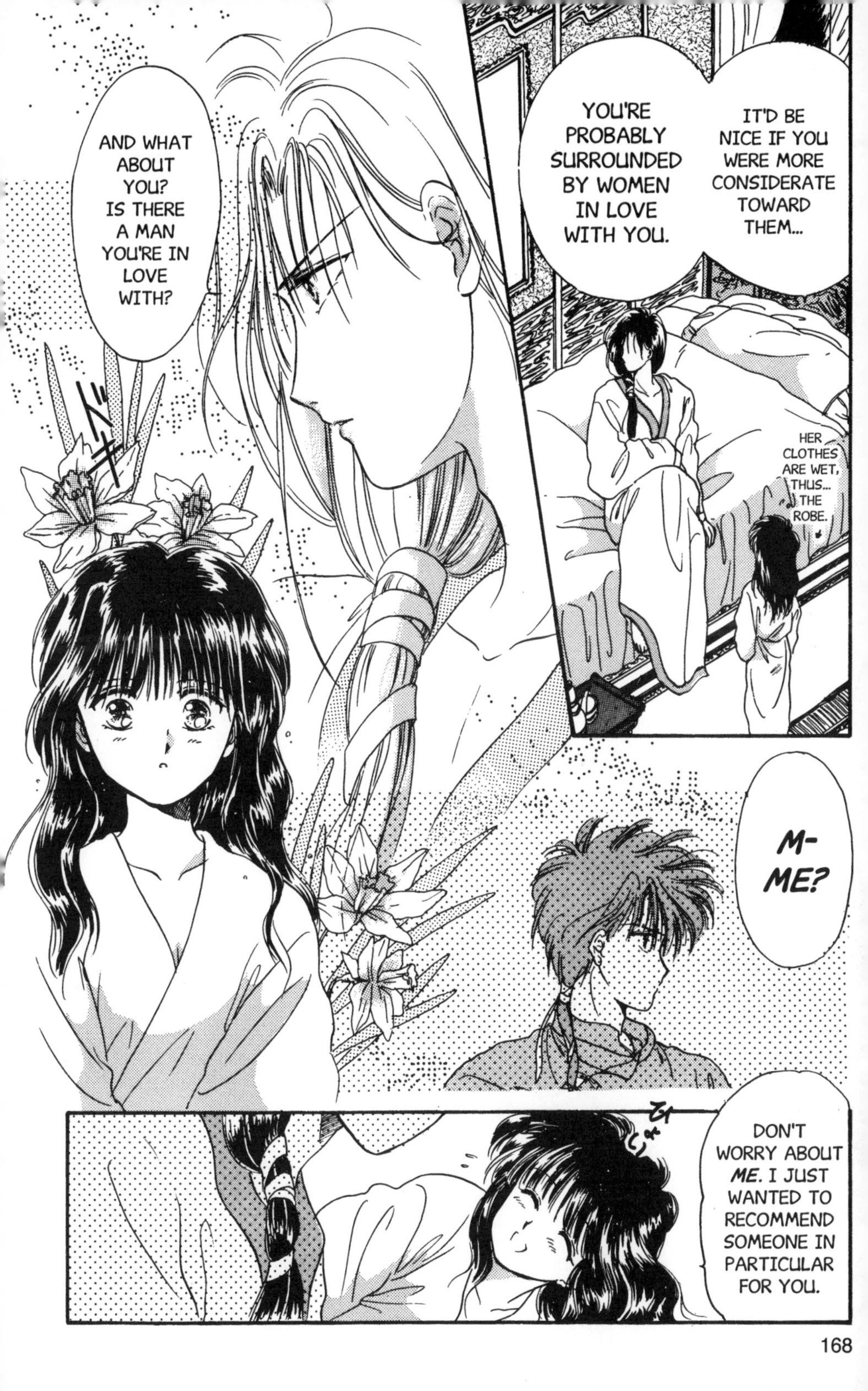
YOU'RE PROBABLY SURROUNDED BY WOMEN IN LOVE WITH YOU.
IT'D BE NICE IF YOU WERE MORE CONSIDERATE TOWARD THEM...
HER CLOTHES ARE WET, THUS... THE ROBE.
AND WHAT ABOUT YOU? IS THERE A MAN YOU'RE IN LOVE WITH?
ドキ
M-ME?
DON'T WORRY ABOUT *ME*. I JUST WANTED TO RECOMMEND SOMEONE IN PARTICULAR FOR YOU.

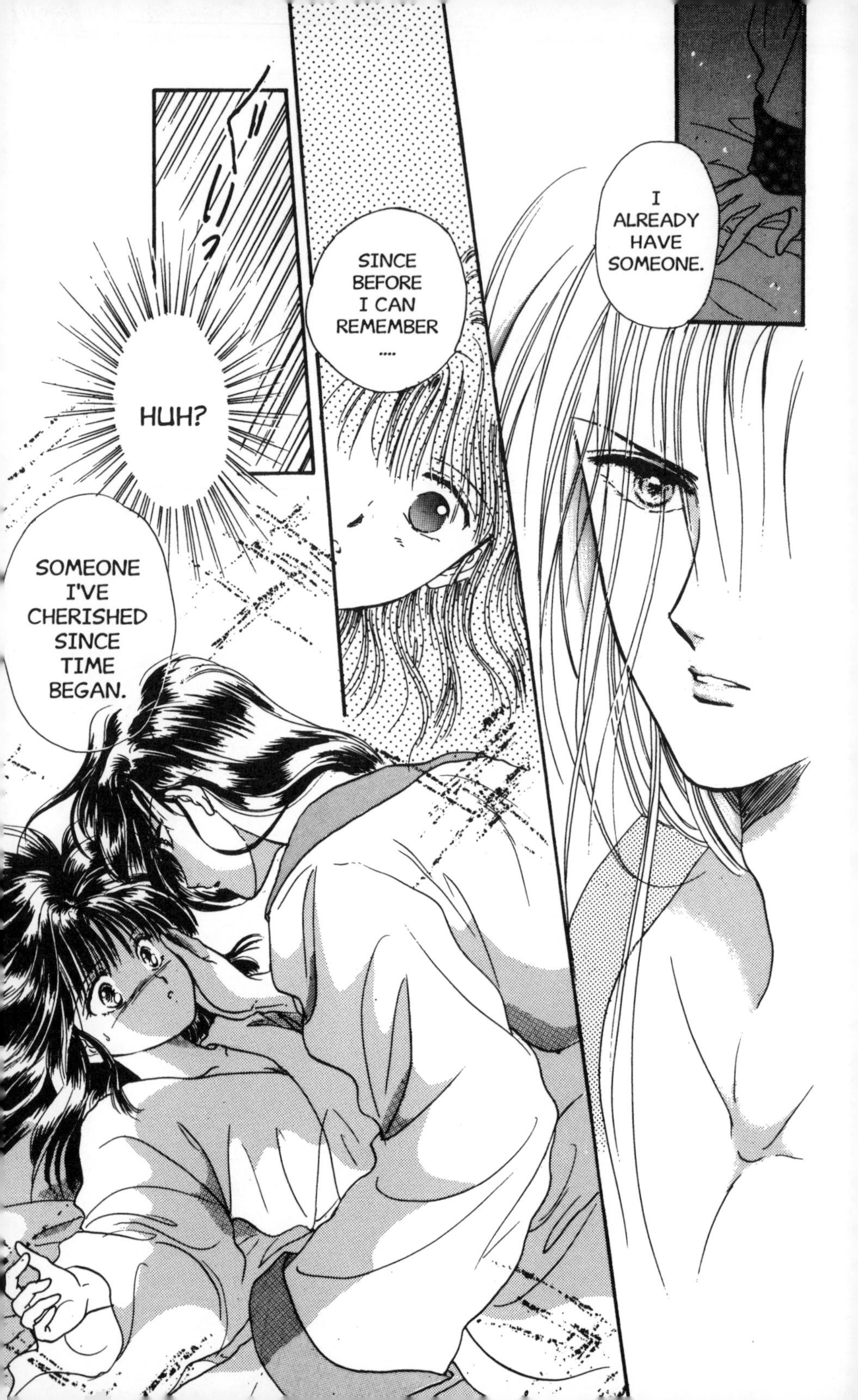
I ALREADY HAVE SOMEONE.
SINCE BEFORE I CAN REMEMBER ....
HUH?
SOMEONE I'VE CHERISHED SINCE TIME BEGAN.

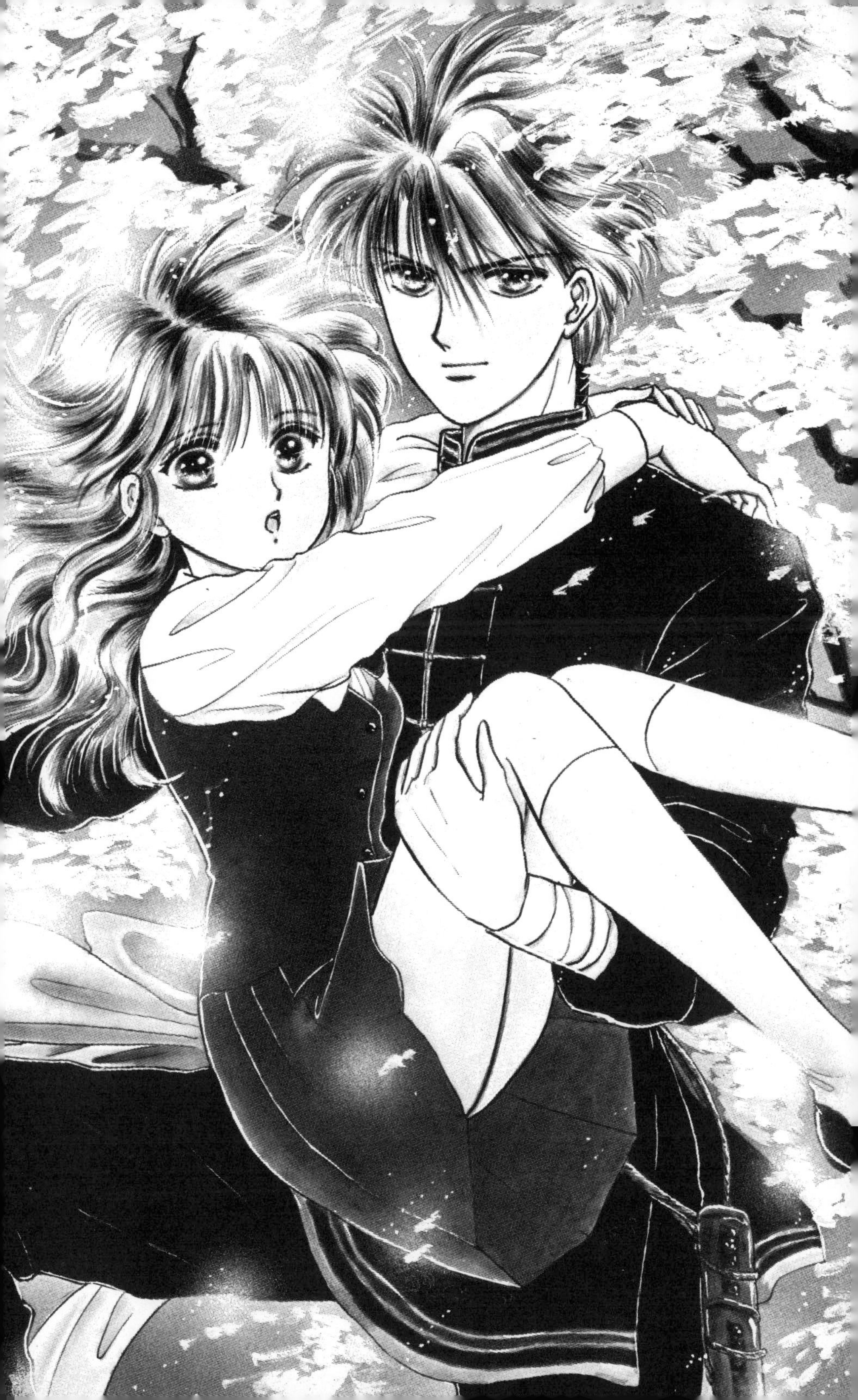

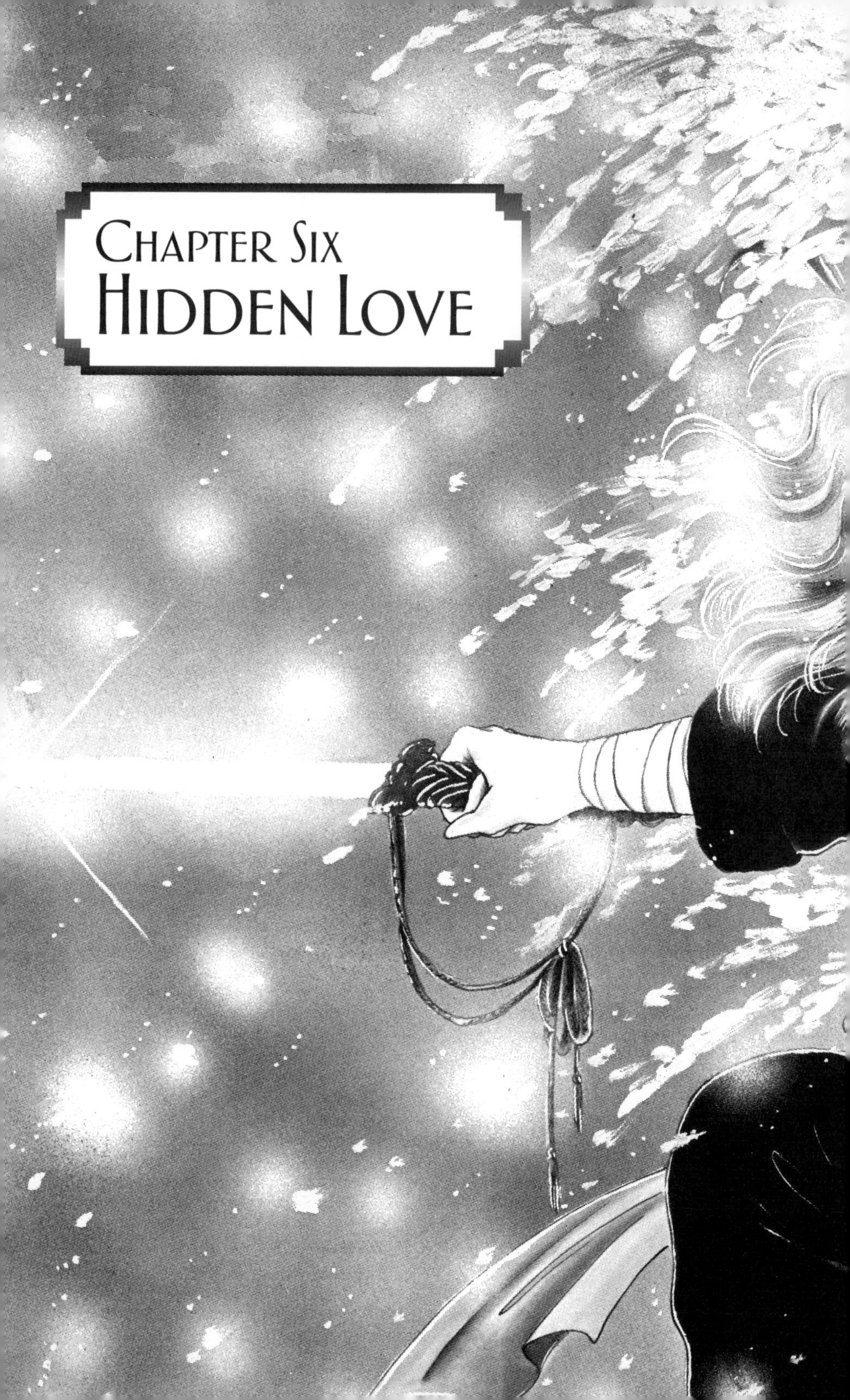
Chapter Six
Hidden Love

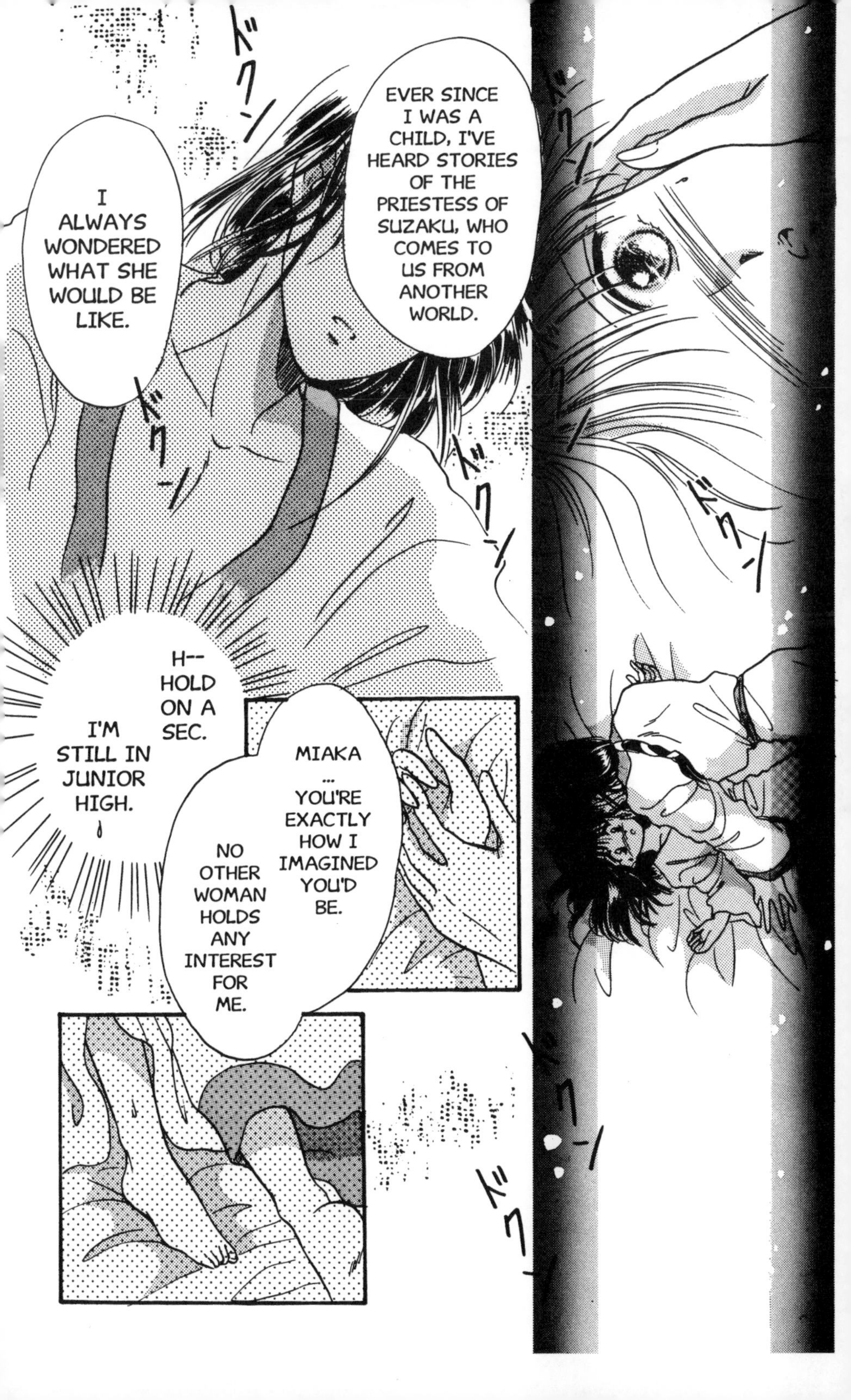

EVER SINCE I WAS A CHILD, I'VE HEARD STORIES OF THE PRIESTESS OF SUZAKU, WHO COMES TO US FROM ANOTHER WORLD.
I ALWAYS WONDERED WHAT SHE WOULD BE LIKE.
MIAKA ... YOU'RE EXACTLY HOW I IMAGINED YOU'D BE.
NO OTHER WOMAN HOLDS ANY INTEREST FOR ME.
H-- HOLD ON A SEC.
I'M STILL IN JUNIOR HIGH.

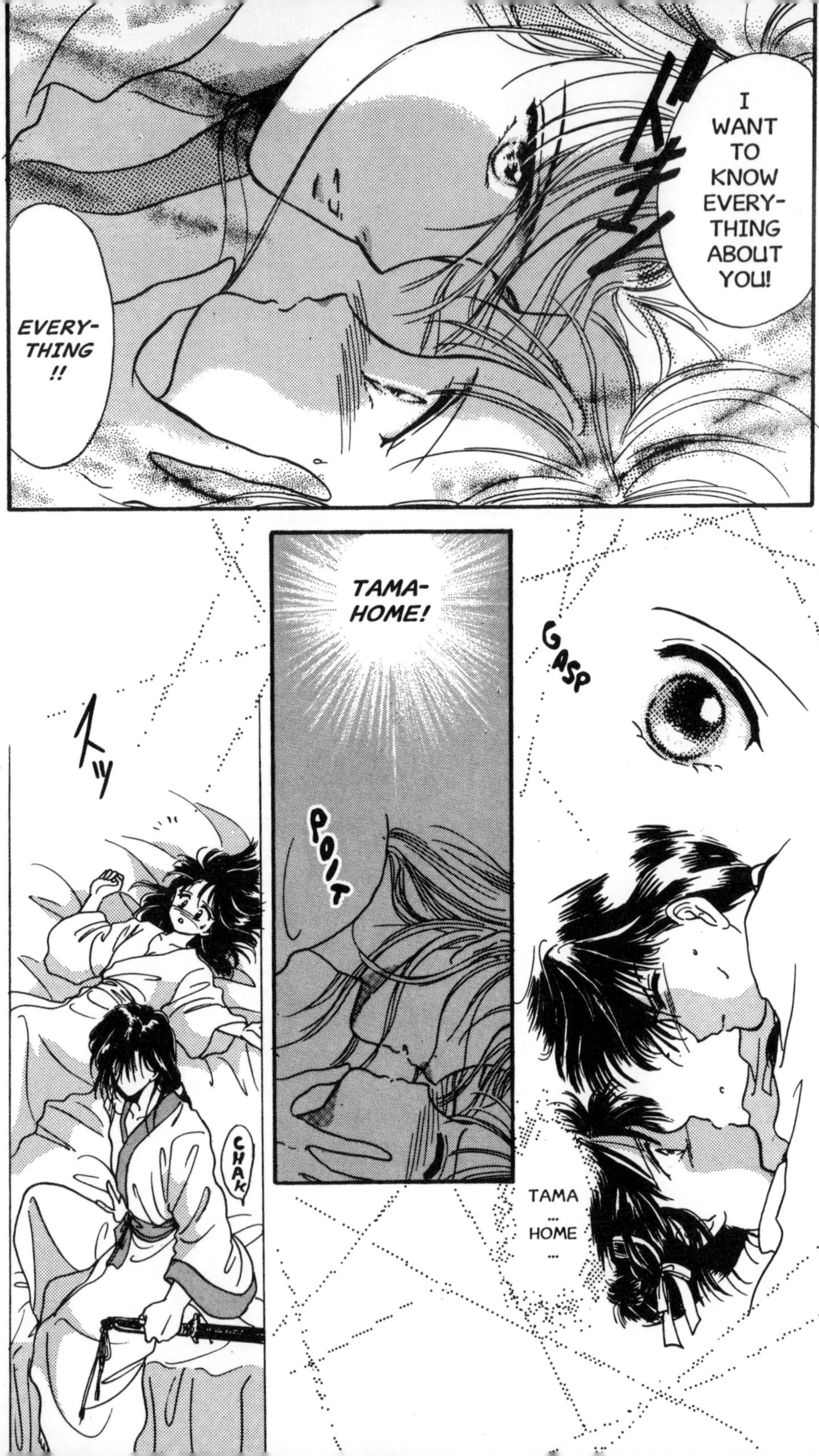
I WANT TO KNOW EVERY-THING ABOUT YOU!
EVERY-THING !!
GASP
TAMA ... HOME ...
TAMA-HOME!
POIT
CHAK

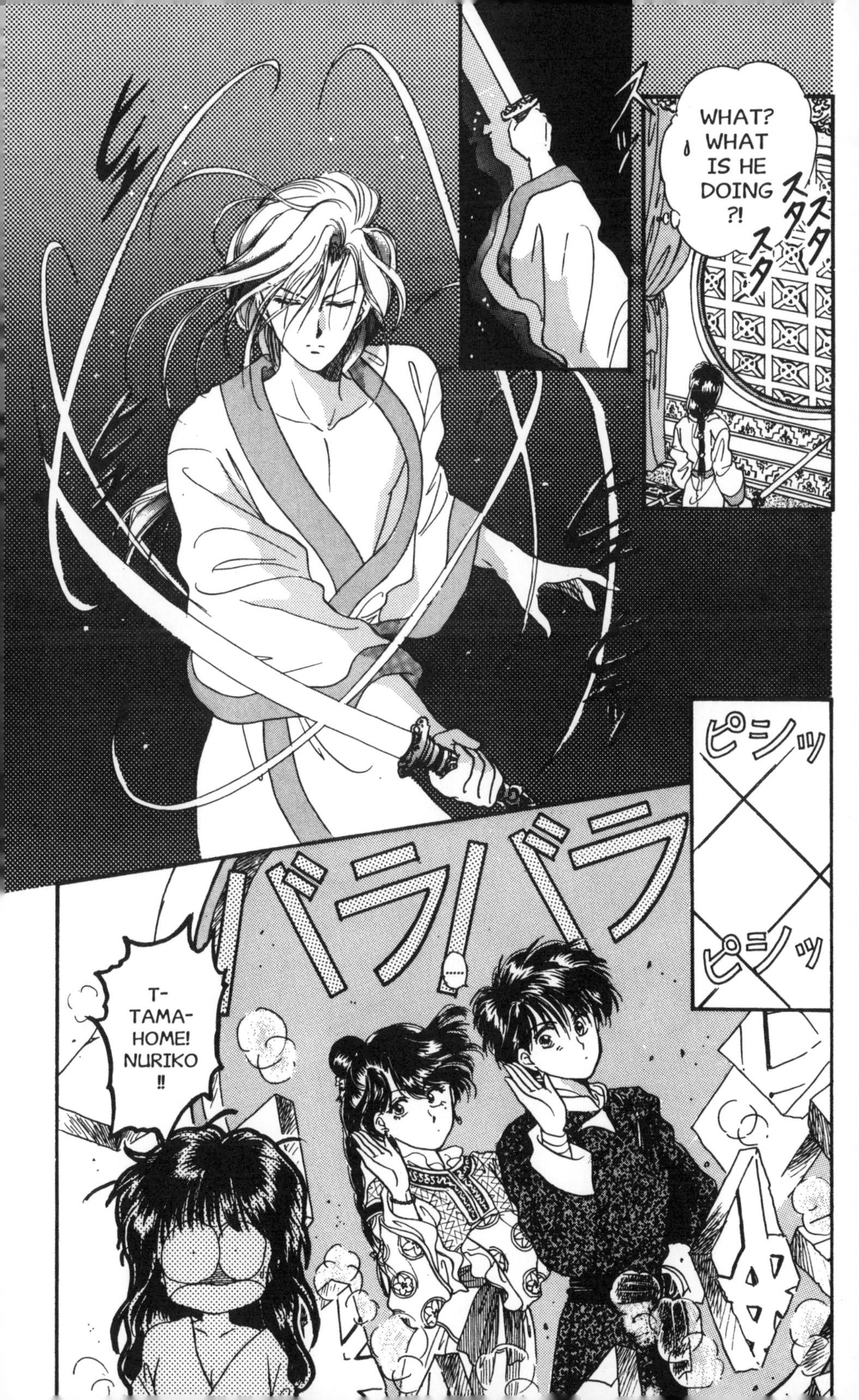
WHAT? WHAT IS HE DOING?!
スタスタ
スタ
ピシッ
ピシッ
バラバラ
......
T-TAMA-HOME! NURIKO!!

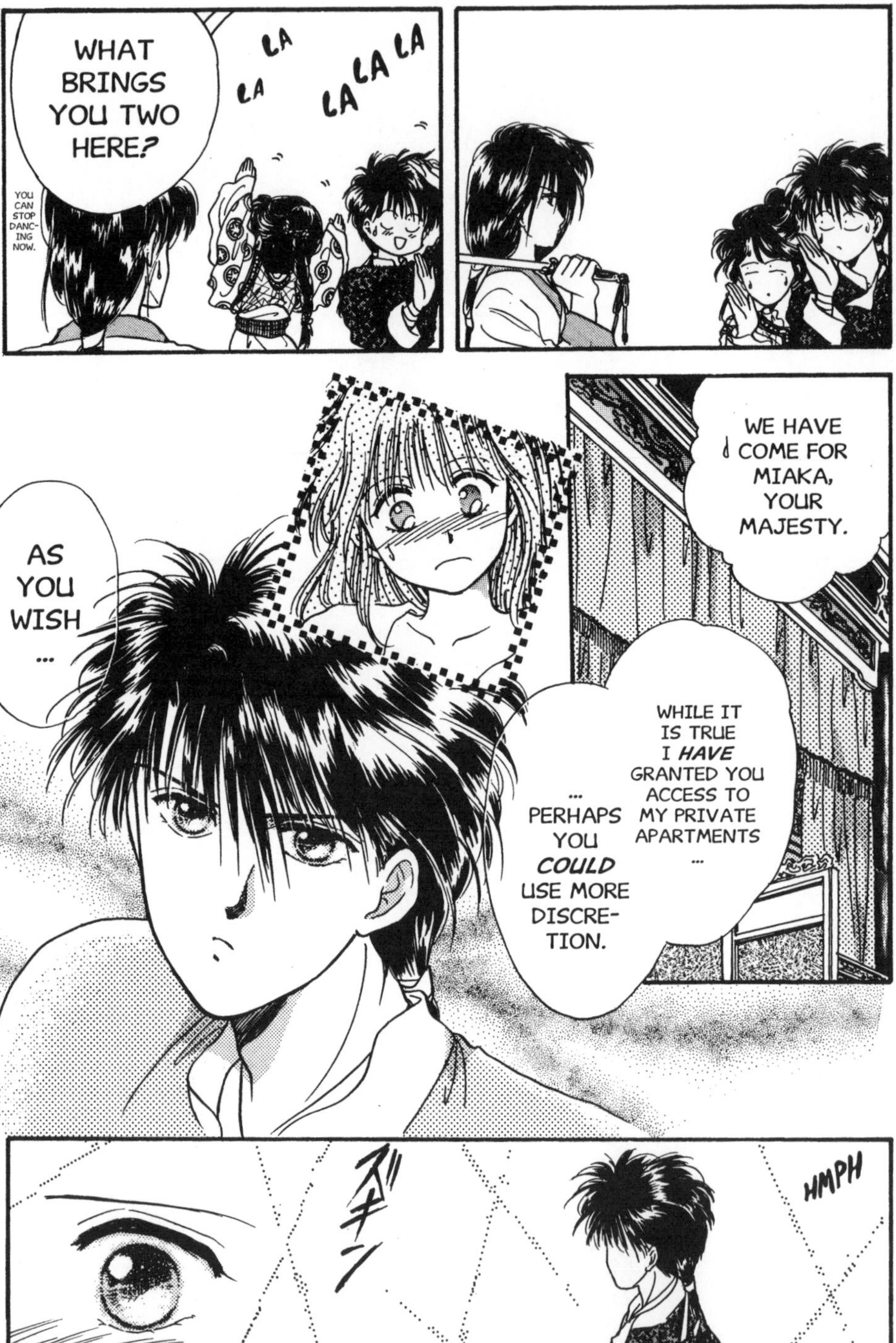
LA LA LA LA LA LA
WHAT BRINGS YOU TWO HERE?
YOU CAN STOP DANCING NOW.
WE HAVE COME FOR MIAKA, YOUR MAJESTY.
WHILE IT IS TRUE I *HAVE* GRANTED YOU ACCESS TO MY PRIVATE APARTMENTS...
...PERHAPS YOU *COULD* USE MORE DISCRETION.
AS YOU WISH...
HMPH
ズキン

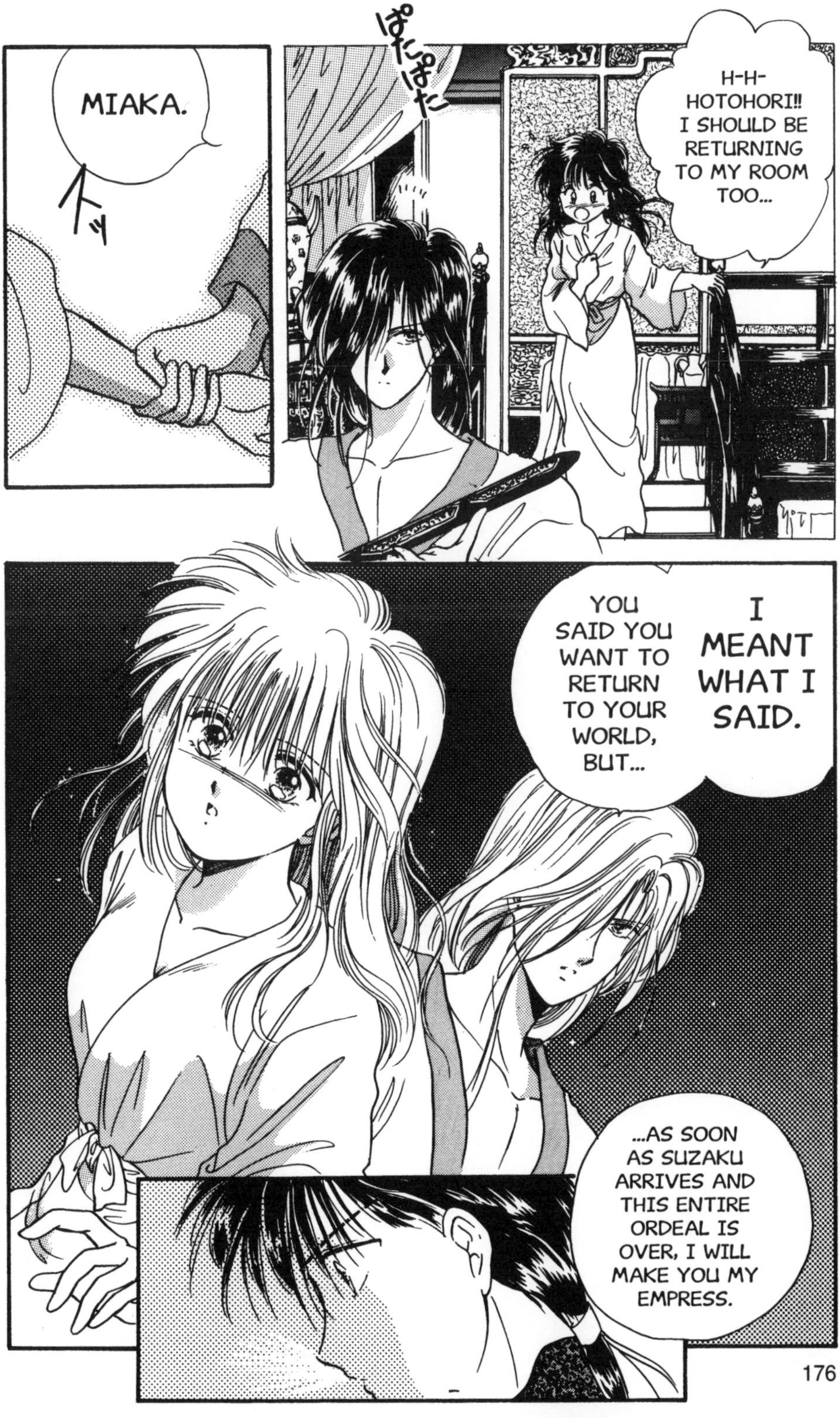
ぽたぽた
H-H-HOTOHORI!! I SHOULD BE RETURNING TO MY ROOM TOO...
MIAKA.
I MEANT WHAT I SAID.
YOU SAID YOU WANT TO RETURN TO YOUR WORLD, BUT...
...AS SOON AS SUZAKU ARRIVES AND THIS ENTIRE ORDEAL IS OVER, I WILL MAKE YOU MY EMPRESS.

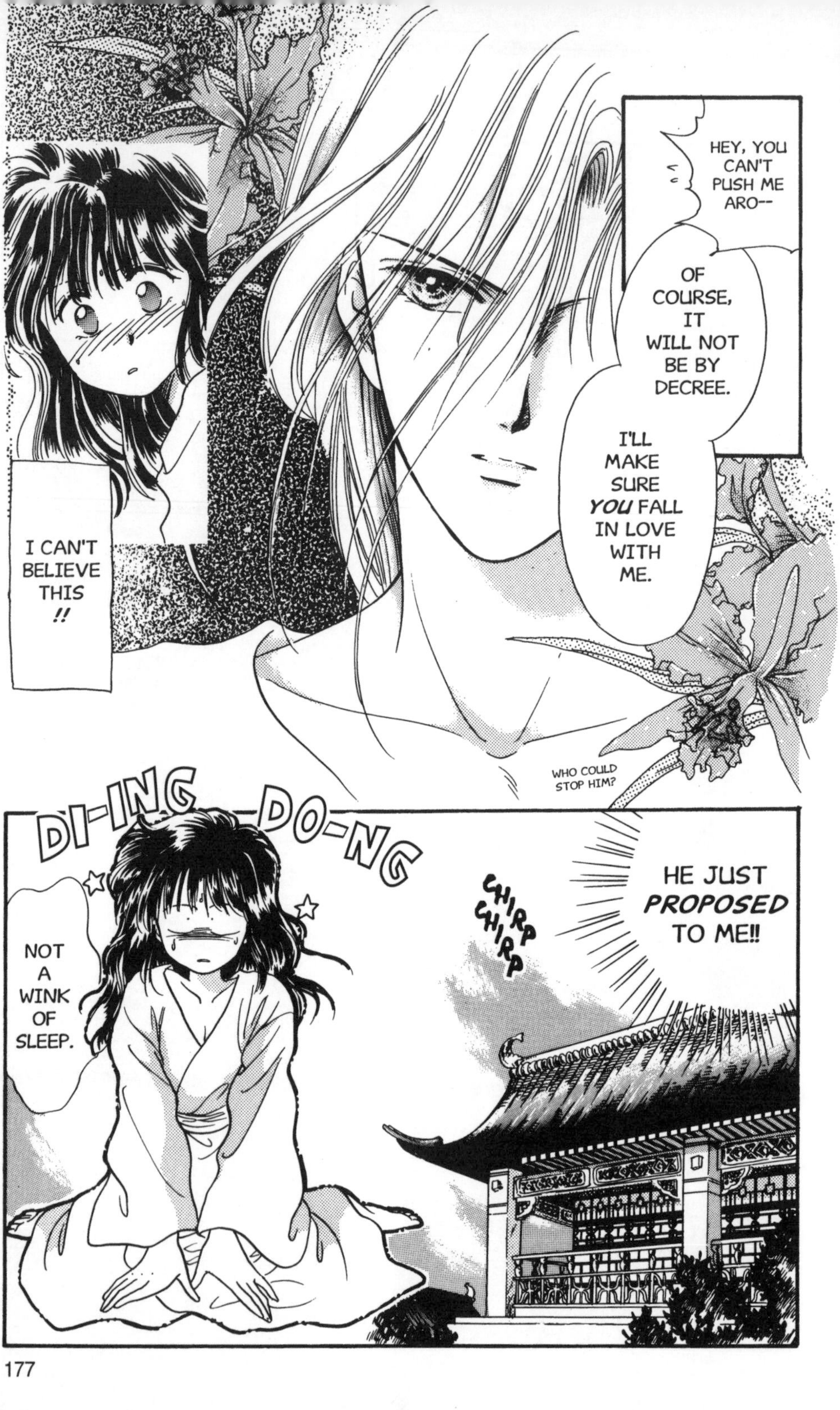
HEY, YOU CAN'T PUSH ME ARO--
OF COURSE, IT WILL NOT BE BY DECREE.
I'LL MAKE SURE *YOU* FALL IN LOVE WITH ME.
I CAN'T BELIEVE THIS!!
WHO COULD STOP HIM?
HE JUST *PROPOSED* TO ME!!
CHIRP CHIRP
DI-ING DO-NG
NOT A WINK OF SLEEP.

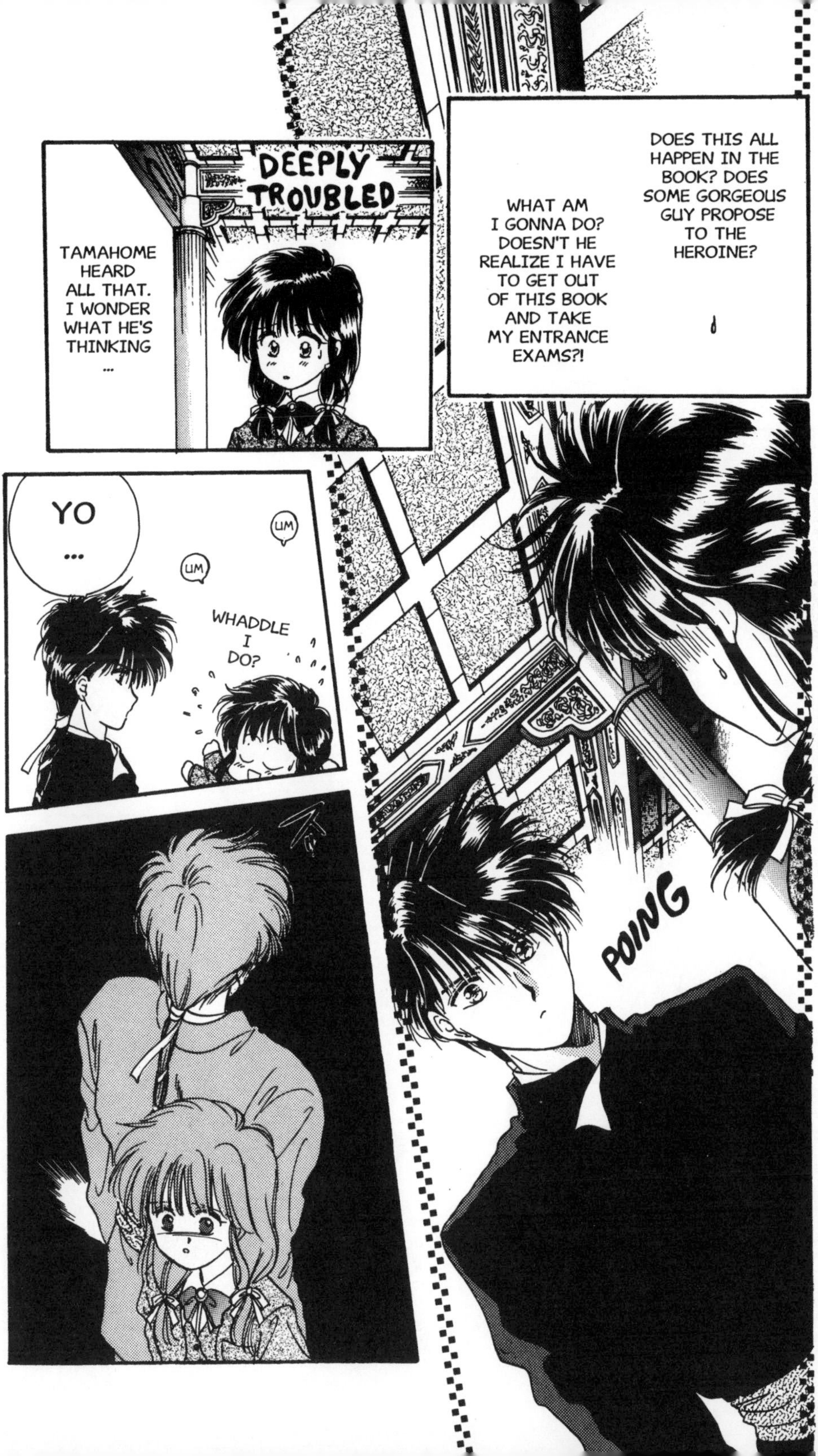
DOES THIS ALL HAPPEN IN THE BOOK? DOES SOME GORGEOUS GUY PROPOSE TO THE HEROINE?
WHAT AM I GONNA DO? DOESN'T HE REALIZE I HAVE TO GET OUT OF THIS BOOK AND TAKE MY ENTRANCE EXAMS?!
DEEPLY TROUBLED
TAMAHOME HEARD ALL THAT. I WONDER WHAT HE'S THINKING ...
POING
YO ...
UM
UM
WHADDLE I DO?

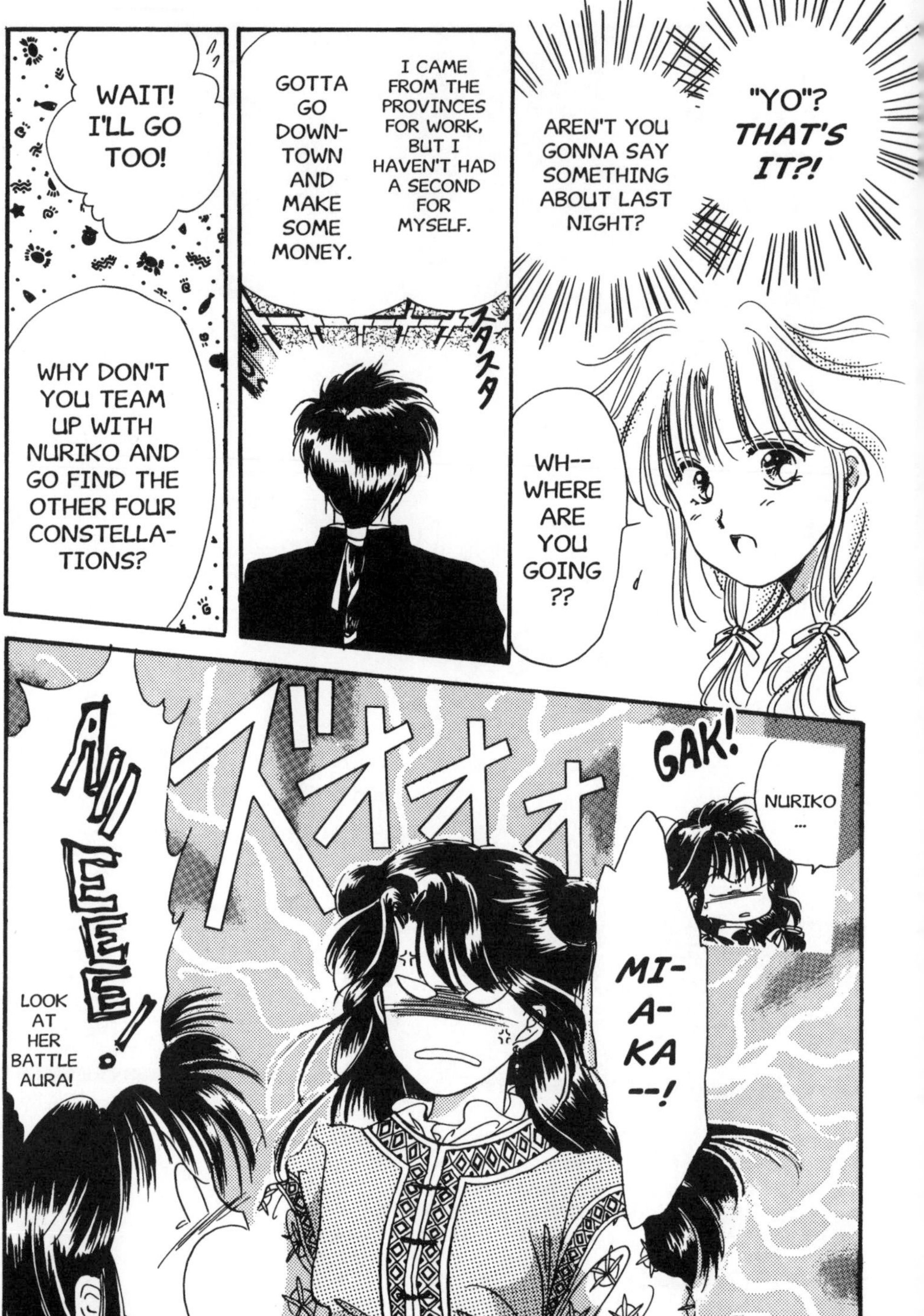
"YO"? THAT'S IT?!
AREN'T YOU GONNA SAY SOMETHING ABOUT LAST NIGHT?
WH-- WHERE ARE YOU GOING ??
I CAME FROM THE PROVINCES FOR WORK, BUT I HAVEN'T HAD A SECOND FOR MYSELF.
GOTTA GO DOWN-TOWN AND MAKE SOME MONEY.
スタスタ
WAIT! I'LL GO TOO!
WHY DON'T YOU TEAM UP WITH NURIKO AND GO FIND THE OTHER FOUR CONSTELLA-TIONS?
GAK!
NURIKO ...
MI-A-KA--!
ズオオオ
AIEEEE!
LOOK AT HER BATTLE AURA!

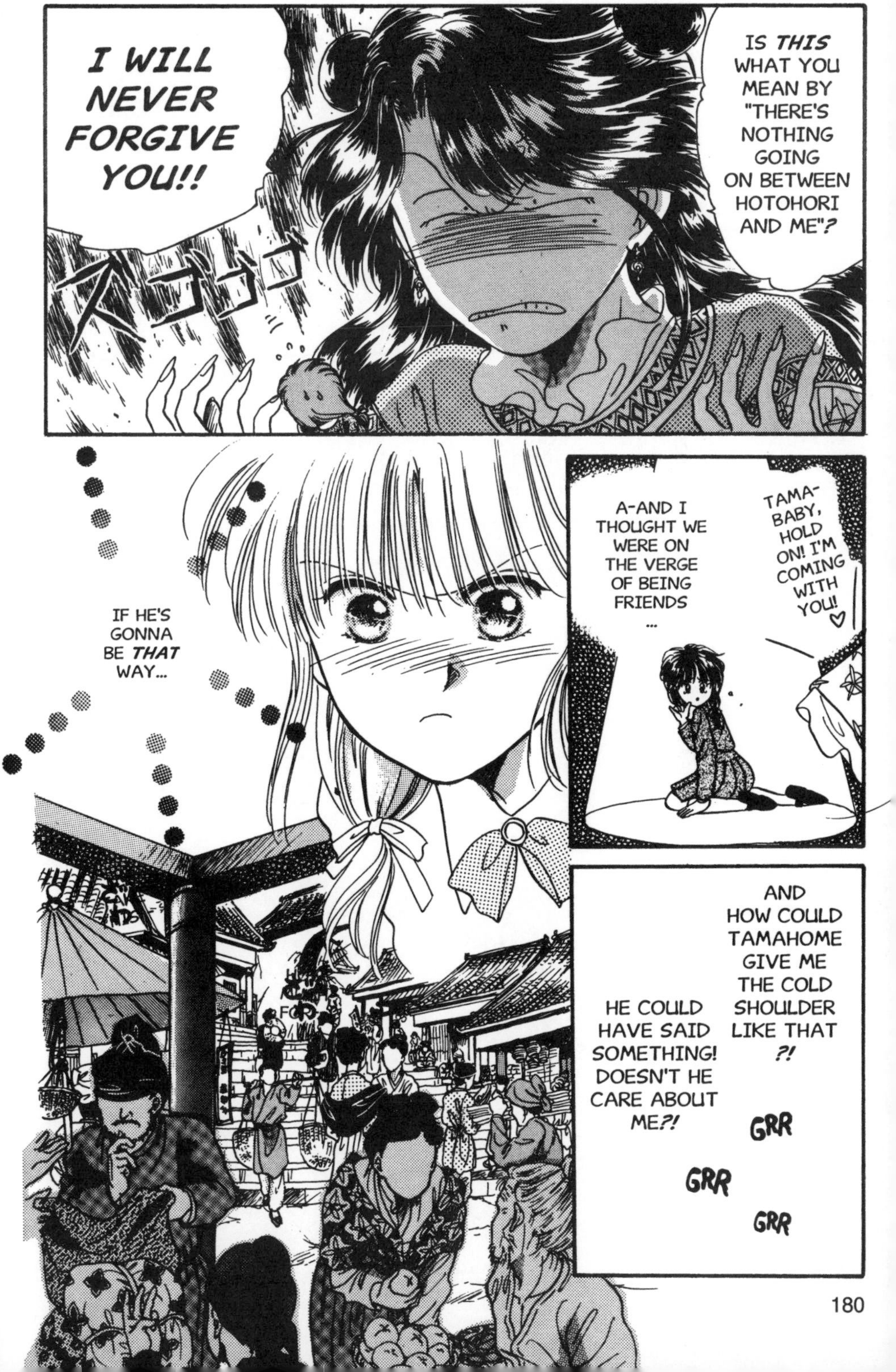
IS *THIS* WHAT YOU MEAN BY "THERE'S NOTHING GOING ON BETWEEN HOTOHORI AND ME"?
I WILL NEVER FORGIVE YOU!!
TAMA-BABY, HOLD ON! I'M COMING WITH YOU! ♡
A-AND I THOUGHT WE WERE ON THE VERGE OF BEING FRIENDS ...
AND HOW COULD TAMAHOME GIVE ME THE COLD SHOULDER LIKE THAT ?!
HE COULD HAVE SAID SOMETHING! DOESN'T HE CARE ABOUT ME?!
GRR
GRR
GRR
IF HE'S GONNA BE *THAT* WAY...

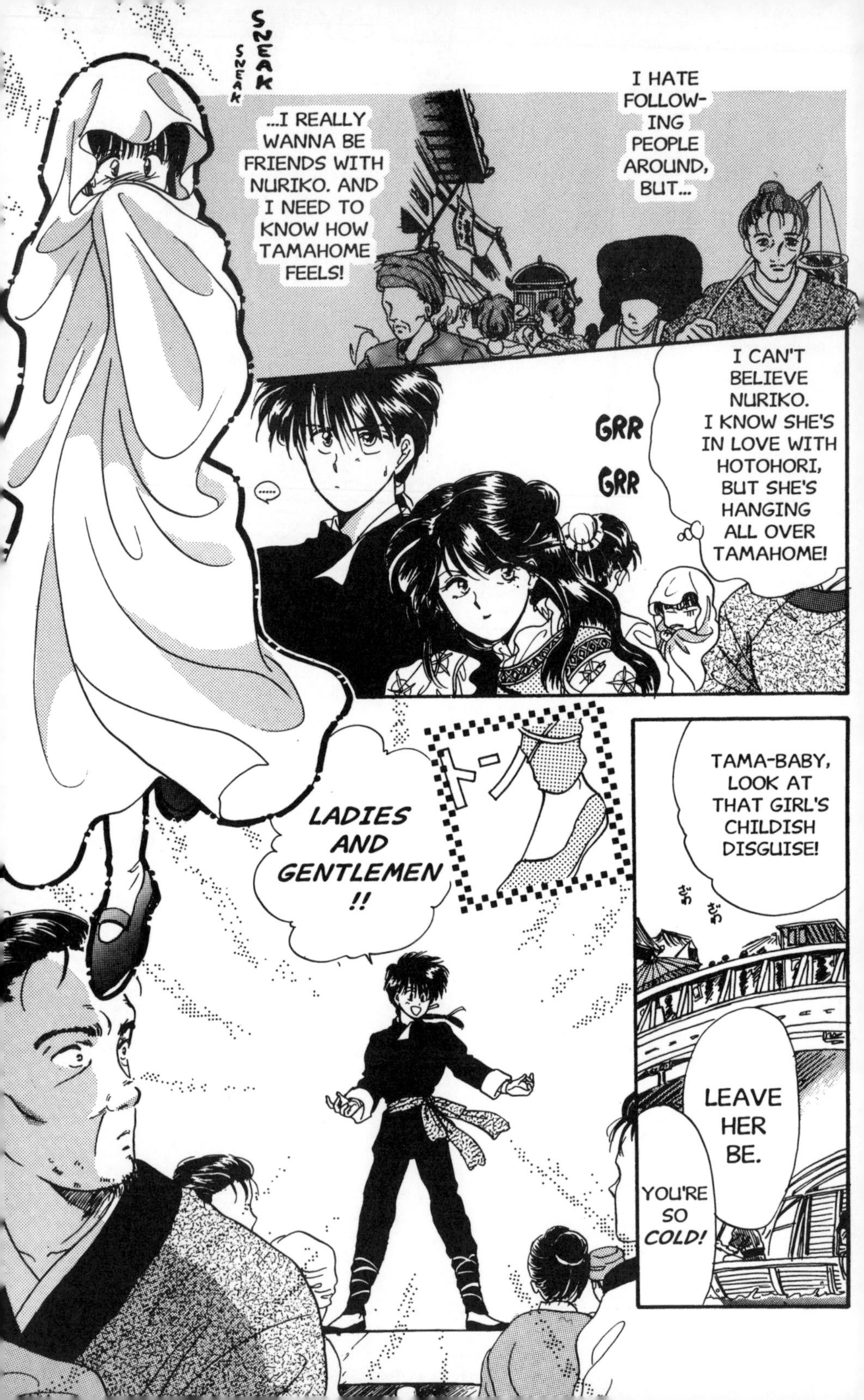
SNEAK SNEAK
I HATE FOLLOWING PEOPLE AROUND, BUT...
...I REALLY WANNA BE FRIENDS WITH NURIKO. AND I NEED TO KNOW HOW TAMAHOME FEELS!
I CAN'T BELIEVE NURIKO. I KNOW SHE'S IN LOVE WITH HOTOHORI, BUT SHE'S HANGING ALL OVER TAMAHOME!
GRR
GRR
......
TAMA-BABY, LOOK AT THAT GIRL'S CHILDISH DISGUISE!
ざわ ざわ
LEAVE HER BE.
YOU'RE SO *COLD!*
LADIES AND GENTLEMEN!!

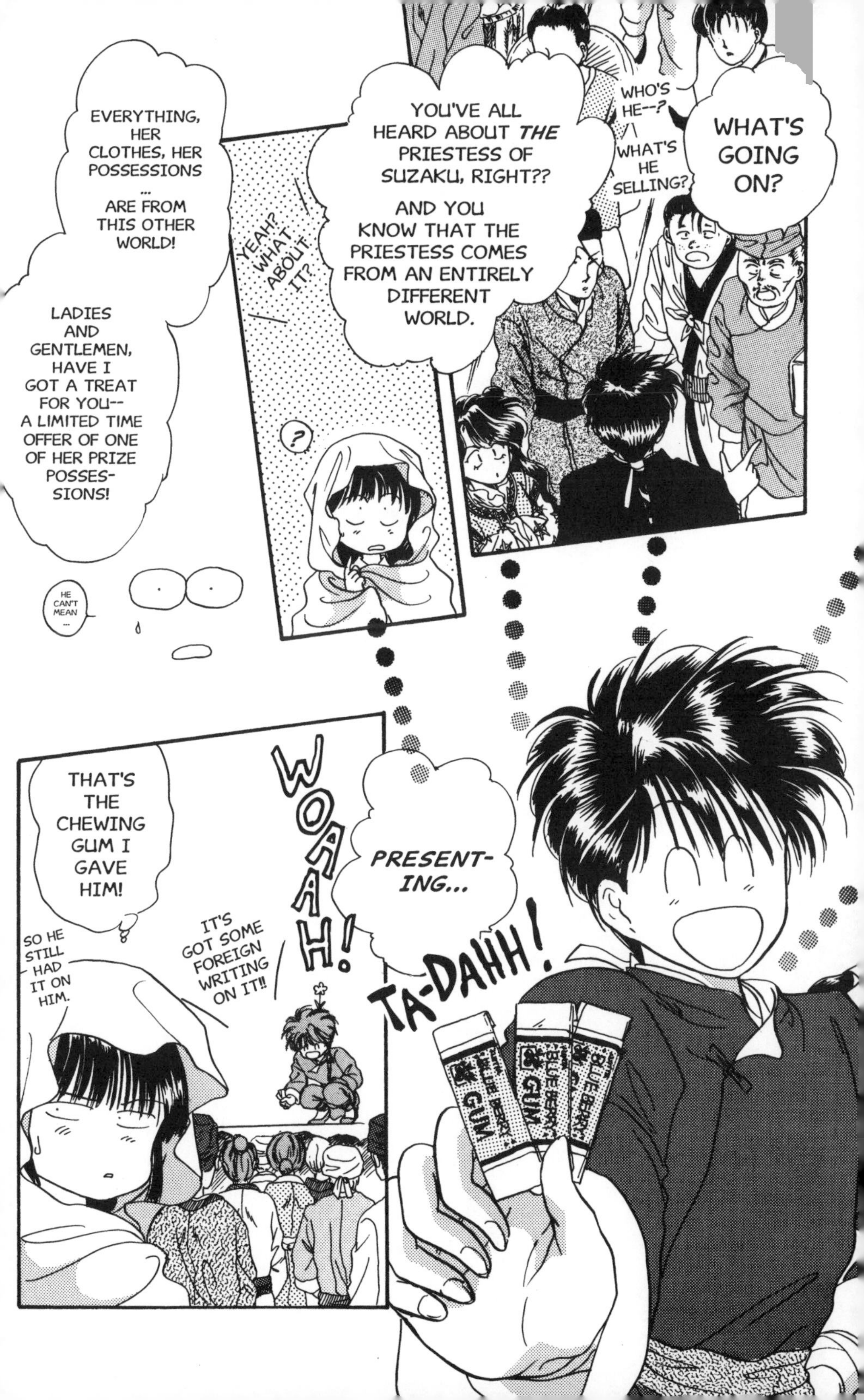
WHAT'S GOING ON?
WHO'S HE--?
WHAT'S HE SELLING?
YOU'VE ALL HEARD ABOUT *THE* PRIESTESS OF SUZAKU, RIGHT??
AND YOU KNOW THAT THE PRIESTESS COMES FROM AN ENTIRELY DIFFERENT WORLD.
YEAH? WHAT ABOUT IT?
?
EVERYTHING, HER CLOTHES, HER POSSESSIONS ... ARE FROM THIS OTHER WORLD!
LADIES AND GENTLEMEN, HAVE I GOT A TREAT FOR YOU-- A LIMITED TIME OFFER OF ONE OF HER PRIZE POSSES-SIONS!
HE CAN'T MEAN ...
PRESENT-ING...
TA-DAHH!
BLUE BERRY GUM
WOAAAH!
IT'S GOT SOME FOREIGN WRITING ON IT!!
THAT'S THE CHEWING GUM I GAVE HIM!
SO HE STILL HAD IT ON HIM.

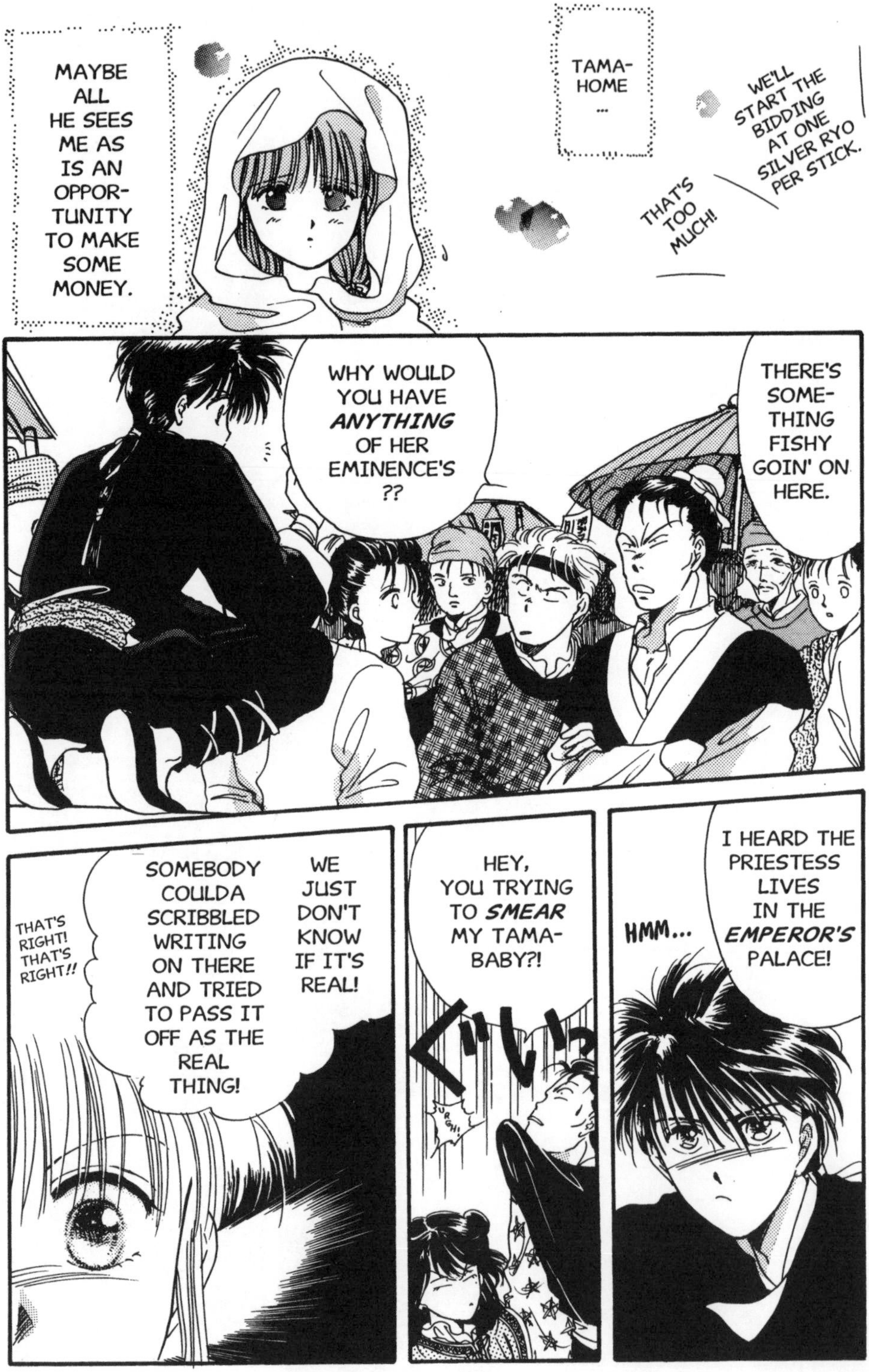
WE'LL START THE BIDDING AT ONE SILVER RYO PER STICK.
THAT'S TOO MUCH!
TAMA-HOME ...
MAYBE ALL HE SEES ME AS IS AN OPPORTUNITY TO MAKE SOME MONEY.
THERE'S SOMETHING FISHY GOIN' ON HERE.
WHY WOULD YOU HAVE *ANYTHING* OF HER EMINENCE'S??
I HEARD THE PRIESTESS LIVES IN THE *EMPEROR'S* PALACE!
HMM...
HEY, YOU TRYING TO *SMEAR* MY TAMA-BABY?!
ぐいっ
URGH!
WE JUST DON'T KNOW IF IT'S REAL!
SOMEBODY COULDA SCRIBBLED WRITING ON THERE AND TRIED TO PASS IT OFF AS THE REAL THING!
THAT'S RIGHT! THAT'S RIGHT!!

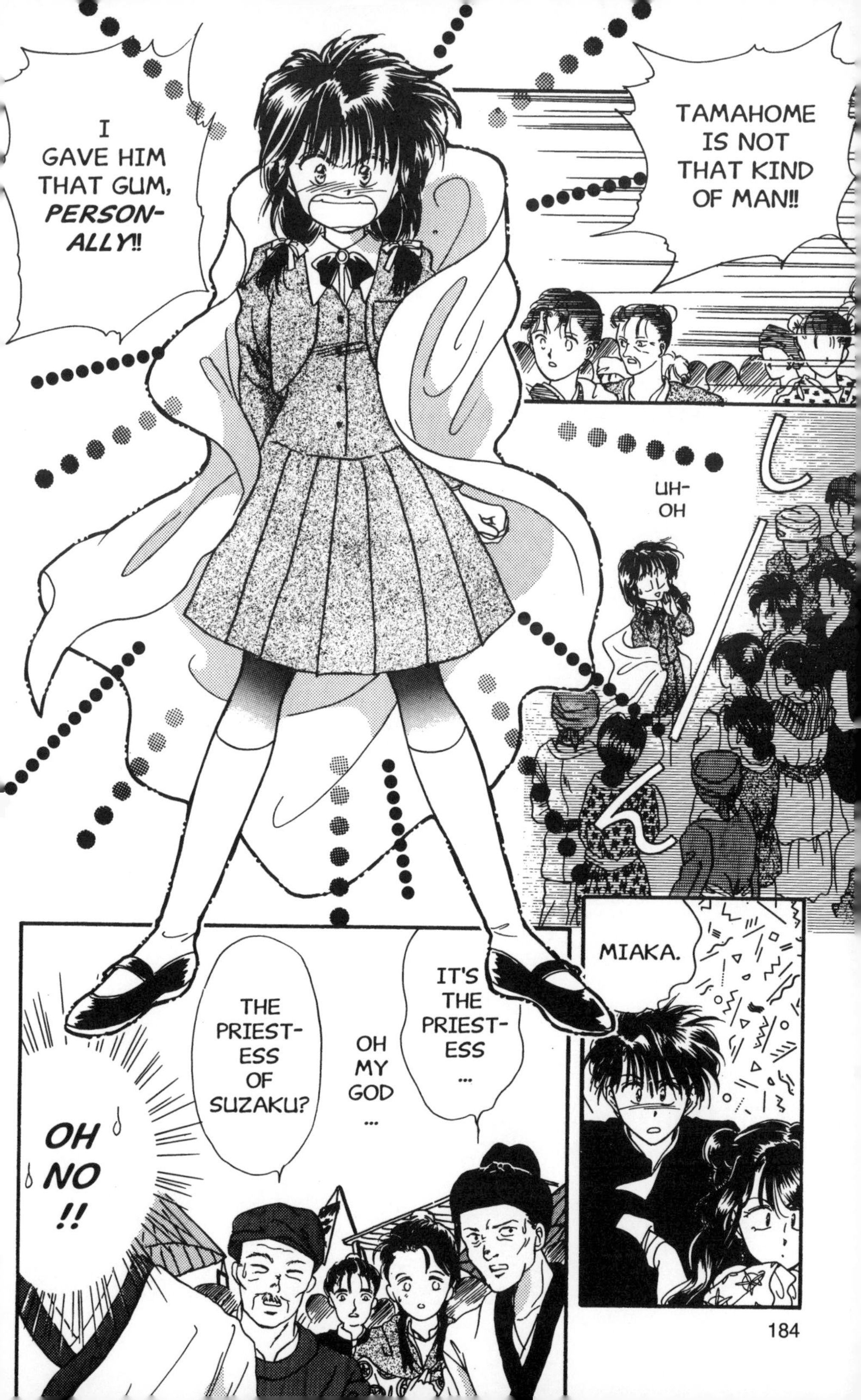
TAMAHOME IS NOT THAT KIND OF MAN!!
UH-OH
I GAVE HIM THAT GUM, *PERSONALLY*!!
MIAKA.
IT'S THE PRIEST-ESS ...
OH MY GOD ...
THE PRIEST-ESS OF SUZAKU?
OH NO !!

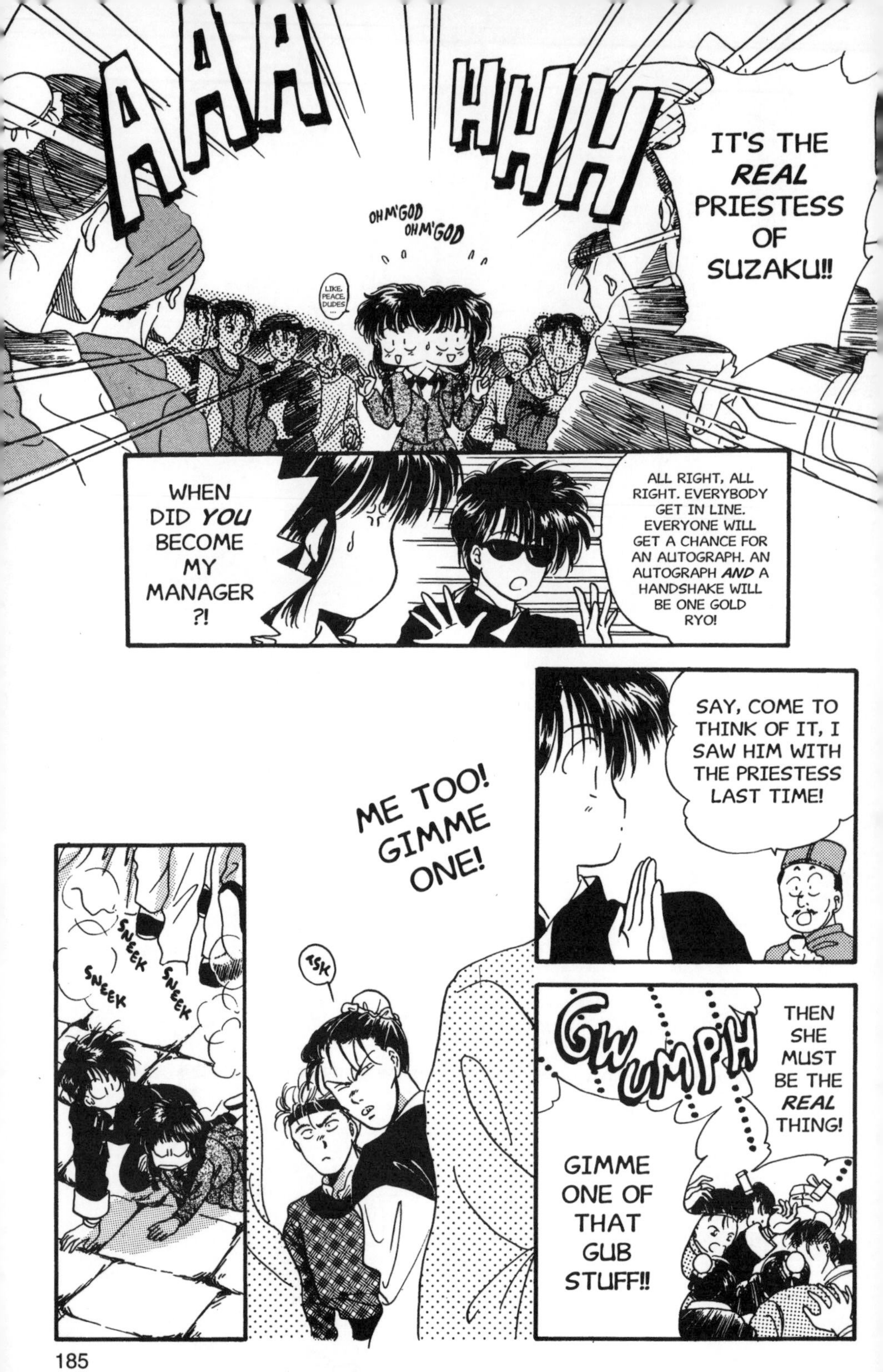
IT'S THE *REAL* PRIESTESS OF SUZAKU!!
AAAHHH
OHM'GOD OHM'GOD
LIKE, PEACE, DUDES...
ALL RIGHT, ALL RIGHT. EVERYBODY GET IN LINE. EVERYONE WILL GET A CHANCE FOR AN AUTOGRAPH. AN AUTOGRAPH *AND* A HANDSHAKE WILL BE ONE GOLD RYO!
WHEN DID *YOU* BECOME MY MANAGER ?!
SAY, COME TO THINK OF IT, I SAW HIM WITH THE PRIESTESS LAST TIME!
ME TOO! GIMME ONE!
THEN SHE MUST BE THE *REAL* THING!
GWUMPH
GIMME ONE OF THAT GUB STUFF!!
TSK
SNEEK
SNEEK
SNEEK

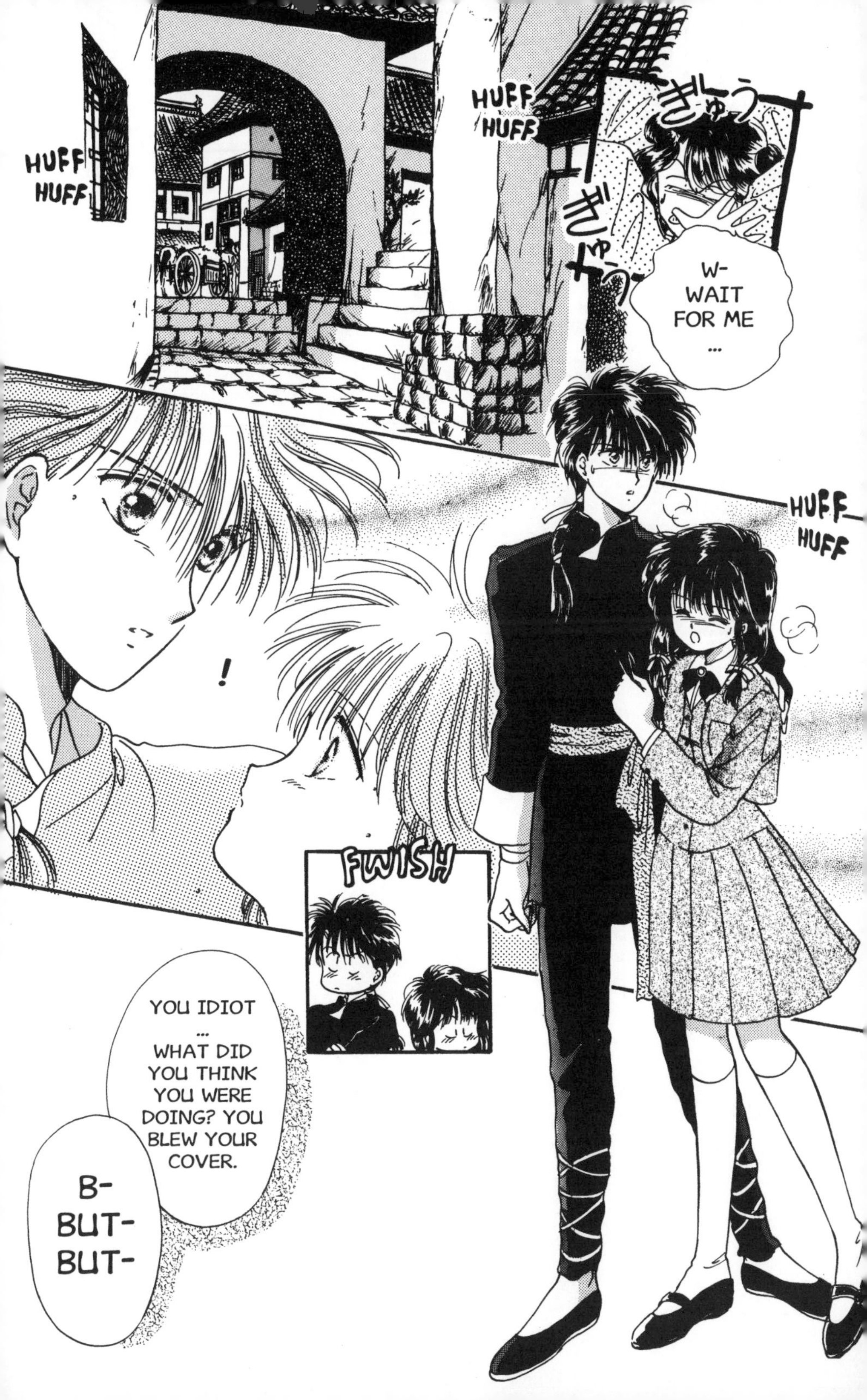
HUFF HUFF
ぎゅう
ぎゅう
W- WAIT FOR ME ...
HUFF HUFF
HUFF HUFF
FWISH
!
YOU IDIOT ... WHAT DID YOU THINK YOU WERE DOING? YOU BLEW YOUR COVER.
B- BUT- BUT-

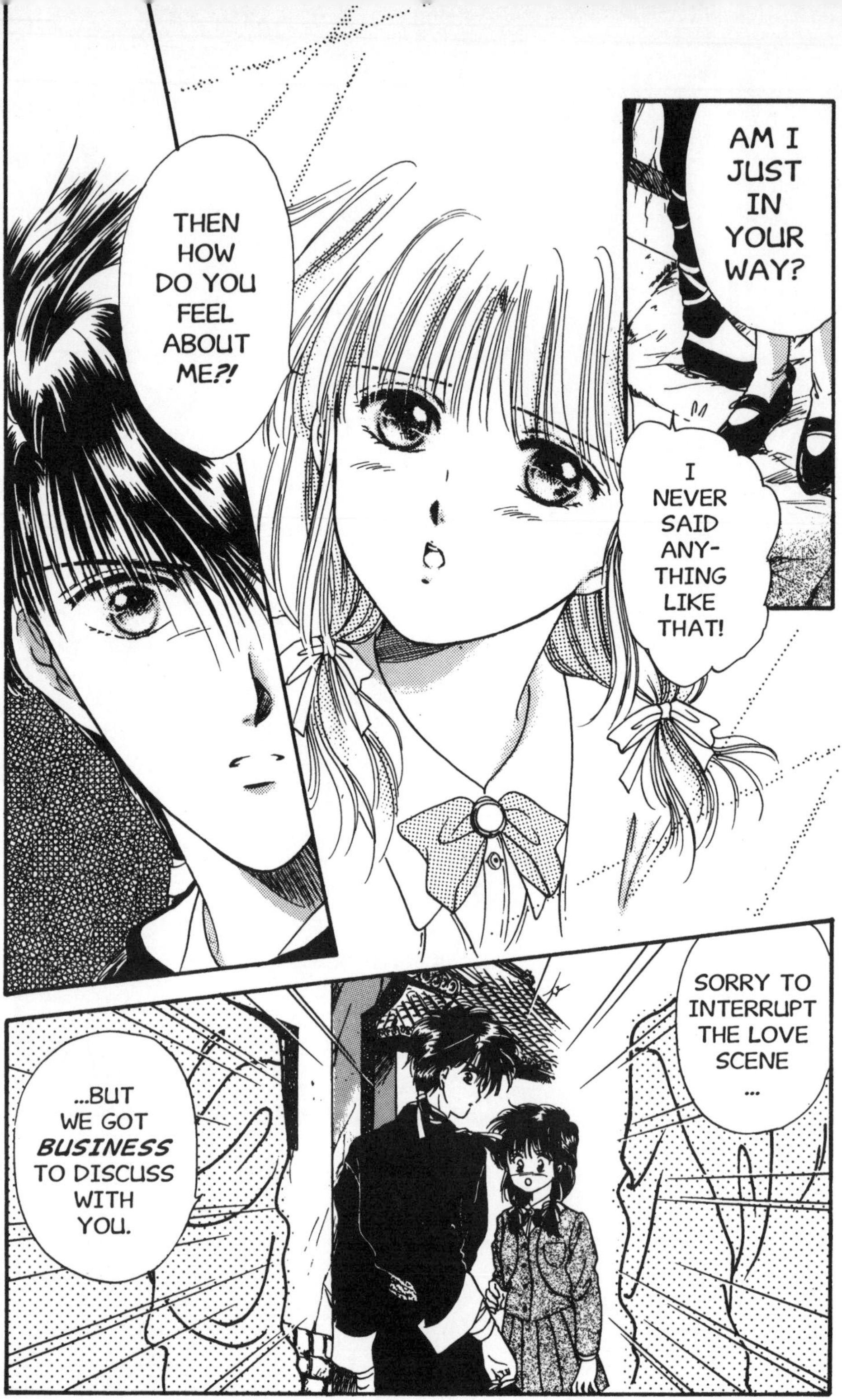
AM I JUST IN YOUR WAY?
I NEVER SAID ANY-THING LIKE THAT!
THEN HOW DO YOU FEEL ABOUT ME?!
SORRY TO INTERRUPT THE LOVE SCENE ...
...BUT WE GOT ***BUSINESS*** TO DISCUSS WITH YOU.

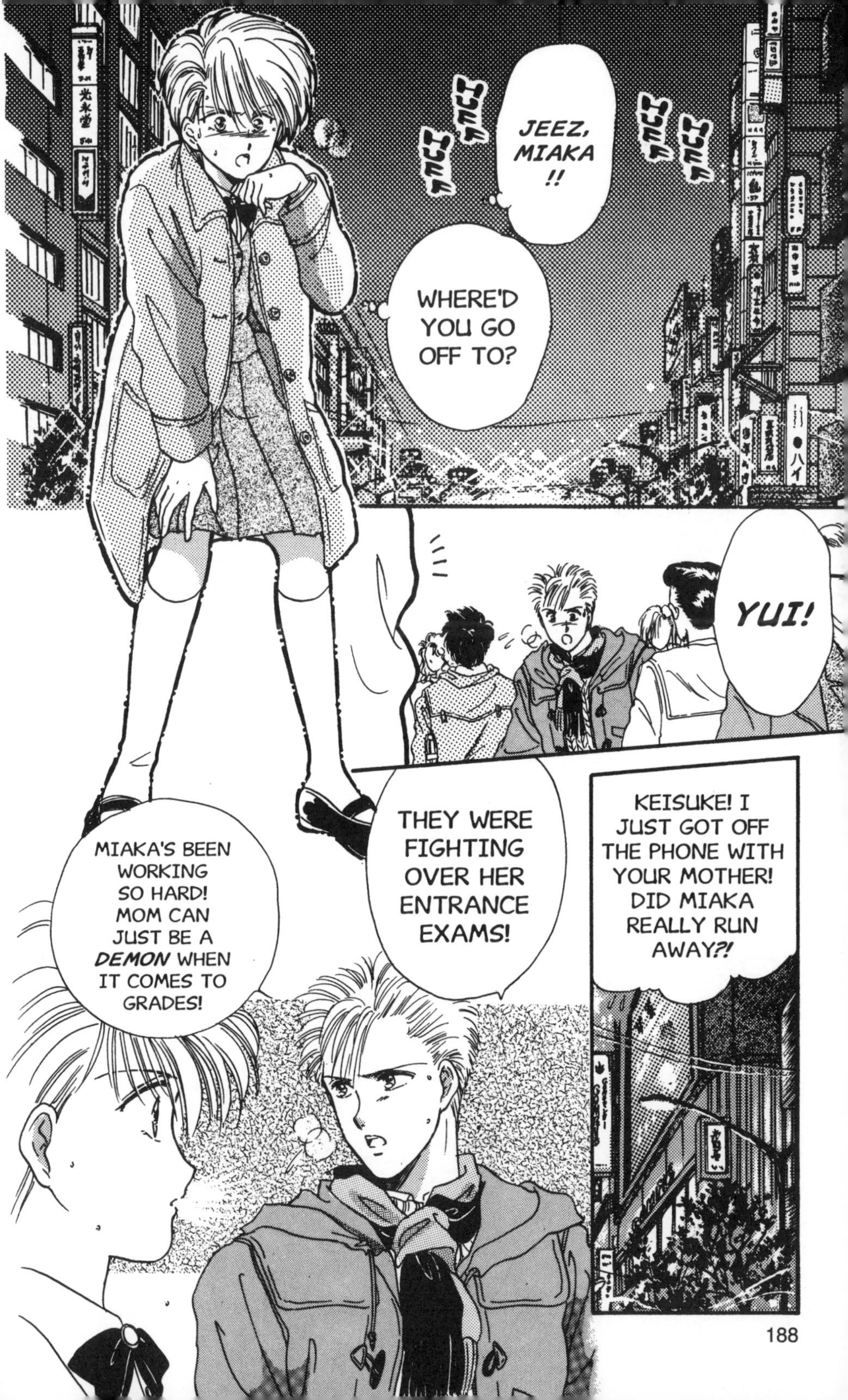
HUFF HUFF
JEEZ, MIAKA!!
HUFF HUFF
WHERE'D YOU GO OFF TO?
YUI!
KEISUKE! I JUST GOT OFF THE PHONE WITH YOUR MOTHER! DID MIAKA REALLY RUN AWAY?!
THEY WERE FIGHTING OVER HER ENTRANCE EXAMS!
MIAKA'S BEEN WORKING SO HARD! MOM CAN JUST BE A *DEMON* WHEN IT COMES TO GRADES!

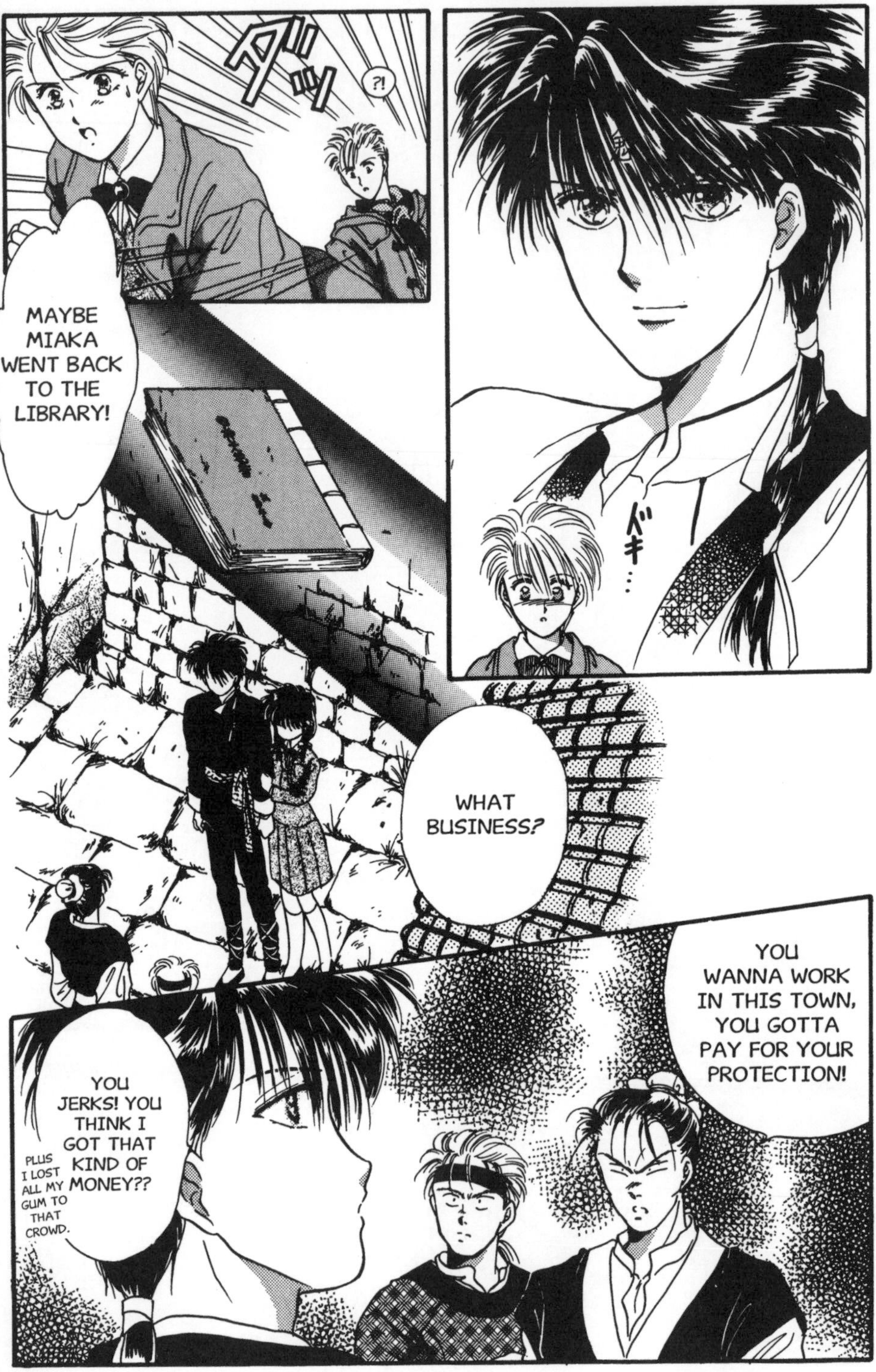
ドキ…
?!
MAYBE MIAKA WENT BACK TO THE LIBRARY!
WHAT BUSINESS?
YOU WANNA WORK IN THIS TOWN, YOU GOTTA PAY FOR YOUR PROTECTION!
YOU JERKS! YOU THINK I GOT THAT KIND OF MONEY??
PLUS I LOST ALL MY GUM TO THAT CROWD.

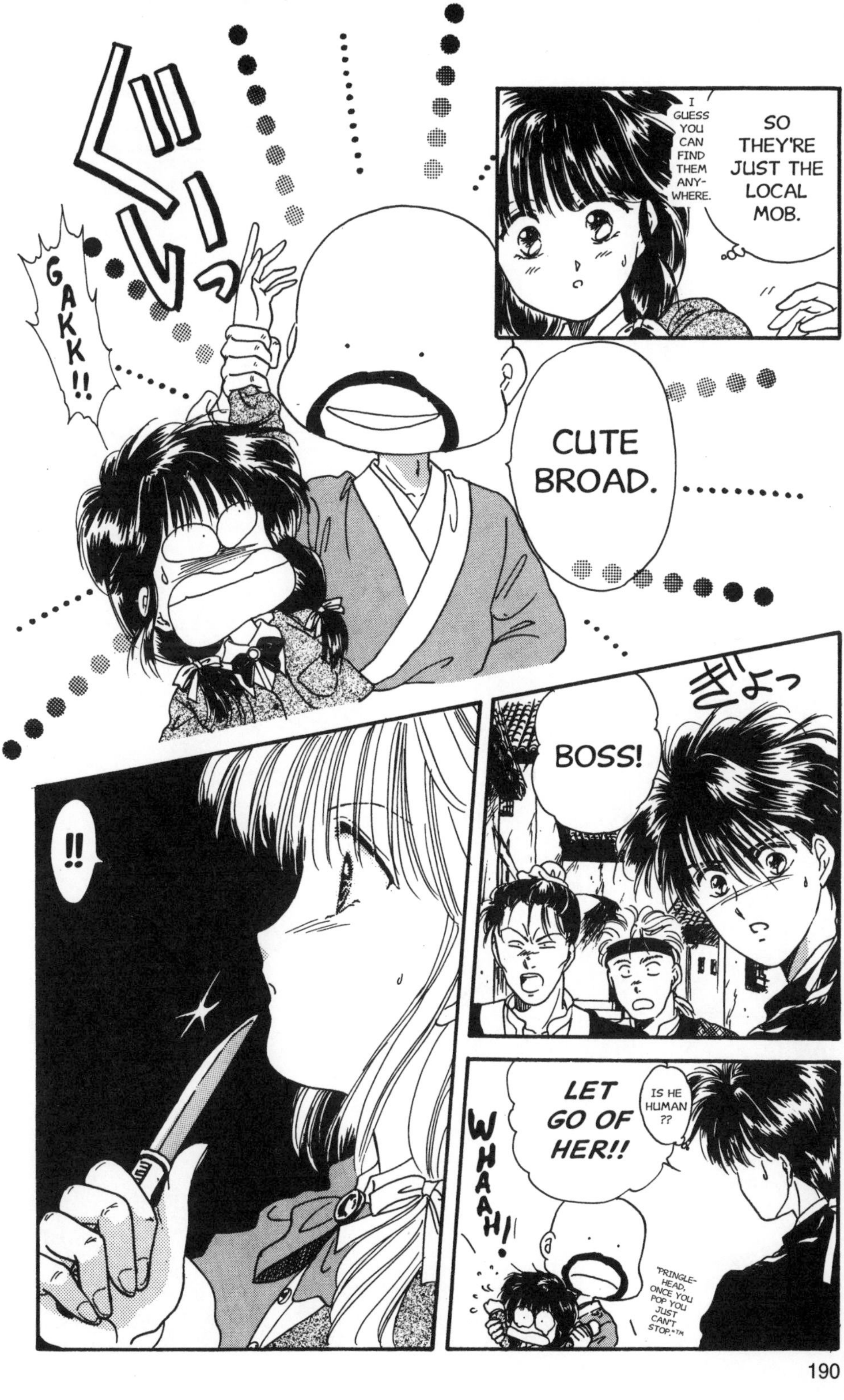
SO THEY'RE JUST THE LOCAL MOB.
I GUESS YOU CAN FIND THEM ANY-WHERE.
ぐいーっ
CUTE BROAD.
GAKK!!
ぎょっ
BOSS!
LET GO OF HER!!
IS HE HUMAN??
WHAAAH!
"PRINGLE-HEAD, ONCE YOU POP YOU JUST CAN'T STOP."™
!!

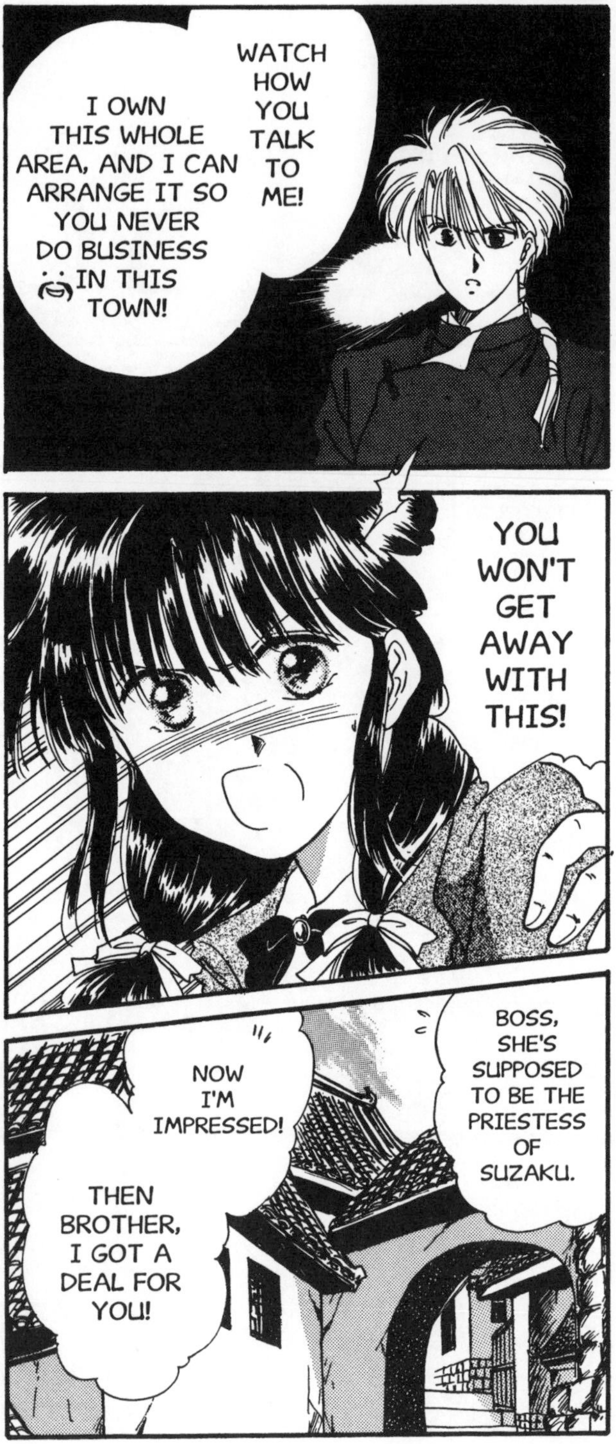
WATCH HOW YOU TALK TO ME!
I OWN THIS WHOLE AREA, AND I CAN ARRANGE IT SO YOU NEVER DO BUSINESS IN THIS TOWN!
YOU WON'T GET AWAY WITH THIS!
BOSS, SHE'S SUPPOSED TO BE THE PRIESTESS OF SUZAKU.
NOW I'M IMPRESSED!
THEN BROTHER, I GOT A DEAL FOR YOU!

Oops, my handwriting's getting sloppy again. Now here's something that caught me by surprise! I never thought you guys would like Tamahome with long hair!! When Tamahome's hair was trimmed shorter in this chapter, the complaints came rushing in! I thought you'd prefer short hair, but boy was I wrong!! Tama's action scenes are hard to draw with his long hair. Don't worry, I'll never cut Hotohori's hair. (My assistants and I call him "Ho-ri".) Apparently the fans are divided between the Tamahome faction and Hotohori faction. I would never have believed your average junior high (and elementary) school student would be into Hotohori. Surprise! Which one will Miaka choose? I really can't portray a girl who can't decide on the guy she's in love with. I like a girl who's got her mind set on one guy. ♥♥ To say you like both guys equally only means that you aren't really in love with either of them. Although she herself might not even be aware of it. Well, let's not be too judgmental here.

I know I've said that I don't want any official fan club, but there are still people who want to join! Hmm, some people insisted on forming their own club and asked me how to let the entire country know about it. I got an idea! I'll print your address right here so everybody can see it! What do you think??

TA-DAHH.

Just kidding. You'd be so flooded with applications that you'd have a heart attack! (I'm not really that popular, though). Anyway, for your sake I won't mention it. Now, I heard there're people making their own *Fushigi Yûgi* dojinshi manga. That's okay, but be sure you send them to me too, okay? I'll be waiting to see them.♥

Until we meet again.

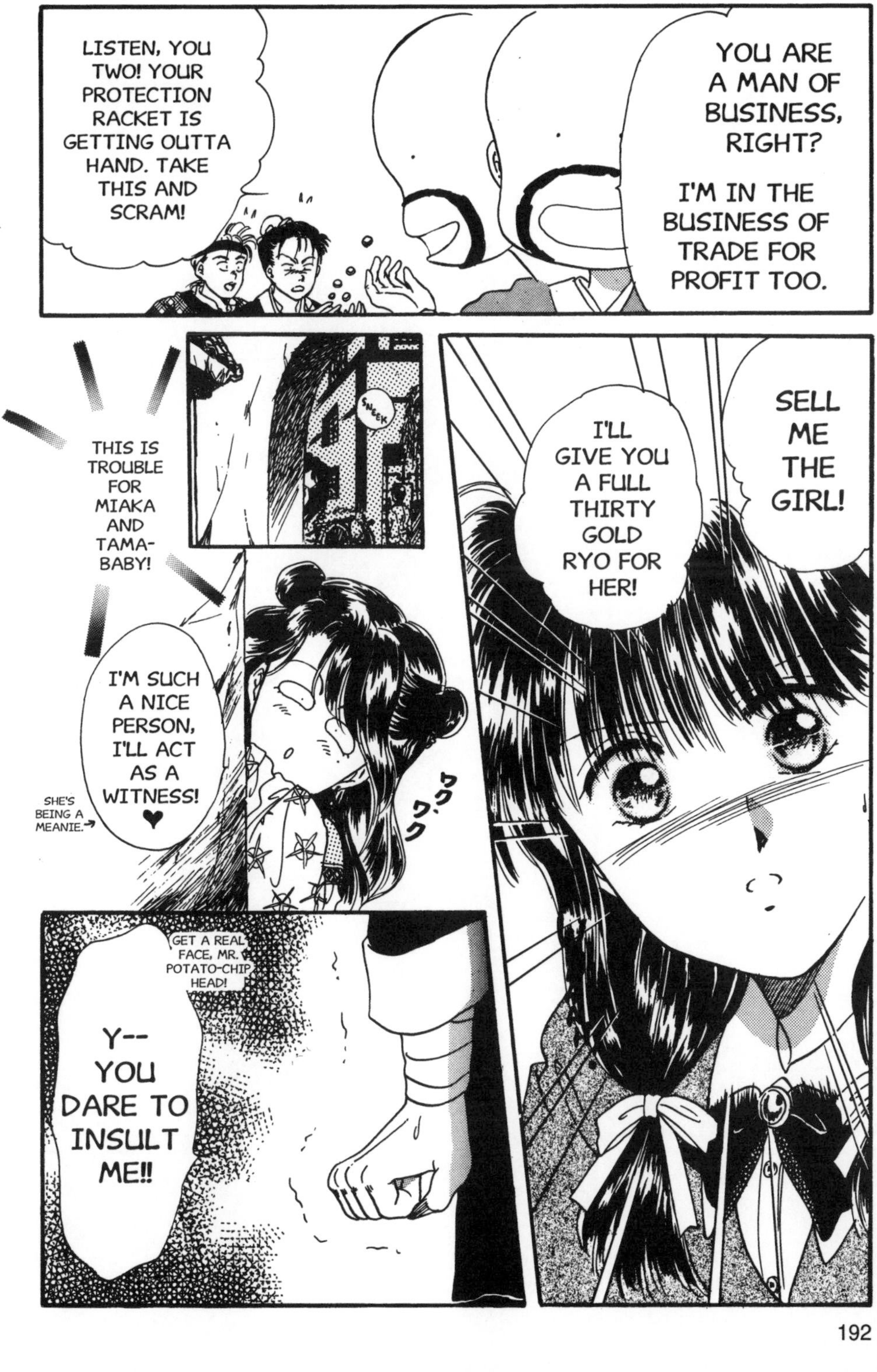
YOU ARE A MAN OF BUSINESS, RIGHT?
I'M IN THE BUSINESS OF TRADE FOR PROFIT TOO.
LISTEN, YOU TWO! YOUR PROTECTION RACKET IS GETTING OUTTA HAND. TAKE THIS AND SCRAM!
SELL ME THE GIRL!
I'LL GIVE YOU A FULL THIRTY GOLD RYO FOR HER!
SNEEK
THIS IS TROUBLE FOR MIAKA AND TAMA-BABY!
I'M SUCH A NICE PERSON, I'LL ACT AS A WITNESS! ❤
SHE'S BEING A MEANIE.
GET A REAL FACE, MR. POTATO-CHIP HEAD!
Y-- YOU DARE TO INSULT ME!!

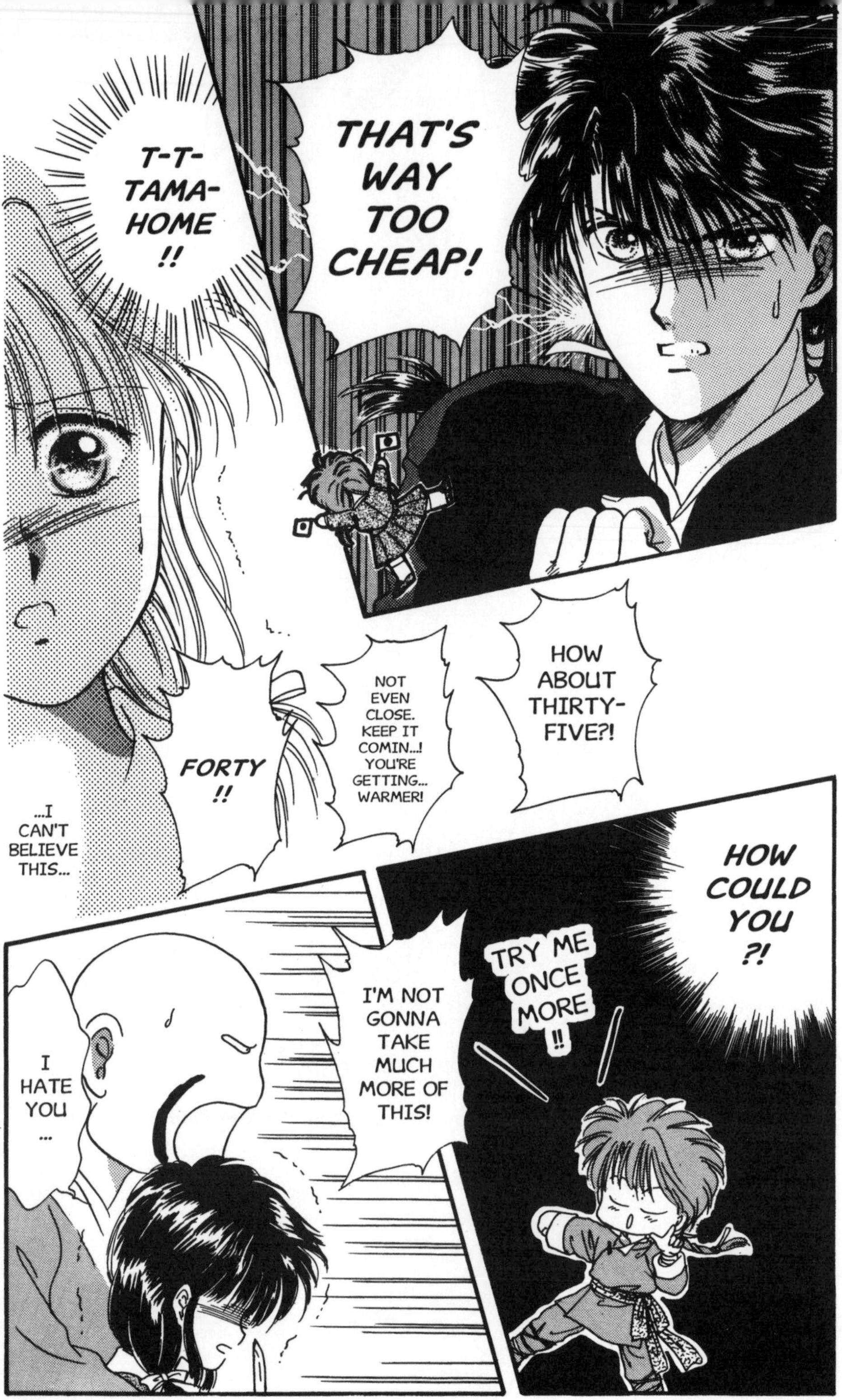
THAT'S WAY TOO CHEAP!
T-T-TAMA-HOME !!
HOW ABOUT THIRTY-FIVE?!
NOT EVEN CLOSE. KEEP IT COMIN...! YOU'RE GETTING... WARMER!
FORTY !!
...I CAN'T BELIEVE THIS...
HOW COULD YOU ?!
TRY ME ONCE MORE !!
I'M NOT GONNA TAKE MUCH MORE OF THIS!
I HATE YOU ...

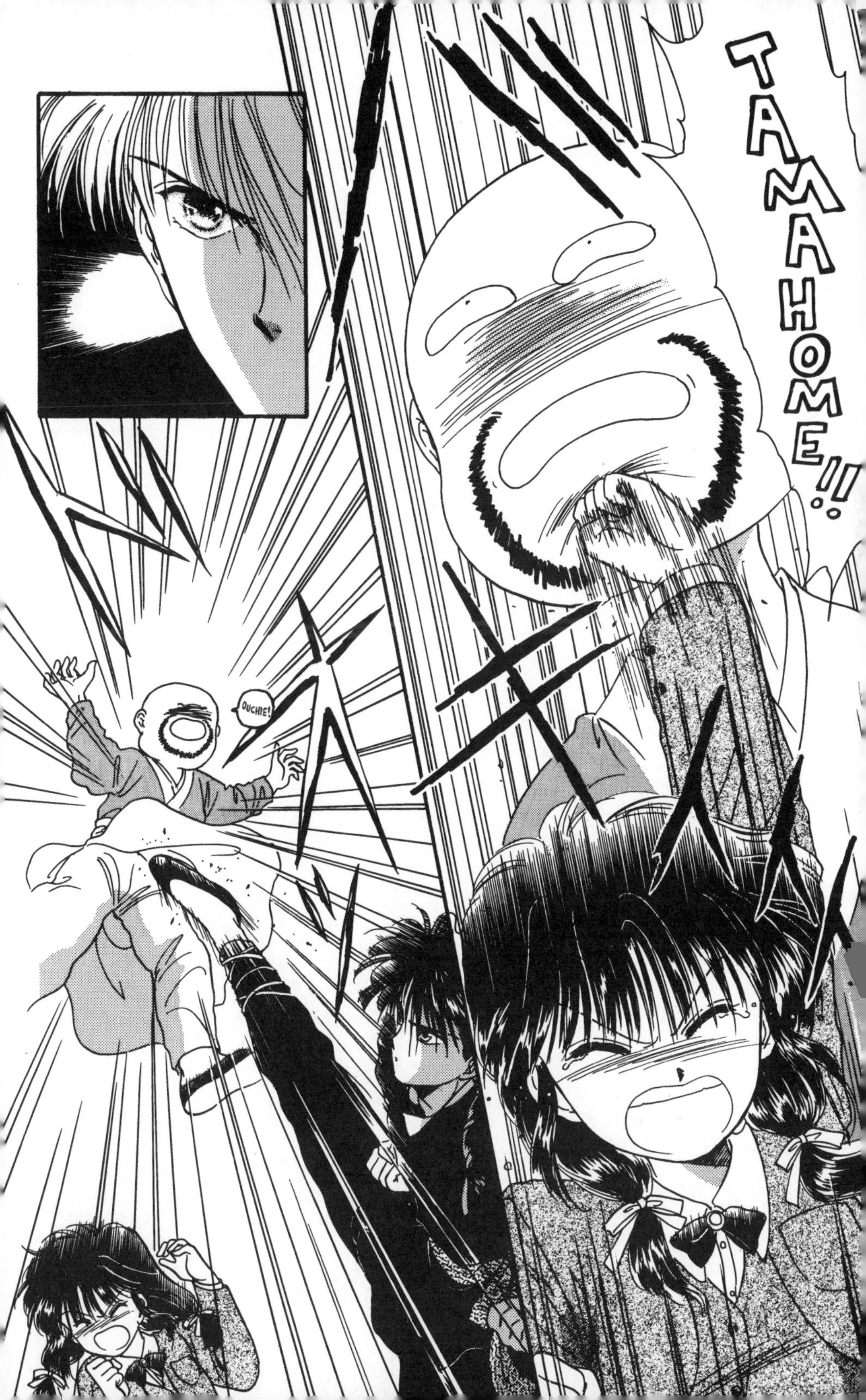
TAMAHOME!!
OUCHIE!

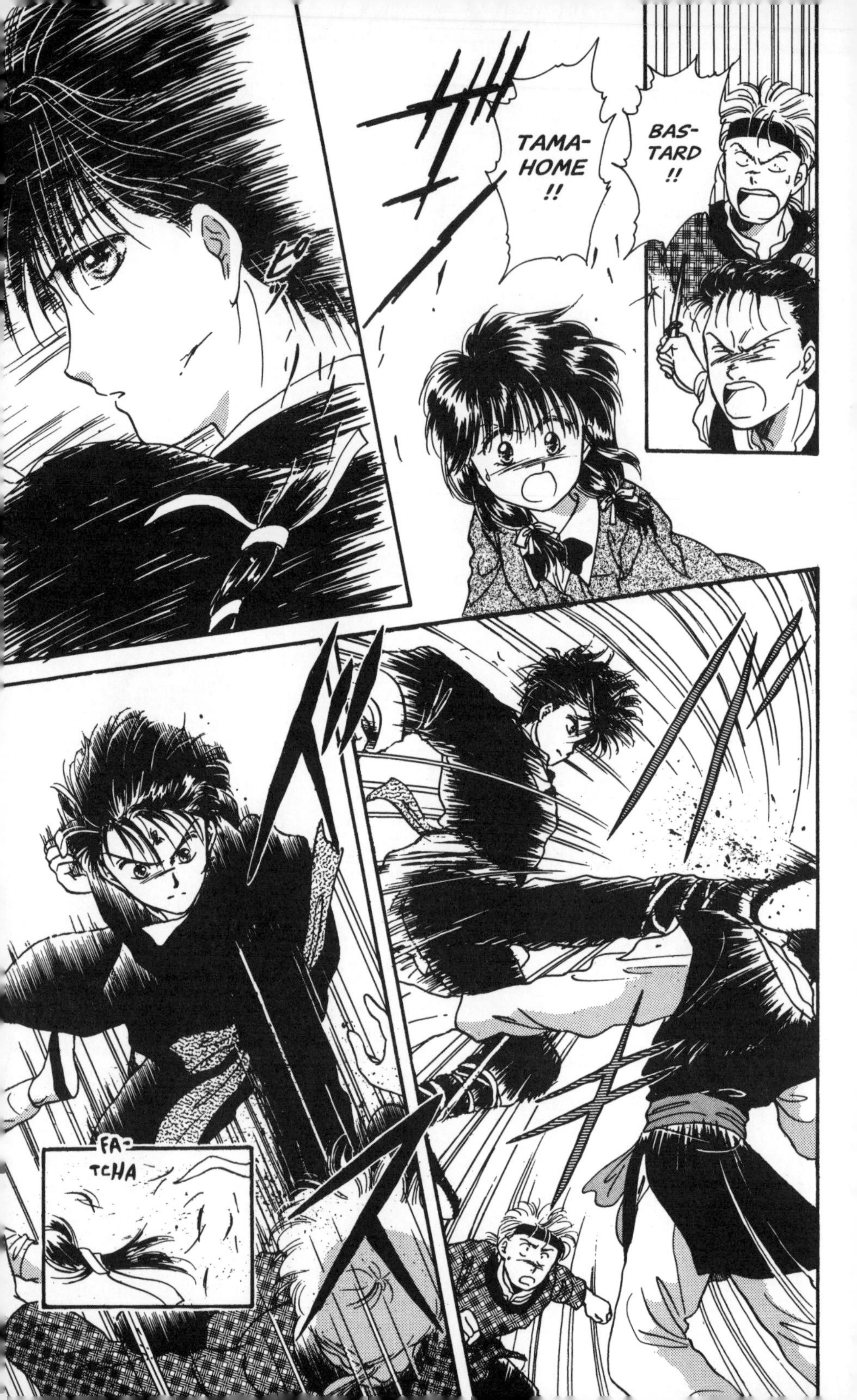
BAS-TARD!!
TAMA-HOME!!
FA-TCHA

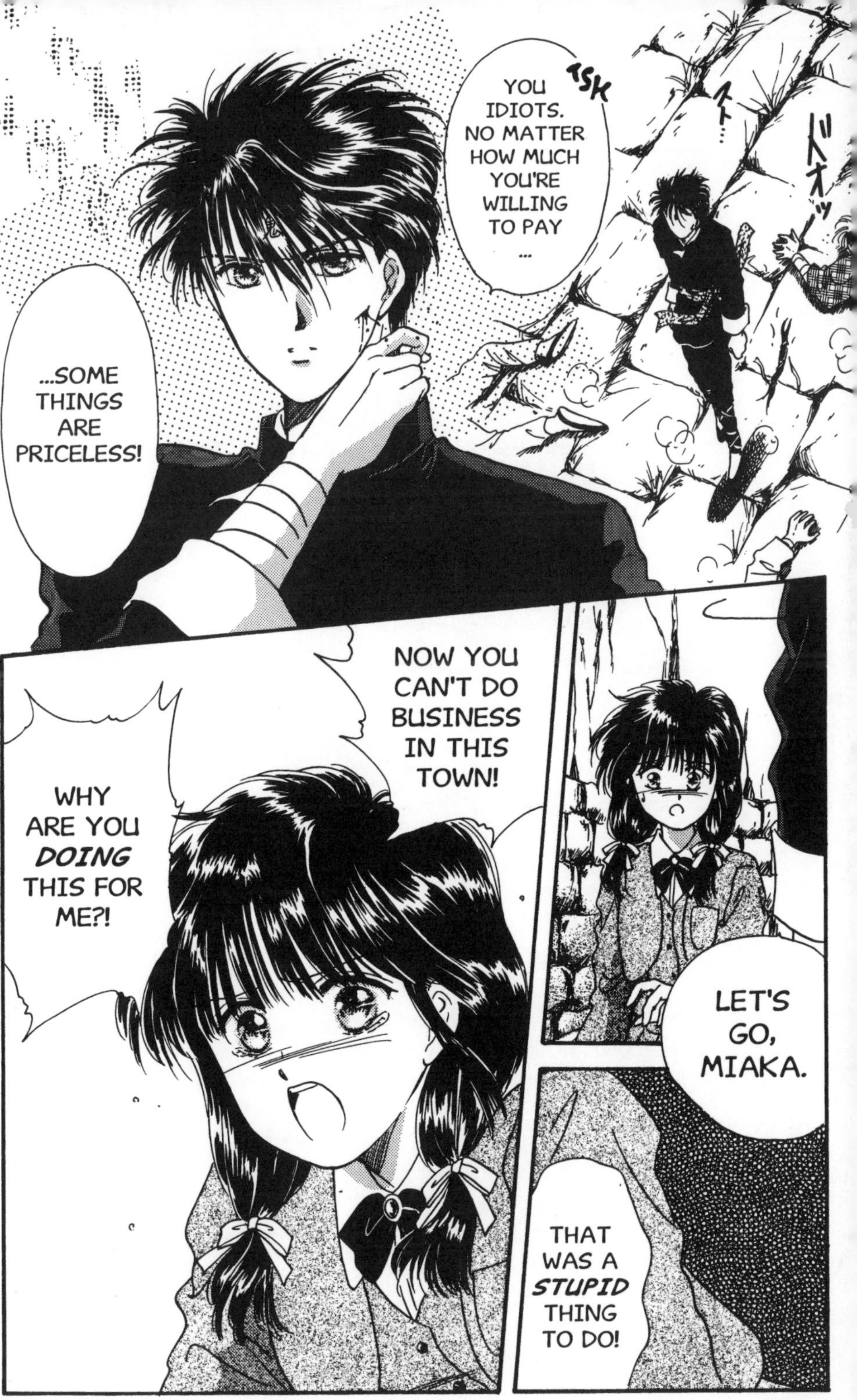
TSK
YOU IDIOTS. NO MATTER HOW MUCH YOU'RE WILLING TO PAY ...
ドオッ
...SOME THINGS ARE PRICELESS!
LET'S GO, MIAKA.
THAT WAS A *STUPID* THING TO DO!
NOW YOU CAN'T DO BUSINESS IN THIS TOWN!
WHY ARE YOU *DOING* THIS FOR ME?!

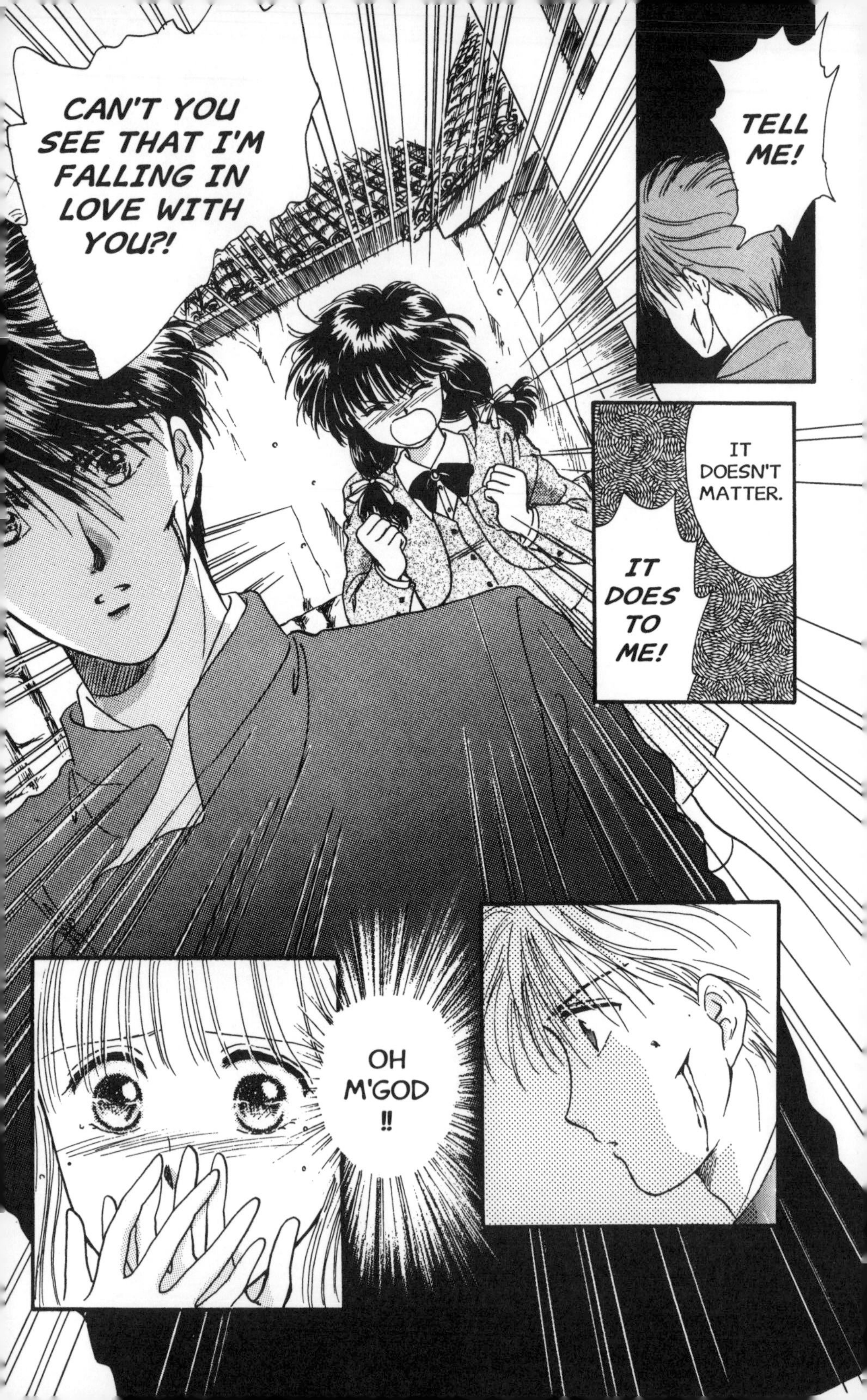
TELL ME!
IT DOESN'T MATTER.
IT DOES TO ME!
CAN'T YOU SEE THAT I'M FALLING IN LOVE WITH YOU?!
OH M'GOD !!

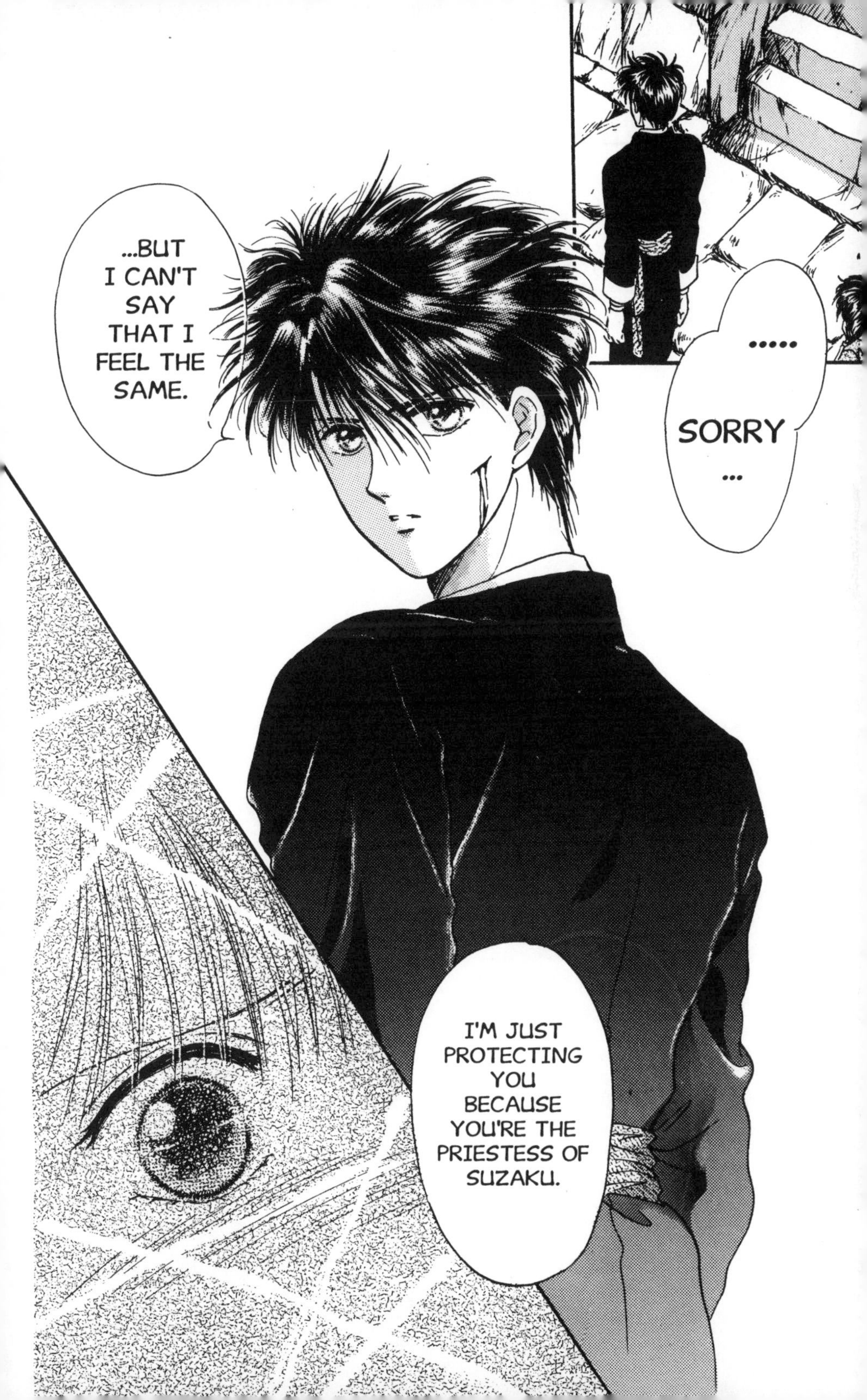
.....
SORRY ...
...BUT I CAN'T SAY THAT I FEEL THE SAME.
I'M JUST PROTECTING YOU BECAUSE YOU'RE THE PRIESTESS OF SUZAKU.

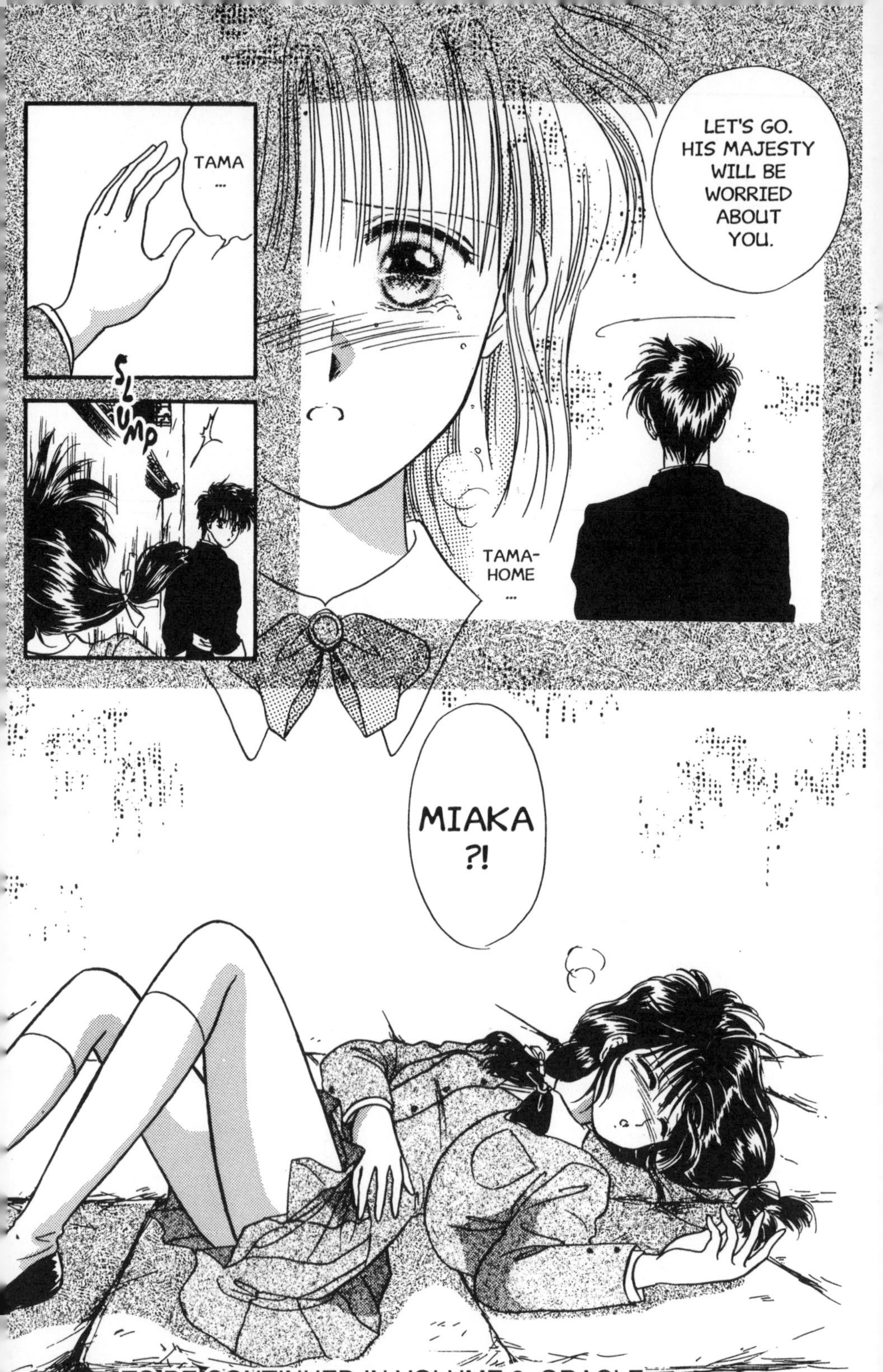
LET'S GO. HIS MAJESTY WILL BE WORRIED ABOUT YOU.
TAMA-HOME ...
TAMA ...
SLUMP
MIAKA ?!
TO BE CONTINUED IN VOLUME 2: ORACLE

FUSHIGI YÛGI

Volume 2: **Oracle**

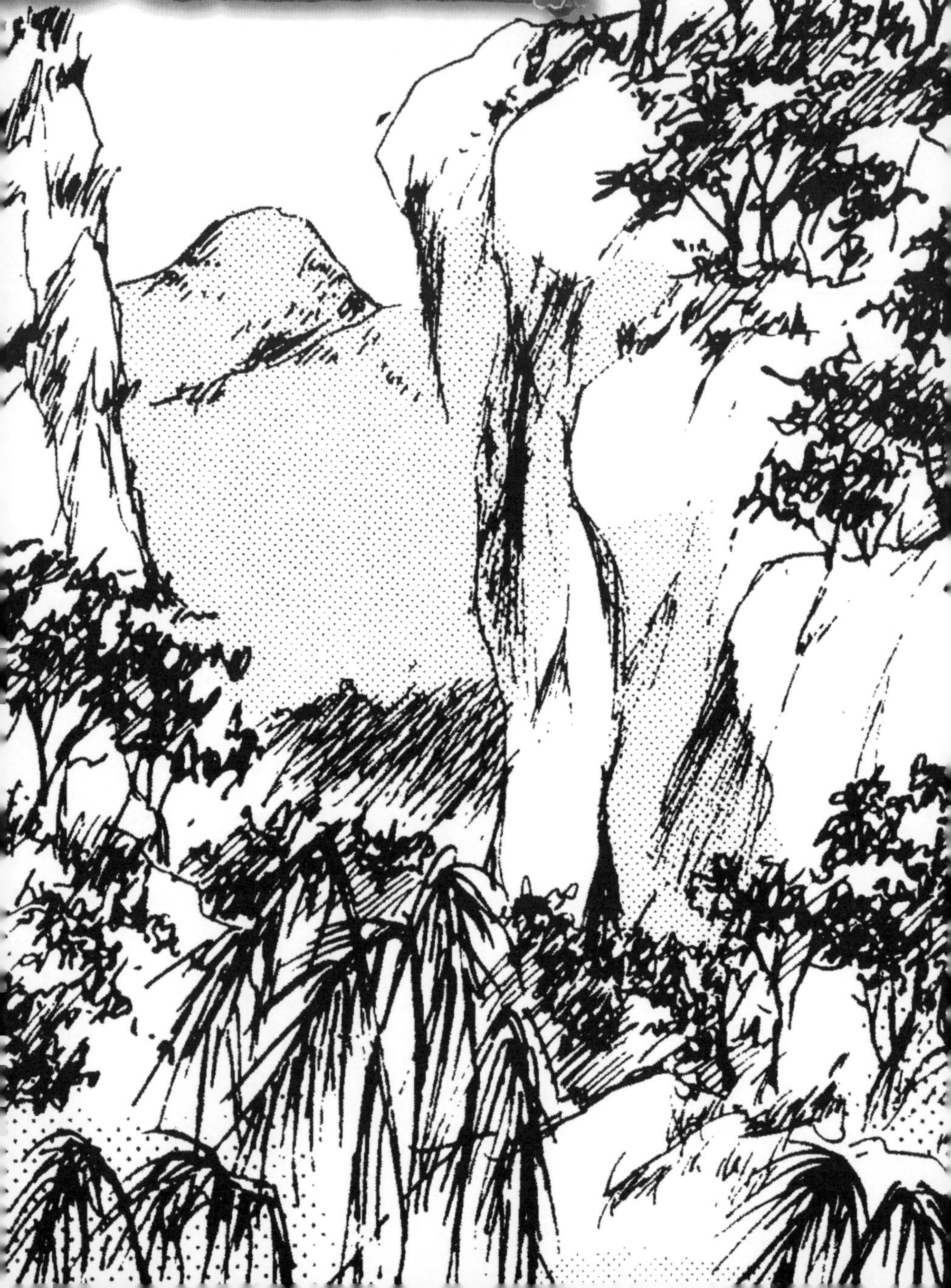

CHAPTER SEVEN
THE AIMLESS HEART

MIAKA YUKI

夕　城　美　朱

M I A K A

- Born in Tokyo. Age 15.
- Third District Junior High School, 9th grade, class 4, seat number 18.
- Resides with her mother and her brother (a college student).
- Height: 5'2", weight: 106lb. Slightly pudgy.
- (But she manages to avoid getting fat.)
- Hobbies: Reading manga, eating, and baking cookies.
- Personality: Outgoing and optimistic. Amicable with everyone. Tends to be guileless and sentimental. Never suspicious. Naïve, but sometimes she surprises adults with an insightful comment. Can be unassuming. Magnanimous and courageous but somewhat unsophisticated. Seems to give the impression she always needs help so she always seems to have someone looking after her. Believes herself to be considerate.

Flower Circle
Seal of Approval

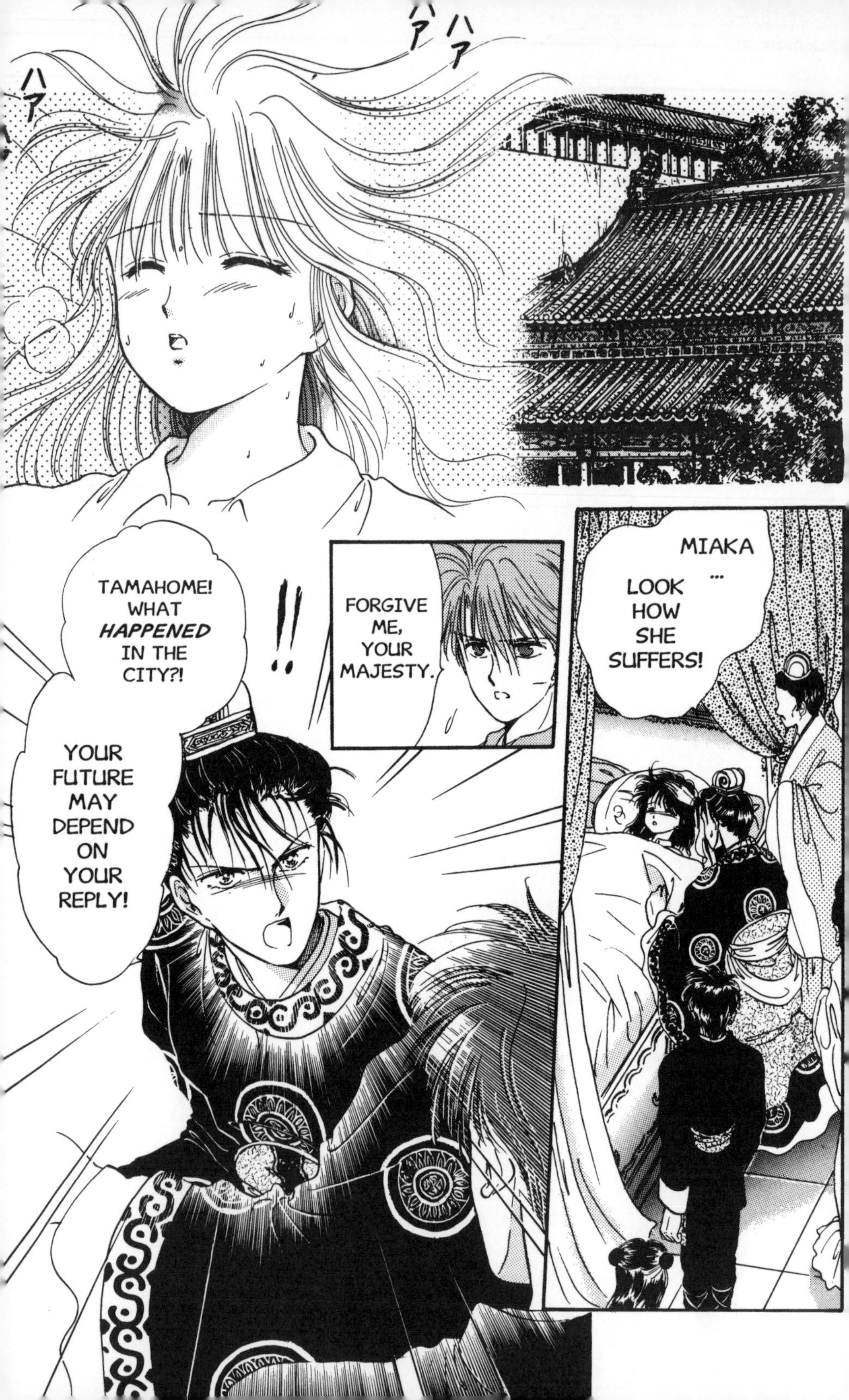
ハァ
ハァ
ハァ
MIAKA ...
LOOK HOW SHE SUFFERS!
TAMAHOME! WHAT *HAPPENED* IN THE CITY?!
!!
YOUR FUTURE MAY DEPEND ON YOUR REPLY!
FORGIVE ME, YOUR MAJESTY.

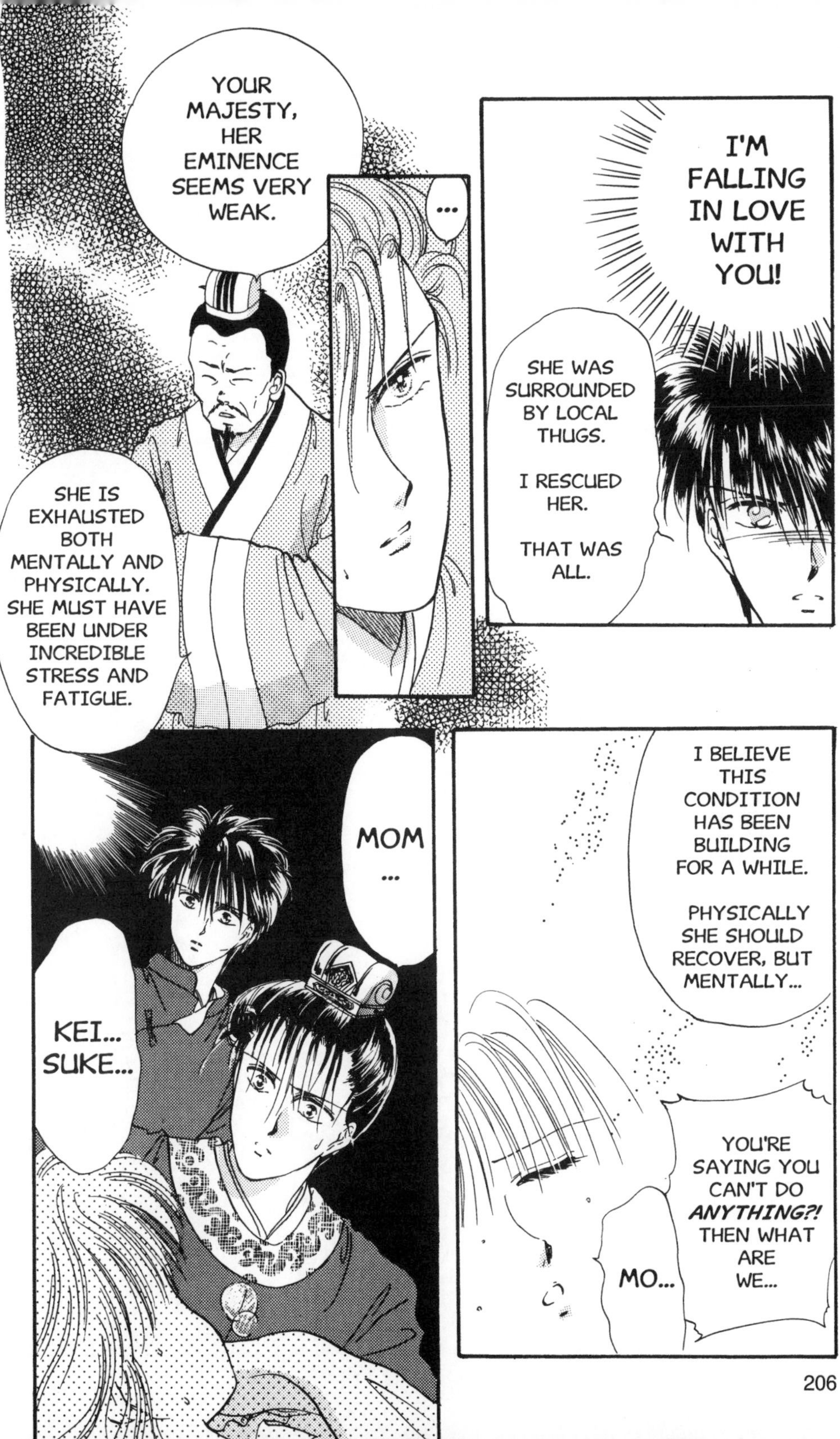
I'M FALLING IN LOVE WITH YOU!
SHE WAS SURROUNDED BY LOCAL THUGS.
I RESCUED HER.
THAT WAS ALL.
...
YOUR MAJESTY, HER EMINENCE SEEMS VERY WEAK.
SHE IS EXHAUSTED BOTH MENTALLY AND PHYSICALLY. SHE MUST HAVE BEEN UNDER INCREDIBLE STRESS AND FATIGUE.
I BELIEVE THIS CONDITION HAS BEEN BUILDING FOR A WHILE.
PHYSICALLY SHE SHOULD RECOVER, BUT MENTALLY...
YOU'RE SAYING YOU CAN'T DO *ANYTHING?!* THEN WHAT ARE WE...
MO...
MOM ...
KEI... SUKE...

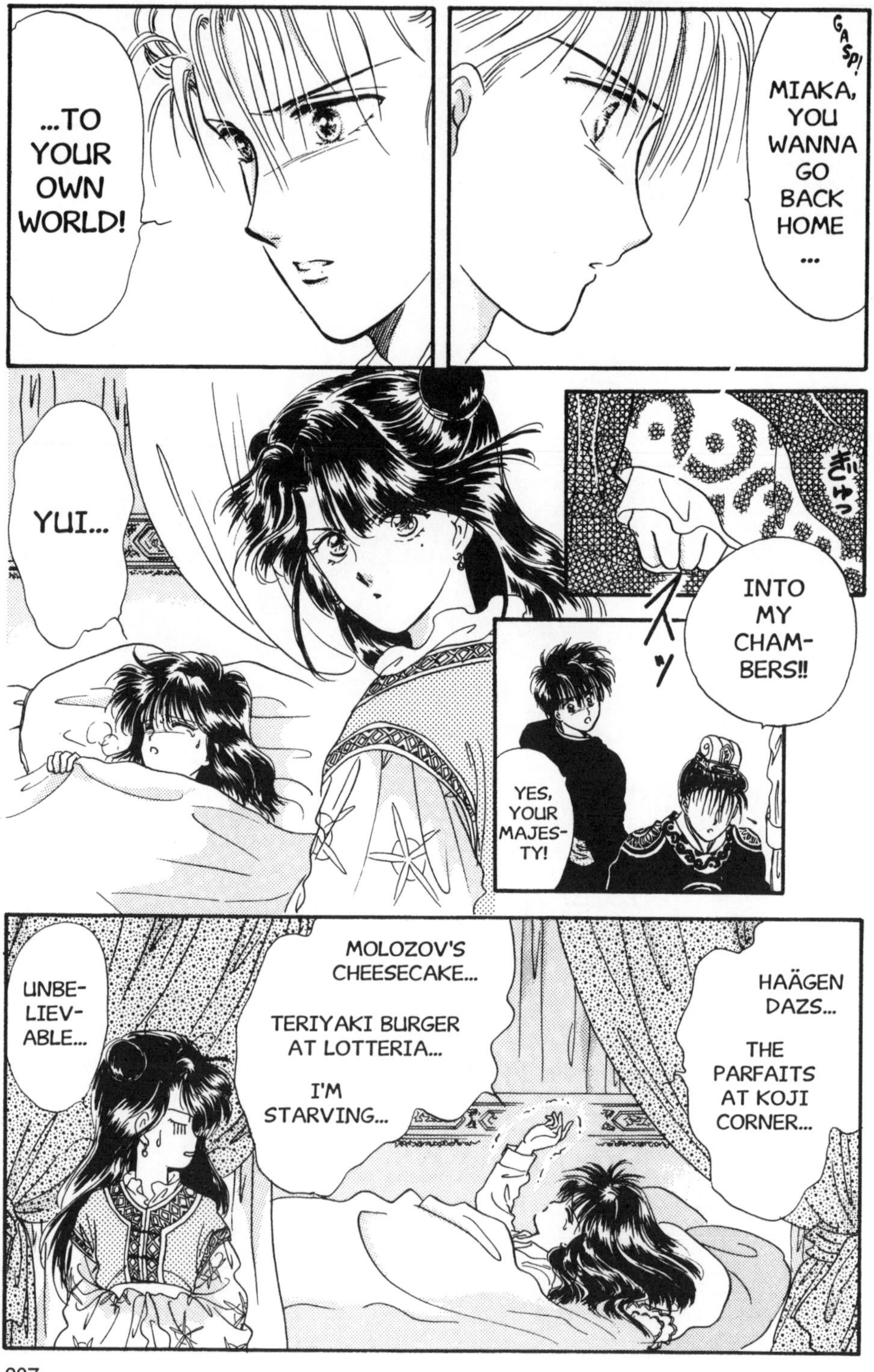
GASP!
MIAKA, YOU WANNA GO BACK HOME...
...TO YOUR OWN WORLD!
ぎゅっ
ッ
INTO MY CHAM-BERS!!
YES, YOUR MAJES-TY!
YUI...
HAÄGEN DAZS...
THE PARFAITS AT KOJI CORNER...
MOLOZOV'S CHEESECAKE...
TERIYAKI BURGER AT LOTTERIA...
I'M STARVING...
UNBE-LIEV-ABLE...

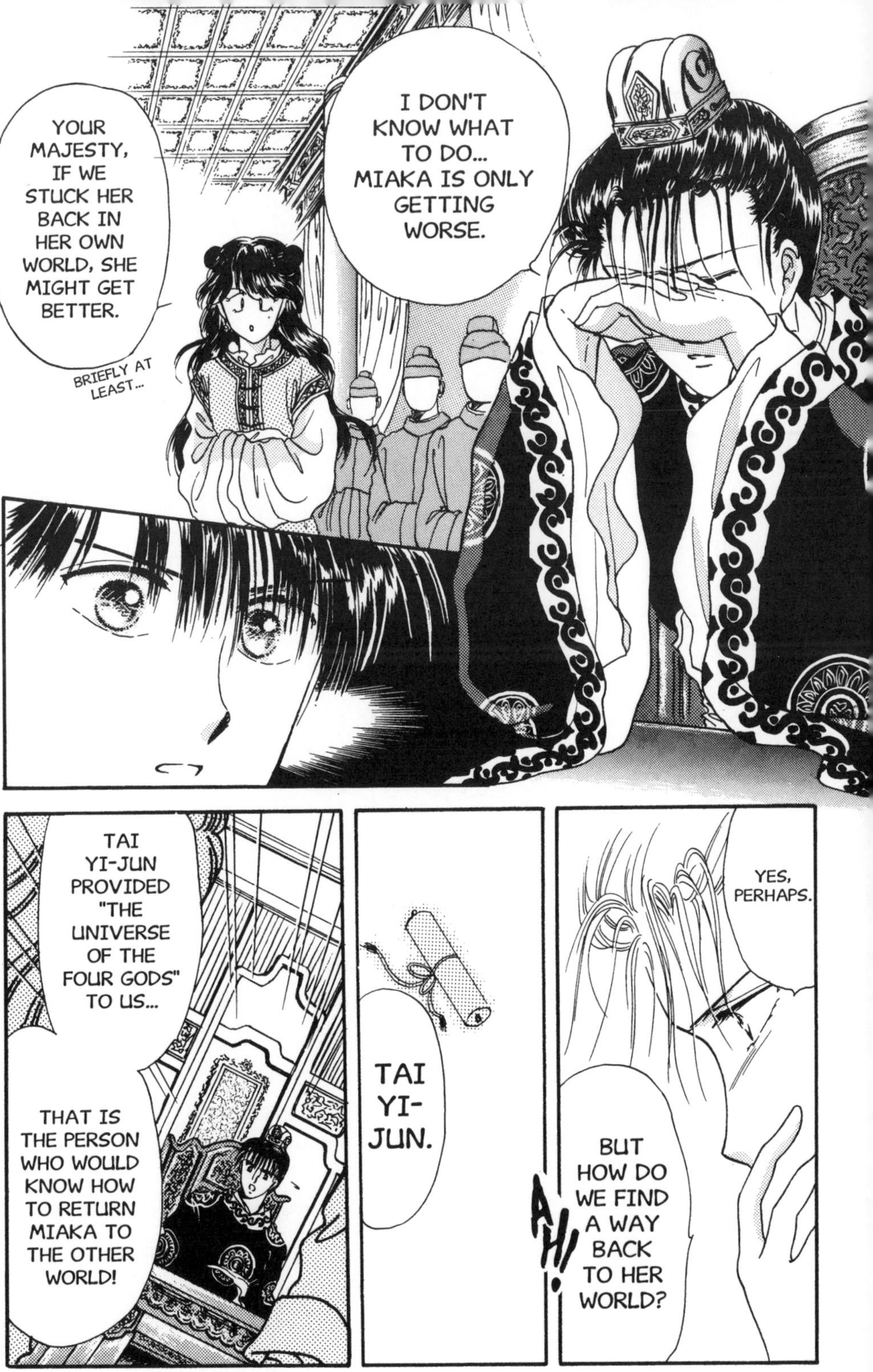
I DON'T KNOW WHAT TO DO... MIAKA IS ONLY GETTING WORSE.
YOUR MAJESTY, IF WE STUCK HER BACK IN HER OWN WORLD, SHE MIGHT GET BETTER.
BRIEFLY AT LEAST...
YES, PERHAPS.
BUT HOW DO WE FIND A WAY BACK TO HER WORLD?
AH!
TAI YI-JUN.
TAI YI-JUN PROVIDED "THE UNIVERSE OF THE FOUR GODS" TO US...
THAT IS THE PERSON WHO WOULD KNOW HOW TO RETURN MIAKA TO THE OTHER WORLD!

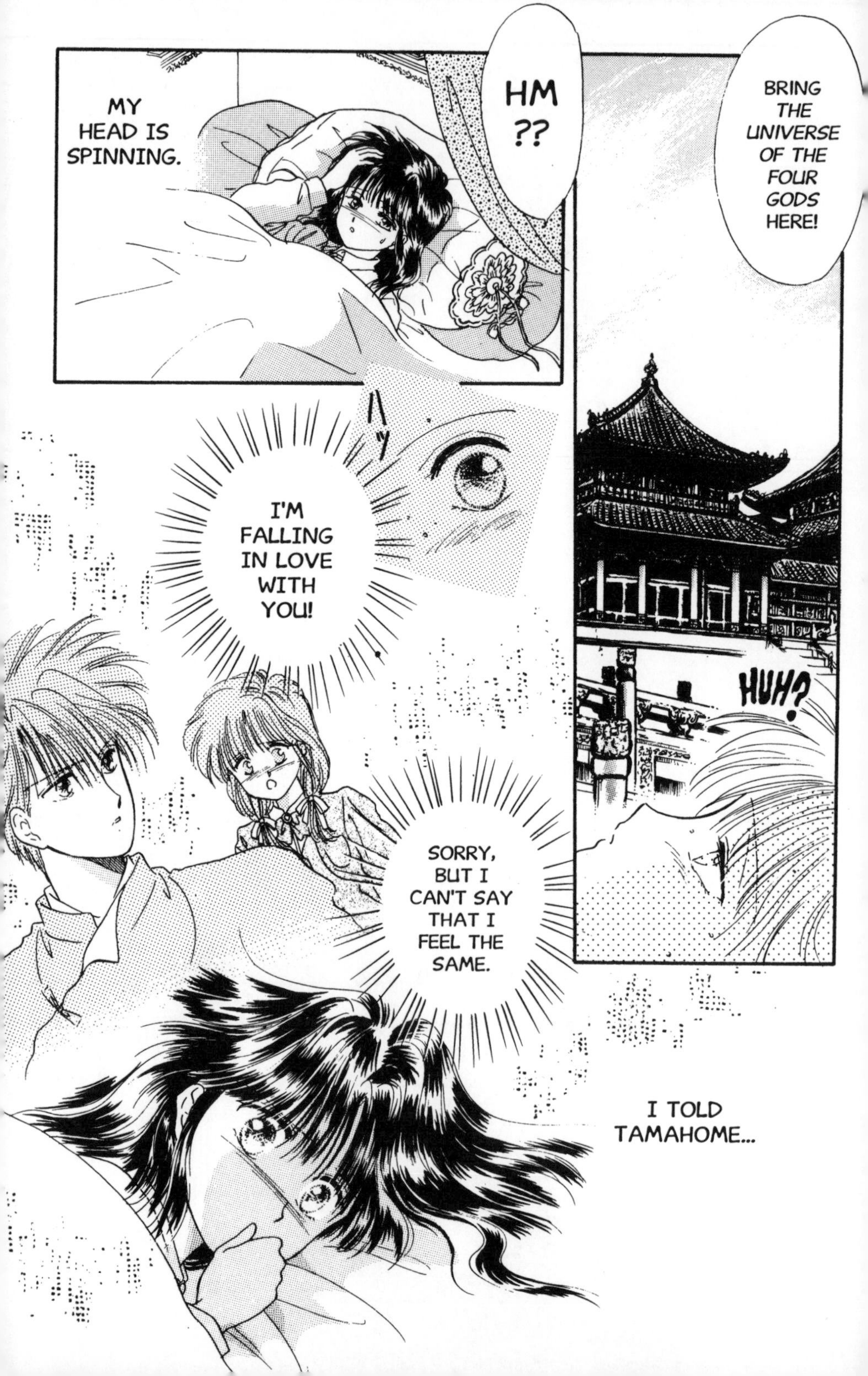
BRING THE UNIVERSE OF THE FOUR GODS HERE!
HUH?
HM ??
MY HEAD IS SPINNING.
ハッ
I'M FALLING IN LOVE WITH YOU!
SORRY, BUT I CAN'T SAY THAT I FEEL THE SAME.
I TOLD TAMAHOME...

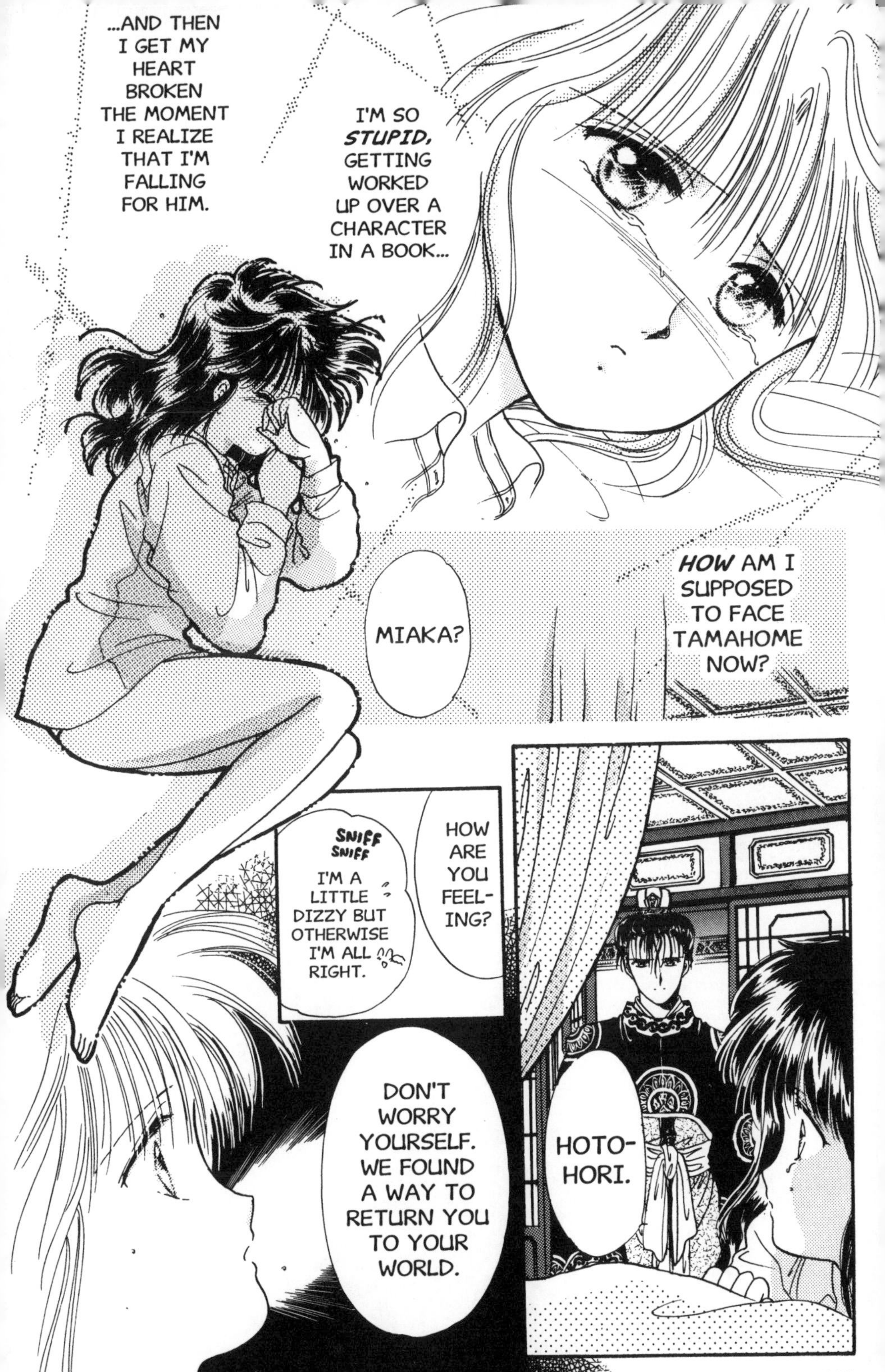
I'M SO *STUPID,* GETTING WORKED UP OVER A CHARACTER IN A BOOK...
...AND THEN I GET MY HEART BROKEN THE MOMENT I REALIZE THAT I'M FALLING FOR HIM.
HOW AM I SUPPOSED TO FACE TAMAHOME NOW?
MIAKA?
HOTO-HORI.
HOW ARE YOU FEEL-ING?
SNIFF SNIFF
I'M A LITTLE DIZZY BUT OTHERWISE I'M ALL RIGHT.
DON'T WORRY YOURSELF. WE FOUND A WAY TO RETURN YOU TO YOUR WORLD.

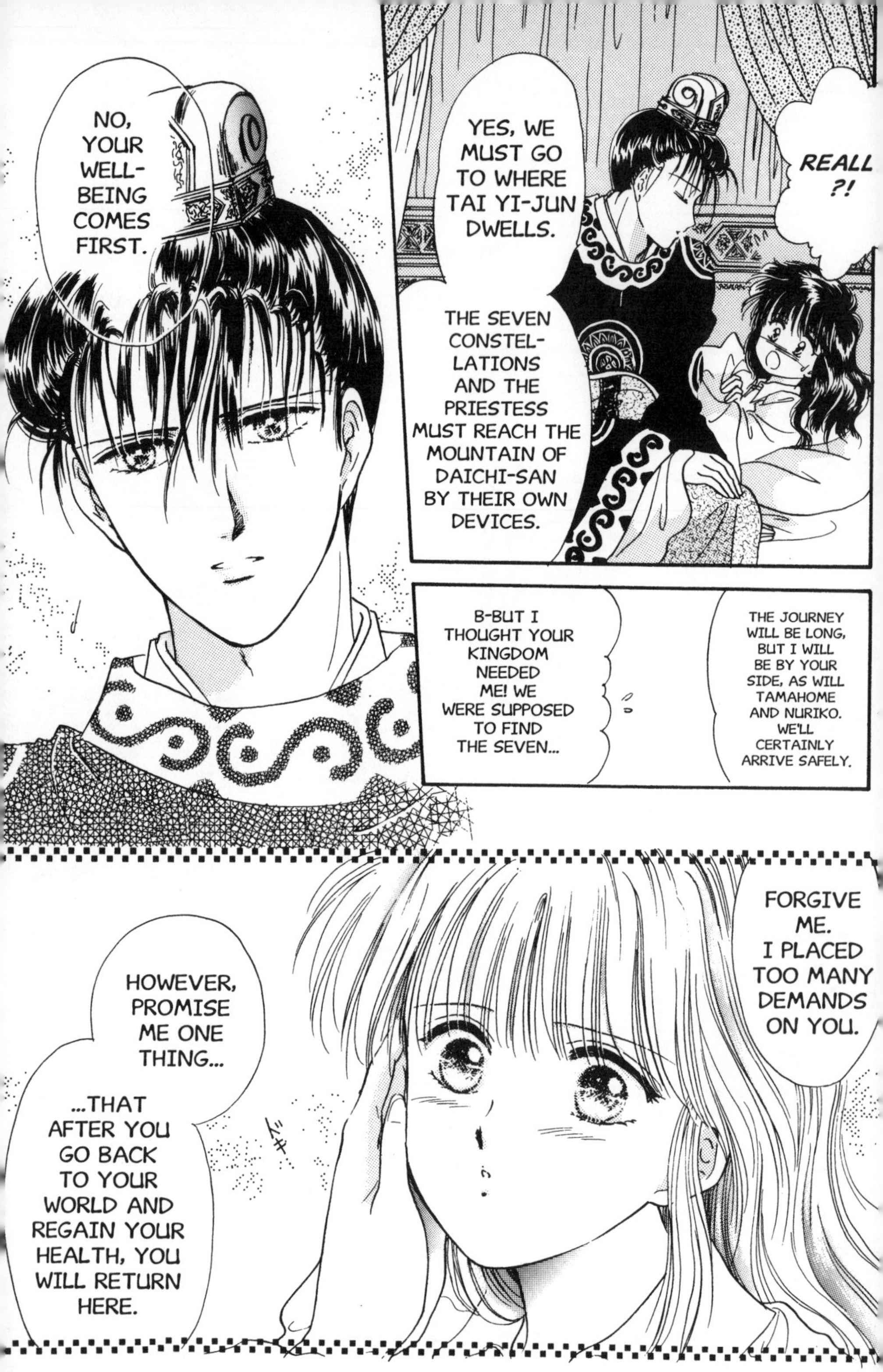
REALL ?!
YES, WE MUST GO TO WHERE TAI YI-JUN DWELLS.
THE SEVEN CONSTEL-LATIONS AND THE PRIESTESS MUST REACH THE MOUNTAIN OF DAICHI-SAN BY THEIR OWN DEVICES.
THE JOURNEY WILL BE LONG, BUT I WILL BE BY YOUR SIDE, AS WILL TAMAHOME AND NURIKO. WE'LL CERTAINLY ARRIVE SAFELY.
B-BUT I THOUGHT YOUR KINGDOM NEEDED ME! WE WERE SUPPOSED TO FIND THE SEVEN...
NO, YOUR WELL-BEING COMES FIRST.
FORGIVE ME. I PLACED TOO MANY DEMANDS ON YOU.
HOWEVER, PROMISE ME ONE THING...
...THAT AFTER YOU GO BACK TO YOUR WORLD AND REGAIN YOUR HEALTH, YOU WILL RETURN HERE.

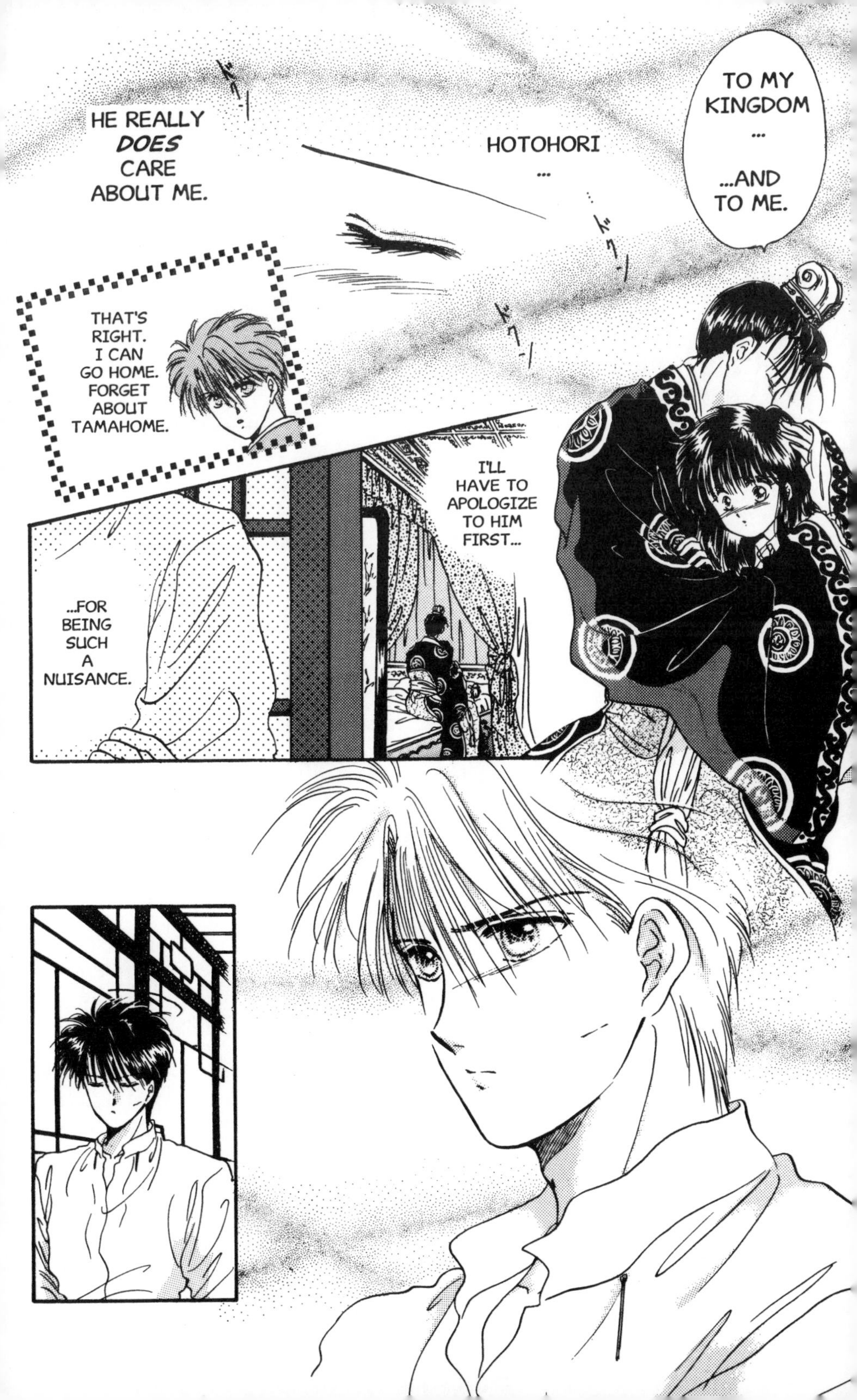
TO MY KINGDOM ... ...AND TO ME.
HOTOHORI ...
HE REALLY DOES CARE ABOUT ME.
THAT'S RIGHT. I CAN GO HOME. FORGET ABOUT TAMAHOME.
I'LL HAVE TO APOLOGIZE TO HIM FIRST...
...FOR BEING SUCH A NUISANCE.

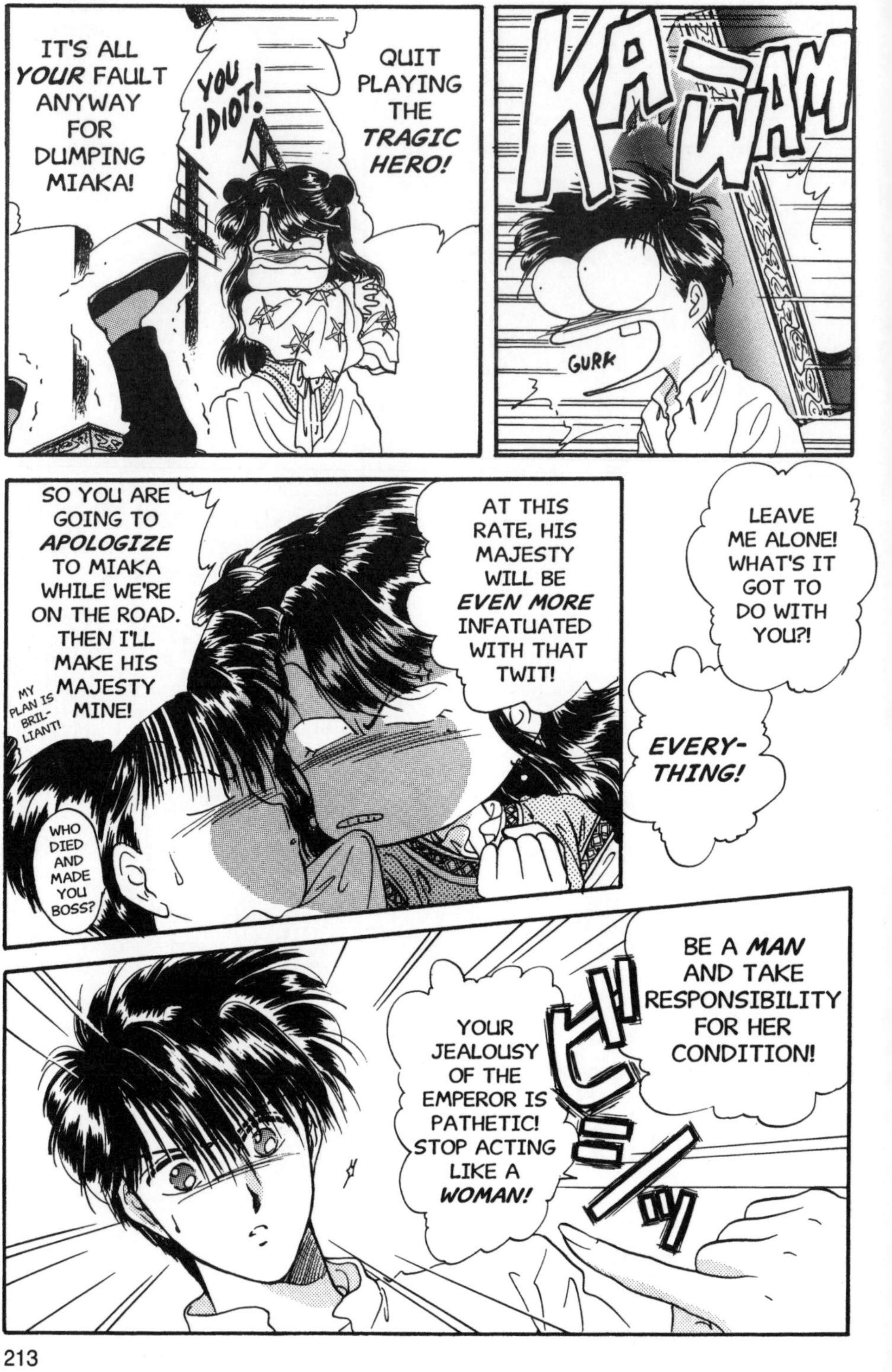
KA-WAM
GURK
QUIT PLAYING THE TRAGIC HERO!
YOU IDIOT!
IT'S ALL YOUR FAULT ANYWAY FOR DUMPING MIAKA!
LEAVE ME ALONE! WHAT'S IT GOT TO DO WITH YOU?!
EVERYTHING!
AT THIS RATE, HIS MAJESTY WILL BE EVEN MORE INFATUATED WITH THAT TWIT!
SO YOU ARE GOING TO APOLOGIZE TO MIAKA WHILE WE'RE ON THE ROAD. THEN I'LL MAKE HIS MAJESTY MINE!
MY PLAN IS BRILLIANT!
WHO DIED AND MADE YOU BOSS?
BE A MAN AND TAKE RESPONSIBILITY FOR HER CONDITION!
YOUR JEALOUSY OF THE EMPEROR IS PATHETIC! STOP ACTING LIKE A WOMAN!

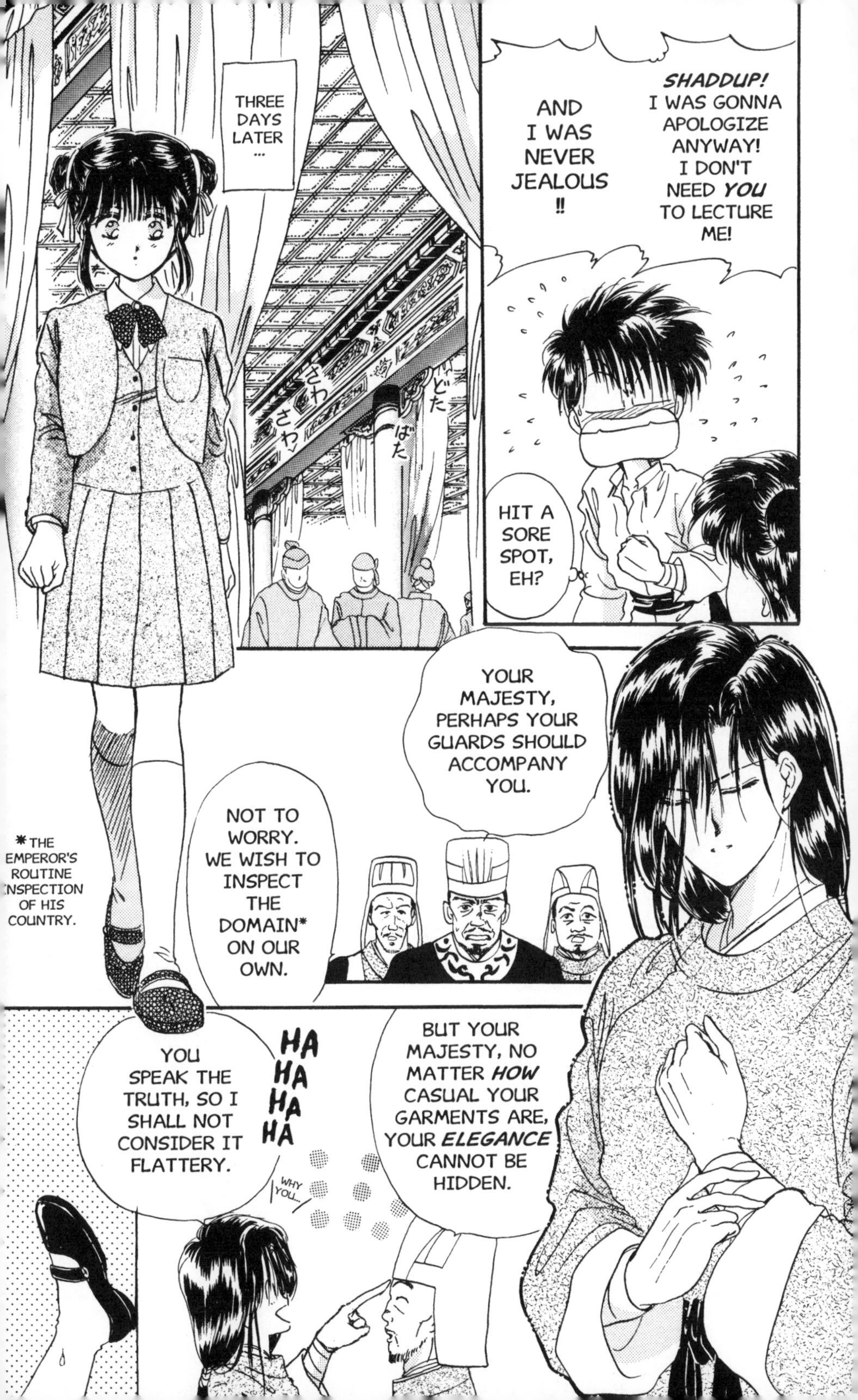
SHADDUP! I WAS GONNA APOLOGIZE ANYWAY! I DON'T NEED YOU TO LECTURE ME!
AND I WAS NEVER JEALOUS!!
HIT A SORE SPOT, EH?
THREE DAYS LATER...
さわさわ
どたばた
YOUR MAJESTY, PERHAPS YOUR GUARDS SHOULD ACCOMPANY YOU.
NOT TO WORRY. WE WISH TO INSPECT THE DOMAIN* ON OUR OWN.
*THE EMPEROR'S ROUTINE INSPECTION OF HIS COUNTRY.
BUT YOUR MAJESTY, NO MATTER HOW CASUAL YOUR GARMENTS ARE, YOUR ELEGANCE CANNOT BE HIDDEN.
HA HA HA HA HA
YOU SPEAK THE TRUTH, SO I SHALL NOT CONSIDER IT FLATTERY.
WHY YOU...

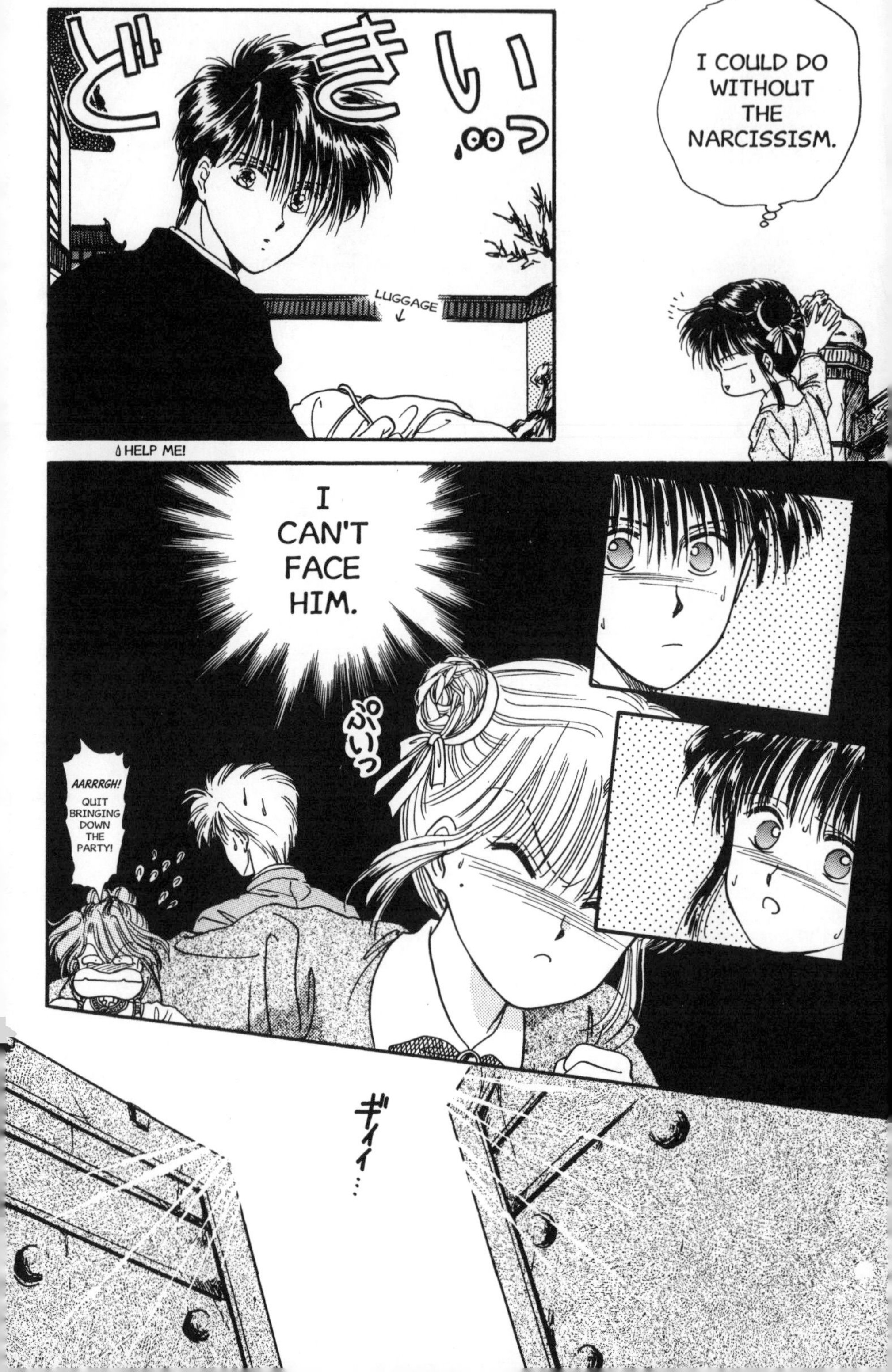
I COULD DO WITHOUT THE NARCISSISM.
どきいっ
LUGGAGE
HELP ME!
I CAN'T FACE HIM.
ぷいっ
AARRRGH! QUIT BRINGING DOWN THE PARTY!
ギイイ…

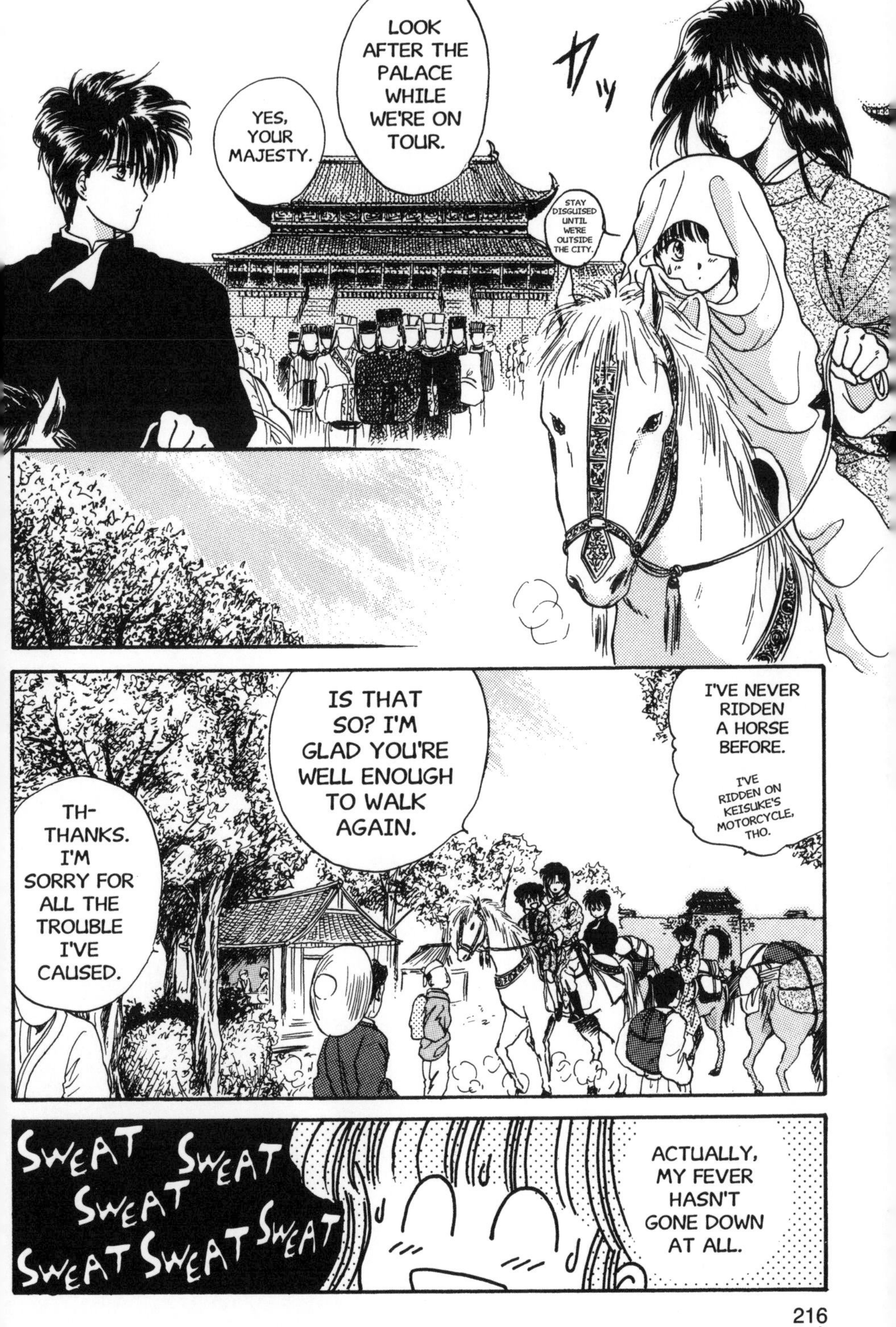
ガッ
LOOK AFTER THE PALACE WHILE WE'RE ON TOUR.
YES, YOUR MAJESTY.
STAY DISGUISED UNTIL WE'RE OUTSIDE THE CITY.
I'VE NEVER RIDDEN A HORSE BEFORE.
I'VE RIDDEN ON KEISUKE'S MOTORCYCLE, THO.
IS THAT SO? I'M GLAD YOU'RE WELL ENOUGH TO WALK AGAIN.
TH- THANKS. I'M SORRY FOR ALL THE TROUBLE I'VE CAUSED.
ACTUALLY, MY FEVER HASN'T GONE DOWN AT ALL.
SWEAT SWEAT SWEAT SWEAT SWEAT SWEAT

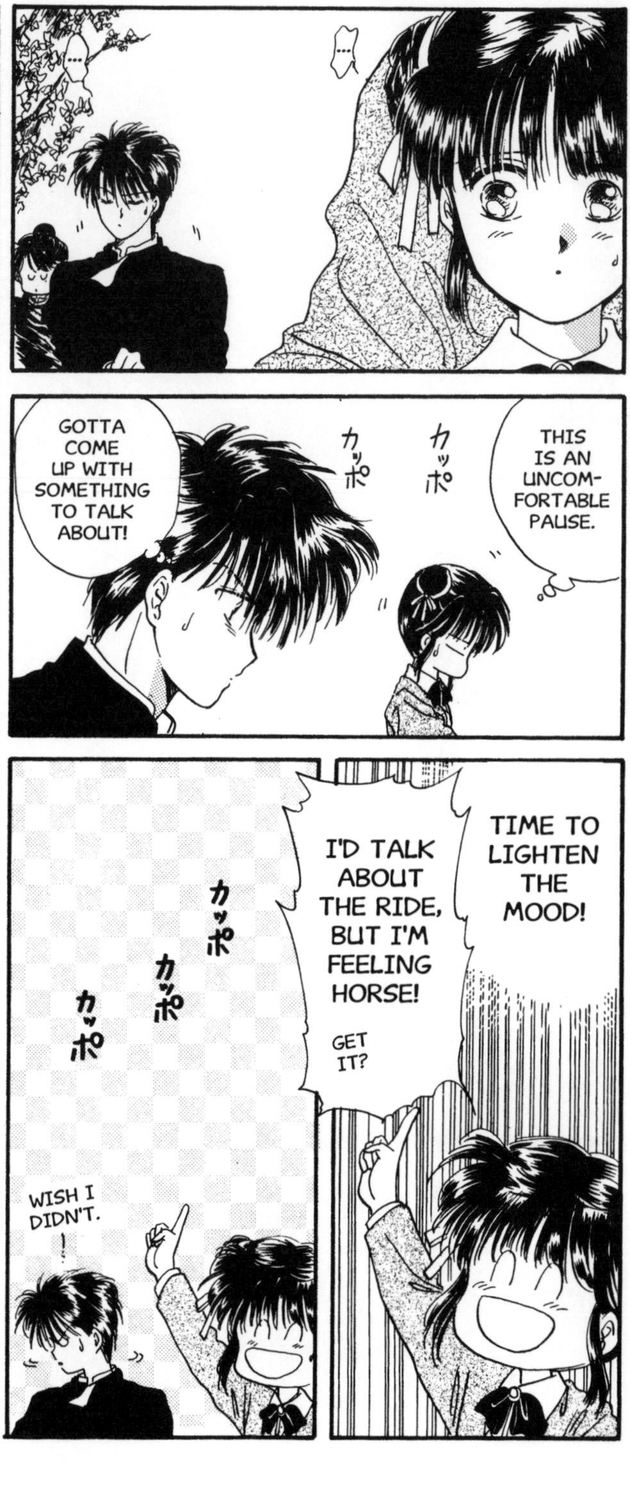
...
...
THIS IS AN UNCOMFORTABLE PAUSE.
カッポ
カッポ
GOTTA COME UP WITH SOMETHING TO TALK ABOUT!
TIME TO LIGHTEN THE MOOD!
I'D TALK ABOUT THE RIDE, BUT I'M FEELING HORSE!
GET IT?
カッポ
カッポ
カッポ
WISH I DIDN'T.
!

I've been a little tired lately. How are you all doing? I've been writing these chat sections for every chapter, but nowadays nobody else is doing them. I thought of quitting, but they told me, "Your fans buy the books to read the chat sections." So I'm stuck and I gotta write them. (sniff, sniff)

From *Prepubescence* on, I've been writing a lot of stuff in manga because I get so many questions from the fans. (Everybody wants to become a manga artist!). But I've only been a pro for three years. A real veteran manga artist might say that I'm not telling you the right things. I may talk about drawing or other parts of manga, but I'm not the artist I want to be yet. And I can't hide my emotions. Whether I'm angry or happy, it always shows right on my face. And that gets me into trouble.

Suddenly my thoughts have come to a halt. I've decided not to think about this stuff anymore. My readers should be priority No. 1! No more long essays on manga. Besides, I never thought that other artists read these books, but a few other artists told me they did read it! I was super-embarrassed. I gotta apologize for my know-it-all lectures. Everybody around me knows that I really have no self-confidence. When this series began, I would look over my drawings and feel sick to my stomach. I'd cry and cry while I continued my work!

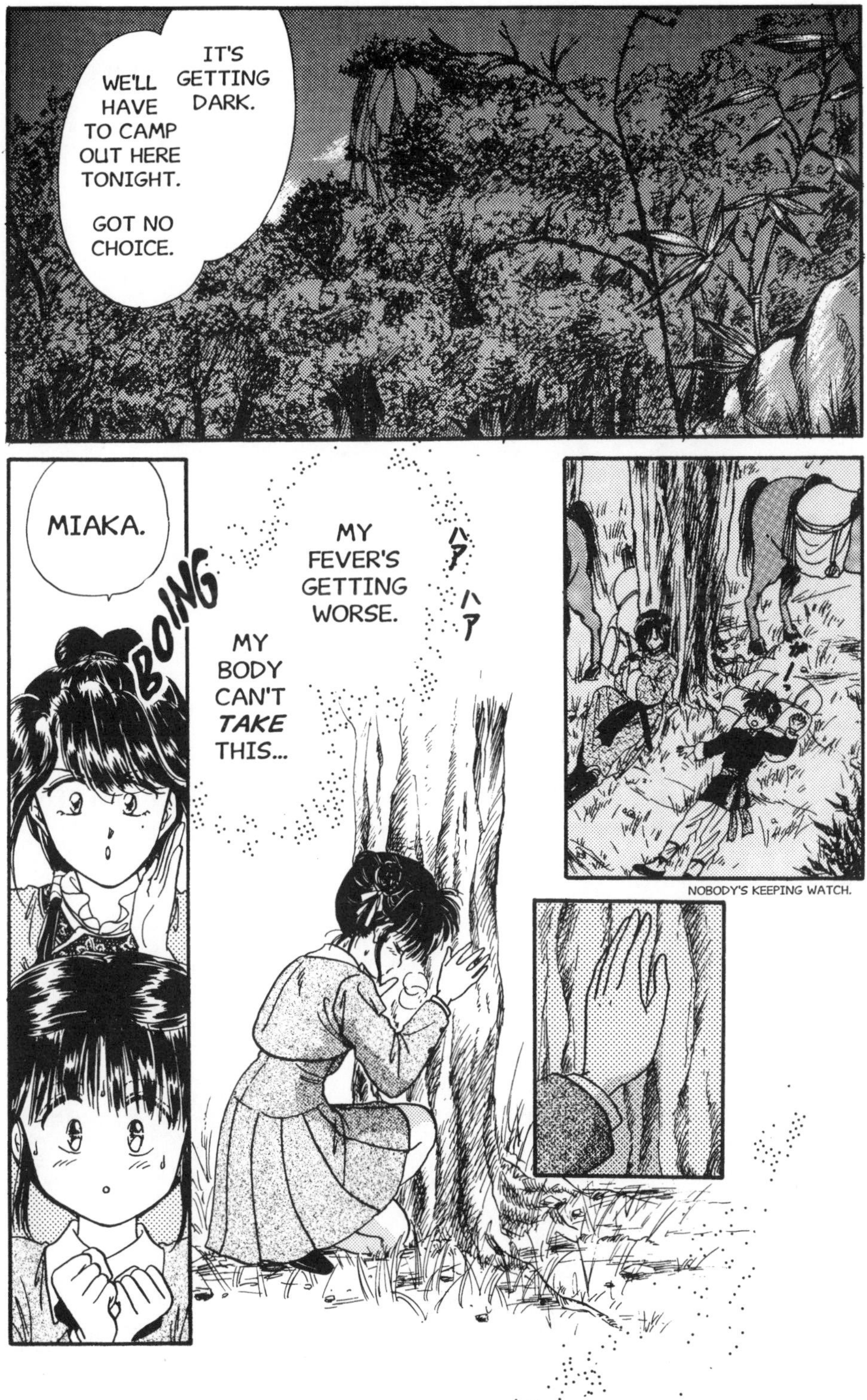
IT'S GETTING DARK.
WE'LL HAVE TO CAMP OUT HERE TONIGHT.
GOT NO CHOICE.
NOBODY'S KEEPING WATCH.
MY FEVER'S GETTING WORSE.
MY BODY CAN'T *TAKE* THIS...
ハア ハア
MIAKA.
BOING

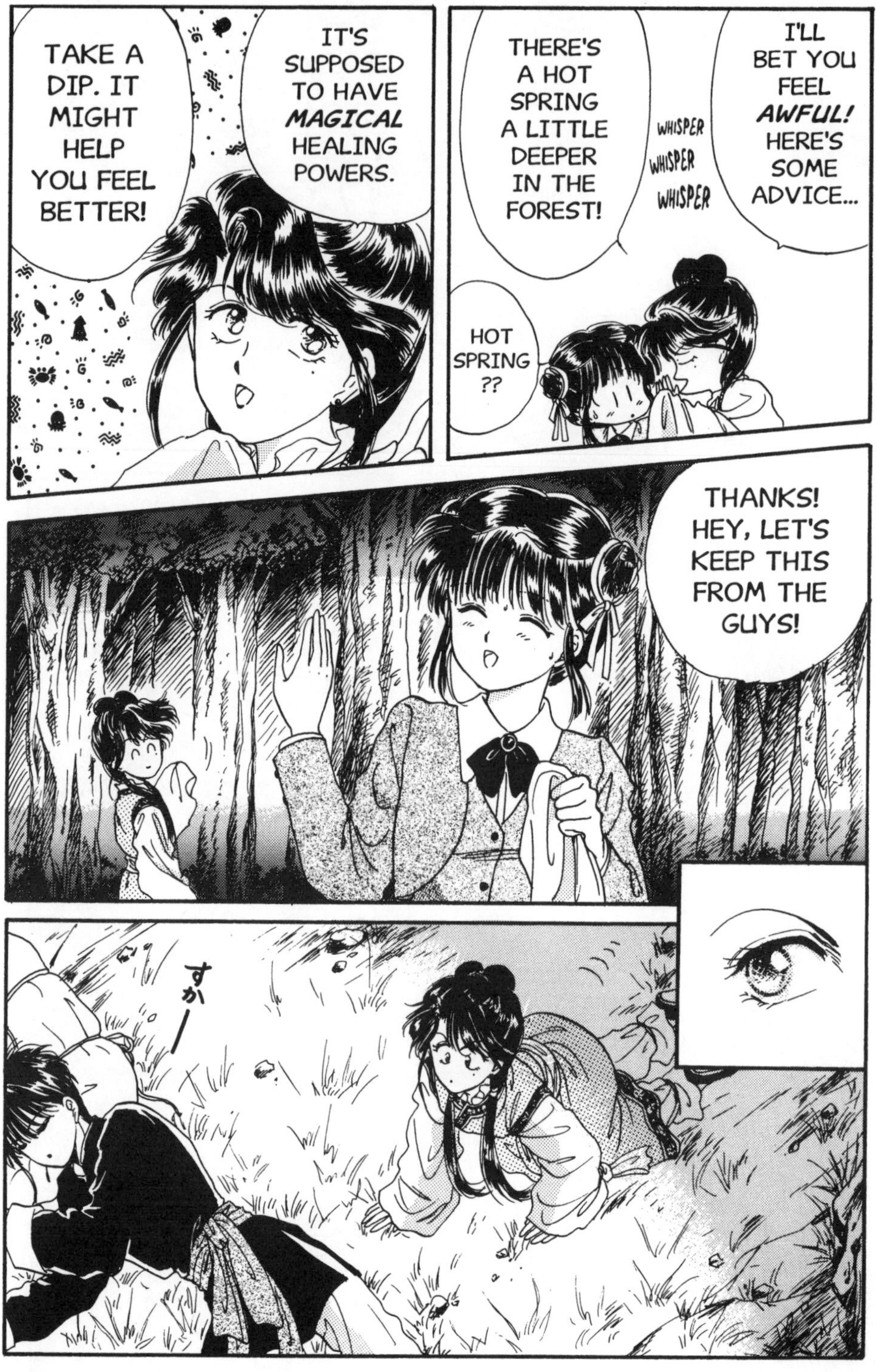
I'LL BET YOU FEEL *AWFUL!* HERE'S SOME ADVICE...
WHISPER
WHISPER
WHISPER
THERE'S A HOT SPRING A LITTLE DEEPER IN THE FOREST!
HOT SPRING ??
IT'S SUPPOSED TO HAVE *MAGICAL* HEALING POWERS.
TAKE A DIP. IT MIGHT HELP YOU FEEL BETTER!
THANKS! HEY, LET'S KEEP THIS FROM THE GUYS!
すかー

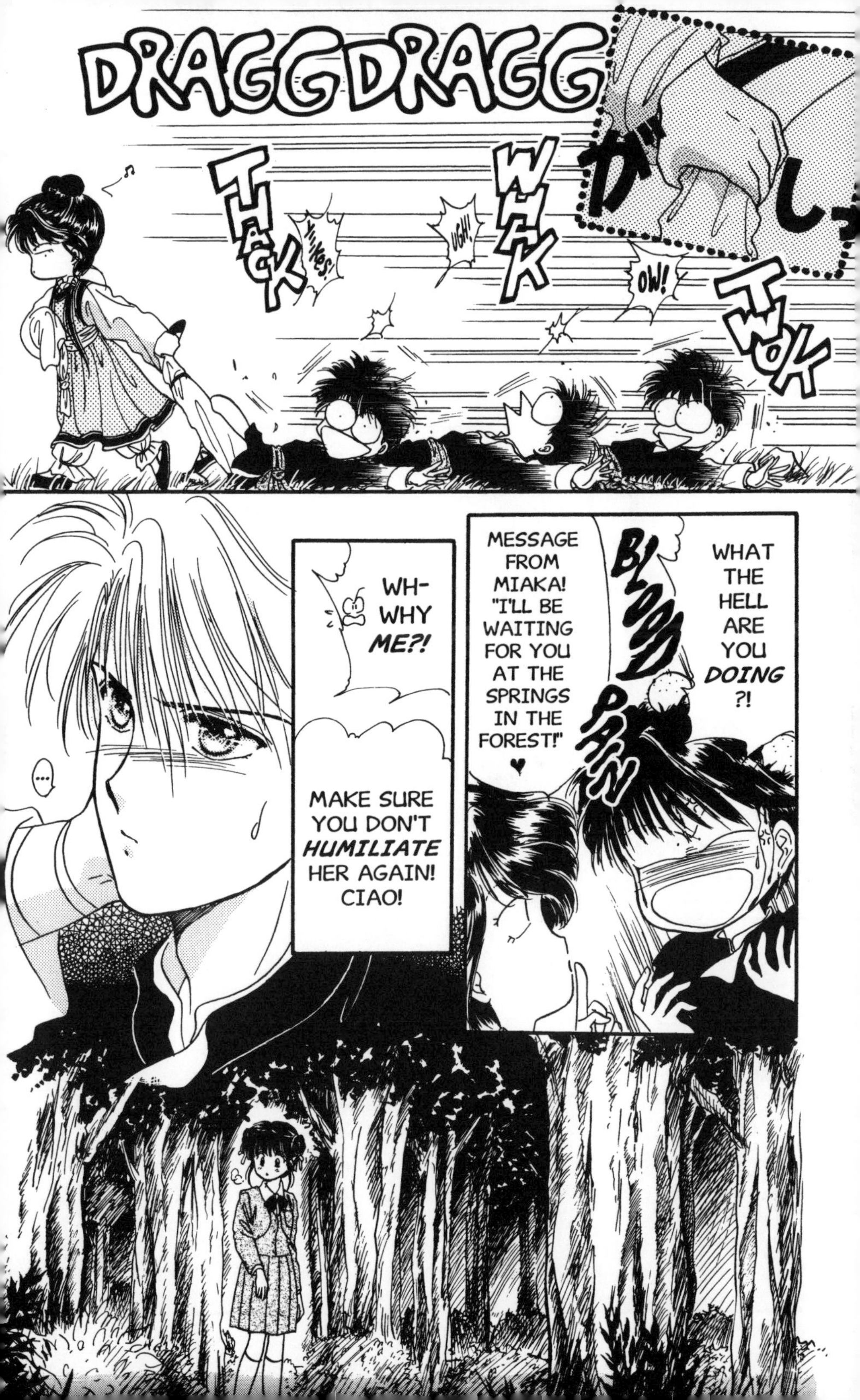

がしっ
DRAGGDRAGG
TWOK
OW!
WHAK
UGH!
YIKES!
THACK
WHAT THE HELL ARE YOU DOING?!
BLOOD PAIN
MESSAGE FROM MIAKA! "I'LL BE WAITING FOR YOU AT THE SPRINGS IN THE FOREST!" ♥
WH-WHY ME?!
MAKE SURE YOU DON'T HUMILIATE HER AGAIN! CIAO!
...

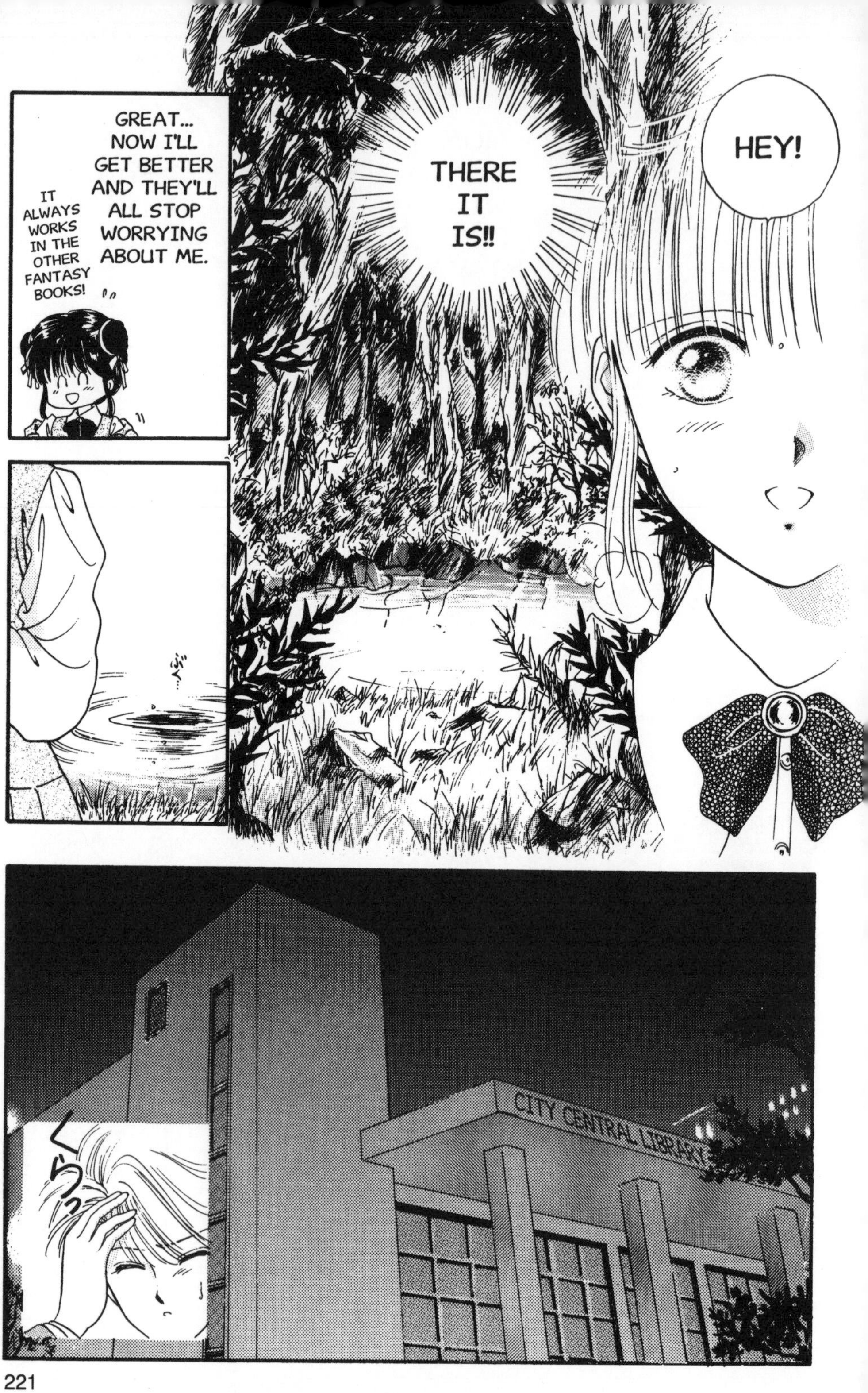
HEY!
THERE IT IS!!
GREAT... NOW I'LL GET BETTER AND THEY'LL ALL STOP WORRYING ABOUT ME.
IT ALWAYS WORKS IN THE OTHER FANTASY BOOKS!
CITY CENTRAL LIBRARY

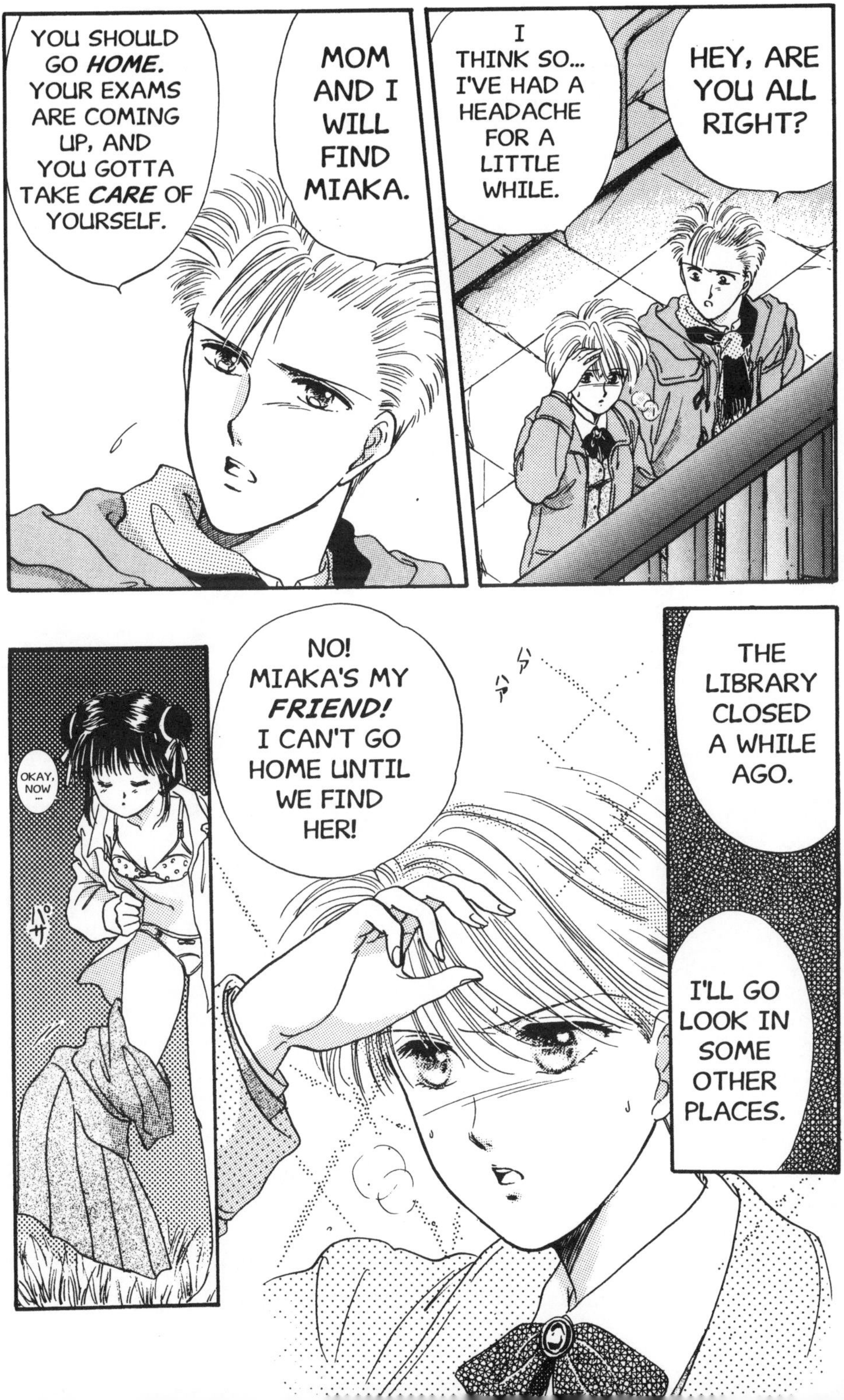
HEY, ARE YOU ALL RIGHT?
I THINK SO... I'VE HAD A HEADACHE FOR A LITTLE WHILE.
MOM AND I WILL FIND MIAKA.
YOU SHOULD GO *HOME.* YOUR EXAMS ARE COMING UP, AND YOU GOTTA TAKE *CARE* OF YOURSELF.
THE LIBRARY CLOSED A WHILE AGO.
NO! MIAKA'S MY *FRIEND!* I CAN'T GO HOME UNTIL WE FIND HER!
I'LL GO LOOK IN SOME OTHER PLACES.
OKAY, NOW...
パサ

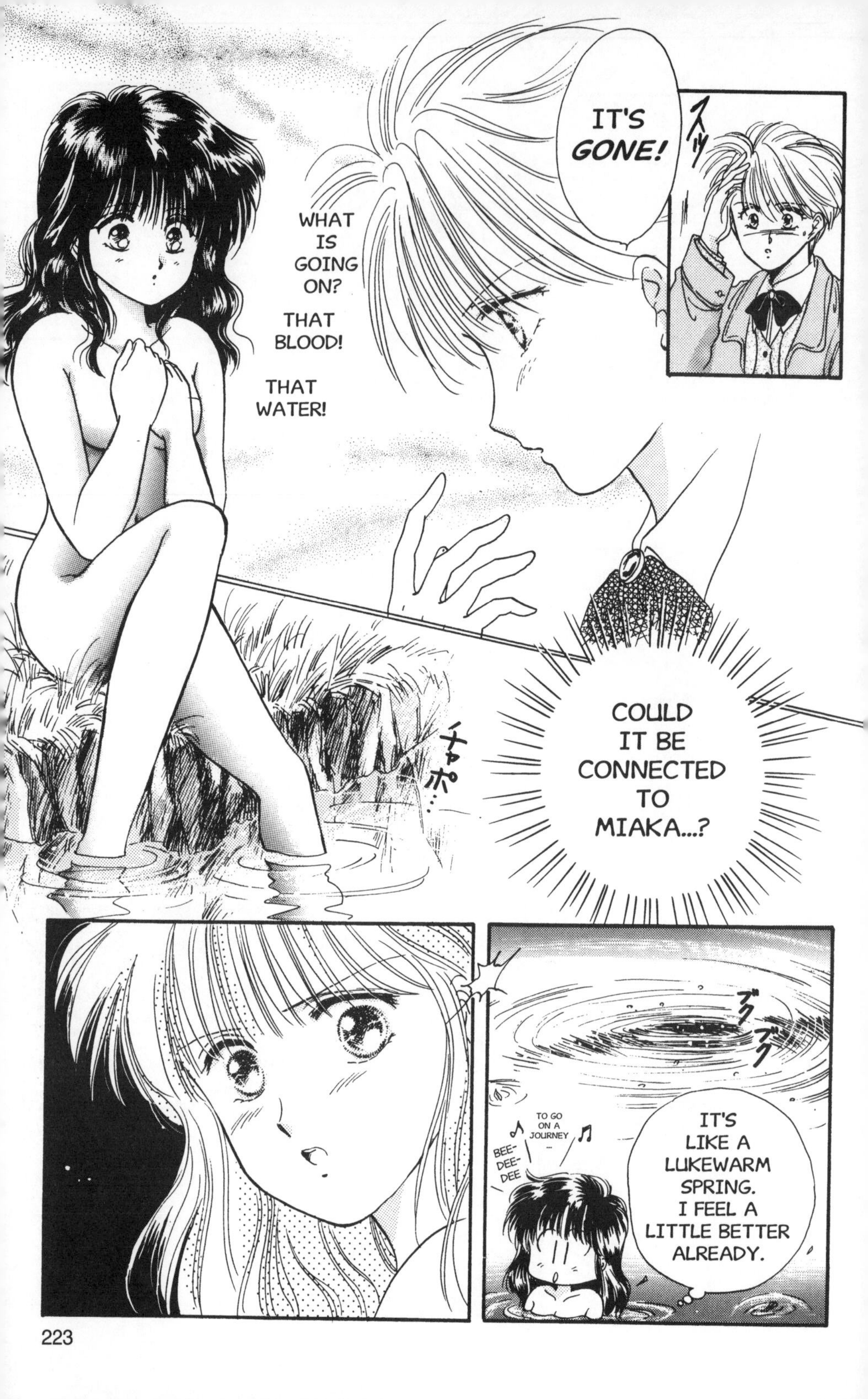
IT'S GONE!
スッ
WHAT IS GOING ON?
THAT BLOOD!
THAT WATER!
COULD IT BE CONNECTED TO MIAKA...?
チャポ...
ブクブク
TO GO ON A JOURNEY ...
BEE-DEE-DEE
IT'S LIKE A LUKEWARM SPRING. I FEEL A LITTLE BETTER ALREADY.

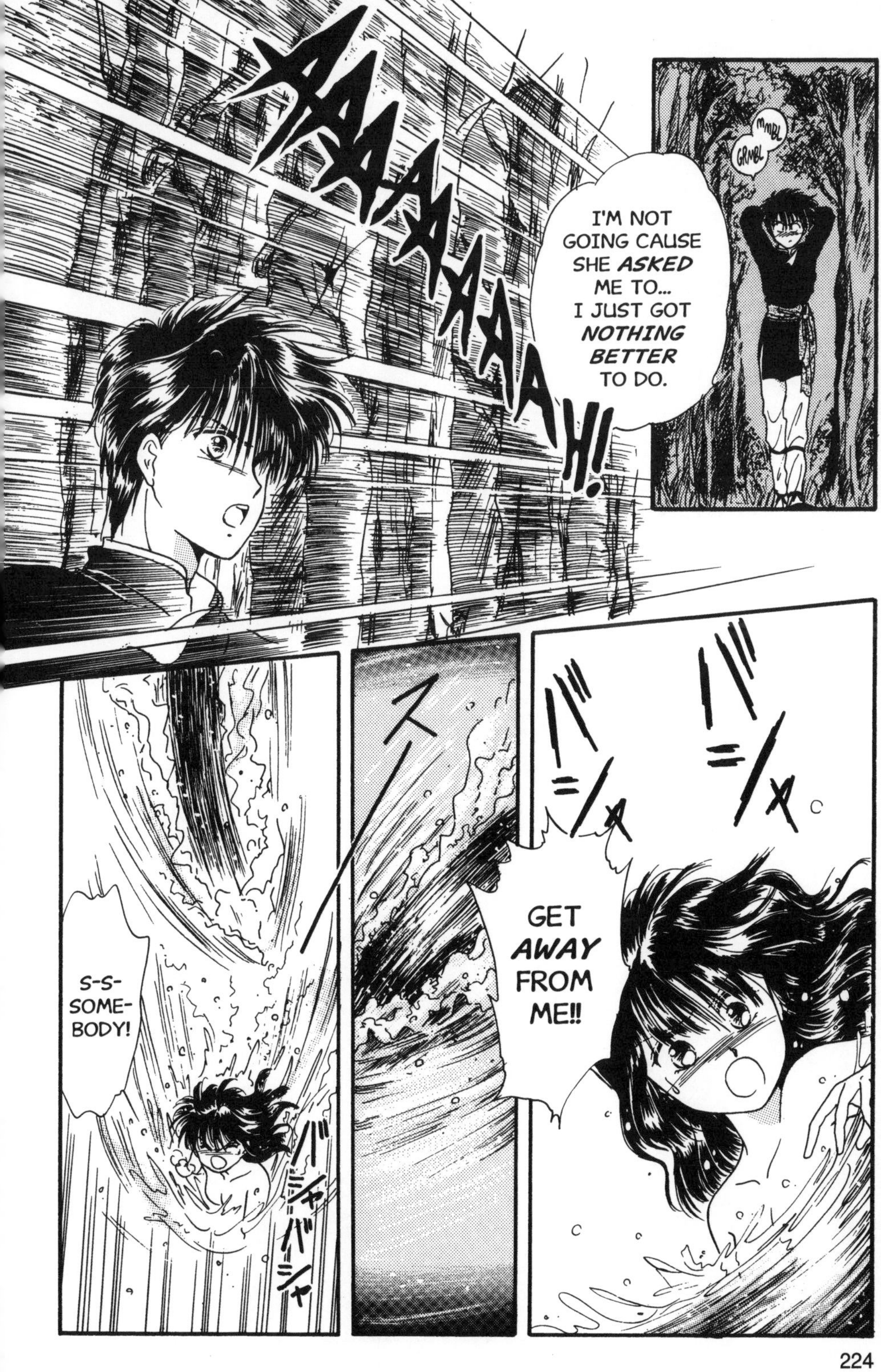
MMBL
GRMBL
I'M NOT GOING CAUSE SHE ASKED ME TO... I JUST GOT NOTHING BETTER TO DO.
AAAAAAAAH!!
GET AWAY FROM ME!!
S-S-SOMEBODY!

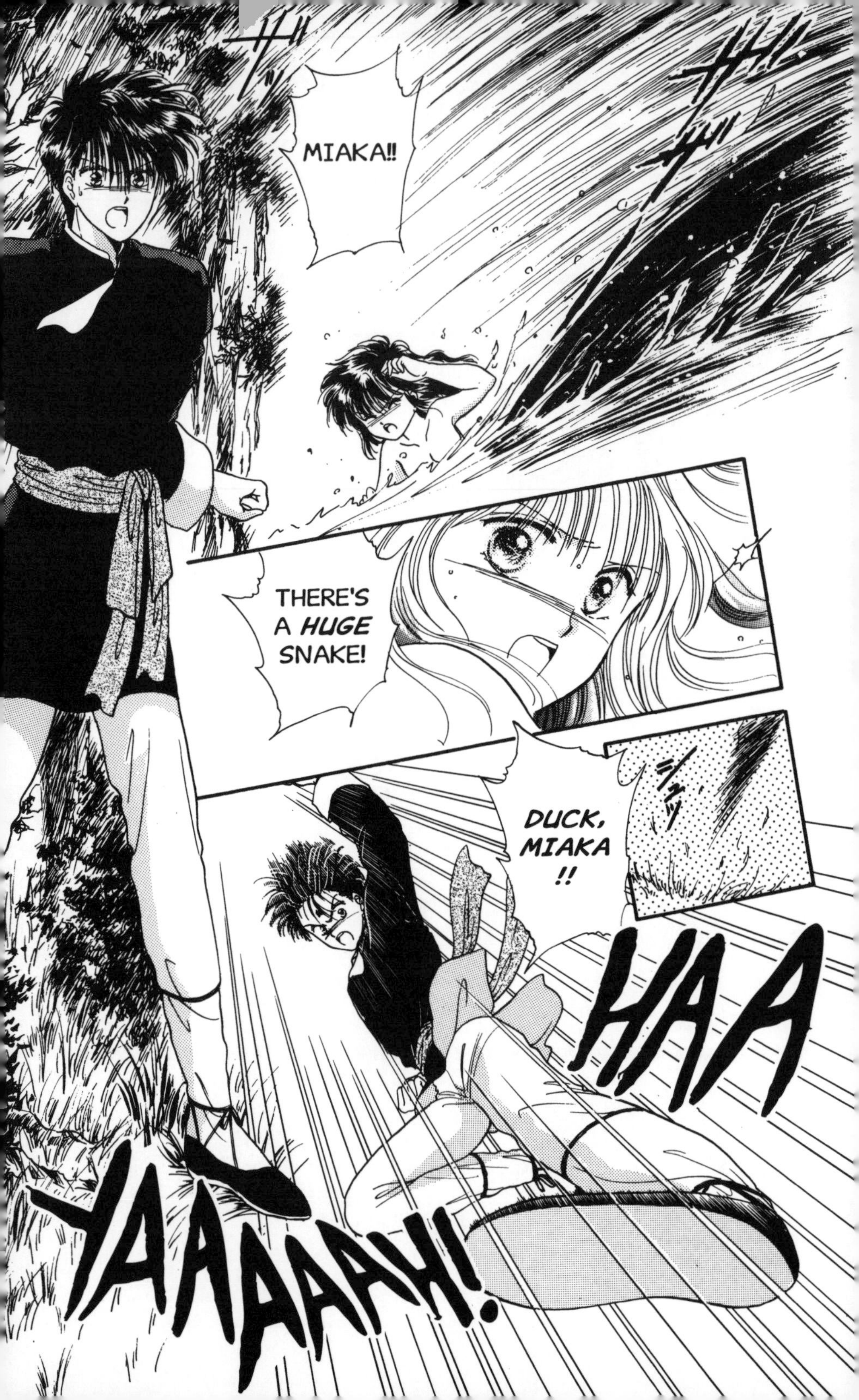
MIAKA!!
THERE'S A *HUGE* SNAKE!
DUCK, MIAKA !!
HAA
YAAAAAH!

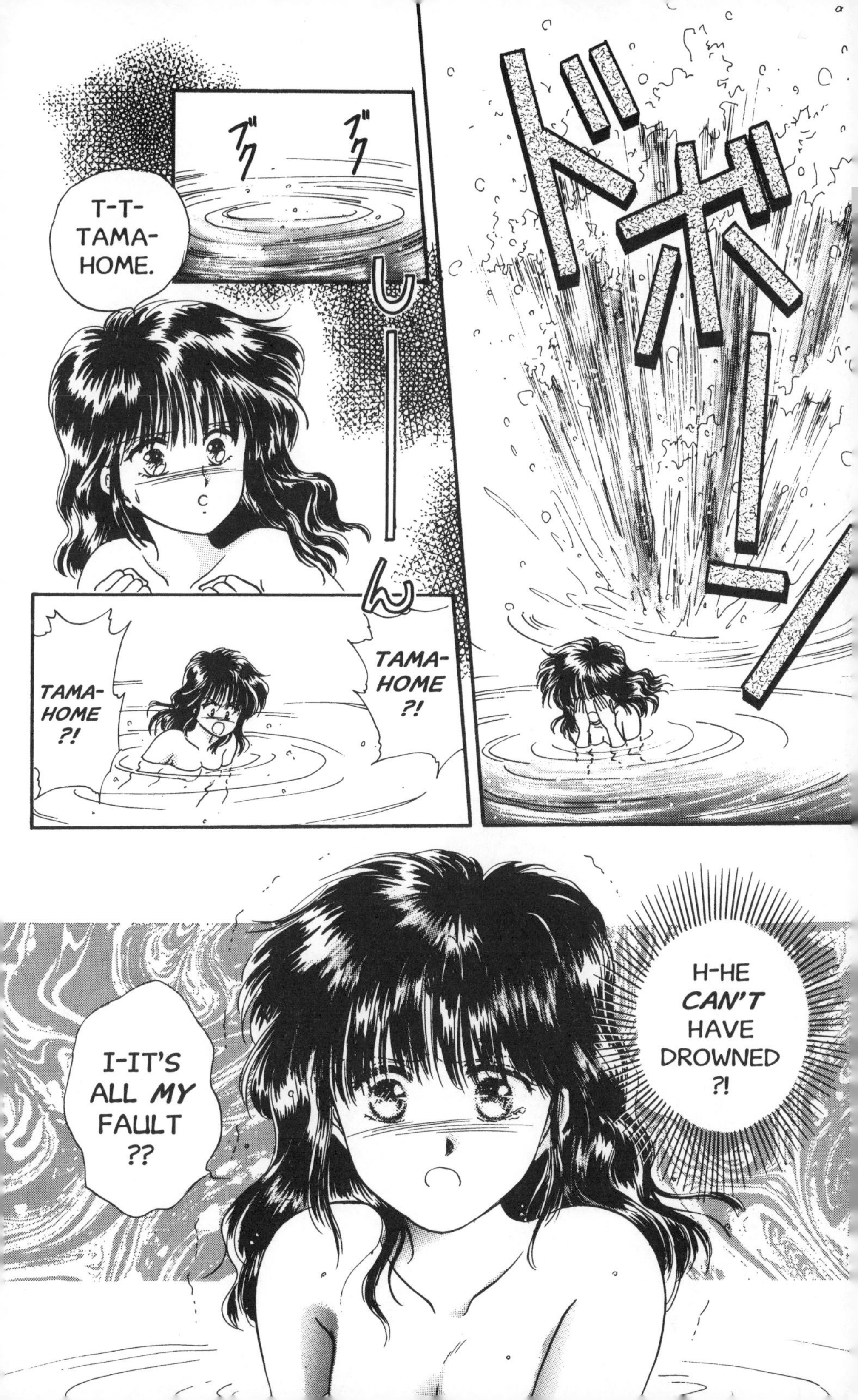
ドボーン
ブク ブク
T-T-TAMA-HOME.
しーん
TAMA-HOME ?!
TAMA-HOME ?!
H-HE *CAN'T* HAVE DROWNED ?!
I-IT'S ALL *MY* FAULT ??

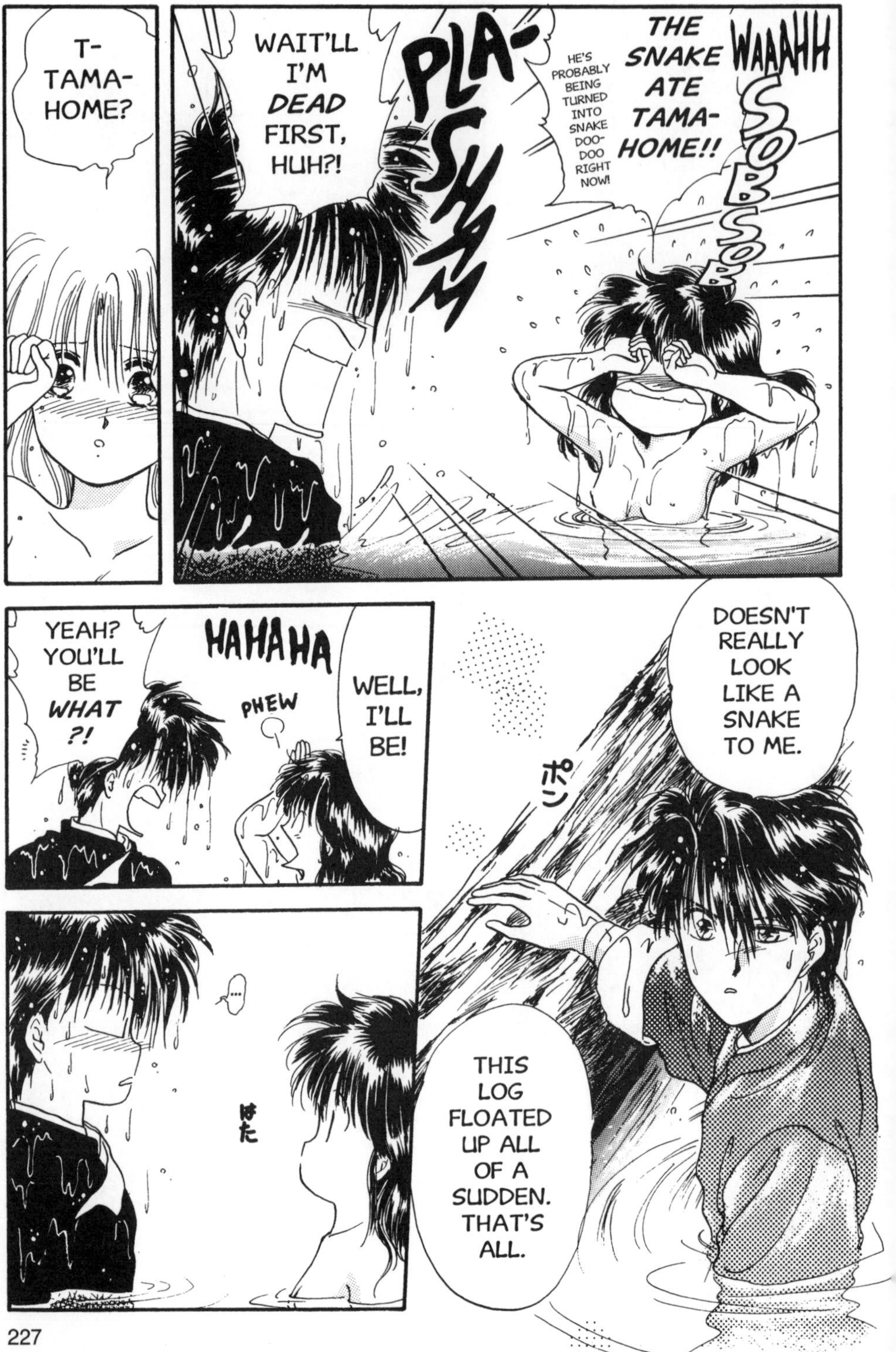
WAAAHH
SOB SOB
THE SNAKE ATE TAMA-HOME!!
HE'S PROBABLY BEING TURNED INTO SNAKE DOO-DOO RIGHT NOW!
PLA-SHAM
WAIT'LL I'M DEAD FIRST, HUH?!
T-TAMA-HOME?
DOESN'T REALLY LOOK LIKE A SNAKE TO ME.
ポン
THIS LOG FLOATED UP ALL OF A SUDDEN. THAT'S ALL.
WELL, I'LL BE!
HAHAHA
PHEW
YEAH? YOU'LL BE WHAT?!
...
はた

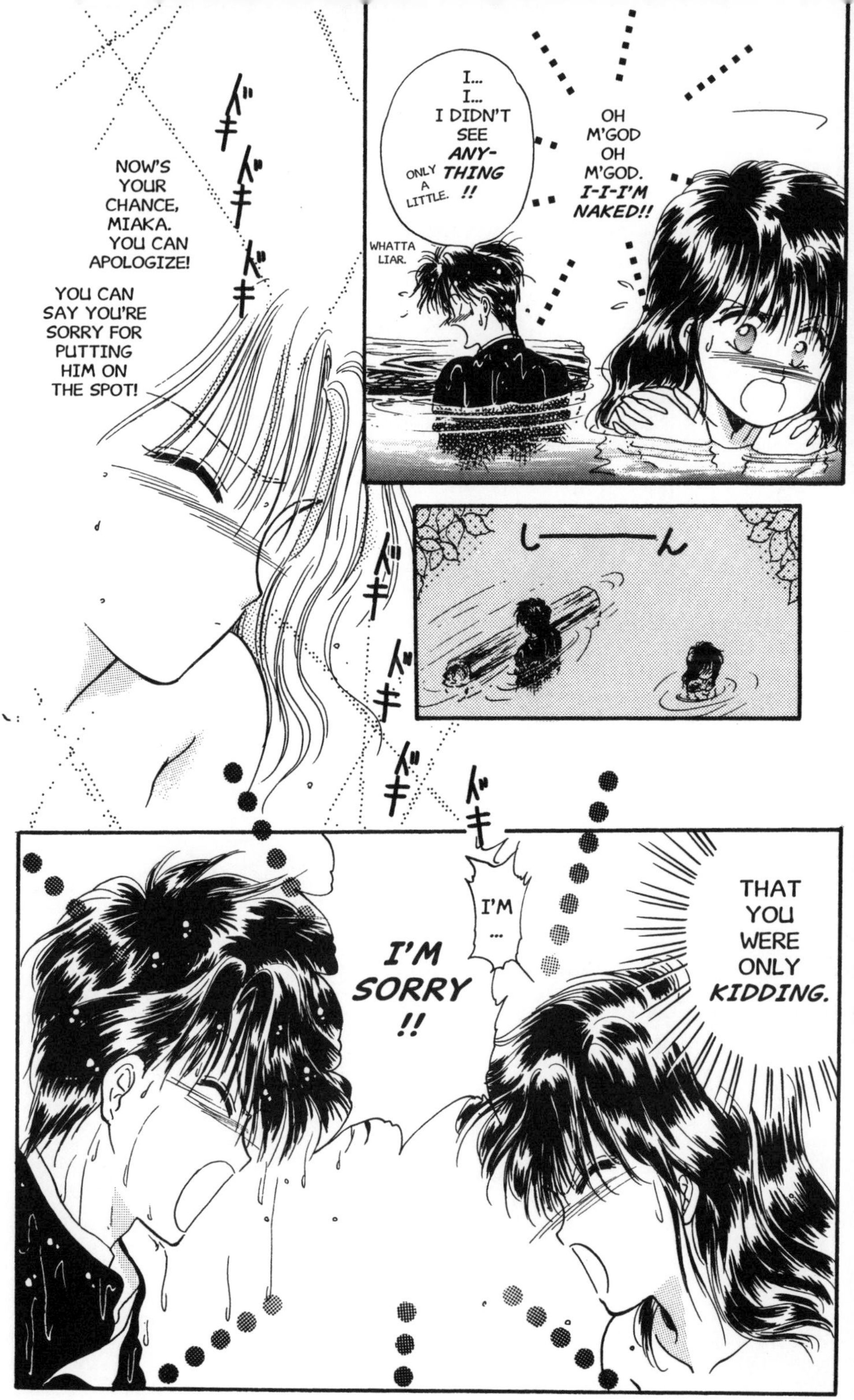

OH M'GOD OH M'GOD. I-I-I'M NAKED!!
I... I... I DIDN'T SEE ANYTHING!!
ONLY A LITTLE.
WHATTA LIAR.
し——ん
ドキ ドキ ドキ
NOW'S YOUR CHANCE, MIAKA. YOU CAN APOLOGIZE!
YOU CAN SAY YOU'RE SORRY FOR PUTTING HIM ON THE SPOT!
ドキ ドキ ドキ ドキ
THAT YOU WERE ONLY KIDDING.
I'M...
I'M SORRY!!

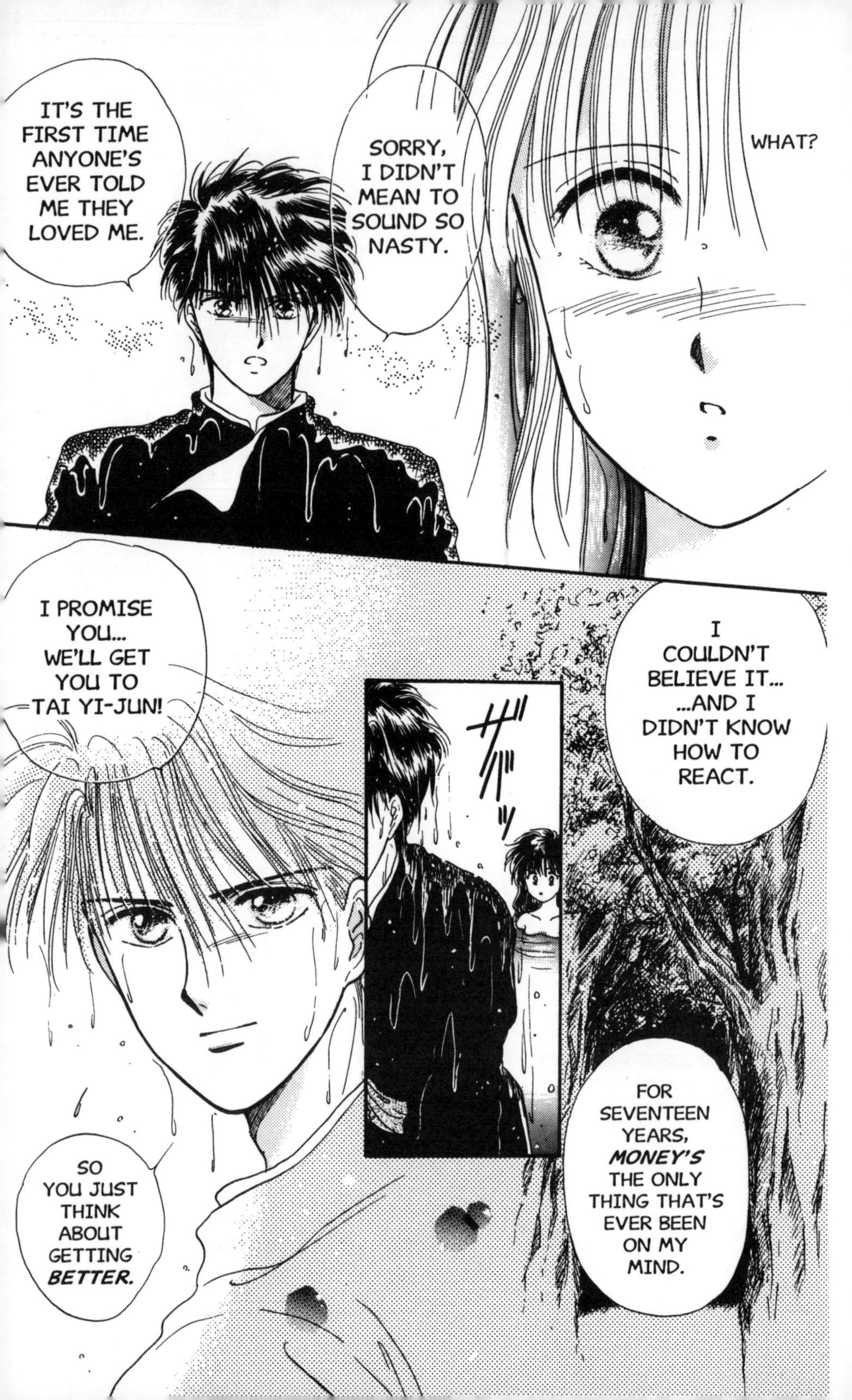
WHAT?
SORRY, I DIDN'T MEAN TO SOUND SO NASTY.
IT'S THE FIRST TIME ANYONE'S EVER TOLD ME THEY LOVED ME.
I COULDN'T BELIEVE IT... ...AND I DIDN'T KNOW HOW TO REACT.
FOR SEVENTEEN YEARS, ***MONEY'S*** THE ONLY THING THAT'S EVER BEEN ON MY MIND.
I PROMISE YOU... WE'LL GET YOU TO TAI YI-JUN!
SO YOU JUST THINK ABOUT GETTING ***BETTER.***

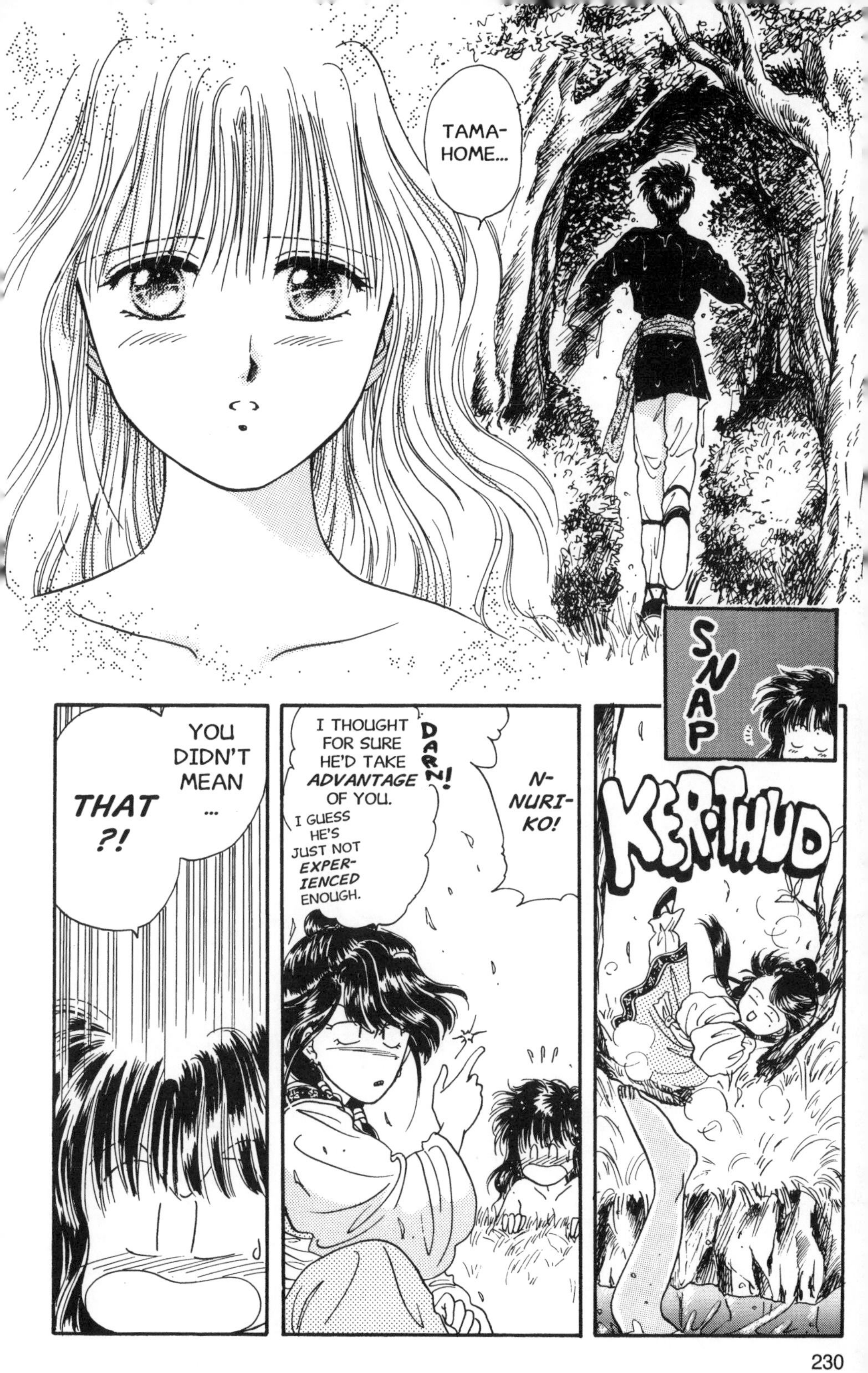
TAMA-HOME...
SNAP
KER-THUD
N-NURIKO!
DARN!
I THOUGHT FOR SURE HE'D TAKE *ADVANTAGE* OF YOU.
I GUESS HE'S JUST NOT *EXPERIENCED* ENOUGH.
YOU DIDN'T MEAN ... *THAT?!*

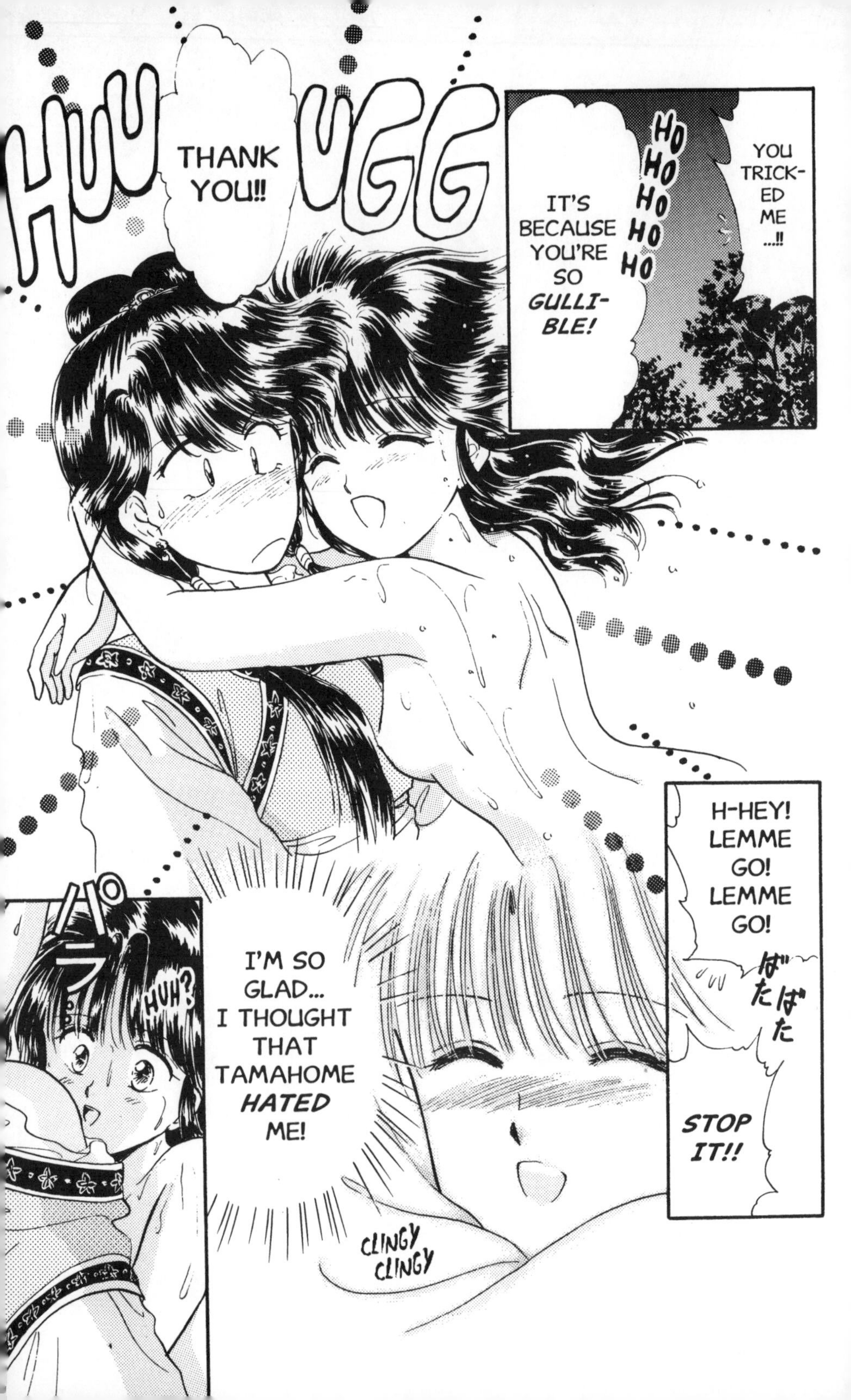

YOU TRICKED ME ...!!
HO HO HO HO HO
IT'S BECAUSE YOU'RE SO *GULLIBLE!*
HUUUGG
THANK YOU!!
H-HEY! LEMME GO! LEMME GO!
ばたばた
STOP IT!!
I'M SO GLAD... I THOUGHT THAT TAMAHOME *HATED* ME!
CLINGY CLINGY
パラ
HUH?

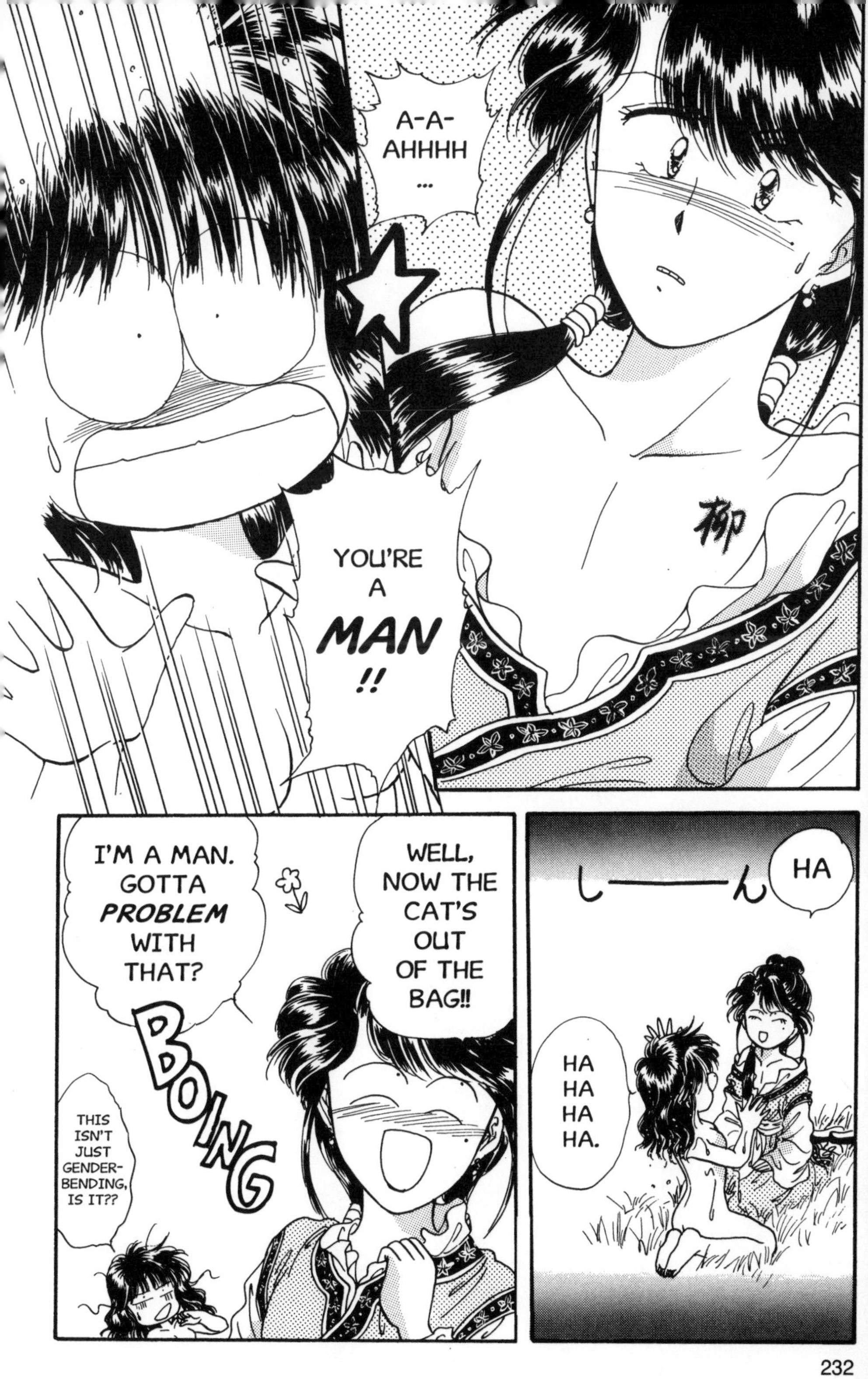

A-A-AHHHH ...
YOU'RE A MAN !!
HA
しーーん
HA HA HA HA.
WELL, NOW THE CAT'S OUT OF THE BAG!!
I'M A MAN. GOTTA PROBLEM WITH THAT?
BOING
THIS ISN'T JUST GENDER-BENDING, IS IT??

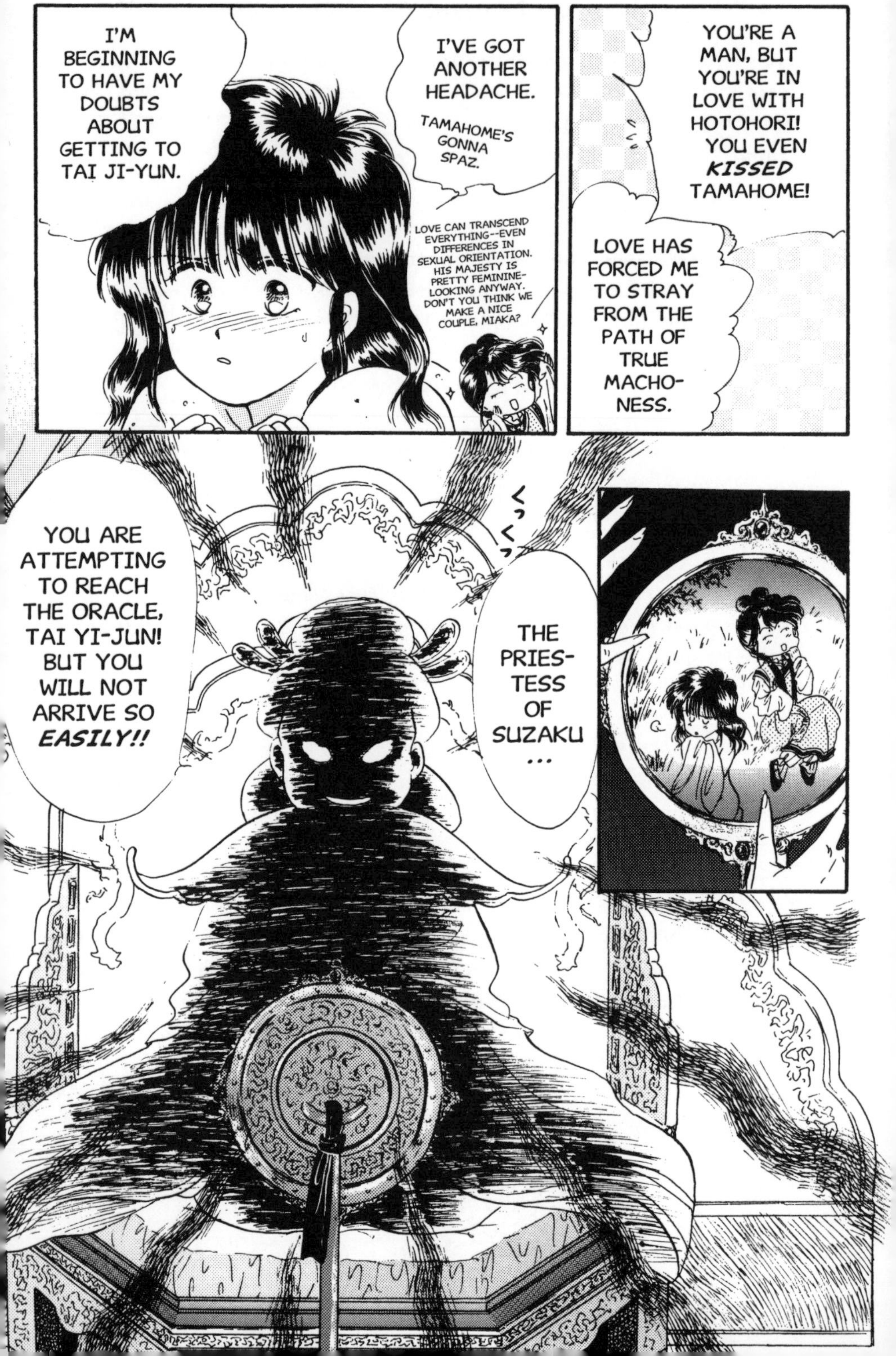
YOU'RE A MAN, BUT YOU'RE IN LOVE WITH HOTOHORI! YOU EVEN *KISSED* TAMAHOME!
LOVE HAS FORCED ME TO STRAY FROM THE PATH OF TRUE MACHO-NESS.
I'M BEGINNING TO HAVE MY DOUBTS ABOUT GETTING TO TAI JI-YUN.
I'VE GOT ANOTHER HEADACHE.
TAMAHOME'S GONNA SPAZ.
LOVE CAN TRANSCEND EVERYTHING--EVEN DIFFERENCES IN SEXUAL ORIENTATION. HIS MAJESTY IS PRETTY FEMININE-LOOKING ANYWAY. DON'T YOU THINK WE MAKE A NICE COUPLE, MIAKA?
くっくっ
THE PRIES-TESS OF SUZAKU...
YOU ARE ATTEMPTING TO REACH THE ORACLE, TAI YI-JUN! BUT YOU WILL NOT ARRIVE SO *EASILY!!*

Surprise! Some thoughts on the
● background music of *Fushigi Yūgi...* ●

- Lately I've been receiving tons of tapes. It makes me so happy! (things like *Romancing Saga, Nadia of the Mysterious Sea*, etc.!) One fan sent me *Urusei Yatsura* and *Ranma* material to be set to *Fushigi*. (Was that really *Ranma?* It was super dark stuff.) (Well done. Thank you.)

- I might also recommend the game music for *Romance of the Three Kingdoms II*. Its sound combines state of the art technology with ethnic music. It's totally my thing. I bought it immediately because Mr. Mukodani from Cassiopeia composed it. ♥ I like the first song that sounds Chinese but the 11th song, "Chosen no Mai," is pretty too. (Better to listen to it on headphones.) But the 14th song doesn't really work for me. I've been skipping it. Sorry, Mr. Mukodani!
 Also the game music to *Madara*. I really like the first song, "Ma Da Ra" (Reminds me of the image of the Suzaku seven stars), and the second song, "Yasuragi no Kimi e" (Comfort in You), reminds me of Miaka. There's only five songs but that's all right.

- Before we began this series, I heard the theme song "Hitomi no Naka no Far Away" (Far Away in Your Eyes) I think! from *Five Star Stories*. (I still haven't seen it.) and it gave me an image idea for this manga. A previous assistant copied "Wo Ai Ni" by 135 for me and I fell in love with it! Another song I love is "Nasuka no Kase" (The Winds of Nasuka)! The voice of that singer sounds as if Tamahome's singing.
 Also Logic System's *To Gen Kyo* (It's a long story so I won't get into how I got hold of it. Maybe I should return it.) The CD cover was modeled after the mountains of Daichi-san! "Coffee Rumba" is on it. Most of the songs are sung in Chinese by a woman. It has lyrics in English, Chinese, and Japanese. ("Rydeen" is sung in Chinese. The lyrics are incredible!) I really like "Shanghai Moonlight" (although I haven't heard much of it). It's got a sad, romantic melody with backing vocals singing "sayonara" in Japanese -- way cool. They're also singing "I love you" in Chinese as well. (The Japanese lyrics remind me of Japanese enka though). The first song is in Chinese, and the 11th song is the controversial "Virtual Reality." There are several instrumentals. Check it out if you can.

SO THE LATEST THING IS TECHNO POP, HUH?

HEY, "O," P-MODEL'S REALLY GOOD.

This is a little retro but the lyrics to "China Town" and "China Boy" have been used for *Koi wa Passion* (Love Is Passion). I don't understand the English lyrics to "Adesso e Fortuna" from *Lodoss Wars*, but I like it a lot too. ⤳ (Sorry if I'm wrong. I'd like to hear this song on a nice system).

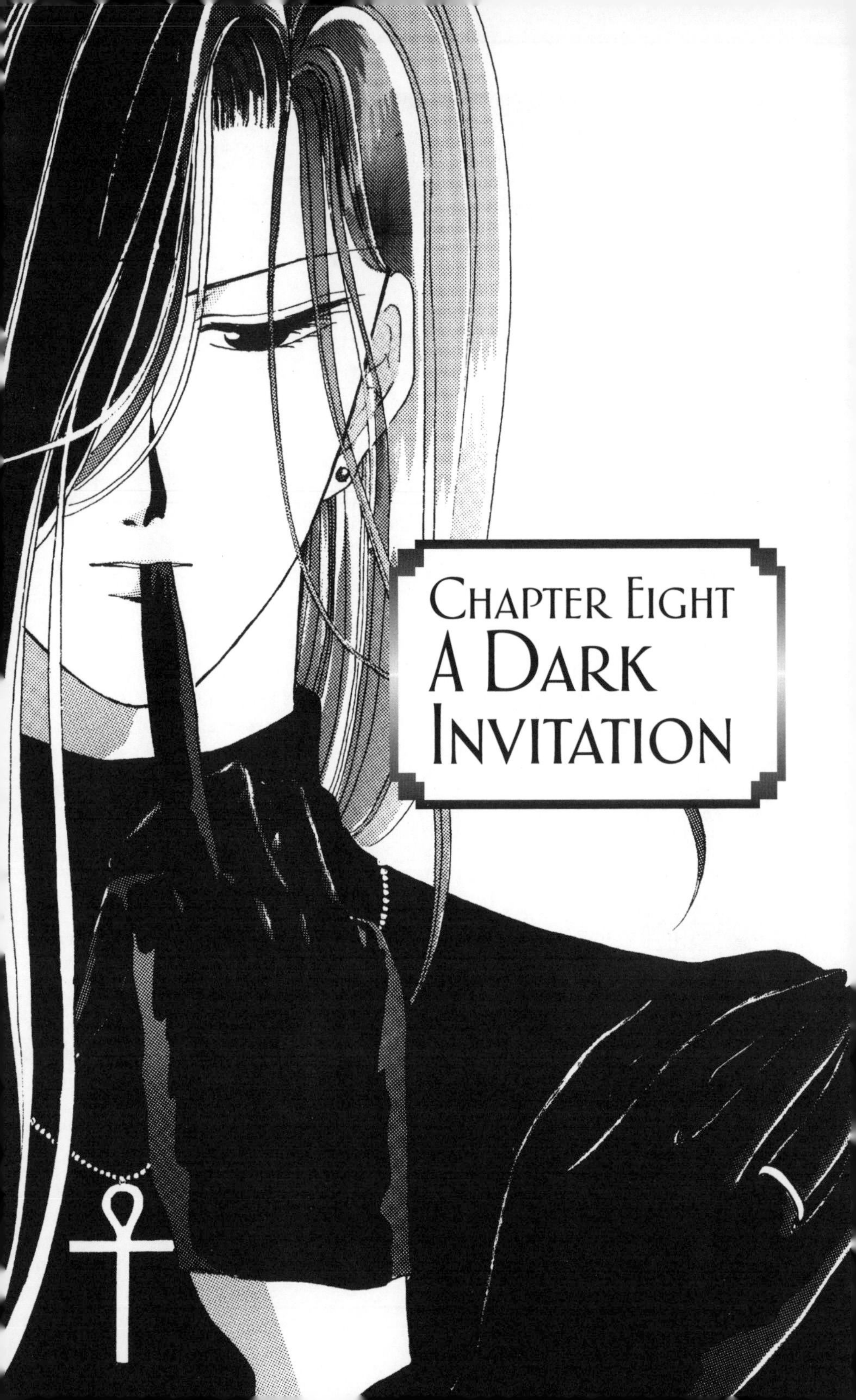
CHAPTER EIGHT
A DARK INVITATION

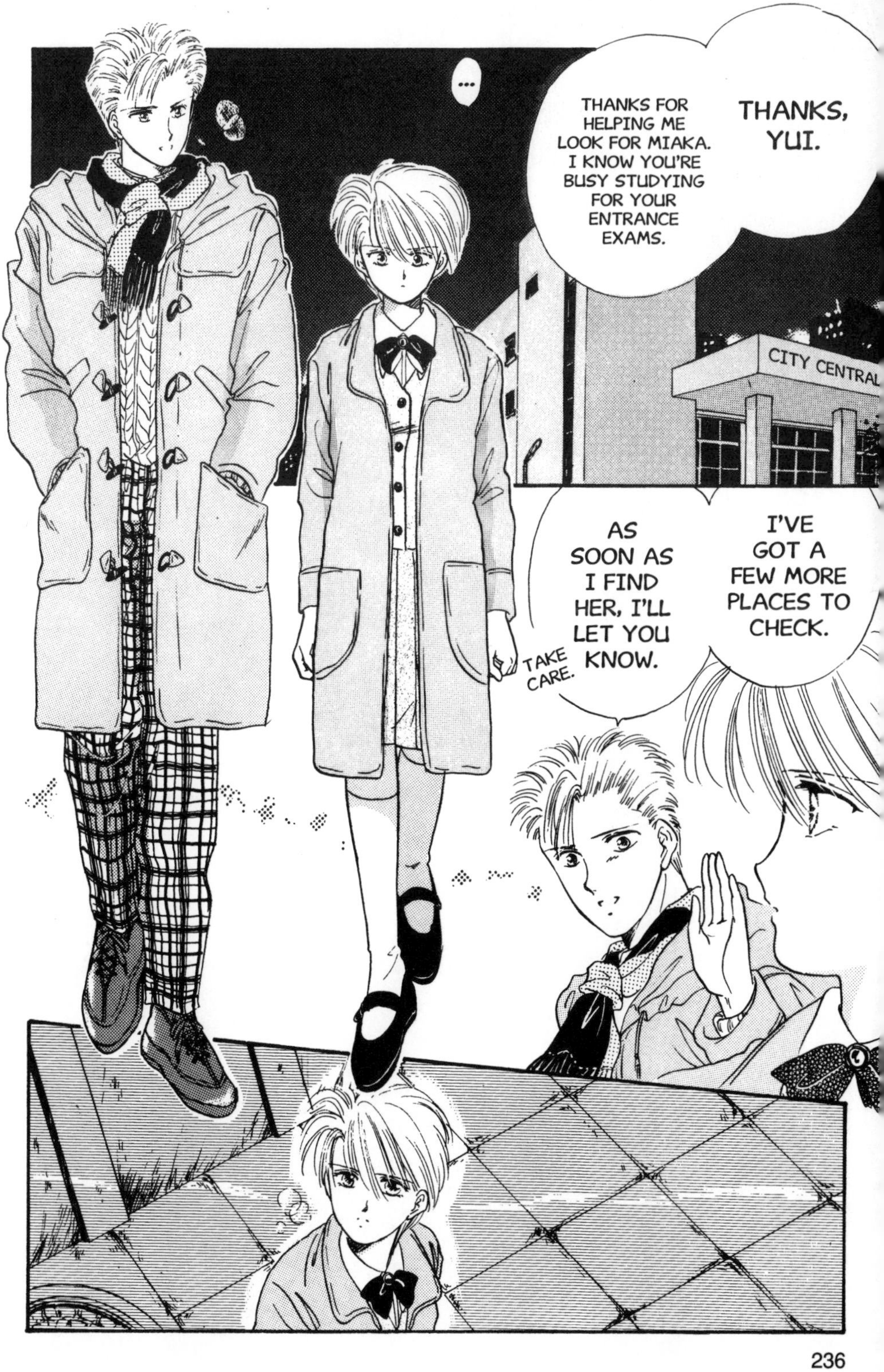
THANKS, YUI.
THANKS FOR HELPING ME LOOK FOR MIAKA. I KNOW YOU'RE BUSY STUDYING FOR YOUR ENTRANCE EXAMS.
CITY CENTRAL
...
I'VE GOT A FEW MORE PLACES TO CHECK.
AS SOON AS I FIND HER, I'LL LET YOU KNOW.
TAKE CARE.

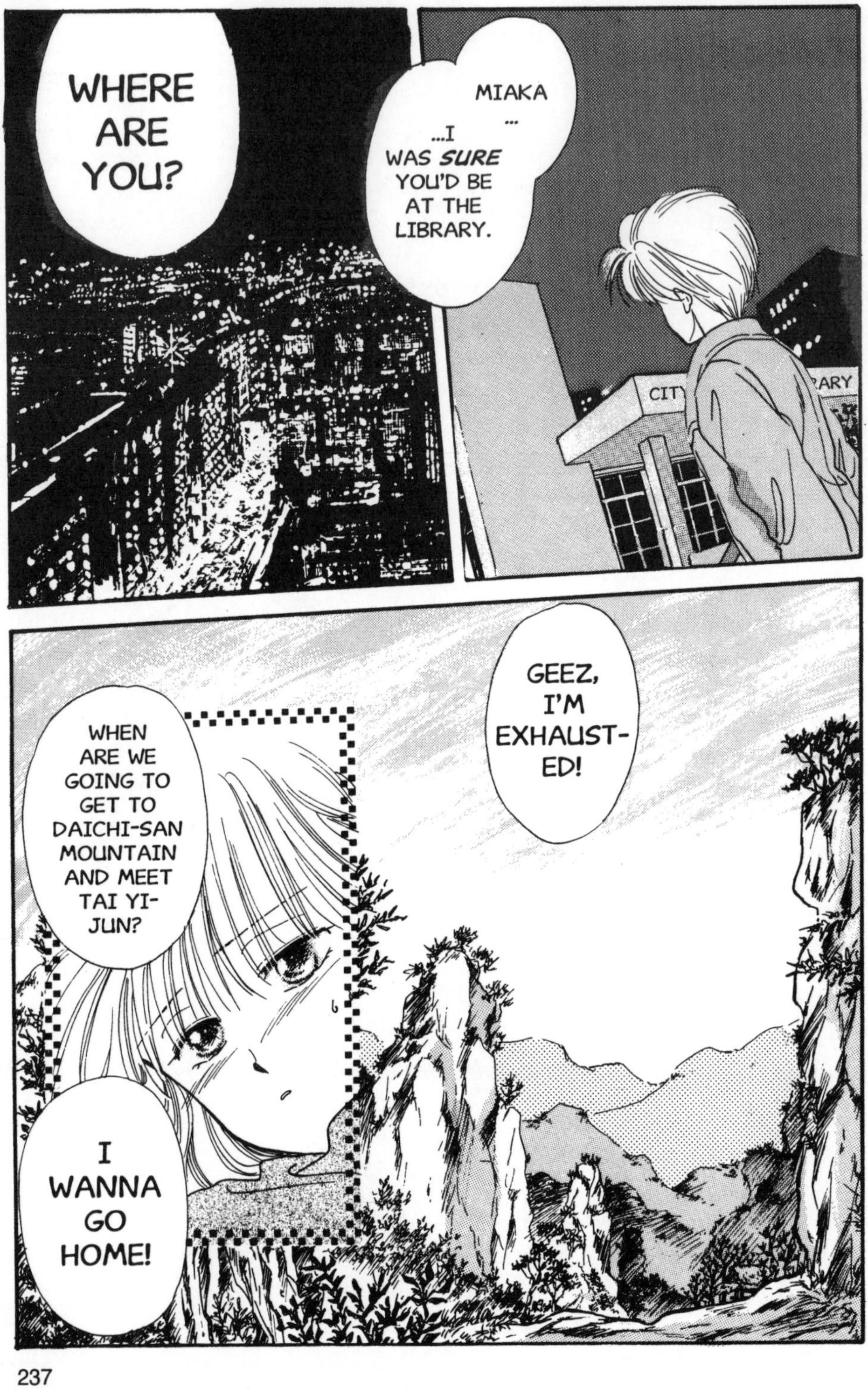
MIAKA ...
...I WAS *SURE* YOU'D BE AT THE LIBRARY.
WHERE ARE YOU?
GEEZ, I'M EXHAUST-ED!
WHEN ARE WE GOING TO GET TO DAICHI-SAN MOUNTAIN AND MEET TAI YI-JUN?
I WANNA GO HOME!

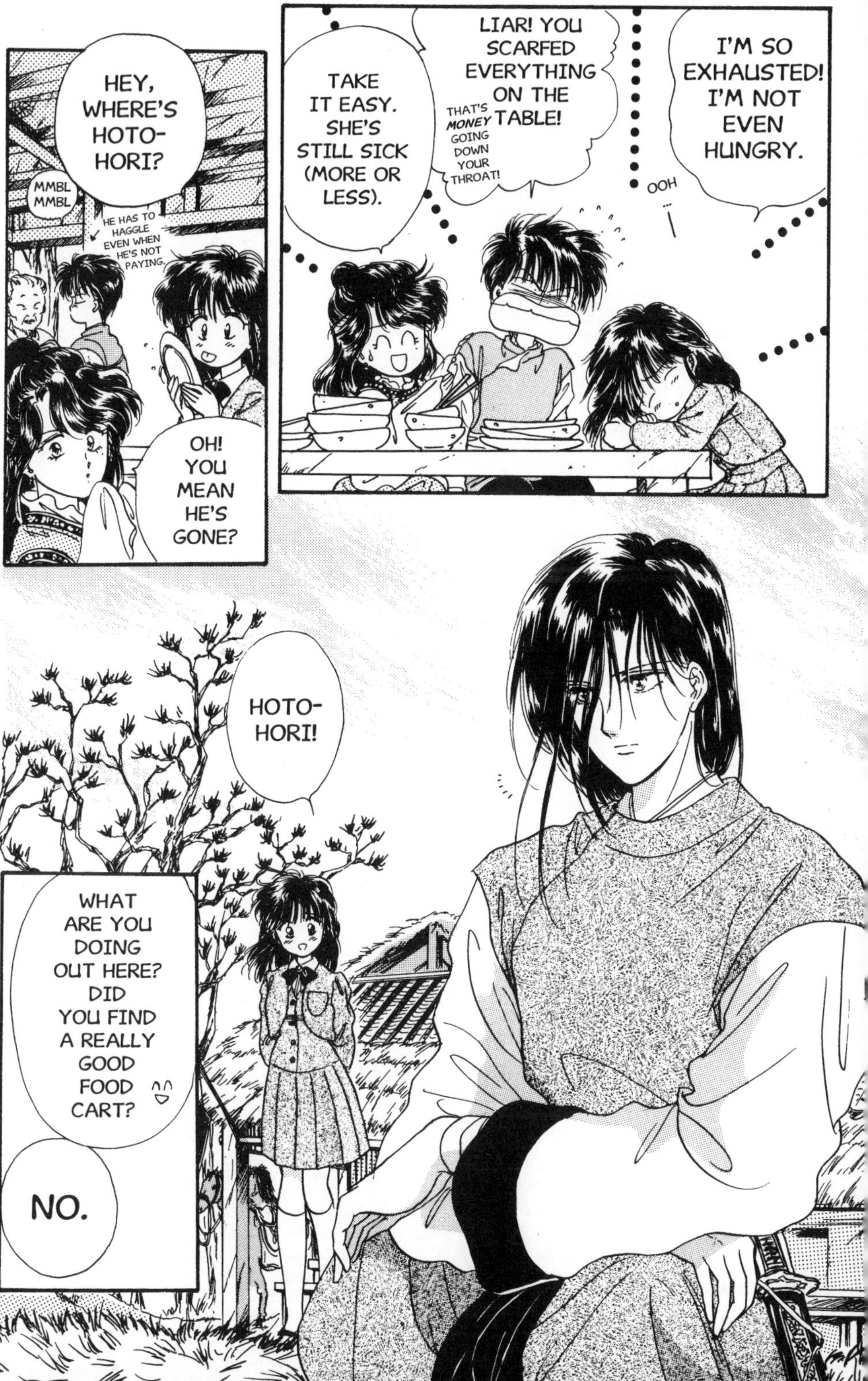
I'M SO EXHAUSTED! I'M NOT EVEN HUNGRY.
OOH...
LIAR! YOU SCARFED EVERYTHING ON THE TABLE!
THAT'S MONEY GOING DOWN YOUR THROAT!
TAKE IT EASY. SHE'S STILL SICK (MORE OR LESS).
HEY, WHERE'S HOTO-HORI?
MMBL MMBL
HE HAS TO HAGGLE EVEN WHEN HE'S NOT PAYING.
OH! YOU MEAN HE'S GONE?
HOTO-HORI!
WHAT ARE YOU DOING OUT HERE? DID YOU FIND A REALLY GOOD FOOD CART?
NO.

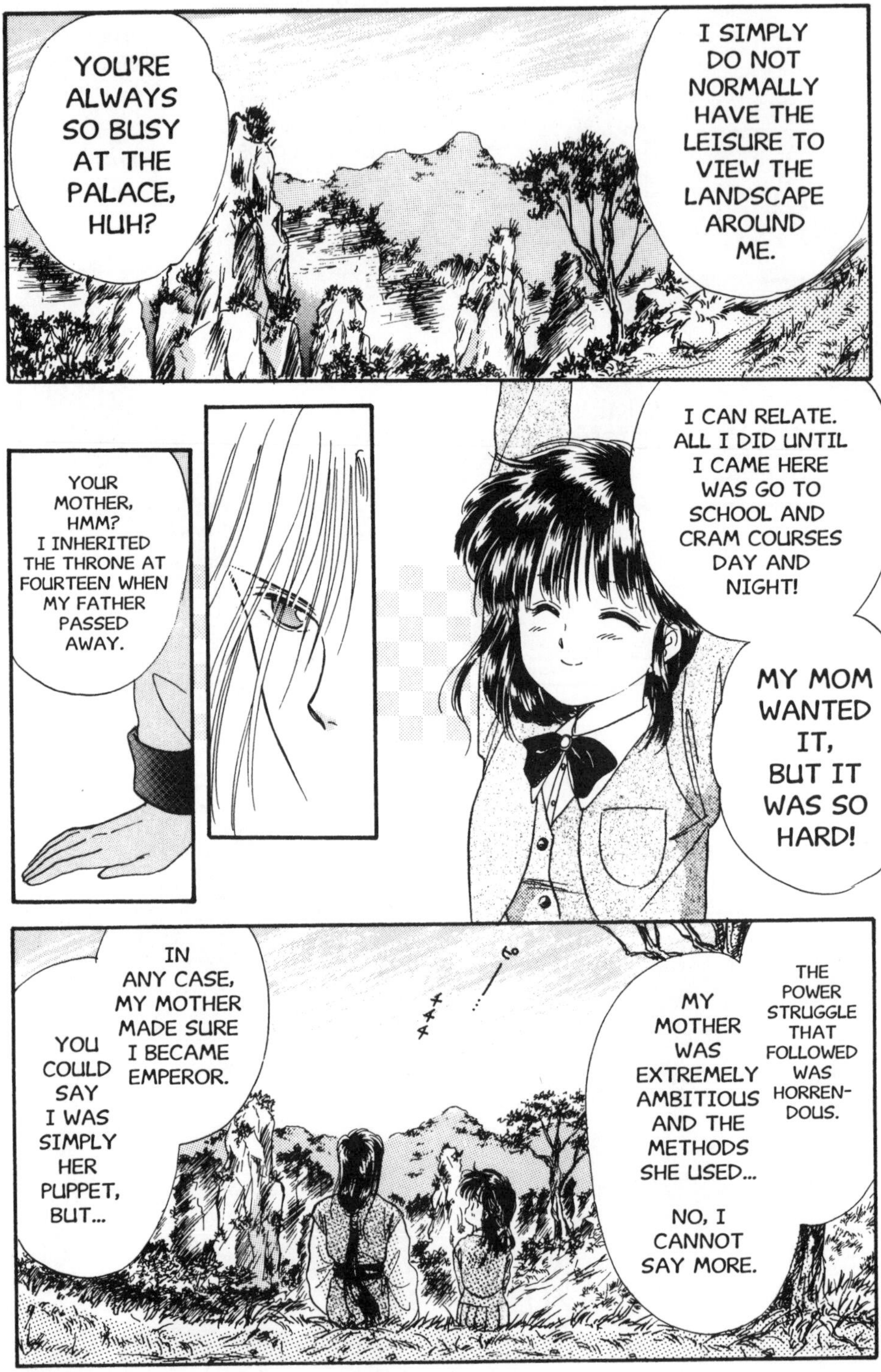
I SIMPLY DO NOT NORMALLY HAVE THE LEISURE TO VIEW THE LANDSCAPE AROUND ME.
YOU'RE ALWAYS SO BUSY AT THE PALACE, HUH?
I CAN RELATE. ALL I DID UNTIL I CAME HERE WAS GO TO SCHOOL AND CRAM COURSES DAY AND NIGHT!
MY MOM WANTED IT, BUT IT WAS SO HARD!
YOUR MOTHER, HMM? I INHERITED THE THRONE AT FOURTEEN WHEN MY FATHER PASSED AWAY.
THE POWER STRUGGLE THAT FOLLOWED WAS HORREN-DOUS.
MY MOTHER WAS EXTREMELY AMBITIOUS AND THE METHODS SHE USED...
NO, I CANNOT SAY MORE.
IN ANY CASE, MY MOTHER MADE SURE I BECAME EMPEROR.
YOU COULD SAY I WAS SIMPLY HER PUPPET, BUT...

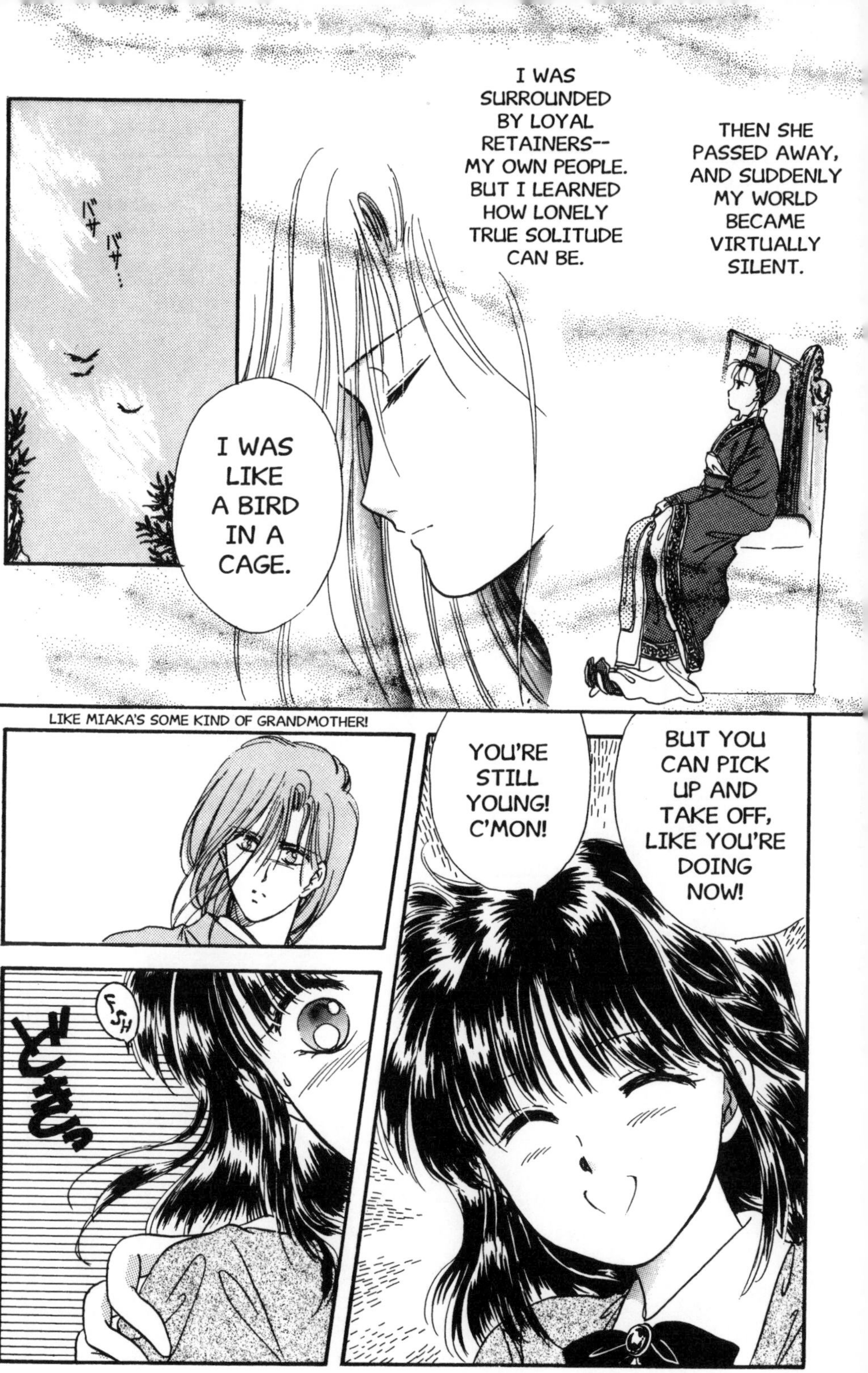

THEN SHE PASSED AWAY, AND SUDDENLY MY WORLD BECAME VIRTUALLY SILENT.
I WAS SURROUNDED BY LOYAL RETAINERS-- MY OWN PEOPLE. BUT I LEARNED HOW LONELY TRUE SOLITUDE CAN BE.
バサ バサ…
I WAS LIKE A BIRD IN A CAGE.
BUT YOU CAN PICK UP AND TAKE OFF, LIKE YOU'RE DOING NOW!
YOU'RE STILL YOUNG! C'MON!
LIKE MIAKA'S SOME KIND OF GRANDMOTHER!

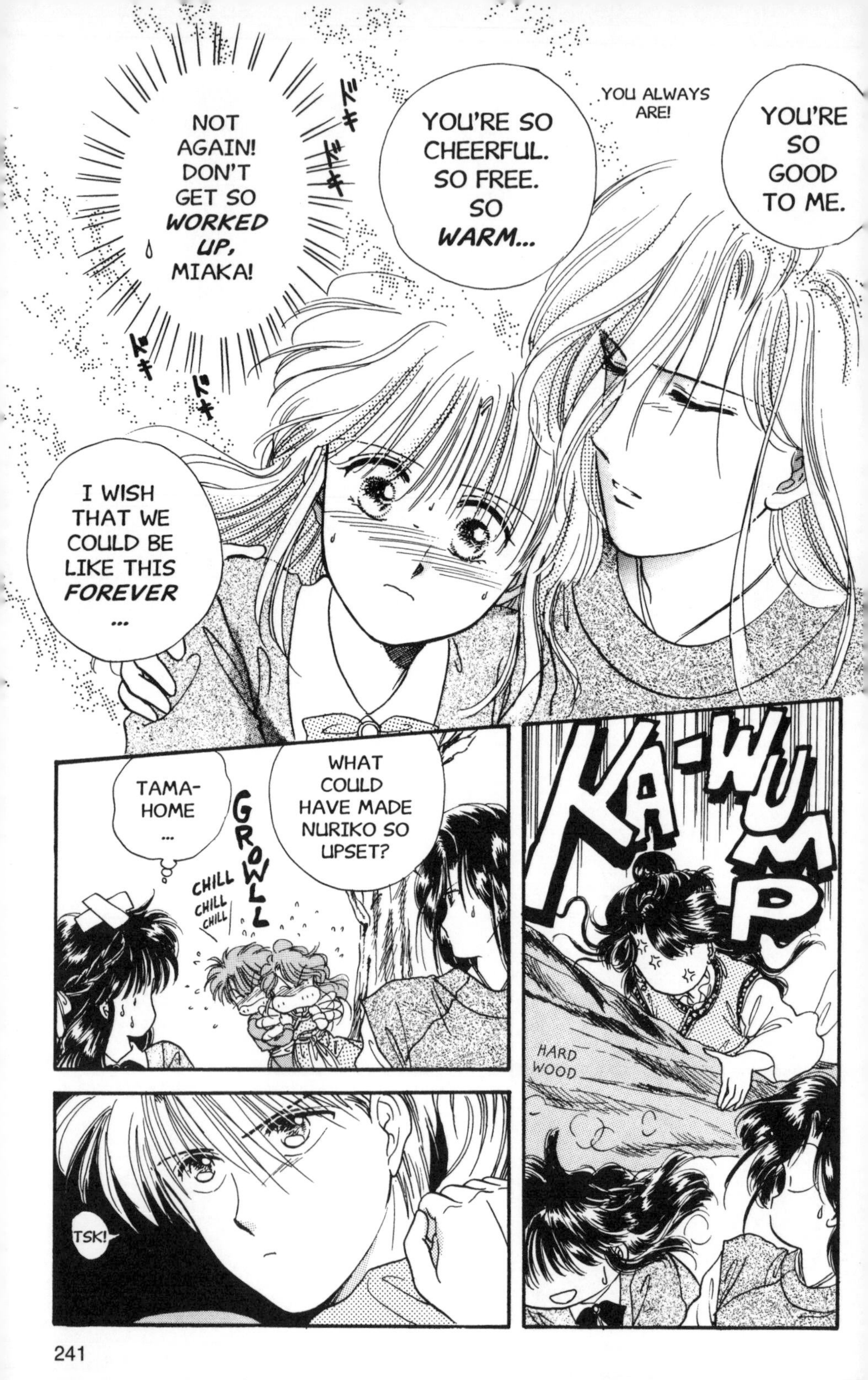

YOU'RE SO GOOD TO ME.
YOU ALWAYS ARE!
YOU'RE SO CHEERFUL. SO FREE. SO *WARM*...
ドキ ドキ
NOT AGAIN! DON'T GET SO *WORKED UP,* MIAKA!
ドキ ドキ
I WISH THAT WE COULD BE LIKE THIS *FOREVER* ...
KA-WUMP
HARD WOOD
WHAT COULD HAVE MADE NURIKO SO UPSET?
GROWLL
TAMA-HOME ...
CHILL CHILL CHILL
TSK!

WELL, WELL.
SHALL WE SEE...
...IF THEY CAN HANDLE A *TEST?*
フッ
クル クル
クル クル
...
...
フッ

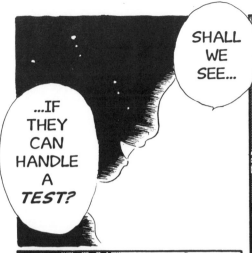

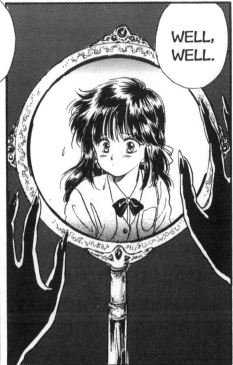

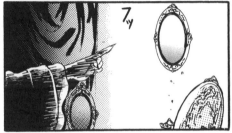

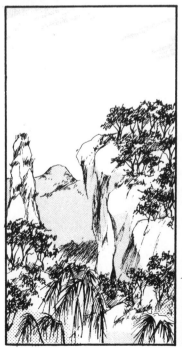

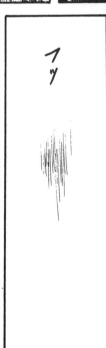

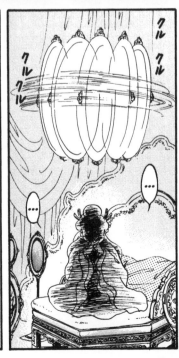

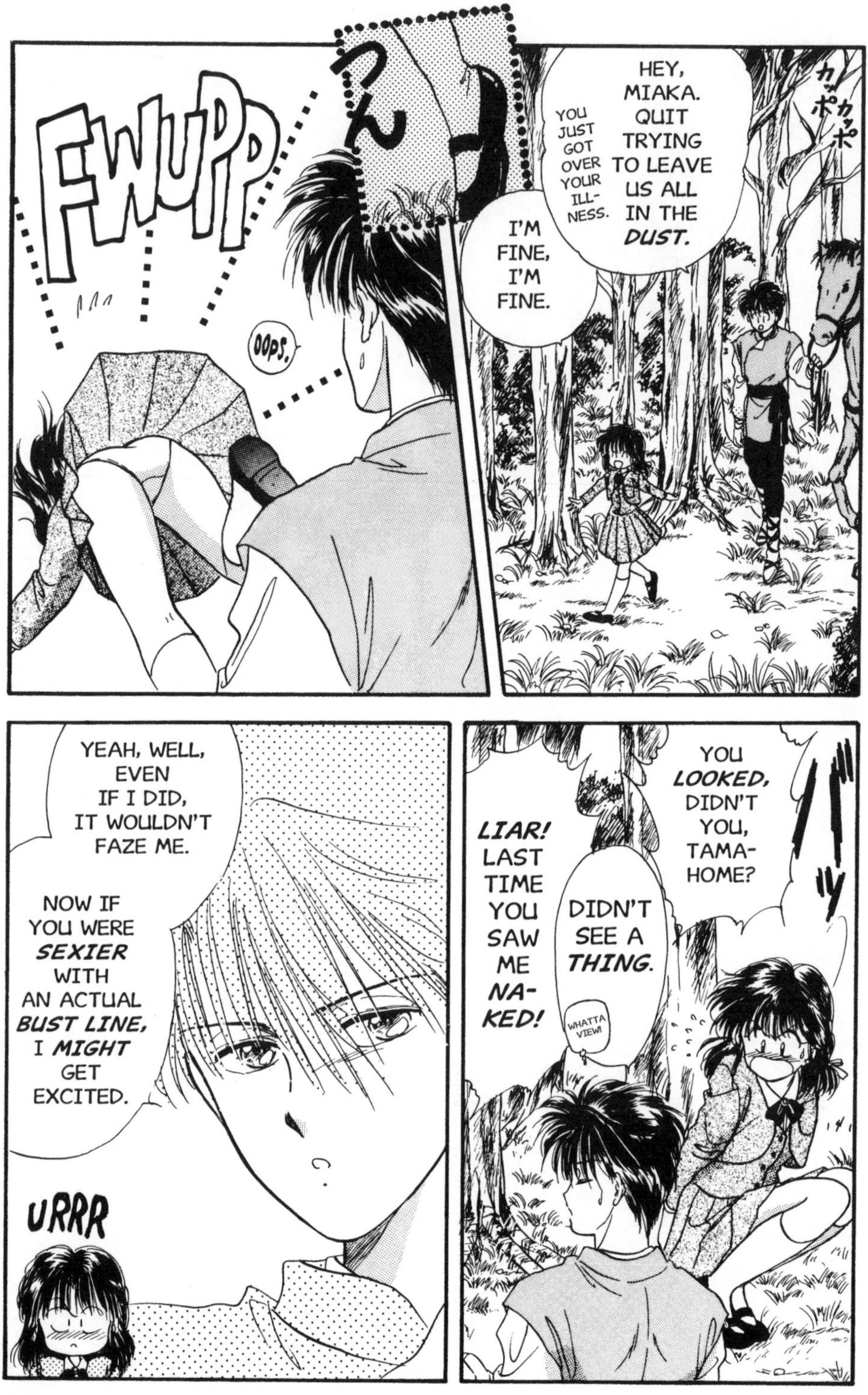
カッポカッポ
HEY, MIAKA. QUIT TRYING TO LEAVE US ALL IN THE *DUST.*
YOU JUST GOT OVER YOUR ILL-NESS.
I'M FINE, I'M FINE.
うん
FWUPP
OOPS.
バッ
YOU *LOOKED,* DIDN'T YOU, TAMA-HOME?
DIDN'T SEE A *THING.*
LIAR! LAST TIME YOU SAW ME *NA-KED!*
WHATTA VIEW!
YEAH, WELL, EVEN IF I DID, IT WOULDN'T FAZE ME.
NOW IF YOU WERE *SEXIER* WITH AN ACTUAL *BUST LINE,* I *MIGHT* GET EXCITED.
URRR

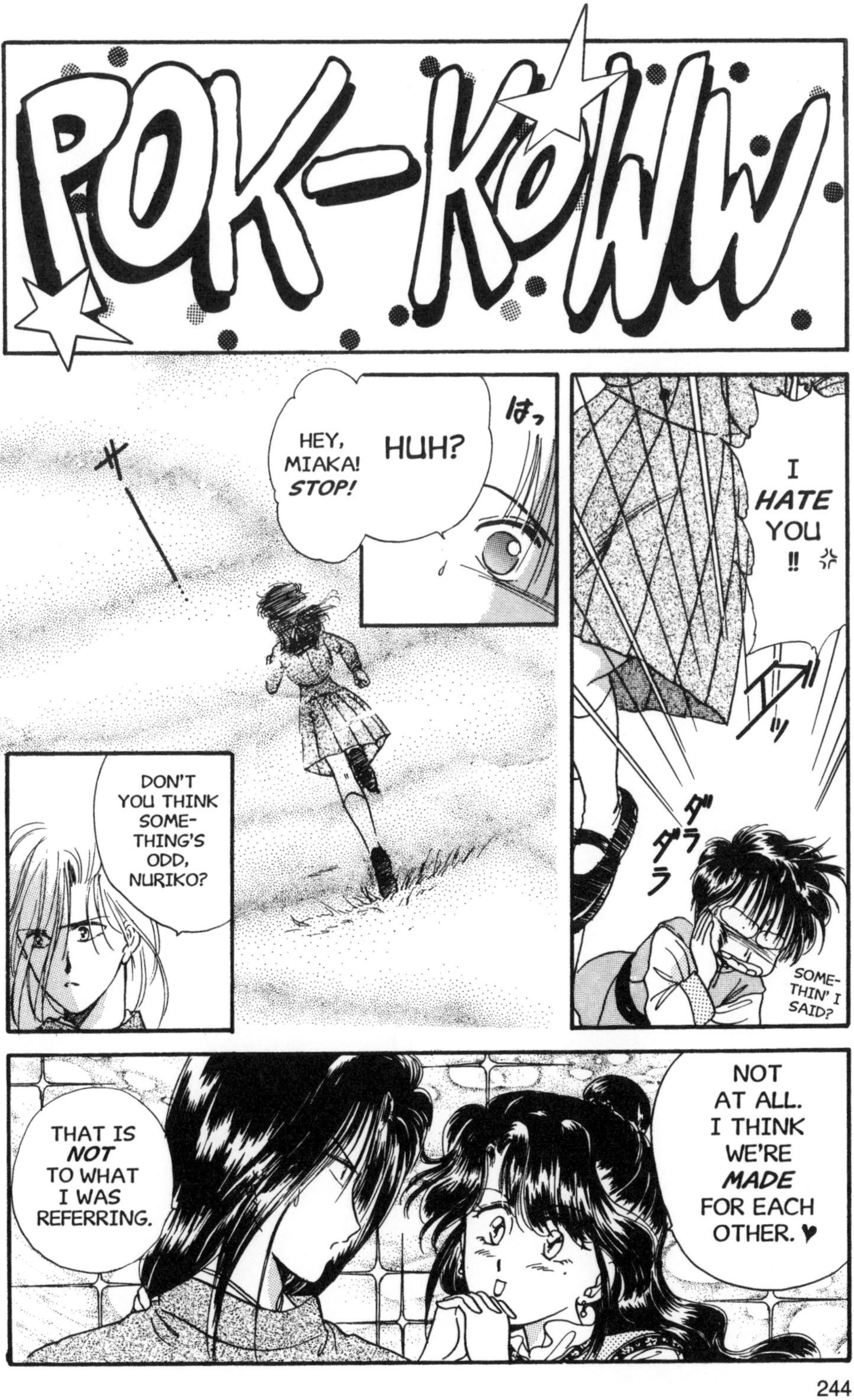
POK-KOWW
I ***HATE*** YOU !!
ダラダラ
SOME-THIN' I SAID?
はっ
HUH?
HEY, MIAKA! ***STOP!***
DON'T YOU THINK SOME-THING'S ODD, NURIKO?
NOT AT ALL. I THINK WE'RE ***MADE*** FOR EACH OTHER. ♥
THAT IS ***NOT*** TO WHAT I WAS REFERRING.

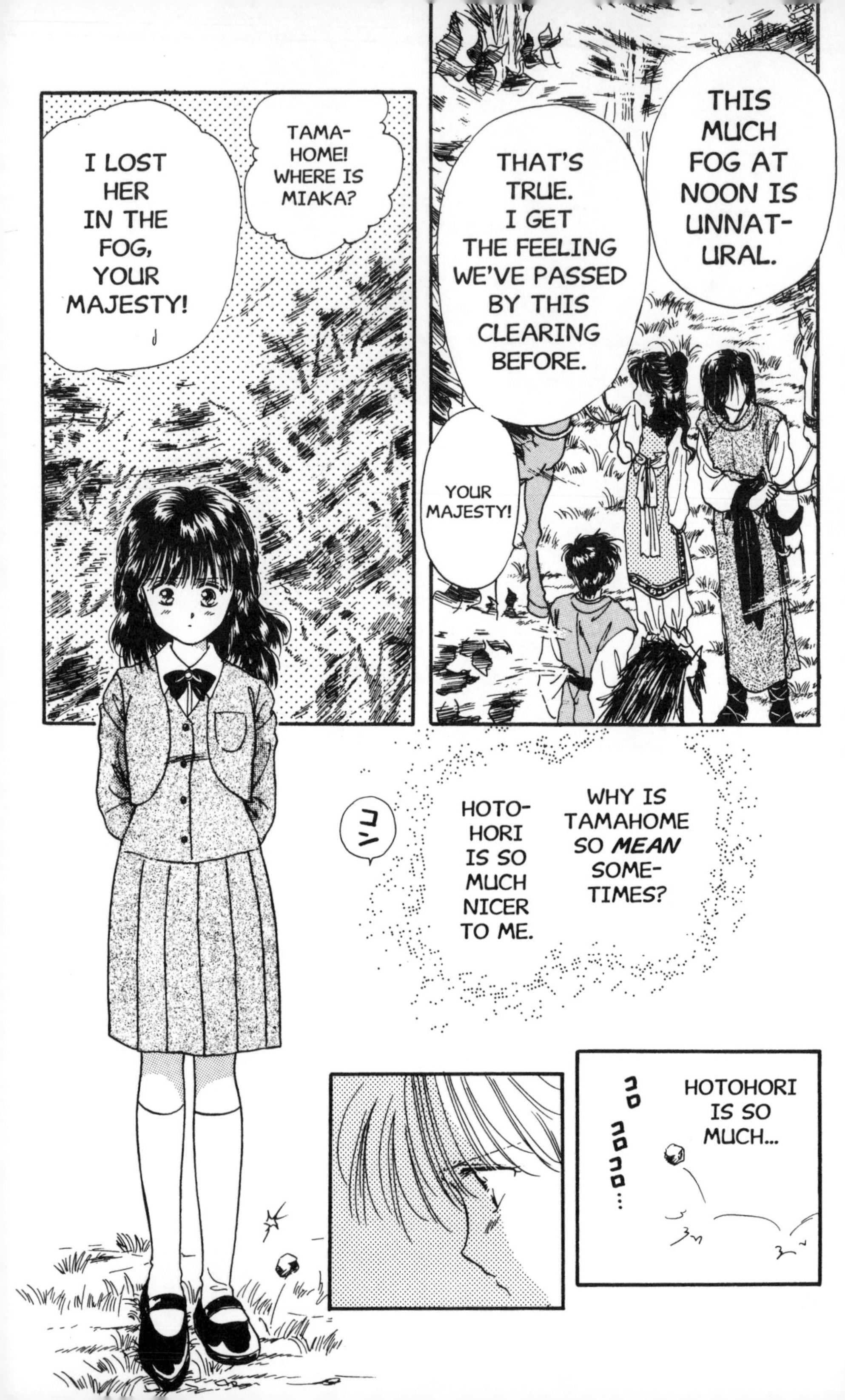
THIS MUCH FOG AT NOON IS UNNATURAL.
THAT'S TRUE. I GET THE FEELING WE'VE PASSED BY THIS CLEARING BEFORE.
YOUR MAJESTY!
TAMA-HOME! WHERE IS MIAKA?
I LOST HER IN THE FOG, YOUR MAJESTY!
WHY IS TAMAHOME SO *MEAN* SOMETIMES?
HOTOHORI IS SO MUCH NICER TO ME.
コン
HOTOHORI IS SO MUCH...
コロ コロコロ...

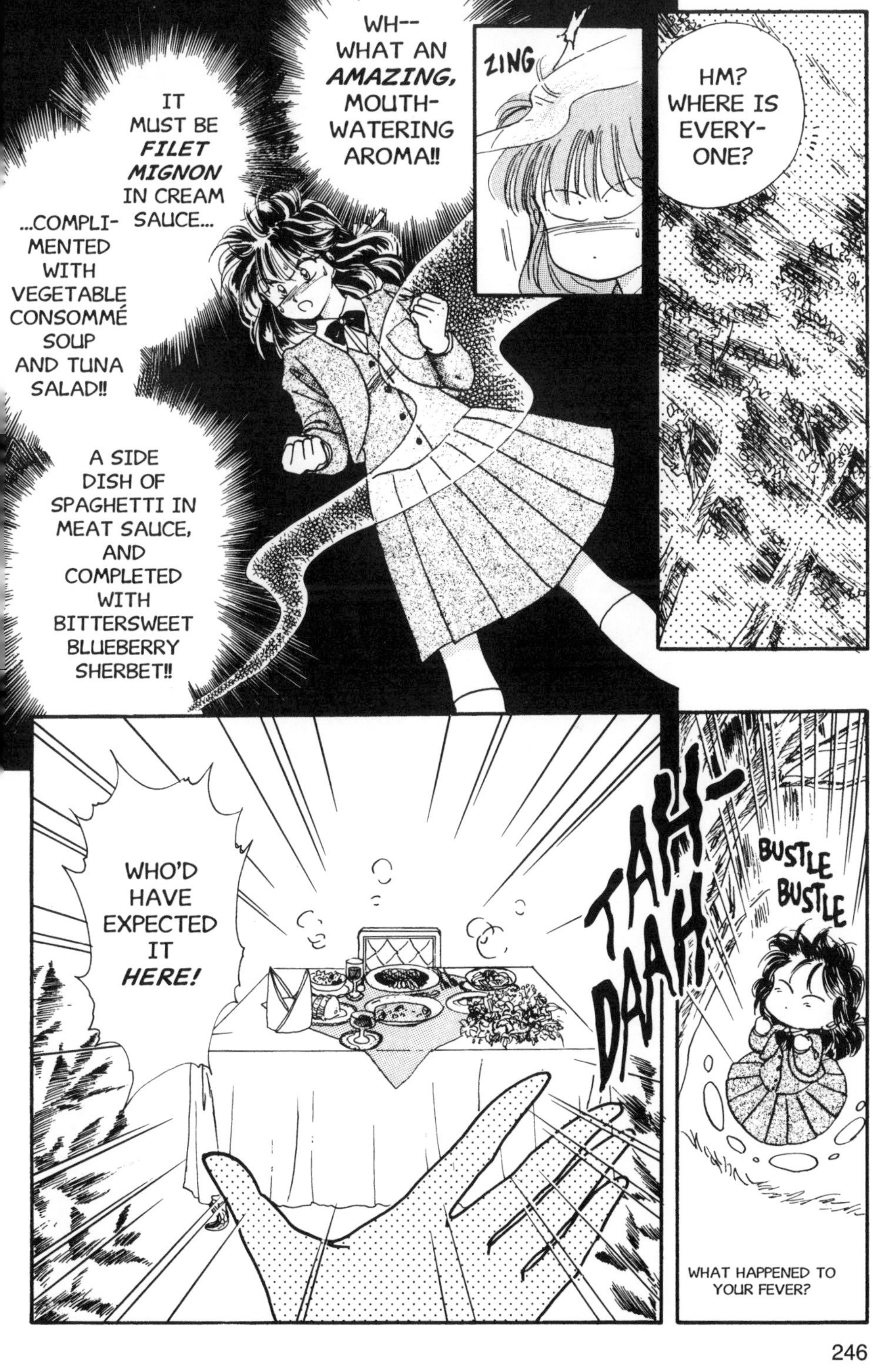
HM? WHERE IS EVERYONE?
ZING
WH-- WHAT AN *AMAZING,* MOUTH-WATERING AROMA!!
IT MUST BE *FILET MIGNON* IN CREAM SAUCE...
...COMPLIMENTED WITH VEGETABLE CONSOMMÉ SOUP AND TUNA SALAD!!
A SIDE DISH OF SPAGHETTI IN MEAT SAUCE, AND COMPLETED WITH BITTERSWEET BLUEBERRY SHERBET!!
BUSTLE BUSTLE
WHAT HAPPENED TO YOUR FEVER?
TAH-DAAH
WHO'D HAVE EXPECTED IT *HERE!*

When I said that I felt sick, I wasn't being modest or begging for sympathy. So don't say, "Oh no, your work is great!!"

Before starting the series, my confidence was at such an all-time low that my stomach really began to ache. My editor told me, "Oh, that. It's an occupational illness." Even now, sometimes when I look at my pages, I just want to tear them to shreds. Or when I'm assigned to do some color pages in the weekly magazine, I ask, "Are you sure you want me to do them?" Or I end up worrying whether they would even put out the first graphic novel. What is wrong with me? My assistant told me I'm weird. Maybe I put down my characters or my work because I lack confidence. By criticizing it, I can be the first to say, "What is this junk?" That's why your letters mean so much to me. I'm so pathetic...

Even when the first graphic novel came out, I was more stressed than happy (which has always been the case with my other manga as well). I would worry that someone would pick it up and say, "What is this junk?" and toss it away. So I'm happy to hear that people are reading it. I'm happy about the *Fushigi Yūgi* CDs as well, but I deal with them the same way. Today is June 30th, the day before the release of volume 2, so it'll already be out by the time you read this. Ugh, how much longer will this go on?

Oh, yes, thanks to those readers receiving the short "Watase Newsletter" for expressing their gratitude (by fan mail, of course). The reason why I had "Yū" in small letters was that my full name is often mistaken for a boy's name, so just to avoid any misunderstanding with your parents, I figured we could pretend to be friends (which might end up creating further misunderstandings).

The "Post-Recording Anecdotes" in the CD booklet was supposed to be "Recording Anecdotes." Human error. No one seemed to notice anyway.

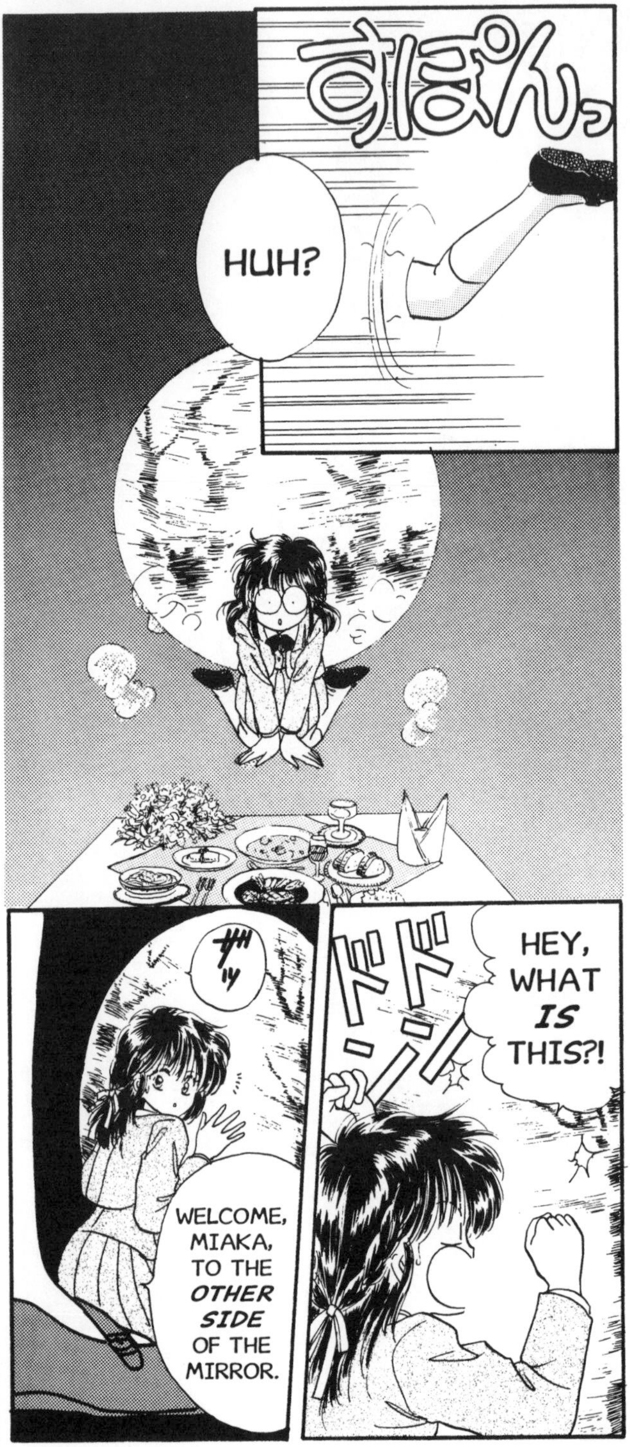
すぽんっ
HUH?
HEY, WHAT *IS* THIS?!
ドドー
ザッ
WELCOME, MIAKA, TO THE *OTHER SIDE* OF THE MIRROR.

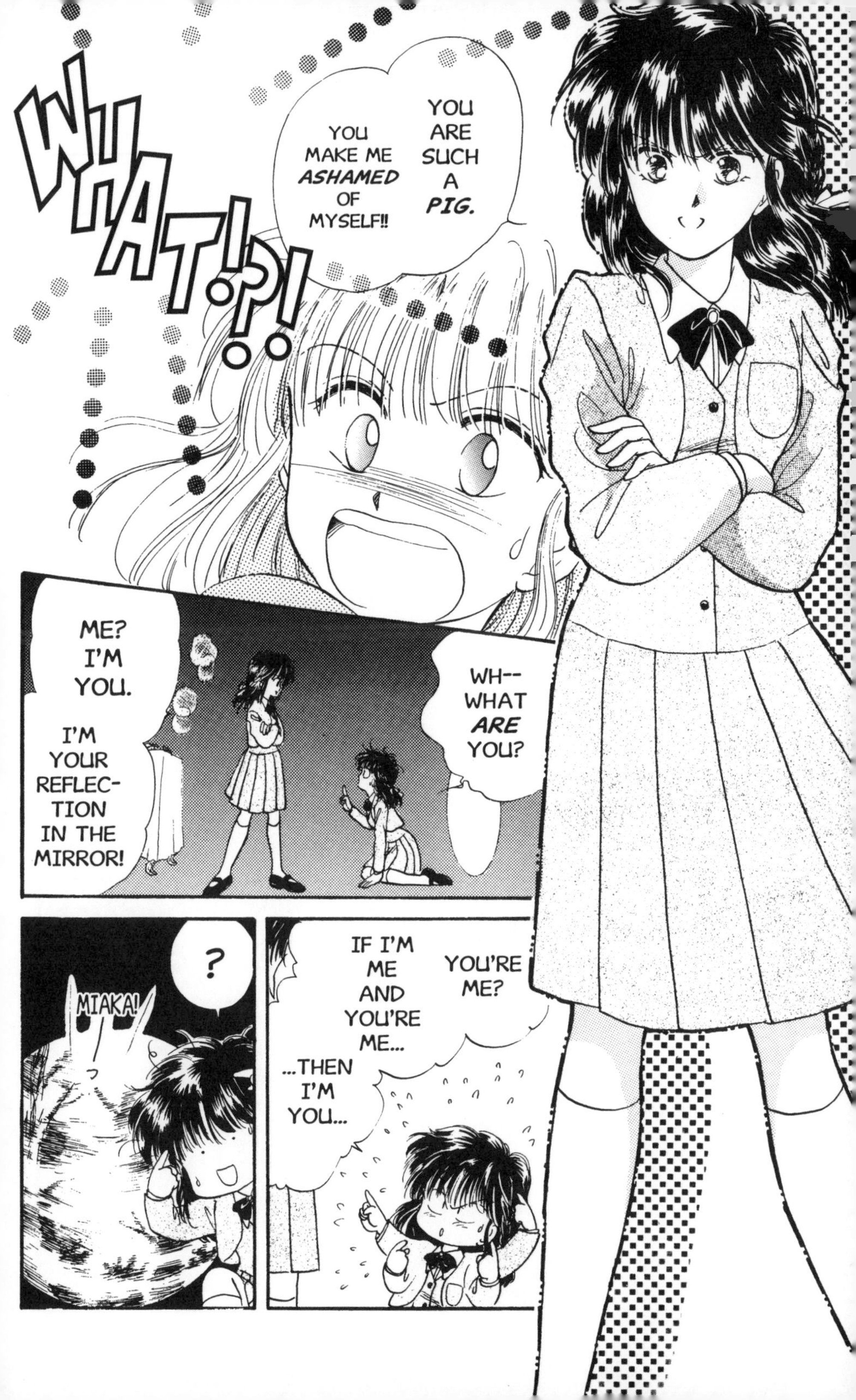
YOU ARE SUCH A *PIG.*
YOU MAKE ME *ASHAMED* OF MYSELF!!
WHAT!?!
WH-- WHAT *ARE* YOU?
ME? I'M YOU.
I'M YOUR REFLECTION IN THE MIRROR!
YOU'RE ME?
IF I'M ME AND YOU'RE ME...
...THEN I'M YOU...
?
MIAKA!

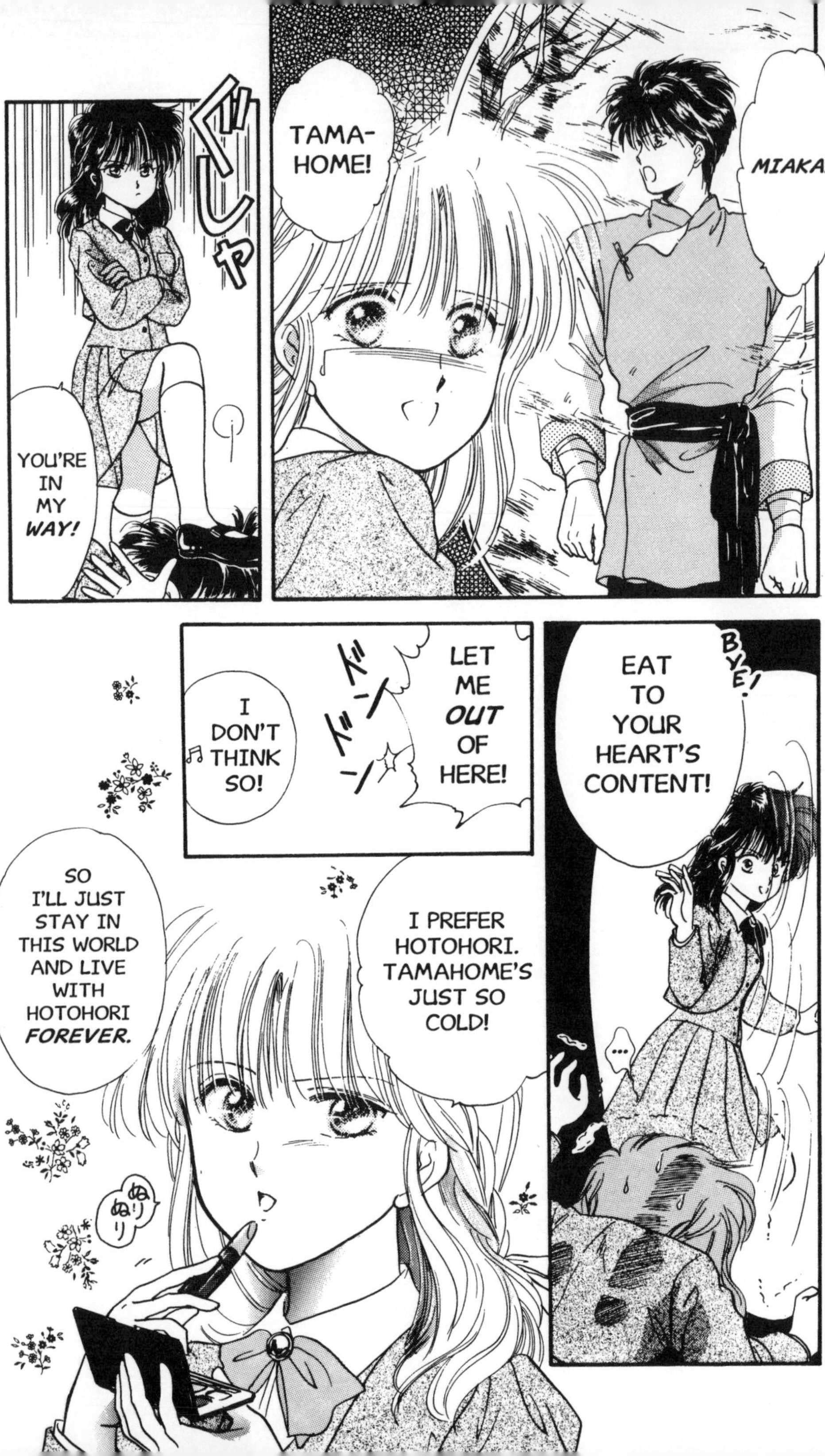
MIAKA!
TAMA-HOME!
ぐしゃ
YOU'RE IN MY WAY!
BYE!
EAT TO YOUR HEART'S CONTENT!
...
LET ME OUT OF HERE!
ドン ドン
I DON'T THINK SO!
I PREFER HOTOHORI. TAMAHOME'S JUST SO COLD!
SO I'LL JUST STAY IN THIS WORLD AND LIVE WITH HOTOHORI FOREVER.
ぬりぬり

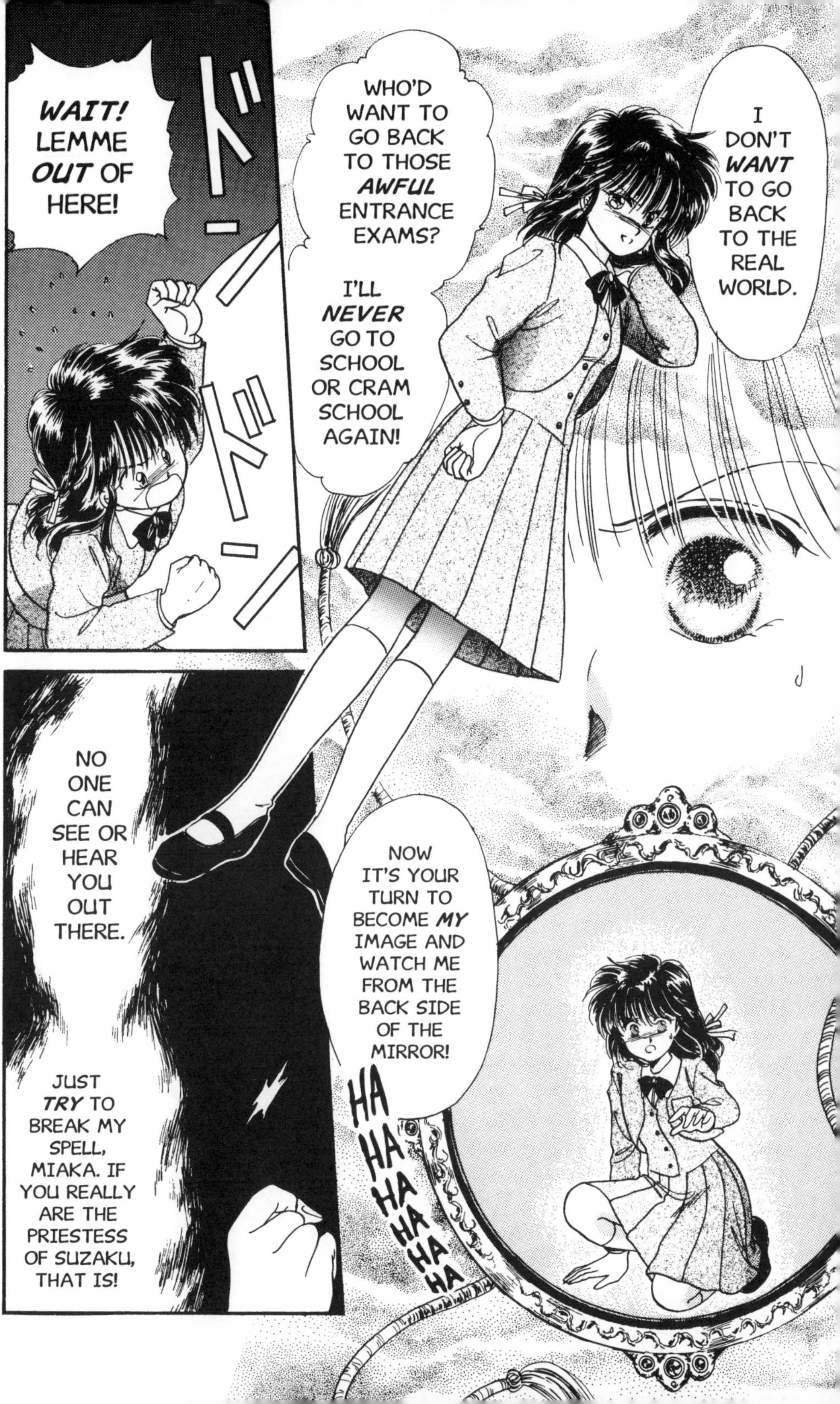
I DON'T *WANT* TO GO BACK TO THE REAL WORLD.
WHO'D WANT TO GO BACK TO THOSE *AWFUL* ENTRANCE EXAMS?
I'LL *NEVER* GO TO SCHOOL OR CRAM SCHOOL AGAIN!
WAIT! LEMME *OUT* OF HERE!
NOW IT'S YOUR TURN TO BECOME *MY* IMAGE AND WATCH ME FROM THE BACK SIDE OF THE MIRROR!
HA HA HA HA HA HA HA HA HA
NO ONE CAN SEE OR HEAR YOU OUT THERE.
JUST *TRY* TO BREAK MY SPELL, MIAKA. IF YOU REALLY ARE THE PRIESTESS OF SUZAKU, THAT IS!

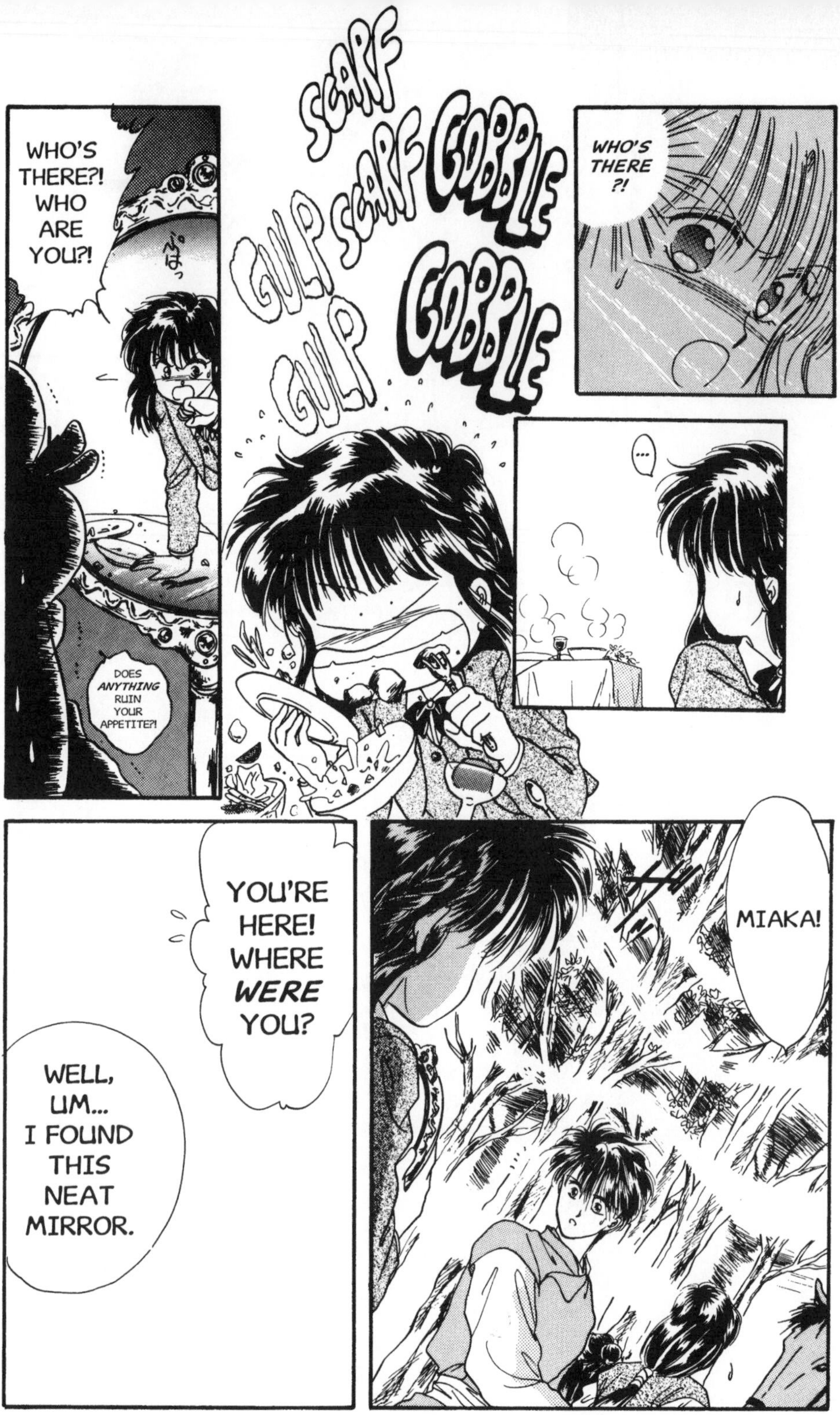
WHO'S THERE ?!
SCARF SCARF GOBBLE GOBBLE
GULP GULP
...
WHO'S THERE?! WHO ARE YOU?!
ぷはっ
DOES *ANYTHING* RUIN YOUR APPETITE?!
MIAKA!
YOU'RE HERE! WHERE *WERE* YOU?
WELL, UM... I FOUND THIS NEAT MIRROR.

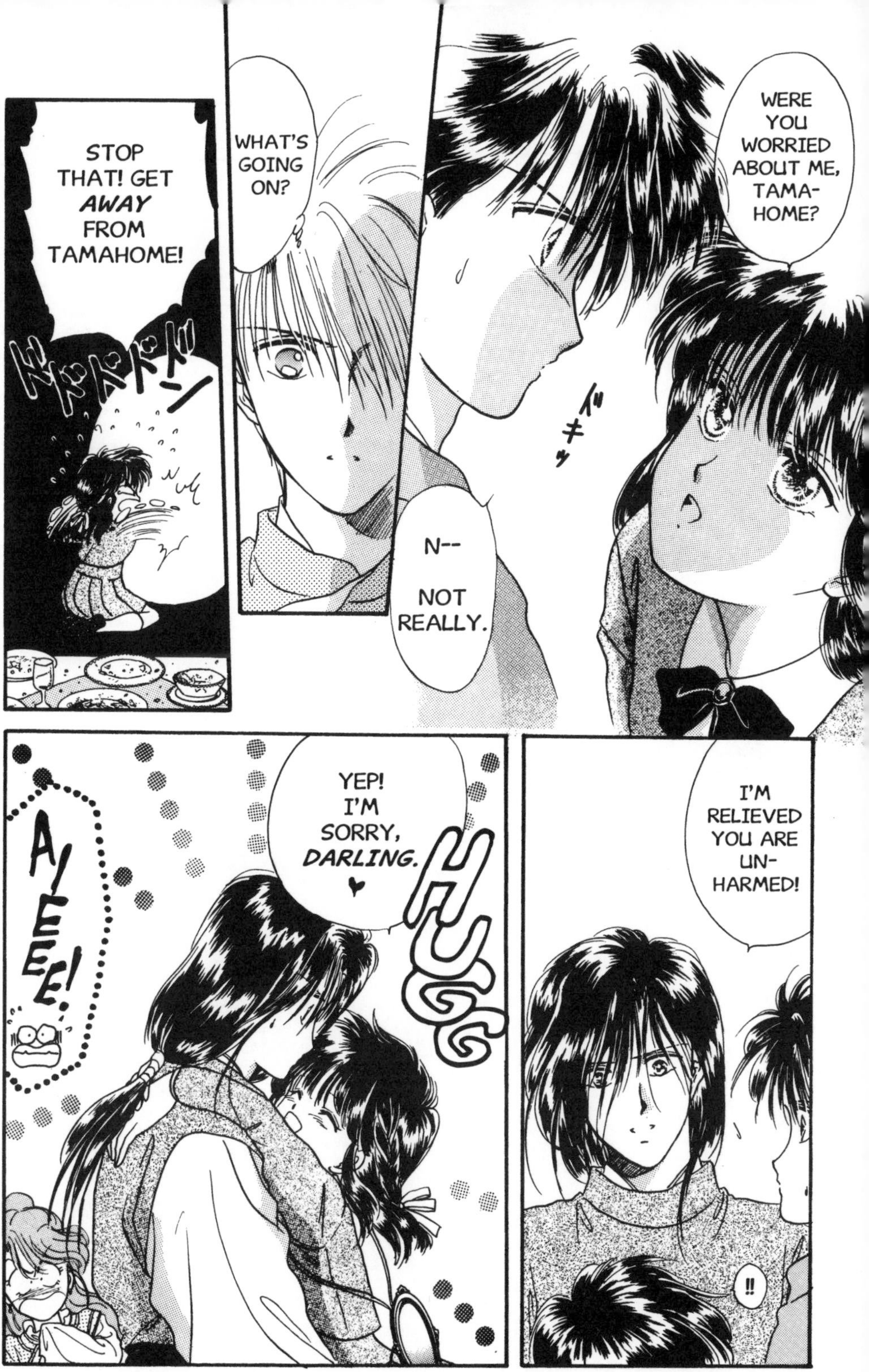
WERE YOU WORRIED ABOUT ME, TAMA-HOME?
N-- NOT REALLY.
WHAT'S GOING ON?
STOP THAT! GET *AWAY* FROM TAMAHOME!
I'M RELIEVED YOU ARE UN-HARMED!
!!
YEP! I'M SORRY, *DARLING.* ♥
HUG
AIEEE!

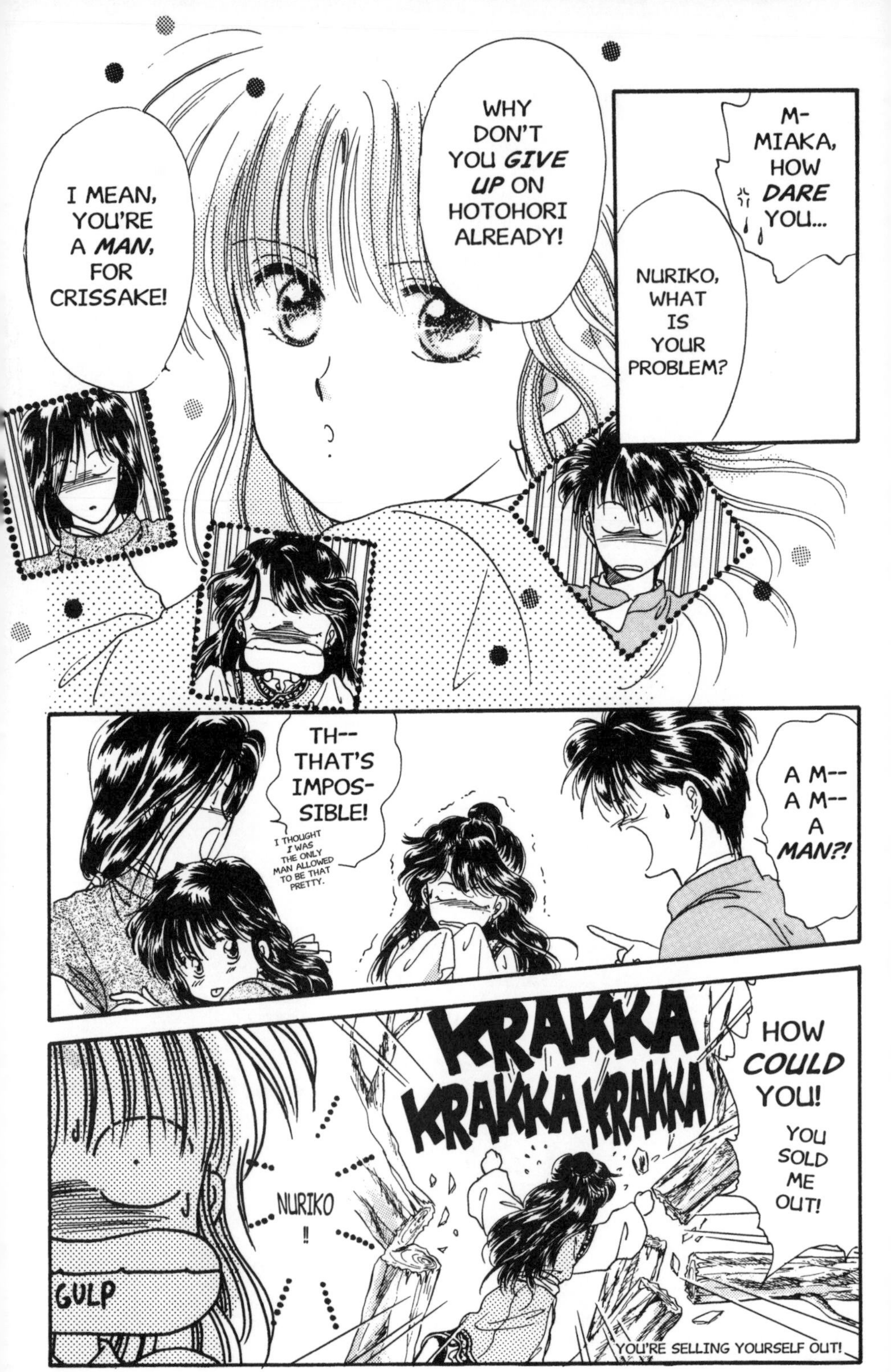
M-MIAKA, HOW DARE YOU...
NURIKO, WHAT IS YOUR PROBLEM?
WHY DON'T YOU GIVE UP ON HOTOHORI ALREADY!
I MEAN, YOU'RE A MAN, FOR CRISSAKE!
A M-- A M-- A MAN?!
TH-- THAT'S IMPOSSIBLE!
I THOUGHT I WAS THE ONLY MAN ALLOWED TO BE THAT PRETTY.
HOW COULD YOU!
YOU SOLD ME OUT!
KRAKKA KRAKKA KRAKKA
YOU'RE SELLING YOURSELF OUT!
NURIKO !!
GULP

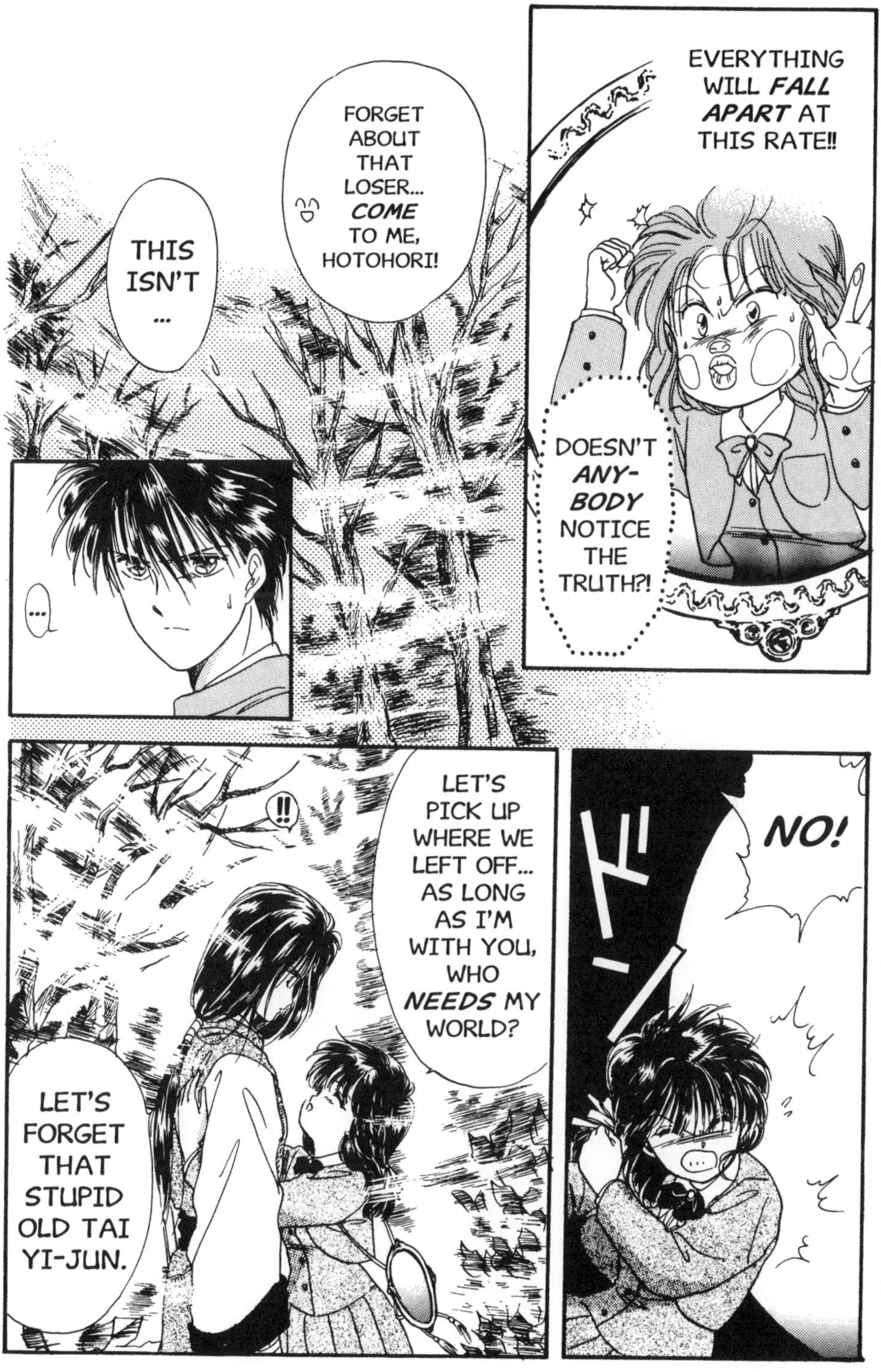
EVERYTHING WILL FALL APART AT THIS RATE!!
DOESN'T ANY-BODY NOTICE THE TRUTH?!
FORGET ABOUT THAT LOSER... COME TO ME, HOTOHORI!
THIS ISN'T ...
...
NO!
LET'S PICK UP WHERE WE LEFT OFF... AS LONG AS I'M WITH YOU, WHO NEEDS MY WORLD?
!!
LET'S FORGET THAT STUPID OLD TAI YI-JUN.

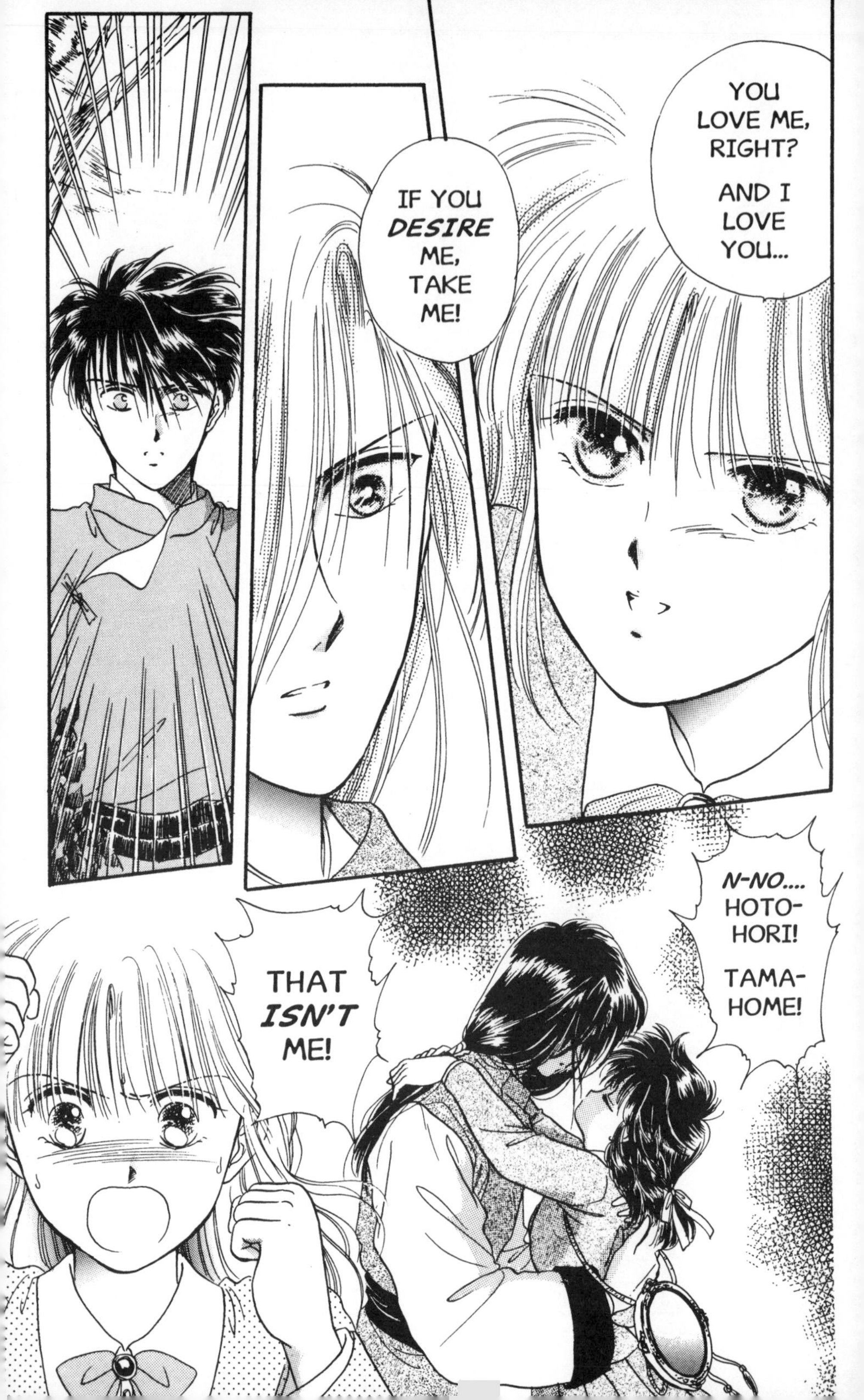
YOU LOVE ME, RIGHT?
AND I LOVE YOU...
IF YOU *DESIRE* ME, TAKE ME!
N-NO.... HOTOHORI!
TAMAHOME!
THAT *ISN'T* ME!

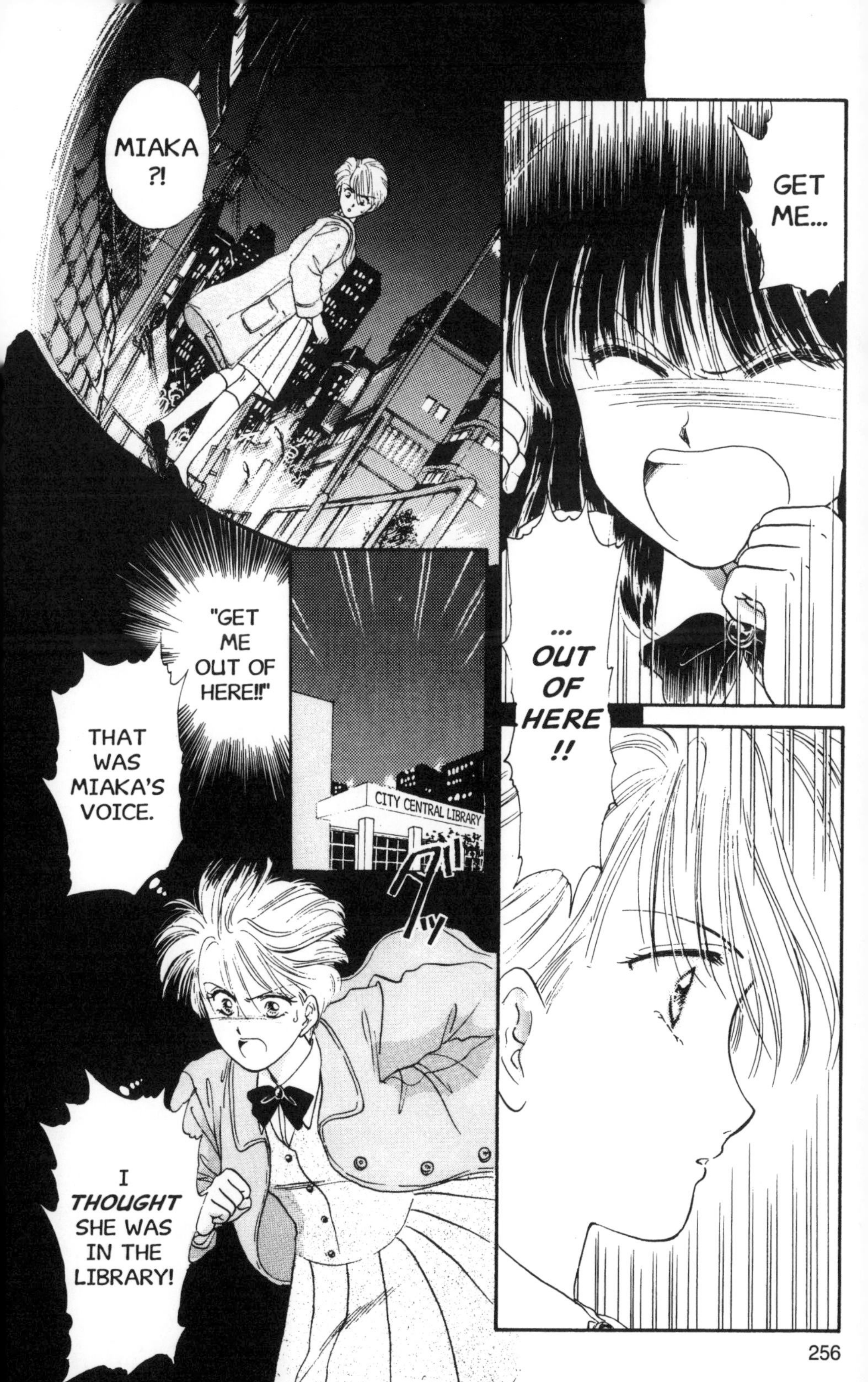
GET ME...
...OUT OF HERE!!
MIAKA?!
"GET ME OUT OF HERE!!"
THAT WAS MIAKA'S VOICE.
CITY CENTRAL LIBRARY
I *THOUGHT* SHE WAS IN THE LIBRARY!

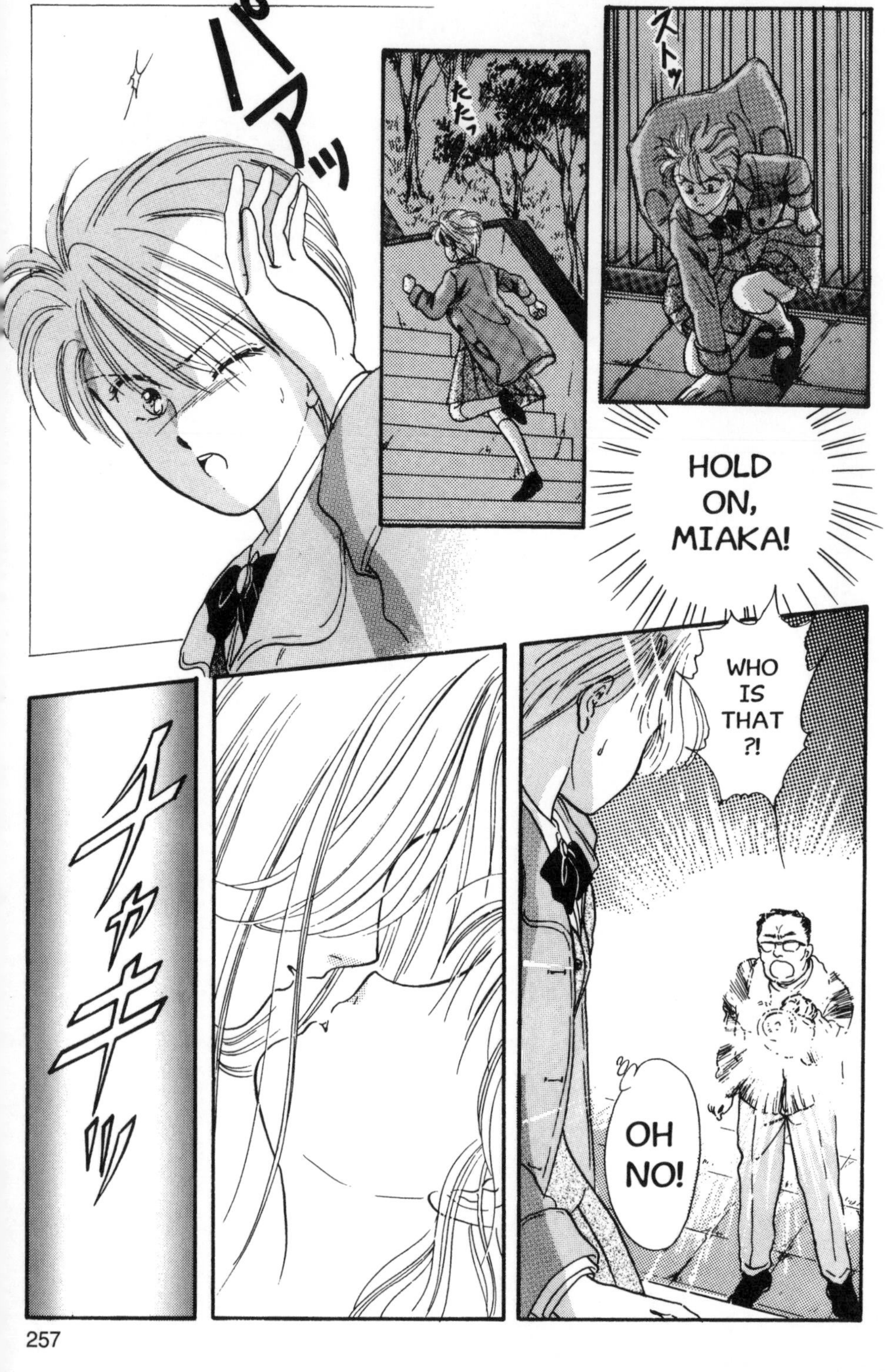
ストッ
たたっ
パアッ
HOLD ON, MIAKA!
WHO IS THAT?!
OH NO!
イャキッ

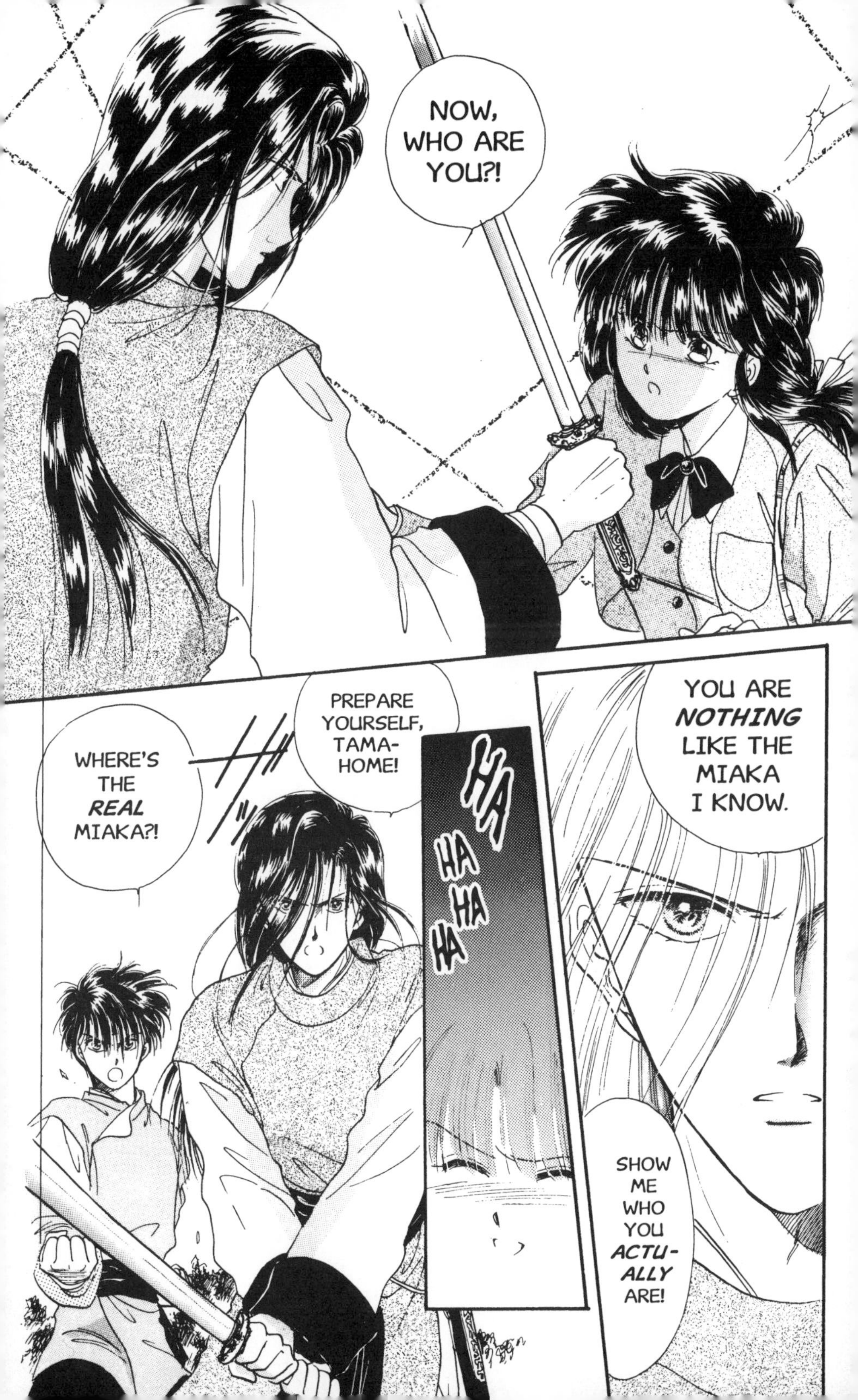
NOW, WHO ARE YOU?!
YOU ARE *NOTHING* LIKE THE MIAKA I KNOW.
SHOW ME WHO YOU *ACTUALLY* ARE!
HA HA HA HA
PREPARE YOURSELF, TAMAHOME!
WHERE'S THE *REAL* MIAKA?!

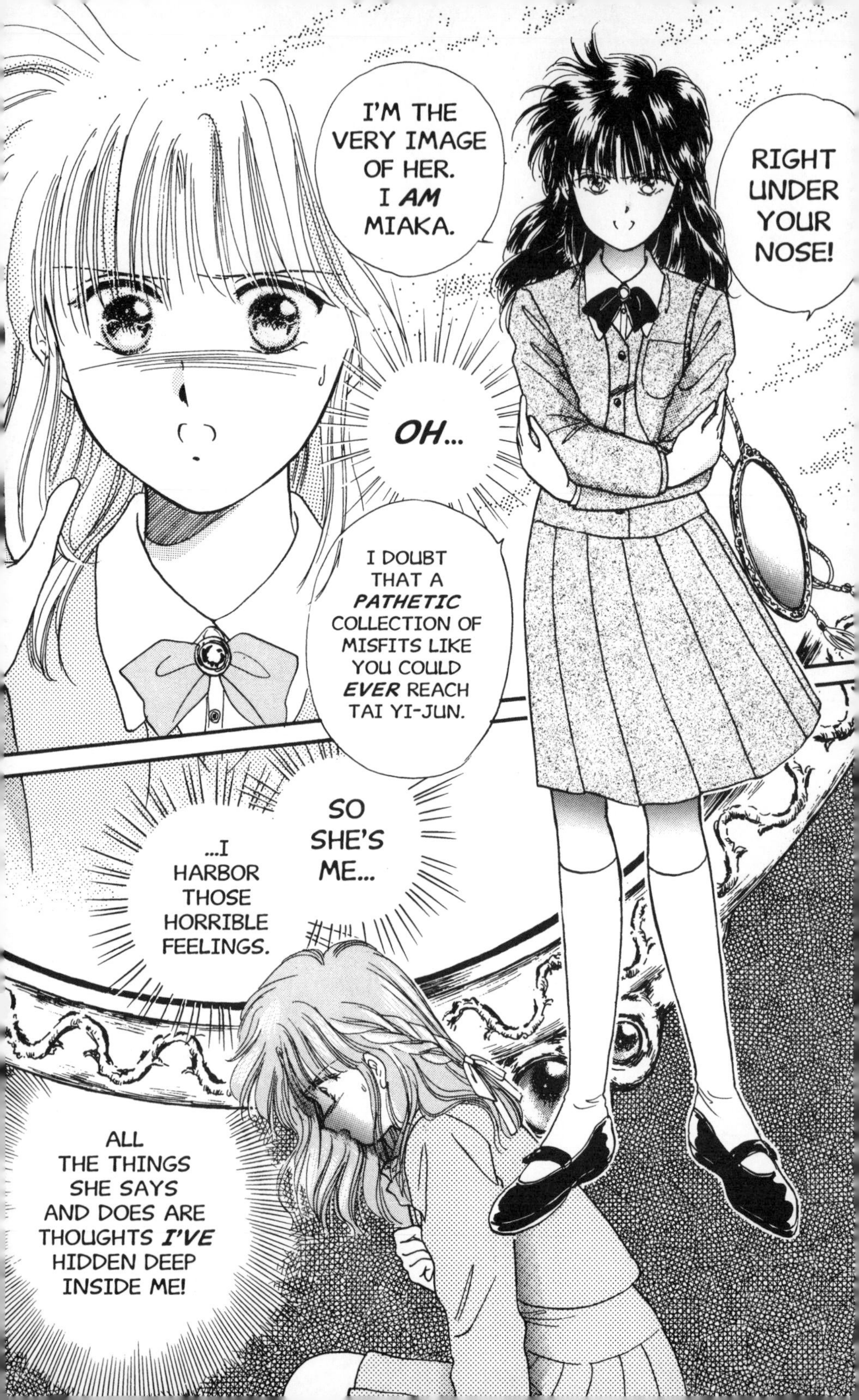
RIGHT UNDER YOUR NOSE!
I'M THE VERY IMAGE OF HER. I *AM* MIAKA.
OH...
I DOUBT THAT A *PATHETIC* COLLECTION OF MISFITS LIKE YOU COULD *EVER* REACH TAI YI-JUN.
SO SHE'S ME...
...I HARBOR THOSE HORRIBLE FEELINGS.
ALL THE THINGS SHE SAYS AND DOES ARE THOUGHTS *I'VE* HIDDEN DEEP INSIDE ME!

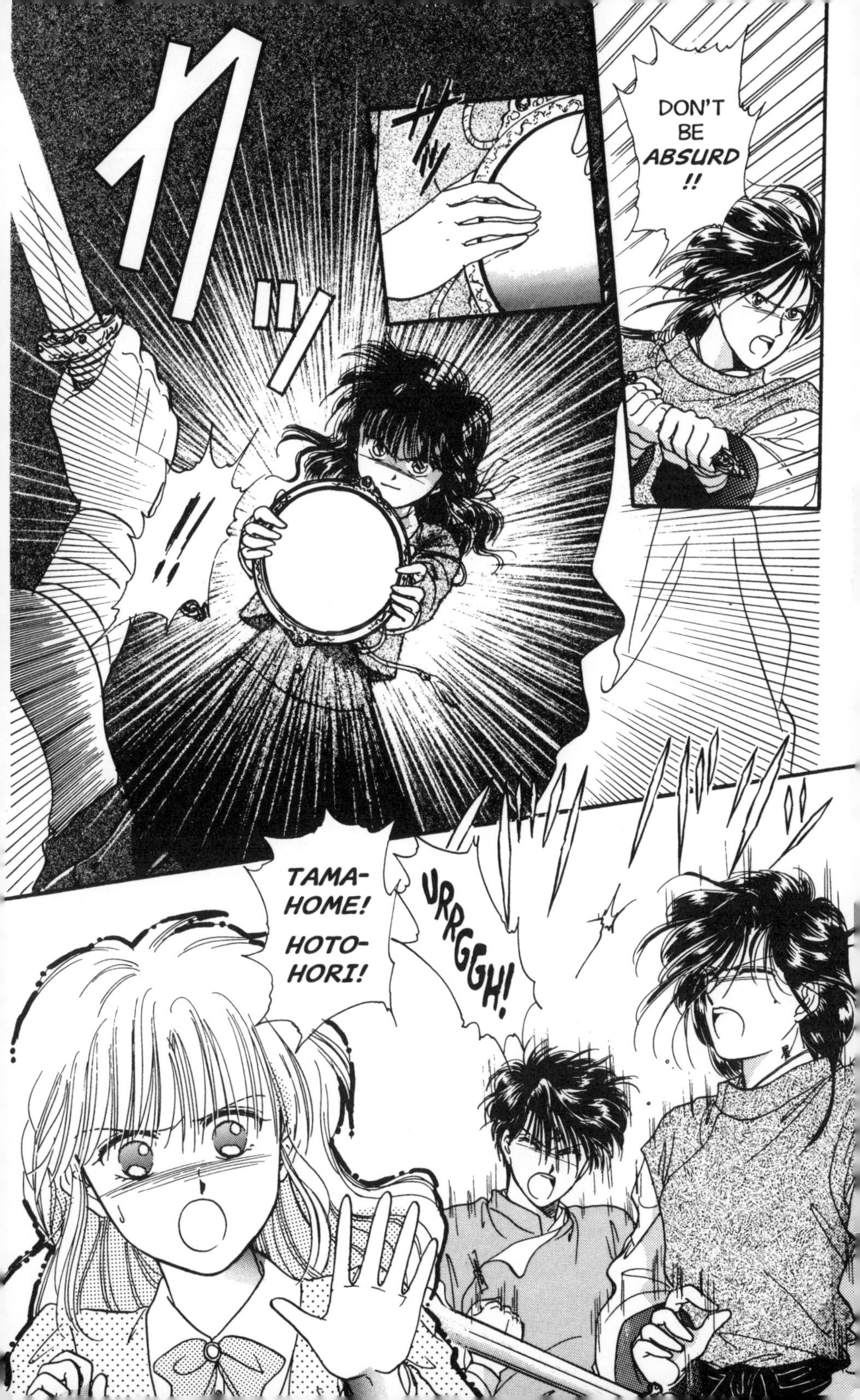
DON'T BE ABSURD!!
URRGGH!
TAMA-HOME! HOTO-HORI!

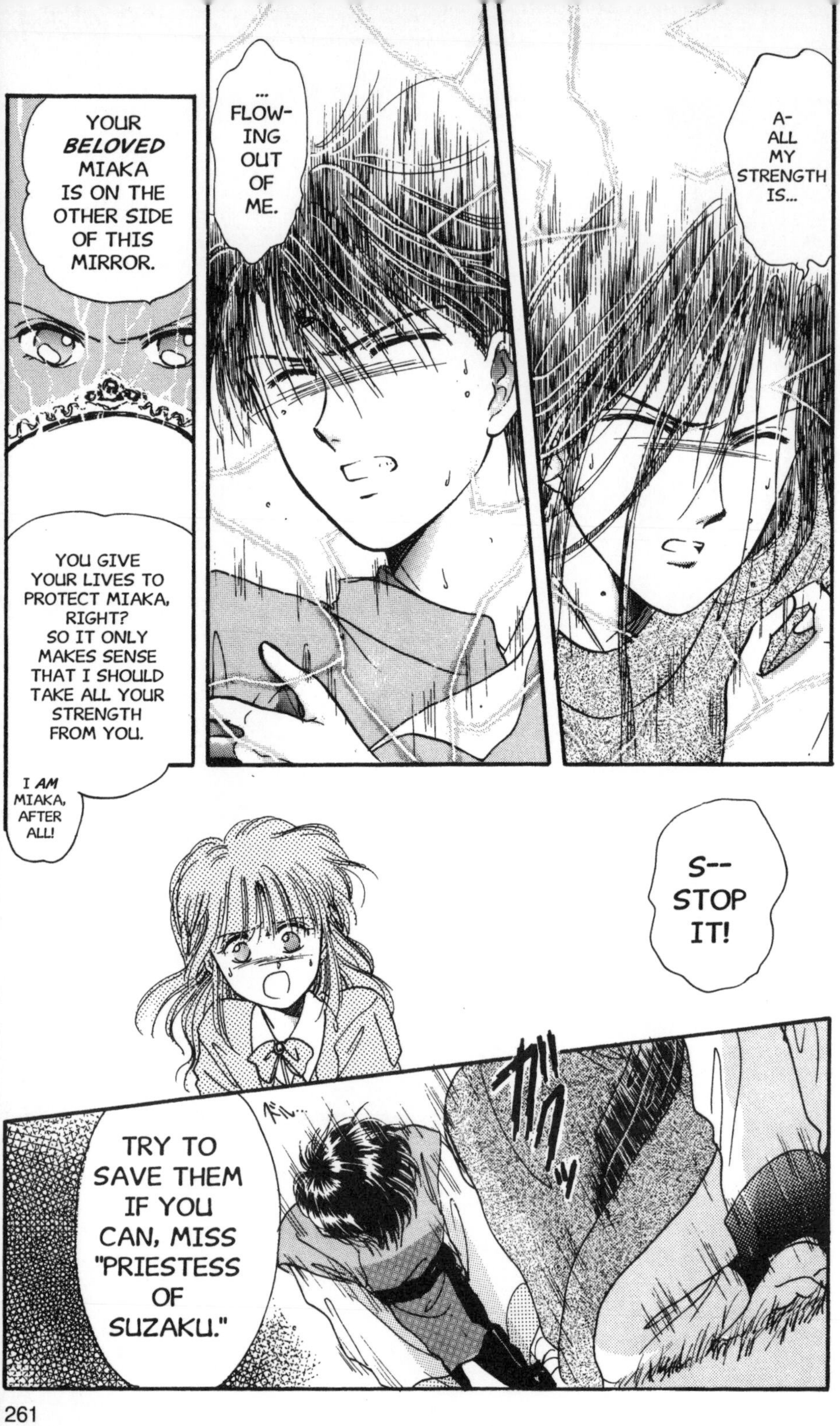
A- ALL MY STRENGTH IS...
... FLOWING OUT OF ME.
YOUR BELOVED MIAKA IS ON THE OTHER SIDE OF THIS MIRROR.
YOU GIVE YOUR LIVES TO PROTECT MIAKA, RIGHT? SO IT ONLY MAKES SENSE THAT I SHOULD TAKE ALL YOUR STRENGTH FROM YOU.
I AM MIAKA, AFTER ALL!
S-- STOP IT!
ガクッ
TRY TO SAVE THEM IF YOU CAN, MISS "PRIESTESS OF SUZAKU."

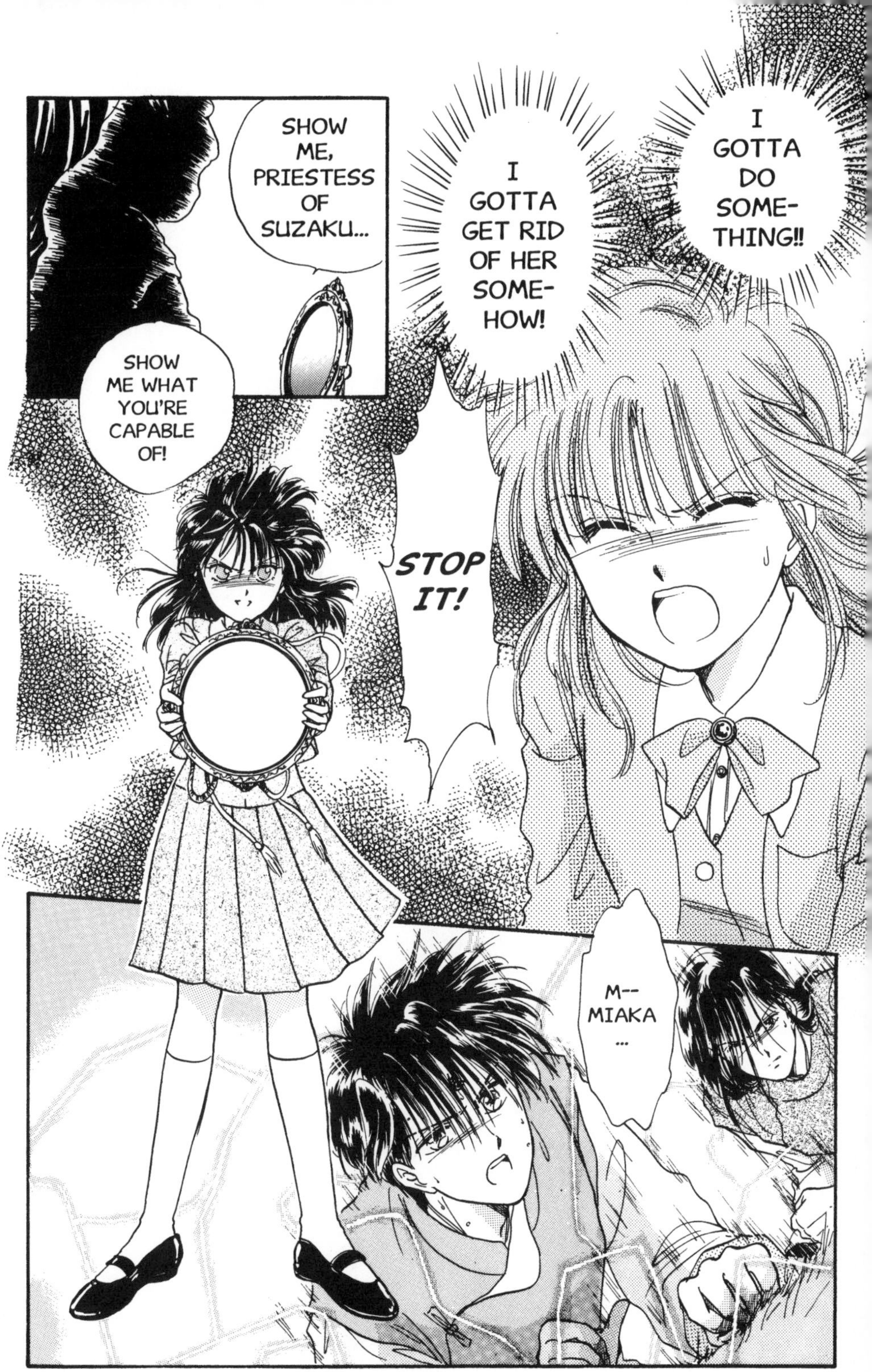
I GOTTA DO SOME-THING!!
I GOTTA GET RID OF HER SOME-HOW!
STOP IT!
SHOW ME, PRIESTESS OF SUZAKU...
SHOW ME WHAT YOU'RE CAPABLE OF!
M-- MIAKA ...

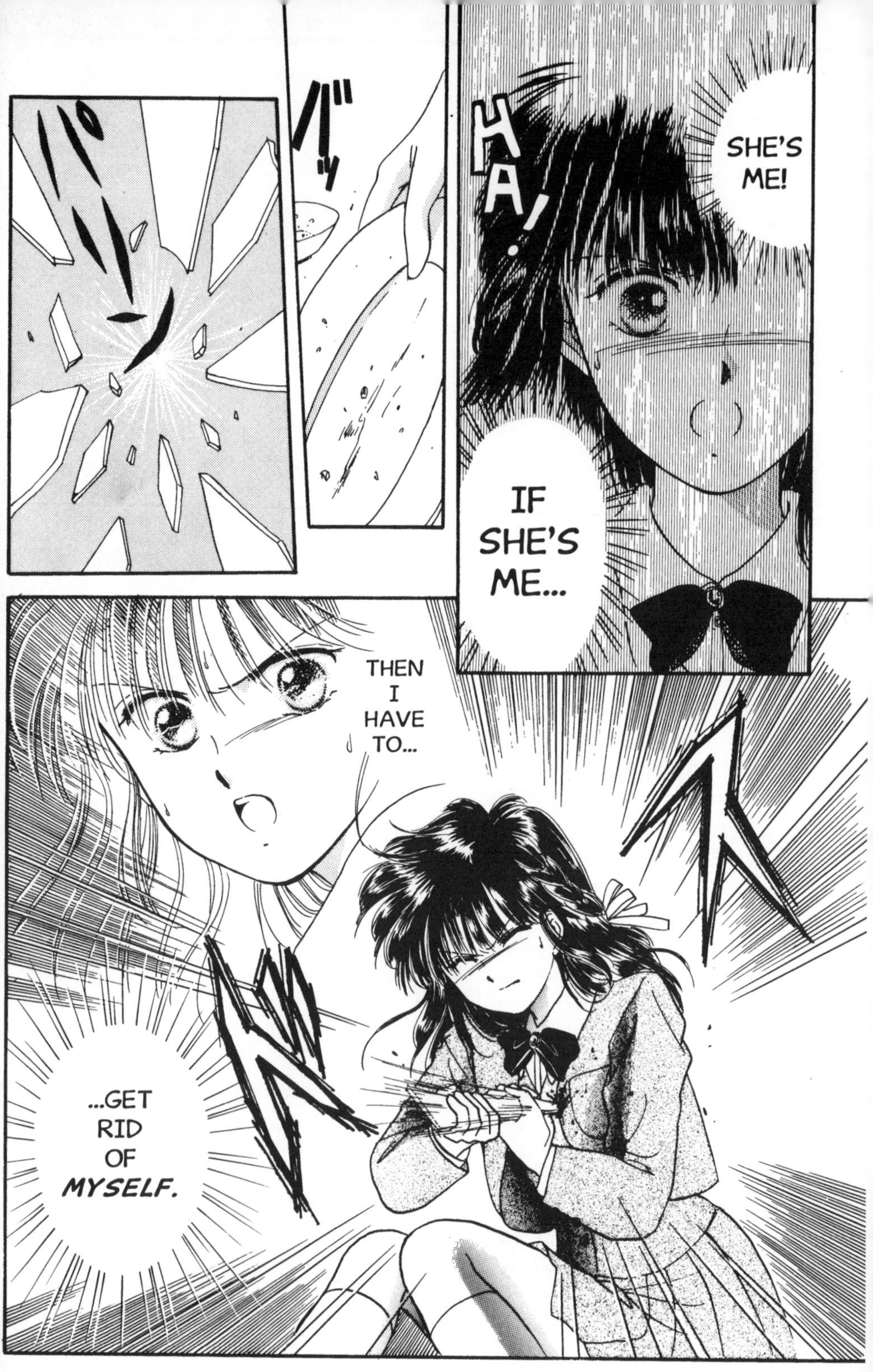
HA!
SHE'S ME!
IF SHE'S ME...
バッ
THEN I HAVE TO...
...GET RID OF *MYSELF.*

PARDON THE PARODY

INCREASING YOUR *FUSHIGI YŪGI* ENJOYMENT BY 100%!

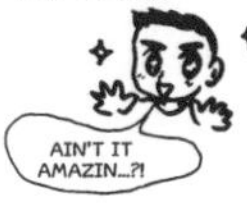
AIN'T IT AMAZIN...?!

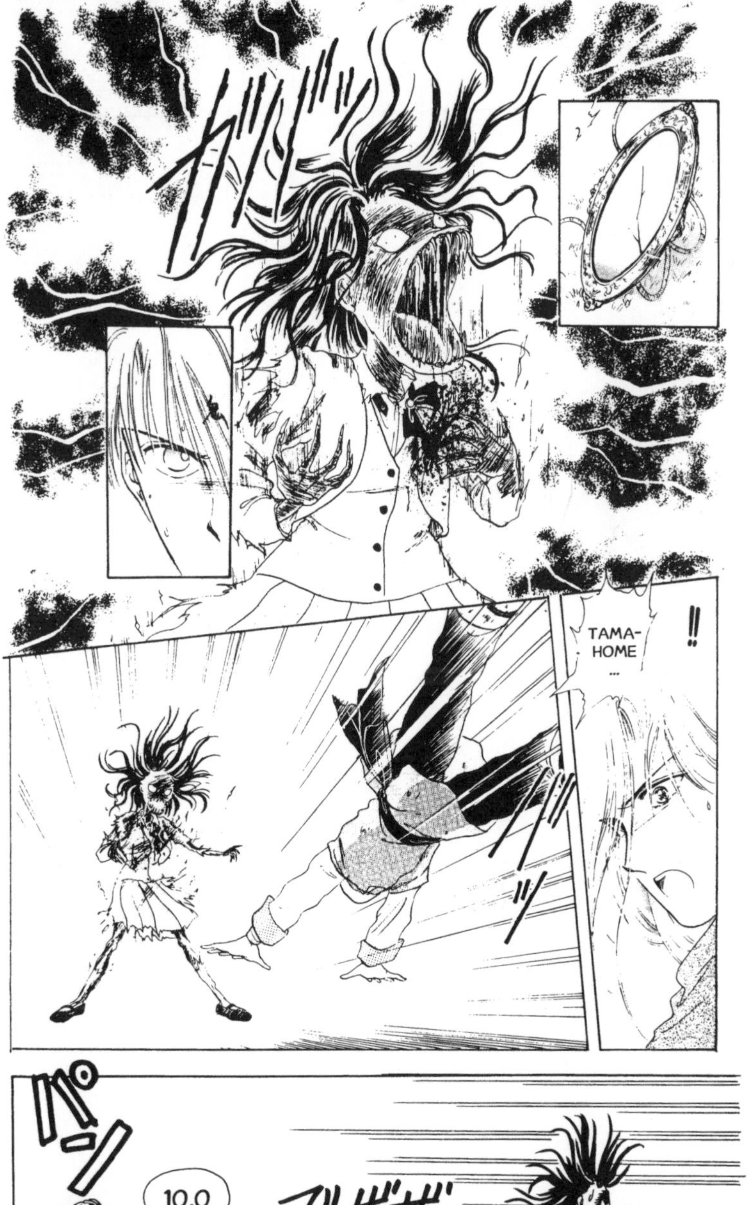
TAMA-HOME ...
!!
10.0

IDEA:
K. OF TOKYO
(A MANGA ASSISTANT)

BY Y.W. ►
(A MANGA ARTIST)

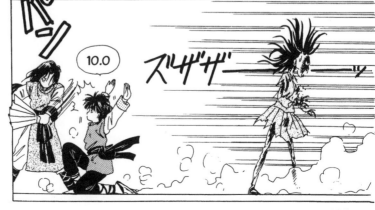

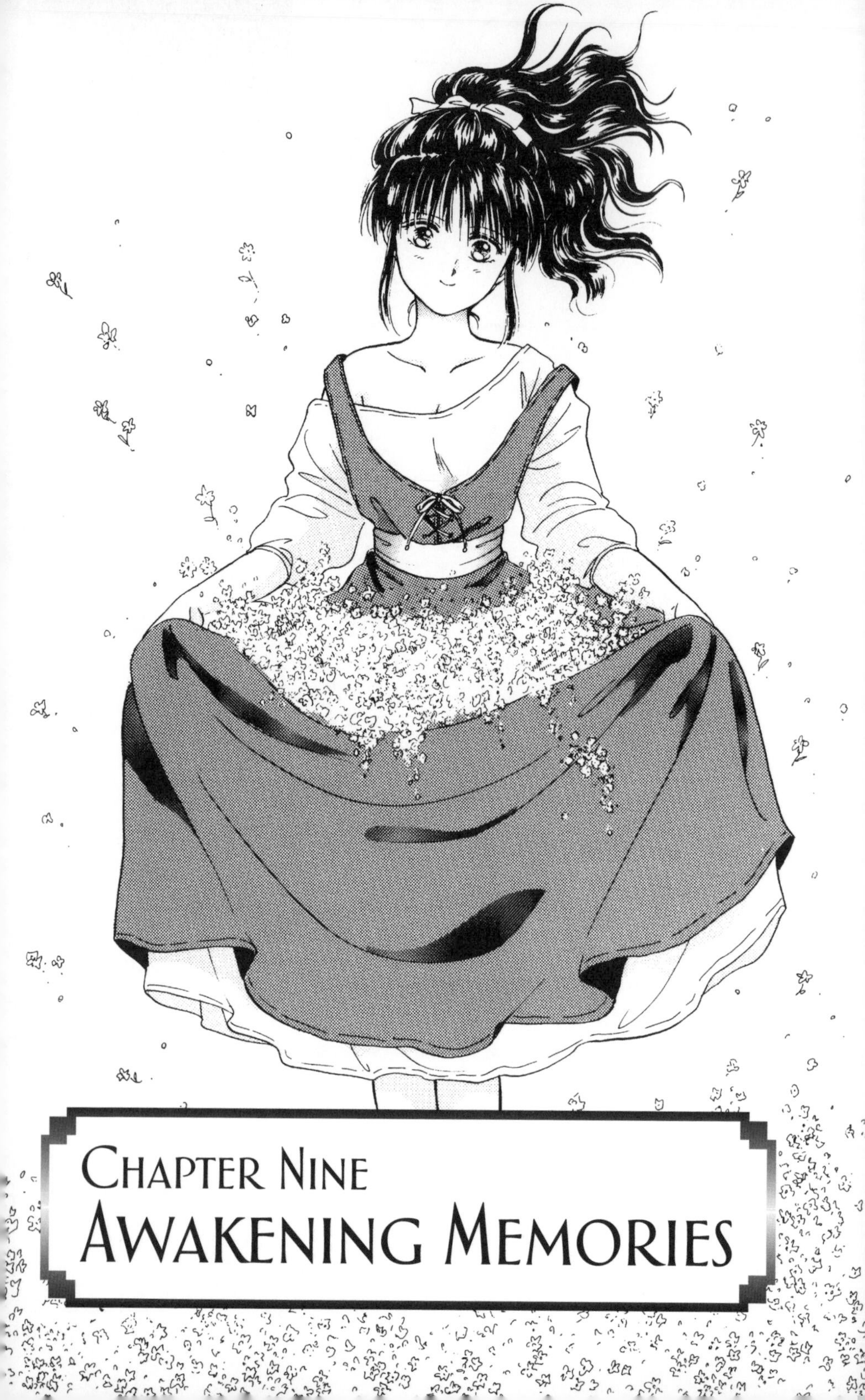

Chapter Nine
Awakening Memories

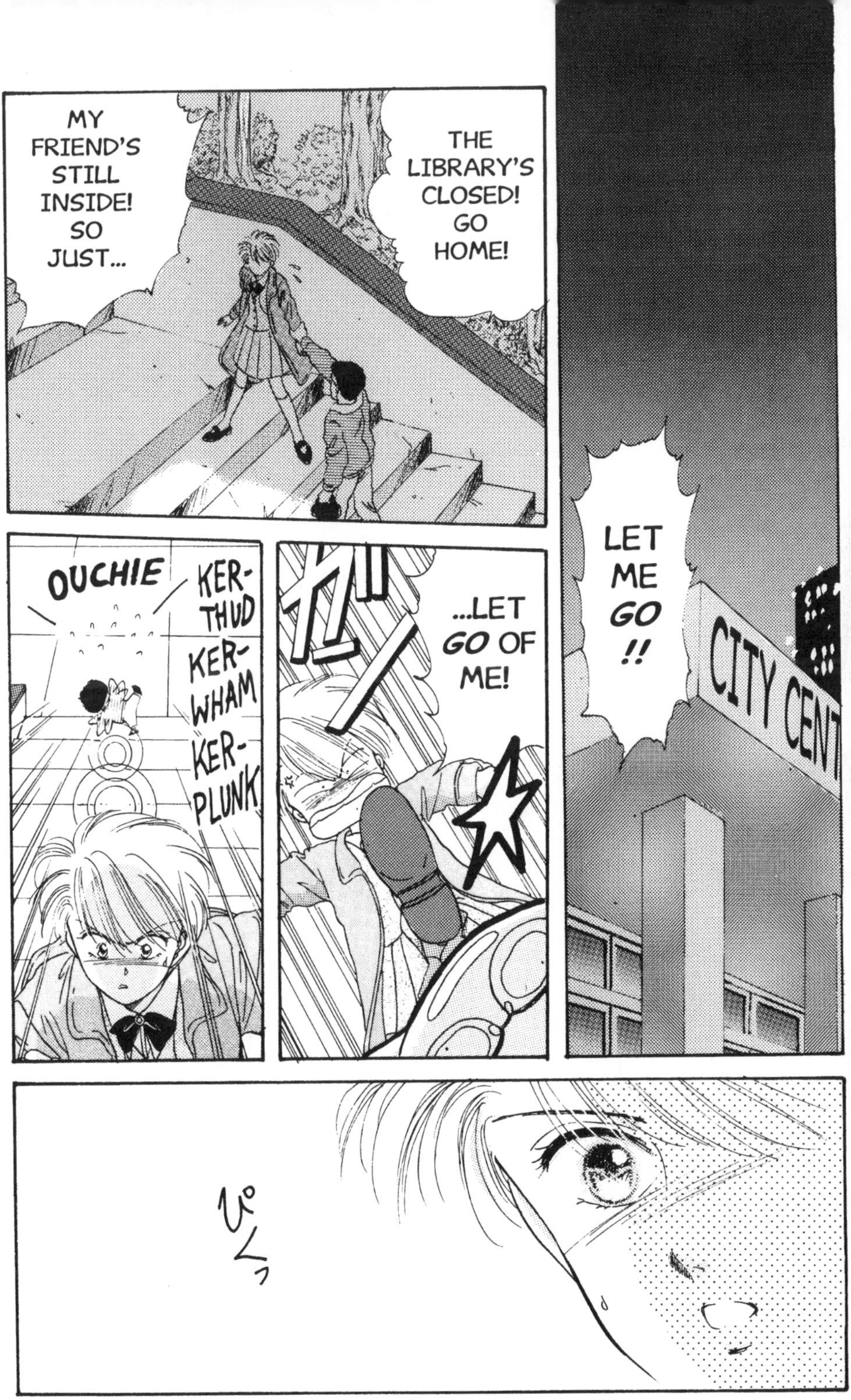
LET ME GO!!
CITY CENT
THE LIBRARY'S CLOSED! GO HOME!
MY FRIEND'S STILL INSIDE! SO JUST...
...LET GO OF ME!
OUCHIE
KER-THUD KER-WHAM KER-PLUNK
ぴくっ

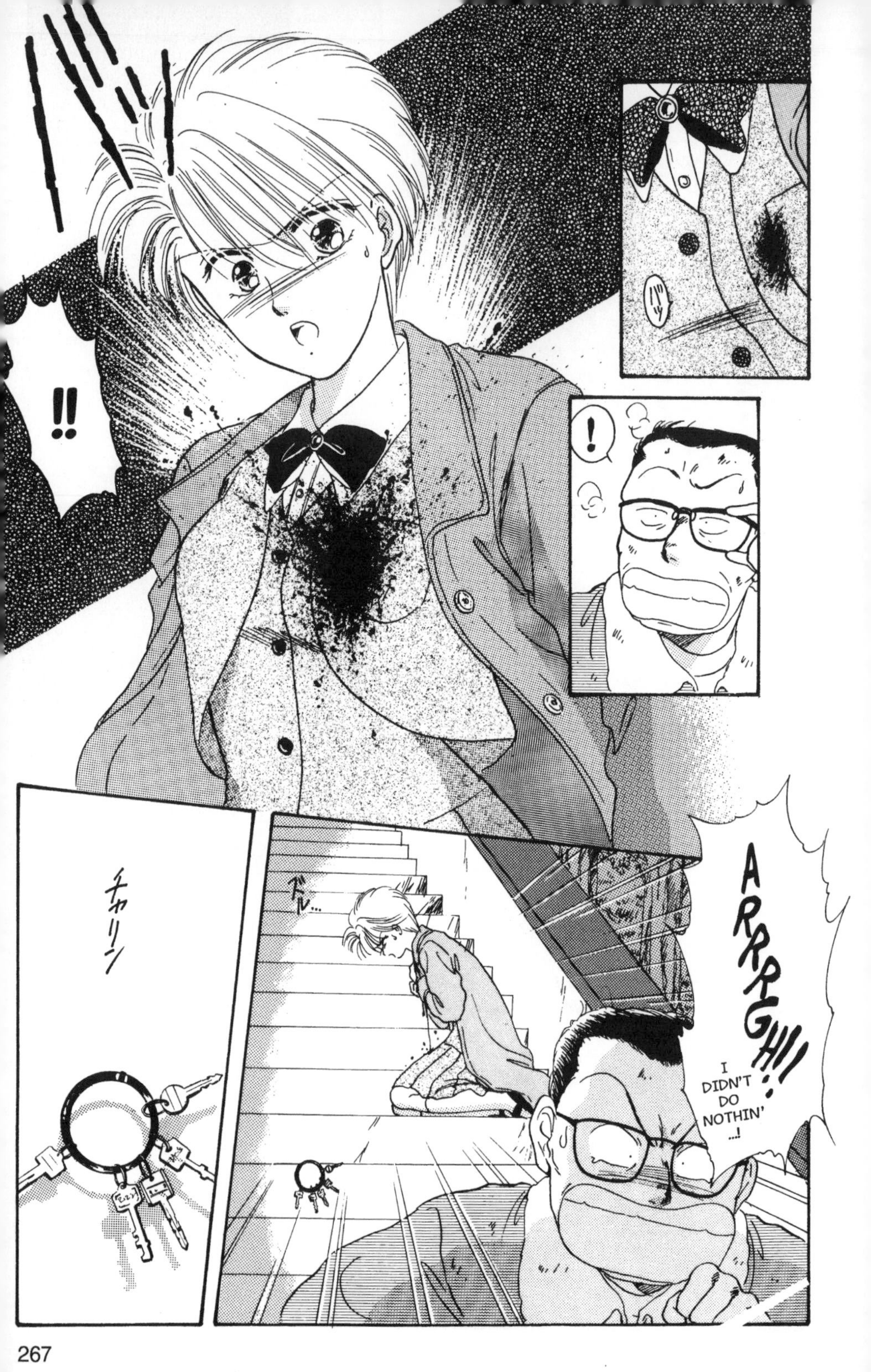
バッ
!!
!
ARRRGH!!!
I DIDN'T DO NOTHIN' ...!
チャリン

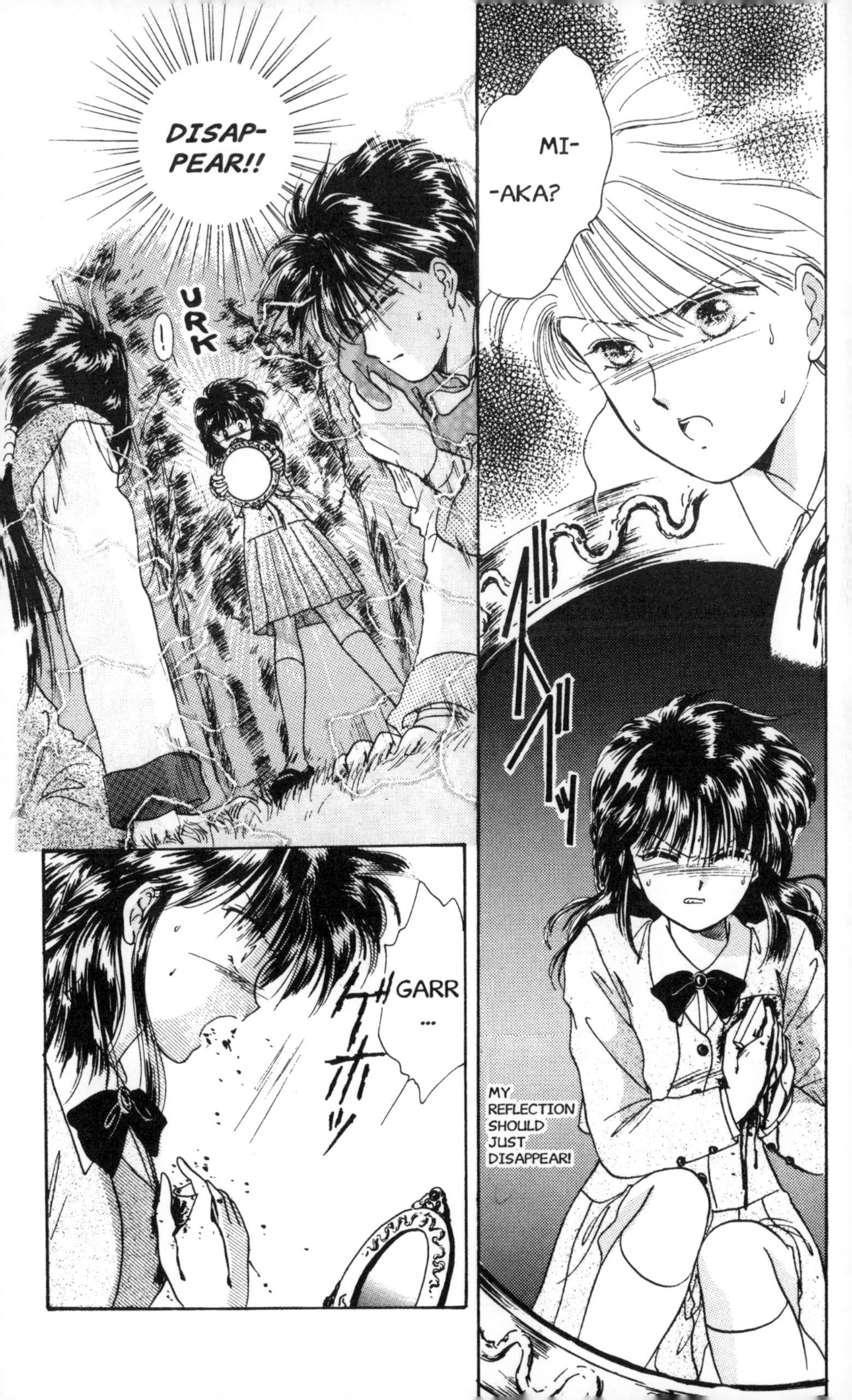
MI- -AKA?
MY REFLECTION SHOULD JUST DISAPPEAR!
DISAP- PEAR!!
!
URK
GARR ...

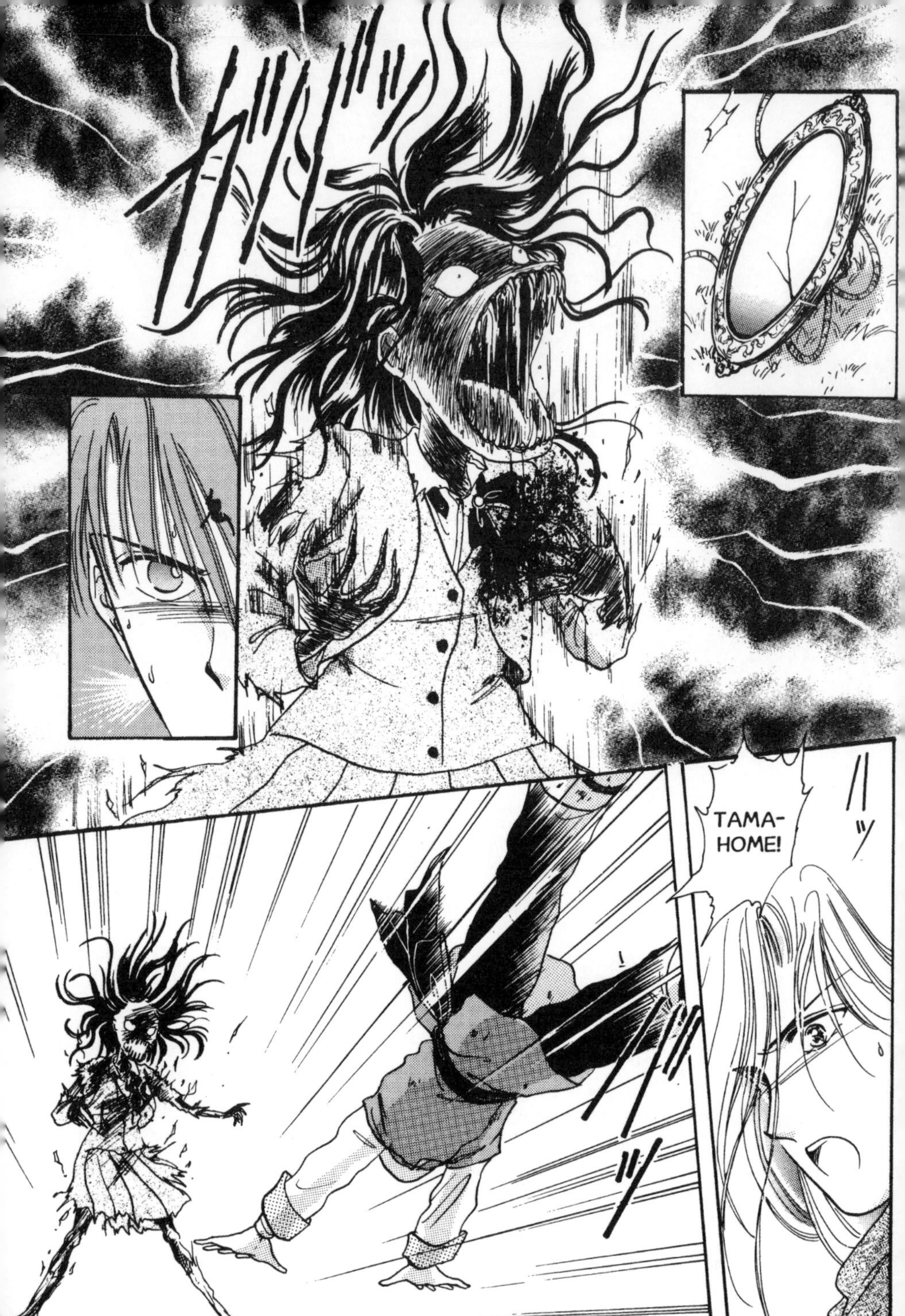
TAMA-
HOME!

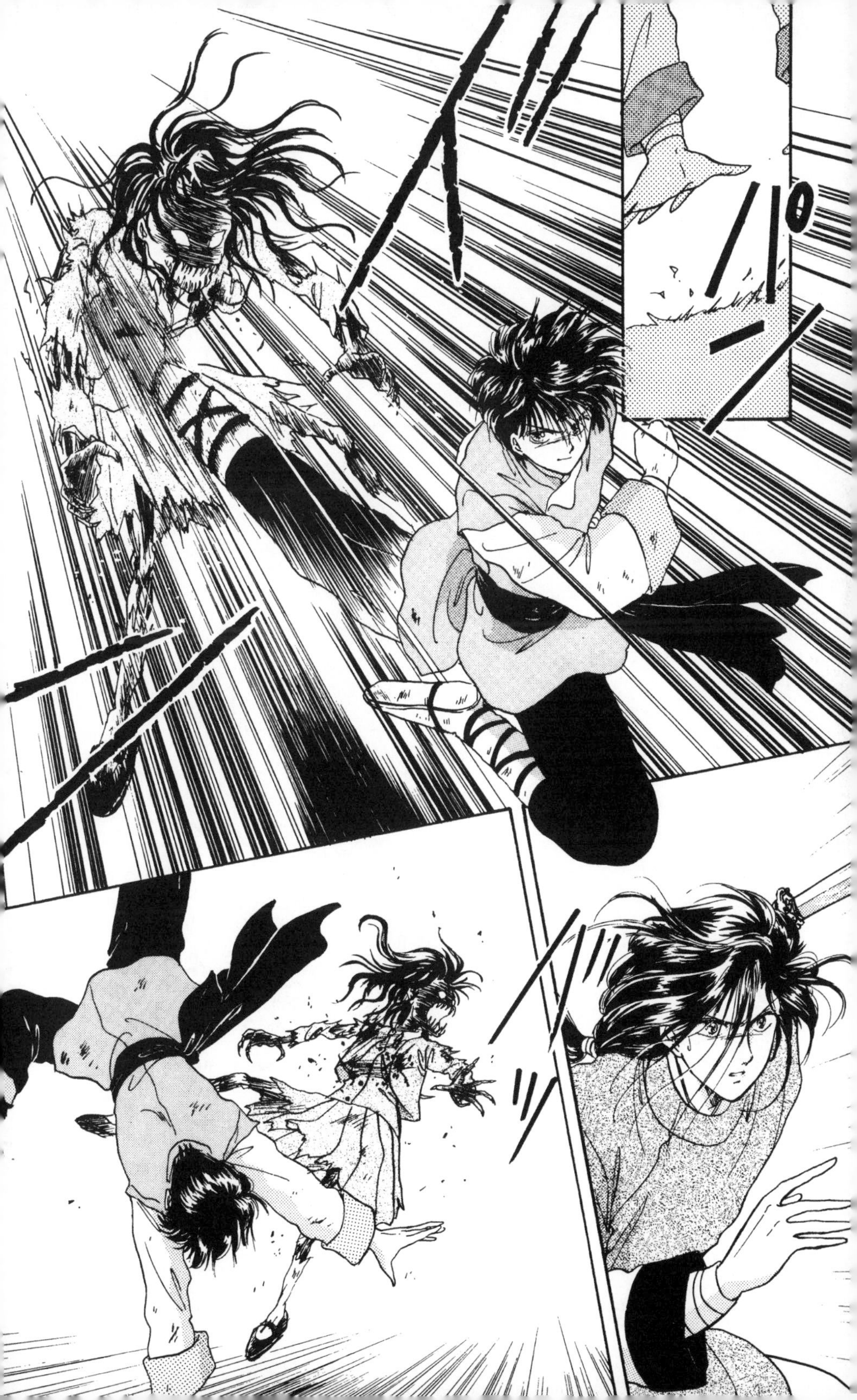

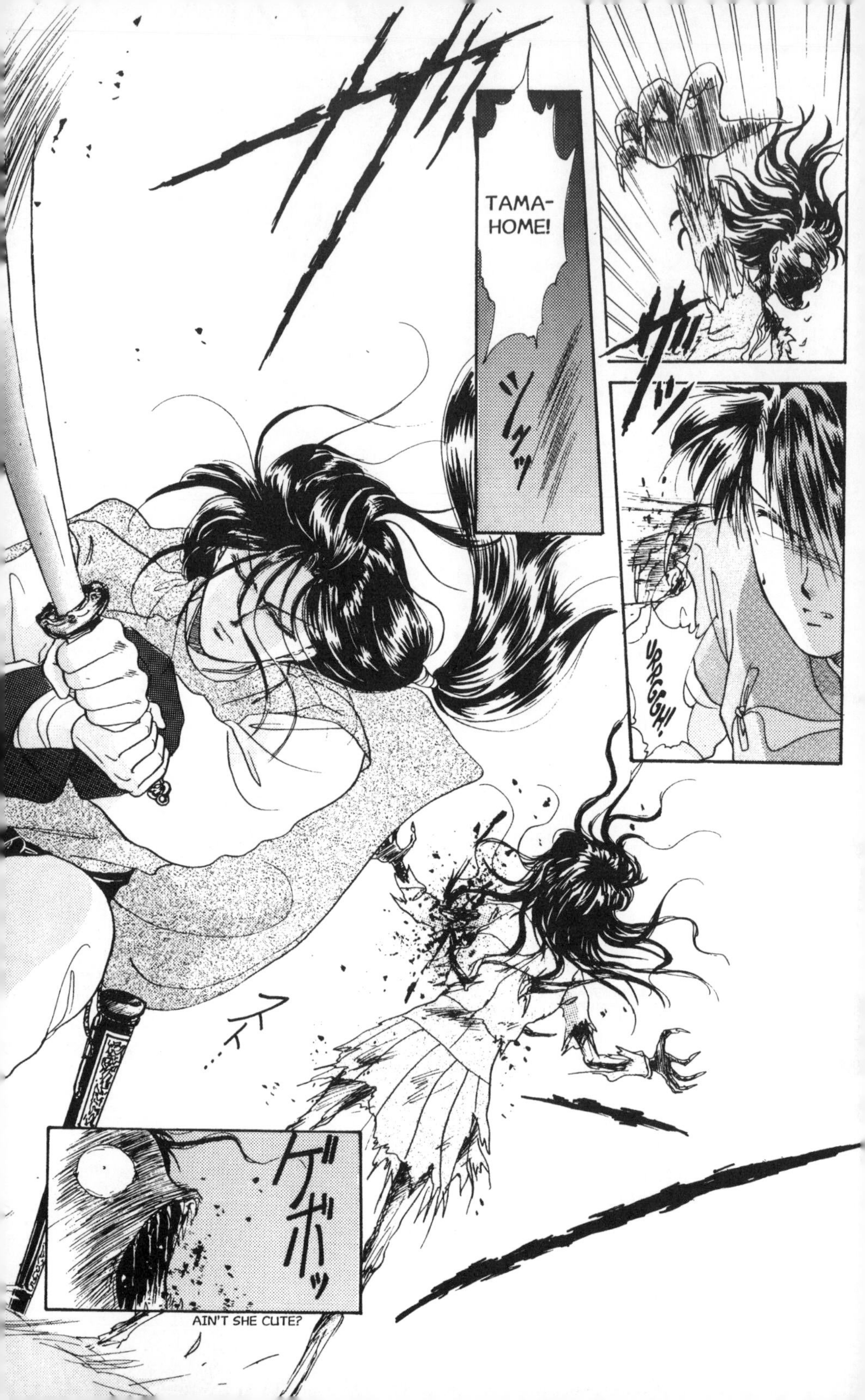
URRGGH!
TAMA-HOME!
AIN'T SHE CUTE?

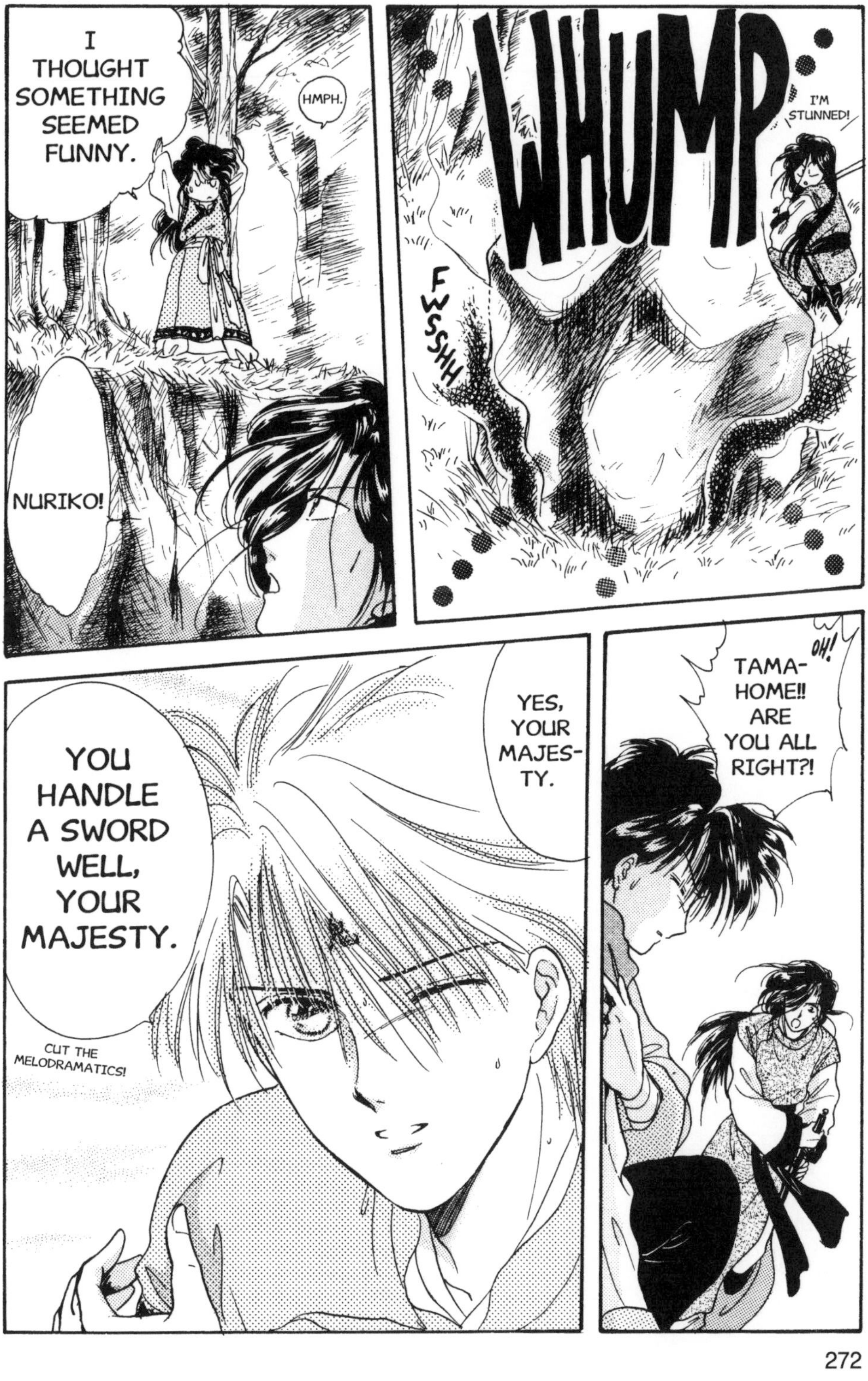
WHUMP
I'M STUNNED!
FWSSHH
I THOUGHT SOMETHING SEEMED FUNNY.
HMPH.
NURIKO!
OH!
TAMA-HOME!! ARE YOU ALL RIGHT?!
YES, YOUR MAJES-TY.
YOU HANDLE A SWORD WELL, YOUR MAJESTY.
CUT THE MELODRAMATICS!

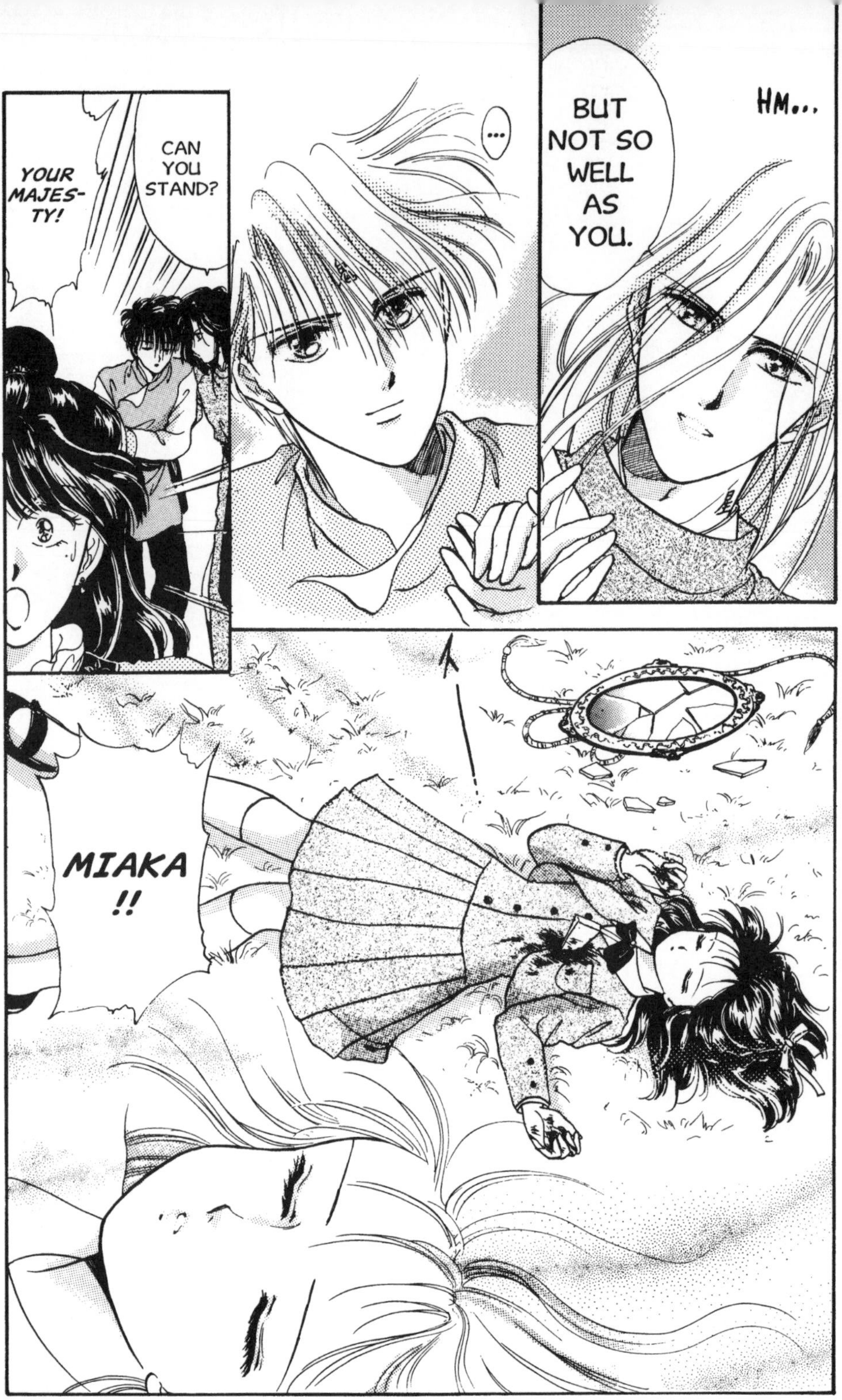
HM...
BUT NOT SO WELL AS YOU.
...
CAN YOU STAND?
YOUR MAJESTY!
MIAKA !!

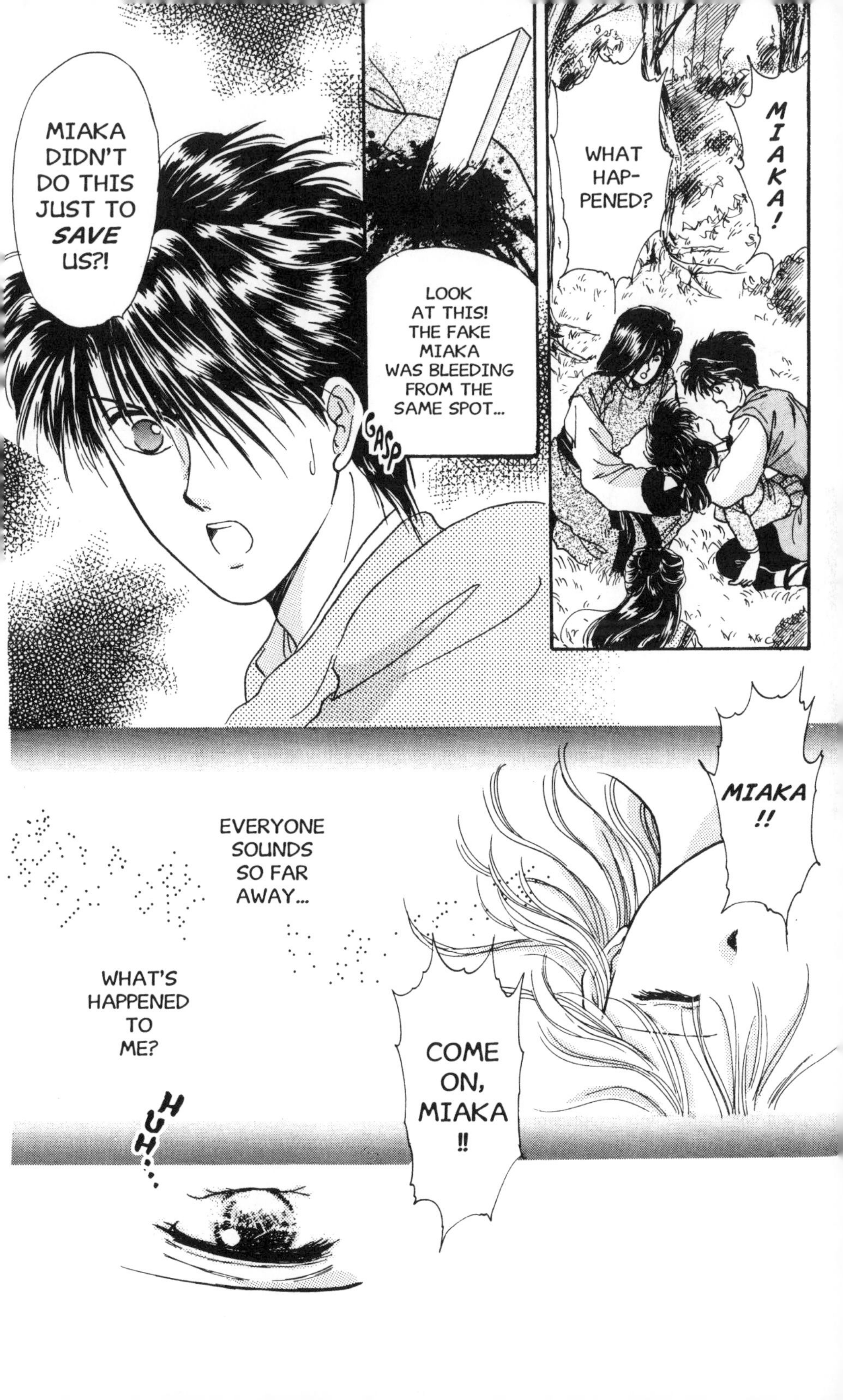
MIAKA!
WHAT HAPPENED?
LOOK AT THIS! THE FAKE MIAKA WAS BLEEDING FROM THE SAME SPOT...
GASP
MIAKA DIDN'T DO THIS JUST TO *SAVE* US?!
MIAKA!!
COME ON, MIAKA!!
EVERYONE SOUNDS SO FAR AWAY...
WHAT'S HAPPENED TO ME?
HUH...

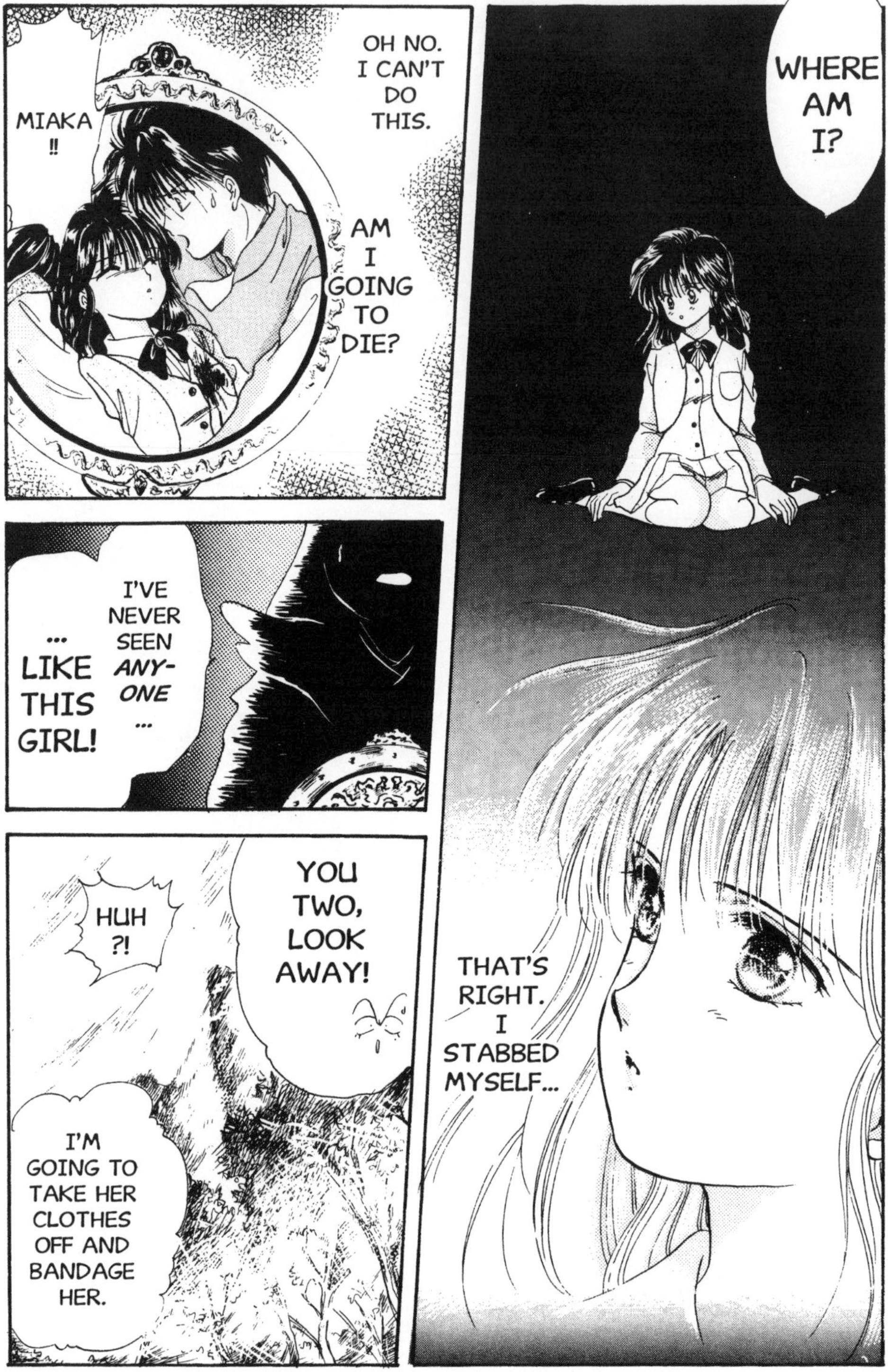
WHERE AM I?
THAT'S RIGHT. I STABBED MYSELF...
OH NO. I CAN'T DO THIS.
MIAKA !!
AM I GOING TO DIE?
I'VE NEVER SEEN *ANYONE*...
...LIKE THIS GIRL!
YOU TWO, LOOK AWAY!
HUH ?!
I'M GOING TO TAKE HER CLOTHES OFF AND BANDAGE HER.

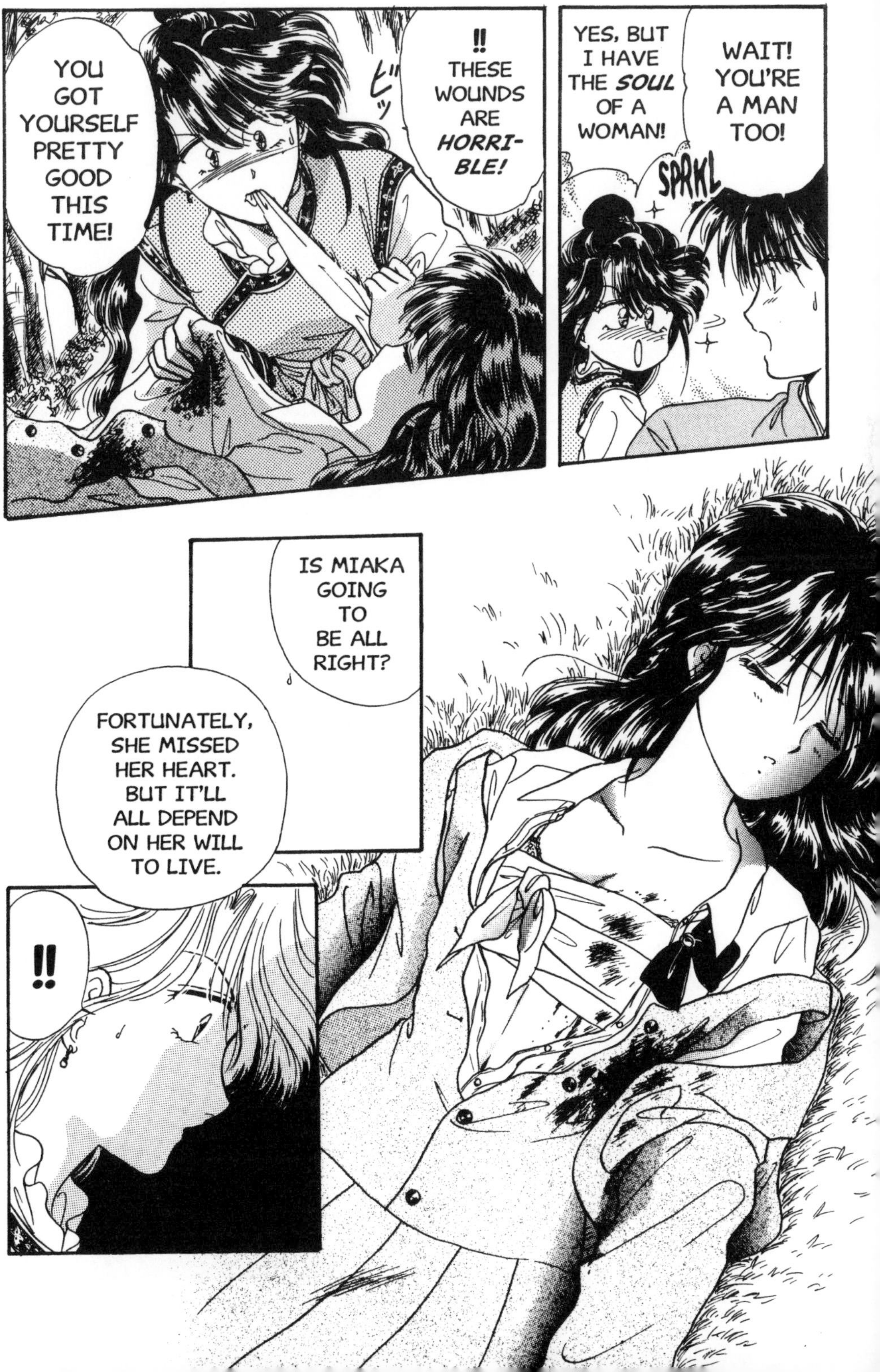
WAIT! YOU'RE A MAN TOO!
YES, BUT I HAVE THE SOUL OF A WOMAN!
SPRKL
!! THESE WOUNDS ARE HORRIBLE!
ビッ
YOU GOT YOURSELF PRETTY GOOD THIS TIME!
IS MIAKA GOING TO BE ALL RIGHT?
FORTUNATELY, SHE MISSED HER HEART. BUT IT'LL ALL DEPEND ON HER WILL TO LIVE.
!!

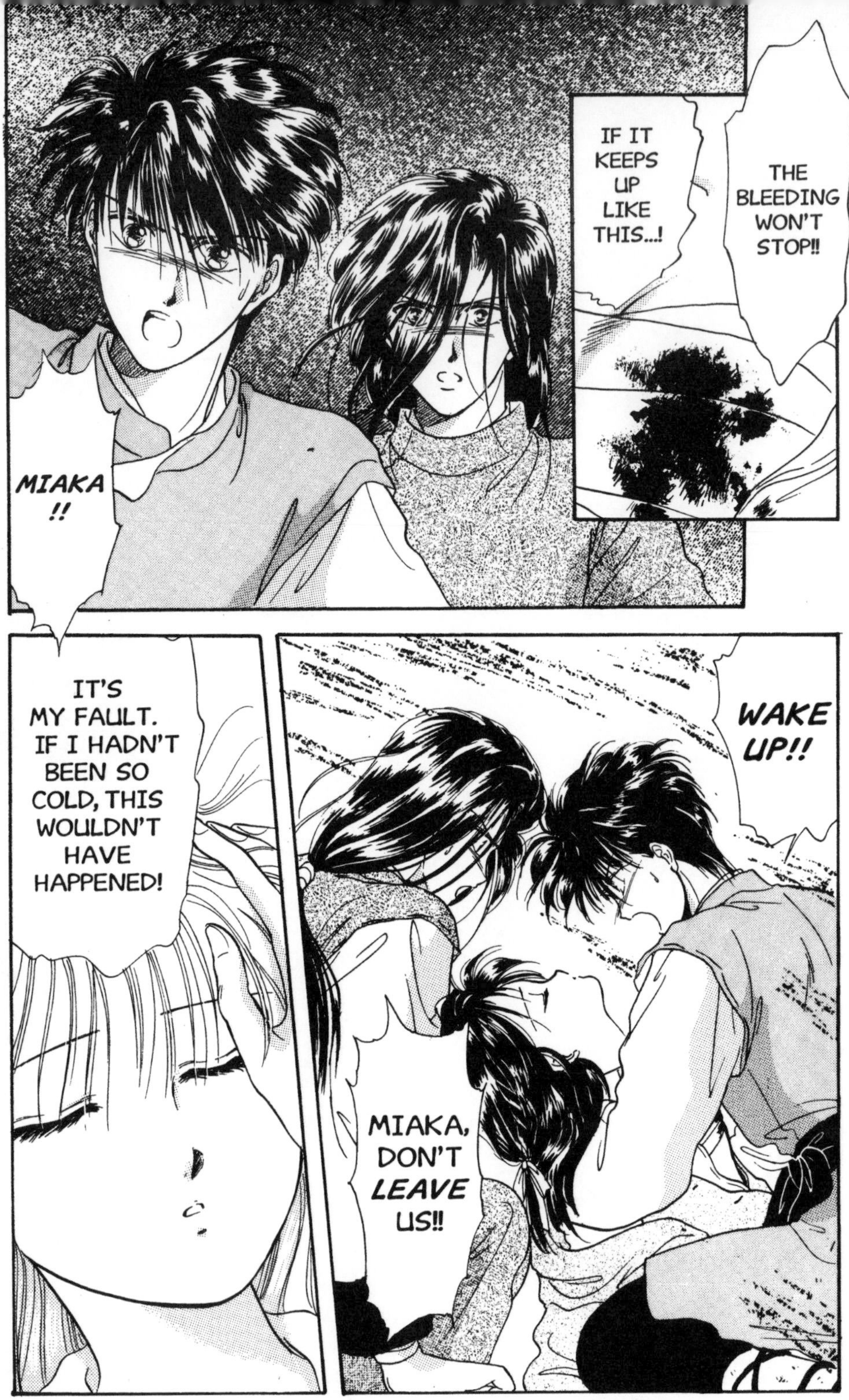
THE BLEEDING WON'T STOP!!
IF IT KEEPS UP LIKE THIS...!
MIAKA!!
WAKE UP!!
MIAKA, DON'T LEAVE US!!
IT'S MY FAULT. IF I HADN'T BEEN SO COLD, THIS WOULDN'T HAVE HAPPENED!

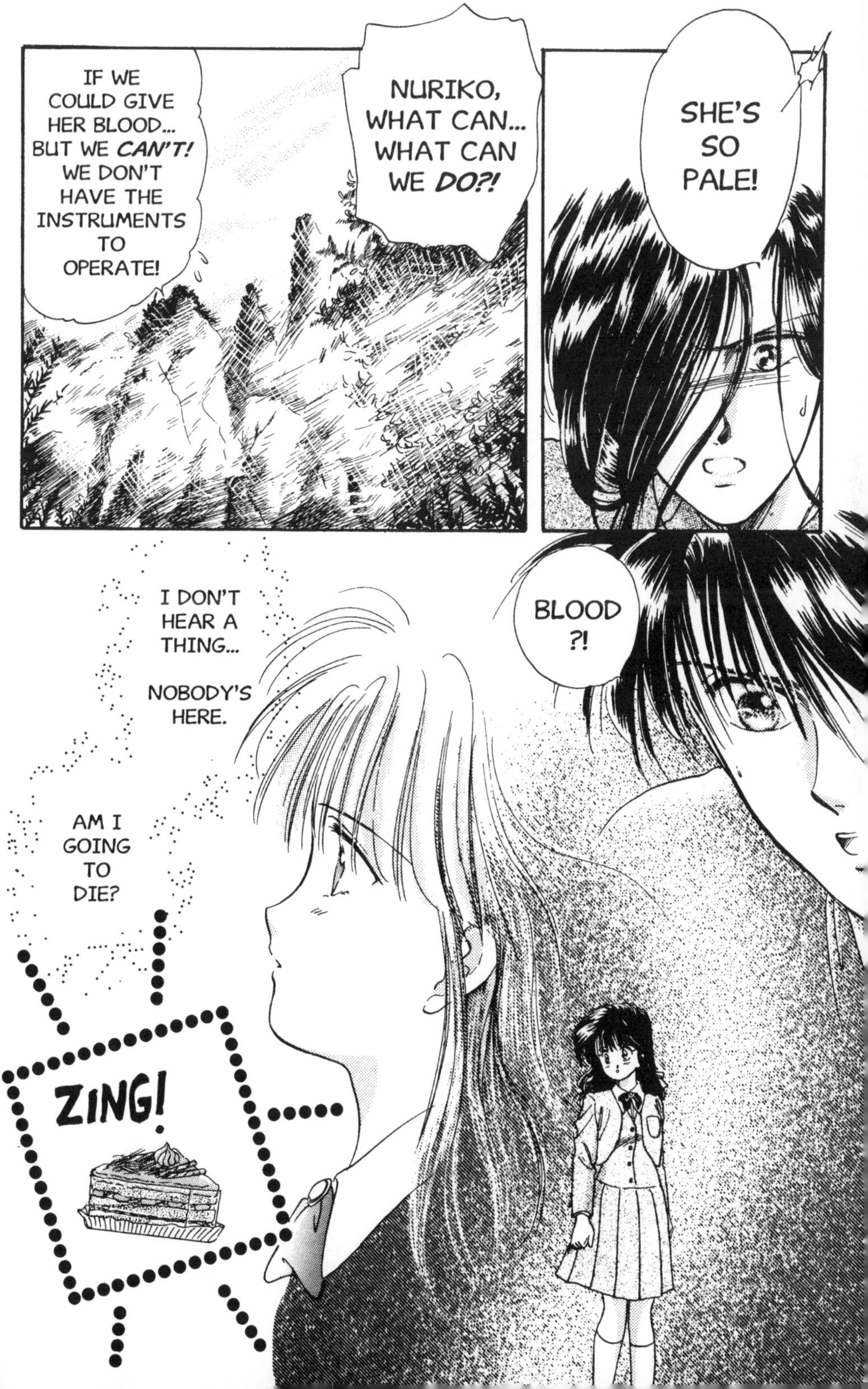

SHE'S SO PALE!
NURIKO, WHAT CAN... WHAT CAN WE *DO?!*
IF WE COULD GIVE HER BLOOD... BUT WE *CAN'T!* WE DON'T HAVE THE INSTRUMENTS TO OPERATE!
BLOOD?!
I DON'T HEAR A THING...
NOBODY'S HERE.
AM I GOING TO DIE?
ZING!

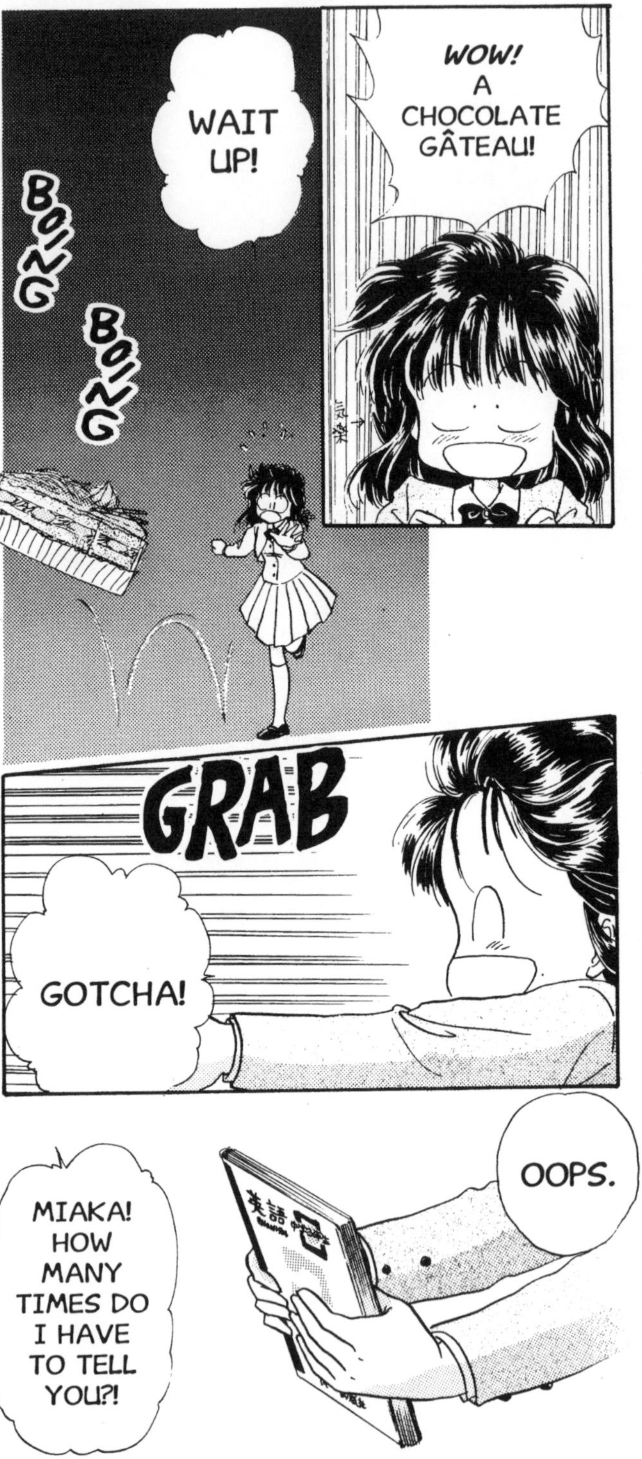
WOW! A CHOCOLATE GÂTEAU!
WAIT UP!
BOING
BOING
GRAB
GOTCHA!
OOPS.
MIAKA! HOW MANY TIMES DO I HAVE TO TELL YOU?!

I just want you to know it's not true! I heard there's been some controversy saying "Watase's a sex fiend!" (Unbelievable!) Let's just get this straight! The only comic that comes close to being sexy is *Prepubescence*. Quite a few readers told me they had dreams about Asuka and the other characters, so I guess the story left a pretty strong impression. On page 141 of volume 7 of *Prepubescence*, I wrote, "I wouldn't want people to think I'm turning into a perv." I didn't mean I was put out by it, I only meant people shouldn't get worked up over this stuff. Teenage girls might get excited and embarrassed and squeal, "Oh m'god! She's so dirty!" but to girls in their twenties, talking about this kind of stuff is common. It's nothing special. So it's not a matter of being a "perv" or not. So this stuff might shock teenage girls. You're so young. (Where am I going with this thought?) If bed scenes are necessary then I have no problem depicting them to the extent that they won't cause any major controversy. But I hate gratuitous sex scenes. Now that the plot is thickening I might have to include a sex scene or two in a serious context. (What? You're happy to hear that?) The characters are developing in volume 1, and in volume 2 they're finally getting to know each other.

But if the sales fall off, I'll have to start drawing autobiographical manga (What the heck would I write about?!). There was quite a bit of...that in the *Prepubescence* side story. ııı but the average age of the readers is pretty high, so I'll be all right. In any case, those scenes represent an expression of love so I don't think they're bad at all. I do think that gratuitous, superficial love scenes might have a bad effect on the reader. What am I talking about?!

Watase: Artist for the boys' comic, *Shônen Perv.*

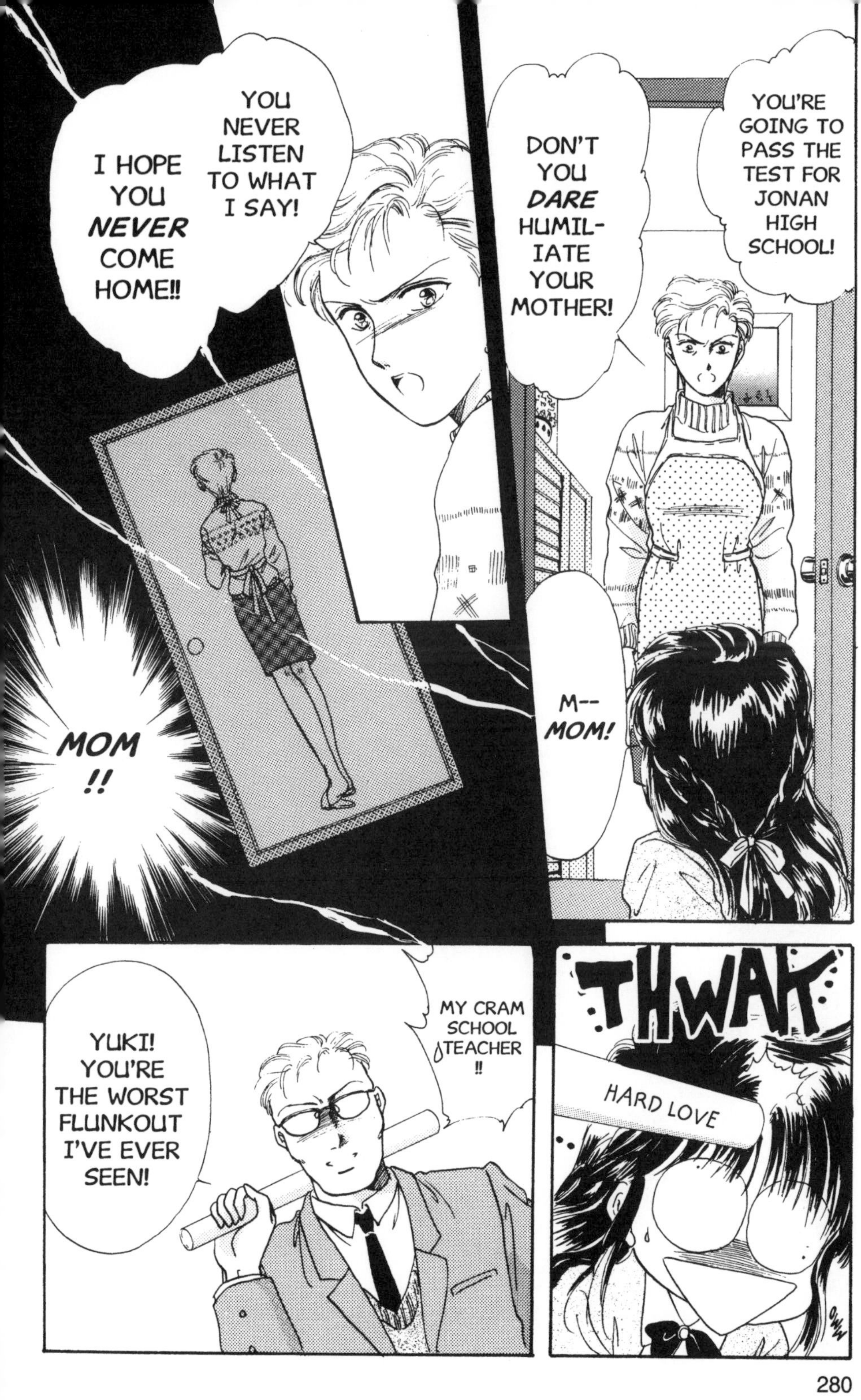
YOU'RE GOING TO PASS THE TEST FOR JONAN HIGH SCHOOL!
DON'T YOU DARE HUMILIATE YOUR MOTHER!
M-- MOM!
YOU NEVER LISTEN TO WHAT I SAY!
I HOPE YOU NEVER COME HOME!!
MOM !!
THWAK
HARD LOVE
MY CRAM SCHOOL TEACHER !!
YUKI! YOU'RE THE WORST FLUNKOUT I'VE EVER SEEN!

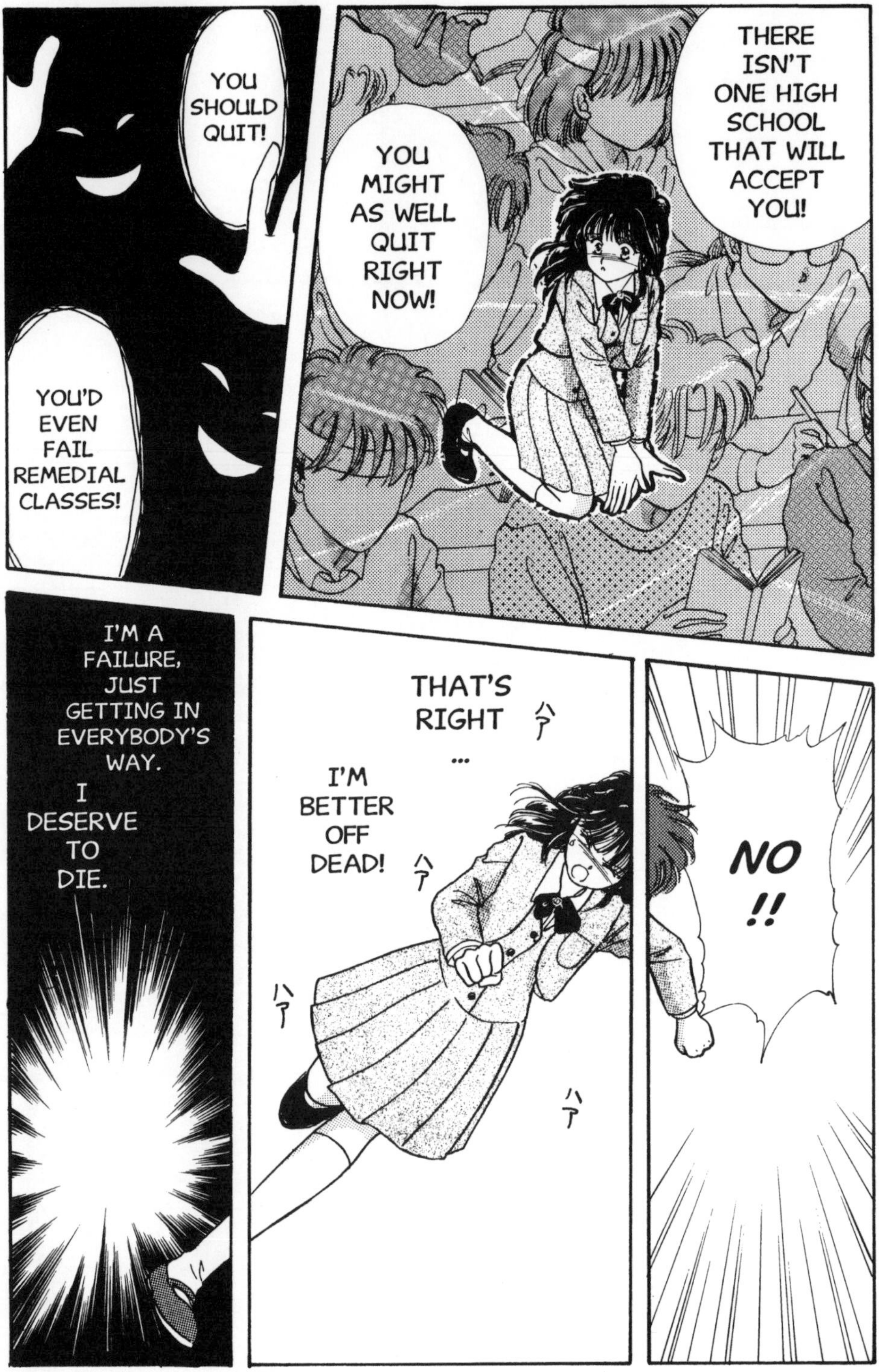
THERE ISN'T ONE HIGH SCHOOL THAT WILL ACCEPT YOU!
YOU MIGHT AS WELL QUIT RIGHT NOW!
YOU SHOULD QUIT!
YOU'D EVEN FAIL REMEDIAL CLASSES!
NO !!
THAT'S RIGHT ...
ハァ
I'M BETTER OFF DEAD!
ハァ
ハァ
ハァ
I'M A FAILURE, JUST GETTING IN EVERYBODY'S WAY.
I DESERVE TO DIE.

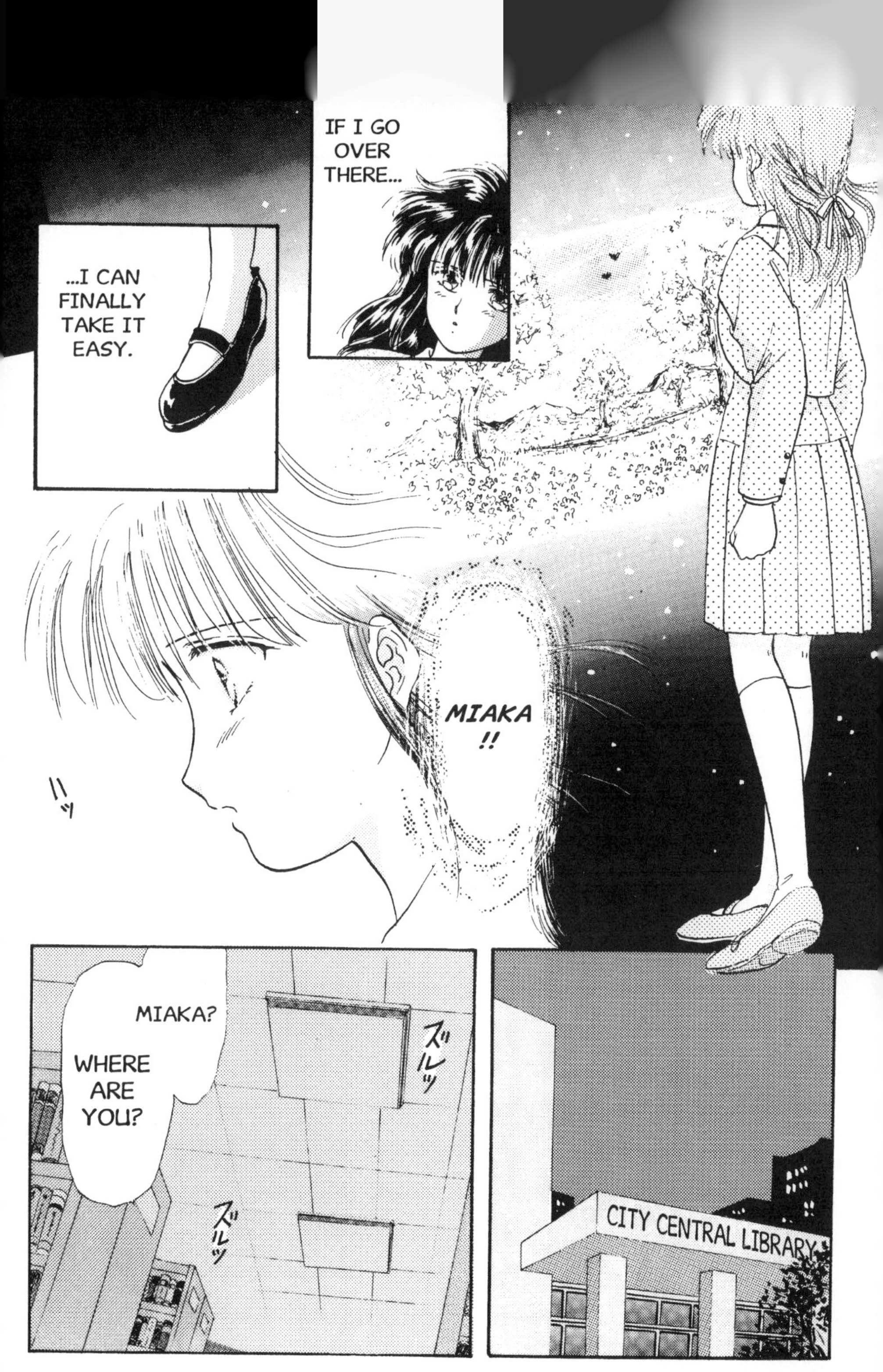
IF I GO OVER THERE...
...I CAN FINALLY TAKE IT EASY.
MIAKA !!
ハッ
CITY CENTRAL LIBRARY
MIAKA?
WHERE ARE YOU?
ズルッ
ズルッ

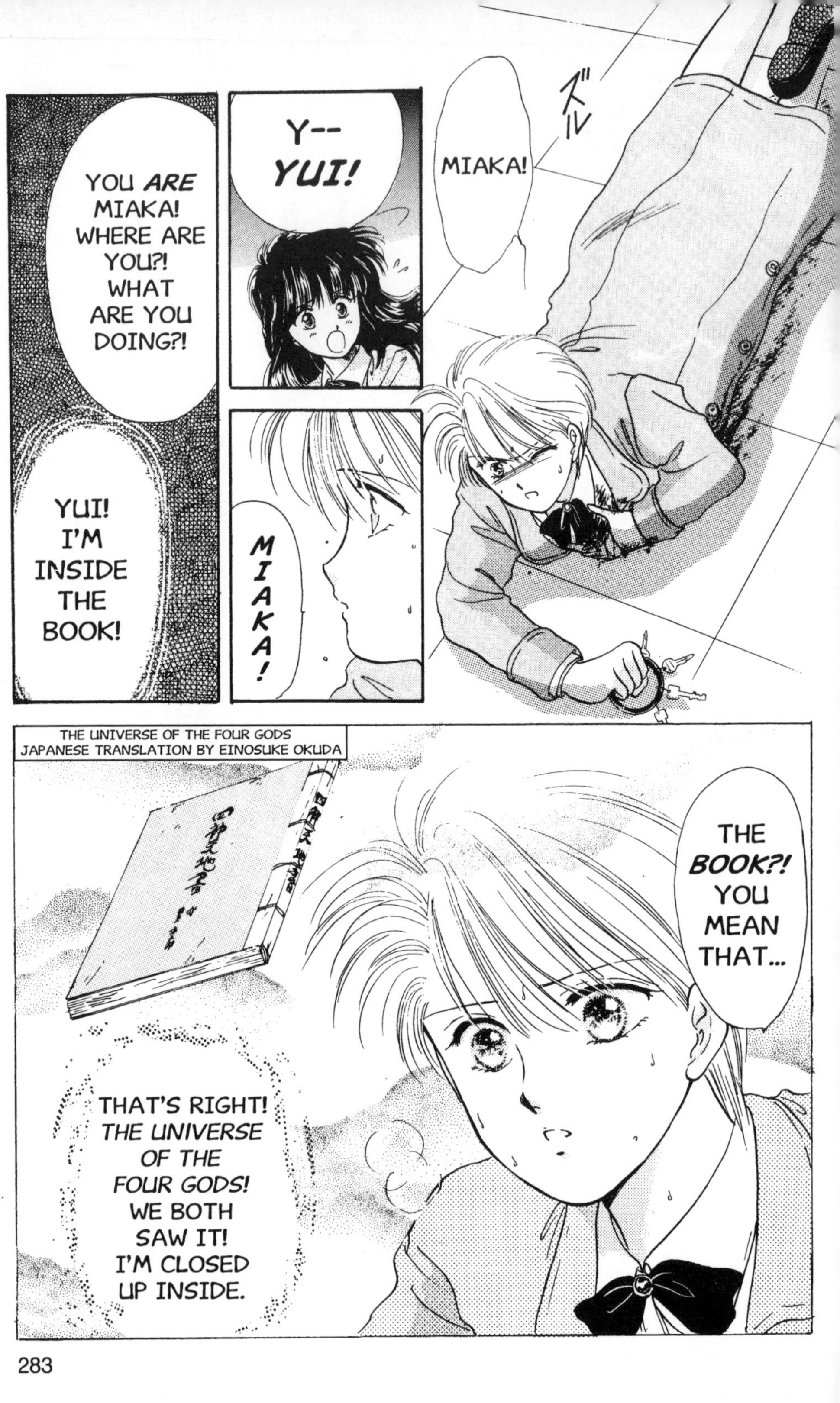
ズル
MIAKA!
Y-- *YUI!*
MIAKA!
YOU *ARE* MIAKA! WHERE ARE YOU?! WHAT ARE YOU DOING?!
YUI! I'M INSIDE THE BOOK!
THE UNIVERSE OF THE FOUR GODS
JAPANESE TRANSLATION BY EINOSUKE OKUDA
THE *BOOK?!* YOU MEAN THAT...
THAT'S RIGHT! *THE UNIVERSE OF THE FOUR GODS!* WE BOTH SAW IT! I'M CLOSED UP INSIDE.

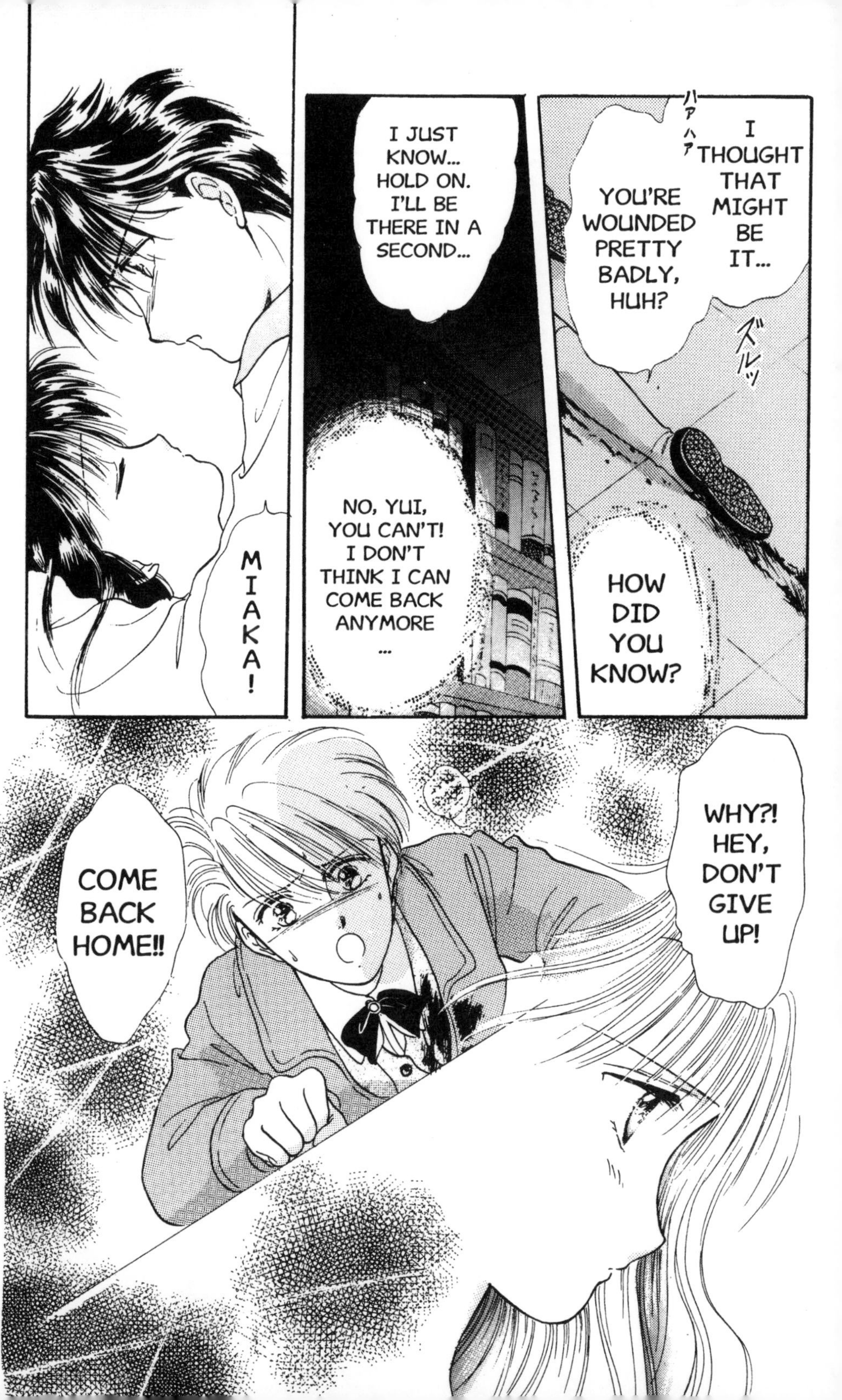
I THOUGHT THAT MIGHT BE IT...
ハァハァ
YOU'RE WOUNDED PRETTY BADLY, HUH?
ズルッ
HOW DID YOU KNOW?
I JUST KNOW... HOLD ON. I'LL BE THERE IN A SECOND...
NO, YUI, YOU CAN'T! I DON'T THINK I CAN COME BACK ANYMORE ...
MIAKA!
WHY?! HEY, DON'T GIVE UP!
COME BACK HOME!!

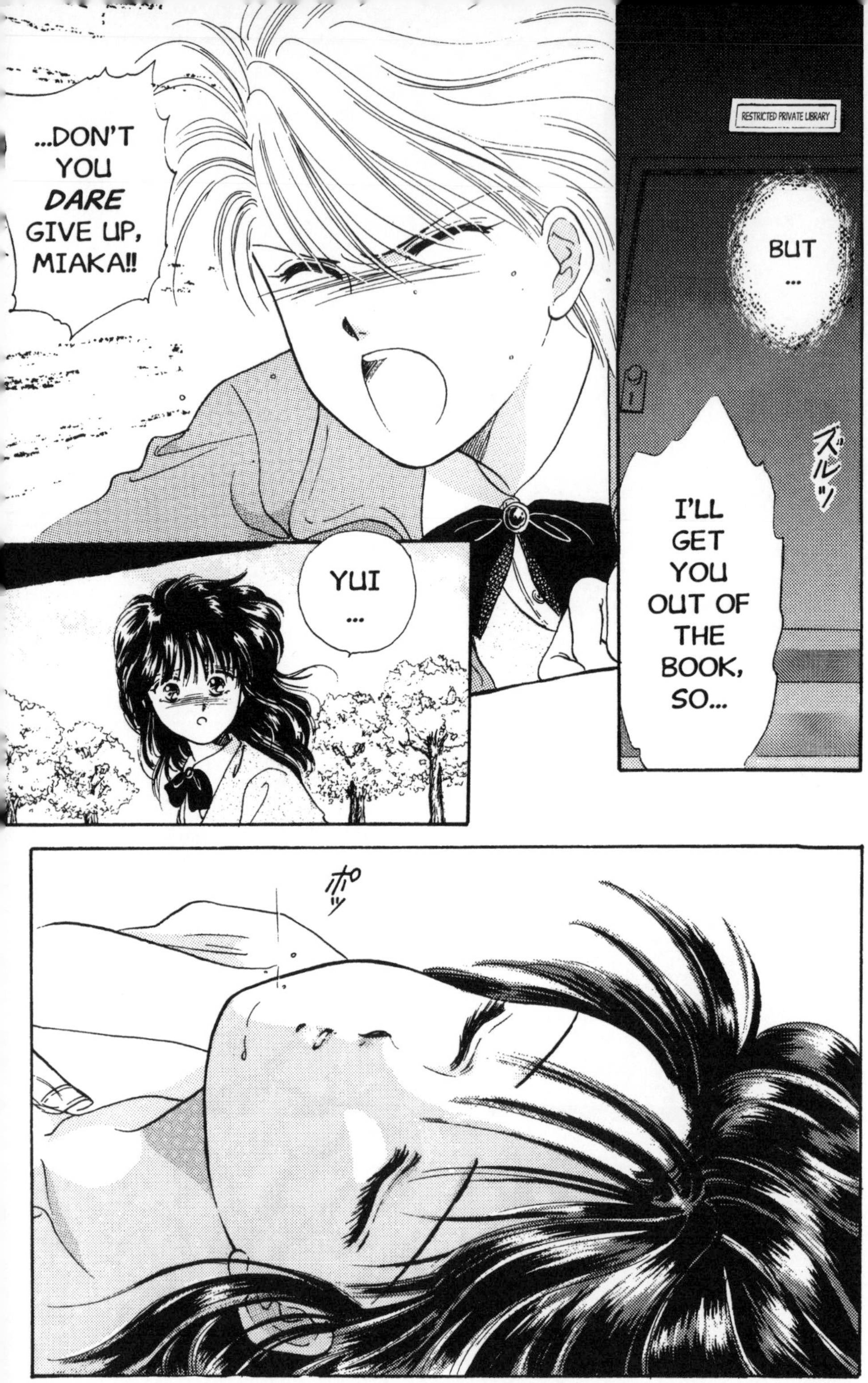
RESTRICTED PRIVATE LIBRARY
BUT...
I'LL GET YOU OUT OF THE BOOK, SO...
ズルッ
...DON'T YOU ***DARE*** GIVE UP, MIAKA!!
YUI...
ポッ

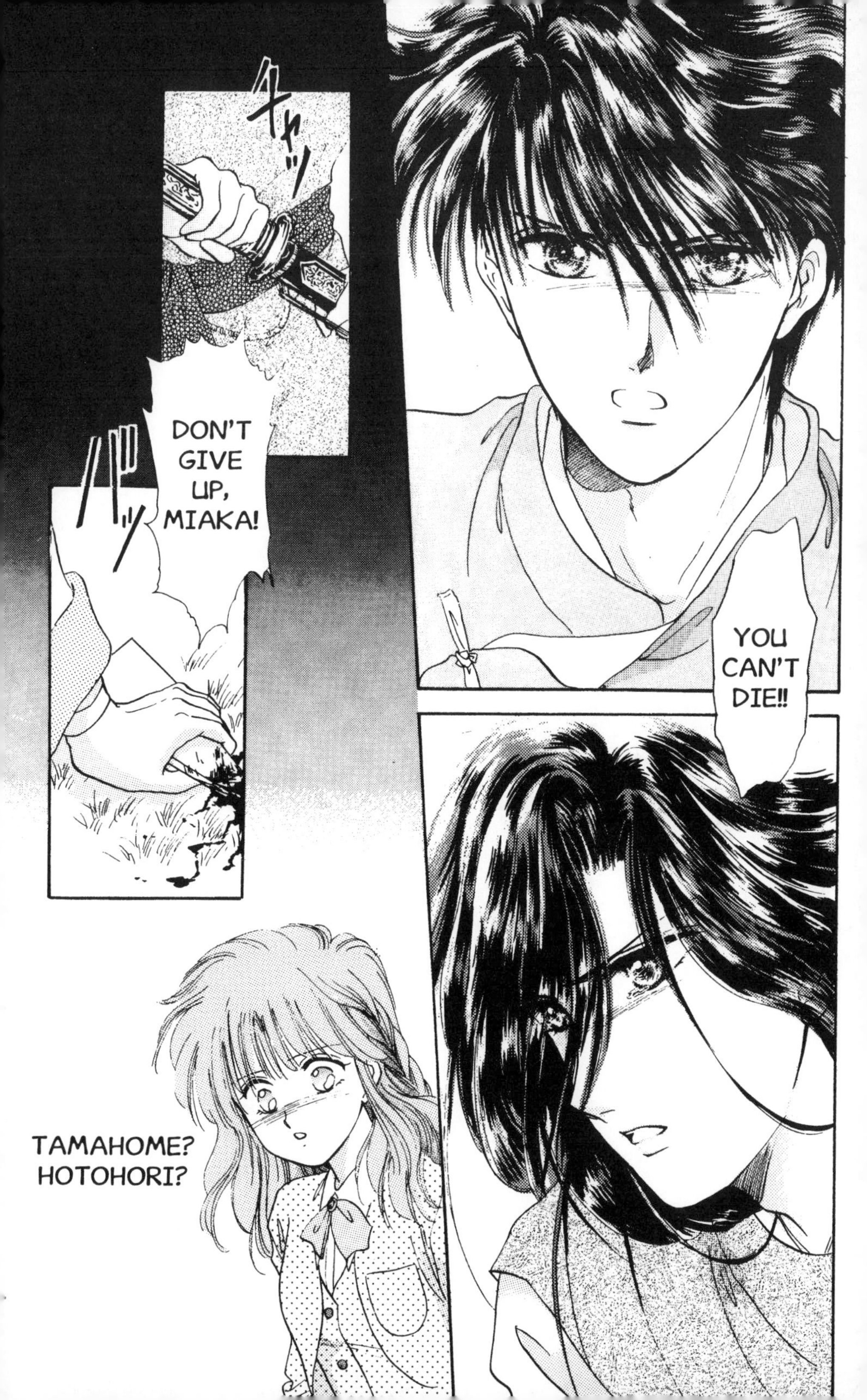
YOU CAN'T DIE!!
DON'T GIVE UP, MIAKA!
TAMAHOME? HOTOHORI?

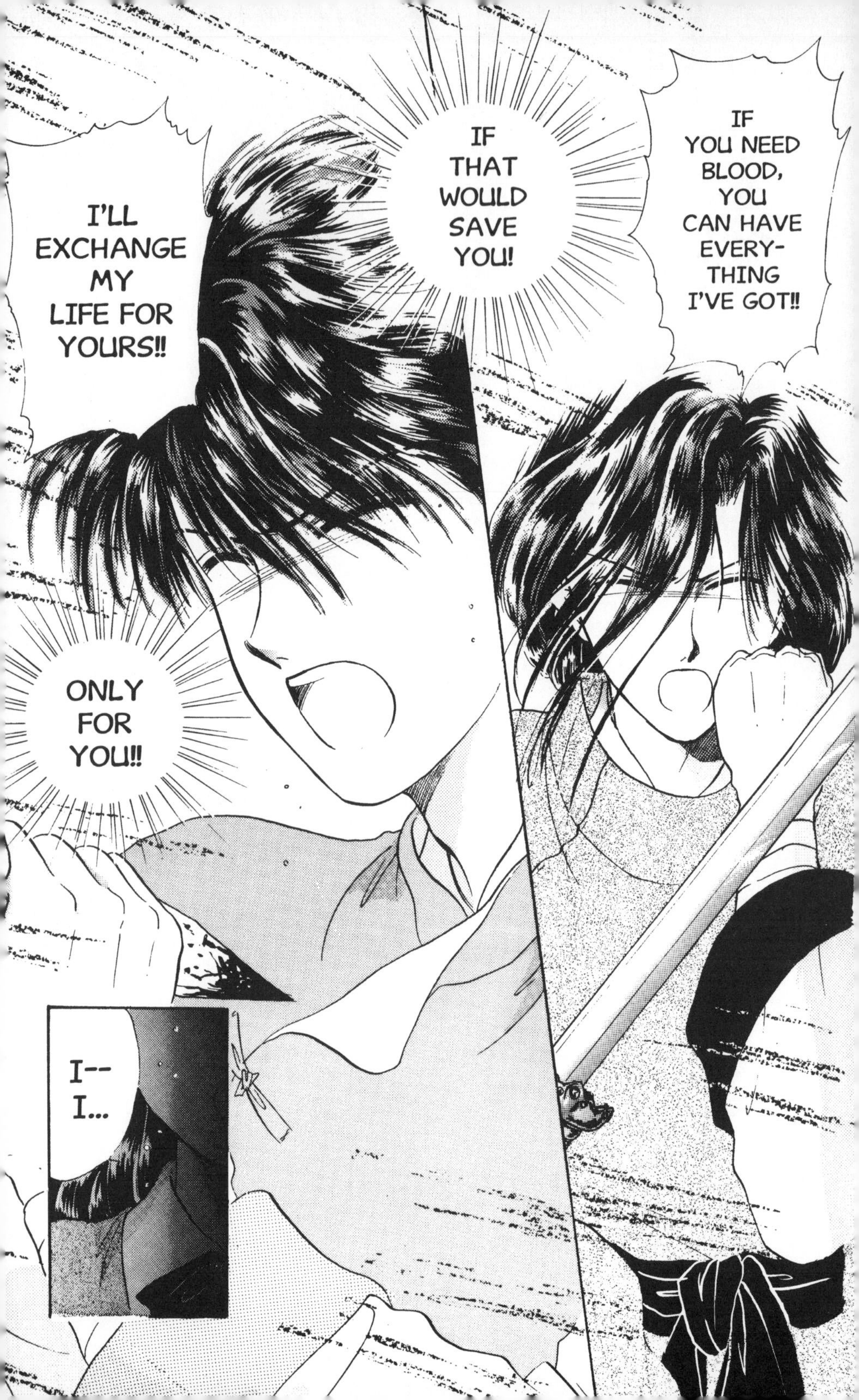
IF YOU NEED BLOOD, YOU CAN HAVE EVERY-THING I'VE GOT!!
IF THAT WOULD SAVE YOU!
I'LL EXCHANGE MY LIFE FOR YOURS!!
ONLY FOR YOU!!
I-- I...

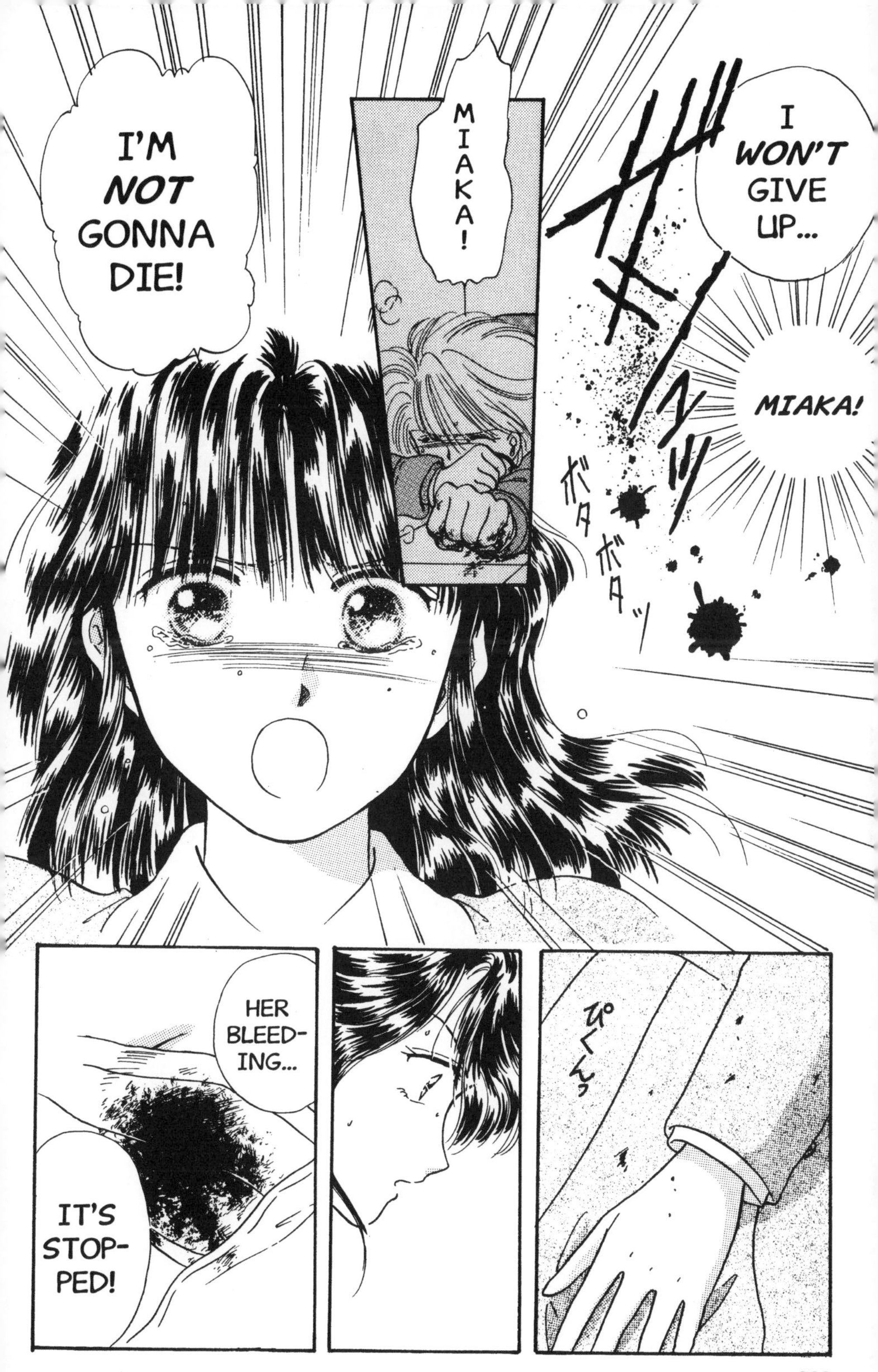
I WON'T GIVE UP...
MIAKA!
ボタボタッ
MIAKA!
I'M NOT GONNA DIE!
ぴくんっ
HER BLEED-ING...
IT'S STOP-PED!

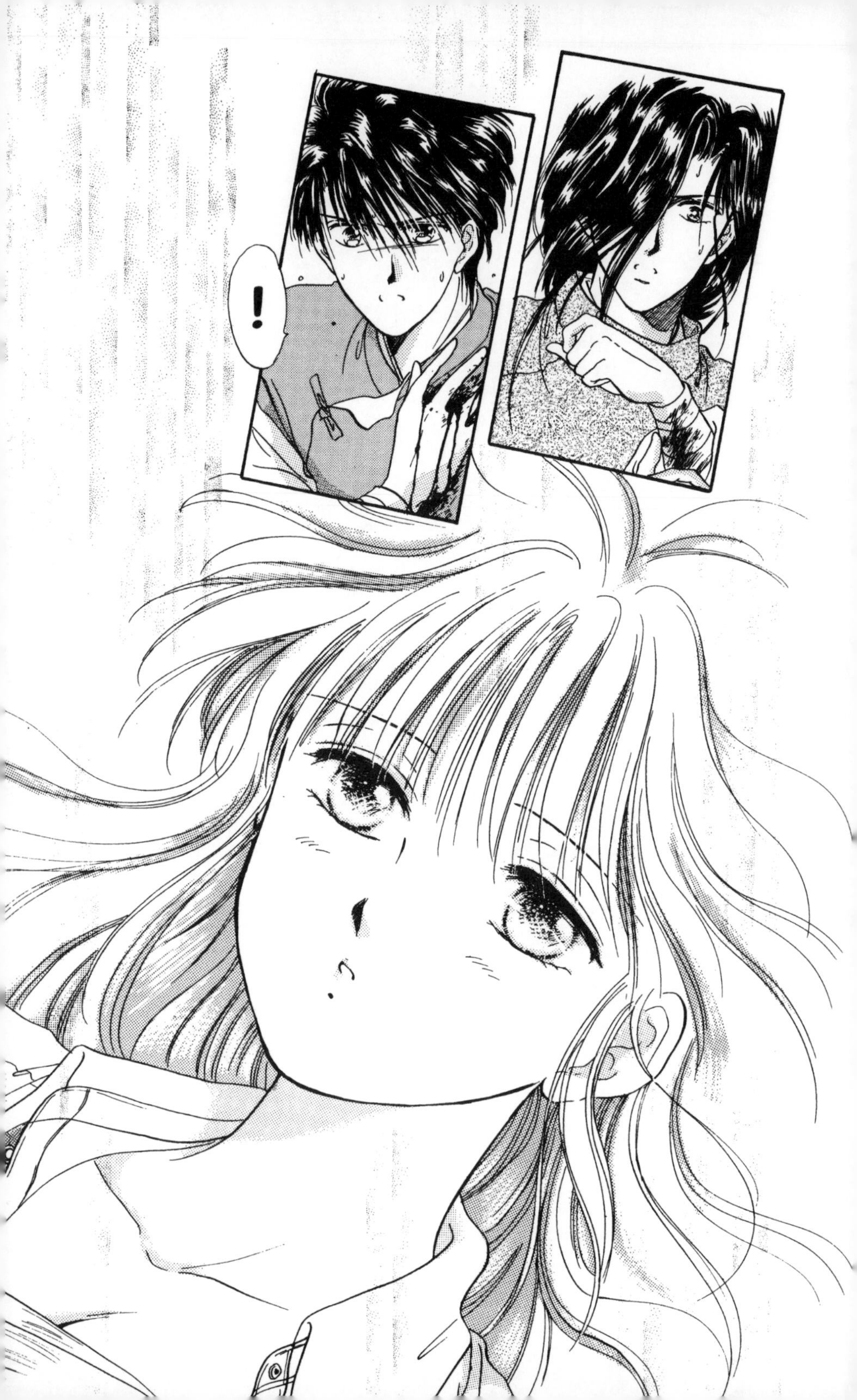
!

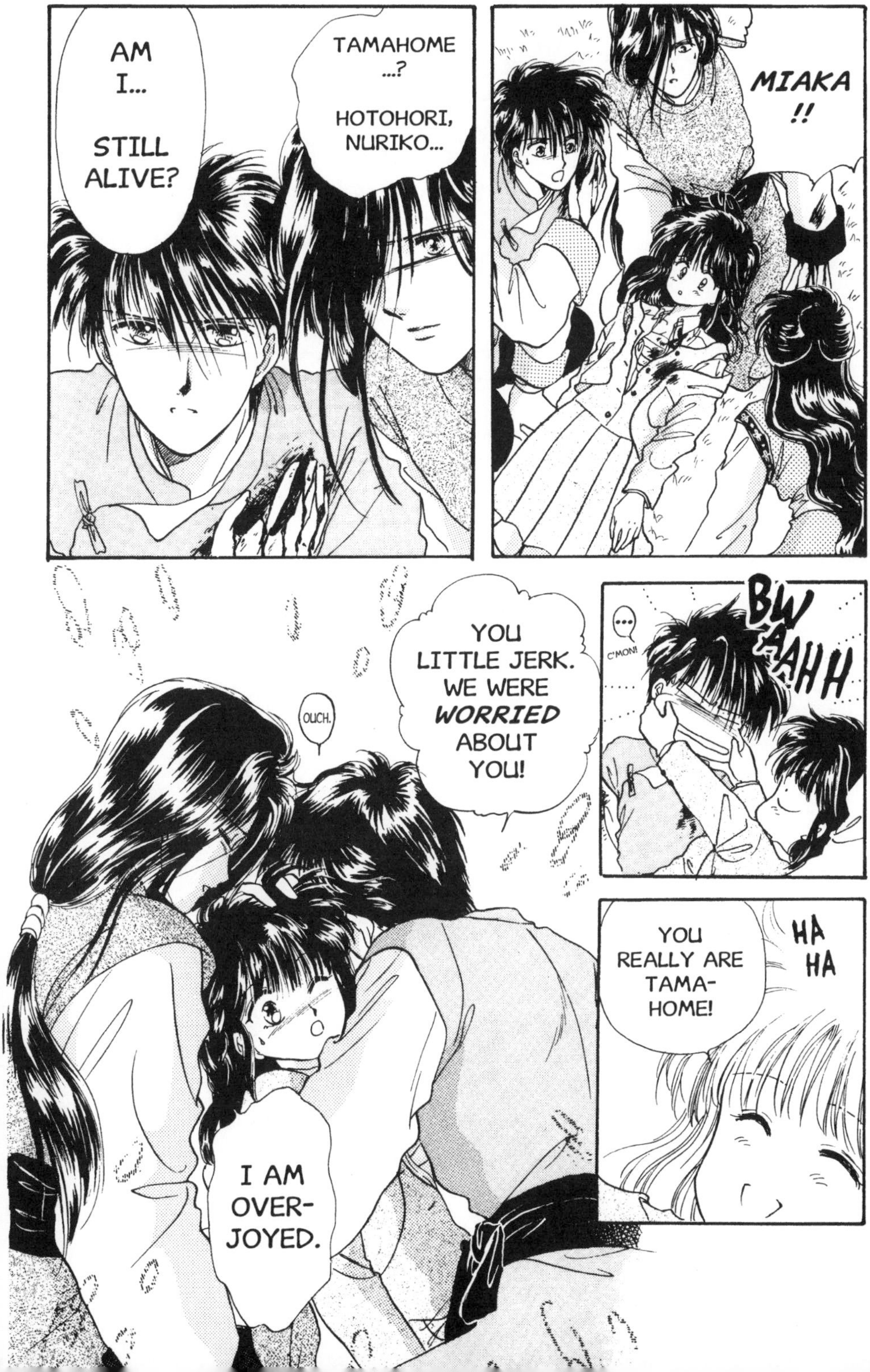
MIAKA!!
TAMAHOME ...? HOTOHORI, NURIKO...
AM I... STILL ALIVE?
BWAAHH
...
C'MON!
HA HA
YOU REALLY ARE TAMA-HOME!
YOU LITTLE JERK. WE WERE ***WORRIED*** ABOUT YOU!
OUCH.
I AM OVER-JOYED.

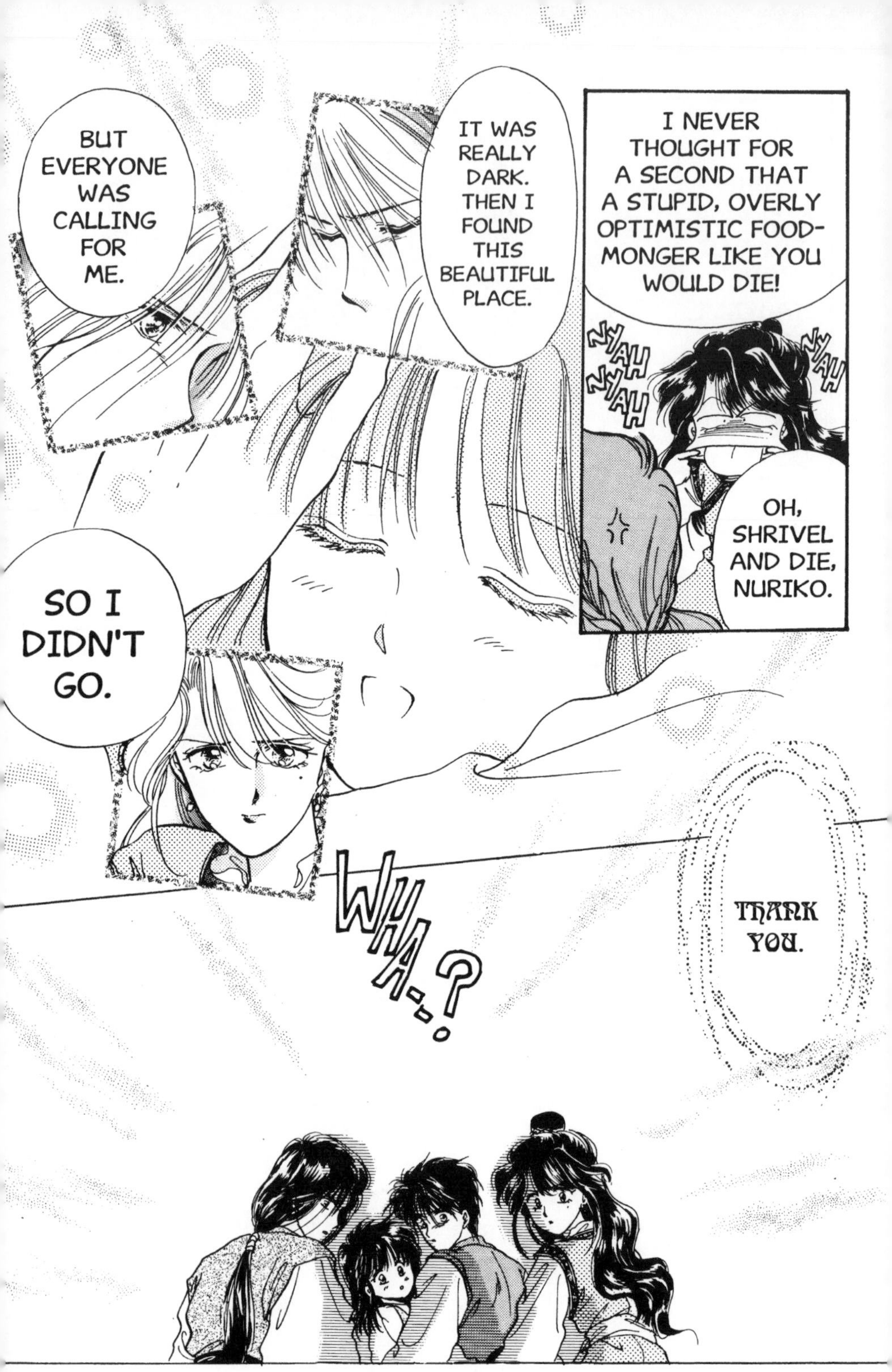
I NEVER THOUGHT FOR A SECOND THAT A STUPID, OVERLY OPTIMISTIC FOOD-MONGER LIKE YOU WOULD DIE!
NYAH NYAH NYAH NYAH
OH, SHRIVEL AND DIE, NURIKO.
IT WAS REALLY DARK. THEN I FOUND THIS BEAUTIFUL PLACE.
BUT EVERYONE WAS CALLING FOR ME.
SO I DIDN'T GO.
THANK YOU.
WHA-?

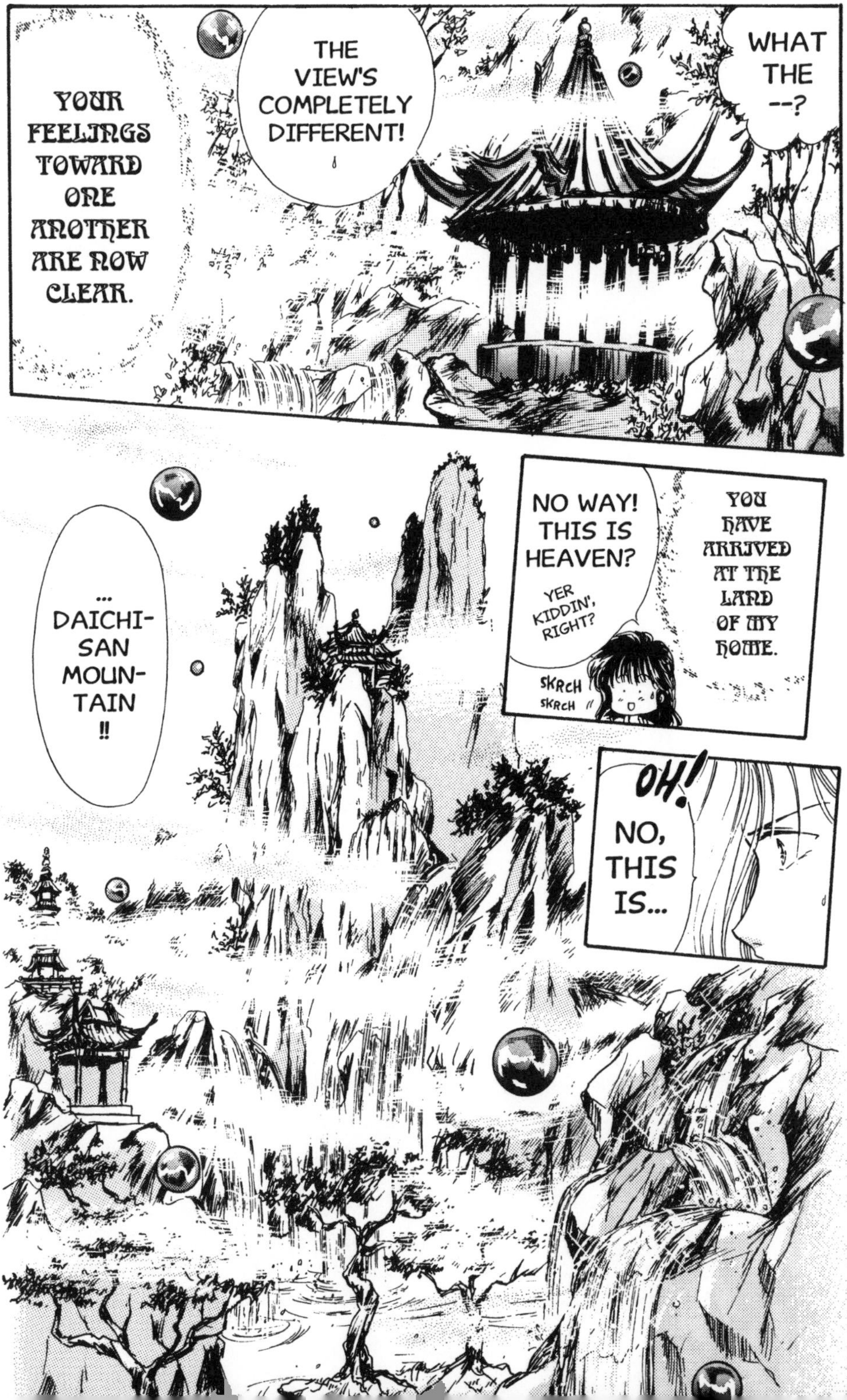
WHAT THE --?
THE VIEW'S COMPLETELY DIFFERENT!
YOUR FEELINGS TOWARD ONE ANOTHER ARE NOW CLEAR.
YOU HAVE ARRIVED AT THE LAND OF MY HOME.
NO WAY! THIS IS HEAVEN?
YER KIDDIN', RIGHT?
SKRCH SKRCH
OH!
NO, THIS IS...
... DAICHI-SAN MOUN-TAIN !!

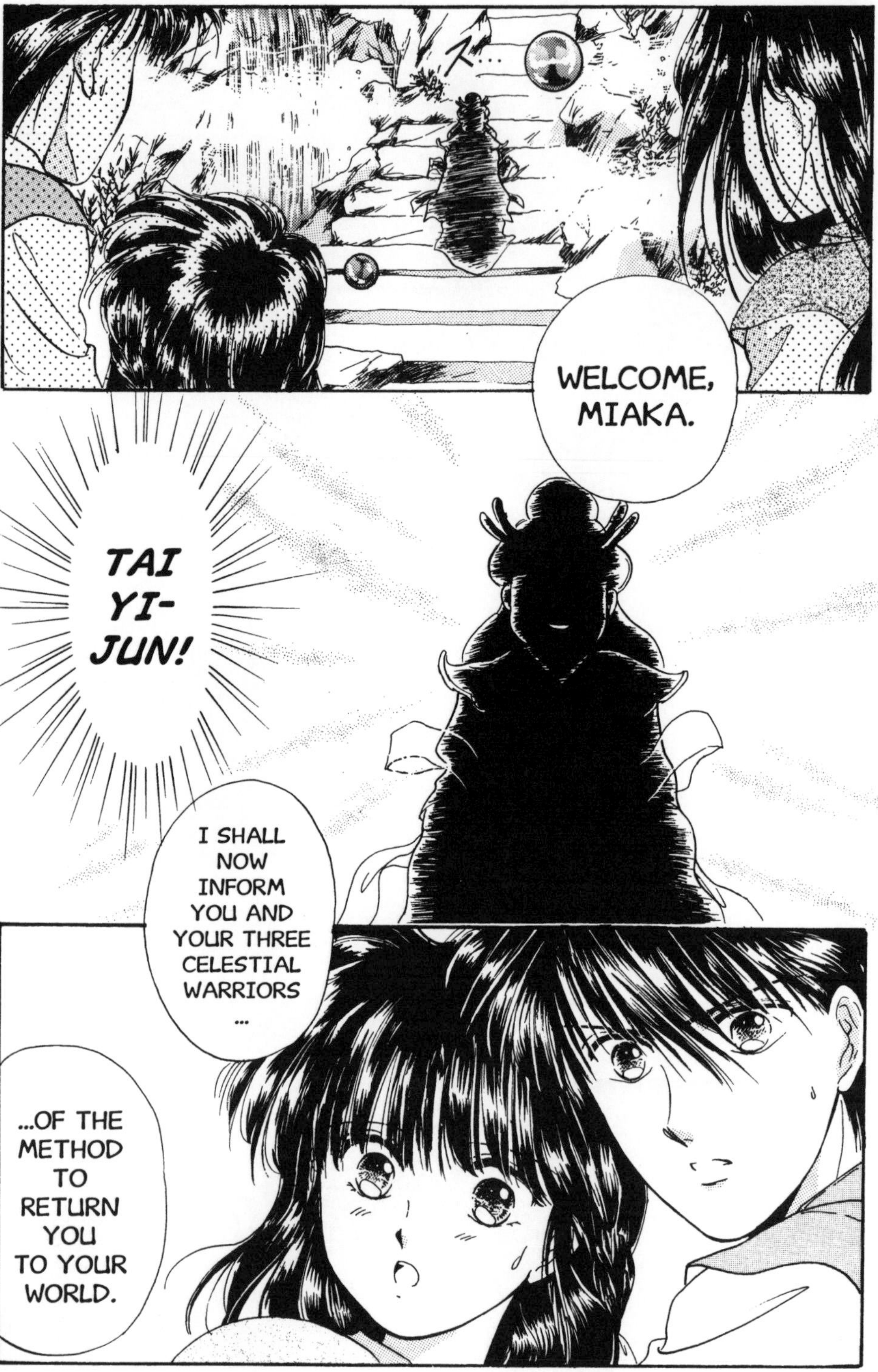

ズ...
WELCOME, MIAKA.
TAI YI-JUN!
I SHALL NOW INFORM YOU AND YOUR THREE CELESTIAL WARRIORS ...
...OF THE METHOD TO RETURN YOU TO YOUR WORLD.

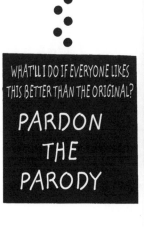

WHAT'LL I DO IF EVERYONE LIKES THIS BETTER THAN THE ORIGINAL?

PARDON THE PARODY

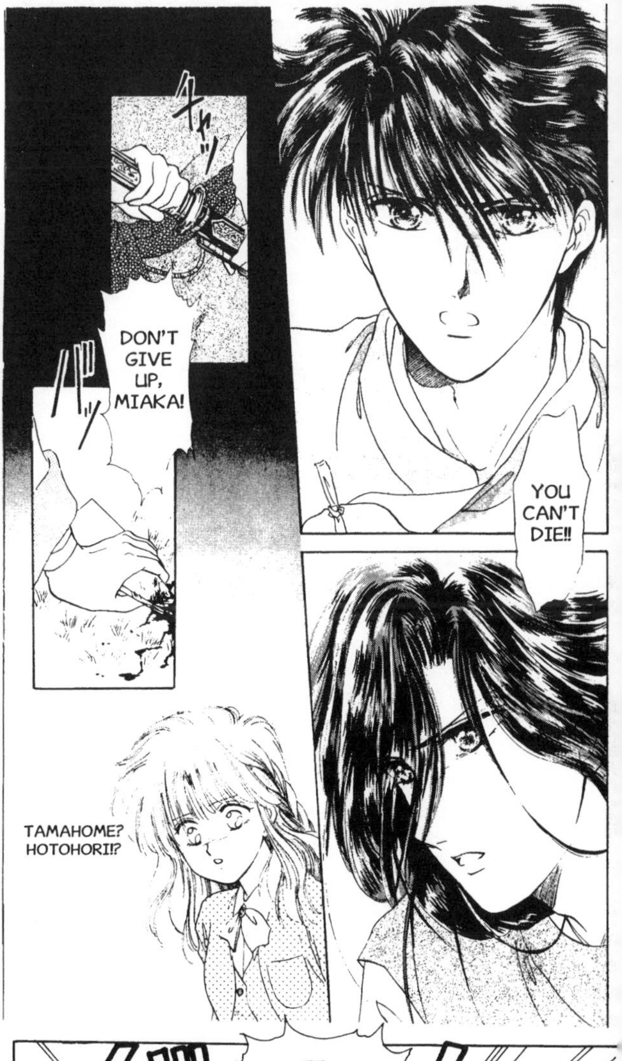
YOU CAN'T DIE!!
TAMAHOME? HOTOHORI!?
DON'T GIVE UP, MIAKA!

IDEA - Y.M.

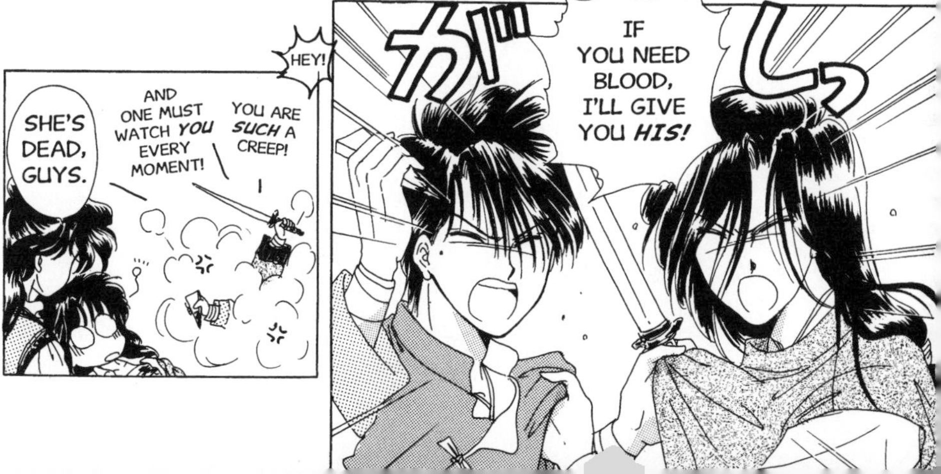
IF YOU NEED BLOOD, I'LL GIVE YOU *HIS!*
HEY!
YOU ARE *SUCH* A CREEP!
AND ONE MUST WATCH *YOU* EVERY MOMENT!
SHE'S DEAD, GUYS.

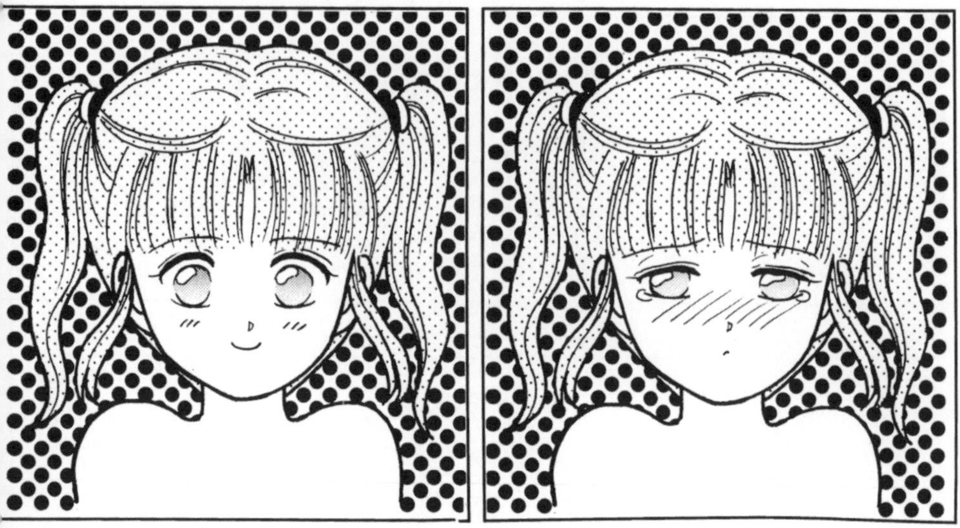

Chapter Ten
Come Back Home

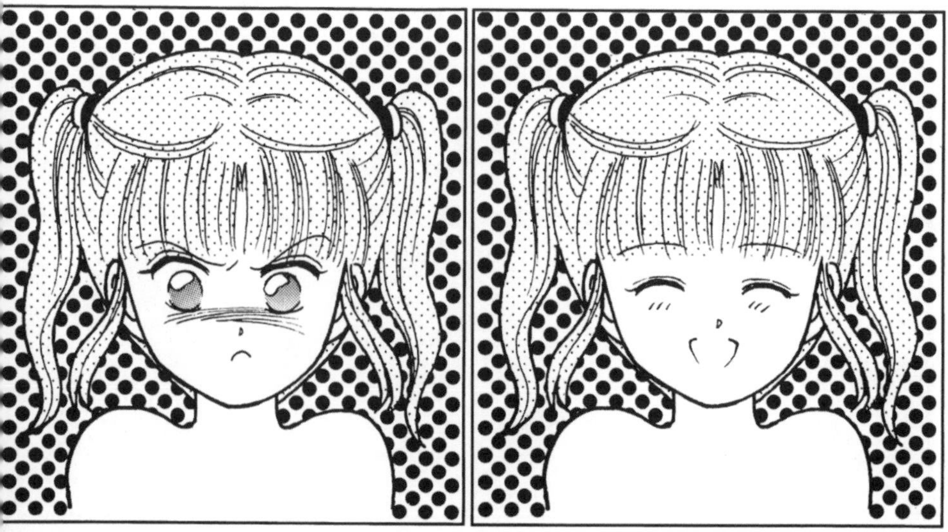

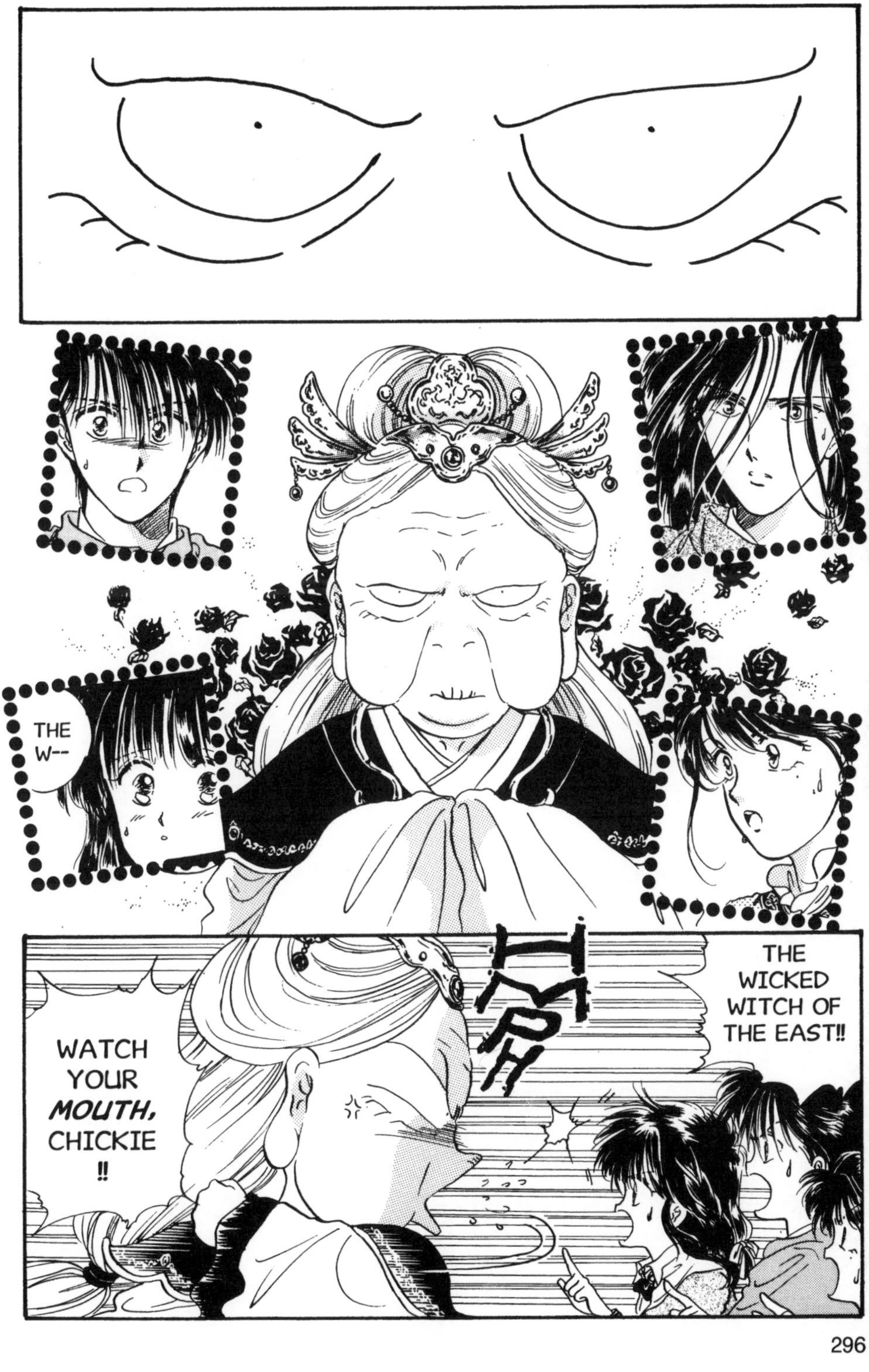
THE W--
THE WICKED WITCH OF THE EAST!!
HMPH!!
WATCH YOUR *MOUTH,* CHICKIE!!

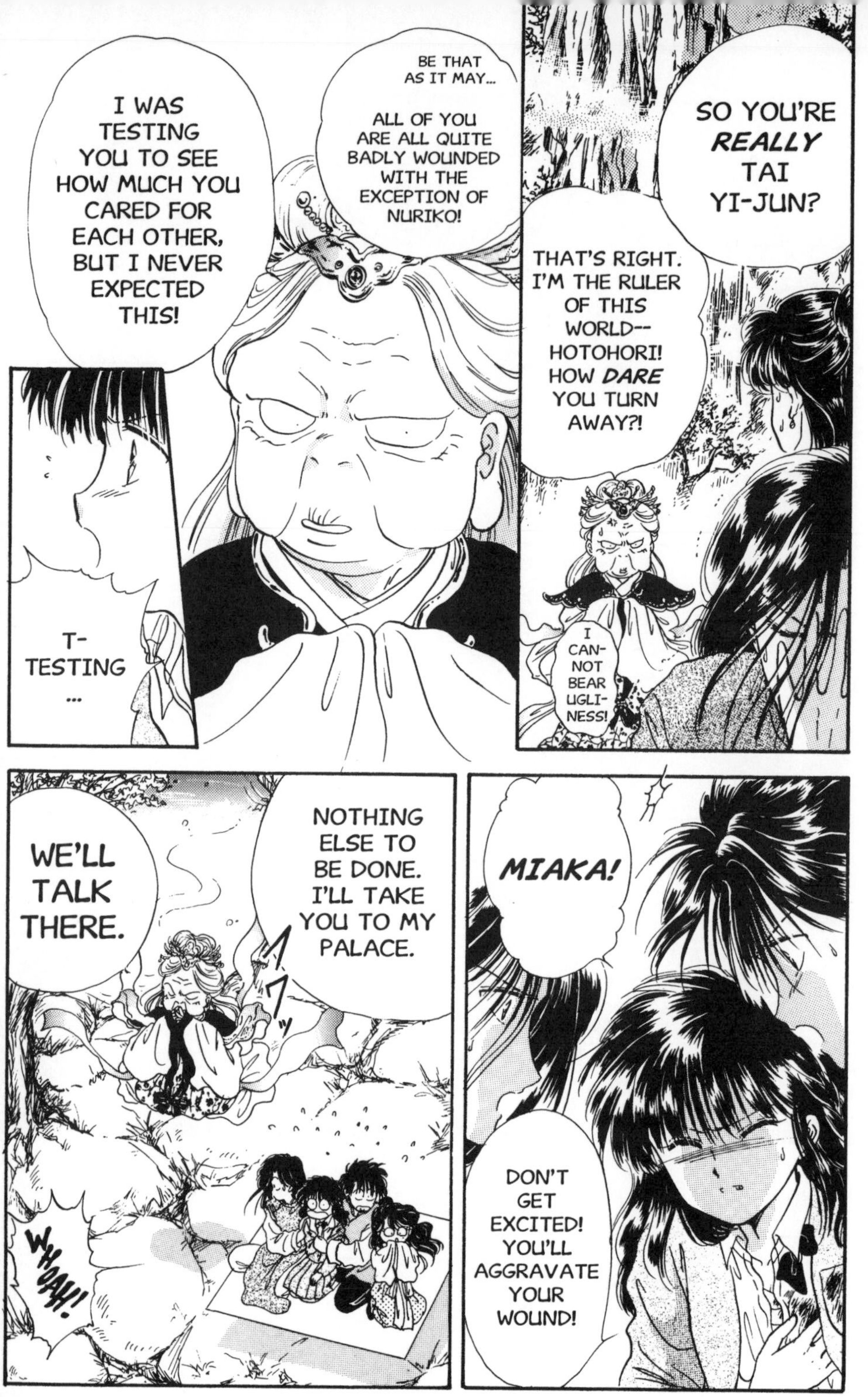
SO YOU'RE *REALLY* TAI YI-JUN?
THAT'S RIGHT. I'M THE RULER OF THIS WORLD-- HOTOHORI! HOW *DARE* YOU TURN AWAY?!
I CANNOT BEAR UGLINESS!
BE THAT AS IT MAY...
ALL OF YOU ARE ALL QUITE BADLY WOUNDED WITH THE EXCEPTION OF NURIKO!
I WAS TESTING YOU TO SEE HOW MUCH YOU CARED FOR EACH OTHER, BUT I NEVER EXPECTED THIS!
T-TESTING...
MIAKA!
DON'T GET EXCITED! YOU'LL AGGRAVATE YOUR WOUND!
NOTHING ELSE TO BE DONE. I'LL TAKE YOU TO MY PALACE.
WE'LL TALK THERE.
WHOAH!

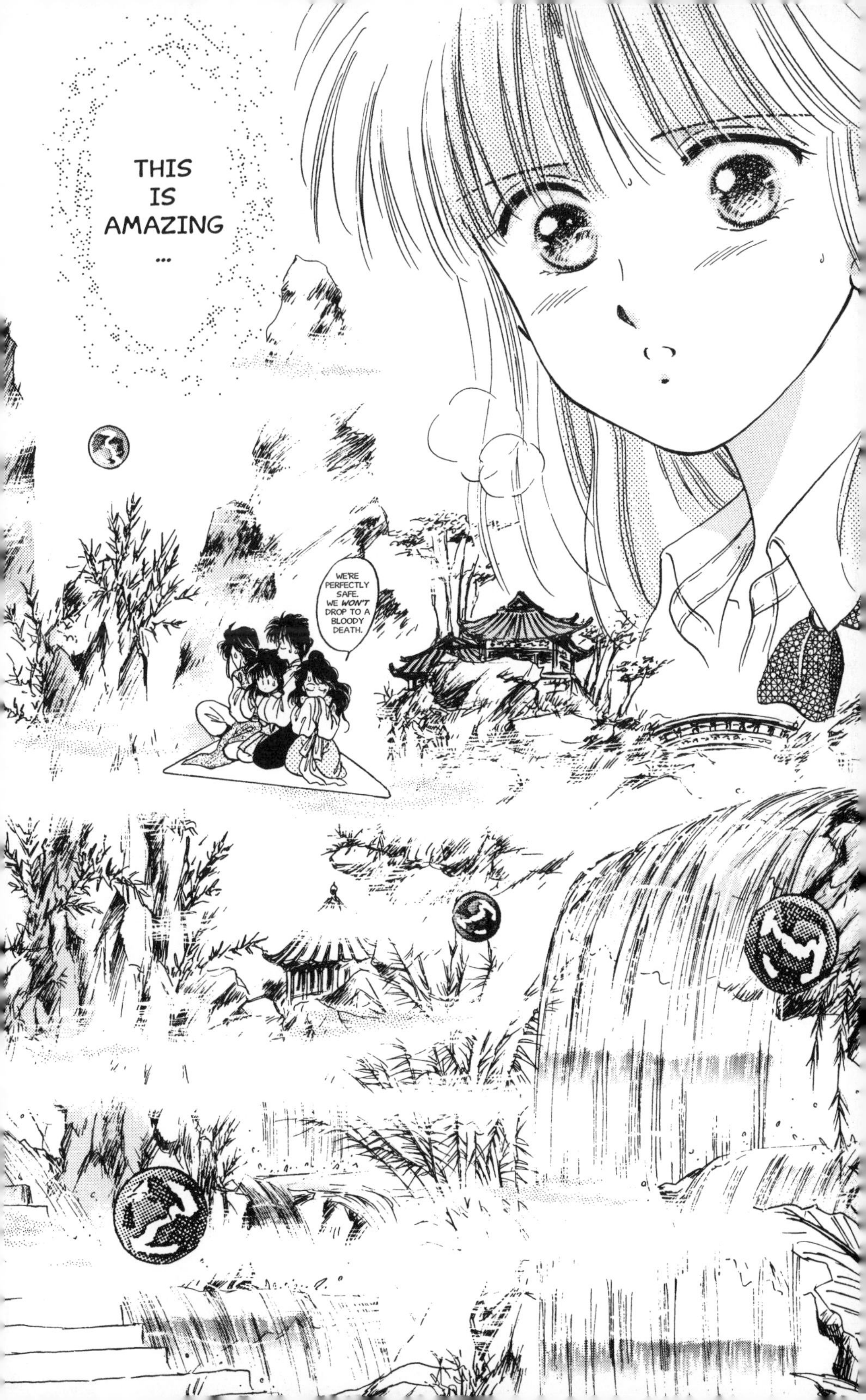
THIS IS AMAZING ...
WE'RE PERFECTLY SAFE. WE *WON'T* DROP TO A BLOODY DEATH.

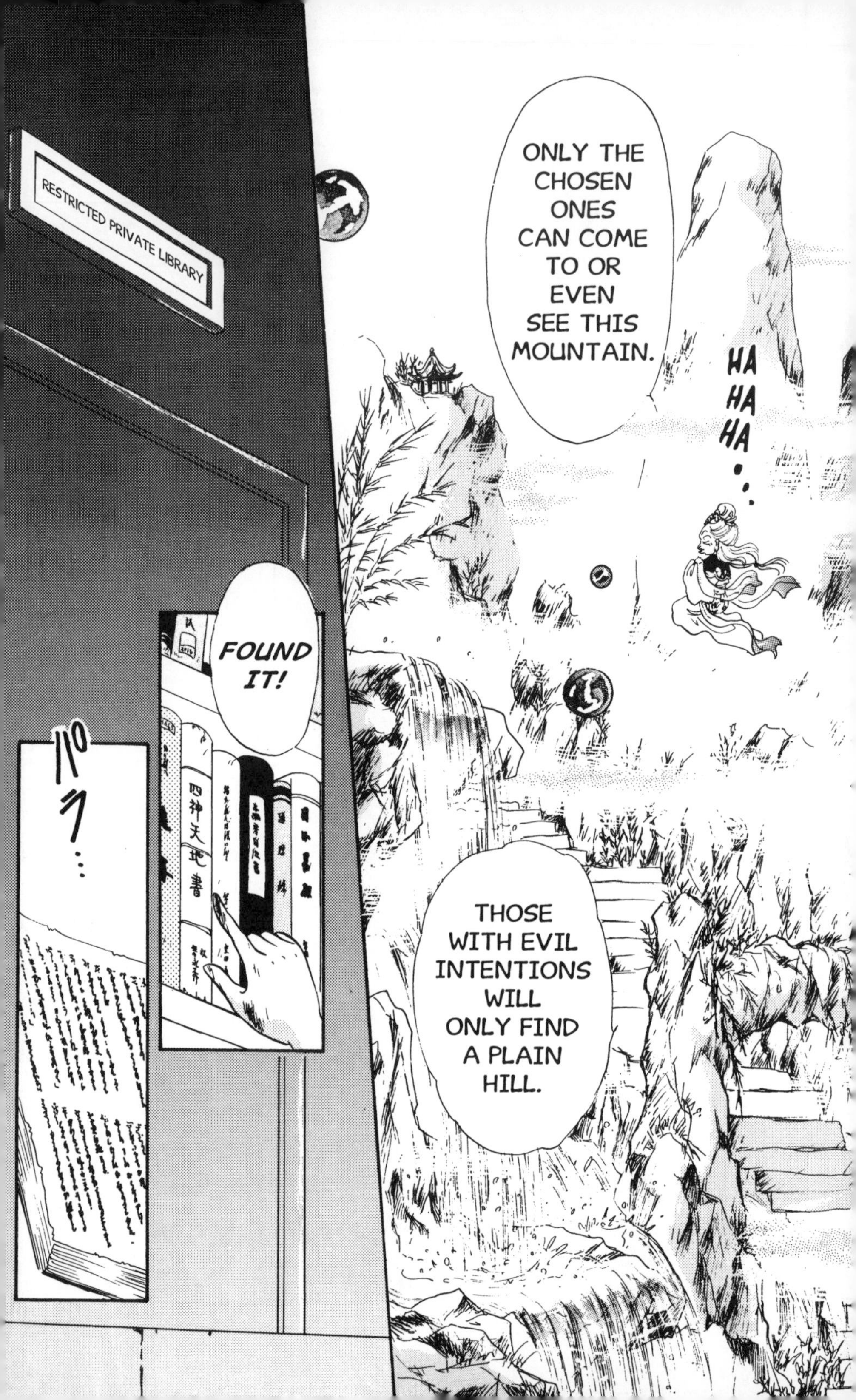
ONLY THE CHOSEN ONES CAN COME TO OR EVEN SEE THIS MOUNTAIN.
HA HA HA...
THOSE WITH EVIL INTENTIONS WILL ONLY FIND A PLAIN HILL.
RESTRICTED PRIVATE LIBRARY
FOUND IT!
四神天地書
パラ…

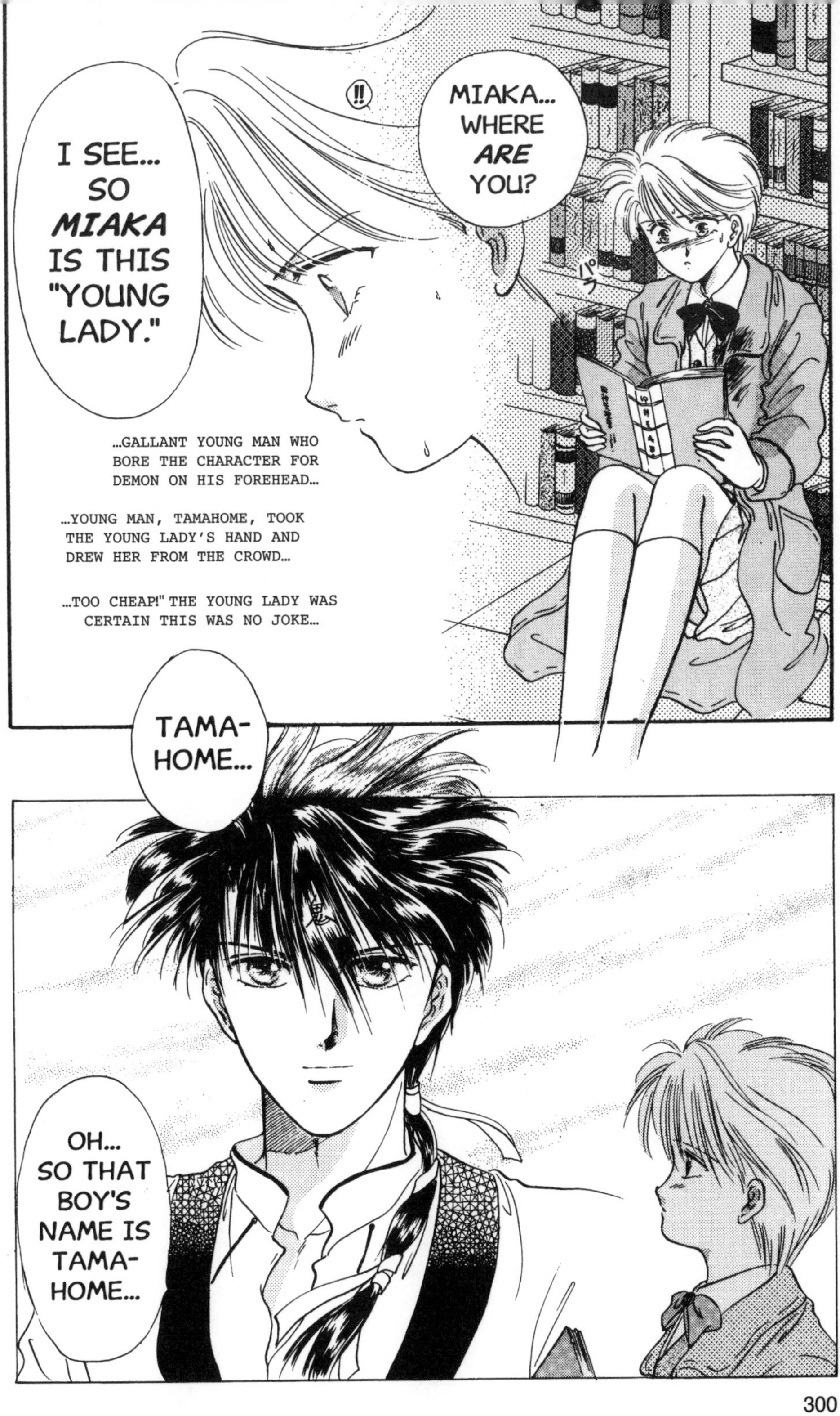
MIAKA... WHERE *ARE* YOU?
!!
I SEE... SO *MIAKA* IS THIS "YOUNG LADY."
...GALLANT YOUNG MAN WHO BORE THE CHARACTER FOR DEMON ON HIS FOREHEAD...
...YOUNG MAN, TAMAHOME, TOOK THE YOUNG LADY'S HAND AND DREW HER FROM THE CROWD...
...TOO CHEAP!" THE YOUNG LADY WAS CERTAIN THIS WAS NO JOKE...
TAMA-HOME...
OH... SO THAT BOY'S NAME IS TAMA-HOME...

By the way, my profile in "The Watase Newsletter" includes something about my leg size, but that's really my shoe size. I can wear a size 25. 25.5 is a loose fit, but 25 is a little too tight. My shoe size is about average for my height. When I mentioned my age in an earlier chat section, someone said, "So you're 26!" Wrong-o! *Prepubescence* began in December of '90, and I started this serial less than a year later. How could I be 26?! I graduated high school only four years ago. sob sob

Oh yeah! Someone from my old high school wrote me! I've had several letters from students there. She's in the Manga Research Club! When I entered high school, I really wished that this club existed! I had no other choice but to join the art club and cinema club. But all they had me doing was ink and paint on Vifam and MinkyMomo cels. I quit both clubs within six months. It seems like ages ago. I still remember it clearly though. According to this letter, a teacher I had during my senior year keeps a copy of my manga in his desk! I never did the chores he assigned and I barely passed his math classes. I was a rotten student, but it was a good school. I heard that the name's been changed to "Sakai Girl's High School." I guess all the badges have different designs now. The one thing I didn't like at school was the winter uniform!! I wanted a ribbon or a tie!! (I've graduated so I can criticize them all I want!) Are the uniforms still ugly? Miaka's uniform is a fan favorite because it's cute. I mean, you have to wear your uniform every day, so cute is good. When I was in school, I was so envious of another Sakai school. They were co-ed. What am I trying to say? My teachers were very committed. (It was a private school, so the rules were strict.) Thanks for all your help! I loved my time in junior high and high school. I'd like to go back--wear my uniform, carry my bag, and joke around with my friends. I'm sure some of you who are still in school say you hate it, but your school days become a great memory.

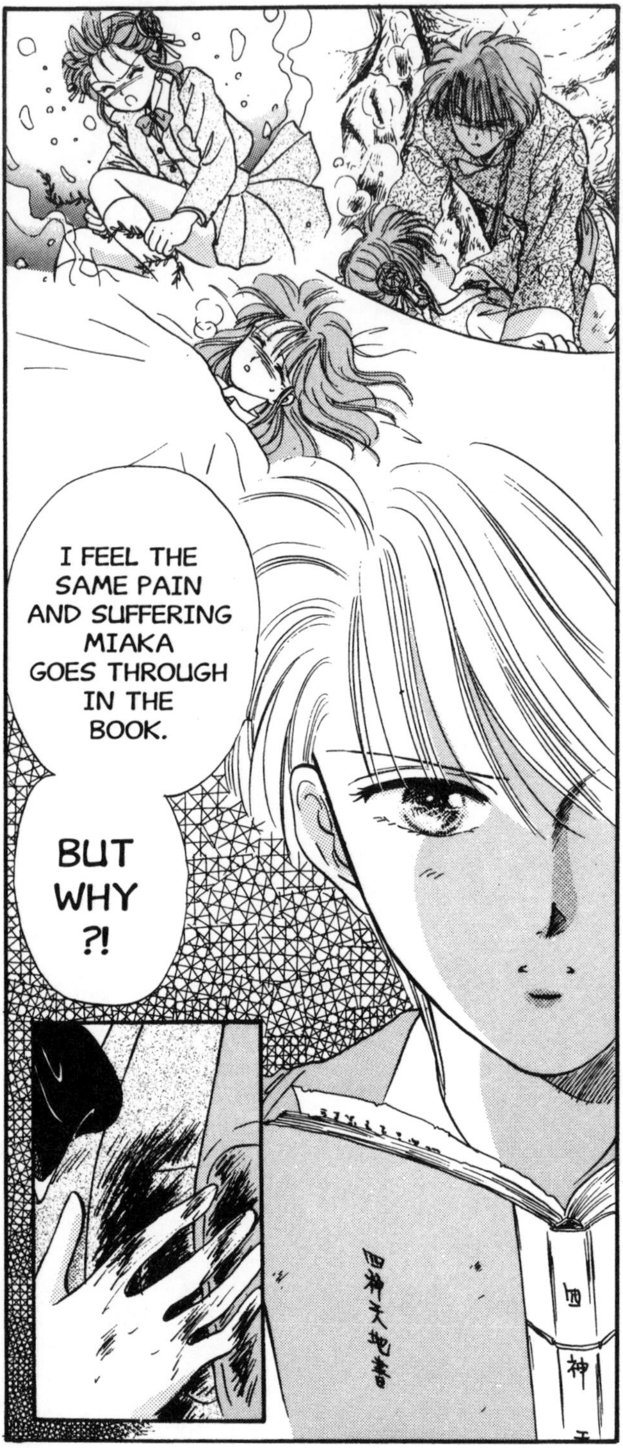
I FEEL THE SAME PAIN AND SUFFERING MIAKA GOES THROUGH IN THE BOOK.
BUT WHY ?!
四神天地書

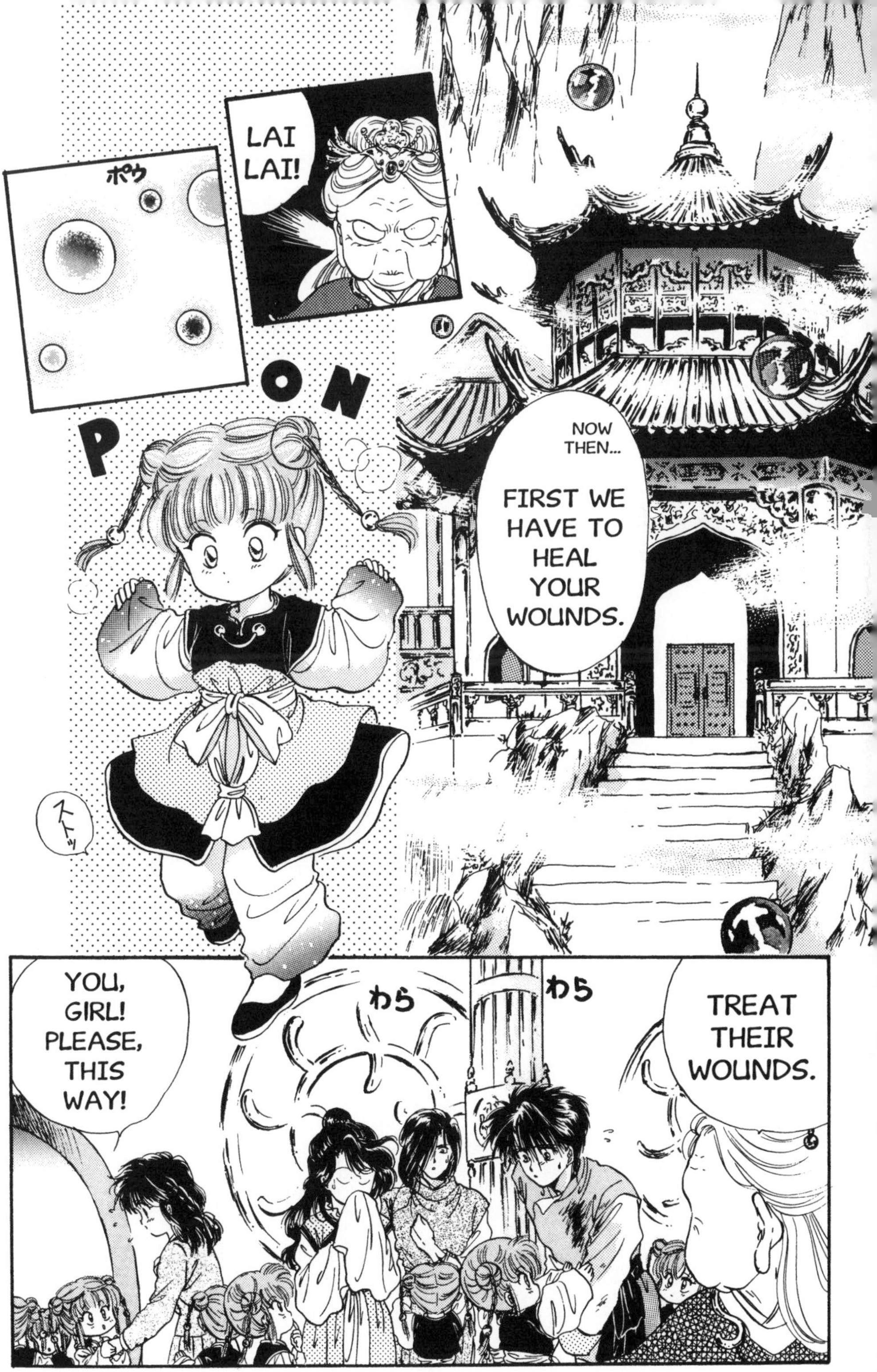
NOW THEN...
FIRST WE HAVE TO HEAL YOUR WOUNDS.
LAI LAI!
ポウ
PON
ストッ
TREAT THEIR WOUNDS.
わら
わら
YOU, GIRL! PLEASE, THIS WAY!

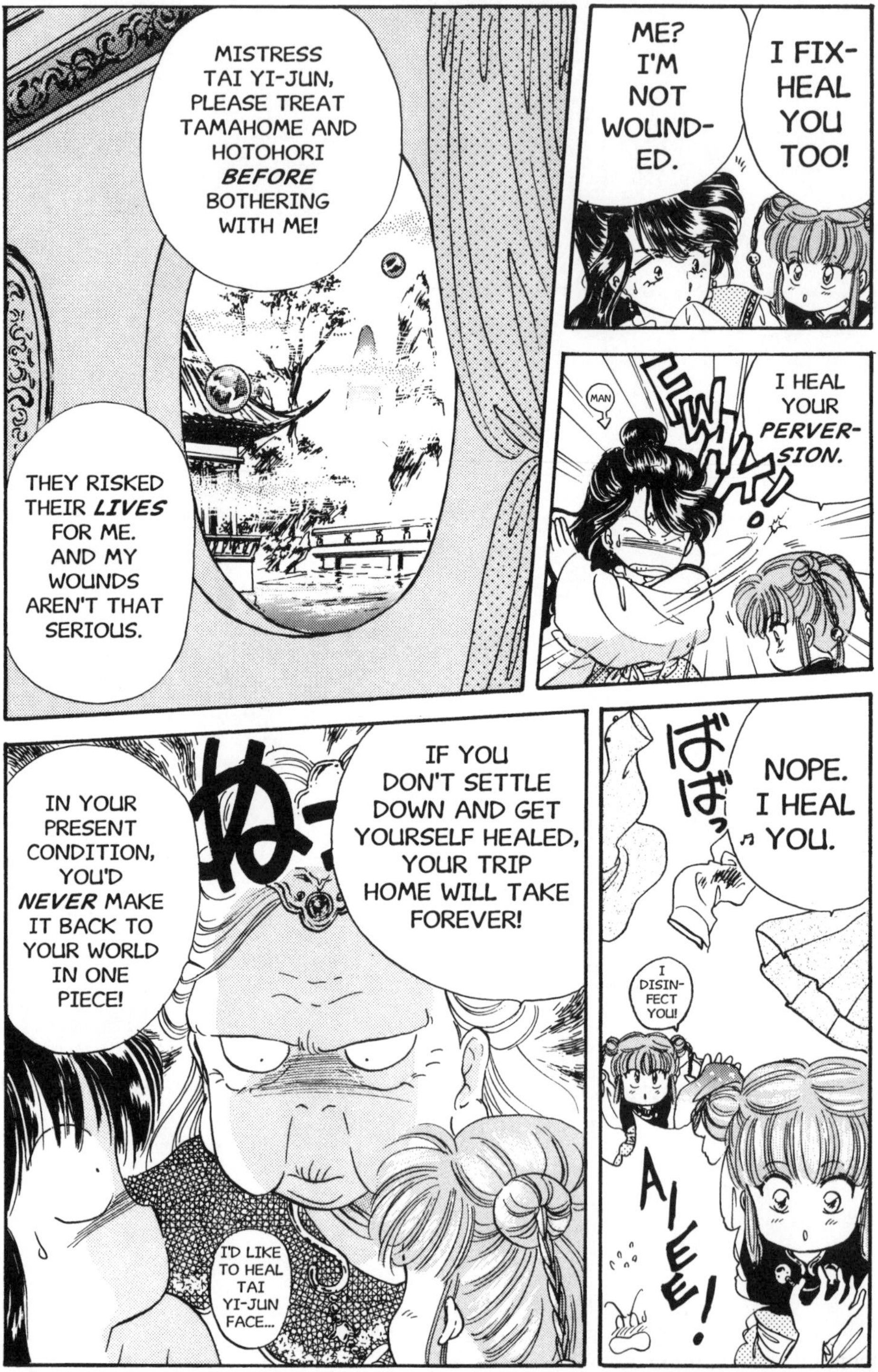
I FIX-HEAL YOU TOO!
ME? I'M NOT WOUNDED.
I HEAL YOUR PERVERSION.
WHAK!
MAN
MISTRESS TAI YI-JUN, PLEASE TREAT TAMAHOME AND HOTOHORI BEFORE BOTHERING WITH ME!
THEY RISKED THEIR LIVES FOR ME. AND MY WOUNDS AREN'T THAT SERIOUS.
NOPE. I HEAL YOU.
ばばっ
I DISINFECT YOU!
AIEE!
IF YOU DON'T SETTLE DOWN AND GET YOURSELF HEALED, YOUR TRIP HOME WILL TAKE FOREVER!
IN YOUR PRESENT CONDITION, YOU'D NEVER MAKE IT BACK TO YOUR WORLD IN ONE PIECE!
ぬっ
I'D LIKE TO HEAL TAI YI-JUN FACE...

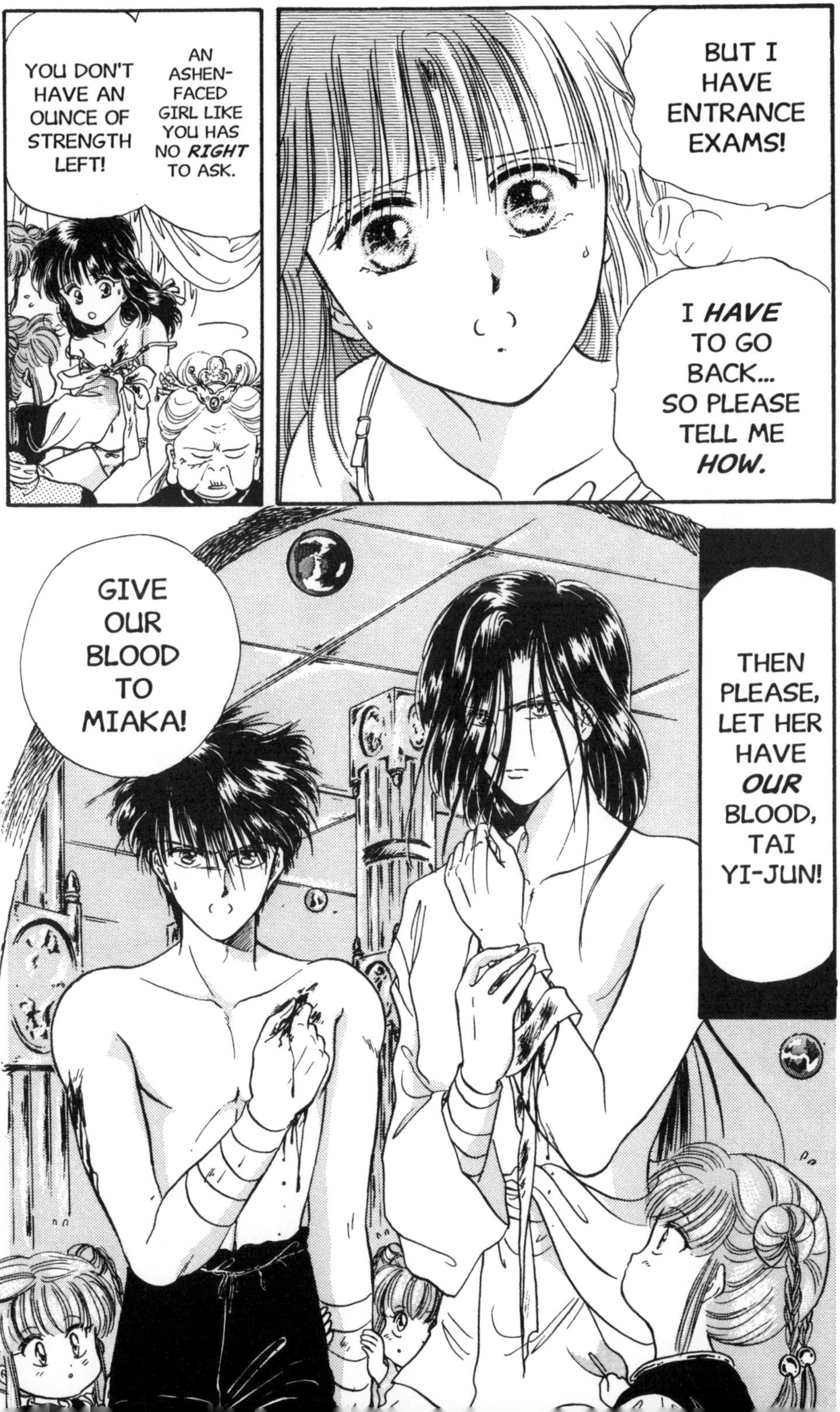
BUT I HAVE ENTRANCE EXAMS!
I HAVE TO GO BACK... SO PLEASE TELL ME HOW.
AN ASHEN-FACED GIRL LIKE YOU HAS NO RIGHT TO ASK.
YOU DON'T HAVE AN OUNCE OF STRENGTH LEFT!
THEN PLEASE, LET HER HAVE OUR BLOOD, TAI YI-JUN!
GIVE OUR BLOOD TO MIAKA!

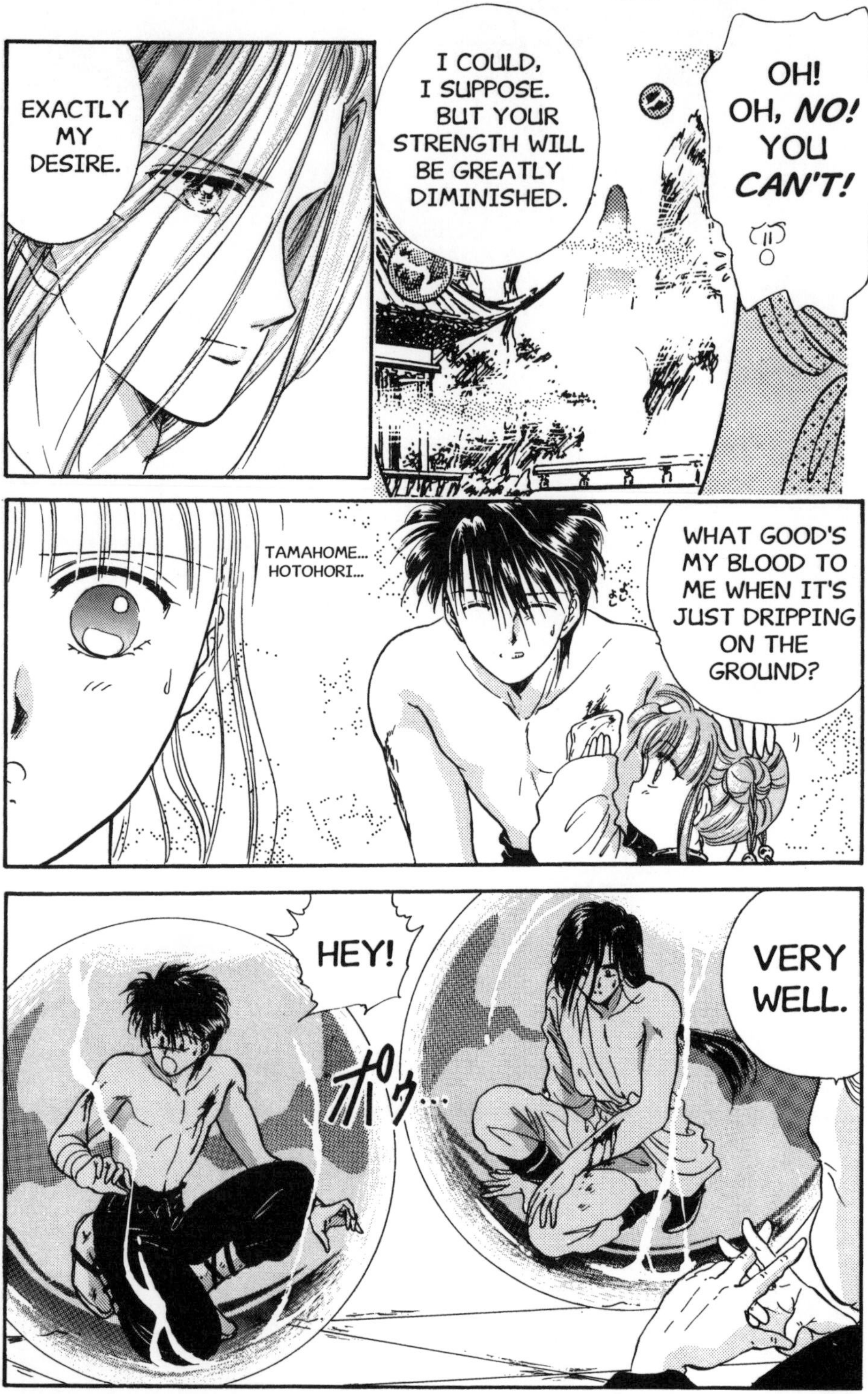
OH! OH, *NO!* YOU *CAN'T!*
I COULD, I SUPPOSE. BUT YOUR STRENGTH WILL BE GREATLY DIMINISHED.
EXACTLY MY DESIRE.
WHAT GOOD'S MY BLOOD TO ME WHEN IT'S JUST DRIPPING ON THE GROUND?
TAMAHOME... HOTOHORI...
VERY WELL.
HEY!
ポゥ...

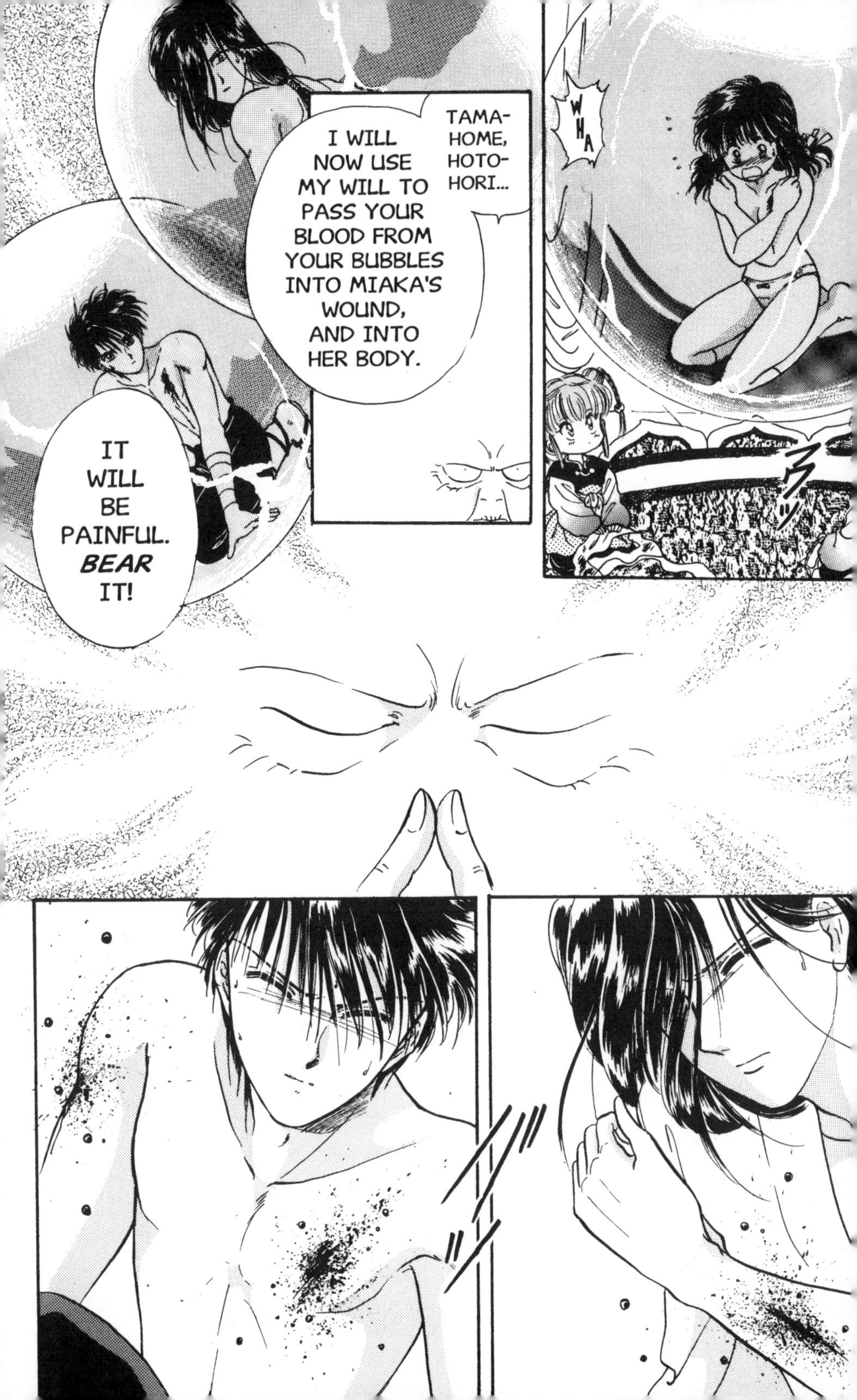
WHA
TAMA-HOME, HOTO-HORI...
I WILL NOW USE MY WILL TO PASS YOUR BLOOD FROM YOUR BUBBLES INTO MIAKA'S WOUND, AND INTO HER BODY.
IT WILL BE PAINFUL. BEAR IT!

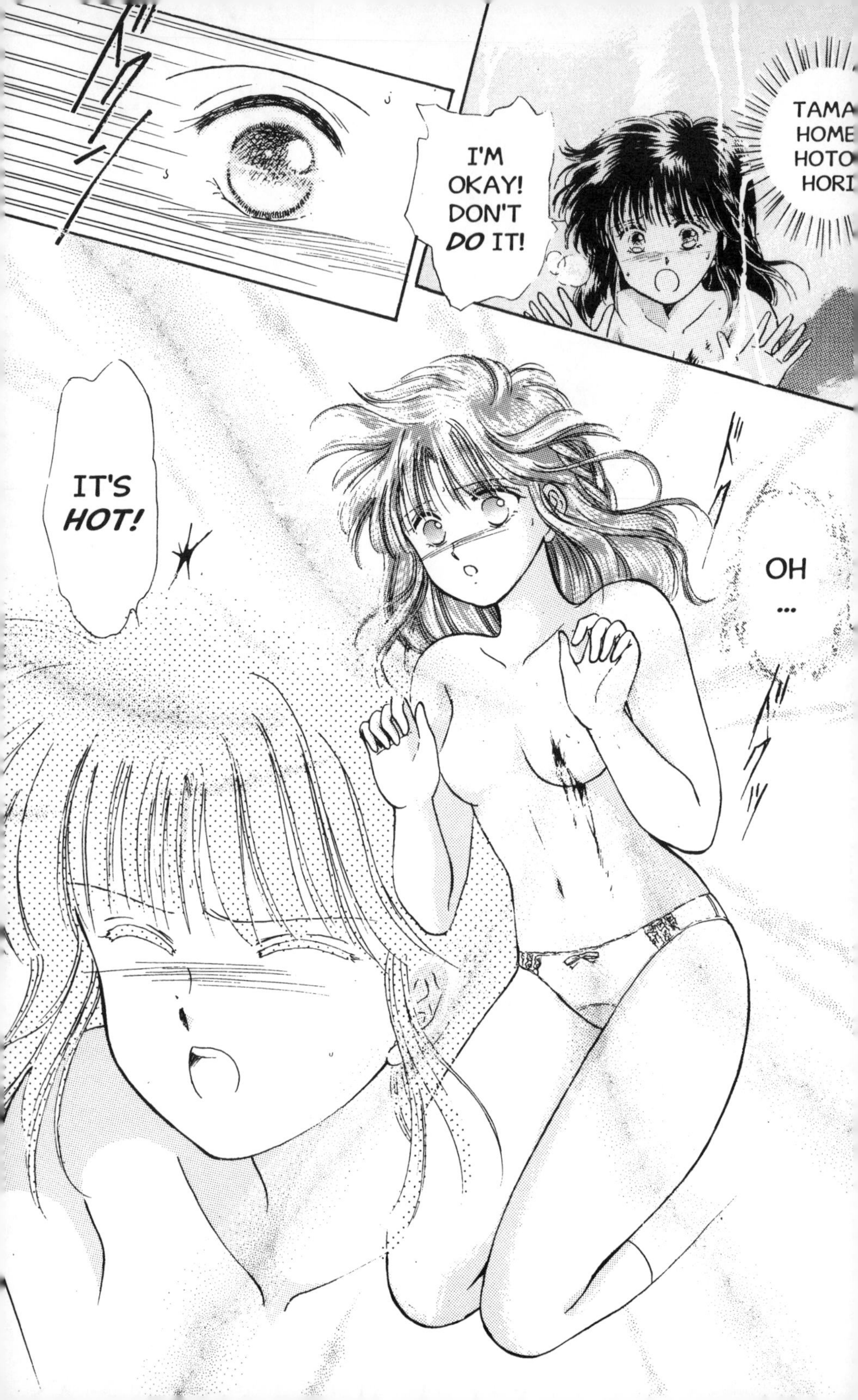
TAMA HOME HOTO HORI
I'M OKAY! DON'T *DO* IT!
OH ...
IT'S *HOT!*

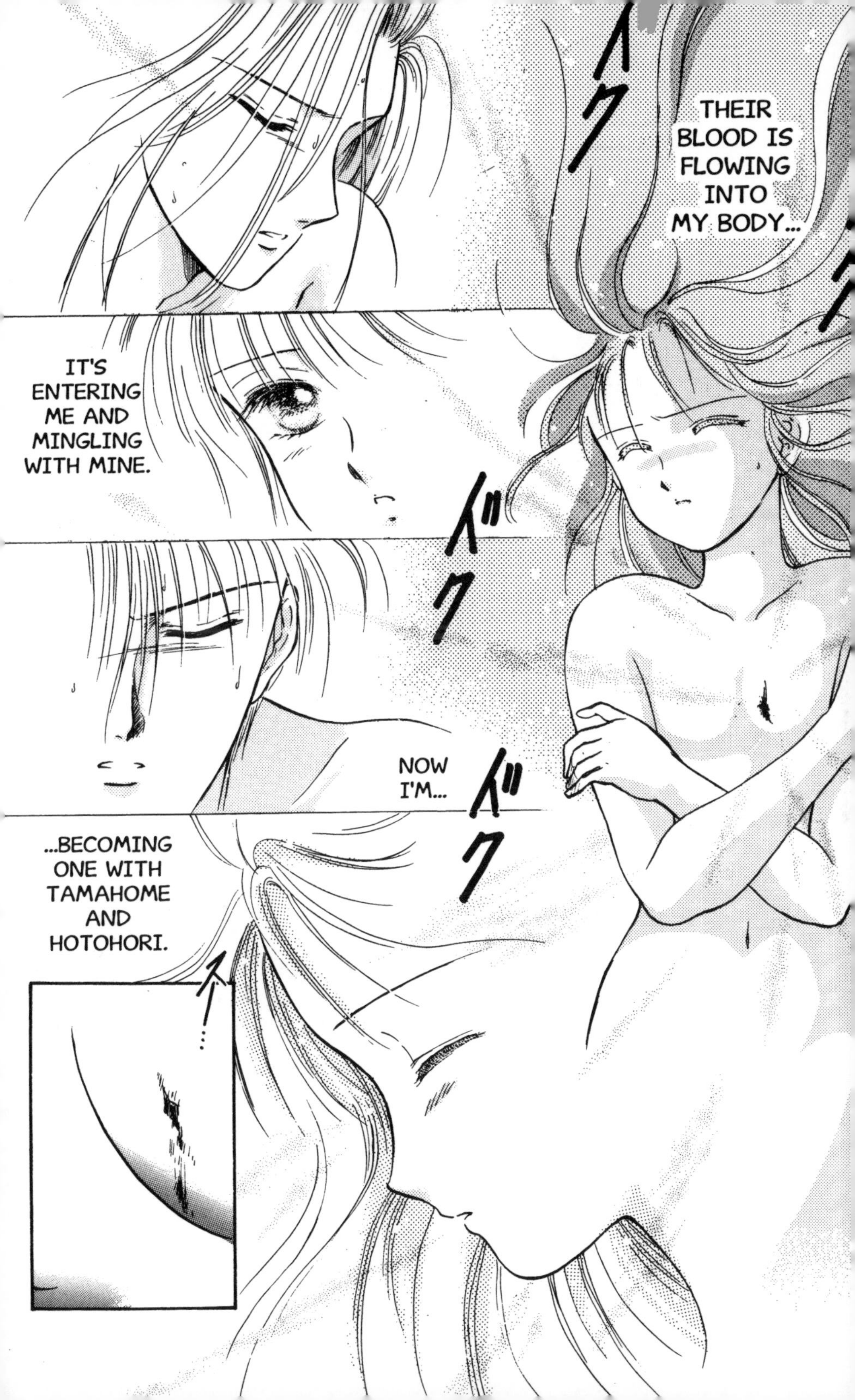

THEIR BLOOD IS FLOWING INTO MY BODY...
IT'S ENTERING ME AND MINGLING WITH MINE.
ドク
NOW I'M...
ドク
...BECOMING ONE WITH TAMAHOME AND HOTOHORI.

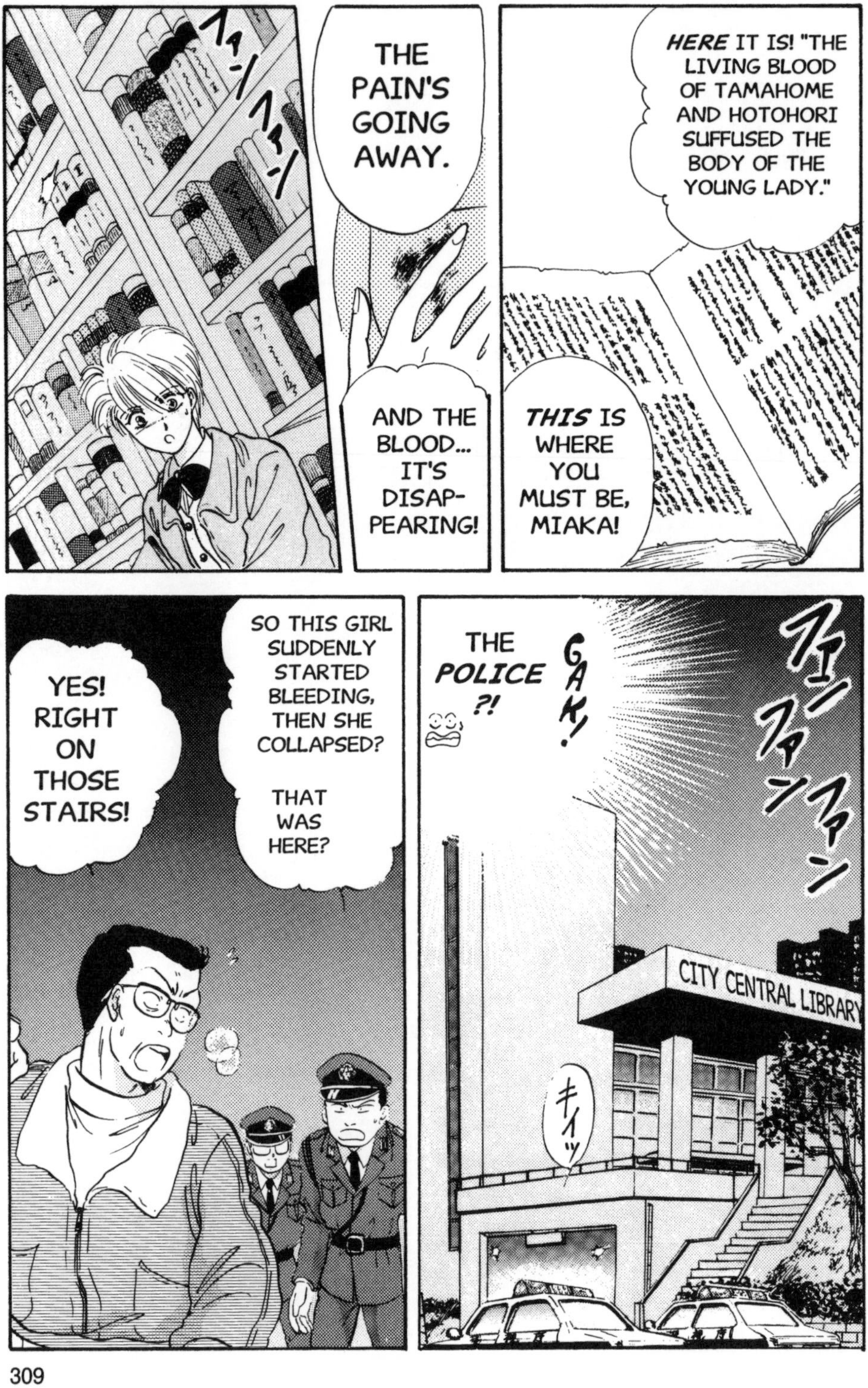
HERE IT IS! "THE LIVING BLOOD OF TAMAHOME AND HOTOHORI SUFFUSED THE BODY OF THE YOUNG LADY."
THIS IS WHERE YOU MUST BE, MIAKA!
THE PAIN'S GOING AWAY.
AND THE BLOOD... IT'S DISAPPEARING!
フィーファンファン
THE POLICE ?!
GAK!
CITY CENTRAL LIBRARY
キイッ
SO THIS GIRL SUDDENLY STARTED BLEEDING, THEN SHE COLLAPSED?
THAT WAS HERE?
YES! RIGHT ON THOSE STAIRS!

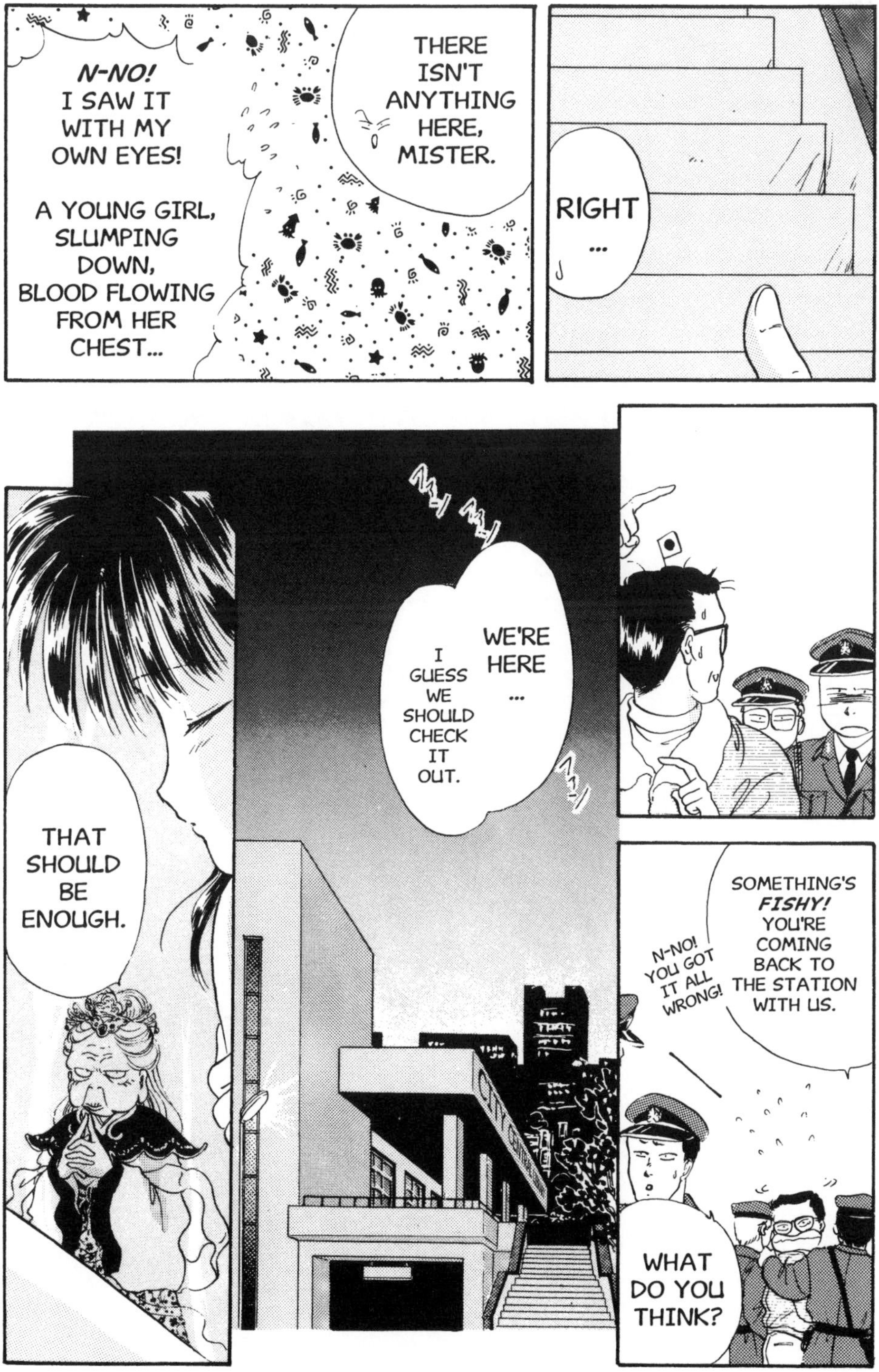
RIGHT ...
THERE ISN'T ANYTHING HERE, MISTER.
N-NO! I SAW IT WITH MY OWN EYES!
A YOUNG GIRL, SLUMPING DOWN, BLOOD FLOWING FROM HER CHEST...
SOMETHING'S *FISHY!* YOU'RE COMING BACK TO THE STATION WITH US.
N-NO! YOU GOT IT ALL WRONG!
WHAT DO YOU THINK?
WE'RE HERE ...
I GUESS WE SHOULD CHECK IT OUT.
THAT SHOULD BE ENOUGH.

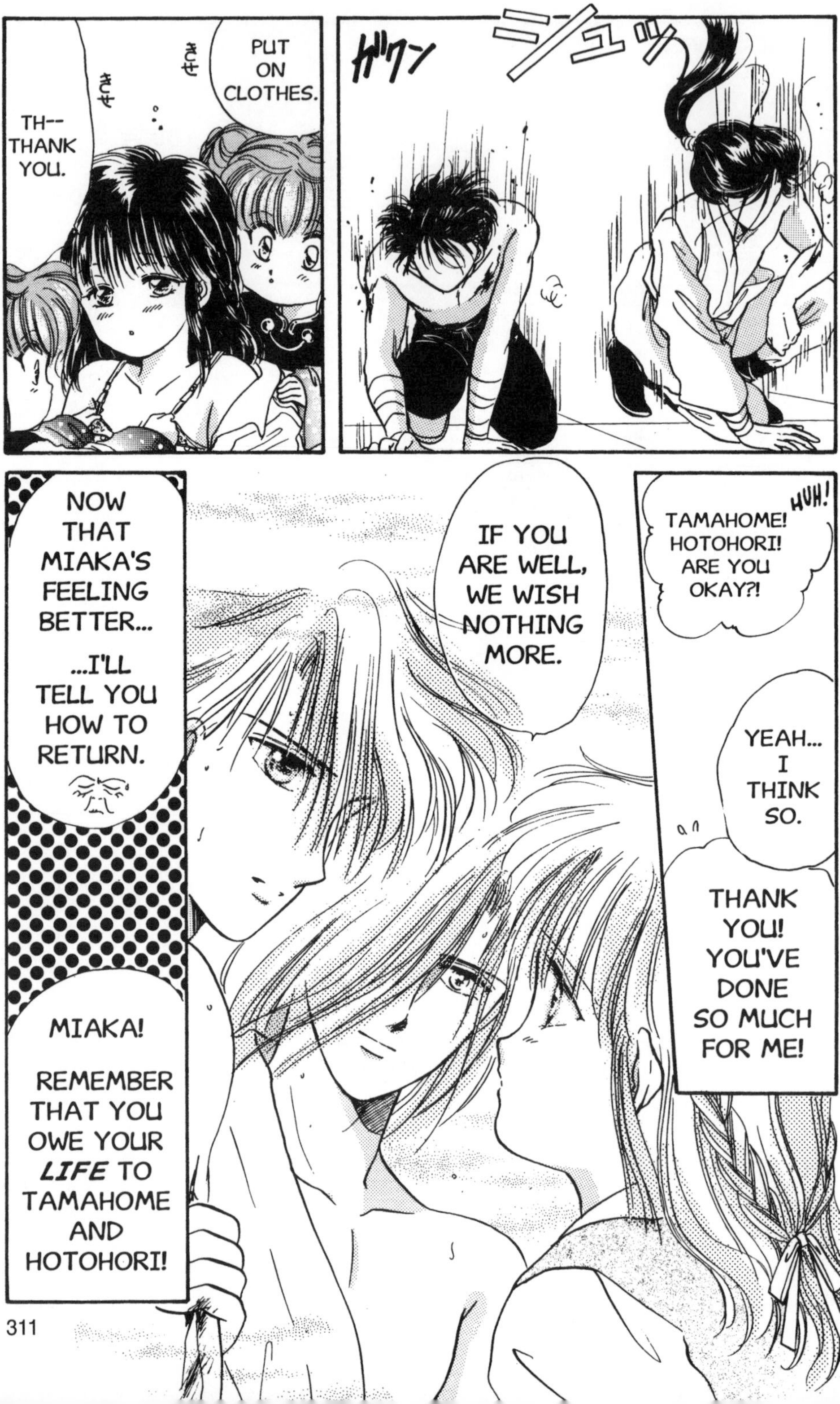
ガクン
シュッ
PUT ON CLOTHES.
TH-- THANK YOU.
HUH!
TAMAHOME! HOTOHORI! ARE YOU OKAY?!
YEAH... I THINK SO.
THANK YOU! YOU'VE DONE SO MUCH FOR ME!
IF YOU ARE WELL, WE WISH NOTHING MORE.
NOW THAT MIAKA'S FEELING BETTER...
...I'LL TELL YOU HOW TO RETURN.
MIAKA!
REMEMBER THAT YOU OWE YOUR *LIFE* TO TAMAHOME AND HOTOHORI!

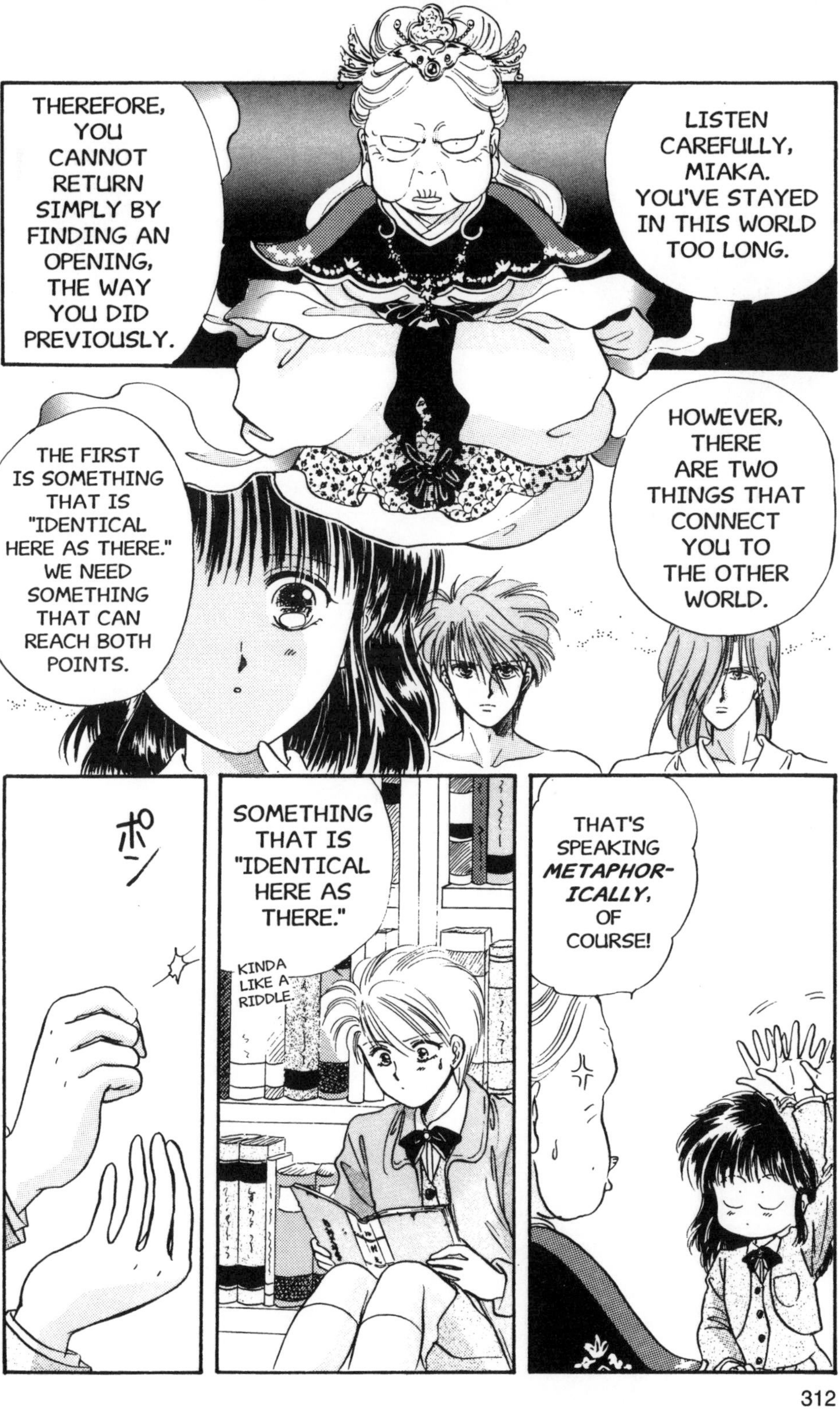
LISTEN CAREFULLY, MIAKA. YOU'VE STAYED IN THIS WORLD TOO LONG.
THEREFORE, YOU CANNOT RETURN SIMPLY BY FINDING AN OPENING, THE WAY YOU DID PREVIOUSLY.
HOWEVER, THERE ARE TWO THINGS THAT CONNECT YOU TO THE OTHER WORLD.
THE FIRST IS SOMETHING THAT IS "IDENTICAL HERE AS THERE." WE NEED SOMETHING THAT CAN REACH BOTH POINTS.
THAT'S SPEAKING *METAPHORICALLY*, OF COURSE!
SOMETHING THAT IS "IDENTICAL HERE AS THERE."
KINDA LIKE A RIDDLE.
ポン

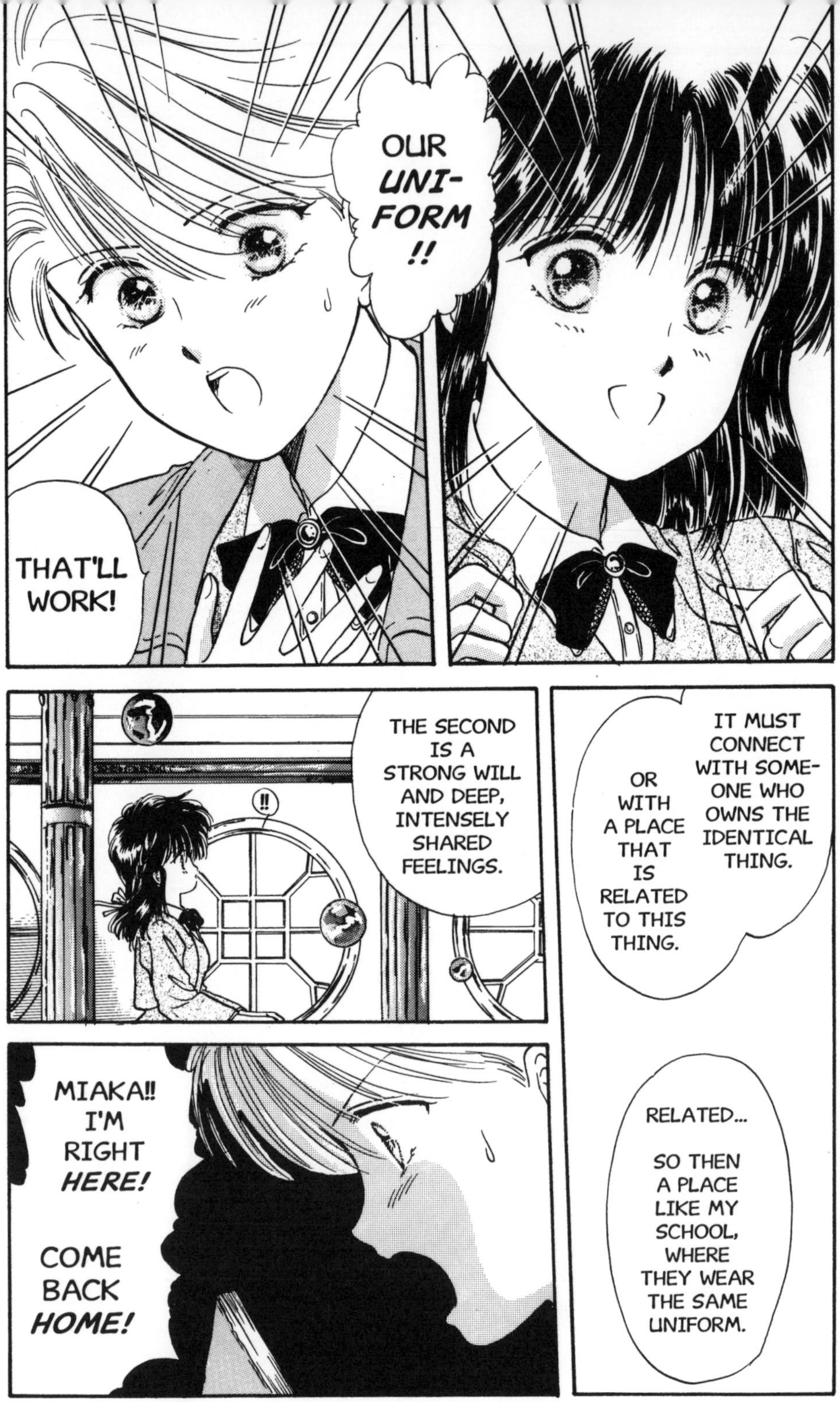
OUR UNI-FORM !!
THAT'LL WORK!
IT MUST CONNECT WITH SOME-ONE WHO OWNS THE IDENTICAL THING.
OR WITH A PLACE THAT IS RELATED TO THIS THING.
RELATED...
SO THEN A PLACE LIKE MY SCHOOL, WHERE THEY WEAR THE SAME UNIFORM.
THE SECOND IS A STRONG WILL AND DEEP, INTENSELY SHARED FEELINGS.
!!
MIAKA!! I'M RIGHT *HERE!*
COME BACK *HOME!*

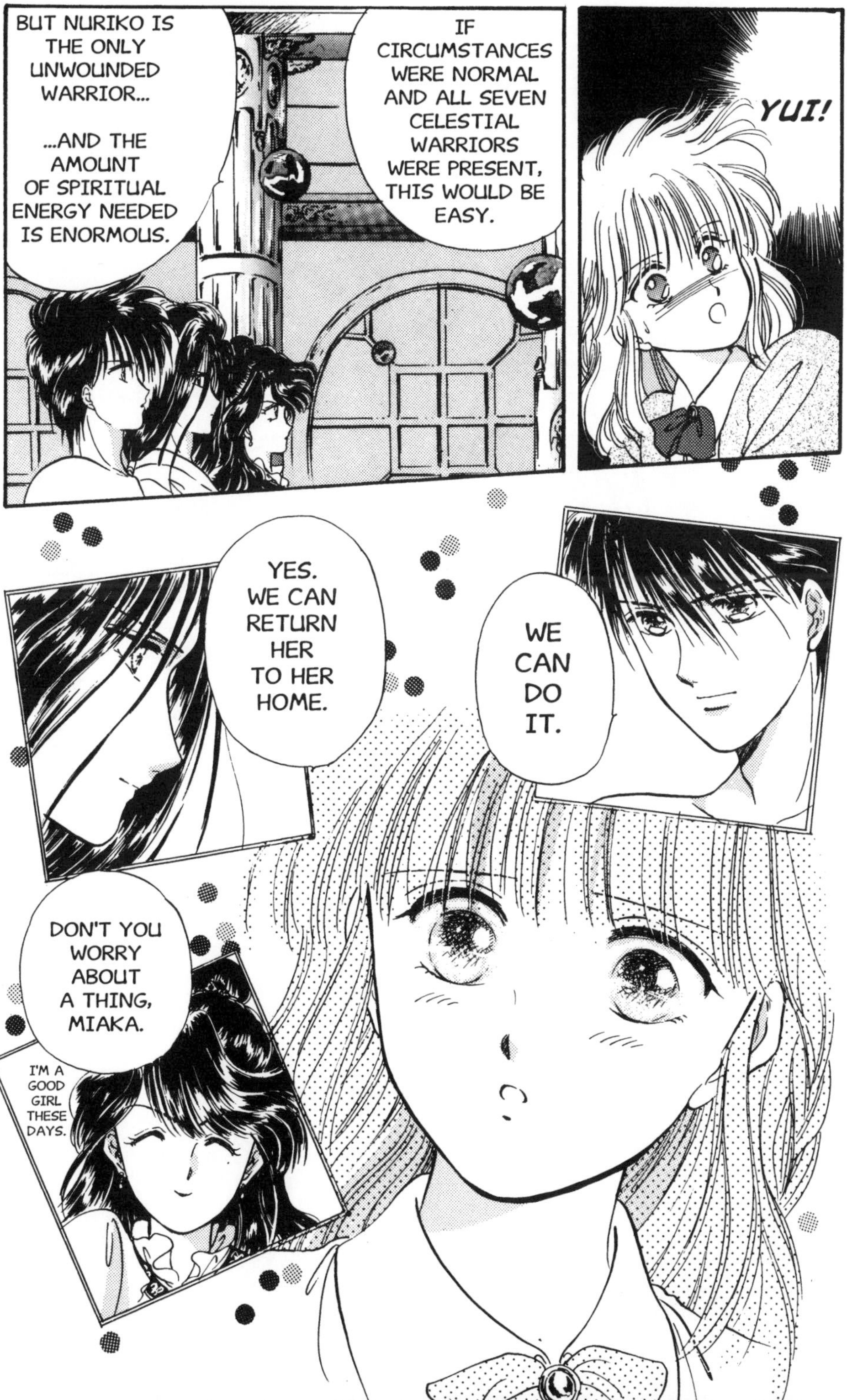
YUI!
IF CIRCUMSTANCES WERE NORMAL AND ALL SEVEN CELESTIAL WARRIORS WERE PRESENT, THIS WOULD BE EASY.
BUT NURIKO IS THE ONLY UNWOUNDED WARRIOR...
...AND THE AMOUNT OF SPIRITUAL ENERGY NEEDED IS ENORMOUS.
WE CAN DO IT.
YES. WE CAN RETURN HER TO HER HOME.
DON'T YOU WORRY ABOUT A THING, MIAKA.
I'M A GOOD GIRL THESE DAYS.

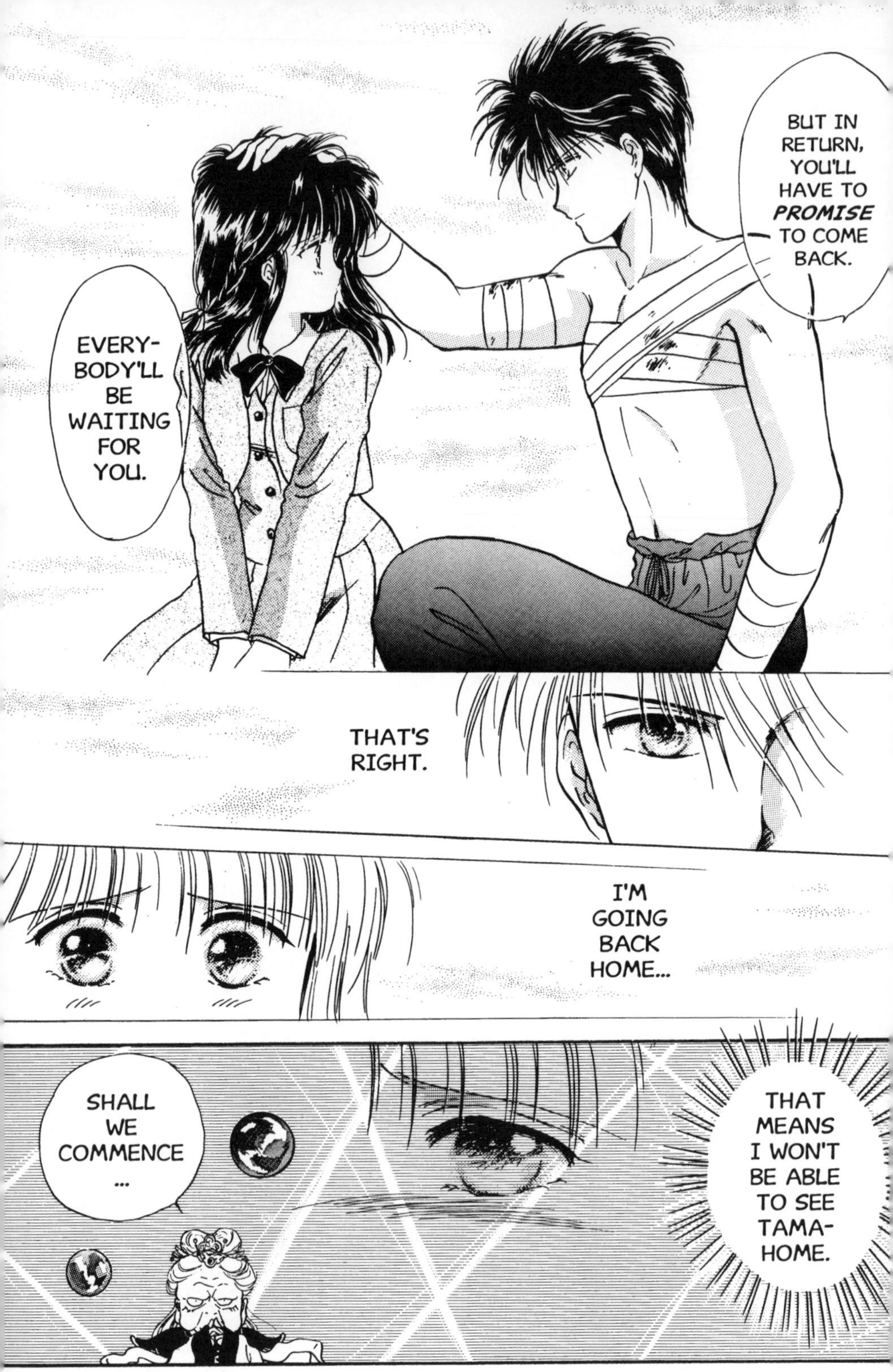
BUT IN RETURN, YOU'LL HAVE TO ***PROMISE*** TO COME BACK.
EVERY-BODY'LL BE WAITING FOR YOU.
THAT'S RIGHT.
I'M GOING BACK HOME...
THAT MEANS I WON'T BE ABLE TO SEE TAMA-HOME.
SHALL WE COMMENCE ...

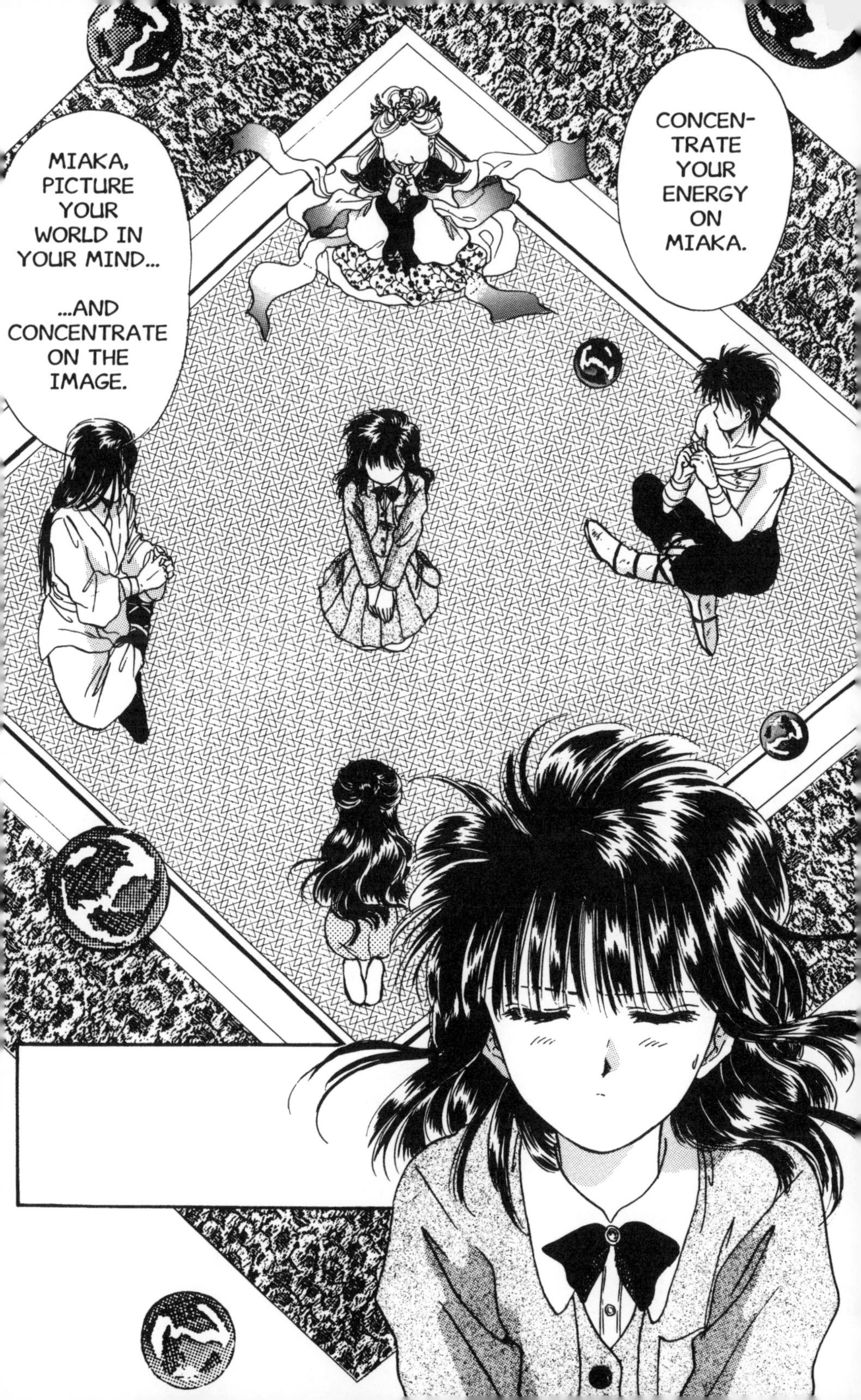
CONCEN-TRATE YOUR ENERGY ON MIAKA.
MIAKA, PICTURE YOUR WORLD IN YOUR MIND...
...AND CONCENTRATE ON THE IMAGE.

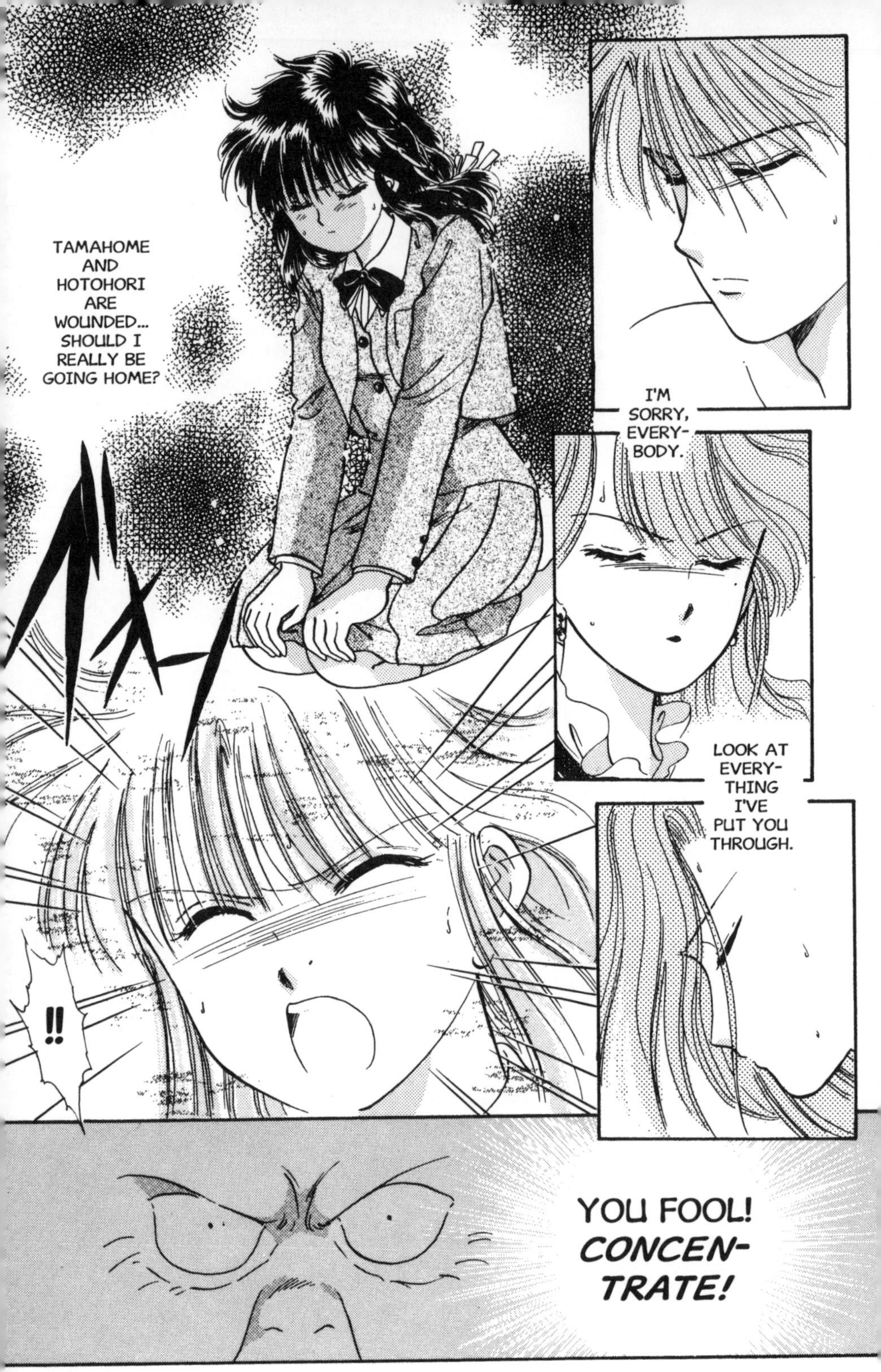
I'M SORRY, EVERY-BODY.
LOOK AT EVERY-THING I'VE PUT YOU THROUGH.
TAMAHOME AND HOTOHORI ARE WOUNDED... SHOULD I REALLY BE GOING HOME?
!!
YOU FOOL! CONCENTRATE!

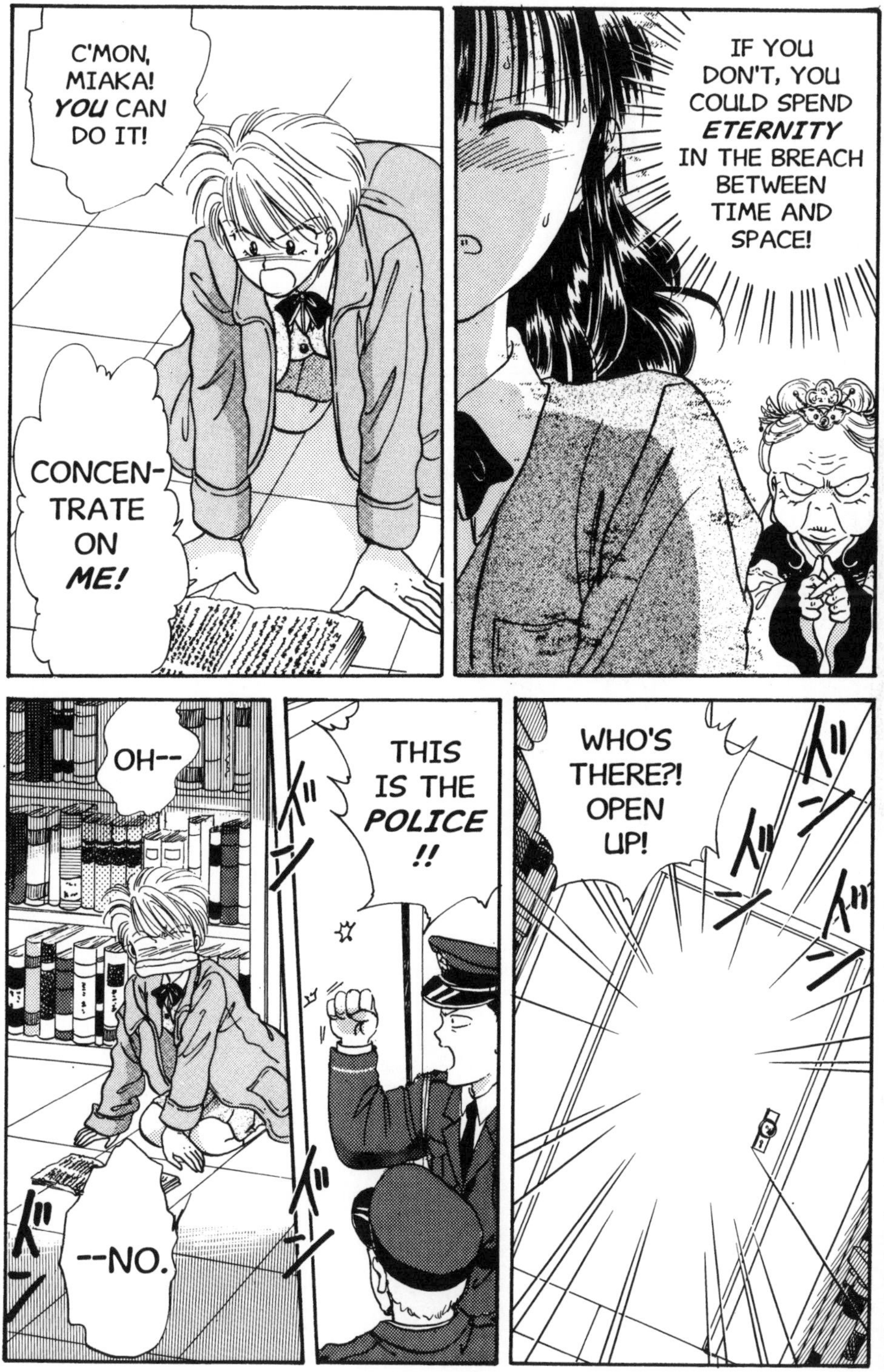
IF YOU DON'T, YOU COULD SPEND *ETERNITY* IN THE BREACH BETWEEN TIME AND SPACE!
C'MON, MIAKA! *YOU* CAN DO IT!
CONCEN-TRATE ON *ME!*
WHO'S THERE?! OPEN UP!
THIS IS THE *POLICE* !!
OH--
--NO.

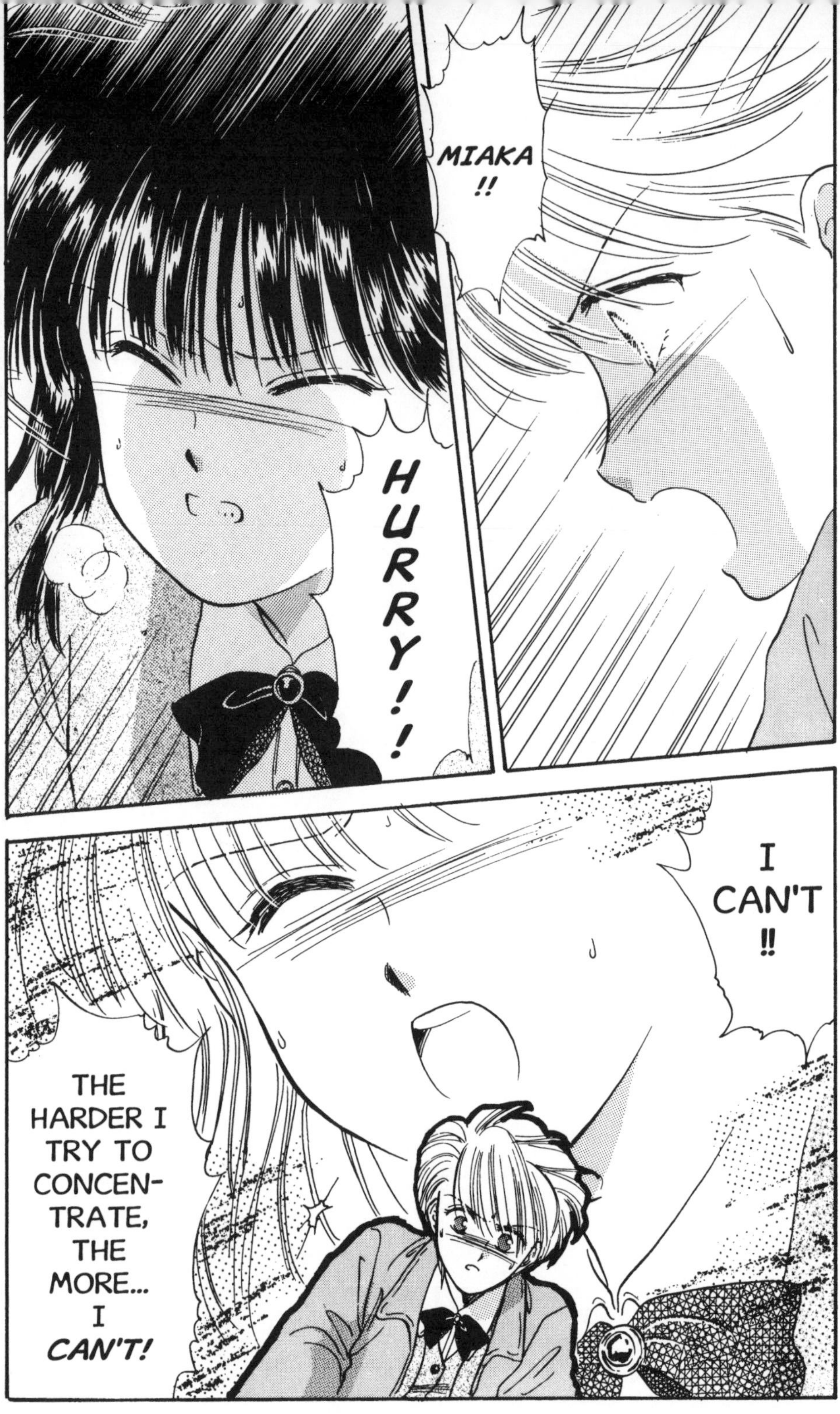
MIAKA!!
HURRY!!!
I CAN'T!!
THE HARDER I TRY TO CONCENTRATE, THE MORE... I *CAN'T!*

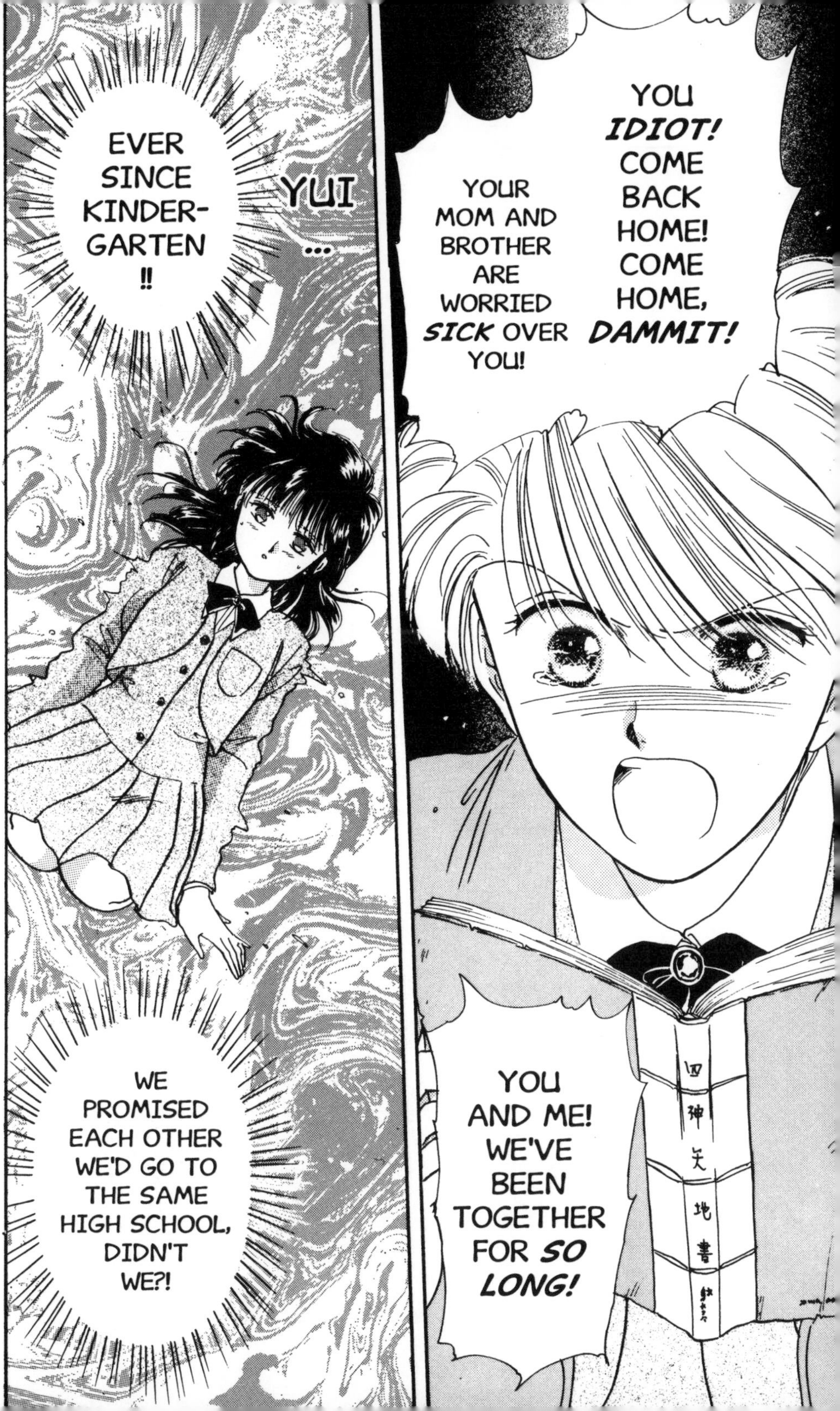
YOU IDIOT! COME BACK HOME! COME HOME, DAMMIT!
YOUR MOM AND BROTHER ARE WORRIED SICK OVER YOU!
四神天地書
YOU AND ME! WE'VE BEEN TOGETHER FOR SO LONG!
EVER SINCE KINDER-GARTEN!!
YUI...
WE PROMISED EACH OTHER WE'D GO TO THE SAME HIGH SCHOOL, DIDN'T WE?!

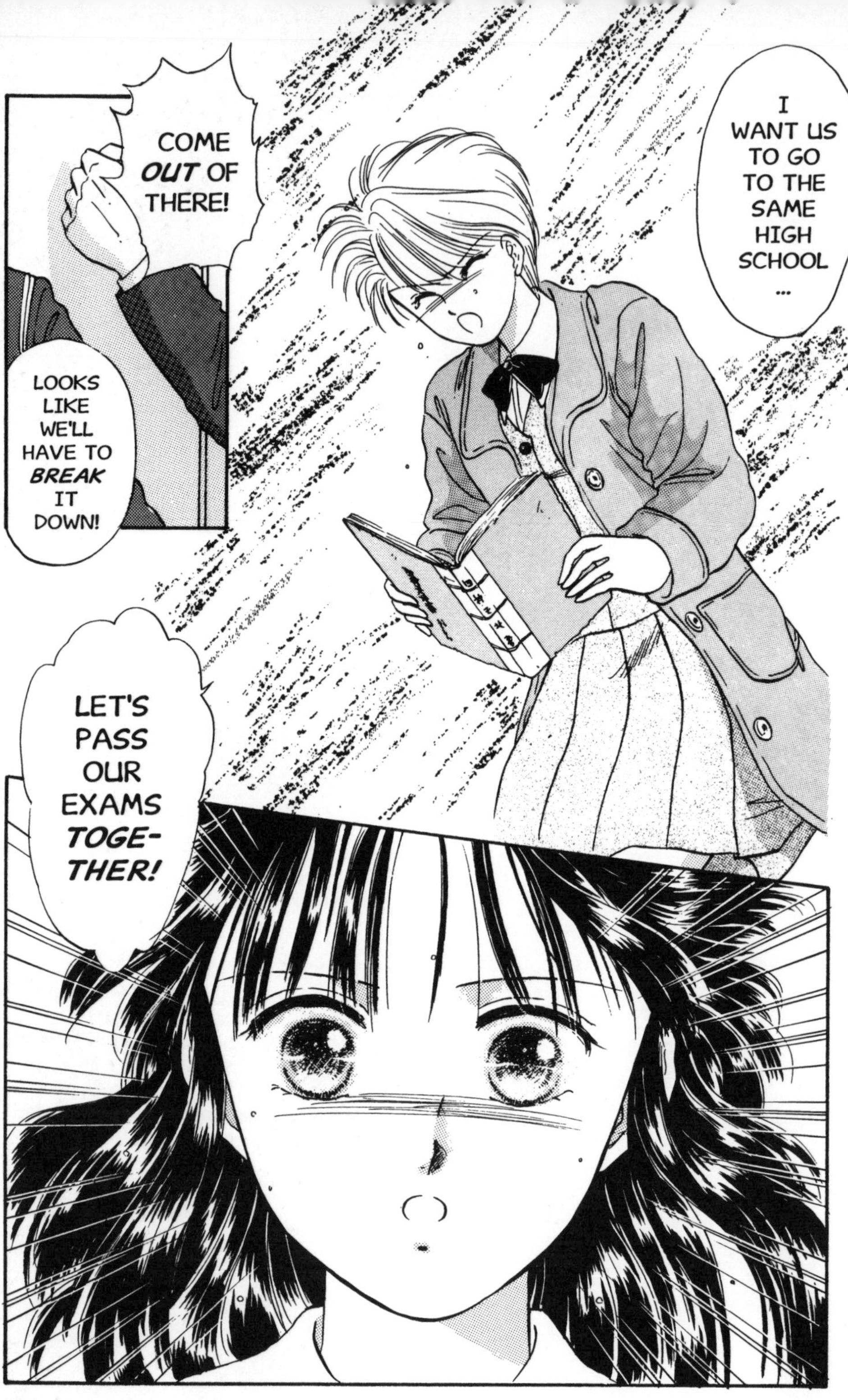
I WANT US TO GO TO THE SAME HIGH SCHOOL ...
LET'S PASS OUR EXAMS TOGE-THER!
COME OUT OF THERE!
LOOKS LIKE WE'LL HAVE TO BREAK IT DOWN!

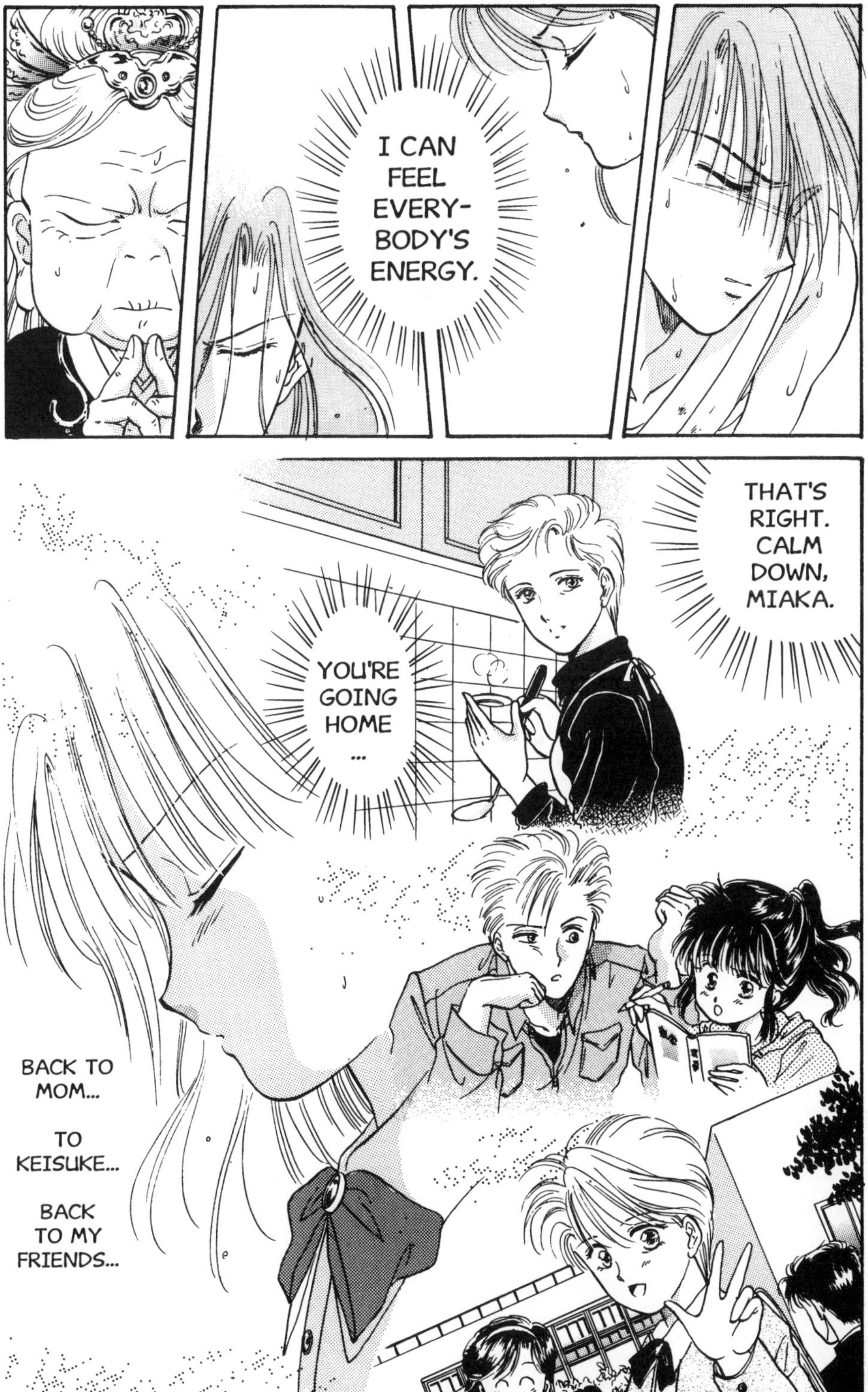
I CAN FEEL EVERY-BODY'S ENERGY.
THAT'S RIGHT. CALM DOWN, MIAKA.
YOU'RE GOING HOME ...
BACK TO MOM...
TO KEISUKE...
BACK TO MY FRIENDS...

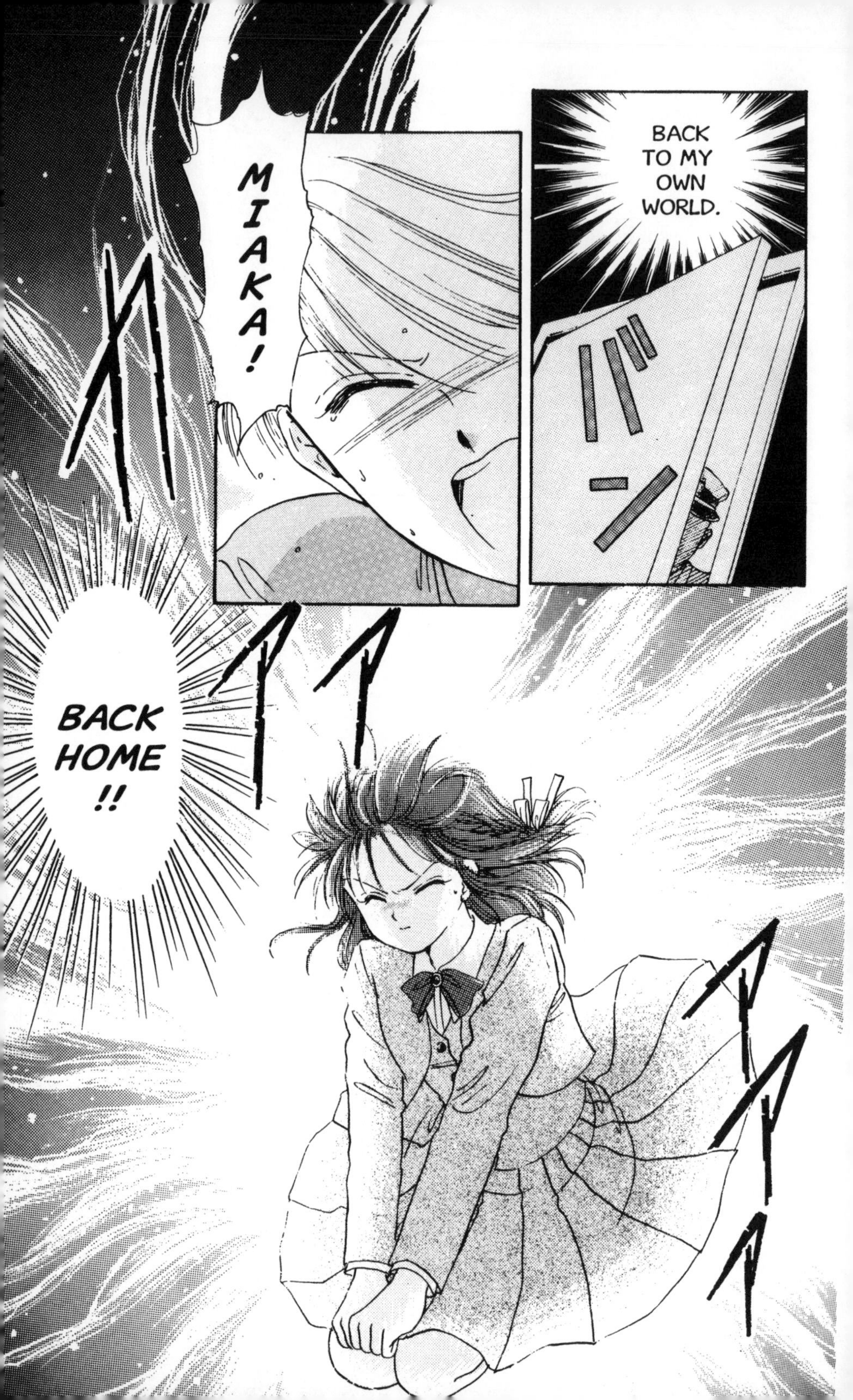
BACK TO MY OWN WORLD.
MIAKA!
BACK HOME !!

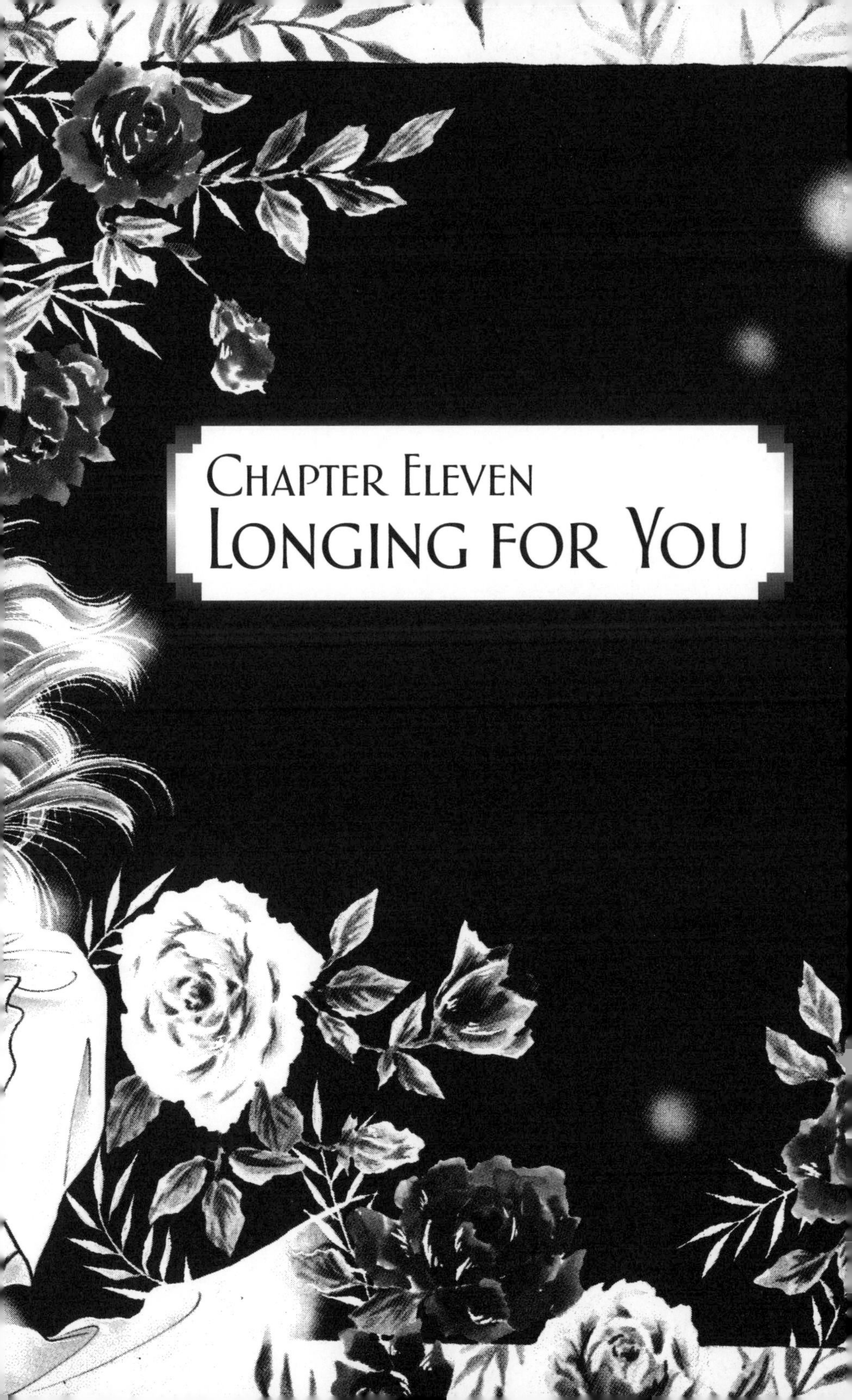
Chapter Eleven
Longing for You

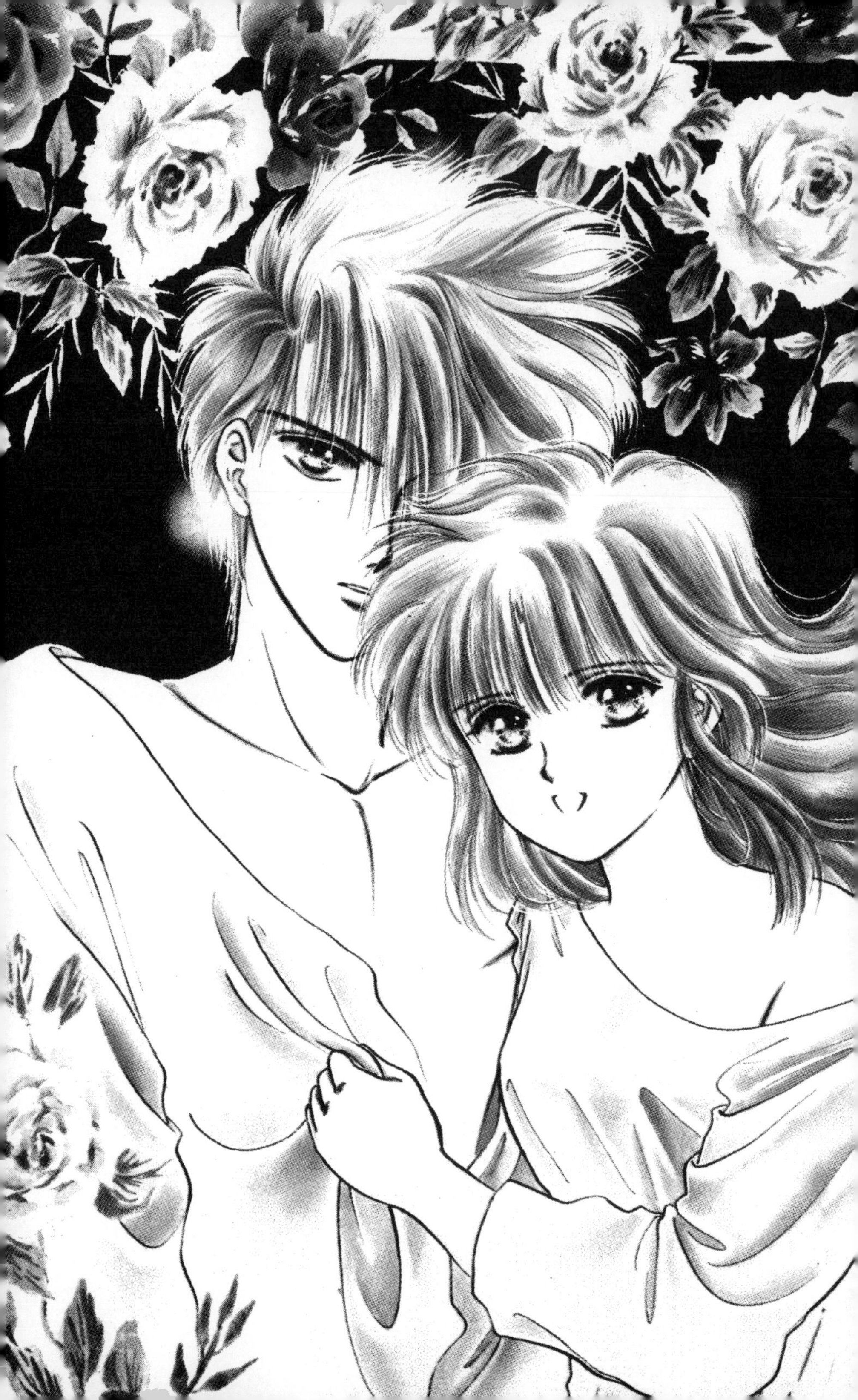

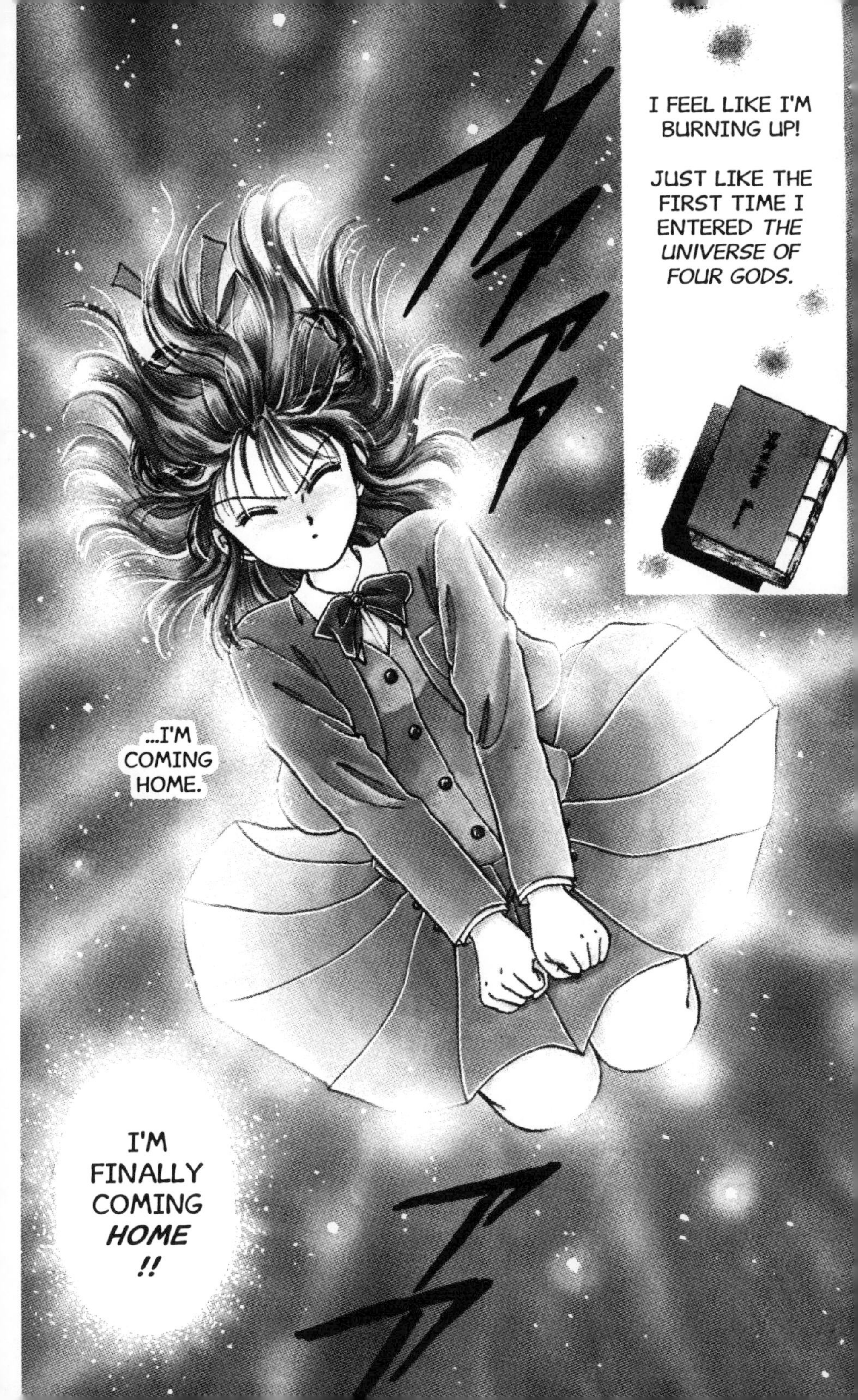
I FEEL LIKE I'M BURNING UP!
JUST LIKE THE FIRST TIME I ENTERED *THE UNIVERSE OF FOUR GODS.*
...I'M COMING HOME.
I'M FINALLY COMING ***HOME*** !!

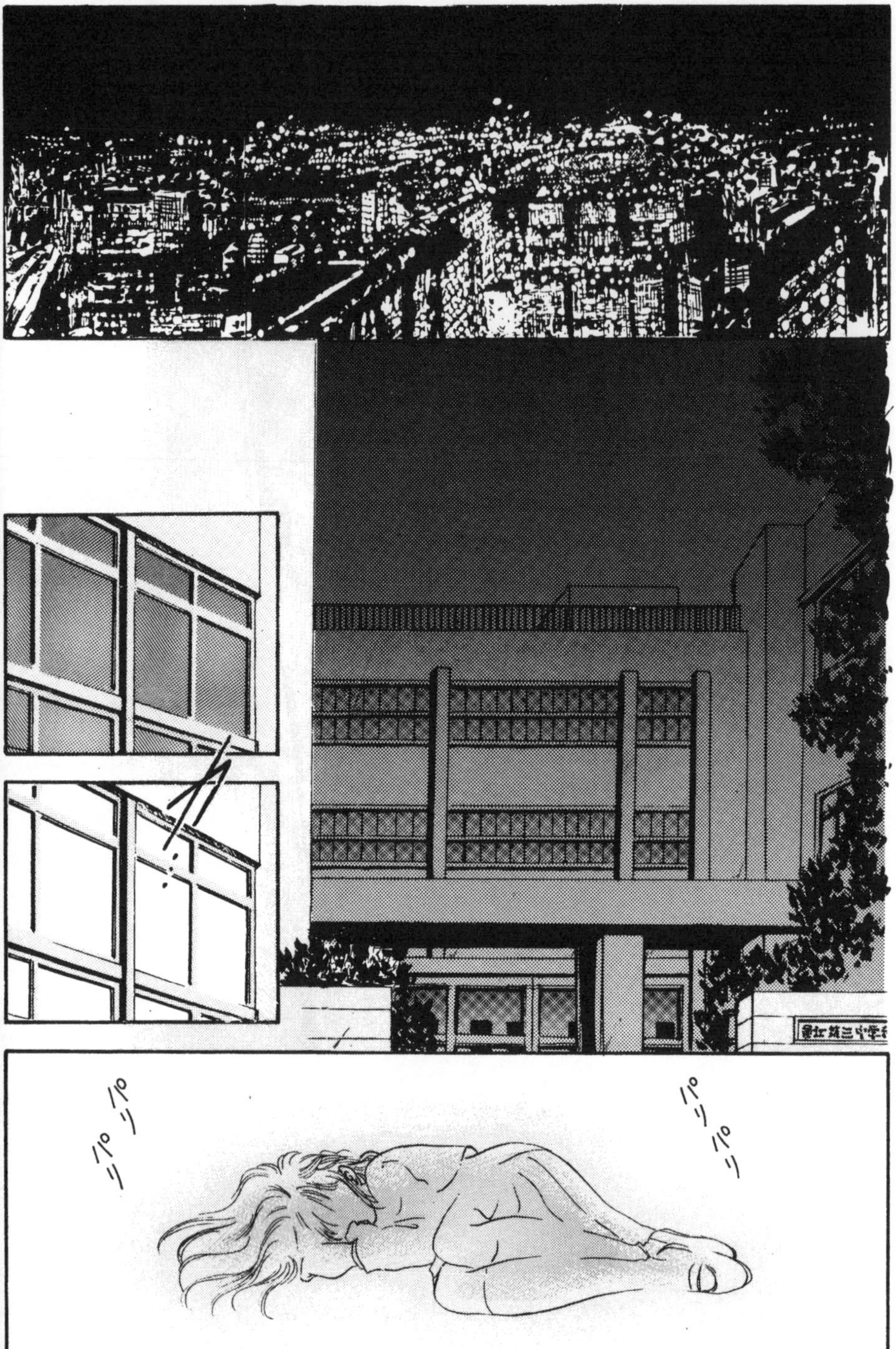
パリ パリ
パリ パリ

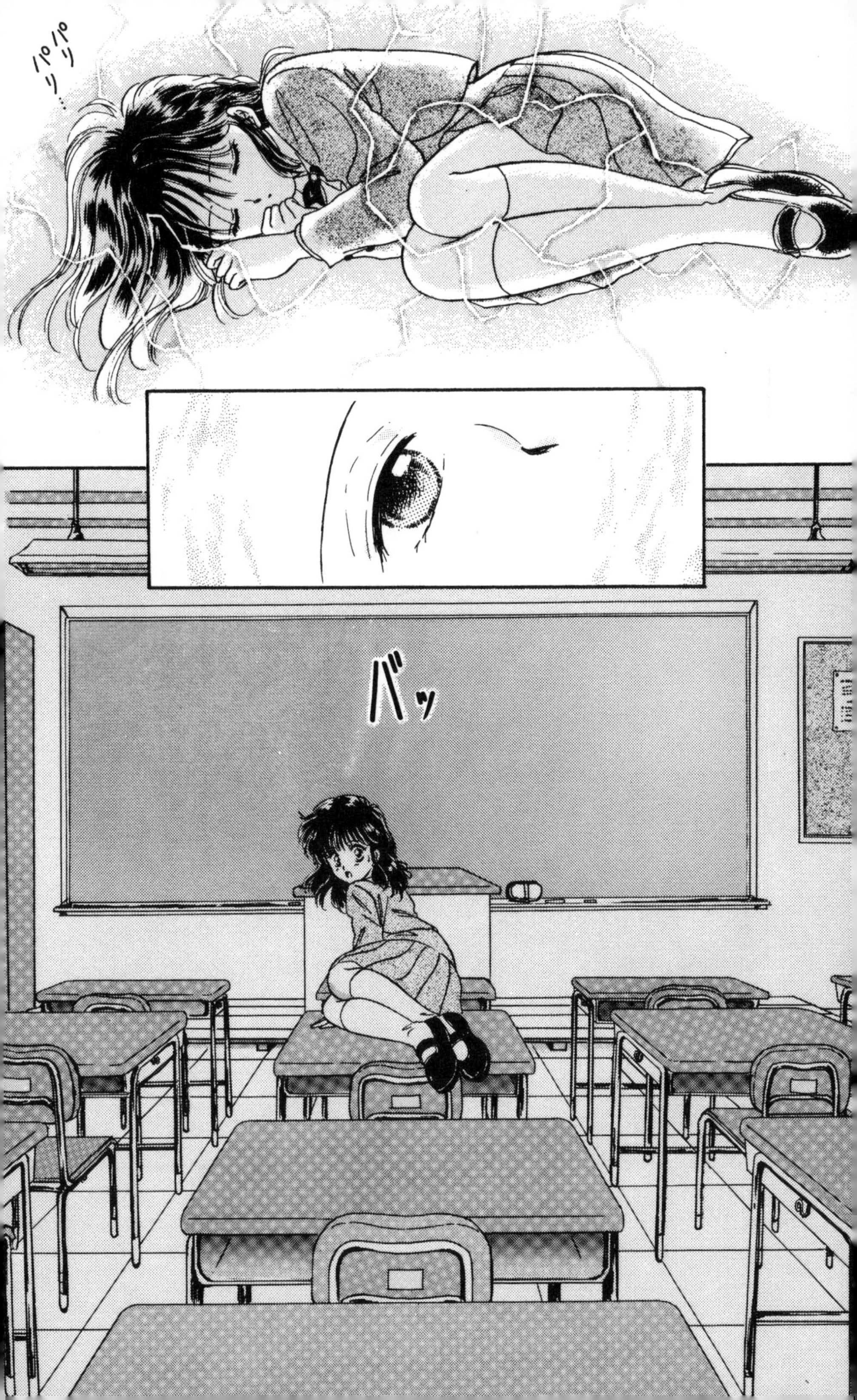
パリパリ…
バッ

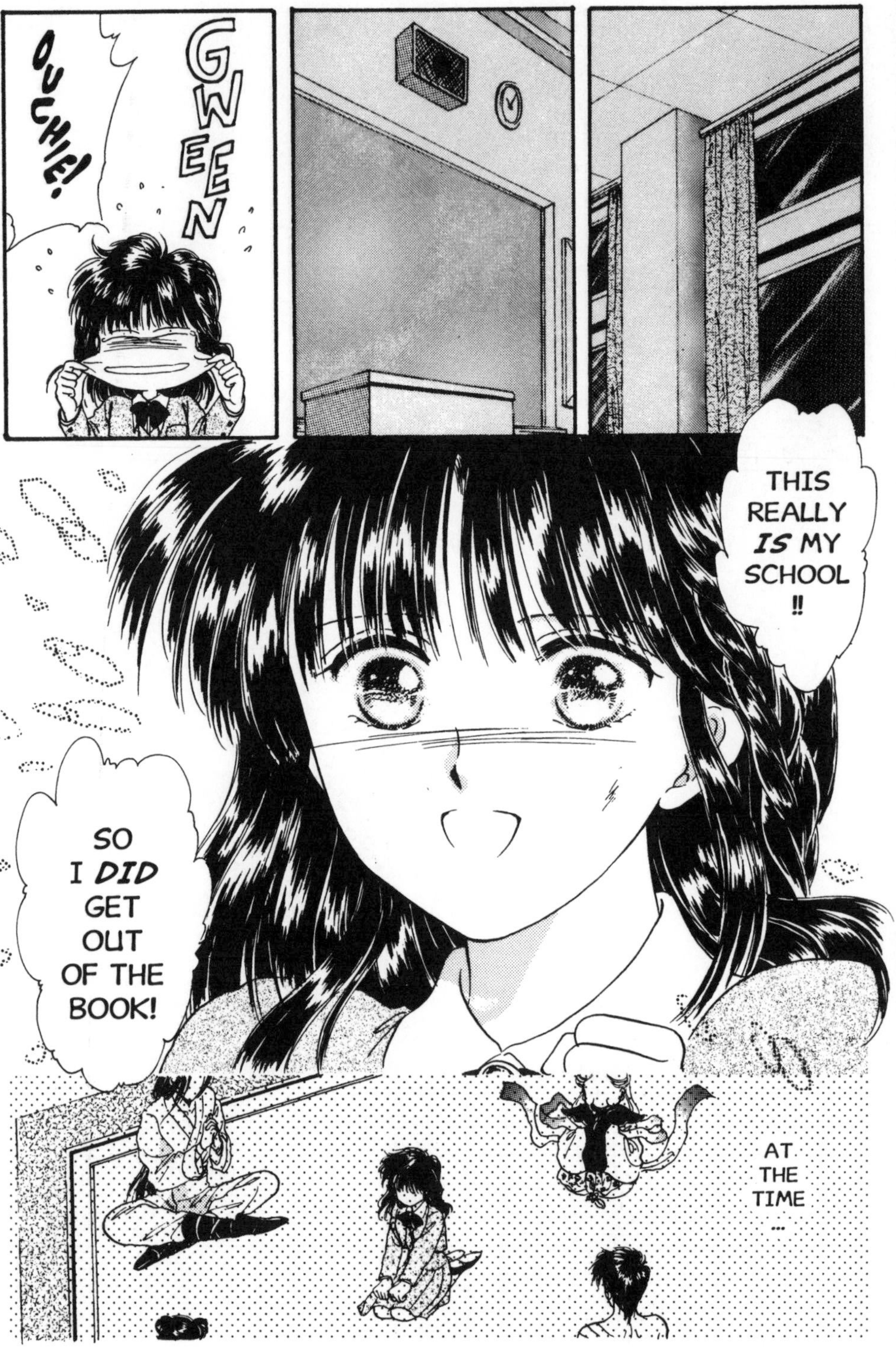
GWEEN
OUCHIE!
THIS REALLY IS MY SCHOOL!!
SO I DID GET OUT OF THE BOOK!
AT THE TIME ...

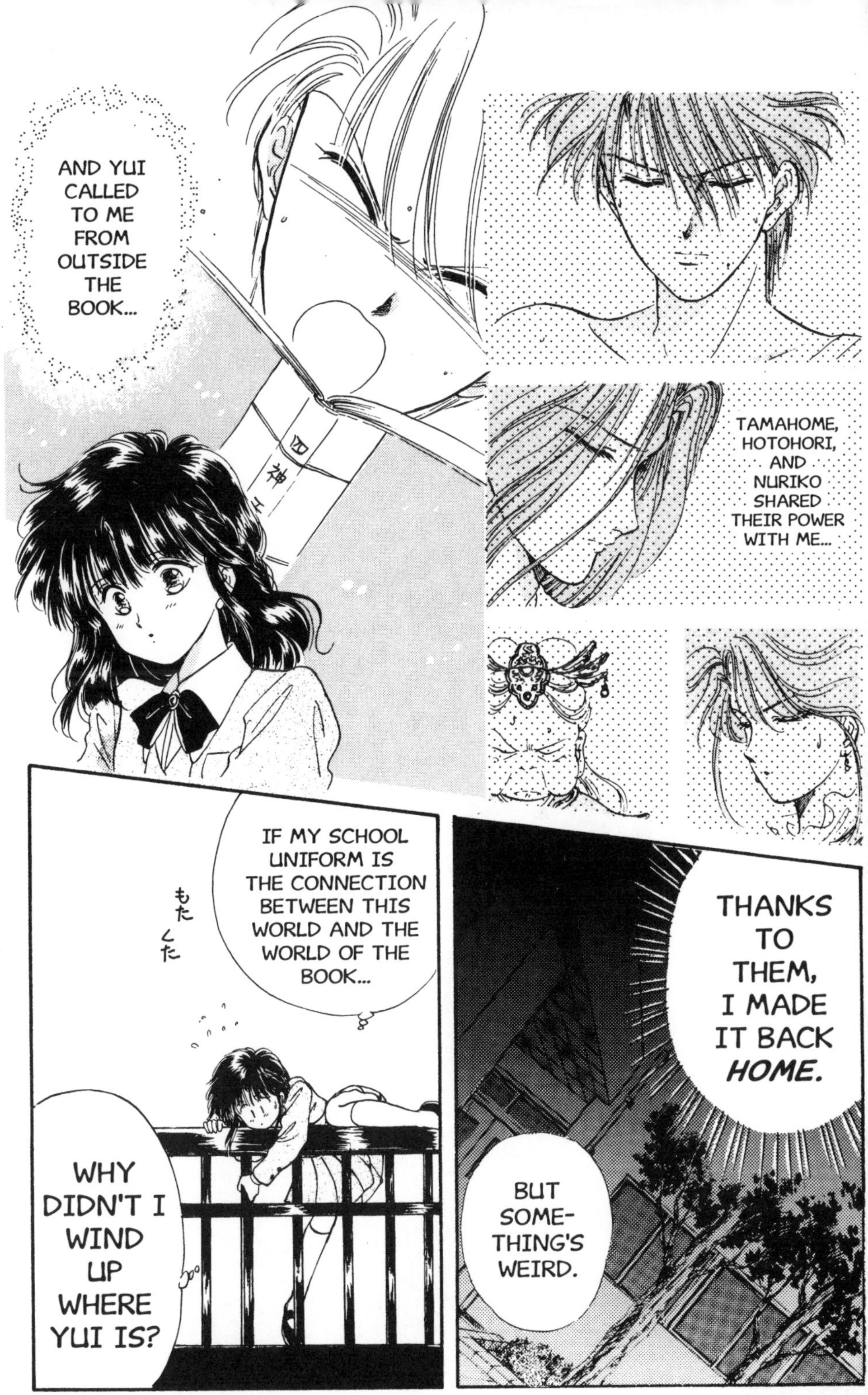
TAMAHOME, HOTOHORI, AND NURIKO SHARED THEIR POWER WITH ME...
AND YUI CALLED TO ME FROM OUTSIDE THE BOOK...
四神天
THANKS TO THEM, I MADE IT BACK *HOME.*
BUT SOME-THING'S WEIRD.
IF MY SCHOOL UNIFORM IS THE CONNECTION BETWEEN THIS WORLD AND THE WORLD OF THE BOOK...
もたくた
WHY DIDN'T I WIND UP WHERE YUI IS?

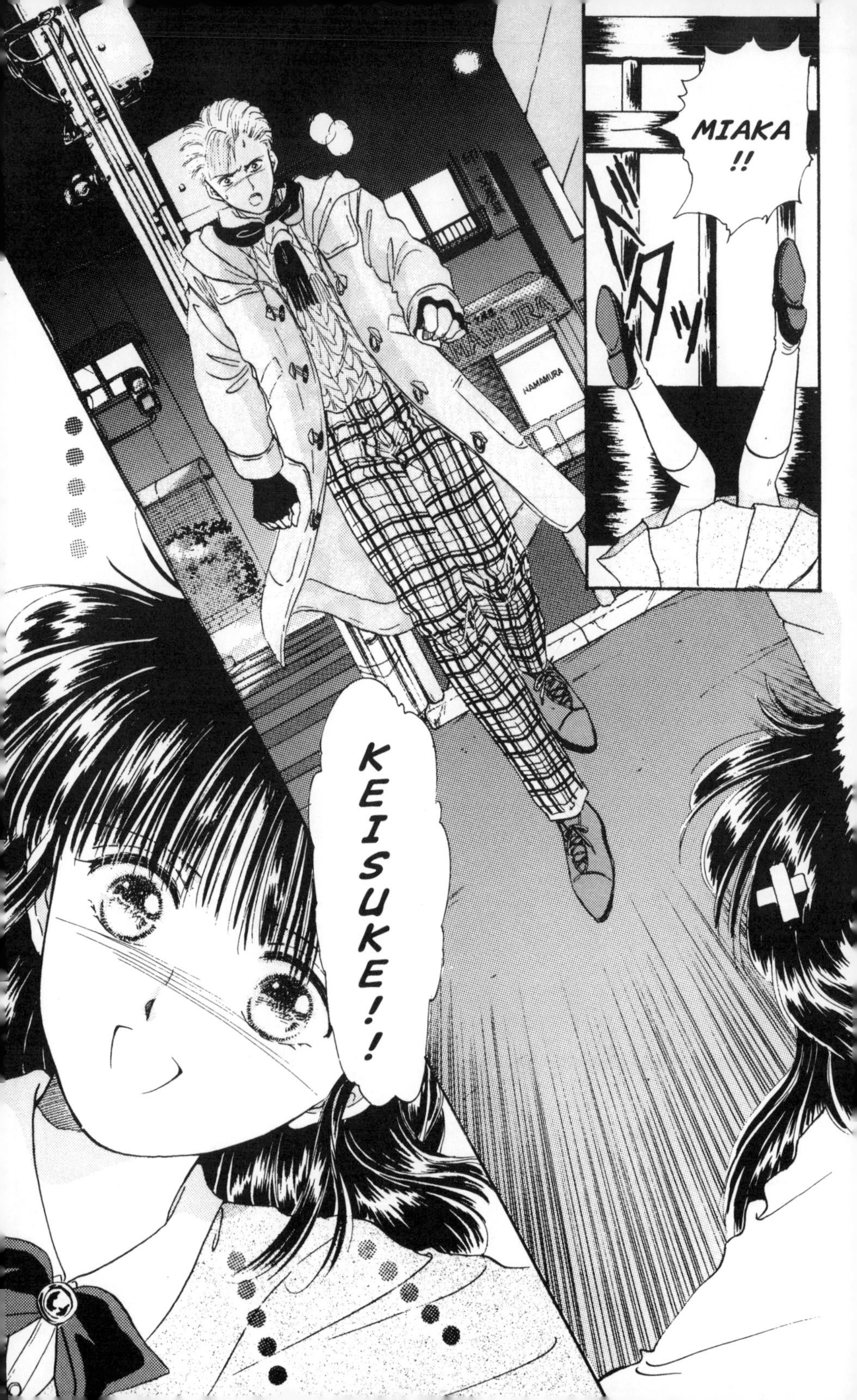
MIAKA !!
KEISUKE!!

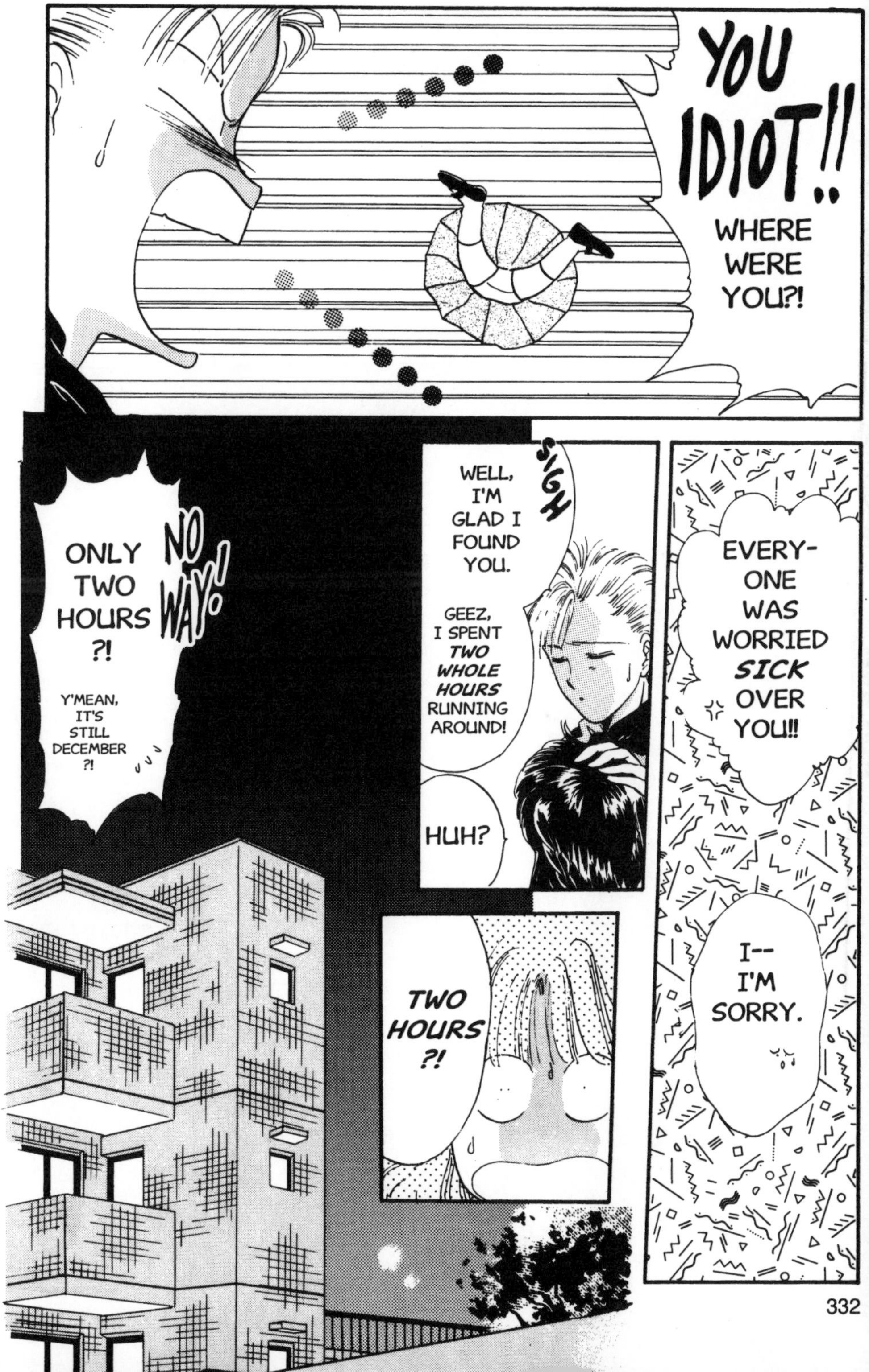
YOU IDIOT!!
WHERE WERE YOU?!
EVERY-ONE WAS WORRIED SICK OVER YOU!!
I-- I'M SORRY.
SIGH
WELL, I'M GLAD I FOUND YOU.
GEEZ, I SPENT TWO WHOLE HOURS RUNNING AROUND!
HUH?
TWO HOURS?!
NO WAY!
ONLY TWO HOURS?!
Y'MEAN, IT'S STILL DECEMBER?!

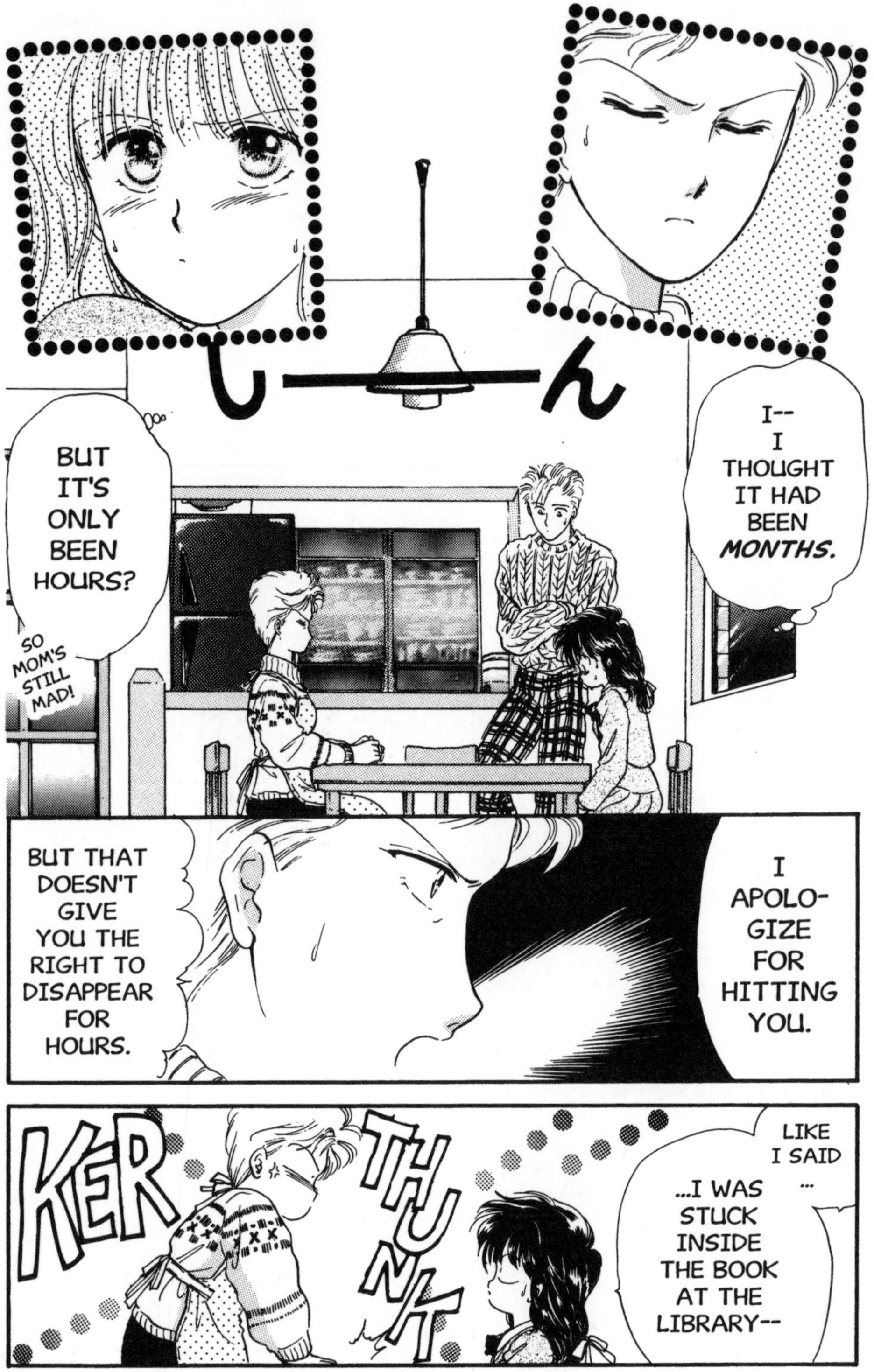

I-- I THOUGHT IT HAD BEEN *MONTHS.*
BUT IT'S ONLY BEEN HOURS?
SO MOM'S STILL MAD!
I APOLOGIZE FOR HITTING YOU.
BUT THAT DOESN'T GIVE YOU THE RIGHT TO DISAPPEAR FOR HOURS.
LIKE I SAID ...
...I WAS STUCK INSIDE THE BOOK AT THE LIBRARY--
KER
THUNK

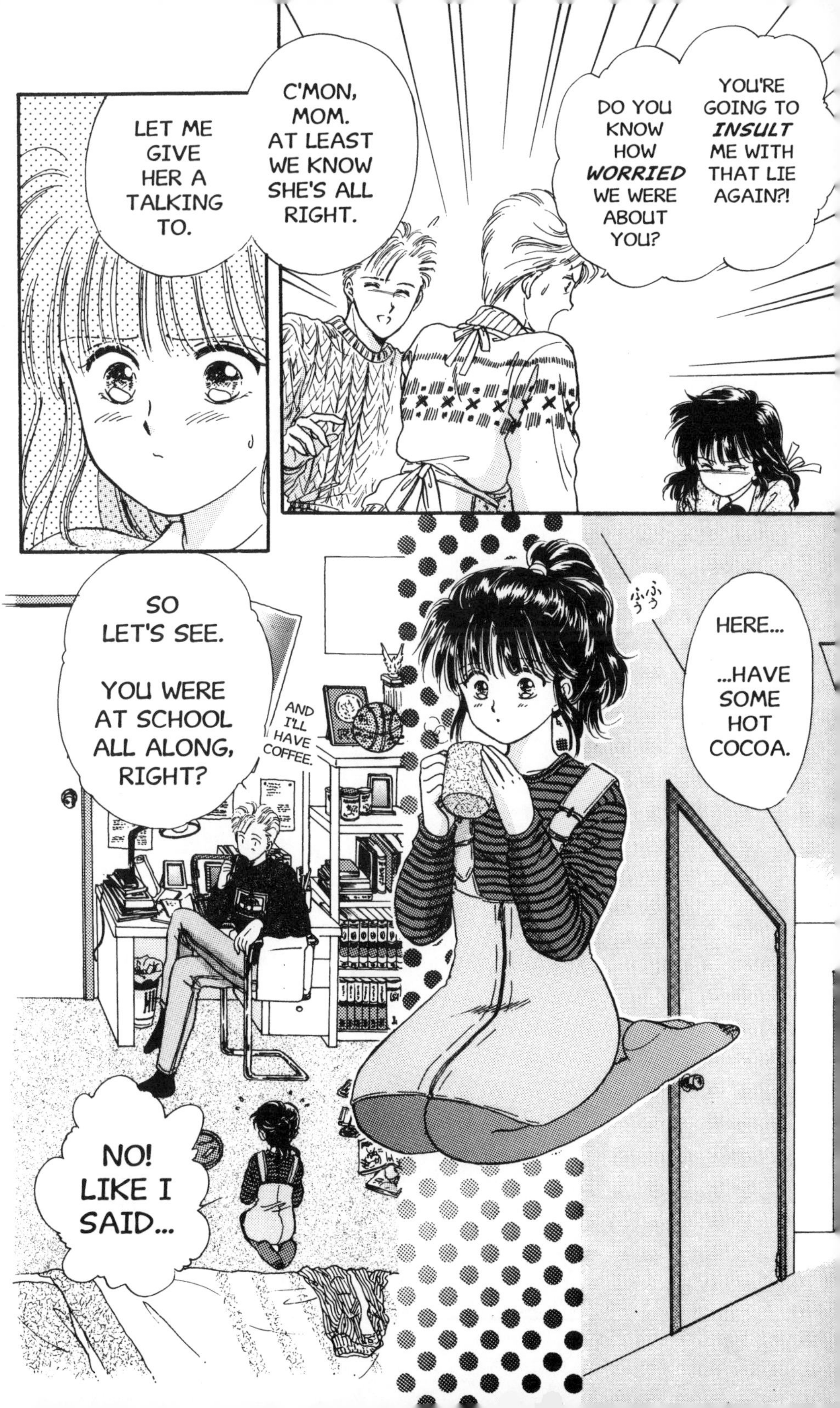

YOU'RE GOING TO *INSULT* ME WITH THAT LIE AGAIN?!
DO YOU KNOW HOW *WORRIED* WE WERE ABOUT YOU?
C'MON, MOM. AT LEAST WE KNOW SHE'S ALL RIGHT.
LET ME GIVE HER A TALKING TO.
HERE... ...HAVE SOME HOT COCOA.
AND I'LL HAVE COFFEE.
SO LET'S SEE. YOU WERE AT SCHOOL ALL ALONG, RIGHT?
NO! LIKE I SAID...

Here's a little confession. I really like Miaka's older brother Keisuke. If he existed, I might really fall for him. His younger classmates would fall for him--he's so nice. He probably would have been the captain of whatever team he was on. If both he and his friend had a crush on the same girl, he would pair the girl up with his friend. He's really fond of his sister (not like she's his pet or anything). My assistant, S., on the other hand, is part of the "Tamahome" faction. I gotta say... Yeah, I like Tamahome too, as a manga character. I guess Tamahome's the most popular among you readers. I heard that one of the reasons for his popularity is that he resembles Manato in *Prepubescence.* S. was totally mortified by this comment, insisting that they had totally different personalities. I suppose Tamahome wouldn't exactly be thrilled to find he was popular because he looked like someone else. Asuka and Miaka are both my main characters and so have the same look, but their personalities are totally different. (But do they look so much alike? Well, maybe they do, but should every manga artist have to draw a different face for every new protagonist?)

I think that Tamahome is more mature than Manato. Manato's an ordinary urban high school boy. He **does** have his lighter side, though. Tamahome, on the other hand, had to work hard and mature, so he's more in control of his feelings. He might seem a little insensitive (e.g., when Nuriko says something outrageous), but that's not his true self at all. In fact, he might be more sensitive than Hotohori. He has some powerful emotions kept inside. I've never written a character like him before. Tamahome is really strong, but he might have some profound weaknesses. He seems really upbeat, when in fact he has a dark side. He can be emotional and yet be cool. He has a childlike face yet he can be so mature. So S. and I think that he is full of contradictory traits...

So that's what he's like!

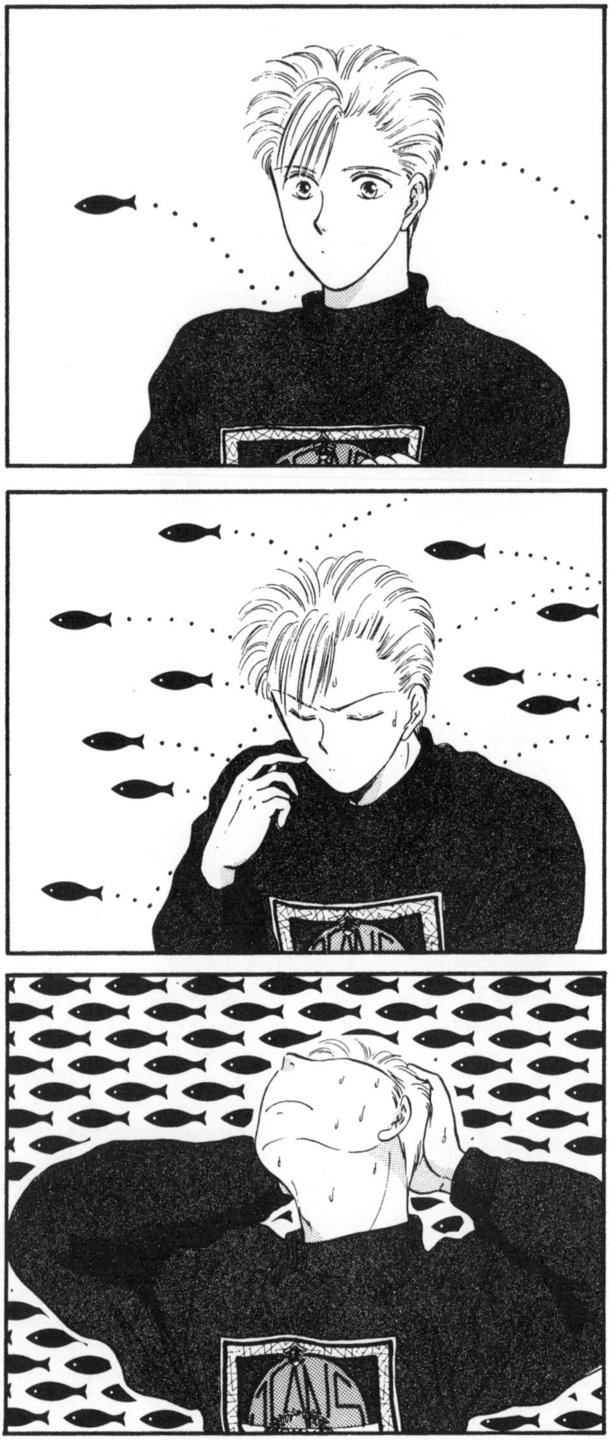

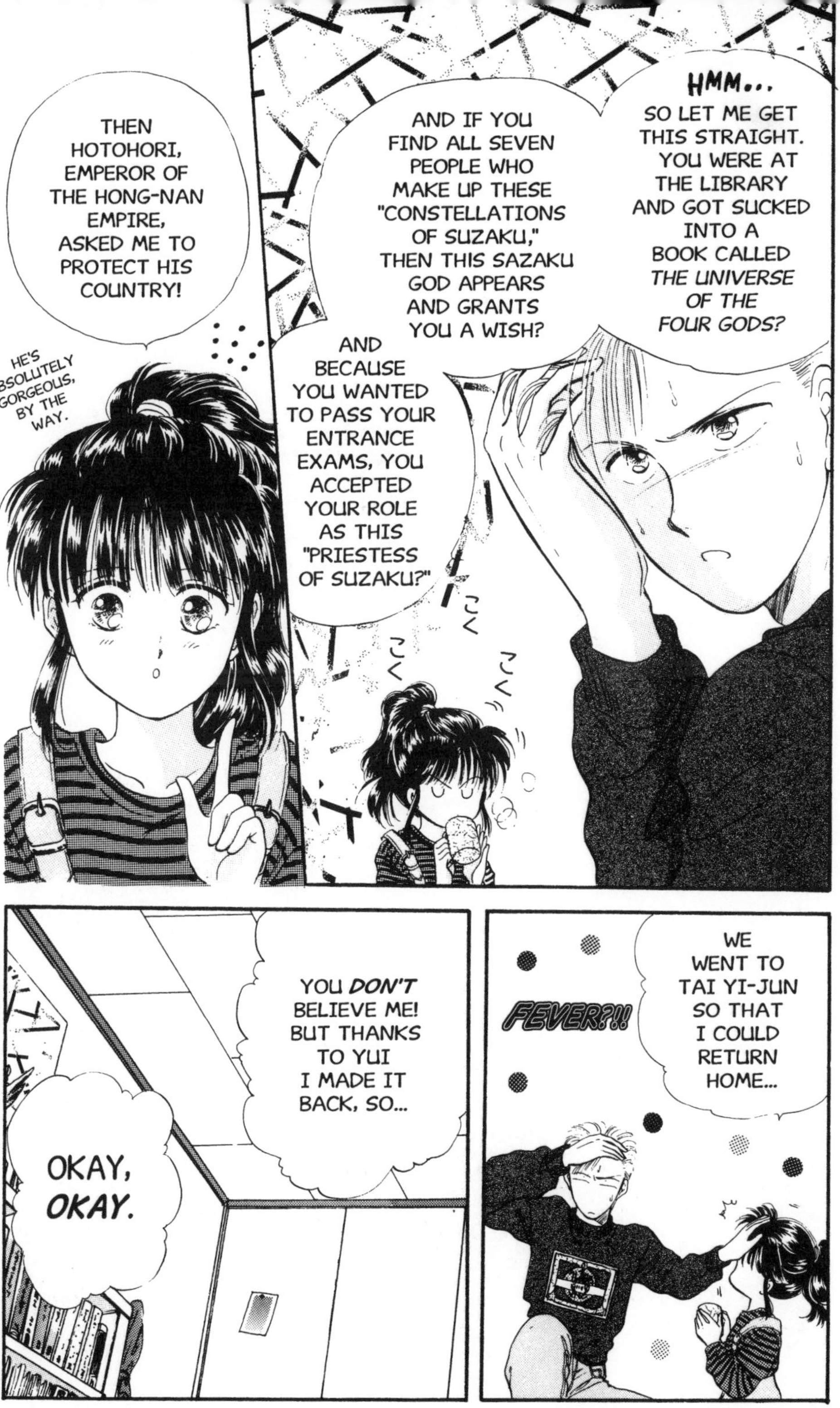
HMM... SO LET ME GET THIS STRAIGHT. YOU WERE AT THE LIBRARY AND GOT SUCKED INTO A BOOK CALLED *THE UNIVERSE OF THE FOUR GODS?*
AND IF YOU FIND ALL SEVEN PEOPLE WHO MAKE UP THESE "CONSTELLATIONS OF SUZAKU," THEN THIS SAZAKU GOD APPEARS AND GRANTS YOU A WISH?
AND BECAUSE YOU WANTED TO PASS YOUR ENTRANCE EXAMS, YOU ACCEPTED YOUR ROLE AS THIS "PRIESTESS OF SUZAKU?"
こく
こく
こく
THEN HOTOHORI, EMPEROR OF THE HONG-NAN EMPIRE, ASKED ME TO PROTECT HIS COUNTRY!
HE'S ABSOLUTELY GORGEOUS, BY THE WAY.
WE WENT TO TAI YI-JUN SO THAT I COULD RETURN HOME...
FEVER?!!
YOU *DON'T* BELIEVE ME! BUT THANKS TO YUI I MADE IT BACK, SO...
OKAY, *OKAY.*

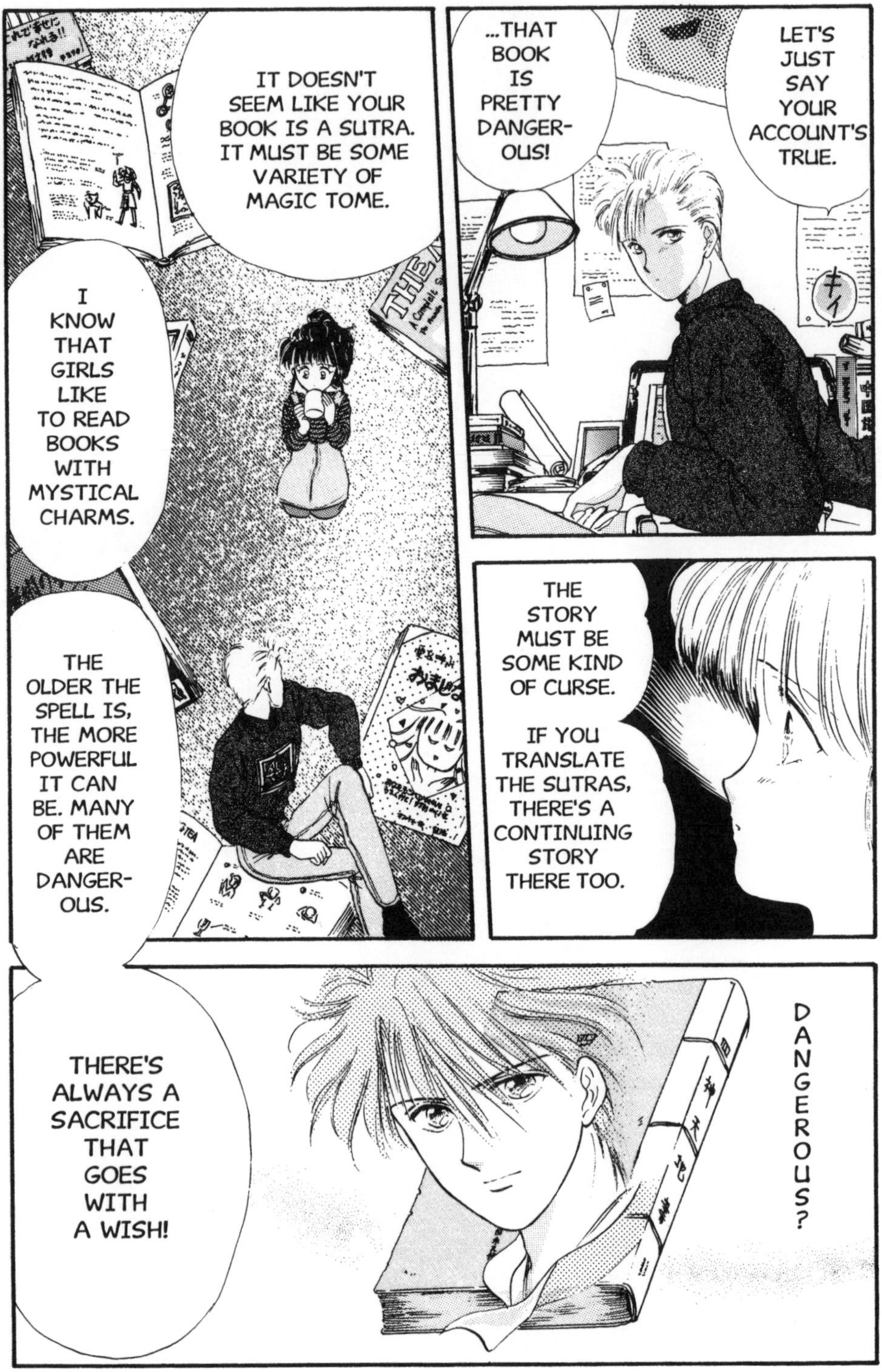
LET'S JUST SAY YOUR ACCOUNT'S TRUE.
...THAT BOOK IS PRETTY DANGER-OUS!
THE STORY MUST BE SOME KIND OF CURSE.
IF YOU TRANSLATE THE SUTRAS, THERE'S A CONTINUING STORY THERE TOO.
IT DOESN'T SEEM LIKE YOUR BOOK IS A SUTRA. IT MUST BE SOME VARIETY OF MAGIC TOME.
I KNOW THAT GIRLS LIKE TO READ BOOKS WITH MYSTICAL CHARMS.
THE OLDER THE SPELL IS, THE MORE POWERFUL IT CAN BE. MANY OF THEM ARE DANGER-OUS.
DANGEROUS?
THERE'S ALWAYS A SACRIFICE THAT GOES WITH A WISH!

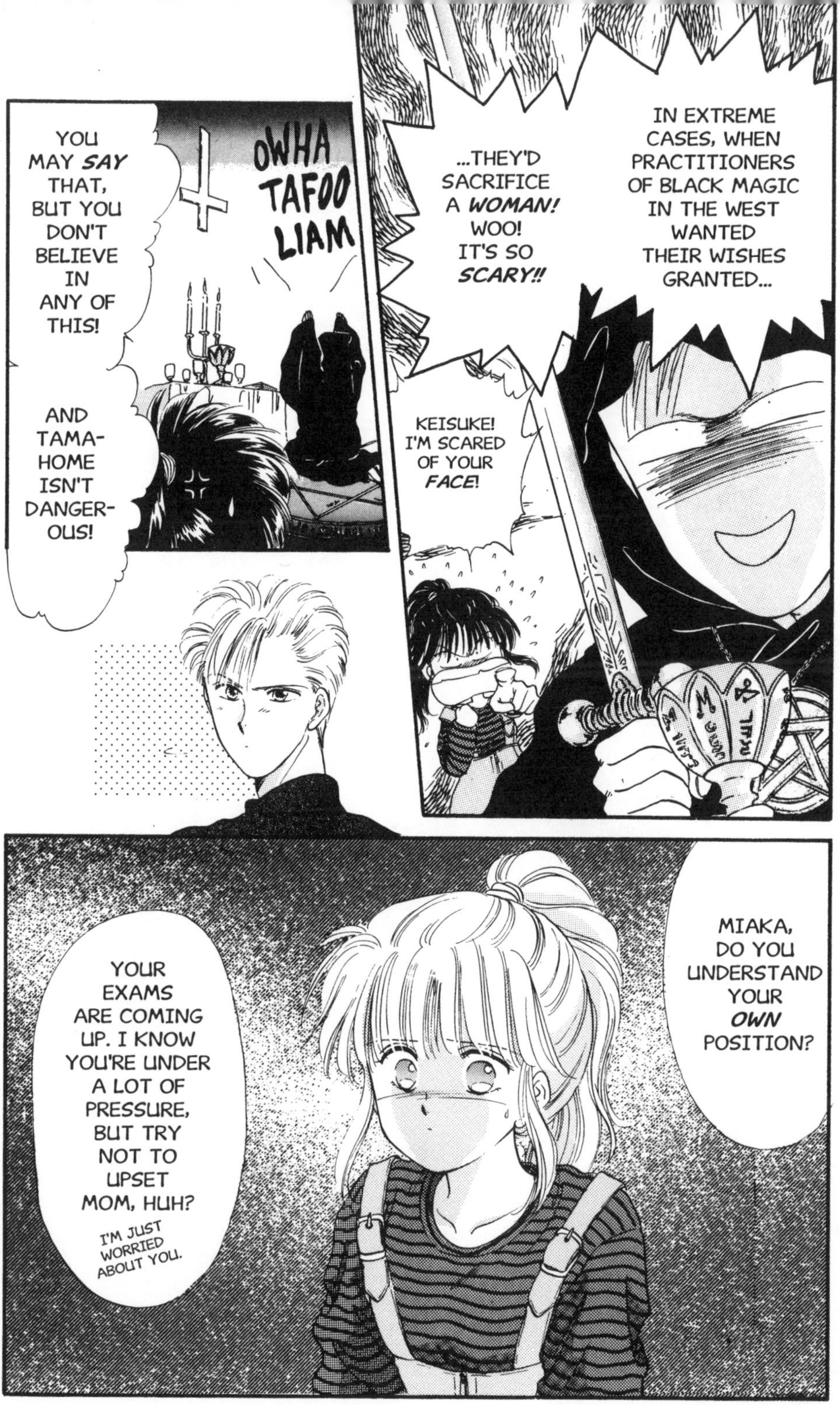
IN EXTREME CASES, WHEN PRACTITIONERS OF BLACK MAGIC IN THE WEST WANTED THEIR WISHES GRANTED...
...THEY'D SACRIFICE A *WOMAN!* WOO! IT'S SO *SCARY!!*
KEISUKE! I'M SCARED OF YOUR *FACE*!
OWHA TAFOO LIAM
YOU MAY *SAY* THAT, BUT YOU DON'T BELIEVE IN ANY OF THIS!
AND TAMAHOME ISN'T DANGEROUS!
MIAKA, DO YOU UNDERSTAND YOUR *OWN* POSITION?
YOUR EXAMS ARE COMING UP. I KNOW YOU'RE UNDER A LOT OF PRESSURE, BUT TRY NOT TO UPSET MOM, HUH?
I'M JUST WORRIED ABOUT YOU.

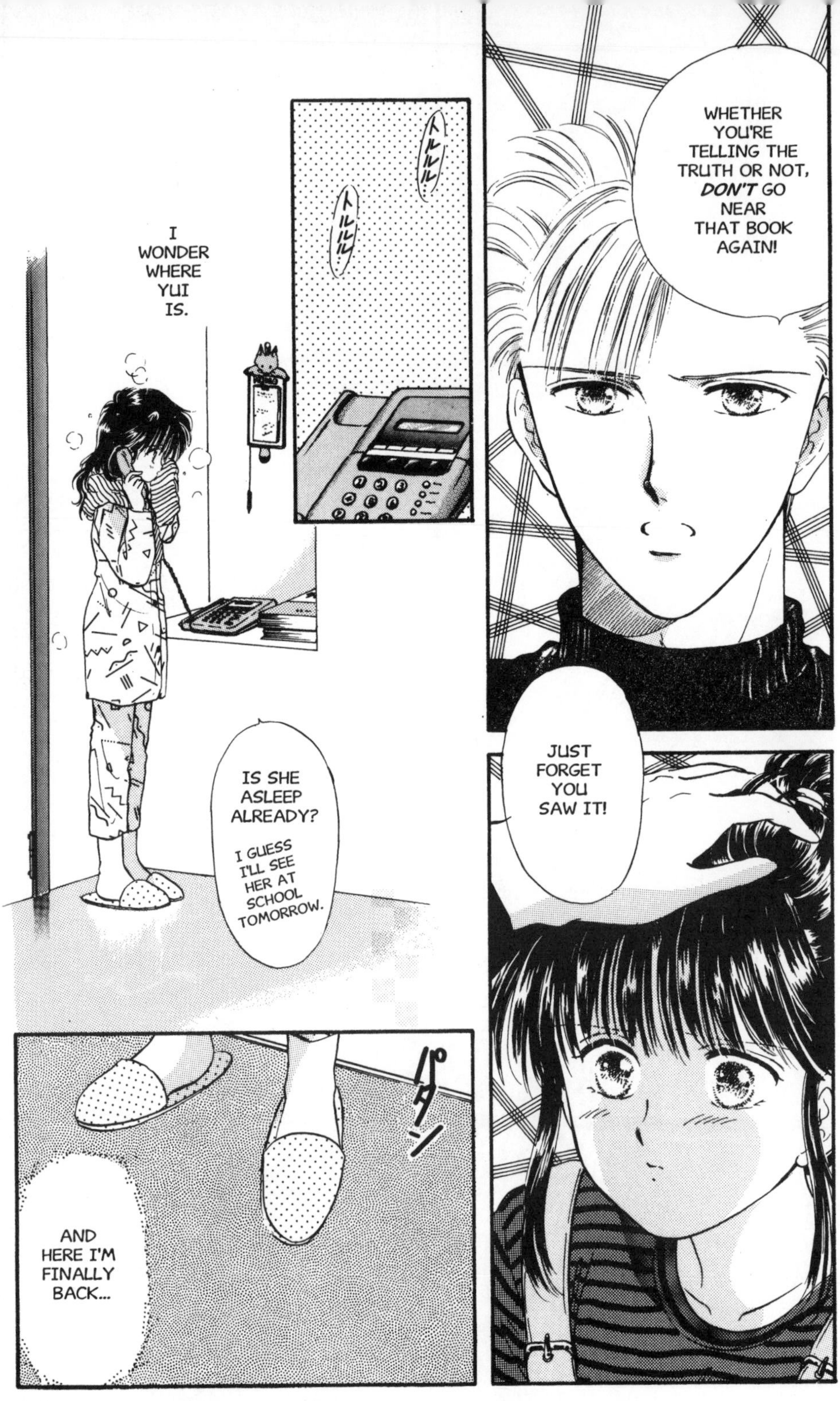
WHETHER YOU'RE TELLING THE TRUTH OR NOT, ***DON'T*** GO NEAR THAT BOOK AGAIN!
JUST FORGET YOU SAW IT!
トルルル…
トルルル…
I WONDER WHERE YUI IS.
IS SHE ASLEEP ALREADY?
I GUESS I'LL SEE HER AT SCHOOL TOMORROW.
パタン
AND HERE I'M FINALLY BACK...

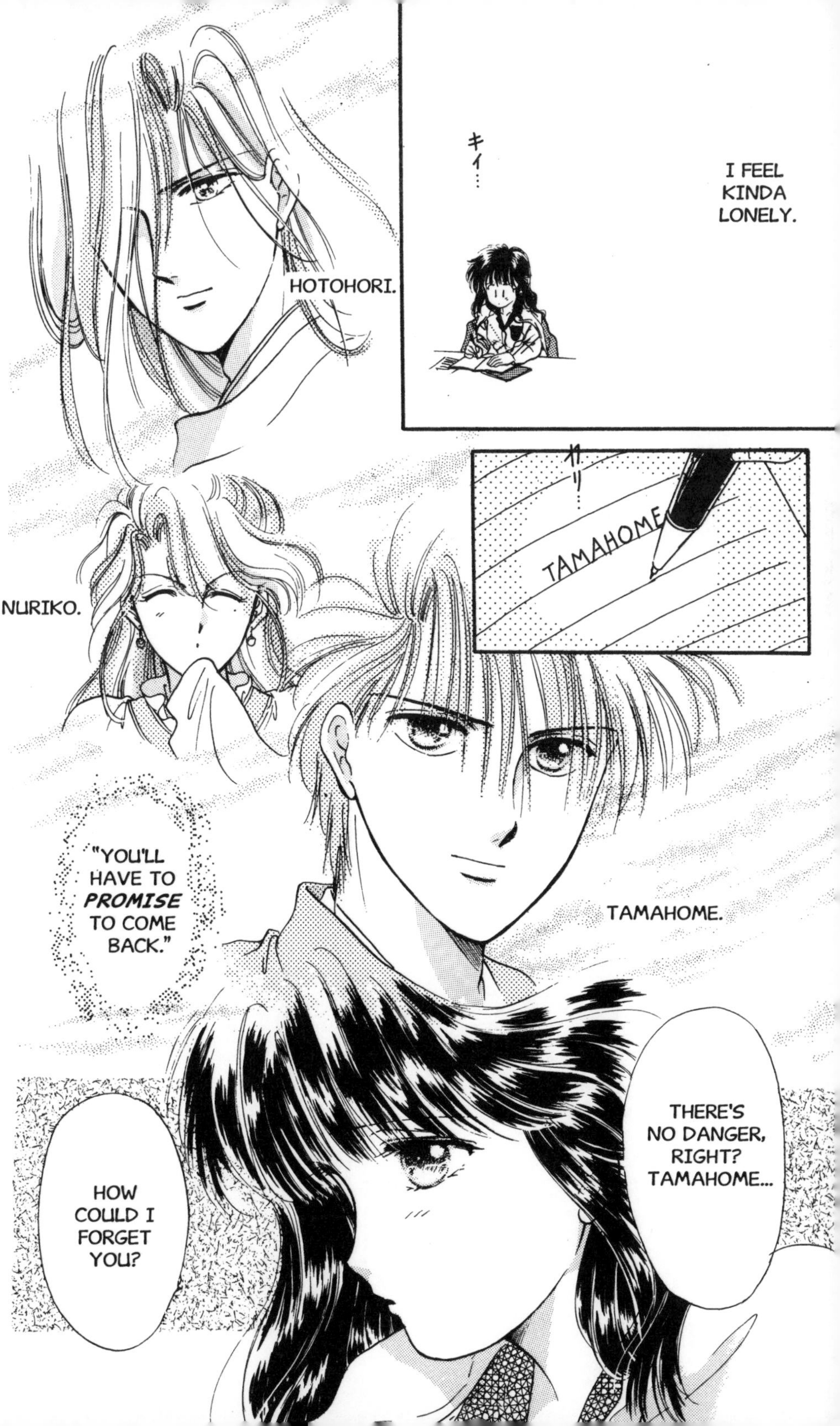

キイ…
I FEEL KINDA LONELY.
HOTOHORI.
カリ…
TAMAHOME
TAMAHOME.
NURIKO.
"YOU'LL HAVE TO PROMISE TO COME BACK."
THERE'S NO DANGER, RIGHT? TAMAHOME...
HOW COULD I FORGET YOU?

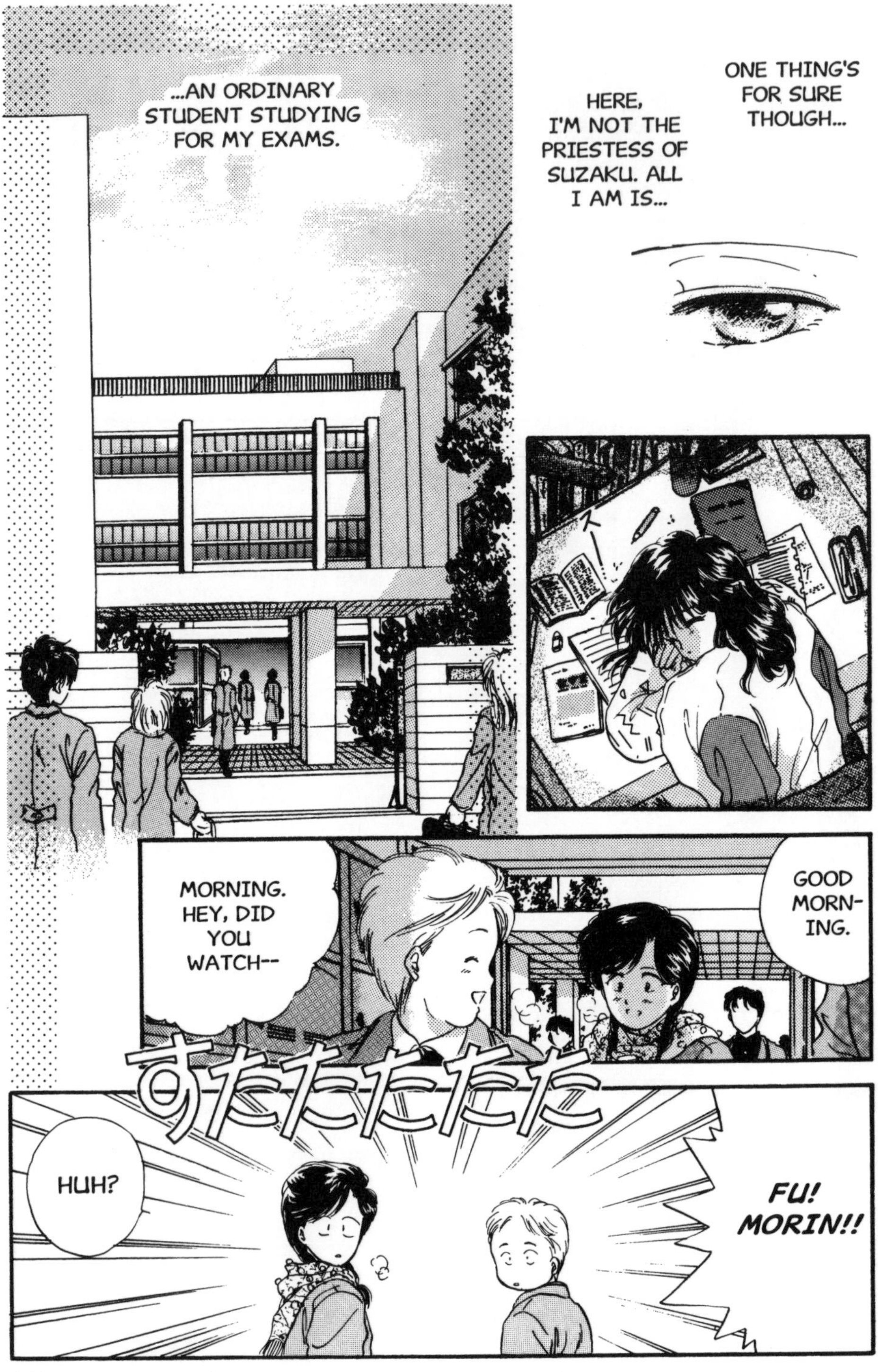
ONE THING'S FOR SURE THOUGH...
HERE, I'M NOT THE PRIESTESS OF SUZAKU. ALL I AM IS...
...AN ORDINARY STUDENT STUDYING FOR MY EXAMS.
GOOD MORNING.
MORNING. HEY, DID YOU WATCH--
すたたたたた
FU! MORIN!!
HUH?

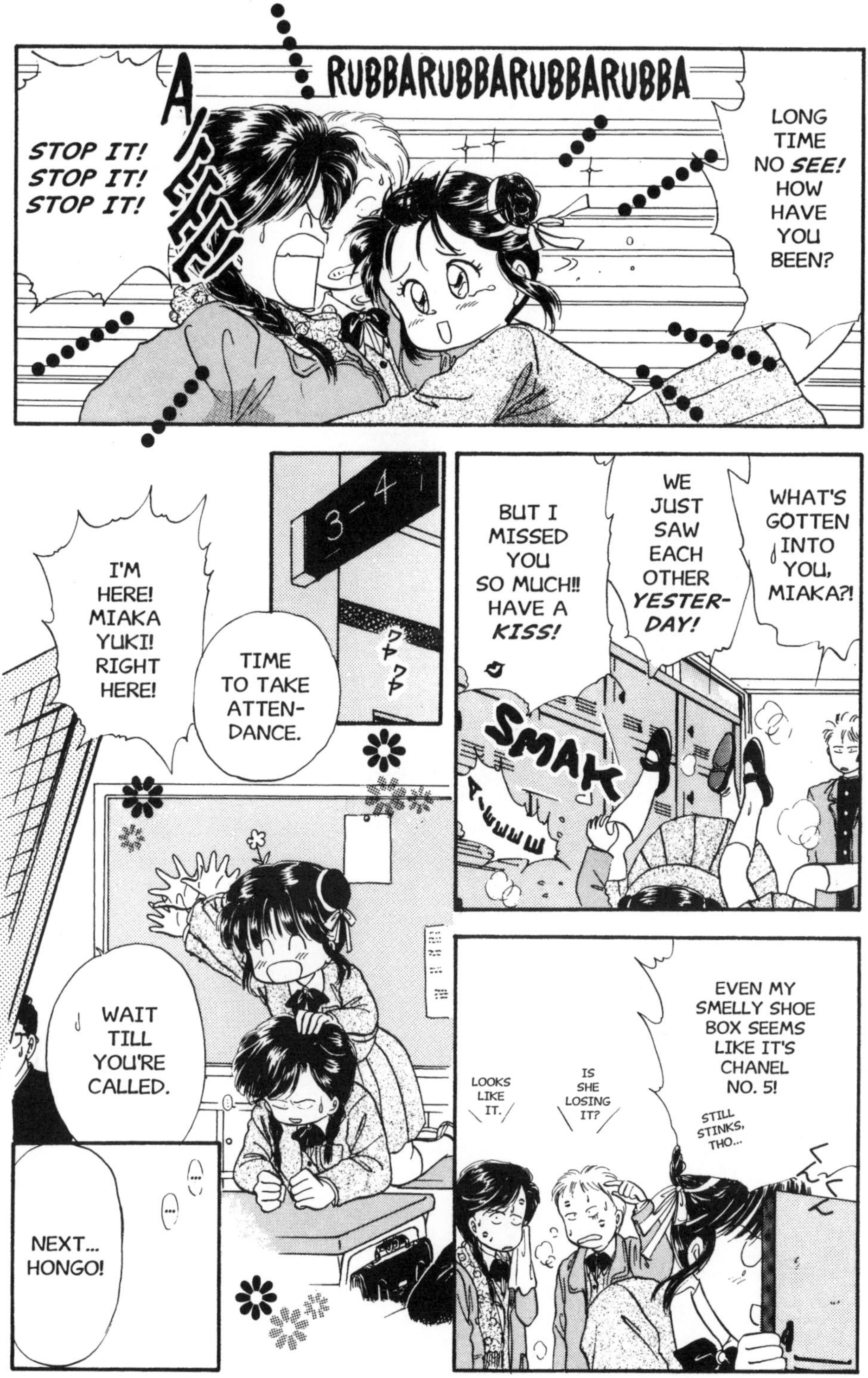
LONG TIME NO SEE! HOW HAVE YOU BEEN?
RUBBARUBBARUBBARUBBA
AIEEEE!
STOP IT! STOP IT! STOP IT!
WHAT'S GOTTEN INTO YOU, MIAKA?!
WE JUST SAW EACH OTHER YESTERDAY!
BUT I MISSED YOU SO MUCH!! HAVE A KISS!
SMAK
MWWWA
EVEN MY SMELLY SHOE BOX SEEMS LIKE IT'S CHANEL NO. 5!
STILL STINKS, THO...
IS SHE LOSING IT?
LOOKS LIKE IT.
TIME TO TAKE ATTENDANCE.
I'M HERE! MIAKA YUKI! RIGHT HERE!
WAIT TILL YOU'RE CALLED.
...
...
NEXT... HONGO!

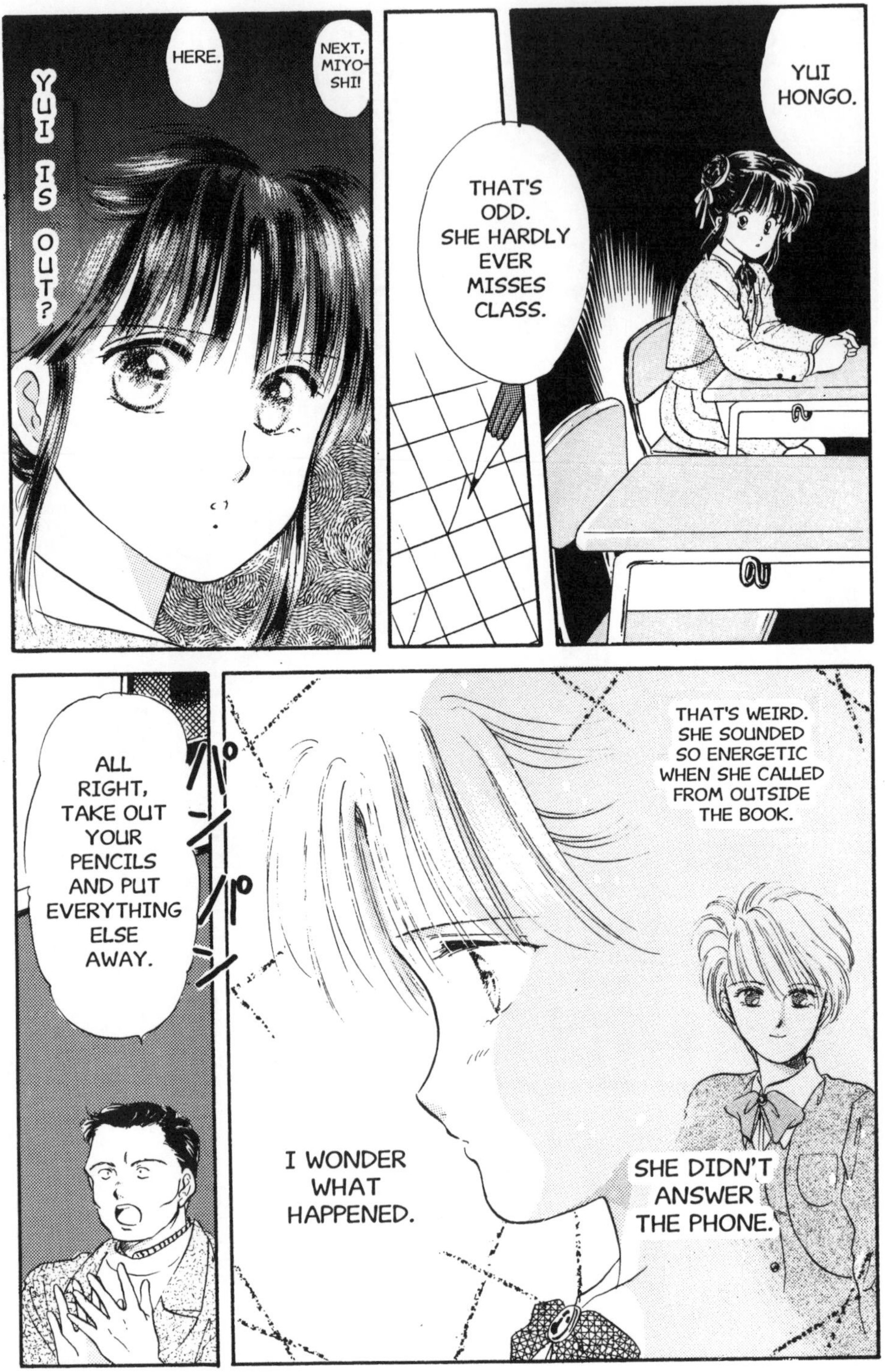
YUI HONGO.
THAT'S ODD. SHE HARDLY EVER MISSES CLASS.
NEXT, MIYO-SHI!
HERE.
YUI IS OUT?
THAT'S WEIRD. SHE SOUNDED SO ENERGETIC WHEN SHE CALLED FROM OUTSIDE THE BOOK.
SHE DIDN'T ANSWER THE PHONE.
I WONDER WHAT HAPPENED.
ALL RIGHT, TAKE OUT YOUR PENCILS AND PUT EVERYTHING ELSE AWAY.

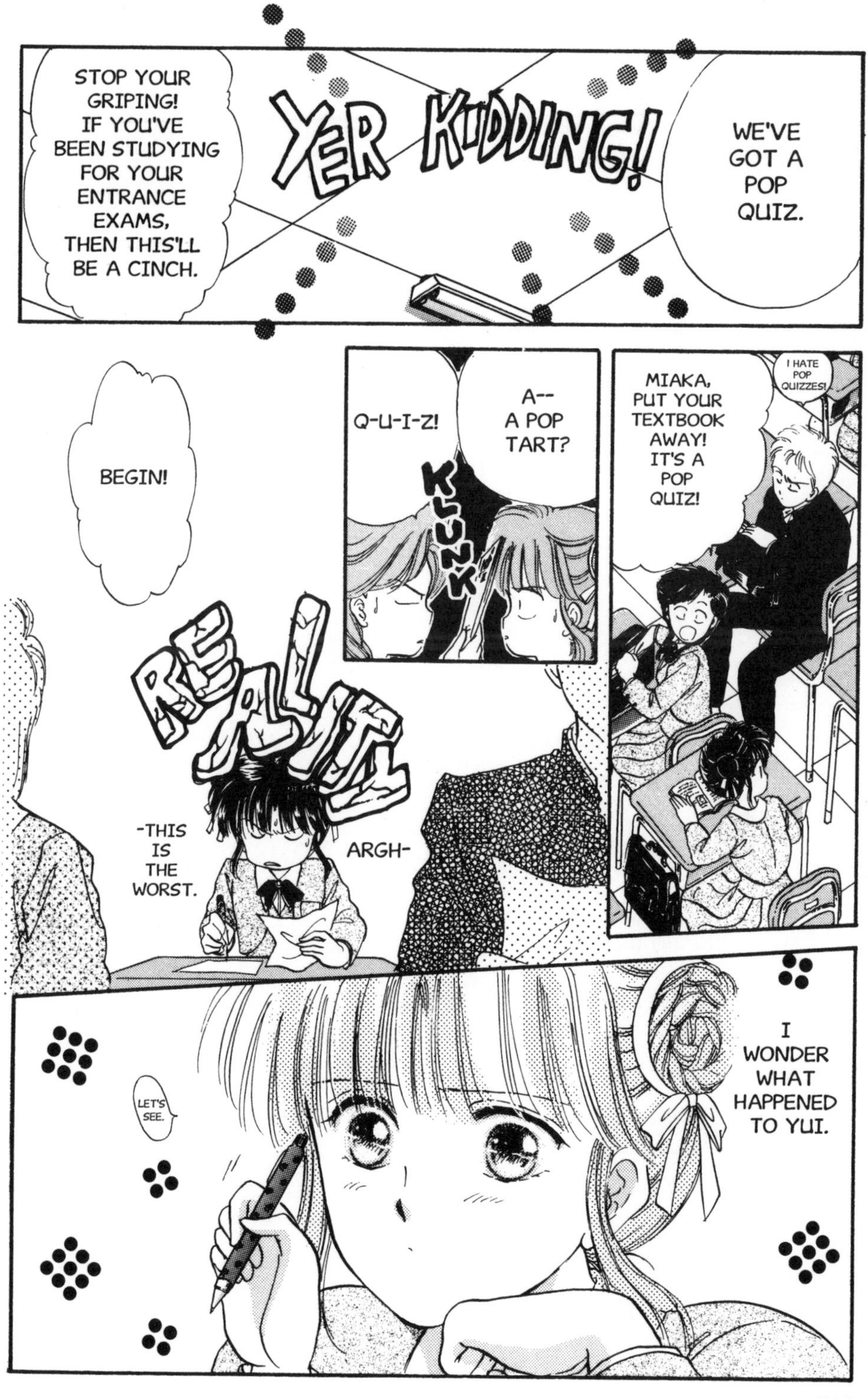
WE'VE GOT A POP QUIZ.
YER KIDDING!
STOP YOUR GRIPING! IF YOU'VE BEEN STUDYING FOR YOUR ENTRANCE EXAMS, THEN THIS'LL BE A CINCH.
I HATE POP QUIZZES!
MIAKA, PUT YOUR TEXTBOOK AWAY! IT'S A POP QUIZ!
A-- A POP TART?
Q-U-I-Z!
KLUNK
BEGIN!
ARGH-
-THIS IS THE WORST.
I WONDER WHAT HAPPENED TO YUI.
LET'S SEE.

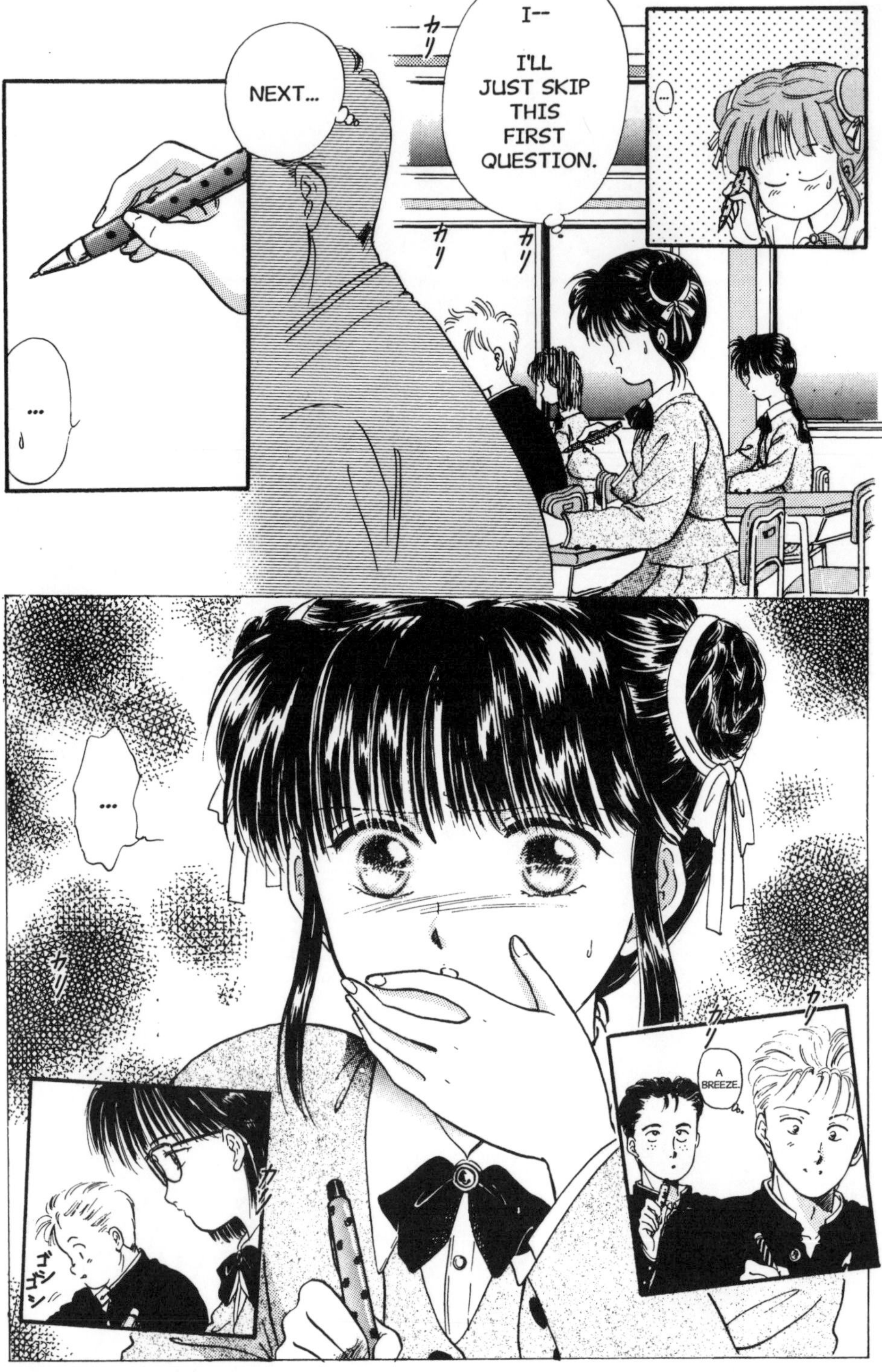
...
I--
I'LL JUST SKIP THIS FIRST QUESTION.
NEXT...
...
...
A BREEZE.

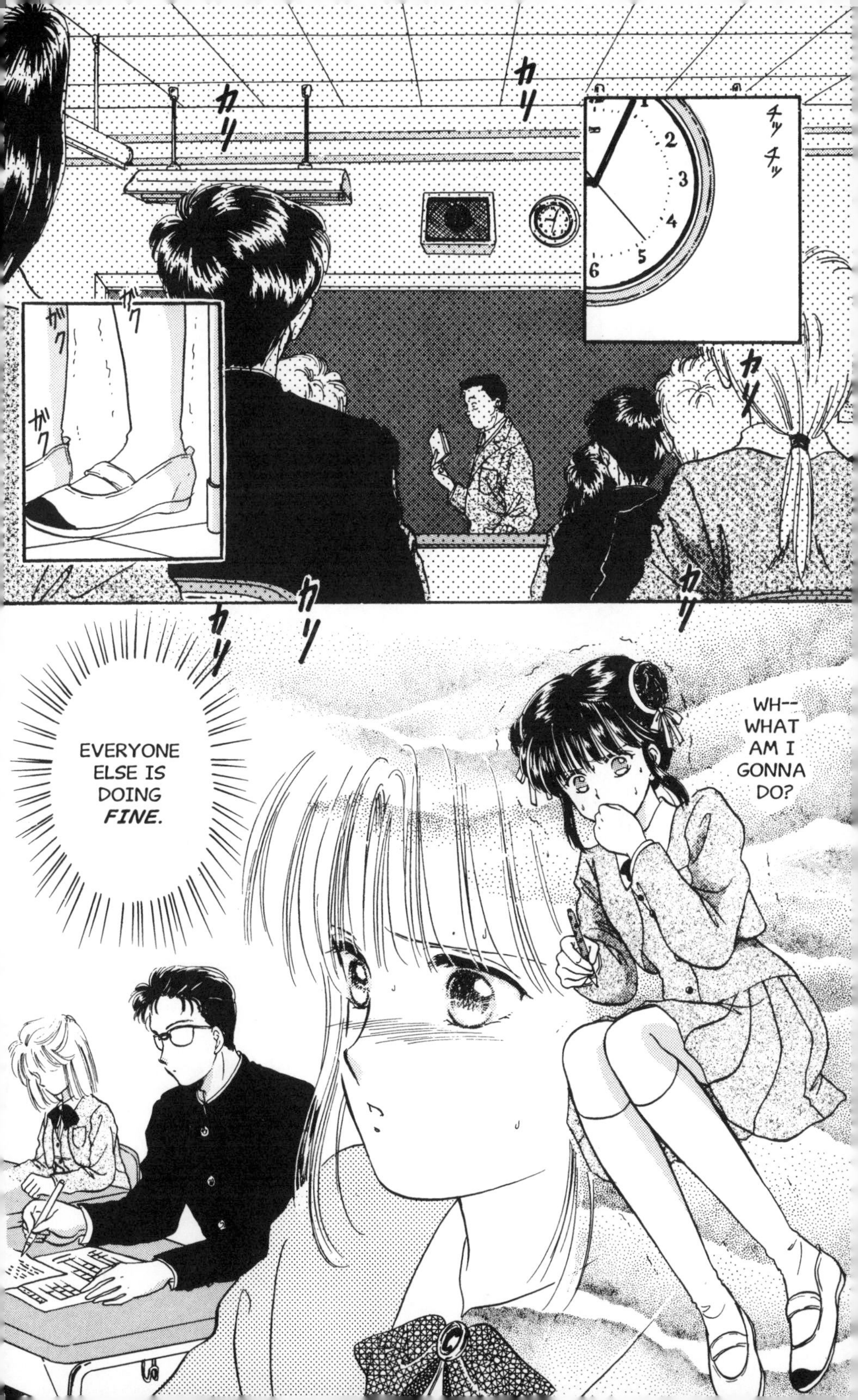
チッ チッ
カリ
カリ
カリ
ガク ガク
カリ
カリ
カリ
WH-- WHAT AM I GONNA DO?
EVERYONE ELSE IS DOING *FINE*.

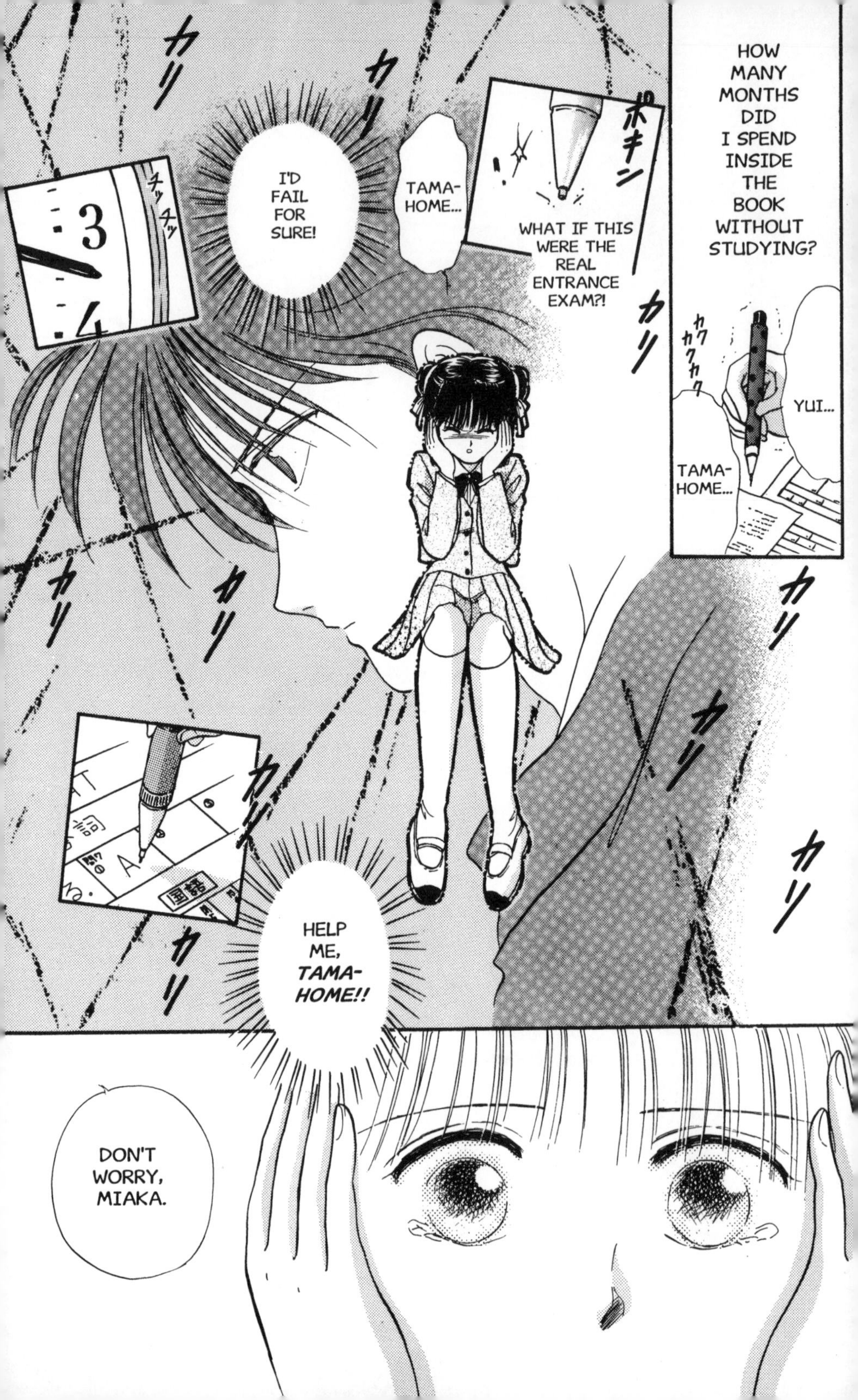
HOW MANY MONTHS DID I SPEND INSIDE THE BOOK WITHOUT STUDYING?
カクカクカク
YUI...
TAMA-HOME...
ポキン
WHAT IF THIS WERE THE REAL ENTRANCE EXAM?!
TAMA-HOME...
I'D FAIL FOR SURE!
チッチッ
カリ
HELP ME, *TAMA-HOME!!*
DON'T WORRY, MIAKA.

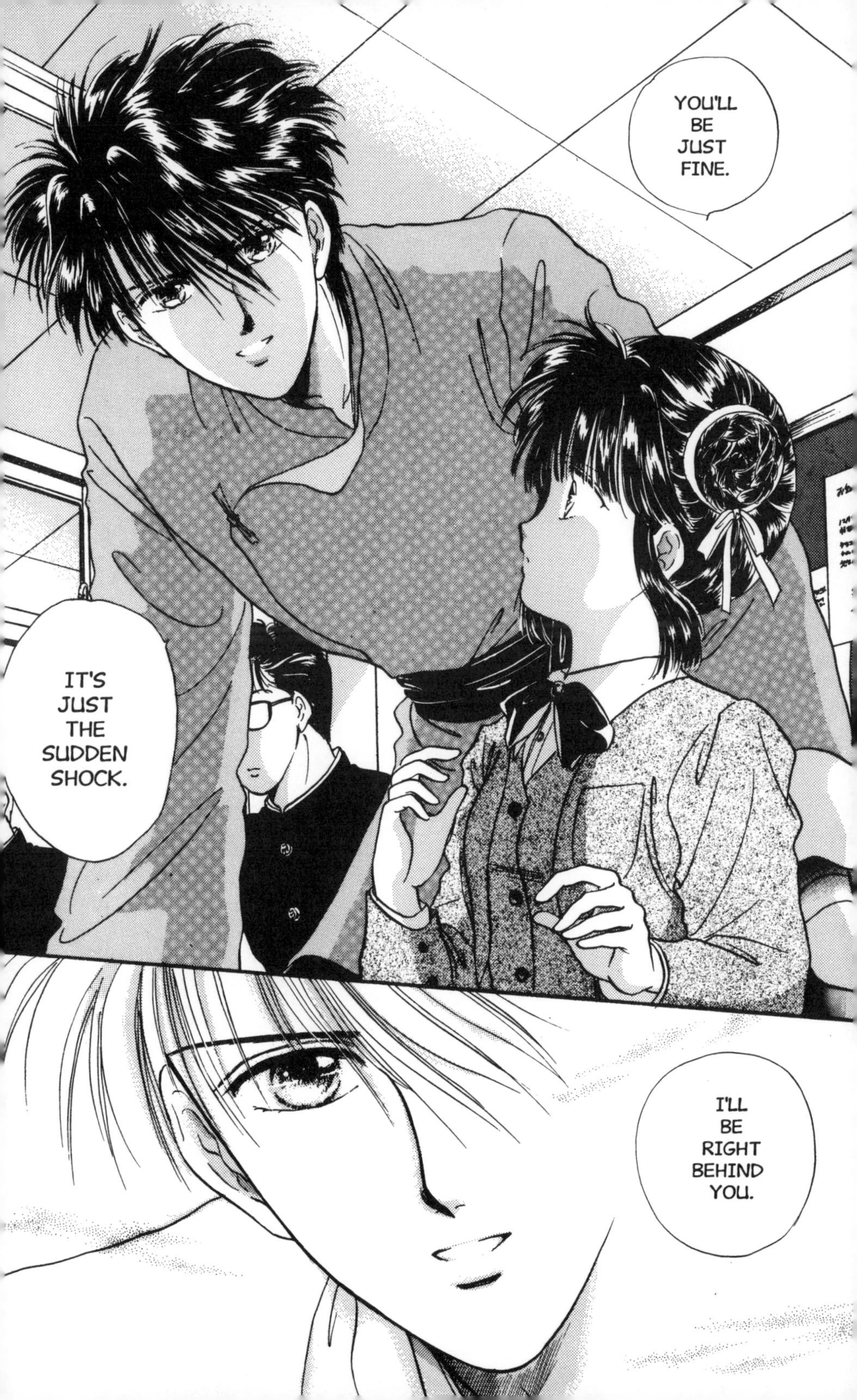
YOU'LL BE JUST FINE.
IT'S JUST THE SUDDEN SHOCK.
I'LL BE RIGHT BEHIND YOU.

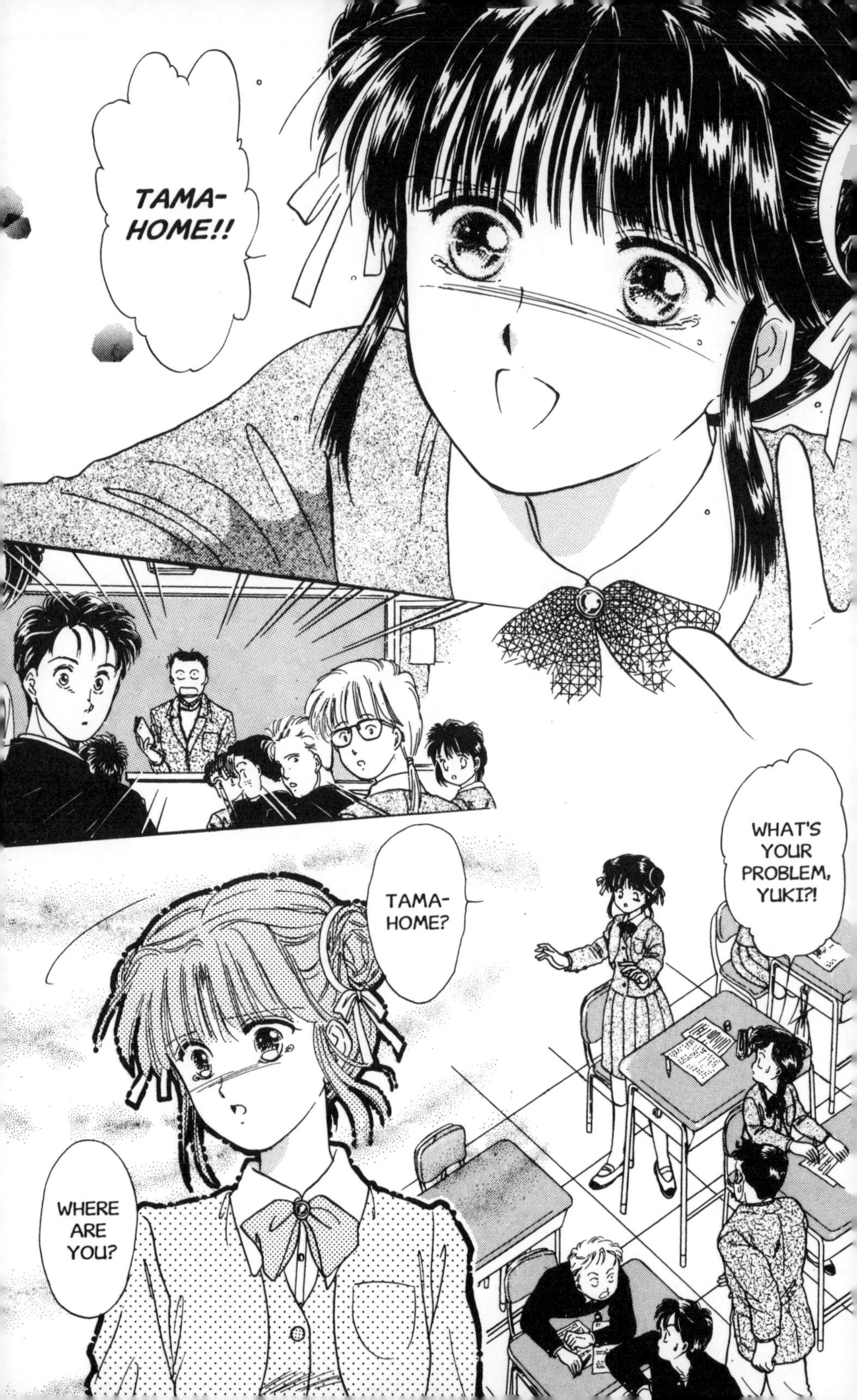
TAMA-HOME!!
WHAT'S YOUR PROBLEM, YUKI?!
TAMA-HOME?
WHERE ARE YOU?

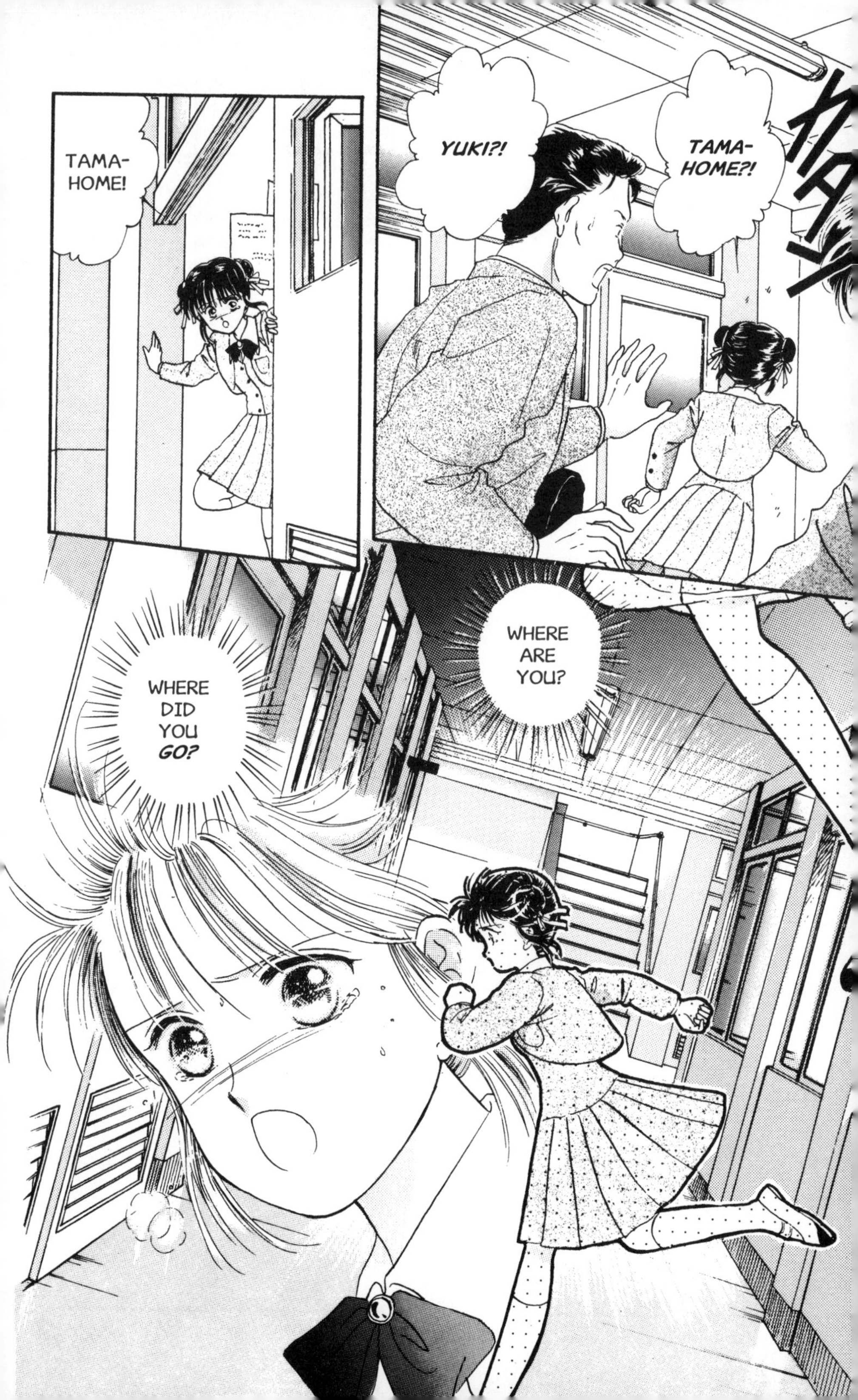
TAMA-
HOME?!
YUKI?!
TAMA-
HOME!
WHERE
ARE
YOU?
WHERE
DID
YOU
GO?

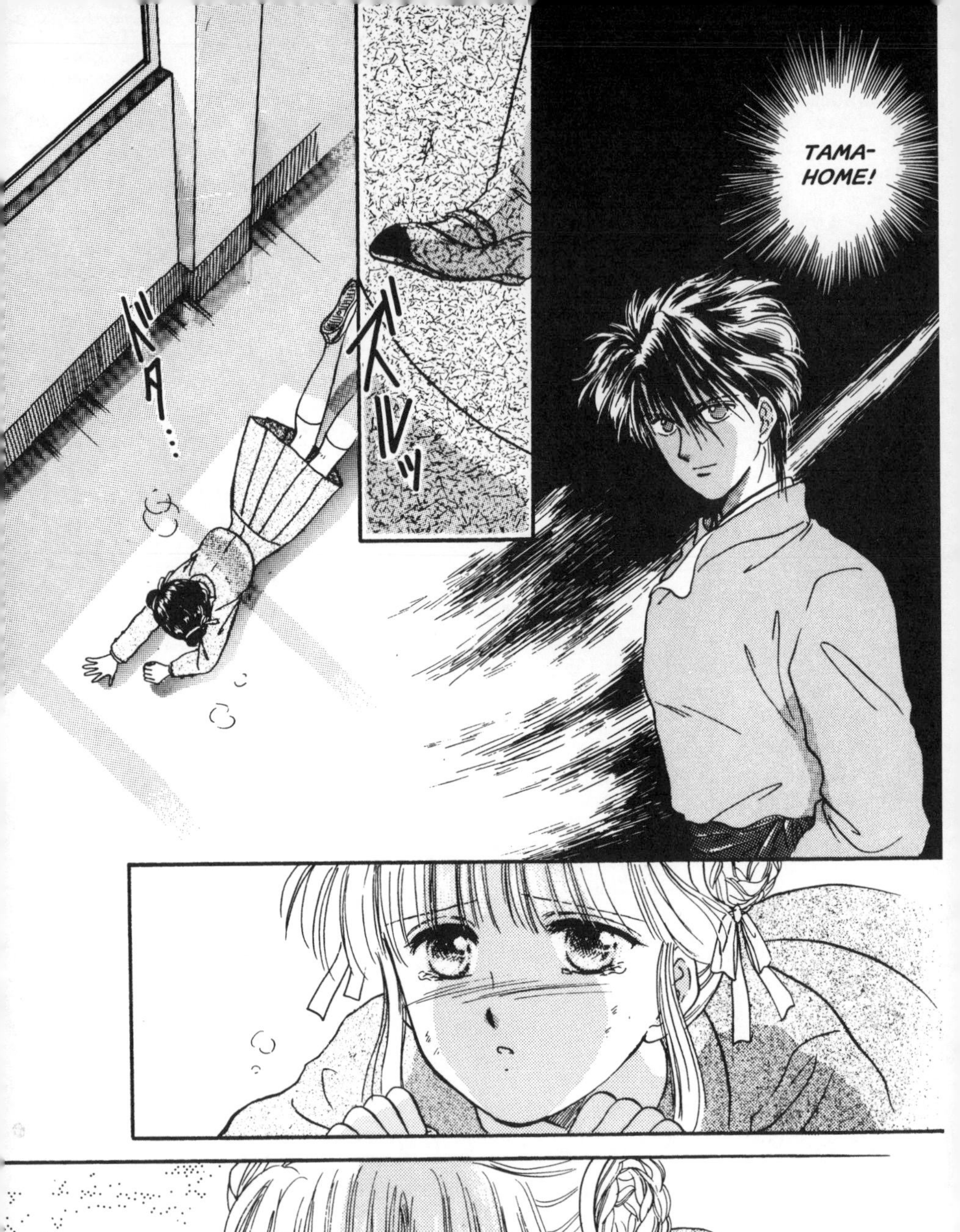
TAMA-
HOME!
ズルッ
ドサ…
HE
ISNT...
...HERE.

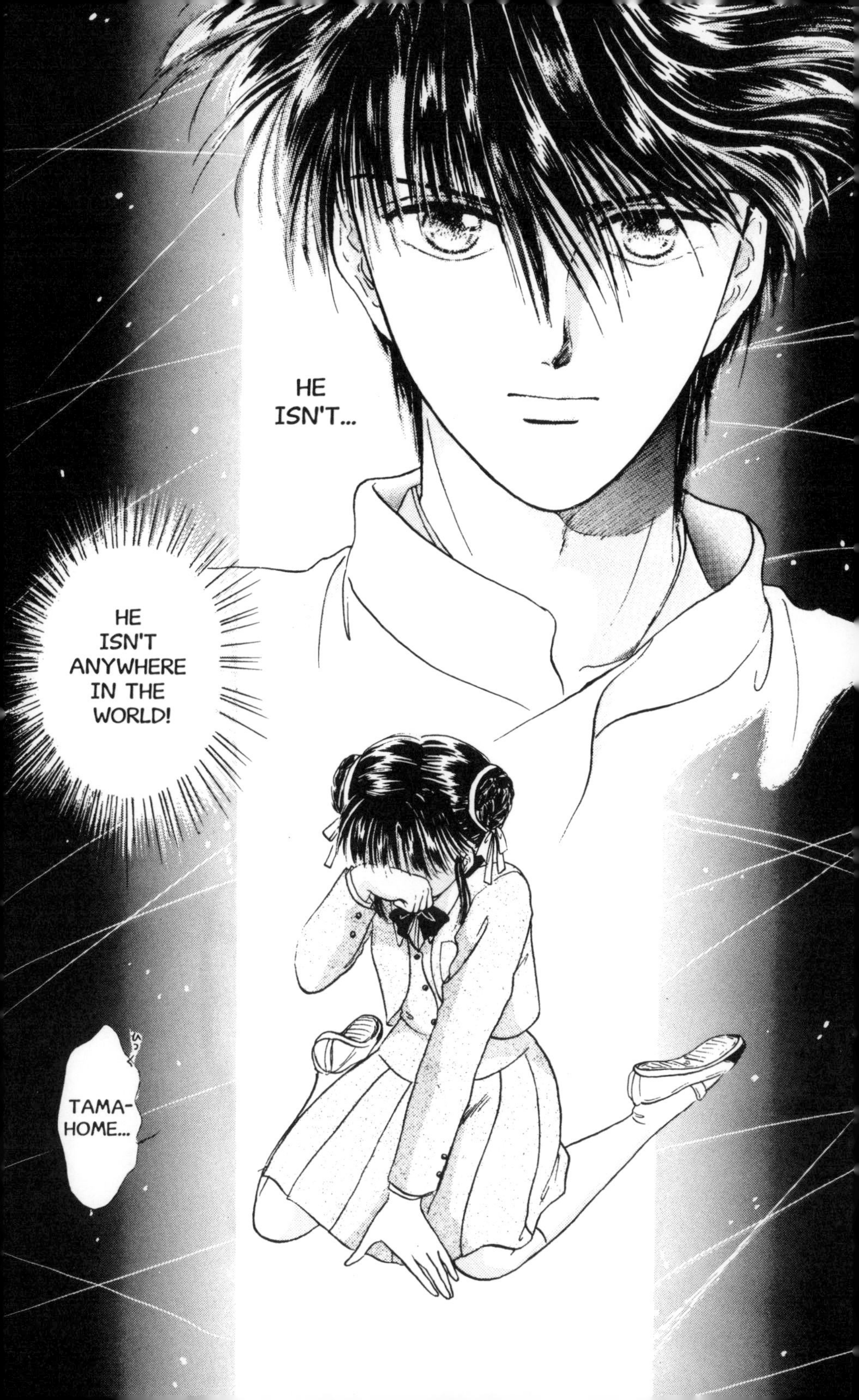
HE ISN'T...
HE ISN'T ANYWHERE IN THE WORLD!
TAMA-HOME...

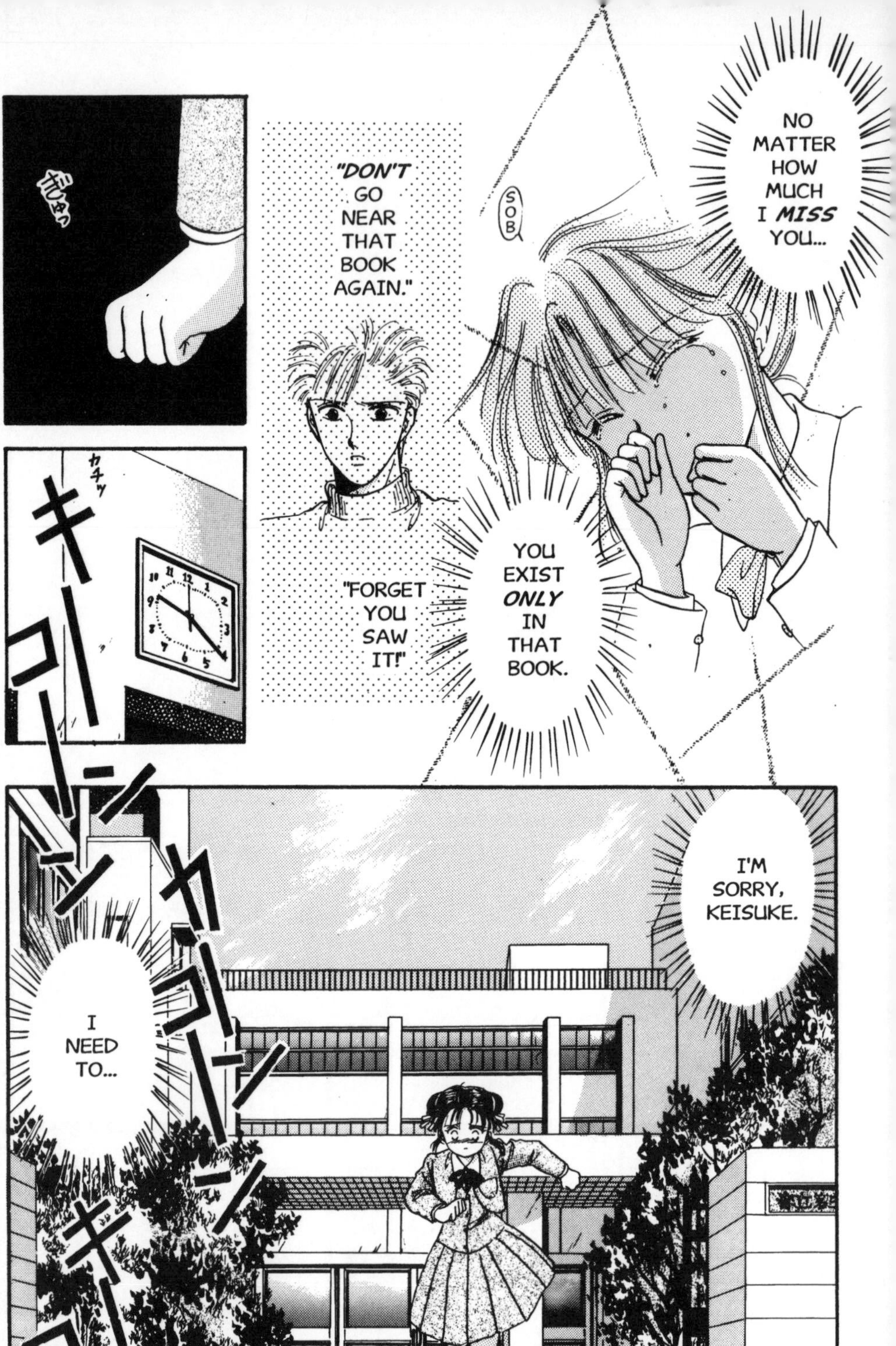
NO MATTER HOW MUCH I *MISS* YOU...
SOB
"*DON'T* GO NEAR THAT BOOK AGAIN."
YOU EXIST *ONLY* IN THAT BOOK.
"FORGET YOU SAW IT!"
ぎゅっ
カチッ
I'M SORRY, KEISUKE.
I NEED TO...

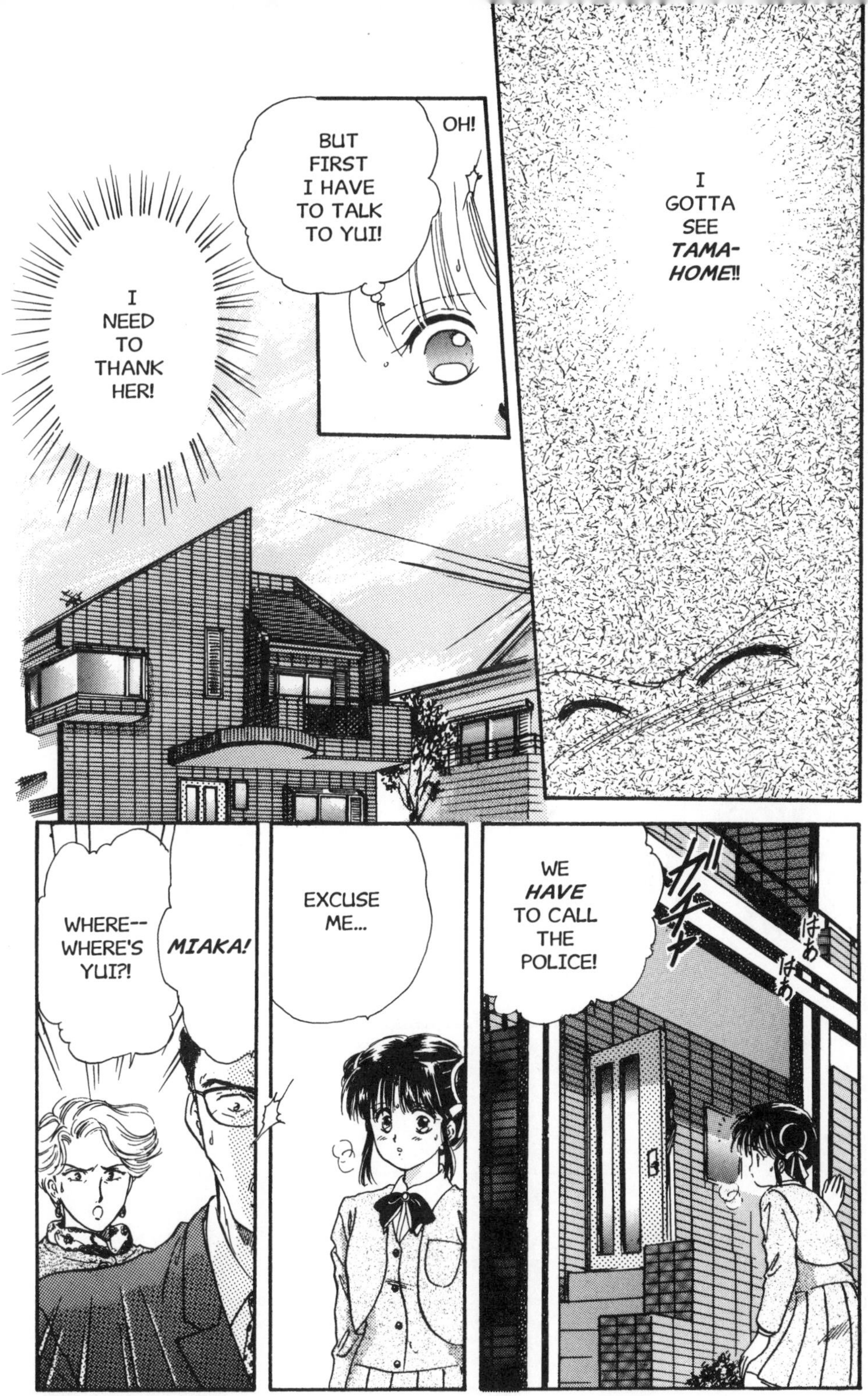
I GOTTA SEE TAMA-HOME!!
OH!
BUT FIRST I HAVE TO TALK TO YUI!
I NEED TO THANK HER!
WE HAVE TO CALL THE POLICE!
はあ はあ
EXCUSE ME...
MIAKA!
WHERE--WHERE'S YUI?!

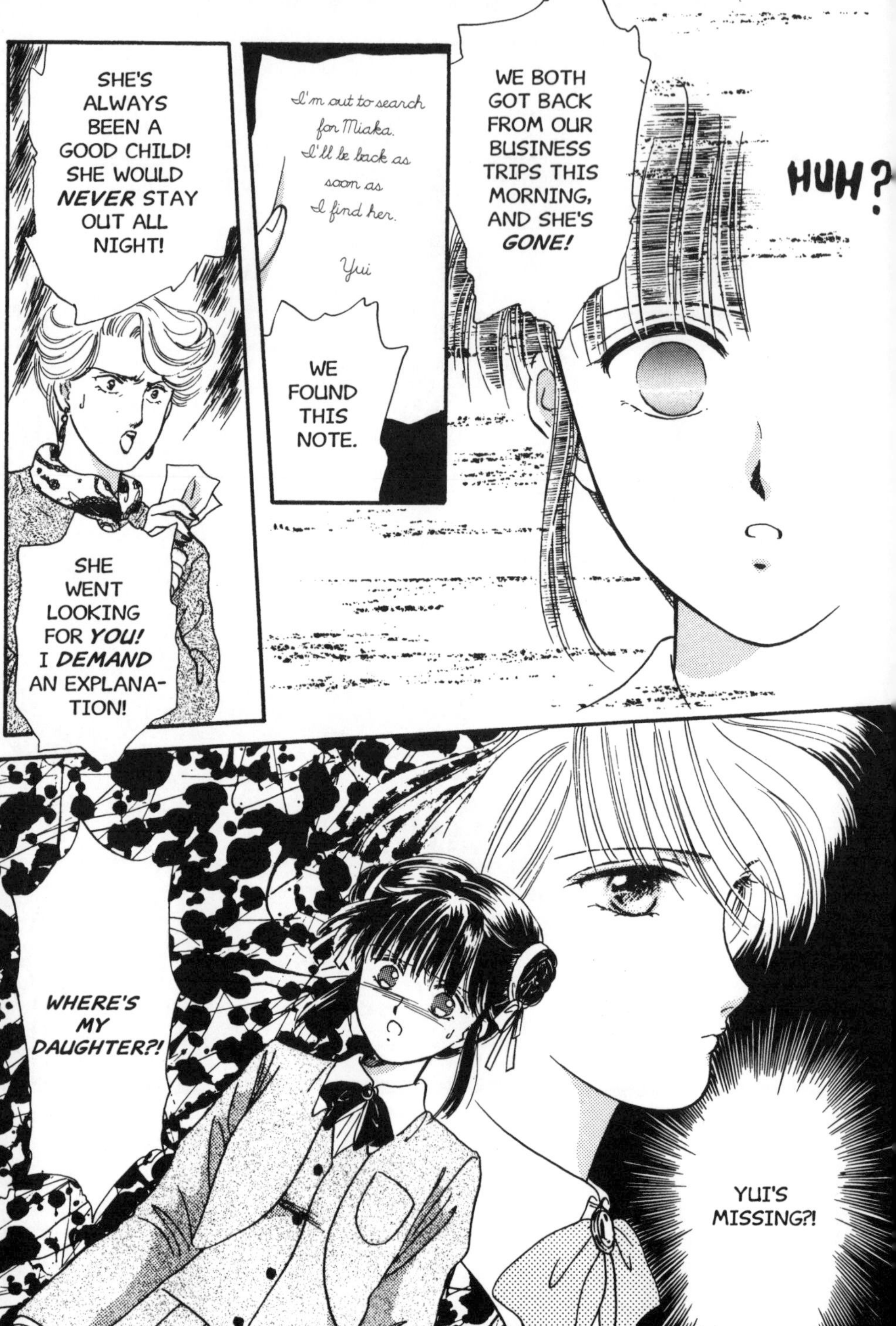

WE BOTH GOT BACK FROM OUR BUSINESS TRIPS THIS MORNING, AND SHE'S ***GONE!***
HUH?
I'm out to search for Miaka. I'll be back as soon as I find her.
Yui
WE FOUND THIS NOTE.
SHE'S ALWAYS BEEN A GOOD CHILD! SHE WOULD ***NEVER*** STAY OUT ALL NIGHT!
SHE WENT LOOKING FOR ***YOU!*** I ***DEMAND*** AN EXPLANATION!
YUI'S MISSING?!
WHERE'S MY DAUGHTER?!

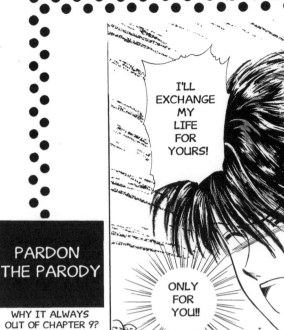

PARDON THE PARODY

WHY IT ALWAYS OUT OF CHAPTER 9?

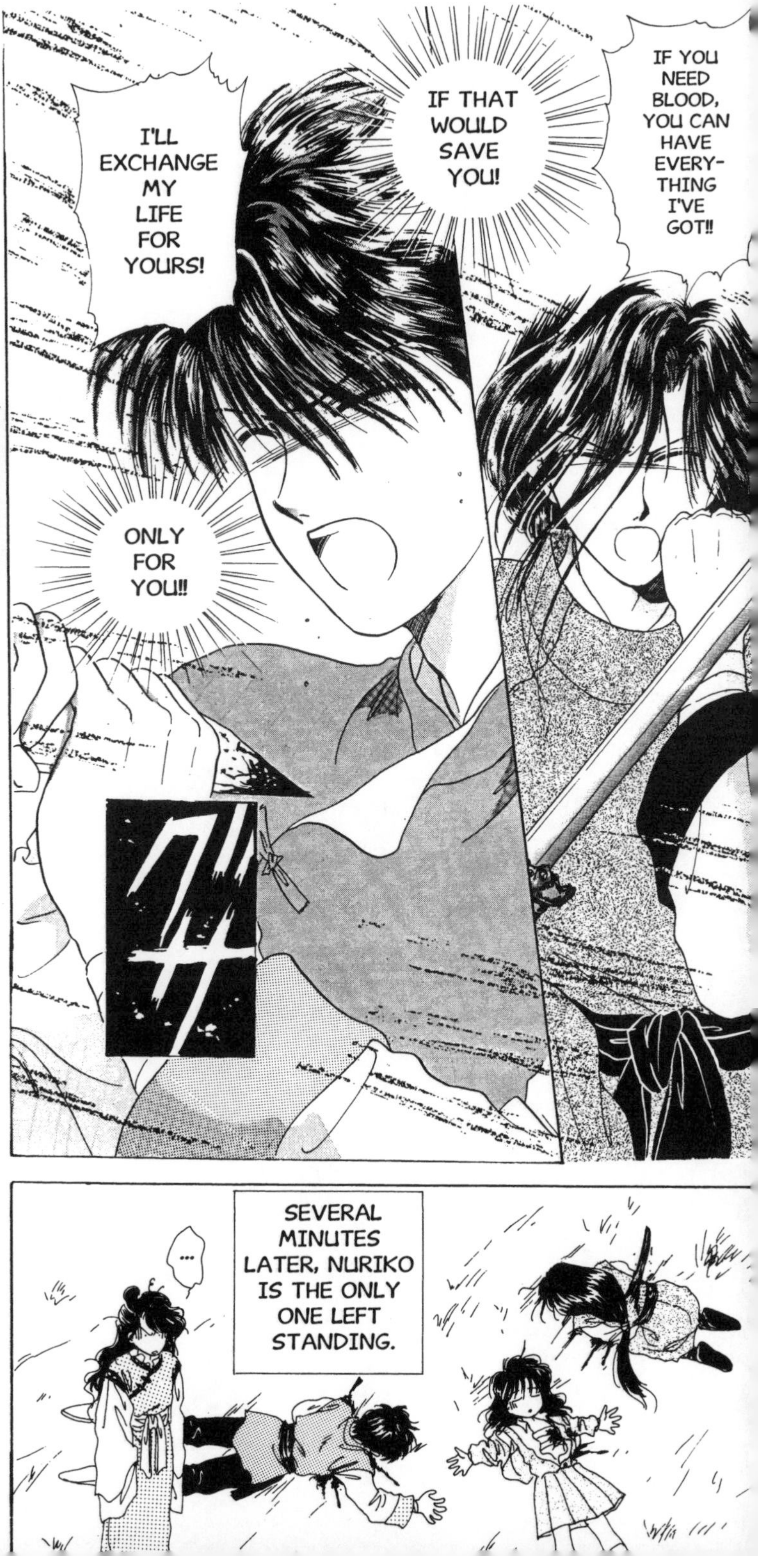
IF YOU NEED BLOOD, YOU CAN HAVE EVERY-THING I'VE GOT!!
IF THAT WOULD SAVE YOU!
I'LL EXCHANGE MY LIFE FOR YOURS!
ONLY FOR YOU!!
グサ
SEVERAL MINUTES LATER, NURIKO IS THE ONLY ONE LEFT STANDING.
...

BY Y. W. (MANGA ARTIST)

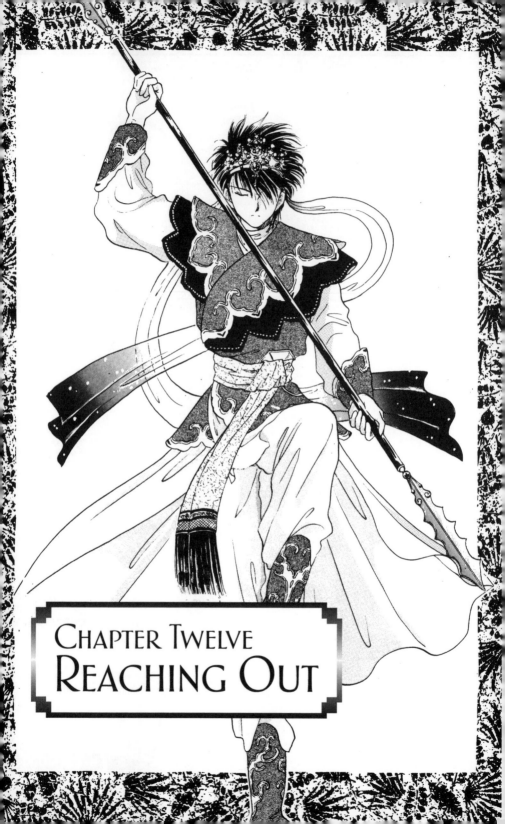

CHAPTER TWELVE
REACHING OUT

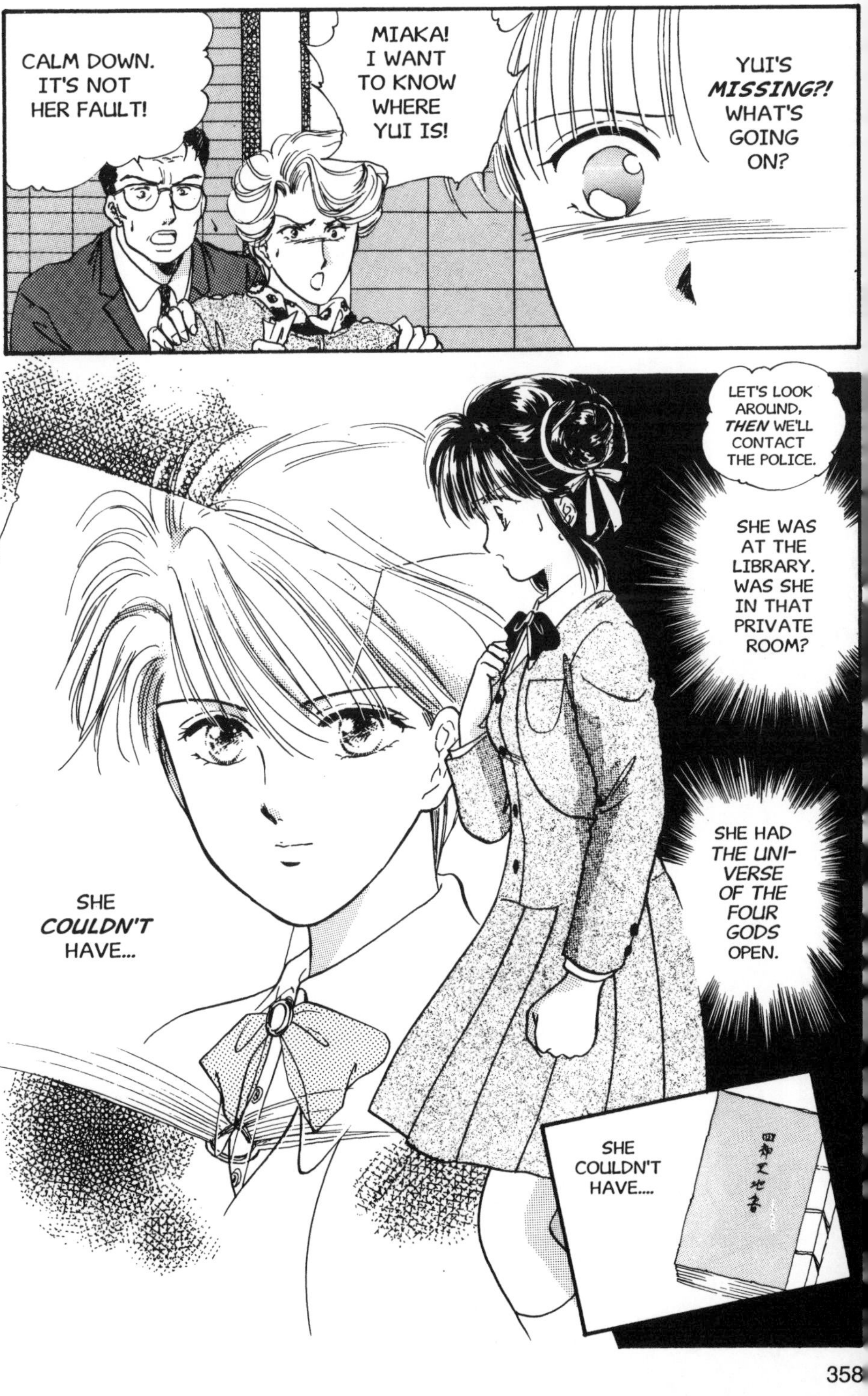
YUI'S *MISSING?!* WHAT'S GOING ON?
MIAKA! I WANT TO KNOW WHERE YUI IS!
CALM DOWN. IT'S NOT HER FAULT!
LET'S LOOK AROUND, *THEN* WE'LL CONTACT THE POLICE.
SHE WAS AT THE LIBRARY. WAS SHE IN THAT PRIVATE ROOM?
SHE HAD *THE UNIVERSE OF THE FOUR GODS* OPEN.
SHE *COULDN'T* HAVE...
SHE COULDN'T HAVE....

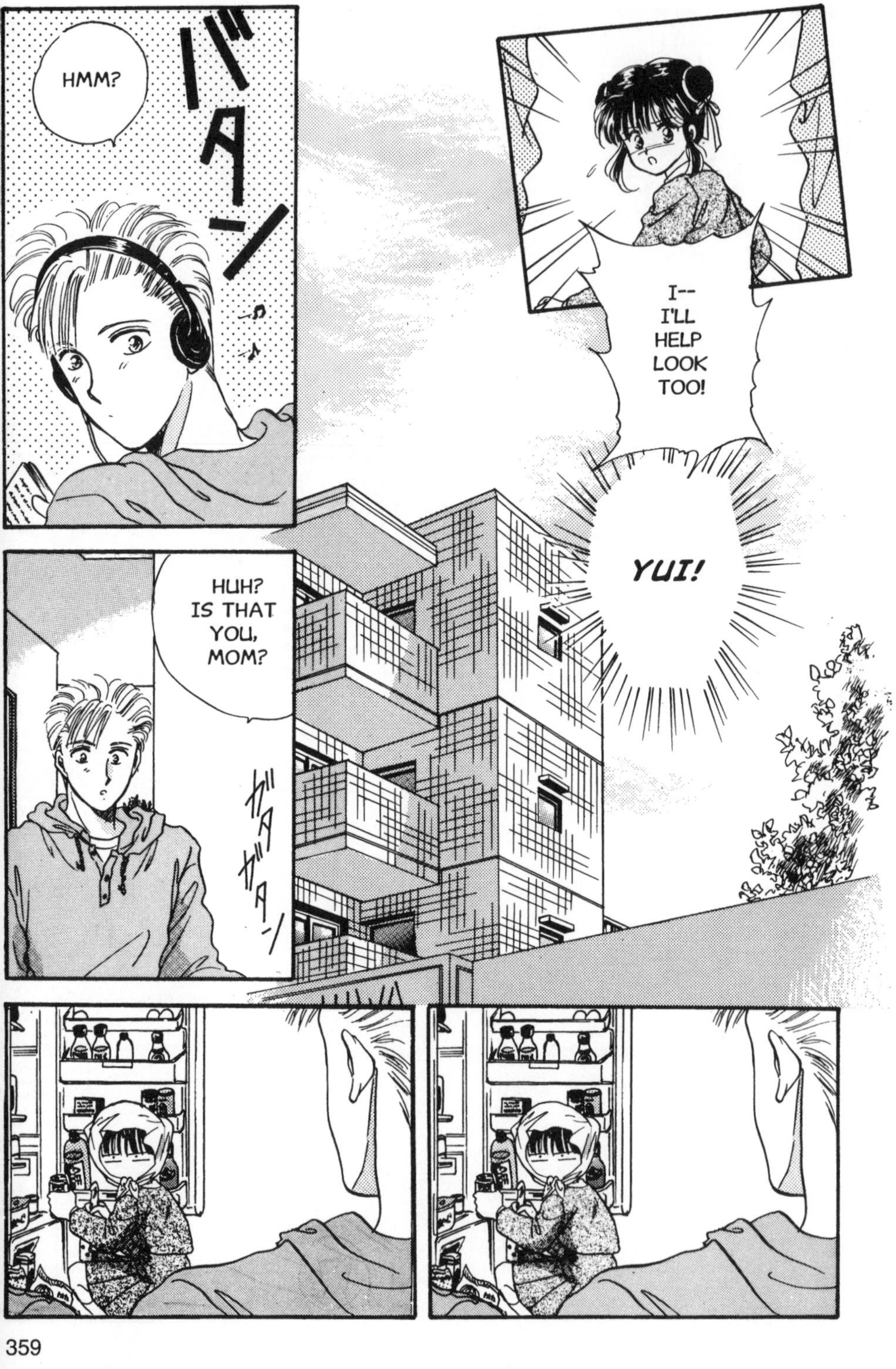
I-- I'LL HELP LOOK TOO!
HMM?
バターン
YUI!
HUH? IS THAT YOU, MOM?
ガタガタン

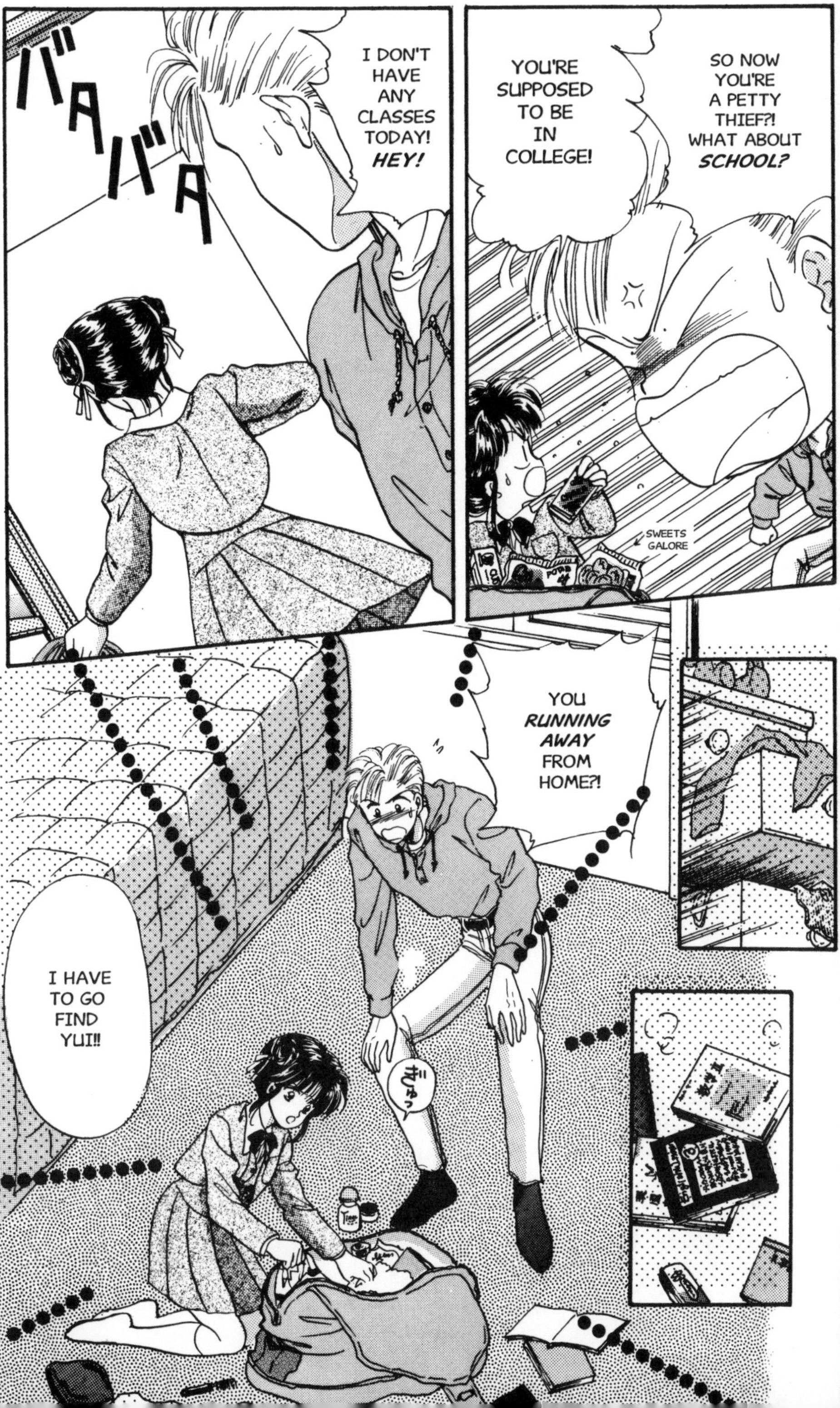
SO NOW YOU'RE A PETTY THIEF?! WHAT ABOUT *SCHOOL?*
YOU'RE SUPPOSED TO BE IN COLLEGE!
SWEETS GALORE
I DON'T HAVE ANY CLASSES TODAY! *HEY!*
バタバタ
YOU *RUNNING AWAY* FROM HOME?!
I HAVE TO GO FIND YUI!!

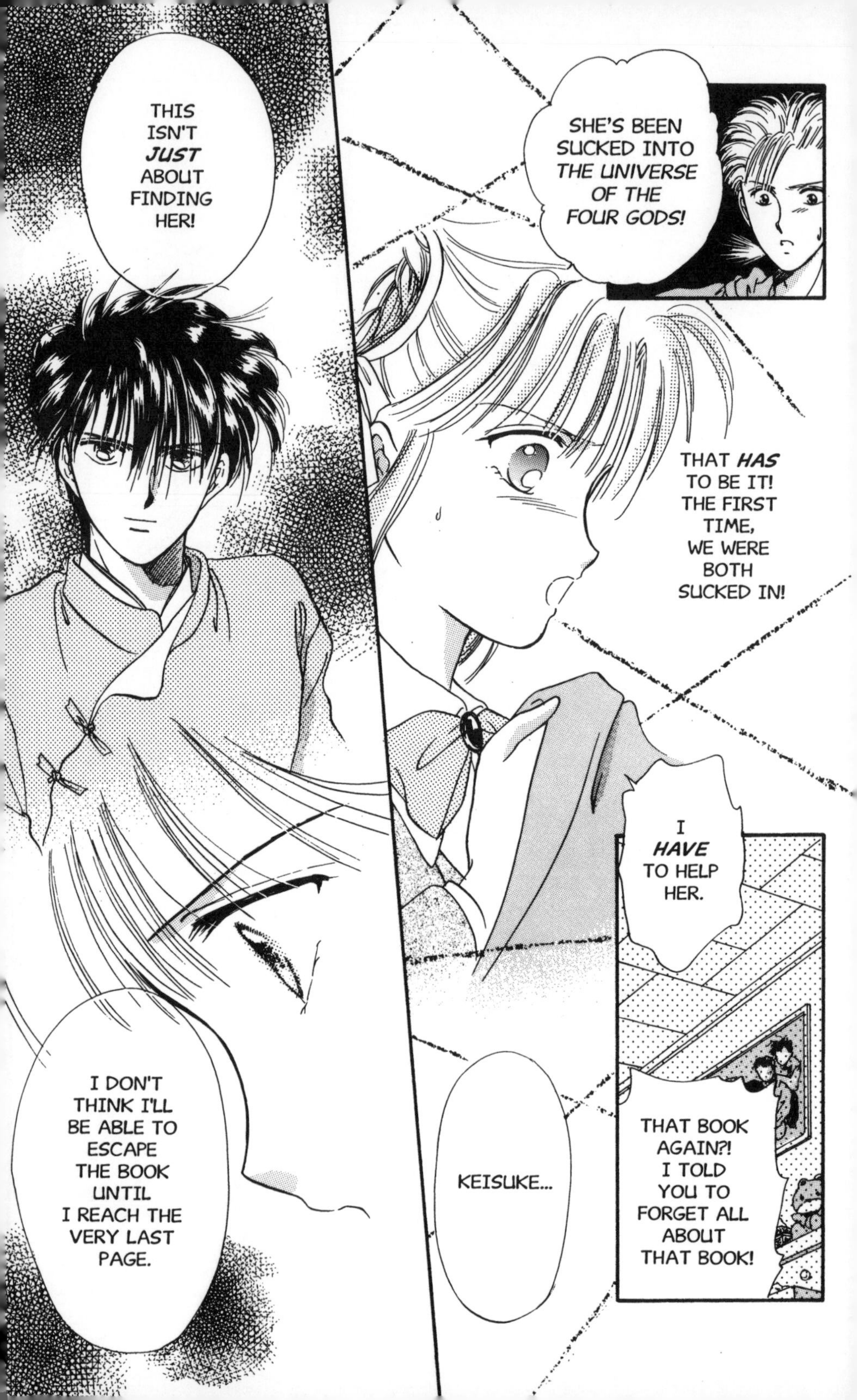
SHE'S BEEN SUCKED INTO THE UNIVERSE OF THE FOUR GODS!
THAT HAS TO BE IT! THE FIRST TIME, WE WERE BOTH SUCKED IN!
I HAVE TO HELP HER.
THAT BOOK AGAIN?! I TOLD YOU TO FORGET ALL ABOUT THAT BOOK!
KEISUKE...
THIS ISN'T JUST ABOUT FINDING HER!
I DON'T THINK I'LL BE ABLE TO ESCAPE THE BOOK UNTIL I REACH THE VERY LAST PAGE.

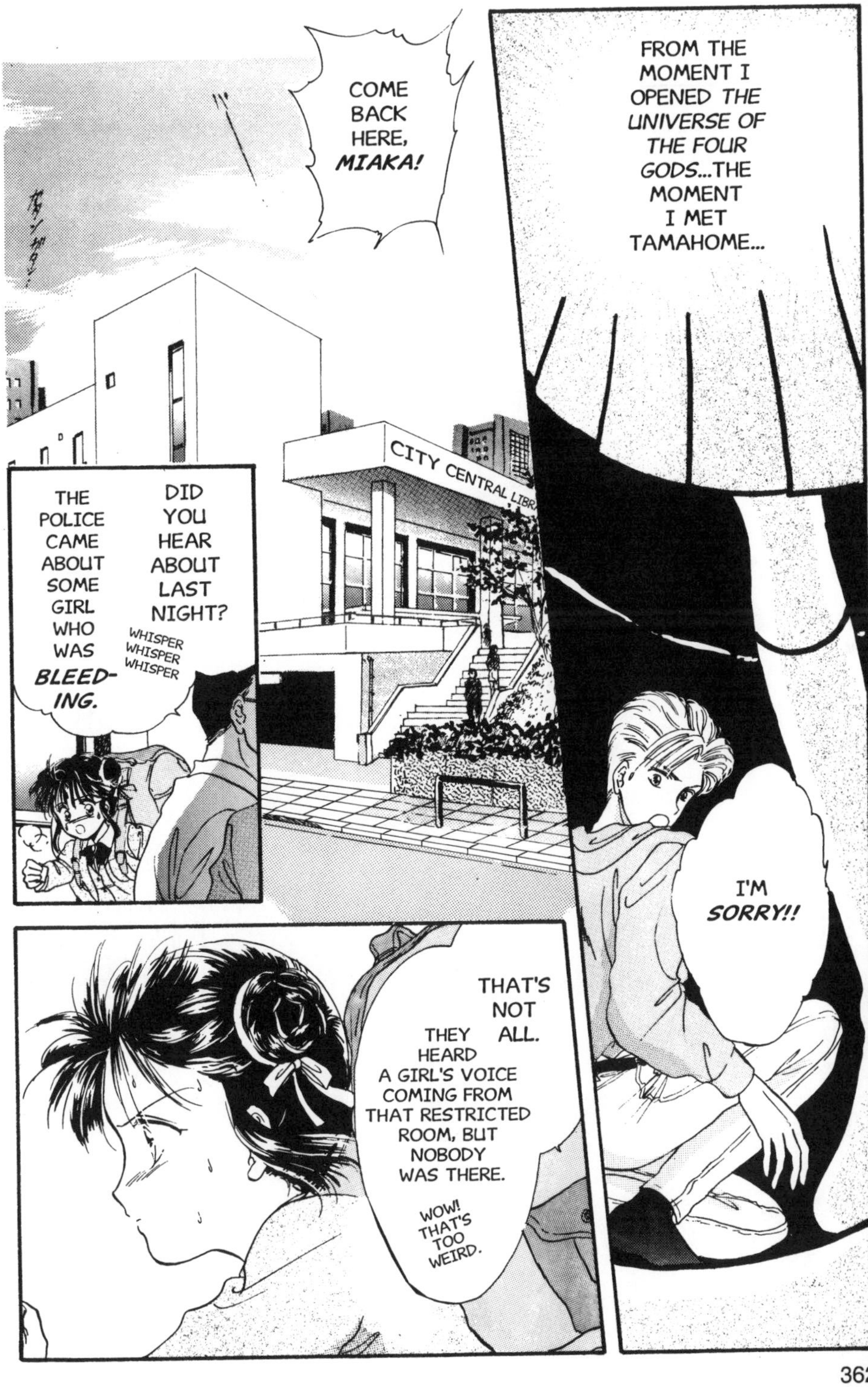
FROM THE MOMENT I OPENED *THE UNIVERSE OF THE FOUR GODS*...THE MOMENT I MET TAMAHOME...
I'M *SORRY!!*
COME BACK HERE, *MIAKA!*
CITY CENTRAL LIBR
DID YOU HEAR ABOUT LAST NIGHT?
WHISPER WHISPER WHISPER
THE POLICE CAME ABOUT SOME GIRL WHO WAS *BLEED-ING.*
THAT'S NOT ALL. THEY HEARD A GIRL'S VOICE COMING FROM THAT RESTRICTED ROOM, BUT NOBODY WAS THERE.
WOW! THAT'S TOO WEIRD.

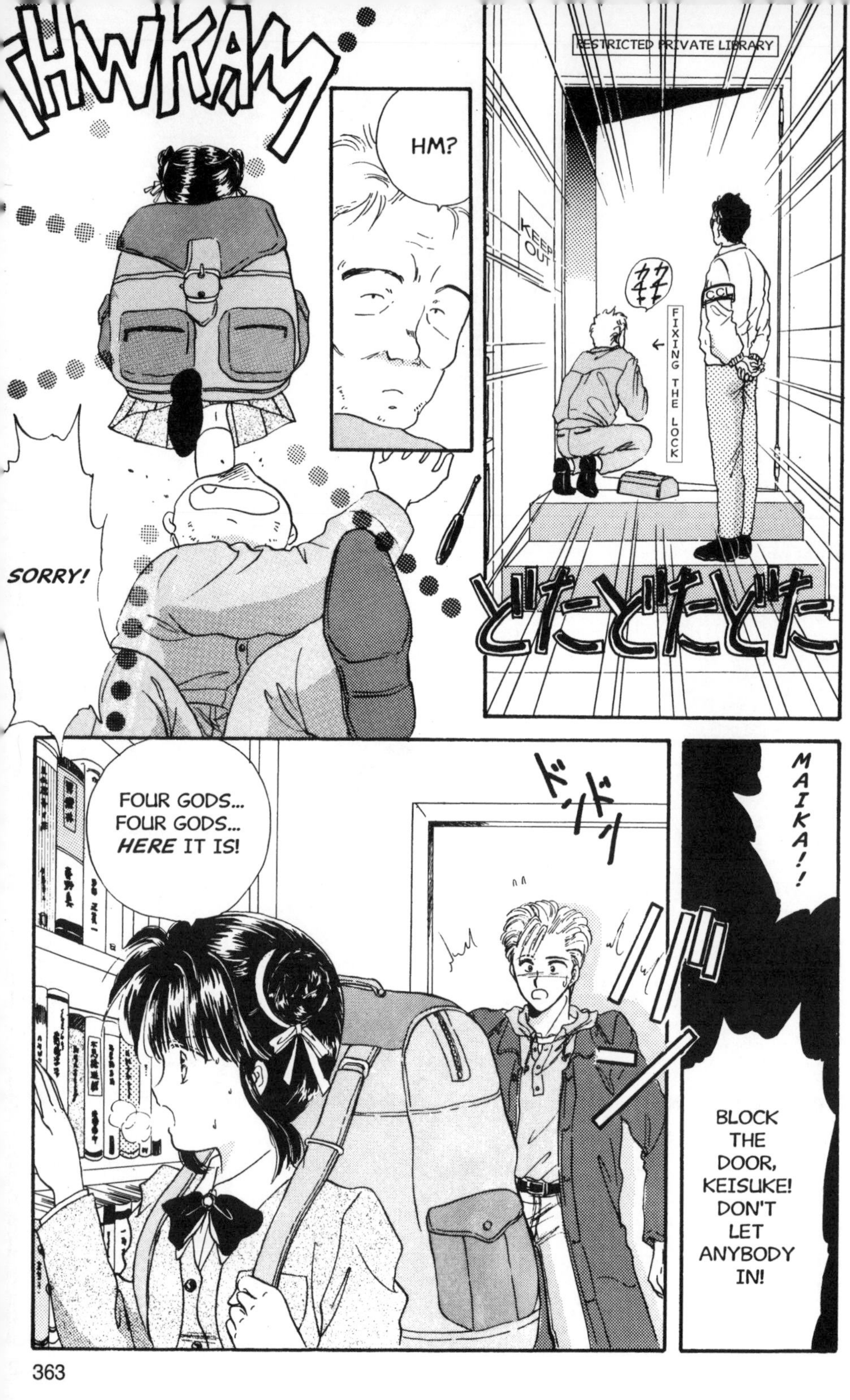
RESTRICTED PRIVATE LIBRARY
KEEP OUT
FIXING THE LOCK
どたーどたーどた
HM?
SORRY!
MAIKA!!
BLOCK THE DOOR, KEISUKE! DON'T LET ANYBODY IN!
ドッドッ
FOUR GODS... FOUR GODS... HERE IT IS!

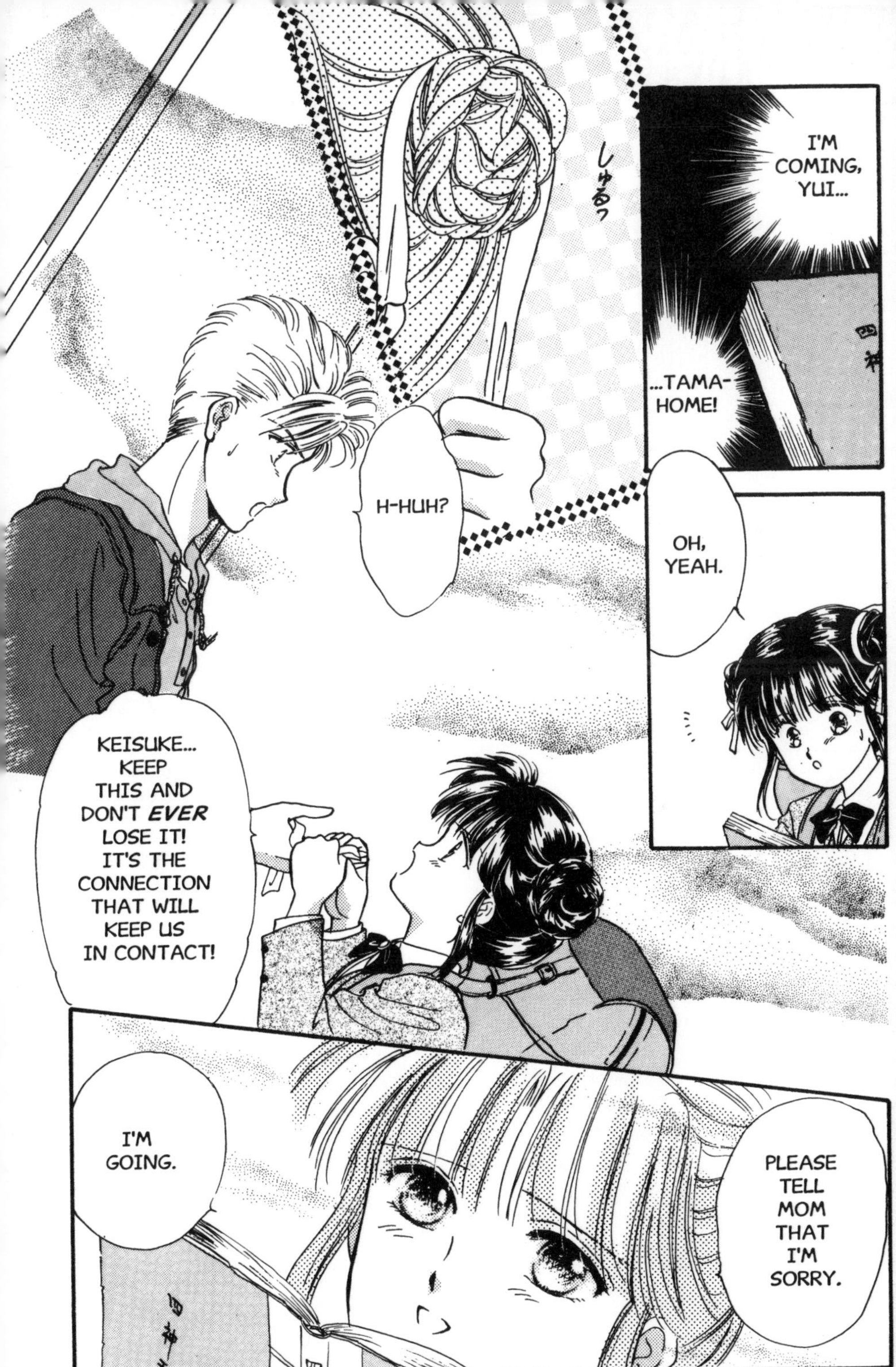
I'M COMING, YUI...
...TAMA-HOME!
OH, YEAH.
しゅるっ
H-HUH?
KEISUKE... KEEP THIS AND DON'T *EVER* LOSE IT! IT'S THE CONNECTION THAT WILL KEEP US IN CONTACT!
PLEASE TELL MOM THAT I'M SORRY.
I'M GOING.

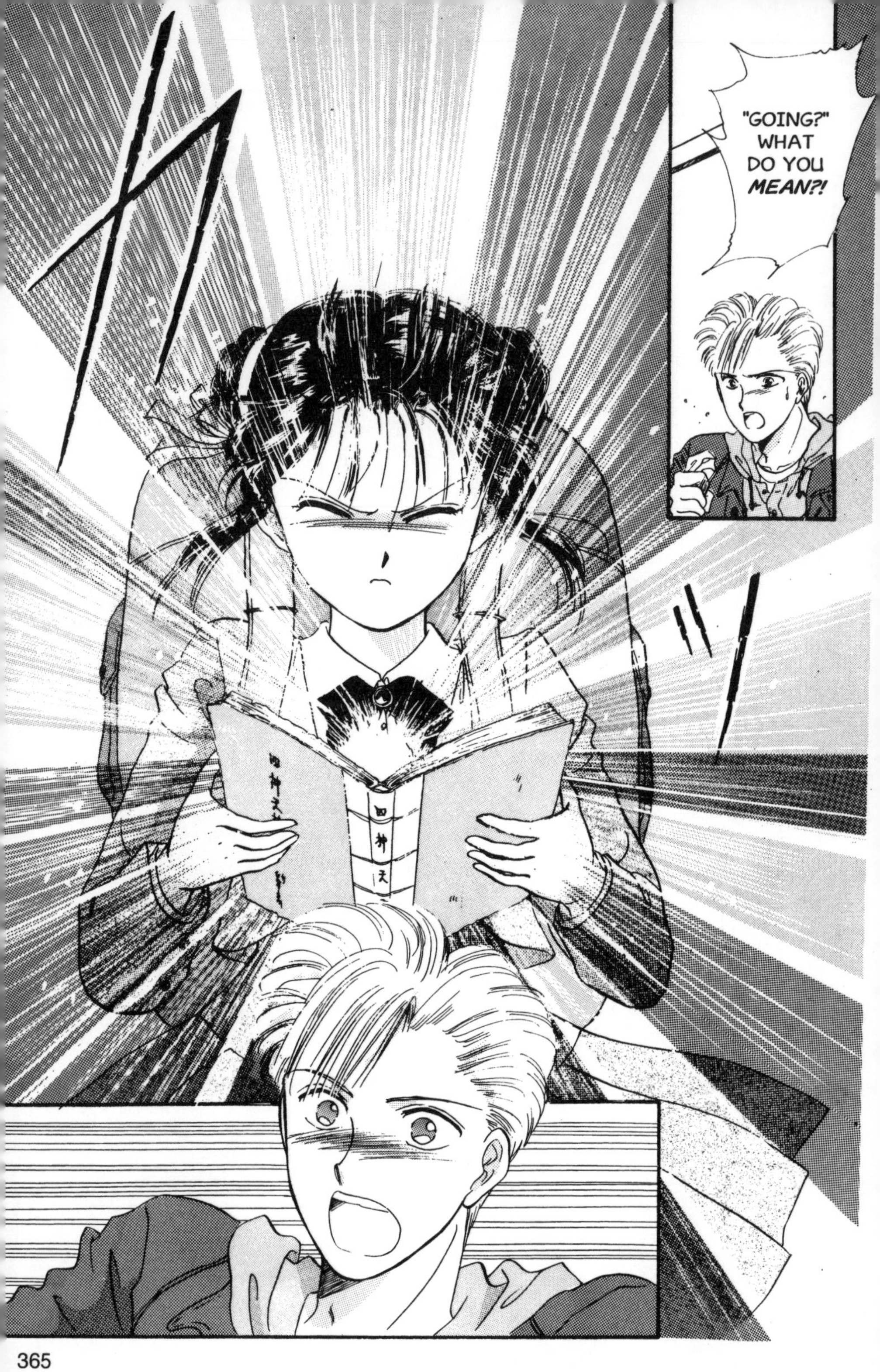
"GOING?" WHAT DO YOU *MEAN?!*

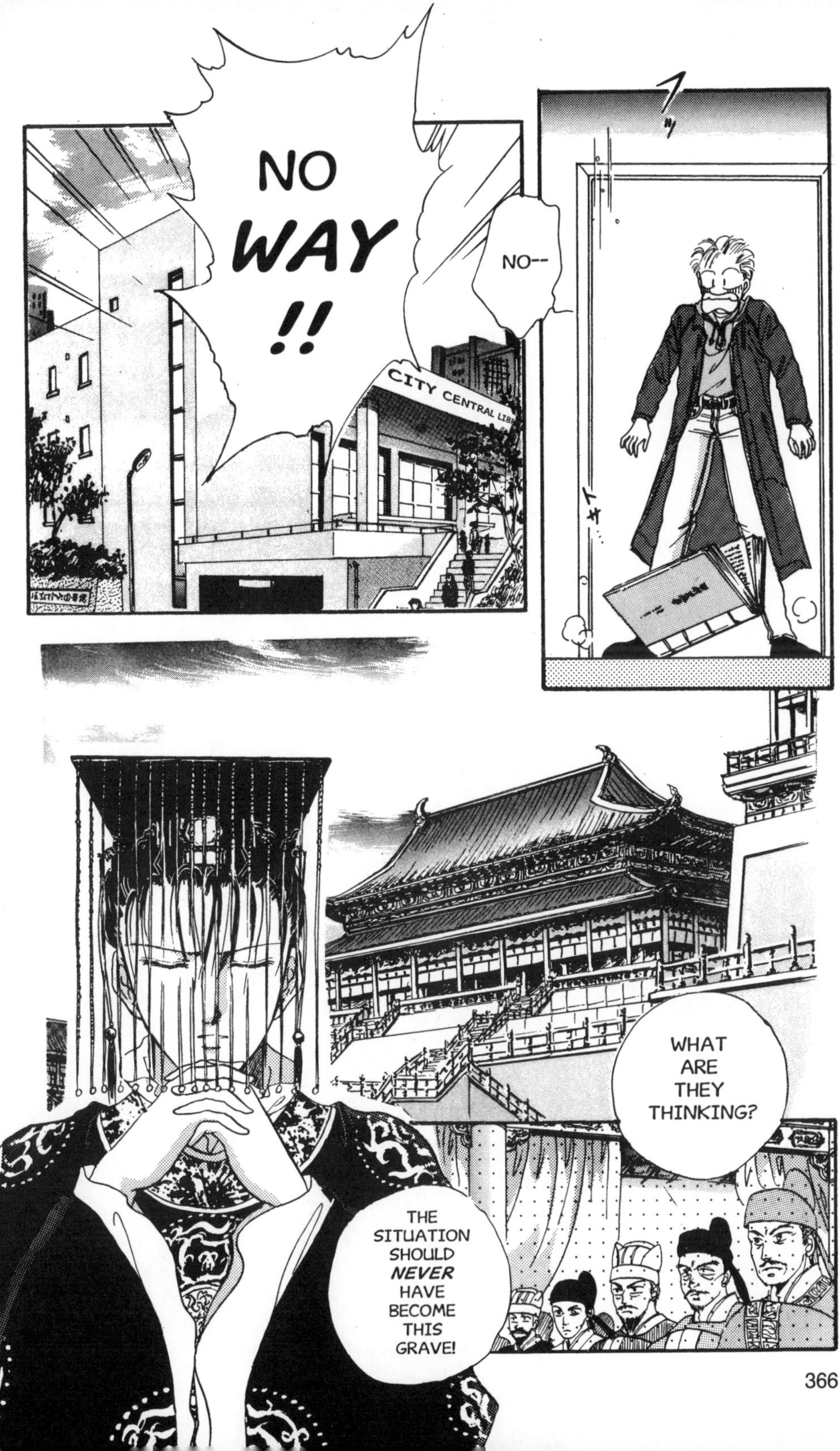
NO--
NO WAY!!
CITY CENTRAL LIB
WHAT ARE THEY THINKING?
THE SITUATION SHOULD NEVER HAVE BECOME THIS GRAVE!

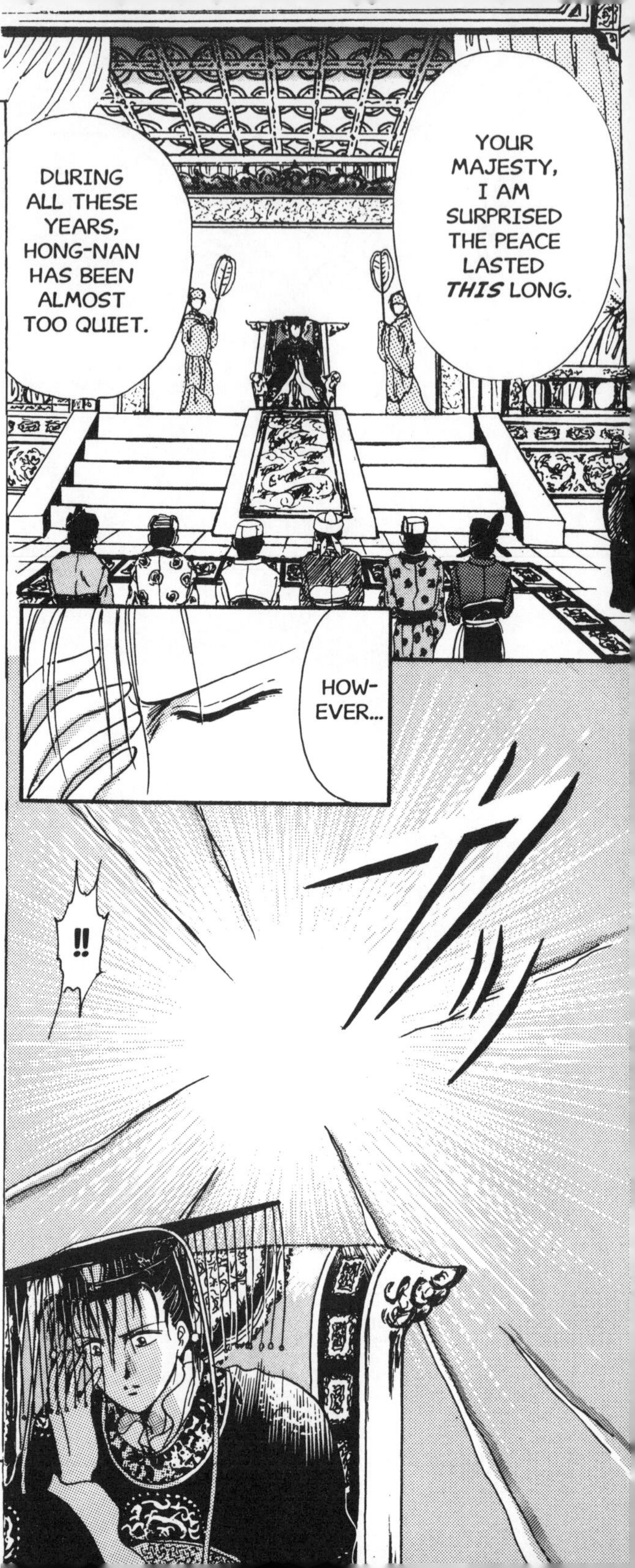
YOUR MAJESTY, I AM SURPRISED THE PEACE LASTED *THIS* LONG.
DURING ALL THESE YEARS, HONG-NAN HAS BEEN ALMOST TOO QUIET.
HOW-EVER...
!!

While Asuka has suffered through many hard times, the only hardship for Miaka is studying for the entrance exams (which are pretty hard, to be sure). She has a nice brother; she's carefree and childish. That's why she'll never have the same mature quality Asuka has. I was wondering why this was, only to realize that they had different upbringings, so their personalities would have to differ. I surprised myself. My protagonists are all the same in their energy and positive outlook. But in terms of her naïveté, Miaka is just an average junior high school girl. Unlike Asuka, who soon finds happiness, Miaka's life is going to get worse and worse. She might mature like Asuka as the story comes to a close. But the pain makes them grow, and growth is something I enjoy seeing. It's interesting to see how these characters grow up on their own. It isn't one of the things I plan. By the way, my friends have started to like either Hotohori or Nuriko. Putting Hotohori aside for a moment... They all hated Nuriko when she (he) kissed Tamahome. Later, they started warming up to him, but once they found out he was gay, they disliked him again. Now that's a busy character! Recently, I'm glad to say that I've been hearing from more and more people who like him. I like him a lot! Children don't like reading about crossdressers, but readers who've graduated middle school seem to like that type of character a lot. This story is going to be really long so I'll do my best to make it through to the end. Stick with me, okay? The situation has been pretty hard up to this point, but this was the easy part! Miaka and Tamahome are really going to suffer. But however much they suffer, it's going to be twice as hard on me! You see, I'm just too nice and sweet a person. Ten demerits to anyone who just threw this book on the floor and stomped on it.

To be continued in the next issue!!

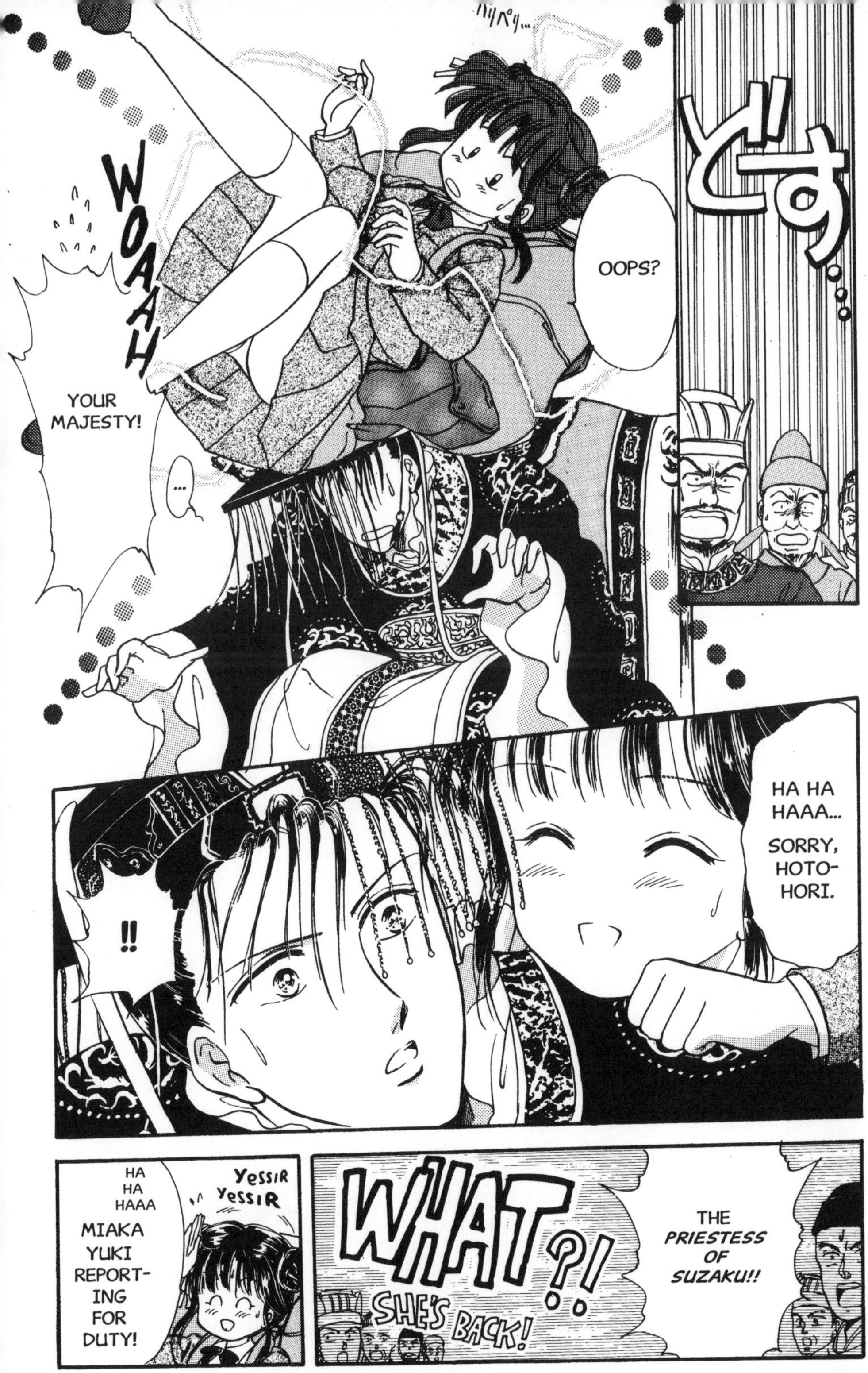
どす…
OOPS?
WOAAAH
YOUR MAJESTY!
...
HA HA HAAA... SORRY, HOTOHORI.
!!
THE *PRIESTESS OF SUZAKU!!*
WHAT?!
SHE'S BACK!
HA HA HAAA
Yessir Yessir
MIAKA YUKI REPORTING FOR DUTY!

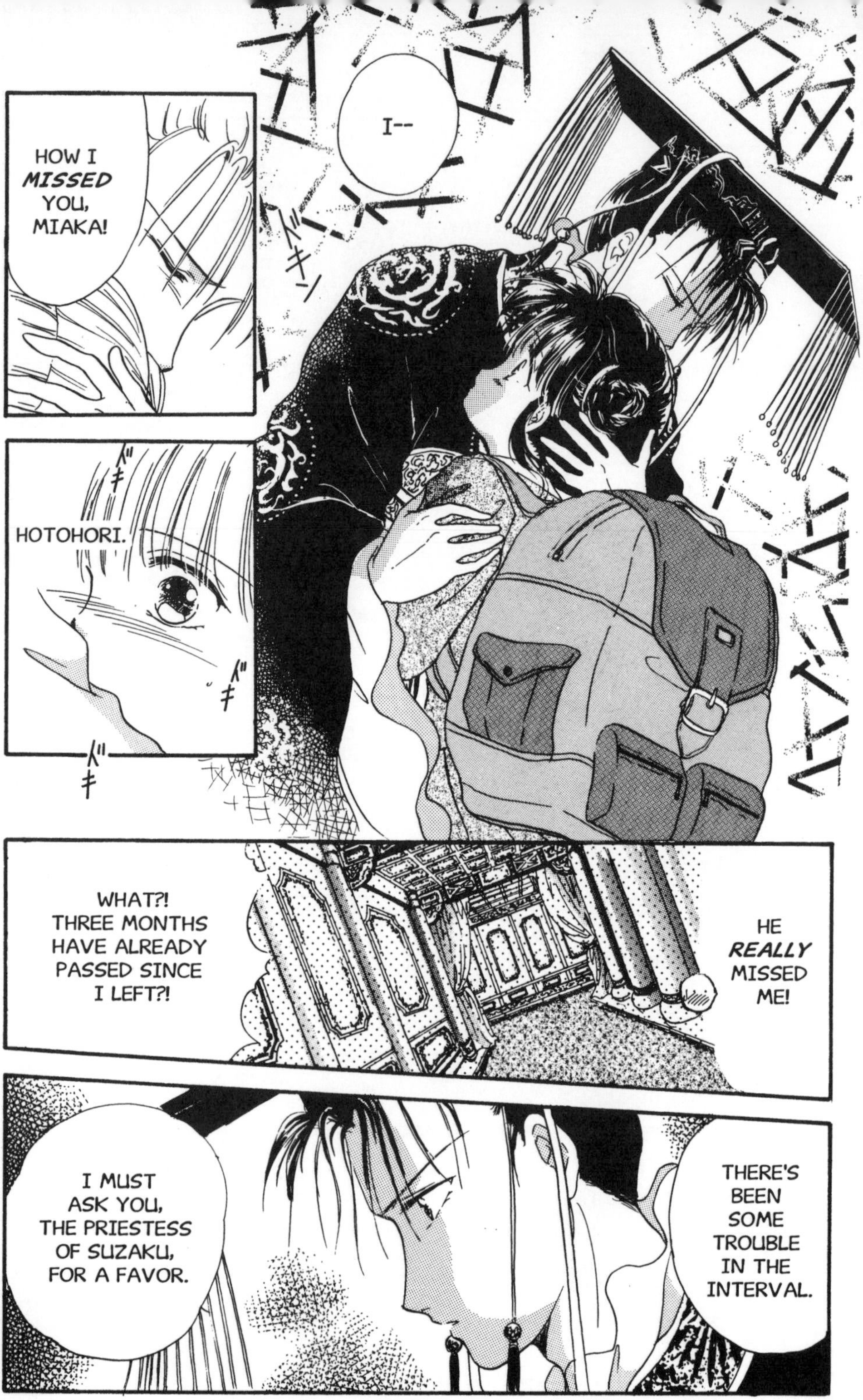
I--
HOW I MISSED YOU, MIAKA!
HOTOHORI.
HE REALLY MISSED ME!
WHAT?! THREE MONTHS HAVE ALREADY PASSED SINCE I LEFT?!
THERE'S BEEN SOME TROUBLE IN THE INTERVAL.
I MUST ASK YOU, THE PRIESTESS OF SUZAKU, FOR A FAVOR.

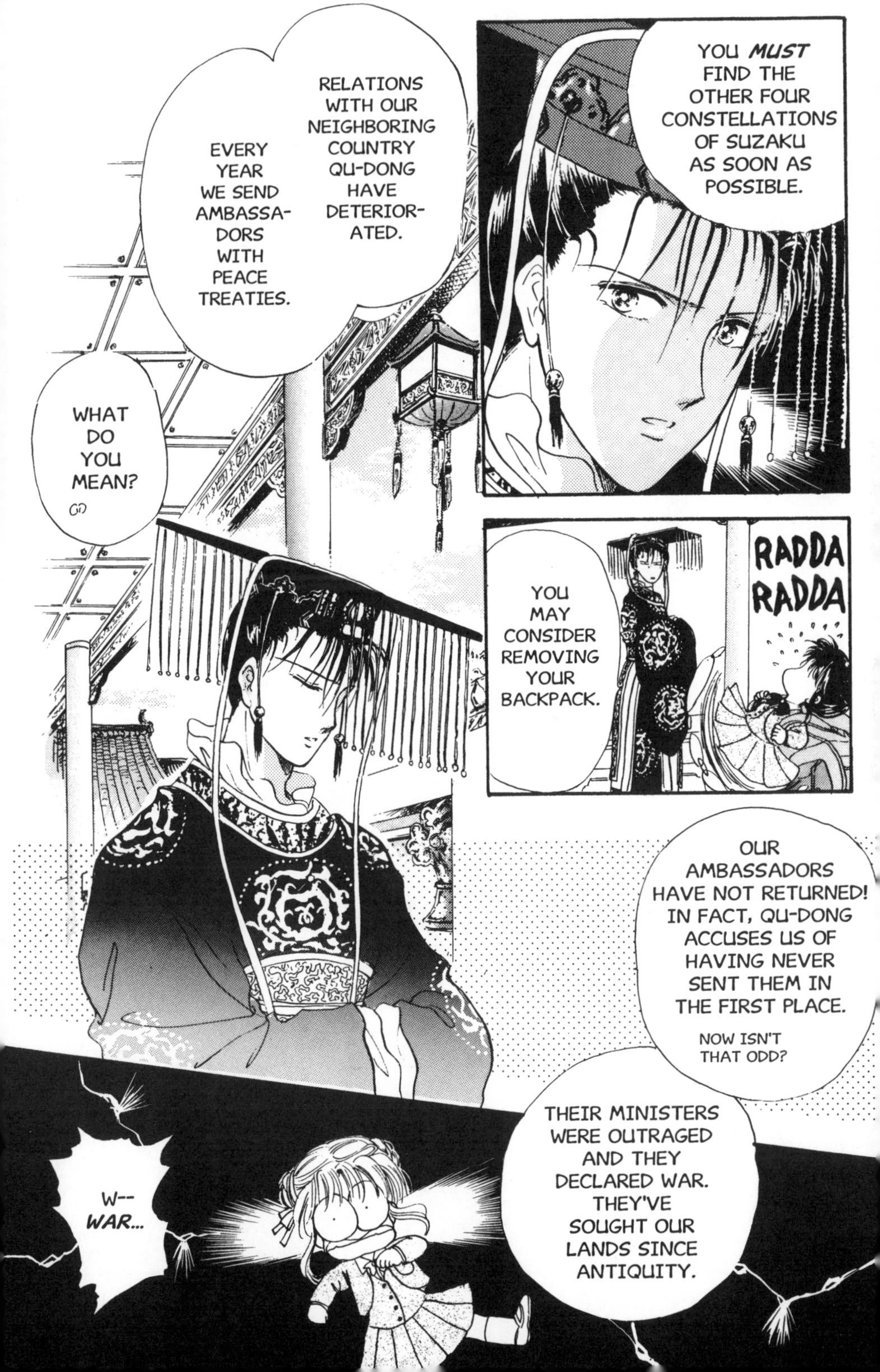
YOU *MUST* FIND THE OTHER FOUR CONSTELLATIONS OF SUZAKU AS SOON AS POSSIBLE.
YOU MAY CONSIDER REMOVING YOUR BACKPACK.
RADDA RADDA
RELATIONS WITH OUR NEIGHBORING COUNTRY QU-DONG HAVE DETERIOR-ATED.
EVERY YEAR WE SEND AMBASSA-DORS WITH PEACE TREATIES.
WHAT DO YOU MEAN?
OUR AMBASSADORS HAVE NOT RETURNED! IN FACT, QU-DONG ACCUSES US OF HAVING NEVER SENT THEM IN THE FIRST PLACE.
NOW ISN'T THAT ODD?
THEIR MINISTERS WERE OUTRAGED AND THEY DECLARED WAR. THEY'VE SOUGHT OUR LANDS SINCE ANTIQUITY.
W-- WAR...

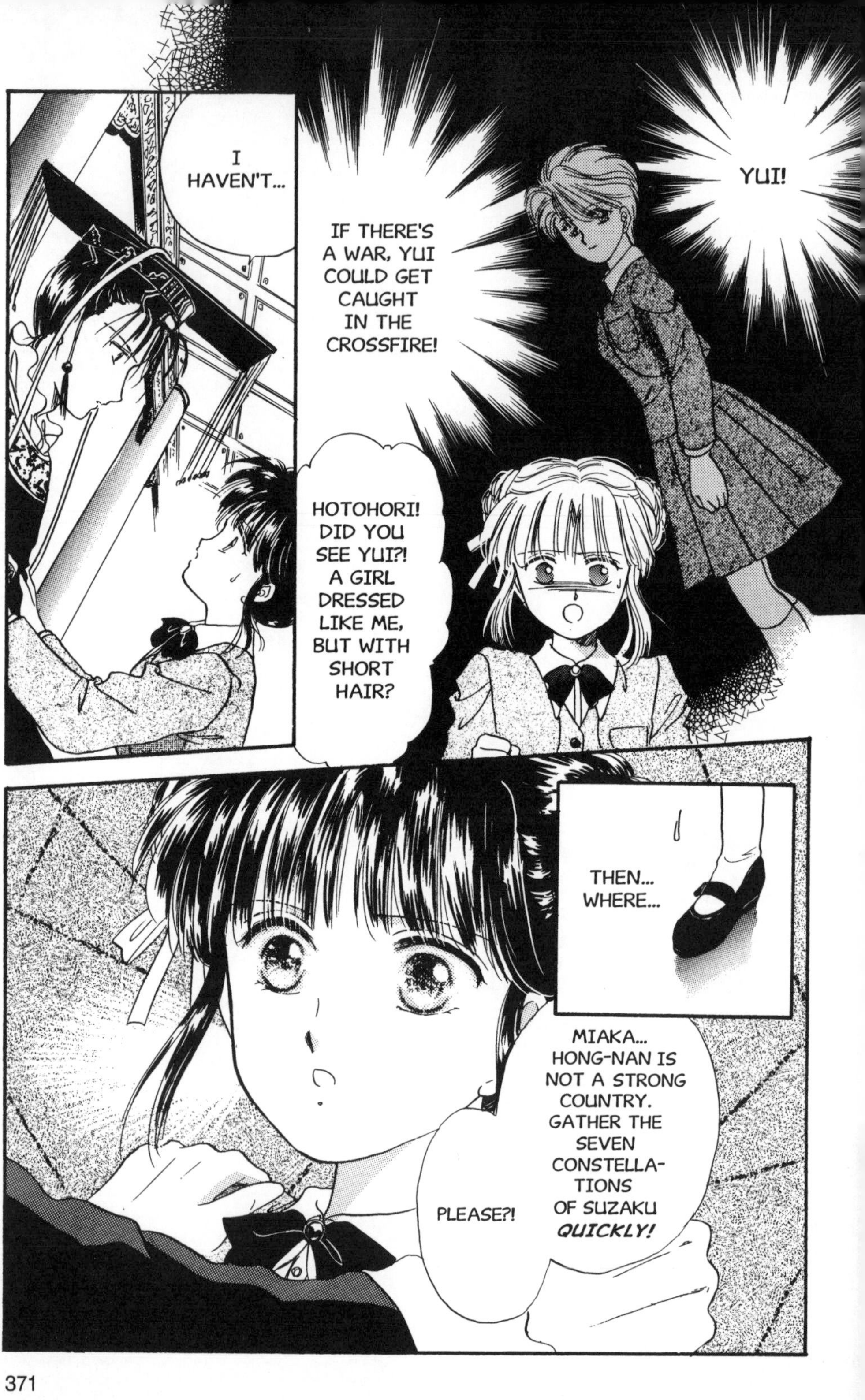
YUI!
IF THERE'S A WAR, YUI COULD GET CAUGHT IN THE CROSSFIRE!
HOTOHORI! DID YOU SEE YUI?! A GIRL DRESSED LIKE ME, BUT WITH SHORT HAIR?
I HAVEN'T...
THEN... WHERE...
MIAKA... HONG-NAN IS NOT A STRONG COUNTRY. GATHER THE SEVEN CONSTELLA-TIONS OF SUZAKU *QUICKLY!*
PLEASE?!

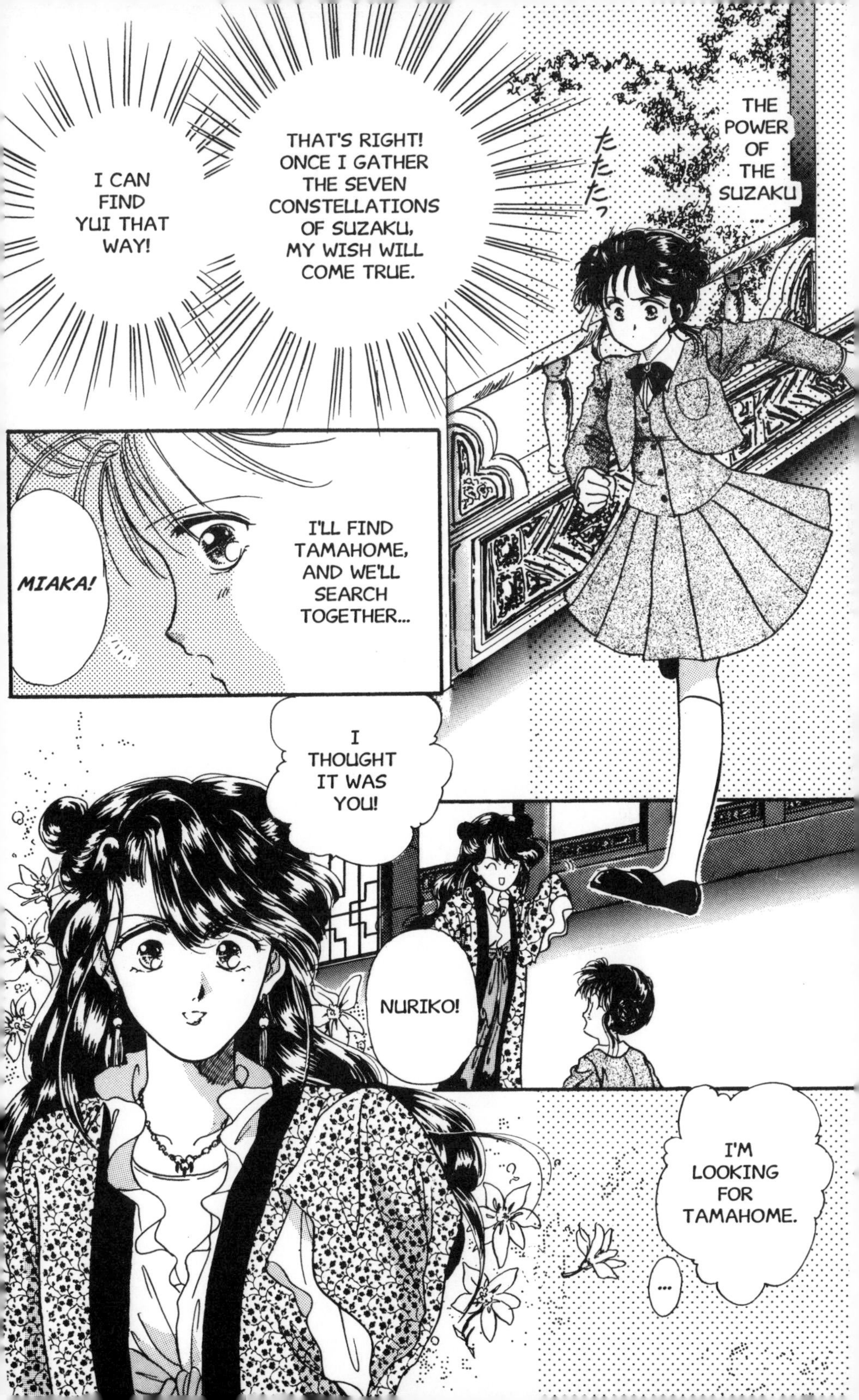
THE POWER OF THE SUZAKU...
たたたっ
THAT'S RIGHT! ONCE I GATHER THE SEVEN CONSTELLATIONS OF SUZAKU, MY WISH WILL COME TRUE.
I CAN FIND YUI THAT WAY!
I'LL FIND TAMAHOME, AND WE'LL SEARCH TOGETHER...
MIAKA!
I THOUGHT IT WAS YOU!
NURIKO!
I'M LOOKING FOR TAMAHOME.
...

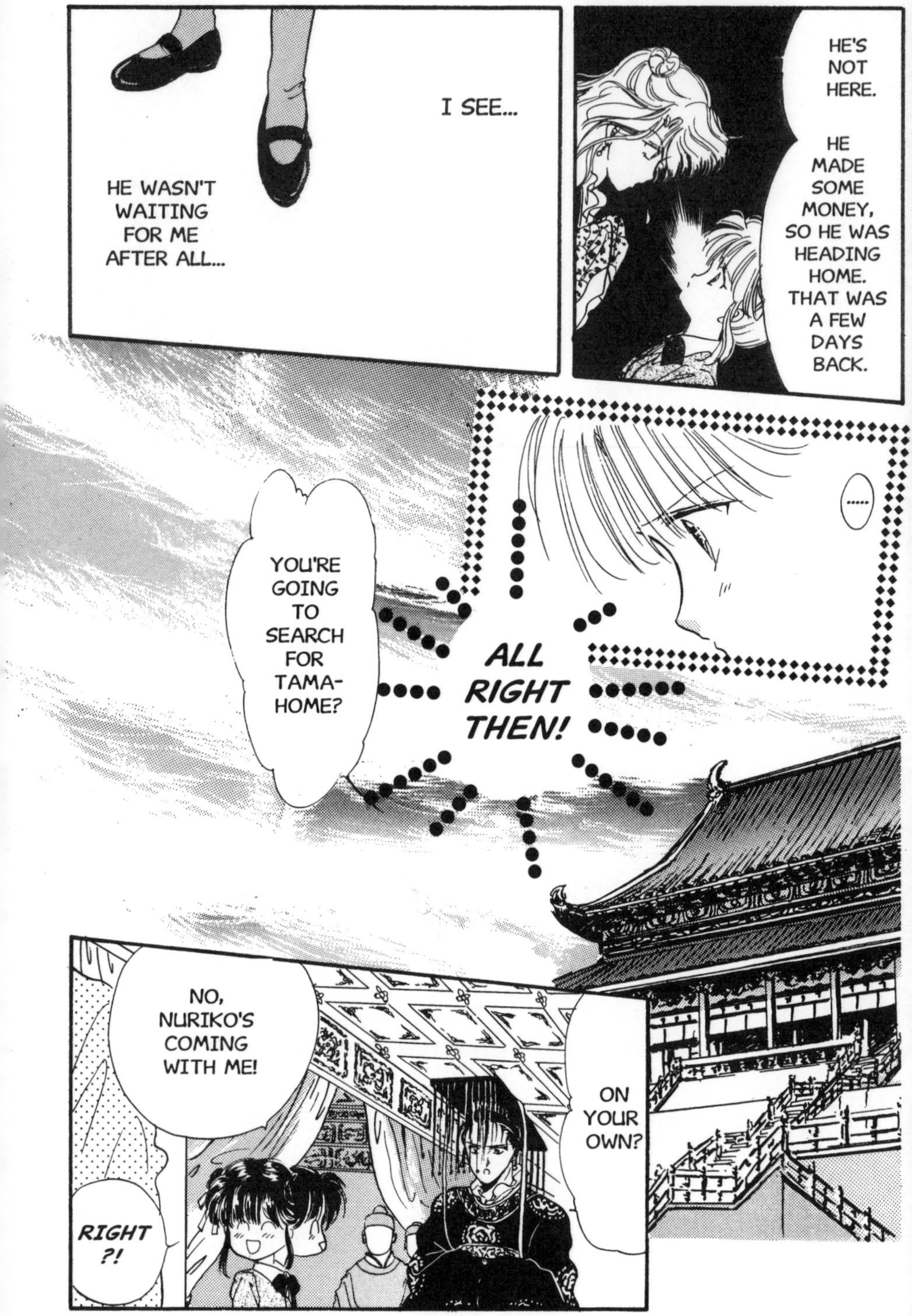
HE'S NOT HERE.
HE MADE SOME MONEY, SO HE WAS HEADING HOME. THAT WAS A FEW DAYS BACK.
I SEE...
HE WASN'T WAITING FOR ME AFTER ALL...
......
ALL RIGHT THEN!
YOU'RE GOING TO SEARCH FOR TAMA-HOME?
ON YOUR OWN?
NO, NURIKO'S COMING WITH ME!
RIGHT ?!

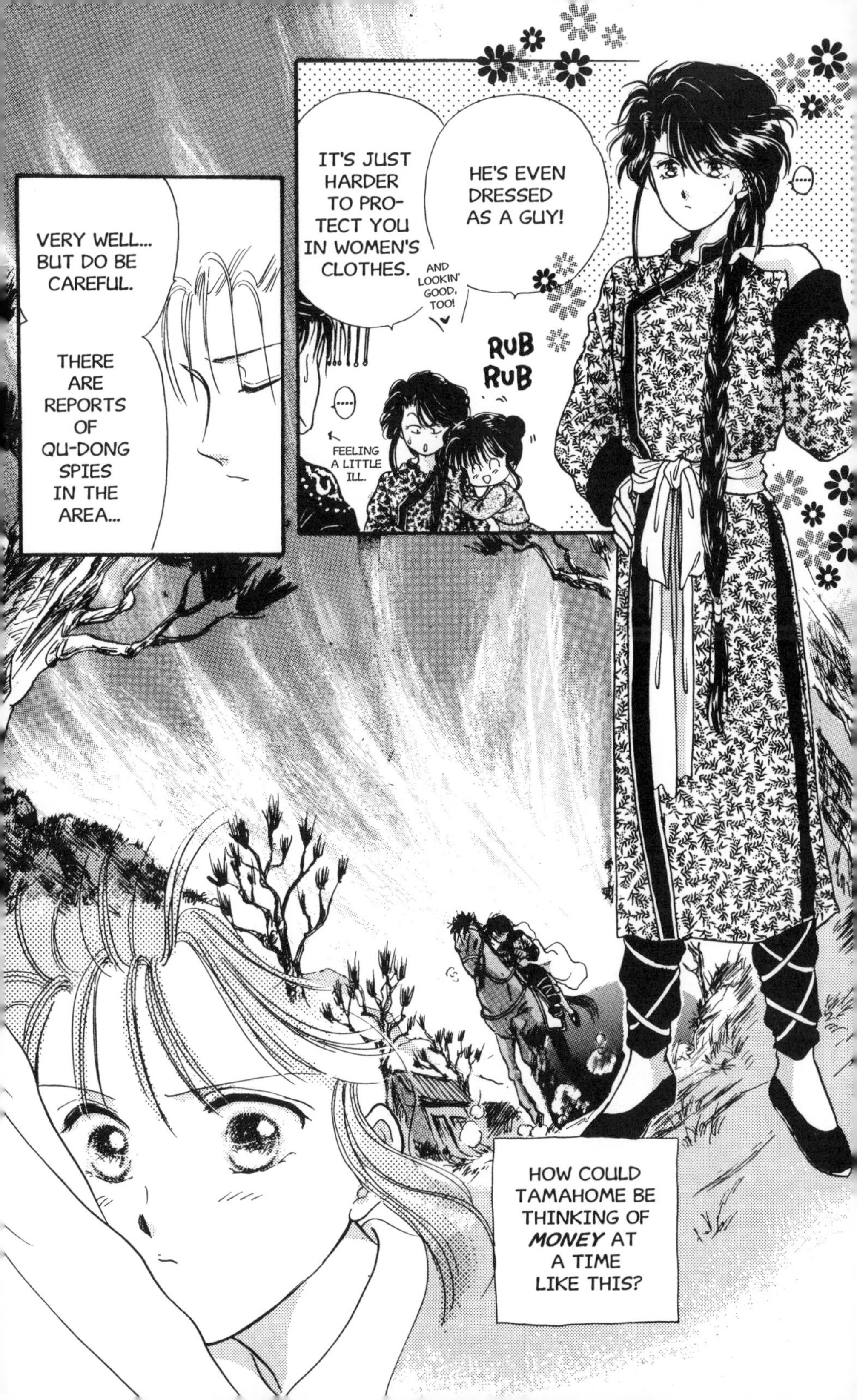
....
HE'S EVEN DRESSED AS A GUY!
IT'S JUST HARDER TO PROTECT YOU IN WOMEN'S CLOTHES.
AND LOOKIN' GOOD, TOO!
RUB RUB
....
FEELING A LITTLE ILL.
VERY WELL... BUT DO BE CAREFUL.
THERE ARE REPORTS OF QU-DONG SPIES IN THE AREA...
HOW COULD TAMAHOME BE THINKING OF *MONEY* AT A TIME LIKE THIS?

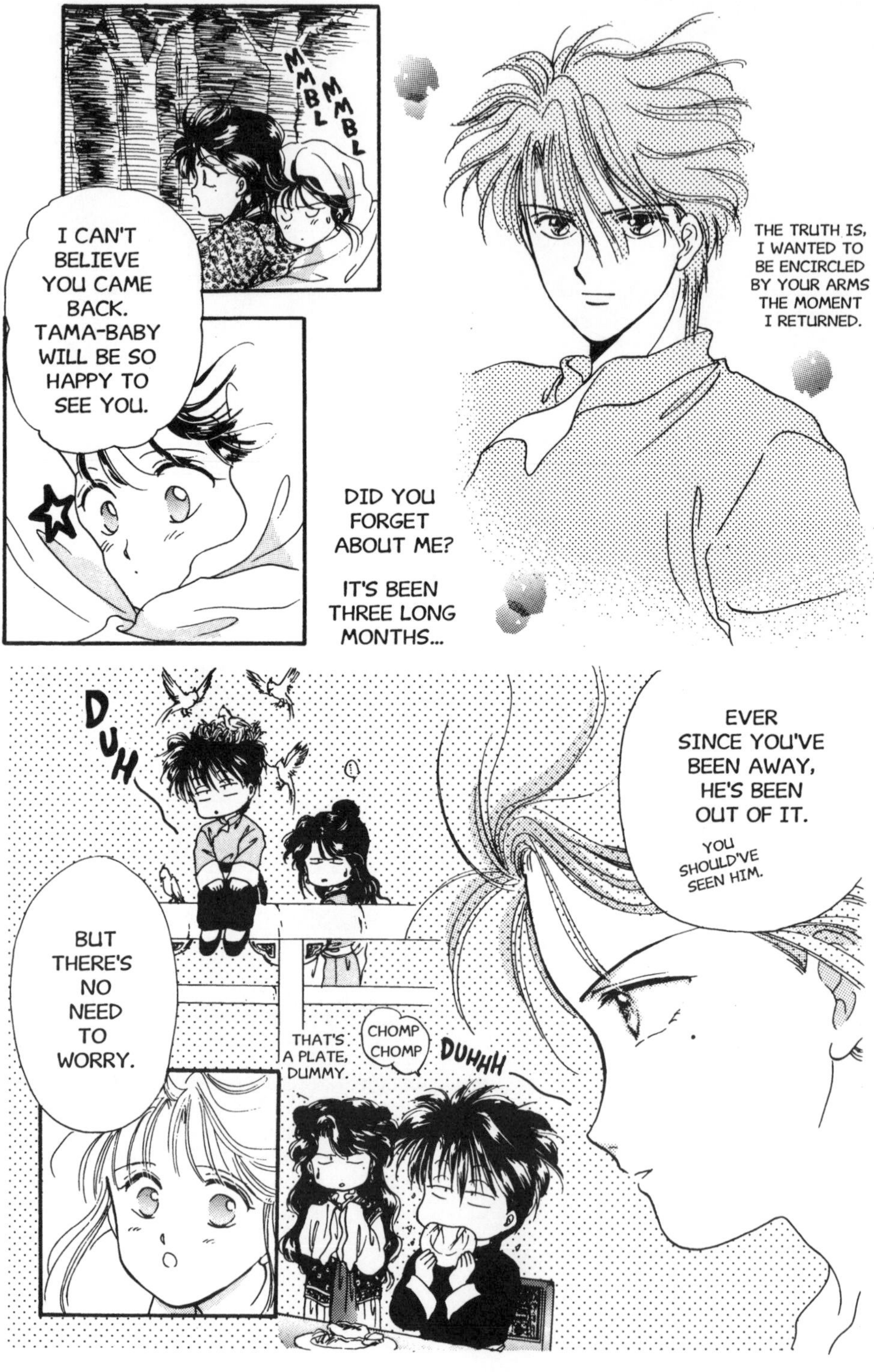
THE TRUTH IS, I WANTED TO BE ENCIRCLED BY YOUR ARMS THE MOMENT I RETURNED.
DID YOU FORGET ABOUT ME?
IT'S BEEN THREE LONG MONTHS...
MMBL MMBL
I CAN'T BELIEVE YOU CAME BACK. TAMA-BABY WILL BE SO HAPPY TO SEE YOU.
EVER SINCE YOU'VE BEEN AWAY, HE'S BEEN OUT OF IT.
YOU SHOULD'VE SEEN HIM.
DUH
BUT THERE'S NO NEED TO WORRY.
CHOMP CHOMP
DUHHH
THAT'S A PLATE, DUMMY.

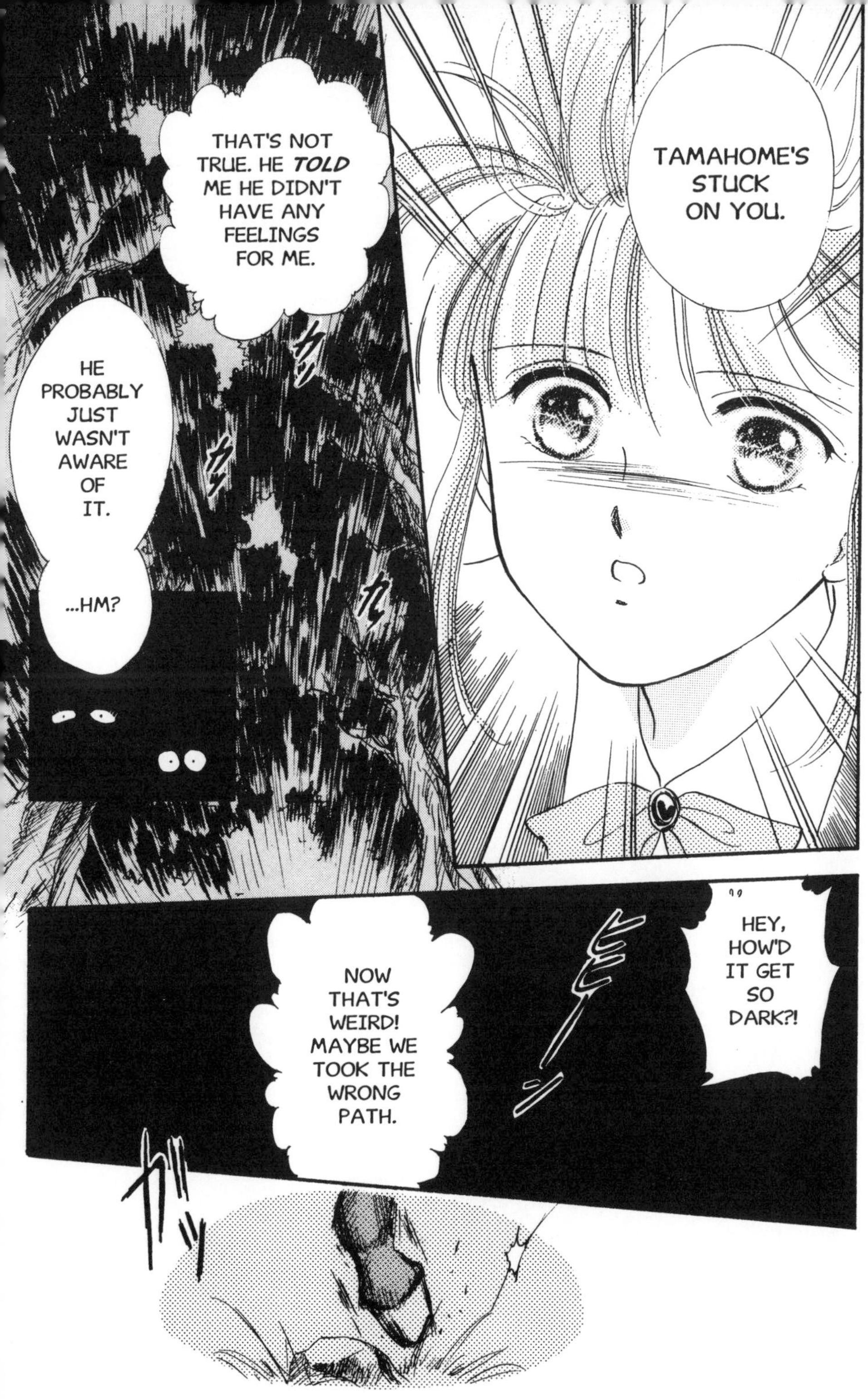
TAMAHOME'S STUCK ON YOU.
THAT'S NOT TRUE. HE *TOLD* ME HE DIDN'T HAVE ANY FEELINGS FOR ME.
HE PROBABLY JUST WASN'T AWARE OF IT.
...HM?
HEY, HOW'D IT GET SO DARK?!
NOW THAT'S WEIRD! MAYBE WE TOOK THE WRONG PATH.

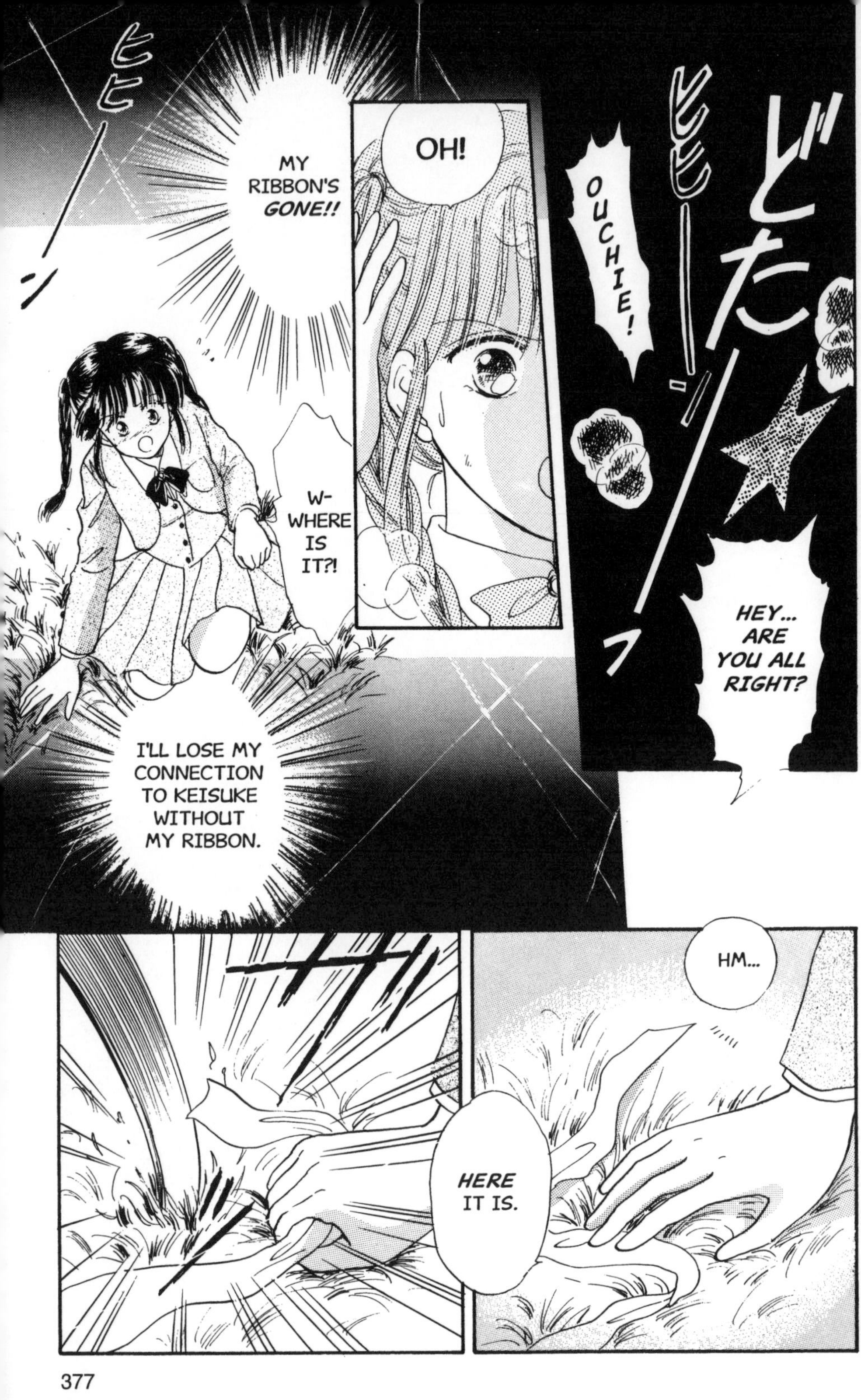
OUCHIE!
HEY... ARE YOU ALL RIGHT?
OH!
MY RIBBON'S *GONE!!*
W-WHERE IS IT?!
I'LL LOSE MY CONNECTION TO KEISUKE WITHOUT MY RIBBON.
HM...
HERE IT IS.

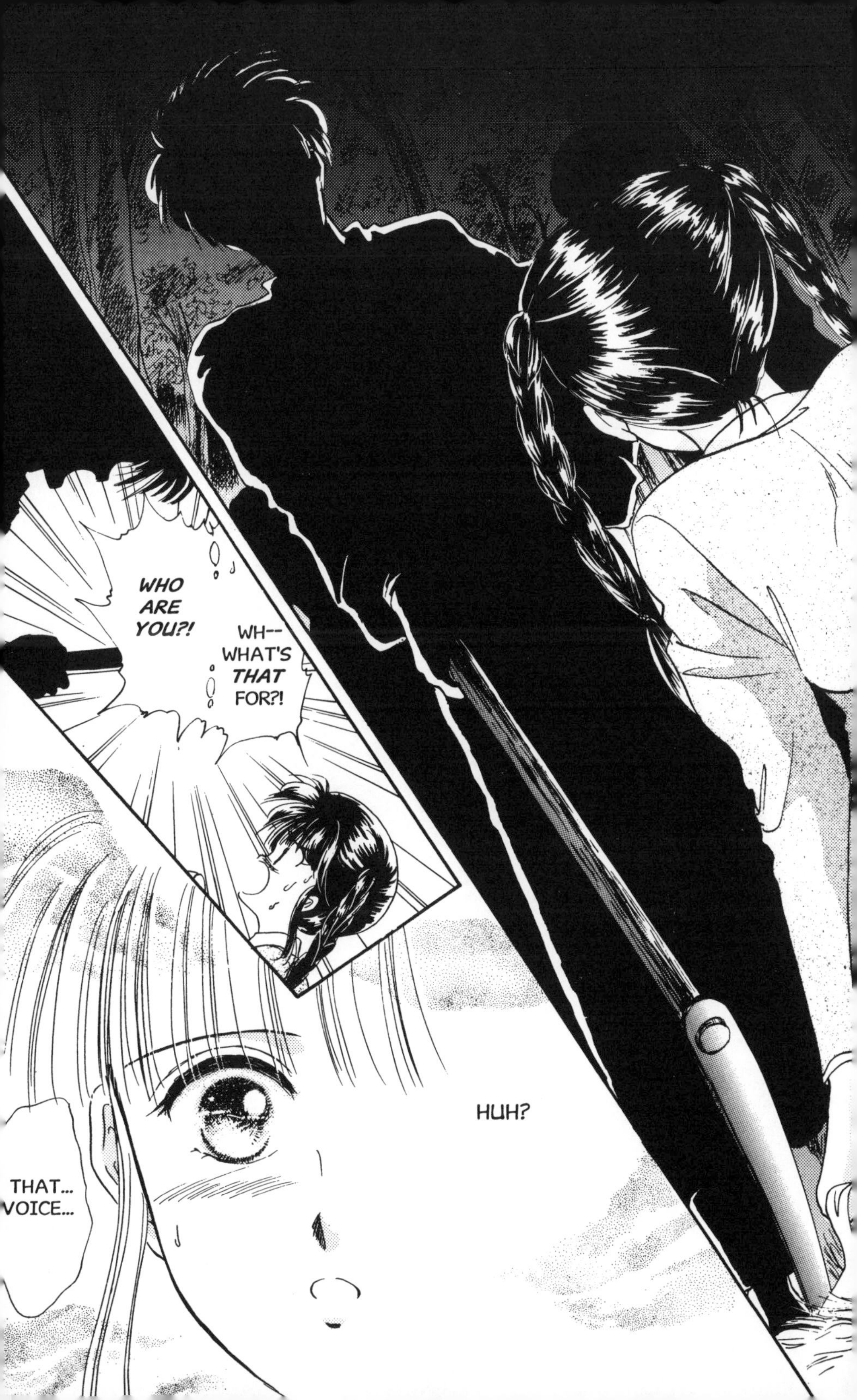

WH-- WHAT'S *THAT* FOR?!
WHO ARE YOU?!
HUH?
THAT... VOICE...

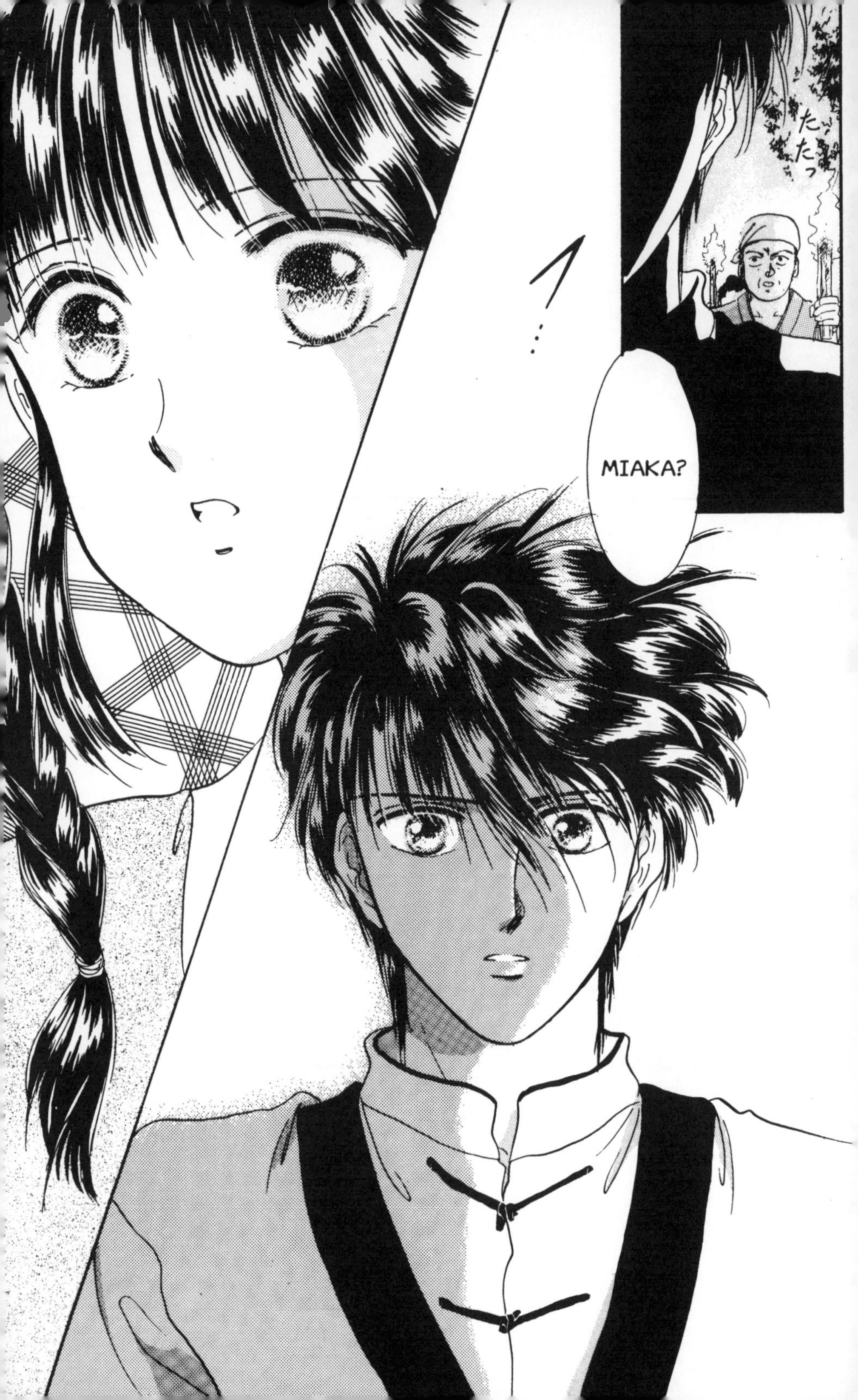
たたっ
MIAKA?

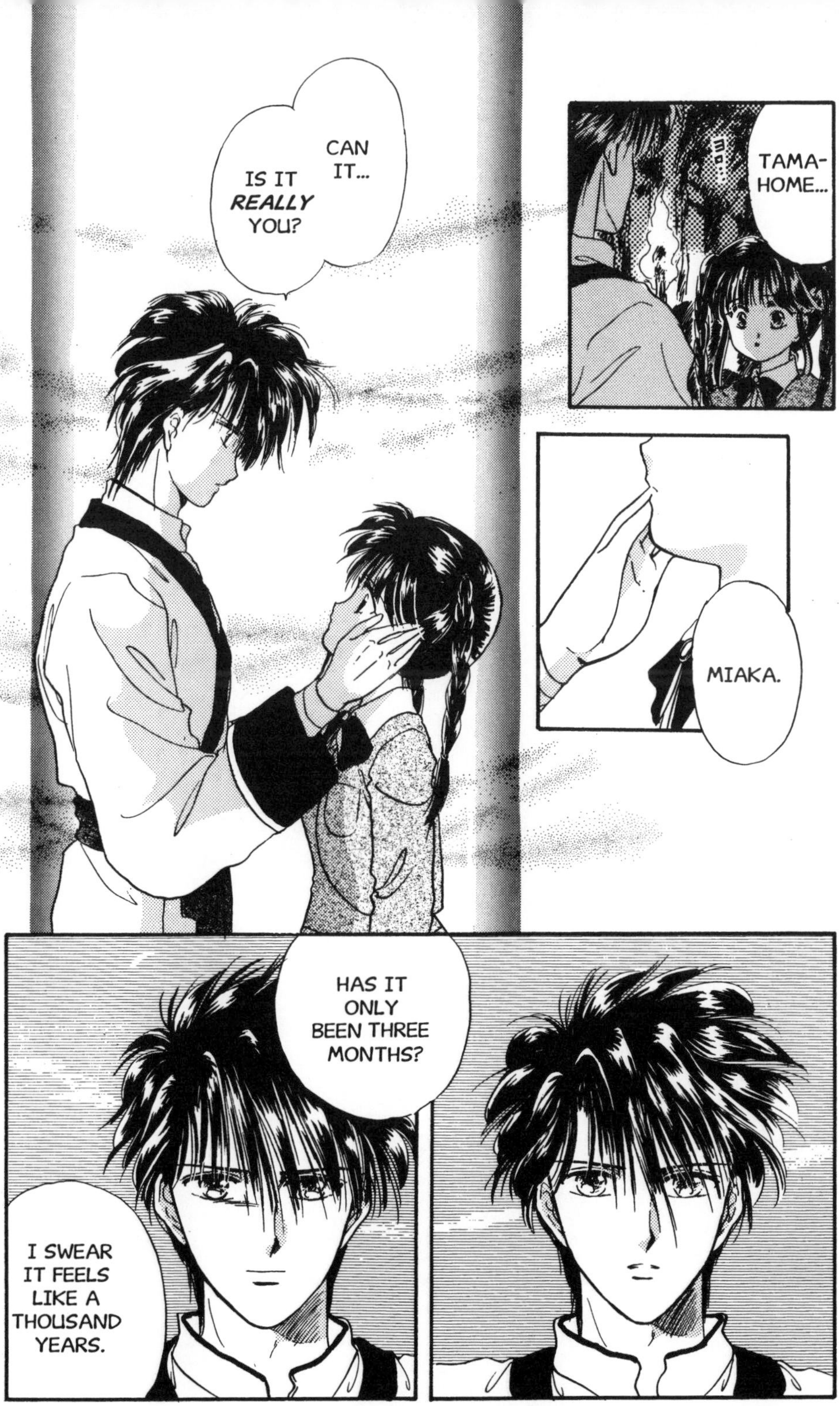
TAMA-HOME...
MIAKA.
CAN IT... IS IT REALLY YOU?
HAS IT ONLY BEEN THREE MONTHS?
I SWEAR IT FEELS LIKE A THOUSAND YEARS.

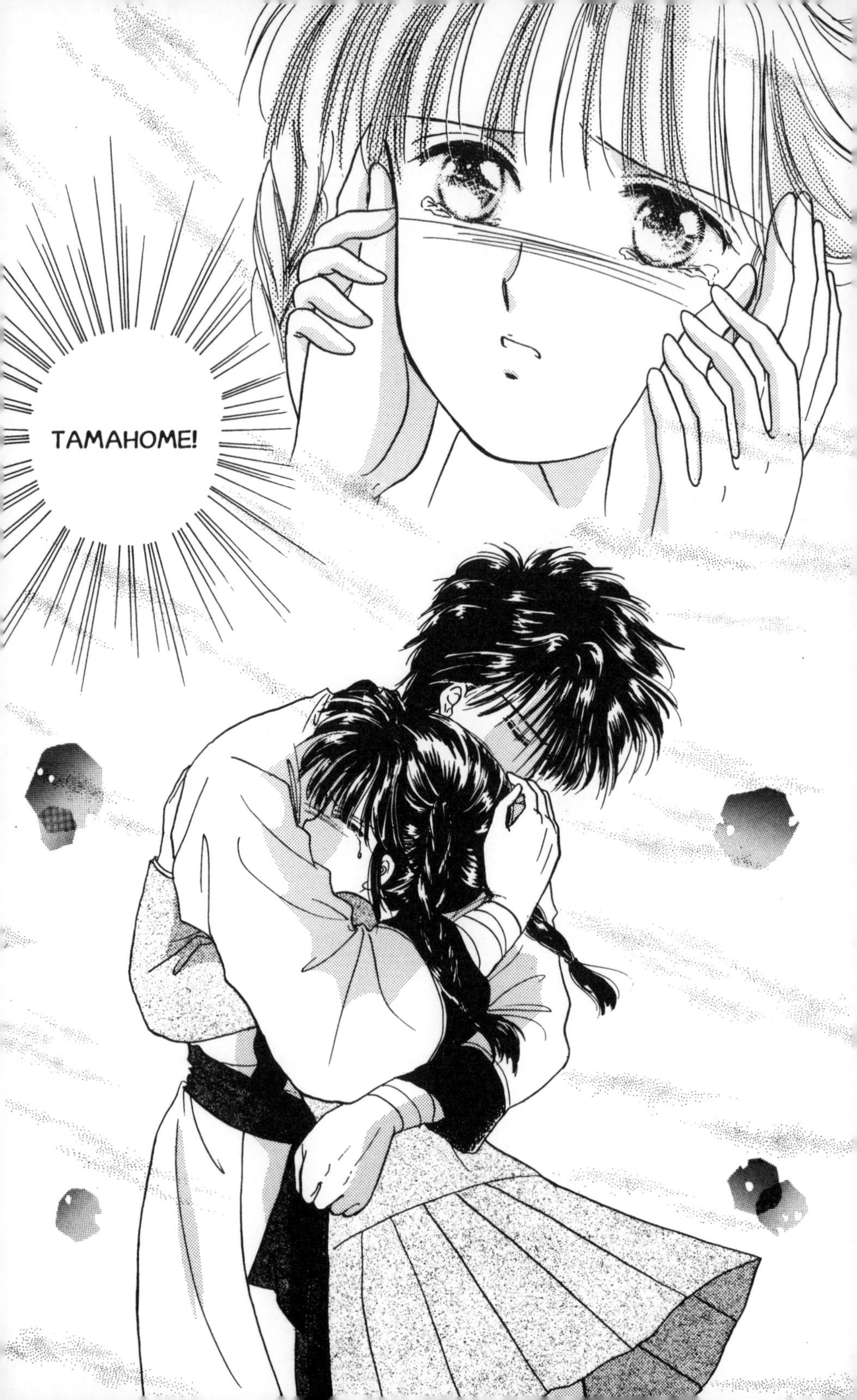
TAMAHOME!

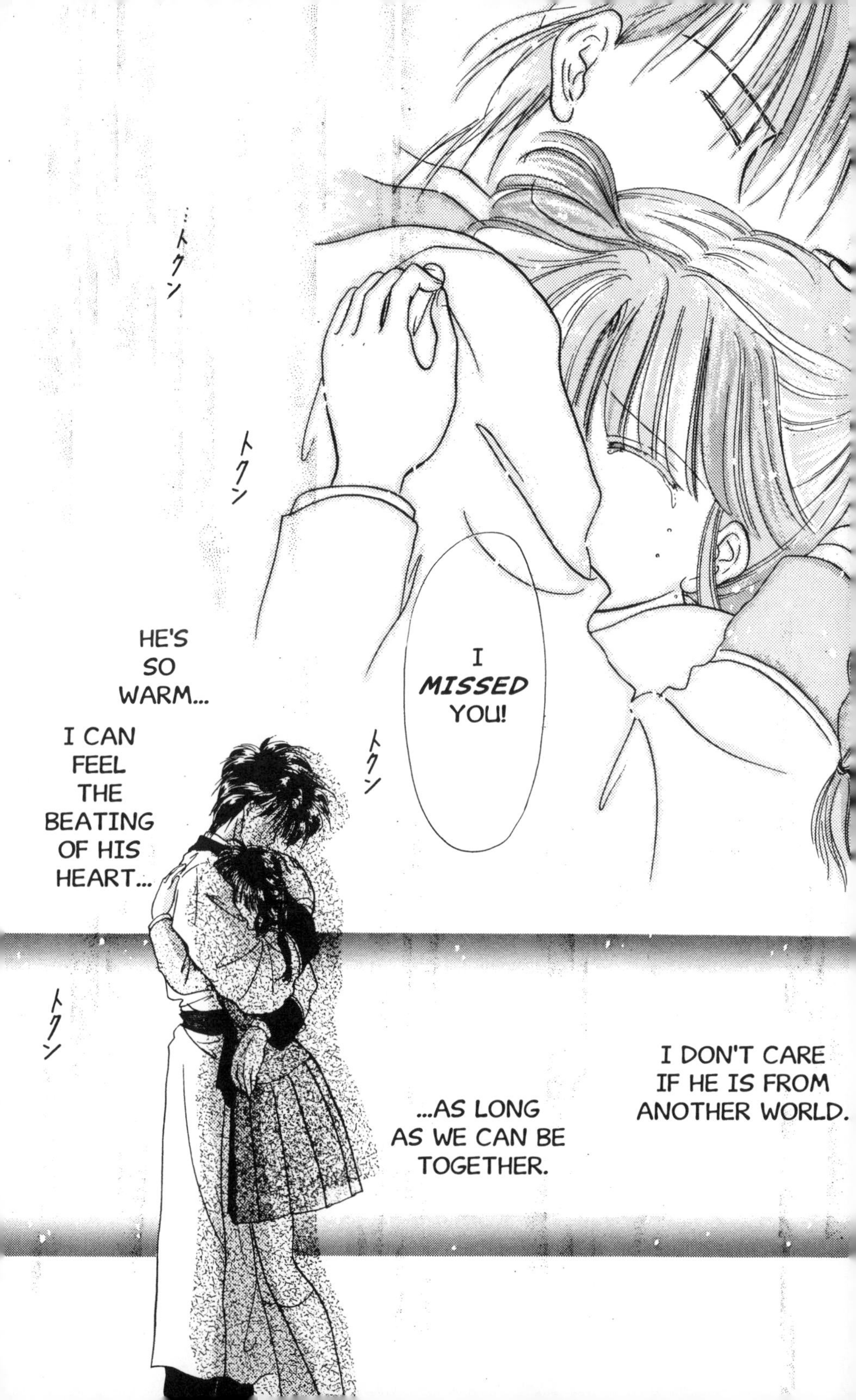
I MISSED YOU!
…トクン
トクン
トクン
HE'S SO WARM...
I CAN FEEL THE BEATING OF HIS HEART...
I DON'T CARE IF HE IS FROM ANOTHER WORLD.
...AS LONG AS WE CAN BE TOGETHER.
トクン

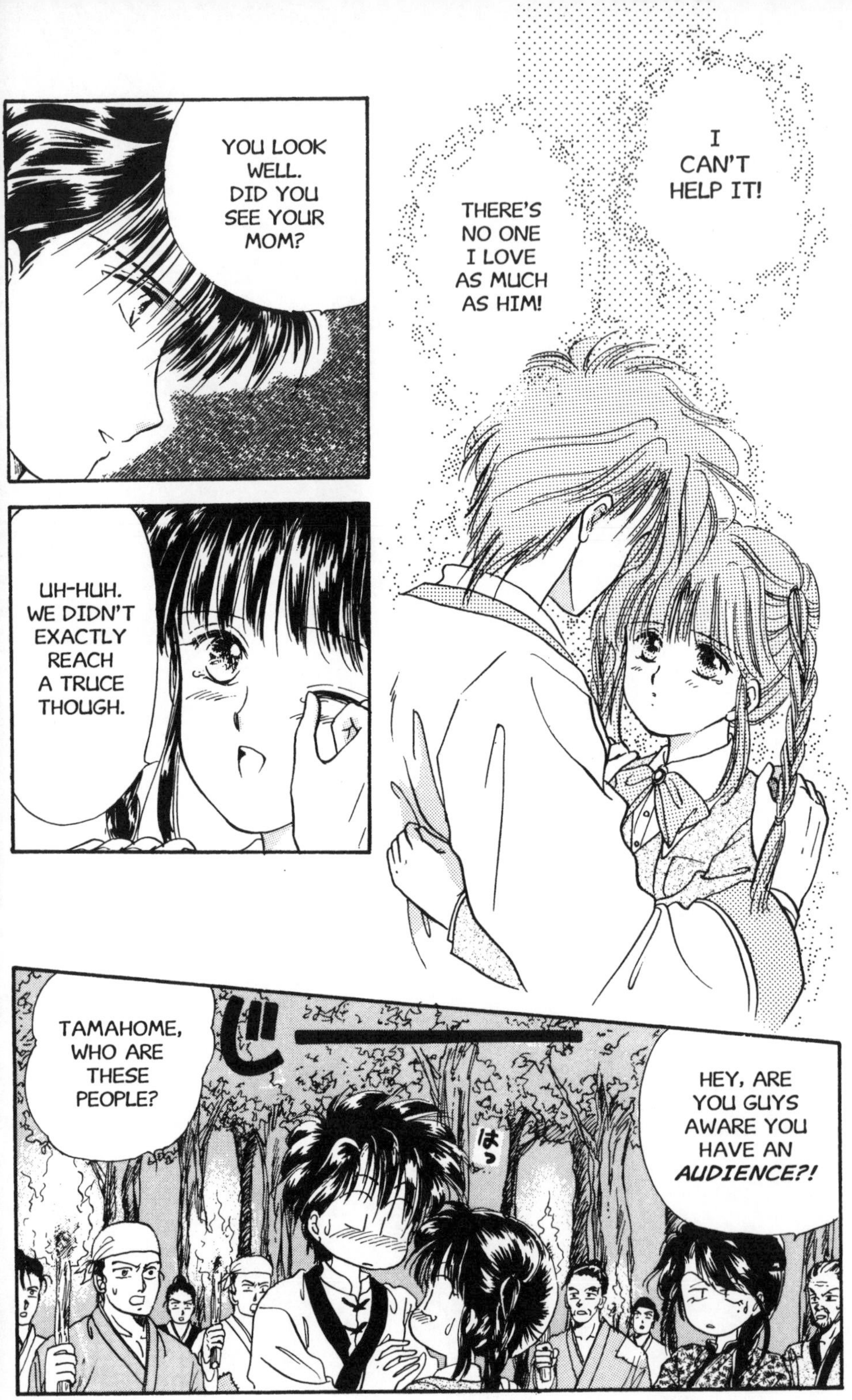
I CAN'T HELP IT!
THERE'S NO ONE I LOVE AS MUCH AS HIM!
YOU LOOK WELL. DID YOU SEE YOUR MOM?
UH-HUH. WE DIDN'T EXACTLY REACH A TRUCE THOUGH.
じー
HEY, ARE YOU GUYS AWARE YOU HAVE AN *AUDIENCE?!*
はっ
TAMAHOME, WHO ARE THESE PEOPLE?

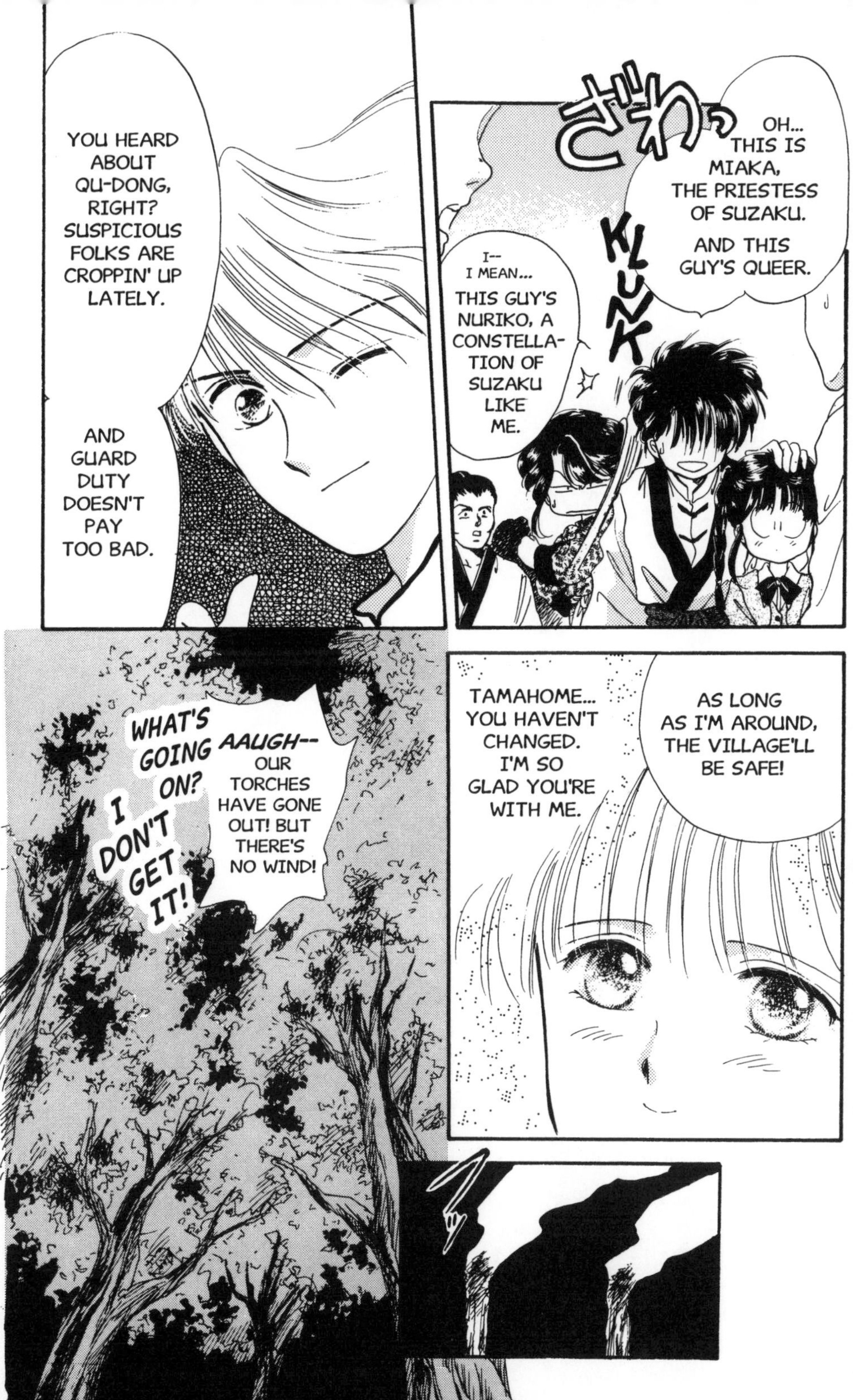
ざわっ
OH... THIS IS MIAKA, THE PRIESTESS OF SUZAKU.
AND THIS GUY'S QUEER.
KLUNK
I-- I MEAN... THIS GUY'S NURIKO, A CONSTELLATION OF SUZAKU LIKE ME.
YOU HEARD ABOUT QU-DONG, RIGHT? SUSPICIOUS FOLKS ARE CROPPIN' UP LATELY.
AND GUARD DUTY DOESN'T PAY TOO BAD.
AS LONG AS I'M AROUND, THE VILLAGE'LL BE SAFE!
TAMAHOME... YOU HAVEN'T CHANGED. I'M SO GLAD YOU'RE WITH ME.
AAUGH-- OUR TORCHES HAVE GONE OUT! BUT THERE'S NO WIND!
WHAT'S GOING ON? I DON'T GET IT!

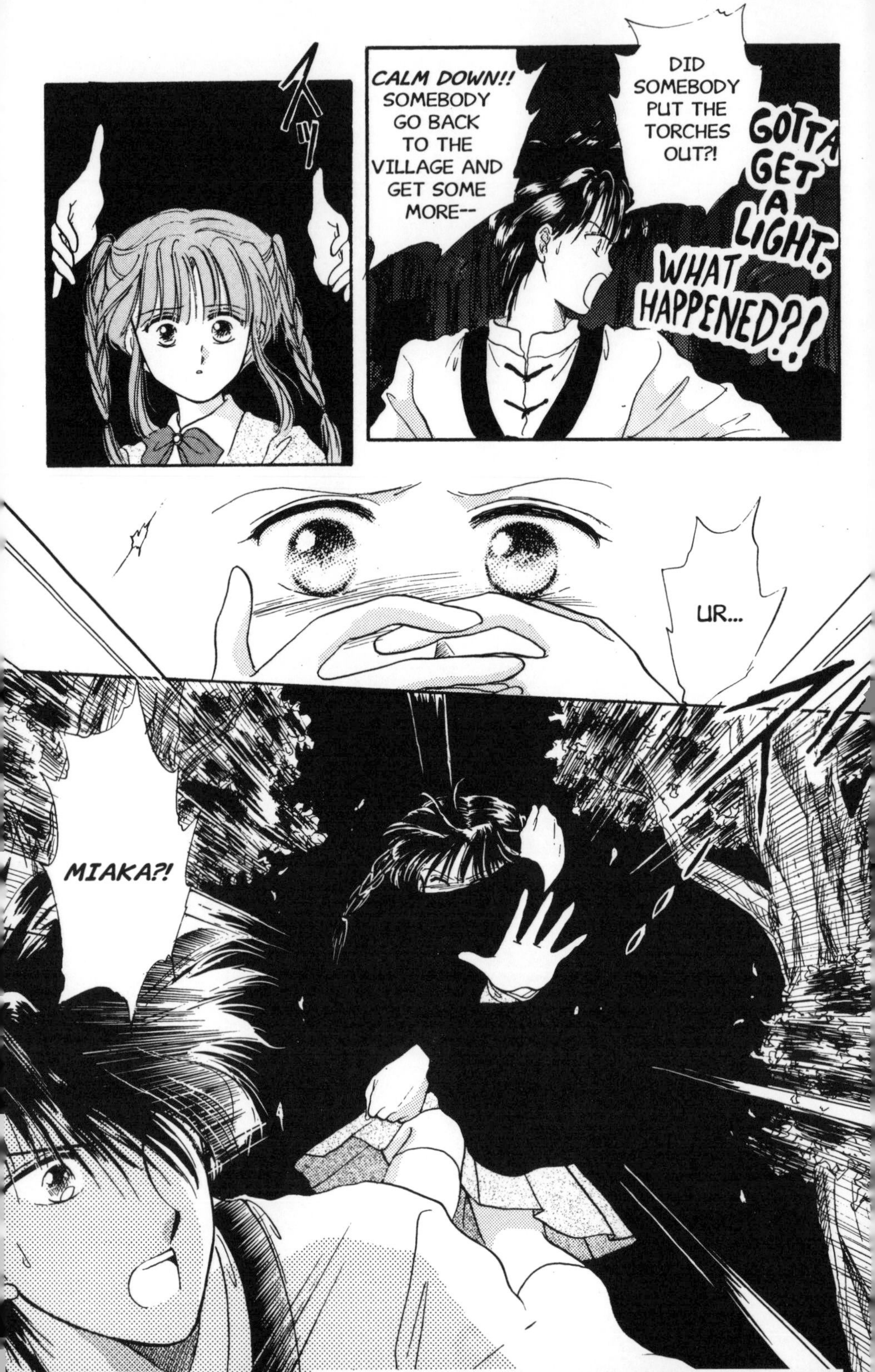
DID SOMEBODY PUT THE TORCHES OUT?!
GOTTA GET A LIGHT. WHAT HAPPENED?!
CALM DOWN!! SOMEBODY GO BACK TO THE VILLAGE AND GET SOME MORE--
UR...
MIAKA?!

TO BE CONTINUED IN VOLUME 3:DISCIPLE

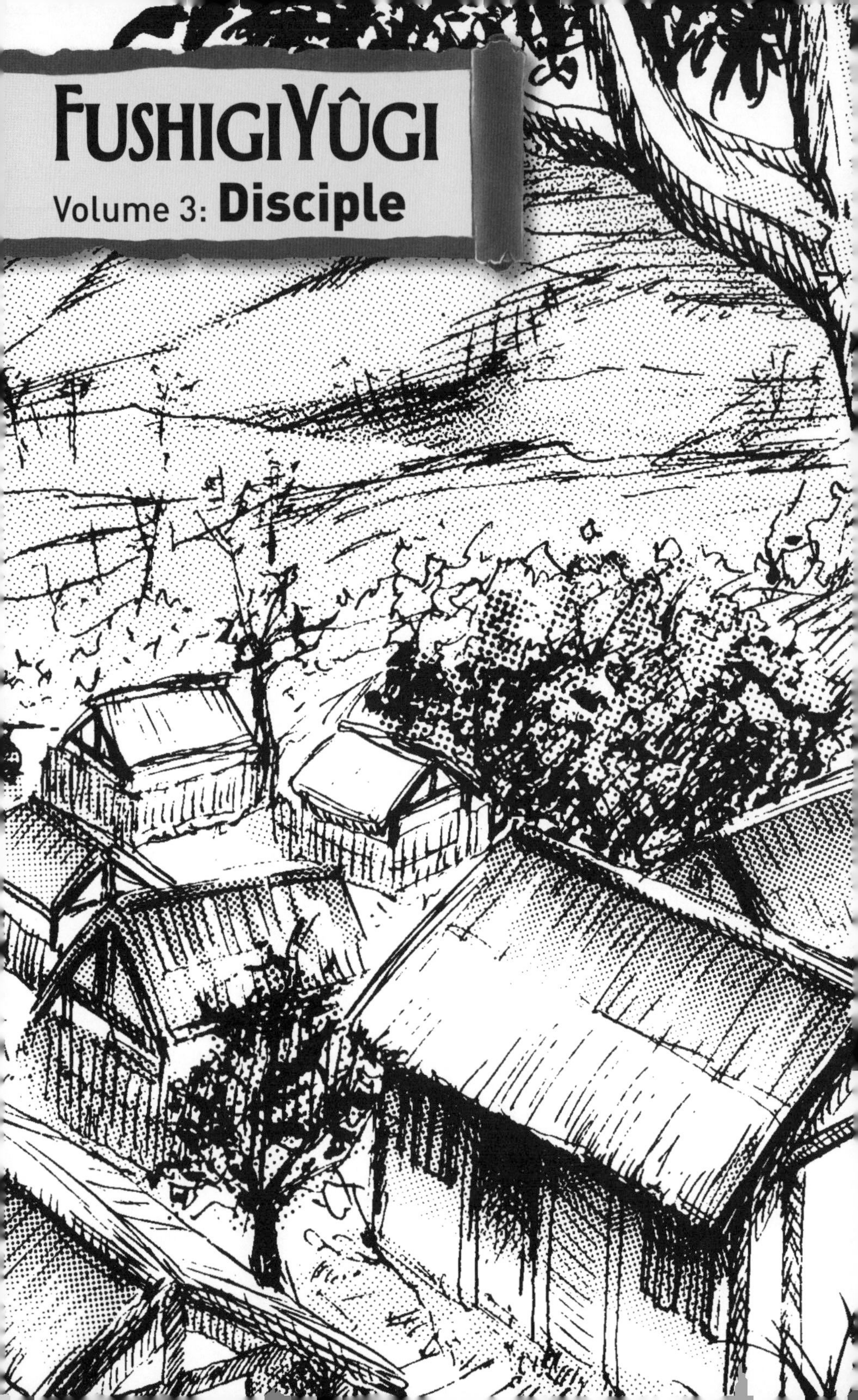
FUSHIGI YÛGI
Volume 3: Disciple

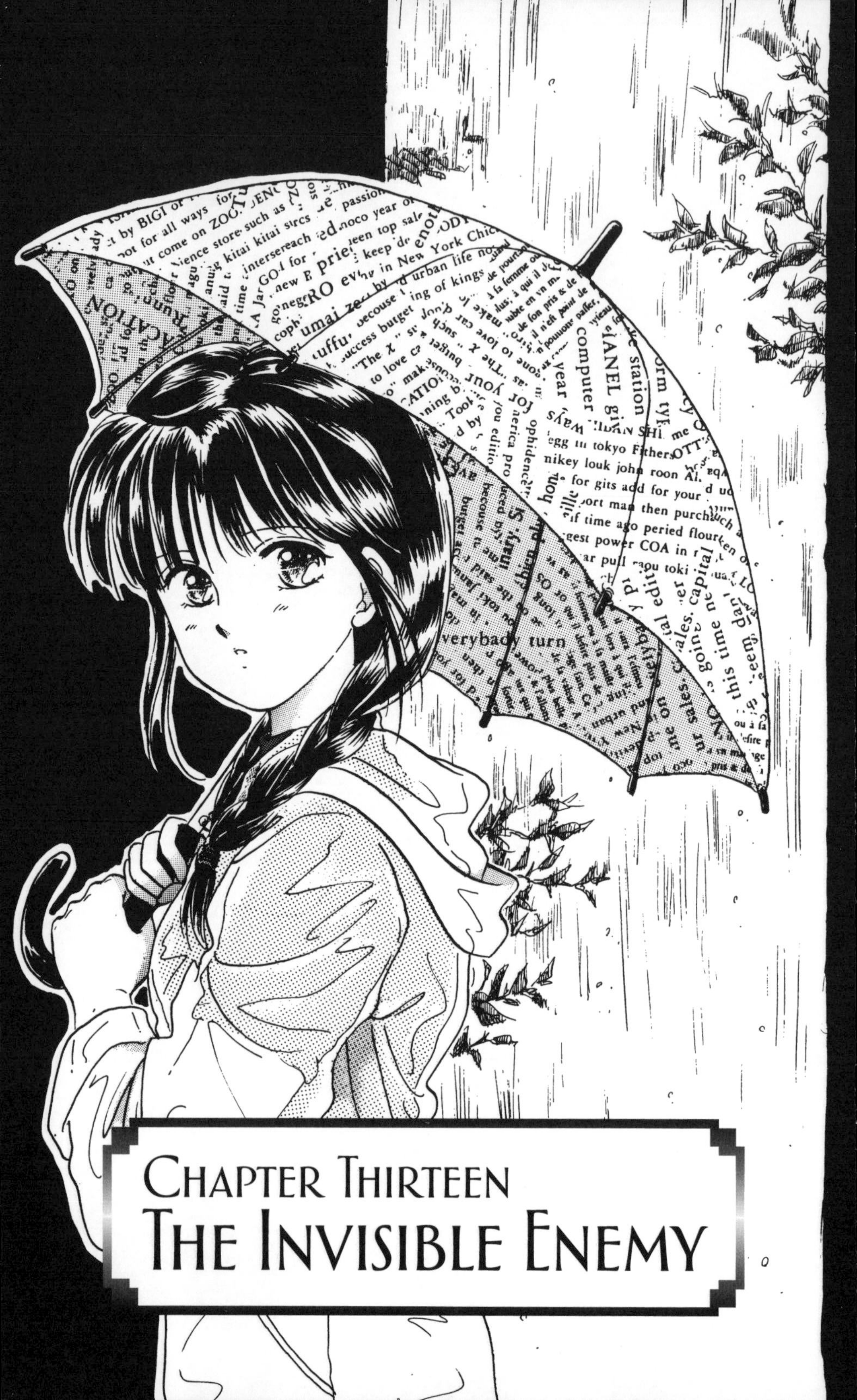

Chapter Thirteen
The Invisible Enemy

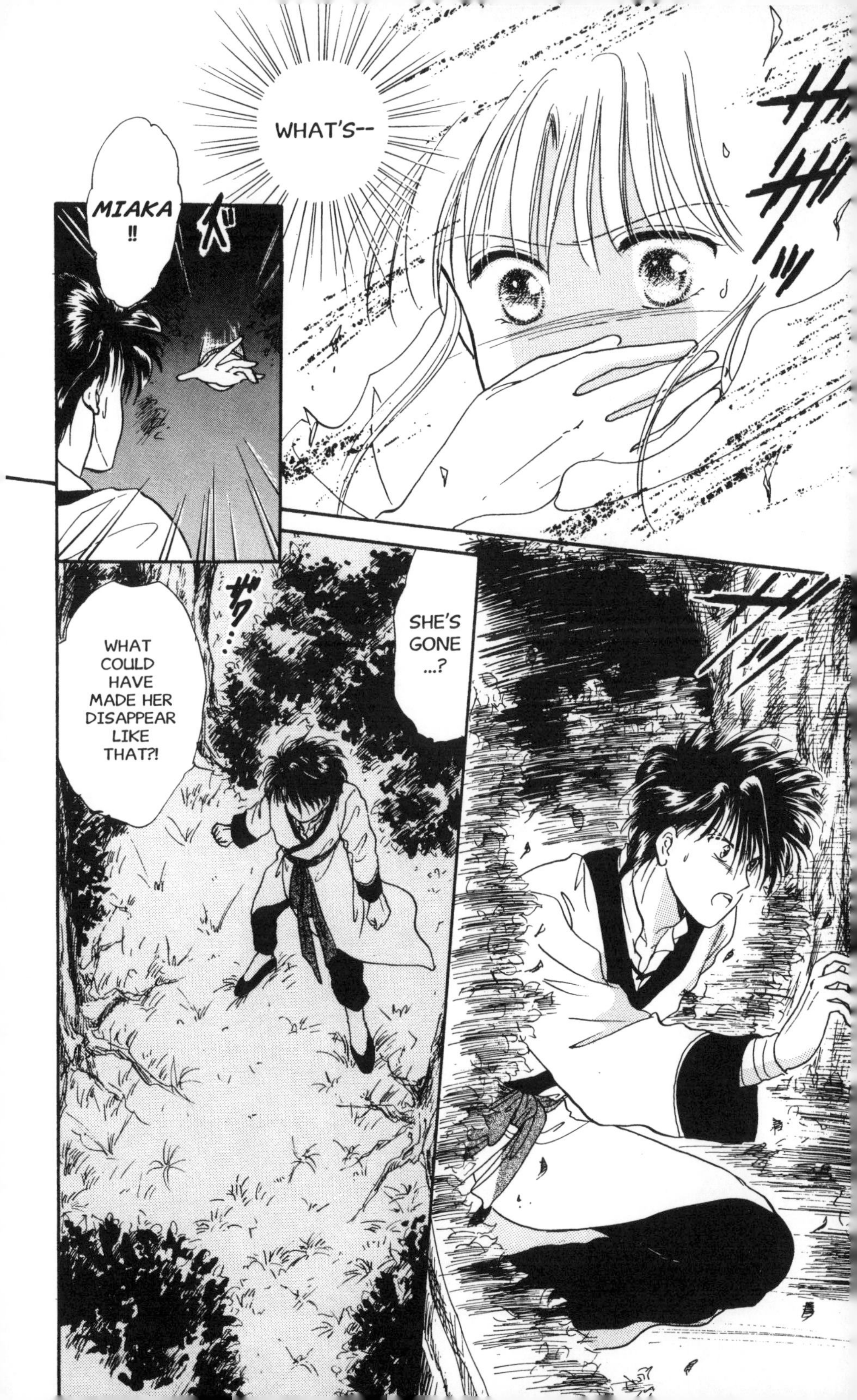
WHAT'S--
MIAKA!!
SHE'S GONE ...?
WHAT COULD HAVE MADE HER DISAPPEAR LIKE THAT?!

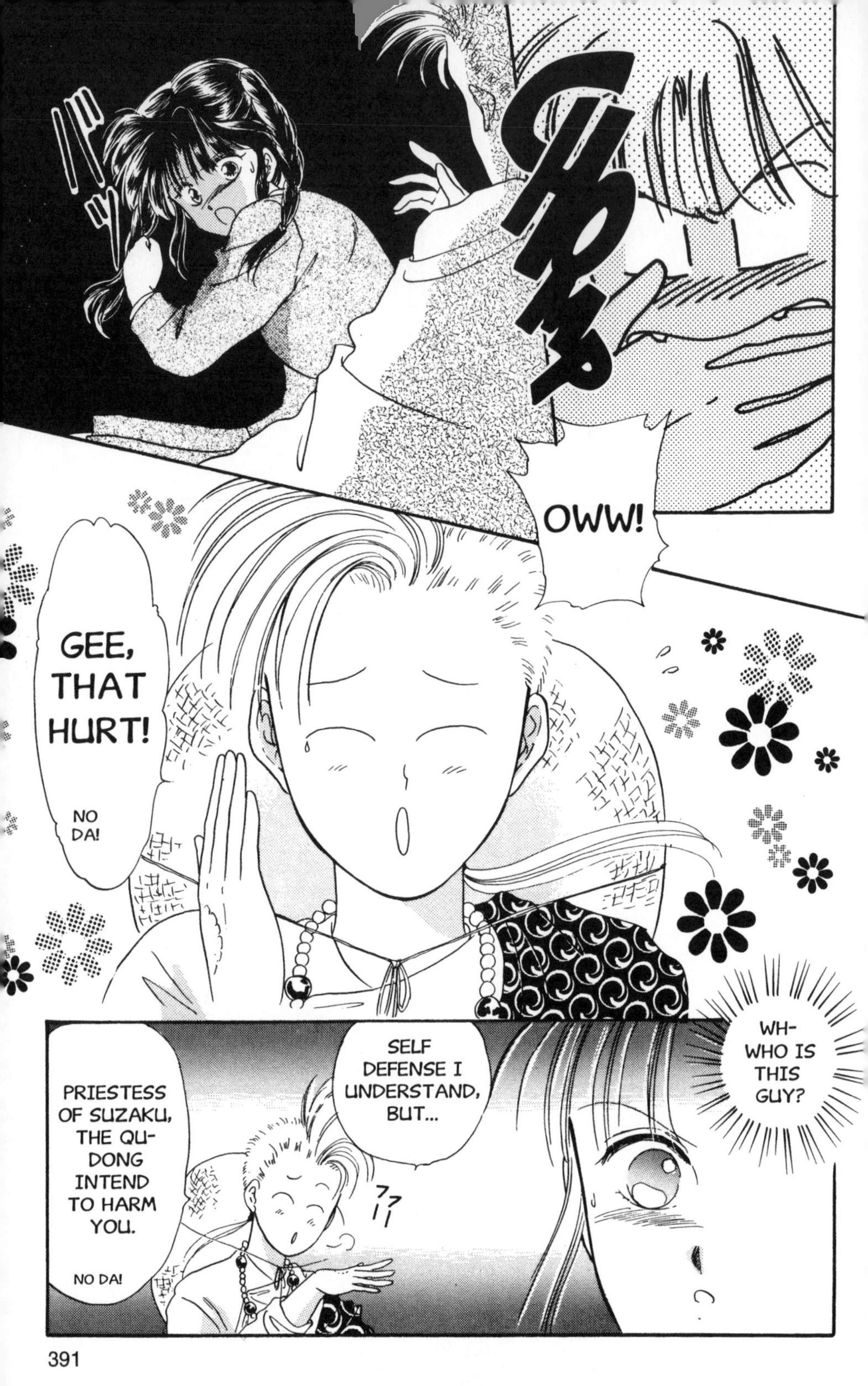
CHOMP
OWW!
GEE, THAT HURT!
NO DA!
WH- WHO IS THIS GUY?
SELF DEFENSE I UNDERSTAND, BUT...
PRIESTESS OF SUZAKU, THE QU-DONG INTEND TO HARM YOU.
NO DA!

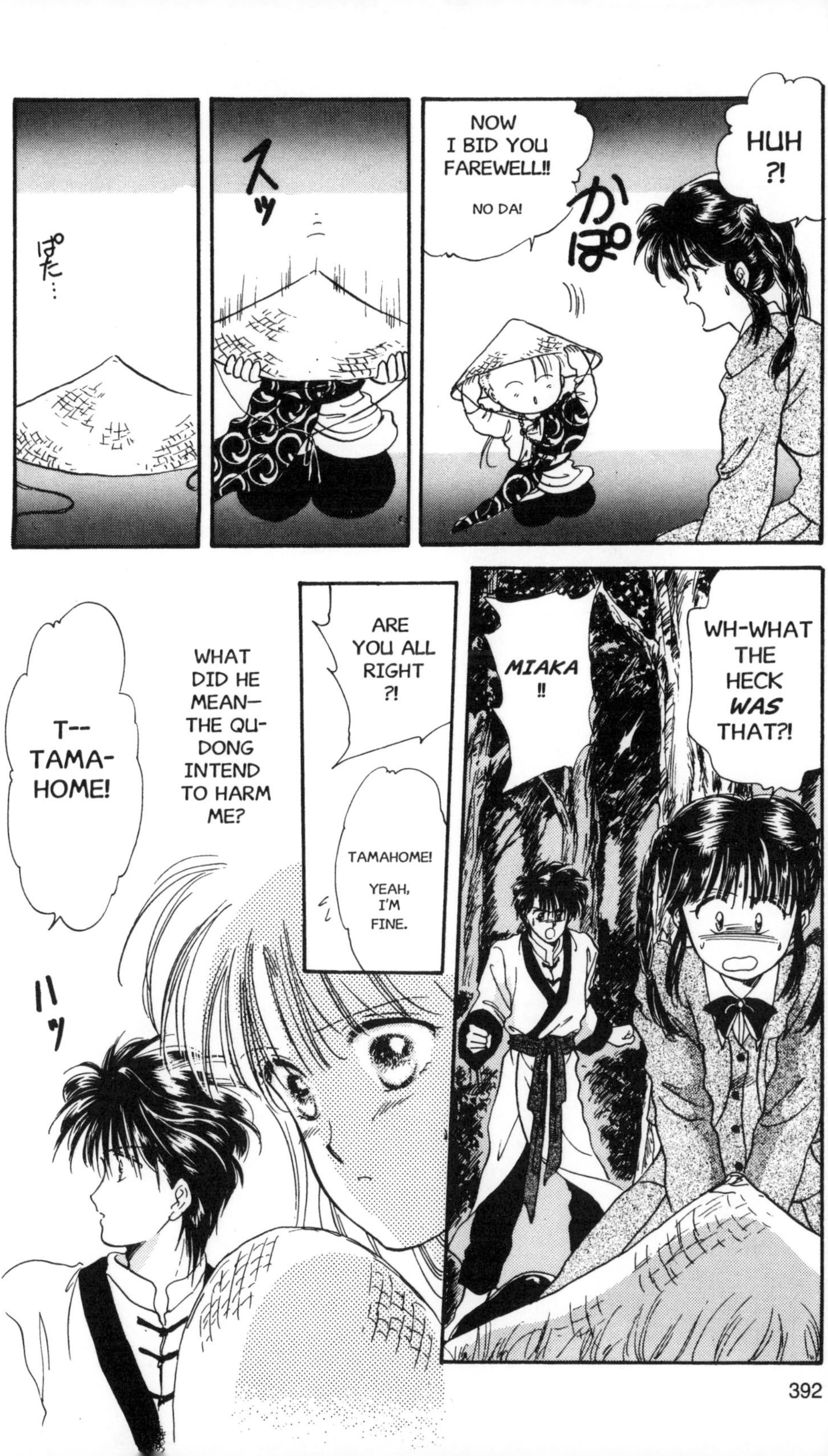
HUH ?!
かぽ
NOW I BID YOU FAREWELL!! NO DA!
スッ
ぱた…
WH-WHAT THE HECK WAS THAT?!
MIAKA !!
ARE YOU ALL RIGHT ?!
TAMAHOME! YEAH, I'M FINE.
WHAT DID HE MEAN— THE QU-DONG INTEND TO HARM ME?
T-- TAMA-HOME!
ハッ

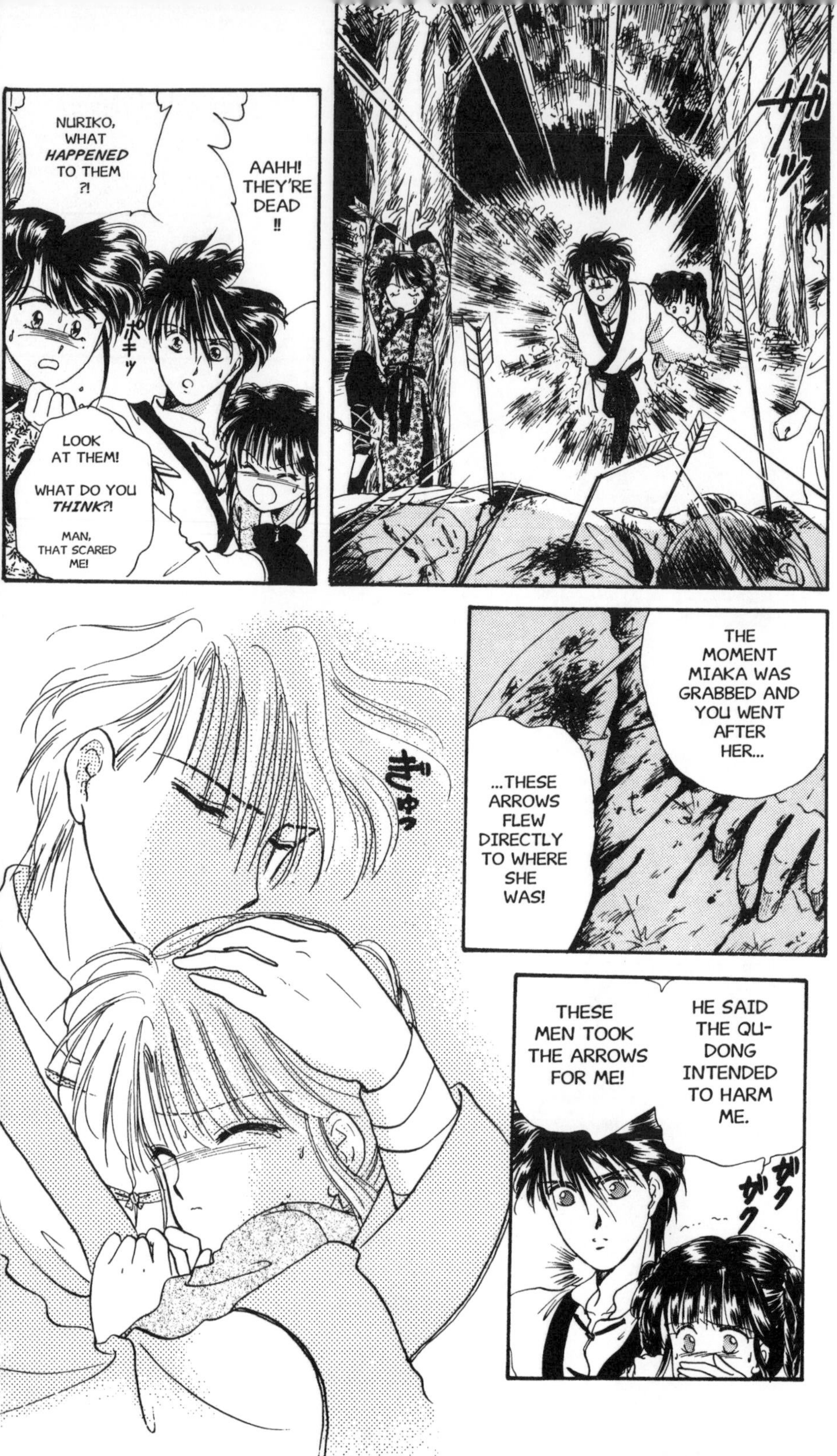
ザッ
NURIKO, WHAT *HAPPENED* TO THEM ?!
AAHH! THEY'RE DEAD !!
ポキッ
LOOK AT THEM!
WHAT DO YOU *THINK*?!
MAN, THAT SCARED ME!
THE MOMENT MIAKA WAS GRABBED AND YOU WENT AFTER HER...
...THESE ARROWS FLEW DIRECTLY TO WHERE SHE WAS!
HE SAID THE QU-DONG INTENDED TO HARM ME.
THESE MEN TOOK THE ARROWS FOR ME!
がく がく
ぎゅっ

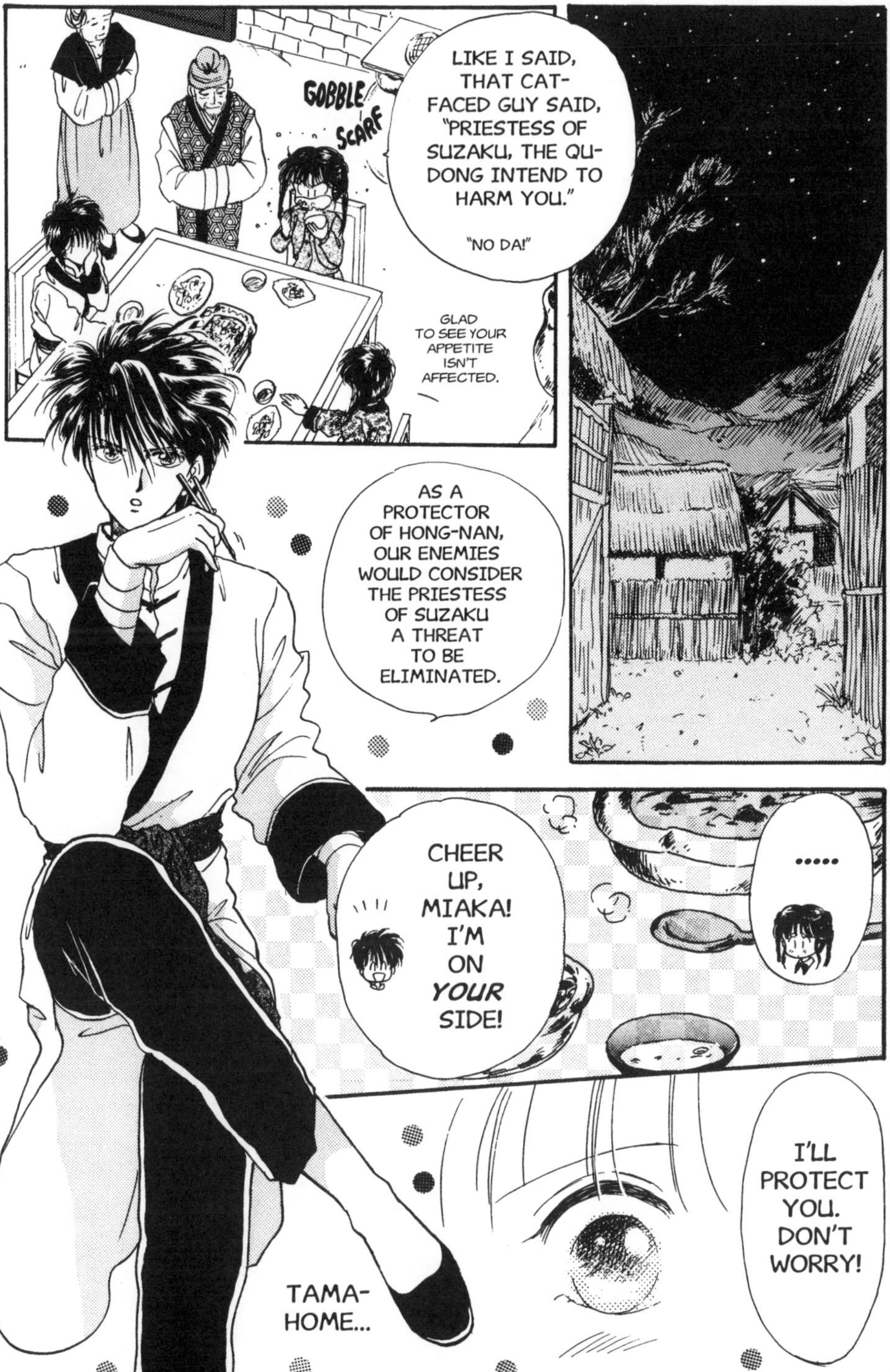
LIKE I SAID, THAT CAT-FACED GUY SAID, "PRIESTESS OF SUZAKU, THE QU-DONG INTEND TO HARM YOU."
GOBBLE
SCARF
"NO DA!"
GLAD TO SEE YOUR APPETITE ISN'T AFFECTED.
AS A PROTECTOR OF HONG-NAN, OUR ENEMIES WOULD CONSIDER THE PRIESTESS OF SUZAKU A THREAT TO BE ELIMINATED.
.....
CHEER UP, MIAKA! I'M ON *YOUR* SIDE!
I'LL PROTECT YOU. DON'T WORRY!
TAMA-HOME...

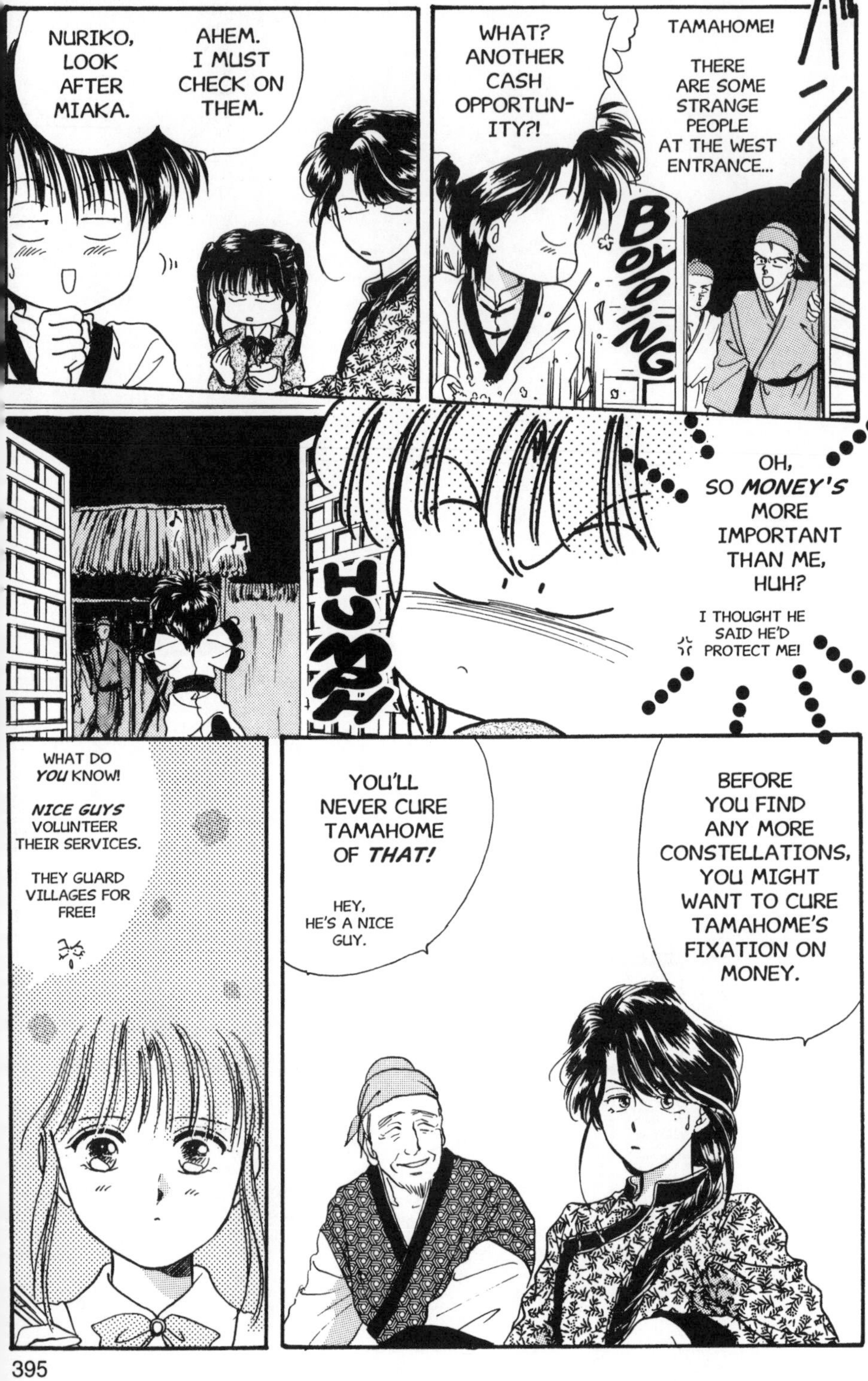
TAMAHOME! THERE ARE SOME STRANGE PEOPLE AT THE WEST ENTRANCE...
WHAT? ANOTHER CASH OPPORTUN-ITY?!
BOYOING
AHEM. I MUST CHECK ON THEM.
NURIKO, LOOK AFTER MIAKA.
OH, SO *MONEY'S* MORE IMPORTANT THAN ME, HUH?
I THOUGHT HE SAID HE'D PROTECT ME!
HUMPH
BEFORE YOU FIND ANY MORE CONSTELLATIONS, YOU MIGHT WANT TO CURE TAMAHOME'S FIXATION ON MONEY.
YOU'LL NEVER CURE TAMAHOME OF *THAT!*
HEY, HE'S A NICE GUY.
WHAT DO *YOU* KNOW! *NICE GUYS* VOLUNTEER THEIR SERVICES. THEY GUARD VILLAGES FOR FREE!

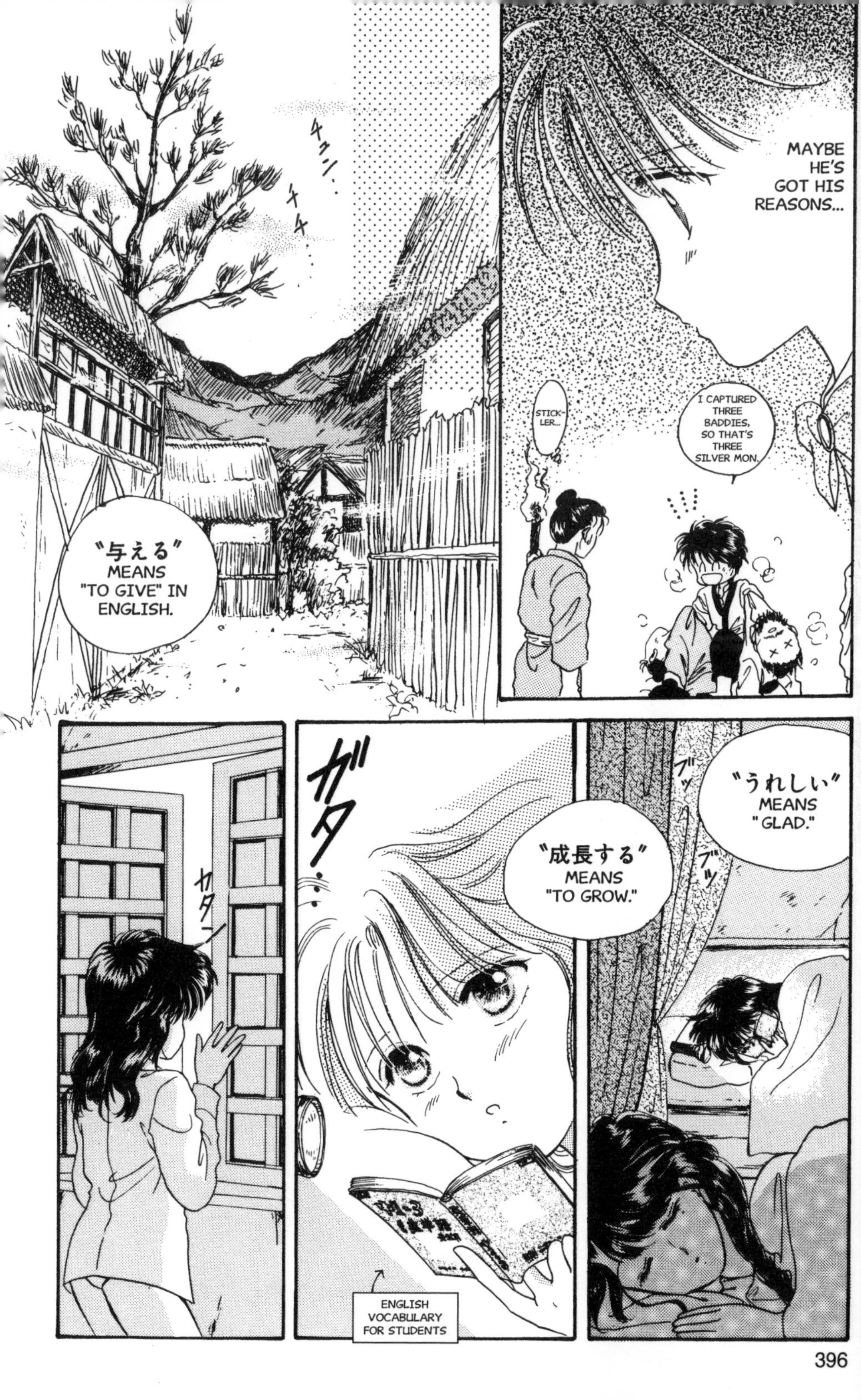
MAYBE HE'S GOT HIS REASONS...
I CAPTURED THREE BADDIES, SO THAT'S THREE SILVER MON.
STICKLER...
チュン..
チチ...
"与える" MEANS "TO GIVE" IN ENGLISH.
"うれしい" MEANS "GLAD."
ブツ
ブツ
ガタ..
"成長する" MEANS "TO GROW."
ENGLISH VOCABULARY FOR STUDENTS
カタン

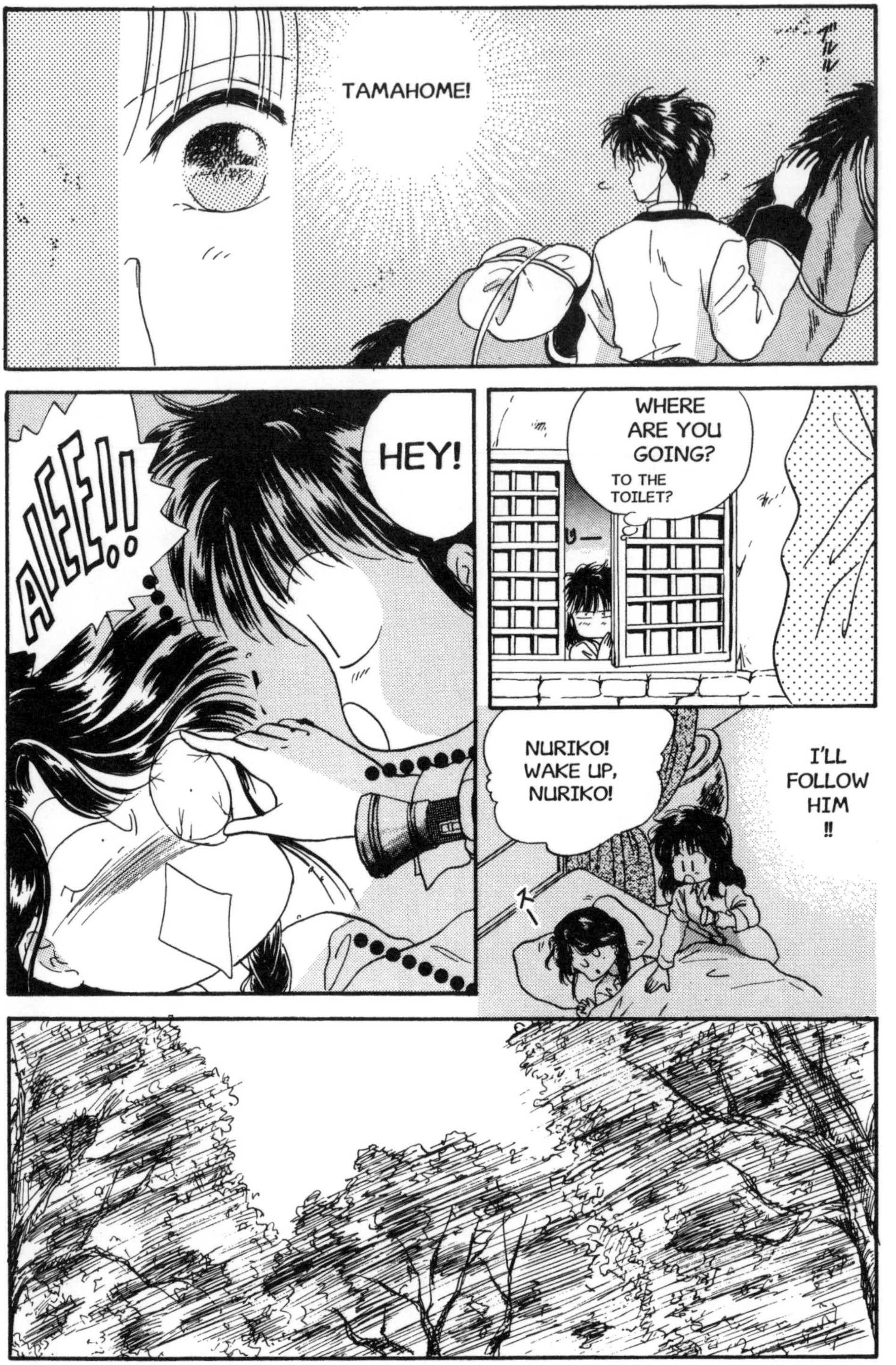
TAMAHOME!
WHERE ARE YOU GOING?
TO THE TOILET?
I'LL FOLLOW HIM!!
NURIKO! WAKE UP, NURIKO!
HEY!
AIEE!!

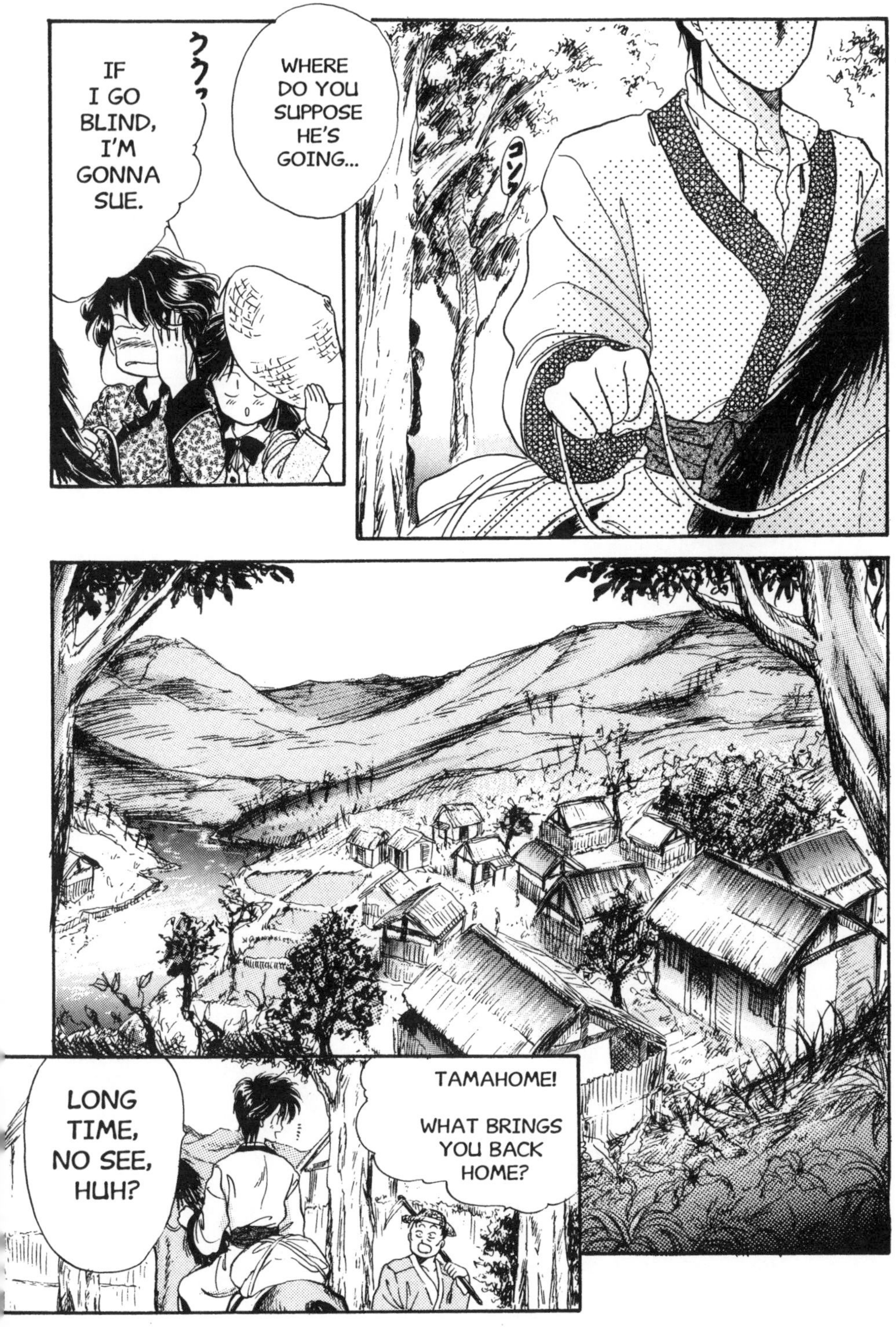
WHERE DO YOU SUPPOSE HE'S GOING...
IF I GO BLIND, I'M GONNA SUE.
TAMAHOME!
WHAT BRINGS YOU BACK HOME?
LONG TIME, NO SEE, HUH?

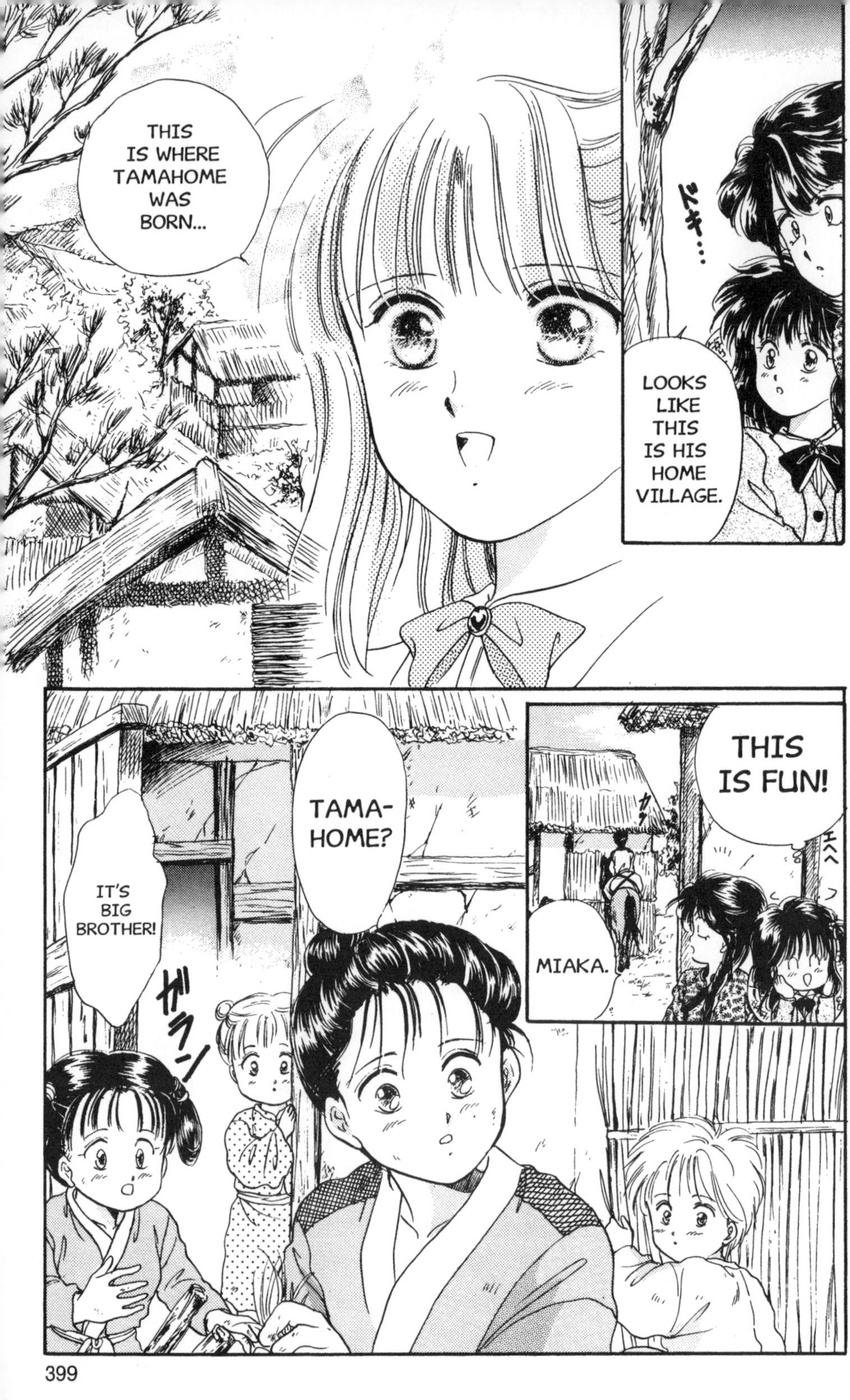
ドキ…
LOOKS LIKE THIS IS HIS HOME VILLAGE.
THIS IS WHERE TAMAHOME WAS BORN...
THIS IS FUN!
エヘヘ
MIAKA.
TAMA-HOME?
IT'S BIG BROTHER!
ガラン

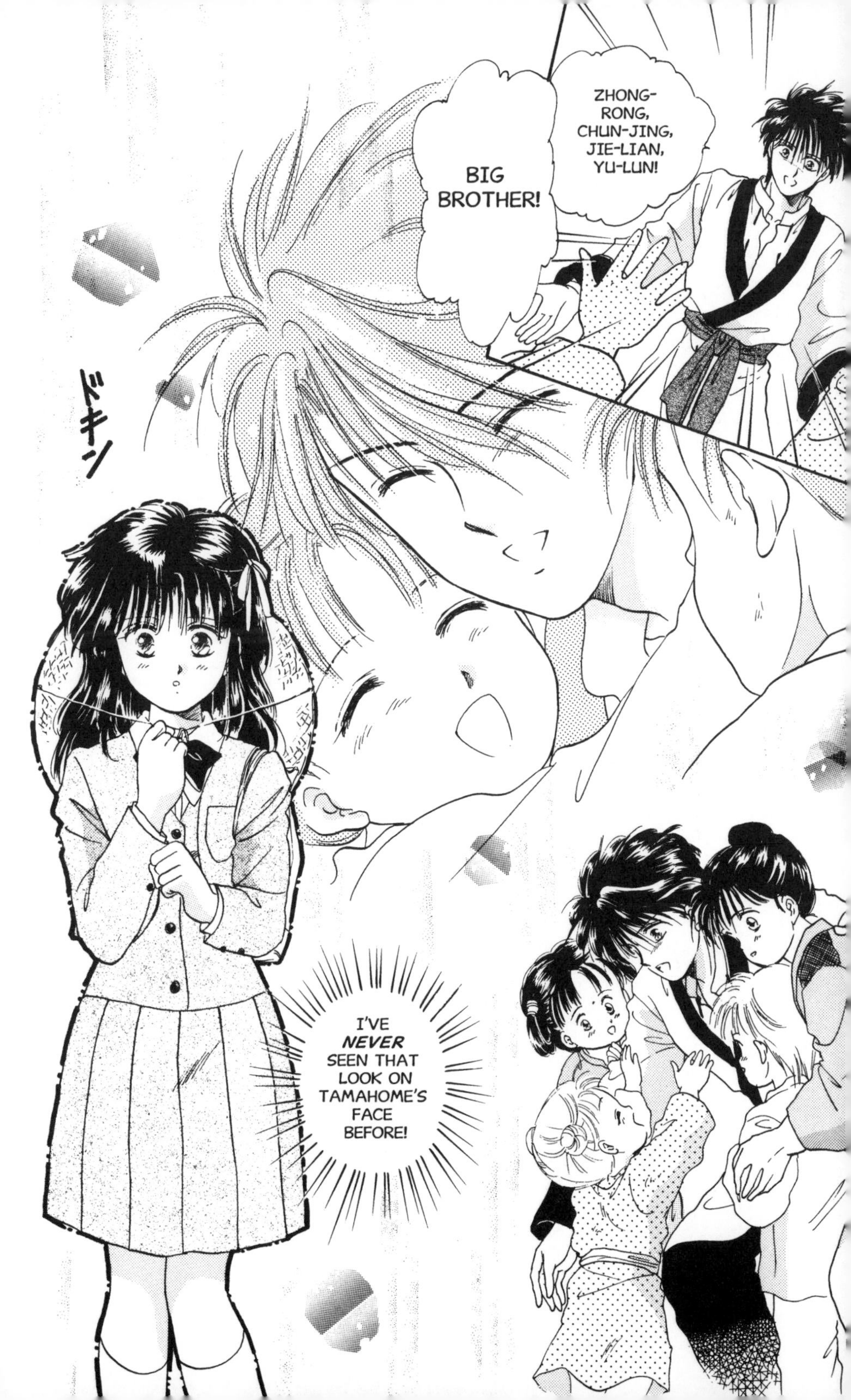
ZHONG-RONG, CHUN-JING, JIE-LIAN, YU-LUN!
BIG BROTHER!
ドキン
I'VE *NEVER* SEEN THAT LOOK ON TAMAHOME'S FACE BEFORE!

How are you all doing? This'll be the start of the third volume!! Time passes quickly. Right now, I'm drawing the last issue of the volume.
I thought at first, given this rapid pace, the story might be completed soon, but that ain't-a gonna happen. (Where'd the old-west sheriff come from?) If I don't watch myself, it could easily go into 10 volumes. That might not even be enough. Enjoy the ride!

I received may letters of encouragement after my whining in volume 2. I really wasn't begging for letters. Sorry to have worried you. I'm all right. I usually don't get depressed at all. Nobody could be depressed and still be a successful manga artist. Usually I draw with a grin on my face. But sometimes I frown when I concentrate.

I like my manga and my drawings! (You can't draw if you hate your own drawings!) When I said I couldn't face my own art, I was just exaggerating. When I see the first printing of my manga, I'm really happy, and I'm always asking for my editor to send me more copies. I was just complaining because my art hasn't fully matured. I'll keep on improving, waiting for that day when I'm perfect. Will it ever really come?
One thing I know for sure: more than anything else, I love drawing manga. Nobody could like drawing manga more than I do! But I'll bet other manga artists say the same thing.
Maybe my readership has gotten wider because I only hear, "I can't stand your manga," once in a very blue moon.

I said I like them--not that I'm any good at them! :)

They can say it if they want. They're just criticizing my entire existence, that's all! I'm crushed!
Recently, several other manga-artist friends and I have come up with the proper response. "Then why don't you try drawing manga, huh!? You can't even draw, you loser!!" Actually this thought occurs to many a manga artist when his or her work is rejected by an editor. (Yeah!) And I've decided to say that to anyone with harsh criticism of my work!

Like I ever could! I'm just acting strong.

sniff

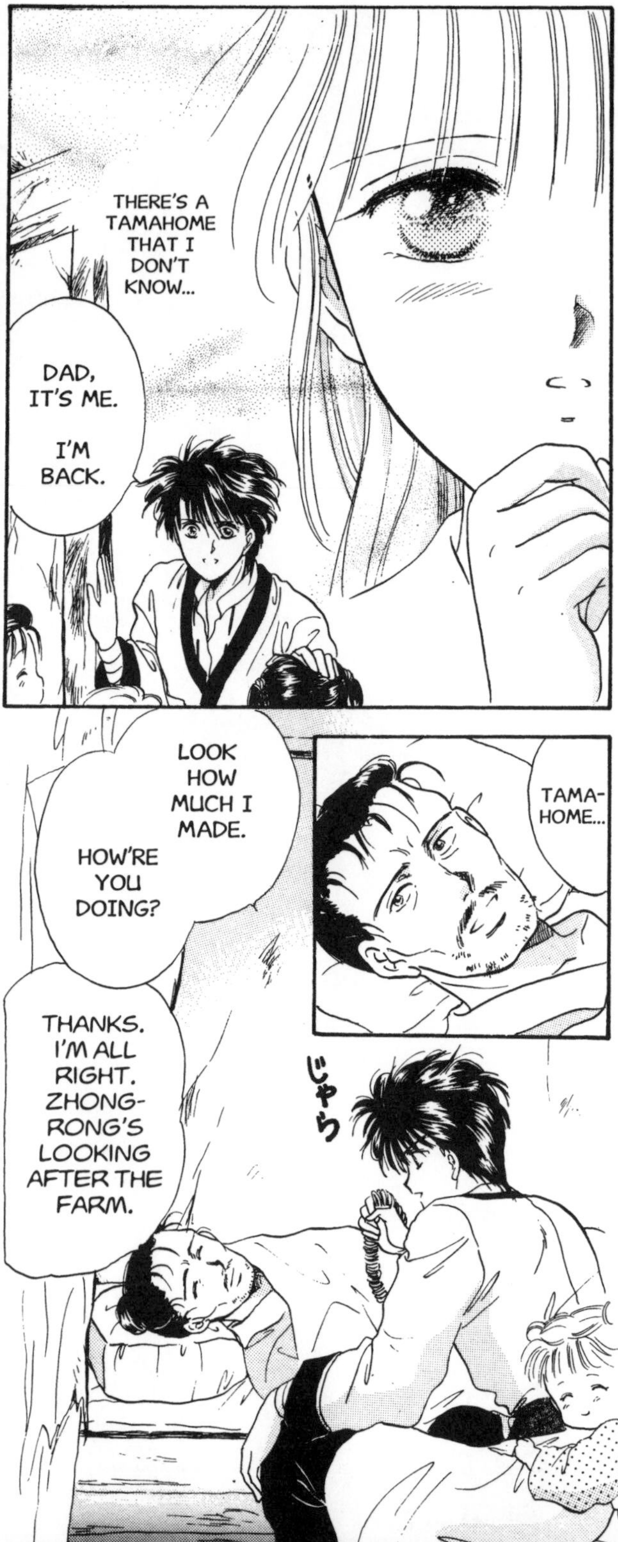
THERE'S A TAMAHOME THAT I DON'T KNOW...
DAD, IT'S ME. I'M BACK.
TAMA-HOME...
LOOK HOW MUCH I MADE.
HOW'RE YOU DOING?
じゃら
THANKS. I'M ALL RIGHT. ZHONG-RONG'S LOOKING AFTER THE FARM.

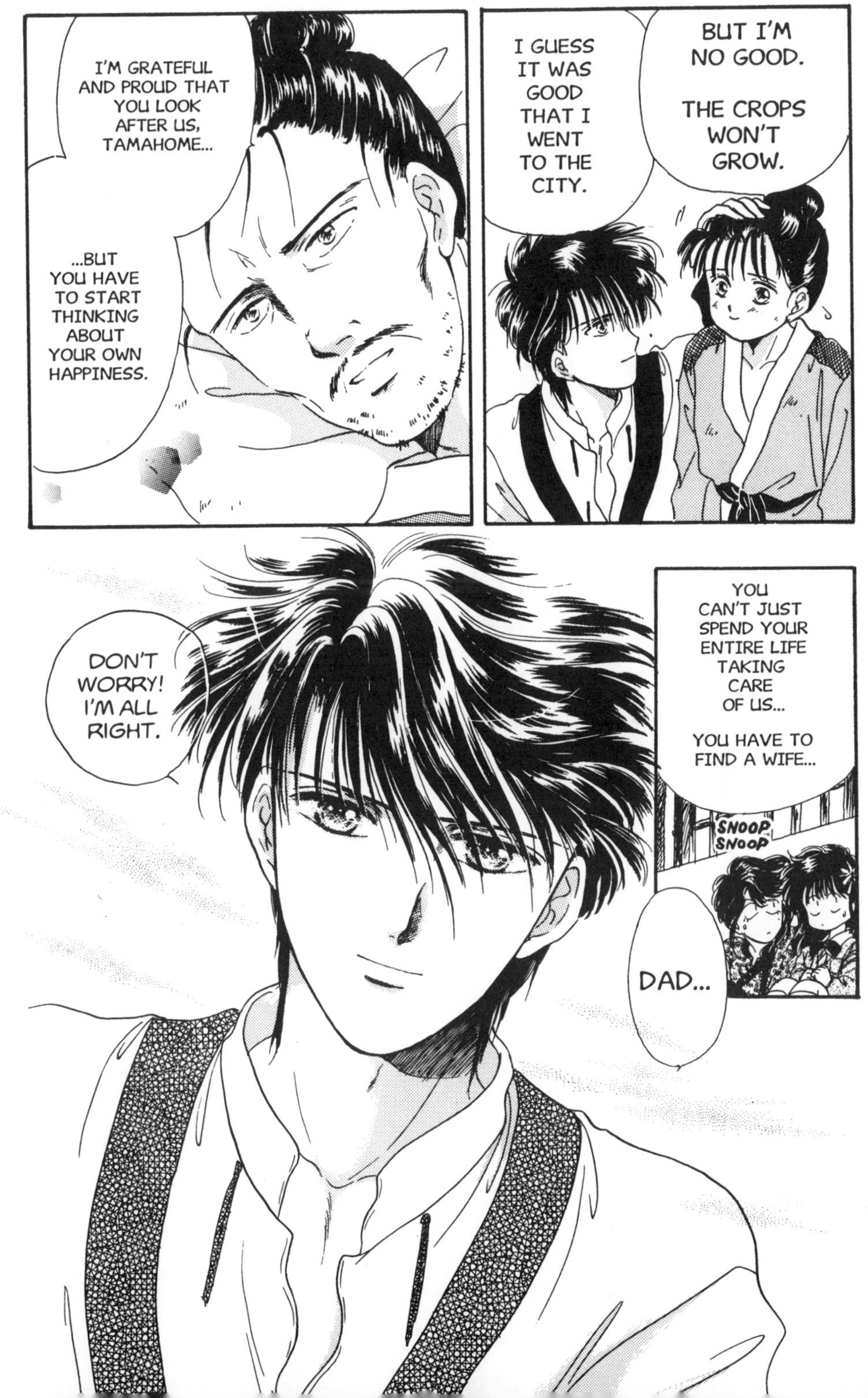
BUT I'M NO GOOD.
THE CROPS WON'T GROW.
I GUESS IT WAS GOOD THAT I WENT TO THE CITY.
I'M GRATEFUL AND PROUD THAT YOU LOOK AFTER US, TAMAHOME...
...BUT YOU HAVE TO START THINKING ABOUT YOUR OWN HAPPINESS.
YOU CAN'T JUST SPEND YOUR ENTIRE LIFE TAKING CARE OF US...
YOU HAVE TO FIND A WIFE...
SNOOP SNOOP
DAD...
DON'T WORRY! I'M ALL RIGHT.

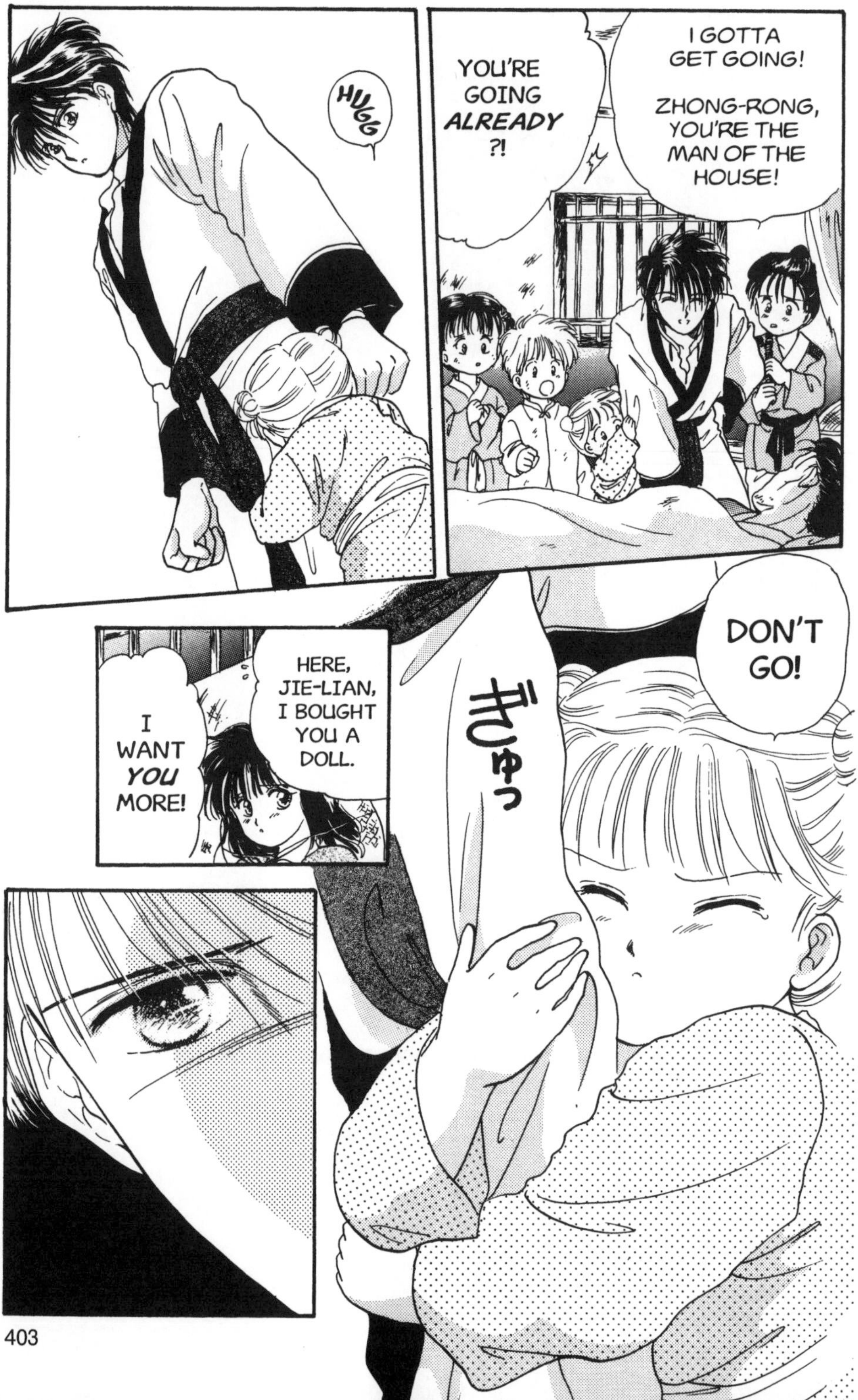
I GOTTA GET GOING!
ZHONG-RONG, YOU'RE THE MAN OF THE HOUSE!
YOU'RE GOING *ALREADY* ?!
HUGG
DON'T GO!
ぎゅっ
HERE, JIE-LIAN, I BOUGHT YOU A DOLL.
I WANT *YOU* MORE!

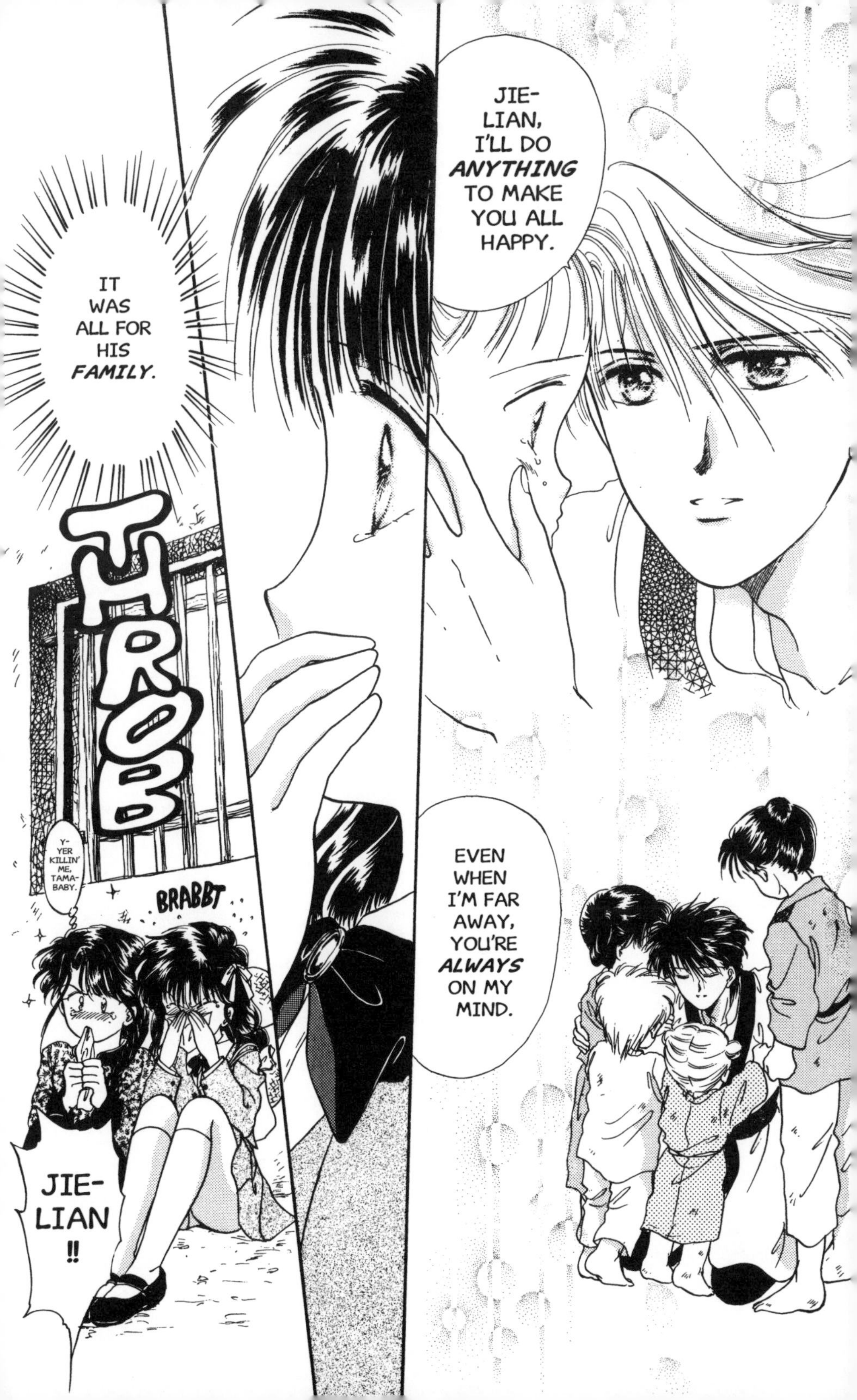
JIE-LIAN, I'LL DO ANYTHING TO MAKE YOU ALL HAPPY.
EVEN WHEN I'M FAR AWAY, YOU'RE ALWAYS ON MY MIND.
IT WAS ALL FOR HIS FAMILY.
THROB
Y-YER KILLIN' ME, TAMA-BABY.
BRABBT
JIE-LIAN!!

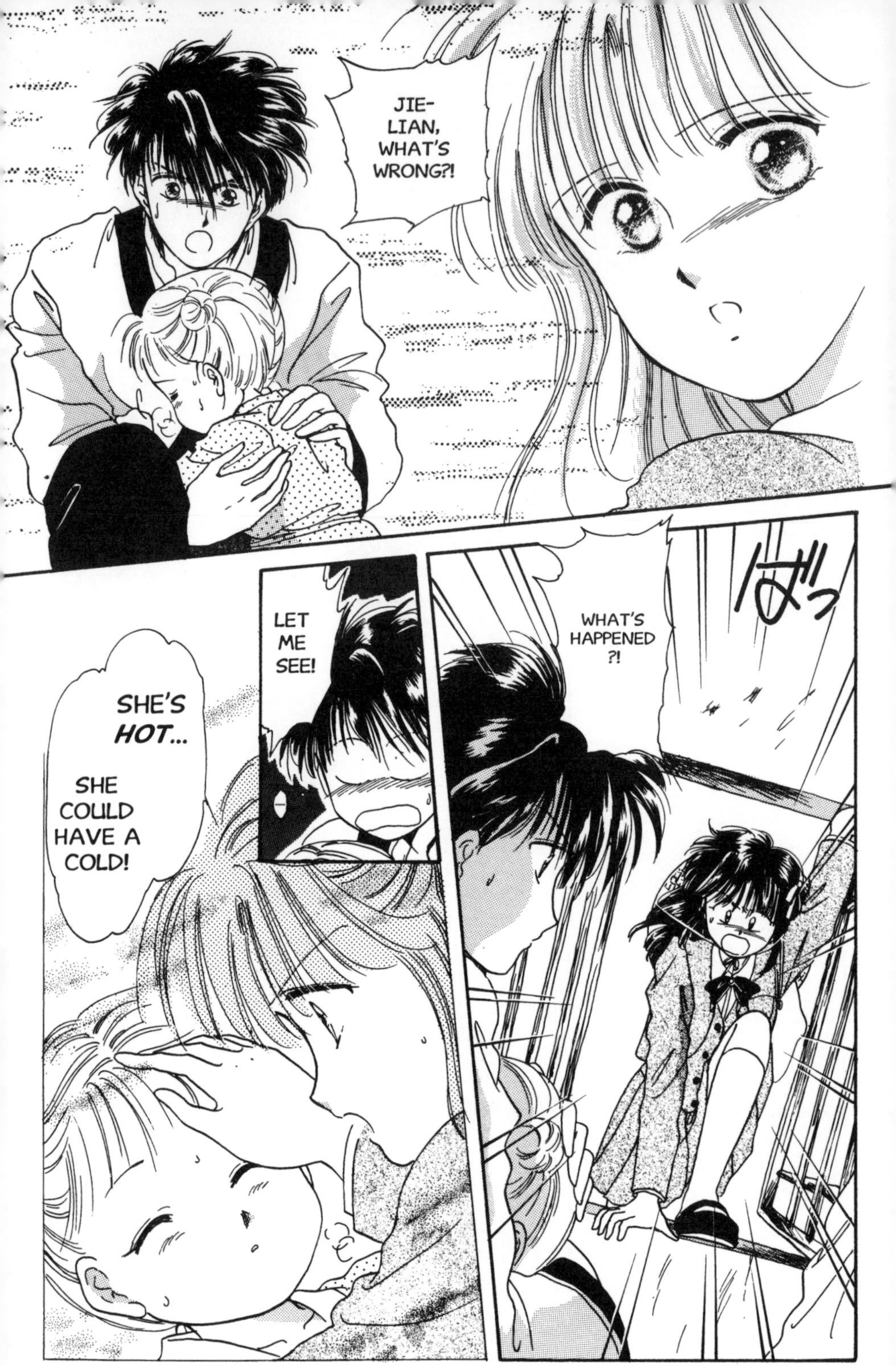
JIE-LIAN, WHAT'S WRONG?!
ばっ
WHAT'S HAPPENED ?!
LET ME SEE!
SHE'S *HOT*...
SHE COULD HAVE A COLD!

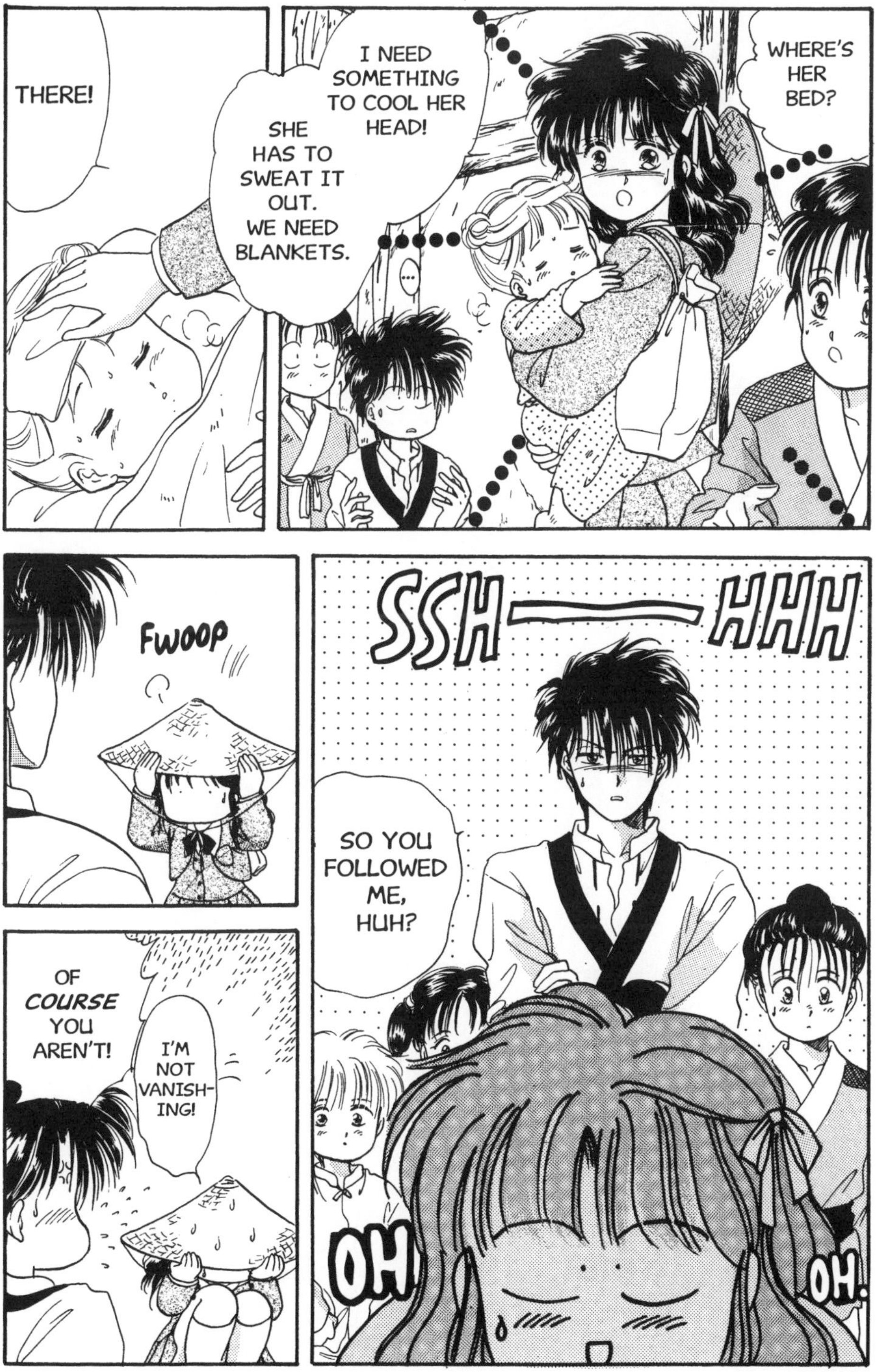
WHERE'S HER BED?
I NEED SOMETHING TO COOL HER HEAD!
SHE HAS TO SWEAT IT OUT. WE NEED BLANKETS.
...
THERE!
SSH——HHH
SO YOU FOLLOWED ME, HUH?
OH.
OH.
FWOOP
I'M NOT VANISHING!
OF *COURSE* YOU AREN'T!

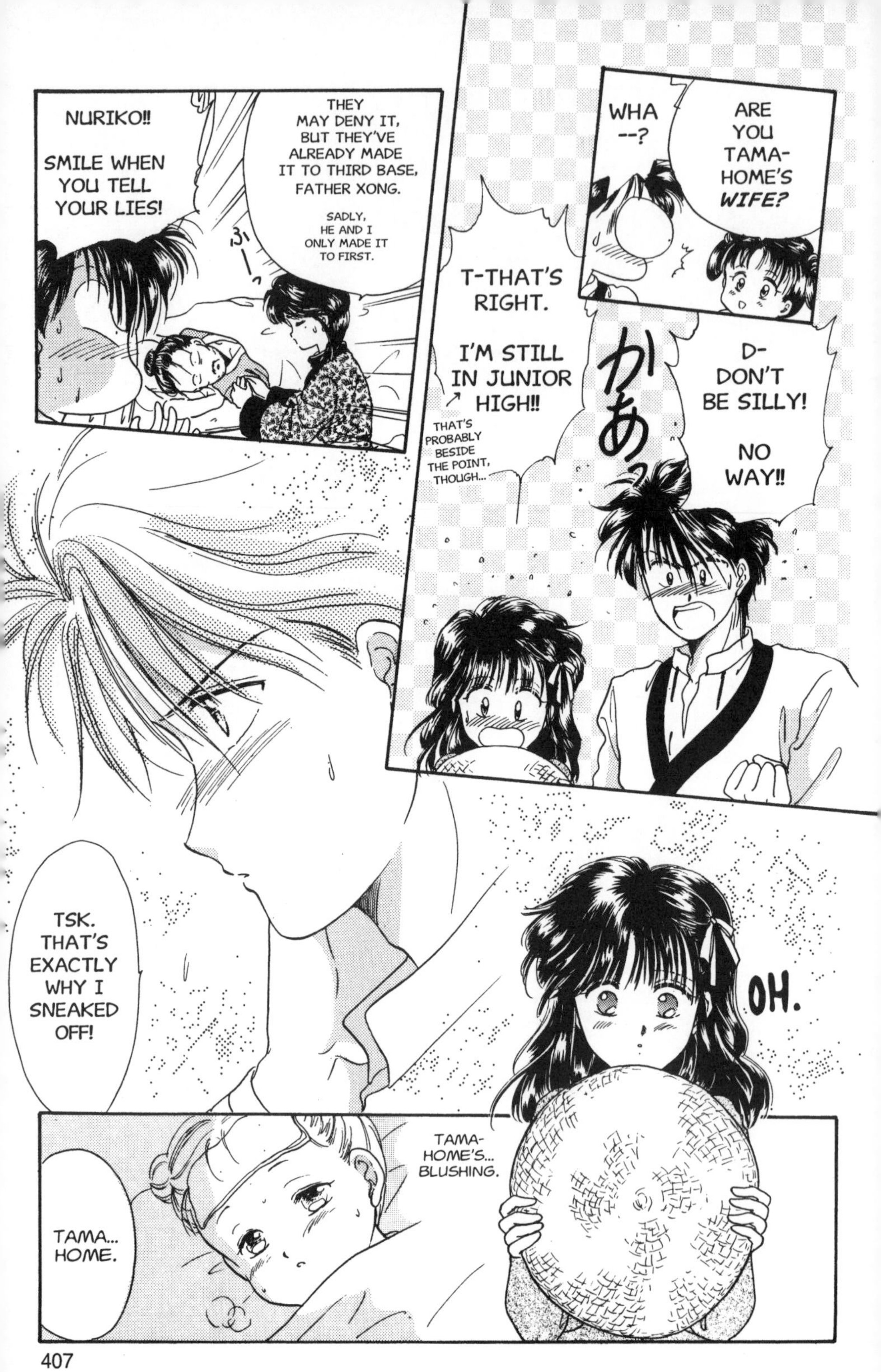
ARE YOU TAMA-HOME'S *WIFE?*
WHA--?
D-DON'T BE SILLY!
NO WAY!!
かあっ
T-THAT'S RIGHT.
I'M STILL IN JUNIOR HIGH!!
THAT'S PROBABLY BESIDE THE POINT, THOUGH...
THEY MAY DENY IT, BUT THEY'VE ALREADY MADE IT TO THIRD BASE, FATHER XONG.
SADLY, HE AND I ONLY MADE IT TO FIRST.
ふ
NURIKO!!
SMILE WHEN YOU TELL YOUR LIES!
OH.
TSK. THAT'S EXACTLY WHY I SNEAKED OFF!
TAMA-HOME'S... BLUSHING.
TAMA... HOME.

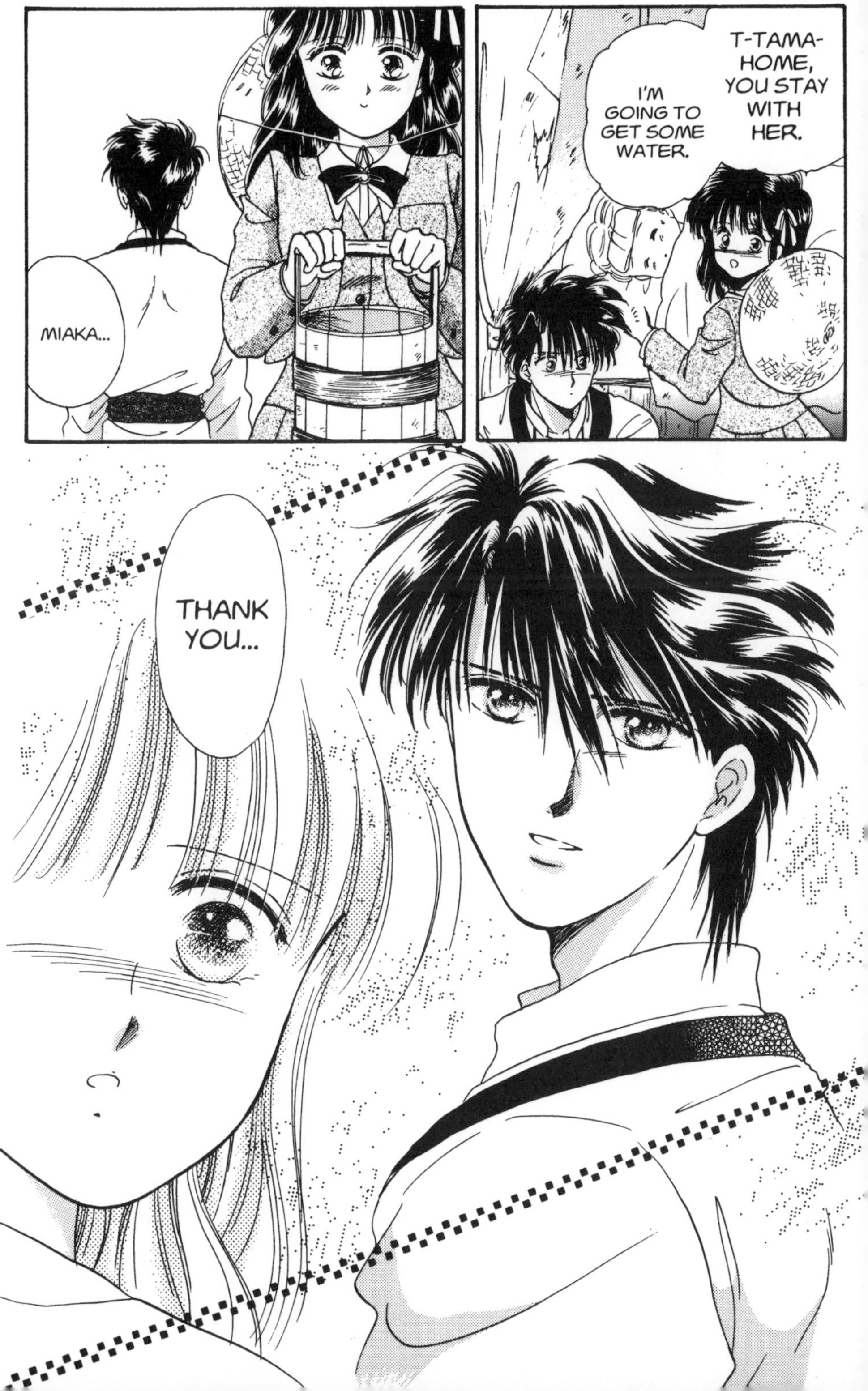
T-TAMA-HOME, YOU STAY WITH HER.
I'M GOING TO GET SOME WATER.
MIAKA...
THANK YOU...

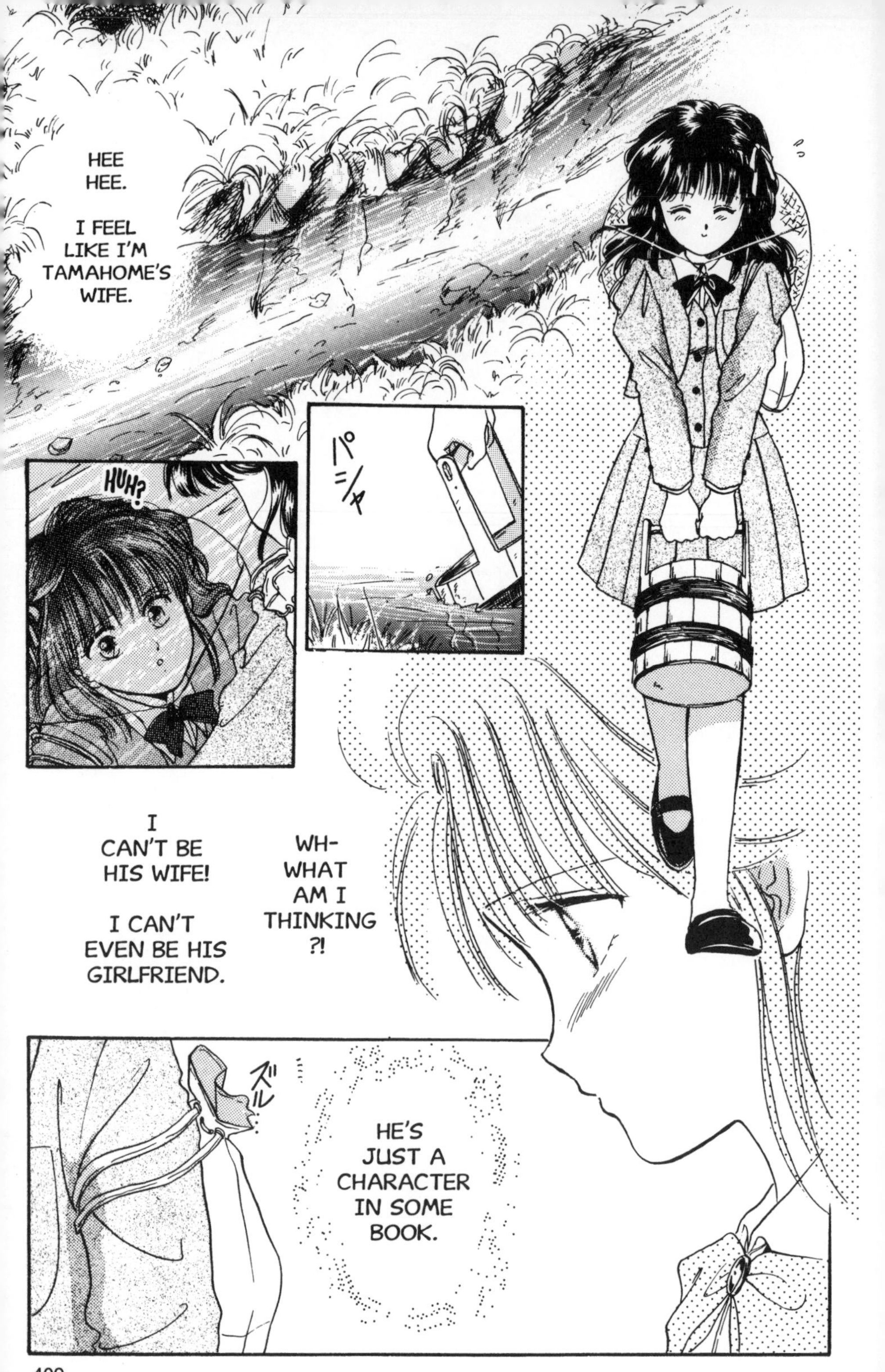
HEE HEE.
I FEEL LIKE I'M TAMAHOME'S WIFE.
パシャ
HUH?
WH- WHAT AM I THINKING?!
I CAN'T BE HIS WIFE!
I CAN'T EVEN BE HIS GIRLFRIEND.
ズル
HE'S JUST A CHARACTER IN SOME BOOK.

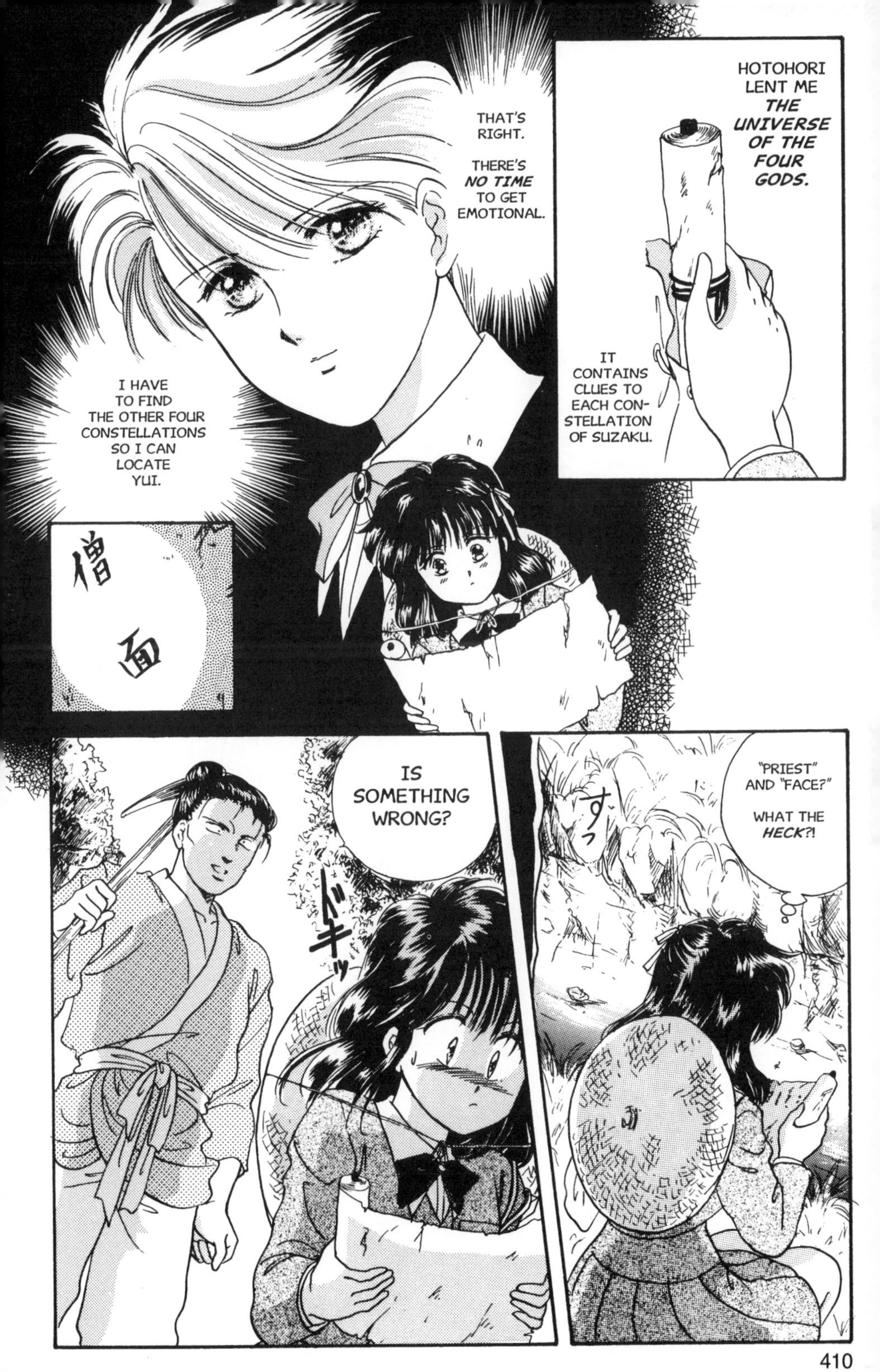
HOTOHORI LENT ME *THE UNIVERSE OF THE FOUR GODS.*
IT CONTAINS CLUES TO EACH CON-STELLATION OF SUZAKU.
THAT'S RIGHT.
THERE'S *NO TIME* TO GET EMOTIONAL.
I HAVE TO FIND THE OTHER FOUR CONSTELLATIONS SO I CAN LOCATE YUI.
僧面
"PRIEST" AND "FACE?"
WHAT THE *HECK*?!
すっ
IS SOMETHING WRONG?
ドキッ

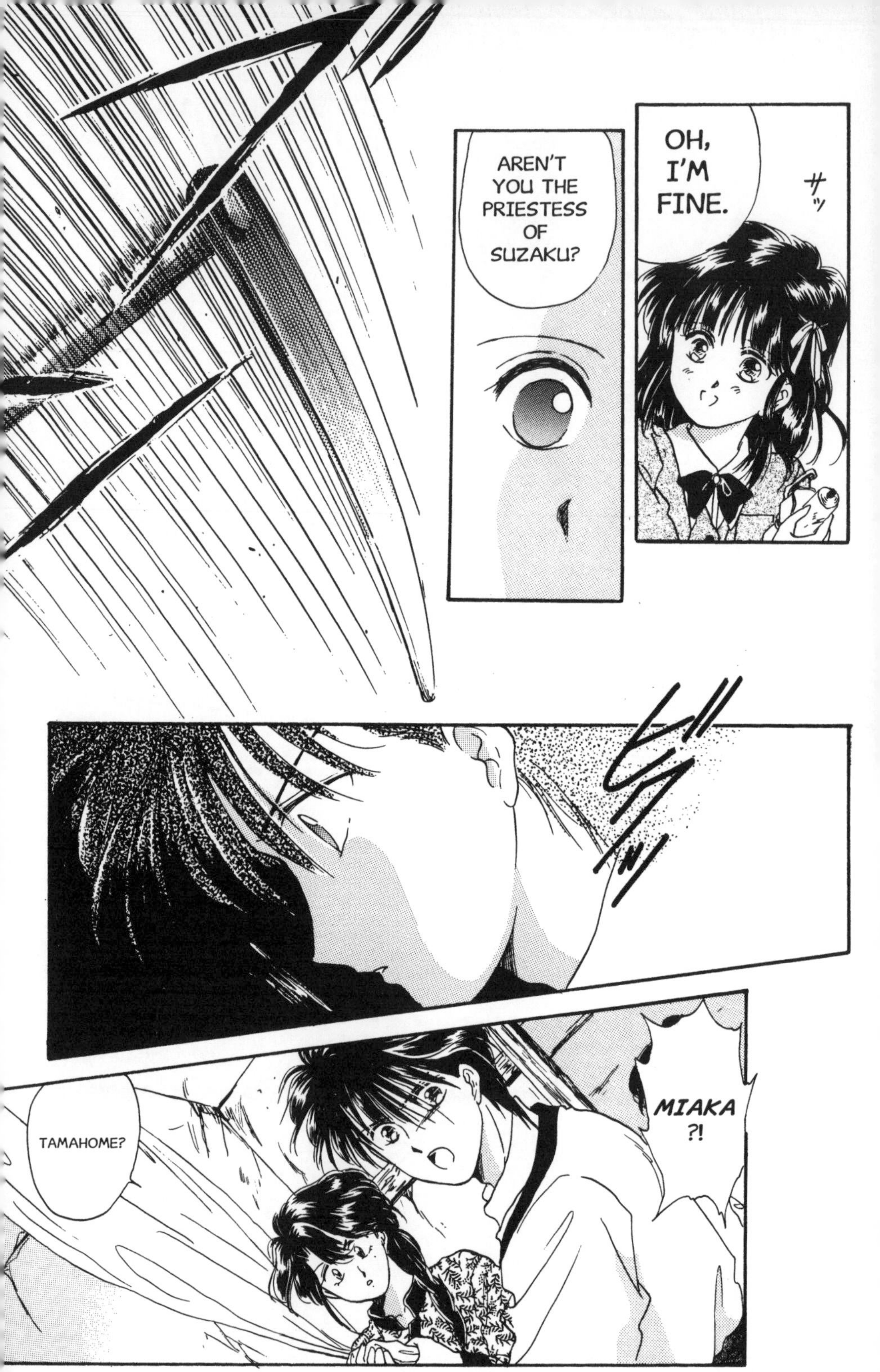

OH, I'M FINE.
サッ
AREN'T YOU THE PRIESTESS OF SUZAKU?
MIAKA ?!
TAMAHOME?

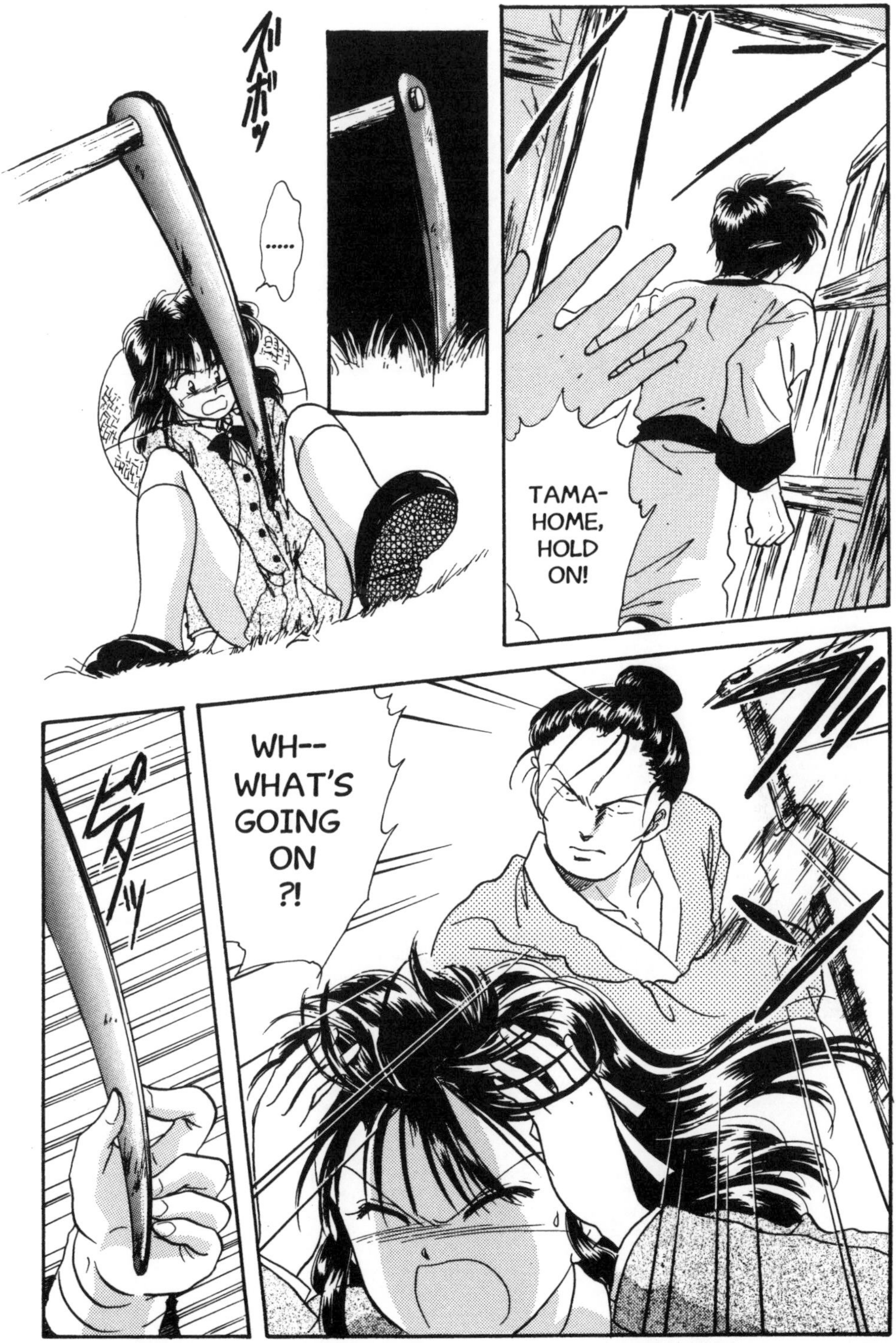
TAMA-HOME, HOLD ON!
ズボッ
......
WH-- WHAT'S GOING ON ?!
ピタッ

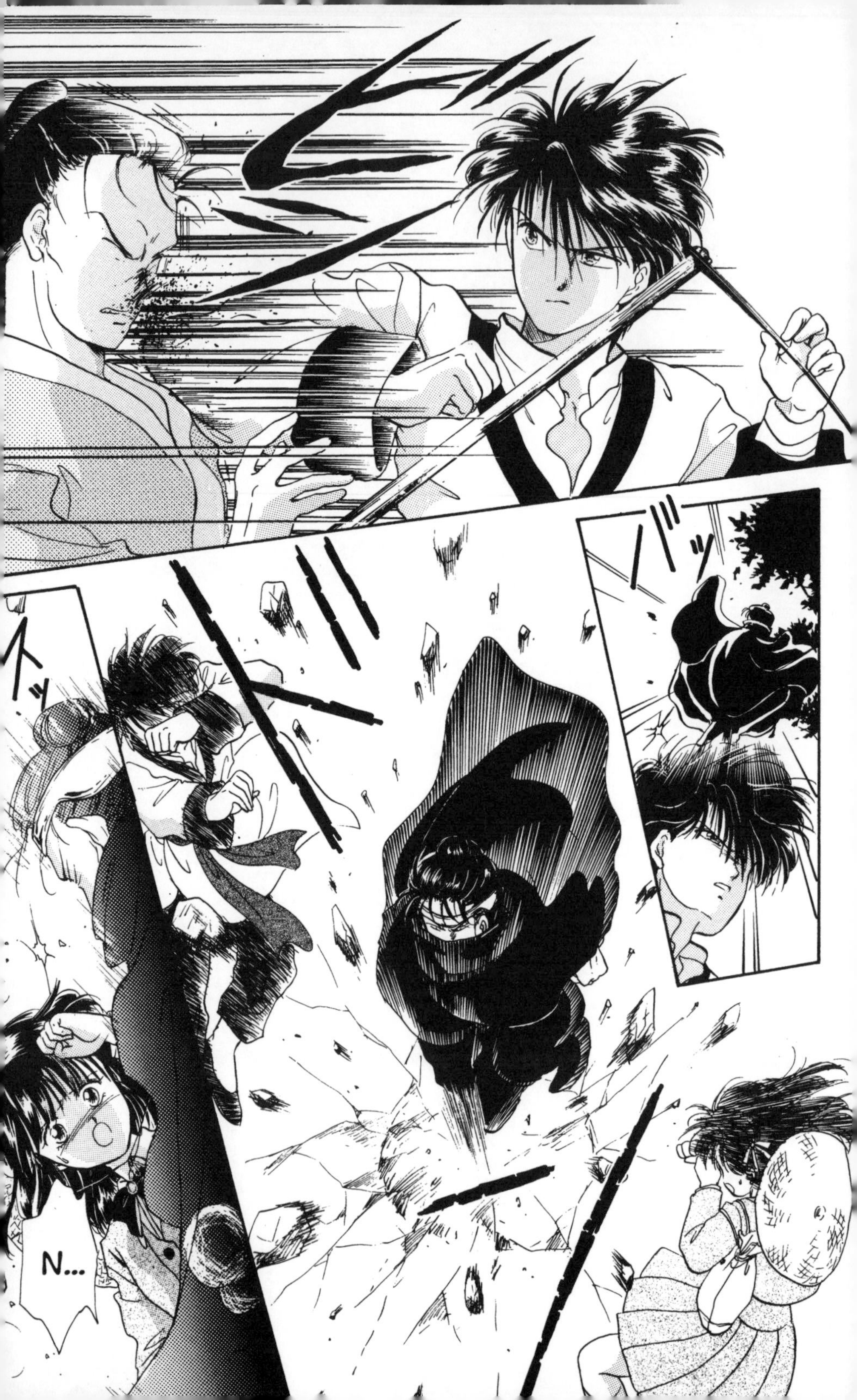
バッ
N...

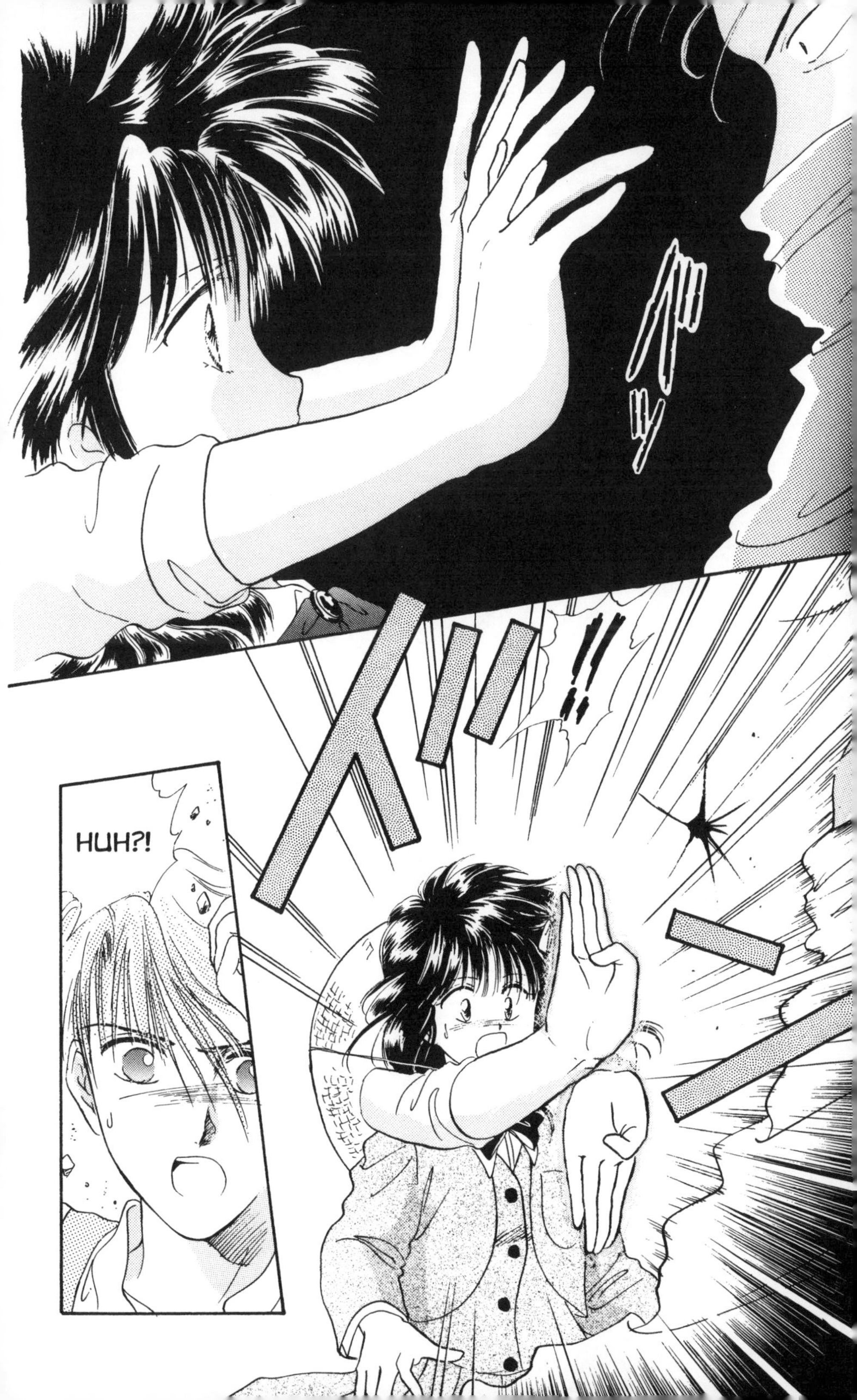
HUH?!

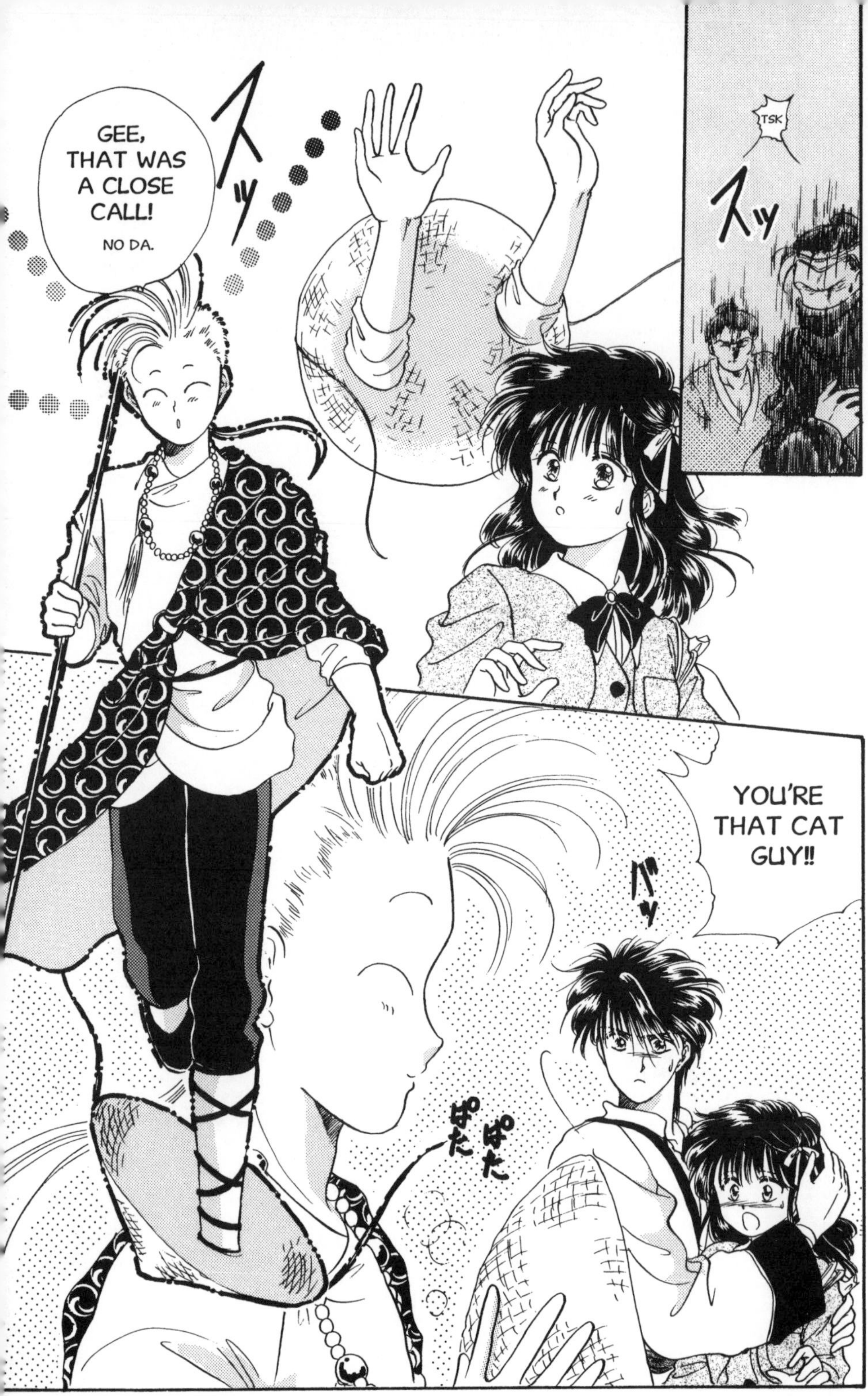
TSK
スッ
スッ
GEE, THAT WAS A CLOSE CALL!
NO DA.
YOU'RE THAT CAT GUY!!
バッ
ぱた ぱた

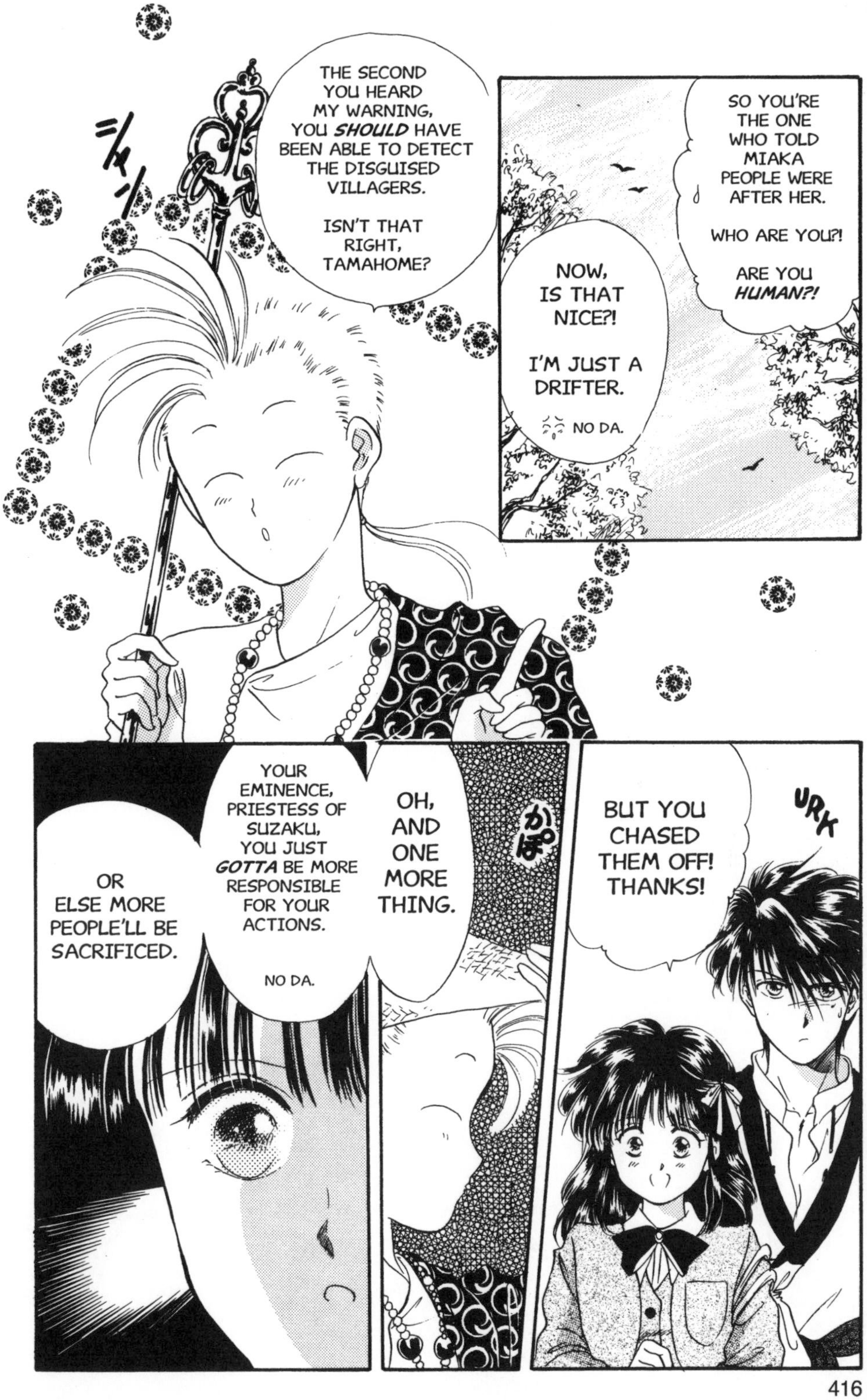
SO YOU'RE THE ONE WHO TOLD MIAKA PEOPLE WERE AFTER HER.
WHO ARE YOU?!
ARE YOU *HUMAN?!*
NOW, IS THAT NICE?!
I'M JUST A DRIFTER.
NO DA.
THE SECOND YOU HEARD MY WARNING, YOU *SHOULD* HAVE BEEN ABLE TO DETECT THE DISGUISED VILLAGERS.
ISN'T THAT RIGHT, TAMAHOME?
URK
BUT YOU CHASED THEM OFF! THANKS!
かぽ
OH, AND ONE MORE THING.
YOUR EMINENCE, PRIESTESS OF SUZAKU, YOU JUST *GOTTA* BE MORE RESPONSIBLE FOR YOUR ACTIONS.
NO DA.
OR ELSE MORE PEOPLE'LL BE SACRIFICED.

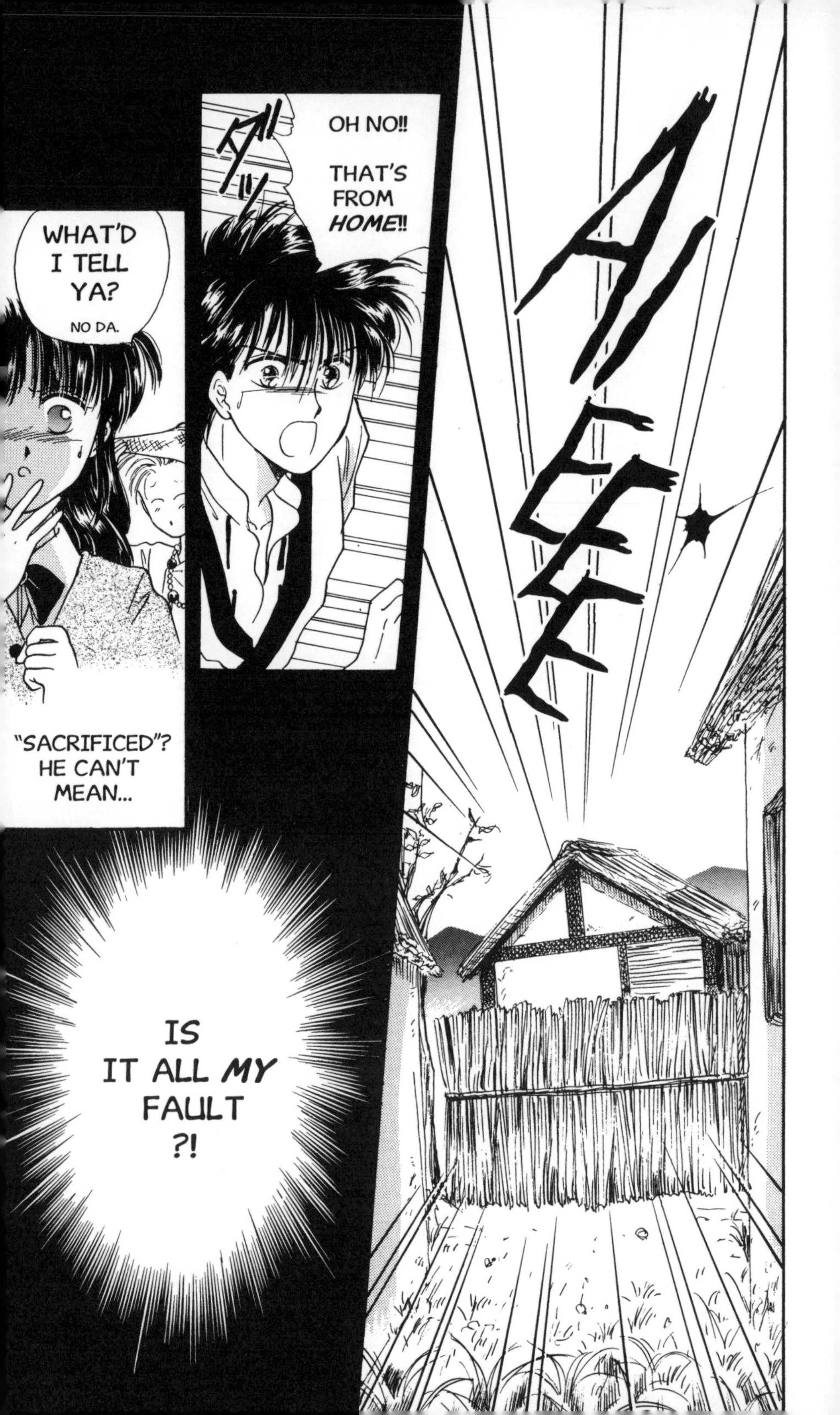
AIEEEE
OH NO!! THAT'S FROM *HOME*!!
WHAT'D I TELL YA?
NO DA.
"SACRIFICED"? HE CAN'T MEAN...
IS IT ALL *MY* FAULT ?!

TELL ME MORE ABOUT *THE UNIVERSE OF THE FOUR GODS*

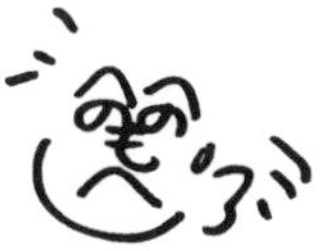

This is one of the questions I hear frequently. If you keep reading the story, you'll find out all about it. But for the impatient who still INSIST! I've decided to expose a few details.

I've never seen constellations attributed to the Four Gods, so I might be the first. (Usually they've been used as compass directions or for the identities of monsters. Other than that, their names have been used for invocations.) The anime OAV *Maryu Senki* used them as monsters. I think Suzaku was female, but this anime gets pretty heavily into erotic-grotesque so I can't recommend it... I'll describe the gods and their constellations. (That way you can find them in the night sky.)

We'll list the Four Gods according to ancient Chinese astrological names rather than geographical areas (which might appear later in the story) or compass directions.

EASTERN SEIRYU SEVEN CONSTELLATIONS (MAY-JULY): Suboshi (Virgo), Amiboshi (Virgo), Tomo (Libra), Soi (Scorpio), Nakago (Scorpio), Ashitare (Scorpio), Mi (Sagittarius)

WESTERN BYAKKO SEVEN CONSTELLATIONS (NOVEMBER-JANUARY): Tokaki (Andromeda), Tatara (Aries), Kokie (Aries), Subaru (Taurus), Amefuri (Taurus), Toroki (Orion), Karasuki (Orion)

SOUTHERN SUZAKU SEVEN CONSTELLATIONS (FEBRUARY-MAY): Chichiri (Gemini), Tamahome (Cancer), Nuriko (Hydra), Chiriko (Hydra), Tasuki (Crater), Mitsukake (Corvus)

NORTHERN GENBU SEVEN CONSTELLATIONS (AUGUST-NOVEMBER): Hikitsu (Sagittarius), Inami (Capricorn), Uruki (Aquarius), Urumiya (Aquarius), Hatsui (Pegasus), Namame (Pegasus)

Usually, when you see the character for Chichiri's name, you read it as "I," and when you see the character for Tamahome's name, you read it as "ki," etc. So most of the tables list the constellation names with the Chinese pronunciations for each of the characters. There are very few which list the Japanese phonetic reading such as "Tamahome," but in the *Buddhaist Philosophy Encyclopedia* I have, the character was listed as "Tamahome." (You'll only find this book at a large bookstore. It costs a whopping ¥80,000!)
The rest I looked up in the constellation tables in the appendices of a Japanese/Chinese dictionary I used in high school. A star in "Hotohori" is second magnitude, and the brightest star is Suzaku (Alpha Hadrae, also known as Alphard or Solitary One. — Ed.)

The names for the Four Gods were taken from these constellation listings. The Southern Seven Star Constellations look like they have short tails so the ancients called them a bird, the Western Seven Star Constellations resemble a tiger, and so on.

Between February and May, you can see the Suzaku constellations appear in the night sky. The brightest star in Cancer is Tamahome.

I love the cosmos, so I get a kick out of naming my characters after constellations.

I've also been told that "Nuriko" is "Meriko," but I think it can be named both ways (most of the time it's called Nuriko). Also, Mitsukake can be read both as Mitsukake and Mitsuuchi. Some said that Tamahome and crew were part of Byakko, but they're mistaken.

Genbu is pretty sad. Dragons like Seiryu are kind of cool, but the idea of a turtle and snake copulating!! Blech! I am not into that!!

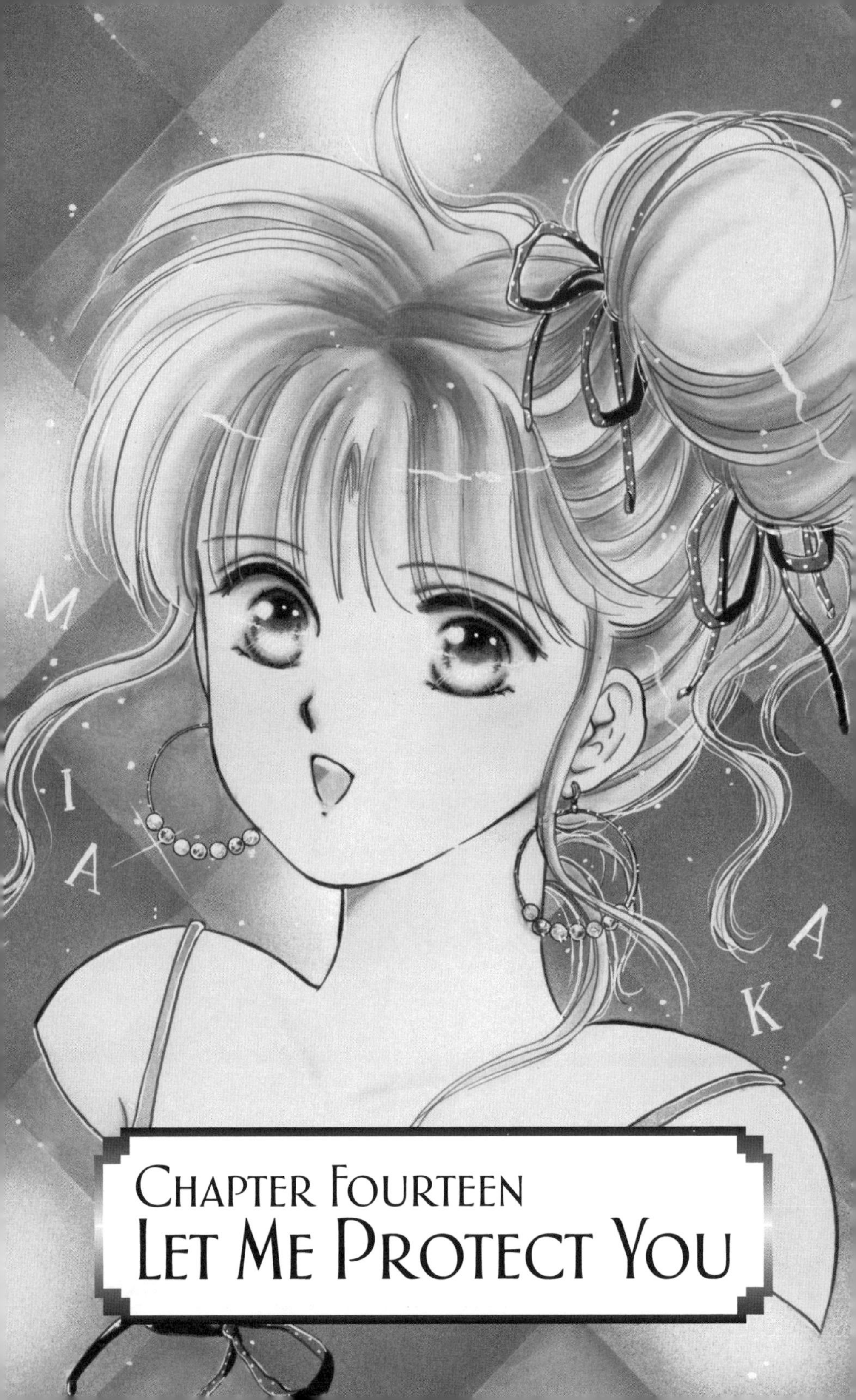
MIAKA

Chapter Fourteen
Let Me Protect You

MEOW MEOW

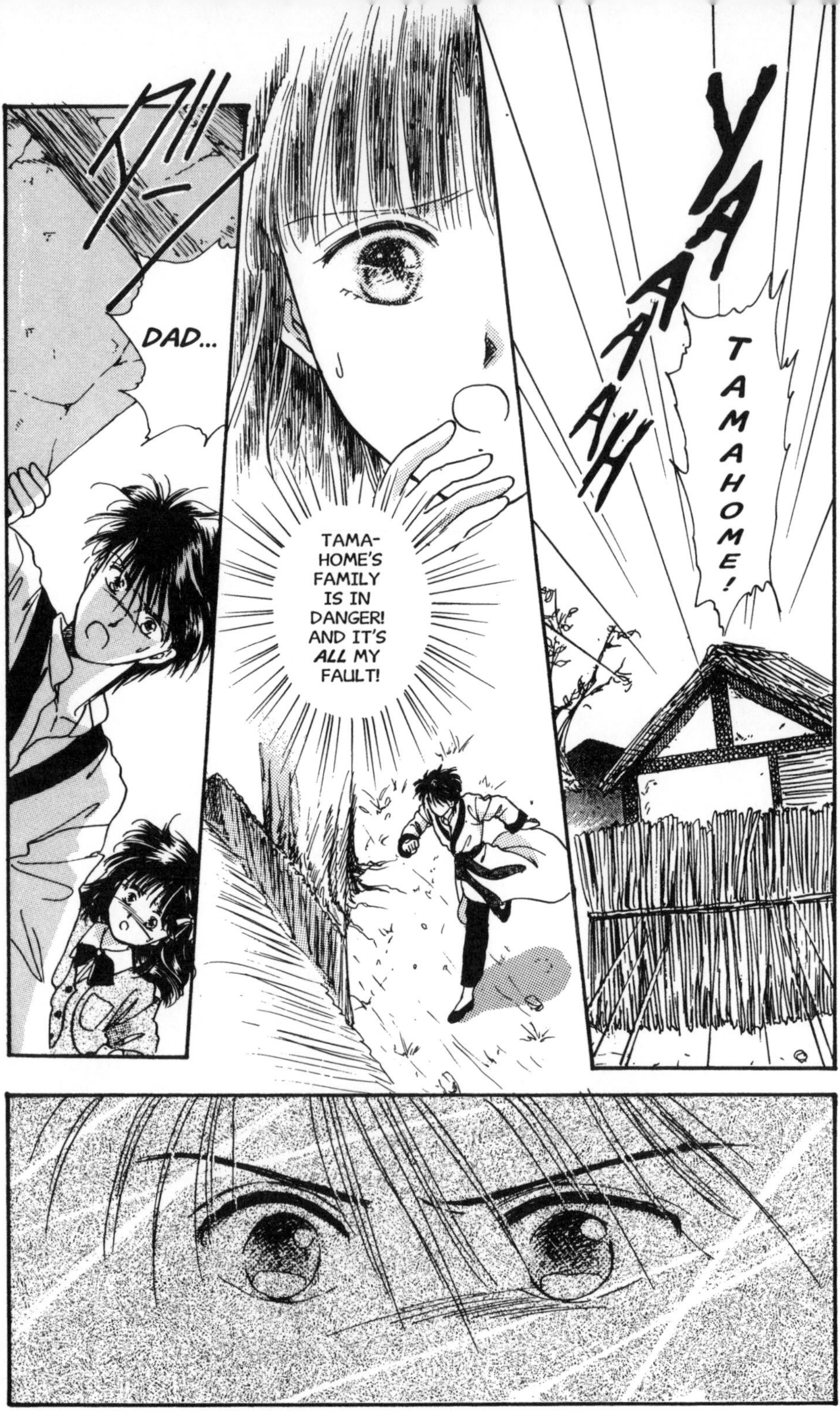
YAAAAH
TAMAHOME!
TAMA-HOME'S FAMILY IS IN DANGER! AND IT'S *ALL* MY FAULT!
DAD...

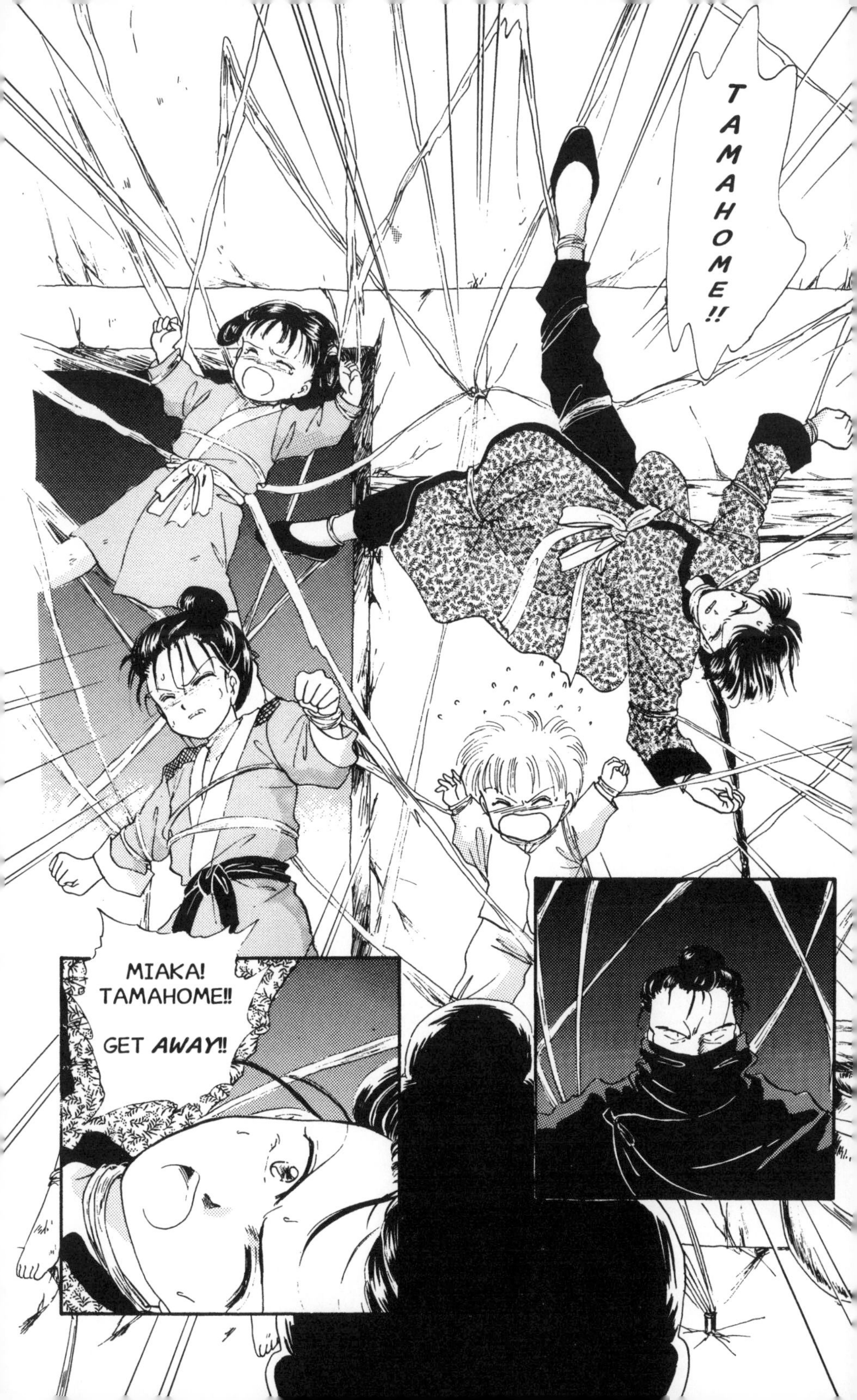
TAMAHOME!!
MIAKA! TAMAHOME!! GET AWAY!!

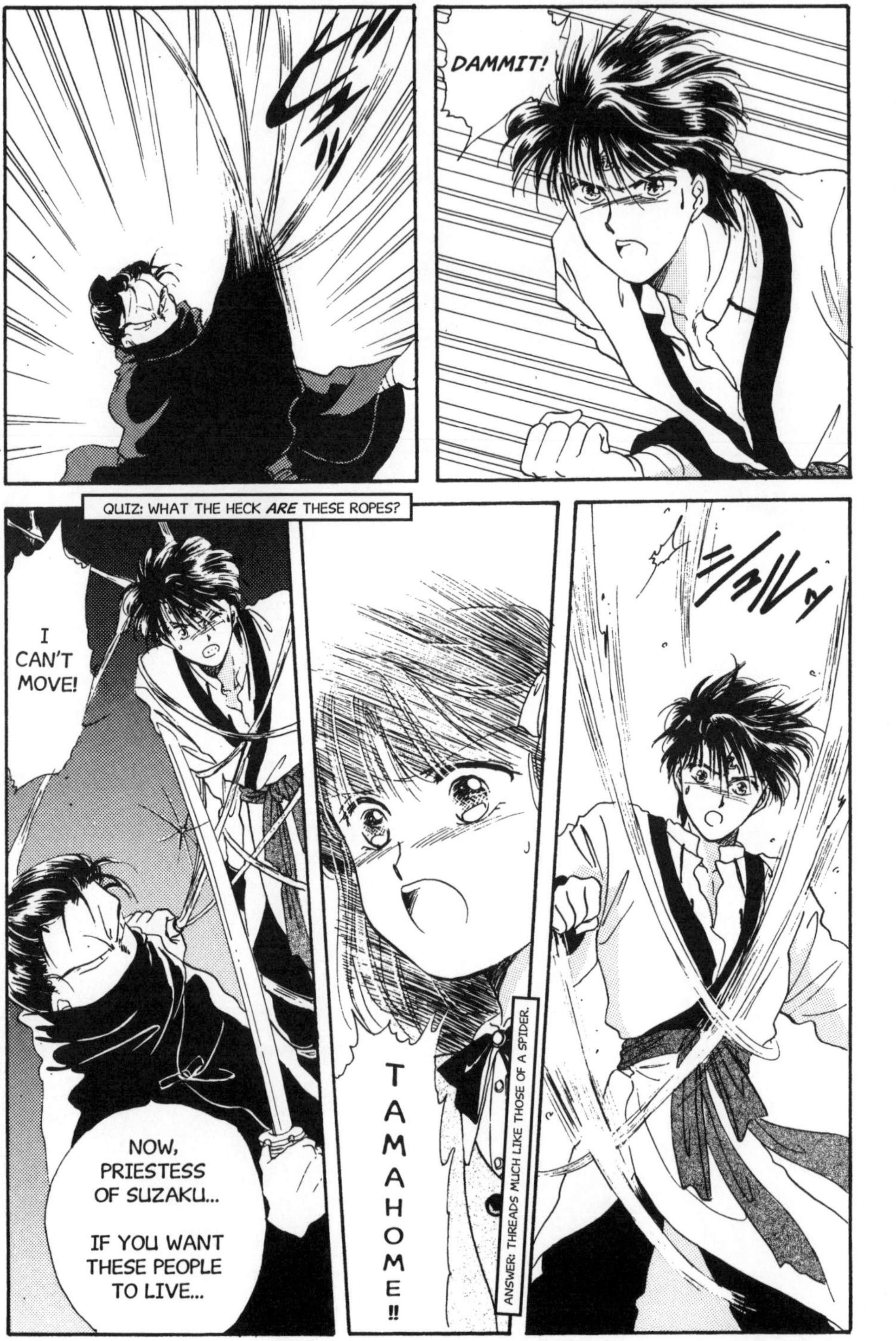
DAMMIT!
TAMAHOME!!
ANSWER: THREADS MUCH LIKE THOSE OF A SPIDER.
QUIZ: WHAT THE HECK *ARE* THESE ROPES?
I CAN'T MOVE!
NOW, PRIESTESS OF SUZAKU...
IF YOU WANT THESE PEOPLE TO LIVE...

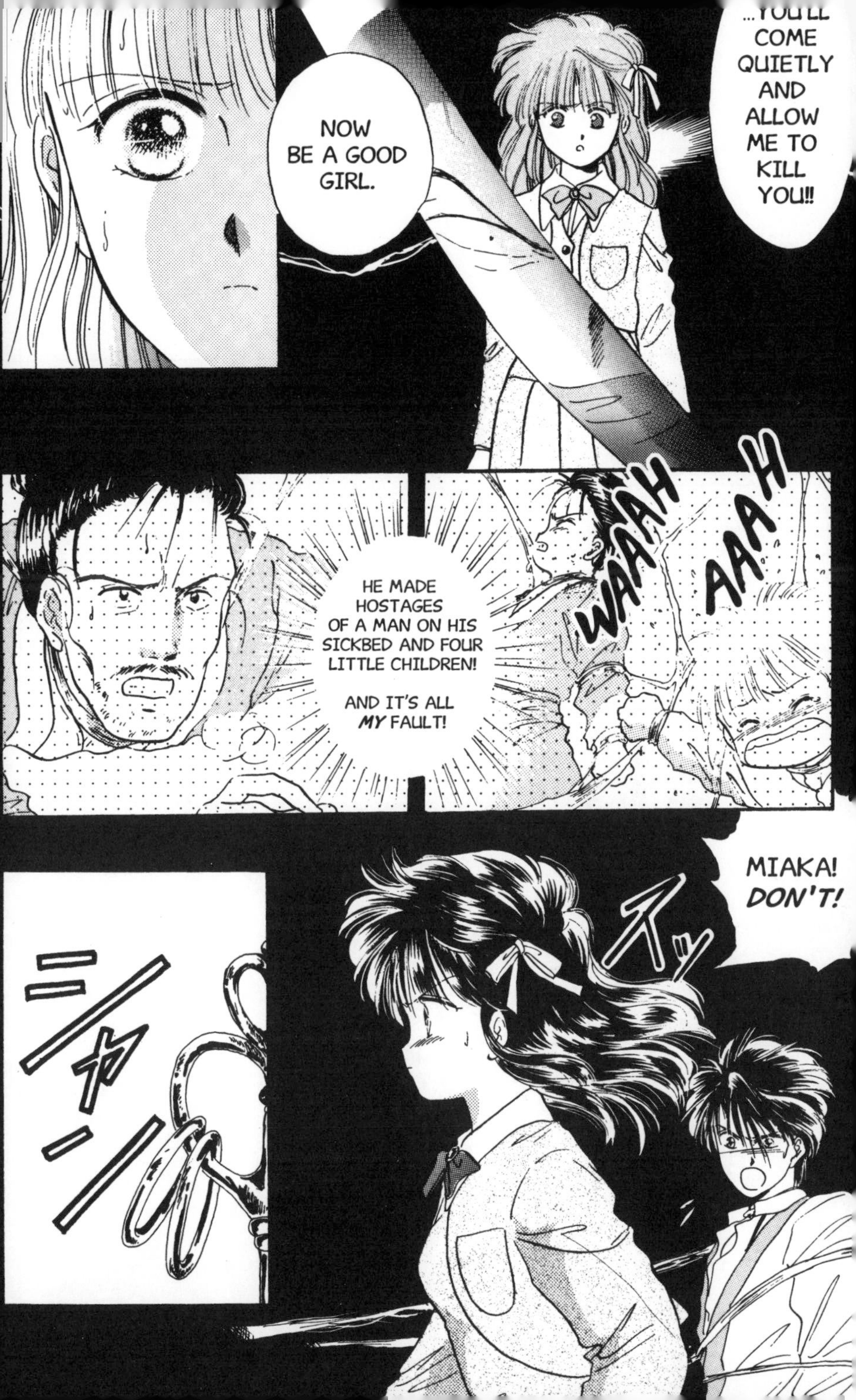
...YOU'LL COME QUIETLY AND ALLOW ME TO KILL YOU!!
NOW BE A GOOD GIRL.
WAAAH
AAAH
HE MADE HOSTAGES OF A MAN ON HIS SICKBED AND FOUR LITTLE CHILDREN!
AND IT'S ALL *MY* FAULT!
MIAKA! *DON'T!*

I mentioned before how I've been reading your fan mail, and I'm surprised at the huge number of questions. You're all so concerned about the remaining warriors in the constellations of Suzaku. Some of you have even sent me illustrations and suggestions for the rest of the warriors. But to tell the truth, I decided on all seven characters before I even started drawing the manga. So I'll introduce them one by one, the same way I envisioned them. I find it fascinating how all the characters get their own fans. The Tamahome fans don't like Hotohori, and the Hotohori fans look down on Tamahome. (There are really very few who like both!) Nuriko's been gaining popularity. Keisuke, Miaka's brother, has a set of fans too. Well, they're all cute so I don't mind. All of my assistants rate their favorites differently. Sometimes they play "Who'd be the best voice actor for each character?" and everyone gets all worked up. Fans have suggested some in their letters, but most of them don't seem right to me. (Sorry!) That's not to say my ideas are any better. We had a dramatic section in "Toy Box '93" so I was allowed to choose the actors for Miaka and Tamahome (but only them). I talked it over with my assistants then made my decision. Give it a listen and see what you think. I like voices that are mature and masculine (and a little erotic). What else? Oh, yes, I heard that all the merchandise at the Animate store sold out! 😢 And we got a lot of complaints! I never got any myself!! The least they could do is save a sample for me!! Did you hear there was a bonus poster with every ¥2,000 purchase?! Gimme!! Calendars (Supposedly, they only display July and August) are posted in bookstores without my knowledge. And I never knew it had been printed!! Speaking of calendars, I think you should know that I had to fight to get an original drawing into that calendar. It also took a lot of work to convince my editor that I should draw for the CD book too.

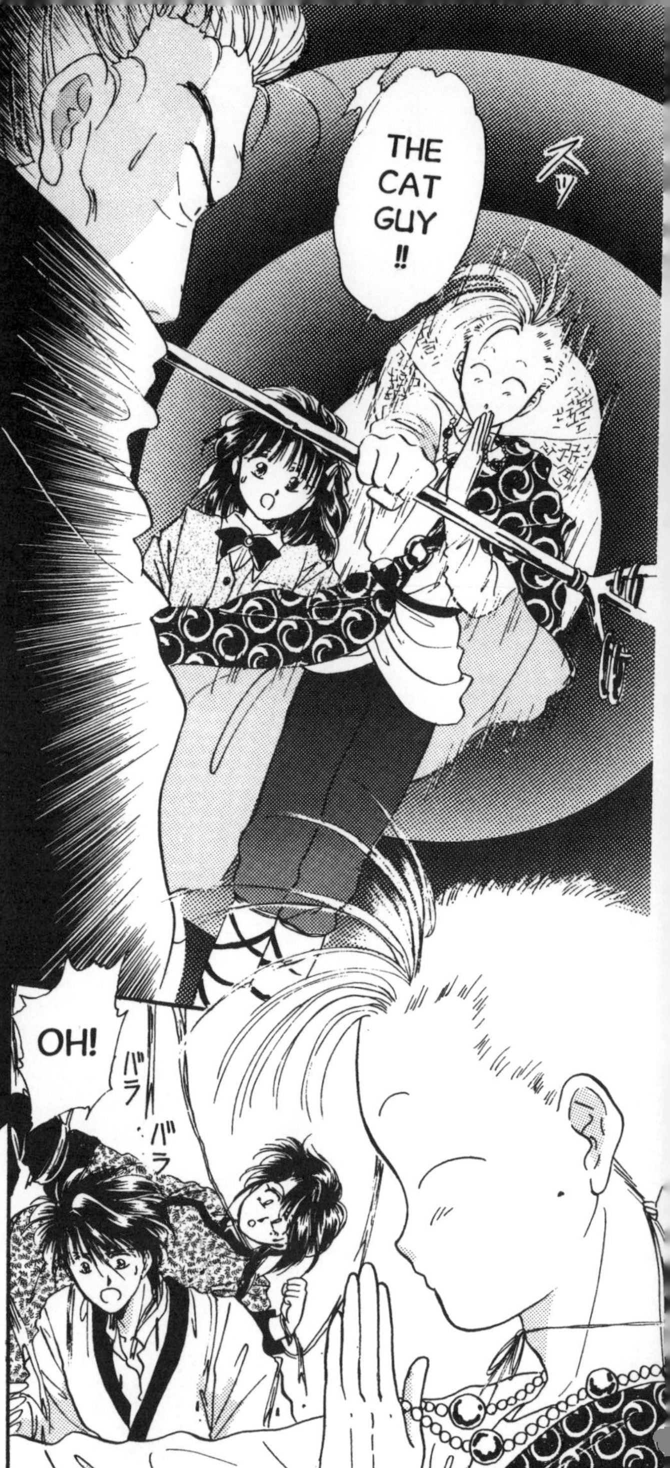
THE CAT GUY!!
スッ
OH!
バラ
バラ

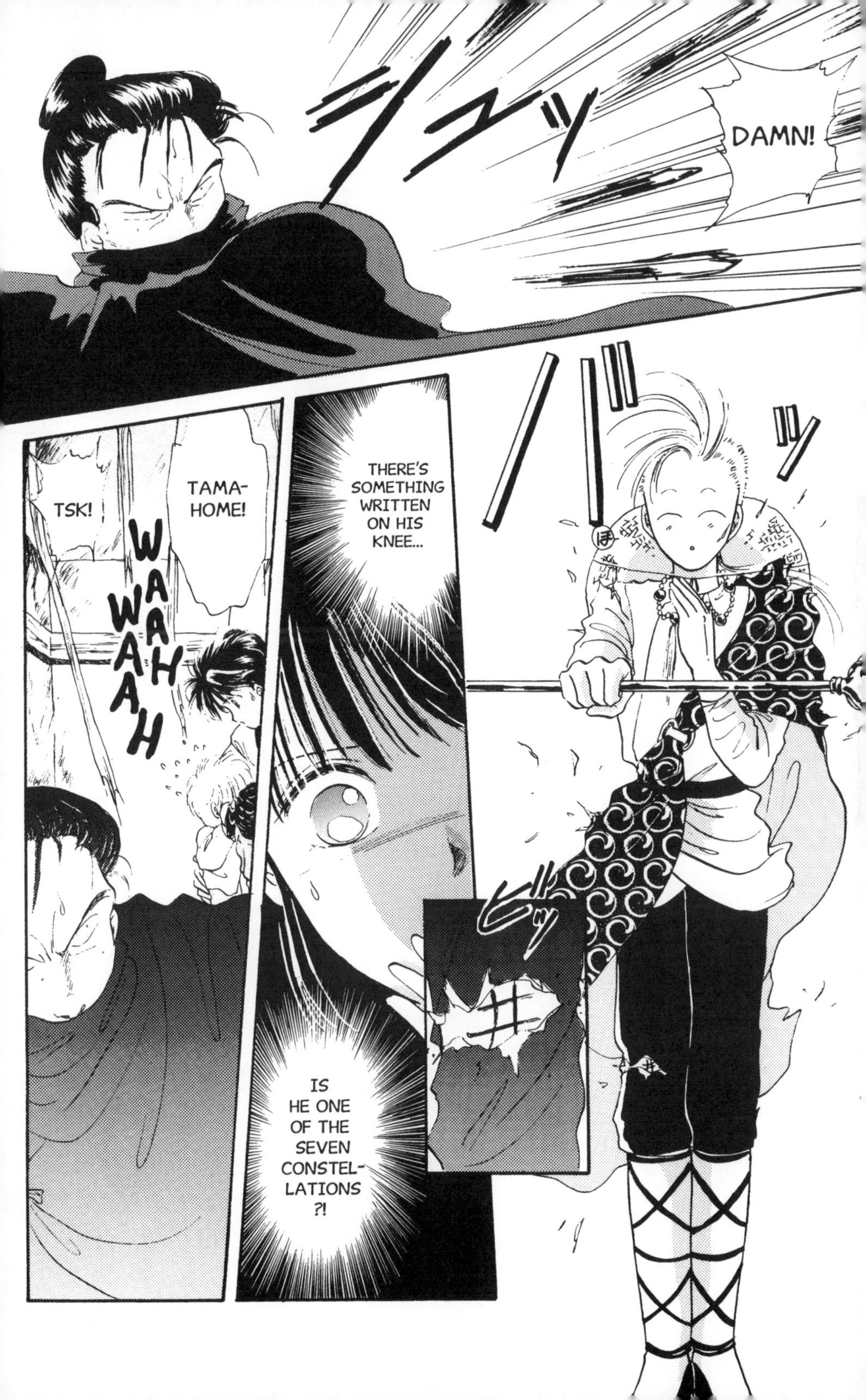
DAMN!
THERE'S SOMETHING WRITTEN ON HIS KNEE...
IS HE ONE OF THE SEVEN CONSTEL-LATIONS ?!
TAMA-HOME!
TSK!
WAAH
WAAAH

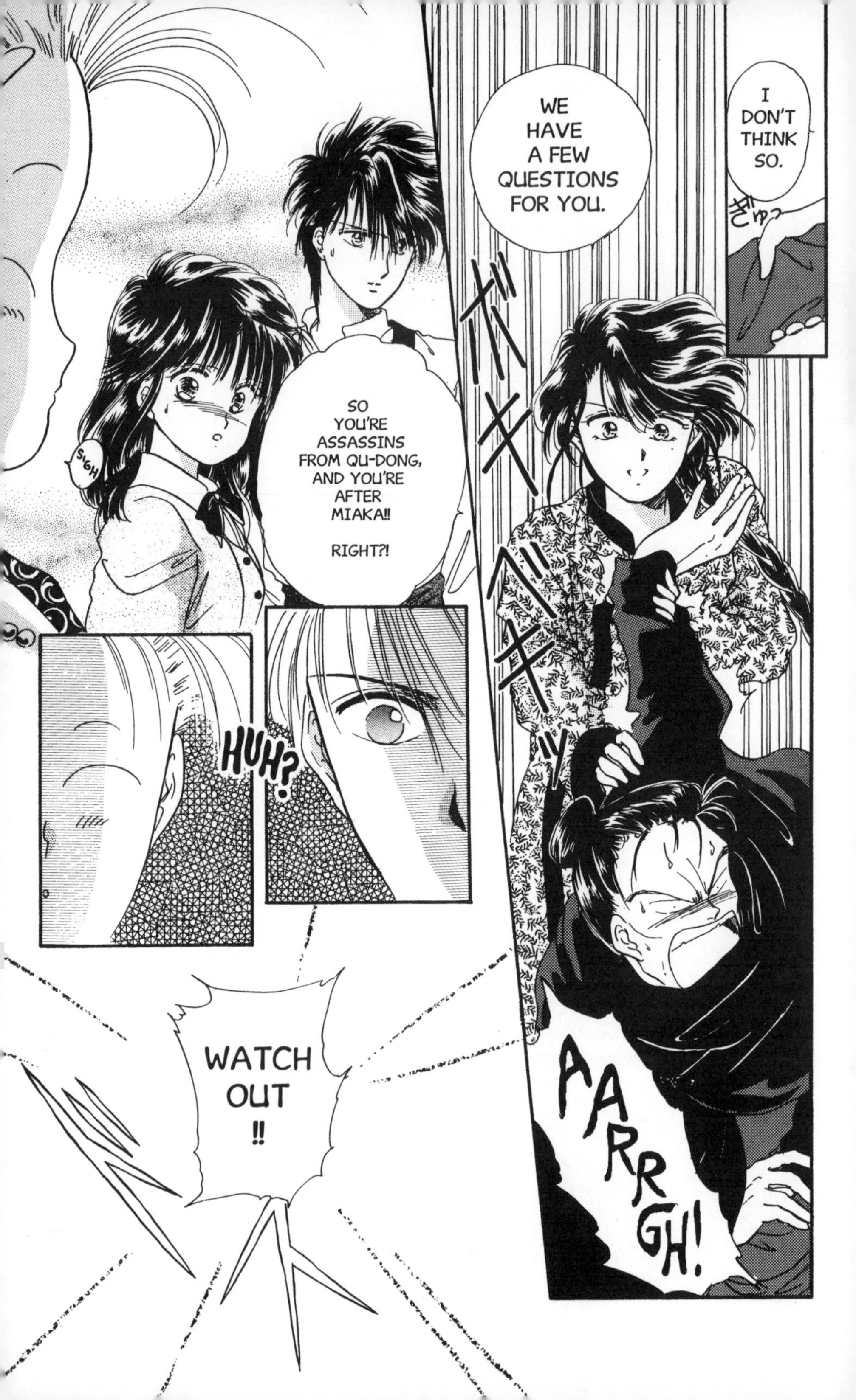

I DON'T THINK SO.
WE HAVE A FEW QUESTIONS FOR YOU.
AARRGH!
SIGH
SO YOU'RE ASSASSINS FROM QU-DONG, AND YOU'RE AFTER MIAKA!! RIGHT?!
HUH?
WATCH OUT !!

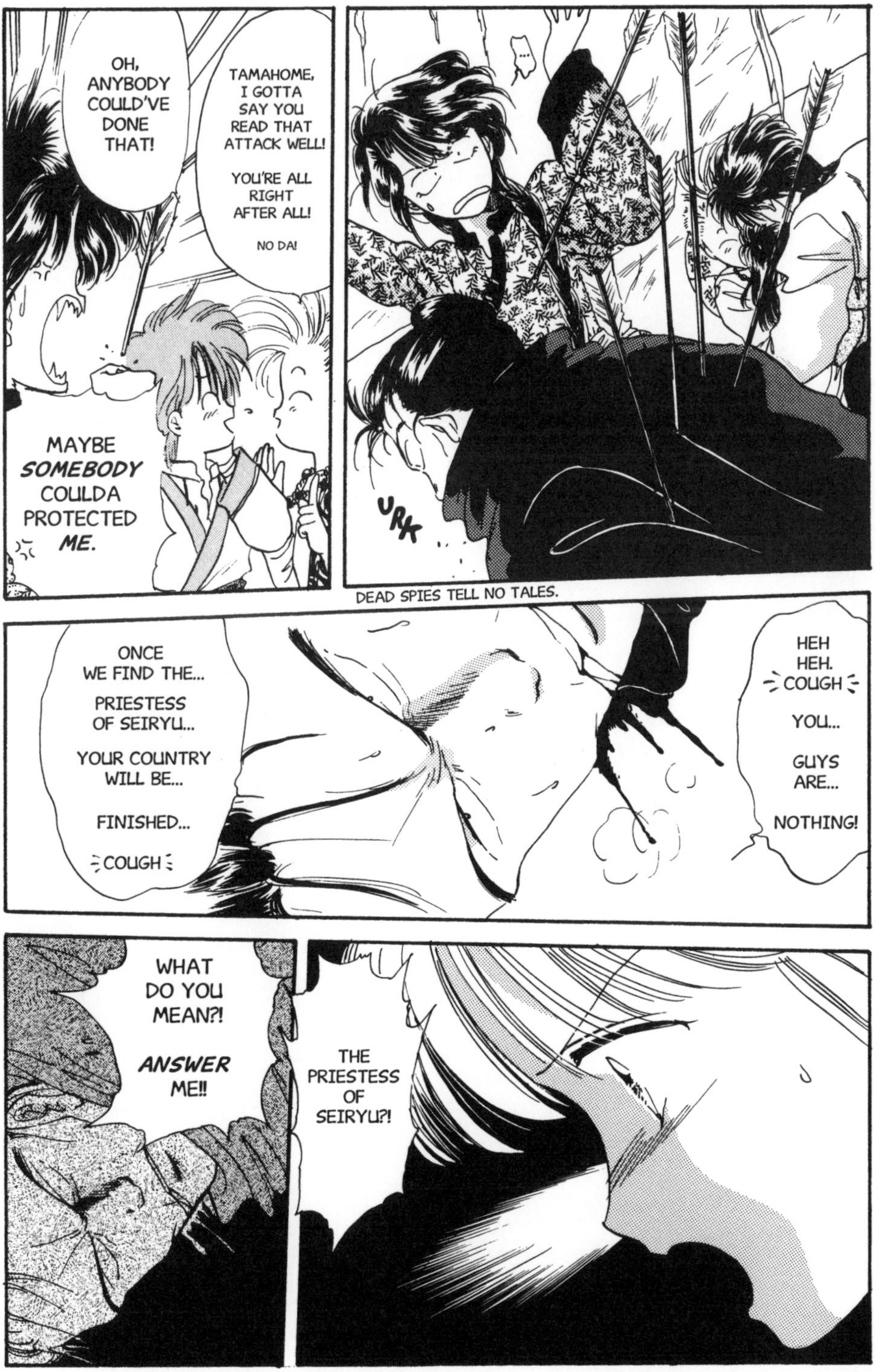
...
URK
DEAD SPIES TELL NO TALES.
TAMAHOME, I GOTTA SAY YOU READ THAT ATTACK WELL! YOU'RE ALL RIGHT AFTER ALL! NO DA!
OH, ANYBODY COULD'VE DONE THAT!
MAYBE *SOMEBODY* COULDA PROTECTED *ME.*
HEH HEH. COUGH YOU... GUYS ARE... NOTHING!
ONCE WE FIND THE... PRIESTESS OF SEIRYU... YOUR COUNTRY WILL BE... FINISHED... COUGH
THE PRIESTESS OF SEIRYU?!
WHAT DO YOU MEAN?! *ANSWER* ME!!

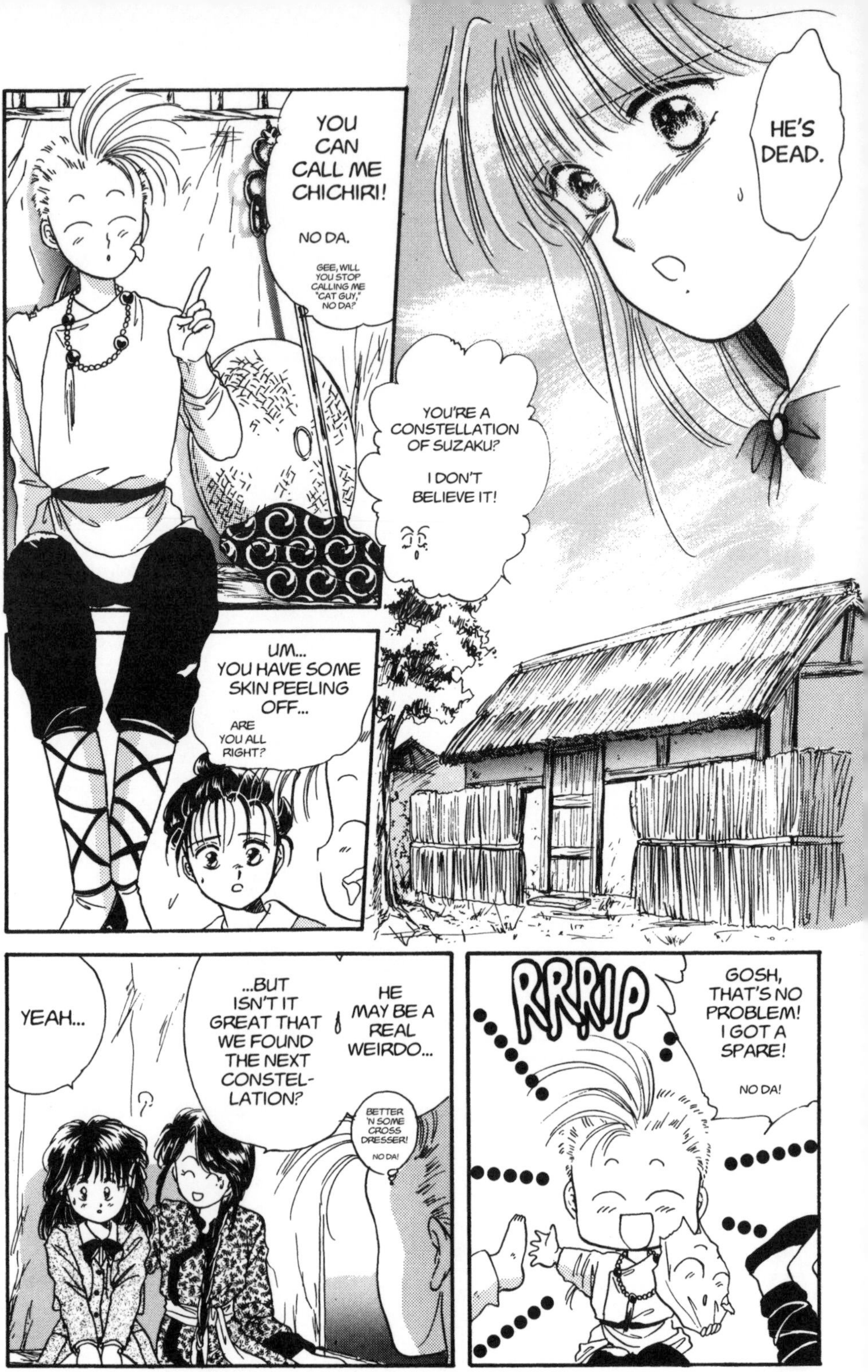
HE'S DEAD.
YOU'RE A CONSTELLATION OF SUZAKU?
I DON'T BELIEVE IT!
YOU CAN CALL ME CHICHIRI!
NO DA.
GEE, WILL YOU STOP CALLING ME "CAT GUY," NO DA?
UM... YOU HAVE SOME SKIN PEELING OFF...
ARE YOU ALL RIGHT?
RRRIP
GOSH, THAT'S NO PROBLEM! I GOT A SPARE!
NO DA!
HE MAY BE A REAL WEIRDO...
...BUT ISN'T IT GREAT THAT WE FOUND THE NEXT CONSTEL-LATION?
YEAH...
BETTER 'N SOME CROSS DRESSER!
NO DA!

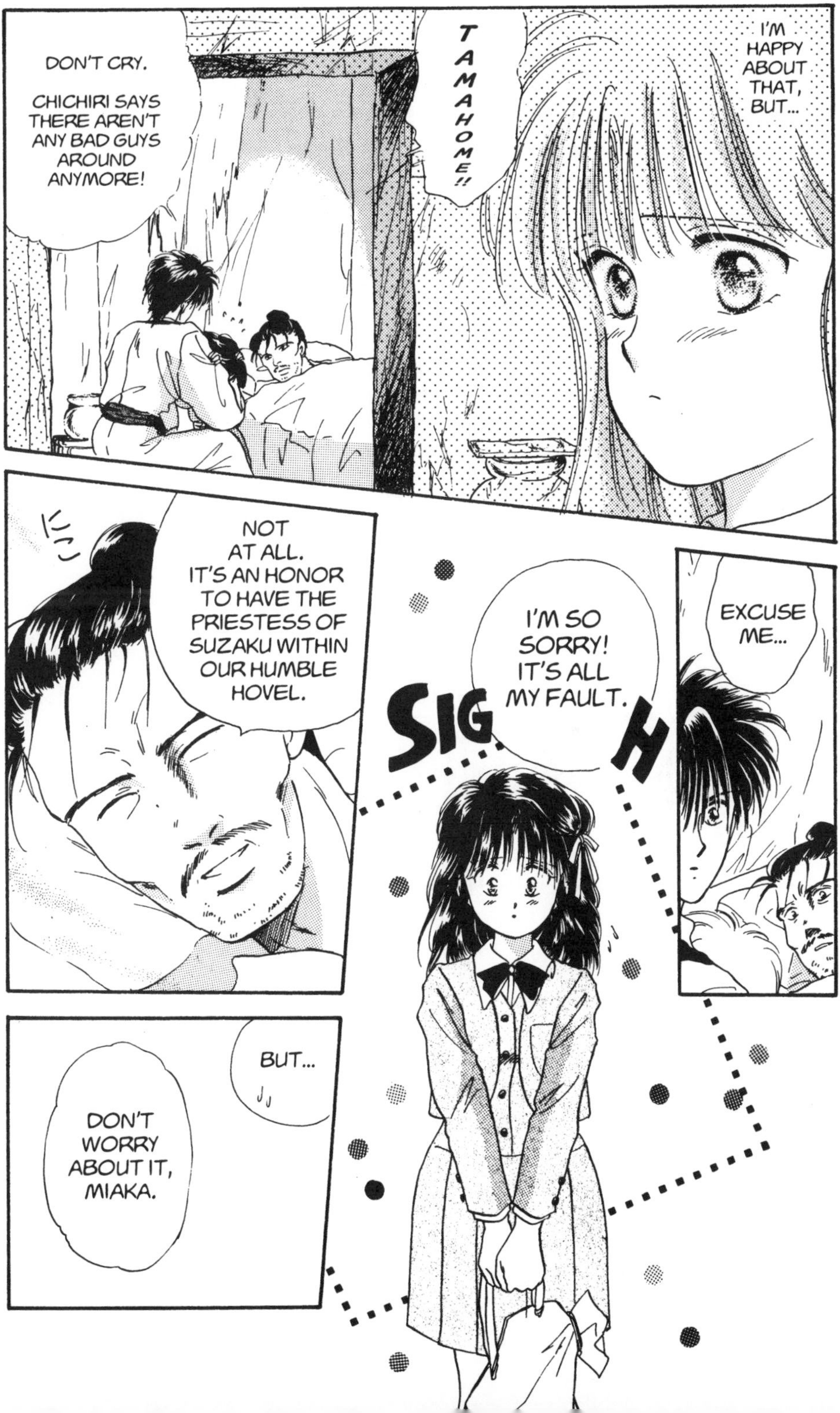

I'M HAPPY ABOUT THAT, BUT...
TAMAHOME!!
DON'T CRY.
CHICHIRI SAYS THERE AREN'T ANY BAD GUYS AROUND ANYMORE!
EXCUSE ME...
I'M SO SORRY! IT'S ALL MY FAULT.
SIGH
NOT AT ALL. IT'S AN HONOR TO HAVE THE PRIESTESS OF SUZAKU WITHIN OUR HUMBLE HOVEL.
BUT...
DON'T WORRY ABOUT IT, MIAKA.

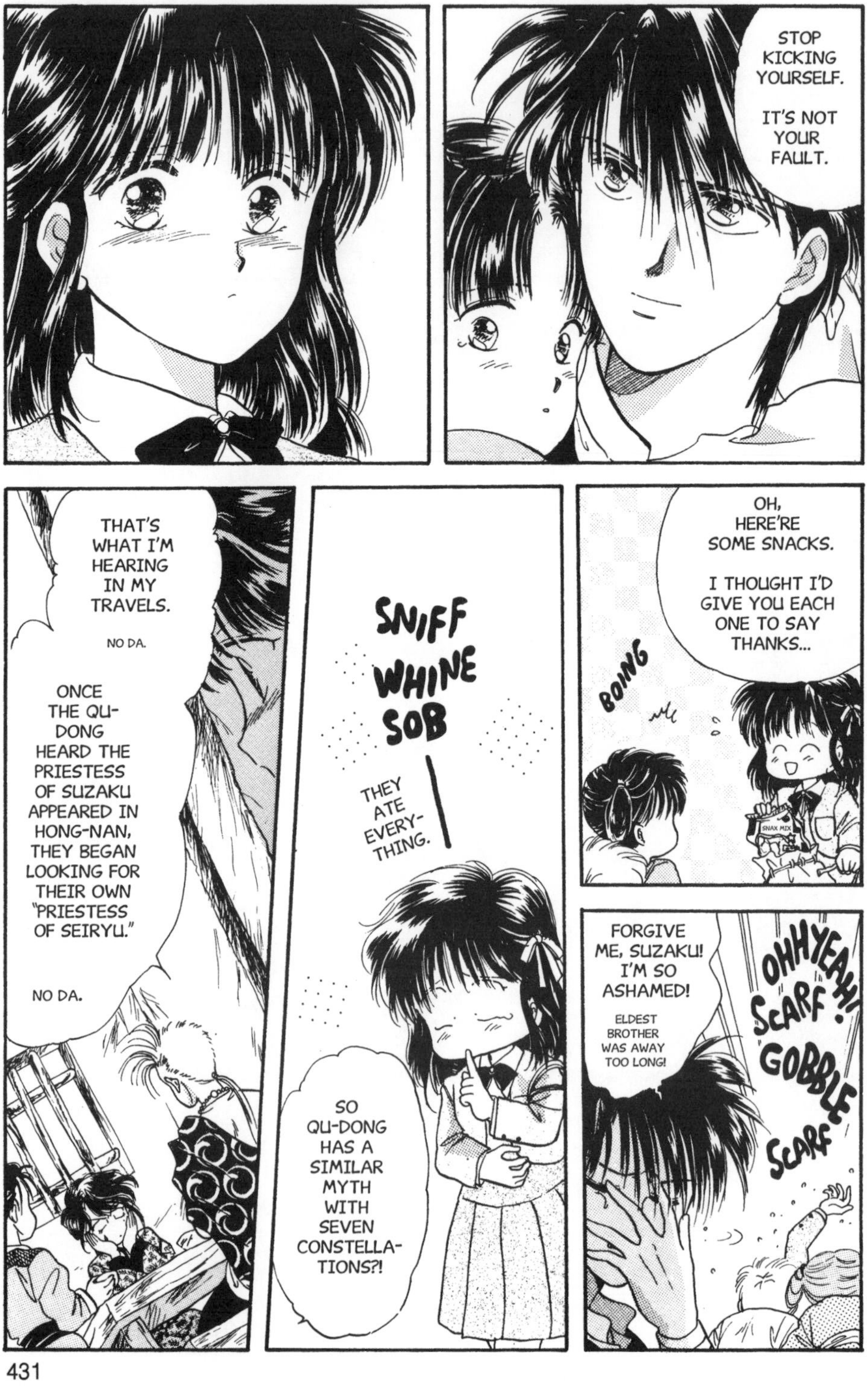
STOP KICKING YOURSELF.
IT'S NOT YOUR FAULT.
OH, HERE'RE SOME SNACKS.
I THOUGHT I'D GIVE YOU EACH ONE TO SAY THANKS...
BOING
SNAX MIX
FORGIVE ME, SUZAKU! I'M SO ASHAMED!
ELDEST BROTHER WAS AWAY TOO LONG!
OHHYEAH!
SCARF!
GOBBLE
SCARF
SNIFF
WHINE
SOB
THEY ATE EVERY-THING.
SO QU-DONG HAS A SIMILAR MYTH WITH SEVEN CONSTELLA-TIONS?!
THAT'S WHAT I'M HEARING IN MY TRAVELS.
NO DA.
ONCE THE QU-DONG HEARD THE PRIESTESS OF SUZAKU APPEARED IN HONG-NAN, THEY BEGAN LOOKING FOR THEIR OWN "PRIESTESS OF SEIRYU."
NO DA.

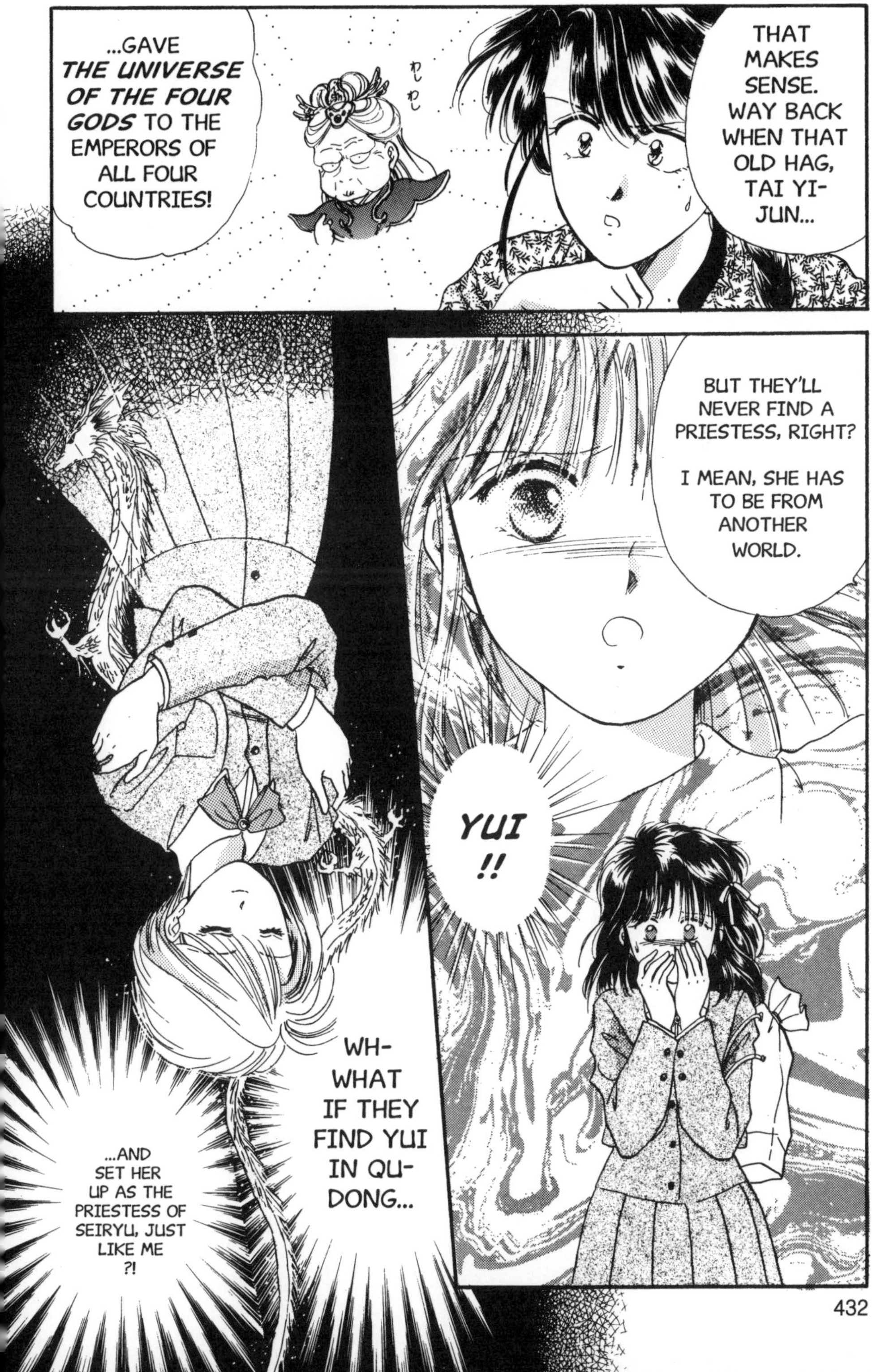
THAT MAKES SENSE. WAY BACK WHEN THAT OLD HAG, TAI YI-JUN...
...GAVE *THE UNIVERSE OF THE FOUR GODS* TO THE EMPERORS OF ALL FOUR COUNTRIES!
BUT THEY'LL NEVER FIND A PRIESTESS, RIGHT?
I MEAN, SHE HAS TO BE FROM ANOTHER WORLD.
YUI!!
WH-WHAT IF THEY FIND YUI IN QU-DONG...
...AND SET HER UP AS THE PRIESTESS OF SEIRYU, JUST LIKE ME?!

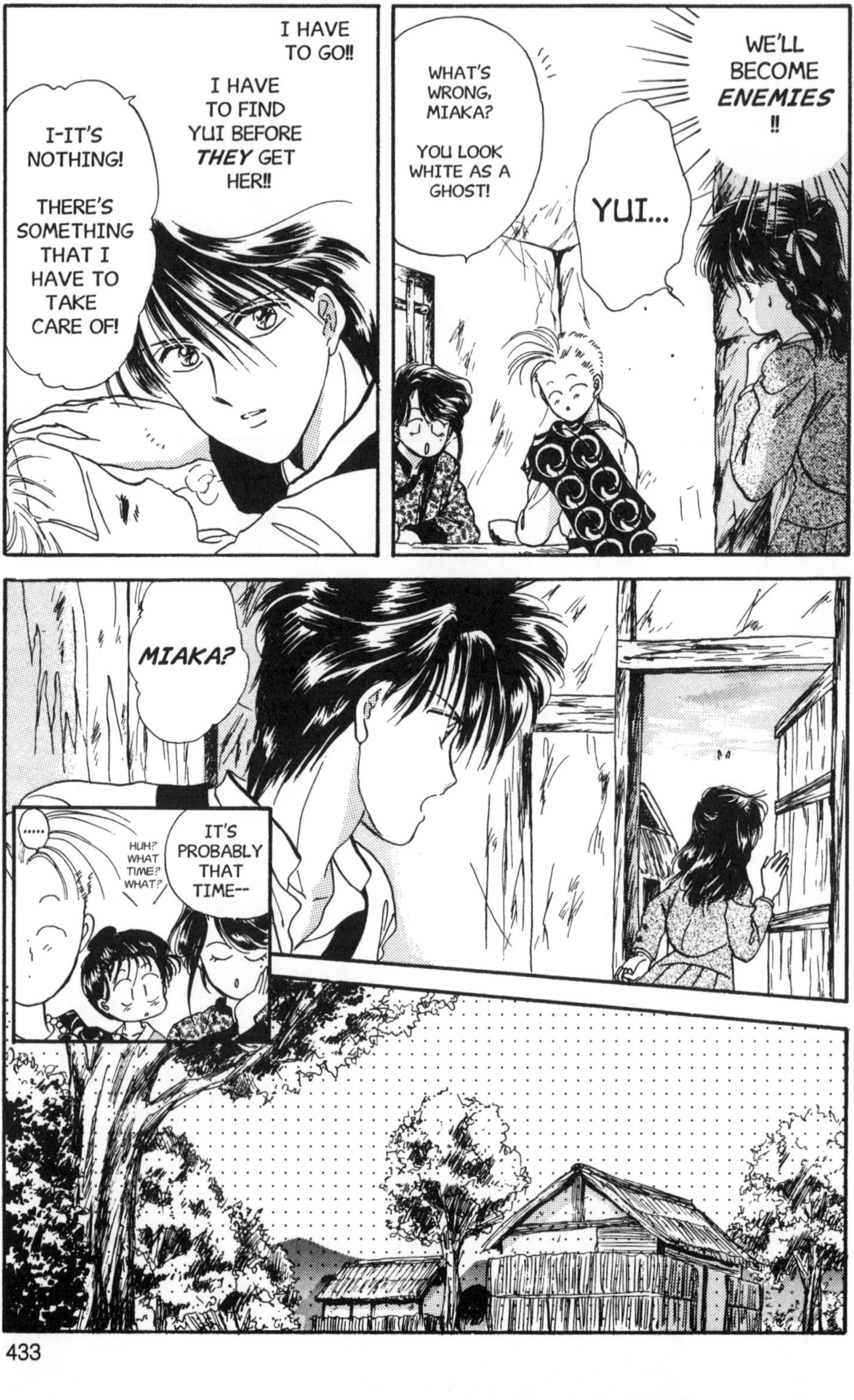
WE'LL BECOME *ENEMIES* !!
YUI...
WHAT'S WRONG, MIAKA? YOU LOOK WHITE AS A GHOST!
I HAVE TO GO!!
I HAVE TO FIND YUI BEFORE *THEY* GET HER!!
I-IT'S NOTHING! THERE'S SOMETHING THAT I HAVE TO TAKE CARE OF!
MIAKA?
IT'S PROBABLY THAT TIME--
HUH? WHAT TIME? WHAT?
......

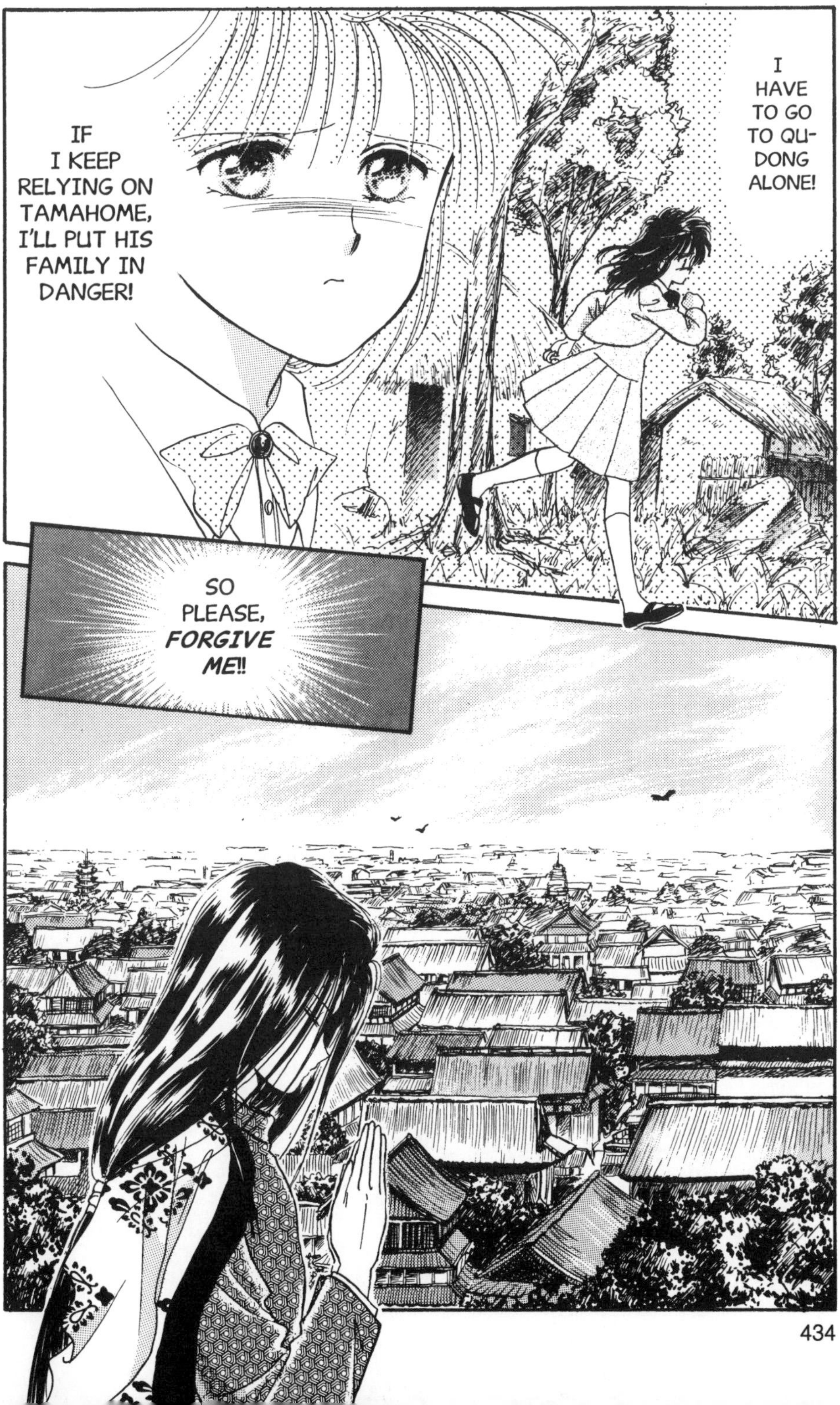
I HAVE TO GO TO QU-DONG ALONE!
IF I KEEP RELYING ON TAMAHOME, I'LL PUT HIS FAMILY IN DANGER!
SO PLEASE, *FORGIVE ME*!!

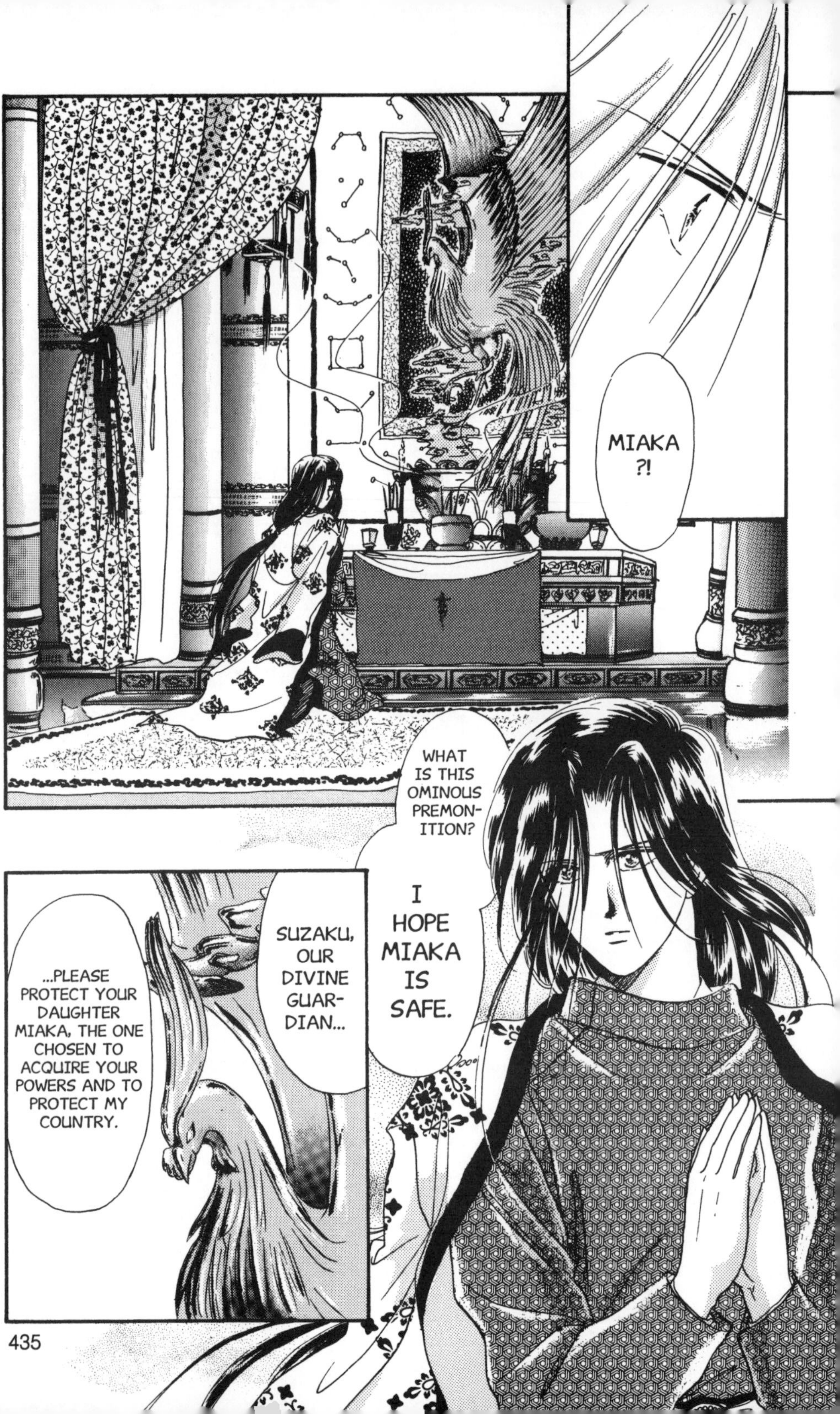
MIAKA ?!
WHAT IS THIS OMINOUS PREMONITION?
I HOPE MIAKA IS SAFE.
SUZAKU, OUR DIVINE GUARDIAN...
...PLEASE PROTECT YOUR DAUGHTER MIAKA, THE ONE CHOSEN TO ACQUIRE YOUR POWERS AND TO PROTECT MY COUNTRY.

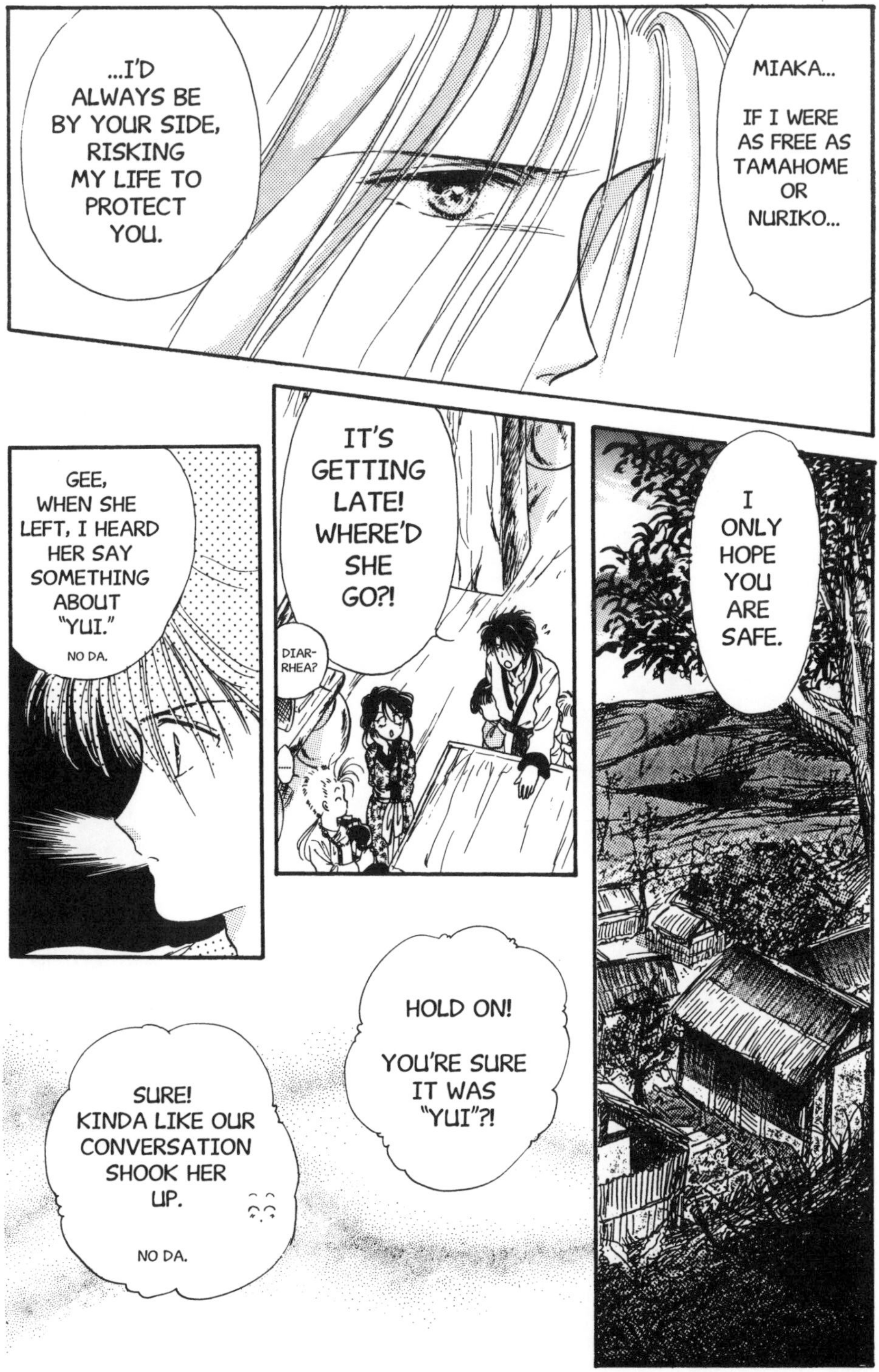
MIAKA... IF I WERE AS FREE AS TAMAHOME OR NURIKO...
...I'D ALWAYS BE BY YOUR SIDE, RISKING MY LIFE TO PROTECT YOU.
I ONLY HOPE YOU ARE SAFE.
IT'S GETTING LATE! WHERE'D SHE GO?!
DIARRHEA?
......
GEE, WHEN SHE LEFT, I HEARD HER SAY SOMETHING ABOUT "YUI."
NO DA.
HOLD ON! YOU'RE SURE IT WAS "YUI"?!
SURE! KINDA LIKE OUR CONVERSATION SHOOK HER UP.
NO DA.

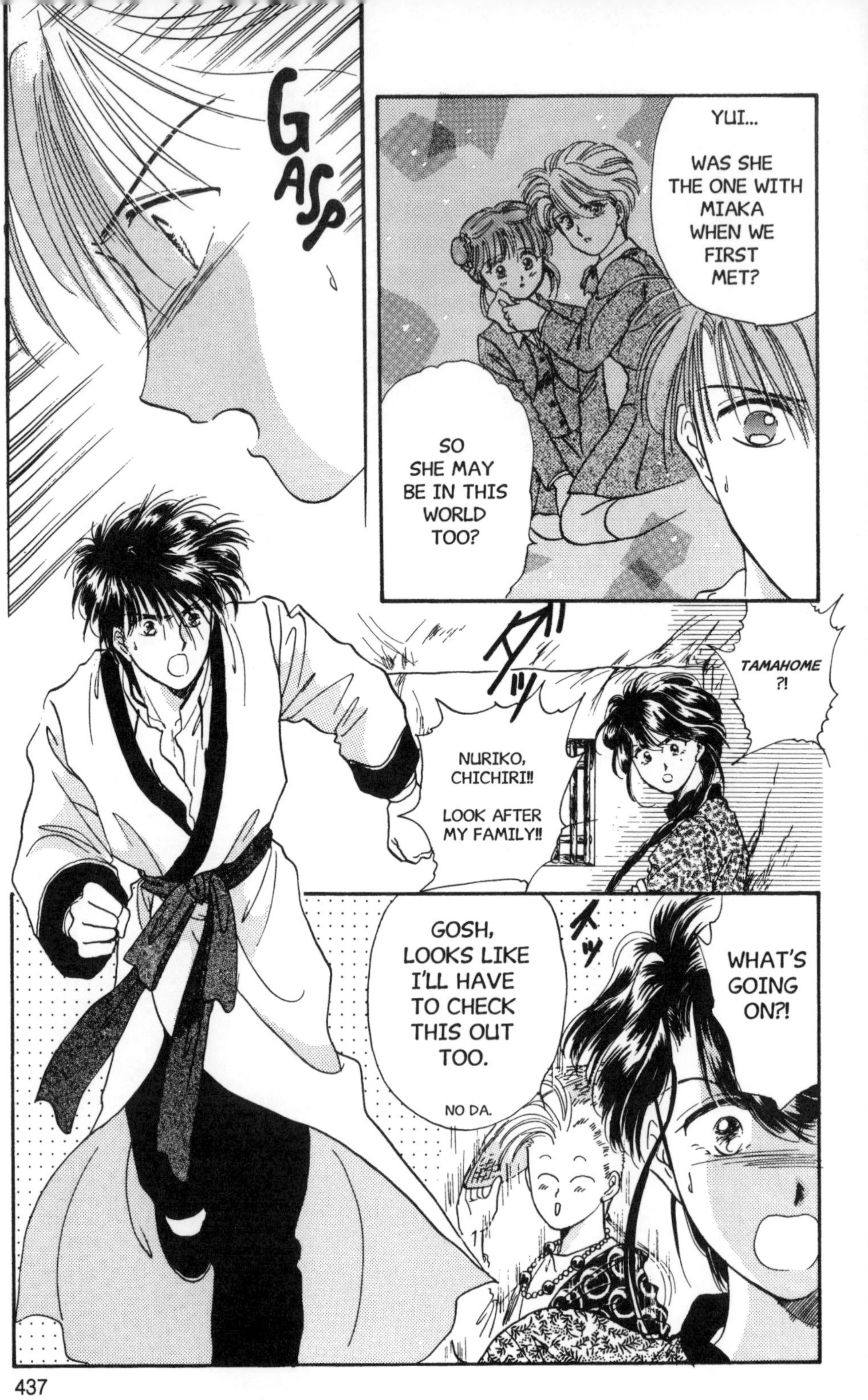
YUI...
WAS SHE THE ONE WITH MIAKA WHEN WE FIRST MET?
SO SHE MAY BE IN THIS WORLD TOO?
GASP
TAMAHOME ?!
ダッ
NURIKO, CHICHIRI!!
LOOK AFTER MY FAMILY!!
WHAT'S GOING ON?!
スッ
GOSH, LOOKS LIKE I'LL HAVE TO CHECK THIS OUT TOO.
NO DA.

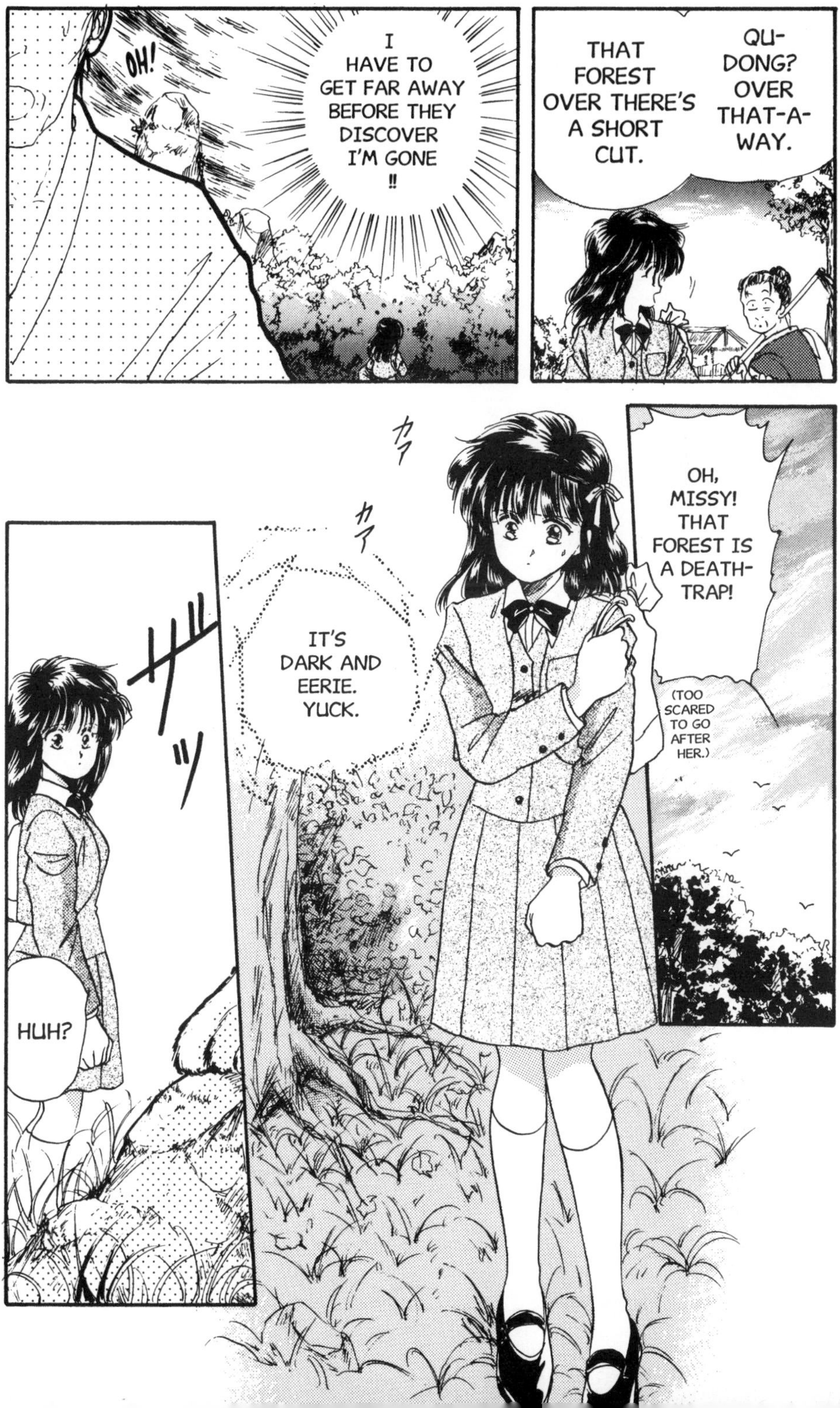
QU-DONG? OVER THAT-A-WAY.
THAT FOREST OVER THERE'S A SHORT CUT.
I HAVE TO GET FAR AWAY BEFORE THEY DISCOVER I'M GONE!!
OH!
OH, MISSY! THAT FOREST IS A DEATH-TRAP!
(TOO SCARED TO GO AFTER HER.)
カァ
カァ
IT'S DARK AND EERIE. YUCK.
ザッ
HUH?

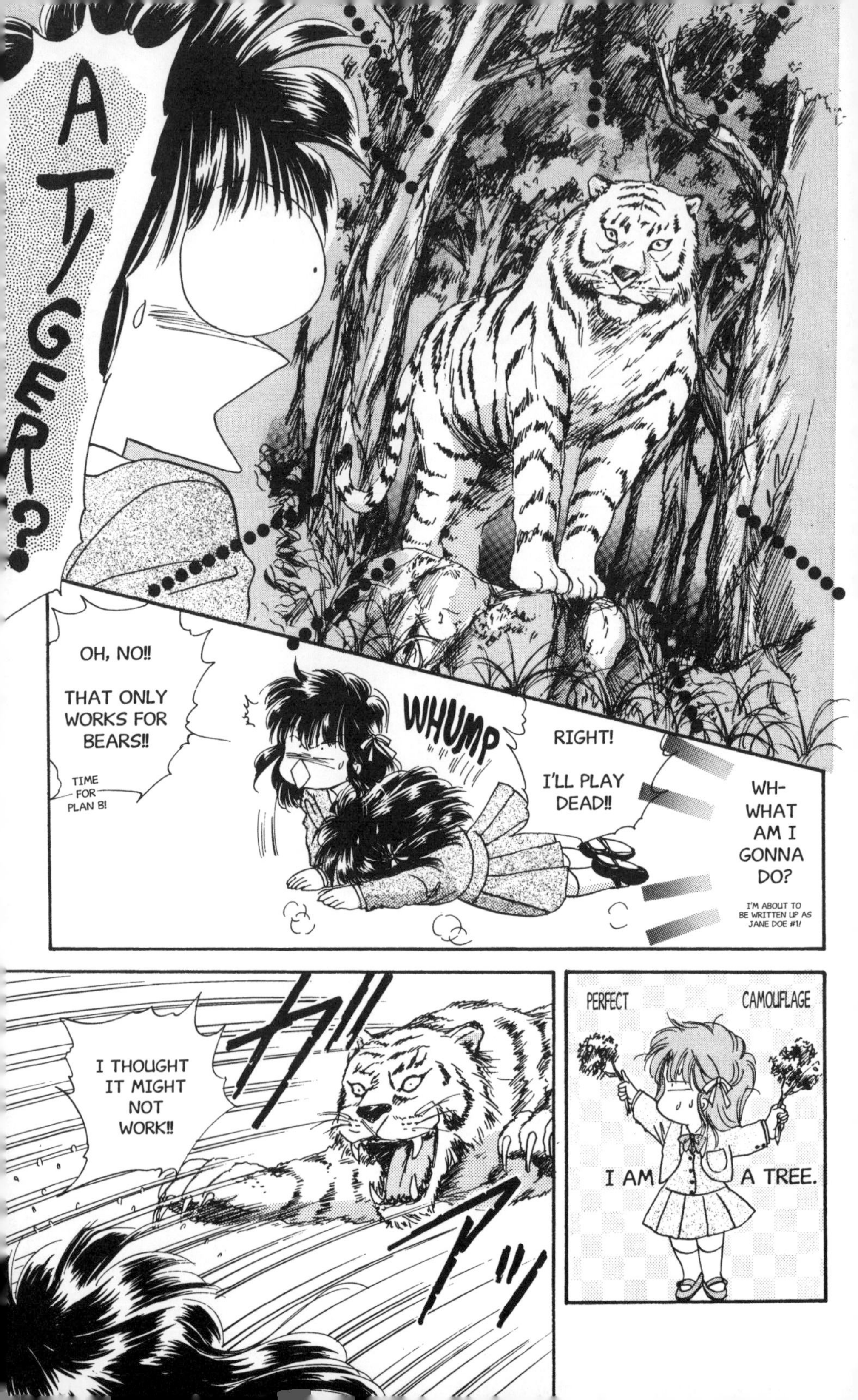
A TIGER?
WH-WHAT AM I GONNA DO?
I'M ABOUT TO BE WRITTEN UP AS JANE DOE #1!
RIGHT! I'LL PLAY DEAD!!
WHUMP
OH, NO!! THAT ONLY WORKS FOR BEARS!!
TIME FOR PLAN B!
PERFECT CAMOUFLAGE
I AM A TREE.
I THOUGHT IT MIGHT NOT WORK!!

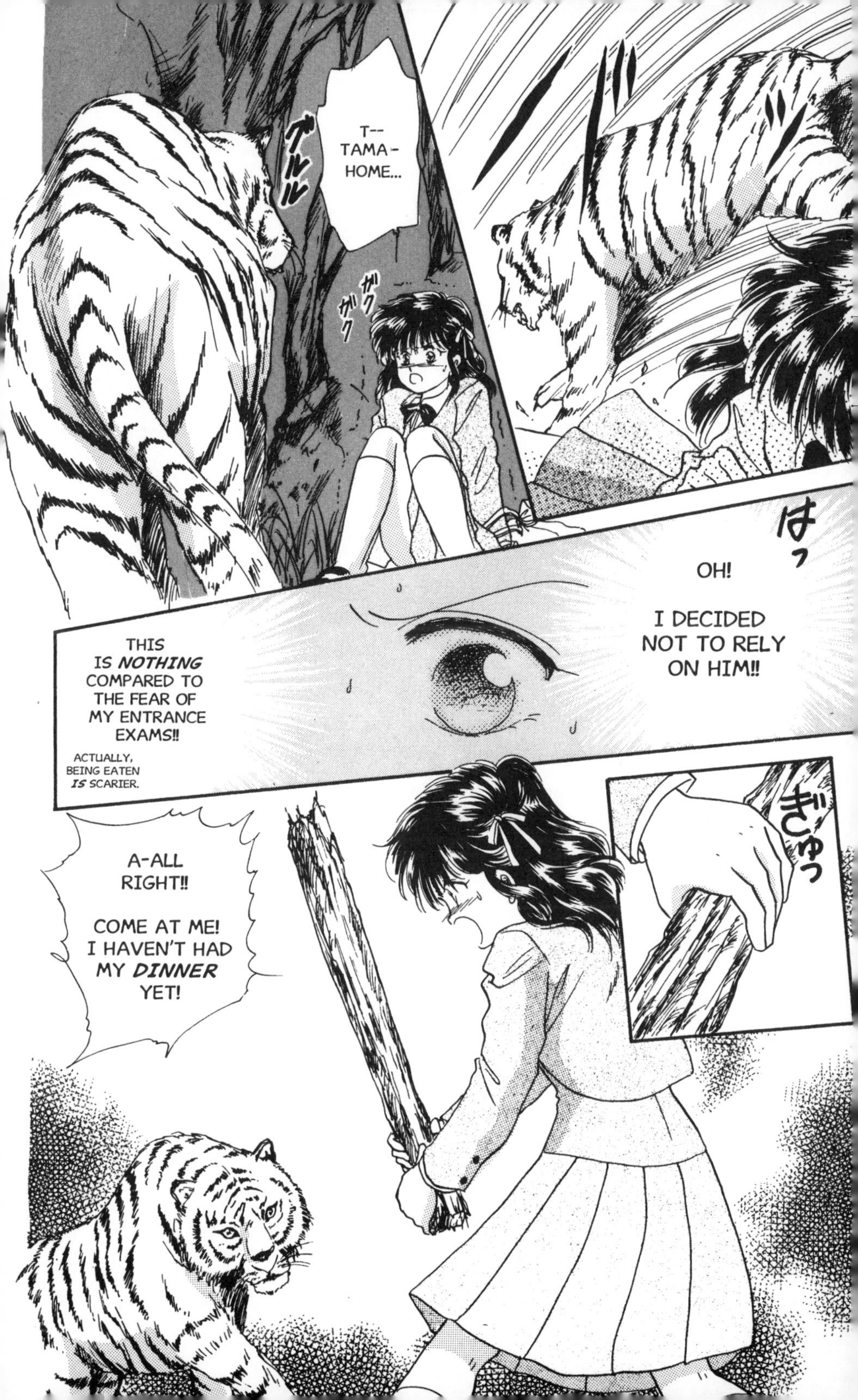
T-- TAMA-HOME...
グルル
がく がく
はっ
OH!
I DECIDED NOT TO RELY ON HIM!!
THIS IS *NOTHING* COMPARED TO THE FEAR OF MY ENTRANCE EXAMS!!
ACTUALLY, BEING EATEN *IS* SCARIER.
ぎゅっ
A-ALL RIGHT!!
COME AT ME! I HAVEN'T HAD MY *DINNER* YET!

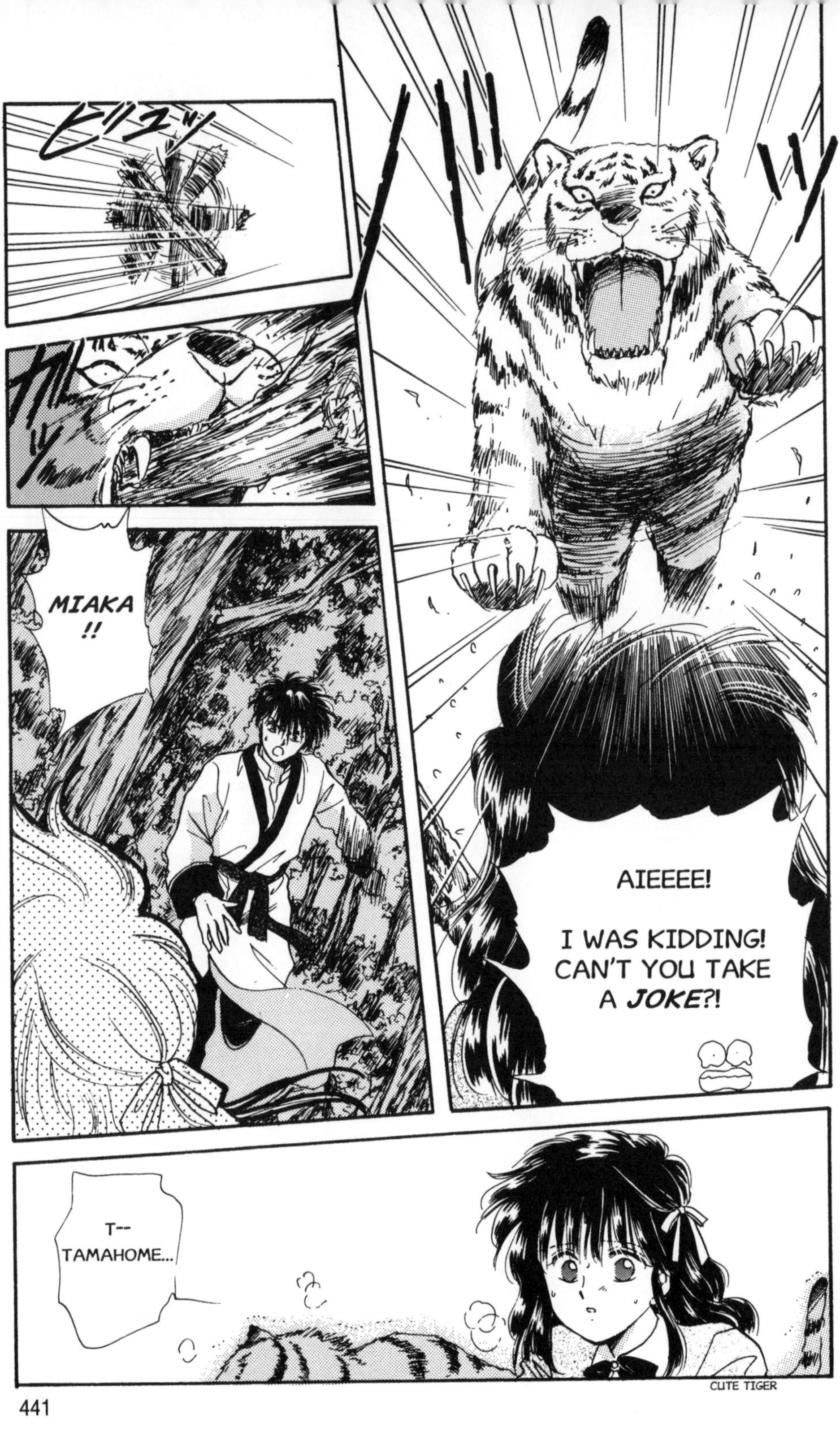
AIEEEE!
I WAS KIDDING! CAN'T YOU TAKE A *JOKE*?!
MIAKA !!
T-- TAMAHOME...
CUTE TIGER

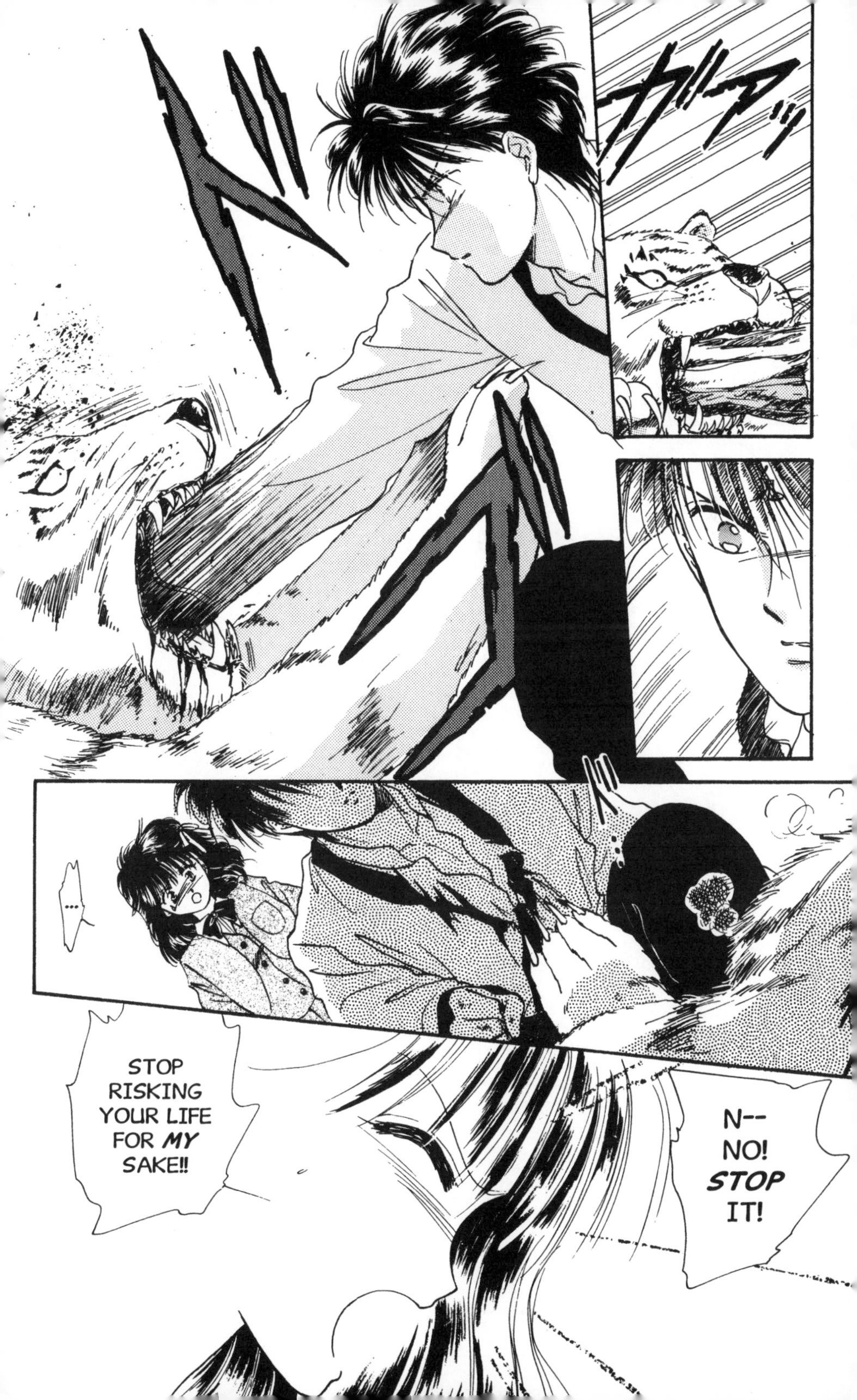
...
N-- NO! *STOP* IT!
STOP RISKING YOUR LIFE FOR *MY* SAKE!!

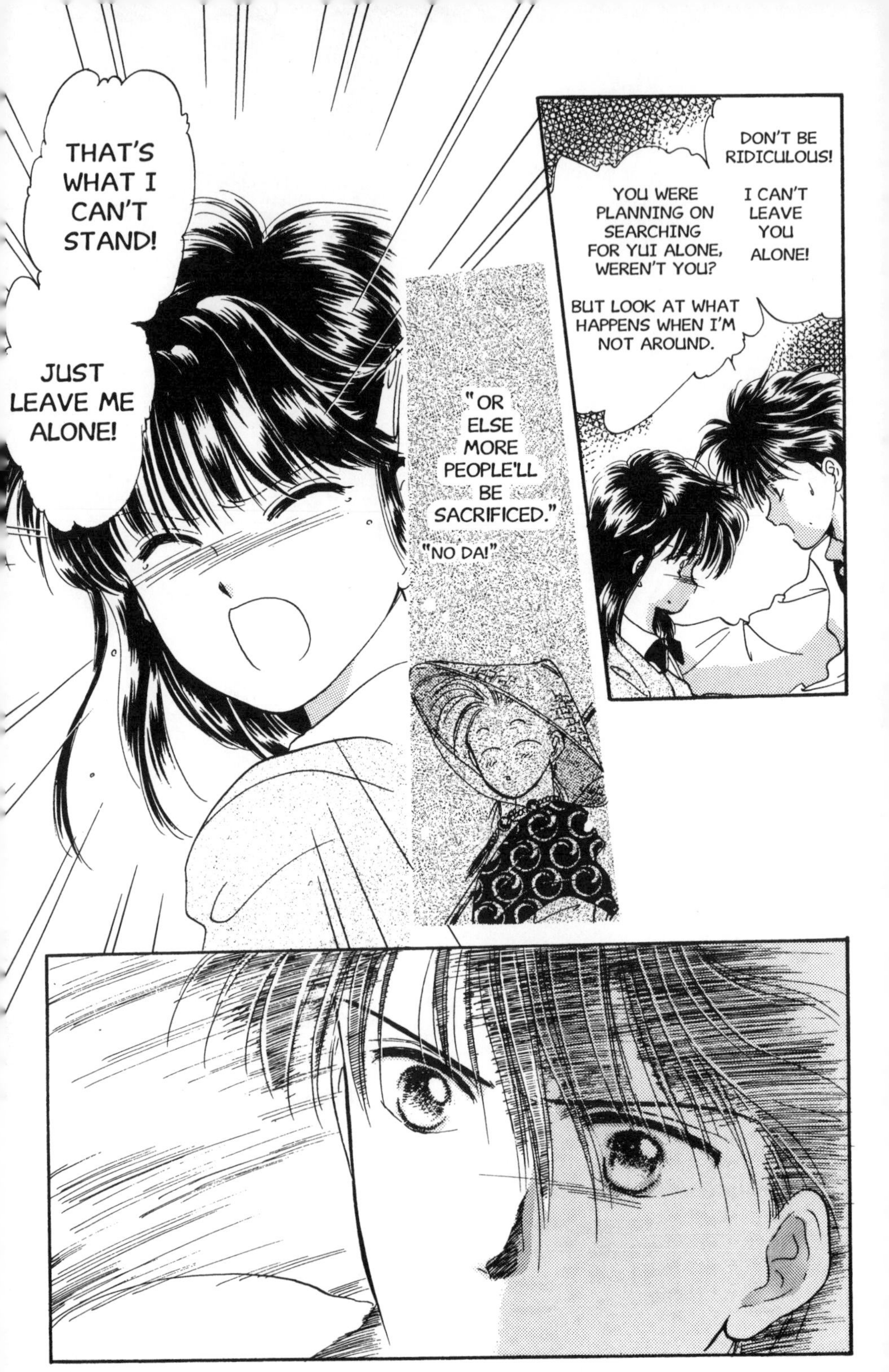
DON'T BE RIDICULOUS!
I CAN'T LEAVE YOU ALONE!
YOU WERE PLANNING ON SEARCHING FOR YUI ALONE, WEREN'T YOU?
BUT LOOK AT WHAT HAPPENS WHEN I'M NOT AROUND.
"OR ELSE MORE PEOPLE'LL BE SACRIFICED."
"NO DA!"
THAT'S WHAT I CAN'T STAND!
JUST LEAVE ME ALONE!

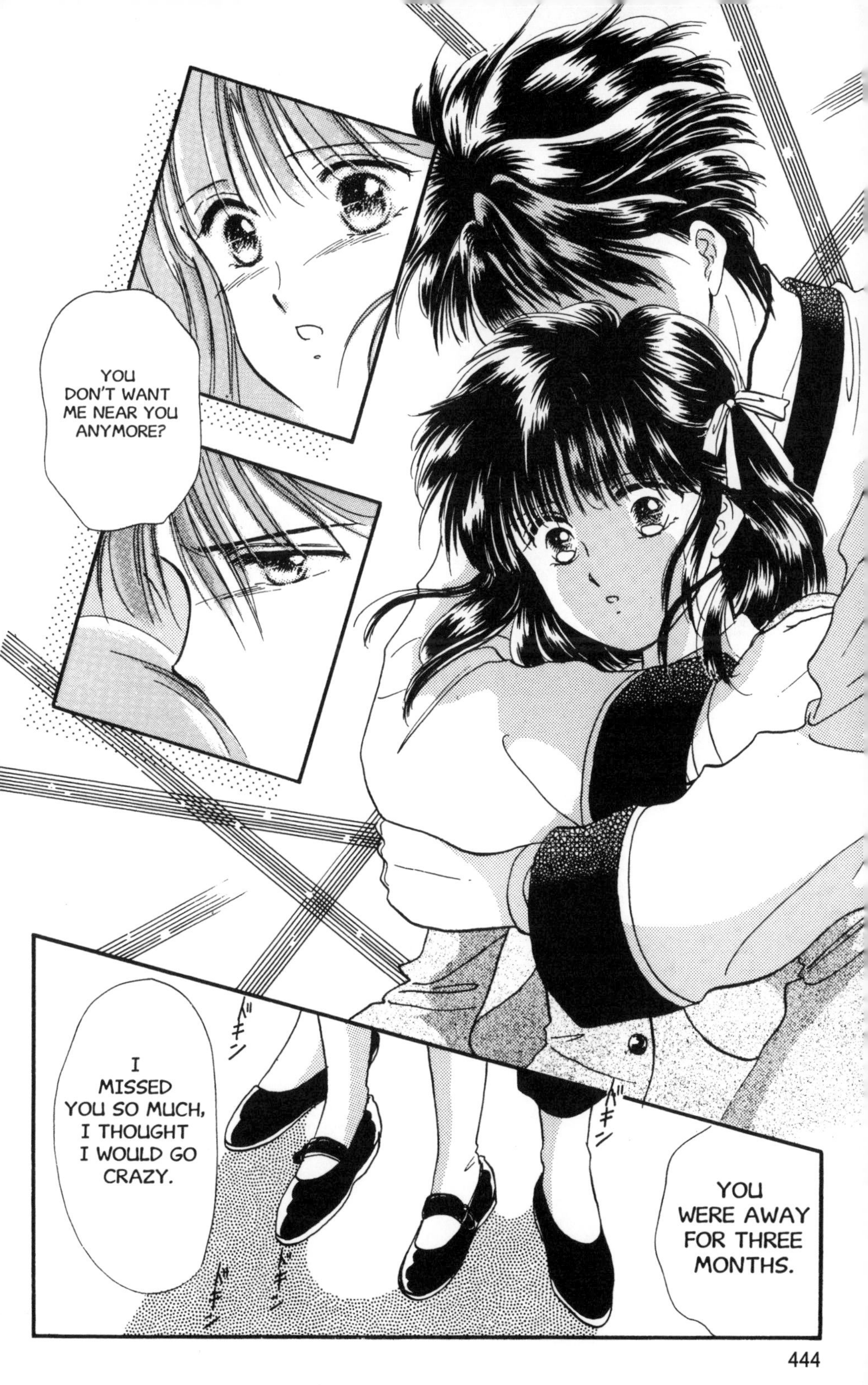
YOU DON'T WANT ME NEAR YOU ANYMORE?
YOU WERE AWAY FOR THREE MONTHS.
I MISSED YOU SO MUCH, I THOUGHT I WOULD GO CRAZY.

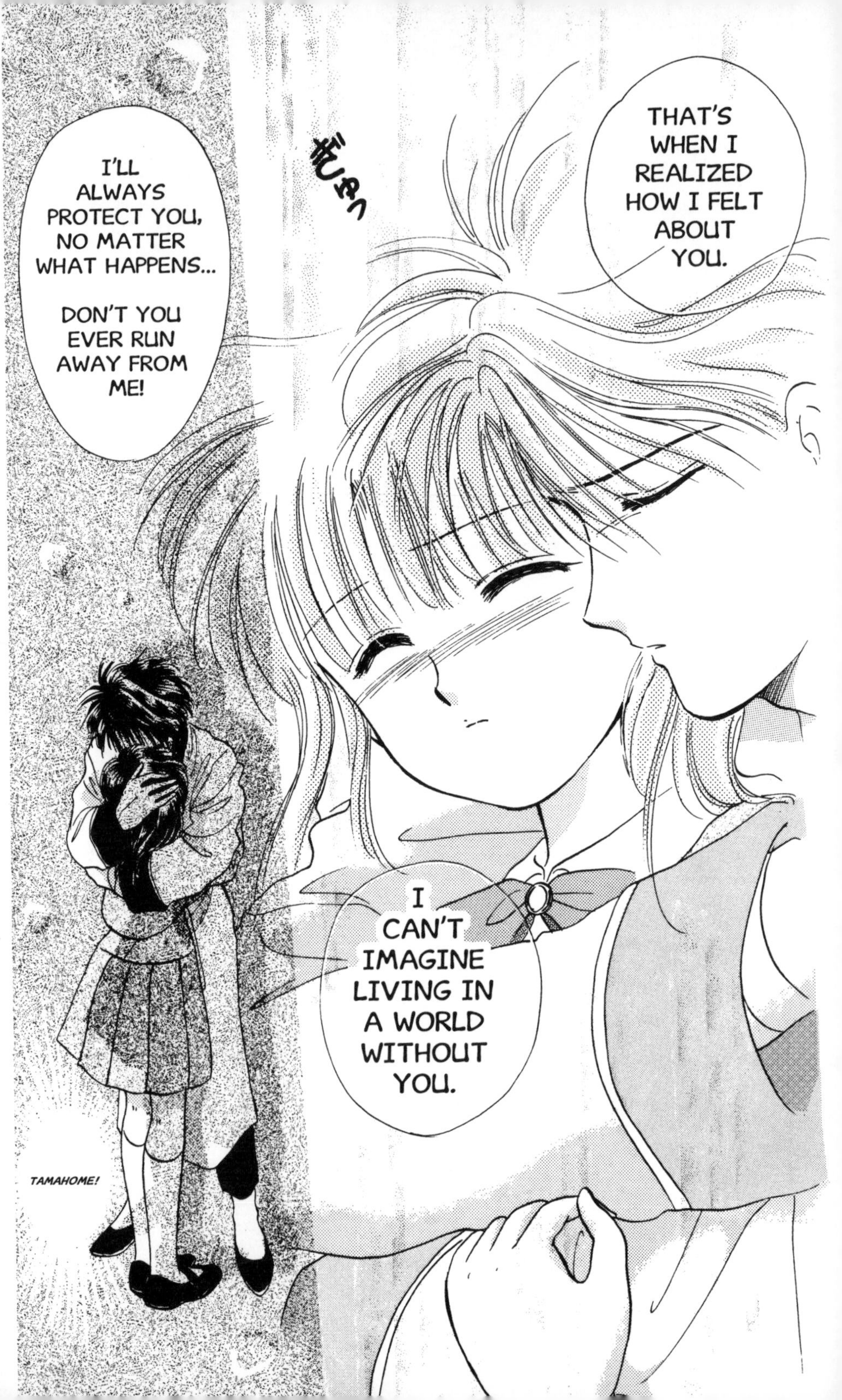
THAT'S WHEN I REALIZED HOW I FELT ABOUT YOU.
ぎゅっ
I'LL ALWAYS PROTECT YOU, NO MATTER WHAT HAPPENS...
DON'T YOU EVER RUN AWAY FROM ME!
I CAN'T IMAGINE LIVING IN A WORLD WITHOUT YOU.
TAMAHOME!

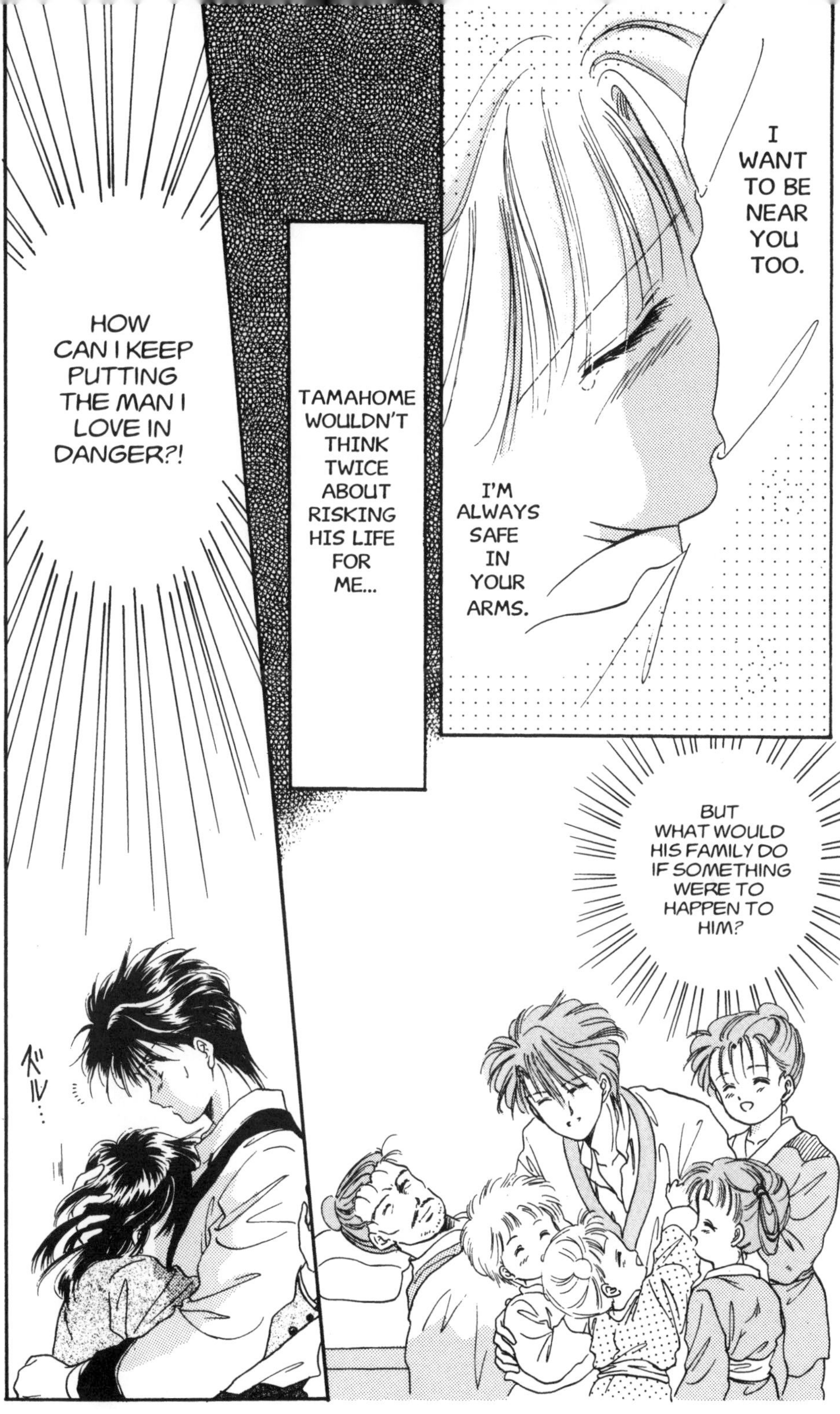
I WANT TO BE NEAR YOU TOO.
I'M ALWAYS SAFE IN YOUR ARMS.
TAMAHOME WOULDN'T THINK TWICE ABOUT RISKING HIS LIFE FOR ME...
BUT WHAT WOULD HIS FAMILY DO IF SOMETHING WERE TO HAPPEN TO HIM?
HOW CAN I KEEP PUTTING THE MAN I LOVE IN DANGER?!
ズル…

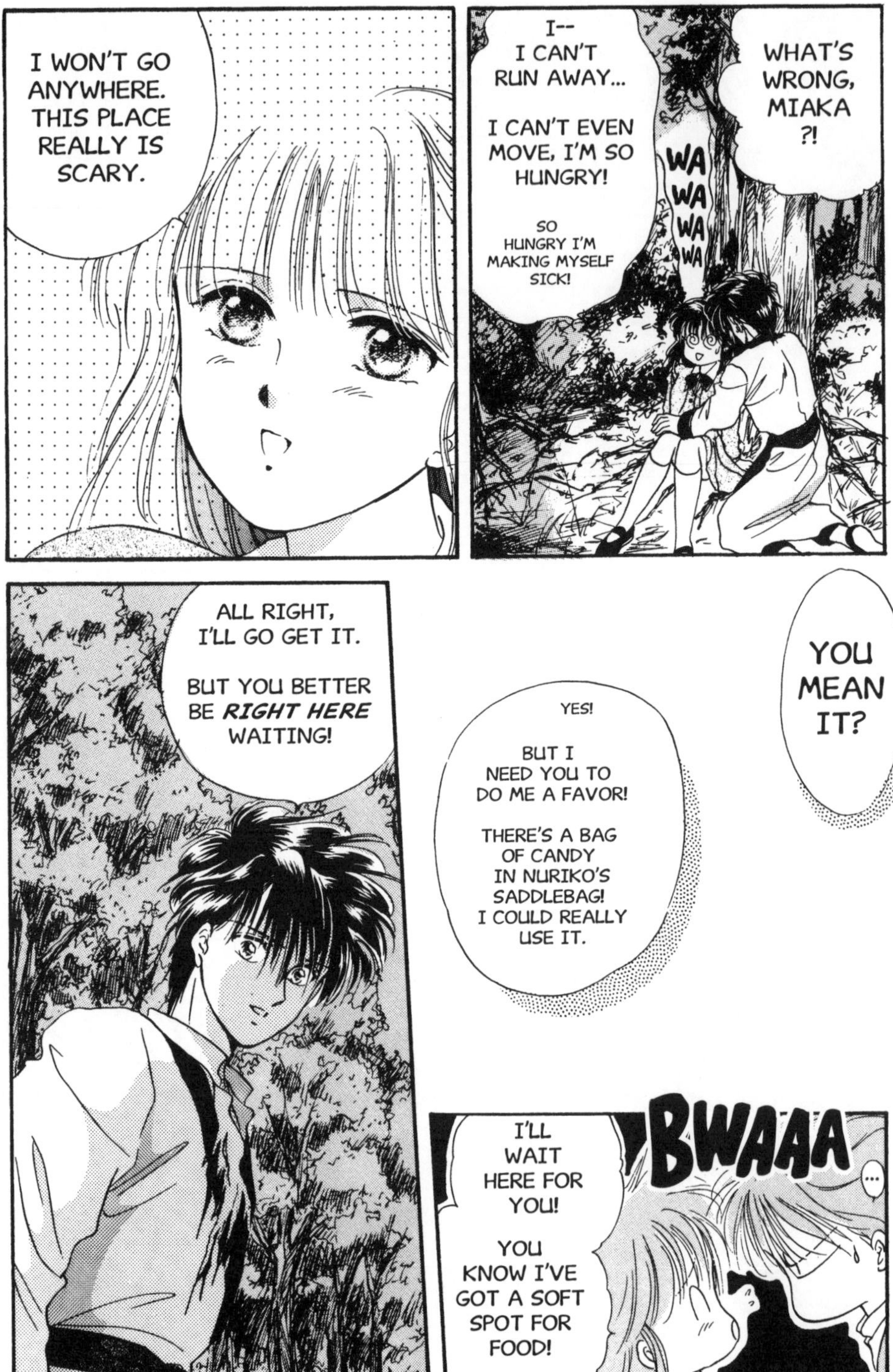
WHAT'S WRONG, MIAKA ?!
I-- I CAN'T RUN AWAY... I CAN'T EVEN MOVE, I'M SO HUNGRY!
WA WA WA WA WA
SO HUNGRY I'M MAKING MYSELF SICK!
I WON'T GO ANYWHERE. THIS PLACE REALLY IS SCARY.
YOU MEAN IT?
YES!
BUT I NEED YOU TO DO ME A FAVOR!
THERE'S A BAG OF CANDY IN NURIKO'S SADDLEBAG! I COULD REALLY USE IT.
BWAAA
...
I'LL WAIT HERE FOR YOU!
YOU KNOW I'VE GOT A SOFT SPOT FOR FOOD!
ALL RIGHT, I'LL GO GET IT.
BUT YOU BETTER BE ***RIGHT HERE*** WAITING!

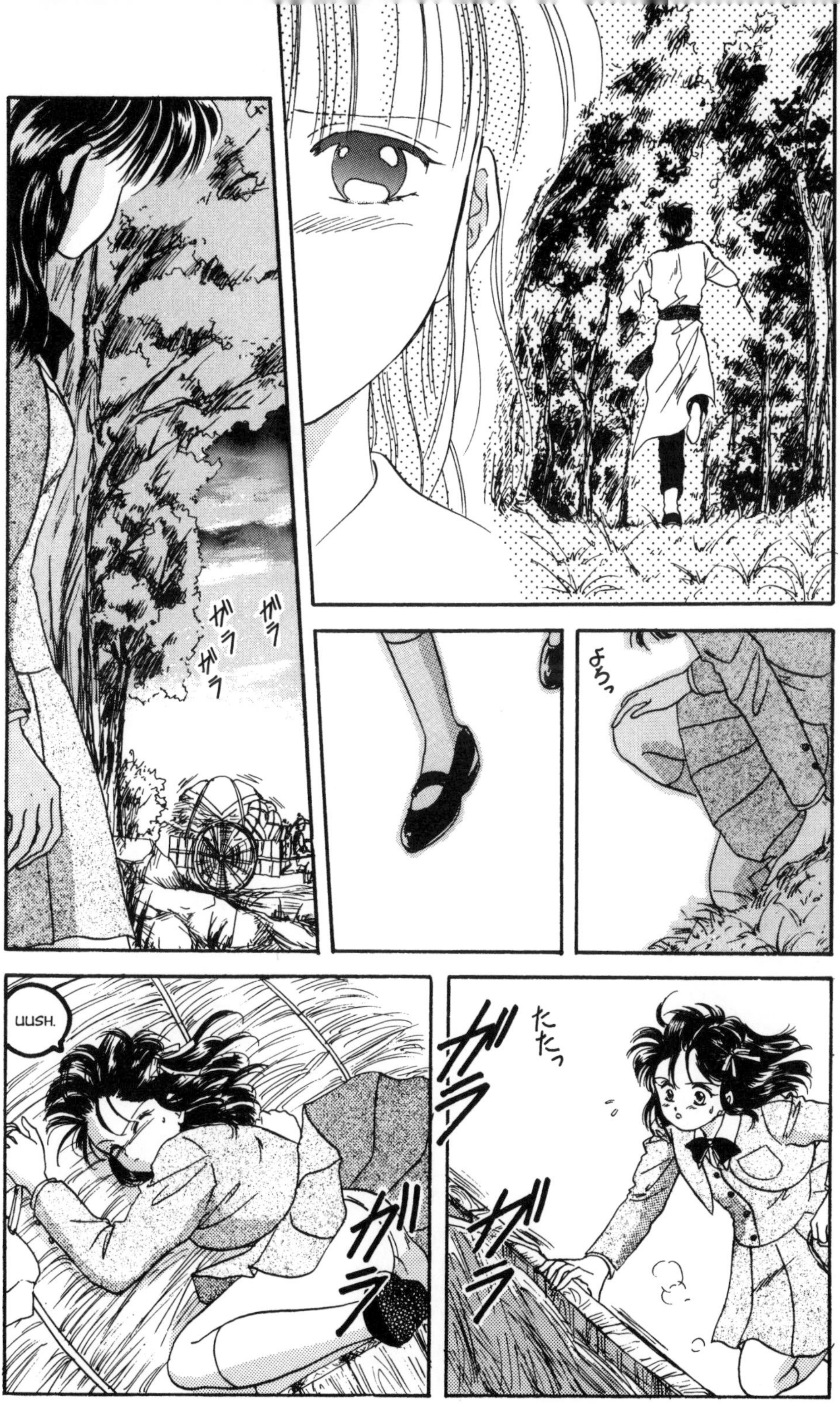
よろっ
ガラ
ガラ
ガラ
たたっ
ガラ
ガラ
ガラ
UUSH.

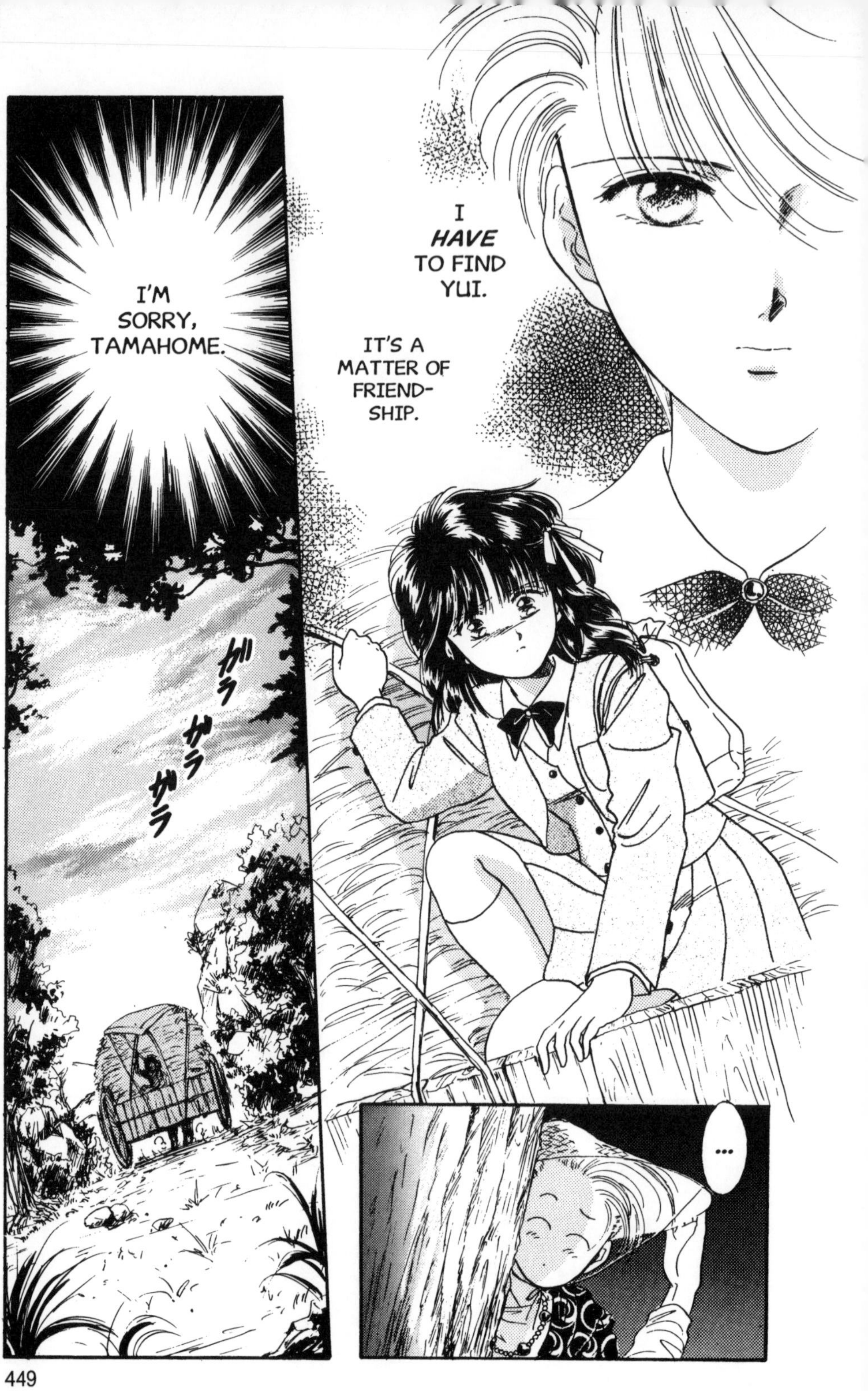
I *HAVE* TO FIND YUI.
IT'S A MATTER OF FRIEND-SHIP.
...
I'M SORRY, TAMAHOME.
ガラ ガラ ガラ

Xong 琮 Gui 鬼 Siu 宿

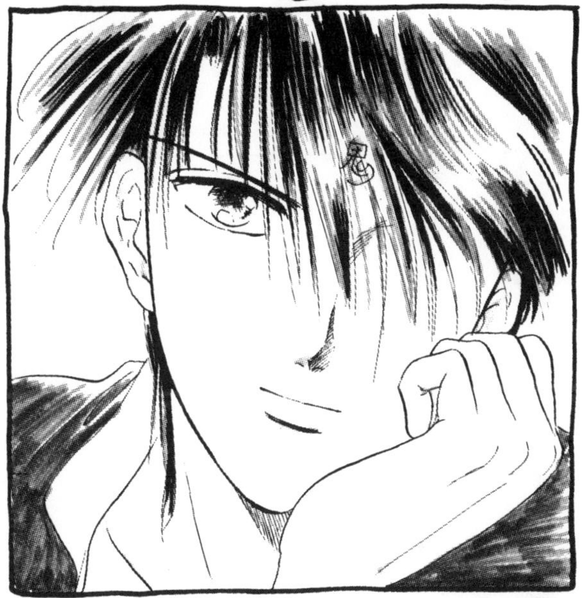

Cancer

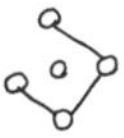

TAMAHOME

- Born in Bai-Jiang Village, Shou-Shuang Prefecture, Hong-Nan.
  Birthday is sometime between February and May (Because he's a constellation of Suzaku).
  Presently 17 years old.
  Relations: father, two brothers, two sisters. Mother: Died when he was 12 years old.
  Strengths: Marital arts (a natural born talent).
- Height: 5'9" Blood-type: O Hobby: Making money
- Eldest son taking the place of his ill father to support his family. Whatta great big brother! He's very caring, but at the same time, he can cause a lot of trouble for others. But everyone cuts him a break. On the outside, he is very chipper, and that leads to some comic expressions. But he's tough on the inside (so he thinks). On the other hand, he is very shy. (He had to become stoic for his family's sake.) That's why he was hard on Miaka in the first issue. Sacrifices himself for the sake of others and won't back down against an enemy.

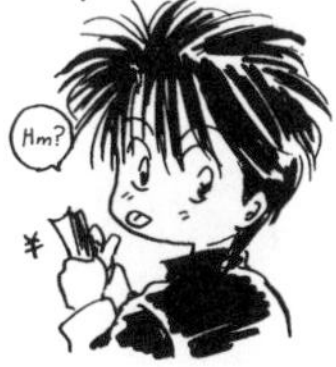
Hm?

It looks like you've all become accustomed to the Tamahome with short hair, but have you noticed how his hair's grown since volume 2? My assistants and I complain about how none of the readers wrote in concerning it.

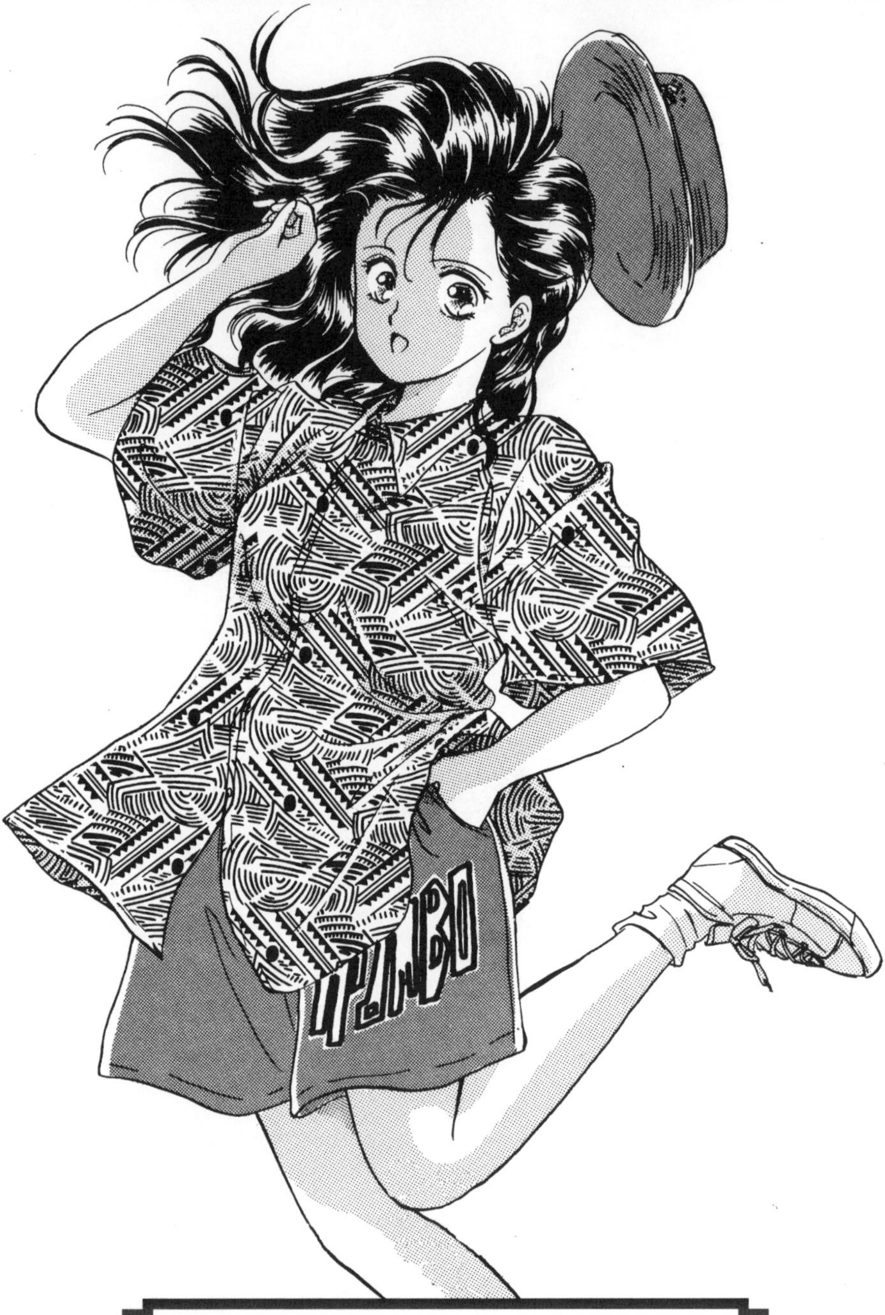

Chapter Fifteen
Captive Women

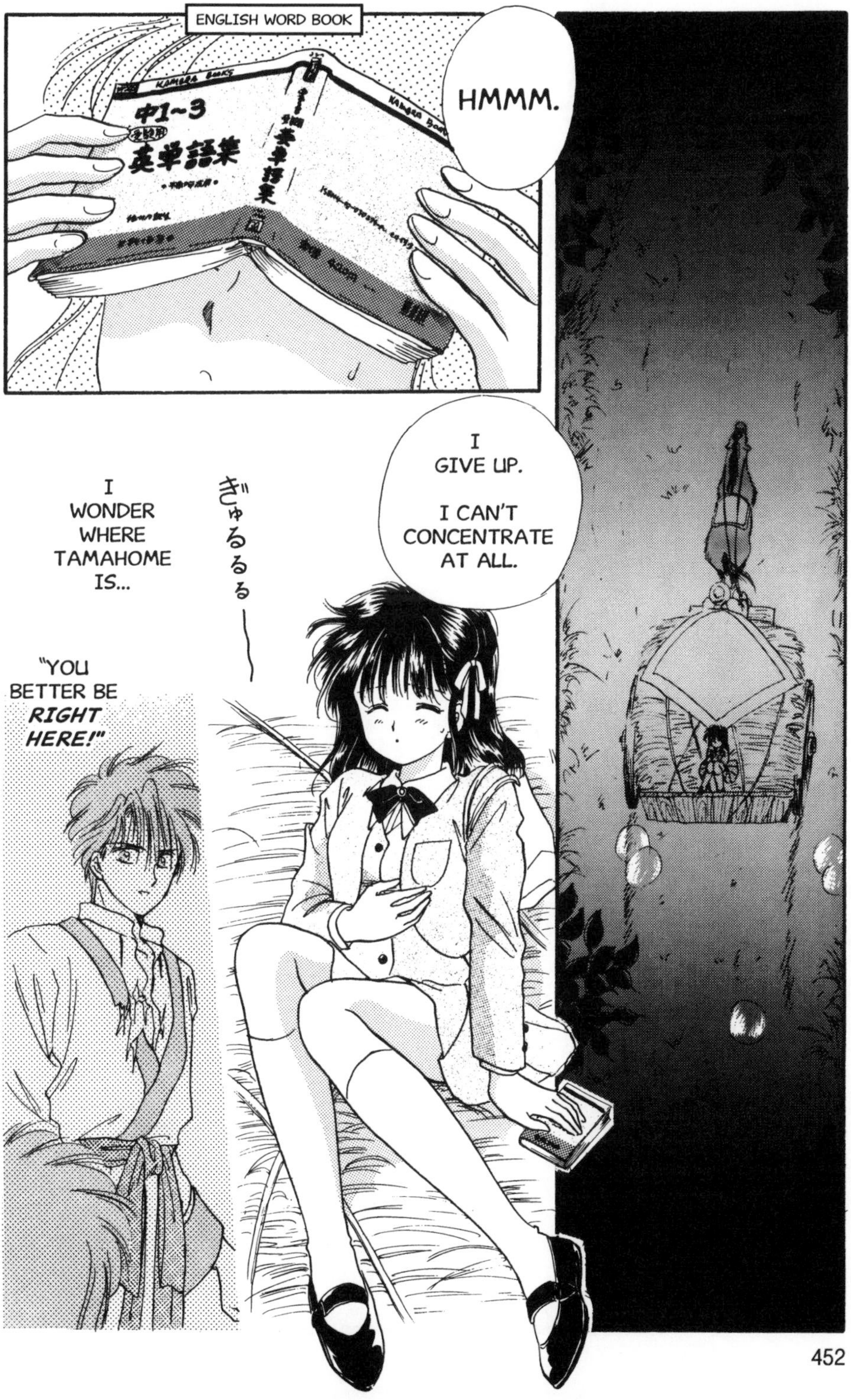

HMMM.
ENGLISH WORD BOOK
I GIVE UP.
I CAN'T CONCENTRATE AT ALL.
ぎゅるるる
I WONDER WHERE TAMAHOME IS...
"YOU BETTER BE RIGHT HERE!"

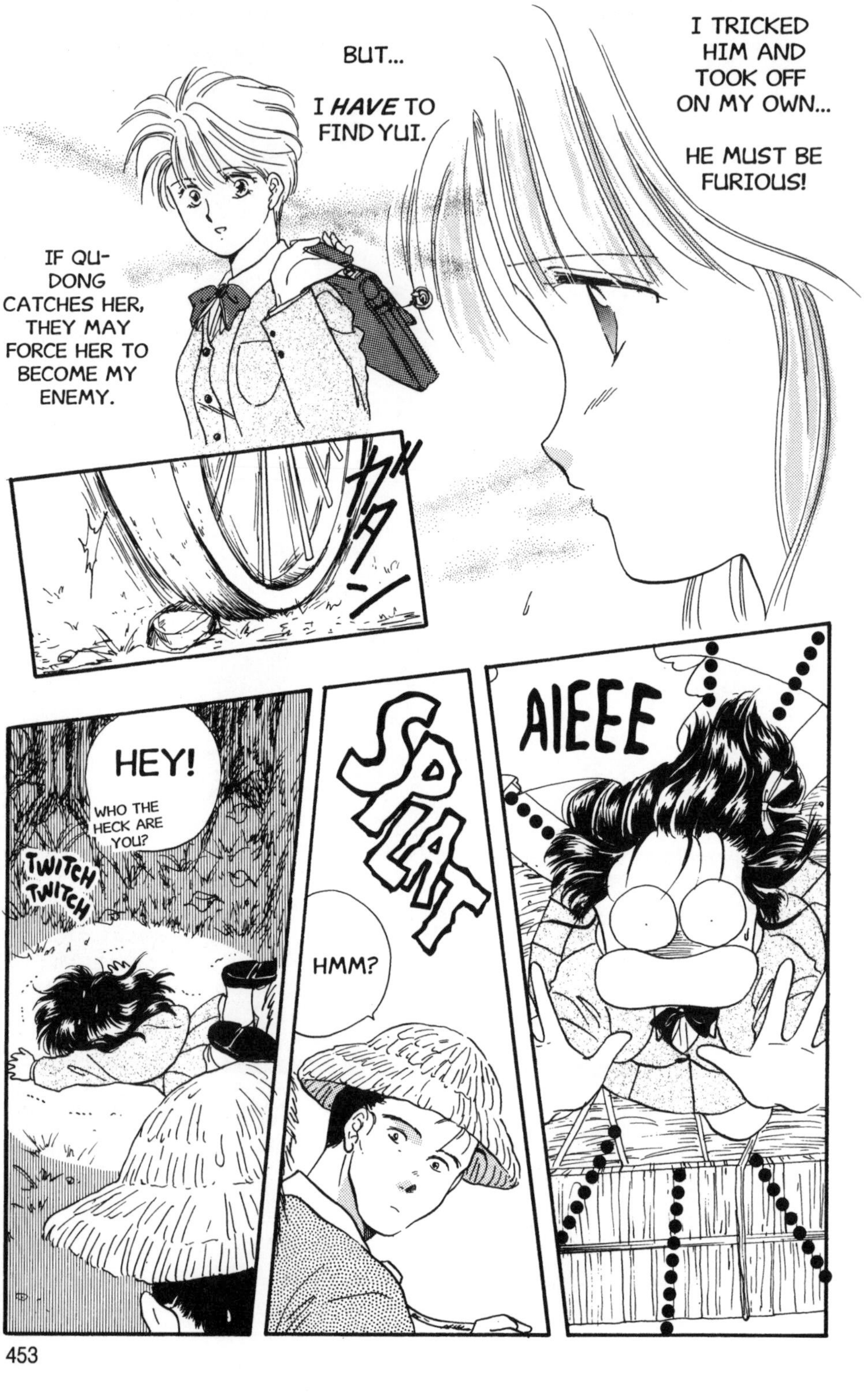
I TRICKED HIM AND TOOK OFF ON MY OWN...
HE MUST BE FURIOUS!
BUT...
I *HAVE* TO FIND YUI.
IF QU-DONG CATCHES HER, THEY MAY FORCE HER TO BECOME MY ENEMY.
ガタン
AIEEE
SPLAT
HMM?
HEY!
WHO THE HECK ARE YOU?
TWITCH TWITCH

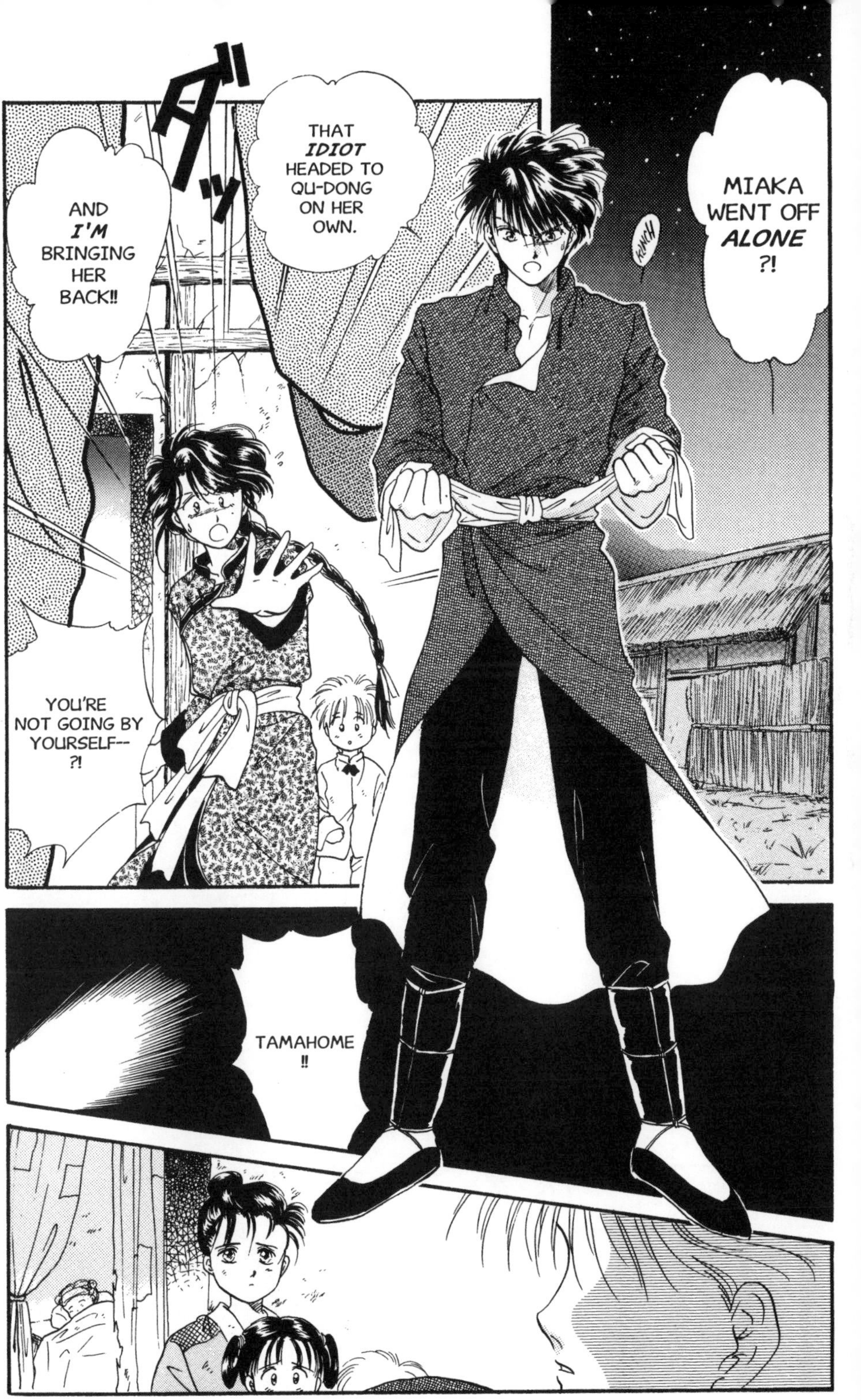
MIAKA WENT OFF ALONE ?!
THAT IDIOT HEADED TO QU-DONG ON HER OWN.
ダッ
AND I'M BRINGING HER BACK!!
YOU'RE NOT GOING BY YOURSELF-- ?!
TAMAHOME !!

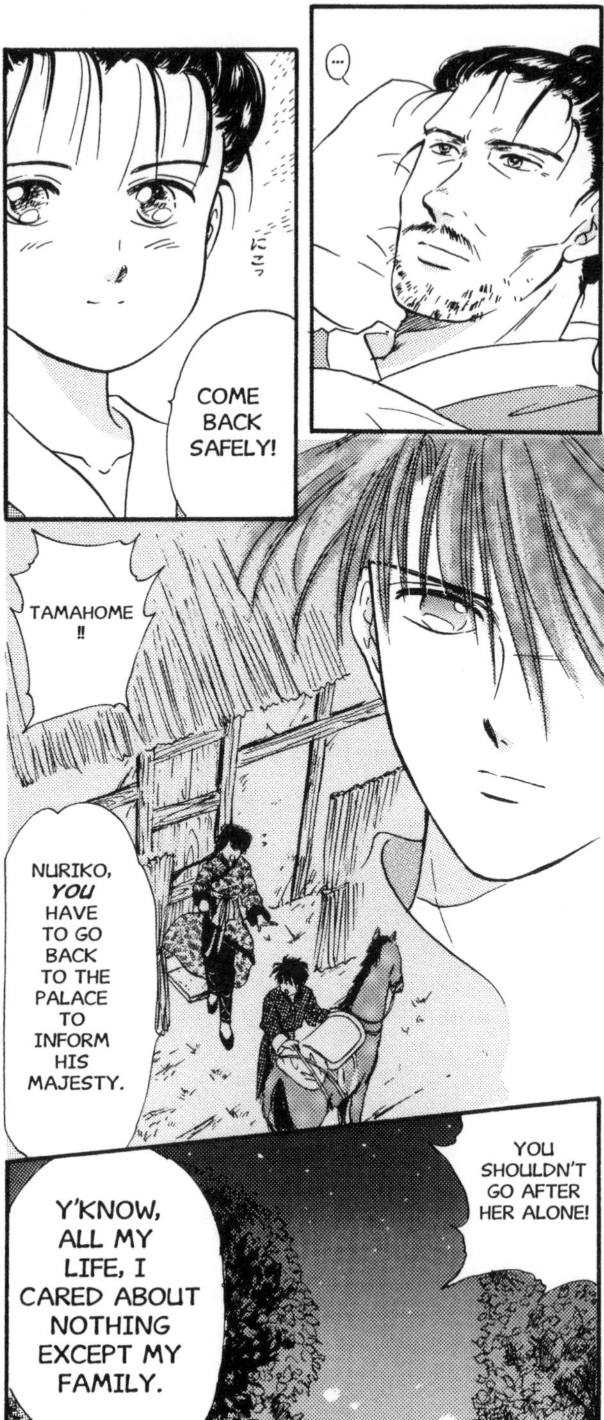
...
COME BACK SAFELY!
TAMAHOME !!
NURIKO, *YOU* HAVE TO GO BACK TO THE PALACE TO INFORM HIS MAJESTY.
YOU SHOULDN'T GO AFTER HER ALONE!
Y'KNOW, ALL MY LIFE, I CARED ABOUT NOTHING EXCEPT MY FAMILY.

I was so busy this year, I wasn't able to go home for the annual festival. But much to my amazement, even though I was in Tokyo, the festivals were given a lot of coverage on TV!! I used to think my area was in the middle of the boonies, but I guess it's becoming famous. But I couldn't look when one of the ceremonial wagons went crashing into a telephone pole, killing seven people! Things were out of control! What's going on Kishi---da?! (Must remain anonymous.)

If I'd gone home, I would've been both furious and terrified. But I have no problem watching it on TV. Hmm. Maybe I should have promoted myself more when I lived there. (Promoted what?!) My little brother really wanted to go back, but my mom isn't too thrilled with the idea. (She's scared.)

My parents were born in Osaka so they're not actually from the town. But the minute I hear the sound of those taiko drums, it starts my blood flowing.

When I was a senior in high school, I always went to the festival wearing a happi coat, but I didn't pull the float. Now guys look pretty good in happi coats. The designs vary from town to town, but our town's design was simple (white lettering on black cloth). The whole town preferred that festival even the New Year's. Town natives who moved away to places over the country to come home all for the festival. (I didn't. Sorry!) They even close down the grade schools for it. Amazing, really! The downtown district has its festival in September, and the uptown district has its in October. The uptown kids (like me) had vacation days for both. The year after I moved to Tokyo when I came back for the festival, my cousin (♀) was pulling the float when she fell, but she held onto the rope for a couple dozen meters. Even though she was scraped and bleeding, she caught her feet and still helped out. If you let go of the rope, you get run over by the float, so you can't let go even if you fall. Of course, some of the older guys act as guardians to save you in case of an accident. It can be scary. Anyway, a lot of famous people are from the area. Kiyohara of the Seibu Lions, the designers, the Koshinos (former neighbors of mine) and a few actors.... I'm the first manga artist to come from there (I think).

I'll go back next year!

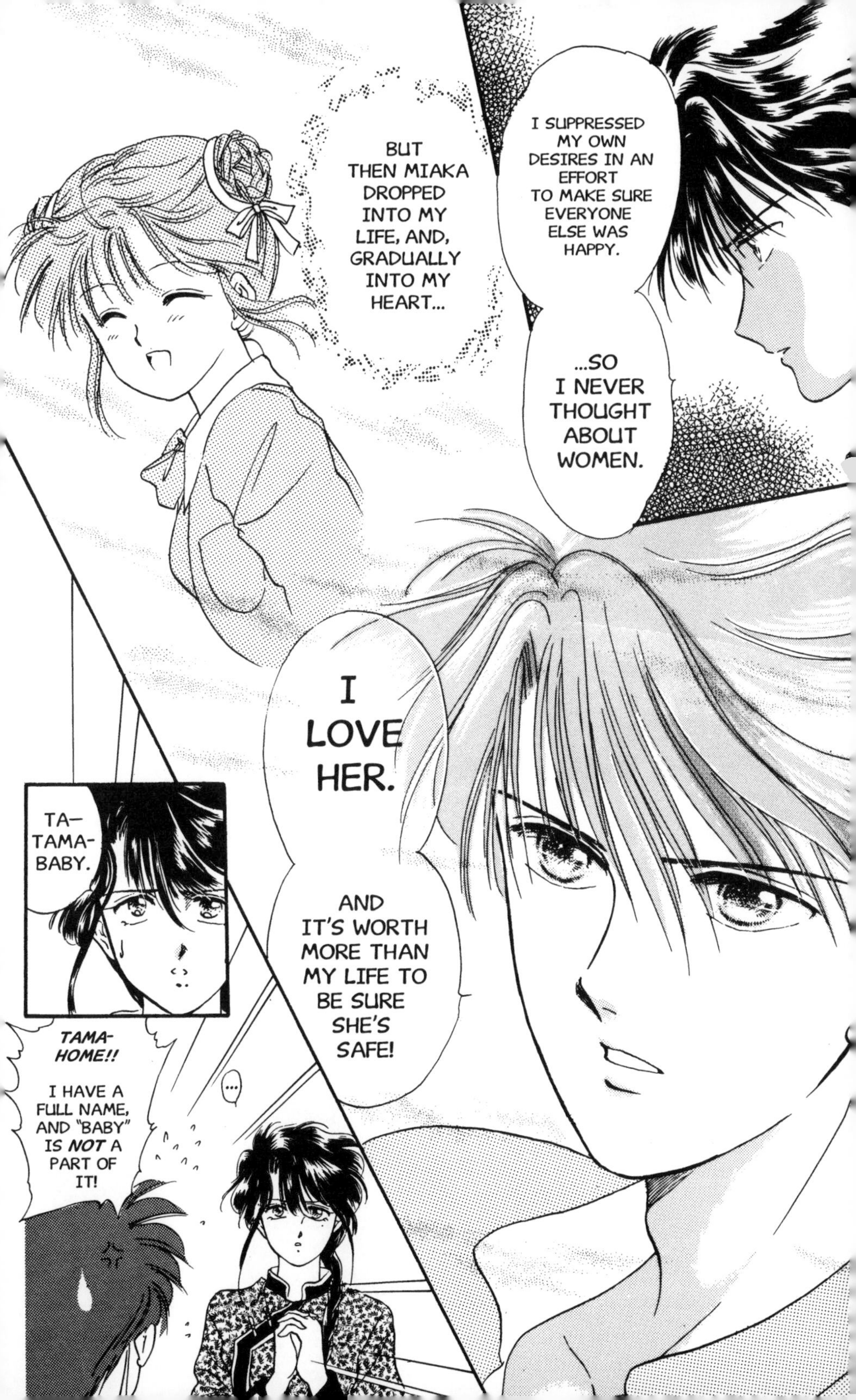
I SUPPRESSED MY OWN DESIRES IN AN EFFORT TO MAKE SURE EVERYONE ELSE WAS HAPPY.
...SO I NEVER THOUGHT ABOUT WOMEN.
BUT THEN MIAKA DROPPED INTO MY LIFE, AND, GRADUALLY INTO MY HEART...
I LOVE HER.
AND IT'S WORTH MORE THAN MY LIFE TO BE SURE SHE'S SAFE!
TA—TAMA-BABY.
...
TAMA-HOME!!
I HAVE A FULL NAME, AND "BABY" IS NOT A PART OF IT!

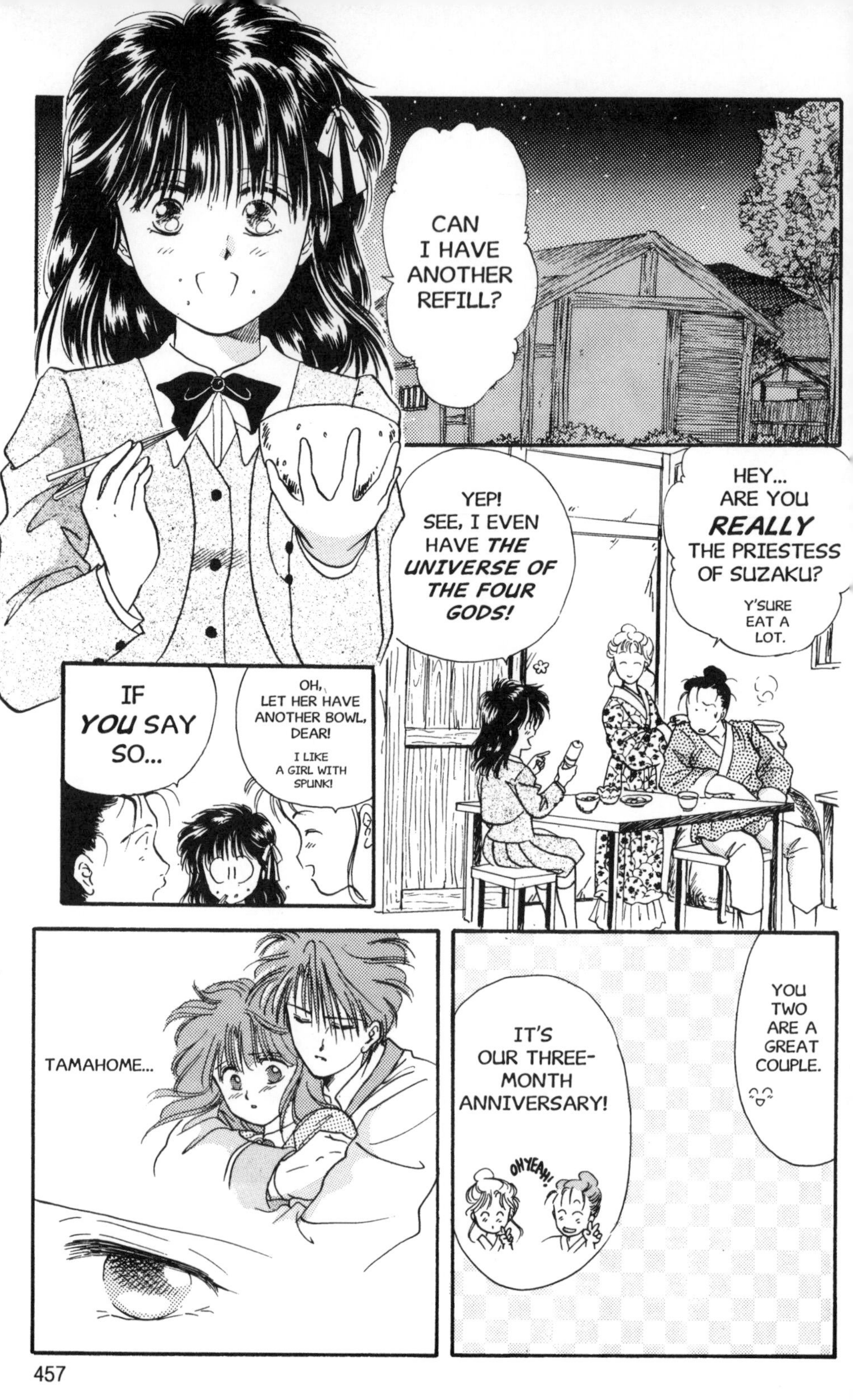
CAN I HAVE ANOTHER REFILL?
HEY... ARE YOU **REALLY** THE PRIESTESS OF SUZAKU?
Y'SURE EAT A LOT.
YEP! SEE, I EVEN HAVE ***THE UNIVERSE OF THE FOUR GODS!***
OH, LET HER HAVE ANOTHER BOWL, DEAR!
I LIKE A GIRL WITH SPUNK!
IF ***YOU*** SAY SO...
YOU TWO ARE A GREAT COUPLE.
IT'S OUR THREE-MONTH ANNIVERSARY!
OH YEAH!
TAMAHOME...

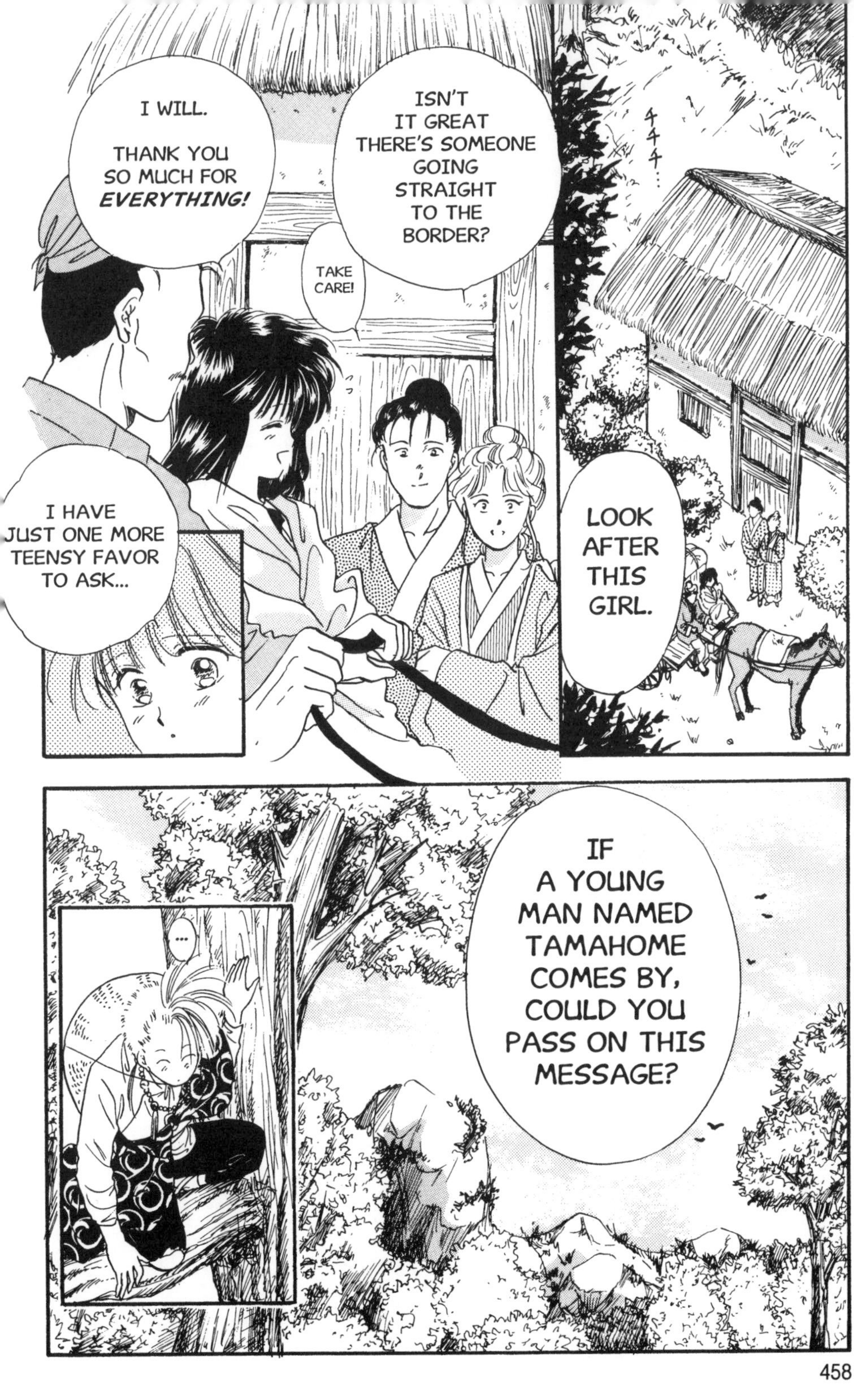
チチチ…
LOOK AFTER THIS GIRL.
ISN'T IT GREAT THERE'S SOMEONE GOING STRAIGHT TO THE BORDER?
I WILL. THANK YOU SO MUCH FOR *EVERYTHING!*
TAKE CARE!
I HAVE JUST ONE MORE TEENSY FAVOR TO ASK...
IF A YOUNG MAN NAMED TAMAHOME COMES BY, COULD YOU PASS ON THIS MESSAGE?
...

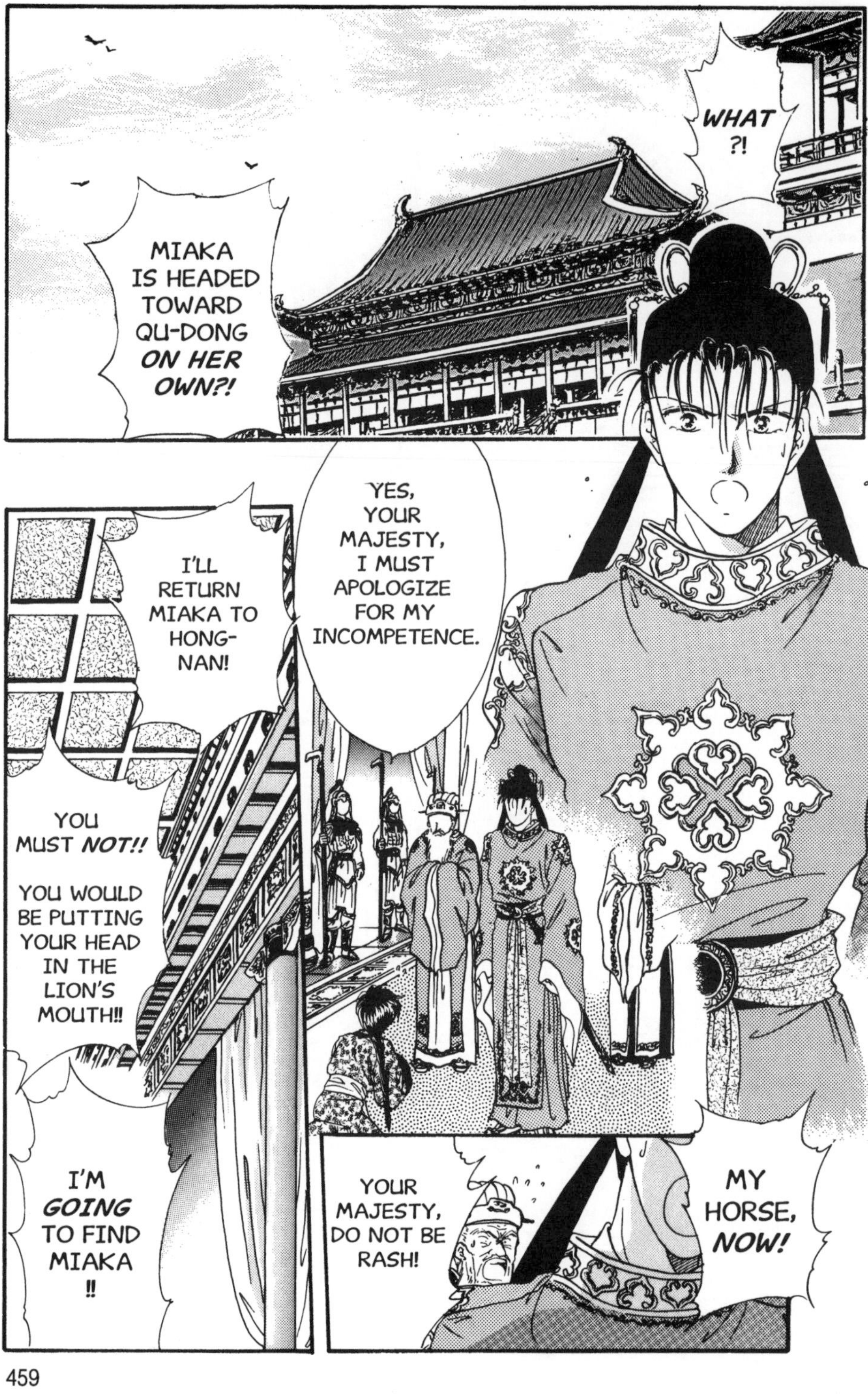
WHAT ?!
MIAKA IS HEADED TOWARD QU-DONG ON HER OWN?!
YES, YOUR MAJESTY, I MUST APOLOGIZE FOR MY INCOMPETENCE.
MY HORSE, NOW!
YOUR MAJESTY, DO NOT BE RASH!
I'LL RETURN MIAKA TO HONG-NAN!
YOU MUST NOT!!
YOU WOULD BE PUTTING YOUR HEAD IN THE LION'S MOUTH!!
I'M GOING TO FIND MIAKA !!

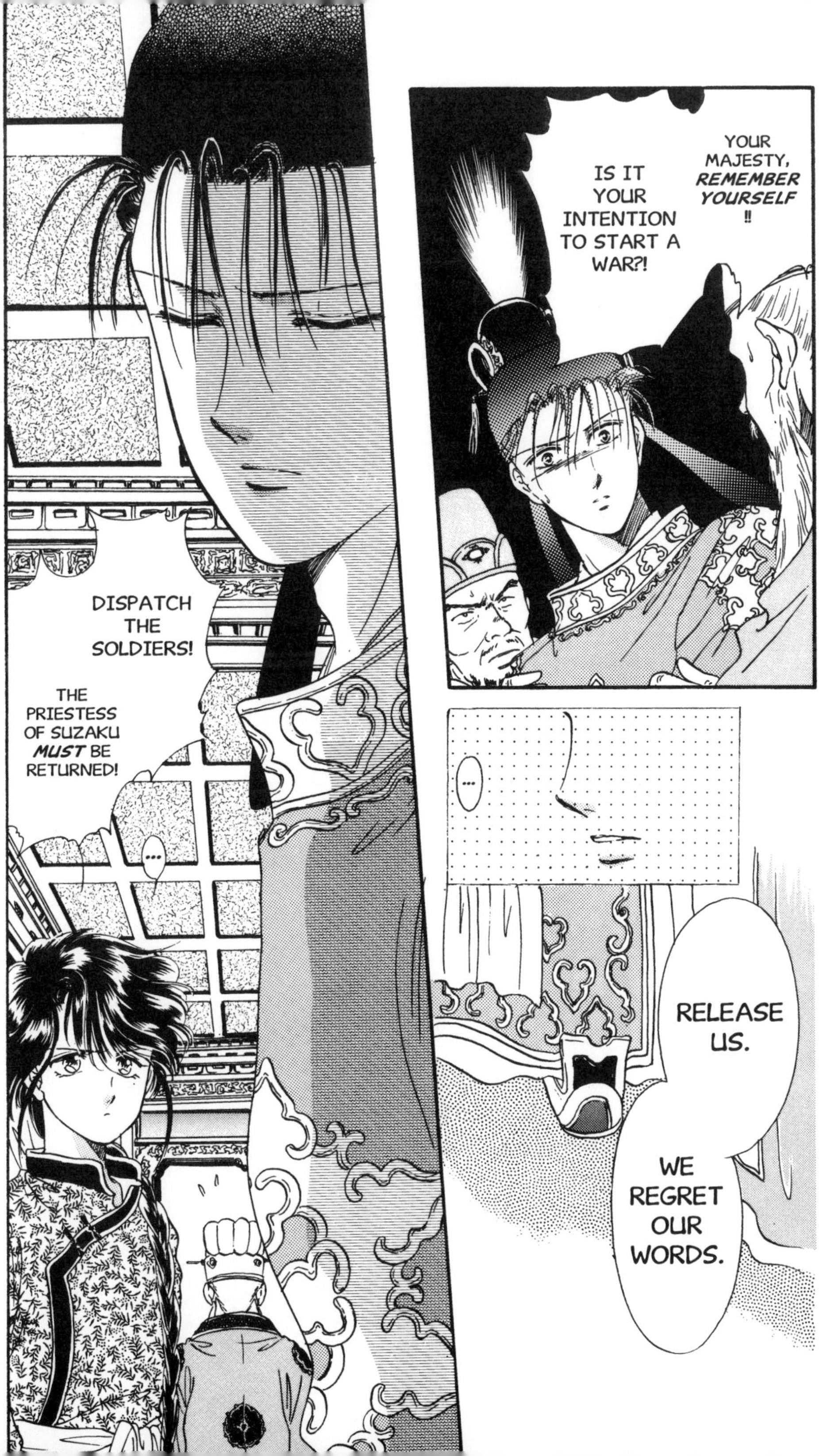

YOUR MAJESTY, *REMEMBER YOURSELF* !!
IS IT YOUR INTENTION TO START A WAR?!
...
RELEASE US.
WE REGRET OUR WORDS.
DISPATCH THE SOLDIERS!
THE PRIESTESS OF SUZAKU *MUST* BE RETURNED!
...

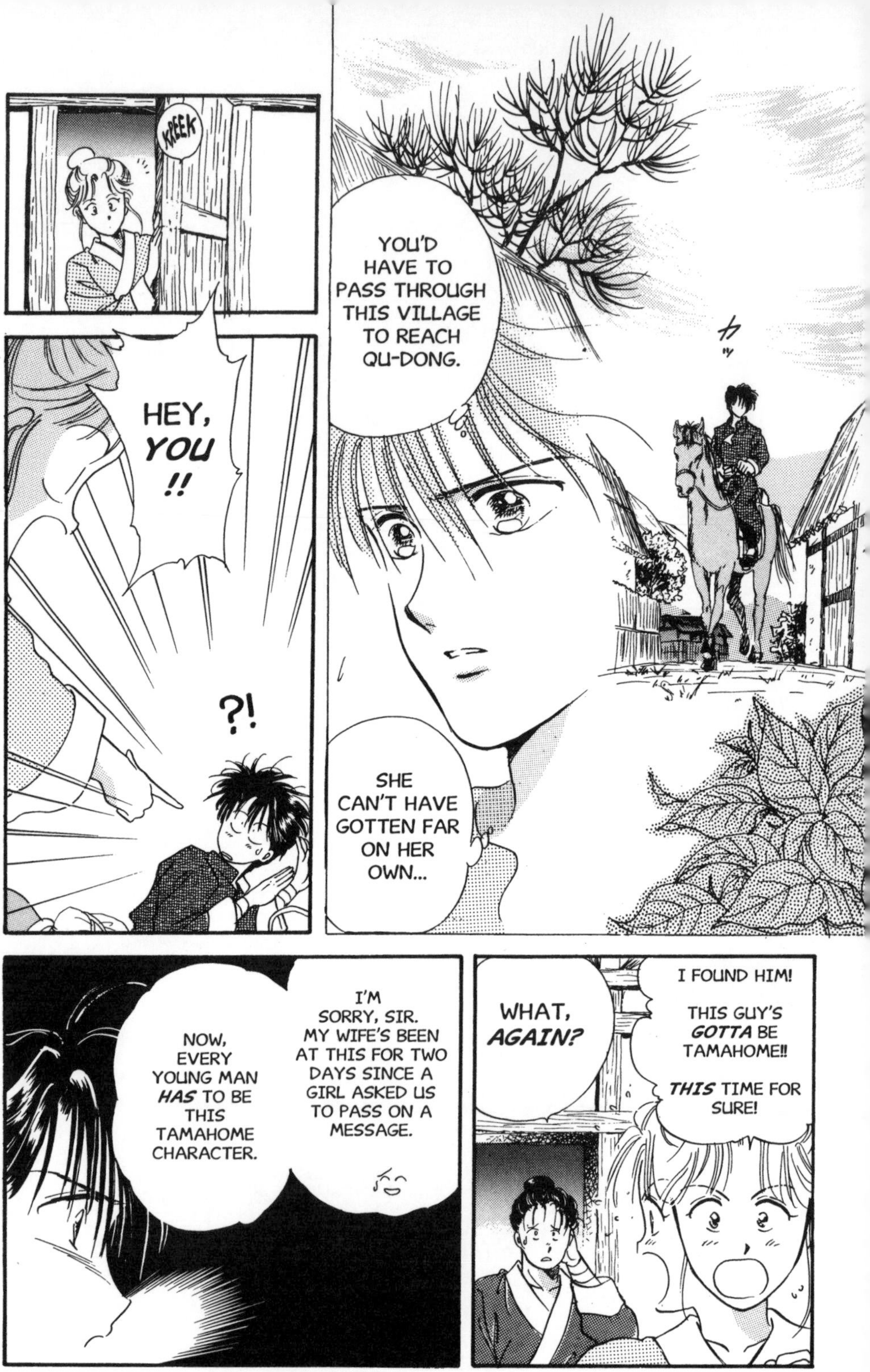
YOU'D HAVE TO PASS THROUGH THIS VILLAGE TO REACH QU-DONG.
カッ
SHE CAN'T HAVE GOTTEN FAR ON HER OWN...
KREEK
HEY, *YOU* !!
?!
I FOUND HIM!
THIS GUY'S *GOTTA* BE TAMAHOME!!
THIS TIME FOR SURE!
WHAT, *AGAIN?*
I'M SORRY, SIR. MY WIFE'S BEEN AT THIS FOR TWO DAYS SINCE A GIRL ASKED US TO PASS ON A MESSAGE.
NOW, EVERY YOUNG MAN *HAS* TO BE THIS TAMAHOME CHARACTER.

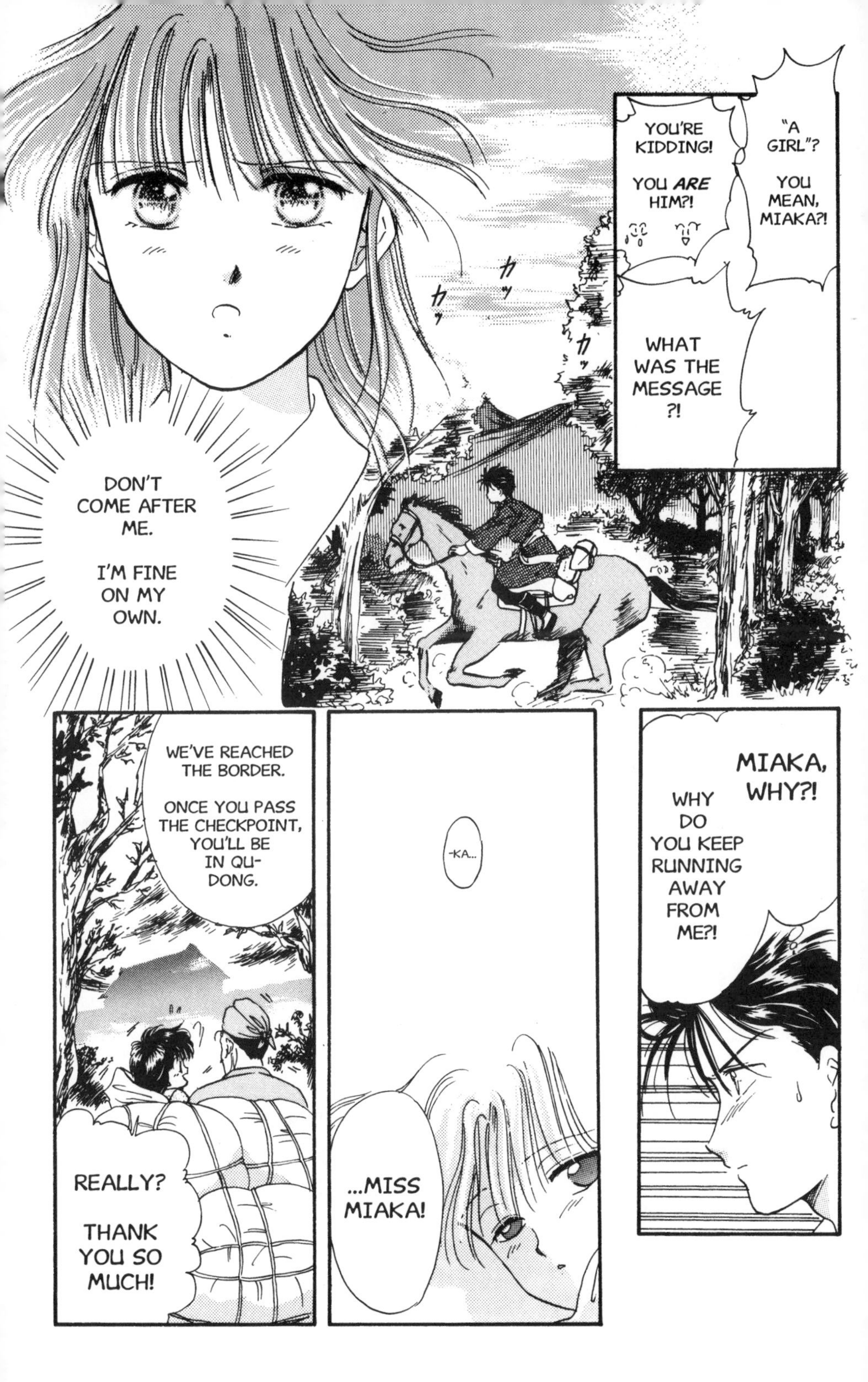
"A GIRL"? YOU MEAN, MIAKA?!
YOU'RE KIDDING! YOU *ARE* HIM?!
WHAT WAS THE MESSAGE ?!
カッ
カッ
カッ
DON'T COME AFTER ME. I'M FINE ON MY OWN.
MIAKA, WHY?!
WHY DO YOU KEEP RUNNING AWAY FROM ME?!
-KA...
...MISS MIAKA!
WE'VE REACHED THE BORDER. ONCE YOU PASS THE CHECKPOINT, YOU'LL BE IN QU-DONG.
REALLY? THANK YOU SO MUCH!

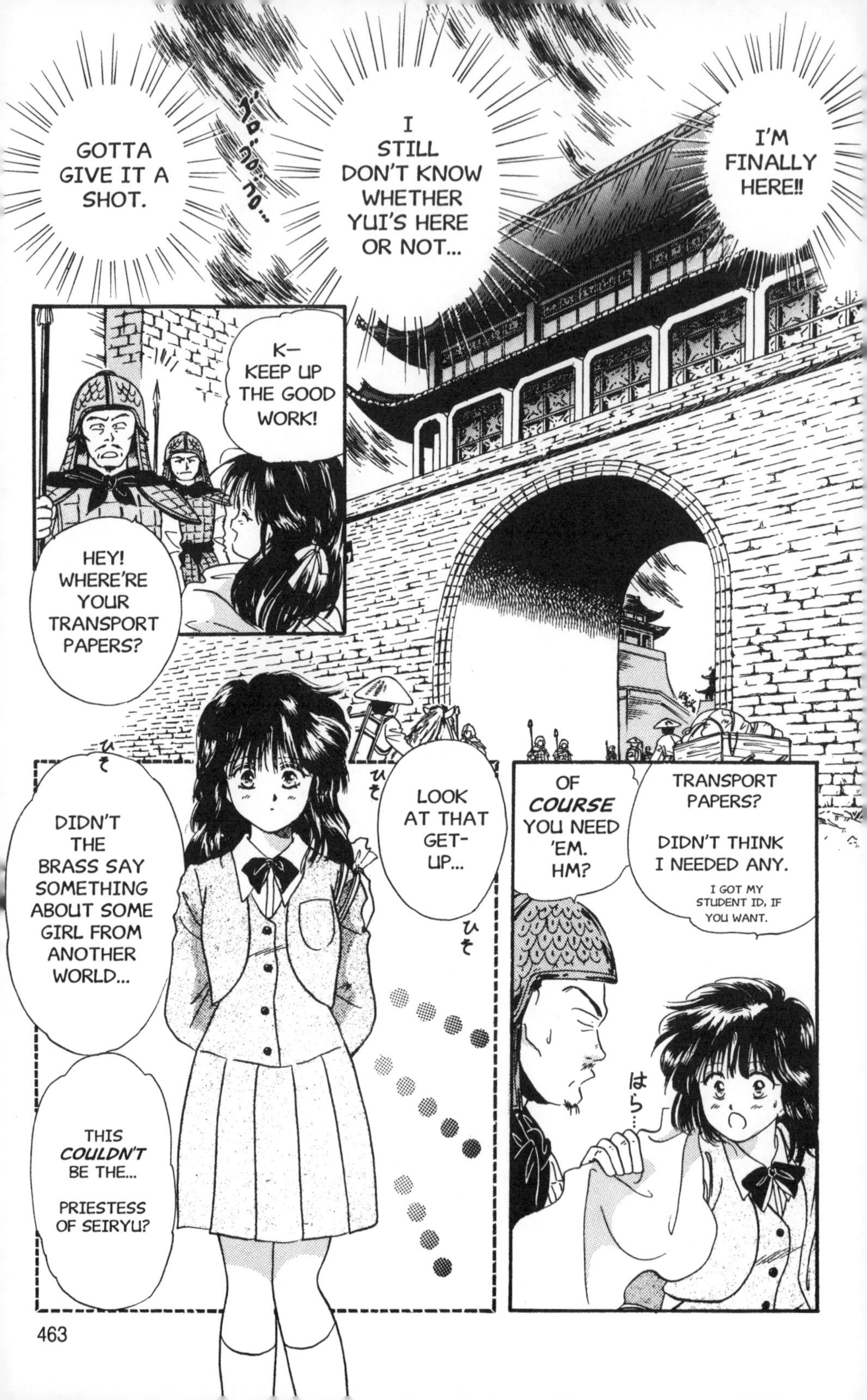
I'M FINALLY HERE!!
ゴゴゴ…
I STILL DON'T KNOW WHETHER YUI'S HERE OR NOT...
GOTTA GIVE IT A SHOT.
K— KEEP UP THE GOOD WORK!
HEY! WHERE'RE YOUR TRANSPORT PAPERS?
TRANSPORT PAPERS? DIDN'T THINK I NEEDED ANY.
I GOT MY STUDENT ID, IF YOU WANT.
OF *COURSE* YOU NEED 'EM. HM?
はら…
ひそ
LOOK AT THAT GET-UP...
ひそ
ひそ
DIDN'T THE BRASS SAY SOMETHING ABOUT SOME GIRL FROM ANOTHER WORLD...
THIS *COULDN'T* BE THE... PRIESTESS OF SEIRYU?

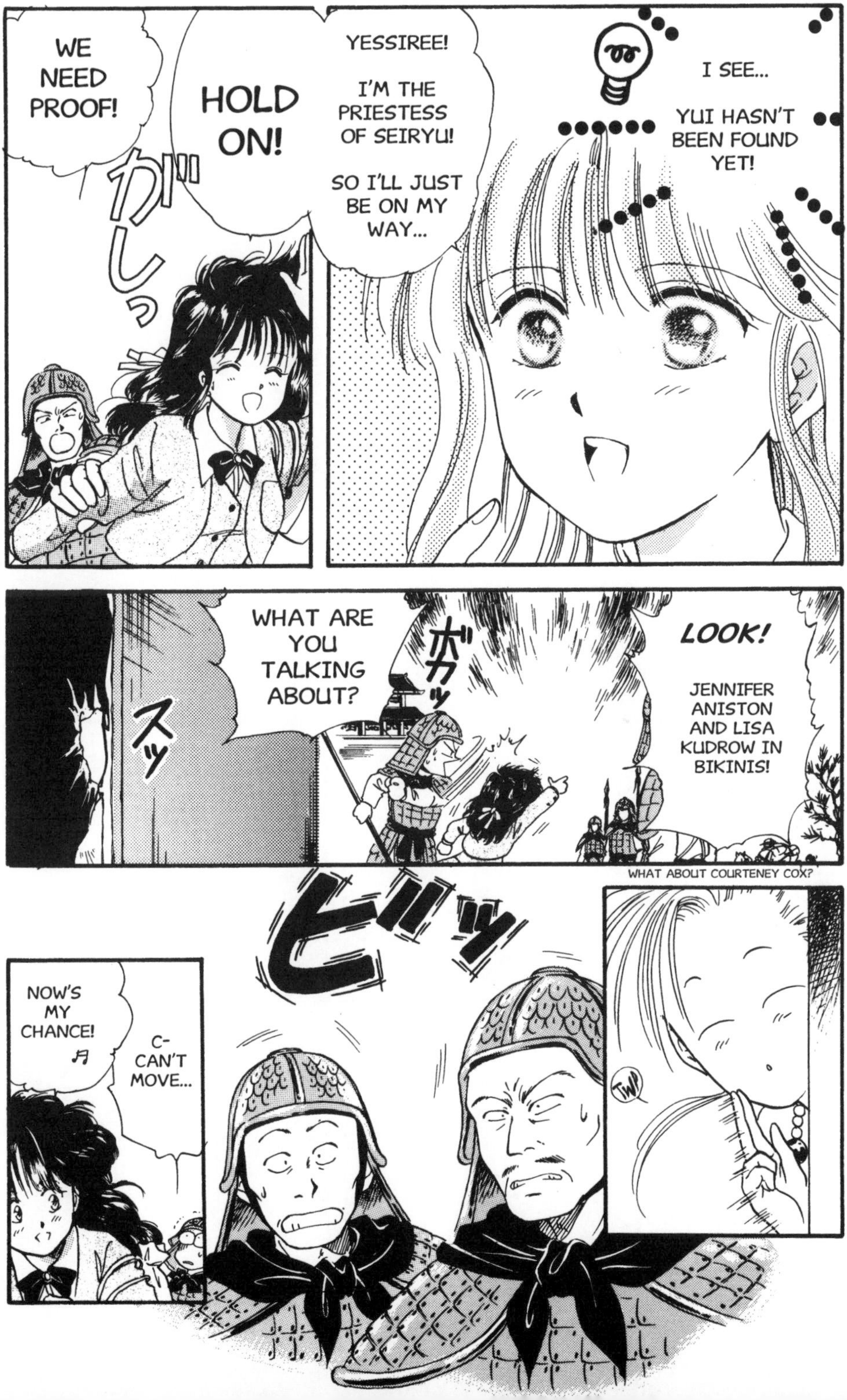
I SEE...
YUI HASN'T BEEN FOUND YET!
YESSIREE!
I'M THE PRIESTESS OF SEIRYU!
SO I'LL JUST BE ON MY WAY...
HOLD ON!
WE NEED PROOF!
がしっ
LOOK!
JENNIFER ANISTON AND LISA KUDROW IN BIKINIS!
WHAT ARE YOU TALKING ABOUT?
ボカッ
スッ
WHAT ABOUT COURTENEY COX?
TWIP
ビッ
NOW'S MY CHANCE! ♪
C-CAN'T MOVE...

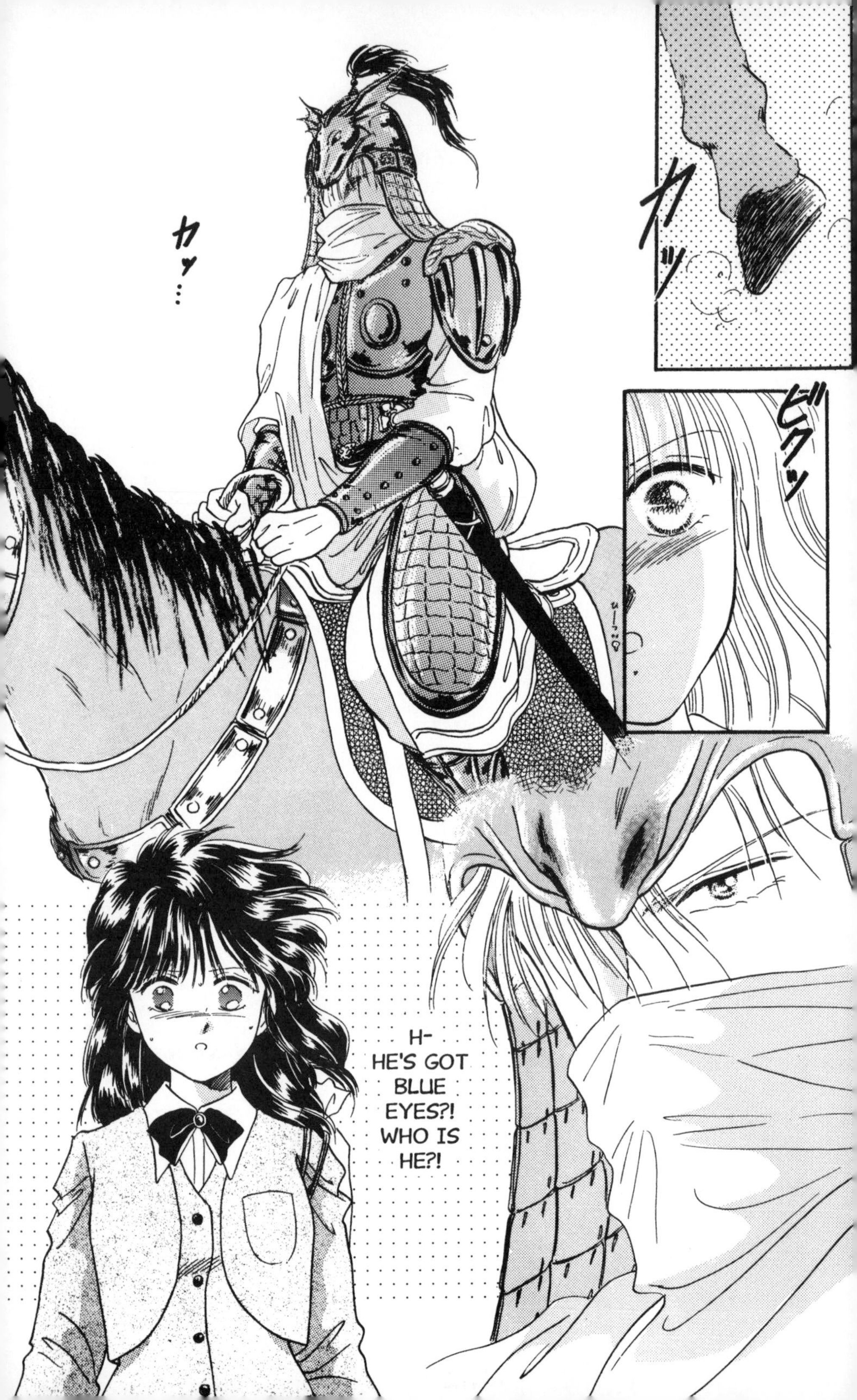
カッ
ビクッ
カッ…
H-
HE'S GOT
BLUE
EYES?!
WHO IS
HE?!

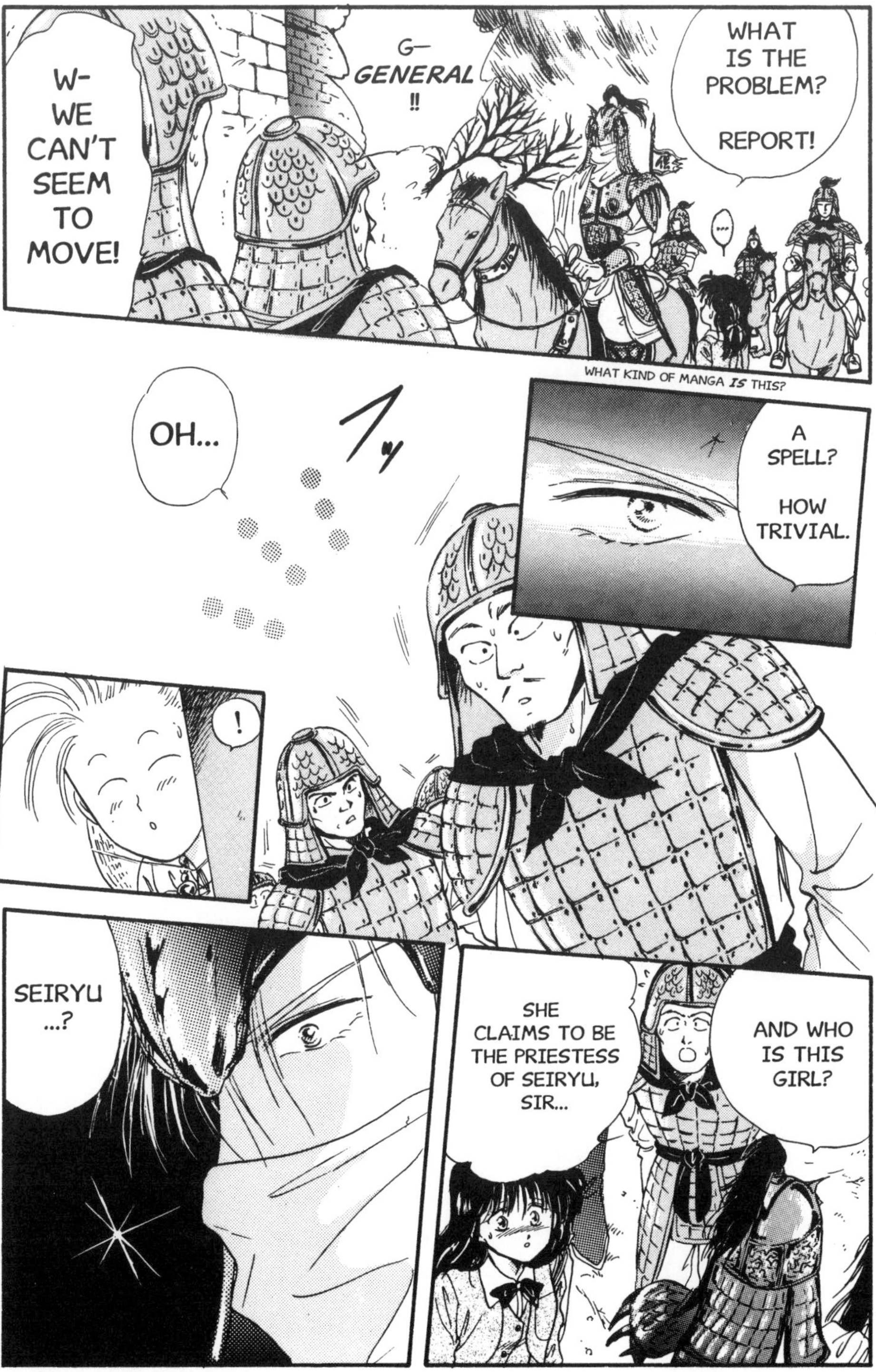
WHAT IS THE PROBLEM? REPORT!
G— GENERAL!!
W- WE CAN'T SEEM TO MOVE!
...
WHAT KIND OF MANGA IS THIS?
A SPELL? HOW TRIVIAL.
OH...
!
AND WHO IS THIS GIRL?
SHE CLAIMS TO BE THE PRIESTESS OF SEIRYU, SIR...
SEIRYU ...?

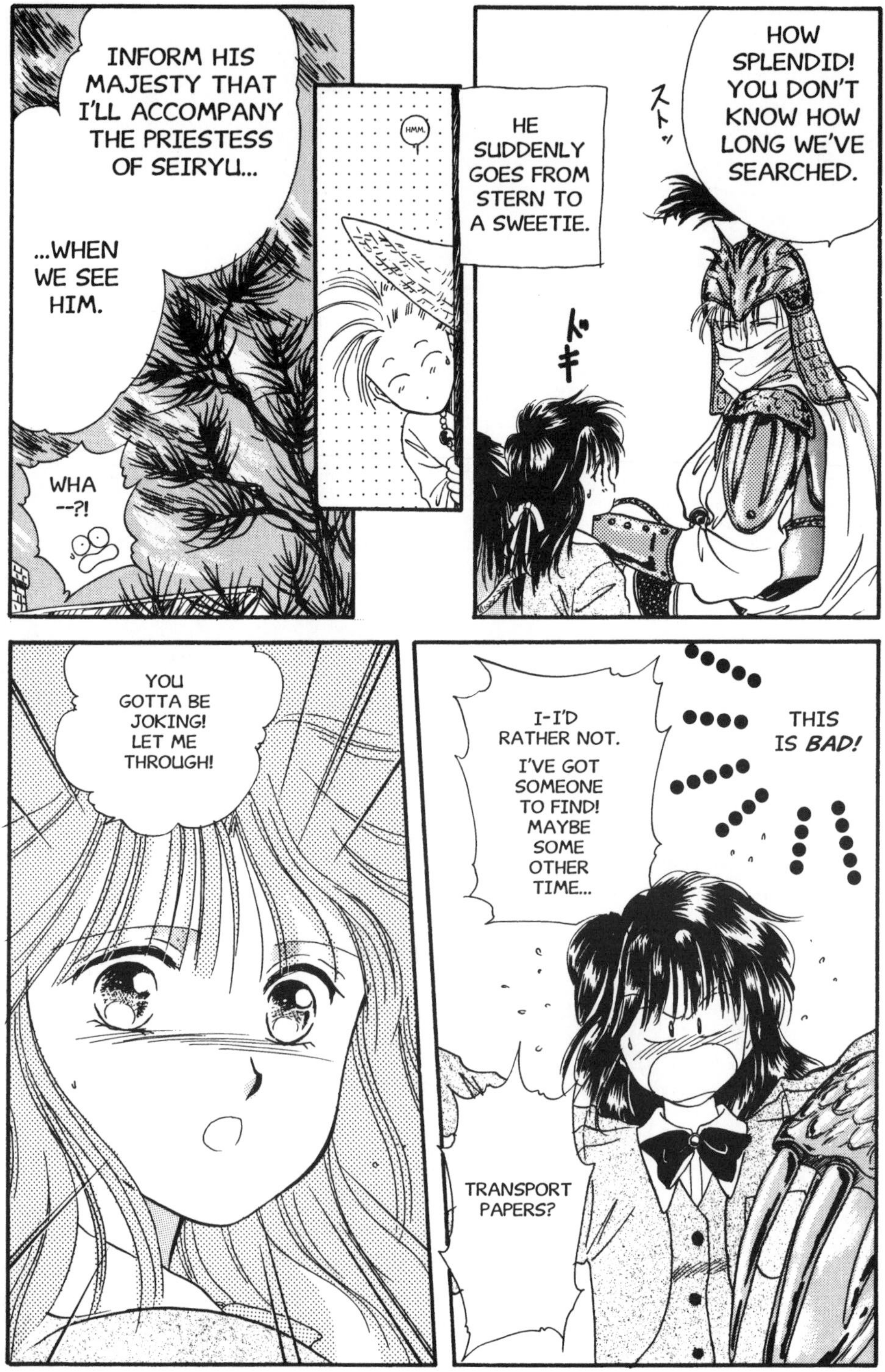
HOW SPLENDID! YOU DON'T KNOW HOW LONG WE'VE SEARCHED.
ストッ
ドキ
HE SUDDENLY GOES FROM STERN TO A SWEETIE.
HMM.
INFORM HIS MAJESTY THAT I'LL ACCOMPANY THE PRIESTESS OF SEIRYU...
...WHEN WE SEE HIM.
WHA --?!
THIS IS *BAD!*
I-I'D RATHER NOT. I'VE GOT SOMEONE TO FIND! MAYBE SOME OTHER TIME...
TRANSPORT PAPERS?
YOU GOTTA BE JOKING! LET ME THROUGH!

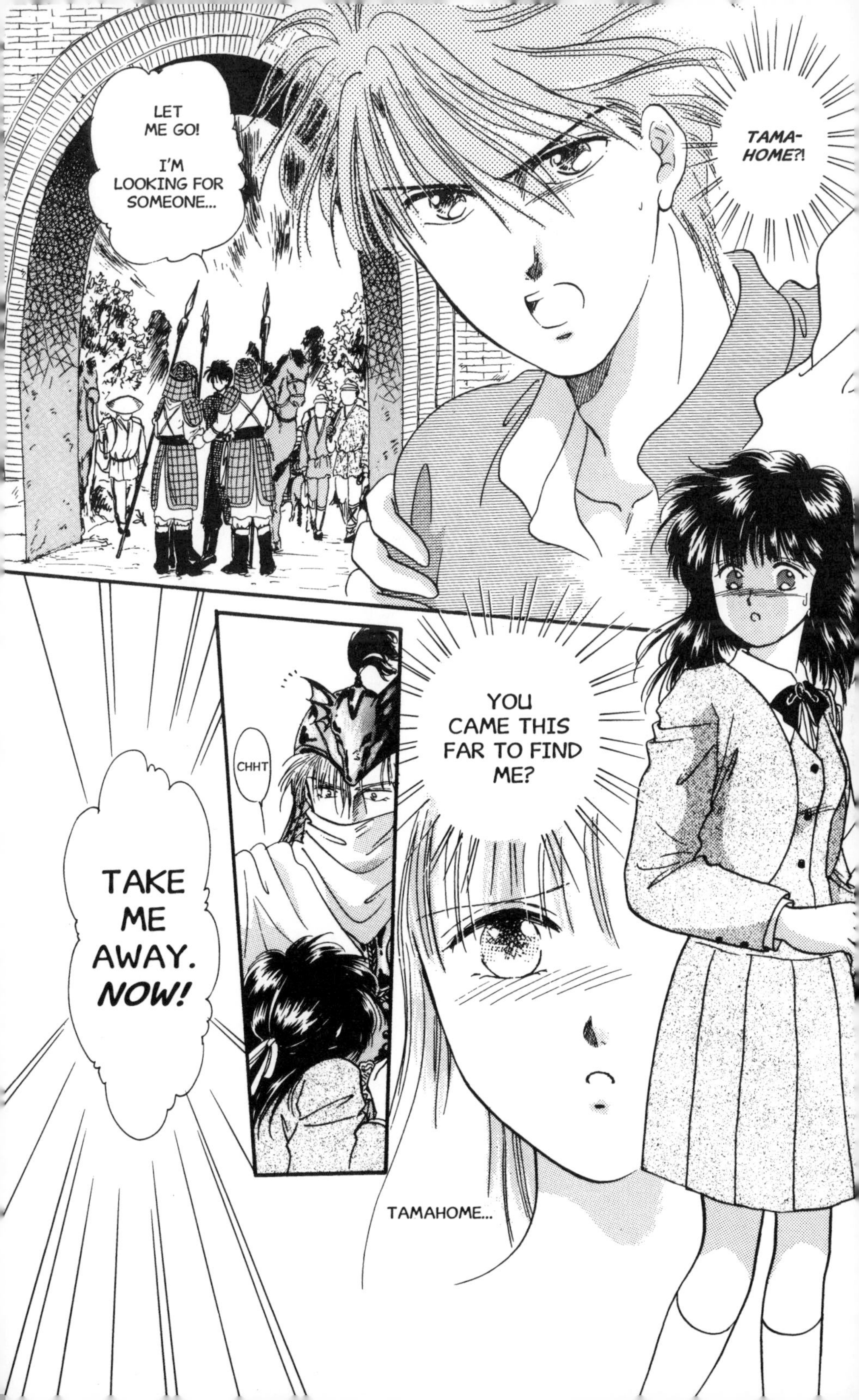
TAMA-HOME?!
LET ME GO! I'M LOOKING FOR SOMEONE...
YOU CAME THIS FAR TO FIND ME?
TAMAHOME...
CHHT
TAKE ME AWAY. *NOW!*

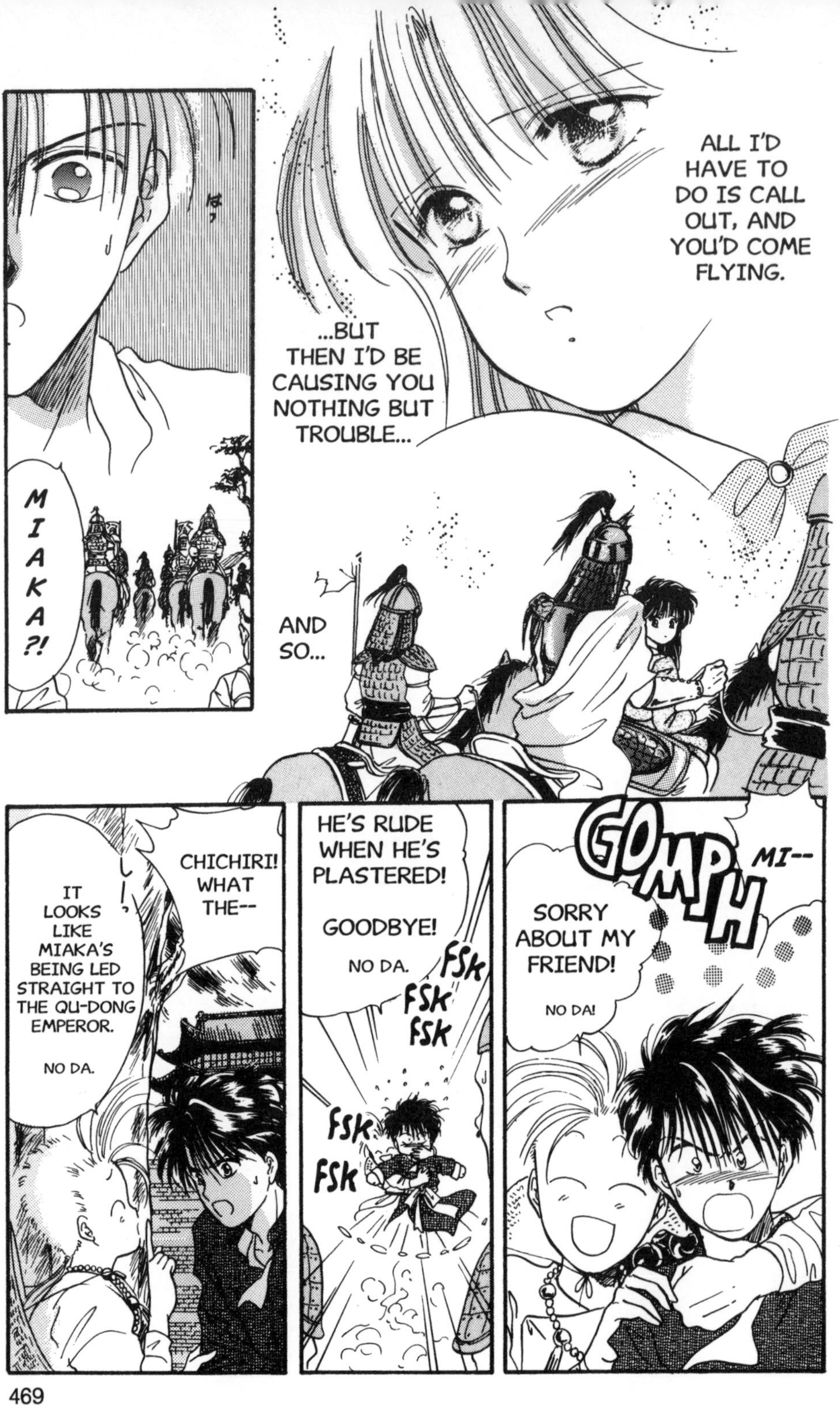
ALL I'D HAVE TO DO IS CALL OUT, AND YOU'D COME FLYING.
...BUT THEN I'D BE CAUSING YOU NOTHING BUT TROUBLE...
AND SO...
はっ
MIAKA?!
GOMPH
MI--
SORRY ABOUT MY FRIEND!
NO DA!
HE'S RUDE WHEN HE'S PLASTERED!
GOODBYE!
NO DA.
FSK FSK FSK
FSK FSK
CHICHIRI! WHAT THE--
IT LOOKS LIKE MIAKA'S BEING LED STRAIGHT TO THE QU-DONG EMPEROR.
NO DA.

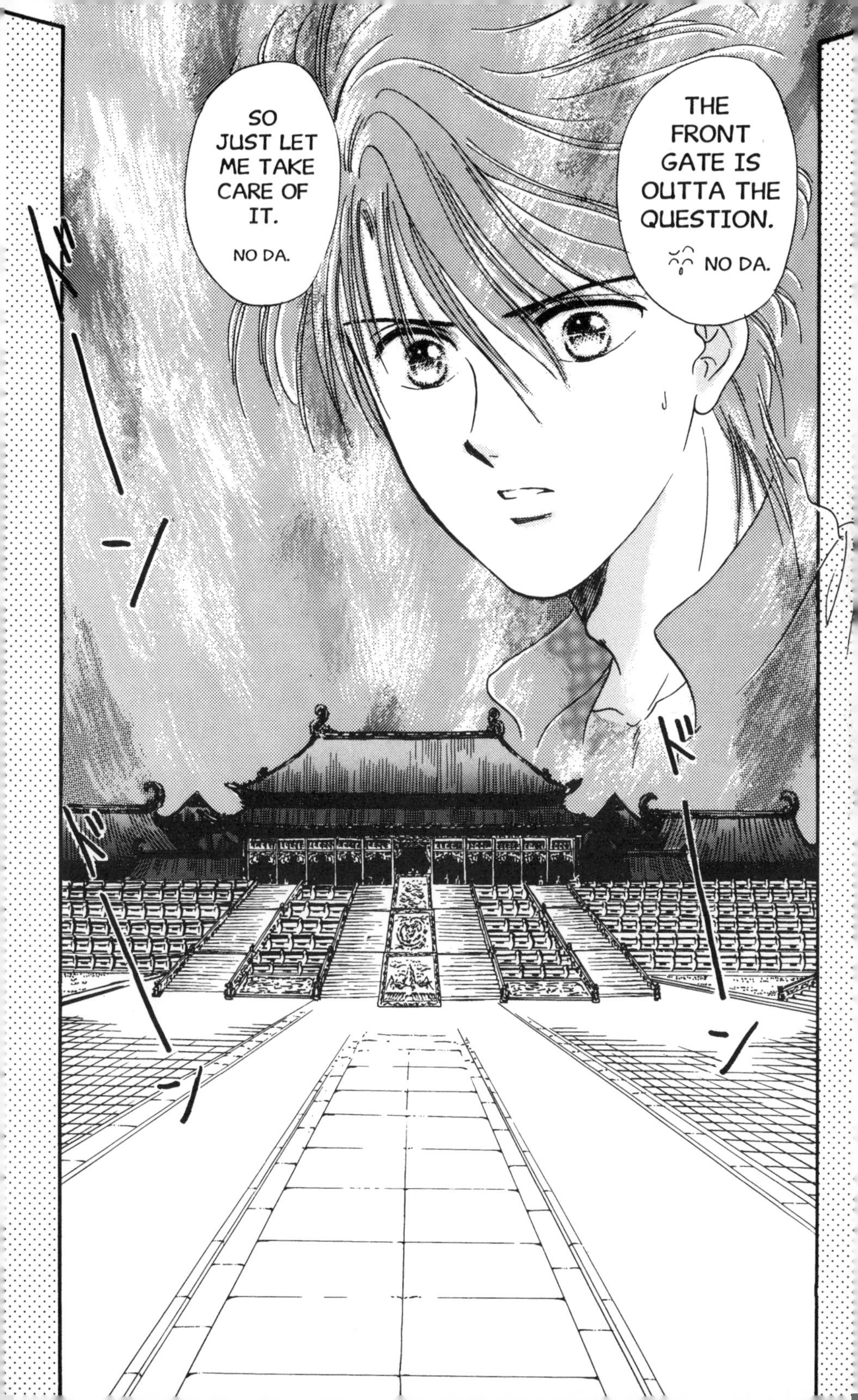
THE FRONT GATE IS OUTTA THE QUESTION.
NO DA.
SO JUST LET ME TAKE CARE OF IT.
NO DA.

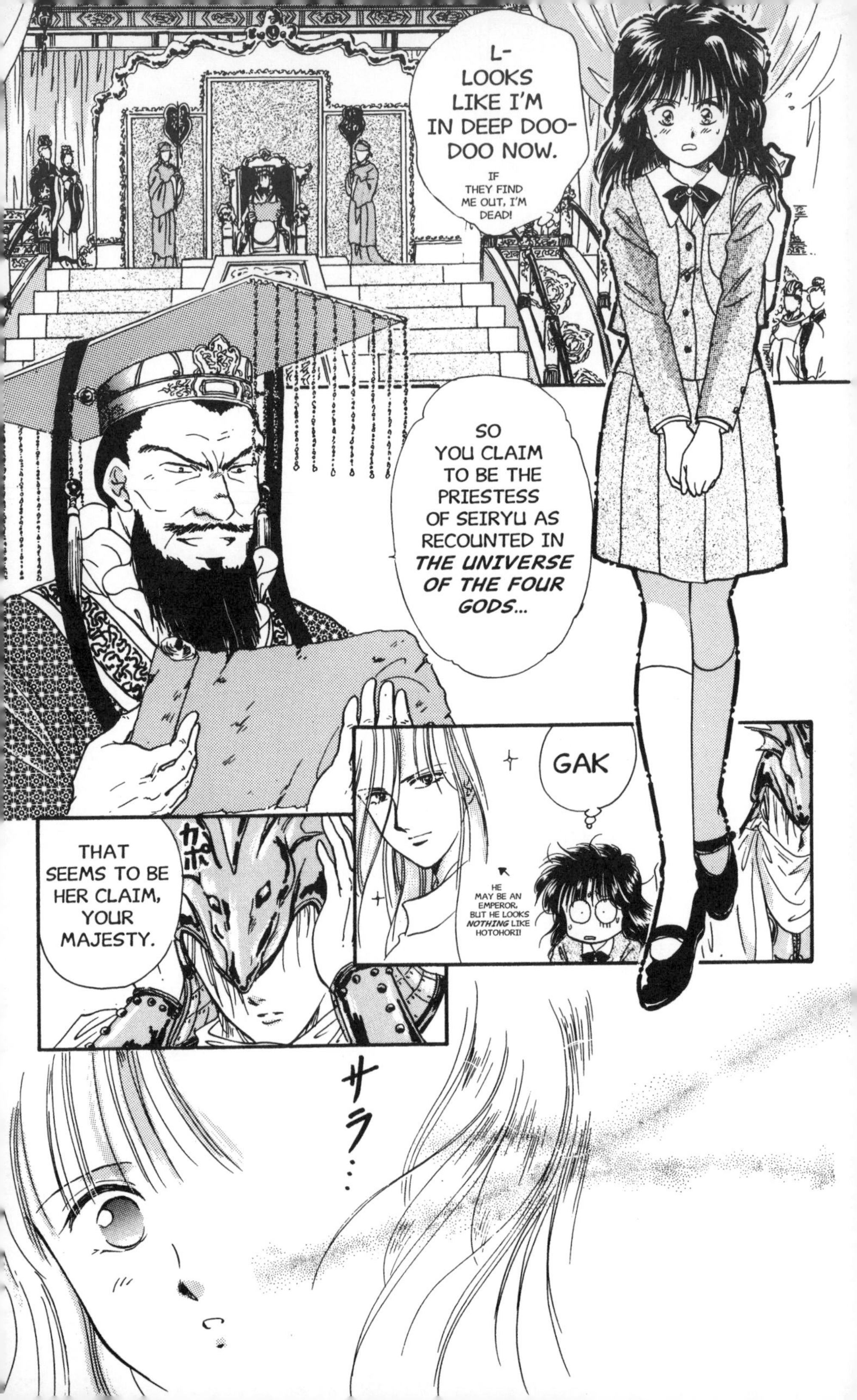

L-LOOKS LIKE I'M IN DEEP DOO-DOO NOW.
IF THEY FIND ME OUT, I'M DEAD!
SO YOU CLAIM TO BE THE PRIESTESS OF SEIRYU AS RECOUNTED IN *THE UNIVERSE OF THE FOUR GODS*...
GAK
HE MAY BE AN EMPEROR, BUT HE LOOKS *NOTHING* LIKE HOTOHORI!
THAT SEEMS TO BE HER CLAIM, YOUR MAJESTY.
カポ
サラ…

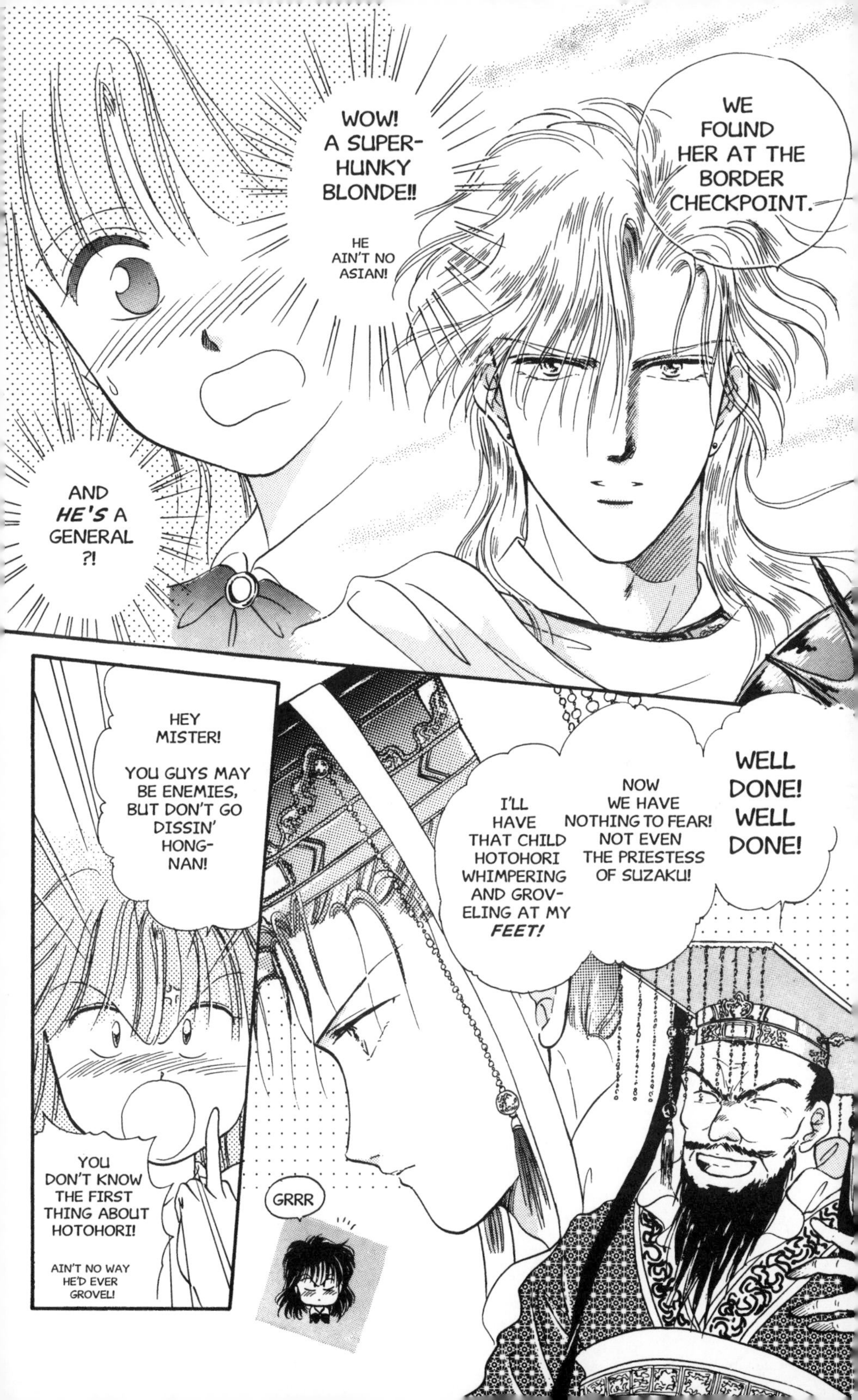
WE FOUND HER AT THE BORDER CHECKPOINT.
WOW! A SUPER-HUNKY BLONDE!!
HE AIN'T NO ASIAN!
AND *HE'S* A GENERAL?!
WELL DONE! WELL DONE!
NOW WE HAVE NOTHING TO FEAR! NOT EVEN THE PRIESTESS OF SUZAKU!
I'LL HAVE THAT CHILD HOTOHORI WHIMPERING AND GROVELING AT MY *FEET!*
GRRR
HEY MISTER!
YOU GUYS MAY BE ENEMIES, BUT DON'T GO DISSIN' HONG-NAN!
YOU DON'T KNOW THE FIRST THING ABOUT HOTOHORI!
AIN'T NO WAY HE'D EVER GROVEL!

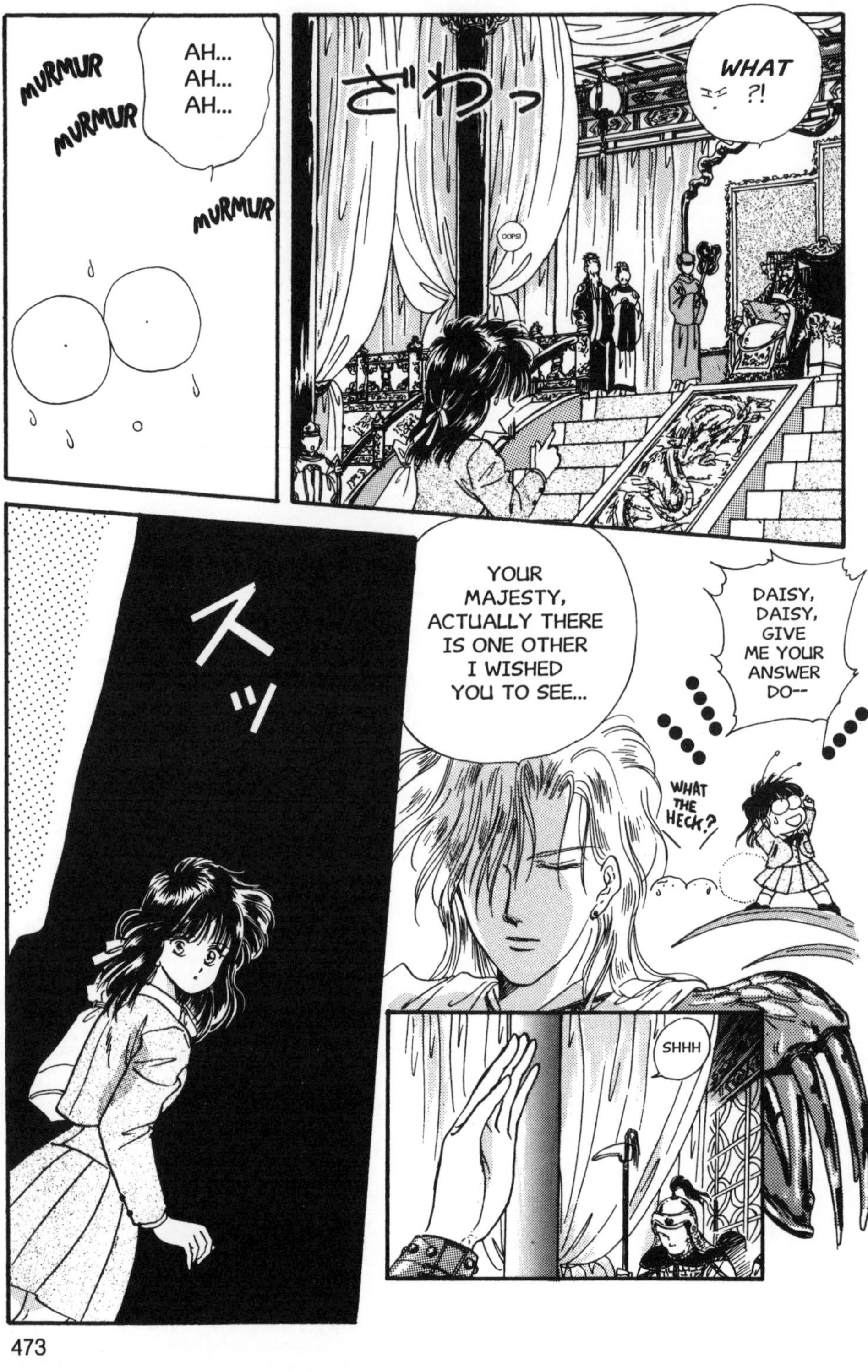
WHAT ?!
ざわっ
OOPS!
MURMUR
MURMUR
AH... AH... AH...
MURMUR
YOUR MAJESTY, ACTUALLY THERE IS ONE OTHER I WISHED YOU TO SEE...
DAISY, DAISY, GIVE ME YOUR ANSWER DO--
WHAT THE HECK?
SHHH
スッ

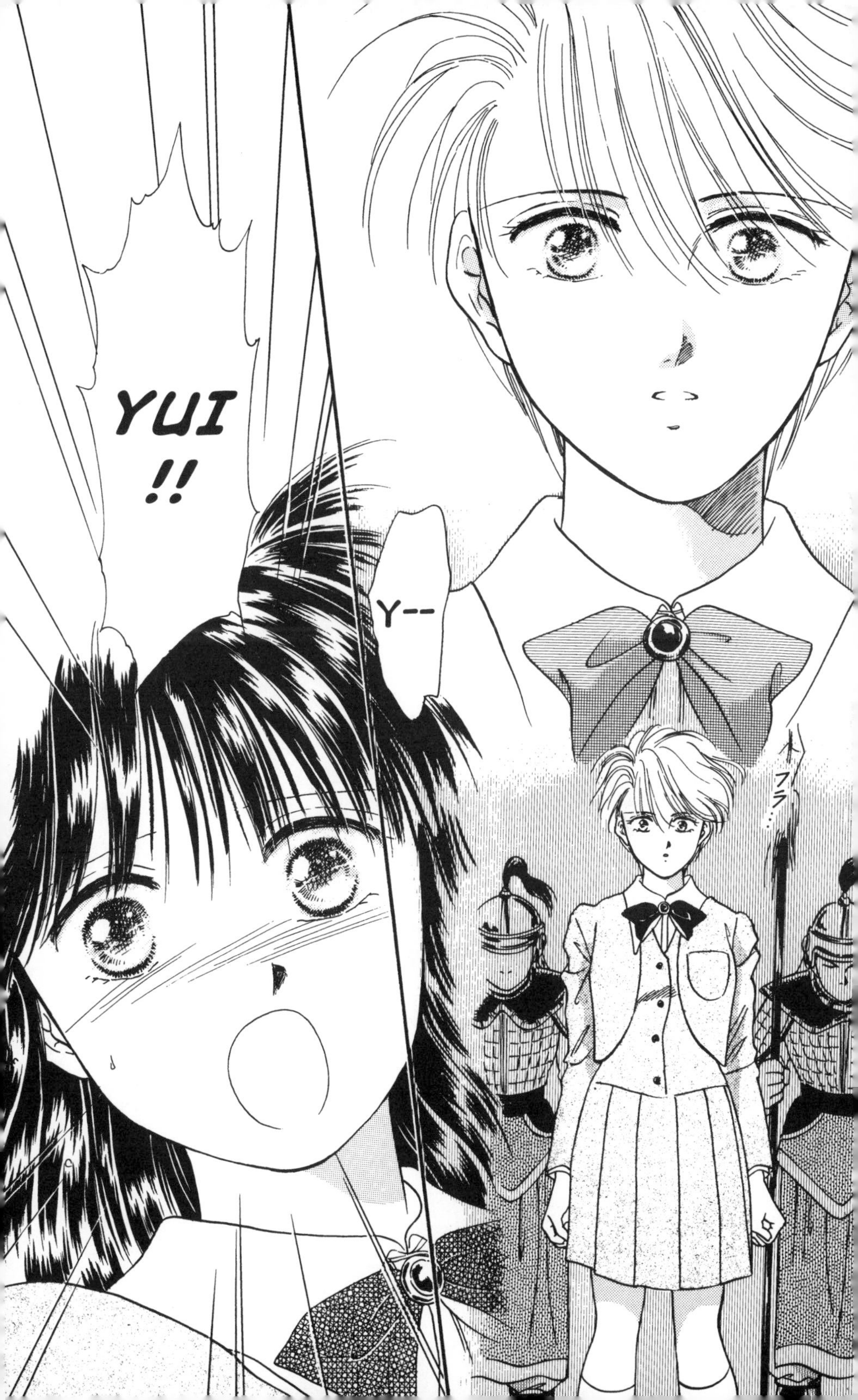
Y--
YUI !!
フラ…

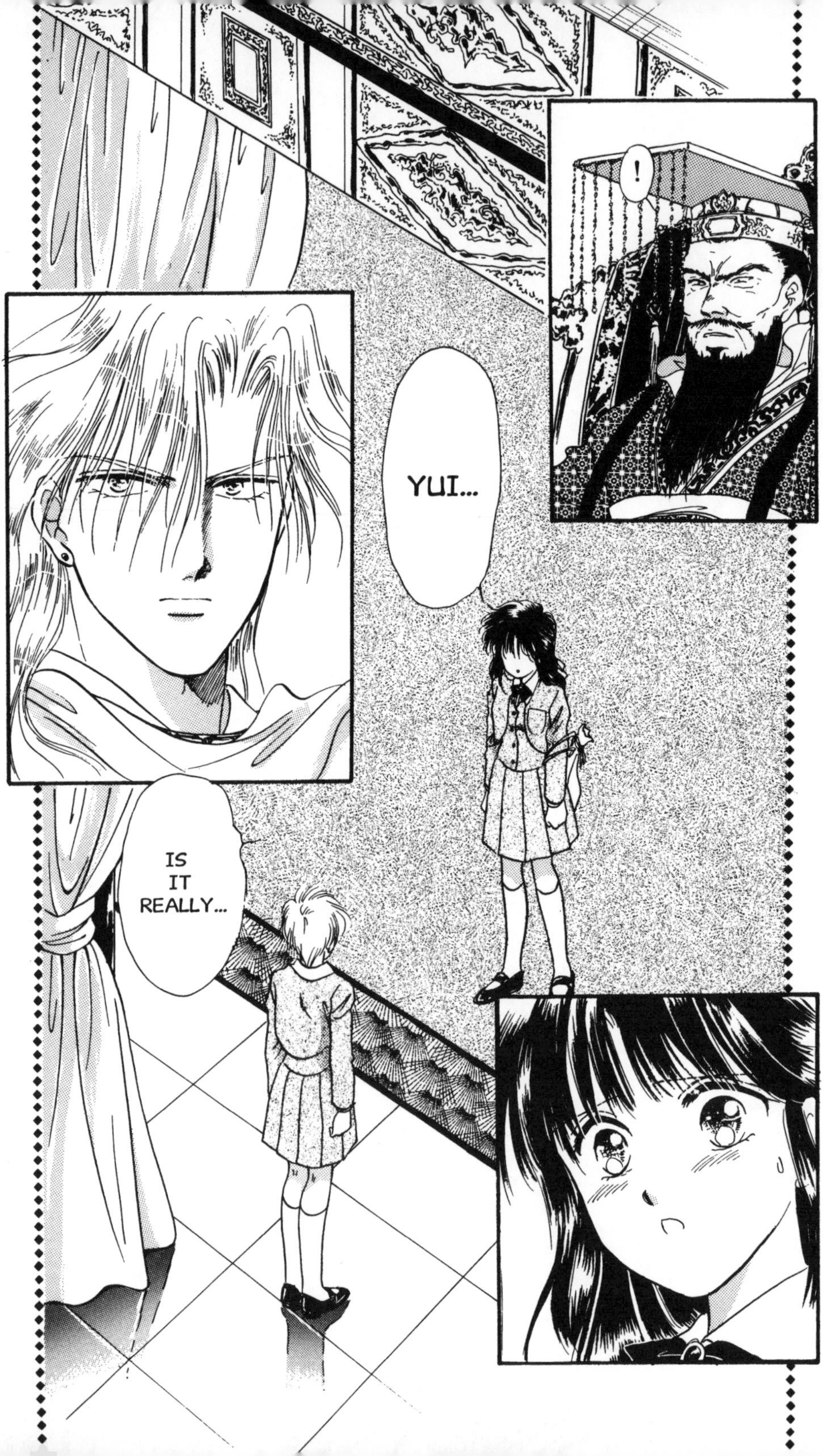
!
YUI...
IS IT REALLY...

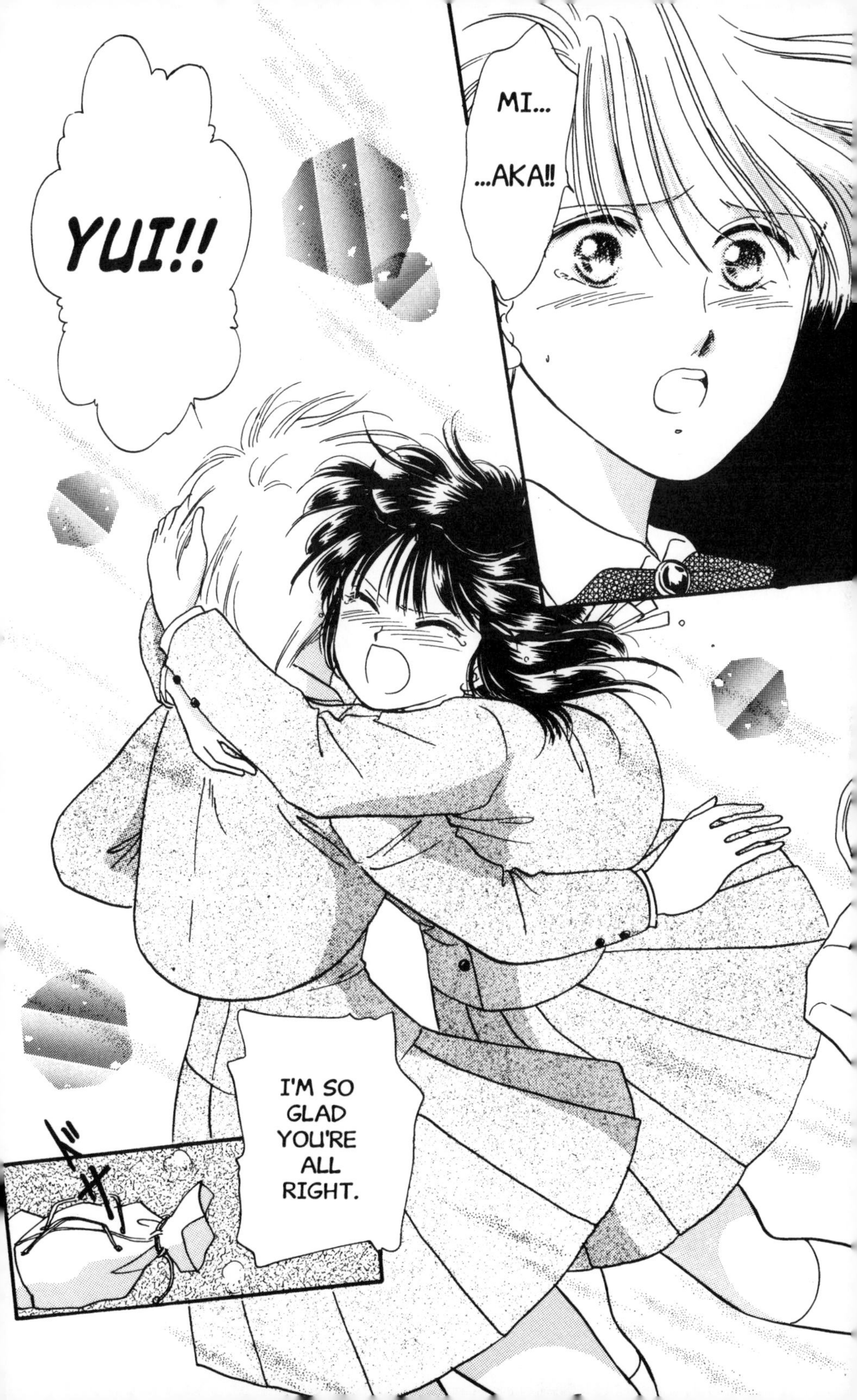
MI...
...AKA!!
YUI!!
I'M SO GLAD YOU'RE ALL RIGHT.
ダッ

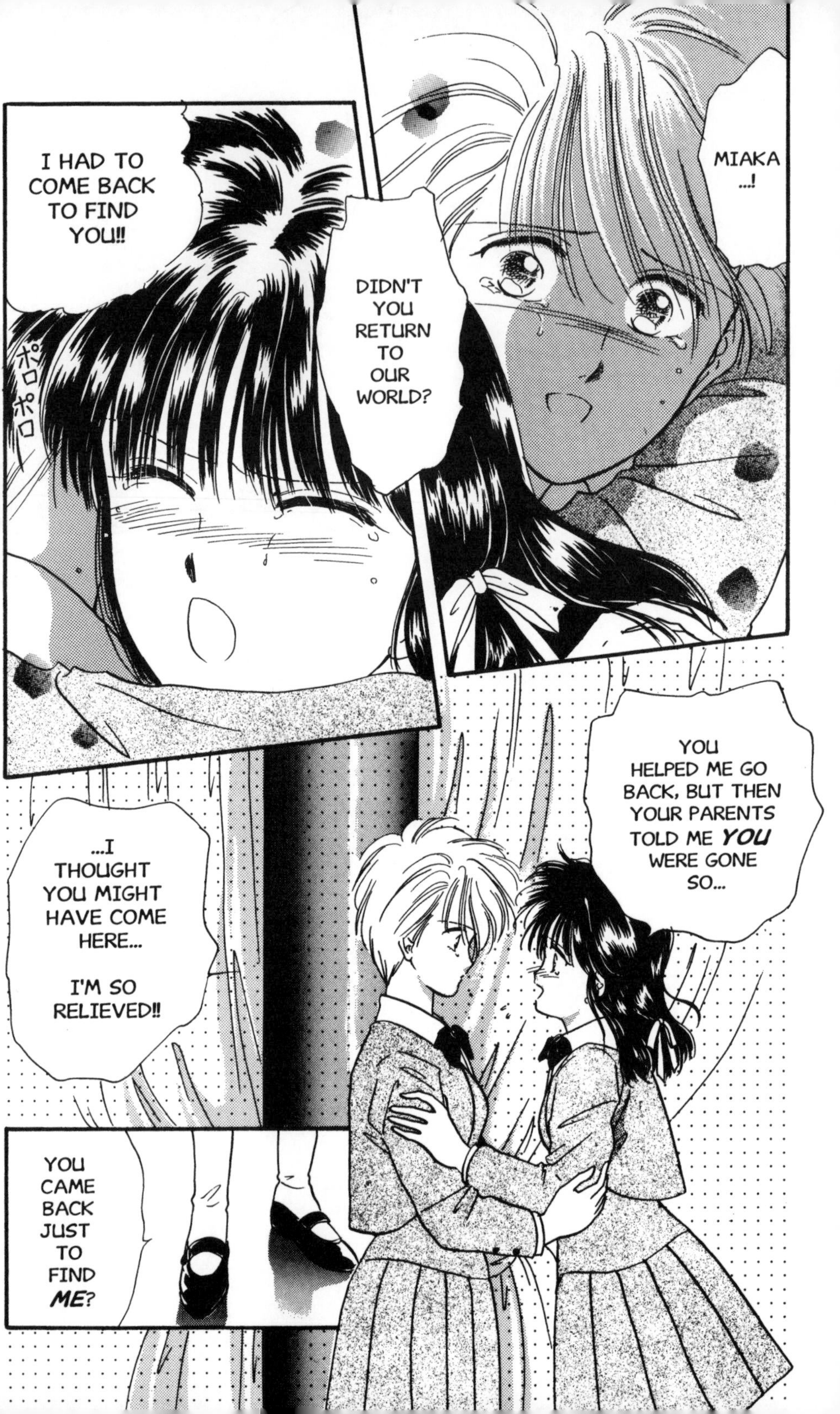
MIAKA ...!
DIDN'T YOU RETURN TO OUR WORLD?
I HAD TO COME BACK TO FIND YOU!!
ポロポロ
YOU HELPED ME GO BACK, BUT THEN YOUR PARENTS TOLD ME *YOU* WERE GONE SO...
...I THOUGHT YOU MIGHT HAVE COME HERE... I'M SO RELIEVED!!
YOU CAME BACK JUST TO FIND *ME*?

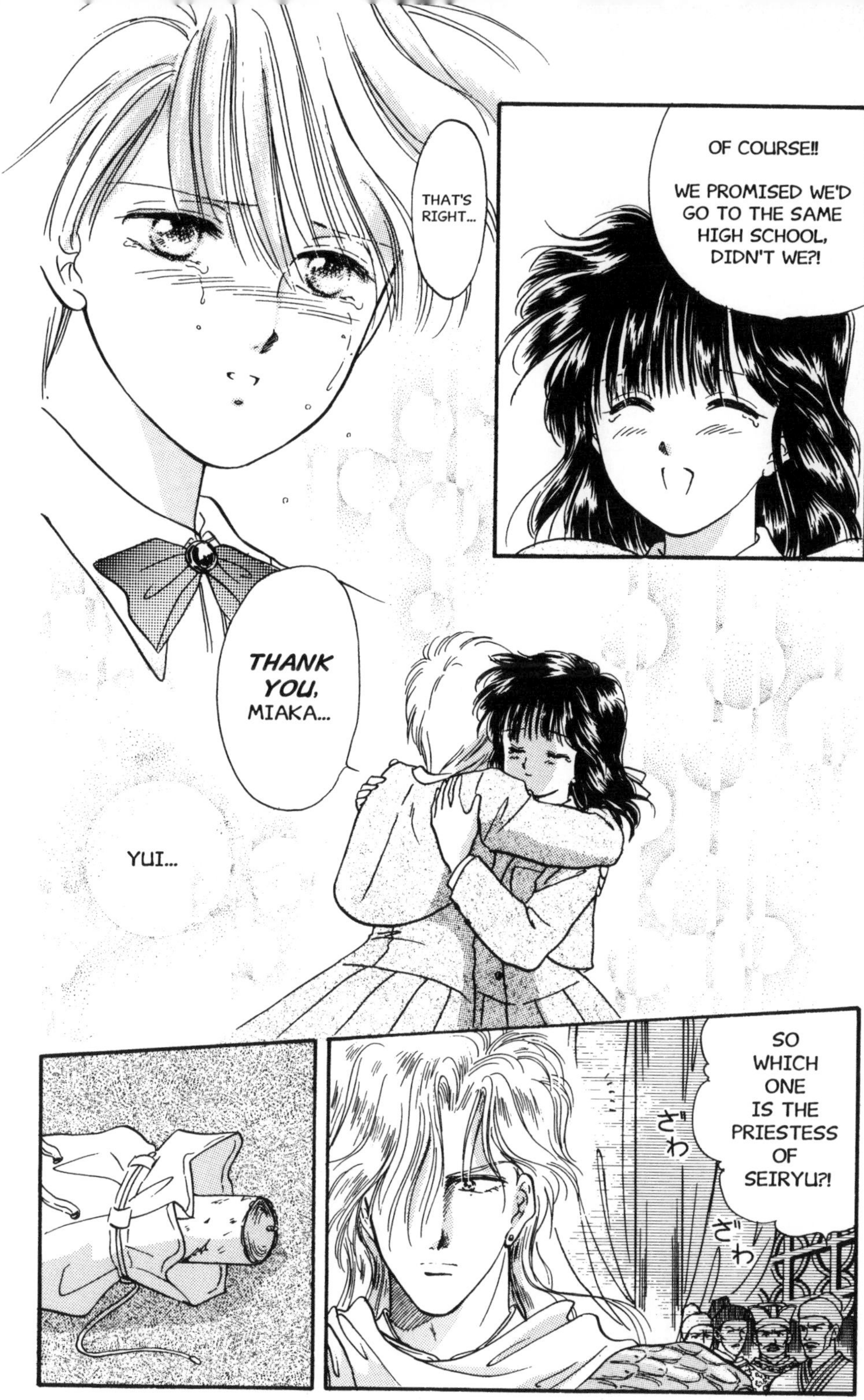
OF COURSE!!
WE PROMISED WE'D GO TO THE SAME HIGH SCHOOL, DIDN'T WE?!
THAT'S RIGHT...
THANK YOU, MIAKA...
YUI...
SO WHICH ONE IS THE PRIESTESS OF SEIRYU?!
ざわ
ざわ

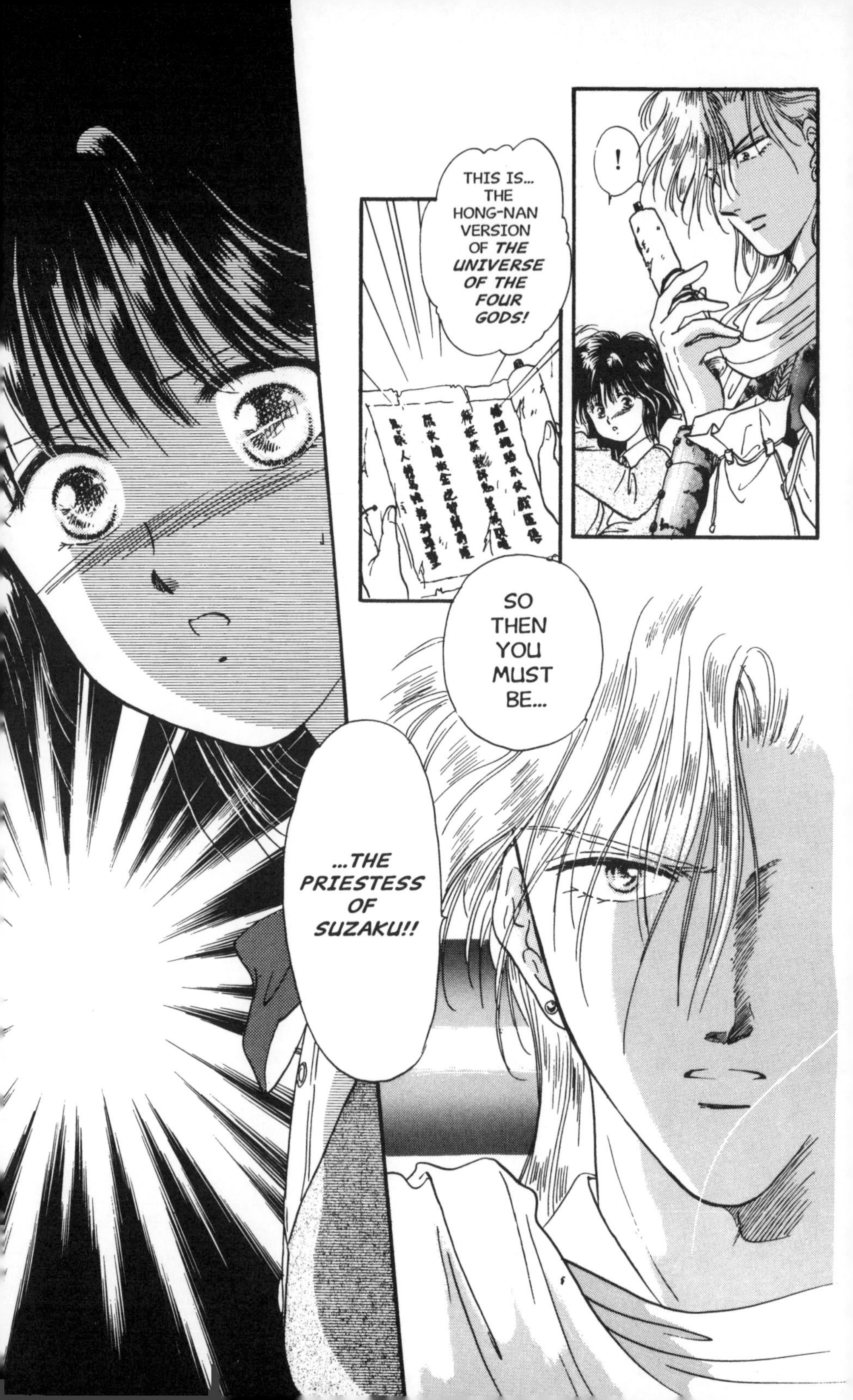
!
THIS IS... THE HONG-NAN VERSION OF *THE UNIVERSE OF THE FOUR GODS!*
SO THEN YOU MUST BE...
...THE PRIESTESS OF SUZAKU!!

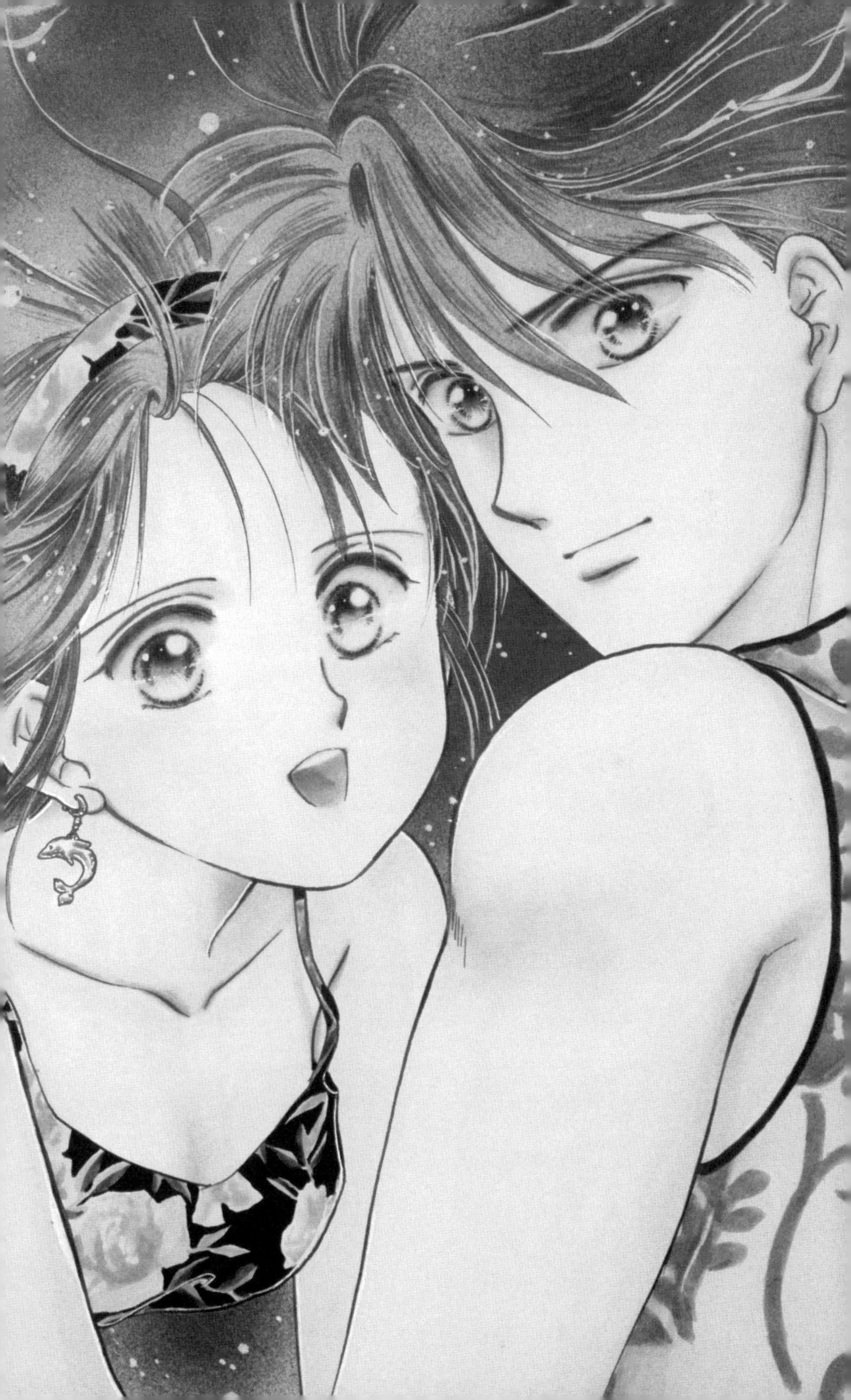

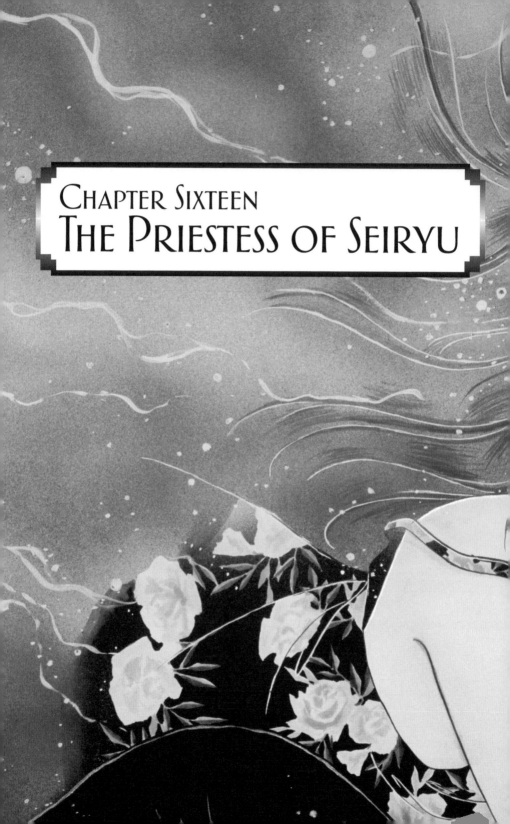

Chapter Sixteen
The Priestess of Seiryu

NICE

YUI WITH LONG HAIR.

SHE HAD IT LONG UNTIL THE 8TH GRADE. SHE CUT IT SHORT TO AVOID ALL THE ATTENTION SHE WAS GETTING FROM THE BOYS.

I'M SO PROUD SHE'S MY FRIEND!

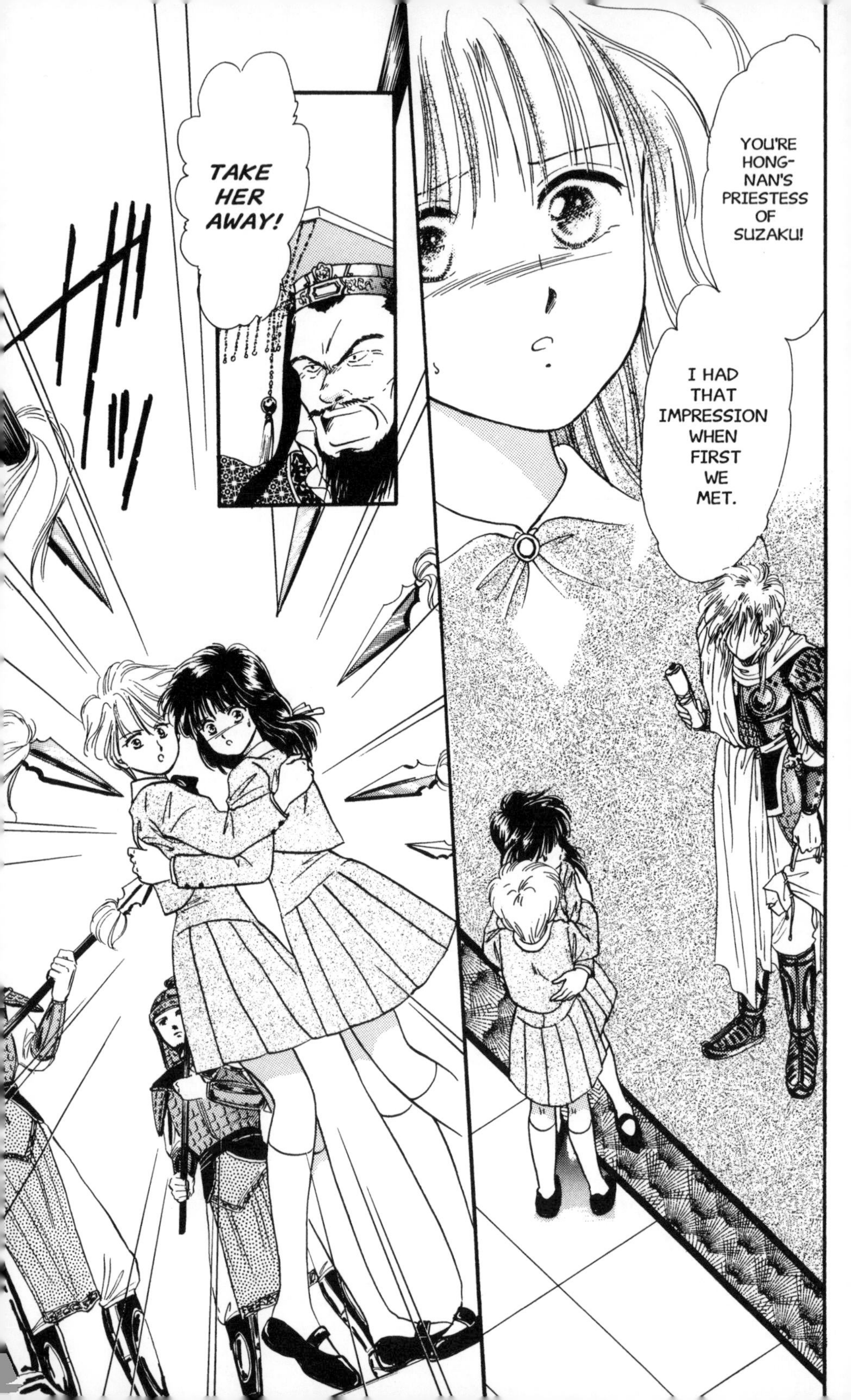
YOU'RE HONG-NAN'S PRIESTESS OF SUZAKU!
I HAD THAT IMPRESSION WHEN FIRST WE MET.
TAKE HER AWAY!

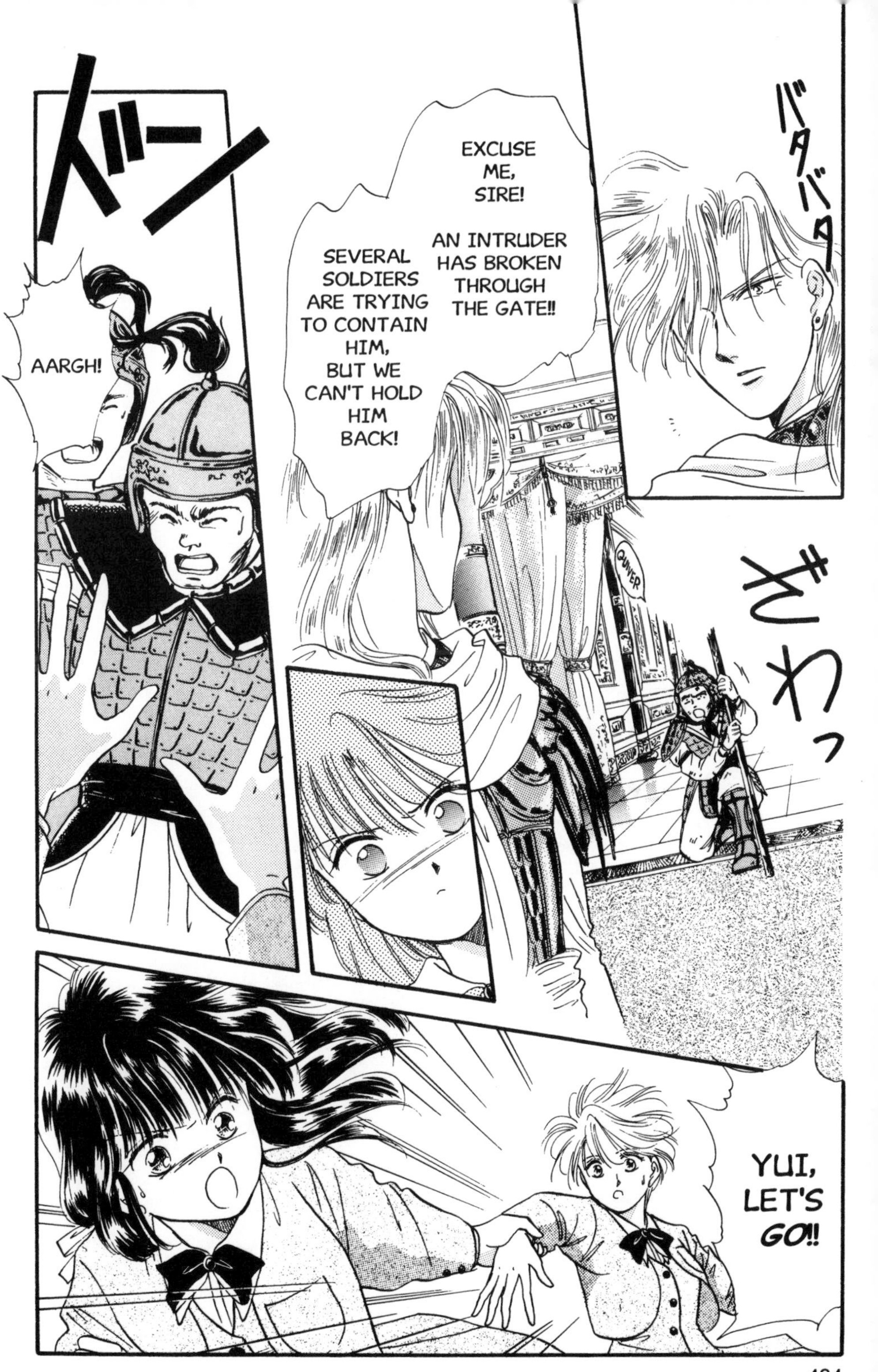
バタバタ
EXCUSE ME, SIRE!
AN INTRUDER HAS BROKEN THROUGH THE GATE!!
SEVERAL SOLDIERS ARE TRYING TO CONTAIN HIM, BUT WE CAN'T HOLD HIM BACK!
QUIVER
ざわっ
AARGH!
YUI, LET'S GO!!

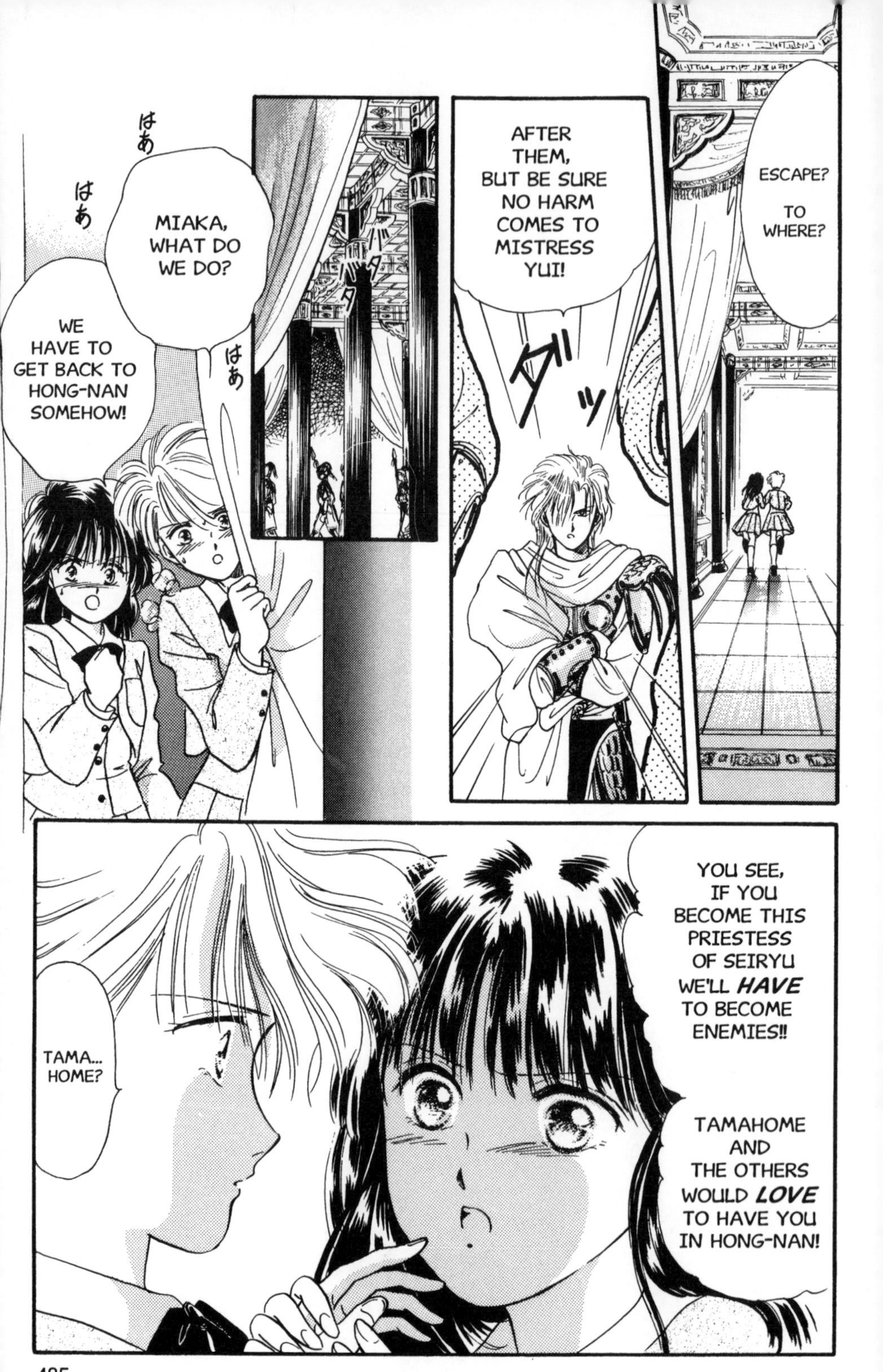
ESCAPE?
TO WHERE?
AFTER THEM, BUT BE SURE NO HARM COMES TO MISTRESS YUI!
ダッ
バタバタ
はあ
はあ
MIAKA, WHAT DO WE DO?
はあ
WE HAVE TO GET BACK TO HONG-NAN SOMEHOW!
YOU SEE, IF YOU BECOME THIS PRIESTESS OF SEIRYU WE'LL ***HAVE*** TO BECOME ENEMIES!!
TAMAHOME AND THE OTHERS WOULD ***LOVE*** TO HAVE YOU IN HONG-NAN!
TAMA... HOME?

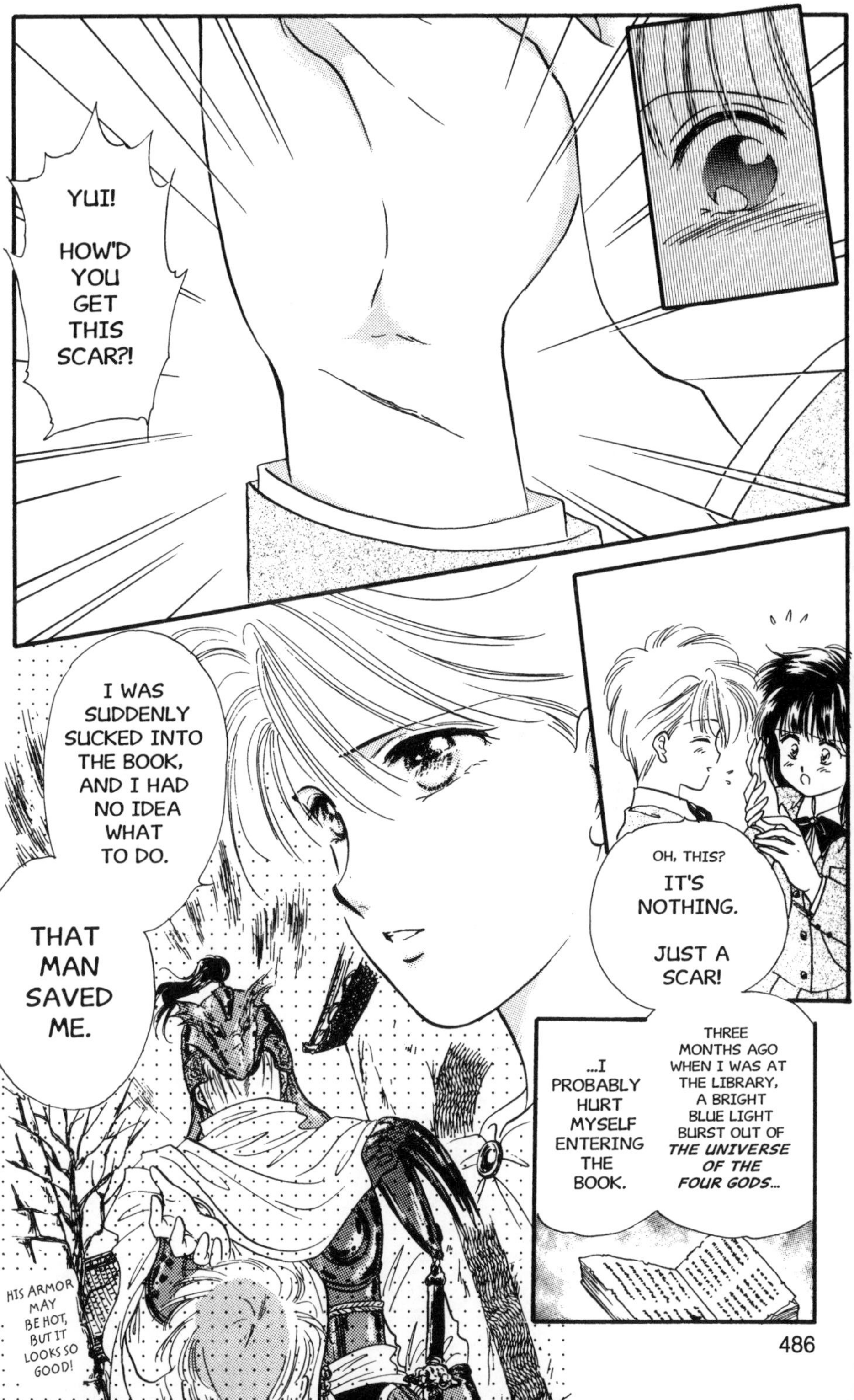

YUI!
HOW'D YOU GET THIS SCAR?!
OH, THIS? IT'S NOTHING. JUST A SCAR!
THREE MONTHS AGO WHEN I WAS AT THE LIBRARY, A BRIGHT BLUE LIGHT BURST OUT OF *THE UNIVERSE OF THE FOUR GODS*...
...I PROBABLY HURT MYSELF ENTERING THE BOOK.
I WAS SUDDENLY SUCKED INTO THE BOOK, AND I HAD NO IDEA WHAT TO DO.
THAT MAN SAVED ME.
HIS ARMOR MAY BE HOT, BUT IT LOOKS SO GOOD!

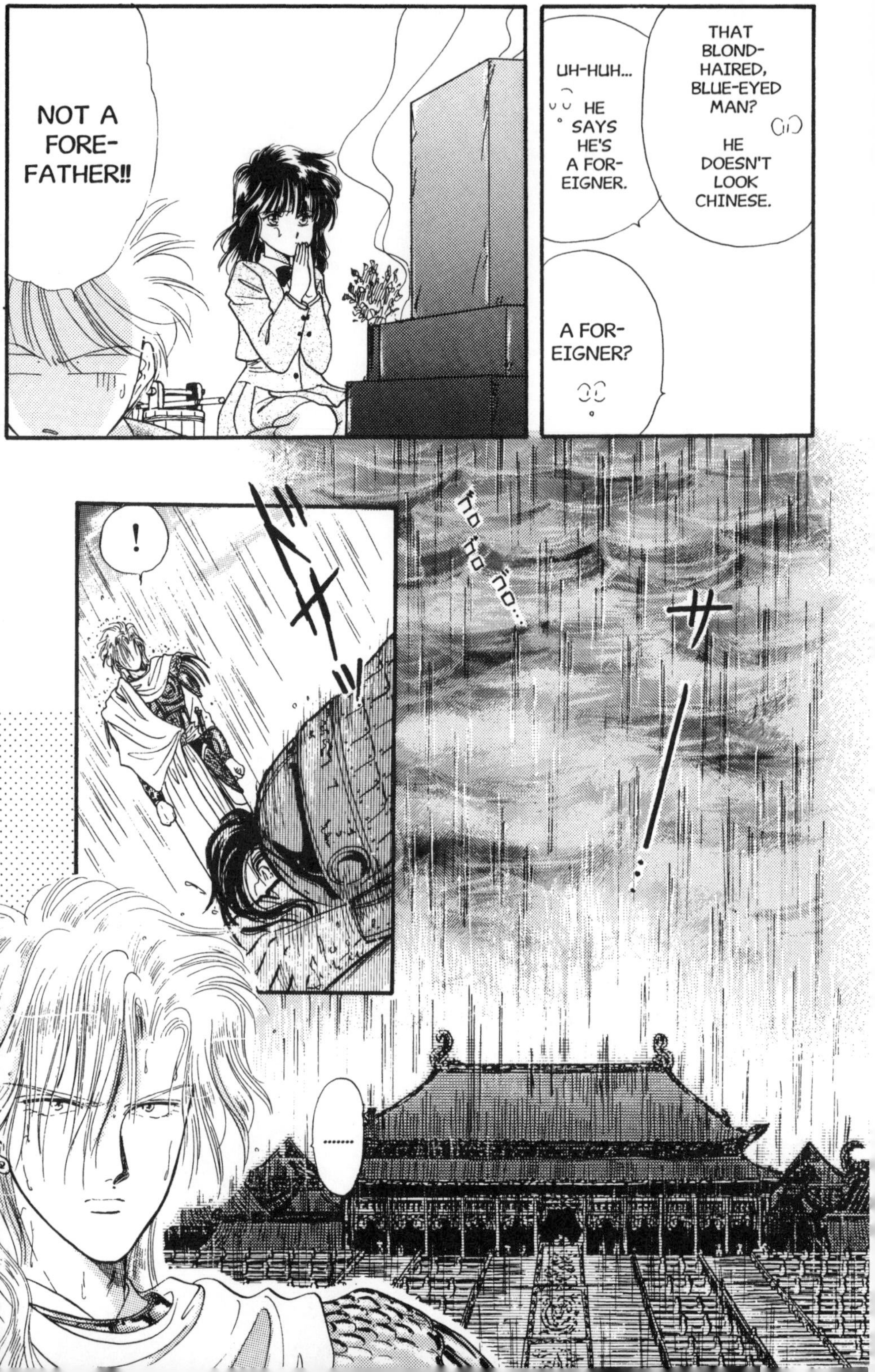
THAT BLOND-HAIRED, BLUE-EYED MAN?
HE DOESN'T LOOK CHINESE.
UH-HUH... HE SAYS HE'S A FOREIGNER.
A FOREIGNER?
NOT A FOREFATHER!!
ゴロゴロゴロ…
サー…
!
......

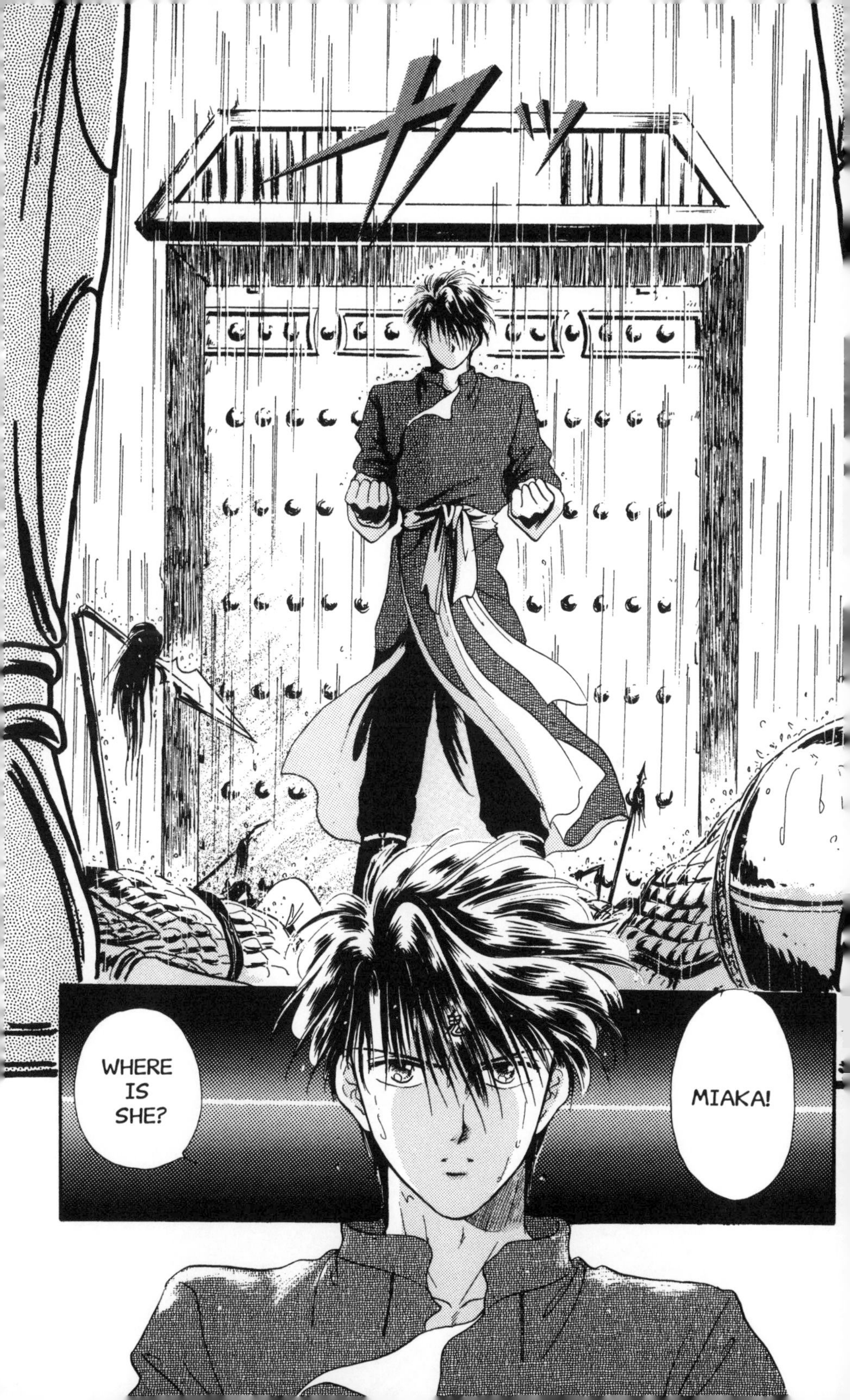
ダッ
MIAKA!
WHERE IS SHE?

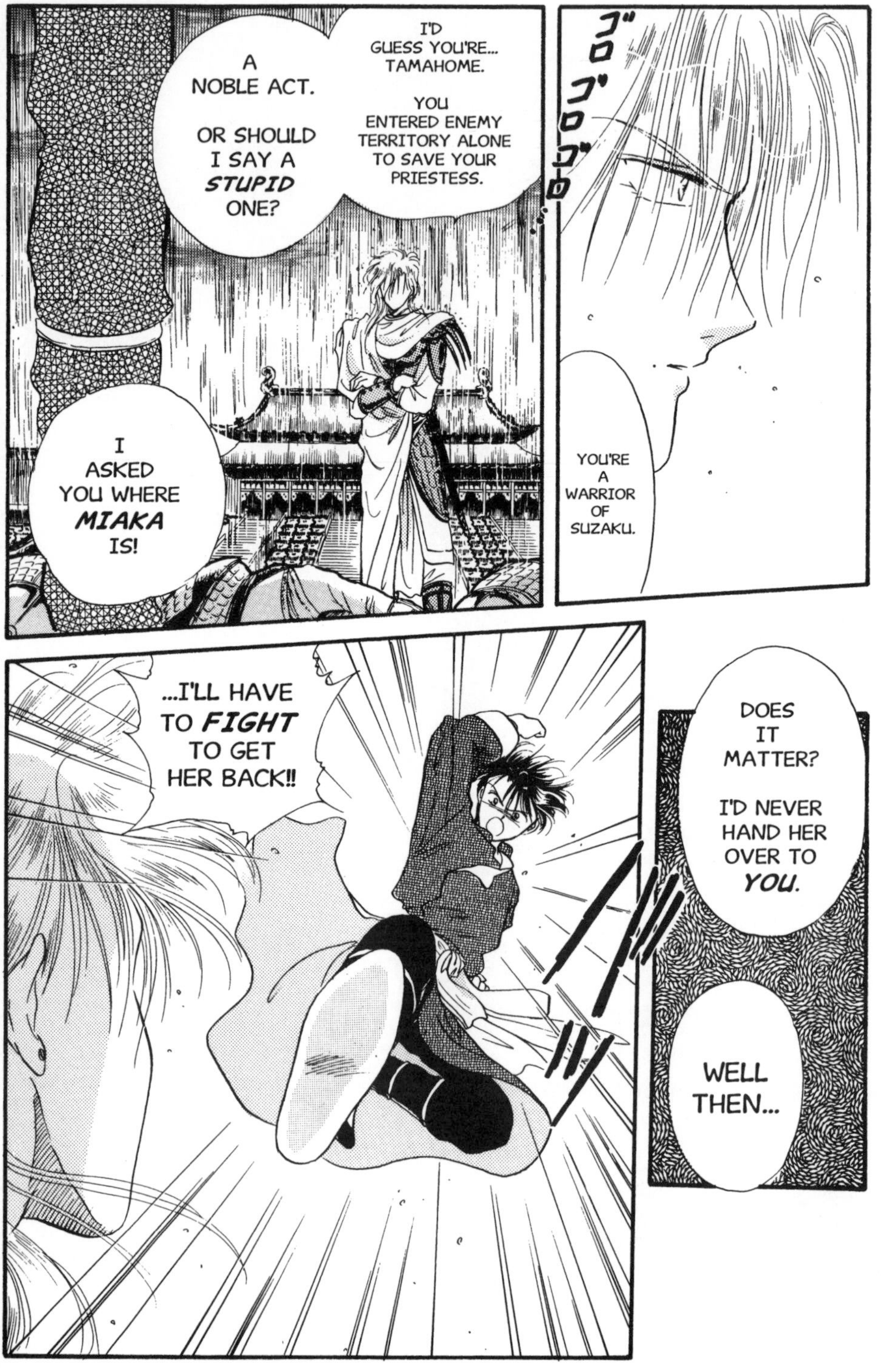
ゴロゴロゴロ
YOU'RE A WARRIOR OF SUZAKU.
I'D GUESS YOU'RE... TAMAHOME.
YOU ENTERED ENEMY TERRITORY ALONE TO SAVE YOUR PRIESTESS.
A NOBLE ACT.
OR SHOULD I SAY A *STUPID* ONE?
I ASKED YOU WHERE *MIAKA* IS!
DOES IT MATTER?
I'D NEVER HAND HER OVER TO *YOU*.
WELL THEN...
...I'LL HAVE TO *FIGHT* TO GET HER BACK!!

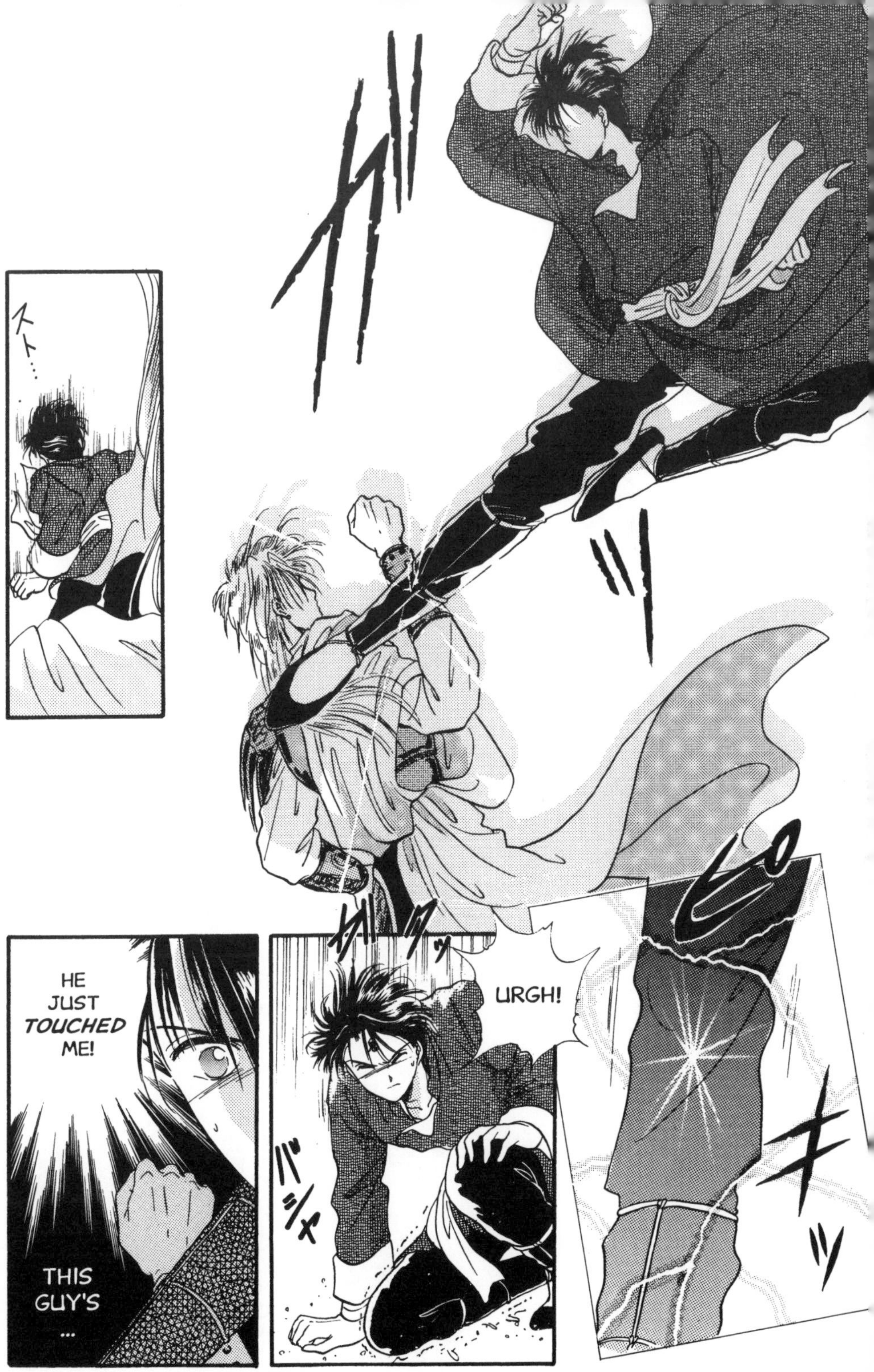
ストト…
URGH!
バシャ
HE JUST *TOUCHED* ME!
THIS GUY'S ...

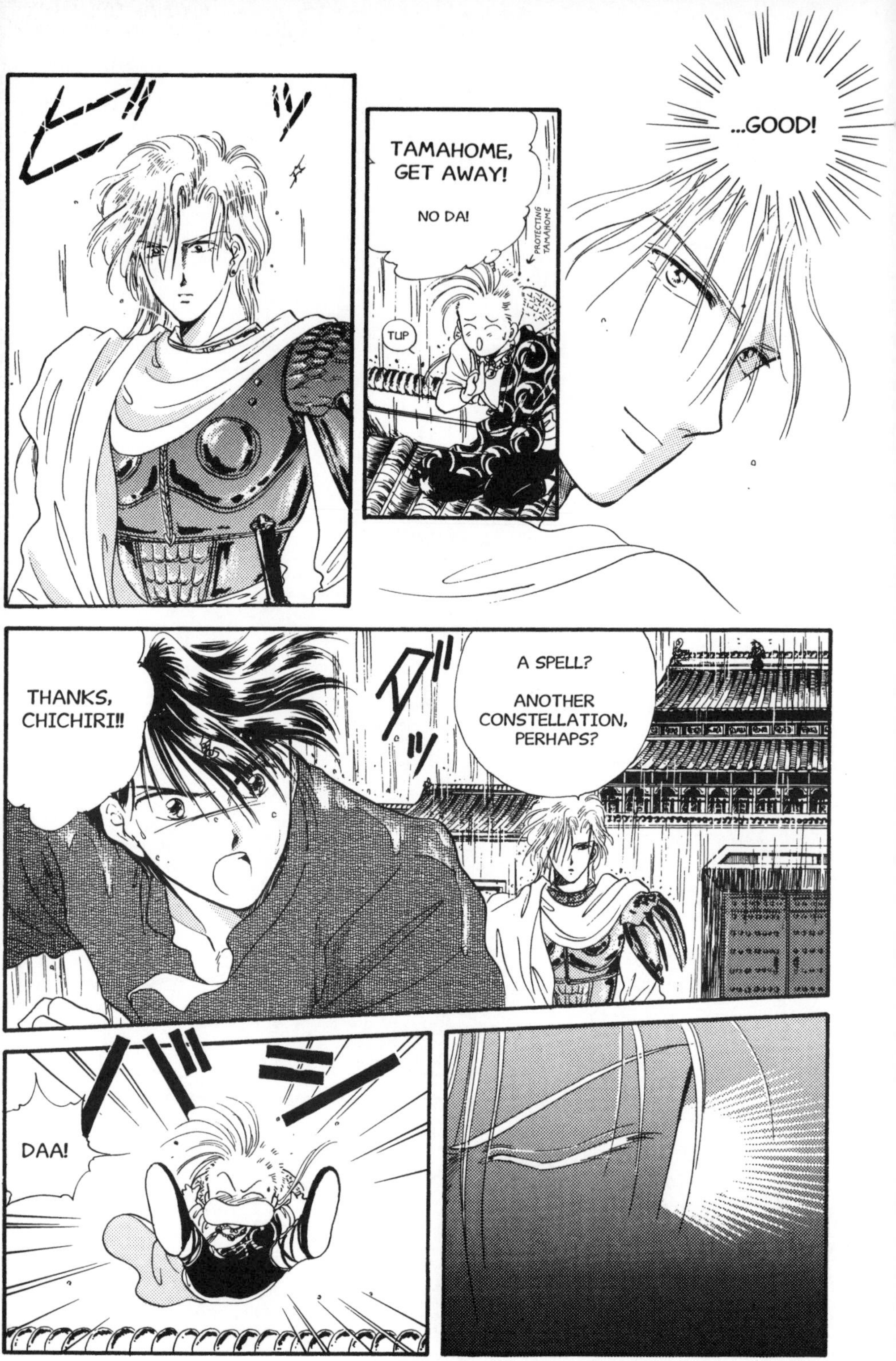
...GOOD!
TAMAHOME, GET AWAY!
NO DA!
PROTECTING TAMAHOME
TUP
A SPELL?
ANOTHER CONSTELLATION, PERHAPS?
THANKS, CHICHIRI!!
DAA!

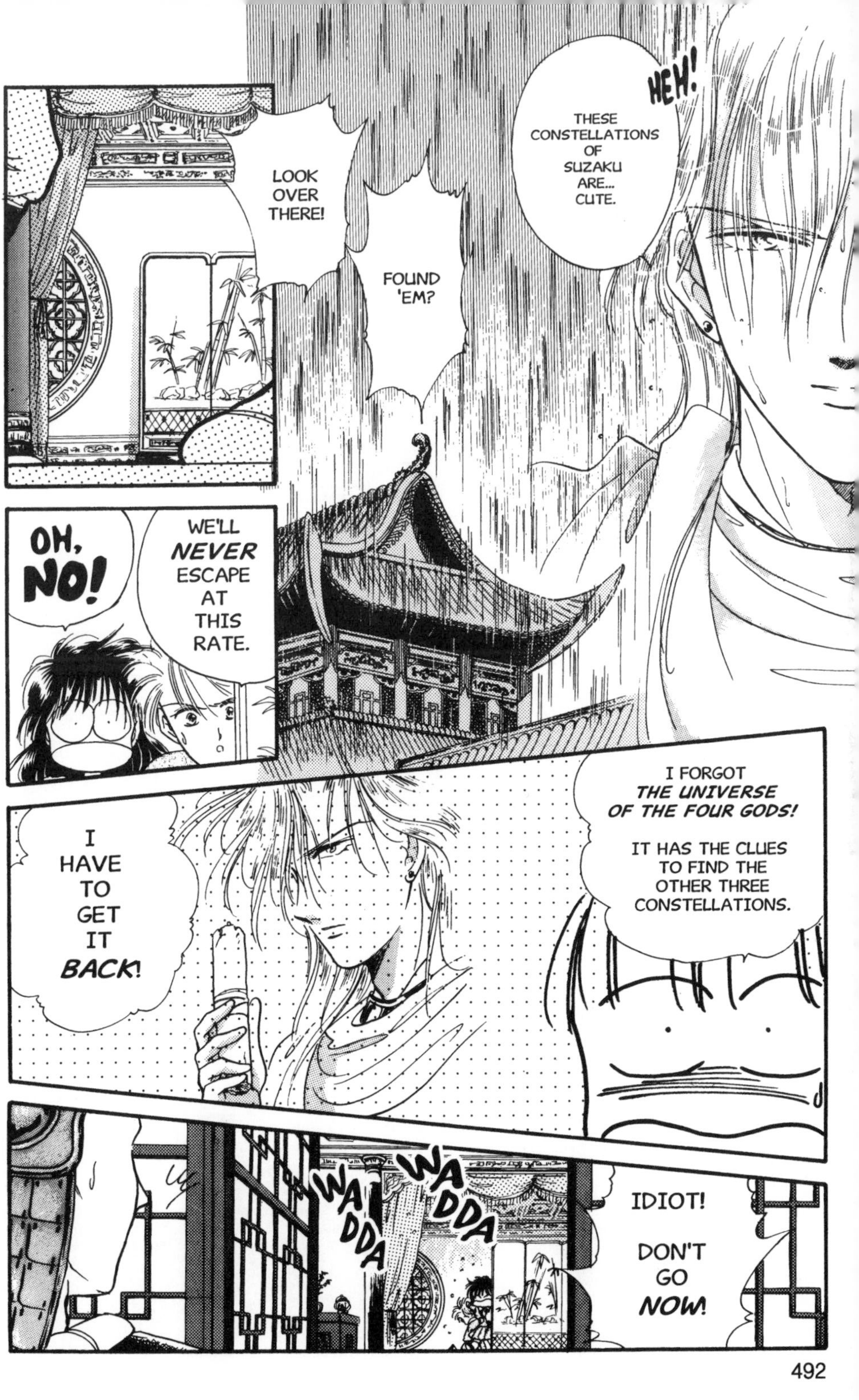
HEH!
THESE CONSTELLATIONS OF SUZAKU ARE... CUTE.
FOUND 'EM?
LOOK OVER THERE!
WE'LL *NEVER* ESCAPE AT THIS RATE.
OH, NO!
I FORGOT *THE UNIVERSE OF THE FOUR GODS!* IT HAS THE CLUES TO FIND THE OTHER THREE CONSTELLATIONS.
I HAVE TO GET IT *BACK*!
IDIOT! DON'T GO *NOW*!
WADDA
WADDA
DDA

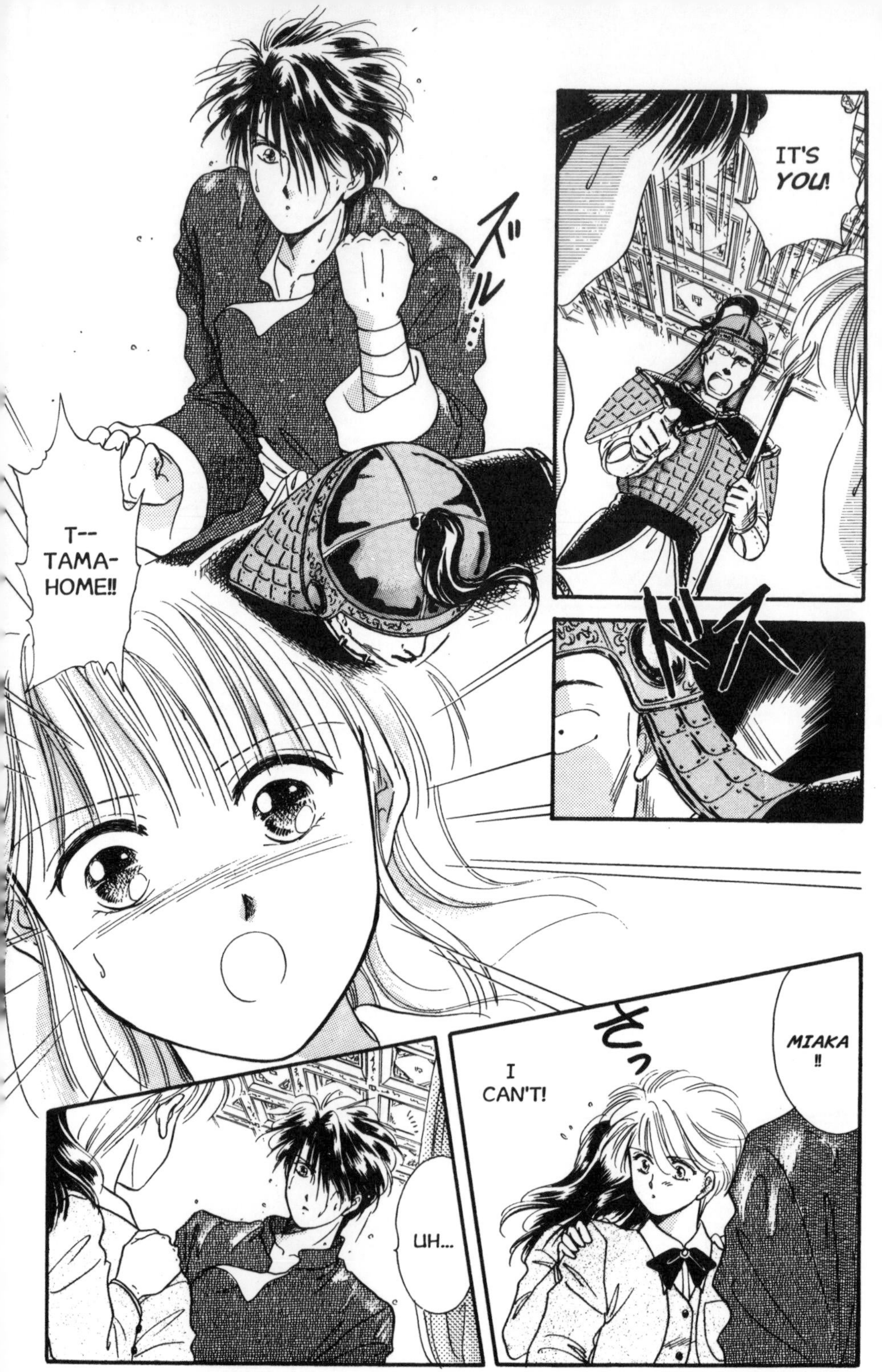
IT'S YOU!
ドス
ズル…
T-- TAMA-HOME!!
MIAKA !!
さっ
I CAN'T!
UH...

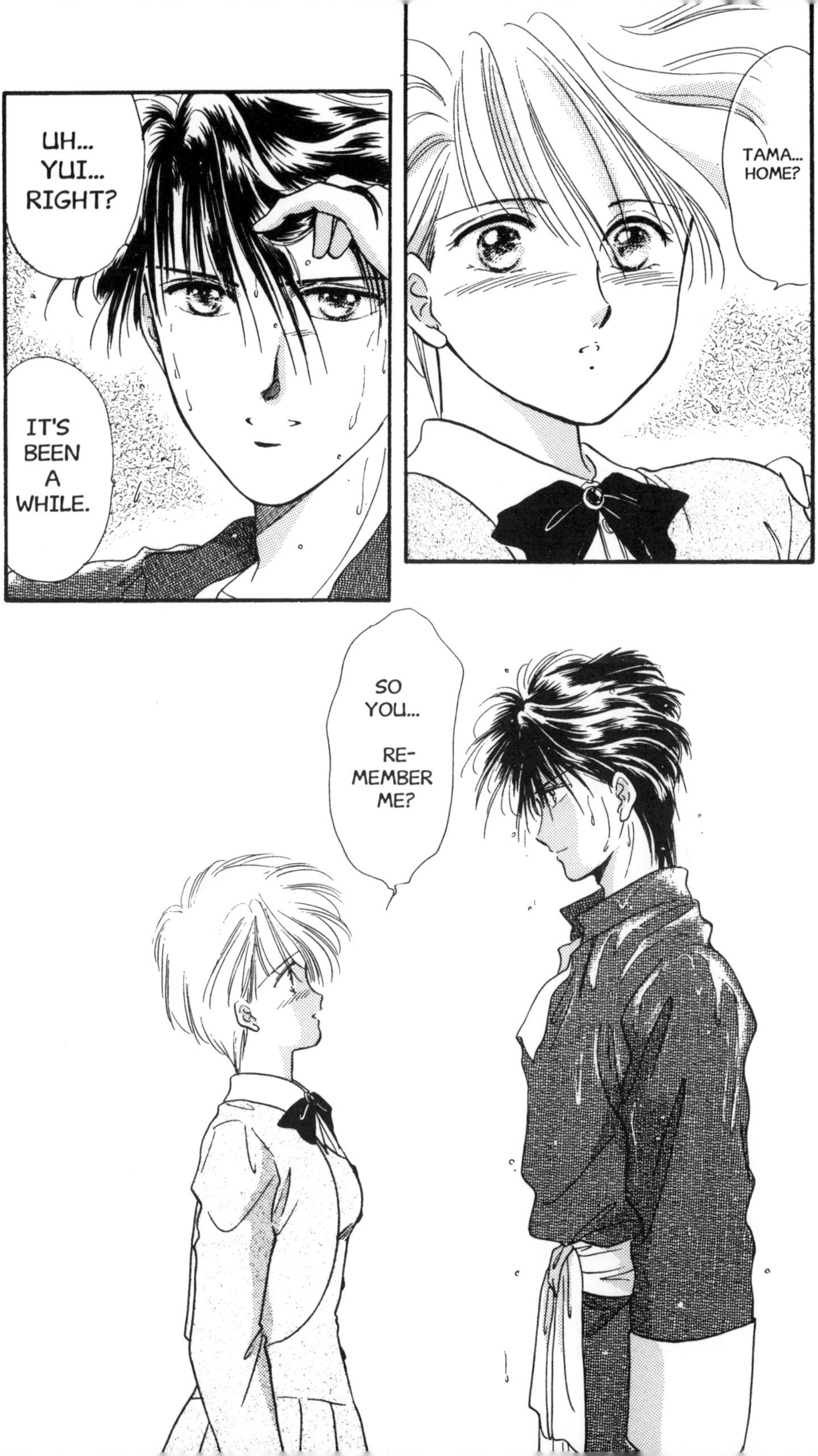
TAMA... HOME?
UH... YUI... RIGHT?
IT'S BEEN A WHILE.
SO YOU... RE-MEMBER ME?

"Where did the title 'Fushigi Yūgi' come from?" I usually don't have trouble coming up with titles, but this one gave me a hard time. I've been planning this story since I was eighteen, but its tentative title, "Suzaku," just didn't seem right, so I had to work really hard for a title that would fit the right image. I looked through a whole bunch of magazines to come up with a good rhyming title, and that's how I came up with "Fushigi Yūgi." I actually think it's a pretty nice title. The kanji for "Yūgi" show up a lot in Hong King films. There's Bruce Lee's "Shibō Yūgi" (The Game of Death), for example. I didn't intend it to mean "frolic," but a nuance more like "game." I guess it would mean "Mysterious Game."*

I was talking about computer games with my assistant M., who insisted that "Fushigi Yūgi" would be a great computer game. We talked about this endlessly. It's not just because we were talking about my story, but because it seemed really fun. Computer games usually begin by introducing the story with drawings, but this one would start with opening the book *The Universe of the Four Gods*. Then a map would come up and you'd see Qu-Dong, Hotohori's palace, Daichi-san, and Tamahome's village. You could follow the plot the same way as the manga, or you could start from any random location and try to find all seven celestial warriors. It'd be an RPG game, so you'd have random enemies appearing, and everybody has different powers and abilities so the way to fight would always change. When you start losing, you could call on Chichiri, who'd suddenly appear and cast a spell. If Tamahome dies (for example), he might be revived at a certain location if he has enough money stored away. Other ideas: If you go to Qu-Dong immediately without gaining enough experience points, you'd get yourself killed. If Miaka's a player-character, you'd have to have a gauge, not just for power, but for love too. Of course, she'd have to lose a lot of love points when she's away from Tamahome. When she returns to reality, that's the end of the game. Miaka could get advice from her brother. The ideas go on and on.

*But something like "Miracle Game" just sounds so corny!

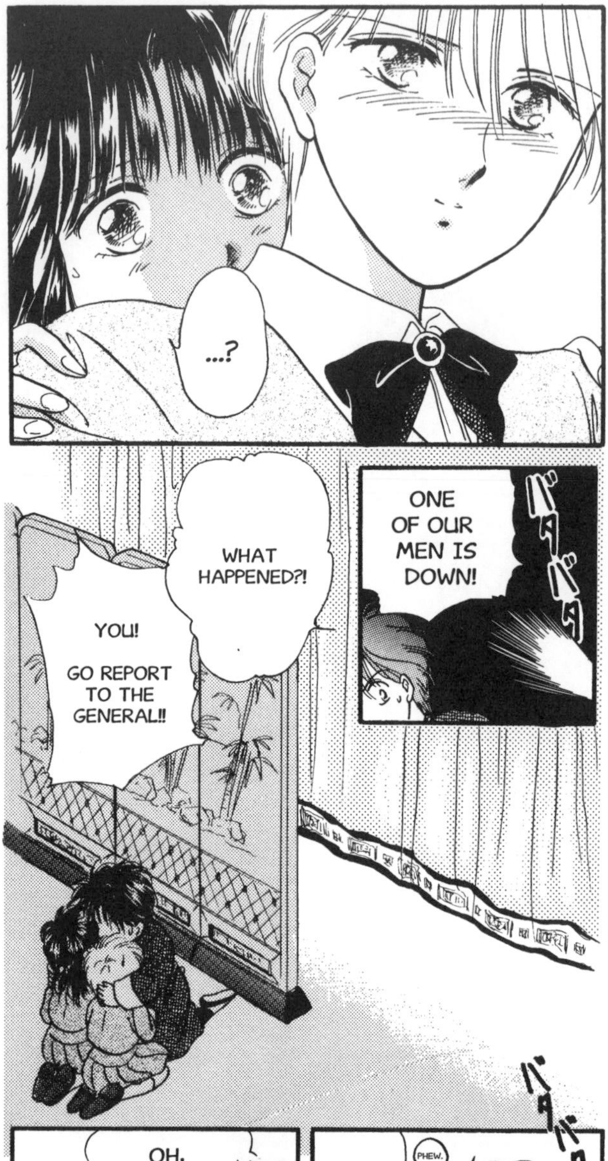

...?
ONE OF OUR MEN IS DOWN!
バタバタ
WHAT HAPPENED?!
YOU!
GO REPORT TO THE GENERAL!!
バタバタ...
PHEW.
U-UMM.
OH, SORRY ABOUT THAT!
WHOOPS
......

To be continued...!

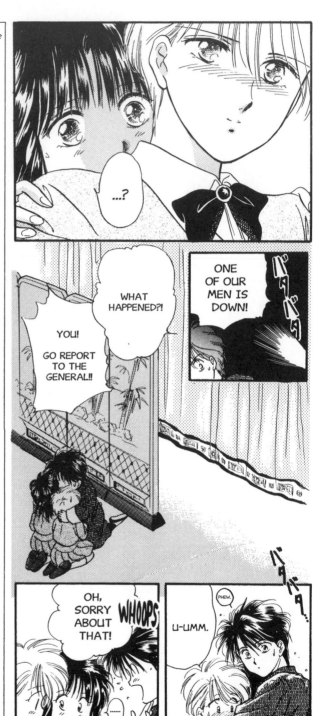

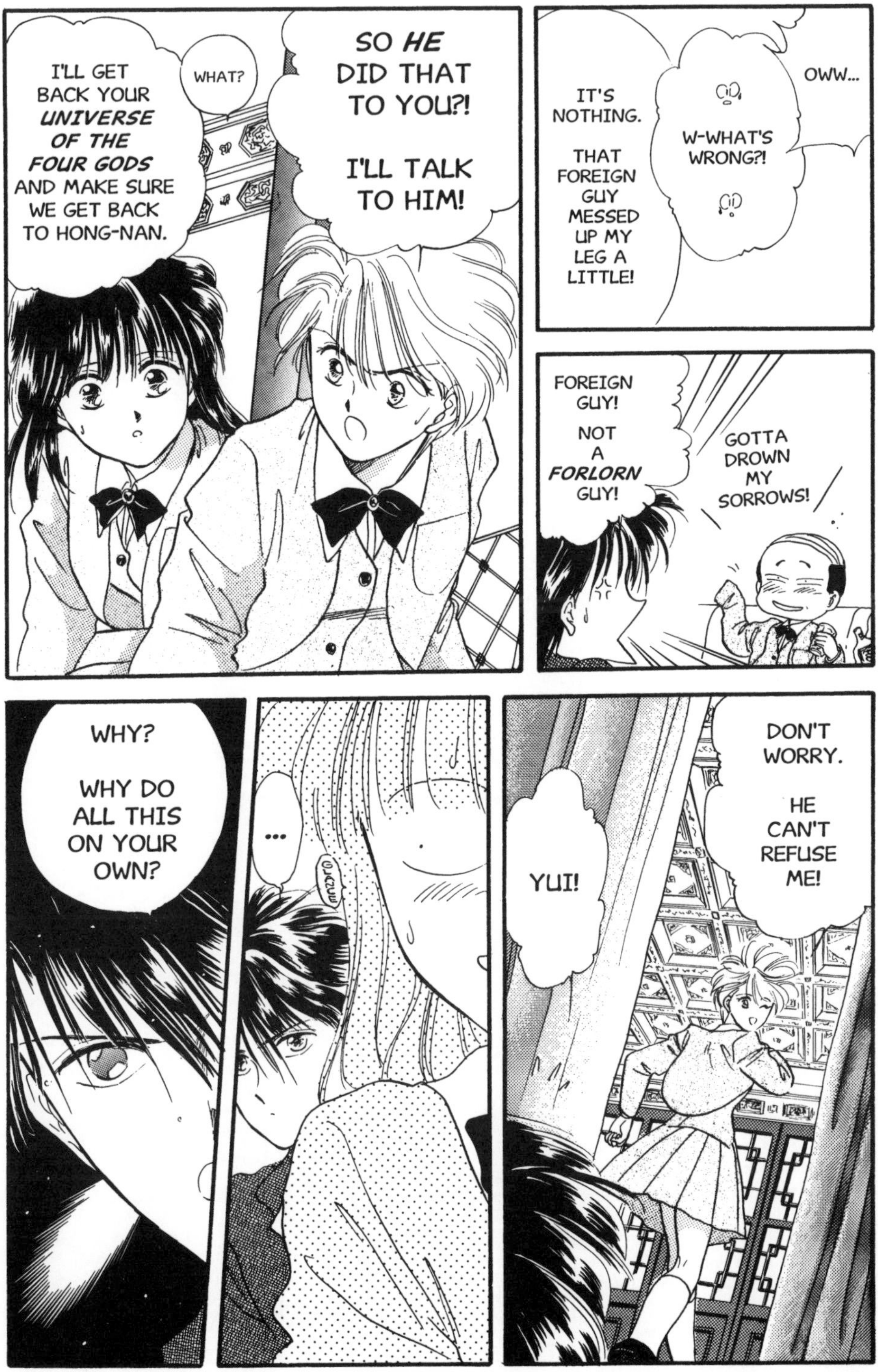
OWW...
W-WHAT'S WRONG?!
IT'S NOTHING. THAT FOREIGN GUY MESSED UP MY LEG A LITTLE!
GOTTA DROWN MY SORROWS!
FOREIGN GUY! NOT A FORLORN GUY!
SO HE DID THAT TO YOU?! I'LL TALK TO HIM!
WHAT?
I'LL GET BACK YOUR UNIVERSE OF THE FOUR GODS AND MAKE SURE WE GET BACK TO HONG-NAN.
DON'T WORRY. HE CAN'T REFUSE ME!
YUI!
...
WHY? WHY DO ALL THIS ON YOUR OWN?

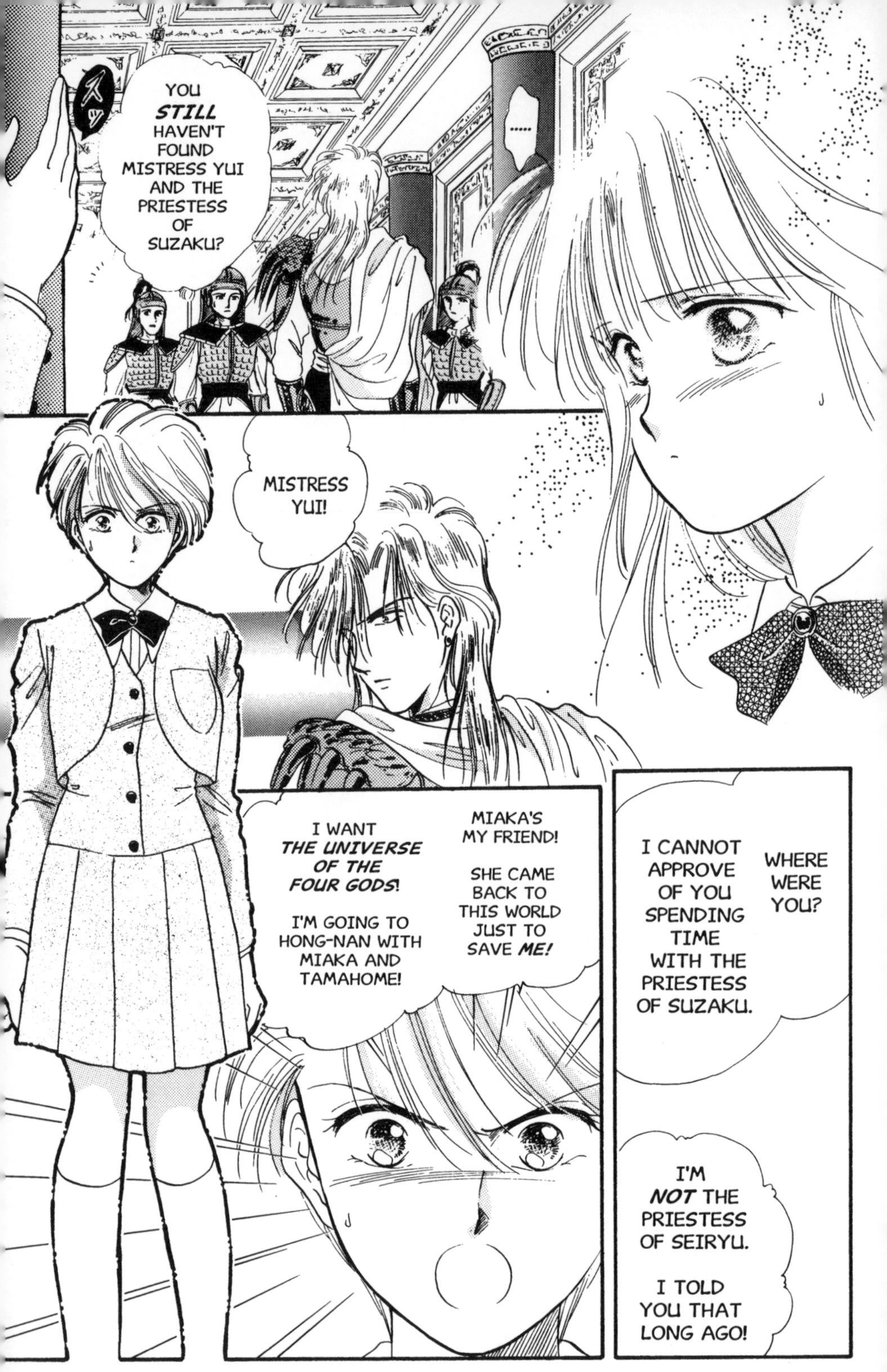
.....
スッ
YOU STILL HAVEN'T FOUND MISTRESS YUI AND THE PRIESTESS OF SUZAKU?
MISTRESS YUI!
WHERE WERE YOU?
I CANNOT APPROVE OF YOU SPENDING TIME WITH THE PRIESTESS OF SUZAKU.
I'M NOT THE PRIESTESS OF SEIRYU.
I TOLD YOU THAT LONG AGO!
MIAKA'S MY FRIEND!
SHE CAME BACK TO THIS WORLD JUST TO SAVE ME!
I WANT THE UNIVERSE OF THE FOUR GODS!
I'M GOING TO HONG-NAN WITH MIAKA AND TAMAHOME!

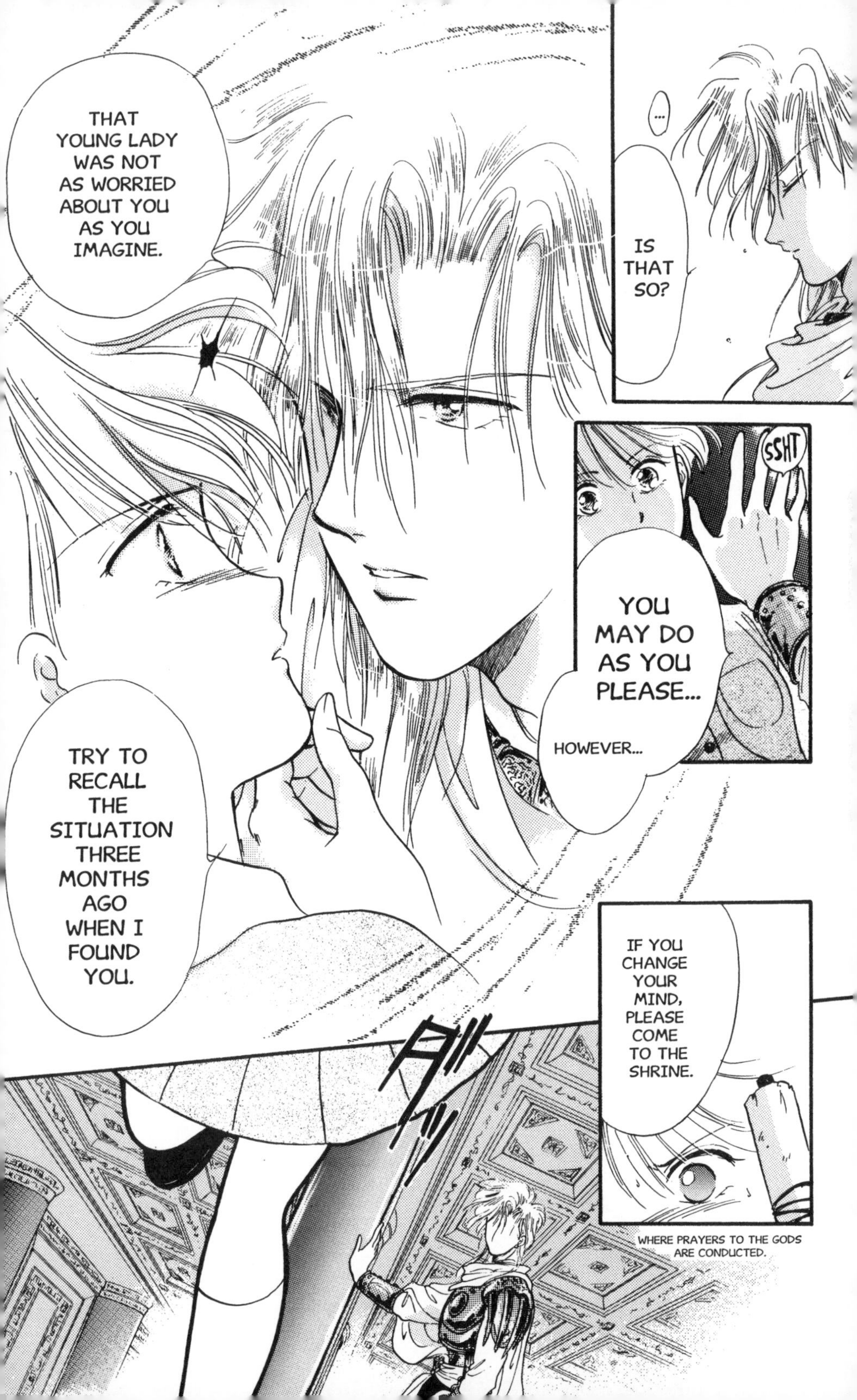
...
IS THAT SO?
SSHT
YOU MAY DO AS YOU PLEASE...
HOWEVER...
IF YOU CHANGE YOUR MIND, PLEASE COME TO THE SHRINE.
WHERE PRAYERS TO THE GODS ARE CONDUCTED.
THAT YOUNG LADY WAS NOT AS WORRIED ABOUT YOU AS YOU IMAGINE.
TRY TO RECALL THE SITUATION THREE MONTHS AGO WHEN I FOUND YOU.

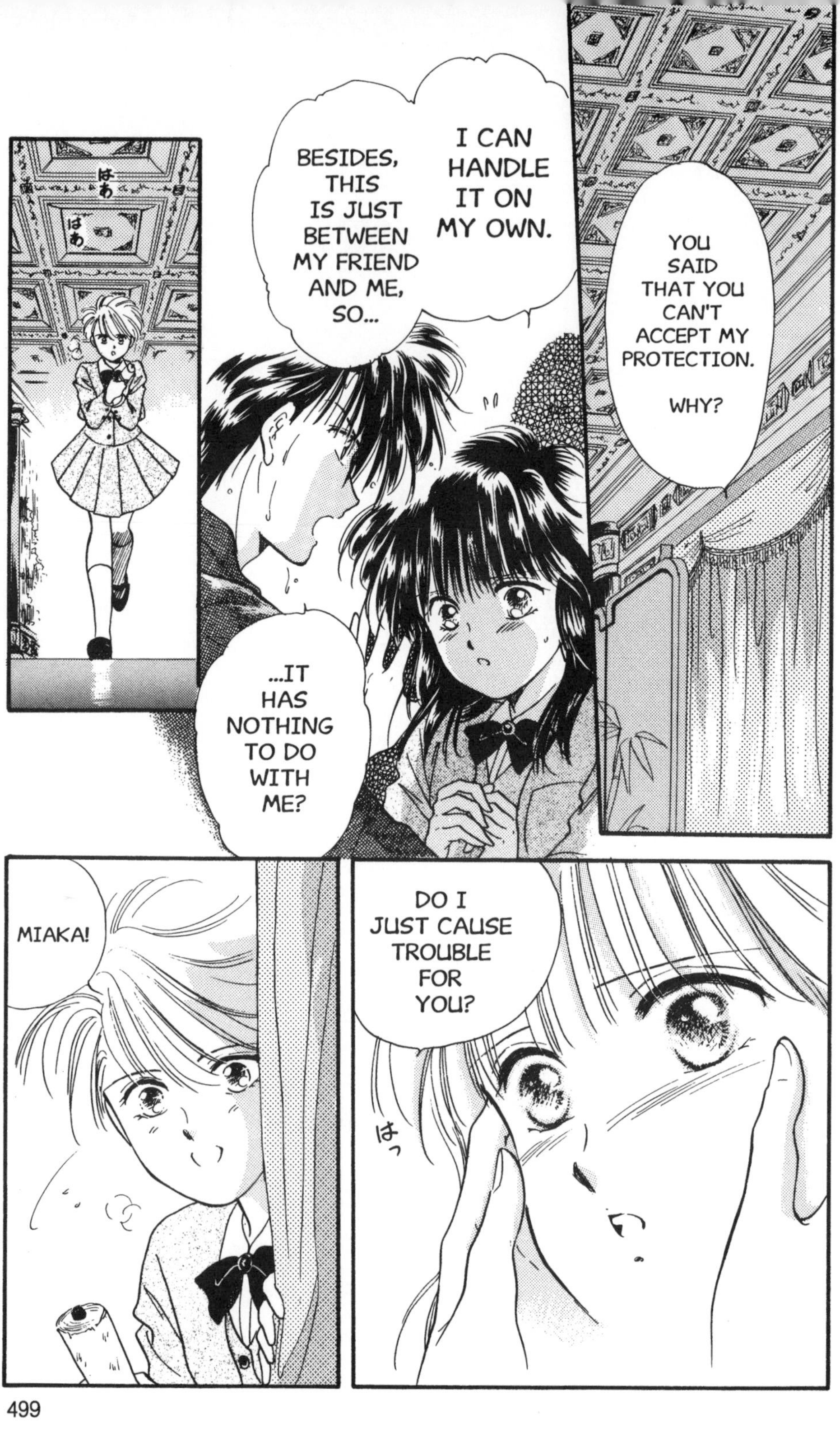
YOU SAID THAT YOU CAN'T ACCEPT MY PROTECTION.
WHY?
I CAN HANDLE IT ON MY OWN.
BESIDES, THIS IS JUST BETWEEN MY FRIEND AND ME, SO...
...IT HAS NOTHING TO DO WITH ME?
はあ
はあ
DO I JUST CAUSE TROUBLE FOR YOU?
はっ
MIAKA!

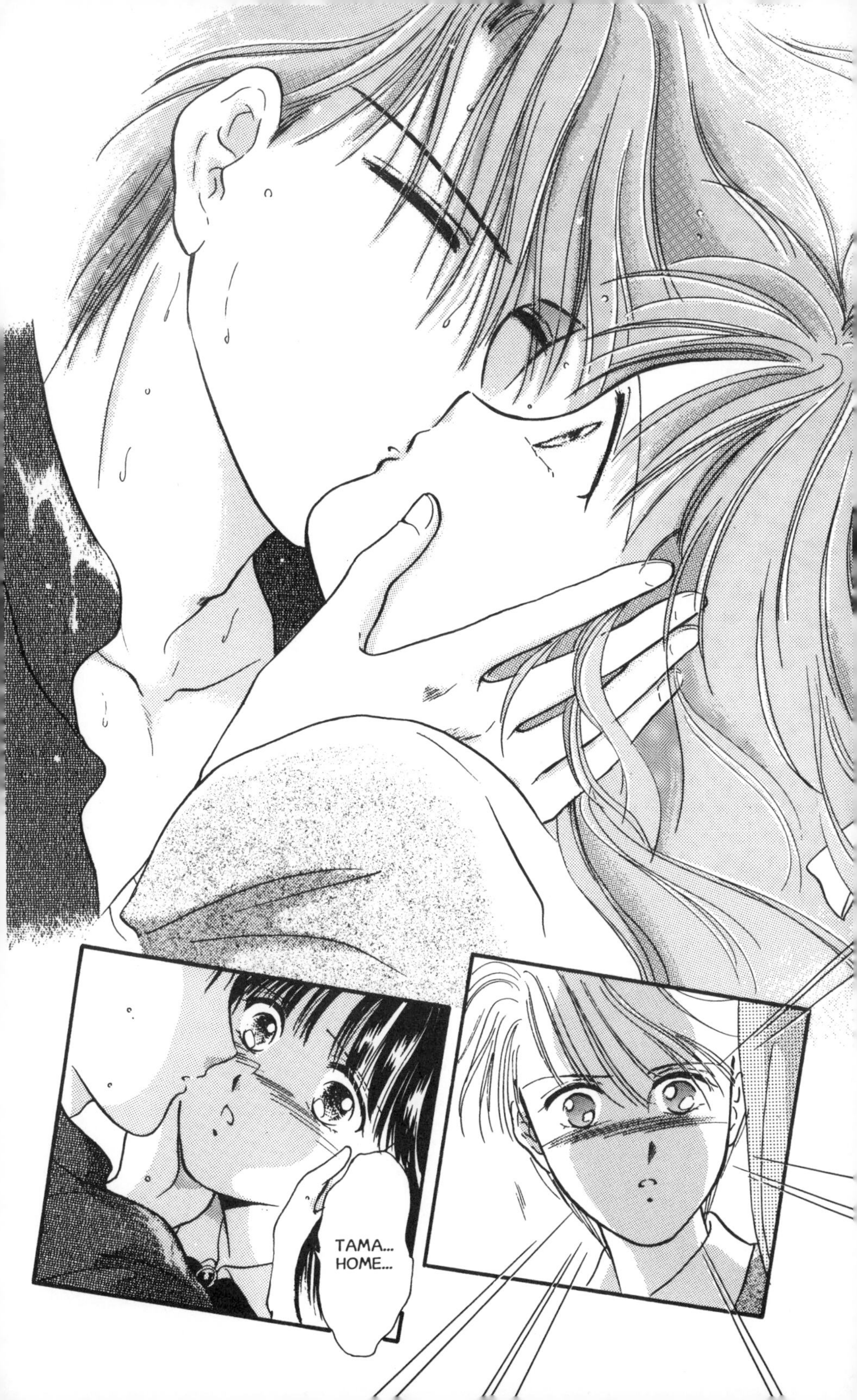
TAMA...
HOME...

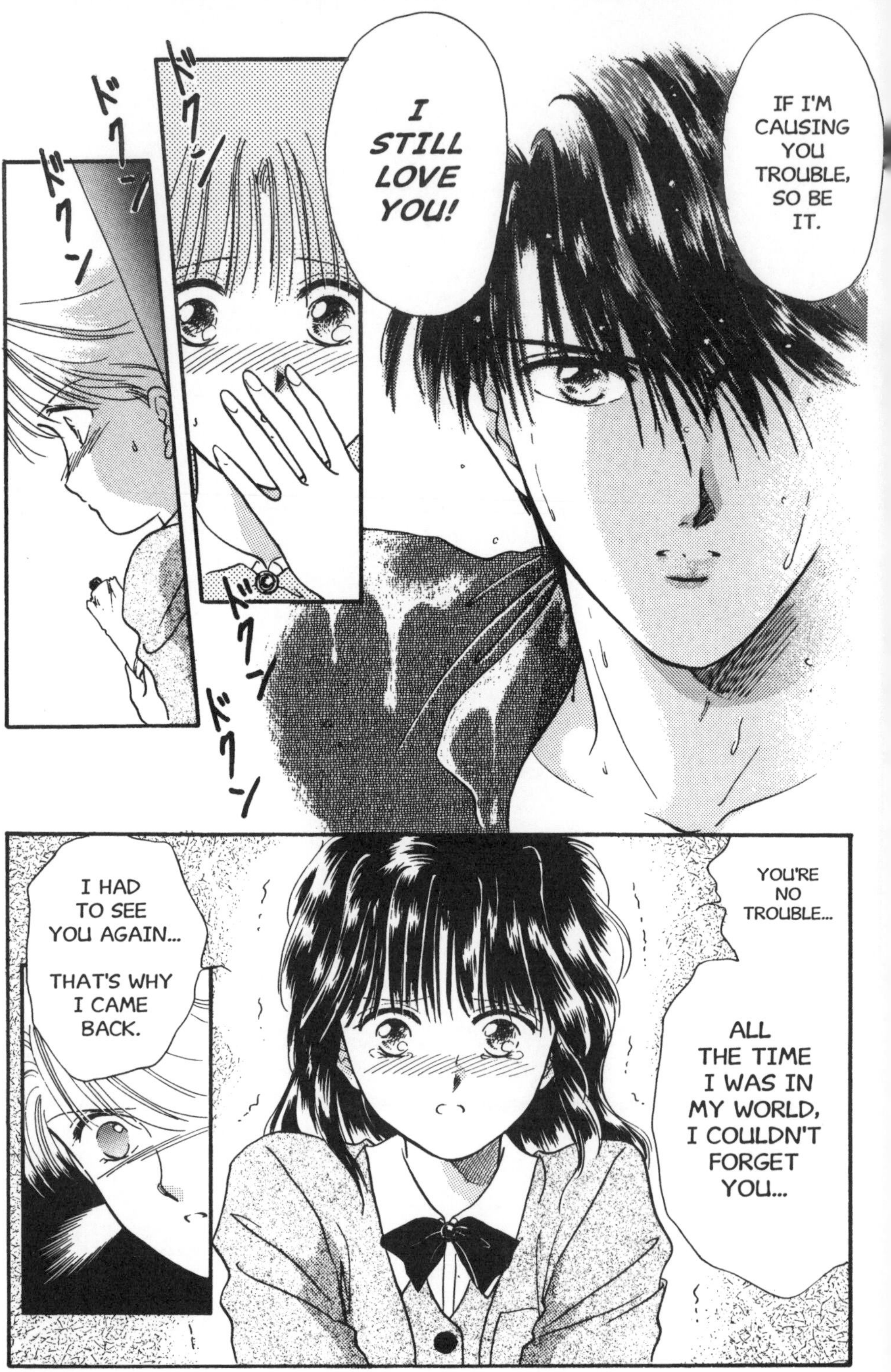
IF I'M CAUSING YOU TROUBLE, SO BE IT.
I STILL LOVE YOU!
ドクン
ドクン
ドクン
ドクン
ドクン
YOU'RE NO TROUBLE...
ALL THE TIME I WAS IN MY WORLD, I COULDN'T FORGET YOU...
I HAD TO SEE YOU AGAIN...
THAT'S WHY I CAME BACK.

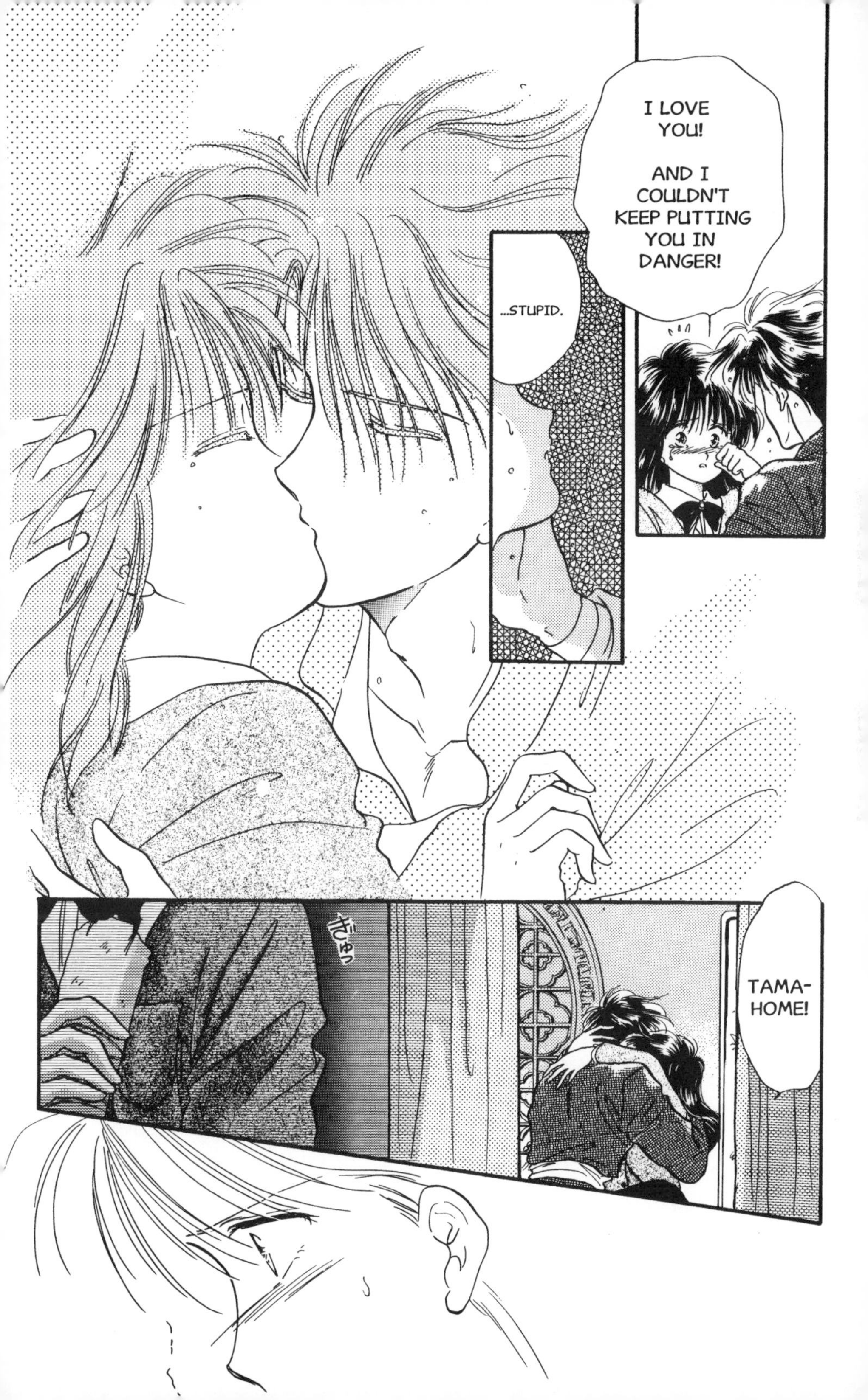
I LOVE YOU!
AND I COULDN'T KEEP PUTTING YOU IN DANGER!
...STUPID.
TAMA-HOME!
ぎゅっ

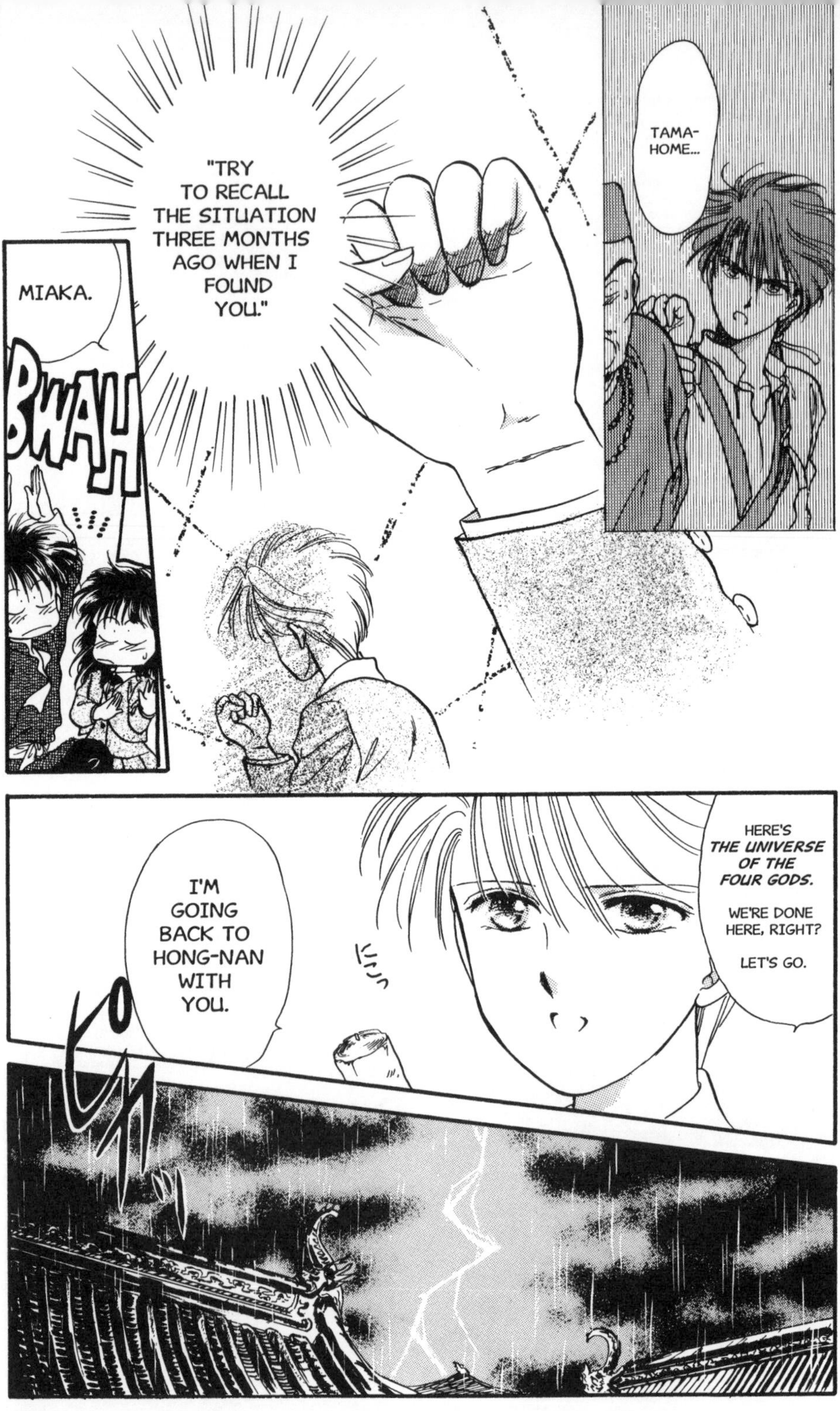
TAMA-HOME...
"TRY TO RECALL THE SITUATION THREE MONTHS AGO WHEN I FOUND YOU."
MIAKA.
BWAH
HERE'S *THE UNIVERSE OF THE FOUR GODS.*
WE'RE DONE HERE, RIGHT?
LET'S GO.
I'M GOING BACK TO HONG-NAN WITH YOU.

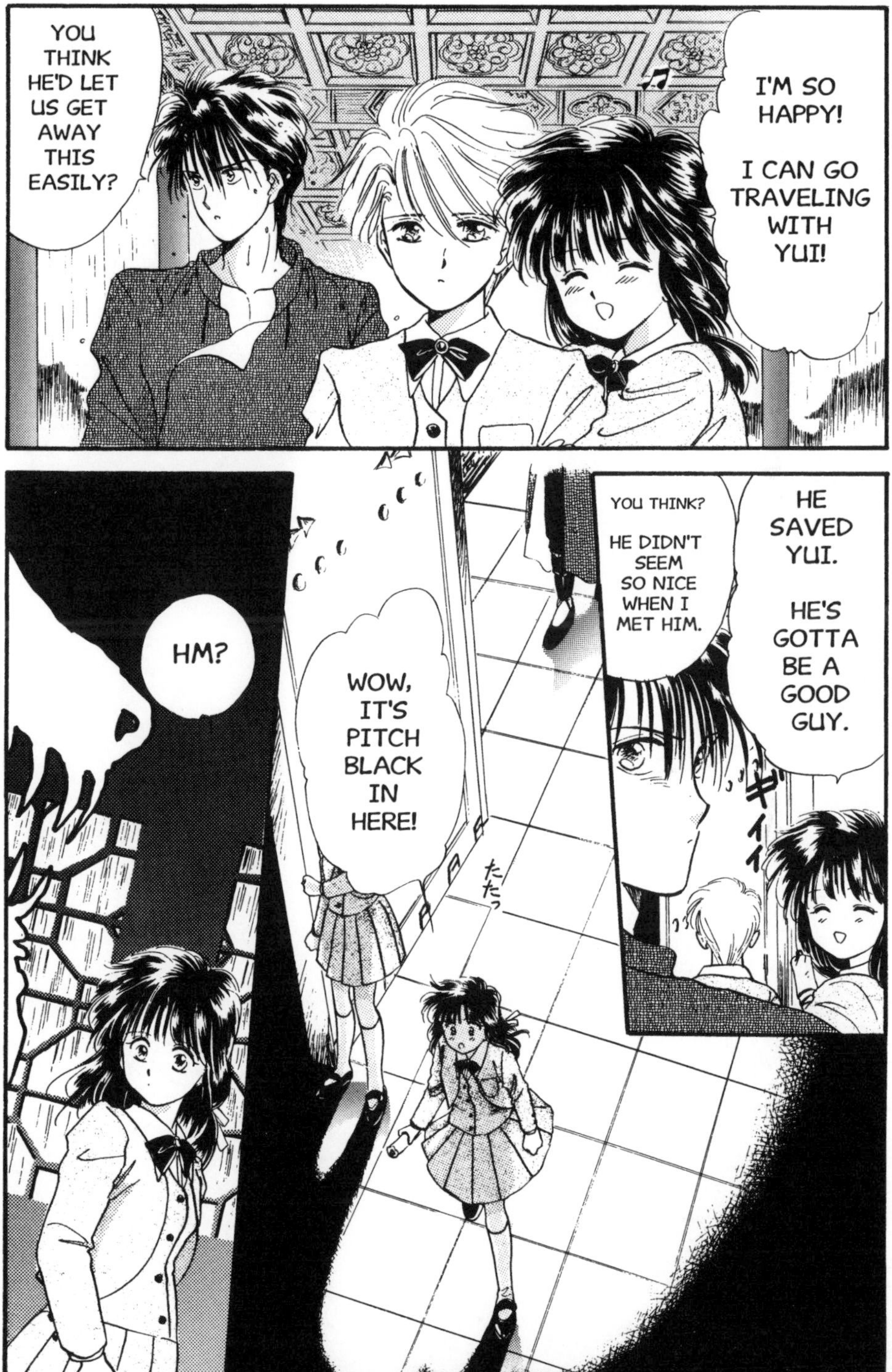
I'M SO HAPPY!
I CAN GO TRAVELING WITH YUI!
YOU THINK HE'D LET US GET AWAY THIS EASILY?
HE SAVED YUI.
HE'S GOTTA BE A GOOD GUY.
ギィィ
YOU THINK?
HE DIDN'T SEEM SO NICE WHEN I MET HIM.
たたっ
WOW, IT'S PITCH BLACK IN HERE!
HM?

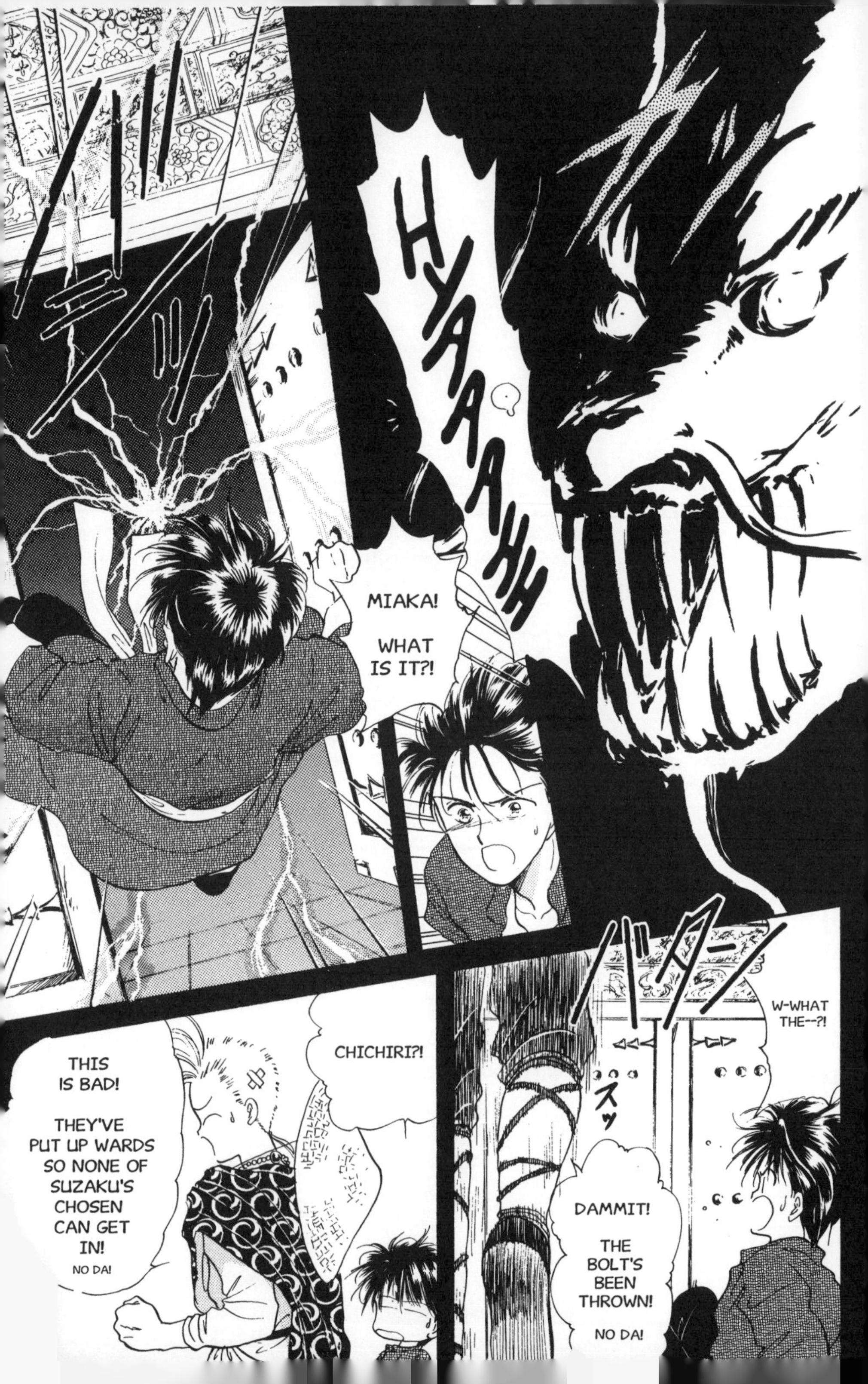
HYAAAAHHH
MIAKA!
WHAT IS IT?!
W-WHAT THE--?!
DAMMIT!
THE BOLT'S BEEN THROWN!
NO DA!
CHICHIRI?!
THIS IS BAD!
THEY'VE PUT UP WARDS SO NONE OF SUZAKU'S CHOSEN CAN GET IN!
NO DA!

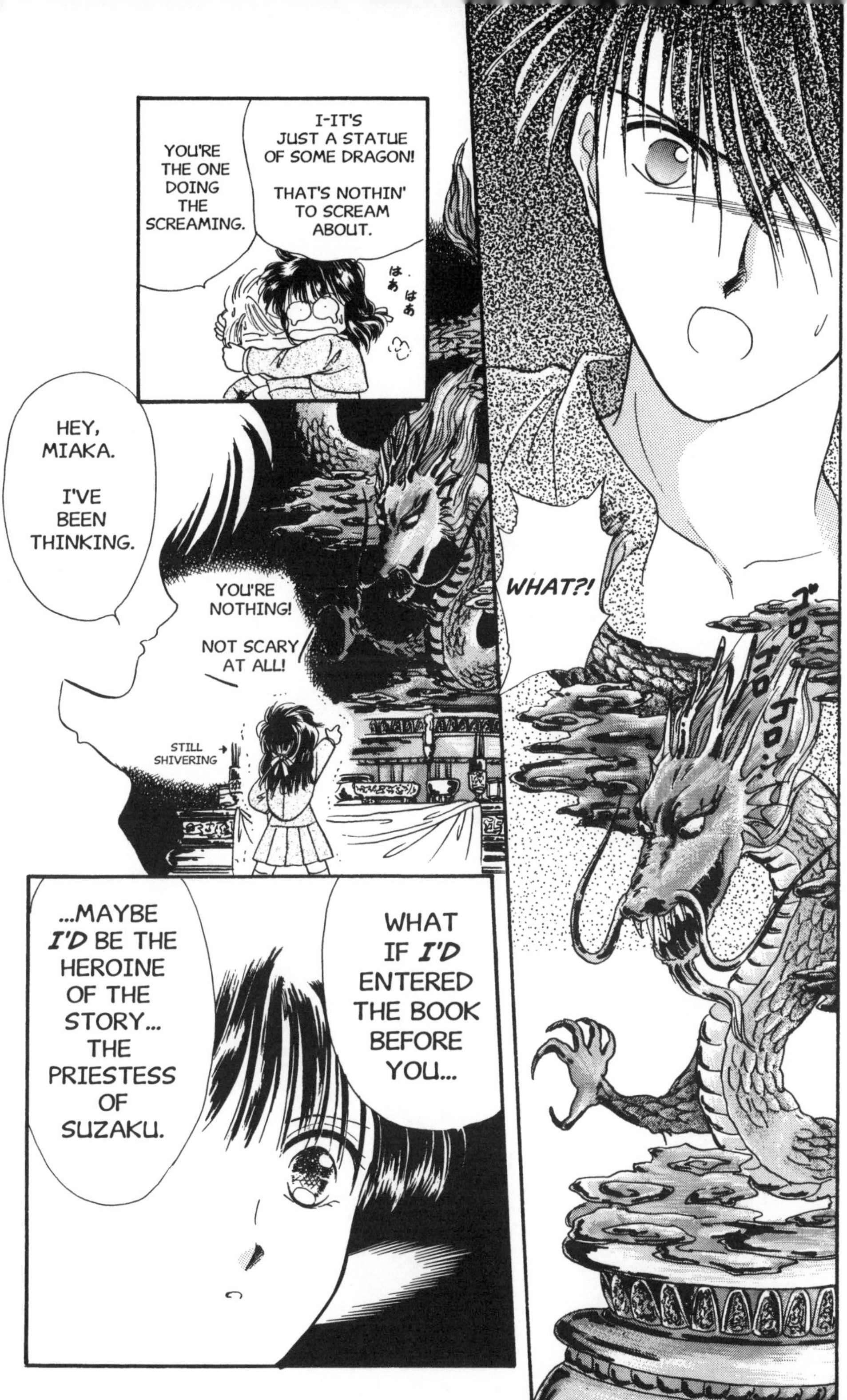
WHAT?!
ゴロゴロゴロ…
I-IT'S JUST A STATUE OF SOME DRAGON! THAT'S NOTHIN' TO SCREAM ABOUT.
YOU'RE THE ONE DOING THE SCREAMING.
はあ はあ
YOU'RE NOTHING! NOT SCARY AT ALL!
STILL SHIVERING
HEY, MIAKA. I'VE BEEN THINKING.
WHAT IF I'D ENTERED THE BOOK BEFORE YOU...
...MAYBE I'D BE THE HEROINE OF THE STORY... THE PRIESTESS OF SUZAKU.

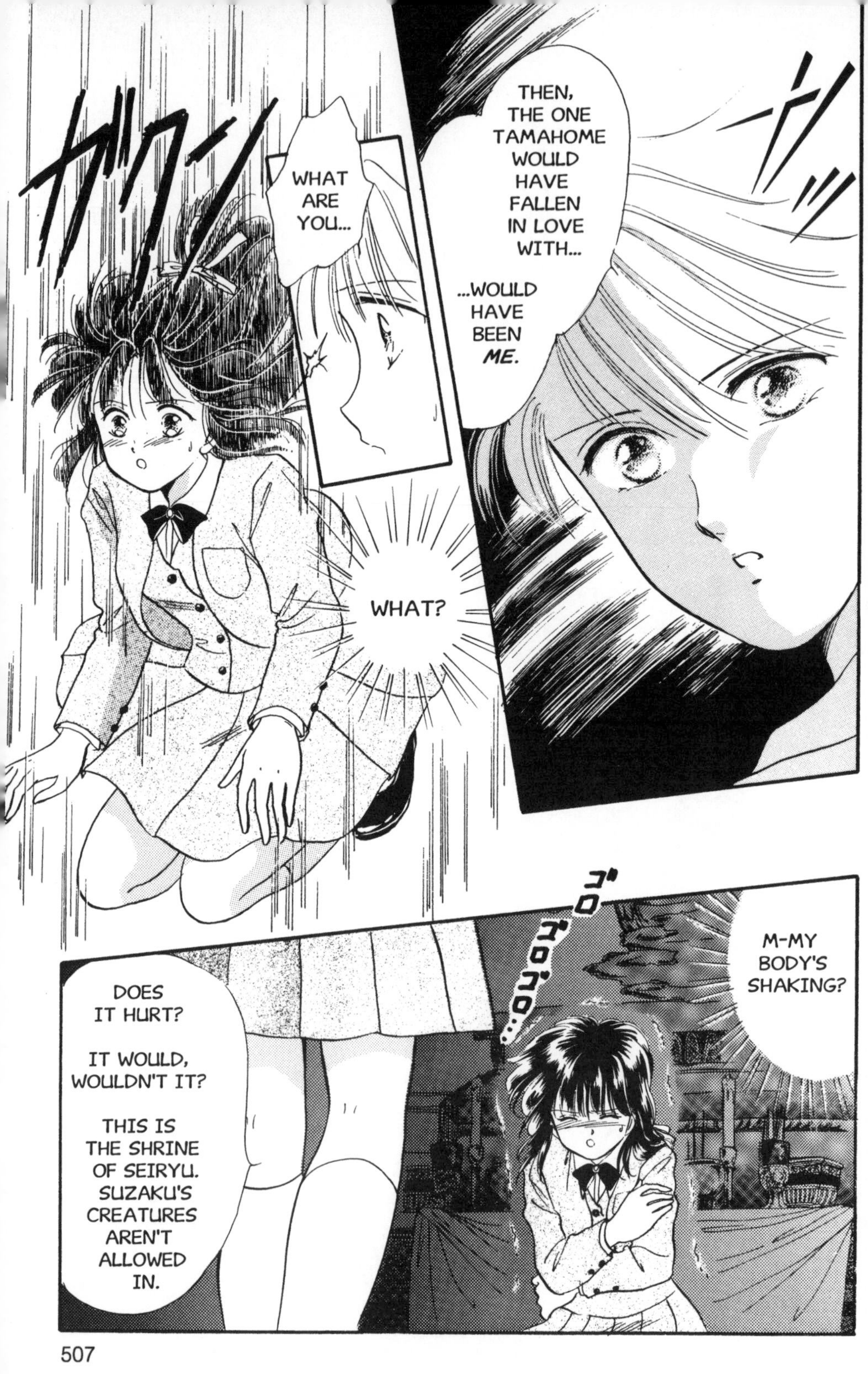
THEN, THE ONE TAMAHOME WOULD HAVE FALLEN IN LOVE WITH...
...WOULD HAVE BEEN *ME.*
WHAT ARE YOU...
WHAT?
M-MY BODY'S SHAKING?
DOES IT HURT?
IT WOULD, WOULDN'T IT?
THIS IS THE SHRINE OF SEIRYU. SUZAKU'S CREATURES AREN'T ALLOWED IN.

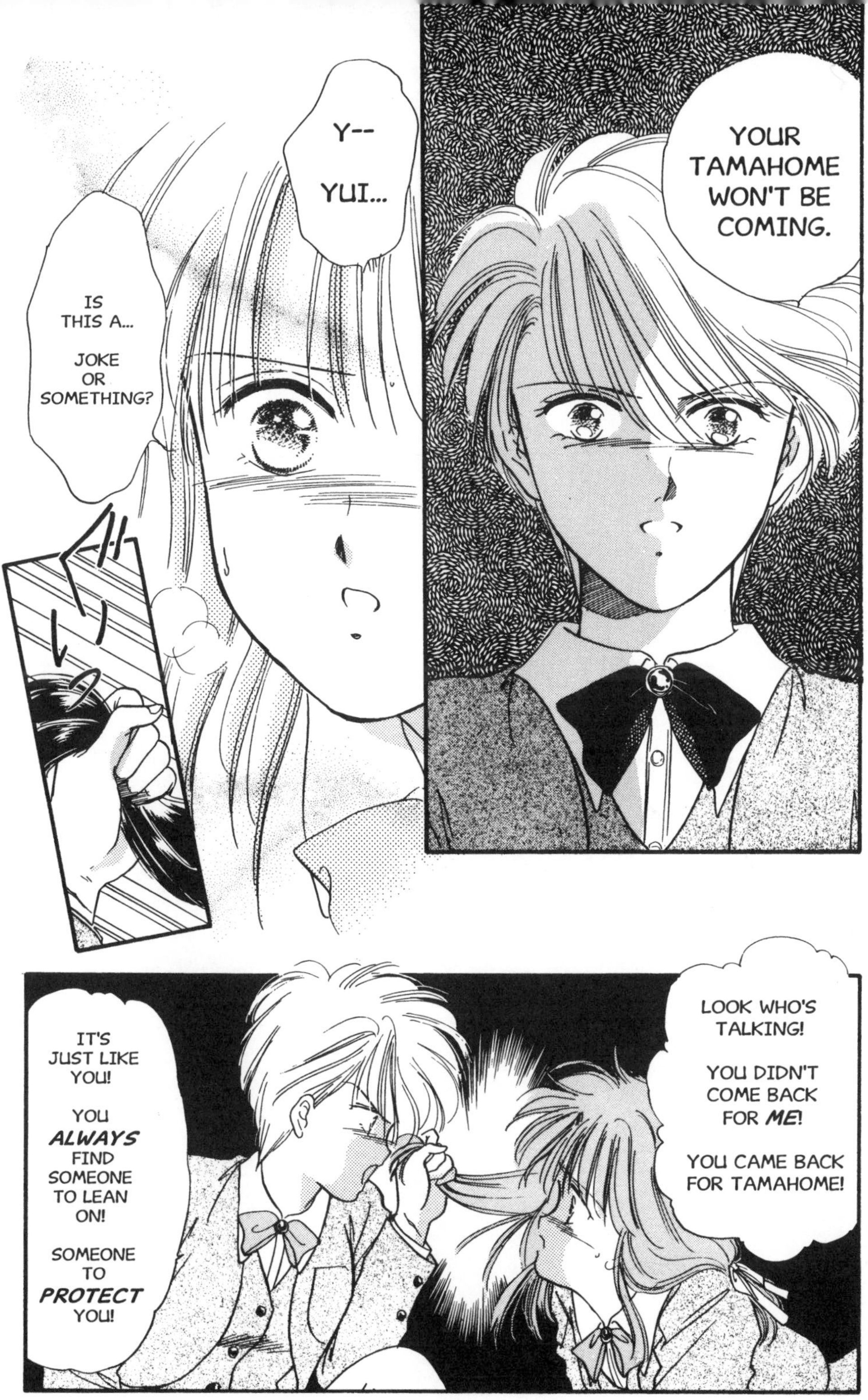
YOUR TAMAHOME WON'T BE COMING.
Y-- YUI...
IS THIS A... JOKE OR SOMETHING?
LOOK WHO'S TALKING! YOU DIDN'T COME BACK FOR *ME*! YOU CAME BACK FOR TAMAHOME!
IT'S JUST LIKE YOU! YOU *ALWAYS* FIND SOMEONE TO LEAN ON! SOMEONE TO *PROTECT* YOU!

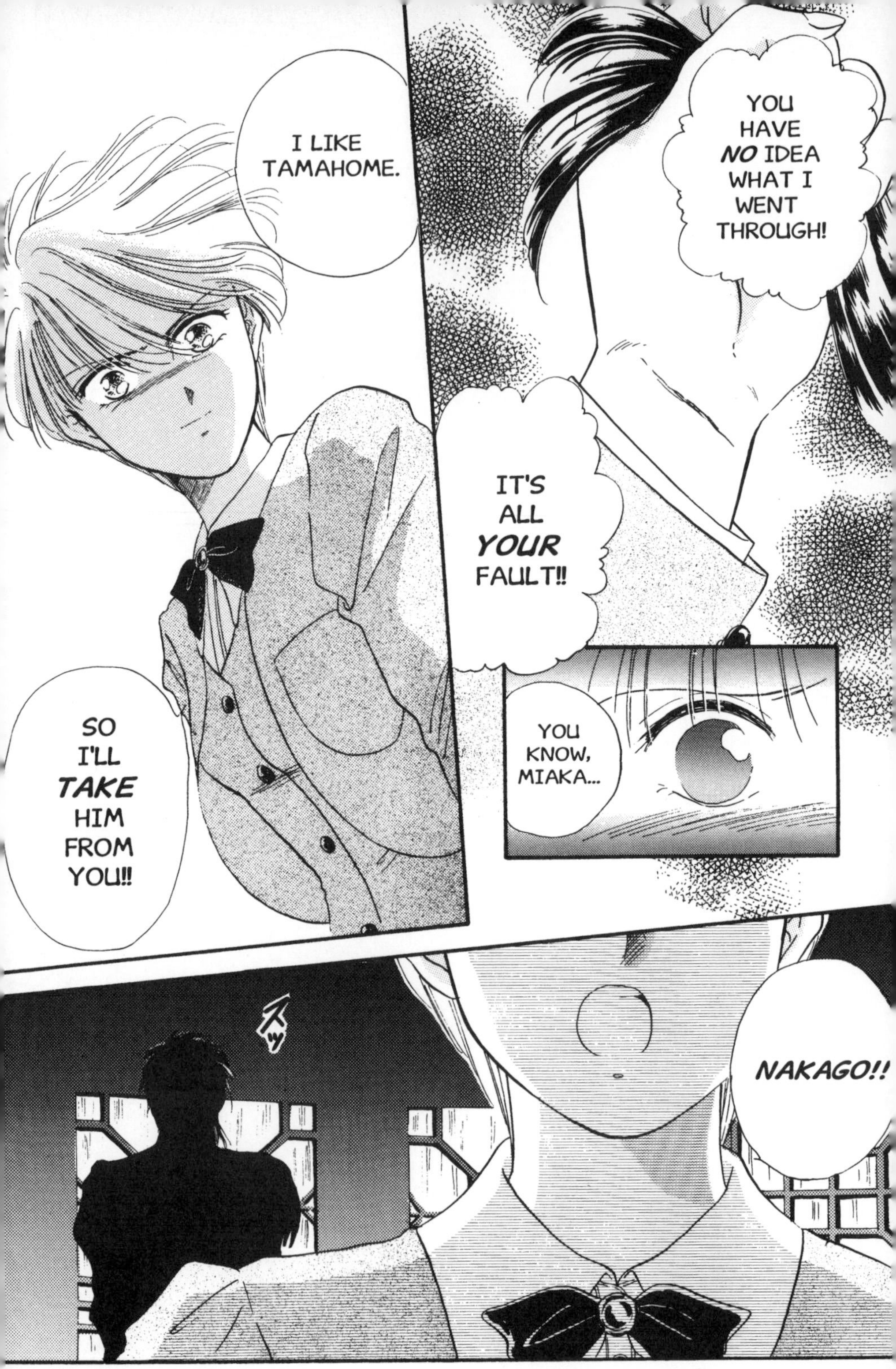
YOU HAVE *NO* IDEA WHAT I WENT THROUGH!
IT'S ALL *YOUR* FAULT!!
YOU KNOW, MIAKA...
I LIKE TAMAHOME.
SO I'LL *TAKE* HIM FROM YOU!!
NAKAGO!!
スッ

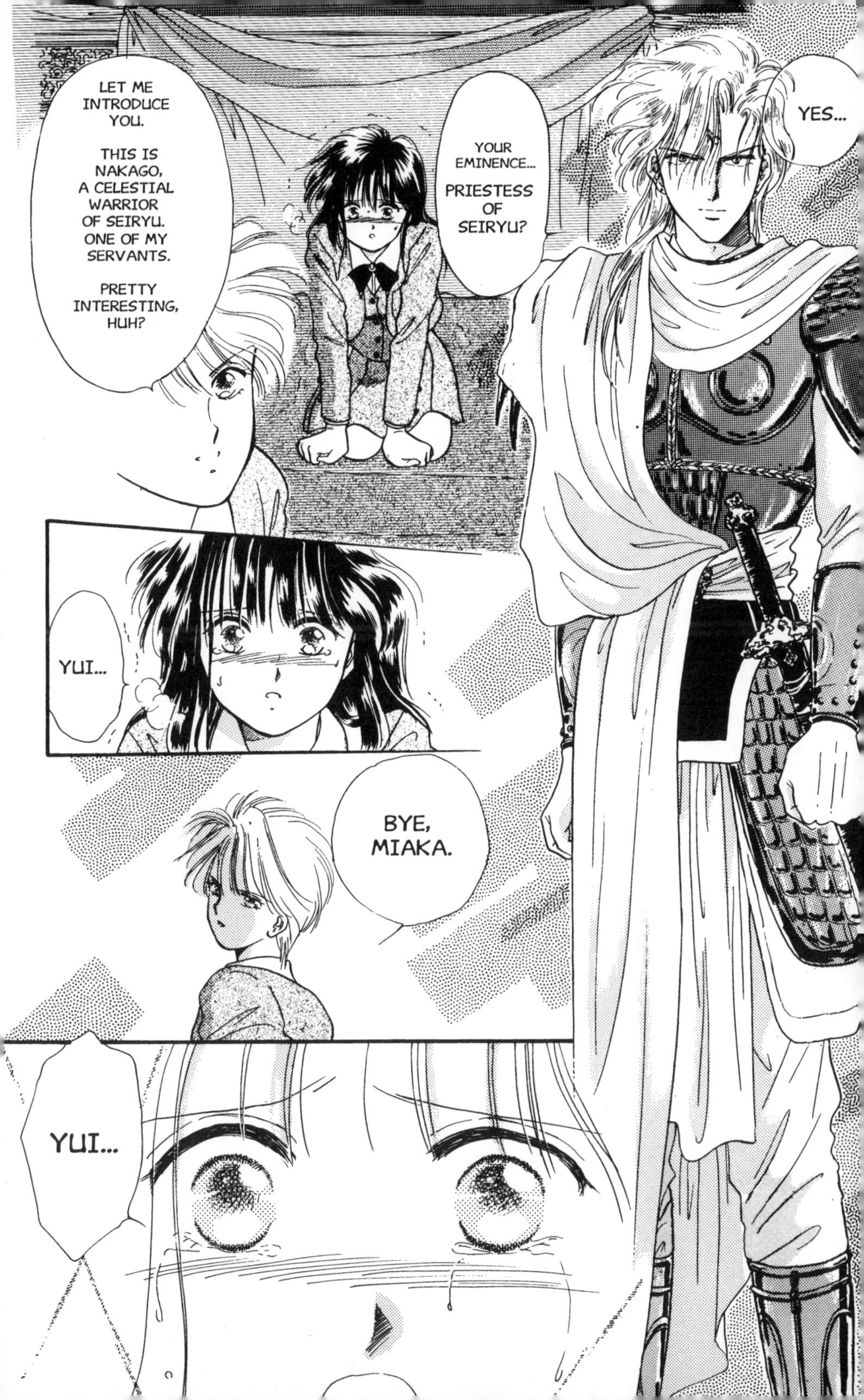
LET ME INTRODUCE YOU. THIS IS NAKAGO, A CELESTIAL WARRIOR OF SEIRYU. ONE OF MY SERVANTS. PRETTY INTERESTING, HUH?
YOUR EMINENCE... PRIESTESS OF SEIRYU?
YES...
YUI...
BYE, MIAKA.
YUI...

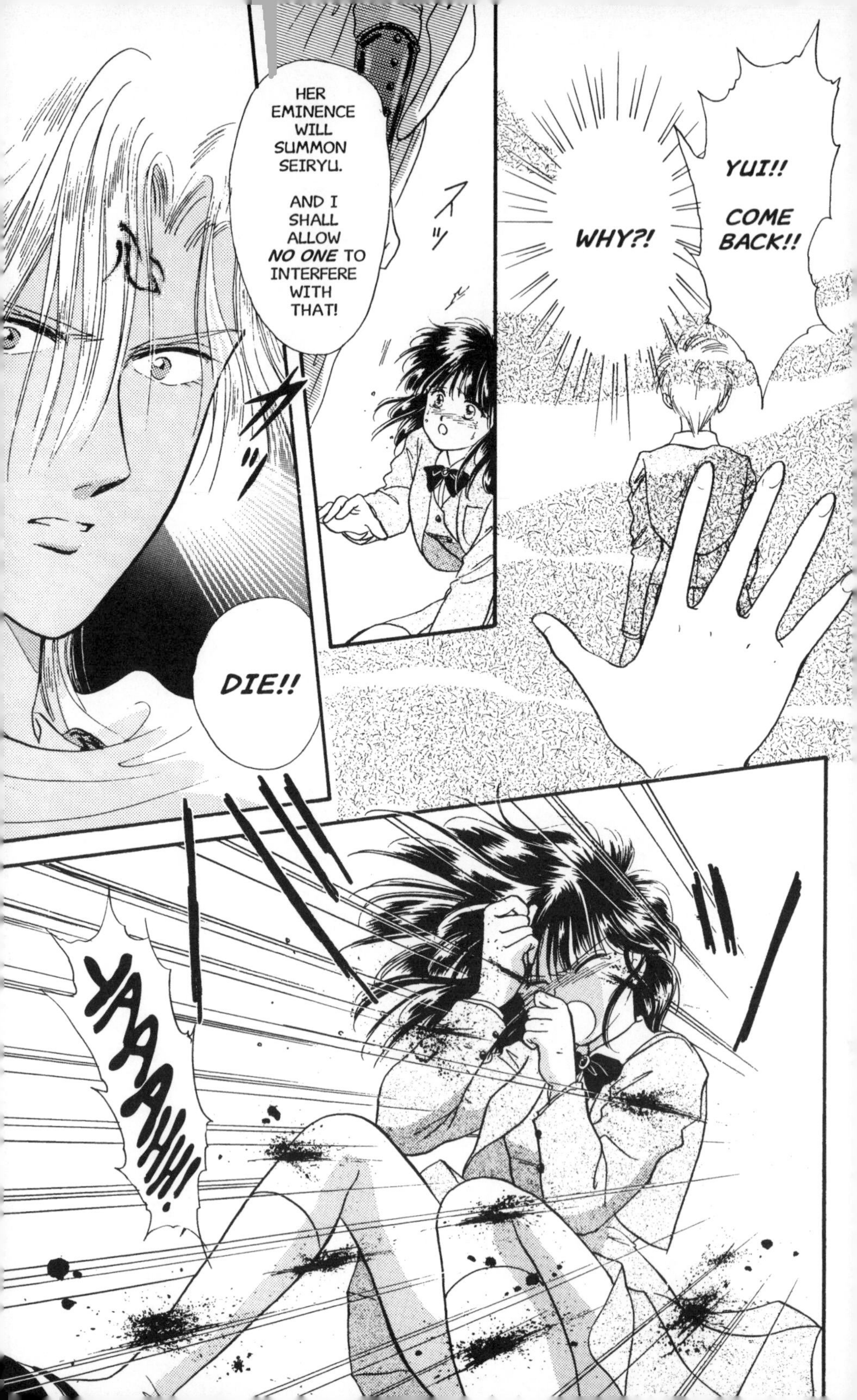
YUI!! COME BACK!!
WHY?!
スッ
HER EMINENCE WILL SUMMON SEIRYU. AND I SHALL ALLOW *NO ONE* TO INTERFERE WITH THAT!
DIE!!
YAAAHH!

BACK BY POPULAR DEMAND
PARDON THE PARODY NEWLY RETITLED AS

FUSHIGI AKUGI ふしぎ悪戯
THE MALICIOUS PLAY

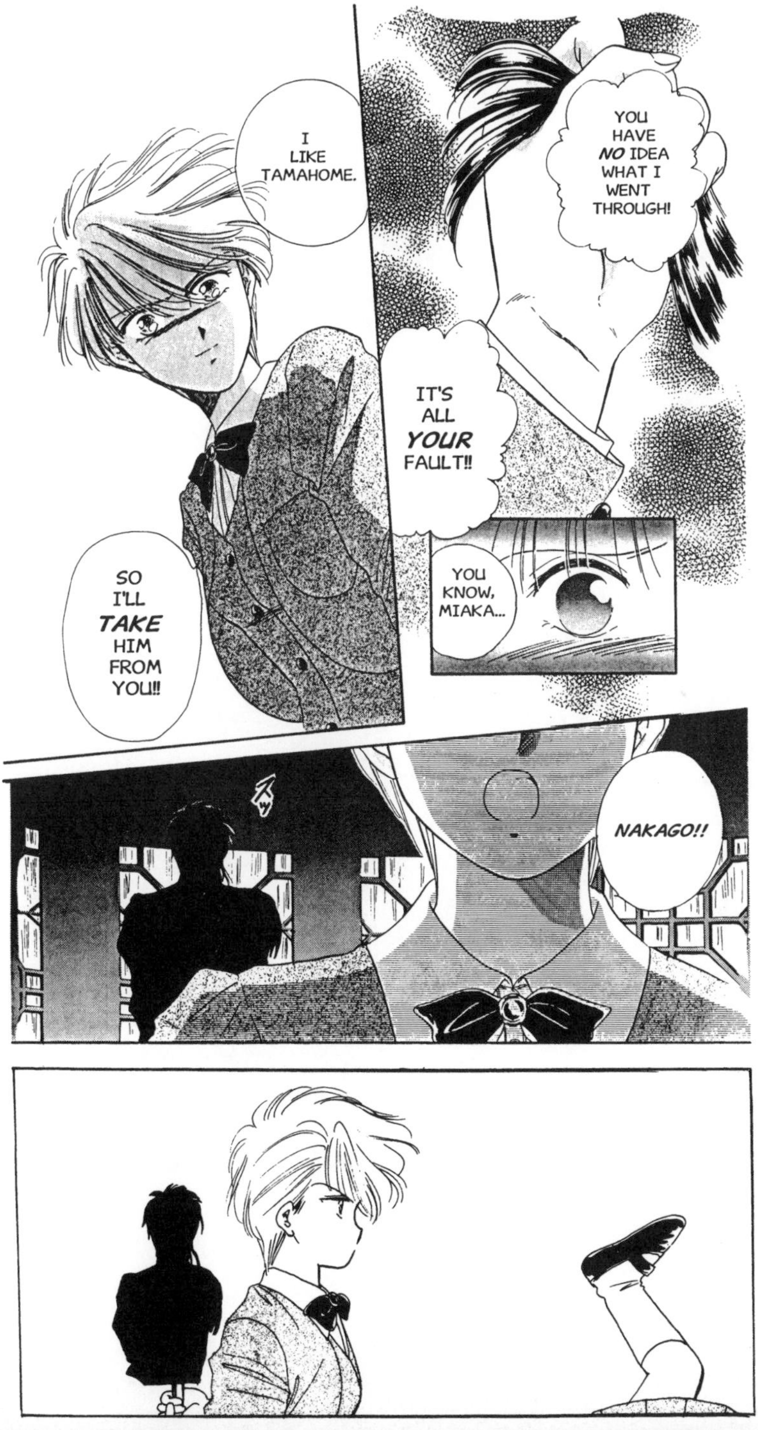
YOU HAVE ***NO*** IDEA WHAT I WENT THROUGH!
IT'S ALL ***YOUR*** FAULT!!
YOU KNOW, MIAKA...
I LIKE TAMAHOME.
SO I'LL ***TAKE*** HIM FROM YOU!!
NAKAGO!!

ANOTHER IDEA ←BY MANGA ARTIST Y.M.

Chapter Seventeen
Souls Drifting Apart

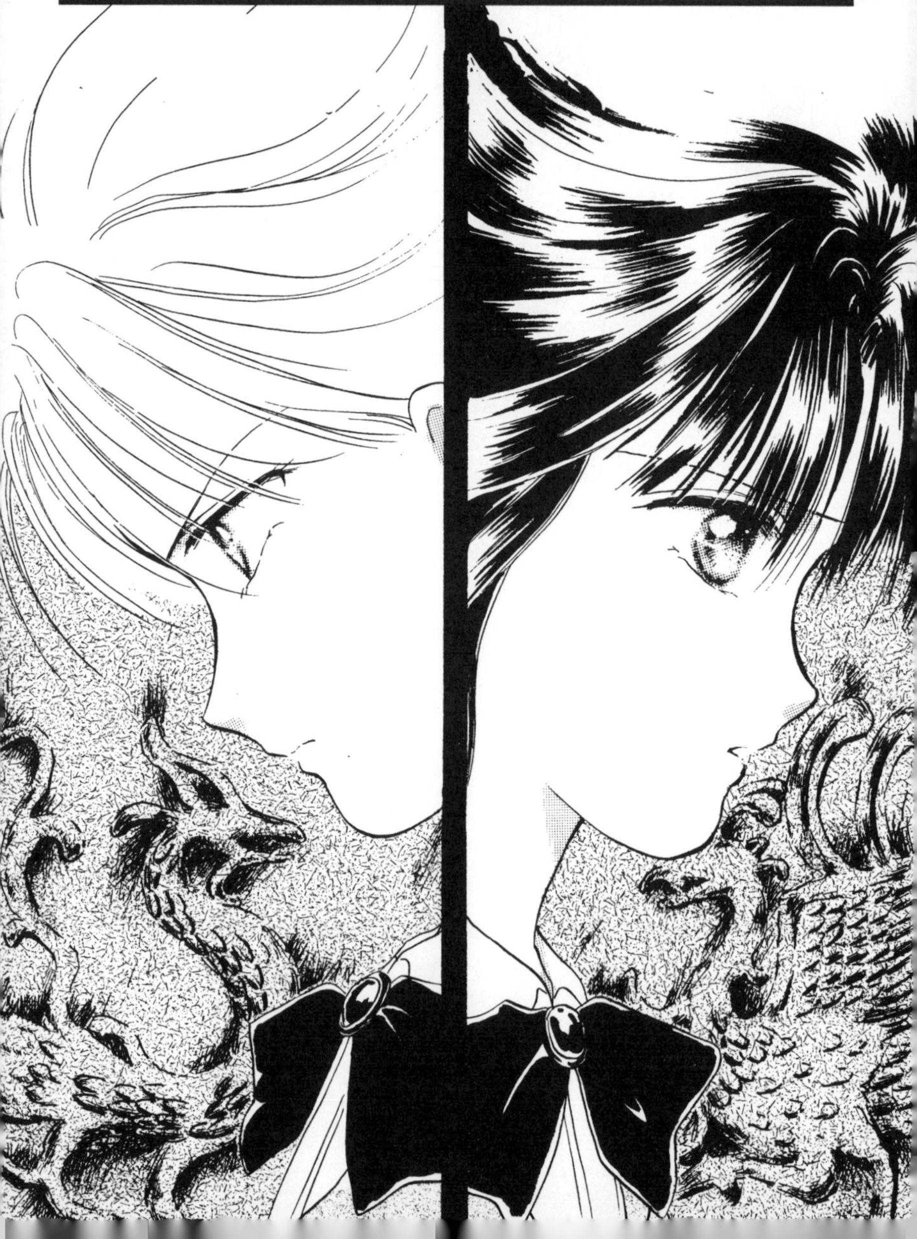

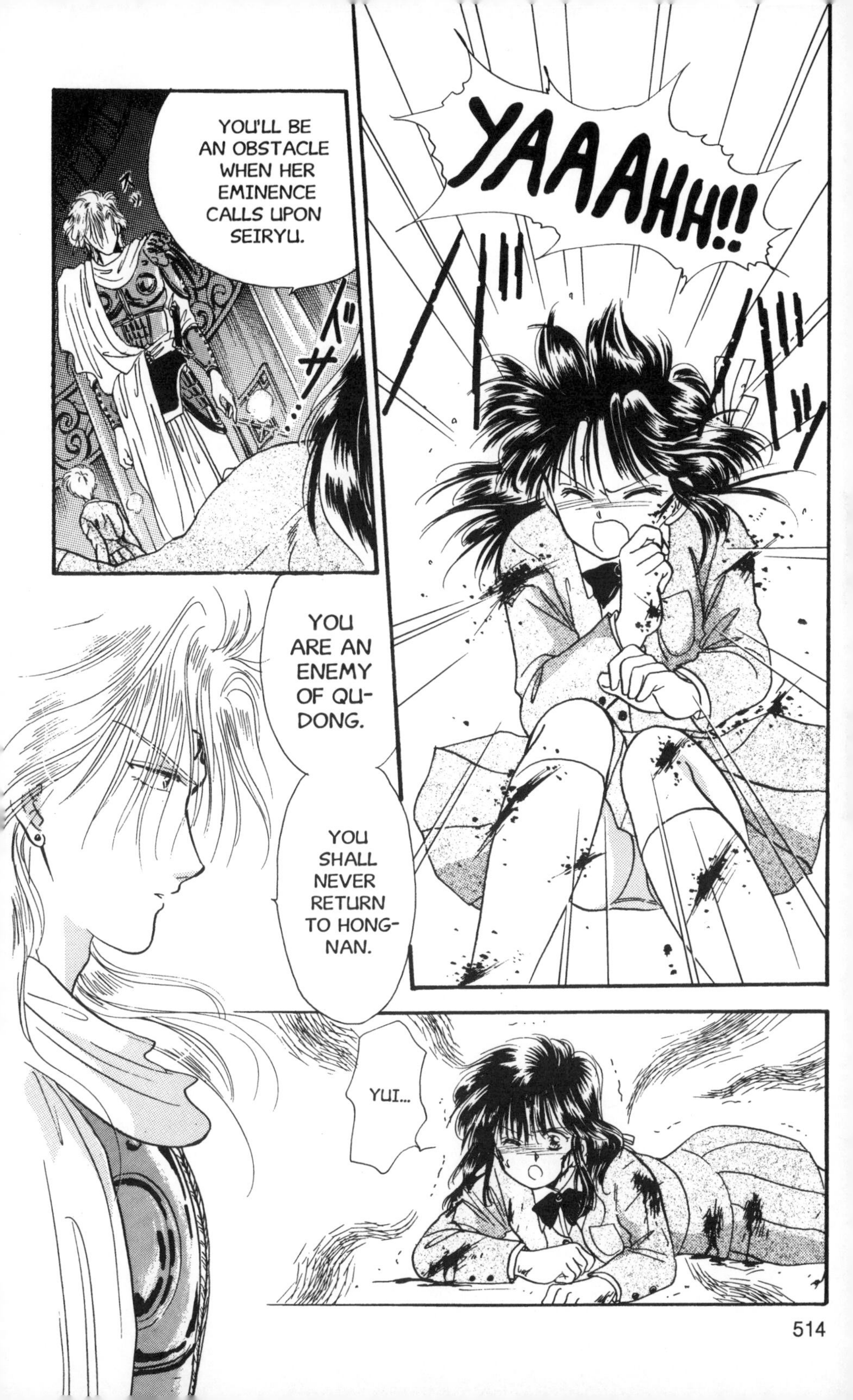
YAAAHH!!
YOU'LL BE AN OBSTACLE WHEN HER EMINENCE CALLS UPON SEIRYU.
YOU ARE AN ENEMY OF QU-DONG.
YOU SHALL NEVER RETURN TO HONG-NAN.
YUI...

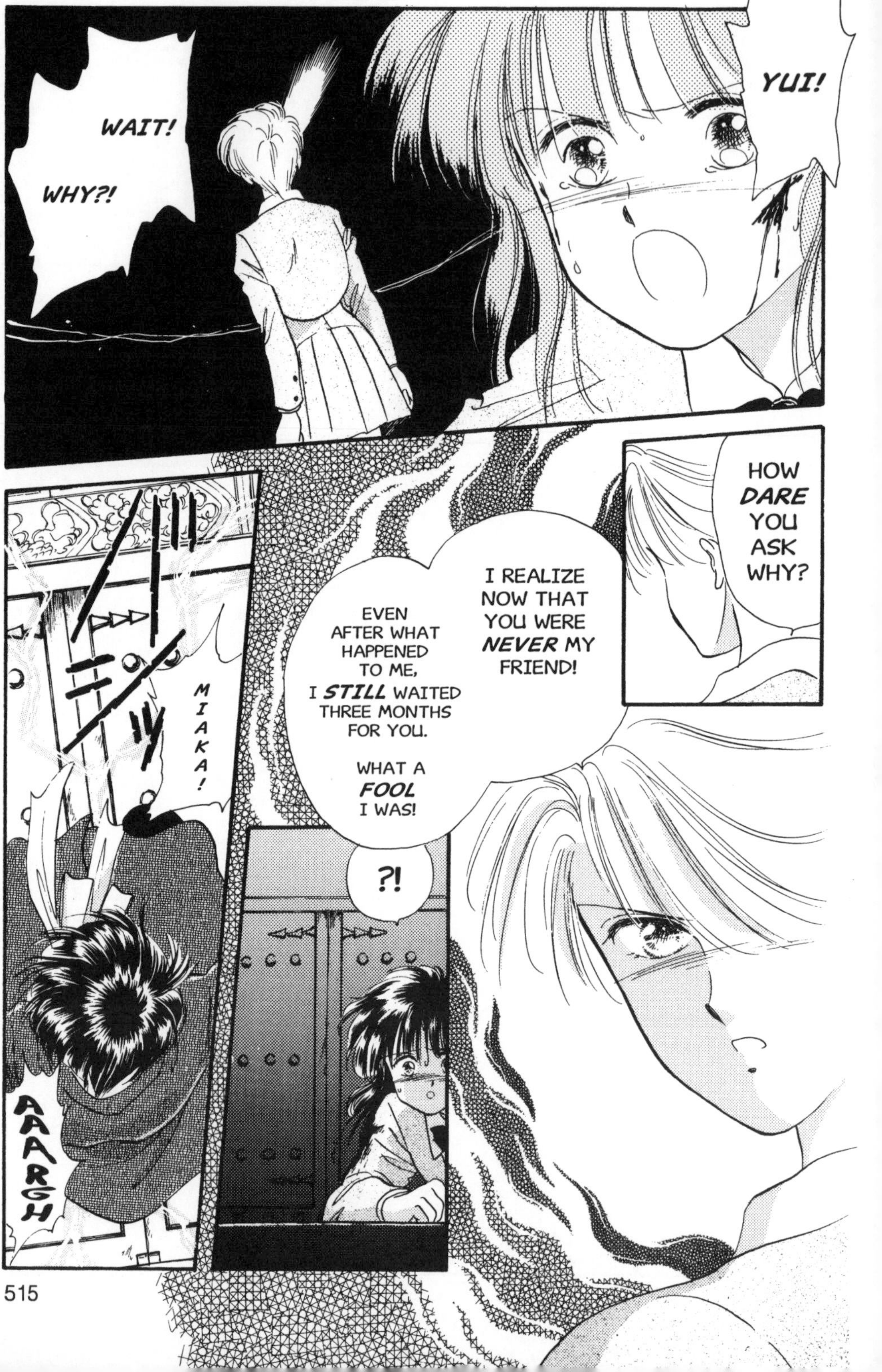
YUI!
WAIT!
WHY?!
HOW DARE YOU ASK WHY?
I REALIZE NOW THAT YOU WERE NEVER MY FRIEND!
EVEN AFTER WHAT HAPPENED TO ME, I STILL WAITED THREE MONTHS FOR YOU.
WHAT A FOOL I WAS!
?!
MIAKA!
AAARGH

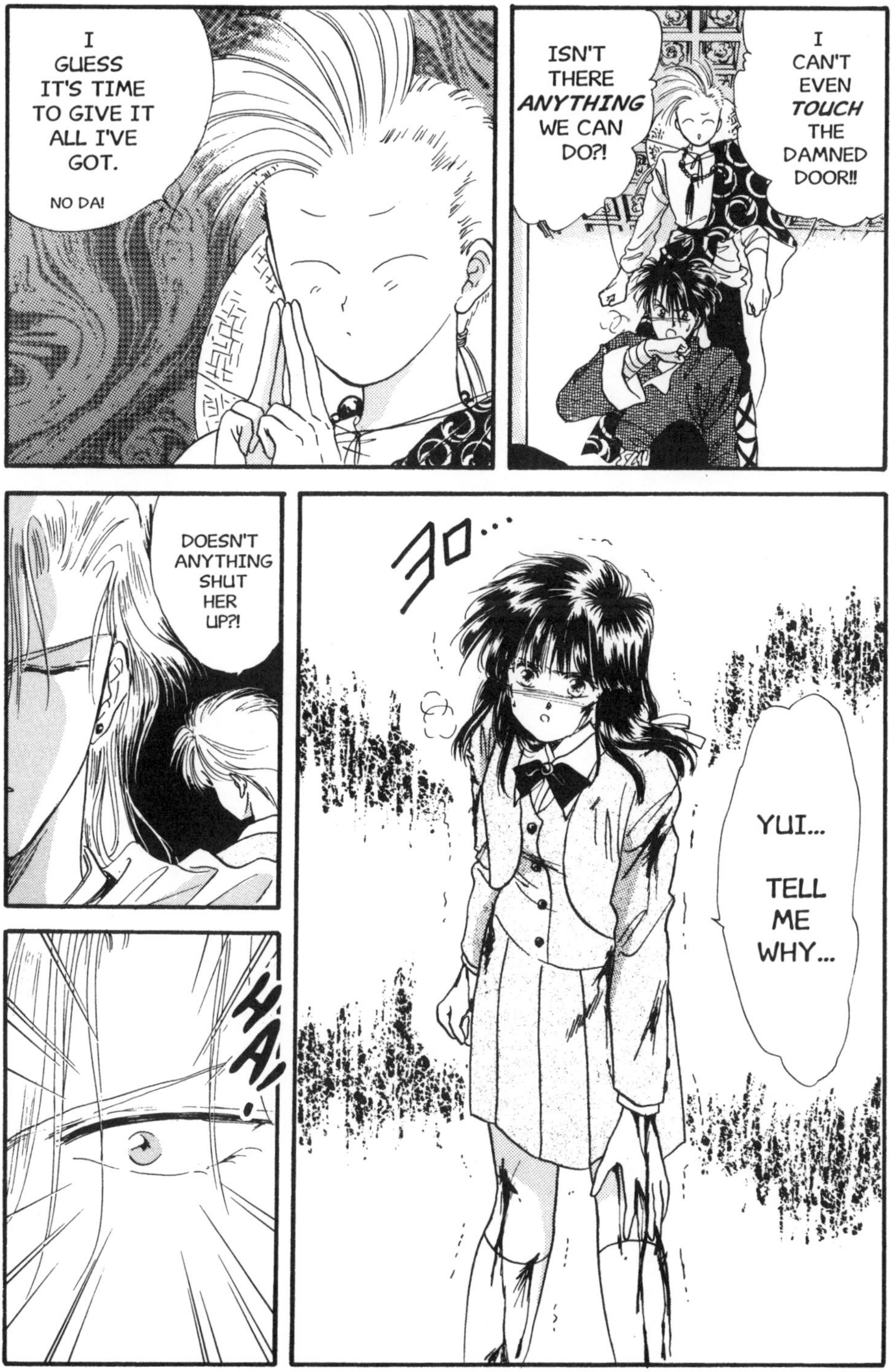
I CAN'T EVEN TOUCH THE DAMNED DOOR!!
ISN'T THERE ANYTHING WE CAN DO?!
I GUESS IT'S TIME TO GIVE IT ALL I'VE GOT.
NO DA!
ヨロ...
YUI... TELL ME WHY...
DOESN'T ANYTHING SHUT HER UP?!
HA!

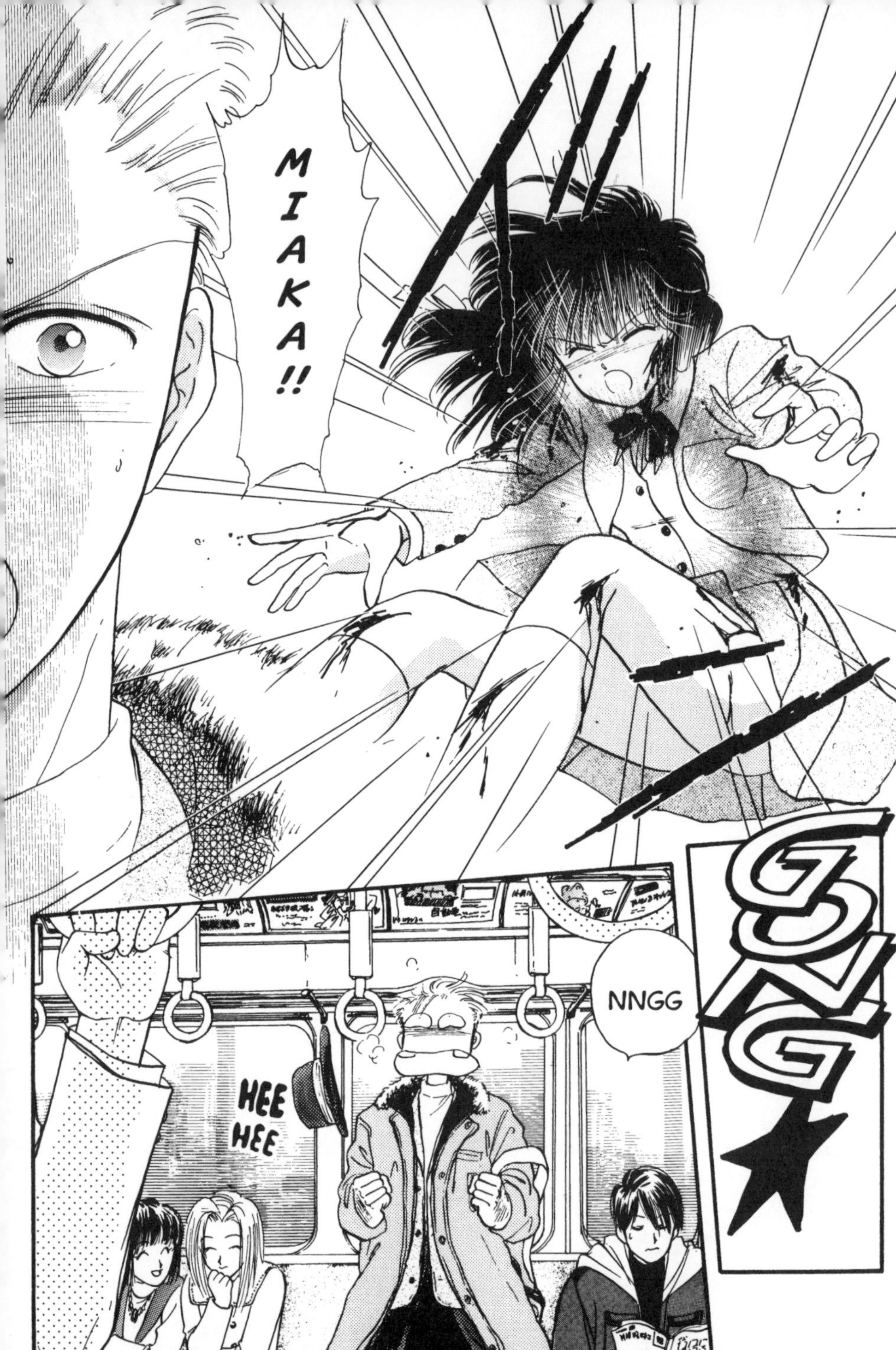
MIAKA!!
GONG
NNGG
HEE HEE

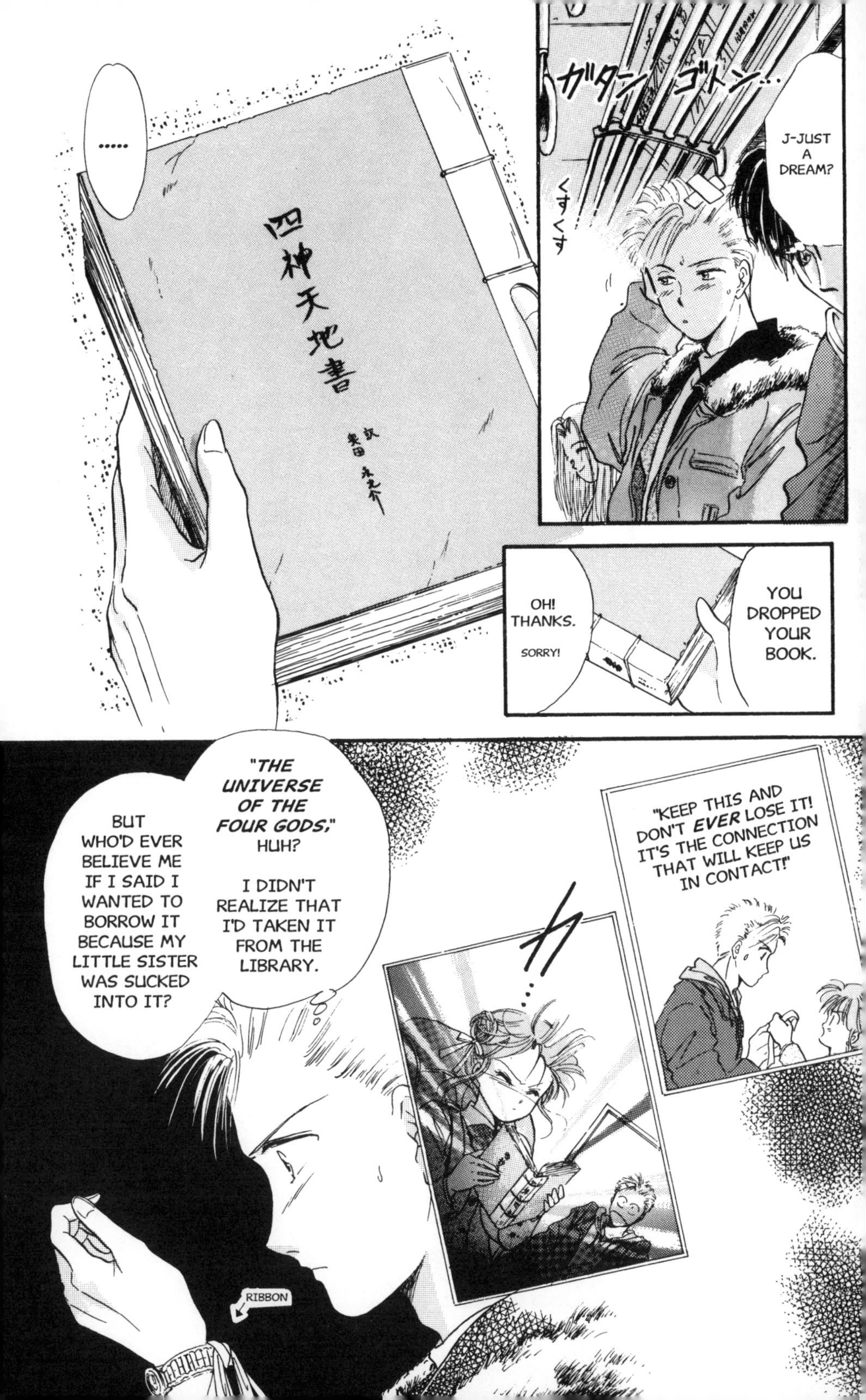

ガタン ゴトン…
くすくす
J-JUST A DREAM?
YOU DROPPED YOUR BOOK.
OH! THANKS.
SORRY!
......
四神天地書
"KEEP THIS AND DON'T EVER LOSE IT! IT'S THE CONNECTION THAT WILL KEEP US IN CONTACT!"
RIBBON
"THE UNIVERSE OF THE FOUR GODS," HUH?
I DIDN'T REALIZE THAT I'D TAKEN IT FROM THE LIBRARY.
BUT WHO'D EVER BELIEVE ME IF I SAID I WANTED TO BORROW IT BECAUSE MY LITTLE SISTER WAS SUCKED INTO IT?

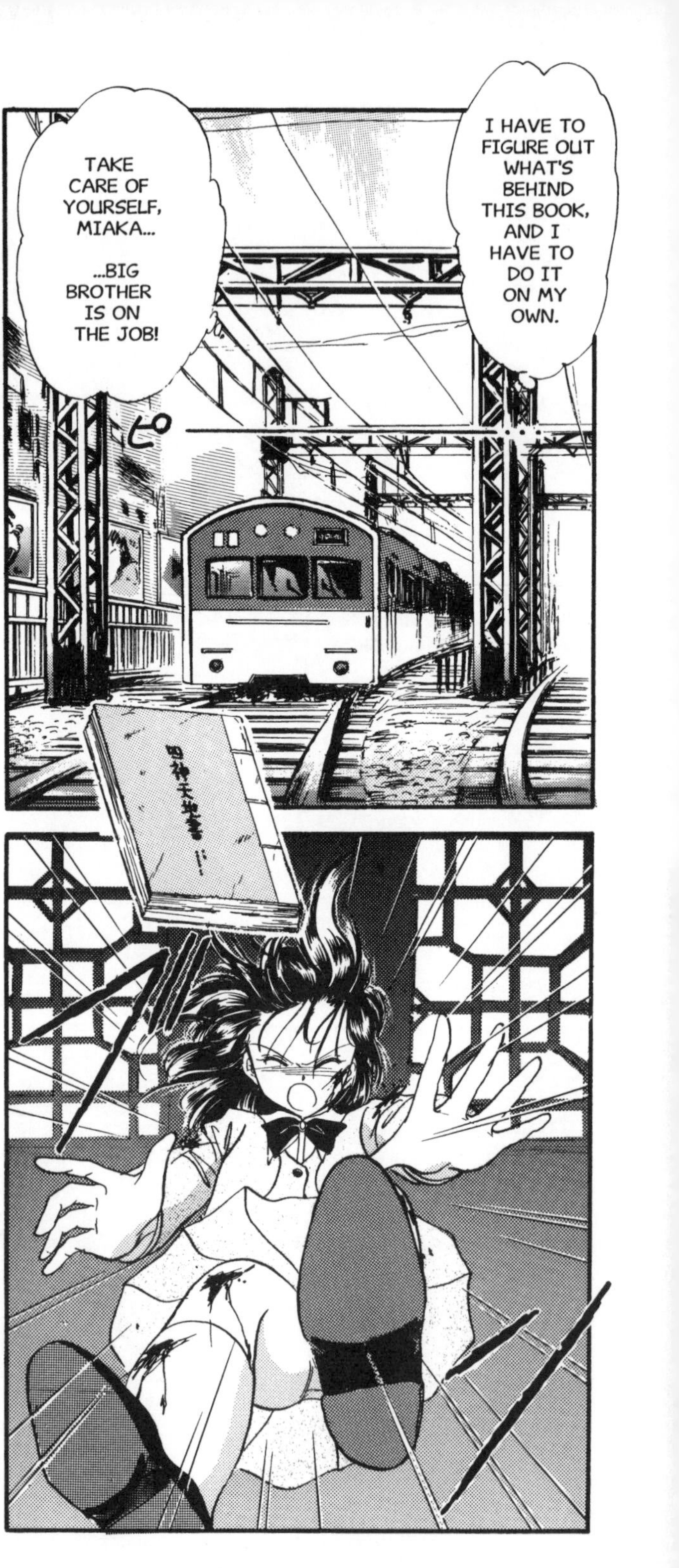
I HAVE TO FIGURE OUT WHAT'S BEHIND THIS BOOK, AND I HAVE TO DO IT ON MY OWN.
TAKE CARE OF YOURSELF, MIAKA... ...BIG BROTHER IS ON THE JOB!
ピ

According to M, the best thing about computer games is the computer graphics. "I look forward to the sequences when you clear each stage." What's to look forward to? Your favorite character stripping! Okay, for women over age 20... If you stroked his ego, Hotohori might be willing to take it all off. But when we realized that most of the players would be guys, our ideas got really out of control. "Fushigi Yūgi Uncensored!" "What if Miaka and Yui were young boys and each of the constellations were different kinds of gorgeous girls!?" "The boys wouldn't be able to resist that!" "Okay, if you finish the entire game the regular way, the special "For Boys" version will appear." Will someone make this game?!

The other thing we thought of was a SD Chichiri doll. When you squeeze it, it says "No da!" I'm sorry for getting so carried away. But these ideas do seem like fun, huh? I'm not serious, of course!

So, now that you've finished chapter 16, it must have been something of a shock. BWA HA HA HA! This was part of my plan all along! I only had the stories through chapter 16 planned at the start, though. Who'da thought this series would have ever gone 15 chapters in the first place?! Now the readers become divided between supporting Miaka or Yui. One thing that made me go "Eh?!" were the letters from readers who wrote in claiming that, "after reading chapter 16, I don't like Miaka because she's a liar!" Please read from chapters 12 to 15 again, okay? Miaka lied to Tamahome in order to find Yui. Are you really reading this story closely? I don't mind it if you've always disliked Miaka. Sometimes people change their minds, and that's interesting in itself. Anyway, I'm taking all your responses into consideration.

By the way, I just remembered, speaking of games (sorry, I'm changing the subject all the time), my game system was disconnected when I moved recently, and I forgot to have it reinstalled!! AARGH! I can't play Final Fantasy! Actually, I don't have any time to play!! Game Boy is more popular at my place anyway. When I'm stuck or need a break, Parodius is good to play. I wish I had time to play more games!!

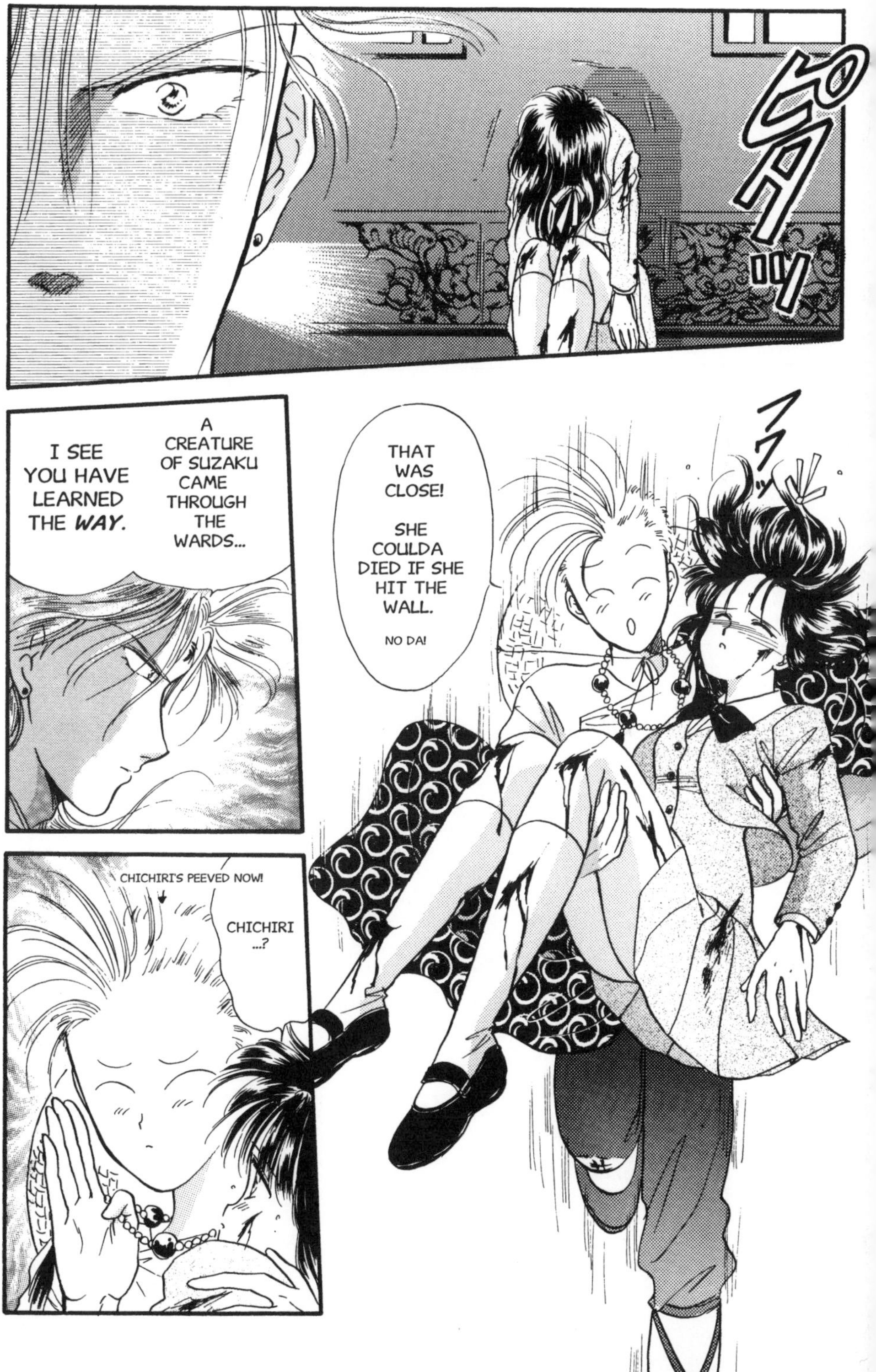

ペタッ
フワッ
THAT WAS CLOSE!
SHE COULDA DIED IF SHE HIT THE WALL.
NO DA!
A CREATURE OF SUZAKU CAME THROUGH THE WARDS...
I SEE YOU HAVE LEARNED THE *WAY*.
CHICHIRI ...?
CHICHIRI'S PEEVED NOW!

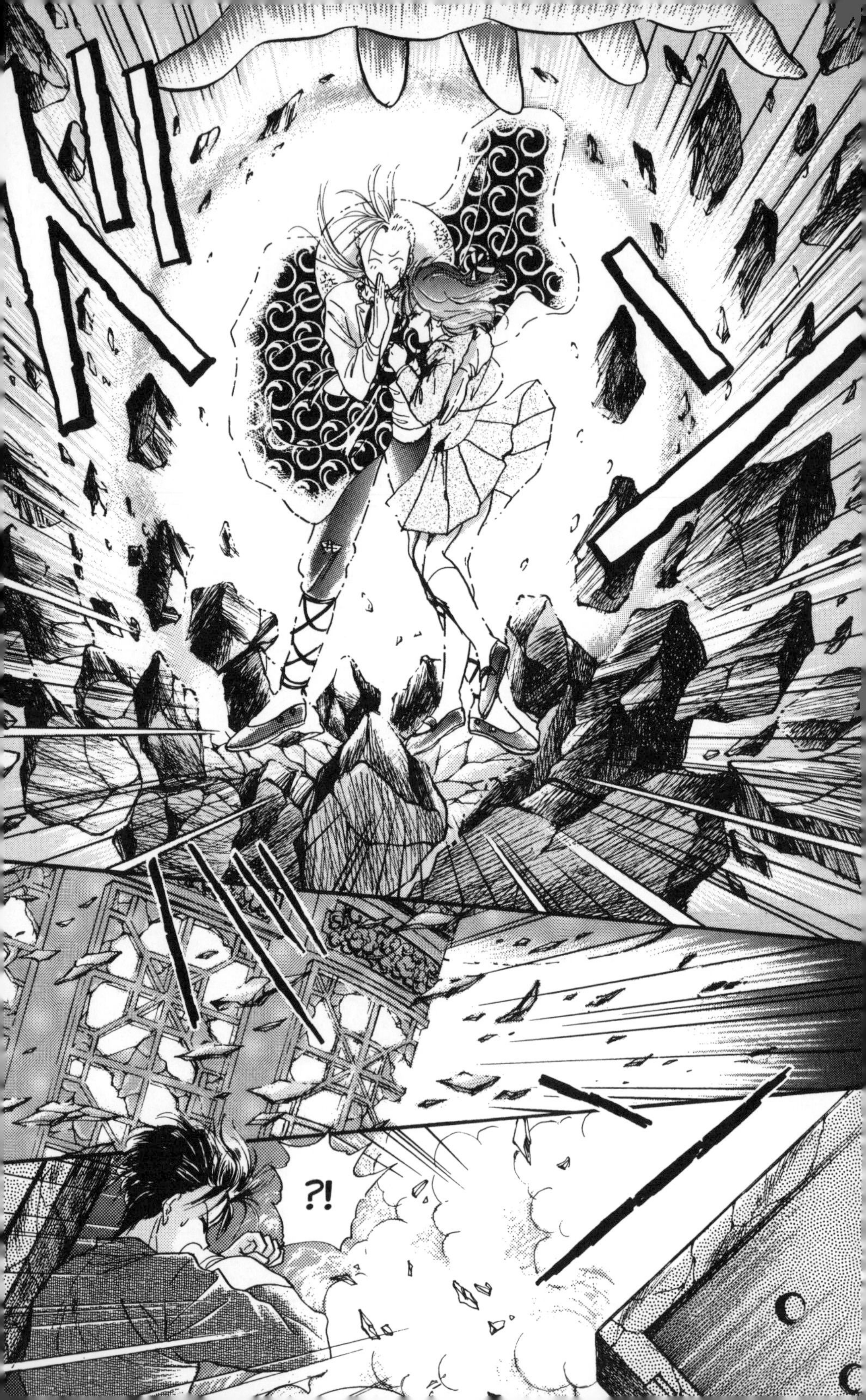
?!

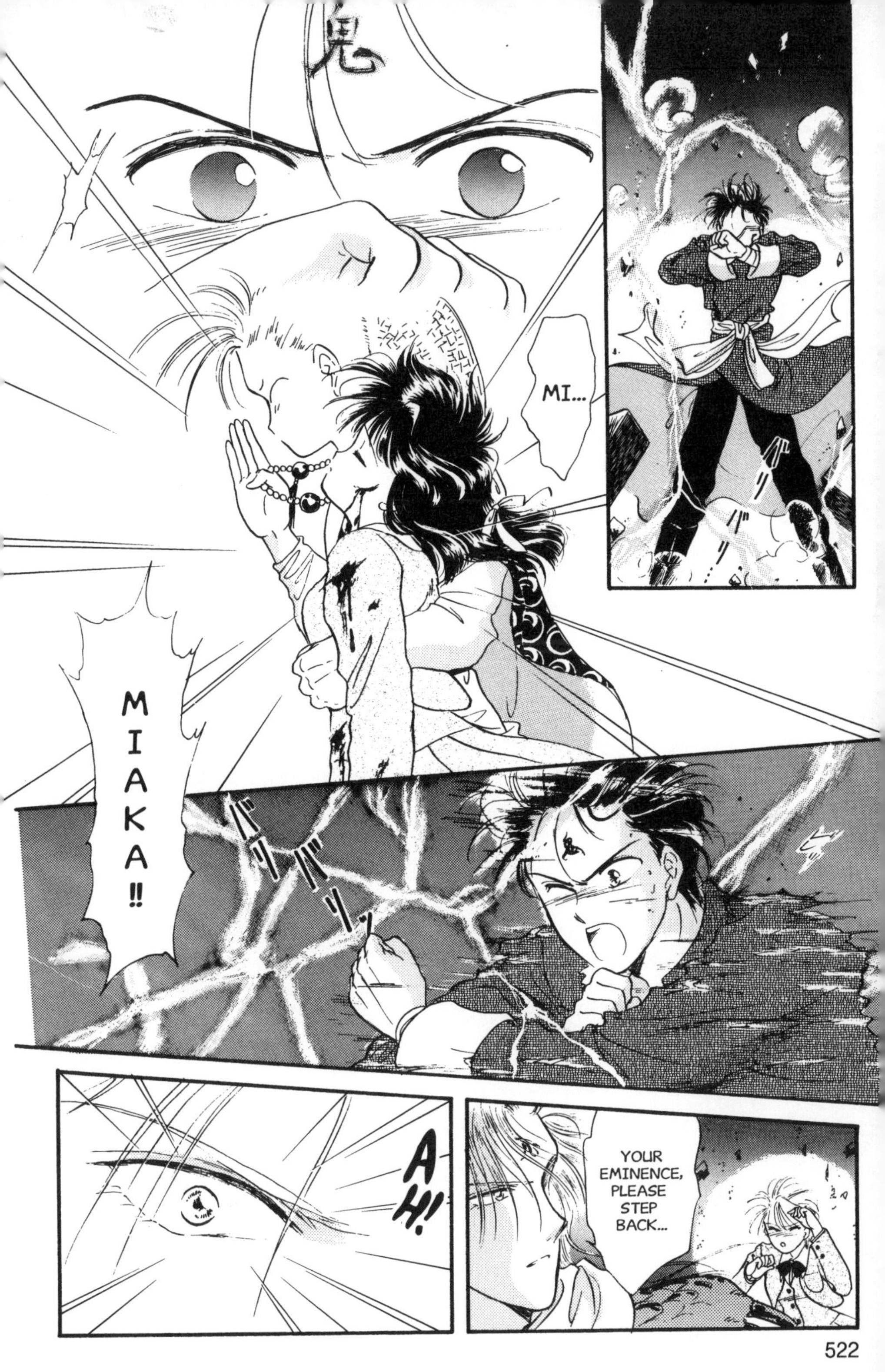
MI...
MIAKA!!
YOUR EMINENCE, PLEASE STEP BACK...
AH!

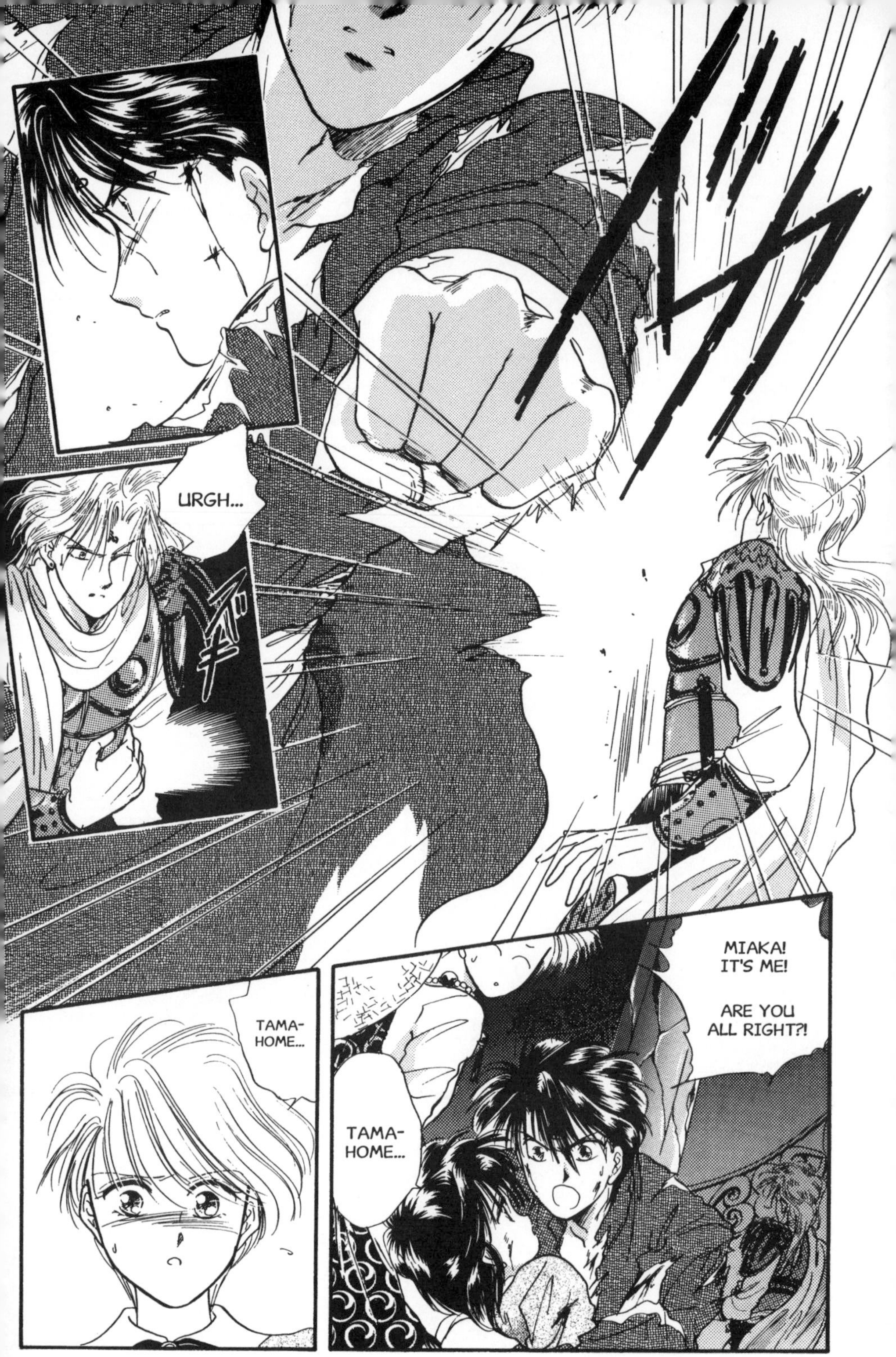
URGH...
MIAKA! IT'S ME!
ARE YOU ALL RIGHT?!
TAMA-HOME...
TAMA-HOME...

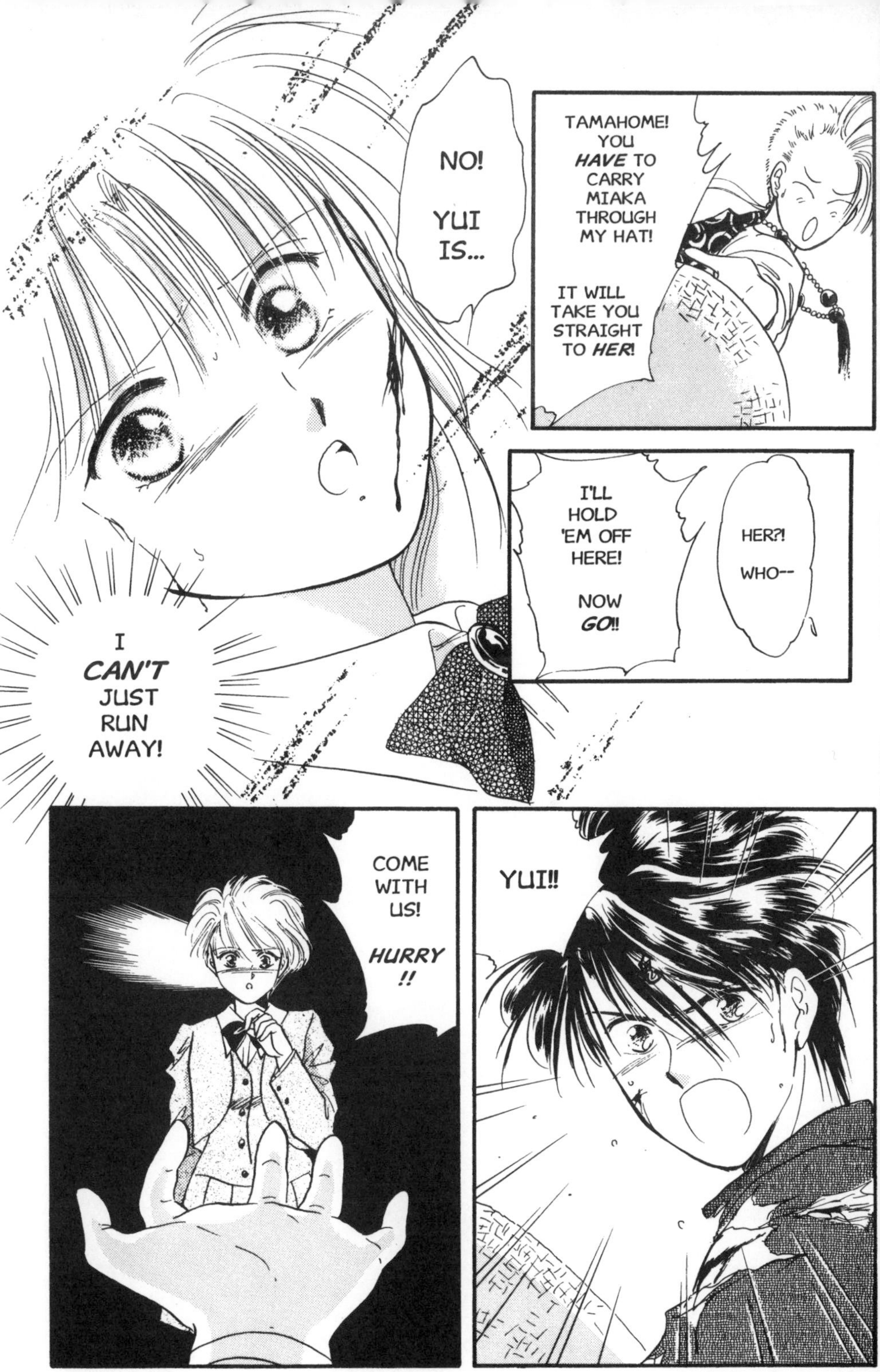
TAMAHOME! YOU HAVE TO CARRY MIAKA THROUGH MY HAT!
IT WILL TAKE YOU STRAIGHT TO HER!
HER?! WHO--
I'LL HOLD 'EM OFF HERE! NOW GO!!
NO! YUI IS...
I CAN'T JUST RUN AWAY!
YUI!!
COME WITH US!
HURRY!!

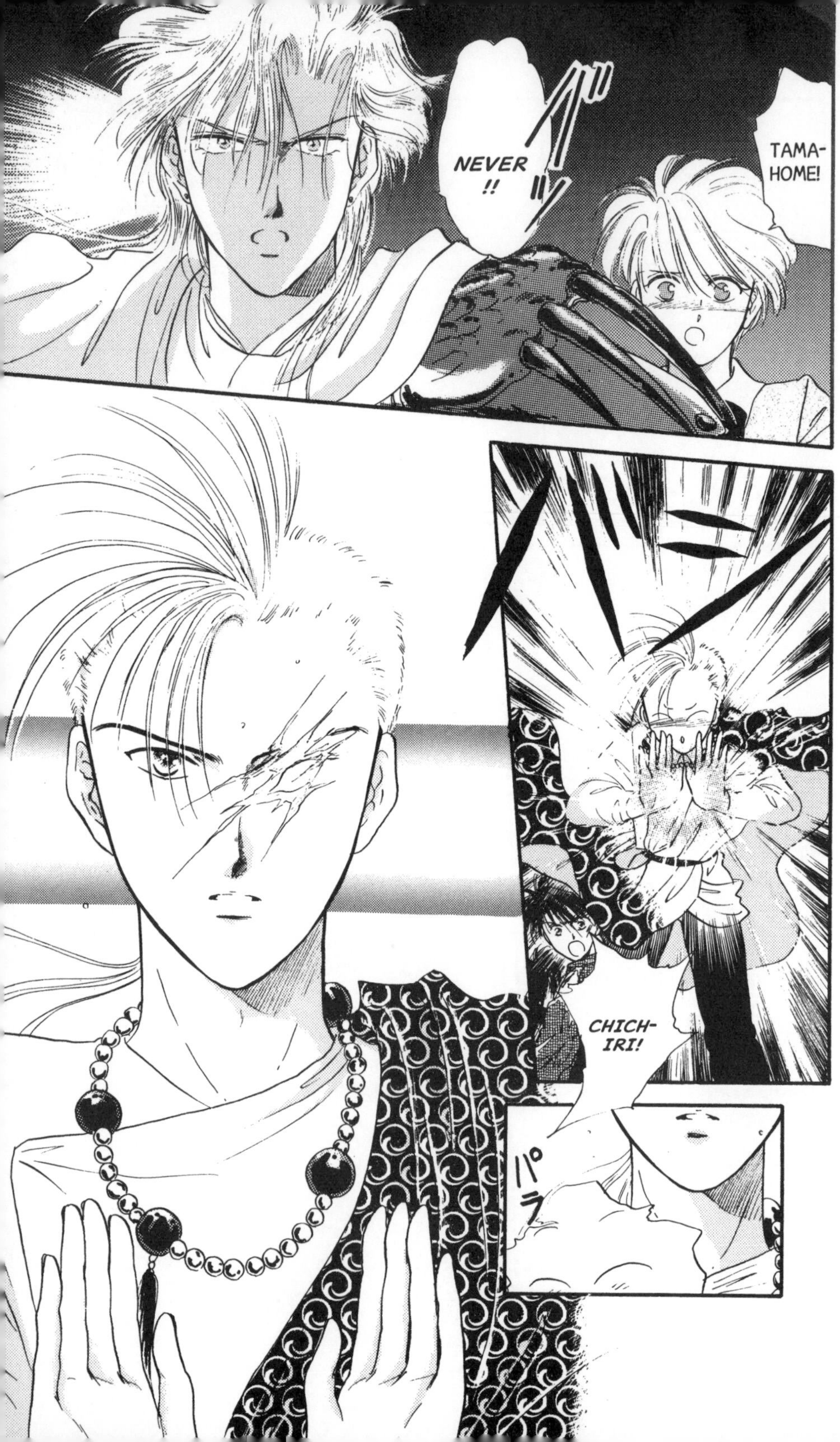

TAMA-HOME!
NEVER !!
CHICH-IRI!
パラ

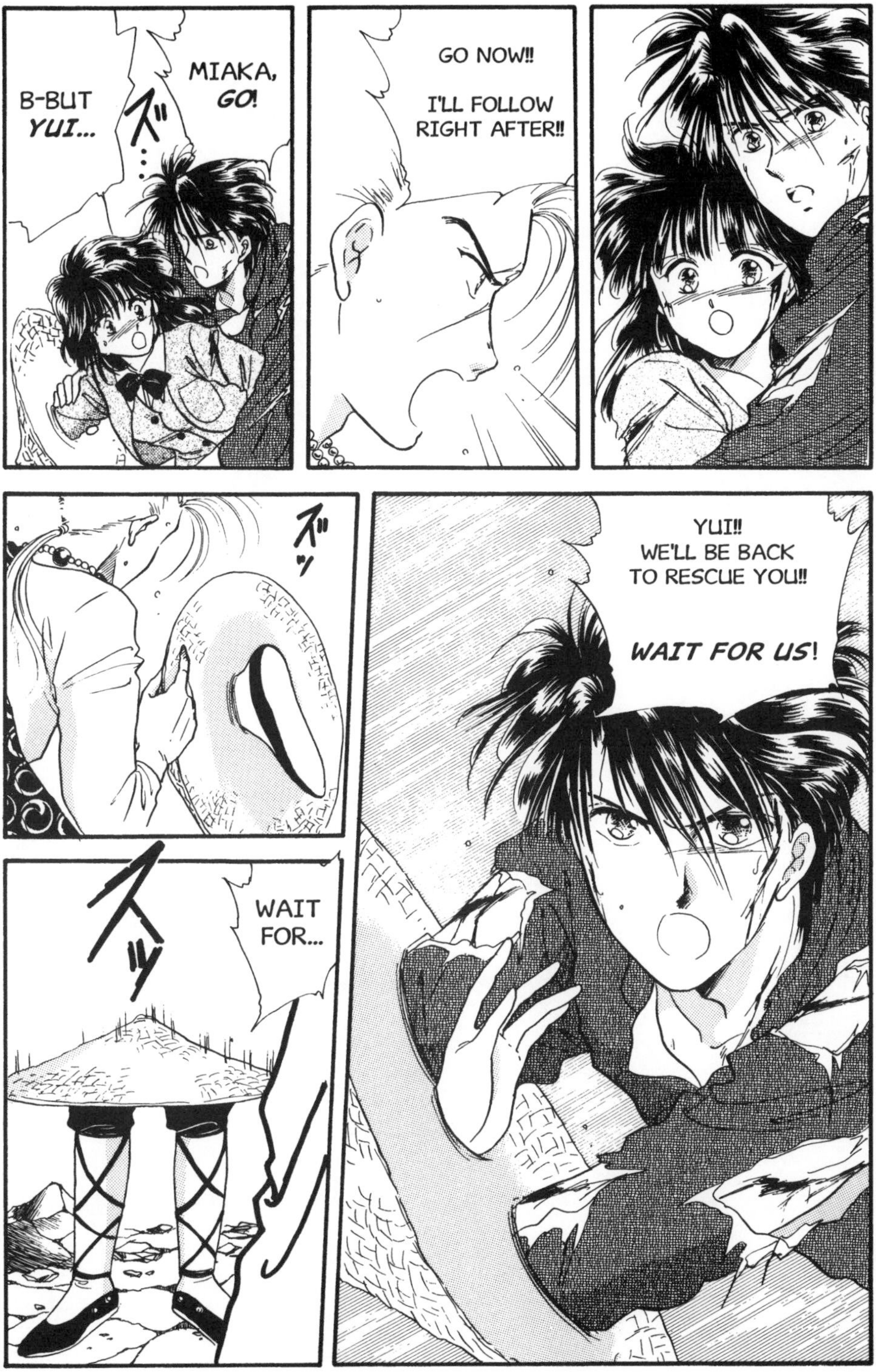
GO NOW!!
I'LL FOLLOW RIGHT AFTER!!
MIAKA, *GO*!
ズ
B-BUT *YUI*...
YUI!! WE'LL BE BACK TO RESCUE YOU!!
WAIT FOR US!
ズッ
スッ
WAIT FOR...

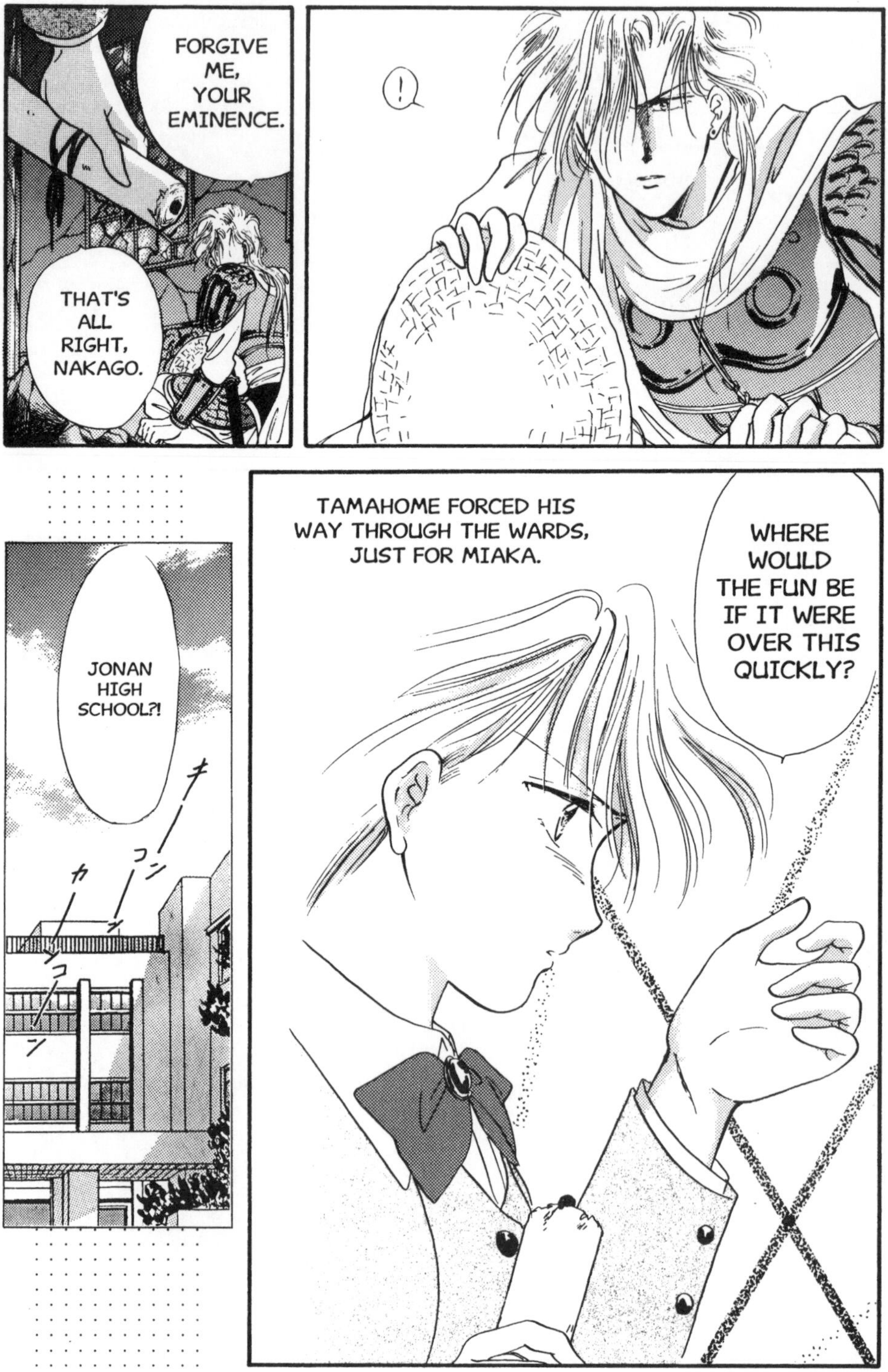
!
FORGIVE ME, YOUR EMINENCE.
THAT'S ALL RIGHT, NAKAGO.
WHERE WOULD THE FUN BE IF IT WERE OVER THIS QUICKLY?
TAMAHOME FORCED HIS WAY THROUGH THE WARDS, JUST FOR MIAKA.
JONAN HIGH SCHOOL?!
キーンコーン
カーンコーン

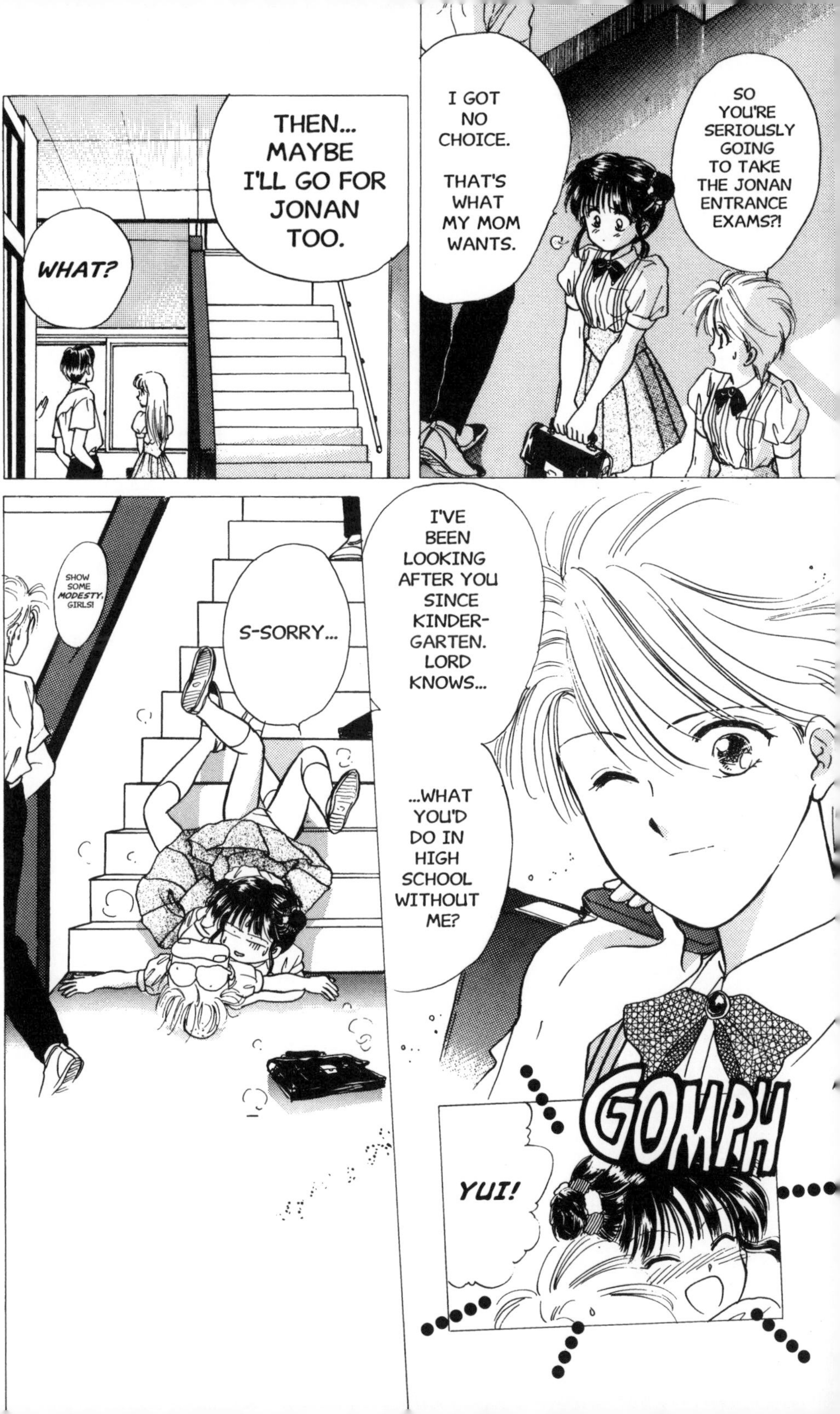
SO YOU'RE SERIOUSLY GOING TO TAKE THE JONAN ENTRANCE EXAMS?!
I GOT NO CHOICE.
THAT'S WHAT MY MOM WANTS.
THEN... MAYBE I'LL GO FOR JONAN TOO.
WHAT?
I'VE BEEN LOOKING AFTER YOU SINCE KINDER-GARTEN. LORD KNOWS...
...WHAT YOU'D DO IN HIGH SCHOOL WITHOUT ME?
GOMPH
YUI!
S-SORRY...
SHOW SOME MODESTY, GIRLS!

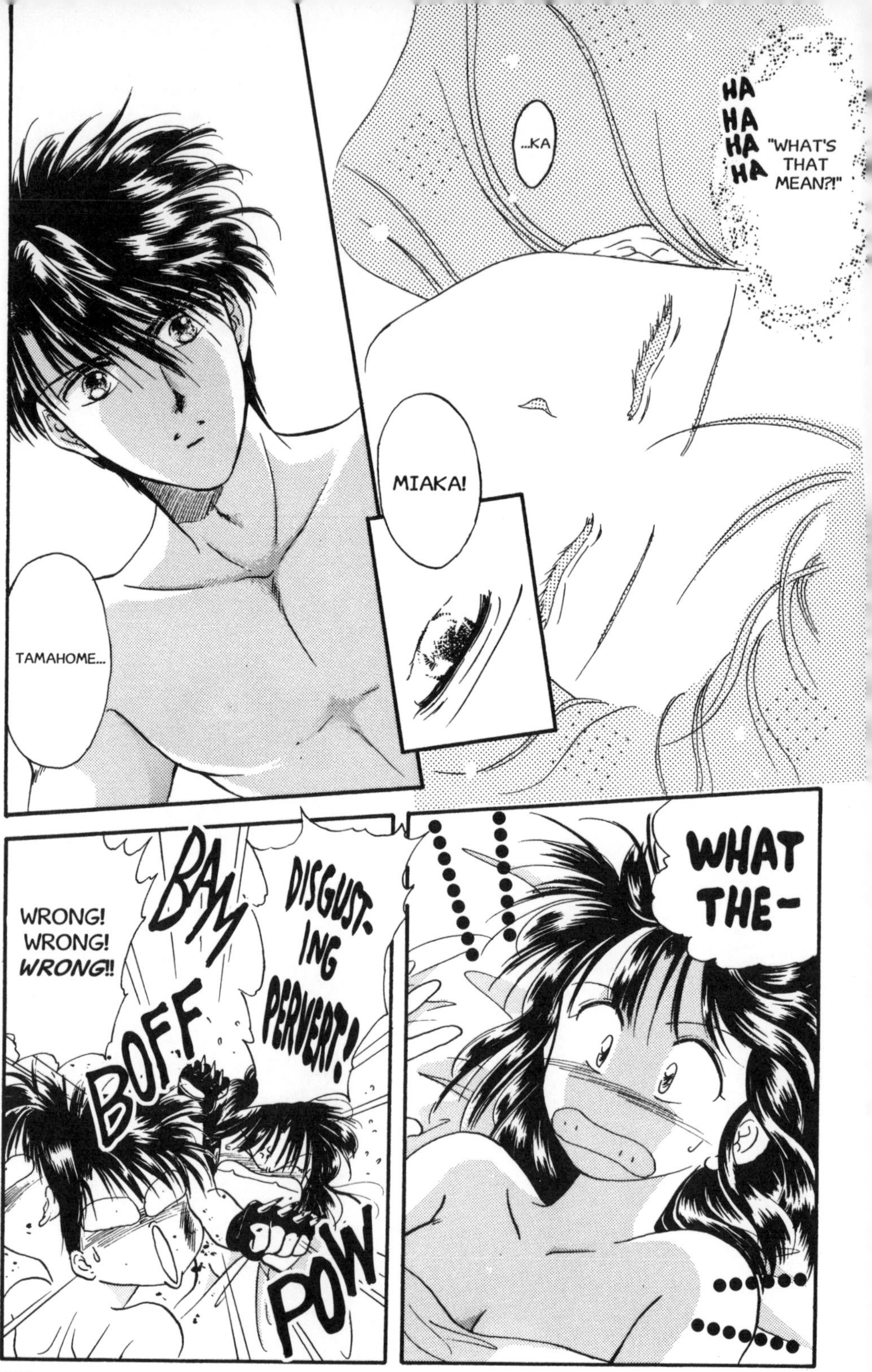
HA HA HA HA
"WHAT'S THAT MEAN?!"
...KA
MIAKA!
TAMAHOME...
WHAT THE-
......
......
......
DISGUST-ING PERVERT!!
BAM
WRONG! WRONG! *WRONG!!*
BOFF
POW

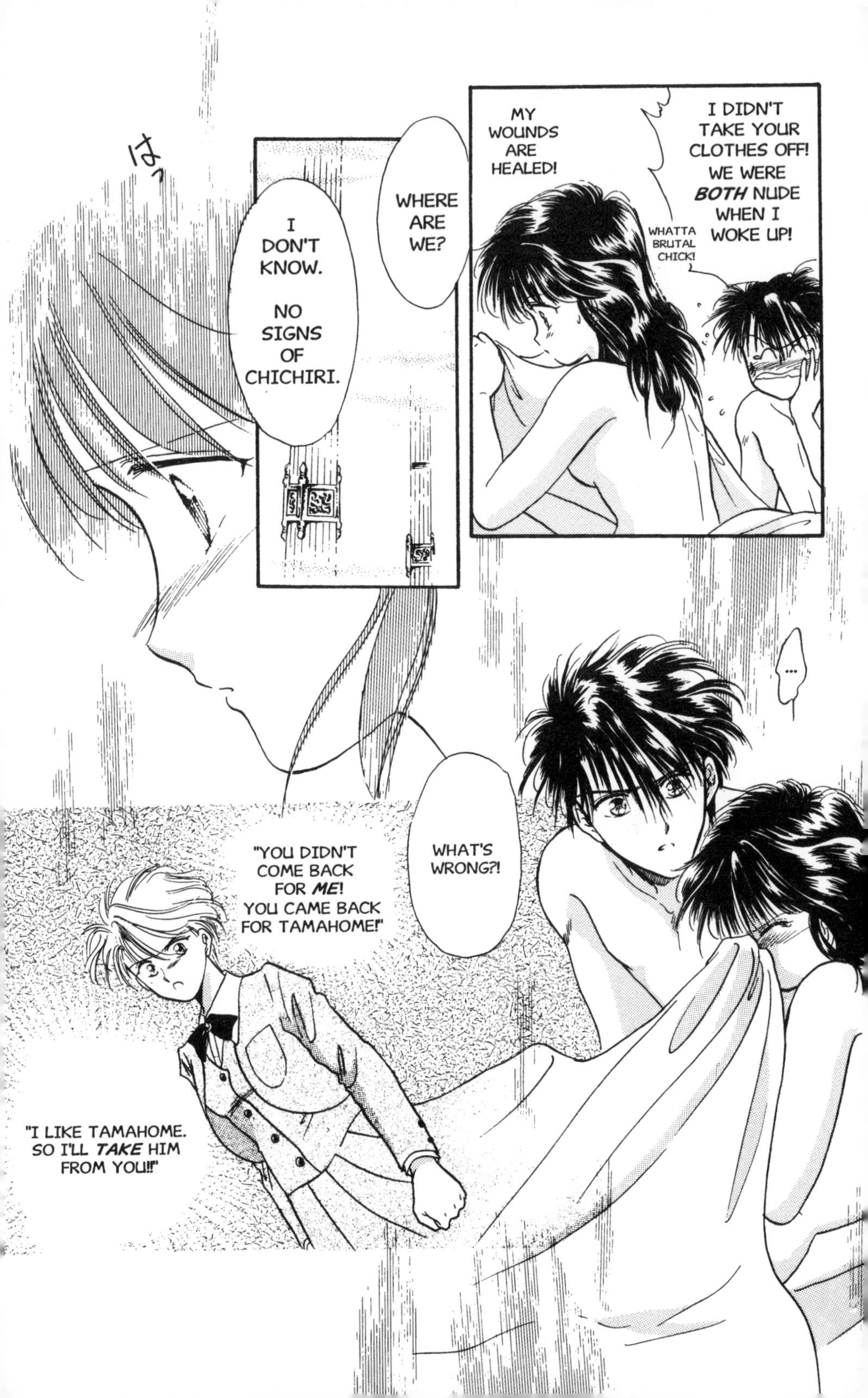
I DIDN'T TAKE YOUR CLOTHES OFF! WE WERE BOTH NUDE WHEN I WOKE UP!
WHATTA BRUTAL CHICK!
MY WOUNDS ARE HEALED!
WHERE ARE WE?
I DON'T KNOW. NO SIGNS OF CHICHIRI.
はっ
...
WHAT'S WRONG?!
"YOU DIDN'T COME BACK FOR ME! YOU CAME BACK FOR TAMAHOME!"
"I LIKE TAMAHOME. SO I'LL TAKE HIM FROM YOU!!"

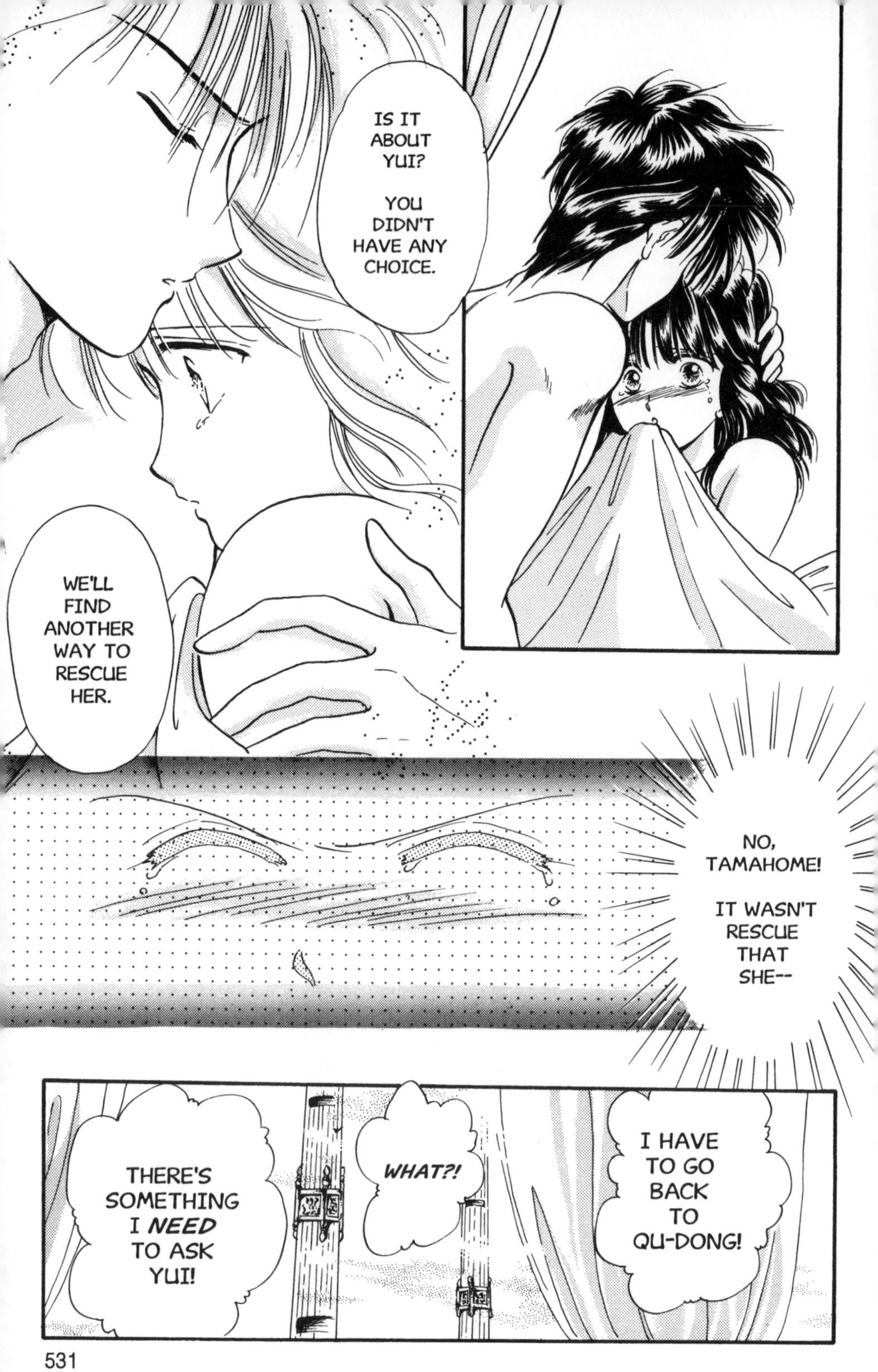
IS IT ABOUT YUI? YOU DIDN'T HAVE ANY CHOICE.
WE'LL FIND ANOTHER WAY TO RESCUE HER.
NO, TAMAHOME! IT WASN'T RESCUE THAT SHE--
I HAVE TO GO BACK TO QU-DONG!
WHAT?!
THERE'S SOMETHING I ***NEED*** TO ASK YUI!

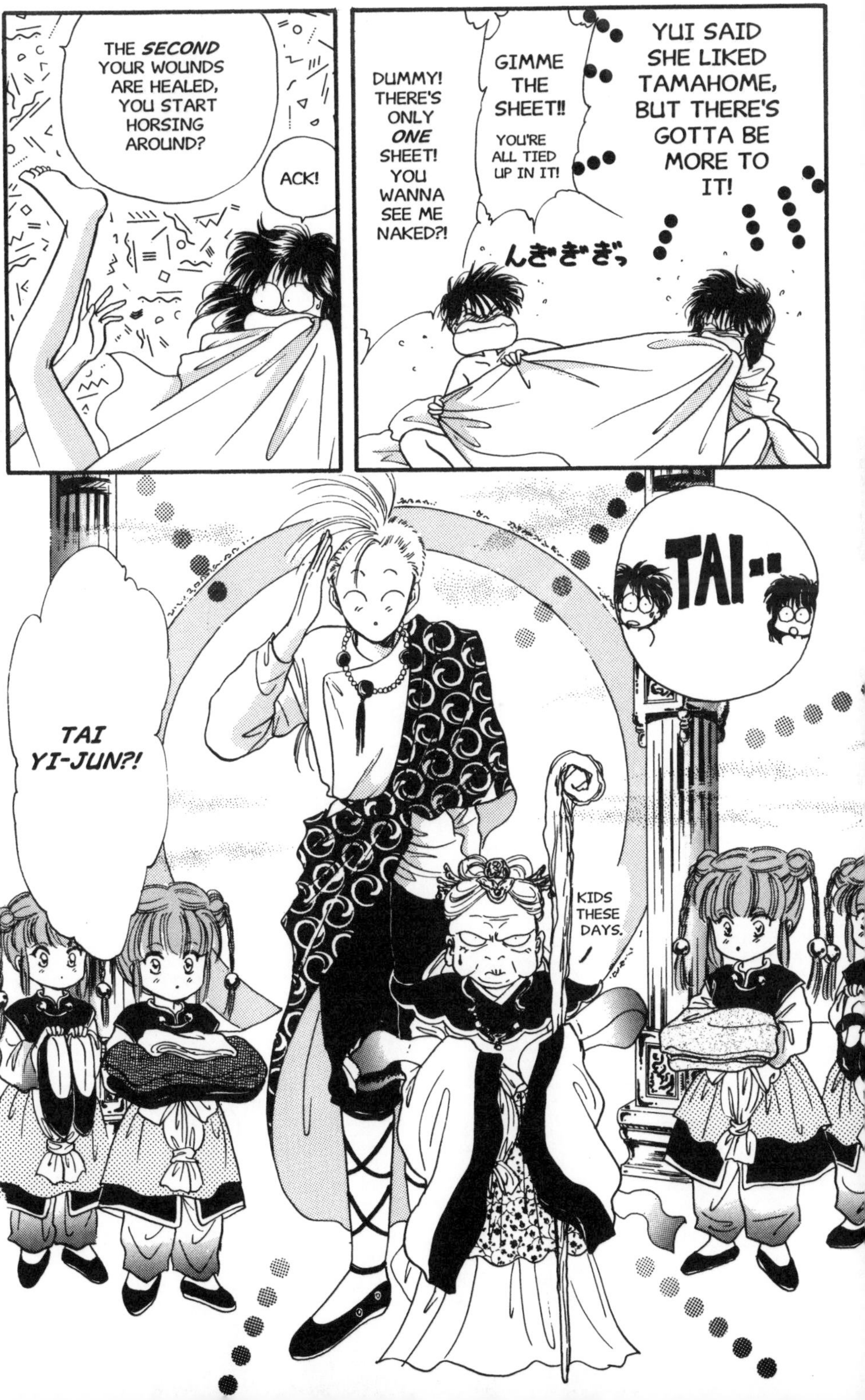
YUI SAID SHE LIKED TAMAHOME, BUT THERE'S GOTTA BE MORE TO IT!
GIMME THE SHEET!!
YOU'RE ALL TIED UP IN IT!
DUMMY! THERE'S ONLY *ONE* SHEET! YOU WANNA SEE ME NAKED?!
んぎぎぎっ
THE *SECOND* YOUR WOUNDS ARE HEALED, YOU START HORSING AROUND?
ACK!
TAI-!!
TAI YI-JUN?!
KIDS THESE DAYS.

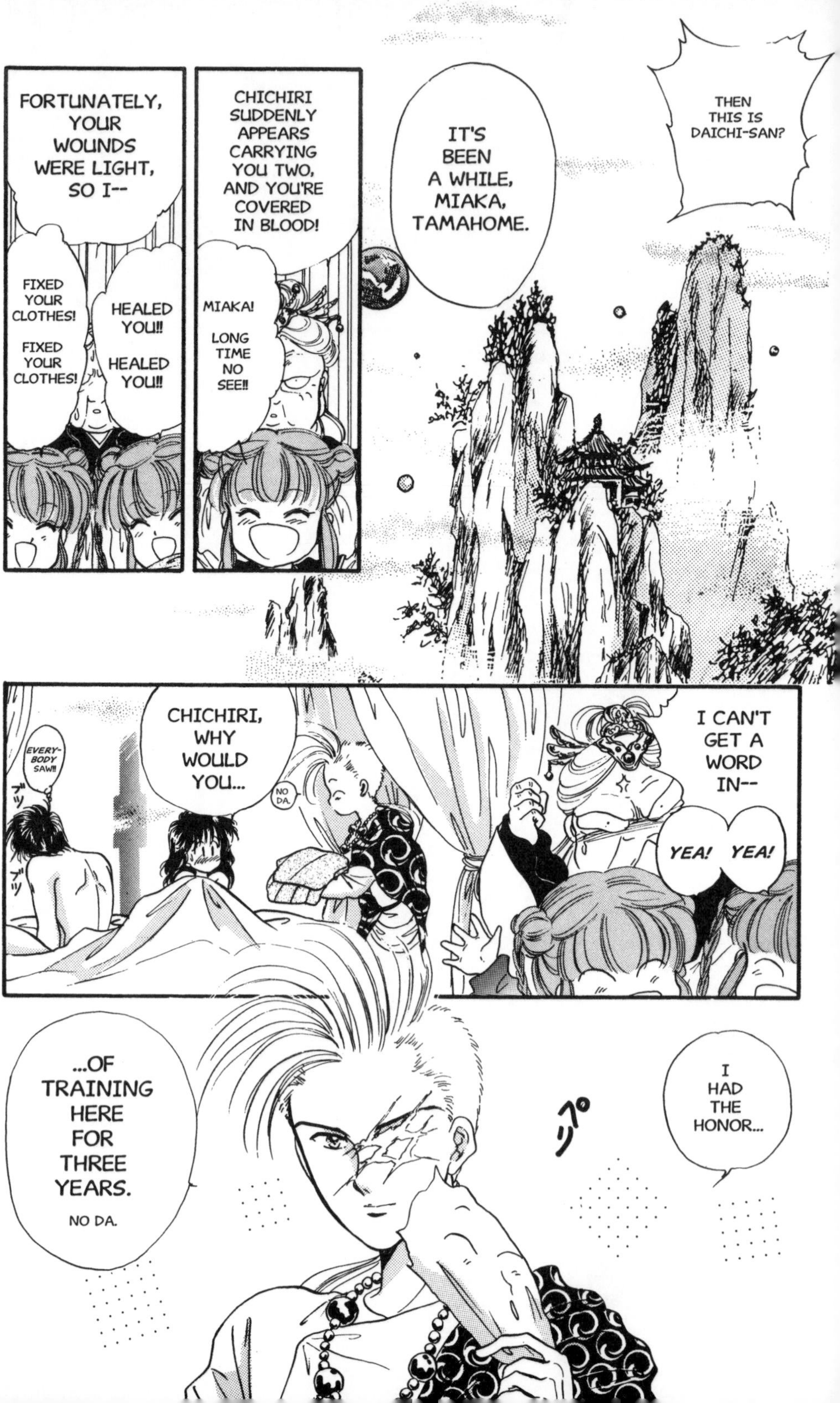
THEN THIS IS DAICHI-SAN?
IT'S BEEN A WHILE, MIAKA, TAMAHOME.
CHICHIRI SUDDENLY APPEARS CARRYING YOU TWO, AND YOU'RE COVERED IN BLOOD!
MIAKA! LONG TIME NO SEE!!
FORTUNATELY, YOUR WOUNDS WERE LIGHT, SO I--
HEALED YOU!! HEALED YOU!!
FIXED YOUR CLOTHES! FIXED YOUR CLOTHES!
I CAN'T GET A WORD IN--
YEA! YEA!
NO DA.
CHICHIRI, WHY WOULD YOU...
EVERY-BODY SAW!!
I HAD THE HONOR...
...OF TRAINING HERE FOR THREE YEARS. NO DA.

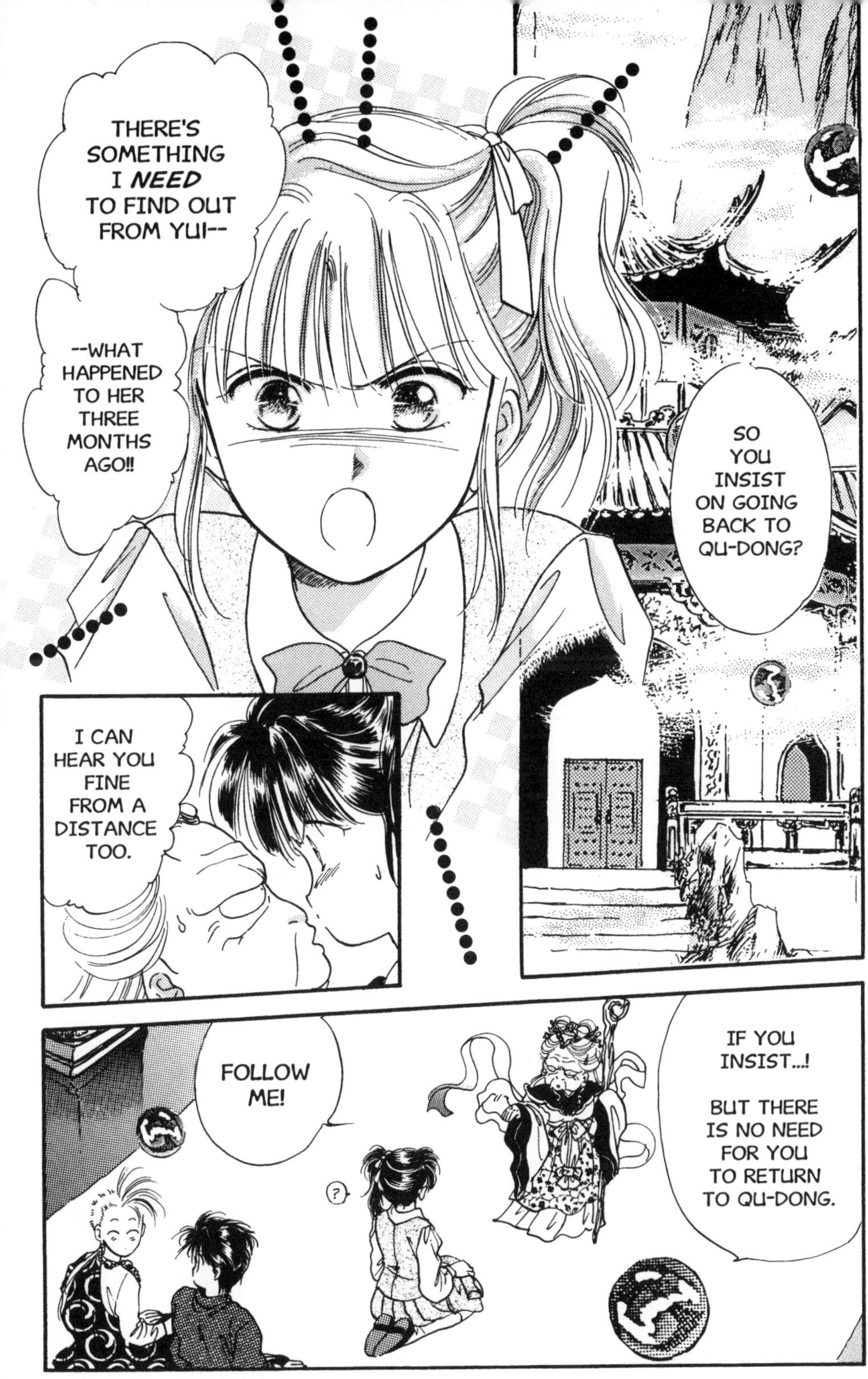
SO YOU INSIST ON GOING BACK TO QU-DONG?
THERE'S SOMETHING I *NEED* TO FIND OUT FROM YUI--
--WHAT HAPPENED TO HER THREE MONTHS AGO!!
I CAN HEAR YOU FINE FROM A DISTANCE TOO.
IF YOU INSIST...!
BUT THERE IS NO NEED FOR YOU TO RETURN TO QU-DONG.
FOLLOW ME!
?

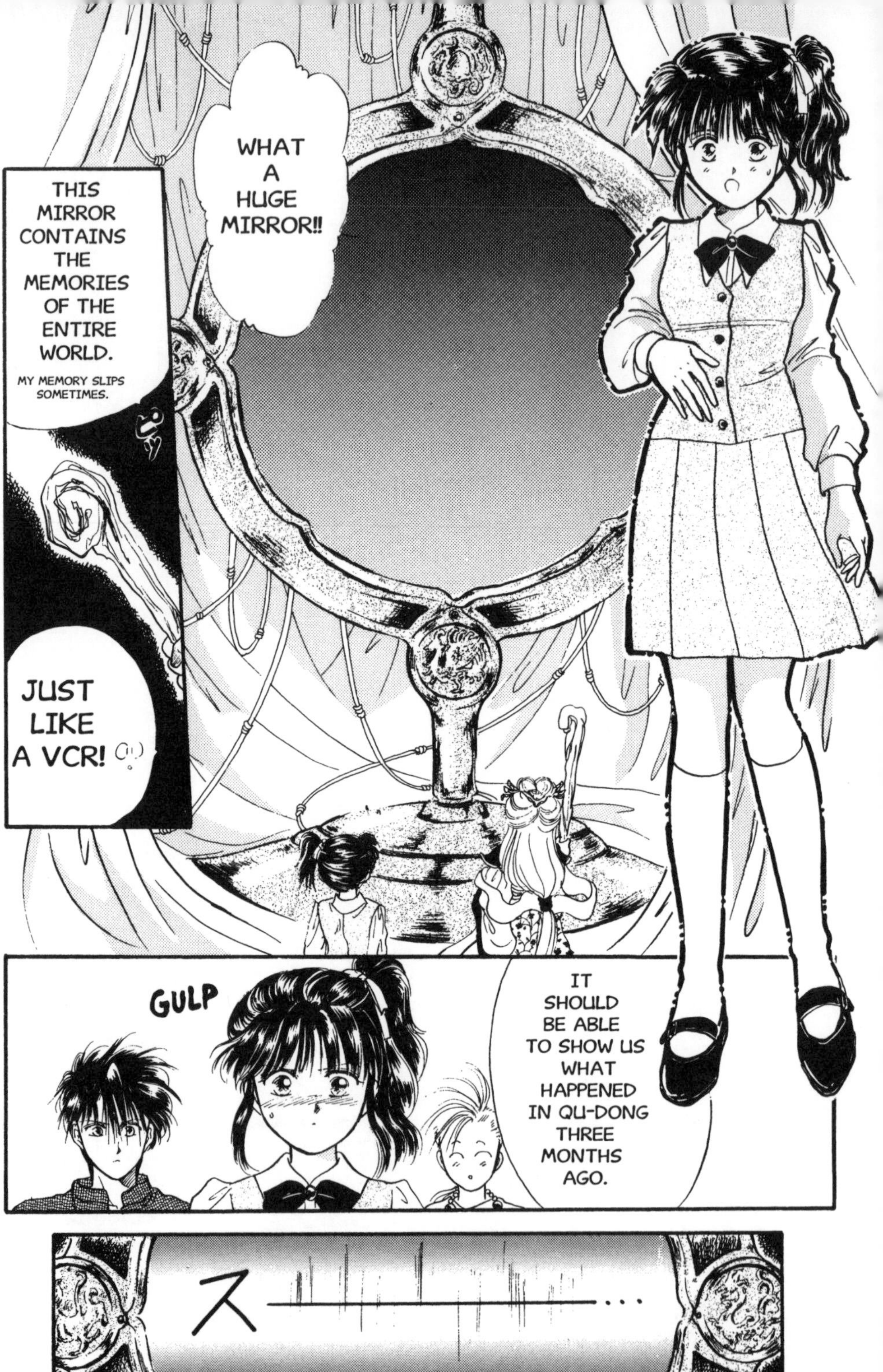
WHAT A HUGE MIRROR!!
THIS MIRROR CONTAINS THE MEMORIES OF THE ENTIRE WORLD.
MY MEMORY SLIPS SOMETIMES.
JUST LIKE A VCR!
IT SHOULD BE ABLE TO SHOW US WHAT HAPPENED IN QU-DONG THREE MONTHS AGO.
GULP
ス———…

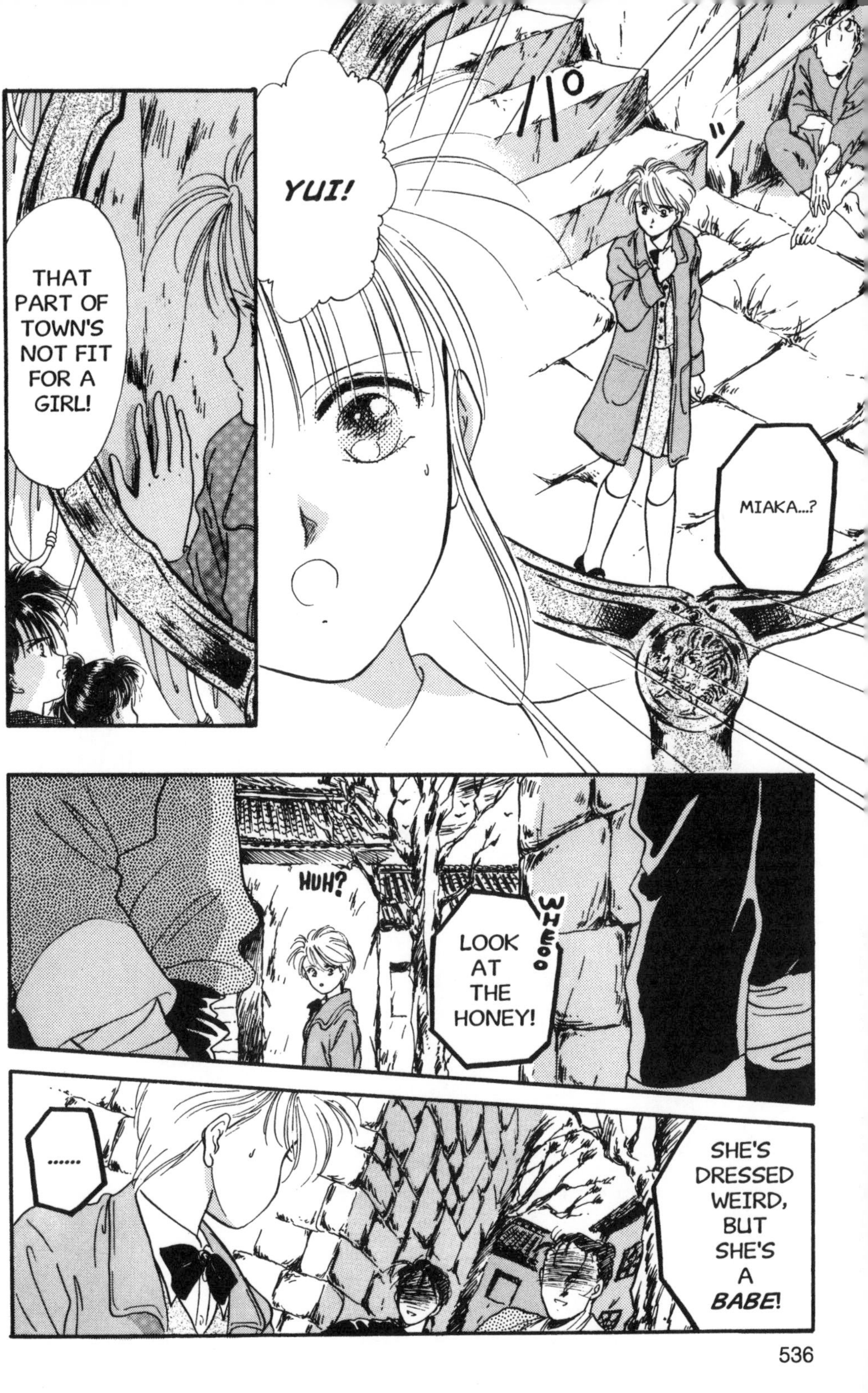
MIAKA...?
YUI!
THAT PART OF TOWN'S NOT FIT FOR A GIRL!
WHEEOO
LOOK AT THE HONEY!
HUH?
SHE'S DRESSED WEIRD, BUT SHE'S A *BABE*!
......

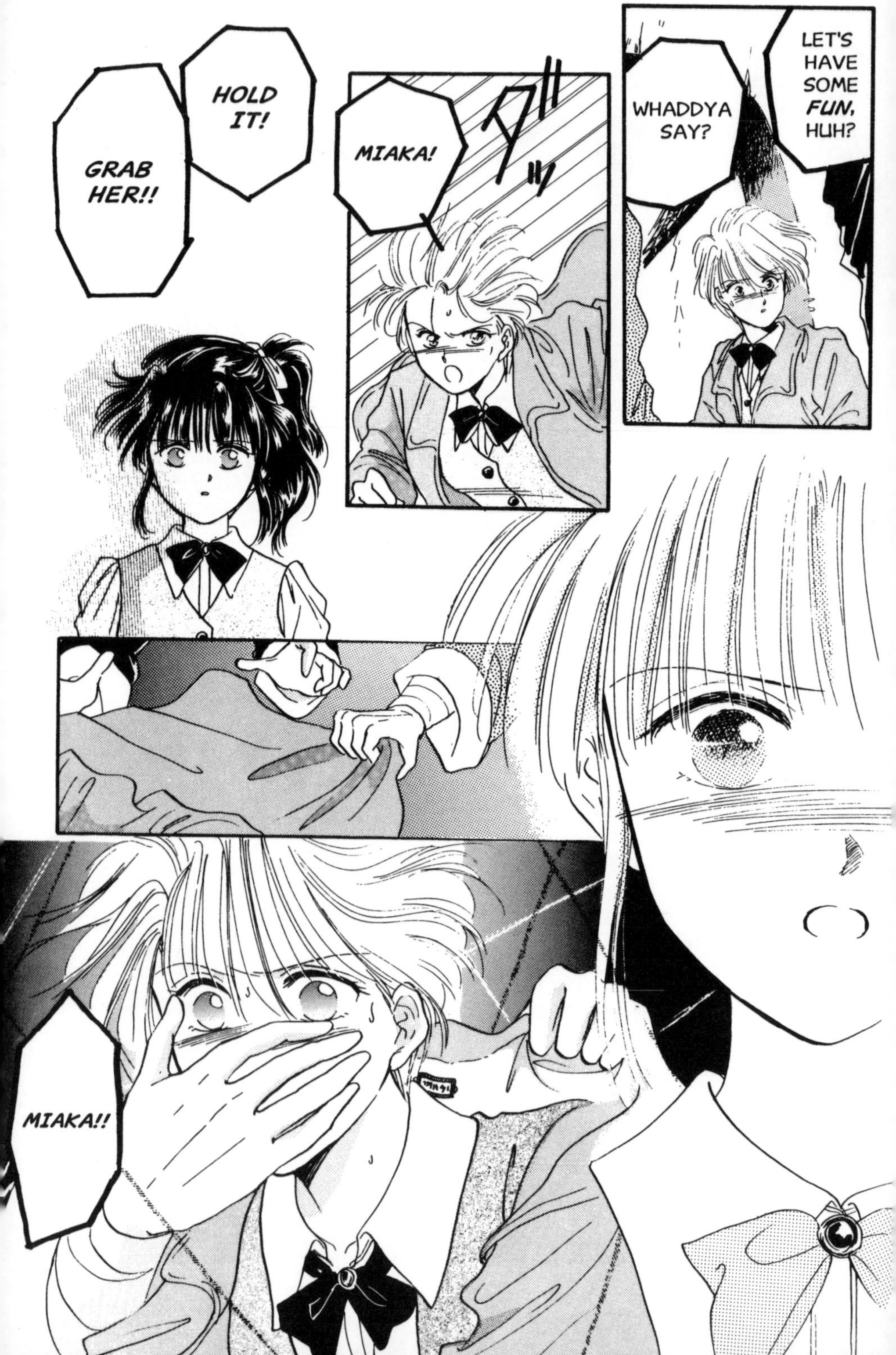
LET'S HAVE SOME *FUN*, HUH?
WHADDYA SAY?
ダッ
MIAKA!
HOLD IT!
GRAB HER!!
MIAKA!!

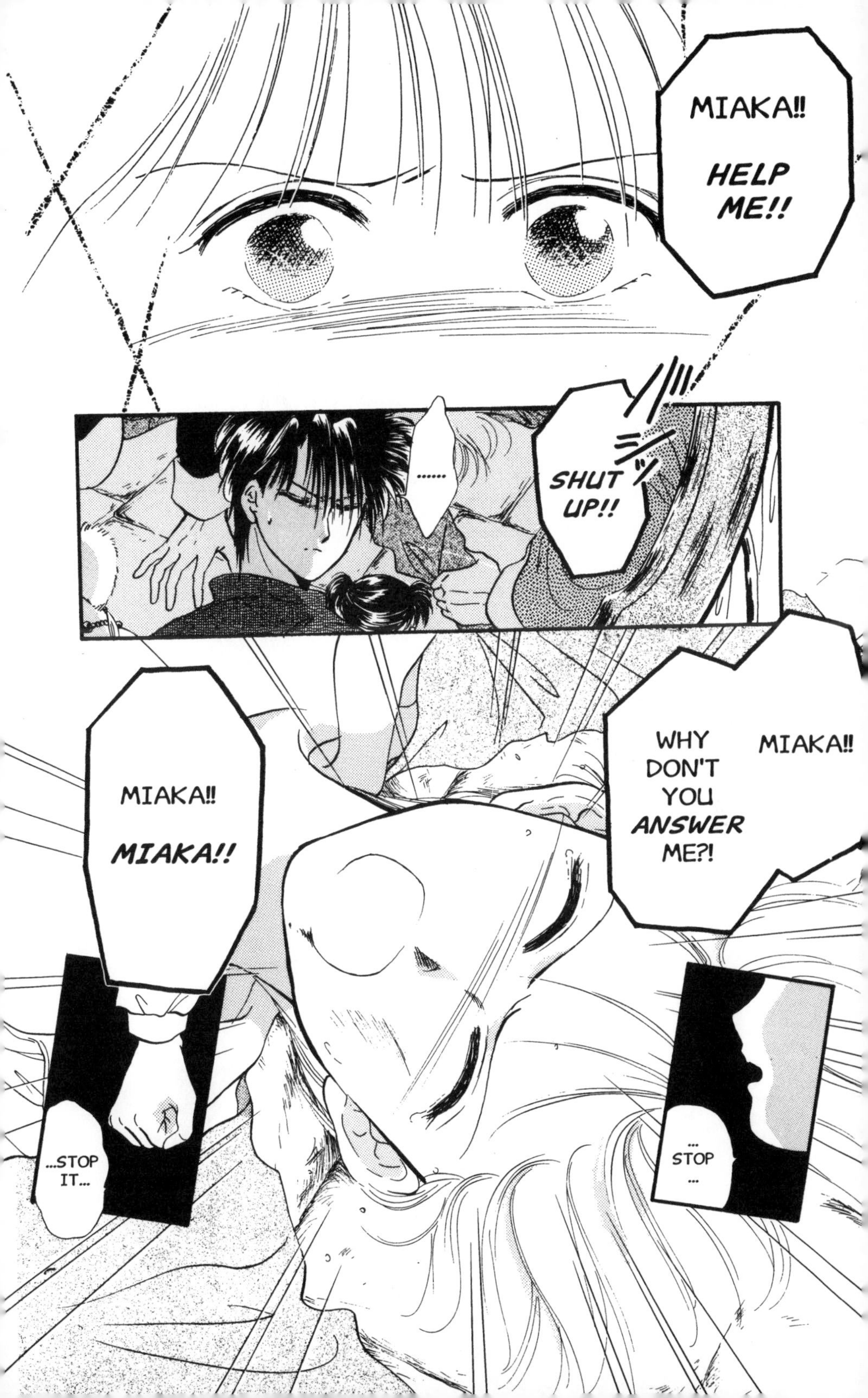
MIAKA!! HELP ME!!
SHUT UP!!
......
MIAKA!!
WHY DON'T YOU ANSWER ME?!
MIAKA!! MIAKA!!
...STOP...
...STOP IT...

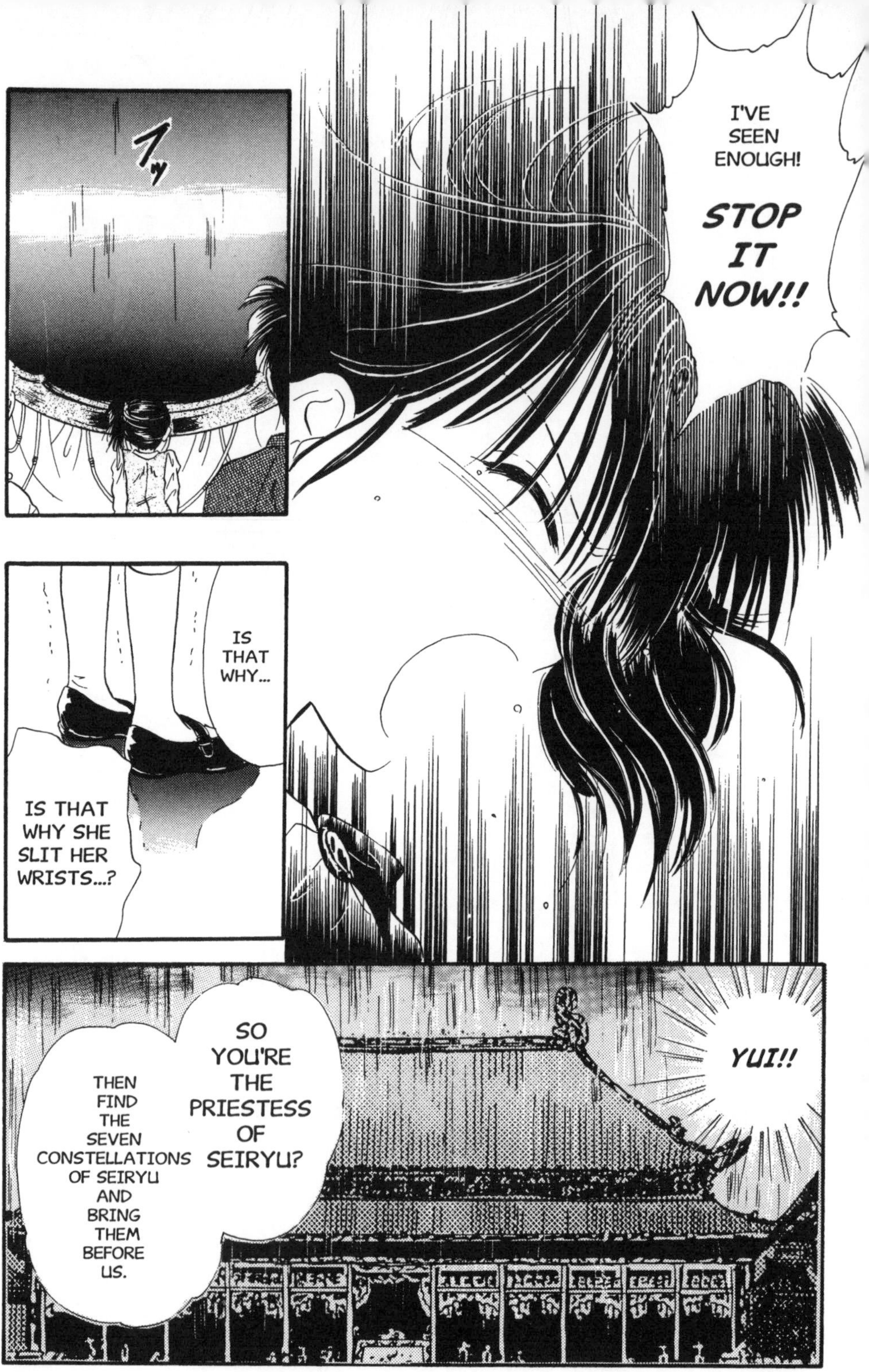
I'VE SEEN ENOUGH!
STOP IT NOW!!
IS THAT WHY...
IS THAT WHY SHE SLIT HER WRISTS...?
YUI!!
SO YOU'RE THE PRIESTESS OF SEIRYU?
THEN FIND THE SEVEN CONSTELLATIONS OF SEIRYU AND BRING THEM BEFORE US.

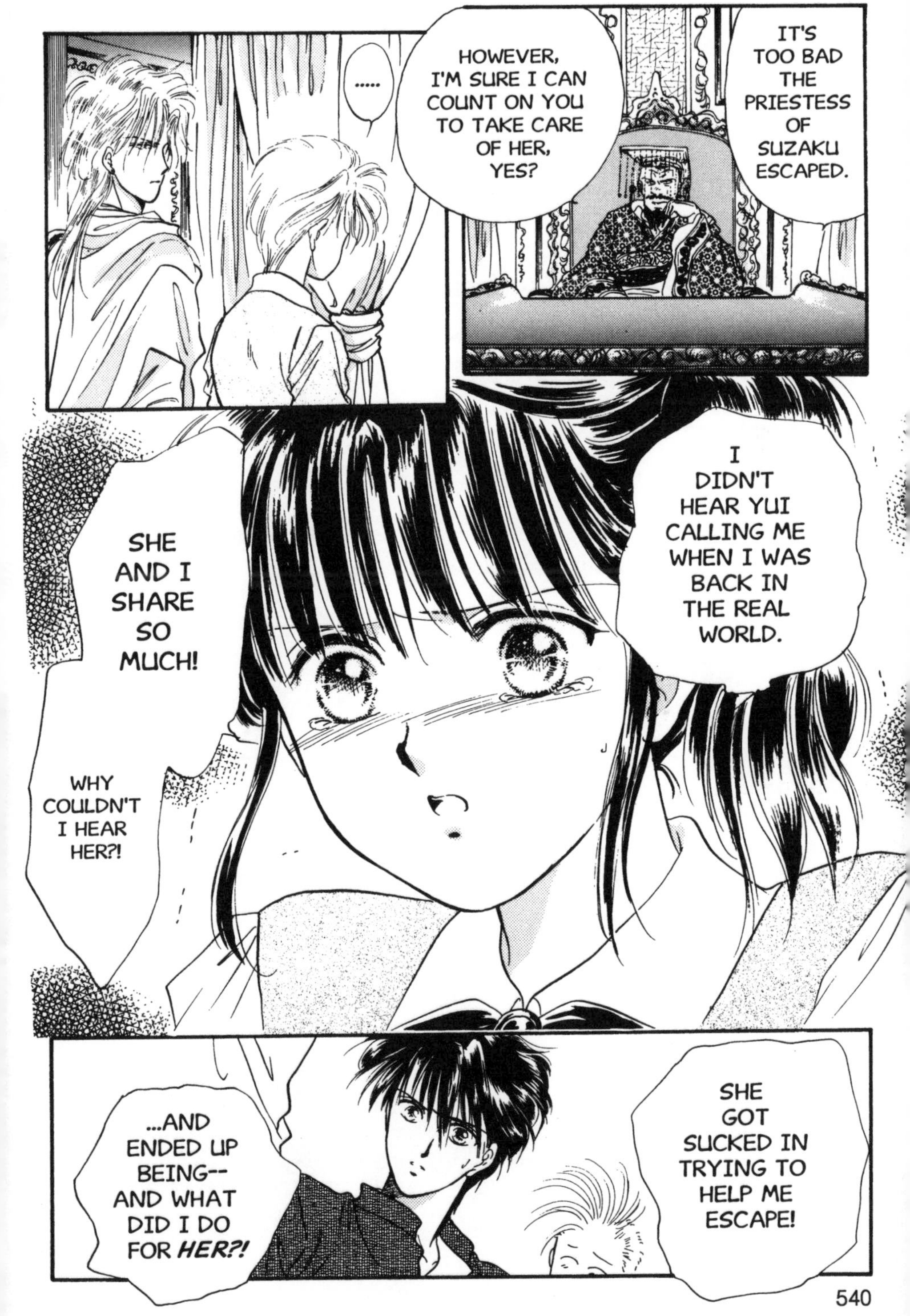
IT'S TOO BAD THE PRIESTESS OF SUZAKU ESCAPED.
HOWEVER, I'M SURE I CAN COUNT ON YOU TO TAKE CARE OF HER, YES?
.....
I DIDN'T HEAR YUI CALLING ME WHEN I WAS BACK IN THE REAL WORLD.
SHE AND I SHARE SO MUCH!
WHY COULDN'T I HEAR HER?!
SHE GOT SUCKED IN TRYING TO HELP ME ESCAPE!
...AND ENDED UP BEING-- AND WHAT DID I DO FOR *HER?!*

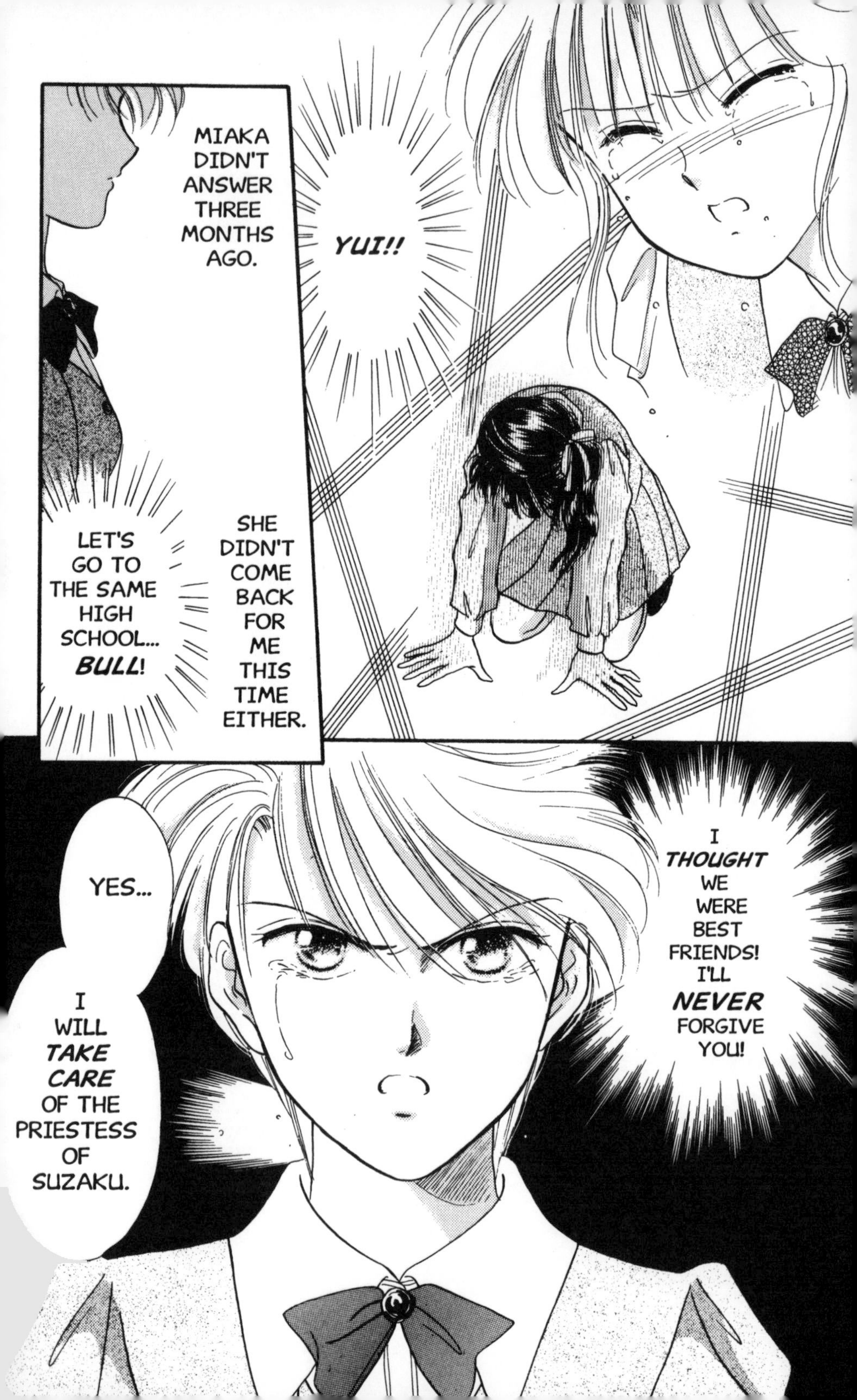
YUI!!
MIAKA DIDN'T ANSWER THREE MONTHS AGO.
SHE DIDN'T COME BACK FOR ME THIS TIME EITHER.
LET'S GO TO THE SAME HIGH SCHOOL... BULL!
I THOUGHT WE WERE BEST FRIENDS! I'LL NEVER FORGIVE YOU!
YES...
I WILL TAKE CARE OF THE PRIESTESS OF SUZAKU.

BACK BY POPULAR DEMAND
PARDON THE PARODY NEWLY RETITLED AS

FUSHIGI AKUGI ふしぎ悪戯
THE MALICIOUS PLAY

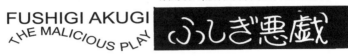

WITH A SLIGHT CHANGE OF WORDING, YOU CAN MAKE THIS INTO SOMETHING YOU'LL FOREVER REGRET!
C'MON, KIDS! TRY THIS AT HOME! (TRY WHAT!?)

......
?
I COULDA SWORN SOMETHING JUST BRUSHED BY ME.
SKR CHA
SKR CHA

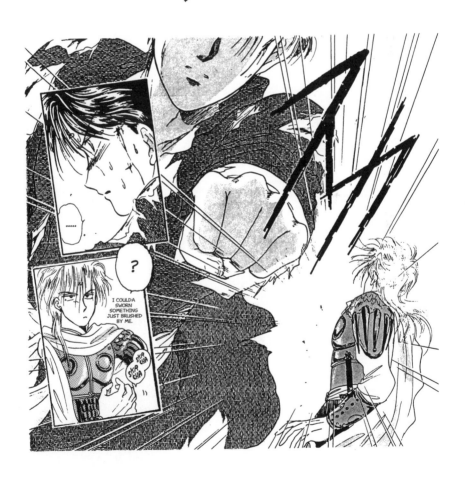

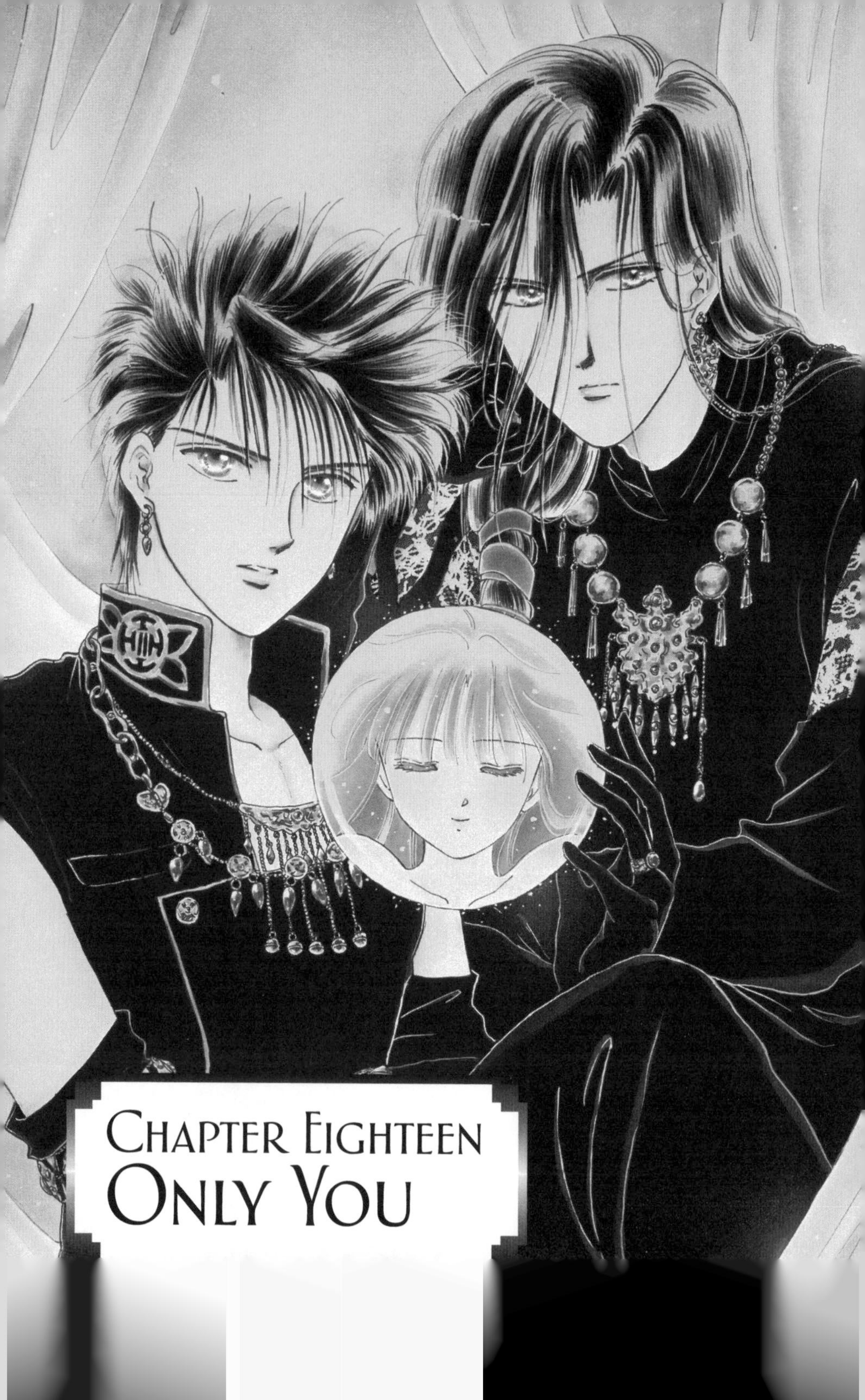
CHAPTER EIGHTEEN
ONLY YOU

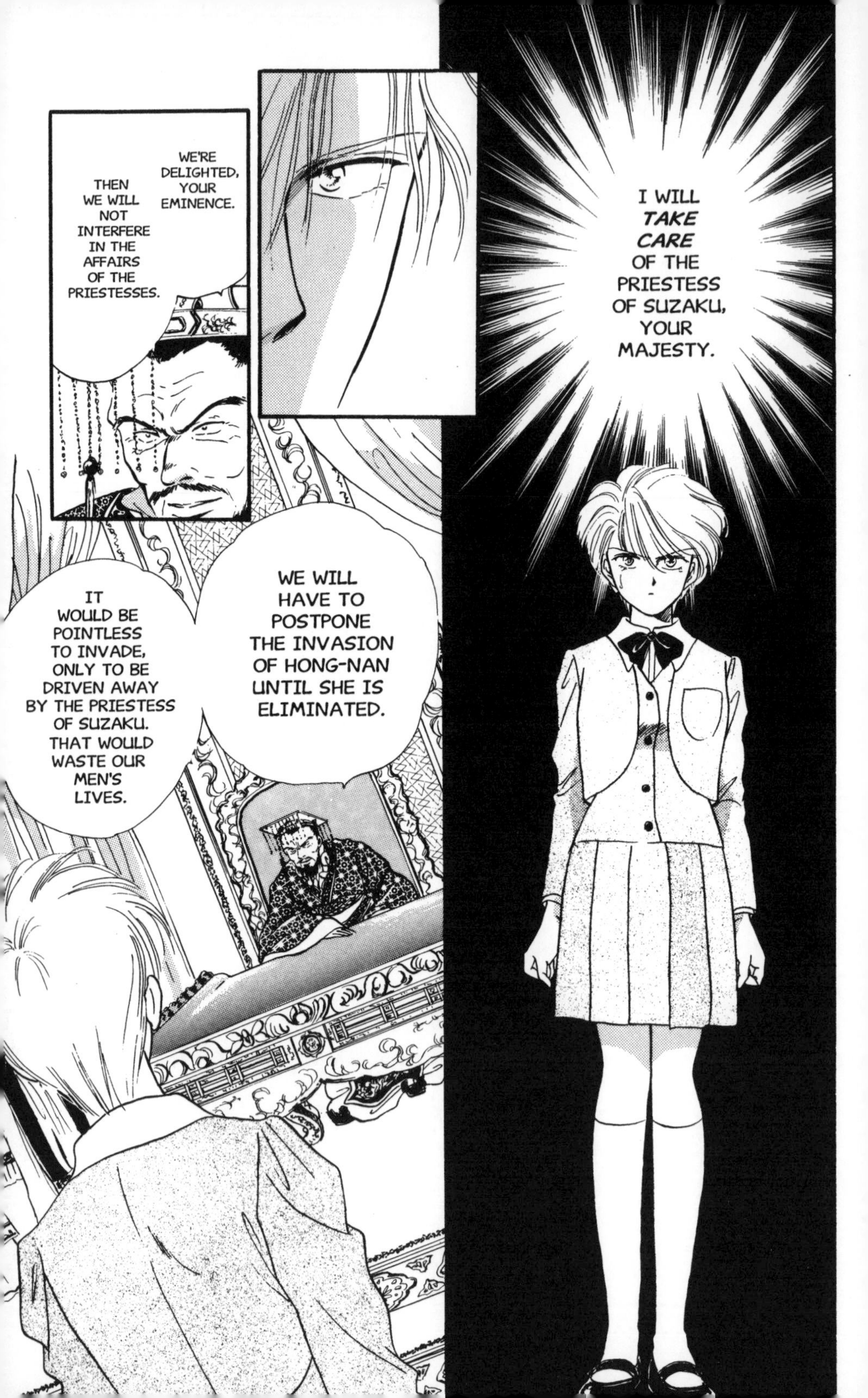

I WILL *TAKE CARE* OF THE PRIESTESS OF SUZAKU, YOUR MAJESTY.
WE'RE DELIGHTED, YOUR EMINENCE.
THEN WE WILL NOT INTERFERE IN THE AFFAIRS OF THE PRIESTESSES.
WE WILL HAVE TO POSTPONE THE INVASION OF HONG-NAN UNTIL SHE IS ELIMINATED.
IT WOULD BE POINTLESS TO INVADE, ONLY TO BE DRIVEN AWAY BY THE PRIESTESS OF SUZAKU. THAT WOULD WASTE OUR MEN'S LIVES.

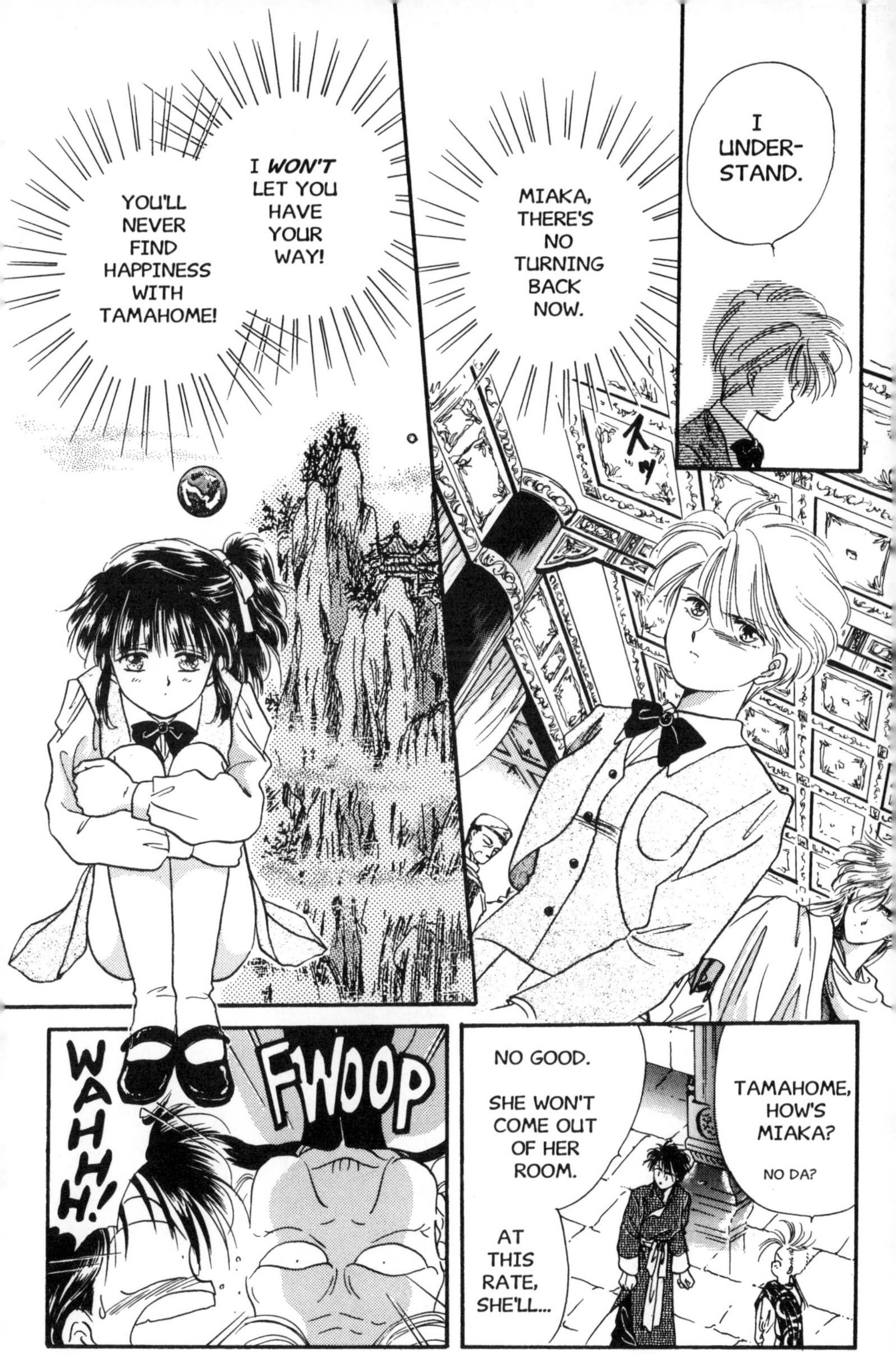
I UNDERSTAND.
MIAKA, THERE'S NO TURNING BACK NOW.
I *WON'T* LET YOU HAVE YOUR WAY!
YOU'LL NEVER FIND HAPPINESS WITH TAMAHOME!
TAMAHOME, HOW'S MIAKA? NO DA?
NO GOOD.
SHE WON'T COME OUT OF HER ROOM.
AT THIS RATE, SHE'LL...
FWOOP
WAHHH!

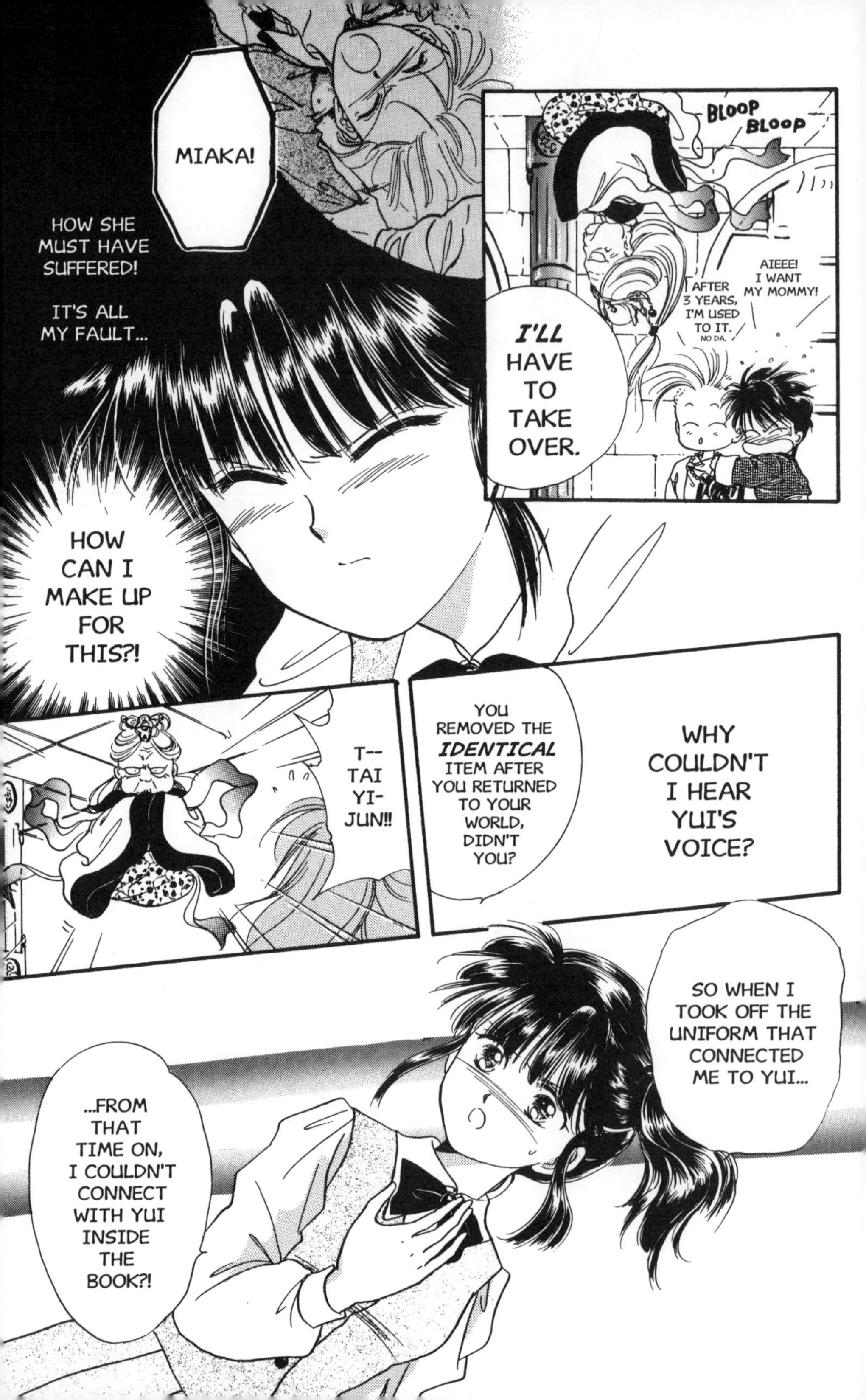
BLOOP BLOOP
AIEEE! I WANT MY MOMMY!
AFTER 3 YEARS, I'M USED TO IT. NO DA.
I'LL HAVE TO TAKE OVER.
MIAKA!
HOW SHE MUST HAVE SUFFERED!
IT'S ALL MY FAULT...
HOW CAN I MAKE UP FOR THIS?!
WHY COULDN'T I HEAR YUI'S VOICE?
YOU REMOVED THE *IDENTICAL* ITEM AFTER YOU RETURNED TO YOUR WORLD, DIDN'T YOU?
T-- TAI YI-JUN!!
SO WHEN I TOOK OFF THE UNIFORM THAT CONNECTED ME TO YUI...
...FROM THAT TIME ON, I COULDN'T CONNECT WITH YUI INSIDE THE BOOK?!

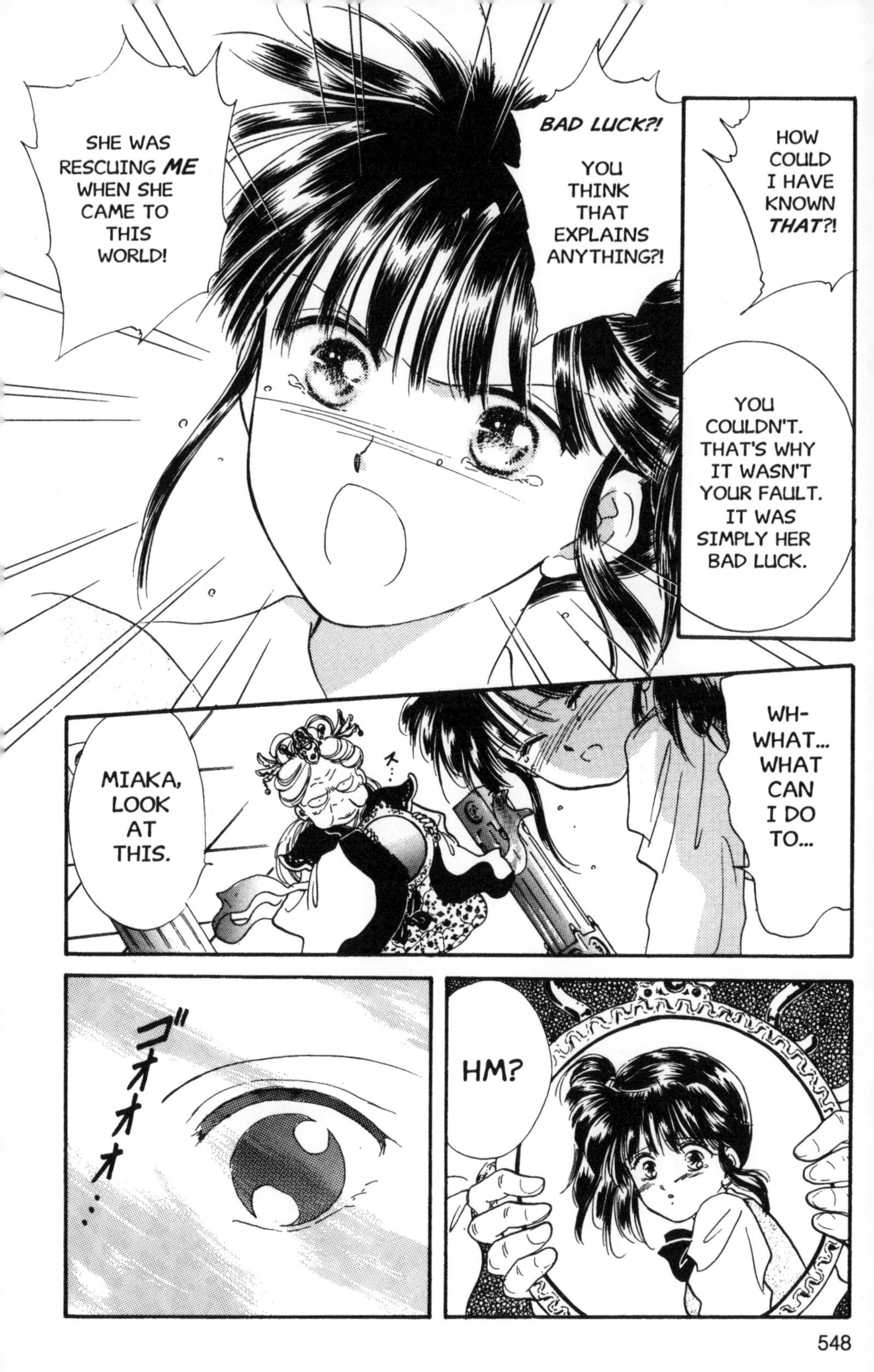
HOW COULD I HAVE KNOWN *THAT*?!
YOU COULDN'T. THAT'S WHY IT WASN'T YOUR FAULT. IT WAS SIMPLY HER BAD LUCK.
BAD LUCK?!
YOU THINK THAT EXPLAINS ANYTHING?!
SHE WAS RESCUING *ME* WHEN SHE CAME TO THIS WORLD!
WH-WHAT... WHAT CAN I DO TO...
ス…
MIAKA, LOOK AT THIS.
HM?
ゴオオオ…

Well, I've been getting responses from you regarding this free chat section. One person wrote in to complain about how I wouldn't give official approval for a project. According to the letter, my failure to give official approval indicated that I was becoming more distant from my readers. But it was my editors' decision. I guess they had problems in the past. I'm not trying to distance myself from my readers! I'm glad to hear that you wouldn't want that, but there's no need to get hung up over getting "official" approval. So don't worry about it, okay? Just because there isn't an official approval doesn't mean that I don't like it. I keep on receiving a lot of fanzines, and I take the time to look through all of them. So go right ahead and make fanzines or dojinshi and send them my way. I thought I'd said that before already. I think it's fine to draw parodies of my work (as long as they're not gross or boring).

Once my story gets published in a magazine, then it becomes part of each reader's imagination, fueled by the way he or she feels about the characters. That's how a work finally becomes complete. I don't know what I'm saying! All I want to say is this book in your hands is your own unique "Fushigi Yūgi." If you see what I mean. Manga is for the reader so... Urgh, I'm getting confused. Those readers who were fans of my work before it merited any "official seal of approval" became the ones that I respect the most. I'm not getting distant! AARGH, I'm getting all jumbled up!

-after a rest-

So fanzines are fine, okay? Oh yeah, I forgot during my rant; I have to apologize for the *Prepubescence Special Edition* not coming out on time. It's not my fault this time! The good news is that a book of illustrations is scheduled to come out next year (I hope). If it doesn't, sorry again! It should be a book of colored illustrations for *Prepubescence* and *Fushigi Yūgi*. You want a story too? Yessir!! I'll do my best.

One last common question: "Do you do illustrations for novels?" I've never had any requests to do one. That's all. This time I answered a lot of questions. Lotta work for those who read through this section.

AIEEEE WHAT-- THE HEEEE- EEECK!!

THIS IS *SCARY!*

549   But who's working hardest here?!

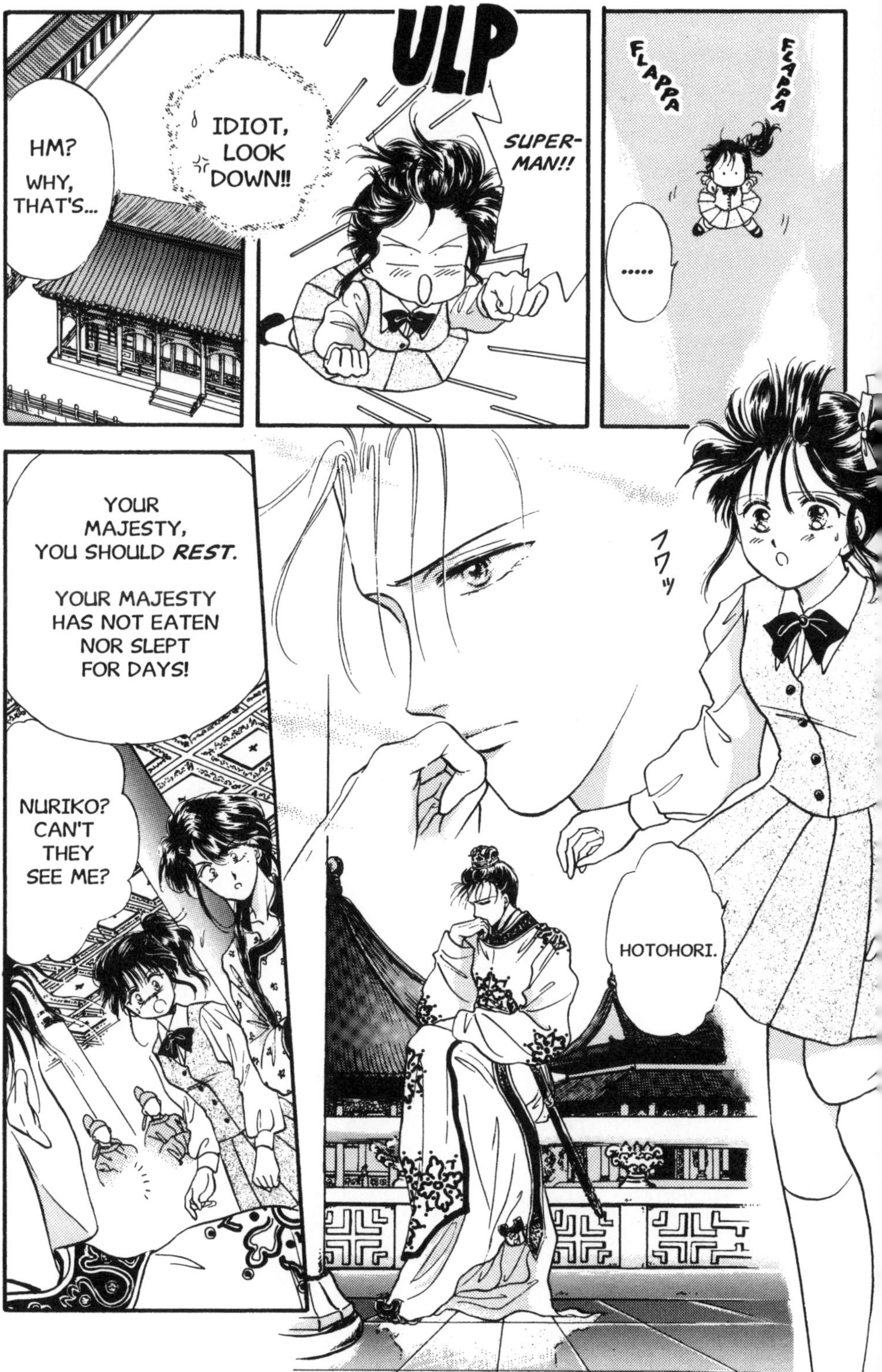
FLAPPA
FLAPPA
......
ULP
SUPER-MAN!!
IDIOT, LOOK DOWN!!
HM? WHY, THAT'S...
フワッ
HOTOHORI.
YOUR MAJESTY, YOU SHOULD *REST*.
YOUR MAJESTY HAS NOT EATEN NOR SLEPT FOR DAYS!
NURIKO? CAN'T THEY SEE ME?

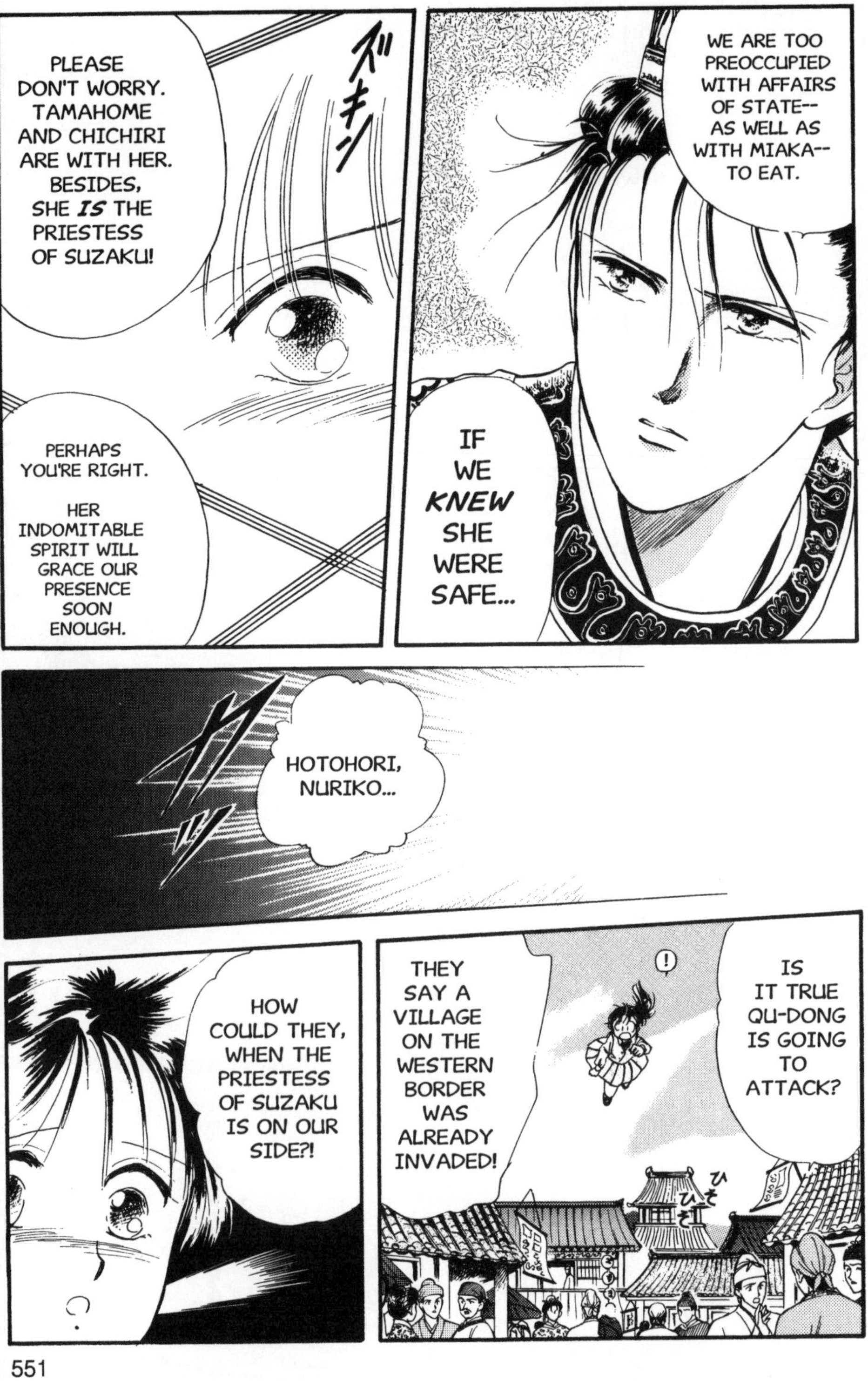
WE ARE TOO PREOCCUPIED WITH AFFAIRS OF STATE-- AS WELL AS WITH MIAKA-- TO EAT.
IF WE *KNEW* SHE WERE SAFE...
ズキン
PLEASE DON'T WORRY. TAMAHOME AND CHICHIRI ARE WITH HER. BESIDES, SHE *IS* THE PRIESTESS OF SUZAKU!
PERHAPS YOU'RE RIGHT.
HER INDOMITABLE SPIRIT WILL GRACE OUR PRESENCE SOON ENOUGH.
HOTOHORI, NURIKO...
ダッ
IS IT TRUE QU-DONG IS GOING TO ATTACK?
!
THEY SAY A VILLAGE ON THE WESTERN BORDER WAS ALREADY INVADED!
ひそ ひそ
HOW COULD THEY, WHEN THE PRIESTESS OF SUZAKU IS ON OUR SIDE?!
?

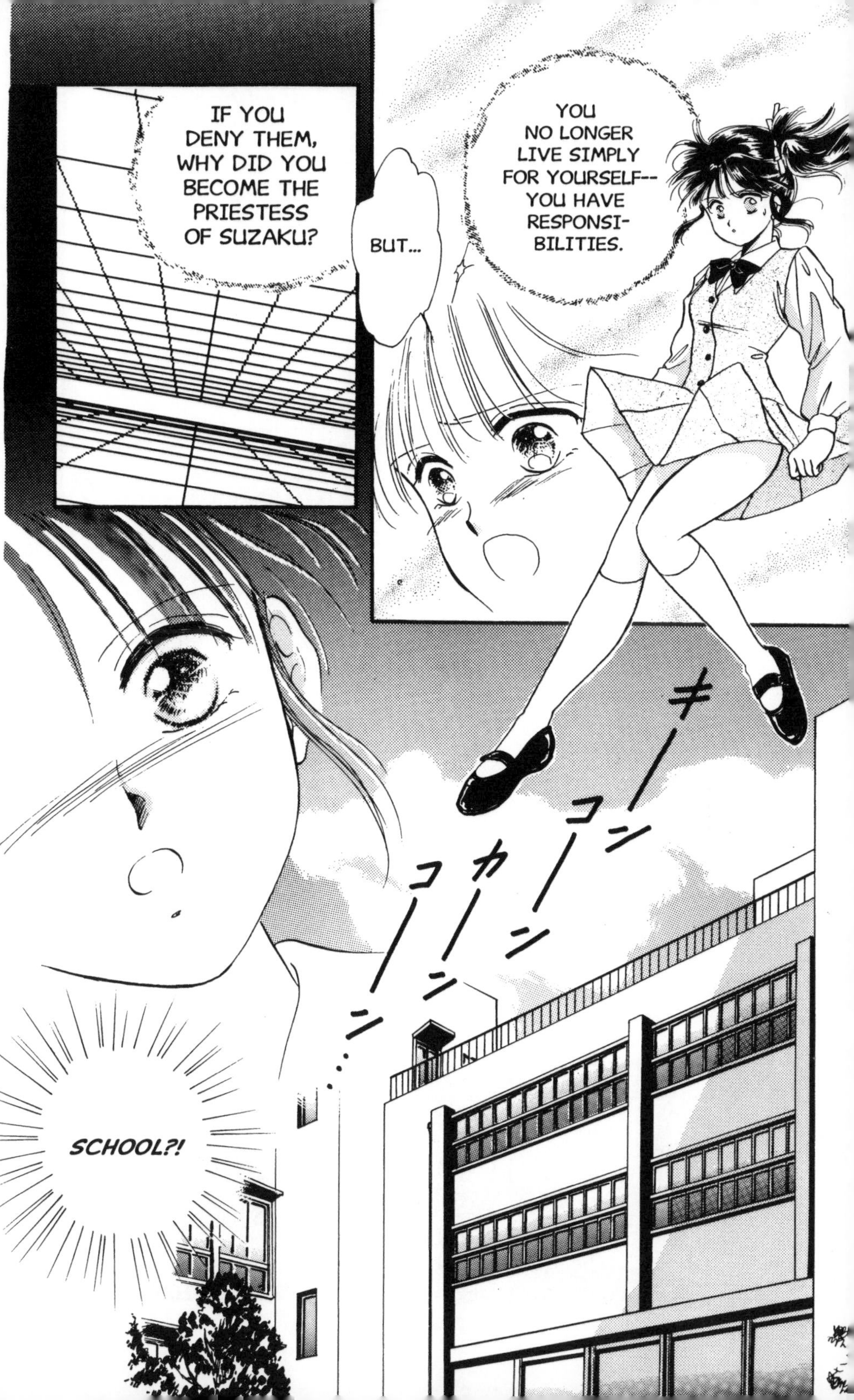
YOU NO LONGER LIVE SIMPLY FOR YOURSELF-- YOU HAVE RESPONSI-BILITIES.
BUT...
IF YOU DENY THEM, WHY DID YOU BECOME THE PRIESTESS OF SUZAKU?
キーンコーン
カーンコーン…
SCHOOL?!

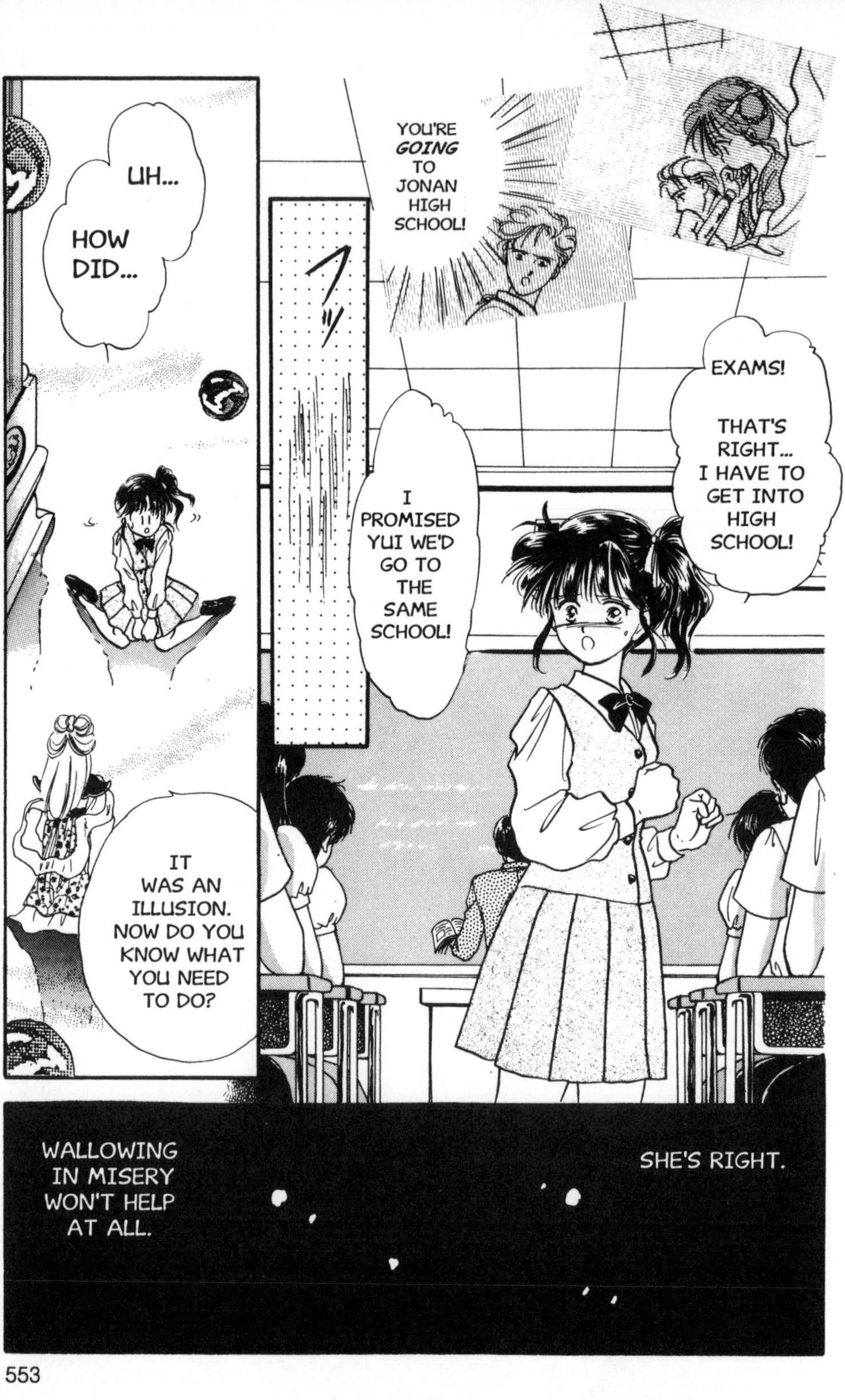
YOU'RE *GOING* TO JONAN HIGH SCHOOL!
EXAMS! THAT'S RIGHT... I HAVE TO GET INTO HIGH SCHOOL!
I PROMISED YUI WE'D GO TO THE SAME SCHOOL!
UH... HOW DID...
IT WAS AN ILLUSION. NOW DO YOU KNOW WHAT YOU NEED TO DO?
SHE'S RIGHT.
WALLOWING IN MISERY WON'T HELP AT ALL.

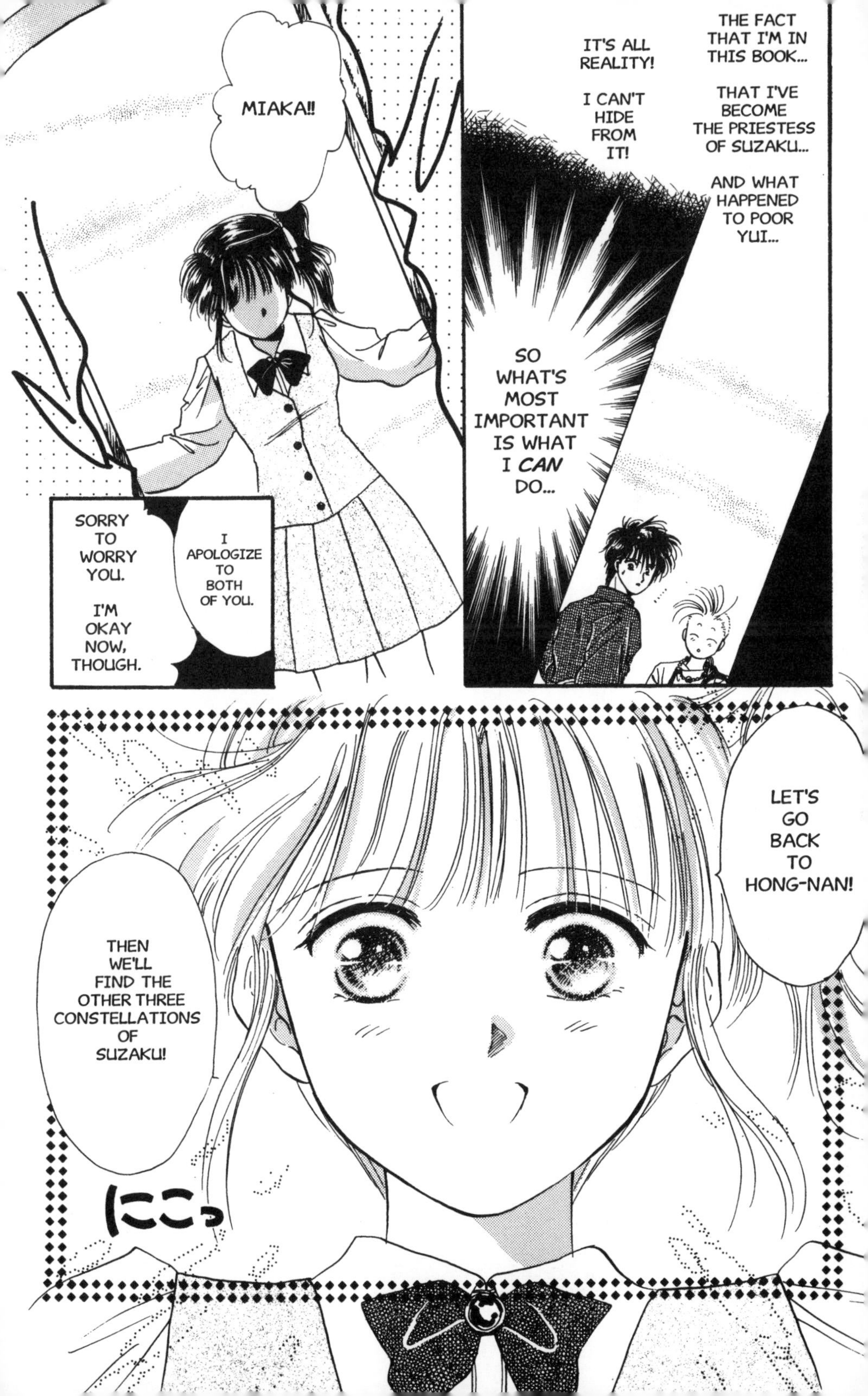
THE FACT THAT I'M IN THIS BOOK...
THAT I'VE BECOME THE PRIESTESS OF SUZAKU...
AND WHAT HAPPENED TO POOR YUI...
IT'S ALL REALITY!
I CAN'T HIDE FROM IT!
SO WHAT'S MOST IMPORTANT IS WHAT I *CAN* DO...
MIAKA!!
I APOLOGIZE TO BOTH OF YOU.
SORRY TO WORRY YOU.
I'M OKAY NOW, THOUGH.
LET'S GO BACK TO HONG-NAN!
THEN WE'LL FIND THE OTHER THREE CONSTELLATIONS OF SUZAKU!
にこっ

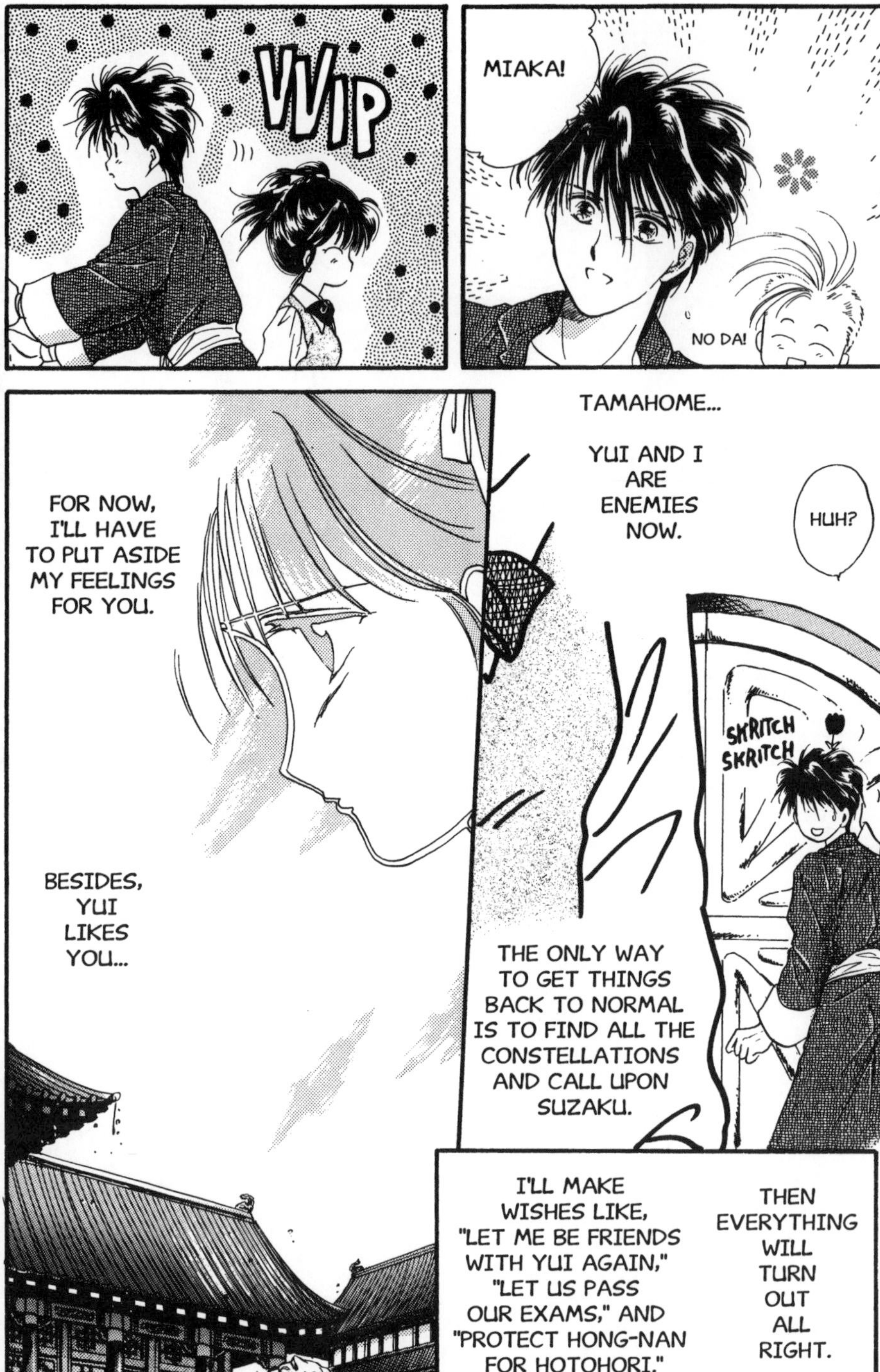

MIAKA!
NO DA!
VVIP
TAMAHOME...
YUI AND I ARE ENEMIES NOW.
HUH?
SKRITCH SKRITCH
THE ONLY WAY TO GET THINGS BACK TO NORMAL IS TO FIND ALL THE CONSTELLATIONS AND CALL UPON SUZAKU.
I'LL MAKE WISHES LIKE, "LET ME BE FRIENDS WITH YUI AGAIN," "LET US PASS OUR EXAMS," AND "PROTECT HONG-NAN FOR HOTOHORI."
THEN EVERYTHING WILL TURN OUT ALL RIGHT.
FOR NOW, I'LL HAVE TO PUT ASIDE MY FEELINGS FOR YOU.
BESIDES, YUI LIKES YOU...

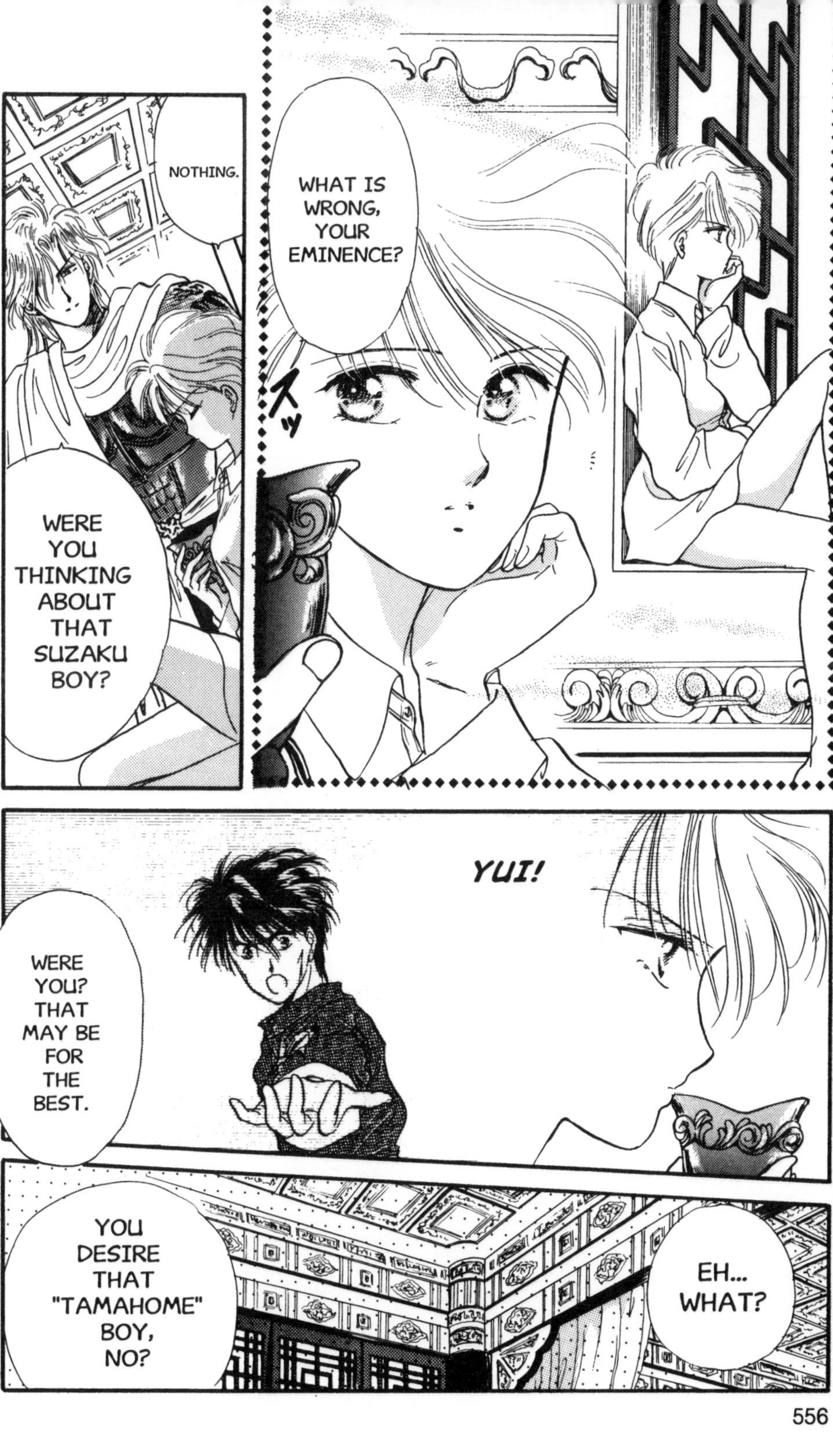
WHAT IS WRONG, YOUR EMINENCE?
スッ
NOTHING.
WERE YOU THINKING ABOUT THAT SUZAKU BOY?
YUI!
WERE YOU? THAT MAY BE FOR THE BEST.
YOU DESIRE THAT "TAMAHOME" BOY, NO?
EH... WHAT?

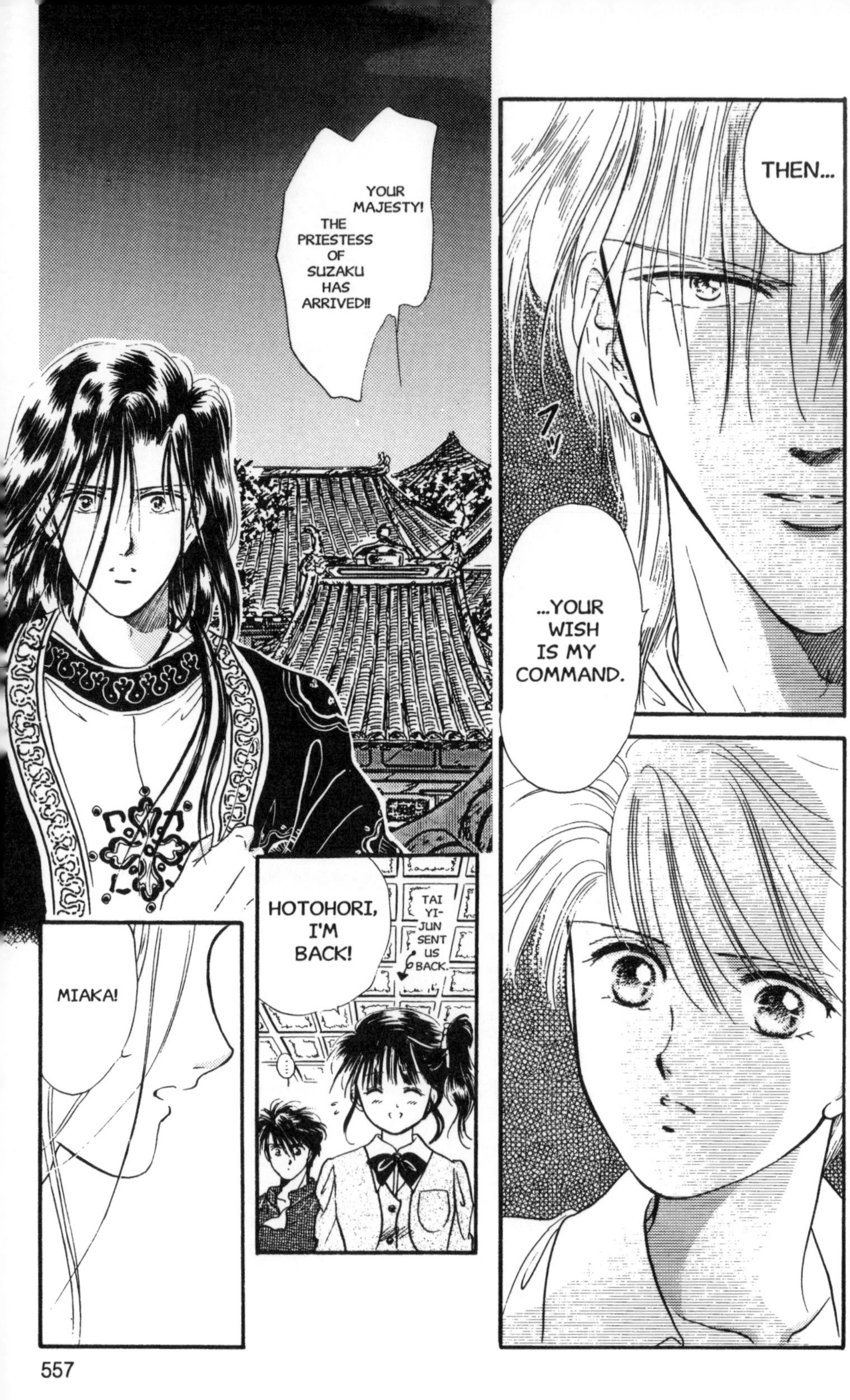
THEN...
...YOUR WISH IS MY COMMAND.
YOUR MAJESTY! THE PRIESTESS OF SUZAKU HAS ARRIVED!!
HOTOHORI, I'M BACK!
TAI YI-JUN SENT US BACK.
...
MIAKA!

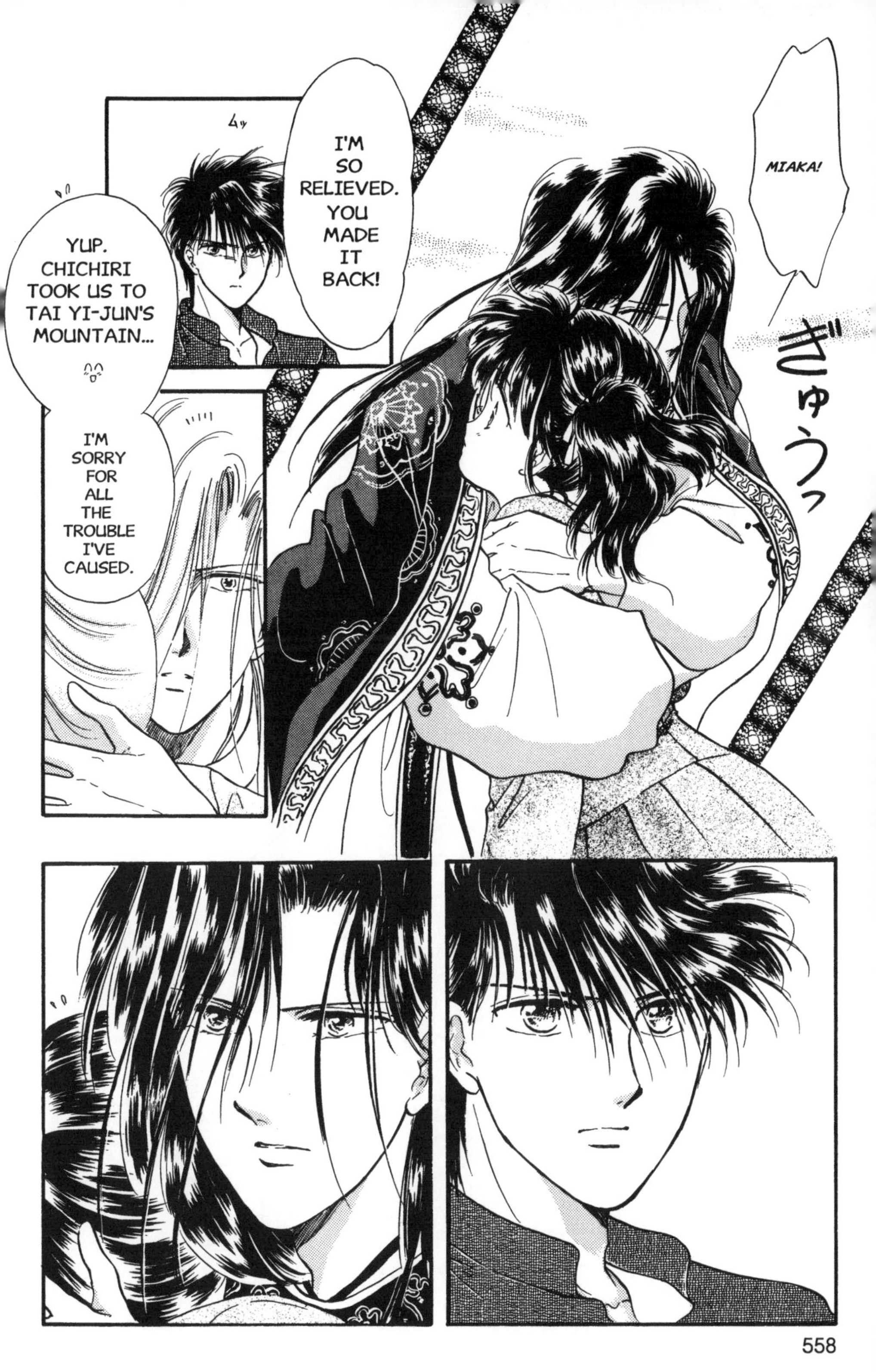
MIAKA!
ぎゅうっ
I'M SO RELIEVED. YOU MADE IT BACK!
ムッ
YUP. CHICHIRI TOOK US TO TAI YI-JUN'S MOUNTAIN...
I'M SORRY FOR ALL THE TROUBLE I'VE CAUSED.

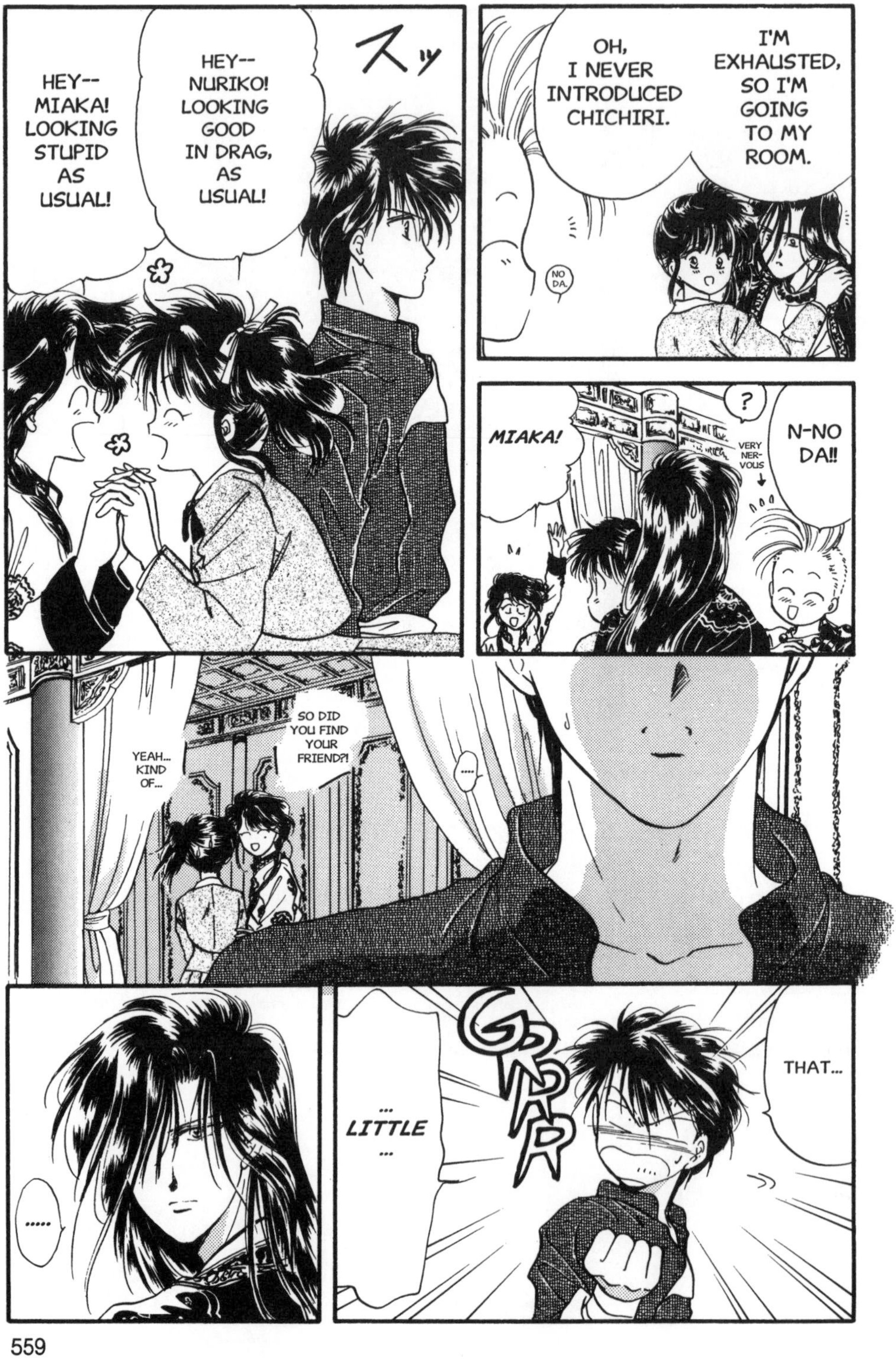
I'M EXHAUSTED, SO I'M GOING TO MY ROOM.
OH, I NEVER INTRODUCED CHICHIRI.
NO DA.
N-NO DA!!
VERY NERVOUS
?
MIAKA!
スッ
HEY-- NURIKO! LOOKING GOOD IN DRAG, AS USUAL!
HEY-- MIAKA! LOOKING STUPID AS USUAL!
.....
SO DID YOU FIND YOUR FRIEND?!
YEAH... KIND OF...
THAT...
GRRR
... LITTLE ...
......

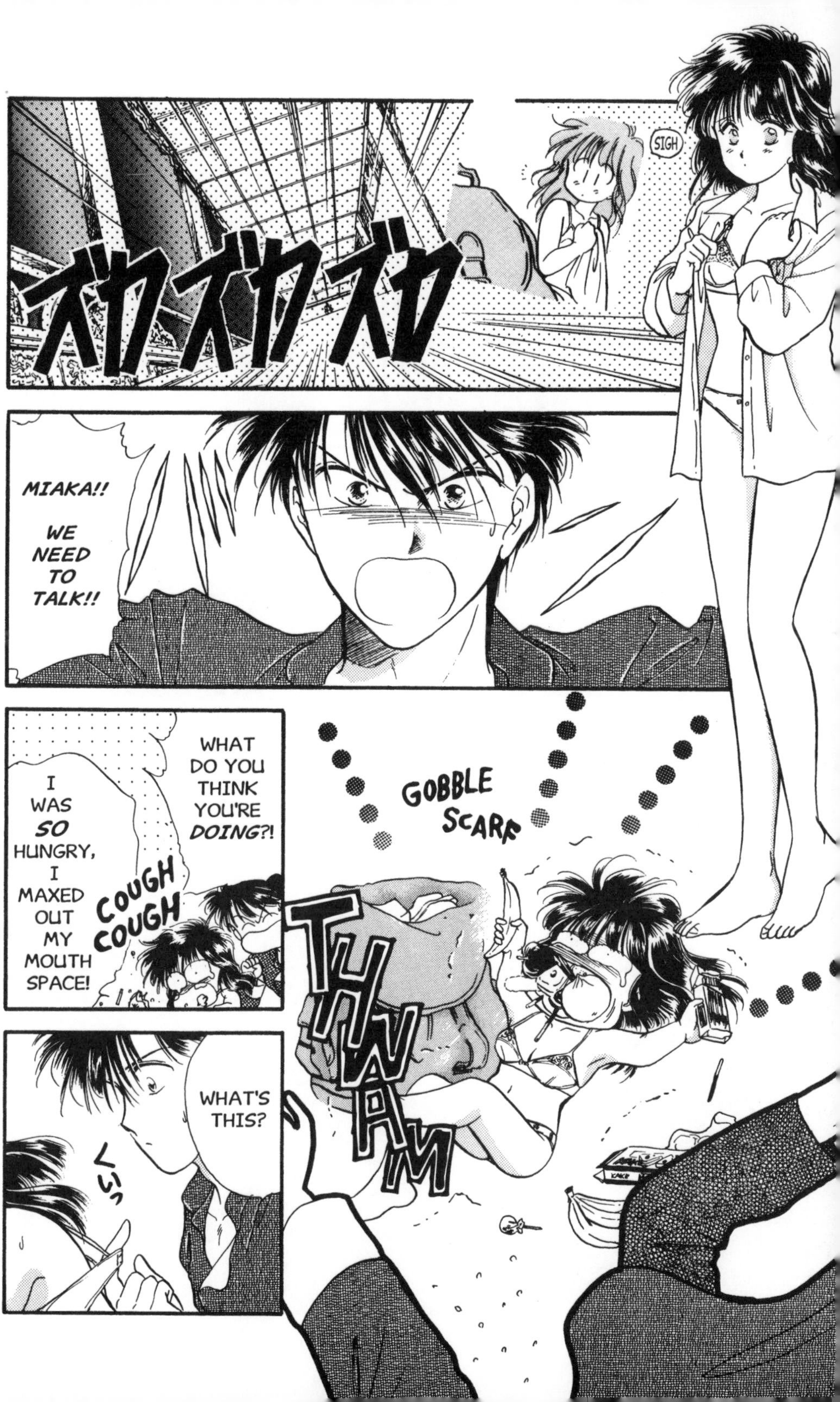
SIGH
ズカズカズカ
MIAKA!! WE NEED TO TALK!!
GOBBLE SCARF
THWAM
WHAT DO YOU THINK YOU'RE *DOING*?!
I WAS *SO* HUNGRY, I MAXED OUT MY MOUTH SPACE!
COUGH COUGH
WHAT'S THIS?

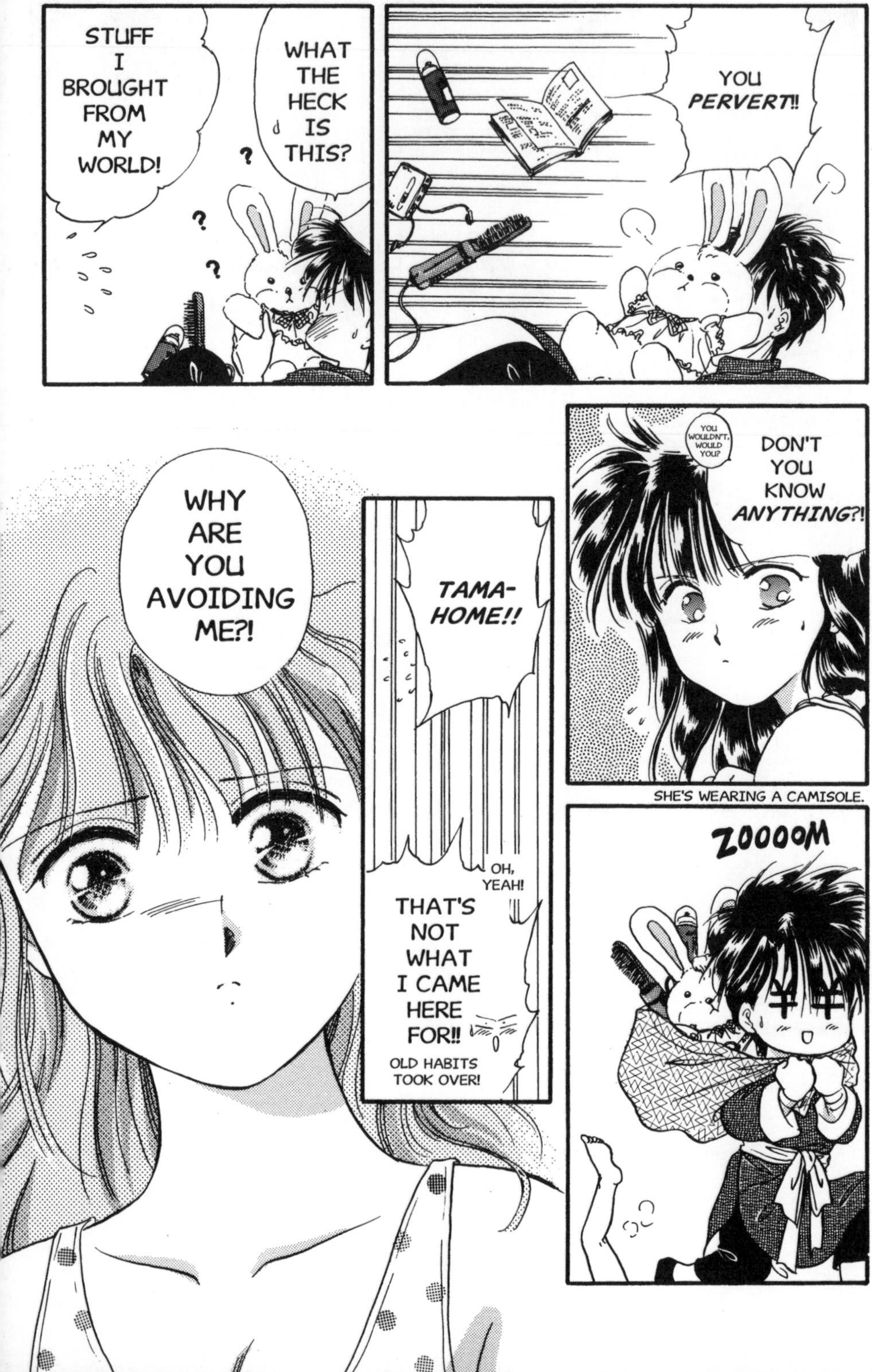
YOU PERVERT!!
WHAT THE HECK IS THIS?
STUFF I BROUGHT FROM MY WORLD!
DON'T YOU KNOW ANYTHING?!
YOU WOULDN'T, WOULD YOU?
SHE'S WEARING A CAMISOLE.
ZOOOOM
TAMA-HOME!!
OH, YEAH!
THAT'S NOT WHAT I CAME HERE FOR!!
OLD HABITS TOOK OVER!
WHY ARE YOU AVOIDING ME?!

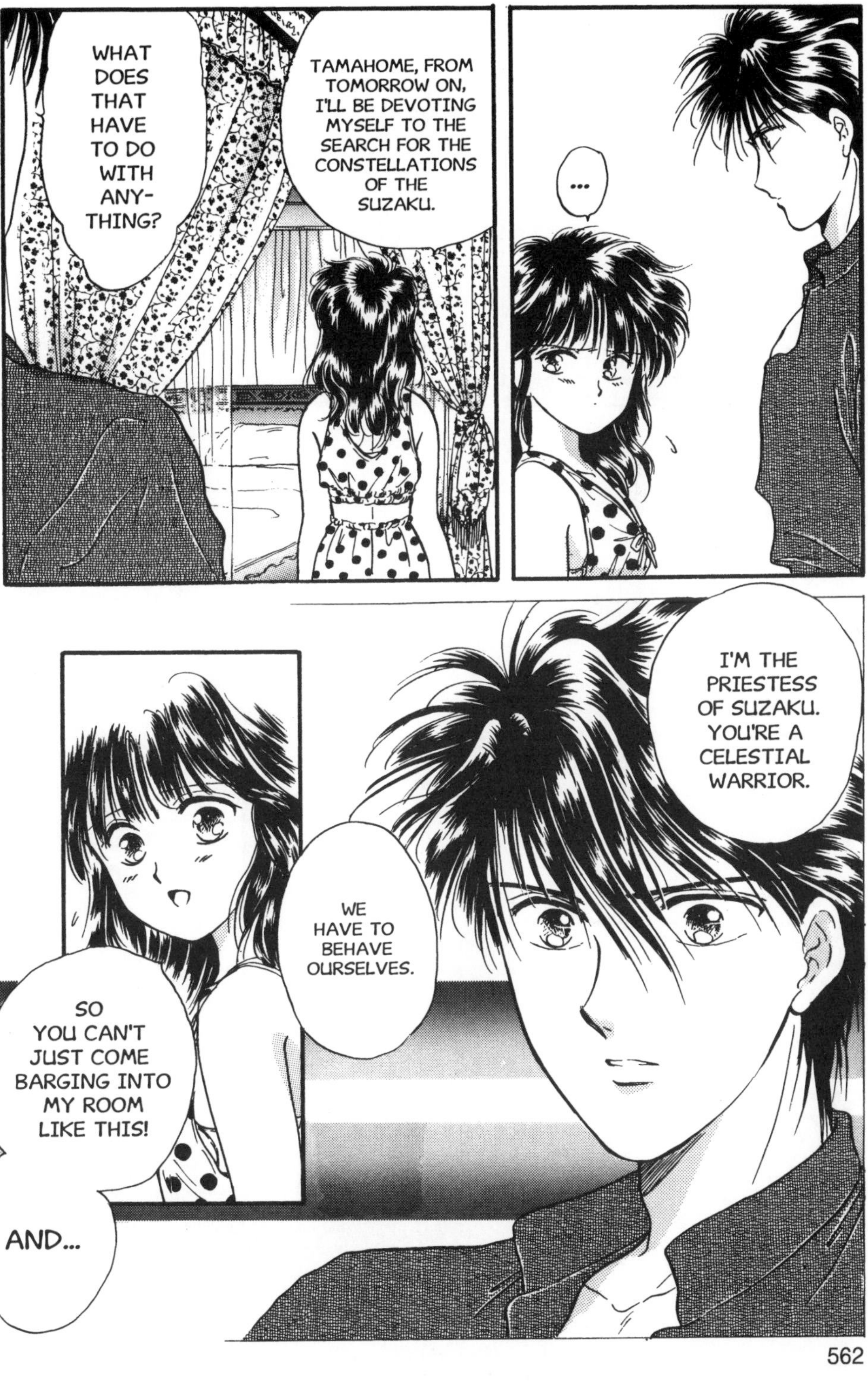
...
TAMAHOME, FROM TOMORROW ON, I'LL BE DEVOTING MYSELF TO THE SEARCH FOR THE CONSTELLATIONS OF THE SUZAKU.
WHAT DOES THAT HAVE TO DO WITH ANYTHING?
I'M THE PRIESTESS OF SUZAKU. YOU'RE A CELESTIAL WARRIOR.
WE HAVE TO BEHAVE OURSELVES.
SO YOU CAN'T JUST COME BARGING INTO MY ROOM LIKE THIS!
AND...

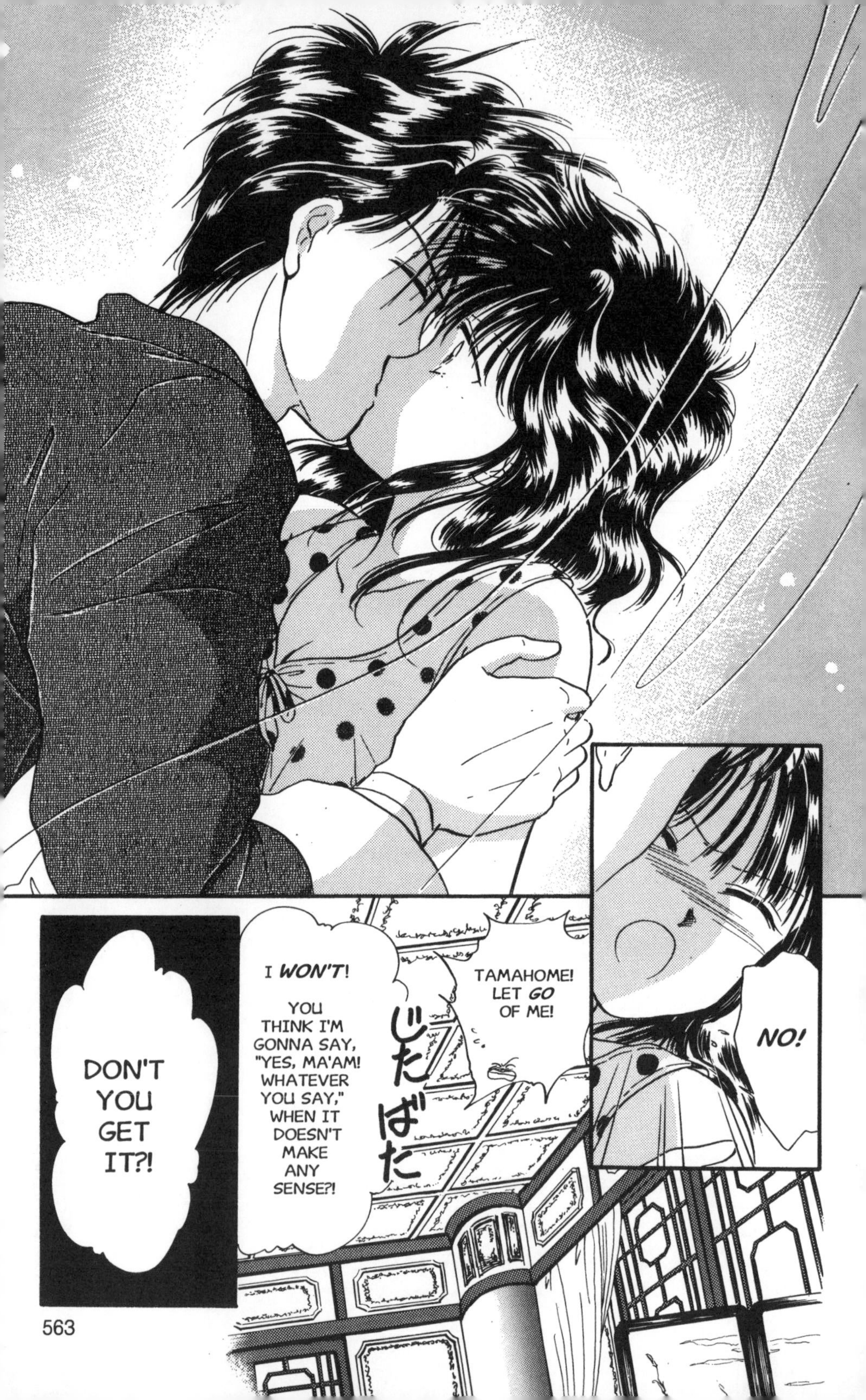
NO!
TAMAHOME! LET GO OF ME!
I WON'T!
YOU THINK I'M GONNA SAY, "YES, MA'AM! WHATEVER YOU SAY," WHEN IT DOESN'T MAKE ANY SENSE?!
じたばた
DON'T YOU GET IT?!

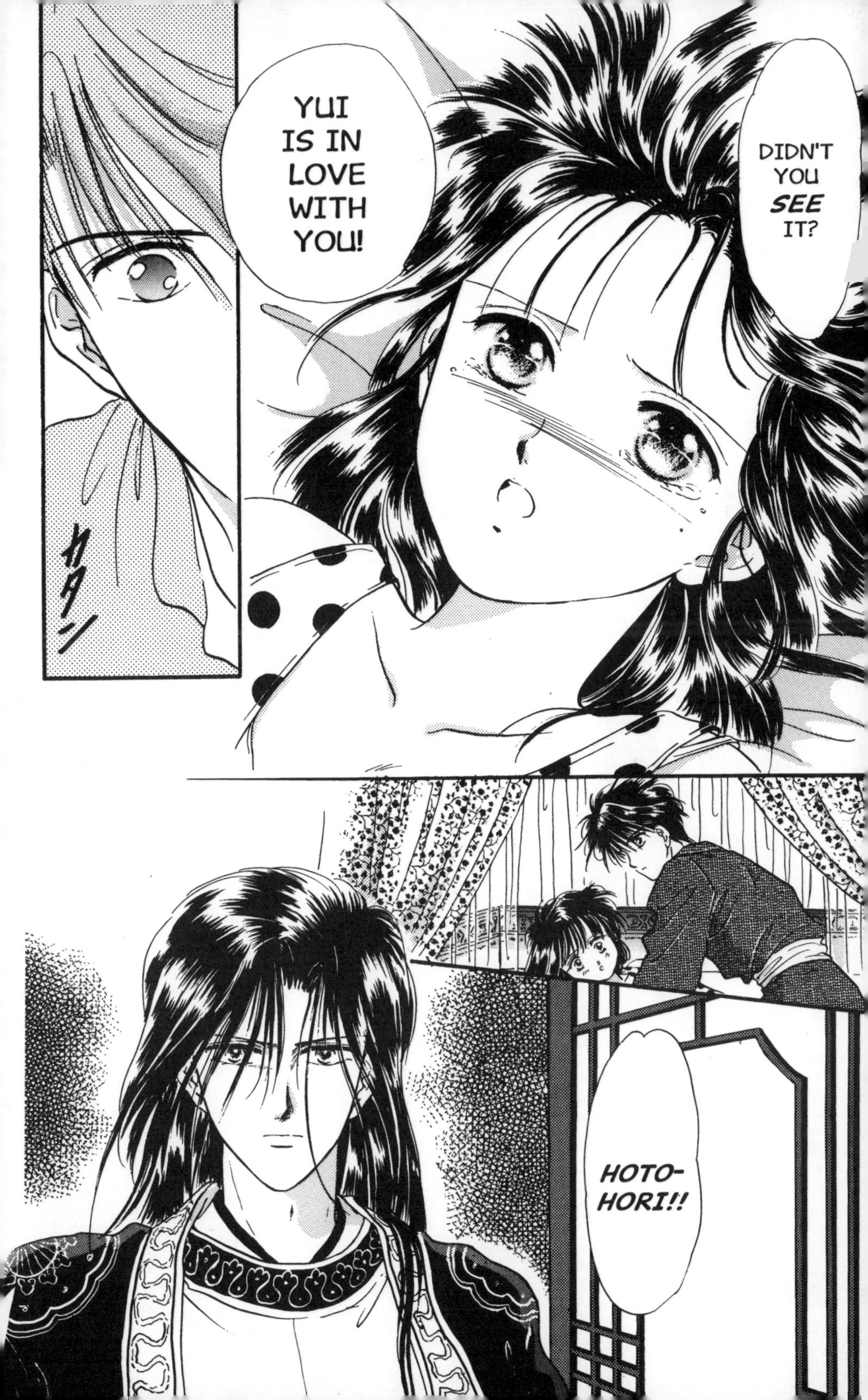
DIDN'T YOU *SEE* IT?
YUI IS IN LOVE WITH YOU!
HOTO-HORI!!

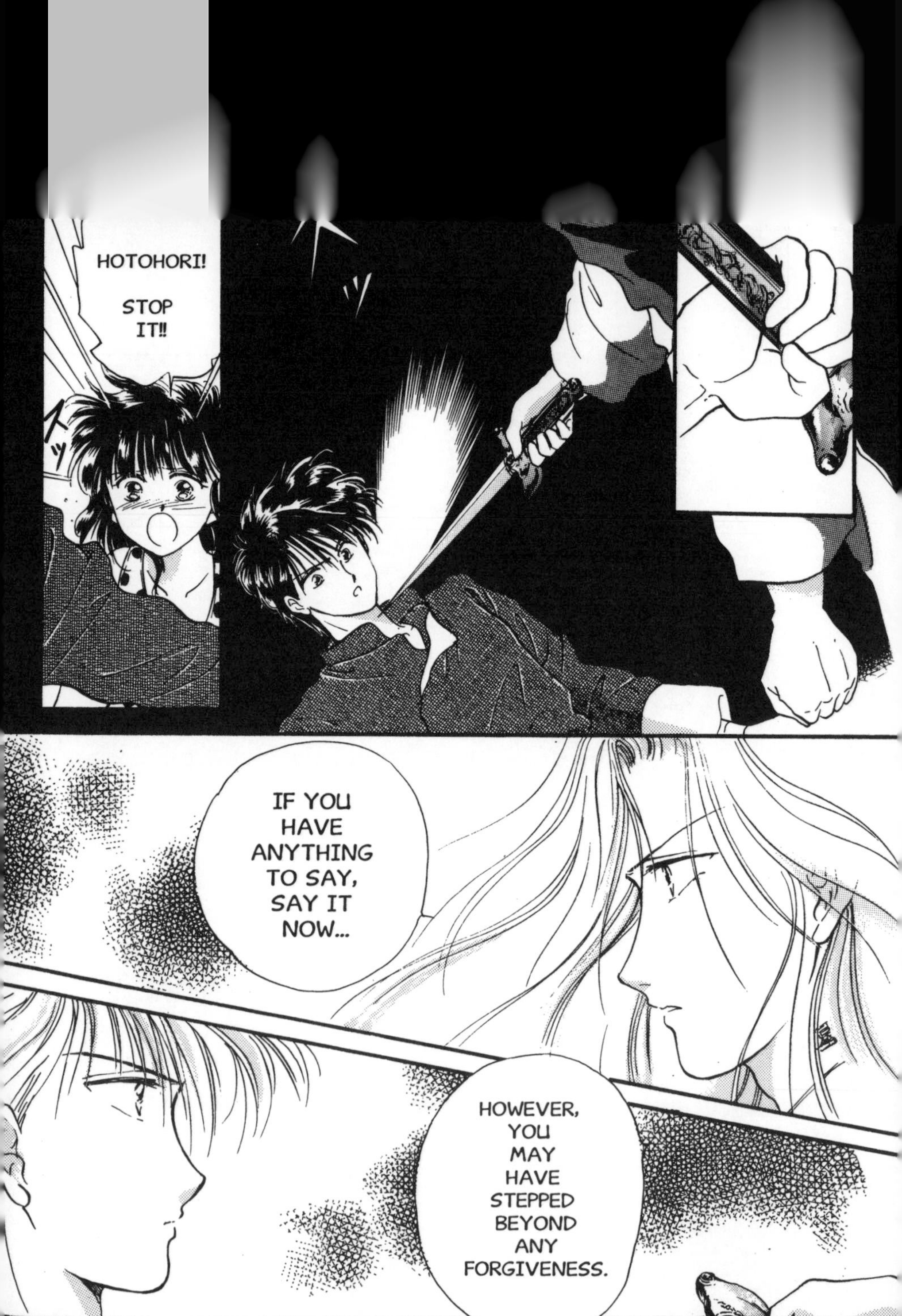
HOTOHORI!
STOP IT!!
IF YOU HAVE ANYTHING TO SAY, SAY IT NOW...
HOWEVER, YOU MAY HAVE STEPPED BEYOND ANY FORGIVENESS.

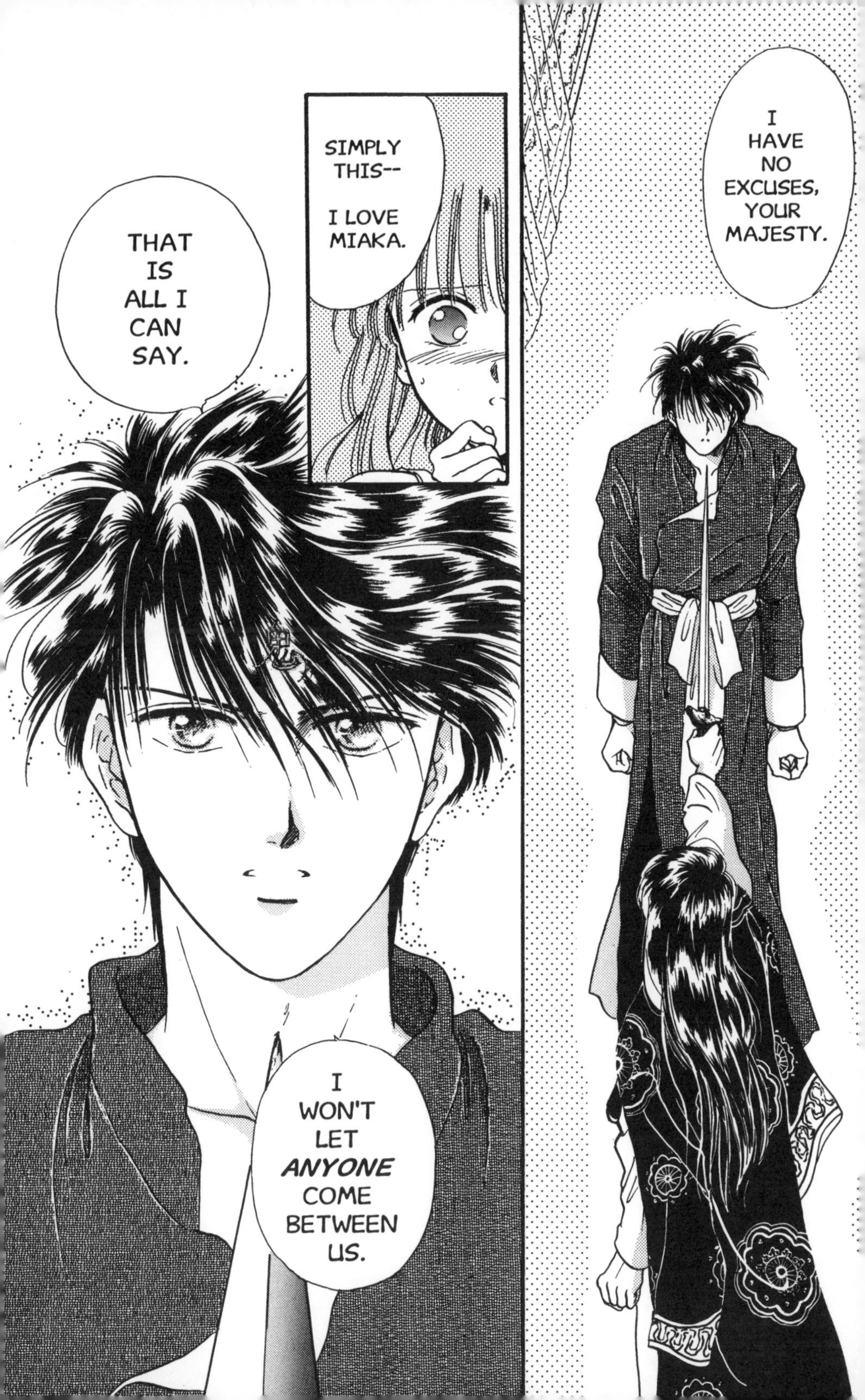
I HAVE NO EXCUSES, YOUR MAJESTY.
SIMPLY THIS-- I LOVE MIAKA.
THAT IS ALL I CAN SAY.
I WON'T LET *ANYONE* COME BETWEEN US.

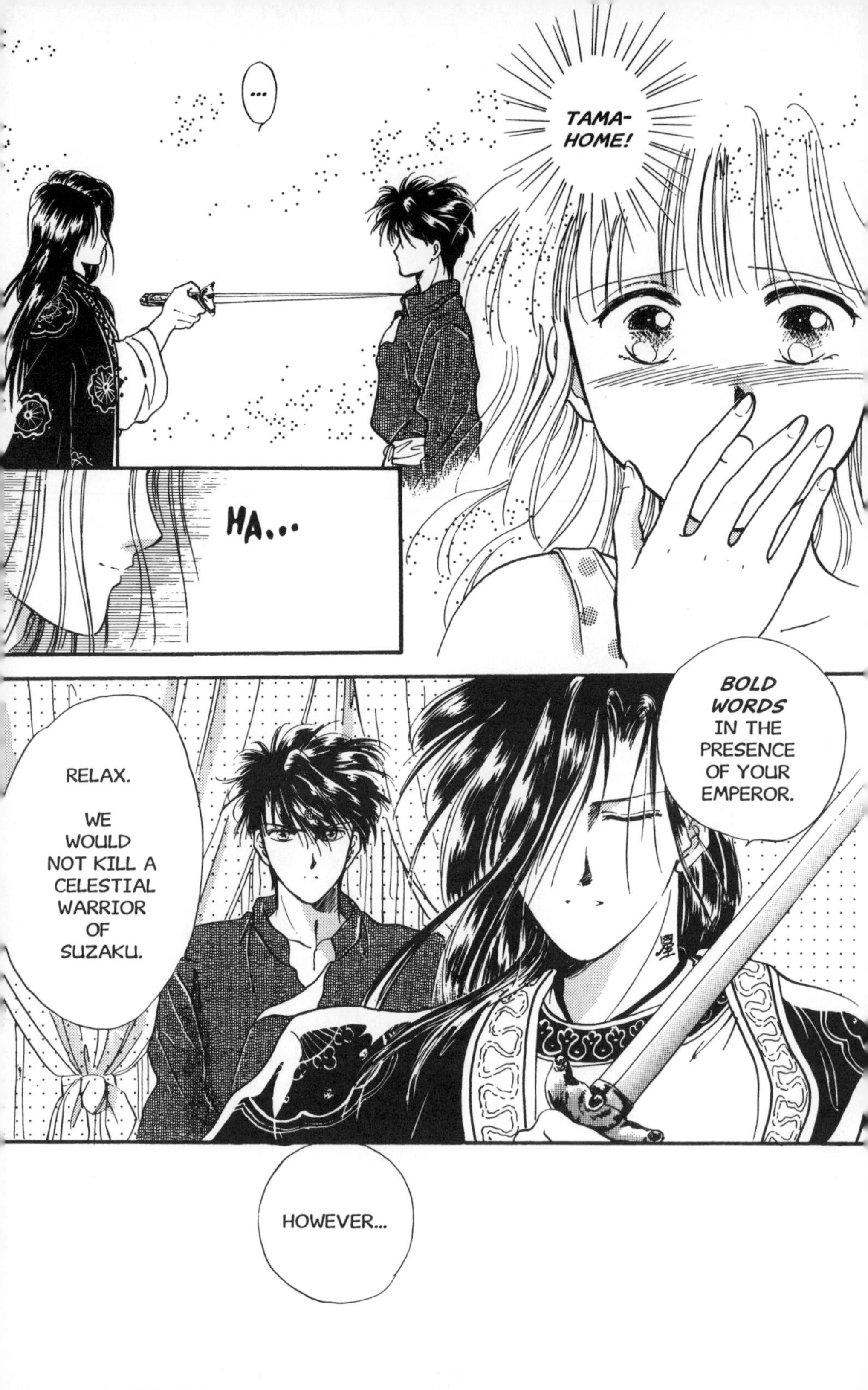
TAMA-HOME!
...
HA...
BOLD WORDS IN THE PRESENCE OF YOUR EMPEROR.
RELAX. WE WOULD NOT KILL A CELESTIAL WARRIOR OF SUZAKU.
HOWEVER...

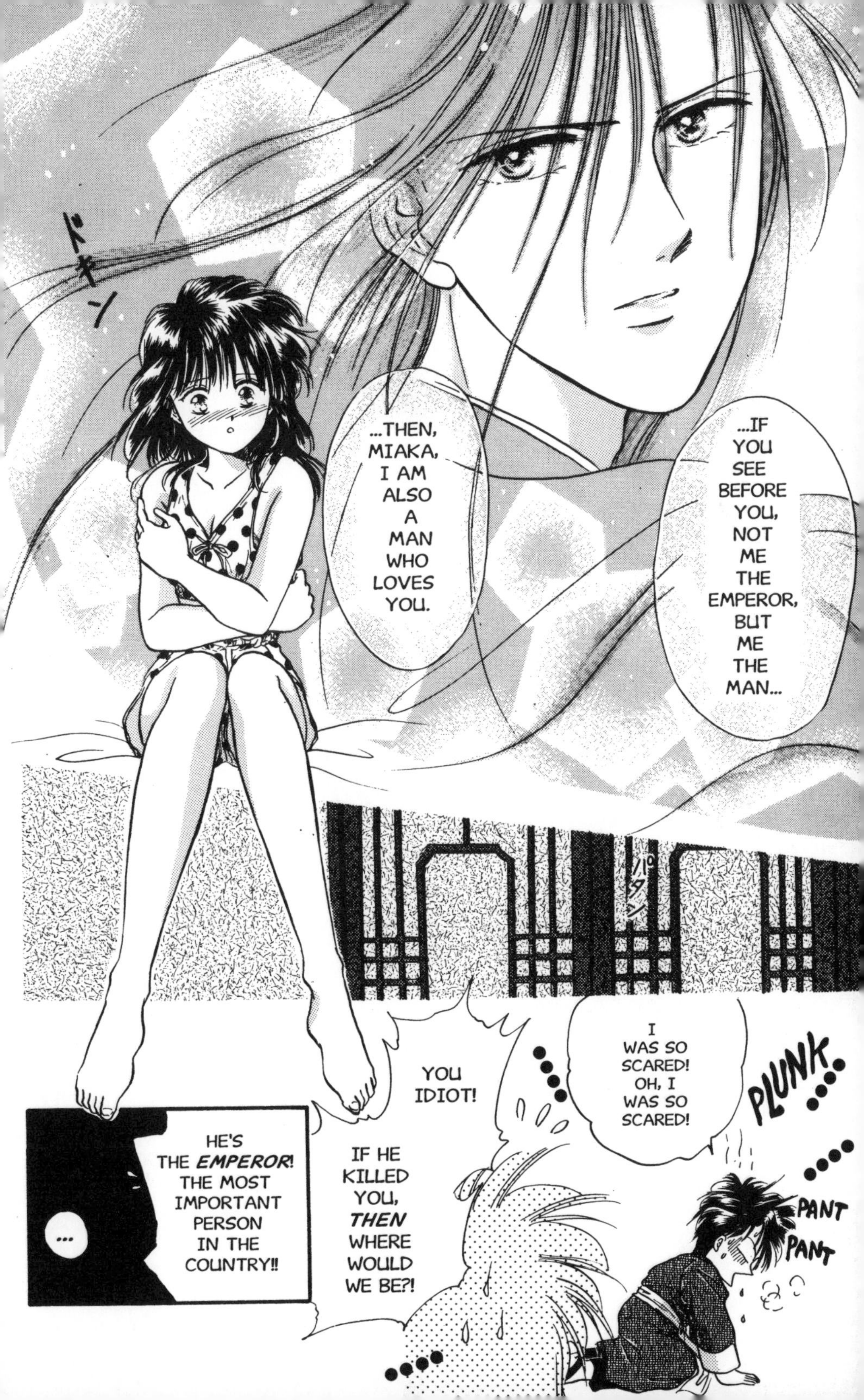

...IF YOU SEE BEFORE YOU, NOT ME THE EMPEROR, BUT ME THE MAN...
...THEN, MIAKA, I AM ALSO A MAN WHO LOVES YOU.
ドキン
パタン
PLUNK
I WAS SO SCARED! OH, I WAS SO SCARED!
PANT PANT
YOU IDIOT!
IF HE KILLED YOU, *THEN* WHERE WOULD WE BE?!
HE'S THE *EMPEROR*! THE MOST IMPORTANT PERSON IN THE COUNTRY!!
...

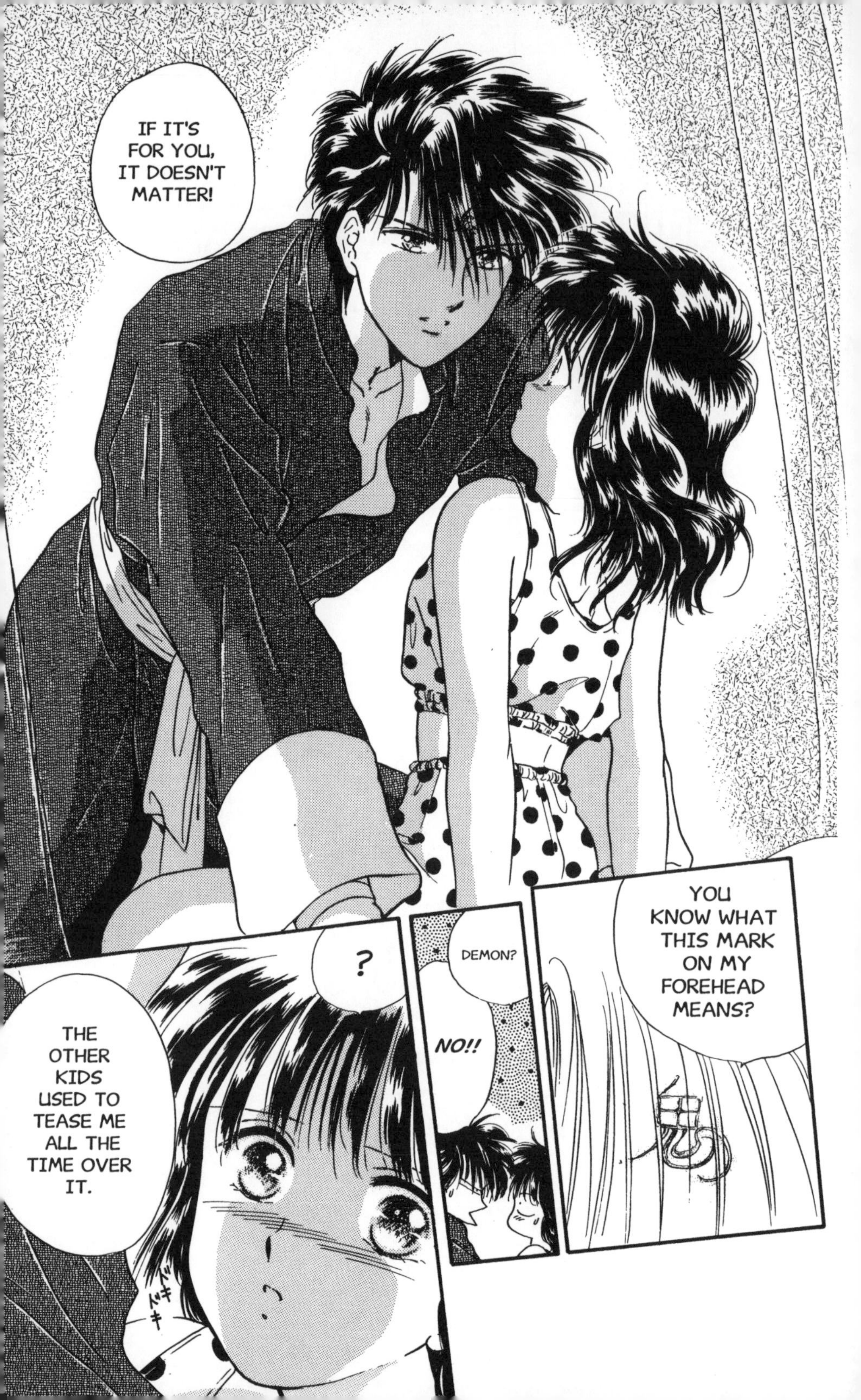
IF IT'S FOR YOU, IT DOESN'T MATTER!
YOU KNOW WHAT THIS MARK ON MY FOREHEAD MEANS?
DEMON?
NO!!
?
THE OTHER KIDS USED TO TEASE ME ALL THE TIME OVER IT.
ドキドキ

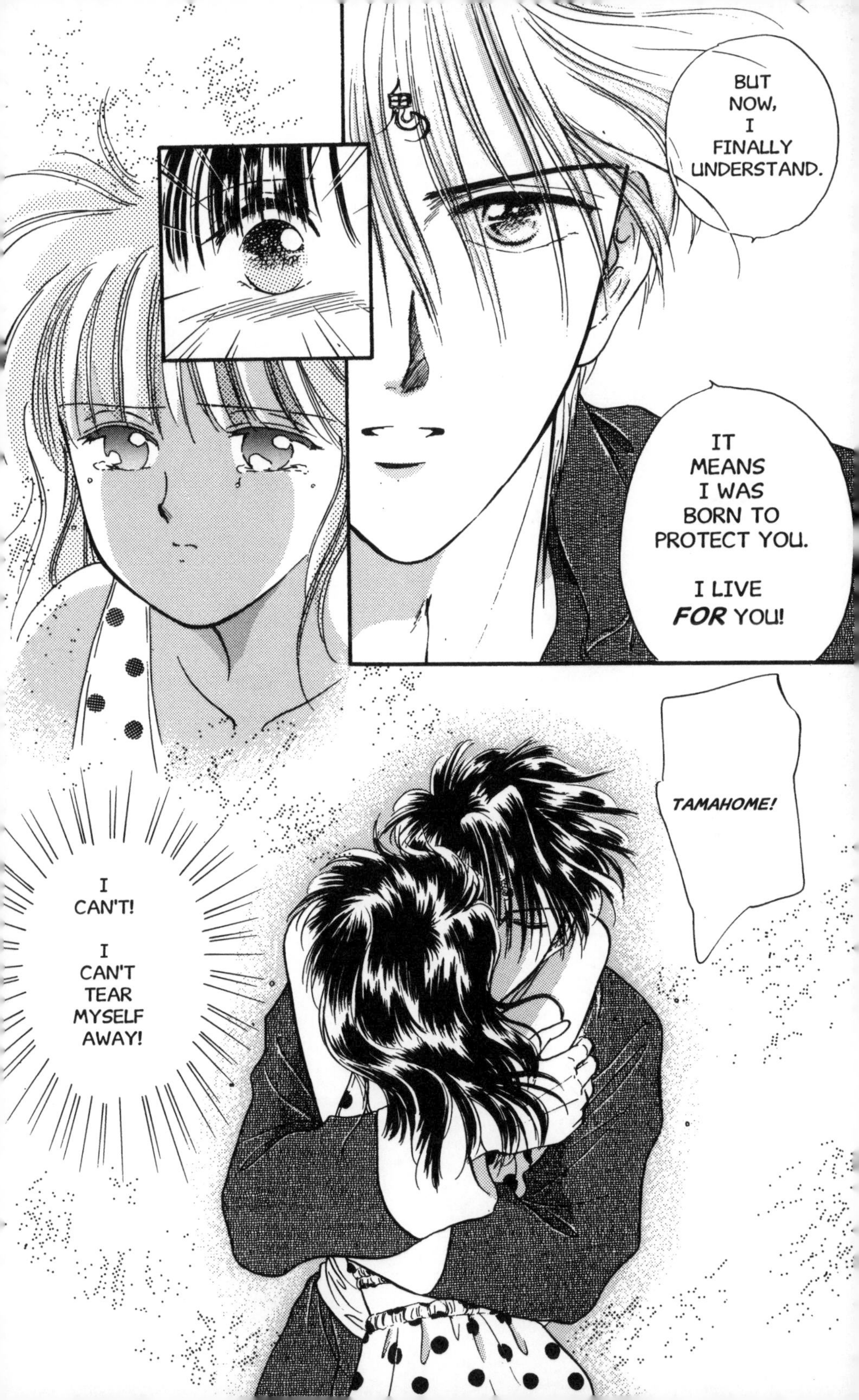
BUT NOW, I FINALLY UNDERSTAND.
IT MEANS I WAS BORN TO PROTECT YOU.
I LIVE ***FOR*** YOU!
TAMAHOME!
I CAN'T!
I CAN'T TEAR MYSELF AWAY!

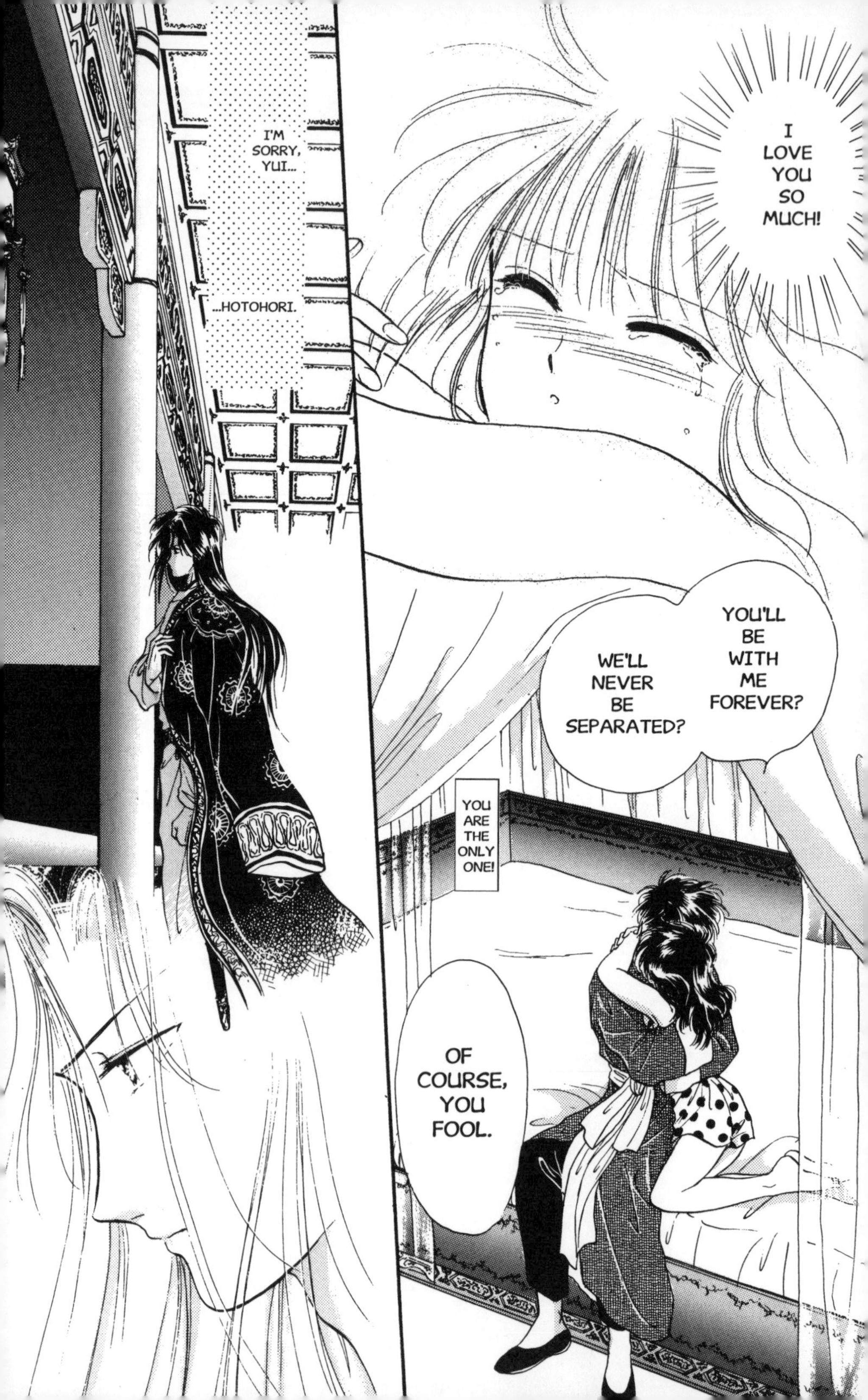
I LOVE YOU SO MUCH!
YOU'LL BE WITH ME FOREVER?
WE'LL NEVER BE SEPARATED?
YOU ARE THE ONLY ONE!
OF COURSE, YOU FOOL.
I'M SORRY, YUI...
...HOTOHORI.

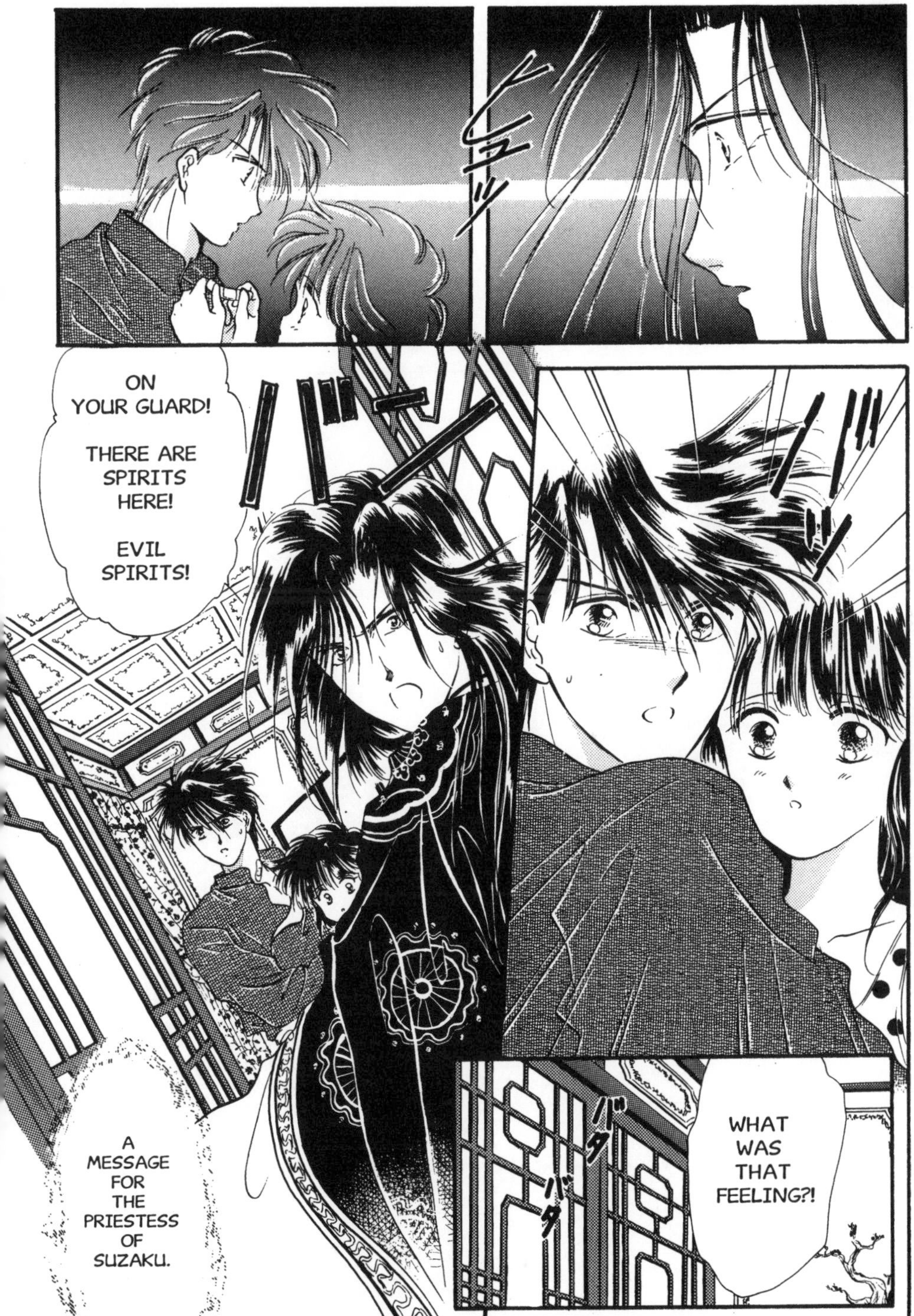
WHAT WAS THAT FEELING?!
バタ バタ
ON YOUR GUARD!
THERE ARE SPIRITS HERE!
EVIL SPIRITS!
A MESSAGE FOR THE PRIESTESS OF SUZAKU.

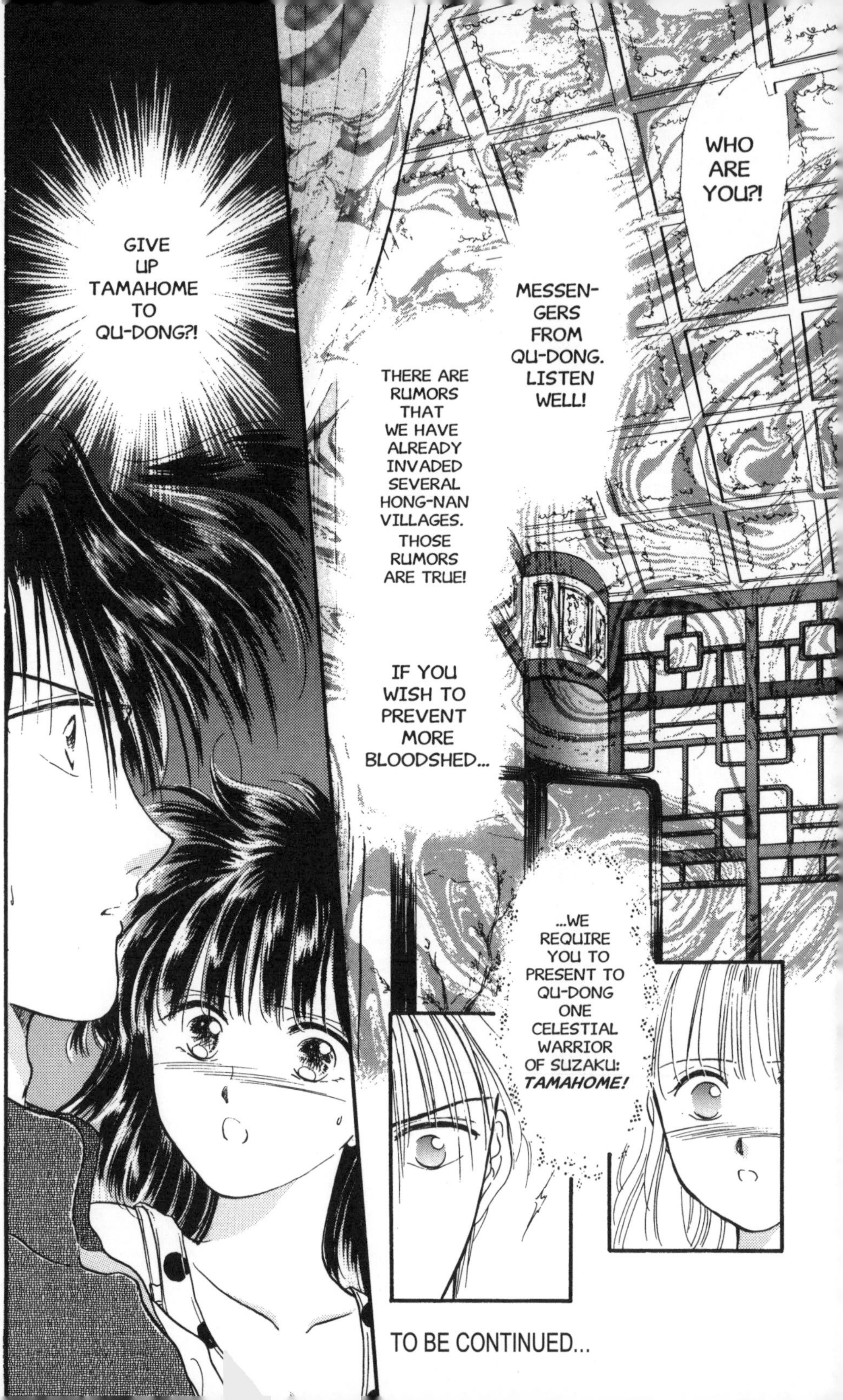
WHO ARE YOU?!
MESSEN-GERS FROM QU-DONG. LISTEN WELL!
THERE ARE RUMORS THAT WE HAVE ALREADY INVADED SEVERAL HONG-NAN VILLAGES. THOSE RUMORS ARE TRUE!
IF YOU WISH TO PREVENT MORE BLOODSHED...
...WE REQUIRE YOU TO PRESENT TO QU-DONG ONE CELESTIAL WARRIOR OF SUZAKU: *TAMAHOME!*
GIVE UP TAMAHOME TO QU-DONG?!
TO BE CONTINUED...

Sound Effects Glossary

Many of the sound effects (FX) in Fushigi Yûgi are as Yuu Watase created them–in the original Japanese. The FX in this glossary are listed by page number, followed by the panel number (e.g., "12.3" is page 12, panel 3).

CHAPTER ONE
THE YOUNG LADY OF LEGENDS

12.3 FX: SU [bowl disappearing]
12.4 FX: SU [bowl disappearing]

13.1 FX: GATAN [desk bumping floor]

14.2 FX: DOKA DOKA [whack whack]
14.3 FX: PITA [stopping in place]

15.2 FX: PAPAAA BUOOO [car horns beeping]
15.3 FX: PAAA [car horn beeping]

17.3 FX: KALI KALI [scribble scribble]

18.3 FX: KOLO KOLO KOLO [roll roll roll]
18.4 FX: GII [creak]

19.5 FX: PALA PALA [flip flip]

21.1 FX: DOKA [whack]
21.3 FX: ZUZU [earth quaking]
FX: ZUZUZUZU [bookshelves and earth shaking]
21.4 FX: BASA BASA BASA [books falling]

22-1.1 FX: BASA [book falling]
22-1.3 FX: BYOOOOOO [wind blowing]

24.1 FX: ELBO [whack]
24.2 FX: APPA [uppercut]

25.3 FX: KULULUN [twirl]

26.1 FX: DON [whump]
FX: GOHO [coughing]
26.2 FX: DOSA [thud]
FX: GEHO GEHO [coughing]
26.3 FX: BASHI [smack]

27.1 FX: GILI [gripping hard]

28.1 FX: BAKI [crack]
28.3 FX: FUWA [hair being lightly blown by a breeze]
28.4 FX: FUKI FUKI [wipe wipe]

29.6 FX: ZUZU [earth shaking]

30.1 FX: GULAAAA [tree leaning over]
FX: MEKI MEKI [tree breaking]
30.2 FX: SHIN [silence]

31.1 FX: BATAN [door slamming open]

33.1 FX: BESHI [slam]

36.2 FX: GILI [gripping hard]

37.2 FX: PAAA [car horn beeping]

38.2 FX: DOKUN DOKUN DOKUN DOKUN DOKUN [ba-dump ba-dump ba-dump ba-dump ba-dump]
FX: DA [dashing off]

39.1 FX: KON KON [tap tap]
39.3 FX: PATAN [click]

40.1 FX: GUI [yank]

42.1 FX: PAN [smack]

43.3 FX: DON [shove]

44.1 FX: BATAAN [slam]
FX: ZUZUZU [sliding down wall]

45.3 FX: KYOLO KYOLO [glance glance]
45.4 FX: KII [creak]
45.5 FX: PATAN [door closing softly]

46.2 FX: PETA [plop]

47.2-3 FX: DOKUN DOKUN DOKUN DOKUN DOKUN [ba-dump ba-dump ba-dump ba-dump ba-dump]

64.1 FX: DOSHEE [shriek]
64.2 FX: DON [thwack]
64.3 FX: DOKA DOKA DOKA [kick kick kick]
64.4 FX: YORO [wobble]
FX: Asia Kong is a pro wrestler in Japan.

65.1 FX: DOTA [thud]
65.2 FX: DAN [wham]
65.3 FX: BATA BATA [struggle struggle]
65.4 FX: SHU [swish]
65.5 FX: BISHI [smack]

66.1 FX: TOSA [whump]
66.2 FX: PASHI PASHI [flipping rock in palm]

67.1 FX: SUTO [landing lightly]
67.3 FX: GYU [squeeze]

68.2 FX: PON [pat]
68.3 FX: PA [quickly letting go]
68.5 FX: SUTA SUTA [stomp stomp]
68.6 FX: BITAN [thud]

69.2 FX: SUTA SUTA SUTA [stomp stomp stomp]
FX: TATA [scamper]

71.1 FX: DA [dash]
FX: BUTTOBI [boing]
71.4 FX: TATATA [running]

72.1 FX: GALA GALA [roll roll]
FX: TATA [walking]

73.1 FX: SHU SHU [small objects being thrown fast]
73.2 FX: BON BON [smoke bombs going off]
73.3 FX: BA [whisking away]
73.4 FX: HIHIIIN [horse whinny]
FX: GEHE GAHA [coughing]
FX: SUTA [landing on the ground]
FX: ZAWA ZAWA [crowd talking]

75.3 FX: POU [glow]
75.4 FX: GEHEGEHE GOHOGOHO [hacking, coughing]

76-5.1 FX: KAAAAAAAA [light emanating]
FX: SUU [becoming transparent]
76-5.2 FX: SUU [becoming transparent]
76-5.4 FX: WAAAAAAH [crowd shouting]
FX: KYAAAAA [woman screaming]

78.1 FX: SUUU [appearing]
78.2 FX: SUUU [appearing]

48.1 FX: KA [flash of light]
48.3 FX: PINPON PINPON [bell chiming]
FX: SAWA SAWA [people filing out]

49.1 FX: PALA PALA [flip flip]

CHAPTER TWO
THE BOY WITH THE DEMON STAR

51.3 FX: SHIN [silence]
51.4 FX: GALA GALA GALA GALA [clip clop clip clop]
51.5 FX: GABA [whoosh]

52.1 FX: GALA GALA GALA GALA [clip clop clip clop]
52.3 FX: ORO ORO [fluster fluster]

53.1 FX: GALA GALA GALA GALA [clip clop clip clop]
53.3 FX: GALA GALA [clop clop]
FX: TON [feet hitting ground]

54.3 FX: ZOLO ZOLO [shuffle shuffle]

55.4 FX: JIRO JIRO [stare stare]

56.1 FX: GUKYULULULU [growling stomach]
56.3 FX: DAAAA [drooling profusely]
56.4 FX: CHALIN [money clinking]

57.1-4 FX: TA TA TA TA TA TA TA [skipping lightly]

58.1 FX: WAAA WAAA [crowd yelling, cheering]
58.2 FX: TEKU TEKU [walking dispiritedly]
58.3 FX: PON [tap]

59.5 FX: ZAWA ZAWA ZAWA [laughing, talking]

60.1 FX: PIKU [ping]
60.2 FX: POLI POLI [crunch crunch]
60.4 FX: SA [swish]
60.5 FX: NIKO [grin]

61.1 FX: SUTA SUTA SUTA SUTA
[stomp stomp stomp stomp]
61.3 FX: PIKA [stop]

62.3 FX: PILA [flip]
62.4 FX: PAN [whack]
62.5 FX: JILI JILI [scratch scratch]

63.2 FX: BA [rolling up sleeve]
63.4 FX: DOKOO [whack]

78.4 FX: HISHI [grasping tightly]
78.5 FX: SHIN [silence]

79.5 FX: JAKI [spears being pointed]

CHAPTER THREE
THE PRIESTESS OF SUZAKU

82.1 FX: GYU [squeeze]
82.3 FX: ZAZA [backing away quickly]

84.3 FX: ZUKIN [stab at heart]
84.5 FX: PEN [slap]

86.2 FX: KASA [putting hand in skirt pocket]

87.4 FX: GASHI [grasp]
87.5 FX: GIII [creak]

88.1 FX: DOKI DOKI DOKI DOKI
[ba-dump ba-dump ba-dump ba-dump]

89.4 FX: FULA FULA [stagger stagger]
89.5 FX: KULU [turn]

90.1 FX: SHIIIN [silence]
90.2 FX: FULA FULA [stagger stagger]

92.1 FX: GAAAAAAN [despair]

93.1 FX: NIKO [smile]
FX: NIKO[smile]
93.3 FX: SUTA SUTA SUTA [stomp stomp stomp]
FX: SUTO [landing lightly]
93.4 FX: NIKKORI [grin]

95.1 FX: HA [gasp]

96.3 FX: SALA [twinkle]
FX: DOKI [ba-dump]

97.1 FX: HA [gasp]
97.4 FX: GA [whack]
97.5 FX: ZA [rushing out of bushes]

98.3 FX: GA [grab]
98.4 FX: DOGA [thwack]
98.5 FX: DOSA [konk]

99.1 FX: SU [symbol appearing on forehead]

100.1 FX: ZAZA [soldiers saluting]

103.5 FX: DOKUN DOKUN DOKUN DOKUN
[ba-dump ba-dump ba-dump ba-dump]

105.3 FX: ZAWA [murmuring]

106.2 FX: ZA [bowing]

108.2 FX: KACHA KACHA [jiggling doorknob]
FX: KOTSU KOTSU [shuffle shuffle]
108.5 FX: PALA PALA [flip flip]

109.2 FX: PATAN [whud]
109.4 FX: HETA [slump]

CHAPTER FOUR
THE SEVEN CONSTELLATIONS OF SUZAKU

111.1 FX: PAPAAA [car horns beeping]
111.2 FX: HA HA [huff huff]
111.3 FX: TATA [running]

114.4 FX: KON [thonk]

116.2 FX: KYU [cuddle]

119.1 FX: SU [pulling shirt aside]

121.5 FX: POKI POKO [cracking knuckles]

122.1 FX: SU [getting into fighting position]
122.3 FX: DOKA GA BISHI [hitting, kicking]

123.1 FX: PITA [stopping suddenly]

125.5 FX: PIKU PIKU [twitch twitch]

126.1 FX: WANA WANA [tremble tremble]
126.2 FX: DON [very angry]
126.3 FX: BUN [punching]
FX: HYOI [jumping out of the way]
126.4 FX: BAKI [breaking off]
FX: SUTATATATA [scurry]
FX: MEKI MEKI MEKI [crack crack crack]
126.5 FX: HAA HAA [pant, gasp]

127.1 FX: DON DOON [objects hitting columns]
127.2 FX: MEKI MEKI [crack crack]

128.2 FX: GALA GALA [crumble crumble]
128.4 FX: ZUDOON [structure imploding]
128.5 FX: PI PI [cha-ching]

129.4 FX: JIWA [blood soaking through skirt]

130.1 FX: ZUKIN [ouch]
130.4 FX: ZAWA ZAWA [murmur murmur]

131.3 FX: GIGIG [column pressing down]

132.2 FX: DOKUN [ba-dump]
132.3 FX: MIKI MIKI MIKI [crack crack crack]

133.3 FX: ZU [massive pressure]
133.4 FX: SU [moving quickly]

134.1 FX: GAKON [moving column]
FX: HYOI [lifting]
134.2 FX: DOON [thud]
134.3 FX: PON PON PON [toss toss toss]
134.4 FX: GAKON [moving column]

136.2 FX: HELON [faint]
136.4 FX: NI [grin]

138.1 FX: NIKO [grin]

139.1 FX: SUI [whoosh]

CHAPTER FIVE
DANGEROUS LOVE

142.3 FX: BATAN [slam]

143.1 FX: JAAA [running water]
FX: GOSHI GOSHI [scrub scrub]
143.2-3 FX: SU [stain vanishing]

144.2 FX: ZUKI [ouch]
144.5 FX: DOTATATA [stomp]

145.1 FX: BAM [slam]
145.3 FX: SHULULU [sash being flung]

146.2 FX: BATAN [slam]
FX: HOHOHOHO [ha ha ha ha]

148.1 FX: HYOI [lifting hair]
148.2 FX: BISHA [splash]

148.6 FX: GAN [gonk]

150.1 FX: GAN [gonk]
150.2 FX: GYUU GYULULUUU [stomach growling]

152.2 FX: GUI [yank]
152.4 FX: DOKIN [ba-dump]

153.3 FX: JI [stare]
153.4 FX: PUPU [heh heh]

158.2 FX: ZA [wind rustling through trees]
158.3 FX: HYOKO HYOKO [limp limp]

159.1 FX: BULU [shiver]
FX: HYOKO [limp]
159.2 FX: BASA BASA [birds flapping wings]
159.3 FX: SHULU [tendril whipping out]
FX: ZAZA [drag]
159.4 FX: ZU [yank]

160.1 FX: PATAN [door closing quietly]
160.2 FX: BISHU [splash]
160.3 FX: POTA POTA [drip drip]

161.3 FX: GABO GABO GABO [gurgling underwater]
FX: GOBO [coughing underwater]
161.4 FX: JIWA [bandages loosening]

162.3 FX: TOTATATA [running]
162.4 FX: ZA [turn]

163.1 FX: BAN [wham]
163.2 FX: GUI [yank]
163.5 FX: BUCHI [snap]

164.2 FX: GA [grab]
164.5 FX: GYUU [clutch]

165.2 FX: POTA POTA [drip drip]
165.3 FX: HYOKO HYOKO [hobble hobble]

166.4 FX: PAN [smack]
166.5 FX: PAN [smack]

168.2 FX: DOKI [ba-dump]
168.3 FX: HYOI [lowering head]

169.4 FX: GUI [tug]

CHAPTER SIX
HIDDEN LOVE

172.1-2 FX: DOKUN DOKUN DOKUN DOKUN DOKUN DOKUN DOKUN DOKUN [ba-dump ba-dump ba-dump ba-dump ba-dump ba-dump ba-dump ba-dump]

173.1 FX: DOKIN [ba-dump]
173.4 FX: SU [moving quickly and quietly]

174.1 FX: SUTA SUTA SUTA [walking briskly]
174.2 FX: SU [drawing sword]
174.3 FX: HYU HYU HYU HYU [slice slice slice slice]
174.4 FX: PISHI PISHI [crack crack]
174.5 FX: BALA BALA [crumble]

175.6 FX: SUI [pang]

176.1 FX: PATA PATA [pitter patter]
176.2 FX: SU [grab]

178.4 FX: SU [walking by]

179.2 FX: SUTA SUTA [stomp stomp]
179.5 FX: ZUOOOOO [anger]

180.1 FX: ZUGOGOGOGO [anger]

181.4 FX: TON [stepping onto platform]

183.4 FX: GUI [whack]

184.2 FX: SHIIIIIN [silence]

186.1 FX: GYU GYU [squash squish]

189.1 FX: DOKI [ba-dump]
189.2 FX: DA [running]

190.2 FX: GUI [grab]
190.3 FX: GYO [shock]

194.1 FX: BAKI [thwack]
194.3 FX: DO [kick]

195.2 FX: ZAN [moving quickly]
195.3 FX: PI [snip]
195.4 FX: BAKI [thwack]
195.5 FX: DOSU [whud]

196.1 FX: SUTO [landing lightly on feet]

CHAPTER SEVEN
THE AIMLESS HEART

205.1 FX: HA HA HA HA [huff huff huff]

207.3 FX: GYU [clench]
207.4 FX: SU [swoosh]

209.3 FX: HA [gasp]

211.4 FX: DOKI [ba-dump]

212.2 FX: DOKUN DOKUN DOKUN [ba-dump ba-dump ba-dump]

213.5 FX: BISHI [vwip]

214.2 FX: DOTA BATA [hustle scramble]
FX: SAWA SAWA [fluster fluster]

215.2 FX: DOKI [ba-dump]
215.5 FX: PUI [twirl]
215.6 FX: GIII [creak]

216.1 FX: KA [clop]

217.2 FX: KAPO KAPO [clop clop]
217.4 FX: KAPO KAPO KAPO [clop clop clop]

218.2 FX: GAAA [snore]
218.4 FX: HAA HAA [huff huff]

219.5 FX: SUKAAA [snore]

220.1 FX: GASHI [clench]

221.3 FX: BUKU [glug]
221.5 FX: KULA [dizzy]

222.4 FX: HA HA [huff huff]
222.5 FX: PASA [slipping out of clothes]

223.1 FX: SU [headache suddenly lifting]
223.3 FX: CHAPO [splorsh]
223.4 FX: BUKU BUKU [glug glug]

224.3 FX: BASHA BASHA [splash splash]
224.4 FX: SUUUUU [swoooosh]
224.5 FX: BASHA BASHA [splash splash]

225.1 FX: ZAZAAAA [splorsh]
FX: ZA [crunch]
225.3 FX: SHU [whoosh]

226.1 FX: DOBOOM [sploosh]
226.2 FX: BUKU BUKU [glug glug]
226.3 FX: SHIIIIN [silence]

227.3 FX: PON [thump]
227.5 FX: HATA [gasp]

228.2 FX: SHIIIIIN [wind blowing]
228.3 FX: DOKI DOKI DOKI DOKI DOKI DOKI DOKI [ba-dump ba-dump ba-dump ba-dump ba-dump ba-dump ba-dump]

229.3 FX: ZABA [sploosh]

231.3 FX: BATA BATA [struggle struggle]
231.5 FX: PALA [slip]

232.3 FX: SHIIIIN [silence]

233.4 FX: KU KU [snicker snicker]

CHAPTER EIGHT
A DARK INVITATION

239.5 FX: PII CHI CHI CHI [tweet chirp chirp chirp]

240.2 FX: BASA BASA [flap flap]
240.5 FX: DOKI [ba-dump]

241.1 FX: DOKI DOKI DOKI DOKI [ba-dump ba-dump ba-dump ba-dump]

242.3 FX: FU [float]
242.4 FX: KULU KULU KULU KULU [whirl whirl whirl whirl]
242.5 FX: FU [mirror disappearing]

243.1 FX: KAPPO KAPPO [clop clop]
243.2 FX: TSUN [trip]
243.4 FX: BA [whoosh]

244.2 FX: DA [dashing off]
FX: DALA DALA [drip drip]
244.4 FX: SAAA [disappearing into the fog]

245.3 FX: KON [kick]
245.4 FX: KOLO KOLO KOLO [roll roll roll]

247.1 FX: SUPON [slipping through barrier]
247.3 FX: DON DON [bam bam]
247.4 FX: ZA [step]

249.2 FX: GUSHA [stomp]
249.4 FX: DON DON [bang bang]
249.5 FX: NULI [shup]

250.2 FX: DON DON [bang bang]

251.4 FX: PUHA [gulp]
251.5 FX: ZA [step]

252.1 FX: DOKI [ba-dump]
252.3 FX: DODODODODON [Ba-ba-bam]

254.4 FX: DON [thud]

256.5 FX: DA [dash]

257.1 FX: SUTO [tump]
257.2 FX: TATA [run]
257.3 FX: PA [flash]
257.6 FX: CHAKI [drawing sword]

258.4 FX: ZA [zhoosh]

260.2 FX: SA [fwoosh]
260.3 FX: KA [flash]
260.4 FX: BALI BALI [zap zap]

261.5 FX: GAKU [thump]
FX: ZULU [slump]

263.2 FX: BA [swoosh]
263.3 FX: PALIN [shatter]
263.4 FX: DOSU [stab]

264.2 FX: GYAAAHH [screech]
264.5 FX: BA [fwoosh]
264.6 FX: SSSSSSSSSKEEECH [screech]
FX: DON [smack]

CHAPTER NINE
AWAKENING MEMORIES

266.3 FX: GAN [boot]
266.5 FX: PIKU [ping]

267.1 FX: BA [blood soaking through]
267.3 FX: BA [goosh]
267.4 FX: ZULU [slump]
267.5 FX: CHALIN [clank]

268.1 FX: ZUBU [stab]
268.3 FX: GEHO [cough]

269.2 FX: GYAAAHH [screech]
269.5 FX: BA [fwoosh]

270.1 FX: PAN [tump]
270.2 FX: DON [thwack]
270.3-4 FX: BA [vwoosh]

271.1-2 FX: ZA [slash]
271.3 FX: SHU [swoosh]
271.4 FX: ZAN [slice]
FX: SUTO [tump]
271.5 FX: GEBO [cough]

273.4 FX: SUUUU [appearing out of thin air]

276.2 FX: BI [rip]

281.4 FX: HA HA HA HA [huff huff huff huff]

282.4 FX: BA [fwoosh]
282.6 FX: ZULU ZULU [drag drag]

283.1 FX: ZULU [drag]

284.1 FX: ZULU [drag]

285.1 FX: ZULU [drag]
285.4 FX: PO [plip]

286.3 FX: CHA [chink]
286.4 FX: BA [clutch]

288.1 FX: ZASHU [slash]
FX: BOTA BOTA [spatter spatter]
288.3 FX: PIKUN [twitch]

293.1 FX: SUU [float]

294.3 FX: CHA [chink]
294.4 FX: BA [clutch]
294.5 FX: GRUNCH [grab]

CHAPTER TEN
COME BACK HOME

297.5 FX: FUWA [float]

299.4 FX: PALA [flip]

300.1 FX: PALA [flip]

302.3 FX: POU [glow]
302.4 FX: SUTO [tump]
302.5 FX: WALA WALA [shuffle shuffle]

303.4 FX: BABA [strip]
303.5 FX: NUUU [wah]

305.4 FX: POU [pong]

306.1 FX: FUWA [float]
306.4-5 FX: BA [vwip]

307.2 FX: DOKUN [ba-dump]
307.3 FX: DOKU DOKU [ba-dump ba-dump]

308.1-4 FX: DOKU DOKU DOKU DOKU
[ba-dump ba-dump ba-dump ba-dump]
308.5 FX: SUUU [wound disappearing]

309.3 FX: FAN FAN [sound of sirens]
309.4 FX: FAN FAN FAN [sound of sirens]
FX: KI [screech]

310.5 FX: FAN FAN FAN [sound of sirens]

311.1 FX: SHU [bubble disappearing]
FX: GAKUN [thud]
311.2 FX: KISE KISE [putting on clothes]

312.5 FX: PON [clap]

317.4 FX: BUON [vwoosh]

318.3 FX: DON DON DON [bang bang bang]
318.4-5 FX: DON DON [bang bang]
318.5 FX: DON [bang]

323.1 FX: BAN [bam]
323.3 FX: KAAAAAAAA [flash]

CHAPTER ELEVEN
LONGING FOR YOU

326.2 FX: KAAAAAAAA [flash]

327.4 FX: KA [flash]
327.5 FX: PALI PALI PALI PALI
[crackle crackle crackle crackle]

328.1 FX: PALI PALI [crackle crackle]
328.3 FX: BA [gasp]

330.7 FX: MOTA KUTA [struggle struggle]

331.1 FX: DOTA [thud]

333.3 FX: SHIIIN [silence]

334.4 FX: FUU FUU [blow blow]

336.1 FX: KOKU KOKU KOKU [nod nod nod]

337.1 FX: KI [creak]

339.2 FX: TOLULU [ring]
FX: TOLULULU [ring]
339.5 FX: PATAN [flop]

340.1 FX: KI [creak]
340.2 FX: KALI [skritch]

341.2 FX: SUU [snore]
341.5 FX: SUTATATATA [tump tump tump tump]

342.3 FX: KUN KUN [sniff sniff]
342.4 FX: ZAWA ZAWA [chatter chatter]

343.5 FX: PAN PAN [clap clap]

345.2 FX: KALI KALI KALI [skritch skritch skritch]
345.4 FX: KALI KALI KALI KALI KALI
[skritch skritch skritch skritch skritch]
345.6 FX: GOSHI GOSHI [erase erase]

346.1 FX: GAKU GAKU GAKU
[tremble tremble tremble]
346.2 FX: KALI KALI KALI [skritch skritch skritch]
346.3 FX: CHI CHI [tick tick]
346.4 FX: KALI KALI KALI [skritch skritch skritch]

347.1 FX: KAKU KAKU KAKU [tremble tremble tremble]
347.2 FX: POKIN [snap]
347.3 FX: CHI CHI [tick tick]
347.4 FX: KALI KALI KALI KALI KALI KALI KALI
[skritch skritch skritch skritch skritch
skritch skritch]

350.1 FX: GATAN [kachunk]

351.2 FX: ZULU [slip]
351.3 FX: DOTA [whud]

352.1 FX: HIKKU [sniffle]

353.3 FX: GYU [clench]
353.4 FX: KACHI KIIIN KOOON [tick bong bong]
353.5 FX: KAAN KOOON KIIN KOON
[bong bong bong bong]

354.4 FX: HA HA [huff huff]
FX: GACHA [kachak]

356.3 FX: ZA [slash]

CHAPTER TWELVE
REACHING OUT

359.3 FX: BATAN [slam]
359.4 FX: GATA GATAN [clank clatter]

360.2 FX: BATA BATA [tump tump]
360.5 FX: GYU [shove]

362.2 FX: BAA [beep]
FX: GATAN GATAN [clack clack]

363.1 FX: KACHA KACHA [rattle rattle]
FX: DOTA DOTA DOTA [thud thud thud]
363.5 FX: DON DON BAN [bang bang bam]

364.3 FX: SHULU [slip]
364.5 FX: PALA [flip]

365.2 FX: KA [flash]

366.1 FX: FU [disappearing]
FX: TOSA [thonk]

367.3 FX: KA [flash]

368.1 FX: DOSU [thud]
368.2 FX: BELI BELI [zzzt zzzt]

369.1 FX: DOKIN [ba-dump]
369.3 FX: DOKI DOKI DOKI
[ba-dump ba-dump ba-dump]

372.1 FX: TA TA [tump tump]

376.2 FX: KA KA KA [clop clop clop]
376.3 FX: HIHIIIIN [neigh]
376.4 FX: GA [trip]

377.1 FX: DOTAAA [thud]
FX: HIHIIIN [neigh]

377.3 FX: HIHIIIN [neigh]
377.5 FX: ZA [slice]

379.1 FX: TA TA [tump tump]
379.2 FX: FU [fwoo]

380.1 FX: YORO [wobble]

382.1 FX: TOKUN TOKUN TOKUN TOKUN [ba-dump ba-dump ba-dump ba-dump]

383.4 FX: JIIII [stare]
FX: HA [gasp]

384.1 FX: ZAWA [murmur]
384.4 FX: ZAWA ZAWA [chatter chatter]

385.2 FX: SU [shwoo]
385.4 FX: SU [shwooosh]

CHAPTER THIRTEEN
THE INVISIBLE ENEMY

390.1 FX: ZAZA [zshaa]
390.2 FX: ZU [zwoosh]
390.3 FX: ZA [zsh]
390.4 FX: ZAWA [rustle]

391.2 FX: BA [yank]

392.1 FX: KAPO [kwop]
392.2 FX: SU [swoosh]
392.3 FX: PATA [pft]

393.1 FX: ZA [zsh]
393.4 FX: GAKU GAKU [tremble tremble]
393.5 FX: GYU [squeeze]

395.1 FX: BAN [bam]

396.2 FX: CHUN CHICHI [chirp chirp]
396.3 FX: BUTSU BUTSU [mumble mumble]
396.4 FX: GATA [gatunk]
396.5 FX: KATAN [katunk]

397.1 FX: BULULU [neeeigh]
397.2 FX: JIII [staaare]
397.3 FX: SUUUU [zzzz]

398.1 FX: KOSO [sneak]

399.1 FX: DOKI [ba-dump]
399.3 FX: EHEHE [hee hee]
399.3 FX: KA [clomp]
399.4 FX: GALAN [glonk]

400.2 FX: DOKIN [ba-dump]

401.3 FX: JALA [clink]

403.3 FX: GYU [squeeze]

405.2 FX: BA [bwah]

407.2 FX: KA [blush]

409.2 FX: PASHA [splosh]
409.5 FX: ZULU [slip]

410.4 FX: SU [shff]
410.5 FX: DOKI [ba-dump]

411.1 FX: SA [shwa]
411.3 FX: BUN [bwoosh]
411.4 FX: BIKU [shudder]

412.1 FX: BAN [bam]
412.3 FX: ZUBO [zvoh]
412.4 FX: BUN [bwoosh]
412.5 FX: PITA [stop]

413.1 FX: BISHI [vwap]
413.2 FX: BA [bwah]
413.3 FX: DON [dwom]
413.4 FX: SU [swish]

414.1 FX: BA [vwip]
414.2 FX: DON [thwakam]

415.1 FX: SU [shwa]
415.2 FX: SU [shwosh]
415.3 FX: BA [grasp]
415.3 FX: PATA PATA [paft paft]

416.2 FX: SHAN [ching]
416.4 FX: KAPO [fwip]

417.2 FX: DA [dash]

CHAPTER FOURTEEN
LET ME PROTECT YOU

421.3 FX: DAN [bam]

423.2 FX: BYU [vwip]
423.3 FX: SHULU [shwwrrsh]

424.5 FX: SU [sshh]
424.6 FX: SHAN [clang]

425.1 FX: SU [shwa]
425.2 FX: BALA BALA [crumble crumble]

426.1 FX: SHU [fwoosh]
426.2 FX: BA [vwah]
426.3 FX: BI [rip]

427.1 FX: GYU [clutch]
427.2 FX: BOKI BEKI [crack snap]
427.6 FX: DOSU [thunk]

430.4 FX: NIKO [grin]

432.1 FX: WASHI WASHI [That's me. Me.]

437.3 FX: DA [dash]
437.4 FX: SU [shwa]

438.4 FX: KA KA [caw caw]
438.5 FX: ZA [zash]

439.4 FX: GA [roooaaar]

440.1 FX: BA [bwosh]
440.2 FX: GAKU GAKU [tremble tremble]
FX: GULULU [grrrrrr]
440.4 FX: GYU [grip]

441.1 FX: BA [pounce]
441.2 FX: BYU [vwish]
441.3 FX: GA [gack]

442.1 FX: GA [roar]
442.3 FX: DOGO [thwack]
442.4 FX: DO [thud]

444.4 FX: DOKIN DOKIN DOKIN
[ba-dump ba-dump ba-dump]

445.1 FX: GYU [squeeze]

446.3 FX: ZULU [slip]

448.2 FX: YORO [wobble]
448.4 FX: GALA GALA GALA [clop clop clop]
448.5 FX: TATA [dash]
448.5-6 FX: GALA GALA GALA [clop clop clop]
448.6 FX: TOSA [twft]

449.3 FX: GALA GALA GALA [clop clop clop]

CHAPTER FIFTEEN
CAPTIVE WOMEN

452.3 FX: GYULULULU [grrrrowwl]

453.2 FX: GATAN [gonk]

454.2 FX: DA [dash]

455.2 FX: NIKO [grin]

458.1 FX: CHICHICHI [chirp chirp]

461.1 FX: KA [clop]

462.2 FX: KA KA [clop clop]

463.1 FX: GOLO GOLO GOLO [rumble rumble rumble]
463.3 FX: HALA [hwaf]
463.4 FX: HISO HISO HISO [whisper whisper whisper]

464.2 FX: GASHI [grab]
464.3 FX: BOKA [bonk]
464.3 FX: SU [shw]
464.5 FX: BI [freeze]

465.1 FX: KA [clop]
465.2 FX: BIKU [jolt]
465.3 FX: KA [clop]

466.3 FX: FU [fwash]

467.1 FX: SUTO [shatunk]
467.2 FX: DOKI [ba-dump]

470.1 FX: DOOON DOOON DOOON
[dooong dooong dooong]

471.4 FX: KAPO [kwoft]
471.5 FX: SALA [shf]

473.1 FX: ZAWA [gasp]
473.5 FX: SU [fht]

474.1 FX: FULA [wobble]

476.3 FX: DOSA [thud]

477.1 FX: POLO POLO [weep weep]

478.3 FX: ZAWA ZAWA [chatter chatter]

CHAPTER SIXTEEN
THE PRIESTESS OF SEIRYU

483.3 FX: ZA [zash]

484.1 FX: BATA BATA [stomp stomp]
484.4 FX: DON [shove]

485.2 FX: DA [dash]
485.3 FX: BATA BATA [dart dash]
485.4 FX: HA HA HA [gasp pant]

487.3 FX: SAAAA [fshhhh]
487.3 FX: GOLO GOLO GOLO [rumble rumble rumble]
487.4 FX: DOSA [thud]

488.1 FX: KA [flash]

489.1 FX: GOLO GOLO GOLO [rumble rumble rumble]
489.4 FX: BA [bwah]

490.1 FX: GA [gonk]
490.2 FX: SUTO [shtk]
490.3 FX: PIKI [pwik]
490.4 FX: GATA [falter]
490.4 FX: BASHA [splosh]

491.3 FX: BI [vwip]
491.4 FX: DA [dash]
491.6 FX: BASHI [vwap]

493.2 FX: DOSU [donk]
493.3 FX: ZULU [topple]
493.4 FX: SA [swish]

495.2 FX: BATA BATA [stomp stomp]
495.4 FX: BATA BATA [stomp stomp]

497.1 FX: SU [shwa]

498.5 FX: DA [dash]

499.3 FX: HA HA [huff huff]
499.4 FX: HA [gasp]

501.2-3 FX: DOKUN DOKUN DOKUN DOKUN DOKUN [ba-dump ba-dump ba-dump ba-dump ba-dump]

502.4 FX: GYU [clench]

503.4 FX: NIKO [grin]
503.5 FX: PIKA [flash]

504.2 FX: GIII [creeeeak]
504.3 FX: TATA [scamper]

505.1 FX: KA [flash]
505.2 FX: BASHI [bzatt]
505.3 FX: BATAN [bam]
505.4 FX: SU [shwa]

506.1 FX: GOLO GOLO GOLO [rumble rumble rumble]
506.2 FX: HA HA [gasp wheeze]

507.1 FX: KA [flash]
507.3 FX: GAKUN [gakunk]
507.4 FX: GOLO GOLO GOLO [rumble rumble rumble]

508.3 FX: GUI [yank]

509.4 FX: SU [shwa]

511.2 FX: SU [shwa]
511.3 FX: KA [krah]
511.4 FX: BA [vwish]

512.5 FX: SU [shwa]

CHAPTER SEVENTEEN
SOULS DRIFTING APART

514.1 FX: BABA [bwatch]
514.2 FX: DOSA [thud]
514.2 FX: SU [step]

515.5 FX: BASHI [bzap]

516.1 FX: HA HA [huff huff]
516.3 FX: YORO [wobble]

CHAPTER EIGHTEEN
ONLY YOU

546.2   FX: SU [stride]

548.3   FX: SU [swsh]
548.5   FX: GOOOOO [gwooooh]

549.1   FX: GOOOOO [gwooooh]

550.5   FX: FUWA [float]

551.2   FX: ZUKIN [zing]
551.3   FX: KA [flash]
551.4   FX: HISO HISO [whisper whisper]

552.3   FX: KIIIN KOOON KAAN KOON
       [diiing doong diiing doong]

553.3   FX: FU [fwosh]

554.5   FX: NIKO [smile]

556.2   FX: SU [shw]

557.1   FX: FU [fha]

558.1   FX: GYUU [embrace]
558.2   FX: MU [grr]

559.3   FX: SU [swish]

560.2   FX: ZUKA ZUKA ZUKA [stomp stomp stomp]
560.3   FX: BAN [bam]

563.3   FX: JITA BATA [struggle struggle]

564.2   FX: KATAN [katunk]

565.1   FX: CHA [chlik]
565.2   FX: SU [swish]

568.2   FX: DOKIN [ba-dump]
568.3   FX: PATAN [pft]

569.4   FX: DOKI DOKI [ba-dump ba-dump]

572.1-2 FX: HYU [hwoosh]
572.3   FX: BA [bwah]
572.4   FX: BATA BATA [dash dash]
572.5   FX: BAN [bam]

517.1   FX: DON [vwamk]

518.1   FX: GATAN GOTON [glonk gatunk]
518.5   FX: KA [flash]

519.1   FX: PIIII [bweeeeep]
519.2   FX: BUN [bam]

520.1   FX: PITA [freeze]
520.2   FX: FUWA [float]

521.1   FX: DON [daboom]
521.2   FX: BAN [bam]

522.1   FX: BALI BALI [crackle bzzzap]
522.3   FX: BALI BALI [crackle bzzzap]

523.1   FX: DOKA [punch]
523.3   FX: ZUKI [zing]

525.1   FX: BA [bwah]
525.2   FX: BASHI [bwam]
525.3   FX: PALA [fwip]

526.3   FX: ZU [zwip]
526.5   FX: ZU [zwop]
526.6   FX: SU [swish]

527.4   FX: KIIN KOON KAAN KOON
       [diiing doong diing doong]

530.3   FX: HA [gasp]

533.4   FX: BUTSU BUTSU [mumble grumble]
533.5   FX: PELI [rip]

535.2   FX: PI [point]
535.4   FX: SUUU [shwaaa]

536.1   FX: PA [flash]
536.3   FX: BOSO [mutter]

537.1   FX: HA [gasp]
537.2   FX: DA [dash]

538.2   FX: BASHI [slap]

539.2   FX: FU [fwosh]

542.1   FX: SUKA [skoosh]

CHINESE-TO-JAPANESE GLOSSARY

The *Universe of the Four Gods* is based on ancient China, but Japanese pronunciation of Chinese names differs slightly from their Chinese equivalents.

Chinese	Japanese	Person, Place, or Object	Meaning
Xong Gui-Siu	Sô Kishuku	Tamahome	Demon Constellation
Hong-Nan	Konan	Southern Kingdom	Crimson South
Gong Wu	Kyûbu	Clue	Palace Strength
Tai Yi-Jun	Tai Itsukun	Oracle	Preeminent Person
Kang-Lin	Kôrin	Lady of Hong-Nan	Peaceful Jewel
Daichi-San	Daikyokuzan	Mountain	Greatest Mountain
Lai Lai	Nyan Nyan	Servant	Nanny
Qu-Dong	Kûto	Eastern Kingdom	Gathered East
Zhong-Rong	Chûei	Second Son	Loyalty, Honor
Chun-Jing	Shunkei	Third Son	Spring, Respect
Yu-Lun	Gyokuran	Eldest Daughter	Jewel, Orchid
Jie-Lian	Yuire	Youngest Daughter	Connection, Lotus

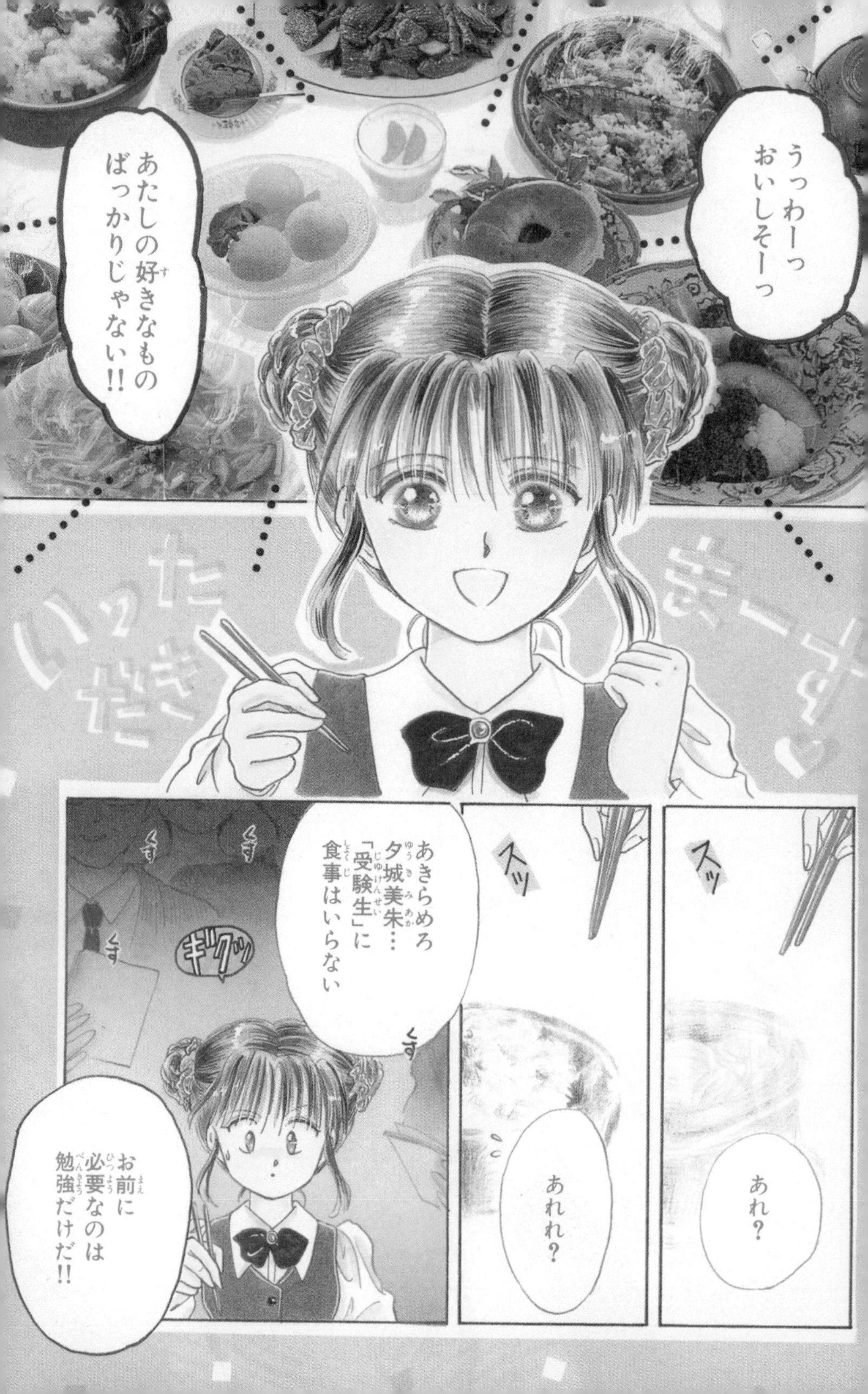
うっわーっ おいしそーっ
あたしの好きなもの ばっかりじゃない!!
いっただきまーす♡
スッ
あれ?
スッ
あれれ?
あきらめろ 夕城美朱… 「受験生」に 食事はいらない
くす くす
ギクッ
くす
くす
お前に 必要なのは 勉強だけだ!!

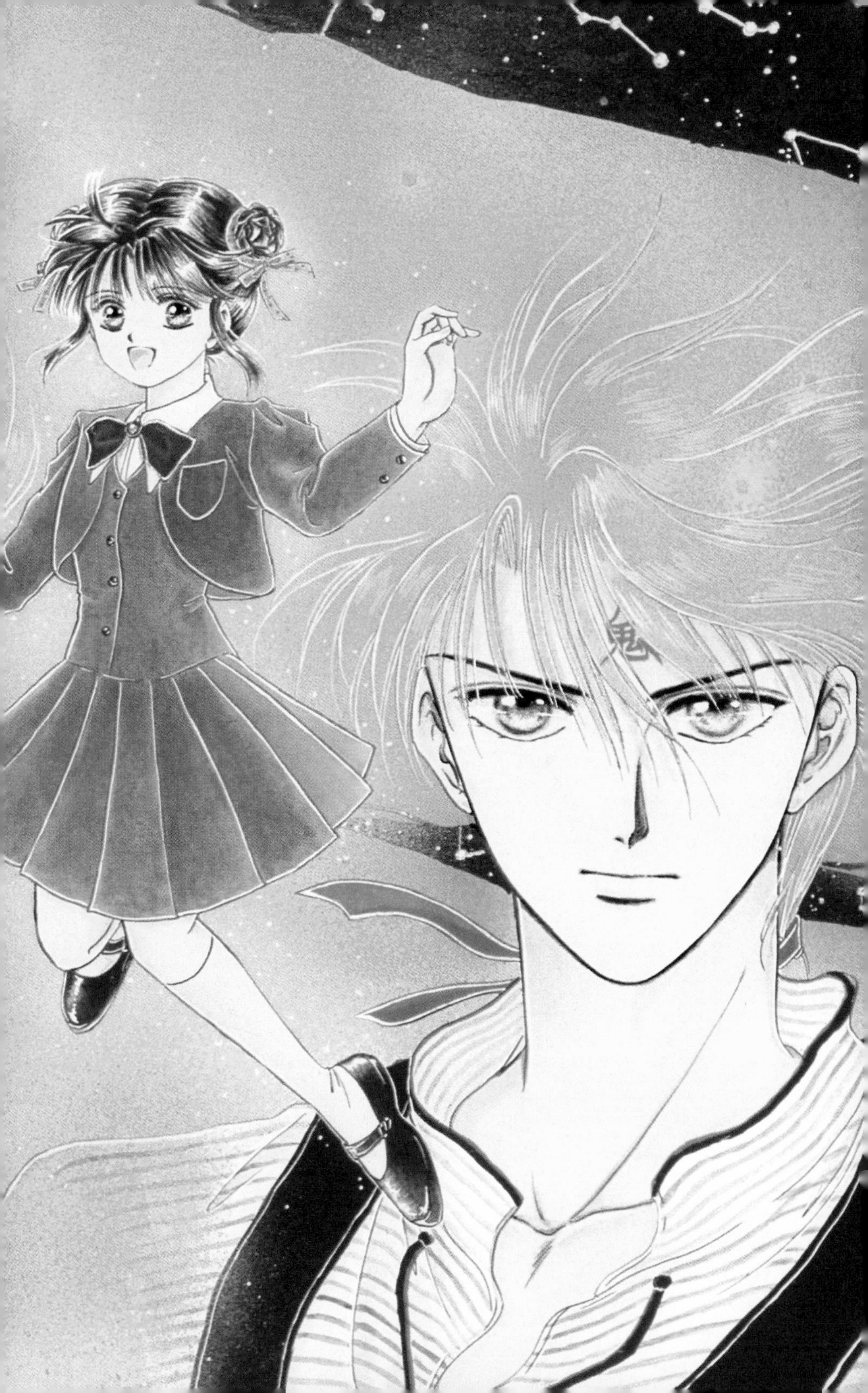
鬼

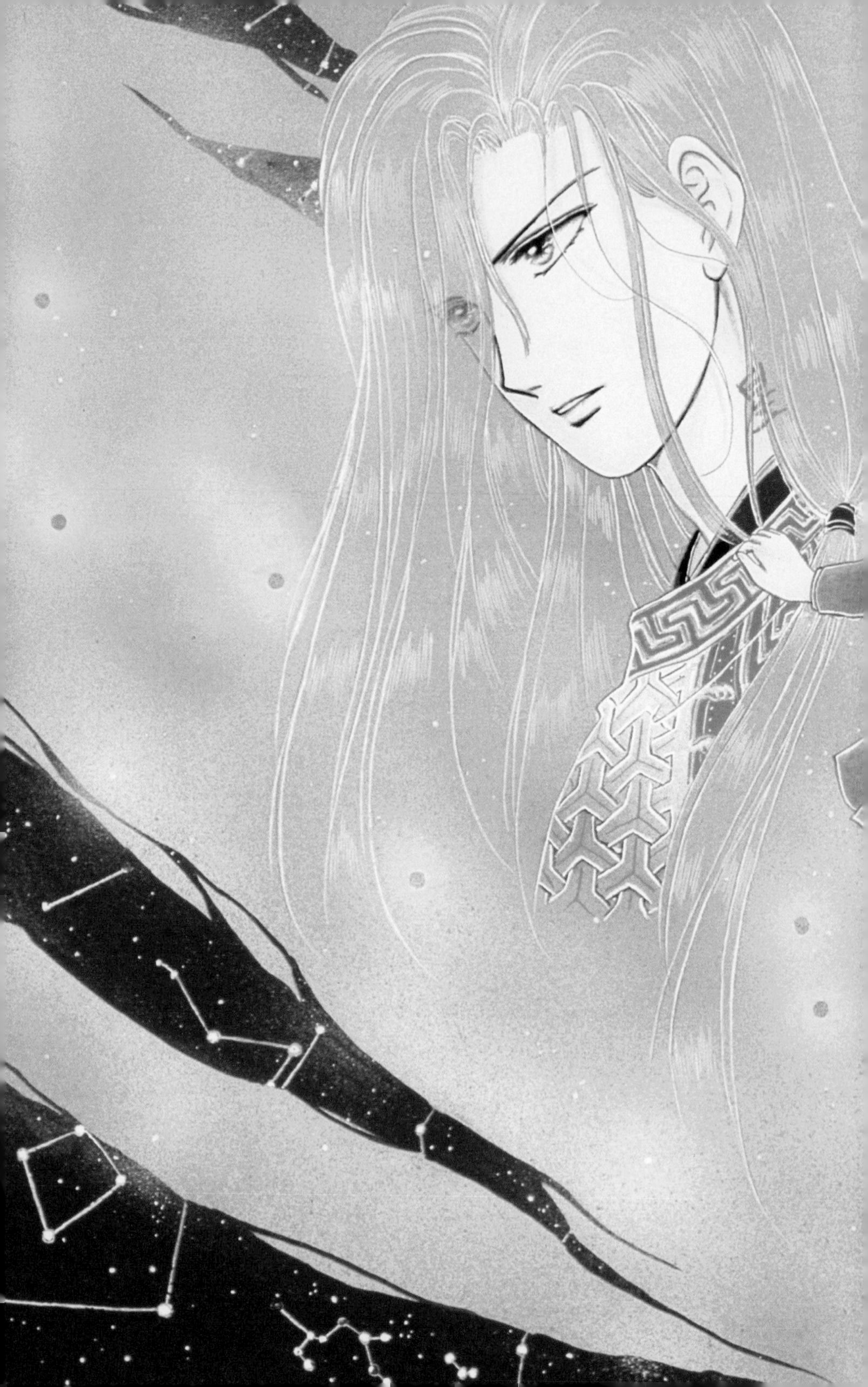

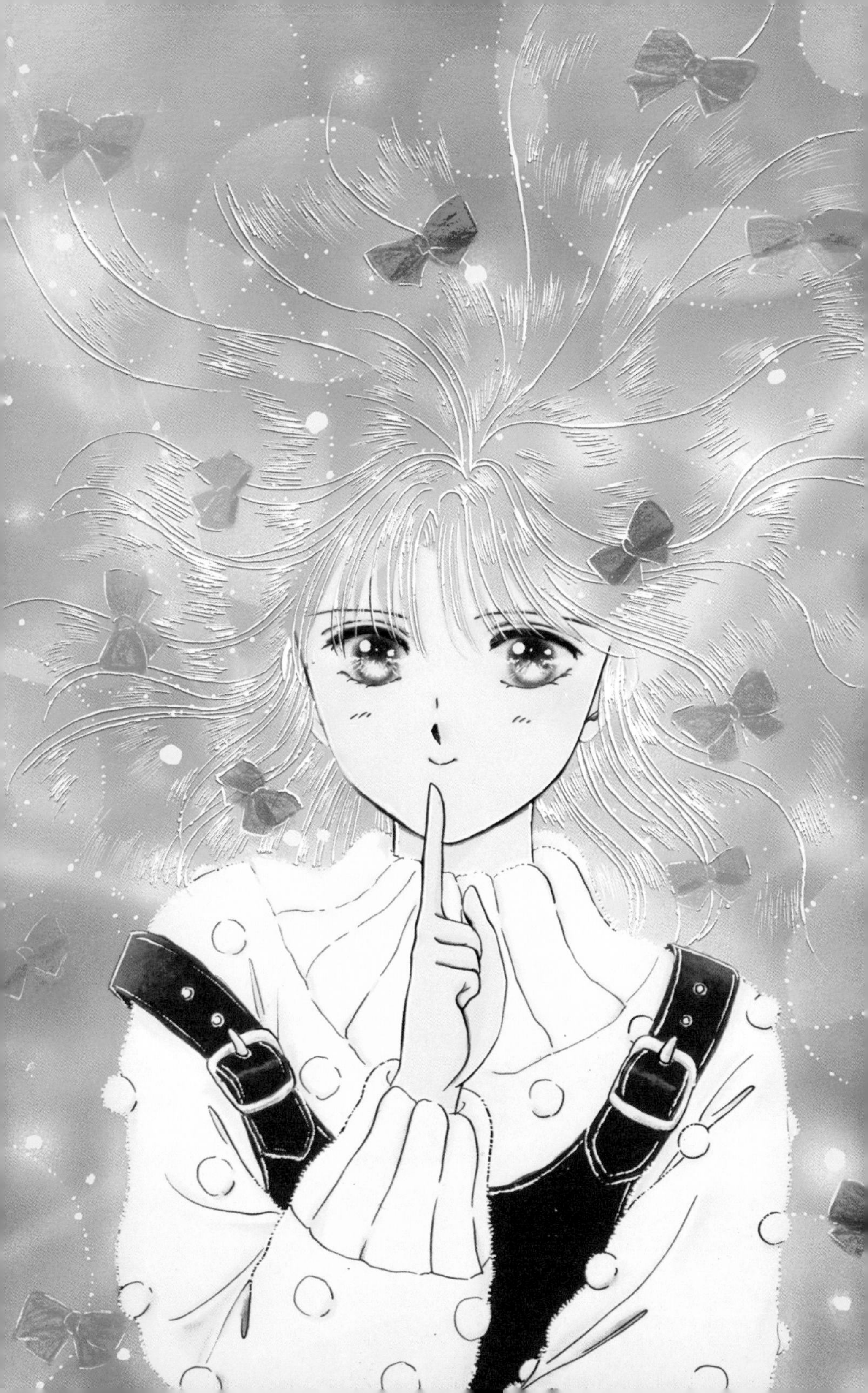

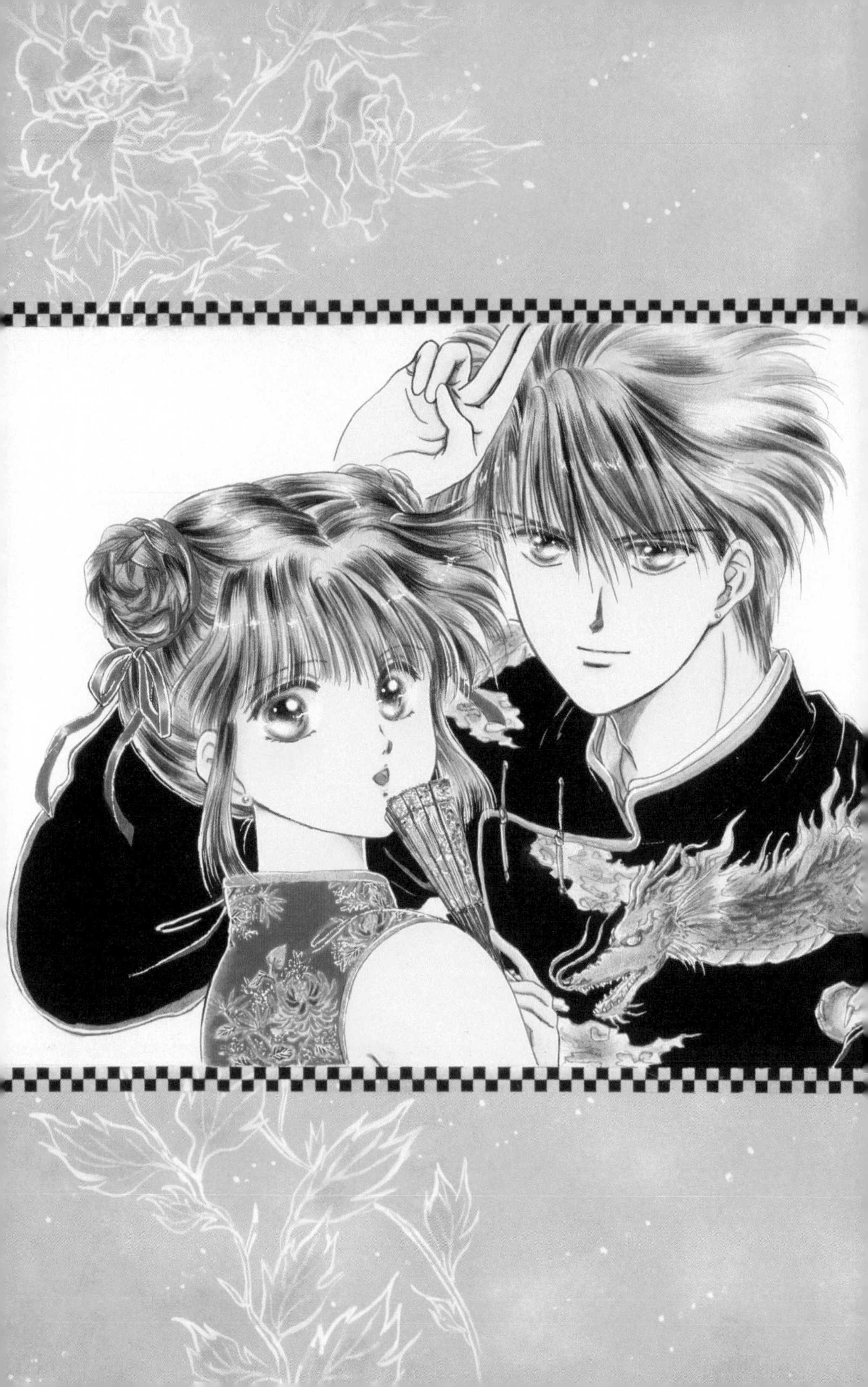

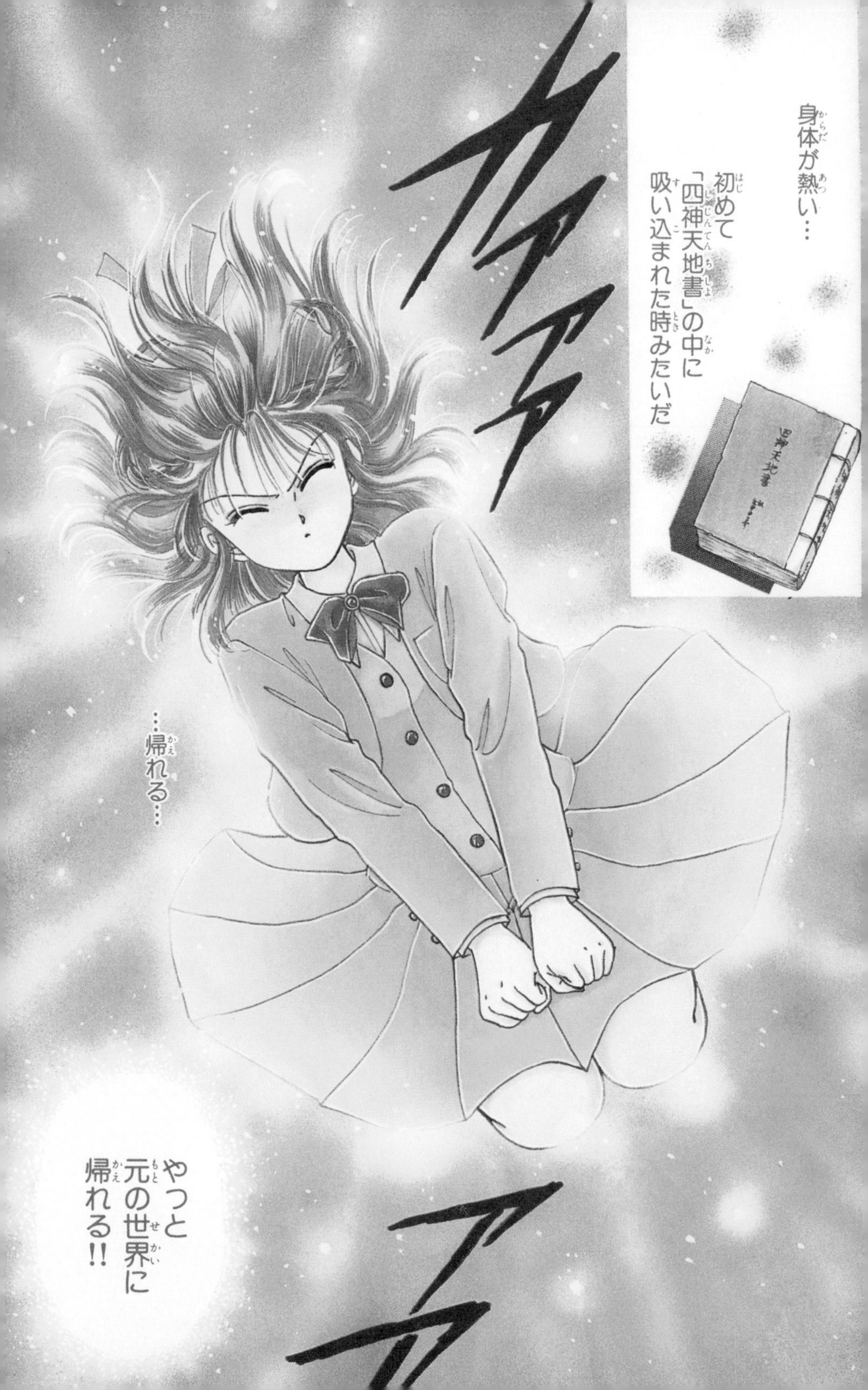
身体が熱い…
初めて「四神天地書」の中に吸い込まれた時みたいだ
四神天地書
カァァァ
…帰れる…
やっと元の世界に帰れる!!
ァァ

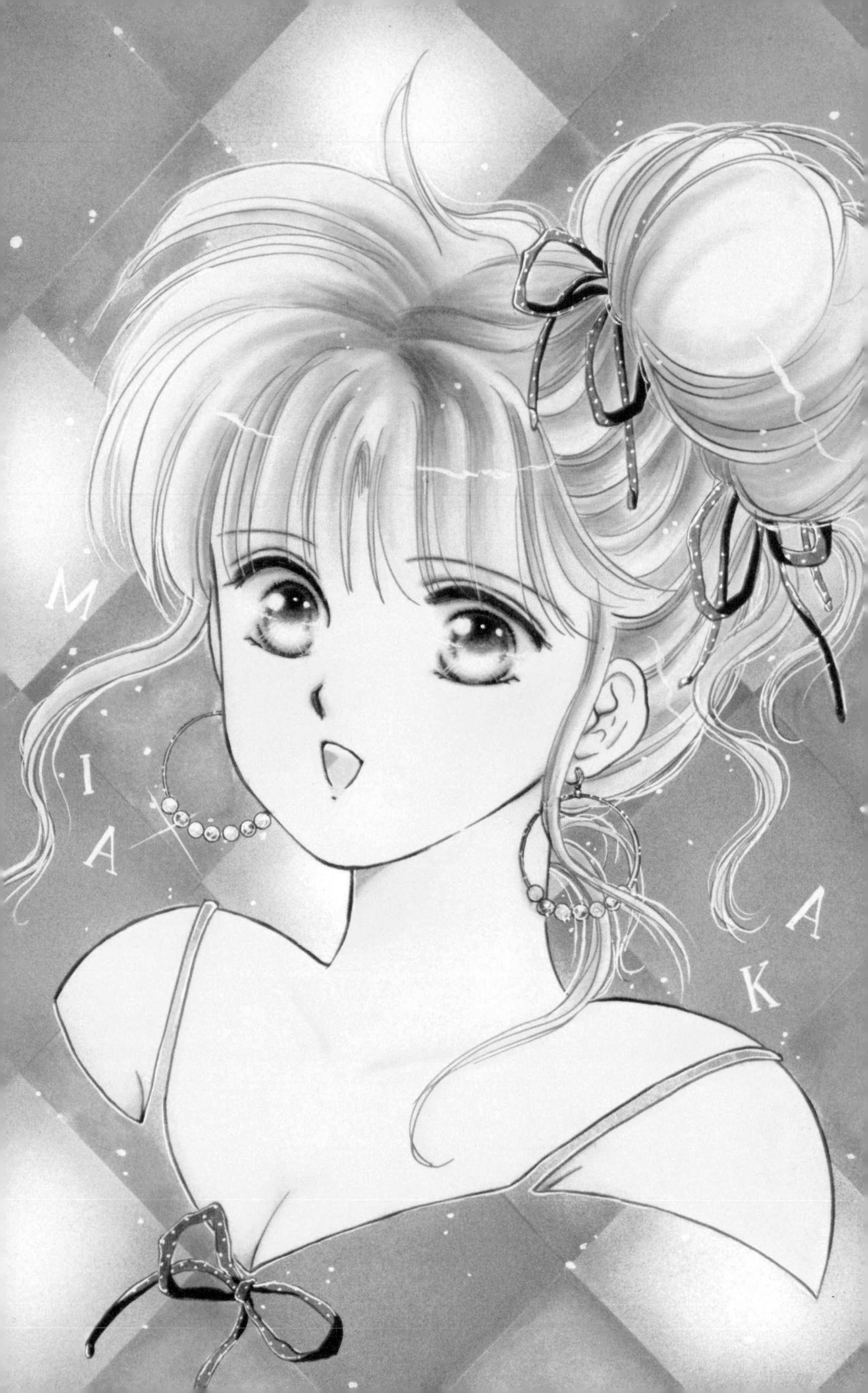
MIAKA

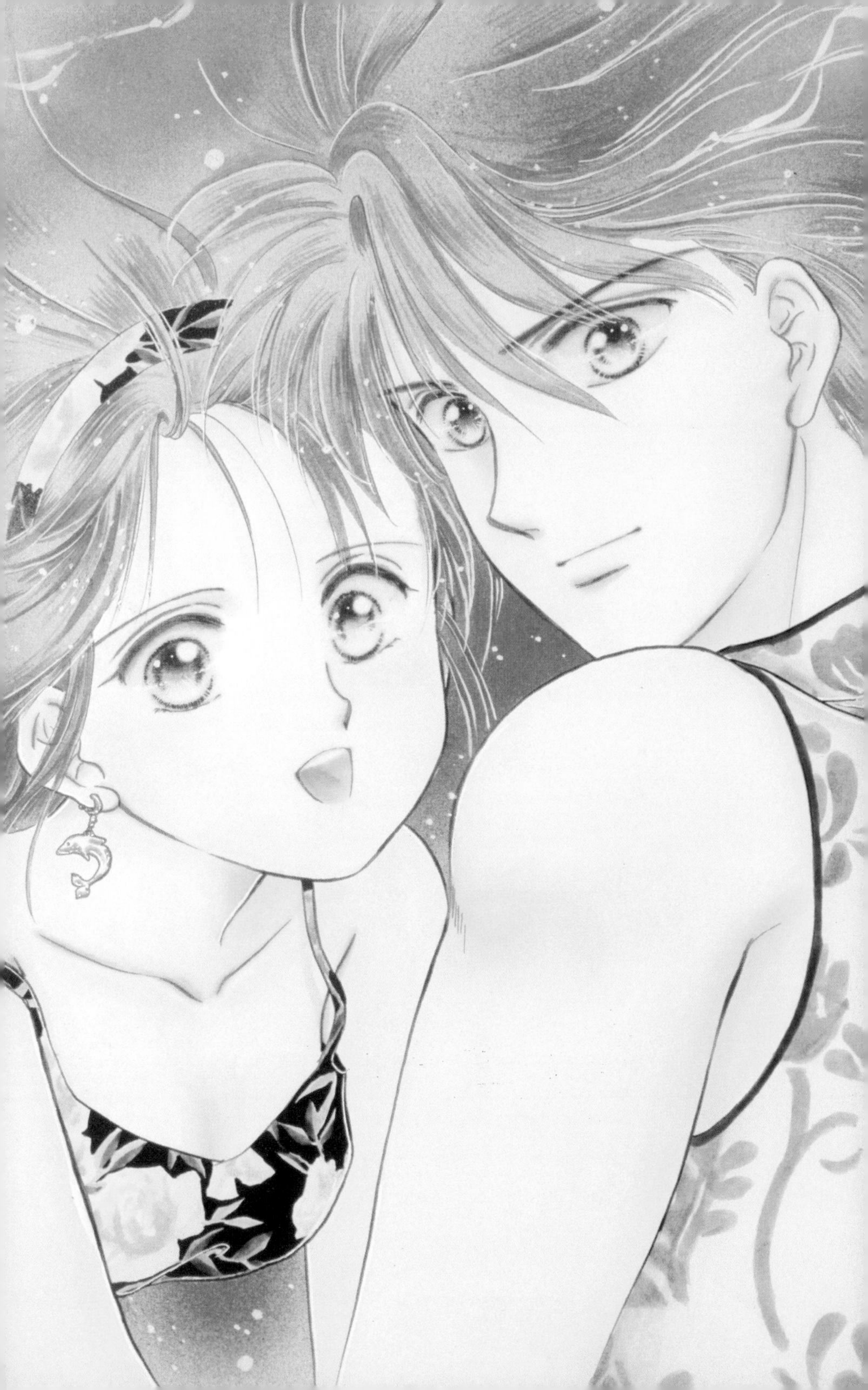

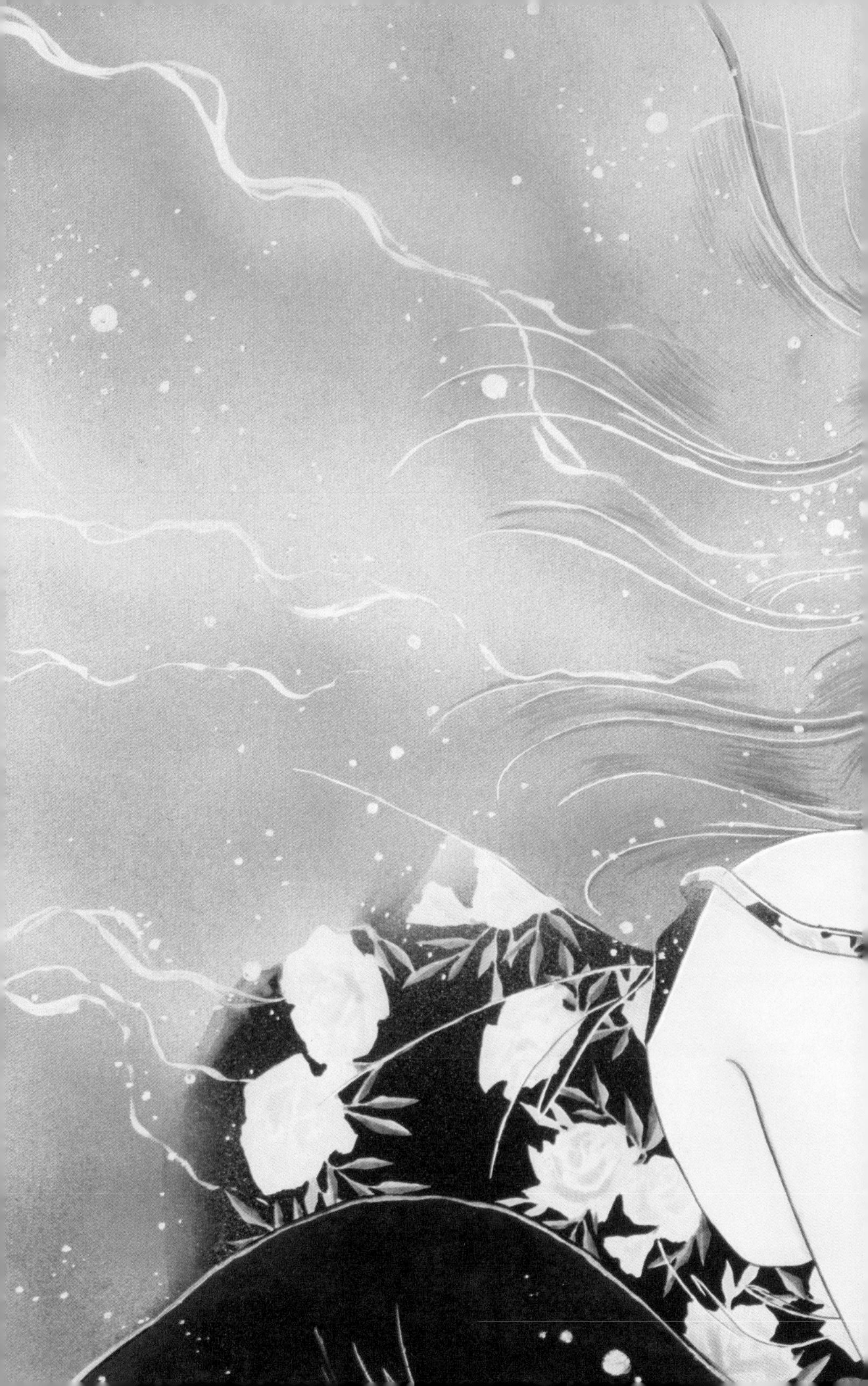

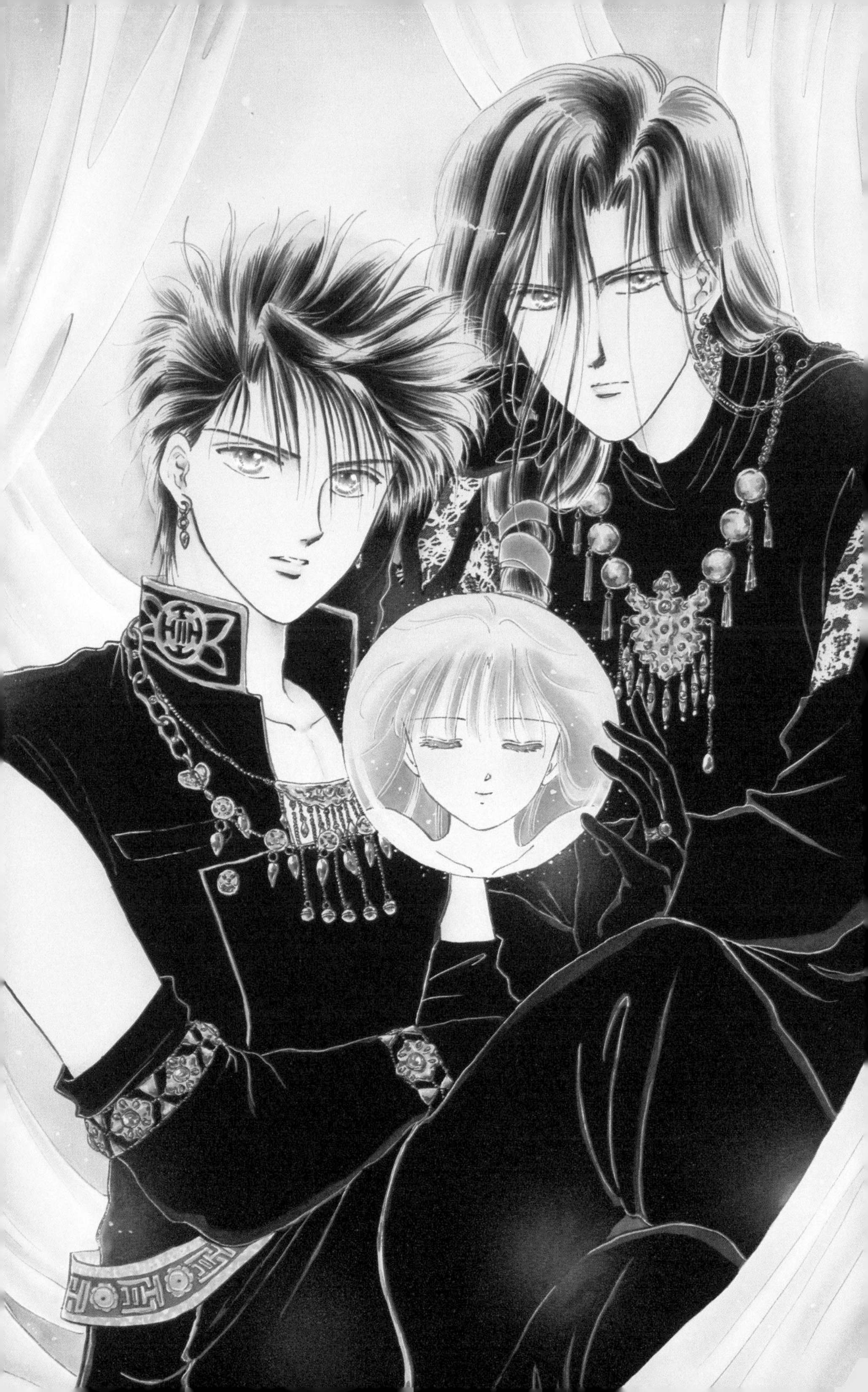

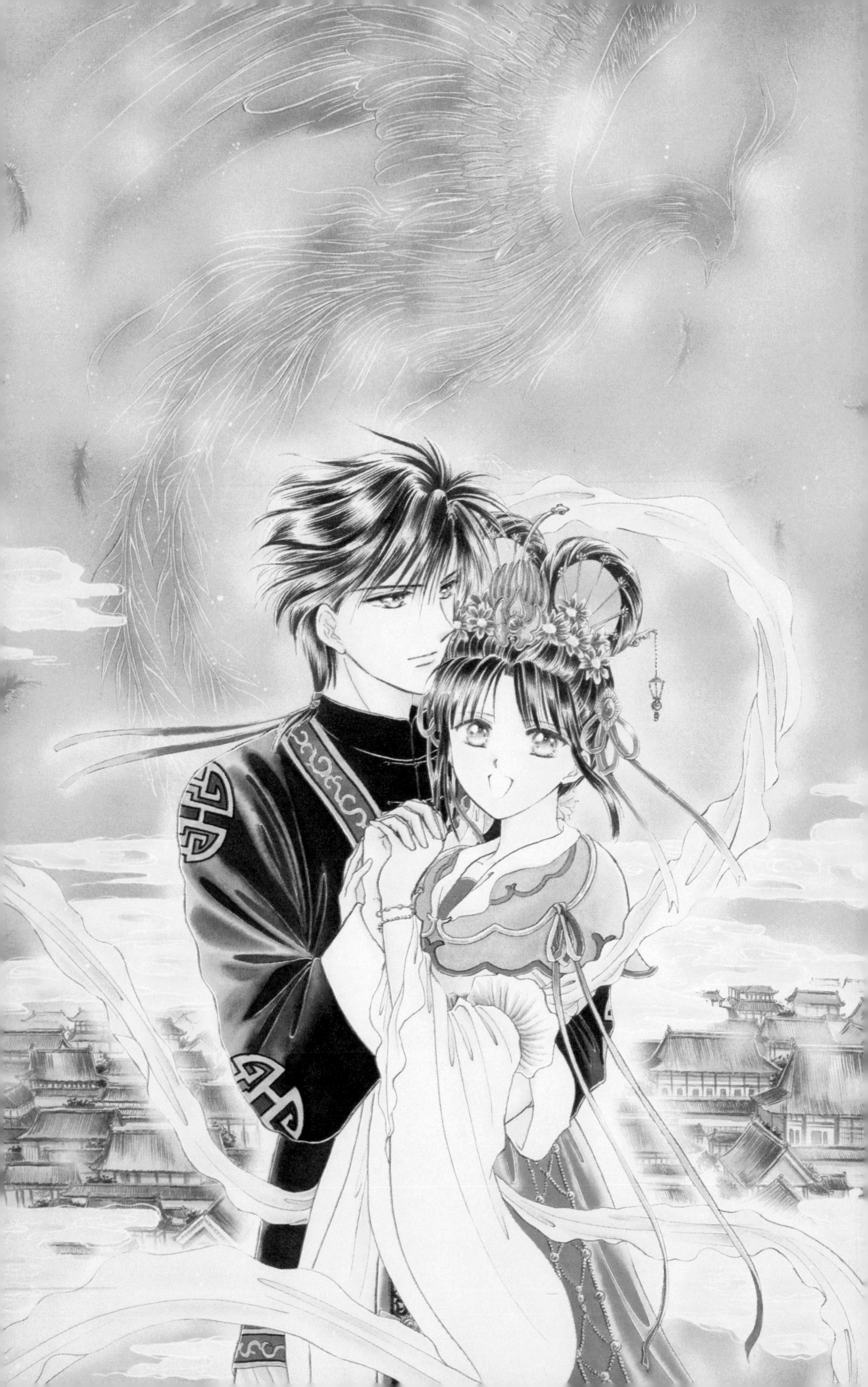

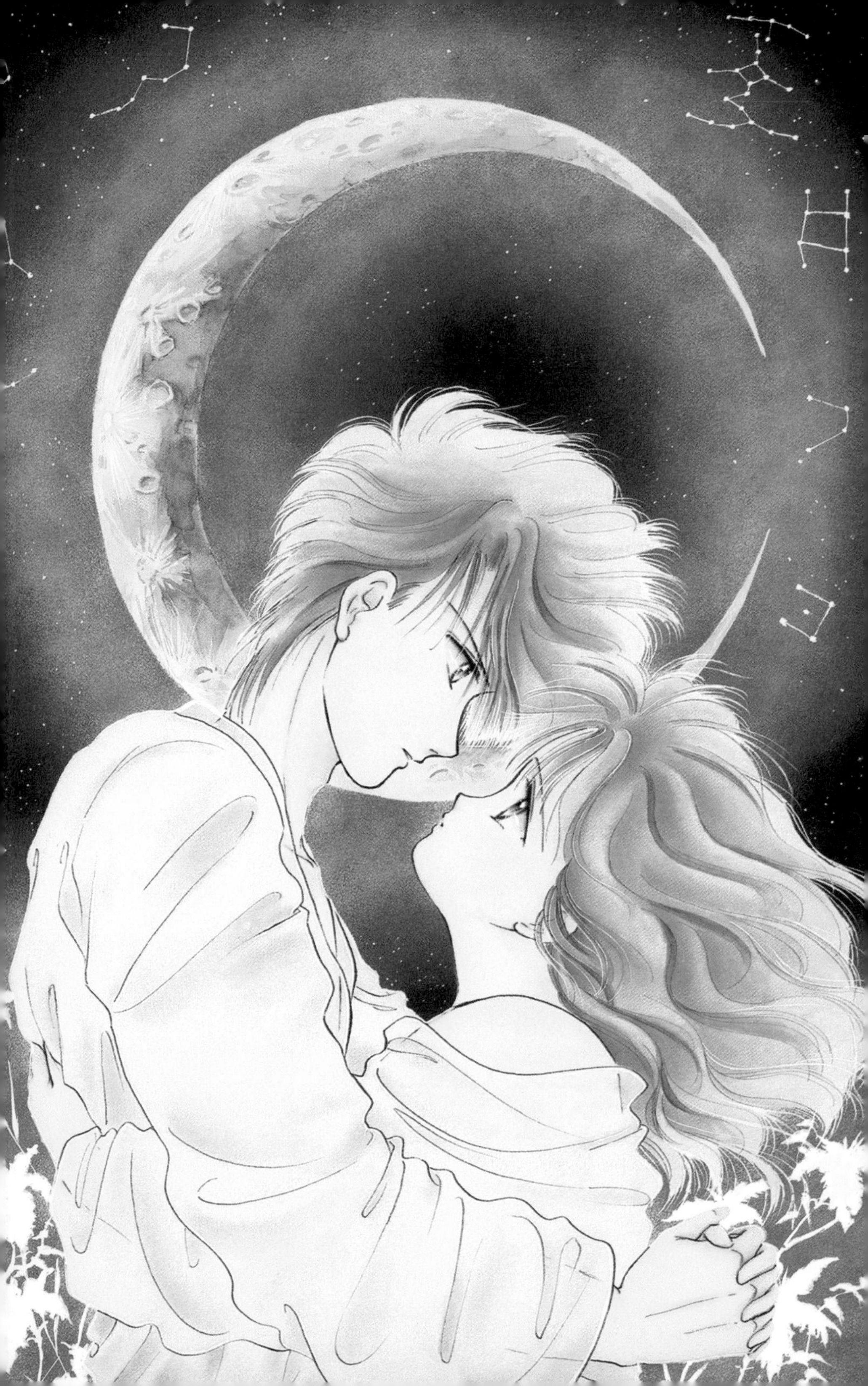

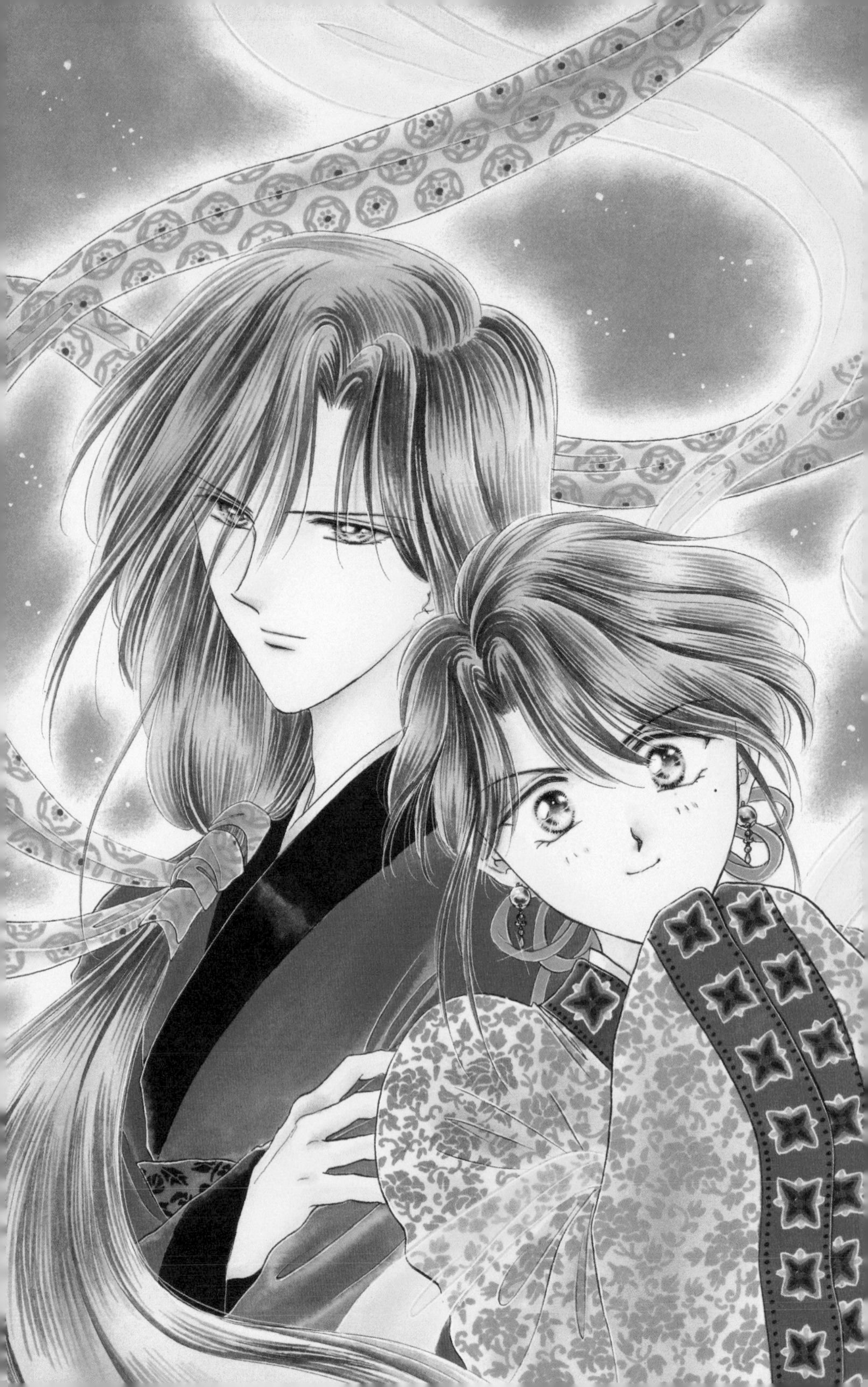